D1353487

Namibia

the Bradt Travel Guide

Chris McIntyre

edition
5

www.bradtguides.com

Bradt Travel Guides Ltd, UK
The Globe Pequot Press Inc, USA

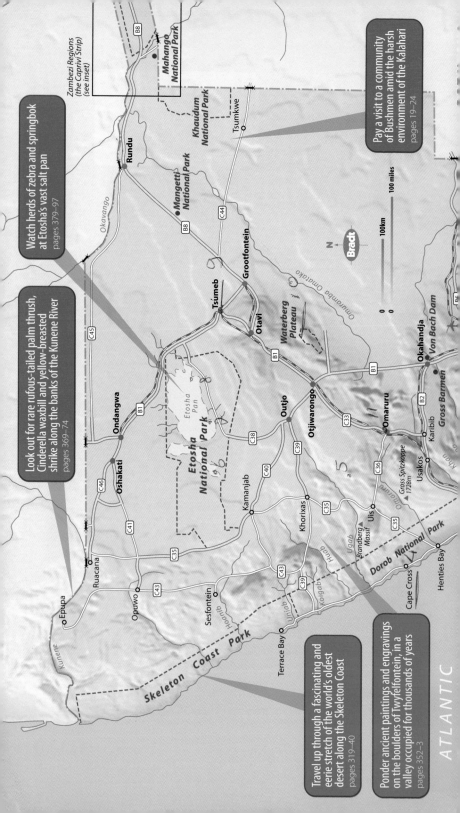

Watch herds of zebra and springbok at Etosha's vast salt pan
pages 379–97

Look out for rare rufous-tailed palm thrush, Cinderella waxbill and yellow-breasted shrike along the banks of the Kunene River
pages 369–74

Pay a visit to a community of Bushmen amid the harsh environment of the Kalahari
pages 19–24

Travel up through a fascinating and eerie stretch of the world's oldest desert along the Skeleton Coast
pages 319–40

Ponder ancient paintings and engravings on the boulders of Twyfelfontein, in a valley occupied for thousands of years
pages 352–3

Zambezi Regions (the Caprivi Strip) (see inset)

Mahango National Park

B8

Khaudum National Park

Tsumkwe

Rundu

Mangetti National Park

B8

C44

C45

Grootfontein

Tsumeb

Otavi

Waterberg Plateau

B1

Omuramba Omatako

Okahandja

Von Bach Dam

B2

Gross Barmen

Ondangwa

B1

Outjo

Otjiwarongo

C33

Omaruru

Karibib

Usakos

Gross Spitzkoppe
1728m

C36

Oshakati

C46

Etosha National Park

Etosha Pan

C38

Kamanjab

C40

C39

C35

Uis

Brandberg Massif

Omaruru

C35

C41

Ruacana

C35

Khorixas

C35

Dorob National Park

Ugab

Epupa

C43

Opuwo

Sesfontein

C43

C39

Hoanib

Hoarusib

Uniab

Cape Cross

Hentiesbaai

Terrace Bay

Skeleton Coast Park

ATLANTIC

N

Bradt

0   100km
0   100 miles

Kunene

Okavango

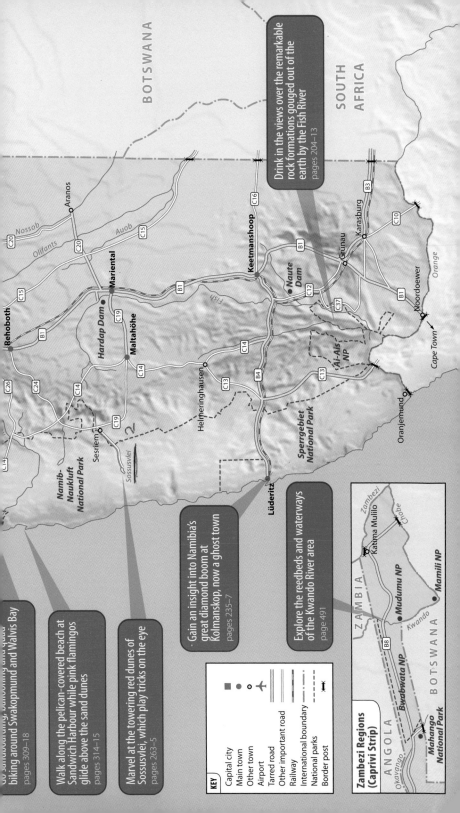

Drink in the views over the remarkable rock formations gouged out of the earth by the Fish River
pages 204–13

Gain an insight into Namibia's great diamond boom at Kolmanskop, now a ghost town
pages 235–7

Explore the reedbeds and waterways of the Kwando River area
page 491

Marvel at the towering red dunes of Sossusvlei, which play tricks on the eye
pages 263–5

Walk along the pelican-covered beach at Sandwich Harbour while pink flamingos glide above the sand dunes
pages 314–15

...sandboarding, ballooning and quad biking around Swakopmund and Walvis Bay
pages 309–18

KEY

■	Capital city
●	Main town
○	Other town
✈	Airport
	Tarred road
	Other important road
	Railway
	International boundary
	National parks
⊣⊢	Border post

Zambezi Regions (Caprivi Strip)

BOTSWANA

SOUTH AFRICA

ANGOLA

ZAMBIA

Katima Mulilo

Mudumu NP

Mamili NP

Bwabwata NP

Mahango National Park

Okavango

Kwando

Zambezi

Chobe

B8

Aranos

Rehoboth

Mariental

Maltahöhe

Hardap Dam

Keetmanshoop

Naute Dam

Karasburg

Grünau

Moordoewer

Oranjemund

Lüderitz

Helmeringhausen

Sesriem

Sossusvlei

Namib-Naukluft National Park

Ai-Ais NP

Sperrgebiet National Park

Cape Town

Nossob

Auob

Olifants

Fish

Orange

C20

C15

C20

C15

C15

C19

C26

C24

C44

C19

C14

C14

C13

B4

C13

C37

C12

B1

B1

B1

B1

B1

B3

C10

C16

Namib

BOTSWANA

Namibia
Don't
miss...

Around Sossusvlei
This is the Namib Desert
at its most dramatic —
towering ochre dunes and
gracefully curving ridges
(ET) pages 256–65

Culture
The Himba live almost entirely in
their traditional areas in remote
Kaokoland (ET) pages 25–6

Fish River Canyon

At 161km long, up to 27km wide, and almost 550m at its deepest, the Fish River Canyon is arguably second in size only to Arizona's Grand Canyon (ML/DT) pages 204–13

Wildlife

Cheetah do exceptionally well in Namibia, which is said to have about 40% of Africa's population (IT/DT) pages 40–1

Rock art

Many of the engravings at Twyfelfontein are of animals and their spoor, or geometric motifs — which have been suggested as maps to water sources (AVZ) pages 352–3

Namibia in colour

above   **At Epupa the river widens to accommodate a few islands, before plunging into a geological fault** (GDP/S) page 370

left   **The ghost town of Kolmanskop is gradually being buried by the surrounding dunes** (ET) pages 235–7

below   **The Skeleton Coast earned its name from treacherous fogs and strong currents that once forced many ships on to the area's uncharted sandbanks that shift underwater** (ET) pages 319–40

How did it all happen? George (my then husband) and I wrote the first Bradt guide – about hiking in Peru and Bolivia – on an Amazon river barge, and typed it up on a borrowed typewriter.

We had no money for the next two books so George went to work for a printer and was paid in books rather than money.

Forty years on, Bradt publishes over 200 titles that sell all over the world. I still suffer from Imposter Syndrome – how did it all happen? I hadn't even worked in an office before! Well, I've been extraordinarily lucky with the people around me. George provided the belief to get us started (and the mother to run our US office). Then, in 1977, I recruited a helper, Janet Mears, who is still working for us. She and the many dedicated staff who followed have been the foundations on which the company is built. But the bricks and mortar have been our authors and readers. Without them there would be no Bradt Travel Guides. Thank you all for making it happen.

Hilary Bradt

AUTHOR

Chris McIntyre went to Africa in 1987, after reading physics at Queen's College, Oxford. He taught with VSO in Zimbabwe for almost three years and travelled around extensively, mostly with a backpack. In 1990 he co-authored the UK's first guide to Namibia and Botswana, published by Bradt, before spending three years as a shipbroker in London.

Since then, Chris has concentrated on what he enjoys most: Africa. He wrote the first guidebook to Zambia for Bradt in 1996, the first edition of this guide in 1998, a new Botswana guide in 2003, co-authored *Zanzibar* with his wife since 2006, and co-authored the 2013 editions of Bradt's two Tanzania guides. While keeping guidebooks up to date, his day job is managing director of Expert Africa – a specialist tour operator which organises high-quality trips throughout Africa for individual travellers from around the world, including a very wide range of trips to Namibia. This also includes the Wild about Africa programme of small, guided groups through Namibia. Obviously Expert Africa isn't the only travel company operating to Namibia – you'll find many other good ones detailed in these pages – but inevitably Chris likes to think it's the best!

Chris maintains a keen interest in development and conservation issues, acting as adviser to various NGOs and projects associated with Africa. He is a Fellow of the Royal Geographical Society and contributes photographs and articles to various publications. Now based in west London, Chris continues to travel and research in Africa regularly; at around the time that this book is published he's due to be in Namibia with his wife, Susan, and their two small children. Chris can usually be contacted by email on **e** chris.mcintyre@expertafrica.com.

PUBLISHER'S FOREWORD

The first Bradt travel guide was written in 1974 by George and Hilary Bradt on a river barge floating down the Amazon. Over the following years, Bradt earned a highly respected reputation as a ground-breaking publisher: its guidebooks were often the first to cover those destinations, and its authors were ahead of the game in promoting responsible travel. Now, over 40 years since the company was founded, Bradt has more than 200 books on its list, ranging from full-country and regional guides to wildlife titles and travel literature. And the pioneering spirit still burns strong. Whether focusing on countries overlooked by other publishers or areas a little more 'mainstream', Bradt seeks out those hidden corners and champions the road less travelled.

Reprinted February 2017

Fifth edition June 2015   First published 1998

Bradt Travel Guides Ltd
IDC House, The Vale, Chalfont St Peter, Bucks SL9 9RZ, England
www.bradtguides.com
Print edition published in the USA by The Globe Pequot Press Inc, PO Box 480,
Guilford, Connecticut 06437-0480

Text copyright © 2015 Chris McIntyre
Maps copyright © 2015 Bradt Travel Guides Ltd
Illustrations copyright © 2015 Individual photographers and artists (see below)
Project Manager: Maisie Fitzpatrick
Cover research: Pepi Bluck, Perfect Picture

ISBN: 978 1 84162 914 8 (print)
e-ISBN: 978 1 78477 126 3 (e-pub)
e-ISBN: 978 1 78477 226 0 (mobi)

British Library Cataloguing in Publication Data
A catalogue record for this book is available from the British Library

Photographs Alamy: Martin Harvey (MH/A); Dreamstime: Anni34 (A/DT), Ecophoto (EP/DT), Itacud (IT/DT), Marylexa (ML/DT), Meunierd (M/DT), Mrallen (MA/DT), Viewapart (VA/DT), Villiers (V/DT); Tricia Hayne (TH); Tracy Lederer (TL); Chris McIntyre (CM); Jeanne Meintjes (JM); Shutterstock: Jan-Dirk Hansen (JDH/S), Grobler du Preez (GDP/S); SuperStock (SS); Piet Swiegers (PS); Emma Thomson (ET); Will Whitford (WW); Martha Young (MY); Ariadne Van Zandbergen (AVZ)

Front cover Gemsbok (*Oryx gazella*)
Back cover Woermann Tower, Swakopmund (ET); Spitzkoppe (EP/DT)
Title page Quivertree (*Aloe dichotoma*) (ET); lilac-breasted roller (*Coracias caudatus*) (MA/DT); colourful houses in Lüderitz (MA/DT)

Illustrations Annabel Milne, Carole Vincer
Maps David McCutcheon FBCart.S. Includes map data © OpenStreetMap contributors

Typeset by Wakewing, High Wycombe, and Ian Spick, Bradt Travel Guides
Production managed by Jellyfish Print Solutions; printed in India
Digital conversion by www.dataworks.co.in

MAJOR CONTRIBUTORS

This book, just as much as the previous editions, has been a team effort, and many have devoted their energy to it. Largest among the contributions to this fifth edition are from the following people.

Emma Thomson (*www.ethomson.co.uk*) is an award-winning travel writer and formerly commissioning editor at Bradt Travel Guides. A member of the British Guild of Travel Writers, she writes for the likes of *The Independent*, *The Telegraph*, *National Geographic Traveller* and *Travel Africa*. She first visited Namibia in 2011 as part of a world-first expedition trekking unaided along the Skeleton Coast, and has been bewitched by the country's open spaces ever since. For this edition she covered the Southern Kalahari and Fish River Canyon, Lüderitz and the southwest, Namib-Naukluft National Park, and Swakopmund and Walvis Bay.

Sue Watt (*www.suewatt.co.uk*) and her partner **Will Whitford** first travelled to Namibia in 2004 as part of an eight-month tour of Africa. They've returned many times since, and Sue is now an experienced travel writer specialising in Africa and regularly published in UK national press and magazines. Will's photography accompanies her features. For this edition, they covered the Central Highlands, the Triangle and the Caprivi Strip, now known as the Kavango/Zambezi regions.

Martha Young has a Geography degree from Leeds University and has lived in various parts of Africa, including Uganda and Kenya where she managed a safari camp in the Maasai Mara, as well as working for a childcare NGO in Cape Town. She has explored extensively and adventurously in Namibia, and off the beaten track in Rwanda, and now puts her experience to good use organising safaris to Namibia for some of Expert Africa's travellers. For this edition, she updated the introductory chapters as well as those on Etosha, Damaraland, Skeleton Coast, Central Corridor, Bushmanland and Ovamboland.

However, this guide has been built very much on the solid foundations laid by contributions for the previous editions from: Philip Briggs, Africa expert and author, who kindly gave an extensive and scholarly basis for the original wildlife section; Purba Choudhury, arts, press and PR professional, who researched and wrote the original arts and crafts section; David Else, expert author and old Africa hand,

UPDATES WEBSITE AND FEEDBACK REQUEST

Namibia is a country that is relatively new to tourism and, although I have endeavoured to make this book as up to date as possible, some things will inevitably change over time. Please help to revise future editions of this book by sending in any information you may have about changes and developments, or simply your own travel experiences in the country, good and bad. Such first-hand feedback is invaluable and all comments will be gratefully received. Please contact Bradt on ☎ 01753 893444 or e info@bradtguides.com. Alternatively, you can add a review of the book to www.bradtguides.com or Amazon.

Periodically, authors post travel updates and reader feedback on the Bradt website. Check www.bradtupdates.com/namibia for any news.

who kindly gave route descriptions for the Naukluft hiking section; Sue Grainger, traveller and writer, who wrote much original material for the Kaokoveld chapter, and commented on more besides; Jonathan Hughes, ecologist, who wrote most of the boxes on survival in the Namib, and gave other valuable critiques; Tricia Hayne, who travelled so much with husband Bob, and has had a hugely positive impact on this book over the years; Angela Griffin, for her work on the fourth edition; and Tracy Lederer, Maruska Adye and Sabina Hekandjo, all Namibia specialists at Expert Africa, who between them have contributed a lot of info and endless fact-checking over the years.

AUTHOR'S STORY

I first visited Namibia in 1989, as the South African administration started to relinquish its grip and the country prepared for independence. By then I had lived in Zimbabwe for several years and travelled widely. Namibia was rumoured to be wonderful; but nobody seemed to know any details. The world knew South West Africa (Namibia) only as a troubled place from news bulletins, nothing more.

So I hired a VW Golf and drove from Namibia's northeastern tip to its southern border in 12 days. Overseas tourism simply didn't exist then. Sesriem had one campsite with just 11 pitches for tents; the Fish River Canyon was deserted. The trip was terribly rushed, but Namibia captivated me. The scale of its wilderness was enchanting, and travelling was remarkably easy.

Six months later I returned to explore – and to research the first English guidebook to the country. While I was there, Namibia's independence arrived, putting the country's troubles into the past. Optimism was tangible, justified by democracy, an implausibly reliable infrastructure and rich mineral resources. I delved a little deeper into its magic and remained entranced. It was this that inspired me to start a travel company, originally focusing on Namibia, and I'm very grateful to be able to keep in close contact with a country that I still love.

Acknowledgements

This fifth edition couldn't have been written without the help of many people who have not yet been mentioned – some who helped with previous editions, and some with this one. Many names I have forgotten, others I never knew. I hope those who aren't named here will forgive me, but some who stand out for their help and input include the following.

The Wilderness Safaris team, Frieda Nefungo, Birgit Bekker, Regina Visher; the community at the remarkable Torra Conservancy; Arno and Estelle Oosthuysen; Jeanne Meintjes of Eco Marine; Russell from Erongo; Donna and the Okonjima team; and, as ever, Kate and Bruno Nebe – without whom Namibia just wouldn't be the same.

The team at Expert Africa sends many hundreds of travellers to Namibia every year, and many of these have helped me with their personal perspectives on the country – through both discussions and some very extensive and detailed feedback reports which they've kindly posted to our website. Meanwhile, back in the office, Tracy, Maruska, Sabina and especially Martha have always been on hand to help with much information and experience. (The support of John, Noel and Dudley with my writing is always appreciated.)

Immense gratitude, as usual, to those who worked on producing the book: Anna Moores, Sally Brock, Ian Spick, David McCutcheon and, especially, Maisie Fitzpatrick – whose hard work made this book possible. That which is good and correct owes much to their care and attention, while errors and omissions remain my own.

Emma Thomson would like to thank her driver, navigator and all-round ace road-trip companion: her father. Marion Schelkle from Lüderitz tourist office, Almuth Styles from Namib tourist information in Swakopmund, and Tricia Hayne – the main updater of previous editions of this guide and beloved Bradt mentor to many.

Sue Watt would like to thank the staff at Olive Exclusive, Erongo Wilderness Lodge, Okonjima, Ghaub Guest Farm, Travel North Namibia in Tsumeb, Tutwa Tourism and Travel in Katima Mulilo, and Nunda River Lodge.

Martha Young would like to thank Kate and Bruno Nebe, Basil Calitz from Brandberg Restcamp, Birgit Bekker, the Wilderness team – particularly Twiitileni Nyamu and Carol Barnard – and Sabina Hekandjo, Tracy Lederer and Angela Griffin at Expert Africa.

Contents

LIST OF MAPS

AUTHOR'S FAVOURITES Finding genuinely characterful accommodation or that unmissable off-the-beaten-track café can be difficult, so the authors and updaters have chosen a few of their favourite places throughout the country to point you in the right direction. These 'author's favourites' are marked with a ✳.

MAPS

Keys and symbols All town maps include alphabetical keys covering the locations of those places to stay, eat or drink that are featured in the book. On regional maps, lodges are marked directly on the map. Please note that maps may not show all hotels and restaurants in the area: other establishments may be located in towns shown on the map.

Grids and grid references Several maps use grid lines to allow easy location of sites. Map grid references are listed in square brackets after the name of the place or sight of interest in the text, with page number followed by grid number, eg: [124 A1].

ACCOMMODATION LISTINGS Where a small group of lodges or hotels come under the same umbrella organisation within a similar area, these have been grouped together. For ease of recognition, the typography used for the 'parent' lodge is as for other lodges, but subsidiaries within the group are noted in small capital letters, with a grey symbol. For example, see Okonjima (see pages 408–10):

🏠 **Okonjima**
🏠 MAIN CAMP
🏠 BUSH CAMP
🏠 OKONJIMA VILLA
⛺ OMBOROKO CAMPSITE

DATUM FOR GPS CO-ORDINATES For GPS co-ordinates given in this guide, note that the datum used is WSG 84 – and you must set your receiver accordingly before copying in any of these co-ordinates.

All GPS co-ordinates in this book have been expressed as degrees, minutes, and decimal fractions of a minute.

For more on wildlife in Namibia, why not check out Bradt's *Southern African Wildlife*? Go to www.bradtguides.com and key in NAMIBIA40 at the checkout for your 40% discount.

Introduction

Namibia has no idyllic sandy beaches, no warm tropical waters or big brassy hotels. However, it does have huge tracts of pristine wilderness, home to some stunning wildlife. Glance around. The Namib Desert has plants and animals found nowhere else on earth. Here is the world's oldest desert, where endemic wildlife has evolved to survive – like the contorted *Welwitschia mirabilis* that lives for millennia, the elusive golden mole and the unique fog-basking beetles.

Namibia's population has always been tiny, a sprinkling of settlements founded by different peoples: some ancient, some colonial. Around these outposts, vast open areas remain protected as national parks, supplemented by conservancies where scattered local communities protect the wildlife in their own areas. Namibia has little industry or pollution, so you look up at the clearest stars you'll ever see.

Best of all, Namibia's wilderness is still easy to explore independently. Choose back roads here and you can drive for hours through endless plains, huge mountain massifs and spectacular canyons without seeing a soul. Even in Etosha, one of Africa's top game parks, driving around is easy, and you can stop beside the waterholes for as long as you like. As animals wander all around, you just sip a cold drink and focus your camera.

Namibia's not an ideal country for backpacking. However, if you can afford to hire a car, then the country is your oyster – and it's not expensive. Good food, wine, beer and cheap camping make the cost of staying in Namibia lower than anywhere else in southern Africa. With just a little more cash to spare, and advanced bookings, you'll find Namibia's lodges, camps and guest farms cost a fraction of the price of similar places elsewhere in the region. Here you can afford comfort and expert guides who will help you discover their own areas, instructing you in everything from tracking black rhino to understanding the native flora.

In the last 25 years I've been lucky enough to make dozens of trips back to Namibia. I've watched tourism gradually develop and change – and on the whole it's done so positively. While there are more visitors now, these are exploring more destinations within Namibia, so the country still seems empty. There are many new lodges and guest farms, but these are spread widely and most remain small, offering personal attention and unique attractions. Namibia is still not a mass-market destination, and there's no sign that it will be.

The contribution to the economy made by visitors is increasing, and the government recognises its importance – which is vital if the wild areas that attract visitors are to be conserved. Even more importantly, the people living in those remote, rural areas are also benefiting from tourism. The Kaokoveld, in particular, is home to some thriving community projects – successes that are rare in most parts of Africa. Elsewhere, new conservancies are sprouting up, where neighbouring farms join forces and return wild game to their land, replacing domestic animals.

Just as Namibia is evolving, so are the ways to travel. At first, flying around was strictly the preserve of those who could afford to charter their own plane. They knew that Namibia's landscapes are often most spectacular from the air, and that flying around gives a whole new perspective on the country. Now it has become less expensive, with tour operators tailor-making fly-in trips around the country, and charging per seat, not per plane. These hops between lodges remain more costly than driving, but they are breathtaking, and allow easy access to even the remotest corners of the Skeleton Coast and Kaokoveld.

So Namibia and trips there are changing. Travel there is also changing on a personal level: as this book is published, I'll be taking my children (aged two and five) there for the first time. Every time I go, I am again surprised at how easy the travelling is, and how remarkable the country – and I can't wait to see the country through their eyes.

Part One

GENERAL INFORMATION

NAMIBIA AT A GLANCE

Location Southwest Africa, astride the Tropic of Capricorn and beside the South Atlantic Ocean. Its main borders are with South Africa, Botswana and Angola, though it also adjoins Zambia.

Size 824,292km²

Climate Subtropical desert climate

Status Republic

Population 2,113,077 (2011 census)

Population growth per year 1.5% (2001 and 2011 census)

Life expectancy at birth 63 years (2014 UN stats estimate)

Capital Windhoek, population 325,858 (2011 census)

Other main towns Swakopmund, Walvis Bay, Rundu, Oshakati, Katima Mulilo

Economy Major earners: mining, including uranium, diamonds and other minerals; agriculture; tourism

GDP US$5,668 per capita (2012 UN stats estimate)

GDP growth rate 5% (2012 UN stats estimate)

Currency Namibian dollar (N$), equivalent to (and interchangeable with) South African rand

Rate of exchange £1 = N$18.17; US$1 = N$12.19, €1 = N$13.03 (March 2015)

Language English (official), Afrikaans, German, several ethnic languages (most in Bantu and Khoisan language groups)

Religion Christianity; traditional beliefs

International telephone code +264

Time Apr–Sep GMT +1, Sep–Mar GMT +2 (except Zambezi Region (formerly Caprivi Strip): GMT +2 all year)

Electricity 220 volts, plugs with three round pins, as in South Africa

Weights and measures Metric

Flag Diagonal red stripe bordered by narrow white stripes separates two triangles: one green; one blue with a yellow sun motif.

Public holidays New Year's Day (1 January), Independence Day (21 March), Good Friday, Easter Monday, Workers' Day (1 May), Cassinga Day (4 May), Africa Day (25 May), Ascension Day (40 days after Easter Sunday), Heroes' Day (26 August), Human Rights Day (10 December), Christmas Day (25 December), Family Day (26 December)

Tourist information www.namibiatourism.com.na

1

History, Politics and Economy

HISTORY

PREHISTORY

Namibia's earliest inhabitants Palaeontologists looking for evidence of the first ancestors of the human race have excavated a number of sites in southern Africa. The earliest remains yet identified are Stone Age tools dated at about 200,000 years old, which have been recovered in gravel deposits around what is now the Victoria Falls. It is thought that these probably belong to *Homo erectus*, whose hand-axes have been dated in Tanzania to half a million years old. These were hunter-gatherer people, who could use fire, make tools, and had probably developed some simple speech.

Experts divide the Stone Age into the middle, early and late periods. The transition from early to middle Stone Age technology – which is indicated by a larger range of stone tools, often adapted for particular uses, and signs that these people had a greater mastery of their environment – was probably in progress around 125,000 years ago in southern Africa. The late Stone Age is characterised by people who used composite tools, those made of wood and/or bone and/or stone used together, and by the presence of a revolutionary invention: the bow and arrow. This first probably appeared about 15,000 years ago, by which time the original Namibians were already roaming the plains of Damaraland and painting on the rocks at Twyfelfontein.

Africa's Iron Age Around 3000BC, late Stone Age hunter-gatherer groups in Ethiopia, and elsewhere in north and west Africa, started to keep domestic animals, sow seeds and harvest the produce: they became the world's first farmers.

By around 1000BC these new pastoral practices had spread south into the equatorial forests of what is now Congo, to around Lake Victoria, and into the northern area of the Great Rift Valley, in northern Tanzania. However, agriculture did not spread south into the rest of central/southern Africa immediately. Only when the technology, and the tools, of iron-working became known did the practices start their relentless expansion southward.

The spread of agriculture and Iron Age culture seems to have been rapid, brought south by Bantu-speaking Africans who were taller and heavier than the existing Khoisan-speaking inhabitants of southern Africa.

BANTU COLONISATION

Khoisan coexistence By around the time of Christ, the hunter-gatherers in Namibia seem to have been joined by pastoralists, the Khoi-khoi (or Nama people), who used a similar language involving clicks. Both belong to the Khoisan language family, as distinct from the Bantu-language family. These were pastoralists who combined keeping sheep, goats and cattle with foraging.

These stock animals are not native to southern Africa and it seems likely that some Khoisan hunters and gatherers acquired stock, and the expertise to keep them, from early Bantu tribes in the Zimbabwe area. As the Bantu spread south, into the relatively fertile Natal area, the Khoisan pastoralists spread west, across the Kalahari into Namibia. Their traditional gathering knowledge, and ability to survive on existing plant foods, meant that they didn't depend entirely on their stock. Hence they could expand across areas of poor grazing which would have defeated the less flexible Bantu.

By around the 9th century another group, the Damara, are recognised as living in Namibia and speaking a Khoisan language. They cultivated more than the Nama, and hence were more settled. Their precise origin is hotly debated, as they have many features common to people of Bantu origin and yet speak a Khoisan language.

The first Bantu people

By the 16th century the first of the Bantu-speaking peoples, the Herero, arrived from the east. Oral tradition suggests that they came south from east Africa's great lakes to Zambia, across Angola, arriving at the Kunene River around 1550. However they got here, they settled with their cattle in the north of the country and the plains of the Kaokoveld. (Note that the Himba people living in the Kaokoveld today are a subgroup of the Herero, speaking the same language.)

Where the Herero settled, the existing people clearly had to change. Some intermarried with the incoming groups; some may even have been enslaved by the newcomers. A few could shift their lifestyles to take advantage of new opportunities created by the Herero, and an unfortunate fourth group (the Bushmen of the time) started to become marginalised, remaining in areas with less agricultural potential. This was the start of a poor relationship between the cattle-herding Herero and the Bushmen.

These iron-working, cattle-herding Herero people were very successful and, as they thrived, so they began to expand their herds southward and into central Namibia.

The early explorers

Meanwhile, in the 15th century, trade between Europe and the East opened up sea routes along the Namibian coast and around the Cape of Good Hope. The first Europeans recorded as stepping on Namibian soil were the Portuguese in 1485. Diego Cão stopped briefly at Cape Cross on the Skeleton Coast and erected a limestone cross. On 8 December 1487, Bartolomeu Dias reached Walvis Bay and then continued south to what is now Lüderitz. However, the coast was so totally barren and uninviting that, even though the Portuguese had already settled in Angola, and the Dutch in the Cape, little interest was shown in Namibia.

It was only in the latter half of the 18th century, when British, French and American whalers began to make use of the ports of Lüderitz and Walvis Bay, that the Dutch authorities in the Cape decided in 1793 to take possession of Walvis Bay – the only good deepwater port on the coast. A few years later, France invaded Holland, prompting England to seize control of the Cape Colony and, with it, Walvis Bay.

Even then, little was known about the interior. It wasn't until the middle of the 19th century that explorers, missionaries and traders started to venture inland, with Francis Galton and Charles John Andersson leading the way.

Oorlam incursions

By the second half of the 18th century, the Dutch settlers in the Cape of South Africa were not only expanding rapidly into the interior, but

THE OORLAM PEOPLE

Originating from the Cape, the Oorlam people were a variety of different groups, all speaking Khoisan languages, who left the Cape because of European expansion there. Some were outlaws, others wanted space far from the Europeans. Many broke away from fixed Nama settlements to join roving Oorlam bands. Under the leadership of *kapteins*, these groups would hunt, trade and steal for survival.

they were also effectively waging war on any of the indigenous people who stood in their way. In *Africa: A Biography of the Continent*, John Reader (see *Appendix 3*) comments:

> Khoisan resistance hardened as the frontier advanced during the 18th century. [The] Government [of the Cape's] edicts empowered [commando groups of settlers]... to wage war against all the region's Khoisan, who were now to be regarded as vermin. Slaughter was widespread. Official records show that commandos killed 503 Khoisan in 1774 alone, and 2,480 between 1786 and 1795. The number of killings that passed unrecorded can only be guessed at.

By 1793 the settler population in the Cape totalled 13,830 people, who between them owned 14,747 slaves.

With this pressure from the south, it is no wonder that mobile, dispossessed bands of Khoisan, known as Oorlam groups, pressed northward over the Orange River and into southern Namibia. They often had guns and horses, and had learned some of the Europeans' ways. However, they still spoke a Khoisan language and were of the same origins as the Nama pastoralists who had already settled in southern Namibia.

At that time, these Nama peoples seem to have settled into a life of relatively peaceful, pastoral coexistence. Thus the arrival of a few Oorlam groups was not a problem. However, around the start of the 19th century more Oorlams came, putting more pressure on the land, and soon regular skirmishes were a feature of the area.

In 1840 the increasingly unsettled situation was calmed by an agreement between the two paramount chiefs: Oaseb of the Nama, and Jonker Afrikaner of the Oorlam people. There was already much intermingling of the two groups, and so accommodating each other made sense – especially given the expansion of Herero groups further north.

The deal split the lands of southern Namibia between the various Nama and Oorlam groups, while giving the land between the Kuiseb and the Swakop rivers to the Oorlams. Further, Jonker Afrikaner was given rights over the people north of the Kuiseb, up to Waterberg.

Nama–Herero conflict By around the middle of the 18th century, the Herero people had expanded beyond Kaokoland, spreading at least as far south as the Swakop River. Their expansion south was now effectively blocked by Oorlam groups, led by Jonker Afrikaner, who won several decisive battles against Herero people around 1835 – resulting in his Afrikaner followers stealing many Herero cattle, and becoming the dominant power in central Namibia. From 1840, Jonker Afrikaner and his Oorlam followers created a buffer zone between the Hereros expanding from the north, and the relatively stable Nama groups in the south.

EUROPEAN COLONISATION

The missionaries In the early 1800s, missionaries were gradually moving into southern Namibia. The London Missionary Society and the German Rhenish and Finnish Lutheran Mission societies were all represented. These were important for several reasons. First, they tended to settle in one place, which became the nucleus around which the local Nama people would permanently settle. Often the missionaries would introduce the local people to different ways of cultivation: a further influence to settle in permanent villages, which gradually became larger.

Secondly, they acted as a focal point for traders, who would navigate through the territory from one mission to the next. This effectively set up Namibia's first trade routes – routes that soon became conduits for the local Nama groups to obtain European goods, from guns and ammunition to alcohol. It seems that the missionaries sometimes provided firearms directly to the local people for protection. While understandable, the net effect was that the whole area became a more dangerous place.

In 1811, Reverend Heinrich Schmelen founded Bethanie, and more missions followed. By December 1842, Rhenish missionaries were established where Windhoek now stands, surrounded by about 1,000 of Jonker Afrikaner's followers. The settlement soon started trading with the coast, and within a few years there was a steady supply of guns arriving.

Nama conflict In 1861 Jonker Afrikaner died while returning from a raid he had mounted on the Ovambo people (a group of Bantu origin who had settled in the far north of the country and displaced some of the Hereros). Jonker's death left a power vacuum in central Namibia.

There were many skirmishes for control during the rest of the 1860s, and much politicking and switching of alliances between the rival Nama groups (some of Oorlam descent). The main protagonists included the Witboois from around Gibeon, the Afrikaners based in Windhoek, the Swartboois, the Bondelswarts, the Topnaar and the Red Nation.

The traders By around 1850 many hunters and traders were penetrating Namibia's interior, in search of adventure and profit – usually in the form of ivory and ostrich feathers. Among these, Charles John Andersson was particularly important, both for his own role in shaping events, and also for the clear documentation that he left behind, including the fascinating books *Lake Ngami* and *The River Okavango* (see *Appendix 3*) – chronicling his great journeys of the late 1850s.

In 1860 Andersson bought up the assets of a mining company, and set up a centre for trading at Otjimbingwe, a very strategic position on the Swakop River, halfway between Walvis Bay and Windhoek. (Now it is at the crossroads of the D1953 and the D1976.) In the early 1860s he traded with the Nama groups in the area, and started to open up routes into the Herero lands further north and east. However, after losing cattle to a Nama raid in 1861, he recruited hunters (some the contemporary equivalent of mercenaries) to expand his operations and protect his interests.

In 1863 the eldest son of Jonker Afrikaner led a foolish raid on Otjimbingwe. He was defeated and killed by Andersson's men, adding to the leadership crisis among the Nama groups. By 1864 Andersson had formed an alliance with the paramount Herero chief, Kamaherero, and together they led a large army into battle with the Afrikaner Namas at Windhoek. This was indecisive, but did clearly mark the end of Nama domination of central Namibia, as well as inflicting a wound on Andersson from which he never fully recovered.

The peace of 1870 During the late 1860s the centre of Namibia was often in a state of conflict. The Hereros under Kamaherero were vying for control with the various Nama clans, as Charles Andersson and his traders became increasingly important by forming and breaking alliances with them all.

After several defeats, the Nama *kaptein* Jan Jonker led an army of Afrikaners to Okahandja in 1870 to make peace with Kamaherero. This was brokered by the German Wesleyan missionary Hugo Hahn – who had arrived in Windhoek in 1844, but been replaced swiftly after Jonker Afrikaner had complained about him, and requested his replacement by his missionary superiors.

This treaty effectively subdued the Afrikaners, and Hahn also included a provision for the Basters, who had migrated recently from the Cape, to settle at Rehoboth. The Afrikaners were forced to abandon Windhoek, and Herero groups occupied the area. Thus the Basters around Rehoboth effectively became the buffer between the Herero groups to the north, and the Namas to the south.

The 1870s was a relatively peaceful era, which enabled the missionaries and, especially, the various traders to extend their influence throughout the centre of the country. This most affected the Nama groups in the south, who began to trade more and more with the Cape. Guns, alcohol, coffee, sugar, beads, materials and much else flowed in. To finance these imports, local Nama chiefs and *kapteins* charged traders and hunters to cross their territory, and granted them licences to exploit the wildlife.

The Hereros, too, traded: but mainly for guns. Their social system valued cattle most highly, and so breeding bigger herds meant more to them than the new Western goods. Thus they emerged into the 1880s stronger than before, while the power of many of the Nama groups had waned.

THE SCRAMBLE FOR AFRICA In the last few decades of the 19th century the Portuguese, the British, the French, and Leopold II of Belgium were starting to embark on the famous 'Scramble for Africa'. Germany had long eschewed the creation of colonies, and Bismarck is widely quoted as stating: 'So long as I am Chancellor we shan't pursue a colonial policy.'

However, in March 1878 the English government of South Africa's Cape formally annexed an enclave around Walvis Bay. (The British had been asked earlier by missionaries to help instil order in the heartland of Namibia, but they didn't feel that it was worth the effort.)

In late 1883 a German merchant called Adolf Lüderitz started to buy land on the coast. He established the town named Lüderitzbucht – usually referred to now as Lüderitz – and began trading with the local Nama groups. (It was news of this act that was said to have finally prompted Britain to make Bechuanaland a protectorate.)

Faced with much internal pressure, Bismarck reversed his policy in May 1884. He dispatched a gunboat to Lüderitz and in July claimed Togo and Cameroon as colonies. By August Britain had agreed to Germany's claims on Lüderitz, from which sprang the German colony of South West Africa. Lüderitz itself was bought out a few years later by the newly formed German Colonial Company for South West Africa, and shortly after that the administration of the area was transferred directly to Germany's control.

In May 1884, Portugal proposed an international conference to address the territorial conflicts of the colonial powers in the Congo. This was convened in Berlin, with no Africans present, and over the next few years the colonial powers parcelled Africa up and split it between them. Among many territorial dealings, mostly involving pen-and-ruler decisions on the map of Africa, a clearly defined border between Britain's new protectorate of Bechuanaland and Germany's South

West Africa was established in 1890 – and Britain ceded a narrow corridor of land to Germany. This was subsequently named after the German Chancellor, Count von Caprivi, as the Caprivi Strip.

German South West Africa After a decade of relative peace, the 1880s brought problems to central Namibia again, with fighting between the Hereros, the Basters, and various Nama groups, notably the Afrikaners and the Swartboois. However, with German annexation in 1884 a new power had arrived. For the first five years, the official German presence in South West Africa was limited to a few officials stationed at Otjimbingwe. However, they had begun the standard colonial tactic of exploiting small conflicts by encouraging the local leaders to sign 'protection' treaties with Germany.

The Hereros, under Chief Maharero, signed in 1885, after which the German Commissioner Göring wrote to Hendrik Witbooi – the leader of the Witbooi Namas who occupied territory from Gibeon to Gobabis – insisting that he desist from attacking the Hereros, who were now under German protection. Witbooi wrote to Maharero, to dissuade him from making a 'pact with the devil' – he was, perhaps, ahead of his time in seeing this German move as an opening gambit in their bid for total control of Namibia.

In 1889 the first 21 German soldiers, Schutztruppe, arrived. More followed in 1890, by which time they had established a fort in Windhoek. That same year Maharero died, which enabled the German authorities to increase their influence in the internal politics of succession which brought Samuel Maharero to be paramount chief of the Herero. By 1892 the first contingent of settlers (over 50 people) had made their homes in Windhoek.

A fair trade? The 1890s and early 1900s saw a gradual erosion of the power and wealth of all Namibia's existing main groups in favour of the Germans. Gradually traders and adventurers bought more and more land from both the Nama and the Herero, aided by credit-in-advance agreements. A rinderpest outbreak in 1897 decimated the Herero's herds, and land sales were the obvious way to repay their debts. Gradually the Herero lost their lands and tension grew. The Rhenish Missionary Society saw the evil, and pressurised the German government to create areas where the Herero *could not* sell their land. Small enclaves were thus established, but these didn't address the wider issues.

THE 20TH CENTURY
Namibian war of resistance 1904–07 As land was progressively bought up, or sometimes simply taken from the local inhabitants by colonists, various skirmishes and small uprisings developed. The largest started in October 1903 with the Bondelswarts near Warmbad, which distracted most of the German Schutztruppe in the south. See *Appendix 3* for details of Mark Cocker's excellent *Rivers of Blood, Rivers of Gold* which gives a full account of this war.

The Herero nation had become increasingly unhappy about its loss of land, and in January 1904 Samuel Maharero ordered a Herero uprising against the German colonial forces. Initially he was clear to exclude as targets Boer and English settlers and German women and children. Simultaneously he appealed to Hendrik Witbooi, and other Nama leaders, to join the battle – they, however, stayed out of the fight.

At first the Hereros had success in taking many German farms and smaller outposts, and in severing the railway line between Swakopmund and Windhoek. However, later in 1904, the German General Leutwein was replaced by von Trotha

– who had a reputation for brutal oppression after his time in east Africa. Backed by domestic German opinion demanding a swift resolution, von Trotha led a large German force including heavy artillery against the Hereros. By August 1904 the Hereros were pushed back to their stronghold of Waterberg, with its permanent waterholes, and von Trotha proposed that the only solution to the problem was to eliminate or expel the Hereros as a nation. On 11 August, over 3,500 Herero warriors and their families assembled expecting peace negotiations, but instead were attacked by 1,500 German soldiers. In what would become known as the Battle of Waterberg it is estimated that 3,000–5,000 Hereros were killed. Those who survived fled east into the desert, and von Trotha set up guard to prevent their return. Immediately following the battle, any Herero that the German troops caught up with was put to death, including women and children. In October 1904, von Trotha stated that the Hereros were no longer German subjects, ordering them to leave Namibia or face death on their capture. This is cited in the UN Whitaker Report on Genocide as one of the earliest examples of genocide in the 20th century. However, in late 1904, following a change of orders, Herero prisoners were sent to concentration camps. Shark Island in Lüderitz is a notorious example, where captured prisoners were made to work as slave labour. Conditions at these camps were very poor, and death rates were high.

Thereafter, somewhat too late to be effective, Hendrik Witbooi's people also revolted against the Germans, and wrote encouraging the other Nama groups to do the same. The Red Nation, Topnaar, Swartbooi and Bondelswarts joined in attacking the Germans, though the last were largely incapacitated after their battles the previous year. The Basters stayed out of the fight.

For several years these Nama groups waged an effective guerrilla campaign against the colonial forces, using the waterless sands of the Kalahari as a haven in which the German troops were ineffective. However, in 1905 Hendrik Witbooi was killed, and January 1907 saw the last fighters sue for peace.

German consolidation With South West Africa under stable German control, there was an influx of German settler families and the colony began to develop rapidly. The settlers were given large plots of the country's most productive lands, the railway network was expanded, and many of the towns began to grow. The non-European Namibians were increasingly marginalised, and simply used as a source of labour.

The building of the railway to Lüderitz led to the discovery of diamonds around there in 1908, and the resulting boom encouraged an influx of prospectors and German opportunists. By that time the mine at Tsumeb was already thriving, and moving its copper produce south on the newly built railway.

The German settlers thrived until the declaration of World War I. Between 1907 and 1914 they were granted self-rule from Germany, a number of the main towns were declared municipalities, and many of Namibia's existing civic buildings were constructed.

World War I At the onset of World War I, Britain encouraged South Africa to push north and wrest South West Africa from the Germans. In July 1915, the German colonial troops surrendered to South African forces at Khorab, where a memorial now marks the spot. At the end of the war, Namibia became a League of Nations 'trust territory', assigned to the Union of South Africa as 'a sacred trust in the name of civilisation' to 'promote to the utmost the material and moral well-being of its inhabitants'. At the same time, the Caprivi Strip was incorporated back into Bechuanaland (now Botswana) – only to be returned 20 years later.

THE FINAL COLONISTS

South African rule After overcoming their initial differences, new colonists from South Africa and the existing German colonists soon discovered a common interest – the unabashed exploitation of the native population whose well-being they were supposed to be protecting.

Gradually more and more of the land in central Namibia was given to settler families, now often Boers from South Africa rather than Germans from Europe. The native population was restricted to various 'native areas' – usually poor land which couldn't be easily farmed by the settlers: Bushmanland and Hereroland in the Kalahari, Damaraland and Kaokoland bordering on the Namib. Much of the rest of the black population was confined to a strip of land in the north, as far from South Africa as possible, to serve as a reservoir of cheap labour for the mines – which South Africa was developing to extract the country's mineral wealth.

In 1947, after World War II, South Africa formally announced to the United Nations its intention to annex the territory. The UN, which had inherited responsibility for the League of Nations trust territories, opposed the plan, arguing that 'the African inhabitants of South West Africa have not yet achieved political autonomy'. Until 1961, the UN insisted on this point. Year after year it was systematically ignored by South Africa's regime.

The struggle for independence Between 1961 and 1968, the UN tried to annul the trusteeship and establish Namibia's independence. Legal pressure, however, was ineffective and some of the Namibian people led by the South West African People's Organisation (SWAPO) chose to fight for their freedom with arms. The first clashes occurred on 26 August 1966.

In 1968, the UN finally declared the South African occupation of the country as illegal and changed its name to Namibia. Efforts by the majority of the UN General Assembly to enforce this condemnation with economic sanctions were routinely vetoed by the Western powers of the UN Security Council – they had vested interests in the multi-national companies in Namibia and would stand to lose from the implementation of sanctions.

The independence of Angola in 1975 affected Namibia's struggle for freedom, by providing SWAPO guerrillas with a friendly rearguard. As a consequence the guerrilla war was stepped up, resulting in increased political pressure on South Africa. But strong internal economic factors also played heavily in the political arena. Right up to independence, the status quo preserved internal inequalities and privileges. Black Africans (approaching 90% of the population) consumed only 12.8% of the gross domestic product (GDP). Meanwhile the inhabitants of European origin (10% of the population) received 81.5% of the GDP. Three-quarters of agricultural production was in the hands of white farmers. Although average income per capita was (and remains) one of the highest in Africa, whites earned on average over 17 times more than blacks. The white population clearly feared they had a great deal to lose if a majority government came to power and addressed itself to these racially based inequalities.

However, external South African economic factors had perhaps the greatest effect in blocking Namibian independence. South African and multi-national companies dominated the Namibian economy and carried massive political influence. Prior to independence, the Consolidated Diamond Mines Company (a subsidiary of Anglo-American) contributed in taxes 40% of South Africa's administrative budget in Namibia. Multi-nationals benefited from extremely generous facilities granted to them by the South African administration in

Namibia. According to one estimate, the independence of Namibia would represent costs for South Africa of US$240 million in lost exports, and additional outlays of US$144 million to import foreign products.

In South Africa the official government view stressed the danger that a SWAPO government might present to Namibia's minority tribes (since SWAPO membership is drawn almost exclusively from the Ovambo ethnic group), while taking few serious steps towards a negotiated settlement for Namibian independence.

On the military side, South Africa stepped up its campaign against SWAPO, even striking at bases in southern Angola. It also supported Jonas Savimbi's UNITA (National Union for the Total Independence of Angola) forces in their struggle against the Soviet/Cuban-backed MPLA (Popular Movement for the Liberation of Angola) government in Luanda. Meanwhile, Cuban troops poured into Angola and aggravated the situation further by threatening the South African forces in Namibia.

Resolution 435 On the diplomatic front, the UN Security Council put forward a proposal (Resolution 435) in 1978, calling for, among other things, the cessation of hostilities, the return of refugees, the repeal of discriminatory legislation and the holding of UN-supervised elections. South Africa blocked this by tying any such agreement to the withdrawal of Cuban troops from Angola, and demanding guarantees that its investments in Namibia would not be affected. SWAPO refused to agree to special benefits for the European population and other minority groups, nor would it accept predetermined limitations to constitutional change following independence.

By 1987, all the states involved in the conflict were showing clear signs of wanting an end to hostilities. After 14 years of uninterrupted war, Angola's economy was on the brink of collapse. (The war is calculated to have cost the country US$13 billion.) On the other side, South Africa's permanent harassment of Angola, and military occupation of Namibia, were costing the regime dearly, both economically and diplomatically.

In December 1988, after prolonged US-mediated negotiations, an agreement was reached between South Africa, Angola and Cuba for a phased withdrawal of Cuban troops from Angola to be linked to the withdrawal of South African troops from Namibia and the implementation of Resolution 435.

INDEPENDENCE The independence process began on 1 April 1989, and was achieved with the help of the United Nations Transition Assistance Group (UNTAG). This consisted of some 7,000 people from 110 countries who worked from nearly 200 locations within the country to ensure free and fair elections and as smooth a transition period to independence as was possible.

In November 1989, 710,000 Namibians (a 97% turnout) voted in the members of the National Assembly that would draft the country's first constitution. SWAPO won decisively, but without the two-thirds majority it needed to write the nation's constitution single-handedly, thereby allaying the fears of Namibia's minorities. The 72 elected members (68 men and four women) of the Constituent Assembly, representing between them seven different political parties, soon reached agreement on a constitution for the new Namibia, which was subsequently hailed as one of the world's most democratic. Finally, at 00.20 on 21 March 1990, I watched as the Namibian flag replaced South Africa's over Windhoek, witnessed by Pérez de Cuéllar, the UN Secretary-General, F W de Klerk, the South African President, and Sam Nujoma, Namibia's first president.

The country's mood was peaceful and, on the day, ecstatic. There was a tremendous feeling of optimism, as (arguably) Africa's last colonial territory had earned its independence – after sustained diplomatic pressure and a bitter liberation struggle that stretched back to the turn of the century.

POLITICS SINCE INDEPENDENCE Since the start there has been every indication that Namibia would stand by its constitution and develop into a peaceful and prosperous state. Walvis Bay, previously disputed by South Africa, was transferred to Windhoek's control on 28 February 1994, and Namibia's relations with neighbouring countries remain good.

An important part of post-independence politics in Namibia is the redistribution of land. These reforms have taken place relatively peacefully and at a fairly slow pace, with land purchased for redistribution based on mutual agreement between buyer and seller. Periodically, with political pressures and upcoming elections, there is talk of increasing the rate of land redistribution. However, unless the constitution is amended to facilitate this change, the land reform programme will continue at its current pace.

In December 1994, general elections for the National Assembly returned SWAPO to power, with 53 out of 72 seats, and extended Sam Nujoma's presidency for a further five years. The main opposition among the remaining six parties was the Democratic Turnhalle Alliance (DTA).

Under the terms of the constitution, the president may serve only two terms in office. Despite that, Sam Nujoma went on to serve a third term, prompting concerns that the carefully crafted constitution was being pushed to one side. It wasn't until 2004 that Nujoma made way for his chosen successor, Hifikepunye Pohamba, while himself remaining head of the party. Five years later, in November 2009, SWAPO was again returned to power with over 74% of the vote, and Pohamba's position as president was consolidated. However, the role of opposition switched to the Rally for Democracy and Progress (RDP), with 11% of the vote and just 8 seats, overtaking the DTA, which is still haunted by the stigma of its co-operation with the former South African regime.

Like Nujoma, who has since retired from politics, Pohamba was a founding member of SWAPO and was head of the party until the 2014 Presidential election. As a leader, he was generally considered to be both liberal and honest, committed to continuing the party's policies and to governing by consensus.

In the run up to the November 2014 election, SWAPO announced plans for a gender-equality quota, referred to as a 'zebra system', where half of its seats in parliament will be held by women. Furthermore, if a minister is a woman, the deputy will be a man, and vice versa – with the implication that the roles will be swapped each election. At the time of writing, before the 'zebra system' was implemented, there were more men than women in parliament so, to avoid these men losing their positions, there are plans to extend parliament to 100 seats total.

2014 ELECTION RESULTS The most recent general election, in November 2014, was the first in Africa to use electronic voting. It saw SWAPO once again elected to power with an overwhelming majority. They won the presidential election with 87% of the vote, and the national assembly vote with 80%, taking 77 out of 96 seats in parliament – the party's highest level of support in any election. The role of largest opposition party switched once again, from the RDP back to the DTA, who won three and five seats.

Hage Geingob took over the presidency from Pohamba, who had reached his term limit. Geingob has been the first Prime Minister of Namibia following its independence in 1990, and held this position until 2002. He then briefly had a ministerial role, as well as working with an African policy group based in Washington. In 2007 he was elected Vice-President of SWAPO, becoming Prime Minister once again in 2012. His success in the 2014 elections was also significant in that he became the first non-Ovambo leader of SWAPO, and Namibia.

GOVERNMENT AND ADMINISTRATION

The Republic of Namibia's modern constitution, adopted on independence in 1990, was hailed as one of the world's most democratic. Its entrenched Bill of Rights provides for freedom of speech, press, assembly, association and religion. It also set up a bicameral Westminster-style parliament, with a strong executive and independent judiciary. General elections for the first house, the National Assembly, are held every five years. The constitution limits the president to a maximum of two terms of office – although Sam Nujoma's third term in office stretched this to breaking point in 1999.

For administrative purposes, the country is divided into 13 regions, replacing the earlier homeland territories that prevailed from 1963 until 1998. The 26 members of the second house, the National Council, are drawn from the regional councils, which are elected every six years.

ECONOMY

Before independence, the South African administration controlled the economy along traditional colonial lines. The country produced goods it did not consume but imported everything it needed, including food. Namibia still exports maize, meat and fish, and imports rice and wheat. However, although about half the workforce is employed in farming, productivity is an issue: the country's commercial agriculture is limited by a lack of water, while large sections of the wetter northern regions are farmed intensively by subsistence farmers.

Namibia inherited a well-developed infrastructure and considerable remaining mineral wealth. Mining is the mainstay of the economy, accounting for over 50% of the country's exports. There are important reserves of uranium, lead, zinc, tin, silver, copper and tungsten, as well as very rich deposits of alluvial diamonds. Oil, coal and iron ore deposits may also be present.

Tourism also plays an important and growing role in the formal economy, forecast to grow at 5.2% a year from 2012 to 2020. In the first years of independence, the number of visitors grew steadily by about 15% per year. Almost two decades later, those numbers had generally stabilised at around 10% a year. In 2011, visitor arrivals from overseas totalled 1,218,234, of whom 21,584 were from the UK, 17,946 from the USA, and 79,721 from Germany. Already tourism is a powerful earner of foreign exchange, a substantial employer, and a vital support for numerous community-development schemes. Namibia's main attractions for visitors are stunning scenery, pristine wilderness areas and first-class wildlife. As long as the country remains safe and its wilderness areas are maintained, then its potential for quality tourism is unrivalled in Africa.

Economically, Namibia remains dependent on South Africa for around a third of its exports – a significant reduction since the early years of independence – and two-thirds of imports. Its other main trading partners are the European Union,

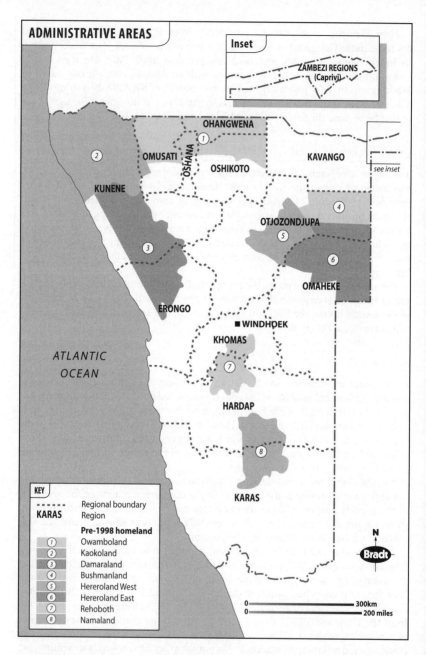

ADMINISTRATIVE AREAS

Inset

ZAMBEZI REGIONS
(Caprivi)

OHANGWENA

OMUSATI

OSHANA

OSHIKOTO

KAVANGO

see inset

KUNENE

OTJOZONDJUPA

OMAHEKE

ERONGO

■ WINDHOEK

KHOMAS

ATLANTIC
OCEAN

HARDAP

KEY

- - - - - Regional boundary
KARAS Region
Pre-1998 homeland
1 Owamboland
2 Kaokoland
3 Damaraland
4 Bushmanland
5 Hereroland West
6 Hereroland East
7 Rehoboth
8 Namaland

KARAS

N

Bradt

0 _____ 300km
0 _____ 200 miles

Angola, Canada and the USA. Realistically, the economy is likely to stay closely involved with that of South Africa, especially while Namibia continues to peg its currency to the value of the South African rand.

The revenue and foreign exchange from mining provide the financial muscle for the government's agenda. The government is developing structural changes to make the economy more equitable, and to diversify its components. Improved

THE GUANO TRADE

A poem quoted in *The River Okavango* by C J Andersson:

> There's an island that lies on West Africa's shore,
> Where penguins have lived since the flood or before,
> And raised up a hill there, a mile high or more.
> This hill is all guano, and lately 'tis shown,
> That finer potatoes and turnips are grown,
> By means of this compost, than ever were known;
> And the peach and the nectarine, the apple, the pear,
> Attain such a size that the gardeners stare,
> And cry, 'Well! I never saw fruit like that 'ere!'
> One cabbage thus reared, as a paper maintains,
> Weighed twenty-one stone, thirteen pounds and six grains,
> So no wonder Guano celebrity gains.

living conditions for the majority of Namibians are being realised by increasing the productivity of the subsistence areas, particularly in the populated north. However, there remains an enormous gap between the rich and the poor – over half the population subsists on US$2 per day – which must be closed if the country is to have a secure and prosperous future.

UPDATES WEBSITE

You can post your comments and recommendations, and read the latest feedback and updates from other readers online at www.bradtupdates.com/namibia.

2

People and Culture

People and Culture ETHNIC GROUPS 2

POPULATION OVERVIEW

At the time of the 2011 census, Namibia's population stood at 2,113,077, an increase of around 15.4% over the previous decade. That's a growth rate of around 1.5% per year. By 2013, the population stood at an estimated 2,303,315 (World Bank).

The effect of HIV/Aids on the Namibian population has been devastating. In 2007, 15.3% of adults were affected, with 5,100 related deaths and 66,000 more orphans. The latest UNAIDS estimates from 2013 suggest that HIV prevalence has fallen to 14.3%, but the number of deaths due to Aids during the year has risen to 6,600 with 96,000 children orphaned as a result. Life expectancy, which averaged 65 years at the turn of the century, fell to just 45 years in 2004, rising only slightly to 51 in 2007, and now, in 2014 it has leapt up again, back to 63 years. Although Namibia's doctor/patient ratio is one of the best in Africa, health provision remains patchy, especially outside urban centres.

While the population is densest in the north (near the Angolan border), where rainfall is heaviest, and in the capital, Windhoek, the overall density is exceptionally low: only around two people per square kilometre. Just over a third of Namibia's people are under 15 years of age, while only 7% are over 60. Around 87.5% of the population are black African in origin, and the remaining 12.5% are mostly of European or mixed race.

Of course, the statistics say nothing of the charm of many Namibians. If you venture into the rural areas you will often find that Namibians are curious about you. Chat to them openly and you will find most to be delightful. They will be pleased to help you where they can, and as keen to help you learn about them and their country as they are interested in your lifestyle and what brings you to their country.

ETHNIC GROUPS

When the colonial powers carved up Africa, the divisions between the countries bore virtually no resemblance to the traditional areas of the various ethnic groups, many of which therefore ended up split between two or more countries. As you will see, there are cultural differences between the groups in different parts of Namibia, but they are only a little more pronounced than those between the states of the USA, or the regions of the (relatively tiny) UK.

There continues to be a great deal of intermarriage and mixing of these various peoples and cultures – perhaps more so than there has ever been, because of the efficiency of modern transport systems. Generally, there is very little friction between these communities (whose boundaries, as we have said, are indistinct) and Namibia's various peoples live peacefully together.

In Namibia, which is typical of any large African country, historians identify numerous ethnic groups. The main ones, detailed below, are arranged alphabetically. Apart from Afrikaans, their languages fall into two main families: Khoisan and Bantu. The population sizes given are based on surveys done during the 1980s, and adjusted according to estimated average growth rates since then.

BASTERS These Afrikaans-speaking people are descendants of indigenous Nama – or Hottentot – women and the Dutch settlers who first arrived at the Cape in the early 17th century. The original 'coloured' or 'bastard' children found themselves rejected by both the white and the black communities in the Cape, so keeping together they relocated themselves further north away from the colonialists. Proudly calling themselves 'Basters', they set up farming communities and developed their own distinct social and cultural structures.

During the 1860s, white settlers began to push into these areas so, to avoid confrontation, the Basters crossed the Orange River in 1868 and moved northward once again. Trying to keep out of the way of the warring Hereros and Namas, they founded Rehoboth in 1871 and set up their own system of government under a *kaptein* (headman) and a *volksraad* (legislative council). Their support of the German colonial troops during the tribal uprisings brought them later protection and privileges.

Demands for self-rule and independence were repressed until the Rehoboth Gebiet was granted the status of an independent state in the 1970s. This move by the

SOCIAL GROUPS OR 'TRIBES'

The people of Africa are often viewed, from abroad, as belonging to a multitude of culturally and linguistically distinct 'tribes' – which are often portrayed as being at odds with each other. While there is certainly an enormous variety of different ethnic groups in Africa, most are closely related to their neighbours in terms of language, beliefs and way of life. Modern historians eschew the simplistic tags of 'tribes', noting that such groupings change with time.

Sometimes the word tribe is used to describe a group of people who all speak the same language; it may be used to mean those who follow a particular leader or to refer to all the inhabitants of a certain area at a given time. In any case, 'tribe' is a vague word that is used differently for different purposes. The term 'clan' (blood relations) is a smaller, more precisely defined unit – though rather too precise for our broad discussions here.

Certainly groups of people or clans who share similar languages and cultural beliefs do band together and often, in time, develop 'tribal' identities. However, it is wrong to then extrapolate and assume that their ancestors will have had the same groupings and allegiances centuries ago.

In Africa, as elsewhere in the world, history is recorded by the winners. Here the winners, the ruling class, may be the descendants of a small group of intruders who achieved dominance over a larger, long-established community. Over the years, the history of that ruling class (the winners) usually becomes regarded as the history of the whole community, or tribe. Two 'tribes' have thus become one, with one history – which will reflect the origins of that small group of intruders, and not the ancestors of the majority of the current tribe.

South African administration was made with the aim of reinforcing racial divisions among the non-whites – rather like in the South African 'independent homelands'.

Today, Namibia's Basters still have a strong sense of identity and make up around 2% of the population. Most still live and work as stock or crop farmers in the good cattle-grazing land around Rehoboth. Their traditional crafts include products like *karosses* (blankets), rugs, wall-hangings and cushion covers made of cured skins.

BUSHMEN/SAN There is not another social/language group on this planet which has been studied, written about, filmed and researched more than the Bushmen, or San, of the Kalahari, although they currently comprise only about 3% of Namibia's population. Despite this, or indeed because of it, popular conceptions about them, fed by their image in the media, are often strikingly out of step with the realities. Thus they warrant the extended section devoted to them here.

The aim of these next few pages is to try to explain some of the roots of the misconceptions, to look at some of the realities, and to make you think. Although I have spent a lot of time with Bushmen in the Kalahari, it is difficult to separate fact from oft-repeated, glossy fiction. If parts of this discussion seem disparate, it's a reflection of this difficulty.

Recent scientific observations on the Khoisan
Our view of the Bushmen is partly informed by some basic anthropological, linguistic and genetic research, which is worth outlining to set the scene. Most of this research applies to the Khoisan, comprising the various peoples of the Khoi and the Bushmen. All have relatively light golden-brown skin, almond-shaped eyes and high cheekbones. Their stature is generally small and slight, and they are now found across southern Africa.

Anthropology The first fossil records that we have of our human ancestors date back to at least about 60,000 years ago in east Africa. These are likely to have been the ancestors of everyone living today.

Archaeological finds from parts of the Kalahari show that human beings have lived here for at least 40,000 years. These are generally agreed to have been the ancestors of the modern Khoisan peoples living in Botswana today.

Language research Of the world's 20 linguistic families, four are very different from the rest. All these four are African families – and they include the Khoisan and the Niger-Congo (Bantu) languages. This is among the evidence that has led linguists to believe that human language evolved in Africa, and further analysis has suggested that this was probably among the ancestors of the Khoisan.

The Khoisan languages are distinguished by their wide repertoire of clicking sounds. Don't mistake these for simple: they are very sophisticated. It was observed by Dunbar (see *Appendix 3*) that, 'From the phonetic point of view these [the Khoisan languages] are the world's most complex languages. To speak one of them fluently is to exploit human phonetic ability to the full.'

At some point the Khoisan languages diverged from a common ancestor, and today three distinct groups exist: the northern, central and southern. Languages gradually evolve and change as different groups of people split up and move to new areas, isolated from their old contacts. Thus the evolution of each language is specific to each group.

According to Michael Main (see *Appendix 3*), the northern group are San and today they live west of the Okavango and north of Ghanzi, with representatives found as far afield as Angola. The southern group are also San, who live in the area between Kang and Bokspits in Botswana. The central group are the Khoi (or Khoe), who live in central Botswana, extending north to the eastern Okavango and Kasane, and west into Namibia, where they are known as the Nama.

Each of these three Khoisan language groups has many dialects. These have some similarities, but they are not closely related, and some are different to the point where there is no mutual understanding. Certain dialects are so restricted that only a small family group speaks them; it was reported recently that one San language died out completely with the death of the last speaker.

This huge number of dialects, and variation in languages, reflects the relative isolation of the various speakers, most of whom now live in small family groups as the Kalahari's arid environment cannot sustain large groups of people living together in one place as hunter-gatherers.

In Namibia, the three main Bushmen language groups are the Haixom in the northern districts of Otavi, Tsumeb and Grootfontein; the !Kung in Bushmanland; and the Mbarankwengo in west Caprivi. See also page 447 for more information on languages that use clicks.

Genetic discoveries Most genetically normal men have an X and a Y chromosome, while women have two X chromosomes. Unlike the other 22 pairs of (non-sex) chromosomes that each human has, there is no opportunity for the Y chromosome to 'swap' or 'share' its DNA with any other chromosome. Thus all the information in a man's Y chromosome will usually be passed on, without change, to all of his sons.

However, very rarely a single 'letter' in the Y chromosome will be altered as it's being passed on, thus causing a permanent change in the chromosome's genetic sequence. This will then be the start of a new lineage of slightly different Y chromosomes, which will be inherited by all future male descendants.

In November 2000, Professor Ronald Davis and a team of Stanford researchers (see *Appendix 3*) claimed to have traced back this lineage to a single individual man, and that a small group of east Africans (Sudanese and Ethiopians) and Khoisan are the closest present-day relatives of this original man. That is, their genetic make-up is closest to his. (It's a scientific 'proof' of the biblical Adam, if you like.)

This is still a very contentious finding, with subsequent researchers suggesting at least ten original male sources ('Adams') – and so although this is interesting, the jury remains out on the precise details of all these findings. If you're interested in the latest on this, then you'll find a lot about it on the web – start searching with keywords: 'Khoisan Y chromosome'.

Historical and current views of the Bushmen
Despite much evidence and research, our views of the Bushmen seem to have changed relatively little since both the Bantu groups and the first Europeans arrived in southern Africa.

The settlers' view Since the first Bantu farmers started migrating south through east Africa, the range of territory occupied by the foragers, whose Stone Age technology had dominated the continent, began to condense. By the time the first white settlers appeared in the Cape, the Khoisan people were already restricted to Africa's southwestern corners and the Kalahari.

All over the world, farmers occupy clearly demarcated areas of land, whereas foragers will move more and often leave less trace of their presence. In Africa, this made it easier for farmers, first black then white, to ignore any traditional land rights that belonged to foraging people.

Faced with the loss of territory for hunting and gathering, the foragers – who, by this time were already being called 'Bushmen' – made enemies of the farmers by killing cattle. They waged a guerrilla war, shooting poison arrows at parties of men who set out to massacre them. They were feared and loathed by the settlers, who, however, captured and valued their children as servants.

Some of the Khoisan retreated north from the Cape – like the ancestors of Namibia's Nama people. Others were forced to labour on the settlers' farms, or were thrown into prison for hunting animals or birds which had been their traditional prey, but which were now designated property of the Crown.

This story is told by Robert J Gordon in *The Bushman Myth: The Making of a Namibian Underclass* (see *Appendix 3*). He shows that throughout history the hunter-gathering Bushmen have been at odds with populations of settlers who divided up and 'owned' the land in the form of farms. The European settlers proved to be their most determined enemy, embarking on a programme of legislation and massacre. Many Bushmen died in prison, with many more shot as 'vermin'.

Thus the onslaught of farmers on the hunter-gatherers accelerated between the 1800s and the mid-1900s. This helped to ensure that hunter-gathering as a lifestyle continued to be practical only in marginal areas that couldn't be economically farmed – like the Kalahari. Archaeological evidence suggests that hunter-gatherer peoples have lived for about 60,000 years at sites like the Tsodilo Hills in Botswana.

Western views Though settlers in the Cape interacted with Khoisan people, so did Europe and the US, in a very limited way. Throughout the 1800s and early 1900s a succession of Khoisan people were effectively enslaved and brought to Europe and the US for exhibition. Sometimes this was under the guise of anthropology, but usually it didn't claim to be anything more than entertainment.

One of the first was the 'Hottentot Venus' – a woman who was probably of Khoisan extraction who was exhibited around London and Paris from 1810 to 1815, as an erotic curiosity for aristocrats.

A string of others followed. For example, the six Khoisan people exhibited at the Coney Island Pleasure Resort, beside New York, and later in London in the 1880s and billed as the 'missing link between apes and men', and the 'wild dancing Bushman' known as Franz brought to England around 1913 by Paddy Hepston (see Parsons's piece in *Botswana Notes & Records*, detailed in *Appendix 3*).

In the 1950s a researcher from Harvard, John Marshall, came to the Kalahari to study the !Kung San. He described a peaceful people living in harmony with nature, amid a land that provided all their needs. The groups had a deep spirituality and no real hierarchy: it seemed like the picture of a modern Eden (especially when viewed through post-war eyes). Marshall was a natural cameraman and made a film that follows the hunt of a giraffe by four men over a five-day period. It swiftly became a classic, both in and outside of anthropological circles.

Further research agreed, with researchers noting a great surfeit of protein in the diet of the !Kung San and low birth rates akin to modern industrial societies.

Again the Bushmen were seen as photogenic and sources of good copy and good images. Their lives were portrayed in romantic, spiritual terms in the book and film *The Lost World of the Kalahari* by Laurens van der Post (see *Appendix 3*). This documentary really ignited the worldwide interest in the Bushmen and led to subsequent films such as *The Gods Must Be Crazy*. All the images conveyed an idyllic view of the Bushmen as untainted by contact with the modern world.

The reality The reality was much less rosy than the first researchers thought. Some of their major misconceptions have been outlined particularly clearly in chapter 13 of John Reader's *Africa: A Biography of the Continent* (see *Appendix 3*). He points out that far from an ideal diet, the nutrition of the Bushmen was often critically limited, lacking vitamins and fatty acids associated with a lack of animal fat in their diet. Far from a stable population with a low birth rate, it seems likely that there had been a decline in the birth rate in the last few

TRADITIONAL LIFE FOR THE BUSHMEN

Looking at the current lifestyle of the Bushmen who remain in the more remote areas of the Kalahari, it's difficult not to lapse into a romantic view of ignoring present realities. There are too many cultural aspects to cover here, so instead I've just picked out a few that you may encounter.

NOMADS OF THE KALAHARI Perhaps the first idea to dispel is that the Bushmen are nomads. They're not. Bushmen family groups have clearly defined territories, called a *n!ore* (in the Ju/'hoansi language), within which they forage. This is usually centred on a place where there is water, and contains food resources sufficient for the basic subsistence of the group.

Groups recognise rights to the *n!ore*, which is passed on from father to first-born son. Any visiting people would ask permission to remain in these. Researchers have mapped these areas, even in places like the Central Kalahari.

SOCIAL SYSTEM The survival of the Bushmen in the harsh environment of the Kalahari is evidence of the supreme adaptability of humans. It reflects their detailed knowledge of their environment, which provides them not only with food, but with materials for shelter and medicine in the form of plants.

Another very important factor in their survival is the social system by which the Bushmen live. Social interaction is governed by unwritten rules that bind the people in friendship and harmony, which must be maintained. One such mechanism is the obligation to distribute the meat from a large kill. Another is the obligation to lend such few things as are individually possessed, thereby incurring a debt of obligation from the borrower.

The San also practise exogamy, which means they have an obligation to marry outside the group. This creates social bonds between groups. Such ties bind the society inextricably together, as does the system of gift exchange between separate groups.

Owing to environmental constraints a group will consist of between 80 and 120 people, living and moving together. In times of shortage the groups will be much smaller, sometimes consisting of only immediate family – parents, grandparents and children. They must be able to carry everything they possess. Their huts are light constructions of grass, and they have few possessions.

Because no-one owns property, no-one is richer or has more status than another. A group of Bushmen has a nominal leader, who might be a senior member of the group, an expert hunter, or the person who owns the water rights. The whole group takes decisions affecting them, often after vociferous discussions.

HUNTER-GATHERERS Any hunter-gatherer lifestyle entails a dependence on, and extensive knowledge of, the environment and the resident fauna and flora found generations. The likely cause for this was periods of inadequate nourishment during the year when they lost weight from lack of food, stress and the great exertions of their lifestyle.

In fact, it seems likely that the San, whom we now see as foragers, are people who, over the last two millennia, have become relegated to an underclass by the relentless advance of the black and white farmers who did not recognise their original rights to their traditional land.

there. In the Kalahari, water is the greatest need and the Bushmen know which roots and tubers provide liquid to quench thirst. They create sip wells in the desert, digging a hole, filled with soft grass, then using a reed to suck water into the hole, and send it bubbling up the reed to fill an ostrich egg. Water-filled ostrich eggs are also buried at specific locations within the group's 'area'. When necessary the Bushmen will strain the liquid from the rumen of a herbivore and drink that.

Researchers have observed that any hunting is done by the men. When living a basic hunting and gathering lifestyle, with little external input, hunting provides only about 20% of their food. The remaining 80% is provided largely by the women, helped by the children, who forage and gather wild food from the bush. By age 12 a child might know about 200 plant species, and an adult more than 300.

HUNTING The Bushmen in the Kalahari are practised hunters, using many different techniques to capture the game. Their main weapons are a very light bow, and an arrow made of reed, in three sections. The arrowhead is usually poisoned, using one of a number of poisons obtained from specific plants, snakes and beetles. (Though most Bushmen know how to hunt with bows and arrows, the actual practice is increasingly uncommon when it's not done to earn money from observing visitors.)

All the hunters may be involved in the capture of large game, which carries with it certain obligations. The whole group shares in the kill and each member is entitled to a certain portion of the meat.

There are different methods for hunting small game, which only the hunter's family would usually share. One method for catching spring hares involves long (sometimes 4m), flexible poles made of thin sticks, with a duiker's horn (or more usually now a metal hook) fastened to the end. These are rammed into the hare's hole, impaling the animal, which is then pulled or dug out.

TRANCE DANCING Entertainment for the Bushmen, when things are good, usually involves dancing. During some dances, which may often have overtones of ritual or religion, the dancers may fall into a trance and collapse.

These trances are induced by a deliberate breathing technique, with a clear physiological explanation. Dances normally take place in the evening, around a fire. Then the women, children and old people will sit around and clap, while some of the younger men will dance around the circle in an energetic, rhythmic dance. Often this is all that happens, and after a while the excitement dies down and everyone goes to sleep.

However, on fairly rare occasions, the dancers will go into a trance. After several hours of constant exertion, they will shorten their breathing. This creates an oxygen deficiency, which leads to the heart pumping more strongly to compensate. Blood pressure to the brain increases; the dancer loses consciousness and collapses.

The Bushmen and the modern media Though scientific thought has moved on since the 1950s, much of the media has not. The Bushmen are still perceived to be hot news.

The outpost of Tsumkwe is the centre for many of the Bushmen communities in Namibia. It's a tiny crossroads with a school and a handful of buildings, in a remote corner of northeastern Namibia. Despite its isolation, by 2001 this desert outpost was hosting no fewer than 22 film crews per year. Yes, really; that's an average of almost two full-scale film crews each month – not counting a whole host of other print journalists and photographers. These numbers are probably even greater now.

Talk to virtually any of the directors and you'll realise that they arrive with very clear ideas about the images that they want to capture. They all think they're one of the first, they think they're original, and they want to return home with images which match their preconceived ideas about the Bushmen as 'the last primitive hunter-gatherers'.

As an example, you'll often see pictures in the media of Bushmen hunters in traditional dress walking across a hot, barren salt-pan. When asked to do these shoots the Bushman's usual comment is, 'Why? There's no point. We'd never go looking for anything there.' But the shots look spectacular and win prizes… so the photographers keep asking for them. From the Bushmen's perspective, they get paid for the shots, so why not pose for the camera? I'd do the same!

Thus our current image of the San is really one that *we* are constantly recreating. It's the one that we expect. But it doesn't necessarily conform to any reality. So on reflection, popular thinking hasn't moved on much from Marshall's first film in the 1950s.

CAPRIVIAN The Caprivi people, whose language is of the Bantu family, live in the fertile, swampy land between the Chobe and Zambezi rivers – at the eastern end of the Caprivi Strip. The agricultural potential of the area is one of the highest in Namibia, but this potential has been largely unrealised. Before the war with Angola, and the heavy involvement of South African troops (which brought roads and infrastructure), the whole of the Kavango and Caprivi region was one of the least developed in Namibia.

Like the Kavango and the Ovambo, the Caprivians farm a variety of crops, raise livestock, and fish. They make up about 4% of Namibia's population, and most can be considered as members of one of five main groups: the Masubia and Mafwe groups, and the smaller Mayeyi, Matotela and Mbukushu. Their traditional crafts include baskets (extensively used for fish traps and carrying grain), wooden masks and stools, drums, pottery, leather goods and stone carvings.

DAMARA Along with the Nama and the Bushmen, or San, the Damara are presumed to be the original inhabitants of Namibia, speaking a similar 'Khoi' click language (Khoisan family). Like the Nama, the Damara were primarily hunting people who owned few cattle or goats. Traditionally enemies of the Nama and Herero, they supported the German colonial forces at Waterberg against the Herero uprisings and were rewarded for their loyalty by an 'enlarged' homeland from the German authorities: Damaraland, the area adjacent to the Skeleton Coast (now the southern part of the Kunene Region). Of the Damara today, only a quarter manage to survive in this area – the rest work on commercial farms, in mines or as labourers in the towns. They make up about 7% of Namibia's population, sharing their language with the Namas. Damara women share the same Victorian style of dress as the Herero and Nama women.

Traditionally Damara people were thought of as miners, smelters, copper traders, stock farmers and tobacco growers, until the end of the 19th century when they moved to Damaraland and started practising agriculture.

Their traditional crafts include leather goods, glass and metal bead-work, wooden bowls and buckets, clay pipes and bowls, and more recently 'township art' such as wire cars.

HERERO In 1904, the Hereros and the Namas staged a massive uprising against the German colonial troops in South West Africa. It ended in a bloody massacre of over half the total Herero population at the battle of Waterberg (see page 9).

The few Herero that survived fled into the Kalahari, some crossing into what is now Botswana. In 2001, the Herero People's Reparation Corporation, based in Washington, sued the German government and two companies for £2.6 billion. The case was fiercely contested, and was finally dismissed in its entirety.

Today, the Herero constitute the third-largest ethnic group in Namibia, after the Ovambo and Kavango – over 7% of the present population. Their language is Bantu-based. In Botswana, they are a minority group inhabiting Ngamiland, south and west of the Okavango Delta.

Traditionally pastoralists, the Herero prefer raising cattle to growing crops – prestige and influence are dependent on the number of cattle possessed. Today, the majority of Namibian Herero use their cattle-handling skills on commercial farms.

Herero women wear very distinctive long, flowing Victorian gowns and headdresses. Multiple layers of petticoats made from over 12m of material give a voluminous look (two women walking side-by-side occupy the whole pavement!). Missionaries, who were appalled by the Herero's semi-nakedness, introduced this style of dress in the 1800s. Now the Herero continue to wear these heavy garments and it has become their traditional dress – though they will admit just how hot it is if asked.

Traditional Herero crafts include skin and leather products, basketry, jewellery and ornaments, and dolls in traditional Victorian-style dress, which are a very popular curio for visitors.

HIMBA The Himba people share a common ethnic origin and language with the Hereros, having split from the main Herero group on the Namibia–Botswana border and moved west to present-day Kaokoland in the northern Kunene in search of available land. The place they found, however, is mountainous, sparsely vegetated and very arid. Cattle are central to their way of life, with the size of the herd an indication of wealth and prestige – but overgrazing of the poor soils is a major problem. Thus these people are semi-nomadic, moving with their cattle in search of suitable pasture.

The Himba are a minority group in Namibia (numbering less than 1% of the population), and live almost entirely in their traditional areas in remote Kaokoland. Their society is traditionally polygamous, with men having up to eight wives.

Of all Namibia's ethnic groups, the Himba – or at least, Himba women and children – are probably the most photographed. Himba women adorn their skin and hair – and often that of their children – with deep-red ochre powder mixed with fat, both for protection against insects and the sun, and for cleanliness; water for washing is a rarity. Their striking appearance is further enhanced by elaborate headdresses and jewellery, much of it symbolic, while their clothes are limited to a simple goatskin skirt, and – for warmth – a rough blanket. As in many traditional societies, the men tend the cattle, so are usually absent during the day, leaving the bulk of the work to the women.

Traditional Himba crafts include work in skin and leather (headdresses, girdles and aprons), jewellery (copper-wire neckbands and bracelets), musical instruments, wooden neck rests, basketry and pottery.

KAVANGO The Kavango people share their name with the Okavango River, which forms part of the northern border of Namibia with Angola. Not surprisingly, they have based their traditional agricultural and fishing existence on the fertile land and good water supply afforded by this environment.

Many of the Kavango, who used to live on the northern side of the Okavango River in Angola, came south of the river into Namibia during the 1970s, 1980s and early 1990s. They fled from the civil war between South African-backed UNITA rebels and the Soviet/Cuban-backed MPLA regime. As a consequence, the Kavango population in Namibia more than doubled in size during the 1970s, and now forms the second-largest ethnic group in the country, making up almost 10% of the population.

CULTURAL GUIDELINES

Comments here are intended to be a general guide, just a few examples of how to travel more sensitively. They should not be viewed as blueprints for perfect Namibian etiquette. Cultural sensitivity is really a state of mind, not a checklist of behaviour – so here we can only hope to give the sensitive traveller a few pointers in the right direction.

When we travel, we are all in danger of leaving negative impressions with local people whom we meet: by snapping that picture quickly, while the subject is not looking; by dressing scantily, offending local sensitivities; or by just brushing aside the feelings of local people, with the high-handed superiority of a rich Westerner. These things are easy to do, in the click of a shutter, or flash of a large dollar bill.

However, you will get the most representative view of Namibia if you cause as little disturbance to the local people as possible. You will never blend in perfectly when you travel – your mere presence there, as an observer, will always change the local events slightly. However, if you try to fit in and show respect for local culture and attitudes, then you may manage to leave positive feelings behind you.

One of the easiest, and most important, ways to do this is with **greetings**. African societies are rarely as rushed as Western ones. When you first talk to someone, you should greet him or her leisurely. So, for example, if you enter a shop and want some help, do not just ask outright, 'Where can I find…?' That would be rude. Instead you will have a better reception (and better chance of good advice) by saying:

Traveller:	'Good afternoon.'
Namibian:	'Good afternoon.'
Traveller:	'How are you?'
Namibian:	'I am fine, how are you?'
Traveller:	'I am fine, thank you.' (Pause) 'Do you know where I can find…?'

This approach goes for anyone – always greet them first. For a better reception still, learn these phrases of greeting in the local language. English-speakers are often lazy about learning languages, and, while most Namibians understand English, a greeting given in an appropriate local language will be received with delight. It implies that you are making an effort to learn a little of their language and culture, which is always appreciated.

Closely related to the Ovambos, and with a Bantu-based language, the Kavango people are traditionally fishermen, and crop and stock farmers. Their craftwork includes woodcarving (bowls, spoons, mortars, masks, boxes and furniture), basketry, pottery, jewellery (grass bracelets and copper-bead necklaces), mats, spears, daggers, pipes, musical instruments and headdresses.

NAMA The Nama, or Hottentot, people are perhaps the closest in origin to the Bushmen or San, traditionally sharing a similar type of 'click' or Khoisan language, the same light-coloured yellow skin, and a hunter-gatherer way of life. One of the first peoples in Namibia, their tribal areas were traditionally communal property, as indeed was any item unless it was actually made by an individual. Basic differences in the perception of ownership of land and hunting grounds led in the past to frequent conflicts with the Herero people. The 60,000 or so Nama today, making up about 5% of Namibia's population, live mostly in the area that was Namaland, north

Very rarely in the town or city you may be approached by someone who doesn't greet you, but tries immediately to sell you something, or hassle you in some way. These people have learned that foreigners aren't used to greetings, so have adapted their approach accordingly. An effective way to dodge their attentions is to reply to their questions with a formal greeting, and then politely, but firmly, refuse their offer. This is surprisingly effective.

Another part of the normal greeting ritual is **handshaking**. As elsewhere, you would not normally shake a shop-owner's hand, but you would shake hands with someone to whom you are introduced. Get some practice when you arrive, as there is a gentle, three-part handshake used in southern Africa which is easily learnt – but not easily taught in a book.

Your **clothing** is an area that can easily give offence. Skimpy, revealing clothing is frowned upon by most Namibians, especially when worn by women. Shorts are fine for the bush or the beach, but dress conservatively and avoid short shorts, especially in the more rural areas. Respectable locals will wear long trousers (men) or long skirts (women).

Photography is a tricky business. Most Namibians will be only too happy to be photographed – provided you ask their permission first. Sign language is fine for this question: just point at your camera, shrug your shoulders, and look quizzical. The problem is that then everyone will smile for you, producing the type of 'posed' photograph which you may not want. However, stay around and chat for 5 or 10 minutes more, and people will get used to your presence, stop posing and you will get more natural shots (a camera with a quiet shutter is a help). Note that care is needed near government buildings, army bases and similar sites of strategic importance. You must ask permission before snapping photographs or you risk people taking offence.

The specific examples above can teach only so much; they are general by their very nature. But wherever you find yourself, if you are polite and considerate to the Namibians you meet, then you will rarely encounter any cultural problems. Watch how they behave and, if you have any doubts about how you should act, then ask someone quietly. They will seldom tell you outright that you are being rude, but they will usually give you good advice on how to make your behaviour more acceptable.

of Keetmanshoop in the south of Namibia. Nama women share the same Victorian traditional dress as the Herero and Damara women.

The Nama people are traditionally stock farmers, and work mainly on commercial farms. Their crafts include leatherwork (aprons and collecting bags), *karosses* (mantle of animal skins) and mats, musical instruments (eg: reed flutes), jewellery, clay pots and tortoiseshell powder containers.

OVAMBO By far the largest group in Namibia, the Ovambo people (sometimes called Owambo) make up just over half the population. Their language, Oshivambo (sometimes known as Ambo or Vambo), is Bantu-based. The great majority still live in their traditional area of Ovamboland in the remote far north of the country, along the border with Angola. This area receives one of the highest rainfalls in the country, and supports a range of traditional crops as well as allowing good grazing for their extensive cattle herds.

Before independence, the existence of half a million indigenous Namibians on the border with (socialist) Angola seriously perturbed the South African administration. By investing money into the region, the administration hoped to establish a buffer against Angola to protect the areas in the interior. The policy backfired – Ovamboland became the heartland of SWAPO during the struggle for independence. The consequent harassment by the South African Defence Force, and a rapid population increase (exacerbated by a large influx of refugees from Angola), left the area overpressurised and undeveloped, a situation that is now being addressed, with substantial investment being sunk into the region.

Most of the Ovambo belong to one of eight tribes: the Kwanyama, Ndongo, Kwambi, Ngandjera, Mbalantu, Kwaluudhi, Nkolokadhi and Eunda. Typically, they are traders and businessmen.

Traditional Ovambo craftwork includes basketry, pottery, jewellery, wooden combs, wood and iron spears, arrows and richly decorated daggers, musical instruments, fertility dolls, and ivory buttons (*ekipa*) – worn by women and conveying their status and indicating their husband's/family's wealth.

OTHER NAMIBIANS
Coloured Namibians
The term 'coloured' is generally used in southern Africa to describe people of mixed (black–white) origin. These coloured people maintain a strong sense of identity and separateness from either blacks or whites – though they generally speak either Afrikaans or English (or frequently both) rather than an ethnic 'African' language. They are very different in culture from any of Namibia's ethnic groups, white or black.

Most coloureds in Namibia live in the urban areas – Windhoek, Keetmanshoop and Lüderitz. Those in Walvis Bay are mainly fishermen, and some in the south are stock farmers. Their traditional crafts centre mainly on musical instruments, like drums and guitars.

White Namibians
The first whites to settle in Namibia were the Germans who set up trading businesses around the port of Lüderitz in 1884. Within a few years, Namibia formally became a German colony, and German settlers began to arrive in ever-increasing numbers. Meanwhile, white farmers of Dutch origin (the Boers, who first settled on the African continent at the Cape in 1652), were moving northward in search of land free from British interference, following the cession of the Dutch Cape Colony to the British government in 1806. After World War I, when control of German Namibia was transferred to South Africa, Boers (Afrikaners)

moved into Namibia, and soon significantly outnumbered the German settlers.

The first Namibians of European descent came as missionaries, traders and hunters, though they are now found throughout the economy. They live mainly in urban, central and southern parts of the country – though they also own and run most of the commercial farming operations. Virtually all of the tourism industry is managed by white Namibians. Perhaps a legacy of colonialism, they are normally among the more affluent members of society.

The crafts currently produced by the whites include leatherwork (shoes, handbags, belts), German Christmas and Easter decorations, needlework (including embroidery, patchwork and clothing), printed T-shirts, costume jewellery, greetings cards and various classical European art forms.

There is also a significant 'expat' community in Namibia. Typically they stay for two or three years, working on short-term contracts, often for either multi-national companies or aid agencies, but some then choose to take up residence. Most are highly skilled individuals who come to share their knowledge with Namibian colleagues – often teaching skills that are in short supply in Namibia.

LANGUAGE

Namibia's variety of languages reflects the diversity of its peoples – black and white. Following independence, one of the new government's first actions was to make English Namibia's only official language (removing Afrikaans and German). This step sought to unite Namibia's peoples and languages under one common tongue ('the language of the liberation struggle'), leaving behind the colonial overtones of Afrikaans and German. This choice is also helping with international relations and education, as English-language materials are the most easily available.

While English is taught throughout the education system, Afrikaans is still the lingua franca among many of the older generation, and in rural areas Afrikaans tends to be more widely used than English (which may not be spoken at all) – despite the widespread enthusiasm felt for the latter. Virtually all black Namibians also speak one or more African languages, and many will speak several. Many white Namibians (especially those in the commercial farming communities of the central region) regard German as their first language, though they will normally understand English and Afrikaans as well.

Among the indigenous languages there are two basic language groups which bear no relation to each other: Bantu (eg: Ovambo, Herero) and Khoisan (eg: Bushmen, Nama). Linguistics experts have identified at least 28 different languages and numerous dialects among the indigenous population. Although these different language groupings do loosely correspond to what might be described as Namibia's 'tribes', the distinctions are blurred by the natural linguistic ability of most Namibians. Thus, ethnic groupings provide only a rough guide to the many languages and dialects of Namibia's people.

RELIGION

Some 85–90% of the population follows a Christian religion. Dutch Reformed, Roman Catholic, Lutheran, Methodist and Presbyterian churches are all common. However, most black Namibians will also subscribe to some traditional African religious practices and beliefs. Among these are ancestor worship, practised by the Herero and Himba, whose traditional homesteads incorporate a holy fire through which they can communicate with the dead.

EDUCATION

Since independence, the government has poured resources into an expansion of the education system. To assist with this expansion, many foreign teachers came to Namibia with the help of NGOs and overseas aid agencies. Around 86% of children are enrolled in primary school, and adult literacy is estimated at about 89%. There are small primary schools in the most rural of areas, some of them mobile to cater for a semi-nomadic population, while large secondary schools are established in the regional centres. Children in secondary school study for the IGCSE (General Certificate of Secondary Education) and then move on to the HIGCSE. Lessons are taught almost exclusively in English, although some indigenous languages may also be taught. The state-run University of Namibia, established immediately after independence, is based in Windhoek, with 11 satellite campuses nationwide.

CULTURE

Namibia boasts some of the world's oldest rock paintings and engravings, which have been attributed to ancestors of the Bushmen. The scenes are naturalistic depictions of animals, people, hunting, battles and social rituals. Local geology determined the colour usage in the paintings. Some are monochrome pictures in red, but many are multicoloured, using ground-up earth pigments mixed with animal fat to produce 'paints' of red, brown, yellow, blue, violet, grey, black and white. Rock engravings have also been found, often in areas where there is an absence of smooth, sheltered rock surfaces to paint on. Some of the best examples of paintings and engravings are in the Brandberg, Twyfelfontein and Erongo areas.

However, there is more to Namibian creativity than rock paintings and engravings. Traditional arts and crafts include basketry, woodcarving, leatherwork, bead-work, pottery, music-making and dancing. More contemporary arts and crafts encompass textile weaving and embroidery, sculptures, printmaking and theatre.

The annual Bank Windhoek Arts Festival (*www.bankwindhoekarts.com.na*) draws together every aspect of the arts, from music, dance and drama to the visual arts and even creative writing. Events are held primarily in Windhoek, but participants are selected from across the country.

For up-to-date information on cultural events, buy a copy of *The Namibian* and read its 'Arts and Entertainment' section.

CRAFTS AND VISUAL ARTS

Basketry Baskets are typically woven by women and are part of the crafts tradition of the northern Namibian peoples – Caprivi, Himba, Herero, Kavango and Ovambo.

Most baskets are made from strips of makalani palm leaves coiled into a shape that is determined by its purpose: flat, plate shapes for winnowing baskets, large bowl-shaped baskets for carrying things, small closed baskets with lids and bottle shapes for storing liquids. Symbolic geometric patterns are woven into a basket as it is being made, using strips of palm leaves dyed in dark browns, purples and yellows.

Recently, baskets have been made using strips of recycled plastic bags to wind around the palm-leaf strips or grasses.

Woodcarving The northern Namibian peoples – Bushmen, Caprivians, Damara, Himba, Kavango and Ovambo – have a tradition of woodcarving, which is usually practised by men. Wooden objects are carved using adzes, axes and knives; lathe-turned work is not traditional. Carving, incising and burning techniques are used to decorate the wood. A wide range of woodcarving is produced: sculptural headrests, musical instruments such as drums and thumb pianos; masks, walking sticks, toys, animal figurines, bows, arrows and quivers; domestic utensils including oval and round bowls and buckets as well as household furniture.

Leatherwork Leatherwork is practised by all the peoples of Namibia. The leather-workers are usually women, though men also participate if large, heavy skins are being tanned or dyed. The skins of cattle, sheep and game are tanned and dyed using vegetable materials, animal fat and sometimes red ochre. The goods crafted include carrying skins and bags, tobacco pouches, *karosses* (to be used as rugs or blankets) and traditional clothing – headdresses, girdles/aprons and sandals as well as more contemporary fashion accessories like shoes, boots, handbags, belts and jackets.

Bead-work Bead-work is traditionally the domain of the Bushman and Himba peoples. The Bushmen make beads from ostrich-egg shells, porcupine quills, seeds, nuts and branches, and also use commercially produced glass beads. The Himba people use iron beads and shells. In both peoples, men tend to make the beads and the women weave and string them into artefacts. These include necklaces, bracelets, armlets, anklets and headbands. The Bushmen also use bead-work to decorate their leatherwork bags, pouches and clothing – a particularly striking traditional design being the multicoloured circular 'owl's-eye'.

In addition to bead-work, the Himba people make a traditional iron-bead and leather head ornament (*oruvanda*) that all women wear, and belts (*epanda*), worn only by mothers.

Pottery Namibia's more renowned potters are women from the Caprivi, Kavango and Ovambo peoples. Traditionally, geometric patterns of various colours decorate the vessels of different shapes and uses. Contemporary potters are experimenting with decoration by textures and a variety of sculptural motifs.

Textiles Nama women traditionally used patchwork techniques when making dresses and shawls. Now these women utilise their sewing skills in the art of embroidery and appliqué, making table and bed linens, cushion covers and wall-hangings depicting Namibian animals and village scenes.

Another, rather more recent textile craft is the hand-weaving of pure karakul wool into wall-hangings and rugs. The designs are usually geometric patterns or Namibian landscapes, though almost any design can be commissioned, and colours can be matched to your own décor.

Painting, sculpture and prints The work of contemporary Namibian artists, sculptors and printmakers is on display (and often available for sale) in the many galleries in the urban areas. The country's biggest permanent collection is at the National Art Gallery of Namibia (see page 154), which has over 560 works of art dating from 1864 to the present day. There are many landscapes and paintings of wild animals among the earlier works. Every two years the winning entries of the Standard Bank Biennale are exhibited here. Contemporary Namibian visual arts are exhibited in Windhoek at John Muafangejo Art Centre, the Centre for Visual and Performing Arts and House of Art (page 147). There's also Namibian Jewellers and Arts Gallery in Swakopmund (page 291).

Karakuls are central Asian sheep, the young of which have long been prized for their pelts. In 1902, a German fur trader called Paul Thorer shipped 69 of these from Uzbekistan to Germany in the hope of breeding them there. The damper European climes did not suit them, but in 1907 12 of those animals were shipped out to German South West Africa – as Namibia's climate was thought to be similar to that of the dry central Asian areas from where they had come.

They did well, and two years later 278 more animals were brought out from Asia. Later, the South Africans continued the work started by the Germans, when they took over as the reigning colonial power in Namibia. An experimental farm was started near Windhoek, to investigate the farming and breeding of karakuls.

Over the next 50 or 60 years Namibia gradually became one of the three main producers of karakul fur, or 'Persian lamb' as it is often known. Early on, selective breeding in Namibia had developed white pelts, which were not produced in either the USSR or Afghanistan – the competing countries. Then Namibia marketed its fur under the trade name of Swakara, for South West African karakul. Now, one firm markets these as Nakara, for Namibian karakul (see page 148).

The trade grew rapidly, and as early as 1937 the country exported over a million pelts for over £1,200,000. At its peak in 1976, about 2.8 million pelts earned some 50 million rand and the nickname 'black gold' was coined. Then the antifur campaigns of the late 1970s and 1980s slashed the demand for fur, and the prices paid for pelts.

When the market crashed, the biggest single source of income for many farmers in southern Namibia was removed. Given that the fur came only from the slaughter of very young lambs (it is said to be at its softest when they are 36 hours old), it's not surprising that people felt unhappy about buying it. However, these are tough sheep, well suited to Namibia's extremes of temperatures and semi-desert climate, and finding new markets was important. Initially, the production of hand-woven karakul carpets served to increase the demand for the wool of adults, and now the market for pelts has stabilised, too, with interest coming from countries as diverse as Japan, Russia and Italy.

PERFORMING ARTS

Dance Traditional dancing in Namibia is a participatory activity at community gatherings and events like weddings. Hence, a visitor is unlikely to witness any, unless invited by a Namibian. Occasionally, public performances of traditional dancing are to be seen at local arts festivals, or even in traditional villages such as Lizauli (page 496). In Bushmanland, in villages surrounding Tsumkwe, traditional Bushmen dances are performed for tourists – usually for a fee. This is generally a relaxed, uncontrived affair.

Performances of European dance, including ballet, take place at either the National Theatre of Namibia or at the Franco-Namibian Cultural Centre (see page 144).

Music Most of the Namibian peoples have a music-making tradition – singing, and playing drums, bows, thumb pianos and harps. The Namas also have a tradition of religious singing in four-part harmony, a cappella. One group that has taken this to a wider audience is the University of Namibia Choir, which has gained an enviable reputation for performing a range of traditional music in both Namibian and European languages.

Pre-independence colonial influences have resulted in many Namibian musicians performing in the Western tradition. Concerts are regularly performed in Windhoek by the Namibia National Symphony Orchestra, National Youth Choir and touring foreign musicians in the main auditorium of the National Theatre of Namibia. Out of Windhoek, the national tour circuit includes large venues in Swakopmund, Walvis Bay and Okahandja.

Theatre and film Namibian theatre companies come and go, as elsewhere, but there is no shortage of venues for performances – at least in the capital (see page 144).

The best of Namibian theatre (and other arts and crafts) can be seen at the annual Bank Windhoek Arts Festival (see page 30).

SPORT Athletics aficionados will be familiar with the name of Frankie Fredericks, the Namibian 200m sprinter. Slightly overshadowed by Michael Johnson, he nevertheless brought home a string of international medals, the latest of which was in the Commonwealth Games held in Manchester in July 2002, which marked the finale of an international career that spanned well over a decade.

More recently, Namibia has gone football crazy, spurred on by the 2010 Football World Cup held in South Africa. Other sports played in schools include rugby, hockey, netball and, more recently, basketball. The opportunity to take part in endurance sports is here, too, though the Namib Desert Challenge (*www. namibdesertchallenge.com*), a gruelling 200km, five-day event around Sossusvlei, is definitely not for the faint-hearted.

3

The Natural Environment

PHYSICAL ENVIRONMENT

The Republic of Namibia is located in southwest Africa, astride the Tropic of Capricorn and beside the South Atlantic Ocean. Its main borders are with South Africa, Botswana and Angola, though it also adjoins Zambia. Covering about 824,292km², the country is much larger than Kenya, and more than twice the size of Zimbabwe. In Western terms, Namibia is more than a third larger than the UK and Germany combined, or twice the size of California.

CLIMATE Most of Namibia is classified as an arid to semi-arid region (the line being crossed from semi-arid to arid when evaporation exceeds rainfall). Most of it has a subtropical 'desert' climate, characterised by a wide range in temperature (from day to night and from summer to winter), and by low rainfall and humidity. The northern strip follows the same pattern, but has a more moderate, less dry climate.

KIMBERLITE (DIAMOND) PIPES

Diamond is a crystalline form of ordinary carbon created under conditions of extreme pressure and temperature. In nature, such conditions are only found deep below the earth's surface in the lower crust or upper mantle. Under certain circumstances in the past (usually associated with tectonic activity) the rock matrix in which diamonds occurred was subjected to such great pressure that it became fluid and welled up to the earth's surface in a volcanic pipe of fluidised material. The situation is similar to a conventional volcanic eruption, except that instead of basaltic magma being erupted through fissures in the crust, the volcanic material is a peculiar rock called kimberlite. This contains a wide assortment of minerals (including diamond) in addition to large chunks of other rocks that have been caught up in the process.

The pipes are correctly termed kimberlite pipes, and occur throughout southern Africa, from the Cape to the Democratic Republic of Congo. However, only a small proportion of those discovered have proved to contain diamonds in sufficient abundance to be profitably worked. Namibia's diamonds derive not from primary kimberlite pipes, but from secondary diamond deposits – areas where diamonds have been washed down and deposited by old rivers, which have eroded kimberlite pipes in the interior on their way.

Though the Namib is one of the world's oldest deserts, many insist that the Kalahari doesn't qualify for the title 'desert' as it receives much more than 100mm of rain per year. However, the sand sheet that covers the Kalahari results in virtually no surface water, and evidence suggests that it may once have been much more arid than it is now. So although it is commonly called a desert, a better description of it would be 'a fossil desert'.

Note that although the terms 'summer' (November to April) and 'winter' (May to October) are sometimes used, they are not as applicable as, say, in a European maritime climate.

Temperatures range widely from very hot to very cold, depending on the height of the land above sea level and the month. From April to September, in the 'dry season', it is generally cool, pleasant, clear and dry. Temperatures average around 25°C during the day, but nights are much colder. Frost is possible in the higher areas and the deserts. October and November are still within the 'dry season' but then the temperatures are higher, especially in the lower-lying and more northerly areas.

Most of Namibia's rain falls in the summer, from around December to March, and it can be heavy and prolonged in the northern regions of Ovamboland and the Caprivi Strip. The further south or west you go, the drier it becomes, with many southern regions of the Kalahari and the whole of the coastal Namib Desert receiving no rainfall at all some years. In this 'rainy' season temperatures occasionally reach above 40°C, and sometimes you may find it humid in the north.

Weather The beginning of the year, in **January** and **February**, is midsummer. Then it's hot and fairly damp with average maximum temperatures around 25–35°C and average minima around 10–20°C (depending exactly where you are). These averages, however, hide peaks of well over 45°C in the desert.

While prolonged rain may occur on occasion, on a typical day during the rains, the sky will start blue and by early afternoon the clouds will appear. In the late afternoon there will be an hour's torrential rain on some days. Such tropical storms are spectacular; everything feels terrifically fresh afterwards, though you wouldn't want to be caught outside. By the early evening the sky will usually begin to clear again.

The frequency of the rains decreases, and they cease around **March** or **April**. From then the heat is waning and the land gradually cools and dries out. As the skies clear, the nights quickly become cooler, accentuating the temperature difference with the bright, hot days. **May** is a lovely month: there is minimal chance of rain, nights are not yet too cold, and many of the summer's plants are still lush and green.

By **June** the nights are cold, approaching freezing in desert areas where night game drives can be bitter. **July** and **August** are winter, when the average maximum temperatures are around 15–25°C and the average minima around 0–10°C. That said, you may still find yourself wearing shorts and a T-shirt during the day, and getting sunburnt if you are not careful. Clouds will be a rare sight for the next few months.

September is another super month, dry and clear, yet not too hot. By then most green vegetation is fading as the heat begins to build. Everything is dry. All through **October** the heat mounts, and by **November** it is very hot during the day. However, the humidity is still exceedingly low, so even the high temperatures feel quite pleasant.

By November the air seems pregnant with anticipation. Everything is dry, awaiting the rains. Though the clouds often build up in the afternoon, they won't usually deliver until at least **December**. When (and if) the rains do arrive, they are a huge relief, dropping the temperatures at a stroke, clearing the air and reviving the vegetation. Despite all this, the traditional seasons are no longer as reliable as they once were. In 2009, for example, the rains in the north started in mid-October, unseasonably early; climate change is a reality in Namibia, too.

The coastal strip Temperatures on the Namibian coast follow a similar overall pattern, though it may seem very different from one day to the next. Here the climate is largely determined by the interaction between warm dry winds from inland and the cold Benguela Current. The sea is too cold for much evaporation to take place and, consequently, rain-bearing clouds don't form over the coast. Most of the coast is classified as desert – rainfall is an extremely low 15mm per annum on average, and in some years there may be none.

However, hot air from the interior mixes regularly with cold sea air to produce a moist fog that penetrates up to 60km inland. This happens regardless of season, and has done for millennia. It is this periodic morning fog which provides the desert's only dependable source of moisture, and the Namib's endemic flora and fauna have evolved to take advantage of it.

GEOLOGY Geologically, Namibia forms part of an extremely old region, with Precambrian granitic and metamorphic rocks dating back over two billion years. These shield or 'basement' rocks are usually covered by more recent sedimentary rocks, mostly deposited during the Mesozoic era (65–235 million years ago). Tectonic activity or movement in the earth's crust over the last 100 million years or so created a number of rifts through which magma was able to reach the surface (see box, *Kimberlite (diamond) pipes*, page 35) and resulted in the uplifting of most of the area above sea level.

TOPOGRAPHY The topography of Namibia can be divided into four regions. At 2,000m, the highest land is the central plateau that runs roughly from north to south, from south of Keetmanshoop to north of Otjiwarongo. This is hilly, verdant country where most of Namibia's best farmland is concentrated.

To the west of this plateau, the land falls off in a dramatic escarpment down to the Namib Desert, one of the world's oldest deserts, which stretches for 1,600km beside the Atlantic Ocean. The escarpment, and the incisions that have been cut through it by river action over the years, provides some of Namibia's most spectacular scenery. Below, the Namib is a flat coastal plain whose profile is broken only by shifting dunes and the odd towering inselberg (see page 247).

East of the central plateau, the land slopes off much more gradually, merging into the great sand sheet of the Kalahari Desert. A plateau standing at about 1,000m, stretching from Namibia into Botswana and even beyond, this is rolling country with vegetated sand dunes.

Sand dunes
Barchan or crescentric dunes These arise wherever sand-laden wind deposits sand on the windward (upwind) slopes of a random patch on the ground. The mound grows in height until a 'slip-face' is established by sand avalanching down on the sheltered leeward (downwind) side. The resulting dune is therefore in a state of constant (if slow) movement – sand is continuously being deposited and blown up the shallow windward slope and then falling down the steep leeward slope. This slow movement, or migration, is more rapid at the edges of the dune (where there

is less wind resistance) than in the centre, which results in the characteristic 'tails' of a mature barchan.

Fairly constant winds from the same direction are essential for the growth and stability of barchan dunes, which can migrate from anything up to 6m a year for high dunes to 15m a year for smaller dunes. Probably Namibia's best examples of barchan dunes occur in the Skeleton Coast, where some of the dune crests are highlighted by a purple dusting of garnet sand. You'll see them 'marching' across the road near where the C39 turns from the main C34 coastal road.

Seif dunes Where the prevailing wind is interrupted by crosswinds driving in sand from the sides, a long seif or longitudinal dune is formed, instead of a swarm of barchans. The shape of seif dunes is that of a long ridge with high crests, parallel to the direction of the prevailing wind. They commonly occur in long parallel ranges, such as those south of the Kuiseb River which show up so clearly on satellite photographs.

Star dunes When the winds blow from several different directions, a tall pyramidal structure or star dune is formed, with three or more arms or ridges that radiate away from the top. Several dunes of this type are to be found in the Namib Desert around Sossusvlei.

Sand sheets Sand sheets occur when the land is vegetated with grass and scrub, or is covered with rocks and pebbles. Then the force of the wind is broken and it becomes less homogenous. In such situations poorly developed seif dunes or irregular barchans form, and may often join together to some extent, making an undulating sand sheet. From this platform of coarser sand, more erratic dunes often rise.

Sand sheets, in one form or another, are the most common dune formation in southern Africa, since the 'textbook' conditions needed to form perfect barchan or seif dunes are rare. However, the principles remain the same and 'imperfect' dunes of barchan or seif origin are widespread throughout the Kalahari and Namib deserts.

FLORA AND FAUNA

Despite its aridity, Namibia is full of fascinating wildlife. Its national parks and concession areas have protected their flora and fauna effectively and offer some superb big game, far from the tourist hordes of more conventional safari countries. Namibia has been the most successful country in the world at protecting its black rhino population, and has Africa's largest population of cheetahs.

Because the Namib is one of the world's oldest deserts, the extraordinary way that plants, animals and even human populations have adapted and evolved in order to survive here is fascinating. There are many endemic species: animals and plants not found anywhere else. From beetles and birds to big game like the famous 'desert elephants' and strange welwitschia plants – Namibia has unique and varied wildlife.

VEGETATION TYPES As with animals, each species of plant has its favourite conditions. External factors determine where each species thrives, and where it will perish. These include temperature, light, water, soil type, nutrients, and which other species of plants and animals live in the same area. Species with similar needs are often found together, in communities which are characteristic of that particular environment. Namibia has a number of such communities, or typical 'vegetation types', within its borders – each of which is distinct from the others. East of the desert, some of the more common include the following:

Mopane woodland The dominant tree here is the remarkably adaptable mopane (*Colophospermum mopane*), which is sometimes known as the butterfly tree because of the shape of its leaves. It is very tolerant of poorly drained or alkaline soils and those with a high clay content. This tolerance results in the mopane having a wide range of distribution throughout southern Africa; in Namibia it occurs mainly in the higher, slightly wetter areas including Etosha, the northern Kunene, Caprivi and the Kalahari.

Mopane trees can attain a height of 25m, especially if growing on rich, alluvial soils. However, shorter trees are more common in areas that are poor in nutrients, or have suffered from extensive fire damage. Stunted mopane will form a low scrub, perhaps only 5m tall. All mopane trees are semi-deciduous. The leaves turn beautiful shades of yellow and red before falling between August and October, depending on their proximity to water (the closer the water, the later the leaves fall), then fresh new leaves start unfurling from late October.

Ground cover in mopane woodland is usually sparse – just thin grasses, herbs and the occasional bush. The trees themselves are an important source of food for game, as the leaves have a high nutritional value – rich in protein and phosphorus – which is favoured by browsers and is retained even after they have fallen from the trees. Mopane forests support large populations of rodents, including bush or tree squirrels (*Peraxerus cepapi*), which are so typical of these areas that they are known as 'mopane squirrels'.

Savannah This all-encompassing category refers to those areas of dry, thorny woodland that occur when trees and shrubs have invaded open grassland, often because of some disturbance like cultivation, fire or overgrazing. It could be subdivided further into 'thorntree', 'bush' and 'mixed tree and shrub' savannah.

Some form of savannah covers much of the Namibian highlands, and the dominant families of trees and bushes are the acacia, terminalia (bearing single-winged seeds) and combretum (bearing seeds with four or five wings), but many others are also present.

Teak forest In a few areas of the Kalahari (including some within Khaudum National Park), the Zambezi teak (*Baikaea plurijuga*), forms dry semi-evergreen forests on a base of Kalahari sand. This species is not fire-resistant, so these stands occur only where slash-and-burn cultivation methods have never been used. Below the tall teak is normally a dense, deciduous thicket of vegetation, interspersed with sparse grasses and herbs in the shadier spots of the forest floor.

Moist evergreen forest In areas of high rainfall, or near main rivers and swamps where a tree's roots will have permanent access to water, dense evergreen forest is found. This lush vegetation contains many species and is characterised by having three levels: a canopy of tall trees, a sublevel of smaller trees and bushes, and a variety of ground-level vegetation. In effect, the environment is so good for plants that they have adapted to exploit the light from every sunbeam. In Namibia, this occurs only as riparian forest (sometimes called riverine forest), which lines the country's major rivers.

Vlei A 'vlei' is a shallow grass depression, or small valley, that is either permanently or seasonally wet – though Namibia's vleis are drier than the areas that one would call vleis in countries further east. These open, verdant dips in the landscape usually support no bushes or trees. In higher valleys among hills, they sometimes form the sources of streams and rivers. Because of their dampness, they are rich in species of grasses, herbs and flowering plants. Their margins are usually thickly vegetated by grasses, herbs and smaller shrubs.

Floodplain Floodplains are the low-lying grasslands on the edges of rivers, streams, lakes and swamps that are seasonally inundated by floods. Namibia has only a few floodplains, in the Caprivi area. The best examples are probably beside the Okavango in Mahango, and near the Chobe and Zambezi rivers in the Impalila area. These contain no trees or bushes, just a low carpet of grass species that can tolerate being submerged for part of the year.

Pan Though not an environment for rich vegetation, a pan is a shallow, seasonal pool of water with no permanent streams leading into or from it. The bush is full of small pans in the rainy season, most of which will dry up soon after the rains cease. The Etosha and Nyae Nyae pans are just much larger versions, which attract considerable numbers of migrant birds when full.

DESERT FLORA Weighty tomes have been written on the flora of the Namib Desert, with its endemic plants and multitude of subtly different vegetation zones. One of the easiest to read is Dr Mary Seely's excellent book *The Namib* (see *Appendix 3*, page 531), which is widely sold in Namibia. This is well worth buying when you arrive, as it will increase your understanding and enjoyment of the desert immensely.

Distance from the coast and altitude are crucial to note when looking at the Namib's flora, as both are factors in determining how much moisture a plant receives by way of the fog. This is maximised at an altitude of about 300–600m above sea level, and extends up to about 60km inland. Thus the communities of vegetation can differ widely over very small distances: the plains full of delicate lichens in one place, but empty a kilometre away. Adaptations to the extremes are all around: wax-covered leaves to reduce transpiration, hollow stems to store water, low growth to avoid the wind, slow growth to take advantage of the infrequent moisture.

The species differ too widely to describe here, but are mentioned in the relevant chapters. Many will become familiar to even a casual observer; none could forget the prehistoric welwitschia (*Welwitschia mirabilis*), the kokerbooms silhouetted on rocky mountainsides, or the strange halfmen (*Pachypodium namaquensis*) seen in the far south.

ANIMALS (For more on wildlife in Namibia, check out Bradt's *Southern African Wildife*. See page ix for a special discount offer. See also *Appendix 1*, pages 509–27) Namibia's large mammals are typical of the savannah areas of southern Africa, though those that rely on daily water are restricted in their distributions. With modern game capture and relocation techniques, you may well find animals far out of their natural ranges, like waterbuck and lechwe. (Bontebok, Blesbock and black wildebeest, for example, are native to South Africa but are now found on many ranches in Namibia.) Thus what you may see in a given area may be different from what 'naturally occurs'.

The large predators are all here in Namibia. **Lion** are locally common, but largely confined to the parks, the arid northwest and the Caprivi Area/Zambezi region away from dense human habitation. **Leopard** are exceedingly common throughout the country, and the central highlands provide just the kind of rocky habitat that they love. They are, however, very rarely seen naturally. **Cheetah** do exceptionally well in Namibia, which is said to have about 40% of Africa's population. This is mainly because commercial farmers eradicated lion and hyena (the natural enemies of cheetah) relatively easily, and allow smaller buck, the cheetah's natural prey, to coexist with cattle. Hence the cheetahs thrive on large ranches – having problems only if the farmers suspect them of killing stock, and then they try to eradicate them, too.

Wild dog have their last strongholds in the wild areas in and around Khaudum and the Zambezi region, but are seldom seen elsewhere. They need huge territories in which to roam, and don't survive well on commercially farmed land. Recent attempts to reintroduce them to Etosha have failed; it is hoped that some may succeed in the future.

The social **spotted hyena** is common in the north and northwest of the country, and even occurs down into the Namib's central desert areas and the Naukluft Mountains – though it is relatively unusual here. Much more common and widespread is the solitary, secretive **brown hyena**, which scavenges by the coast among the seal colonies, though is rarely seen.

Buffalo occur in protected national parks in the Caprivi/Zambezi region, and have been reintroduced to Bushmanland and Waterberg from South Africa, but are not found elsewhere in Namibia.

Elephant occur widely in the north, in Khaudum, Caprivi/Zambezi region and Etosha. A separate population has its stronghold in the Kunene Region. Many venture right down the river valleys and live in desert areas: these are the famous 'desert elephants'. They survive there by knowing exactly where the area's waterholes are, and where water can be found in the rivers. This ancestral knowledge, probably passed down the generations, is easily lost, although in recent years various conservation/development schemes in the area have been so successful that these 'desert-adapted' elephants are now thriving.

Black rhino occur in similar areas, but poaching now effectively limits them to some of the main national parks, and the less accessible areas of the Kunene Region. Their numbers are increasing slowly but, as elsewhere, have recently suffered due to poaching. As a prevention method against this, most of the rhino in the areas worst affected by poaching have been dehorned. Those in the Kunene form one of Africa's only increasing black rhino populations: success indeed for an area outside any national park where only community conservation schemes stand between the poachers and their quarry. **White rhino** have been reintroduced to Waterberg and Etosha, where they are thriving.

Antelope are well represented, with springbok, gemsbok and kudu being numerically dominant depending on the area. The rare endemic **black-faced impala** is a subspecies found only in northwestern Namibia and southern Angola, and can be seen in Etosha.

Roan antelope are found in the Caprivi/Zambezi region, Waterberg and with luck in Etosha. **Sable** occur only in the Zambezi region, with excellent numbers often seen on the Okavango's floodplains on the edge of Mahango. In the Zambezi region's wetter areas there are also **red lechwe, reedbuck** and the odd **sitatunga**.

Red hartebeest are widespread in the east, though common nowhere. **Blue wildebeest** are found only in Etosha. **Eland** occur in Etosha and the Kalahari, while **kudu** seem the most adaptable of the large antelope, occurring everywhere apart from the coastal desert strip.

Among the smaller antelope, **duiker** are common everywhere apart from the desert, as are **steenbok**. **Klipspringer** occur throughout Namibia's mountains. Namibia's smallest antelope, the **Damara dik-dik** can be found in most rocky areas north and west of Windhoek, and Etosha, particularly around Namutoni.

Giraffe are fairly widespread and can be seen from the Namib-Naukluft park all the way up to the Kunene River, but are most common in Etosha.

For further details of wildlife, see *Appendix 1*, pages 509–27.

Animal tracks A good guide can make animal tracks come alive, helping you to make sense of what you see in the bush. Showing you, for example, that cats' tracks have three lobes at the bottom, whereas dog and hyena tracks feature only two; pointing out the cheetah's claws, usually absent from other cat tracks; or the direction in which an elephant is walking from small scuff marks around its track.

The more you learn, the more you'll enjoy about the bush. The tracks illustrated on pages 512–13 are shown in relation to each other, sizewise, and are intended as a simple introduction to the many signs of wildlife that may be seen around a waterhole, or in the sand.

BIRDLIFE Much of Namibia is very dry, and thus hasn't the variation in resident birds that you might find in lusher environments. However, many of those dry-country birds have restricted distributions, and so are endemic, or close to being so. Further, where Namibia's drier interior borders on to a wetter area, as within Mahango National Park, or along the Kunene and Okavango rivers to the north, the species count shoots up.

In addition to its residents, Namibia receives many migrants. In September and October the Palaearctic migrants appear (ie: those that come from the northern hemisphere – normally Europe), and they remain until around April or May. This is also the peak time to see the intra-African migrants, which come from further north in Africa.

The coastal wetland sites, most notably around Walvis Bay and Sandwich Harbour, receive visits from many migrating species, as well as seabird species that aren't normally seen in the interior of southern Africa. So trips including the coast, as well as the country's interior and riverine borders, make Namibia an excellent and varied destination for birders.

Inevitably the rains from December to around April see an explosion in the availability of most birds' food: seeds, fruits and insects. Hence this is the prime time for birds to nest, even if it is also the most difficult time to visit the more remote areas of the country.

FIELD GUIDES Finding field guides to plants, animals and birds while in Namibia is relatively easy; though it can be difficult outside of the country.

There are some comprehensive little hardback guides on the flora of various areas, including *Namib Flora* and *Damaraland Flora* published by Gamsberg Macmillan in Windhoek. These are sold in Namibia both in bookshops and at some tourist lodges. The Shell guides to *The Namib* and *Waterberg* are excellent for appreciating the area's flora and fauna.

The standard birding guides to travel with are the established Newman's *Birds of Southern Africa*, and the newer Sasol-sponsored guide of the same name, both of which are widely available overseas. For mammals, Chris and Tilde Stuart's *Field Guide to Mammals of Southern Africa* is generally very good. See *Appendix 3* for details of all these books.

CONSERVATION

A great deal has been written about conservation in Africa, much of it oversimplistic and intentionally emotive. As an informed visitor you are in the unique position of being able to see some of the issues at first hand, and to appreciate the perspectives of local people. So abandon your preconceptions, and start by appreciating the complexities of the issues involved. Here I shall try to develop a few ideas, touched on only briefly elsewhere in the book, which are common to most current thinking on conservation.

First, *conservation* must be taken within its widest sense if it is to have meaning. Saving animals is of minimal use if the whole environment is degraded, so best practice in modern conservation is to aim to conserve the flora and fauna of environment and ecosystems, not just the odd isolated species or individual animal.

Observe that land is regarded as an asset by most societies, in Africa as it is elsewhere. (In common with most hunter-gatherer groups worldwide, the Bushmen used to be perhaps a notable exception to this.) To 'save' the land for the animals and to use it merely for the recreation of a few privileged foreign tourists – while the local people remain in poverty – is a recipe for huge social problems. Local people in Namibia have hunted game for food for centuries. They have always killed those animals that threatened them or ruined their crops. If we now try to proclaim animals in a populated area as protected, without addressing the concerns of the people, then our efforts will fail.

The only pragmatic way to conserve Namibia's wild areas is to see the *conservation* of animals and the environment as inseparably linked to the *development* of the local people. In the long term one will not work without the other. Conservation without development leads to resentful local people who will happily, and frequently, shoot, trap and kill animals. Development without conservation will simply repeat the mistakes that most developed countries have already made: it will lay waste a beautiful land, and kill off its natural heritage. Look at the tiny areas of natural vegetation which survive undisturbed in the UK, the USA or Japan, to see how unsuccessful they have been at long-term conservation over the last 500 years.

As an aside, the local people in Namibia – and other developing countries – are sometimes wrongly accused of being the only agents of degradation. Observe the volume of tropical hardwoods imported by the industrialised countries to see that the West plays no small part in this.

In conserving some of Namibia's natural areas, and helping its people to develop, the international community has a vital role to play. It could use its aid projects to encourage the Namibian government to practise sustainable long-term strategies, rather than grasping for the short-term fixes which politicians seem universally to prefer. But such strategies must have the backing of the people themselves, or they will fall apart when foreign funding eventually wanes.

Most Namibians are more concerned about where they live, what they can eat, and how they will survive, than they are about the lives of small, obscure species of antelope that taste good when roasted. To get backing from the local communities, it is not enough for a conservation strategy to be compatible with development: it must actually promote it and help the local people to improve their own standard of living. If that situation can be reached, then rural populations can be mobilised behind long-term conservation initiatives.

Governments are the same. As one of Zambia's famous conservationists once commented, 'governments won't conserve an impala just because it is pretty'. But they will work to save it *if* they can see that it is worth more to them alive than dead.

The best strategies tried so far on the continent attempt to find lucrative and sustainable ways to use the land. They then plough much of the revenue back into the surrounding local communities. Once the people see revenue from conservation being used to help them improve their lives – to build houses, clinics and schools, and to offer paid employment – then such schemes stand a chance of getting their backing and support. It can take a while...

Carefully planned, sustainable tourism is one source of income that can work effectively. For success, the local people must understand that visitors pay because they want the wildlife and thus that the existence of wildlife directly improves their income. Then they will strive to conserve it. It isn't enough for them to see that the wildlife helps the government to get richer; that won't dissuade a local hunter from shooting a duiker for dinner. However, if that hunter benefits directly from the visitors, who come to see the animals, then he has a vested interest in saving that duiker.

It matters little to the Namibian people, or ultimately to the wildlife in general terms, whether these visitors come to shoot the animals with a camera or with a gun – as long as any hunting is done on a sustainable basis (ie: that only a few of the oldest 'trophy' animals are shot each year, and the size and genetic diversity of the animal population remains largely unaffected). Photographers may claim the moral high ground, but should remember that hunters pay far more for their privileges. Hunting operations generate large revenues from few guests, who demand minimal infrastructure and so cause little impact on the land. Photographic operations need more visitors to generate the same revenue, and so may have greater negative effects on the country. In practice, there is room for both types of visitor in Namibia: the photographer and the hunter. The main challenge in allowing sustainable hunting is in implementing the regulations designed to keep it sustainable.

PROTECTED AREAS Over 40% of Namibia's land falls under private or state protection. There are very few countries in Africa where land is being returned to a more natural state, with fewer livestock and more indigenous game, and so Namibia is a great success story.

National parks and private reserves
The country's national parks and other protected areas – covering a total land area of over 135,000km² – are designated for photographic visitors, and no hunting is allowed. The first to be gazetted was Etosha in 1907; the most recent, the Sperrgebiet National Park south of Lüderitz, in 2009. In 2010, the National West Coast Tourist Recreational Area was renamed Dorob National Park. Thus Namibia's entire coastal strip is now protected within the Namib-Skeleton Coast National Park, stretching for 1,570km from the country's northern border on the Kunene River right down to the Orange River in the south.

Many private farms and reserves now have game on their land, and have adopted a similar policy, encouraging photographic tourists to visit as a means of supporting wildlife conservation. Others, however, style themselves as 'hunting farms'. These attract mainly overseas hunters (primarily from Germany and the USA), who pay handsomely for the privilege. The livelihood of these farms depends on hunting, and so they generally practise it sustainably.

Government protection has recently extended to the sea, with the proclamation of the Namibian Islands' Marine Protected Area. Stretching along 400km of coastline, from Meob Bay in the Namib-Naukluft National Park to Chamais Bay in the Sperrgebiet National Park, it is designed to protect the small islands and islets that provide refuge for seals and seabirds, as well as the surrounding waters which are breeding grounds for both whales and dolphins.

Conservancies
In 1995 the Namibian Cabinet passed a landmark policy on wildlife management, utilisation and tourism in communal areas (areas occupied by subsistence farmers rather than large-scale commercial ranches). Many interested groups, including the IRDNC (see box, opposite) were closely involved with the

IRDNC

Integrated Rural Development and Nature Conservation (*www.irdnc.org.na*) is a small organisation directed by Garth Owen-Smith, a Namibian nature conservator, and Dr Margaret Jacobsohn, a Namibian anthropologist who worked for years among the Himba people. Since the mid-1980s their goal has been to ensure the sustainable social, economic and ecological development of Namibia's communal areas. The directors have received several international environmental prizes. Typical of their low-key approach, they emphasise that they have always worked as part of a team with the government, various NGOs, community groups and like-minded organisations in the private sector. (Namibia's Save the Rhino Trust is another notable player in much of this work; see box, page 360.)

The IRDNC was one of the pioneers of the **Community Game Guard** scheme set up in 1983 in the Kaokoveld, now the Kunene Region. In its simplest form, a community game guard is appointed from each community, and is paid to ensure that no member of the community hunts any animal that they are not allowed to hunt. Originally called the Auxiliary Game Guard scheme, it has been behind the phenomenal recovery of the desert-adapted populations of elephant and black rhino in the area.

Later, the organisation helped to set up some of the **community campsites** in the same region. It facilitated the important projects to return money from lodges to local communities at Lianshulu and Etendeka, and was also involved with setting up the joint venture between the community and Wilderness Safaris that is behind Damaraland Camp.

In a more recent initiative, IRDNC has been involved in the establishment of **conservancy-owned safaris**, helping to test the concept and to facilitate conservancy involvement. The first company under this umbrella, involving five conservancies, is Kunene Conservancy Safaris (see page 366), and the second, Caprivi Conservancy Safaris, is now also running a small programme (contact details as for Kunene Conservancy Safaris).

The IRDNC now employs a staff of around 60, most of them rural Namibians, and currently works with more than 40 conservancies in both the Kunene and Zambezi regions, each of which in turn employs several community workers.

formulation of this policy, which encouraged the linking of 'conservation with rural development by enabling communal farmers to derive financial income from the sustainable use of wildlife and from tourism'. It also aimed to 'provide an incentive to the rural people to conserve wildlife and other natural resources, through shared decision-making and financial benefit'.

Put simply, this gave a framework for local communities to take charge of the wildlife in their own areas for sustainable utilisation – with decisions made by the local communities, for the community.

The visitor travelling through the more isolated areas of Namibia will frequently come across signs demarcating the boundaries of these communal conservancies. One of the first was the Torra Conservancy in southern Damaraland, which is home to Damaraland Camp. By March 2013, 79 communal conservancies had been registered, with more in the pipeline. With the establishment of Conservancy Safaris Namibia (see box, *IRDNC*, above) comes a new opportunity to learn about the individual conservancies at first hand.

Entirely separate are private conservancies, created by commercial farmers who have joined forces with neighbouring farms to protect the environment – and the wildlife – within their boundaries. Among these are the NamibRand Nature Reserve and the Erongo Mountain Nature Conservancy.

TOURISM Namibia lies far from Africa's 'original' big-game safari areas of east Africa, Kenya and Tanzania, and from the newer destinations of Zimbabwe and Zambia. Aside from Etosha and Caprivi, Namibia doesn't have the density of game that visitors would expect for such a trip, or the warm tropical shores that they would expect for a beach holiday (anyone who has been to Lüderitz will surely agree). Thus the country doesn't generally attract first-time visitors who simply want to tick off game, or see game and lie on a beach – a combination that accounts for much volume in the travel business. Therefore few cheap charter planes arrive in Namibia, and there is still only a small number of large hotels, most of which aim more for businesspeople than tourists.

The main area of growth in Namibia's tourism is in individual self-drive trips and small-group tours and, most recently, in fly-in safaris. These are perfect for the small lodges and guest farms, and have encouraged many small-scale tourist ventures to develop and thrive – utilising not only the few famous national parks, but also old cattle ranches and otherwise unproductive sections of desert.

In the long term, this is a huge advantage for the country. With tourism continuing to grow slowly but steadily, it is hoped that Namibia will avoid the boom-then-bust experienced by countries like Kenya. Every month new small camps, lodges and guest farms open for visitors; most try hard to retain that feeling of 'wilderness' which is so rare in more densely populated countries, and much sought after by visitors. Namibia has so much space and spectacular scenery that, provided the developments remain small-scale and responsible, it should have a very long and profitable career in tourism ahead.

Perhaps Namibia's most promising developments in this field are its successes in linking tourism with community-development projects. Tourism is a vital source of revenue for many of these projects and, if it helps to provide employment and bring foreign exchange into Namibia, this gives the politicians a reason to support environmental conservation.

Community campsites Tourists who are camping would do well to seek out community campsites, and support them. These sites aim to enable local communities to benefit directly from passing tourists. The community sets up a campsite, and then a central community fund receives the money generated – and the whole community decides how that revenue is spent. Once the tourists have stopped to camp, it also gives the community a chance to earn money by guiding the visitors on local walks, selling curios or firewood, or whatever else seems appropriate in the area. Even travellers on a lower budget can thus have a direct impact on some of Namibia's smaller, rural communities.

There are now several community campsites in the Kunene Region, and an increasing number in the Caprivi area. Many of the most successful ventures are run under the auspices of NACSO (*www.nacso.org.na*) – the Namibian Association of CBNRM (Community-Based Natural Resource Management) Support Organisations. NACSO has essentially taken up the role of the former NACOBTA, which was a nonprofit organisation working with communities seeking to develop tourism initiatives at local level. A partner of NACSO, Community Conservation Namibia (*www.namibiawildlifesafaris.com*) offers helpful profiles and contact information for many community campsites across Namibia, though they cannot assist with making reservations.

Lodges A few operators have really excellent, forward-thinking ways of helping their local communities. The success of Etendeka and then Damaraland Camp opened up the possibility for other ventures along similar lines, with more recent initiatives including Doro Nawas and Grootberg. Some others make a form of 'charity' donation to local communities, but otherwise only involve local people as workers. While this is valuable, much more is needed. Local people must gain greater and more direct benefits from tourism if conservation is going to be successful in Africa, and Namibia is no exception.

If you're staying in lodges, asking the right questions can go a long way towards encouraging Namibia's operators to place development initiatives higher on their list of priorities. For example, how much of the lodge's revenue goes directly back to the local community? How do the local people benefit directly from the visitors staying at *this* camp? How much of a say do they have about what goes on in the area where *these* safaris are operated? If enough visitors did this, it would make a big difference.

HUNTING Big-game hunting, where visiting hunters pay large amounts to kill trophy animals, is a practical source of revenue for many 'hunting farms' that accept guests. Some also accept nonhunters or 'photographic' guests.

Although many find hunting distasteful, it does benefit the Namibian economy greatly, and encourages farms to cultivate natural wildlife rather than introduced livestock. Until there are enough photographic guests to fill all the guest farms used for hunters, pragmatic conservationists will encourage the hunters.

If you don't hunt, but choose to stay at these places, ensure either that you are comfortable with hunting per se, or that there are no hunters on the farm while you are there. Arguments over dinner are surprisingly common.

4

Planning and Preparation

In the 25 years since independence, Namibia has seen tourist facilities develop substantially. While the original restcamps, developed for South African visitors driving their own vehicles, are still thriving, there has been a real boom in lodges and bushcamps, and many once-marginal farms are thriving again as guest farms. Such small, individual places cater largely for overseas visitors, who often have little time but a relatively high budget. They don't suit large tours or high-volume tour operators, who use only large hotels for their big groups. Therefore, the future for Namibia, the way that tourism is growing, is in self-drive trips and fly-in safaris by independent visitors who actively seek out these smaller places rather than joining a large tour or a big group.

At the more economic end of the spectrum, there is also a significant number of first-time visitors travelling around Namibia on small-group camping trips, led by a driver/guide. This arrangement can offer great flexibility, and a real taste of the country at pretty low cost. Often people who first visit with a group like this will then return for their own individual self-drive trip – or even fly-in safari.

And then there are those who really want to get under the country's skin and are fairly self-sufficient. For them, the growing network of community campsites offers exceptional opportunities for independent exploration at leisure.

Namibia is fortunate: its roads are good, its attractions well signposted, and its national parks well managed. Even the centralised booking system for accommodation in the parks, run by Namibia Wildlife Resorts (NWR), generally works well for advance bookings.

Despite its phenomenal growth, tourism to Namibia is still on a small scale, a fraction of that found in, say, South Africa or Tanzania. So the feeling of wilderness has not been lost; you will still be the only visitors in many corners of the country.

WHEN TO VISIT

Although much of Namibia can seem deserted, individual places can often be very busy, and tourism to the country as a whole picks up considerably around Easter and from late July to the end of October. Then advanced bookings are essential. Many of the lodges and restcamps in and around Etosha, and in the Namib-Naukluft area, are fully booked for August as early as a year in advance.

Avoid coming during the Namibian school holidays if possible. These are generally around 25 April–25 May, 15 August–5 September and 5 December–15 January. Then many places will be busy with local visitors, especially the less expensive restcamps and the national parks.

The main season when overseas visitors come is from around mid-July to mid-October. Outside of this, you'll often find the lodges delightfully quiet and have some of the attractions to yourself.

While there really are neither any 'bad' nor any 'ideal' times to visit Namibia, there are times when some aspects of the country are at their best. You must decide what you are primarily interested in, and what's important to you, and then choose accordingly. See the *Climate* section, pages 35–6, for a more detailed discussion of the weather – perhaps the biggest influence on your decision. Then consider your own specific requirements, which might include some of the following.

PHOTOGRAPHY For photography, Namibia is a stunning country in any month. Even with the simplest of camera equipment you can get truly spectacular results. My favourite time for photography is April to June. Then the dust has been washed out of the air by the rains, the vegetation is still green, and yet the sky is clear blue with only a few wispy white clouds.

GAME VIEWING The latter parts of the dry season, between July and late October, are certainly the best time to see big game. Then, as the small bush pools dry up and the green vegetation shrivels, the animals move closer to the springs or the waterholes and rivers.

During and after the rains, you won't see much game, partly because the lush vegetation hides the animals, and partly because most of them will have moved away from the waterholes (where they are most easily located) and gone deeper into the bush. However, many of the animals you do see will have young, as food (animal or vegetable) is at its most plentiful then.

BIRDWATCHING The last few months of the year witness the arrival of the summer migrant birds from the north, anticipating the coming of the rains. Further, if the rains are good the natural pans in Etosha and Bushmanland will fill with aquatic species, including huge numbers of flamingos. This is an amazing spectacle (see box on *Flamingos*, page 316). However, bear in mind that Namibia's ordinary feathered residents can be seen more easily during the dry season, when there is less vegetation to hide them.

WALKING Daytime temperatures occasionally top 40°C in October and November, and heavy rainstorms are likely during the first two or three months of the year. Hence walkers should try to come between about May and September, when the temperatures are at their coolest, and the chances of rain are minimised. Note that most of the long trails in the national parks are closed between November and March.

DRIVING AROUND Driving usually presents few problems at any time of year. However, visitors in January and February, and occasionally even March or exceptionally April, may find that flooding rivers will block their roads. These usually subside within a matter of hours, and certainly within a day or so, but do provide an extra hazard. A 4x4 may be useful at these times, although taking another route is usually a cheaper alternative! Those mounting 4x4 expeditions to the more remote corners of the country should certainly avoid these months, when large tracts of Bushmanland and Kaokoland, for example, become totally impassable in any vehicle.

For detailed coverage of driving in Namibia, see *Chapter 6*. For suggested itineraries, see pages 94–6.

HIGHLIGHTS

NAMIBIA'S TRADITIONAL CULTURES Get to know people of a radically different cultural background in one of Namibia's more remote areas. Visit a Himba village in the Kunene Region and see how these semi-nomadic desert-dwelling people live, or spend some time in a traditional Bushman village; learning in detail about their hunter-gatherer culture.

CAPRIVI STRIP/ZAMBEZI REGION This stretch of land in the northeast of Namibia offers a great contrast to the rest of the country and some exciting birdlife. Watered by a generous annual rainfall, it's a lush environment; with chances to see wildlife not found elsewhere in Namibia, look out for crocodile, hippo and buffalo, to name a few!

ETOSHA NATIONAL PARK One of Africa's best game reserves, Etosha National Park protects a vast shallow bowl of silvery sand the size of Holland – and its surrounding bush. It excels during the dry season when huge herds of animals can be seen amid some of the most startling and photogenic safari scenery in Africa.

SKELETON COAST Although it is now difficult to visit the northern Skeleton Coast, accessing Namibia's coastline anywhere will give you a feel for just how wild and windy it can be. Expect barren and desolate landscapes and large colonies of Cape fur seals. The occasional remaining shipwreck serves as a reminder of the treacherous fogs and strong currents found offshore.

TWYFELFONTEIN The slopes of Twyfelfontein, amid flat-topped mountains typical of Damaraland, conceal one of the continent's greatest concentrations of rock art. When you first arrive, they seem like any other hillsides strewn with rocks. But the boulders that litter these slopes are dotted with thousands of paintings and ancient engravings. It was made a UNESCO World Heritage Site in 2007.

SOSSUSVLEI The classic desert scenery around Sesriem and Sossusvlei is the stuff that postcards are made of – enormous apricot dunes with gracefully curving ridges, invariably pictured in the sharp light of dawn with a photogenic oryx or feathery acacia adjacent. Climb the dunes at sunrise to catch the best light for your photos.

KOLMANSKOP This ghost town, once the principal town of the local diamond industry, was abandoned over 45 years ago and now gives a fascinating insight into the area's great diamond boom. Many of the buildings are left exactly as they were deserted, and now the surrounding dunes are gradually burying them. It's a very photogenic spot!

FISH RIVER CANYON The Fish River Canyon is the second-largest canyon in the world, and approaching it from the north is like driving across Mars. The vast rocky landscape breaks up into a series of spectacular cliffs, formed by the Fish River as it meanders between boulders over half a kilometre below. Its size is impressive: 161km long, up to 27km wide and almost 550m at its deepest.

HOW TO TRAVEL AND BUDGETING

Obviously your style of travel around Namibia depends on your budget, though more expensive doesn't always guarantee a better trip.

NOTES FOR TRAVELLERS WITH MOBILITY PROBLEMS
Gordon Rattray

A vast land of sand, strewn with rocks and pitted by rivers and ravines sounds inadvisable for people who have trouble walking, and downright impossible for wheelchair users. Surprisingly, the opposite is true. Namibia is one of Africa's most accessible destinations, with decent infrastructure, facilities catering to most needs and operators ranging from 'ready and efficient' to 'experienced and specialised'.

Granted, depending on your needs, a lot of research and effort may be necessary to get the best from your trip, but Namibians love a challenge and, as other travellers have shown, almost anything is possible.

ACCOMMODATION Namibia has (for Africa) an unusually high proportion of accessible accommodation. The three NWR restcamps within Etosha (pages 386–7) have adapted rooms, and this awareness is echoed throughout the country – albeit on a lesser scale. The adapted rooms at the NWR camps have varying degrees of accessibility – at Okaukuejo and Halali adapted rooms have wider doorways, extra space in the rooms to allow easy movement in a wheelchair, the toilet has handrails, and there is a pull-down seat in the shower. At Dolomite, there is one adapted room with similar access adaptations and handrails in the bathroom, but no seat in the shower. At Namutoni, the rooms are wheelchair friendly as above, but they are not equipped with any other features such as handrails in the bathroom. Many proprietors are easily contactable by email (see individual listings), so you can discuss your requirements beforehand.

TRANSPORT
By air If you need assistance then let the airline know in advance and arrive early for your departure. During the flight, anyone who uses a pressure-relieving wheelchair cushion should consider using it instead of (or on top of) the fitted seat cushion.

Windhoek's Hosea Kutako International Airport has wheelchairs, an aisle chair and staff to assist with transfers. It also has roomy, step-free toilets for both sexes with grab rails. More provincial airports won't guarantee such 'luxuries', but if needed, aisle chairs can usually be ordered.

By road Unless you choose a specialised operator, most tour companies use 4x4s and minibuses, which are higher than normal cars, usually making entry more difficult. Similarly, buses and minibuses have no facilities for wheelchairs, and getting off and on can be a hectic affair. But that does not necessarily mean these options are to be discounted; drivers, guides and fellow passengers are usually prepared to assist. Do remember, however, that they are not trained in these skills so you must thoroughly explain your needs and stay in control of the situation.

BACKPACKING Backpacking around Namibia is very limiting. You need private transport to see most of the national parks, and will be missing out on a lot if you don't have it. However, if you can splash out on a few days' car hire here, and a couple of guided trips from a hostel there, you might get by on £25/US$40 per day for the rest of your time.

It may be worth taking an assistant for the guide with you on a tour, enabling the guide to focus on the traditional aspects of guiding, and the assistant to help as required with a wheelchair or other access needs.

HEALTH AND INSURANCE Namibian hospitals and pharmacies in urban areas are usually well equipped, but those in rural regions can be basic, so if possible, take all essential medication and equipment with you. It is advisable to pack this in your hand luggage during flights in case your main bags don't arrive immediately. Doctors will know about 'everyday' illnesses, but you must understand and be able to explain your own particular medical requirements. Depending on the season it can also be hot; if this is a problem for you then try to book accommodation and vehicles with fans or air conditioning. A plant-spray bottle is a useful cooling aid.

Travel insurance can be purchased in the UK from Age Concern (↘ *0800 389 4852; www.ageconcern.org.uk*), who have no upper age limit, and Free Spirit (↘*0845 230 5000; www.free-spirit.com*), who cater for people with pre-existing medical conditions, and also have no upper age limit. Most insurance companies will insure disabled travellers, but it is essential that they are made aware of your disability.

In the USA, most travel insurance companies offer a 'pre-existing condition waiver' as an incentive if the traveller purchases trip insurance within a certain time period (typically one to two weeks) of paying the deposit on their trip. Travelex Insurance Services (↘ *1 800 228 9792;* e *customerservice@travelex-insurance.com; www.travelex-insurance.com*) advertise that they have no upper or lower age limits.

SECURITY For anyone following the usual security precautions (see pages 82–4) the chances of robbery are greatly reduced. In fact, as a disabled person I often feel more 'noticed' when in public places, and therefore a less attractive target for thieves. But the opposite may also apply, so do stay aware of where your bags are and who is around you, especially when transferring to another car or similar activities.

SPECIALIST OPERATOR
Endeavour Safaris 23 Lark Crescent, Flamingo Vlei, Yable View 7441, Cape Town, South Africa; ↘ +27 (0)21 556 6114; e info@endeavour-safaris.com; www.endeavour-safaris.com. Specialists in accessible travel for people with disabilities.

FURTHER INFORMATION
www.globalaccessnews.com Searchable database of disability travel information.
www.rollingrains.com Searchable website advocating disability travel.
www.youreable.com UK-based general resource for disability information, with an active forum.
www.apparelyzed.com Dedicated to spinal injury, but containing information that those with other disabilities will find useful. It also hosts a hugely popular forum.

SELF-DRIVE TRIPS The best way to see the country is certainly to have your own vehicle. Whether you opt to use camps, lodges and restcamps, or bring your own camping kit, is then merely a matter of style. The questions of what, how and where to hire a vehicle, and how much it will cost, are extensively covered in *Chapter 6*, pages 85–96.

If you have a tight budget, a much better bet than backpacking would be to find four people to share the car, and camp everywhere. Then you could keep costs to around £40/US$65 per person per day.

For a less basic self-drive trip, with two people sharing the car and staying in a variety of small lodges and restcamps, expect a cost of about £100/US$165 each per day. If you choose more expensive lodges, with guided activities included, then this might rise to about £250–400/US$400–650 – but should guarantee a first-class trip.

GROUP TOURS Another option is to take a scheduled, guided group tour around the country. These suit single travellers as they provide ready-made companions, those who may not feel confident driving, and those who really do want the input of a guide for their trip – often without spending too much money. In either case, provided that you are happy to spend your whole holiday with the same group of people, such a trip might be ideal. Guided trips with larger groups are generally less expensive than self-drive trips which follow the same itinerary and use the same accommodation, and taking a guided trip that includes some nights camping can help to bring costs down substantially.

Generally, the smaller the vehicle used and the group size, the better and the more expensive the trip becomes. On a cheaper trip, expect to camp, with a group size of 12–15 people, for around £80/US$130 per day, based on a 12-day itinerary. For something less basic, using smaller vehicles with fewer people, and staying in luxury mobile camps, a trip of one to two weeks will cost around £200/US$330 a day, per person sharing, including all meals and activities. Several operators run guided accommodated trips for those who do not fancy camping but like the idea of a small-group trip. These cost around £150–300/US$250–500 per person per night, depending on the quality of the lodges used.

PRIVATE GUIDED TRIPS If money is not so restricted, and especially if you're travelling in your own small group with four or more people (eg: a family trip), consider a private guided trip. Your group would then have its own vehicle and guide for the whole trip. You might sleep in existing lodges and camps, or use camping kits supplied by your guide – or might even stay at luxury private tented camps set up just for you. The choice will be yours when you arrange the trip. This isn't a cheap way to travel, especially for smaller groups, but can be well worth the price tag. As an example, two people might expect to pay around £380/US$620 per person per night, whereas for a group of six people that cost would fall to around £260/US$425. Other factors that will affect costs are the standard of accommodation and style of camping.

FLY-IN TRIPS Finally, if your budget is very flexible (and especially if your time is very limited), then consider doing some or all of your trip as a fly-in safari. Small private charter flights can be arranged to many of the smaller lodges and guest farms; it's a very easy way to travel. It is also the only way to get to some of the more inaccessible corners, like the northern section of the Skeleton Coast.

A very popular combination is to fly down to the Sesriem area for three or four nights, hop up to Swakopmund, and then pick up a hire car to drive yourself north to Damaraland and Etosha. Another place commonly visited on short fly-in trips is the Fish River Canyon.

Expect to pay upwards of about £350/US$570 per person per night for a full fly-in trip, and note that your choice of lodges will be restricted to those that can arrange all your activities for you.

ORGANISING YOUR TRIP

Most visitors who come to Namibia for a holiday use the country's guest farms, lodges and restcamps – often combining them into a self-drive tour around the country. Such trips are quite complex, as you will be using numerous hotels, camps and lodges in your own particular sequence. Many of these places are small (and so easily filled), and organise their own logistics with military precision. Finding space at short notice is often difficult.

To arrange everything, it's best to use a reliable, independent tour operator based in your own country. Although many operators sell trips to Namibia, few really know the country well. Insist on dealing directly with someone who does. Namibia changes so fast that detailed local knowledge is vital in putting together a trip that runs smoothly and suits you. Make sure that whoever you book with is fully bonded, so that your money is protected if they go broke; and, ideally, pay with a credit card. Never book a trip from someone who doesn't know Namibia personally: you are asking for problems.

Trips around Namibia are not cheap, though they are currently cheaper (and also better value in many cases) than in any other country in southern Africa. Expect to pay around the same to an operator as you would have to pay directly: from about £650–1,800/US$1,100–2,950 per person per week, including car rental, but excluding airfares. At this price you can expect a good level of service while you are considering the options and booking the trip. If you don't get it, go elsewhere.

Booking directly with Namibian safari operators or agencies is possible, but telephone communication can be more difficult and you will have no recourse if anything goes wrong. European and US operators usually work on commission for the trips that they sell, which is deducted from the basic cost that the visitor pays. Thus you should end up paying about the same whether you book through an overseas operator or talk directly to someone in Namibia.

TOURIST INFORMATION AND NATIONAL PARKS

TOURIST OFFICE The national tourist board, Namibia Tourism (☏ +264 (0)61 290 6000; e info@namibiatourism.com.na; www.namibiatourism.com.na), based in Windhoek, is worth contacting for information before your trip. They have overseas representation in the UK, South Africa, Germany, France, Italy and China.

China Beijing c/o DPS Consulting Co Ltd, Room 416, ShengBao Building, No 2 Tuanjiehu Beilu, Chaoyang 100026; ☏+86 10 844 66463; e huhm@dps-china.com Shanghai c/o Oriental Gateway Consultancy, 3/F, #2150, Jinxuxiu Road 200127; ☏+86 21 5059 6888; e zhuzheng0312@yahoo.com
France 31 Boulevard Suchet, 75016, Paris; ☏+33 1 405 08863; e ntbfrance@orange.fr
Germany Schiller Strasse 42–44, D-60313 Frankfurt am Main; ☏+49 69 133 7360; e info@namibia-tourism.com

Italy c/o Airconsult, Via Adolpho Rava 106, 00142, Rome; ☏+39 06 542 42542; e namibiatourism@airconsult.it
South Africa Ground Flr, The Pinnacle, Burg St, Cape Town 8000; ☏+27 21 422 3298; e namibia@saol.com
UK c/o H B Portfolio, Colechurch Hse, 1 London Bridge Walk, London SE1 2SX; ☏+44 (0)20 7367 0965; e namibia@hbportfolio.co.uk

NATIONAL PARKS The Ministry of the Environment and Tourism (**MET**; *www. met.gov.na*) is the government department responsible for the national parks, but most parks' accommodation is run by Namibia Wildlife Resorts (**NWR**; *Central Reservations: P Bag 13378, Windhoek;* ☎ *061 285 7200;* e *reservations@nwr.com.na; www.nwr.com.na*). Both are generally efficient, if sometimes apparently overzealous about bureaucracy.

Reservations for accommodation must be made in advance, either online or through the NWR offices in Windhoek or Swakopmund; you can, theoretically, book by post or fax too. Advance payment, which can be made by credit card to the reservations office, is required. Alternatively, book in advance through a tour operator that understands the system.

Entry permits for most parks are available at the gates, provided that you're there before they close and that there is space left. The exceptions are permits for the restricted areas of the Namib-Naukluft, such as the Welwitschia Plains, which must be bought in advance from the MET's office in Windhoek or Swakopmund.

Entrance to the major national parks – Etosha, Namib-Naukluft (Sesriem entrance), Waterberg, Ai-Ais Transfrontier and the Skeleton Coast – is currently N$80 per person per day (under 16s free), plus N$10 per vehicle. At other parks, the entrance fee is N$40 per person, but the vehicle fee remains N$10. Note that accommodation fees do not include park entrance fees; both are payable.

If you have booked accommodation in advance through the NWR, it's worth confirming this just before your trip. Despite the best of intentions, there have been occasions when visitors have arrived to find prebooked accommodation closed for reasons such as flooding or a presidential visit, so it's wise to be cautious.

TOUR OPERATORS

As Namibia has become better known, many overseas tour operators have seized the opportunity to put together programmes without knowing what they're doing. Often they are just selling tours that someone in Namibia has designed and marketed. Few have spent much time in the country themselves, and fewer still can give detailed first-hand guidance on all of the country, let alone a wide range of guest farms, camps and lodges.

Don't be talked into thinking that there are only a handful of places to visit and a few camps to stay in. There are many, all individual and different. Ask about ones mentioned in these chapters; a good operator will know the vast majority of them and be able to describe them to you.

Here I must, as the author, admit a personal interest in the tour-operating business: I organise and run the African operations of the UK-based operator Expert Africa, including Wild about Africa (see page 58). Together we are the leading operator to Namibia for English-speaking travellers from Europe and America – with the widest choice of Namibian lodges and camps available anywhere. In Namibia, Expert Africa concentrates on flexible self-drive trips and fly-in safaris; starting at about £850/US$1,400 per person for 11 nights, including car hire, accommodation and some meals – but excluding international flights (typically £1,100 return from the UK). Wild about Africa focuses on guided small-group trips, starting at around £1,700. Booking with a tour operator like us will cost you the same as or less than if you contact Namibia's camps directly – plus you have independent advice, financial protection, and arrangements made for you by experts.

For a fair comparison, tour operators that feature Namibia include:

UK

Aardvark Safaris Aspire Business Centre, Ordnance Rd, Tidworth, Hants SP9 7QD; ☎01980 849160; e mail@aardvarksafaris.com; www. aardvarksafaris.co.uk. Small, upmarket operator featuring much of Africa & Madagascar.

Abercrombie & Kent St George's Hse, Ambrose St, Cheltenham, Glos GL50 3LG; ☎0845 485 1524; e info@abercrombiekent.co.uk; www. abercrombiekent.co.uk. Long-established, large & posh operator worldwide, with a wide choice of Africa trips – which include its own lodges.

Africa Explorer (See ad, page 16) ☎020 8987 8742; e john@africa-explorer.co.uk; www.africa-explorer.co.uk. Tiny but knowledgeable company, run by the jovial John Haycock.

Africa Travel 227 Shepherds Bush Rd, Hammersmith, London W6 7AS; ☎020 7843 3500; e info@africatravel.co.uk; www.africatravel.co.uk. Featuring east & southern Africa, with a special emphasis on sports travel.

Audley Travel New Mill, New Mill Lane, Witney, Oxon OX29 9SX; ☎01993 838500; e africa@ audleytravel.com; www.audleytravel.com. Tailor-made operator with worldwide coverage including Namibia.

Cazenove & Loyd Argon House, Argon Mews, Fulham Broadway, London SW6 1BJ; ☎020 3553 7965; e info@cazloyd.com; www.cazloyd.com. Old-school, established tailor-made specialists to east/southern Africa, Asia, Indian Ocean, & Central/ South America.

Cedarberg African Travel Long Cottage, King Henrys Rd, Lewes BN7 1BU; ☎020 8898 8533; e web@cedarberg-travel.com; www. cedarbergtravel.com. South African specialist with some knowledge of Namibia.

Cox & Kings 6th Floor, 30 Millbank, London SW1P 4EE; ☎020 7873 5000; e sales@ coxandkings.co.uk; www.coxandkings.co.uk. Old company renowned for India, now also featuring Latin America, Indian Ocean, Middle East, China, Asia & Africa, including some Namibian trips.

Expert Africa (See ads, pages i & 340) 9 & 10 Upper Sq, Old Isleworth, Middx TW7 7BJ; ☎020 8232 9777; e info@expertafrica.com; www. expertafrica.com. Started trips to Namibia in 1992, & now has the most comprehensive programme to the country, run by Chris McIntyre – this book's author.

Explore! Nelson Hse, 55 Victoria Rd, Farnborough, Hants GU14 7PA; ☎0843 775 5687; e res@explore.co.uk; www.explore.co.uk. A relatively large company specialising in escorted small-group tours & tailor-made trips throughout the world. Currently has 5 Namibia-only tours.

Gane & Marshall (See ad, page 48) Aldenham, 2 Deer Park Lane, Tavistock, Devon PL19 9HD; ☎01822 600600; e info@ganeandmarshall.com; www.ganeandmarshall.com. Tailor-made trips to east & southern Africa & the Indian Ocean.

Hartley's Safaris The Old Chapel, Chapel Lane, Hackthorn, Lincs LN2 3PN; ☎01673 861600; e info@hartleysgroup.com; www.hartleys-safaris.co.uk. Old-school, established tailor-made specialists to east/southern Africa.

Intrepid Wessex Hse, 40 Station Rd, Westbury, Wilts BA13 3JN; ☎0808 274 5111; e ask@ intrepidtravel.com; www.intrepidtravel.com. Offers a wide range of group trips worldwide, including southern Africa.

Nomad African Travel 4 Broughton Cl, Walton St, BA16 9RS; ☎01458 898272; e nomadat@ onetel.com; www.nomadafricantravel.co.uk. Set-itinerary & tailor-made safaris for all budgets in southern Africa, including Namibia.

Okavango Tours & Safaris White Lion Hse, 64A Highgate High St, London N6 5HX; ☎020 8347 4030; e info@okavango.com; www.okavango. com. Small, long-established specialists to east/ southern Africa, Madagascar & the Indian Ocean islands.

Original Travel 21 Ransome's Dock, 35–37 Parkgate Rd, London SW11 4NP; ☎020 3627 3237; e ask@originaltravel.co.uk; www.originaltravel. co.uk. Bespoke worldwide operator now incorporating Tim Best's Africa programme.

Rainbow Tours (See ad, 3rd colour section) 2 Waterhouse Sq, 138–140 Holborn, London EC1N 2ST; ☎020 7666 1250; e info@ rainbowtours.co.uk; www.rainbowtours.co.uk. Established operator to southern, east & west Africa, Madagascar, the Indian Ocean & Oman.

Safari Consultants Africa House, 2 Cornard Mills, Mill Tye, Gt Cornard, Suffolk CO10 0GW; ☎01787 888590; e info@safariconsultantuk. com; www.safari-consultants.co.uk. Old-school tailor-made specialists to east, central & southern Africa, including Namibia, & the Indian Ocean islands.

Safari Drive (See ad, page xii) Windy Hollow, Sheepdrove, Lambourn, Berks RG17 7XA; ☎01488 71140; e info@safaridrive.com; www.safaridrive.

com. Self-drive expeditions using very well-equipped Land Rovers in east & southern Africa, & Oman.

Scott Dunn Fovant Mews, 12 Noyna Rd, London SW17 7PH; ☎020 3432 5717; e enquiries@ scottdunn.com; www.scottdunn.com. Worldwide luxury operator featuring Asia, Latin America, ski chalets, Mediterranean villas & Africa, including Namibia.

Steppes Travel 51 Castle St, Cirencester, Glos GL7 1QD; ☎01285 880980; e enquiry@ steppestravel.co.uk; www.steppestravel.co.uk. Founded as Art of Travel, this posh tailor-made specialist now has worldwide coverage, including Namibia.

Wild about Africa Sunvil House, Upper Sq, Old Isleworth, Middx TW7 7BJ; ☎020 8758 4717; e safari@wildaboutafrica.com; www. wildaboutafrica.com. Sister company of Expert Africa offers a wide choice of small-group guided trips in Namibia, Tanzania & some of Botswana & Zambia, from inexpensive camping trips to privately guided expeditions.

Wildlife Worldwide Capitol Hse, 12–13 Bridge St, Winchester, Hants SO23 0HL; ☎0845 130 6982; e reservations@wildlifeworldwide.com; www. wildlifeworldwide.com. Wide-ranging small operator with tailor-made & tour programmes across the globe, including options that feature Namibia.

Zambezi Safari & Travel Africa Hse, Modbury, Devon PL21 0QJ; ☎01548 830059; e info@ zambezi.co.uk; www.zambezi.co.uk. Tailor-made specialist to a range of east, central & southern African destinations.

Overland specialists

Dragoman Camp Green, Debenham, Stowmarket, Suffolk IP14 6LA; ☎01728 861133; e info@dragoman.co.uk; www.dragoman.co.uk. Overland truck & small-group tours worldwide, including Africa.

Exodus Grange Mills, Weir Rd, London SW12 0NE; ☎0845 287 7620; e sales@exodus.co.uk; www.exodus.co.uk. Overland truck & set tours worldwide, including 5 Namibia-only options.

FRANCE
Makila Voyages 4 place de Valois, 75001 Paris; ☎01 42 96 80 00; e info@makila.fr; www.makila. fr. Tailor-made trips worldwide, with a focus on southern Africa.

USA
Africa Adventure Company 2601 East Oakland Park Bd, Suite 600, Fort Lauderdale, FL 33306, USA; ☎+1 800 882 9453; e safari@africanadventure. com; www.africa-adventure.com. One of the older Africa travel companies in the USA, run by the irrepressible Mark Nolting.

SOUTH AFRICA
Drifters ☎011 888 1160; e drifters@drifters. co.za; www.drifters.co.za. Established specialists in overland trips.

Jenman African Safaris ☎021 683 7826; e info@jenmansafaris.com; www.jenmansafaris.com

Pulse Africa (See ad, page 48) ☎011 325 2290; e info@pulseafrica.com; www.pulseafrica.com. Tailor-made trips to east & southern Africa & Indian Ocean islands.

RED TAPE

Currently all visitors require a passport which is valid for at least six months after they are due to leave, a completely blank page for Namibian immigration to stamp, and an onward ticket of some sort. In practice, the third requirement is rarely even considered if you look neat, respectable and fairly affluent.

At present, British, Irish and US citizens can enter Namibia without a visa for 90 days or less for a holiday or private visit, as can nationals of the following countries: Angola, Australia, Austria, Belgium, Botswana, Brazil, Canada, Cuba, Denmark, Finland, France, Germany, Hong Kong, Iceland, Italy, Japan, Kenya, Lesotho, Liechtenstein, Luxembourg, Macau, Malawi, Malaysia, Mauritius, Mozambique, the Netherlands, New Zealand, Norway, Portugal, Russian Federation, Singapore, South Africa, Spain, Swaziland, Sweden, Switzerland, Tanzania, Zambia and Zimbabwe.

That said, it is *always* best to check with your local Namibian embassy or high commission before you travel. If you have difficulties in your home country, contact the Ministry of Home Affairs and Immigration in Windhoek (*Cohen Bldg, Kasino St, P Bag 13200, Windhoek;* ☏ *061 2922111*).

The 90-day tourist visa can be extended by application in Windhoek. You will then probably be required to show proof of the 'means to leave', like an onward air ticket, a credit card, or sufficient funds of your own. The current cost of a tourist or business visa is £30/US$50.

EMBASSIES AND HIGH COMMISSIONS

A list of the foreign embassies in Windhoek can be found on page 150. Namibia's diplomatic representatives overseas are as follows:

❸ **Angola** (embassy) Rua da Liberdade No 20, Vila Alice, PO Box 953, Luanda; ☏ +244 222 321 241/952/136; f +244 222 322 008/323 848; e embnam@netangola.com

❸ **Austria** (embassy) Zuckerkandlgasse 2, A-1190 Vienna; ☏ +431 402 9371/2/3; f +431 402 9370; e nam.emb.vienna@speed.at, www.embnamibia.at

❸ **Belgium** (embassy) Av de Tervuren 454, B1150 Brussels; ☏ +32 2 771 1410; f +32 2 771 9689; e nam.emb@brutele.be

❸ **Botswana** (high commission) PO Box 987, Plot 186 Morara Cl, Gaborone; ☏ +267 390 2181; f +267 390 2248; e namibhc@botsnet.bw

❸ **Brazil** (embassy) SHIS QI09, Conjunto 08, Casa 11, Lago Sul, Brasilia df, CEP: 71.625-080; ☏ +55 61 3248 6274/7621; f +55 61 3248 7135; e info@embassyofnamibia.org.br; www. embassyofnamibia.org.br

❸ **China** (embassy) 2-9-2 Ta Yuan, Diplomatic Office Bldg, Beijing 100600; ☏ +86 10 653 22211/24810; f +86 10 653 24549; e namemb@ eastnet.com.cn

❸ **Congo** (embassy) 138 Boulevard du 30 Juin, PO Box 8934, Satelite, Kinshasa 1/Gombe; ☏ +243 81 555 9840/9841; f +873 762 927561; e namembassy_drc@ic.cd

❸ **Cuba** (embassy) Calle 36 No 504, Between 5th Ave and 5th A St, Miramar, Playa, Havana; ☏ +53 7 204 1430/28; f +53 7 204 1431; e namembassycuba@hotmail.com

❸ **Egypt** (embassy) Villa No 60 El Nahda St, Maadi, Cairo; ☏ +202 235 84467; f +202 235 98170; e namembcai@link.net

❸ **Ethiopia** (embassy) Bole Road W17 k19, House No 002, PO Box 1443, Addis Ababa; ☏ +251 116611966/2055; f +251 116612677; e nam. emb@ethionet.et

❸ **France** (embassy) 80 Av Foch, 17 Square de l'Av Foch, Paris 75016; ☏ +33 1 44 17 32 65/76;

f +33 1 44 17 32 73; e info@embassyofnamibia.fr; www.embassyofnamibia.fr

❸ **Germany** (embassy) Reichsstrasse 17, 14052 Berlin; ☏ +49 30 254 0950; f +49 30 254 09555; e namibiaberlin@aol.com; www.namibia-botschaft.de

❸ **India** (high commission) B 8/9, Vascant Vihar, New Delhi 110 057; ☏ +91 11 261 40389/40890; f +91 11 261 46120; e nam@nhcdelhi.com

❸ **Japan** (embassy) 3-5-7 Amerex Building, 4th Floor, Azabudai, Minato-Ku, Tokyo 1060041; ☏ +81 3 6426 5460; f +81 3 6426 5461; e embassy@ namibiatokyo.or.jp

❸ **Malaysia** (high commission) Suite 15-01, Level 15, Menara HLA, No 3 Jalan Kia Peng, 50450, Kuala Lumpur; ☏ +60 3 216 46520/28950; f +60 3 216 88790/88657; e namhckl@streamyx.com; embnam@netangola.com

❸ **Nigeria** (high commission) 16 T Y Danjuma Street, Asokoro District, P M B 5097, Wuse Zone 3, Abuja; ☏ +234 9 780 9441/5485; e info@ namibiahc.com.ng; www.namibiahc.com.ng

❸ **Russia** (embassy) 2nd Kazachy Lane, Hse No 7, Moscow; ☏ +7 499 230 3275/2041; f +7 499 230 2274; e moscow@mfa.gov.na

❸ **South Africa** (high commission) 197 Blackwood St, Arcadia, Pretoria; ☏ +27 12 481 9100; f +27 12 343 7294; e secretary@namibia.org.za

❸ **Sweden** (embassy) Luntmakargatan 86–8, PO Box 19151, 11351 Stockholm; ☏ +46 8 442 9800/9805; f +46 8 612 6655; e info@ embassyofnamibia.se; www.embassyofnamibia.se

❸ **Tanzania** (high commission) 54 Msasani/ Masaki, Upanga Area, PO Box 80211, Dar-es-Salaam; ☏ +255 22 260 1903; f +255 22 260 2003; e namhcdar@gmail.com

❸ **UK** (high commission) 6 Chandos St, London W1G 9LU; ☏ +44 20 7636 6244; f +44 20 7637

5694; e info@namibiahc.org.uk; www.namibiahc.
org.uk
e USA (embassy) 1605 New Hampshire Av NW,
Washington, DC 20009; ☏ +1 202 986 0540; f +1
202 986 0443; e info@namibianembassyusa.org;
www.namibianembassyusa.org

e Zambia (high commission) 30B Mutende Rd,
360407/8 Woodlands, Lusaka; ☏ +260 211 260 407/8;
f +260 211 263 858; e namibia@coppernet.zm
e Zimbabwe (embassy) Lot 1 of 7A, Borrowdale
Estates, 69 Borrowdale Rd, Harare; ☏ +263 4
885841/882709/853218; f +263 4 885800;
e secretary@namibianembassy.co.zw

GETTING THERE AND AWAY

BY AIR

From Europe Several reliable airlines fly to southern Africa from Europe, with onward connections to Windhoek. Most fly overnight, so you can fall asleep on the plane in London and wake in the southern hemisphere ready to explore. The time difference between western Europe and Namibia is minimal, so there's no jet lag.

Air Namibia's (SW; *www.airnamibia.com.na*) only direct flight to Windhoek from Europe is from Frankfurt, with connections to London on British Airways. Flights depart from Frankfurt for Windhoek, and return every evening. Air Namibia also operates connecting flights to/from Johannesburg and Cape Town to link up with most of their intercontinental flights to/from Windhoek.

For many European travellers, the best choice is to fly via Johannesburg. There's a whole host of other options here, from many European airports. British Airways (BA; *www.britishairways.com*) and South African Airways (SA; *www.flysaa.com*) have daily overnight services from London, and both operate add-on connections to Windhoek, run by their subsidiaries. Virgin (VS; *www.virgin-atlantic.com*) also services the Johannesburg route, though their add-on prices to Windhoek are not usually as competitive.

Expect to pay from around £850/US$1,400 return if booked direct with the airline. Prices rise significantly for departures during Easter, July and August, and peak from mid-December to mid-January, when you can expect to pay upward of £1,600/US$2,600. The quietest periods are mid-April to the end of June, and November.

Finding cheap tickets, and the right flights, is an art in itself. Your first stop should probably be to research the possibilities and costs on some of the large online travel agents (OTAs) – companies like Kayak (*www.kayak.co.uk*), Skyscanner (*www.skyscanner.net*) and Expedia (*www.expedia.co.uk*). That should tell you what routes and flights are available, and give you a broad idea of their costs. You might also want to look at these same flights on the websites of the airlines concerned, and perhaps a local flight specialist if there is one.

If you plan to hire a car and arrange accommodation in advance, then also speak to a specialist tour operator (pages 56–8) *before* you book your flights. They will usually quote one cost for your whole trip – flights, car and accommodation. The best operators will usually be cheaper than booking the various components directly, and be able to guide you so that organising your trip becomes a lot less hassle. However, if you're on a very tight budget and want to fly in and backpack around, then go straight to an OTA.

From the Americas South African Airways operates direct flights between New York and Johannesburg, code-sharing with United (*www.united.com*), which connects with numerous regional flights to Windhoek. Delta (*www.delta.com*) operates direct flights between Atlanta and Johannesburg. Alternatively, many travellers from the US approach southern Africa using connections via Europe,

IMPORTS AND EXPORTS

Since Namibia is a member of the Southern African Customs Union (SACU), there are few import and export restrictions between Namibia and either Botswana or South Africa. If you wish to export animal products, including skins or legally culled ivory, make sure you obtain a certificate confirming the origin of every item bought. Remember: even with such a certificate, the international CITES convention prohibits the movement of some things across international borders. Do consider the ethics of buying any animal products that might be covered by CITES.

Visitors can reclaim the VAT on any purchases for export at Hosea Kotako Airport in Windhoek, though note that a commission of N$75 is charged on each transaction.

joining Air Namibia's flights in Frankfurt, or travelling on one of the many carriers servicing Johannesburg, and then connecting through to Windhoek. As in Europe, start your research online.

Given the duration of these flights, travellers often include a few days in Europe as they transit. However, do allow a day or so in London between the flights, as your flights will not technically 'connect' – and if one is late you don't want to miss the other.

Travellers in Central and South America might use the Atlanta or European gateways, or the direct flights between São Paulo and Johannesburg, run by South African Airways daily.

From elsewhere From the Far East, there are flights between Johannesburg and most of the major centres in the region, including Hong Kong (with South African Airways or Cathay Pacific) and Singapore (Singapore Airlines). From Australasia, the best route is probably one of the flights from Perth or Sydney to Johannesburg, with South African Airways or Qantas, connecting to Windhoek.

OVERLAND Entering over one of Namibia's land borders is equally easy. Namibia has fast and direct links with South Africa – good tarred roads and railway service.

Crossing borders Namibia's borders are generally hassle-free and efficient. If you are crossing with a hired car, then remember to let the car-hire company know as they will need to provide you with the right paperwork before you set off. Opening hours at the borders – listed clockwise – are as follows. Note, however, that in winter, between April and September, opening times away from the Caprivi Strip may be an hour earlier, and that all times are subject to change.

With Angola

Ruacana – near the hydro-electric station	08.00–19.00
	(07.00–18.00 winter)
Omahenene – north of the C46 between Outapi and Ruacana	08.00–19.00
	(07.00–18.00 winter)
Oshikango – on the B1 north	08.00–19.00
	(07.00–18.00 winter)
Katitwe – off the C45	06.00–18.00
Rundu – cross the river to go north	06.00–18.00

With Zambia
Wenela – just north of Katima Mulilo   06.00–18.00

With Botswana
Impalila Island – over the river from Kasane   07.00–17.00
Ngoma Bridge – on the B8 between Caprivi/Zambezi and Kasane   06.00–18.00
Mohembo – on the C48, on the southern side of Mahango   06.00–18.00
Dobe – between Tsumkwe and Nokaneng   08.00–16.30
                                                                  (08.00–15.30 winter)
Buitepos – on the B6 Gobabis–Ghanzi road   07.00–24.00
                                                                  (06.00–23.00 winter)

With South Africa
Mata-Mata – on the C15, bordering the Kgalagadi Transfrontier Park   08.00–16.30
                                                                  (07.00–15.30 winter)
Klein Menasse – on the C16 Aroab–Rietfontein road   08.00–16.30
                                                                  (07.00–15.30 winter)
Hohlweg – on the D622 southeast of Aroab   08.00–16.30
                                                                  (07.00–15.30 winter)
Ariamsvlei – on the B3 Karasburg–Upington road   24 hours
Velloorsdrif – on the C10 southeast of Karasburg   08.00–16.30
                                                                  (07.00–15.30 winter)
Noordoewer – on the B1 Windhoek–Cape Town road   24 hours
Sendelingsdrift – ferry across the Orange River within Ai-Ais   08.00–16.30
     Richtersveld Transfrontier Park   (07.00–15.30 winter)
Oranjemund – the bridge over the Orange River   06.00–22.00
                                                                  (07.00–23.00 winter)

By rail and coach For details of rail and coach services across the border from South Africa and Zimbabwe, see *Chapter 6*.

WHAT TO TAKE

This is difficult advice to give, as it depends upon how you travel and your own personality. If you intend to do a lot of hitching or backpacking, then you should plan carefully what you take in an attempt to keep things as light as possible. If you have a vehicle for your whole trip, then weight and bulk will not be such an issue.

CLOTHING On most days you will want light, loose-fitting clothing. Cotton (or a cotton-rich mix) is cooler and more absorbent than synthetic fibres. For men, shorts (long ones) are usually fine, but long trousers are more socially acceptable in towns and especially in rural settlements and villages. For women, knee-length skirts or culottes are best. Namibia has a generally conservative dress code. Revealing or scruffy clothing isn't respected or appreciated by most Namibians.

For the evenings, especially for chilly rides in the back of safari vehicles, and during rainstorms, you will need something warm. Night-time temperatures in the winter months can dip below freezing, especially in desert areas. If possible, dress in layers, taking along a light sweater (polar fleeces are ideal) and a long-sleeved jacket, or a tracksuit, and a light but waterproof anorak. Note that some excellent cotton safari wear is produced and sold locally; try the department stores in Windhoek.

Finally, don't forget a squashable sunhat. Cotton is perfect. Bring one for safety's sake, even if you hate hats, as it will greatly reduce the chance of your getting sunstroke when out walking.

OTHER USEFUL ITEMS See *Chapter 7, Camping and walking in the bush*, pages 103–10, for information on recommended types of camping equipment to take. In addition, below I have outlined a few of my own favourites and essentials, just to jog your memory:

- sunblock and lipsalve – vital for protection from the sun
- sunglasses – essential – ideally dark with a high UV absorption
- insect repellent, especially if travelling to the north or during the rains
- binoculars – essential for watching game and birds
- camera – a long lens is vital for good wildlife shots
- 'Leatherman' multi-purpose tool
- electrical insulating tape – remarkably useful for general repairs
- basic sewing kit, with at least some really strong thread for repairs
- cheap waterproof watch (leave expensive ones, and jewellery, at home)
- couple of paperback novels
- CDs to play in hire cars
- large plastic 'bin-liner' (garbage) bags, for protecting your luggage from dust
- simple medical kit
- magnifying glass, for looking at some of the smaller attractions
- a couple of cheap walkie-talkies if travelling in convoy
- torch (flashlight) – LED Lenser torches are particularly good and worth the investment.

And for backpackers, useful extras might include:

- concentrated, biodegradable washing powder or liquid
- long-life candles – African candles are often soft, and burn quickly
- nylon 'paracord' – at least 20m for emergencies and washing lines
- good compass and a whistle
- more comprehensive medical kit (see page 76)
- universal plug

MAPS AND NAVIGATION A reasonable selection of maps is available in Europe and the USA from specialised outlets. The Michelin map of east and southern Africa (sheet 995) sets the standard for the whole subcontinent, but is not really detailed enough for Namibia. Better maps are those published by Map Studio and Globetrotter, which both contain town plans. For online maps, it is worth taking a look at www.map-of-namibia.com, an offshoot of the exhaustive website www.namibia-1on1.com. Imported maps are obtainable in Britain from Stanfords in Long Acre, Covent Garden, London (✆ *020 7836 1321; www.stanfords.co.uk*) or in the USA at East View Geospatial, Minneapolis, Minnesota (✆ *+1 952 252 1205; www.geospatial.com*). Another useful source is one of the bookshops at Johannesburg airport.

An excellent range of detailed, albeit very old, 'Ordnance Survey' type maps of Namibia is available cheaply in Windhoek from the Surveyor General's office (see page 120). If you are planning a 4x4 expedition, then you may need to buy some of these before you head out into the bush. However, for most normal visitors on

If you are heading into one of the more remote parks in your own vehicle, then you really should invest in a hand-held GPS (global positioning system). These can fix your latitude, longitude and elevation to within about 10m, using a network of American military satellites that constantly pass in the skies overhead. They will work anywhere on the globe.

Although many smartphones incorporate GPS receivers, don't be fooled into thinking that they're anywhere near as good as a dedicated GPS unit in the more rural areas – they're not.

WHAT TO BUY Commercial hand-held GPS units cost from around £80/US$150 in Europe or the USA. As is usual with high-tech equipment, their prices are falling and their features are expanding as time progresses. Alternatively, consider hiring locally from Be Local Tourism (see page 122).

I have been using a variety of Garmin GPS receivers for years now. The early ones ate batteries at a great rate and often took ages to 'fix' my position; more recent models not only have endless new functions and far better displays, but also use fewer batteries, fix positions much more quickly, and usually even work when sitting on the car's dashboard. Whatever make you buy, you don't need a top-of-the-range machine.

WHAT A GPS CAN DO A GPS should enable you to store 'waypoints' and build a simple electronic picture of an area, as well as working out basic latitude, longitude and elevation. So, for example, you can store the position of your campsite and the nearest road, making it much easier to be reasonably sure of navigating back without simply retracing your steps.

It will also enable you to programme in points, using the co-ordinates given throughout this book and by some of the maps listed above, and use these for navigation. Thus you should be able to get an idea of whether you're going in the right direction, and how far away your destination is.

self-drive or guided trips, these maps are *far* too detailed and unwieldy to use. Much better is the TASA map, with a street plan of Windhoek, which is perfectly adequate for self-drive trips on Namibia's roads. It is available from some of the better specialist tour operators, as well as fairly widely in shops and fuel stations in Namibia.

Many overland travellers with a GPS (see box, above) would be lost (sometimes quite literally) without Tracks4Africa (*www.tracks4africa.co.za*), a digital mapping software package that covers the whole continent, or you can download the regional maps separately.

ELECTRICITY Sockets usually supply alternating current at 220/240V and 50Hz. These are the same as South African sockets (the very old standard British design) with three round pins. Adaptors for these are usually easiest to find in Jo'burg Airport or Windhoek; you may struggle to find them elsewhere.

PHOTOGRAPHY Namibia's scenery and wildlife are a big draw for photographers, but the country's harsh environment creates its own problems.

When you return home, if you have a fast internet connection then knowing the GPS co-ordinates for a place will enable you to see satellite images of the place using programmes like Google Maps and Google Earth. See Expert Africa's website (*www.expertafrica.com*) for a demonstration of the satellite images of lodges that are possible.

WHAT A GPS CAN'T DO First, a GPS isn't a compass and, when you're standing still, it can't tell you which direction is which. It can only tell you a direction if you're moving. (That said, some of the more expensive GPS units do now incorporate electronic compasses that can do just this!)

Secondly, it can give you a distance and a bearing for where you might want to go but it can't tell you how to get there. You'll still need to find a track. You should NEVER just set out across the bush following a bearing; that's a recipe for disaster.

Finally, it can't replace a good navigator. You still need to be able to navigate and think to use a GPS effectively. If you're clueless on navigation then driving around any unfamiliar place, including Namibia, you may get you into a mess, with or without a GPS.

ACCESSORIES Most GPS units use quite a lot of battery power, so bring plenty of spare batteries with you. Also get hold of a cigarette lighter adaptor for your GPS when you buy it. This will enable you to power it from the car while you're driving, and thus save batteries.

WARNING Although a GPS may help you to recognise your minor errors before they are amplified into major problems, note that such a gadget is no substitute for good map work and navigation. They're great fun to use, but shouldn't be relied upon as a sole means of navigation. You MUST always have a back-up plan – and an understanding of where you are – or you will be unable to cope if your GPS fails.

Camera insurance Most travel insurance policies are poor at covering valuables, including cameras. If you are taking valuable camera equipment abroad, then include it in your house insurance policy, or cover it separately with a specialist.

MONEY

The Namibian dollar (N$) is divided into 100 cents. This is freely convertible in Namibia; there's no black market and no customs regulations applicable to moving it across borders. It is currently tied to the South African rand (R) so that N$1 = R1. Rand can be used freely in Namibia – nobody even notices. It is, however, often difficult to change Namibian dollars once you leave Namibia. Even in South Africa, you must change the dollars at a bank, and may be charged a small premium for doing so.

It is not possible to get Namibian dollars outside of Namibia. Exchange your currency for South African rand, and use that instead. You can get Namibian dollars out of local cash machines. Try to use up any Namibian change while you're still there; you won't be able to exchange it once you're home.

If the rand plummets in the future, then the government in Windhoek could take full control of its currency and allow it to float free from the rand. Namibia's economy is probably strong enough to make this a very positive move. Check the latest situation with one of the bigger banks before you leave.

For most of the late 1990s the rand slowly but steadily devalued, slipping from about £1 = R6 in 1996 to £1 = R12 in 2001. Then in late 2001 it tumbled down to almost £1 = R20, only to recover back to £1 = R12 in 2003. It remained around the £1 = R11–12 until 2012, and has been devaluing steadily to the time of research. In March 2015, the rates of exchange were:

£1   = N$18.17
US$1   = N$12.19
€1   = N$13.03

Despite the volatility, travel in Namibia for the Western visitor remains largely good value compared with the rest of the region.

Prices in Namibia are subject to VAT at 15%.

HOW TO TAKE YOUR MONEY The best system is always to have some cash Namibian dollars (or rand – remember they are interchangeable) with you, while conserving these by using credit cards where you can. You can gradually withdraw more money from your credit or debit cards as your trip progresses. However, it's important to remember that there are long distances between towns and lodges, so be sure to assess your needs thoroughly in advance, and always make sure that your Namibian dollars will last until you can get to a bank or reliable ATM.

Cash in the form of Namibian dollars or South African rand is essential for buying fuel (credit cards are not always accepted) as well as for small items, and in remote areas. It is also useful for tipping when staying at lodges.

The major **credit cards** (Visa and MasterCard) are widely accepted by lodges, hotels, restaurants and shops, but American Express and Diners Club cards are often not accepted. Even the smaller towns now have ATMs, either as part of a bank, or inside a supermarket, and withdrawing cash by this means is usually no harder than at home. That said, Visa cards are easier to use than most. Whether you are using a debit card or a credit card, you should enter 'credit card account' and not 'bank account' when an ATM asks you where you want your money to come from. It is advisable to take at least two cards, and to notify your bank of your travel plans in advance of departure, in case of any attempted fraud while you're travelling.

The use of **travellers' cheques** has decreased substantially. You may find some banks still exchanging travellers' cheques, but don't rely on them. Cash and cards are much more reliable and the norm, so you will be fine with these.

For details of changing money, see below.

BANKS Namibia's major banks are FNB, Standard, Bank Windhoek and Nedbank, and most town-centre branches have ATMs. Note that FNB has close links with Barclays in the UK, and is best for Visa transactions, but if you're using MasterCard, then Standard is generally a better bet.

Changing money at any of the commercial banks is as easy and quick as it is in Europe. Normal banking hours are 09.00–15.30 weekdays and sometimes 09.00–11.00 Saturdays, depending upon the town; in major centres a few branches open seven days a week. Banks give cash advances on credit cards, though the clearance required for a cash advance may take 30 minutes or so. Note that you may need to take a passport, even just to change currency. Be aware, too, that at the end of the month, when many government employees are paid, queues at the bank can be several hours long.

BUDGETING Namibia genuinely offers something to suit travellers of every budget, with accommodation ranging from backpackers' hostels to luxurious lodges, with everything in-between. For an indication of budgeting for various styles of trip, see *How to travel and budgeting*, pages 52–5.

TIPPING Tipping is a very difficult and contentious topic that is worth thinking about carefully; thoughtlessly tipping too much is just as bad as tipping too little.

Always ask locally what's appropriate; suitable levels of tipping vary significantly, so my guidance here can only be general. Helpers with baggage might expect a couple of Namibian dollars for their assistance. Restaurants will often add an automatic service charge to the bill, in which case an additional tip is not usually given. If they do not do this, then 10% would certainly be appreciated if the service was good.

At upmarket lodges, tipping is not obligatory, despite the destructive assumptions of some visitors that it is. If a guide has given you really good service, then a tip of about N$150 (US$14/£9) per guest per day would be a generous reflection of this. If the service hasn't been that good, then don't tip. Always tip at the end of your stay, not at the end of each day/activity, which can lead to the guides only trying hard when they know there's a tip at the end of the morning. Such camps aren't pleasant to visit and this isn't the way to encourage top-quality guiding. Give what you feel is appropriate in one lump sum, though before you do this find out if tips go into one box for all of the camp staff, or if the guides are treated differently. Then ensure that your tip reflects this – with perhaps as much again divided between the rest of the staff.

ACCOMMODATION

HOTELS, PENSIONS, LODGES AND CAMPS Namibia's hotels are without exception fairly clean and safe. Unless you choose a really run-down old-style hotel in one of the smaller towns, you're unlikely to find anywhere that's dirty. Generally you'll get what you pay for, with the level of choice outside Windhoek and Swakopmund improving year on year. All places in this guide have en-suite shower or bathroom unless otherwise stated.

Establishments are licensed as hotels, lodges, restcamps, etc, according to their facilities, though the distinction between a hotel and a lodge depends on its location – a hotel must fall within a municipal area; a lodge will be outside. Similarly, a guest farm must be a working farm, otherwise it will be classified as a lodge. They are also graded by stars, from one to five, but the system is more a guide to their facilities and size than the quality or service. A 'T' alongside the star rating indicates that the place has been judged suitable for tourists, while the number of 'Y's reflects the type of licence to serve alcohol (three 'Y's being a full licence).

Most bush camps and lodges are of a high standard, though their prices – and atmosphere – vary wildly. Price is a guide to quality here, though not a reliable one. Often the places that have better marketing (ie: you've heard of them) cost more than their less famous neighbours that are equally good. Prices in this guide were correct at the time of research, but inevitably many will rise during the life of the guide.

GUEST FARMS These are private, working farms that host small numbers of guests, usually arranged in advance. They are often very personal and you'll eat all your meals with the hosts and be taken on excursions by them during the day.

Most have some game animals on their land and conduct their own game drives. One or two have interesting rock formations, or cave paintings to visit. Those listed in this guide usually encourage mainly 'photographic' visitors – those with a general interest in the place and its wildlife. Others that concentrate on hunters coming to shoot trophy animals have generally not been included. Many guest farms focus on German-speaking visitors, though those mentioned here also welcome English-speaking guests (and will often make enormous efforts to make you feel at home).

Their prices vary, but are rarely less than N$500 per person per night – usually nearer N$850. They include half board and sometimes a trip around the farm.

CAMPING Wherever you are in Namibia, you can usually find a campsite nearby. Even in remote areas, there may be a community campsite (see page 46) although, if you're far from any settlements, nobody bothers if you just sleep by the road.

The campsites that are dotted all over the country generally have good ablution blocks, which vary from a concrete shed with toilets and cold shower, to an immaculately fitted out set of changing rooms with toilets and hot showers. The more organised ones will also have facilities for washing clothes, barbecue stands and electric points.

Prices nowadays are usually per person rather than per pitch, although at NWR sites in Etosha and Waterberg there is still a site fee as well. Rates vary widely, from around N$60 per person per night at a community campsite, to N$150 or more. There is sometimes an extra charge for a vehicle.

CHILDREN Many of Namibia's hotels, lodges and camps offer special rates for children, which can range from discounts to free accommodation to those

ACCOMMODATION PRICE CODES

This guide uses two sets of price codes: one for hotels based in towns, the other for lodges and guest farms in rural areas. Rates for town establishments are based on a standard double room with breakfast in high season. Rates for rural establishments are based on a double room with dinner, bed and breakfast (DBB); those that are full board (ie: include activities) are noted. Single supplements may apply, averaging 20%, but often significantly higher. While the prices given at the end of the lodge accommodation listings were correct at the time of going to print, these are likely to change over the life of this edition. The price codes are intended to give an enduring indication of how the cost of a night's stay at one establishment is likely to compare with others.

TOWN ACCOMMODATION PRICE CODES

Luxury	$$$$$	£112+; US$173+; N$2,000+
Upmarket	$$$$	£84–112; US$129–173; N$1,500–2,000
Mid-range	$$$	£45–84; US$69–129; N$800–1,500
Budget	$$	£17–45; US$26–69; N$300–800
Shoestring	$	up to £17; up to US$26; up to N$300

RURAL LODGES PRICE CODES

Top-end	LLLLL	£197+ ; US$302+; N$3,500+
Quality	LLLL	£140–197 ; US$216–302; N$2,500–3,500
Mid-range	LLL	£84–140; US$129–216; N$1,500–2,500
Economy	LL	£45–84; US$69–129; N$800–1,500
Basic	L	up to £45; up to US$69; up to N$800

sharing a room with their parents. Some go out of their way to cater for children, too, perhaps with a family room that has loft accommodation. Conversely, a few venues are not suitable for youngsters. It's always worth checking for the availability of any 'family rooms' when making your initial enquiries, as well as ensuring that your chosen location is suitable for children. However, don't expect anywhere to be completely free of risks for children; they will always need to be supervised to some extent.

EATING AND DRINKING

FOOD Traditional Namibian cuisine is rarely served for visitors, so the food at restaurants tends to be European in style, with a bias towards German dishes and seafood. It is at least as hygienically prepared as in Europe, so don't worry about stomach upsets. Restaurant prices are generally lower than you would expect for an equivalent meal in Europe, with a light lunch with drink at N$70–80, and main courses at N$85–110 being fairly standard in Windhoek and Swakopmund restaurants (assuming that you're not splashing out on a seafood platter).

Travellers with special dietary requirements, for example coeliacs, should bring their own gluten-free breads and snacks – there are one or two dining options offering gluten-free meal options in Swakopmund, but elsewhere options are non-existent.

Namibia is a very meat-orientated society, and many menu options will feature steaks from one animal or another. If you eat fish and seafood you'll be fine; menus often feature white fish such as kingklip and kabeljou, as well as lobster in coastal areas. Otherwise, most restaurants offer a small vegetarian selection, and lodge chefs will usually go out of their way to prepare vegetarian dishes if given notice.

In the larger supermarkets you'll find meat, fresh fruit and vegetables (though the more remote the areas you visit, the smaller your choice), and plenty of canned foods, pasta, rice, bread, etc. Most of this is imported from South Africa, and you'll probably be familiar with some of the brand names.

Traditional foodstuffs eaten in a Namibian home may include the following:

eedingu	dried meat
eendunga	fruit of the makalane palm, rather like a rusk
kapana	bread
mealiepap	form of porridge, most common in South Africa
omanugu	also known as mopane worms (*Imbrassia belina*) – these are fried caterpillars, often cooked with chilli and onion
ombindi	spinach
oshifima	doughlike staple made from millet
oshifima ne vanda	millet with meat

DRINK

Alcohol Because of a strong German brewing tradition, Namibia's lagers are good, the Hansa draught being a particular favourite. In cans or bottles, Windhoek Export and Tafel – at around N$12 – provide a welcome change from the Lion and Castle brands that dominate the rest of the subcontinent.

The wine available is mainly South African, with little imported from elsewhere. At its best, this matches the best that California or Australia have to offer, and at considerably lower prices. You can get a bottle of palatable wine from a *drankwinkel* (off-licence) for N$60, or a good bottle of vintage estate wine from N$150.

Soft drinks Canned soft drinks, from Diet Coke to sparkling apple juice, are available ice cold from just about anywhere – which is fortunate, considering the amount that you'll need to drink in this climate. They cost about N$5–6 each, and can be kept cold in insulating polystyrene boxes made to hold six cans. These cheap containers are invaluable if you are on a self-drive trip, and are not taking a large cool box with you. They are available from some big hardware or camping stores for about N$50.

In an Ovambo home you may be offered *oshikundu*, a refreshing breakfast drink made from fermented millet and water.

Water The water in Namibia's main towns is generally safe to drink, though it may taste a little metallic if it has been piped for miles. Natural sources should usually be purified, though water from underground springs and dry river-beds seldom causes any problems. (See *Chapter 5*, page 77, for more detailed comments.)

SHOPPING With the exception of supermarkets and convenience stores at fuel stations, shops are typically open ⊕ 08.30–17.00 Monday to Friday, and on Saturday mornings. The larger supermarkets often stay open all day Saturday and sometimes on Sunday mornings, too, but this is by no means always the case. In general, Namibia's towns become ghostlike at weekends – so if you're self-catering, do make sure that you plan ahead.

PUBLIC HOLIDAYS

During Namibia's public holidays the towns shut down, though the national parks and other attractions just carry on regardless.

COMMUNITY CAMPSITES

With the backing of the government and the IRDNC (see box, page 45), several communities have opened small campsites, many under the auspices of NACSO (*www.nacso.org.na*) – the Namibian Association of CBNRM (Community-Based Natural Resource Management) Support Organisations.

Supporting these communities, by staying there and paying for their crafts, and by using their skills as guides to the local area, is a practical way in which visitors can help some of the poorest of rural people to raise both money and pride.

Many of these sites have only rudimentary facilities and simple ablutions, while others are more elaborate – but in almost all you will need a self-contained 4x4 with your own food and supplies.

New Year's Day	1 January
Independence Day	21 March
Good Friday	variable
Easter Monday	variable
Workers' Day	1 May
Cassinga Day	4 May
Africa Day	25 May
Ascension Day	40 days after Easter Sunday
Heroes' Day	26 August
Human Rights Day	10 December
Christmas Day	25 December
Family Day	26 December

SHOPPING

To access the whole range of Namibian regional arts and crafts in one place, visit the Namibia Craft Centre (see page 147) in Windhoek. Outside of the capital, many towns have street markets selling curios, and numerous lodges showcase local arts and crafts, albeit sometimes at rather inflated prices. At grass-roots level, the number of local communities that have set up small-scale craft projects is growing, bringing employment and attracting revenue back to where both are needed. Many of these are within the fold of the Namibian Association of CBNRM (Community-Based Natural Resource Management) support organisations (*www.nacso.org.na*), and are well worth seeking out.

Many professional artists choose to sell their work at street markets rather than pay a gallery commission on any items sold, so high-quality arts and crafts can often be found by the roadside and on the pavements. In Kavango and Caprivi/Zambezi, you'll find good **woodcarvings** sold on small stalls by the side of the road. However, the best selection is at the two huge street markets on either side of Okahandja (see page 166). There are also some good buys to be had from street stalls in Windhoek.

Bushman crafts are best bought either locally in the Tsumkwe area or at the Tsumeb Arts and Crafts Centre (see page 434).

Authentic **Himba crafts** are easiest to find in Kaokoland, where you will often be offered crafts by local villagers.

The best examples of **basketwork** are found in the northern arts and crafts co-operatives, which include Khorixas Community Craft Centre (see page 349); Tsumeb Arts and Crafts (see page 434); Mashi Crafts, beside the B8 in Kongola (see page 491); and the Caprivi Arts Centre in Katima Mulilo (see page 504).

Swakopmund has several shops sellings crafted **leatherwork**. One of the best selections of **pottery** is found at the Caprivi Arts Centre (see page 504).

Karakul rugs can be found at the Namibia Craft Centre, but specialists are Swakopmund's Karakulia and Kirikara Arts and Crafts (see page 291) and Kiripotib near Dordabis (see page 178).

For more on crafts, see *Chapter 2*, pages 30–1.

CRYSTALS AND GEMSTONES With rich deposits of natural minerals, Namibia can be a good place for the enthusiast to buy crystals and gems – but don't expect many bargains, as the industry is far too organised. For the amateur, the desert roses (sand naturally compressed into forms like flowers) are unusual and often cheap, while iridescent tiger's eye is rare elsewhere and very attractive. If you're really interested, forget the agates on sale and look for the unusual crystals – in Windhoek, the House of Gems (see page 147) and the Diamond Works (see page 147) is a must, and the Johnstons in Omaruru (see page 401) have a fascinating collection. There's also Swakopmund's Stonetique (see page 291) and Kristall Galerie (see page 295).

MEDIA AND COMMUNICATIONS

POST The postal service, Namib Post, is efficient and reasonably reliable. A postcard or airmail letter to Europe or the USA costs N$8–10; delivery to Europe takes about a fortnight. For larger items, sending them by sea is much cheaper, but it may take up to three months and isn't recommended for fragile items. Philatelists might like to note that Namibia's stamps feature numerous designs, often focusing on wildlife.

Post offices are normally open Monday to Friday ⊕ 08.00–16.30, and those in towns also on Saturdays ⊕ 08.00–noon.

TELEPHONE AND FAX Dialling into Namibia, the country code is 264. Dialling out, the international access code is 00. In both cases, omit the first 0 of the area code. You can dial internationally, without going through the operator, from any public phone box, provided you've enough coins or a phonecard (although note that most public phones take only cards). Phonecards (Telecards) are available from post offices and several shops, including many supermarkets. That said, they are slowly becoming obsolete, and finding a working payphone is increasingly difficult.

Almost all areas have direct-dial numbers, preceded by three-digit area codes like 061, 063 and 064.

If faxing from abroad, always dial the number yourself, with your fax machine set to manual. Wait until you are properly connected (listen for a high-pitched tone), and then try to send your fax.

Note that '**a/h**' written next to a phone number means 'after hours' – ie: a number where the person is reachable in the evenings and at weekends. Often this is included for emergency contact, not for casual enquiries.

Mobile and satellite phones
Mobiles work in much of Namibia, though not in the more remote areas of the country. If you plan to use your own mobile phone without a Namibian SIM card, contact your service provider to make sure you are set for global roaming including Namibia. However, unless you plan to use it only for emergencies, it's far cheaper to buy a local SIM card on arrival in Namibia and use this for the duration of your trip. Alternatively, mobile phones can be rented from various locations, including Windhoek International and Walvis Bay airports.

The main Namibian service provider, Mtc, provides excellent coverage in almost all towns and in some (but not all) remote areas. SIM cards for Mtc cost N$7, including N$5 airtime with top-up cards of varying values available. If you plan to visit the more remote regions independently, it may be worth considering taking a satellite phone for emergencies (to hire one, try Be Local Tourism, page 122).

INTERNET Although only 12% of the population is said to have access to the internet, email is common among business users. That said, services are not always up to standard, so don't expect swift responses to all emails sent to Namibia. There are plenty of internet cafés in major towns, and many hotels and backpackers' lodges have internet facilities too – many with Wi-Fi access.

THE PRESS There are no official press restrictions in Namibia, and generally there's a healthy level of debate and criticism in some of the media, although that's not to say that important issues don't sometimes escape public scrutiny because of powerful pressures on editors. In short, it's just like back home!

There is a choice of about seven commercial newspapers, which are easiest to obtain in the larger cities. Getting them elsewhere often means that you will be a few days out of date. *The Namibian* (*www.namibian.com.na*) has the widest circulation and is probably the best during the week, and the *Windhoek Observer* on Sunday is also good. Of the others, there's the daily *Namibian Economist* and the state-owned *New Era* (*www.newera.com.na*), as well as a couple published in Afrikaans and German.

Additionally, there are various colour magazines aimed at the tourist, of which two stand out: *Flamingo*, the in-flight magazine of Air Namibia, is available online (*www.venturepublications.com.na*), while *Travel Namibia*, an offshoot of the well-respected *Travel Africa* (*www.travelafricamag.com*), is published quarterly with features also posted online.

RADIO AND TELEVISION The government-sponsored Namibian Broadcasting Corporation (NBC; *www.nbc.na*) accounts for most of the radio and all of Namibia's normal TV stations. They broadcast radio in six languages from Windhoek, and in three languages from transmitters in the north of the country.

There are currently five local commercial radio stations in Windhoek, all of which are primarily music-based: Radio Wave, Kudu FM, Radio Energy, Radio 99, and the Afrikaans Kosmos 94.1. Away from Windhoek and the larger centres, the radio and public television can be difficult to receive so, if you're travelling around by car, make sure you bring lots of music CDs.

NBC broadcasts one public television channel, and there are several commercial networks. These satellite channels offer a variety of international news, sport and movie channels – the same the world over. By far the most common is the South African-based Mnet TV, which is installed in many of the larger hotels.

TRAVELLING POSITIVELY

Visitors spending significant amounts of money on their trip to Namibia are usually, by their mere presence, making some financial contribution to development and conservation in Namibia. Should you wish to do more, there are numerous organisations working to improve the lot of Namibia's most disadvantaged. Among the most worthwhile are the following, any of which would be delighted to suggest a worthwhile home for your donation – where every cent of your money will be put to good use, without causing any damage to the people that you are trying to help.

IRDNC (see page 45)
The Nyae Nyae Conservancy (see page 443)
Save the Rhino Trust (see page 360)

There are also countless individual projects worthy of support. Seek out your own, or consider the **Bernhard Nordkamp Centre** (*Katutura, Windhoek;* m *081 228 5717; www.thebncnamibia.com*). For details, see box, page 157.

Volunteering Namibia hasn't been slow to take advantage of the upsurge in volunteering holidays. If working with animals is something that appeals, consider contacting Harnas Guest Farm (see pages 175–6), who have a volunteer programme. For humanitarian aid, your first stop could be the Bernhard Nordkamp Centre (see box, page 157).

Meanwhile, there are many pitfalls for unwary volunteers, so be sure to do your homework – especially if you are trying to get involved with a local community. An excellent place to start is www.ethicalvolunteering.org, which also has a downloadable pamphlet entitled *The Ethical Volunteering Guide*. Some of the many issues to consider include:

- For every bona fide organisation there will be others who are willing to take your cash without delivering on their side of the deal.
- Try to be realistic about what your skills are; they will probably define what you can usefully contribute. Namibian communities don't need unskilled hobbyists; they need professionals. To teach skills properly takes years of volunteering, not weeks. (How long did *you* take to learn those skills?) So, for example, if you're not a qualified teacher or builder in your home country, then don't expect to be let loose to do any teaching or building in Namibia.
- Most volunteers will learn much more than the members of the communities that they come to 'help'; be aware of this when you describe who is helping whom.
- Make sure that what you are doing isn't effectively taking away a job from a local person.

Time in Namibia will do you lots of good; make sure it's not to the detriment of your hosts.

NAMIBIA ONLINE

You can post your comments and recommendations, and read the latest feedback and updates from other readers, online at www.bradtupdates.com/namibia.

5

Health and Safety

with Dr Felicity Nicholson and Dr Jane Wilson-Howarth

There are always pitfalls when writing about health and safety for the uninitiated visitor. It is all too easy to become paranoid about exotic diseases that you may catch, and all too easy to start distrusting everybody you meet as a potential thief – falling into an unfounded us-and-them attitude towards the people of the country you are visiting.

As a comparison, imagine an equivalent section in a guidebook to a Western country – there would be a list of possible diseases and advice on the risk of theft and mugging. Many Western cities are very dangerous, but with time we learn how to assess the risks, accepting almost subconsciously what we can and cannot do.

It is important to strike the right balance: to avoid being excessively cautious or too relaxed about your health and your safety. With experience, you will find the balance that best fits you and the country you are visiting.

HEALTH

BEFORE YOU GO Sensible preparation will go a long way to ensuring your trip goes smoothly. Particularly for first-time visitors to Africa, this includes a visit to a travel clinic to discuss matters such as vaccinations and malaria prevention. A full list of travel clinic websites worldwide is available at www.itsm.org, and other useful websites for prospective travellers include www.nathnac.org/ds/map_world.aspx and www.netdoctor.co.uk/travel. The Bradt website now carries an African health section (*www.bradtguides.com/africahealth*) to help travellers prepare for their African trip, elaborating on the information below, but the following summary points are worth emphasising:

- Don't travel without comprehensive medical travel insurance that will fly you home in an emergency.
- Having a full set of immunisations takes time, normally at least six weeks, although some protection can be had by visiting your doctor as late as a few days before you travel. No immunisations are required by law for entry into Namibia, unless you are coming from an area where **yellow fever** is endemic. In that case, a vaccination certificate is mandatory. To be valid the vaccination must be obtained at least ten days before entering the country. It is wise to be up to date on **tetanus**, **polio** and **diphtheria** (now given as an all-in-one vaccine, Revaxis, that lasts for ten years), hepatitis A and typhoid. Immunisations against hepatitis B and rabies may also be recommended. Immunisation against cholera is not usually required for trips to Namibia. Vaccination against **rabies** is now recommended for all visitors as there is an international shortage of rabies immunoglobulin (RIG), which is essential if you have not had three doses of vaccine before you travel. Experts differ

over whether a BCG vaccination against **tuberculosis** (TB) is useful in adults: discuss this with your travel clinic.

- There is no vaccine against malaria, but preventative drugs are available, including mefloquine, atovaquone/proguanil (Malarone) and the antibiotic doxycycline. Malarone and doxycycline need only be started two days before entering Namibia, but mefloquine should be started two to three weeks before. Doxycycline and mefloquine need to be taken for four weeks after the trip and Malarone for seven days. It is as important to complete the course as it is to take it before and during the trip. The most suitable drug varies depending on the individual and the country they are visiting, so visit your GP or a specialist travel clinic for medical advice. If you will be spending a long time in Africa, and expect to visit remote areas, be aware that no preventative drug is 100% effective, so carry a cure too. It is also worth noting that no homeopathic prophylactic for malaria exists, nor can any traveller acquire effective resistance to malaria. Those who don't make use of preventative drugs risk their life in a manner that is both foolish and unnecessary.

- Anybody travelling away from major centres should carry a personal first aid kit. Contents might include a good drying antiseptic (eg: iodine or potassium permanganate), Band-Aids, suncream, insect repellent, aspirin or paracetamol, antifungal cream (eg: Canesten), ciprofloxacin or norfloxacin (for severe diarrhoea), antibiotic eye drops, tweezers, condoms or femidoms, a digital thermometer and a needle-and-syringe kit with accompanying letter from a healthcare professional.

- Bring any drugs or devices relating to known medical conditions with you. That applies to those who are on medication prior to departure, and those who are, for instance, allergic to bee stings, or prone to attacks of asthma. Always check with the country website to identify any restricted medications. Carry a copy of your prescription and a letter from your GP explaining why you need the medication.

- Prolonged immobility on long-haul flights can result in deep vein thrombosis (DVT), which can be dangerous if the clot travels to the lungs to cause pulmonary embolus. The risk increases with age, and is higher in obese or pregnant travellers, heavy smokers, those taller than 6ft/1.8m or shorter than 5ft/1.5m, and anybody with a history of clots, recent major operation or varicose veins surgery, cancer, a stroke or heart disease. If any of these criteria apply, consult a doctor before you travel.

TRAVEL CLINICS AND HEALTH INFORMATION A full list of current travel clinic websites worldwide is available on www.istm.org. For other journey preparation information, consult www.nathnac.org/ds/map_world.aspx (UK) or http://wwwnc.cdc.gov/travel/ (US). Information about various medications may be found on www.netdoctor.co.uk/travel. All advice found online should be used in conjunction with expert advice received prior to or during travel.

IN NAMIBIA
Hospitals, dentists and pharmacies Namibia's main **hospitals** are good and will treat you first and ask for money later. However, with comprehensive medical insurance as part of your travel cover, it is probably better go to one of the **private clinics**. The main ones are in Windhoek and Otjiwarongo, and these are capable of serious surgery and a good quality of care. There are also private medical facilities in Swakopmund, Tsumeb and Walvis Bay.

If you've a serious problem outside of Windhoek, then contact **International SOS** (*from a landline, toll free* ✆ *+27 11 541 1300/1350; www.internationalsos.com*), which organises medical evacuations from anywhere. They do insure individual travellers, but many lodges are members, covering you while you are staying there, and it may be that your insurers overseas would ultimately pick up the International SOS bills if their services were needed.

Pharmacies in the main towns stock a good range of medicine, though often not in familiar brands. Bring with you a repeat prescription for anything you may lose or run out of.

Staying healthy
Namibia is probably the healthiest country in sub-Saharan Africa for visitors. It has a generally low population density and a very dry climate, which means there are comparatively few problems likely to affect visitors. The risks are further minimised if you are staying in good hotels, lodges, camps and guest farms, where standards of hygiene are generally at least as good as you will find at home.

The major dangers in Namibia are car accidents caused by driving too fast on gravel roads, and sunburn. Both can also be very serious, yet both are within the power of the visitor to avoid.

The following advice is applicable to travelling anywhere, including Namibia.

Food and storage
Throughout the world, most health problems encountered by travellers are contracted by eating contaminated food or drinking unclean water. If you are staying in safari camps or lodges, or eating in restaurants, then you are unlikely to have problems in Namibia.

However, if you are backpacking and cooking for yourself, or relying on local food, then you need to take more care. Tins, packets and fresh green vegetables (when you can find them) are least likely to cause problems – provided that clean water has been used in preparing the meal. In Namibia's hot climate, keeping meat or animal products unrefrigerated for more than a few hours is asking for trouble.

Water and purification
Tap water in Namibia's major towns and borehole water used in many more remote locations is perfectly safe to drink. However, even the mildest of the local microbes may cause slight upset stomachs for an overseas visitor. Two-litre bottles of mineral water are available from most supermarkets; these are perfect if you're in a car.

If you need to purify water for yourself in the bush, then first filter out any suspended solids, perhaps by passing the water through a piece of closely woven cloth or something similar. Then bring it to the boil, or sterilise it chemically with chlorine dioxide tablets (iodine is not considered to be safe to use any more). Boiling is much more effective, provided that you have the fuel available. By far the easiest solution is to use a filter bottle such as Aquapure, which filters out all microbes and minerals. It is very cost-effective and mean that you can even drink river water if you need to.

Medical problems
Malaria
Malaria is the most dangerous disease in Africa, and the greatest risk to the traveller. It occurs in northern, and occasionally central, Namibia (see map, page 78), so it is essential that you take all possible precautions against it (see box, page 82). Broadly, antimalarial tablets are recommended for the northern third of the country from November to June, and for the Okavango and Kunene rivers all year round.

Since no malaria prophylactic is 100% effective, one should take all reasonable precautions against being bitten by the nocturnal Anopheles mosquitoes that transmit the disease. Malaria usually manifests within two weeks of transmission, but it can be as little as seven days and anything up to a year. Any fever occurring

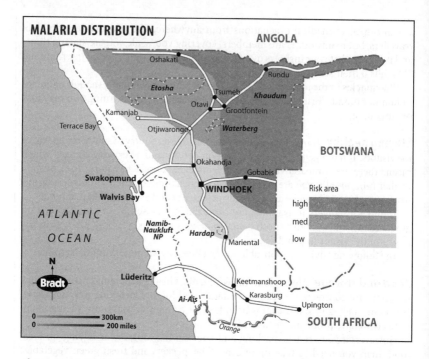

MALARIA DISTRIBUTION

ANGOLA

Oshakati

Rundu

Etosha

Tsumeb

Khaudum

Otavi

Kamanjab

Grootfontein

Terrace Bay

Otjiwarongo

Waterberg

BOTSWANA

Okahandja

Gobabis

Swakopmund

WINDHOEK

Risk area

Walvis Bay

high

ATLANTIC

Namib-Naukluft NP

Hardap

med

OCEAN

Mariental

low

N

Bradt

Lüderitz

Keetmanshoop

Ai-Ais

Karasburg

Upington

0   300km

0   200 miles

Orange

SOUTH AFRICA

after seven days should be considered as malaria until proven otherwise. Symptoms typically include a rapid rise in temperature (over 38°C), and any combination of a headache, flu-like aches and pains, a general sense of disorientation, and possibly even nausea and diarrhoea. The earlier malaria is detected, the better it usually responds to treatment. So if you display possible symptoms, get to a doctor or clinic immediately (in the UK, go to accident and emergency and say that you have been to Africa). A simple test, available at even the most rural clinic in Africa, is usually adequate to determine whether you have malaria. You need three negative tests to be sure it is not the disease. And while experts differ on the question of self-diagnosis and self-treatment, the reality is that if you think you have malaria and are not within easy reach of a doctor, it would be wisest to start treatment.

Travellers' diarrhoea Many visitors to unfamiliar destinations suffer a dose of travellers' diarrhoea, usually as result of imbibing contaminated food or water. Rule one in avoiding diarrhoea and other sanitation-related diseases is to wash your hands regularly, particularly before snacks and meals. As for what food you can safely eat, a useful maxim is: PEEL IT, BOIL IT, COOK IT OR FORGET IT. This means that fruit you have washed and peeled yourself should be safe, as should hot cooked foods. However, raw foods, cold cooked foods, salads, fruit salads prepared by others, ice cream and ice are all risky. It is rarer to get sick from drinking contaminated water but it happens, so stick to bottled water, which is widely available. If you suffer a bout of diarrhoea, it is dehydration that makes you feel awful, so drink lots of water and other clear fluids. These can be infused with sachets of oral rehydration salts, though any dilute mixture of sugar and salt in water will do you good, for instance a bottled soda with a pinch of salt. If diarrhoea persists beyond a couple of days, it is possible it is a symptom of a more serious sanitation-related illness (typhoid, cholera, hepatitis, dysentery, worms, etc), so get to a doctor. If the diarrhoea is greasy and bulky, and is accompanied by sulphurous (eggy) burps, one likely cause is giardia, which is best treated with tinidazole (four x 500mg in one dose, repeated seven days later if symptoms persist).

Rifaximin is a newer treatment for simple traveller's diarrhoea which is not absorbed into the body so is far less likely to cause side effects associated with taking antibiotics. It can only be used in those aged 18 and over but is a useful addition to a medical pack for those who are particularly susceptible to traveller's diarrhoea or for those travelling more remotely. A three-day course is needed and is only available on prescription.

Bilharzia Also known as schistosomiasis, bilharzia is an unpleasant parasitic disease transmitted by freshwater snails most often associated with reedy shores where there is lots of water weed. It cannot be caught in hotel swimming pools or the ocean, but should be assumed to be present in any freshwater river, pond, lake or similar habitat, even those advertised as 'bilharzia free'. The most risky shores will be within 200m of villages or other places where infected people use water, wash clothes, etc. Ideally, however, you should avoid swimming in any fresh water other than an artificial pool. If you do swim, you'll reduce the risk by applying DEET insect repellent first, staying in the water for under 10 minutes, and drying off vigorously with a towel. Bilharzia is often asymptomatic in its early stages, but some people experience an intense immune reaction, including fever, cough, abdominal pain and an itching rash, around four to six weeks after infection. Later symptoms vary but often include a general feeling of tiredness and lethargy. Bilharzia is difficult to diagnose, but it can be tested for at specialist travel clinics, ideally at least six weeks after likely exposure. Fortunately, it is easy to treat at present.

Meningitis This nasty disease can kill within hours of the appearance of initial symptoms, typically a combination of a blinding headache (light sensitivity), blotchy rash and high fever. Outbreaks tend to be localised and are usually reported in newspapers. Fortunately, immunisation with meningitis ACWY vaccine (eg: Menveo, Nimenrix) protects against the most serious bacterial form of meningitis. Nevertheless, other less serious forms exist which are usually viral, but any severe headache and fever – possibly also symptomatic of typhoid or malaria – should be sufficient cause to visit a doctor immediately.

Rabies This deadly disease can be carried by any mammal and is usually transmitted to humans via a bite or a scratch that breaks the skin. In particular, beware of village dogs and monkeys habituated to people, but assume that any mammal that bites or scratches you (or even licks an open wound) might be rabid, even if it looks healthy. First, scrub the wound with soap under a running tap for a good 10–15 minutes, or while pouring water from a jug, then pour on a strong iodine or alcohol solution, which will guard against infections and might reduce the risk of the rabies virus entering the body. Pre-exposure vaccination for rabies is ideally advised for everyone, but is particularly important if you intend to have contact with animals and/or are likely to be more than 24 hours away from medical help. Ideally three doses should be taken over a minimum of 21 days. All three doses are needed in order to change the treatment needed following an exposure.

If you are bitten, scratched or licked over an open wound by a mammal, postexposure prophylaxis should be given as soon as possible, although it is never too late to seek help, as the incubation period for rabies can be very long. Those who have not been immunised before will need four/five doses of rabies vaccine given over 28–30 days and should also receive a product called Human Rabies Immunoglobulin (HRIG). The

HRIG is injected round the wound to try to neutralise any rabies virus present and is a key part of the treatment if you have not had pre-exposure vaccine. HRIG is expensive and may not be readily available as there is a global shortage, so it is important to insist on getting to a place that has it. This is another reason for having good insurance. As a last resort, equine RIG (horse serum) can be used and is definitely better than nothing.

Tell the doctor if you have had pre-exposure vaccine, as this will change the treatment you receive. You will no longer need to have RIG and will only need a couple of doses of vaccine, ideally given three days apart. And remember that, if you do contract rabies, mortality is 100% and death from rabies is probably one of the worst ways to go.

Tetanus Tetanus is caught through deep dirty wounds, including animal bites, so ensure that such wounds are thoroughly cleaned. Immunisation protects for ten years, provided you don't have an overwhelming number of tetanus bacteria on board. If you haven't had a tetanus shot in ten years, or you are unsure, get a booster immediately.

HIV/Aids Rates of HIV/Aids infection are high in most parts of Africa, and other sexually transmitted diseases are rife. Condoms (or femidoms) greatly reduce the risk of transmission.

Tick bites Ticks in Africa are not the rampant disease transmitters that they are in the Americas, but they may spread tick-bite fever along with a few dangerous rarities. They should ideally be removed complete as soon as possible to reduce the chance of infection. The best way to do this is to grasp the tick with your finger nails as close to your body as possible, and pull it away steadily and firmly at right angles to your skin (do not jerk or twist it). If possible douse the wound with alcohol (any spirit will do) or iodine. If you are travelling with small children, remember to check their heads, and particularly behind the ears, for ticks. Spreading redness around the bite and/or fever and/or aching joints after a tick bite imply that you have an infection that requires antibiotic treatment, so seek advice.

Skin infections Any mosquito bite or small nick is an opportunity for a skin infection in warm humid climates, so clean and cover the slightest wound in a good drying antiseptic such as dilute iodine, potassium permanganate or crystal (or gentian) violet. Fungal infections also get a hold easily in hot moist climates so wear 100%-cotton socks and underwear and shower frequently.

Eye problems Bacterial conjunctivitis (pink eye) is a common infection in Africa, particularly for contact-lens wearers. Symptoms are sore, gritty eyelids that often stick closed in the morning. They will need treatment with antibiotic drops or ointment. Lesser eye irritation should settle with bathing in salt water and keeping the eyes shaded. If an insect flies into your eye, extract it with great care, ensuring you do not crush or damage it, otherwise you may get a nastily inflamed eye from toxins secreted by the creature. Small elongated red-and-black blister beetles carry warning colouration to tell you not to crush them anywhere against your skin.

Sunstroke and dehydration Overexposure to the sun can lead to short-term sunburn or sunstroke, and increases the long-term risk of skin cancer. Wear a T-shirt and waterproof sunscreen when swimming. On safari or walking in the direct sun, cover up with long, loose clothes, wear a hat, and use sunscreen. The glare and the dust can be hard on the eyes, so bring UV-protecting sunglasses. A less direct effect of the tropical heat is dehydration, so drink more fluids than you would at home.

Other insect-borne diseases Although malaria is the insect-borne disease that attracts the most attention in Africa, and rightly so, there are others, most too uncommon to be a significant concern to short-stay travellers. These include dengue fever and other arboviruses (spread by day-biting mosquitoes), sleeping sickness (tsetse flies), and river blindness (blackflies). Bearing this in mind, however, it is clearly sensible, and makes for a more pleasant trip, to avoid insect bites as far as possible. Two nasty (though ultimately relatively harmless) flesh-eating insects associated with tropical Africa are tumbu or putsi flies, which lay eggs, often on drying laundry, that hatch and bury themselves under the skin when they come into contact with humans, and jiggers, which latch on to bare feet and set up home, usually at the side of a toenail, where they cause a painful boil-like swelling. Drying laundry indoors and wearing shoes are good ways of deterring this pair of flesh-eaters. Symptoms and treatment of these afflictions are described in detail on Bradt's website (*www.bradtguides.com*).

Prickly heat A fine pimply rash on the trunk is likely to be heat rash; cool showers, dabbing dry, and talc will help. Treat the problem by slowing down to a relaxed schedule, wearing only loose, baggy, 100%-cotton clothes and sleeping naked under a fan; if it's bad you may need to check into an air-conditioned hotel room for a while.

Hepatatis This is a group of viral diseases which generally start with Coca-Cola-coloured urine and light-coloured stools. It progresses to fevers, weakness, jaundice (yellow skin and eyeballs) and abdominal pains caused by a severe inflammation of the liver. There are several forms, of which the two most common are typical of the rest: hepatitis A (or infectious hepatitis) and hepatitis B (or serum hepatitis).

Hepatitis A and hepatitis E are spread by the faecal-oral route, that is by ingesting food or drink contaminated by excrement. They are avoided in the same ways you normally avoid stomach problems: by careful preparation of food and by drinking only clean water. But as there are now excellent vaccines against hepatitis A it is certainly worth getting inoculated before you travel (see page 75). In contrast, the more serious but rarer hepatitis B is spread in the same way as Aids (by blood or body secretions), and is avoided the same way as one avoids Aids. There is also a vaccine against hepatitis B. In most cases, with lots of bed rest and a good low-fat, no-alcohol diet, most people recover within six months. If you are unlucky enough to contract hepatitis of any form, use your travel insurance to fly straight home.

Sleeping sickness or trypanosomiasis This is really a cattle disease, which is rarely caught by people. It is spread by bites from the distinctive tsetse fly – which is slightly larger than a housefly, and has pointed mouth-parts designed for sucking blood. The bite is painful. These flies are easily spotted as they bite during the day, and have distinctive wings which cross into a scissor shape when they are resting. They are not common in Namibia, but do occur occasionally in Bushmanland and the Caprivi. Note that not all tsetses carry the disease. Prevention is easier than cure, so avoid being bitten by covering up. Chemical insect repellents are also helpful. Dark colours, especially blue, are favoured by the flies, so avoid wearing these if possible.

Tsetse bites are nasty, so expect them to swell up and turn red – that is a normal allergic reaction to any bite. The vast majority of tsetse bites will do only this. However, if the bite develops into a boil-like swelling after five or more days, and a fever starts two or three weeks later, then seek immediate medical treatment to avert permanent damage to your central nervous system. The name 'sleeping sickness' refers to a daytime drowsiness which is characteristic of the later stages of the disease.

AVOIDING MOSQUITO AND INSECT BITES

The Anopheles mosquitoes that spread malaria are active at dusk and after dark. Most bites can thus be avoided by covering up at night. This means donning a long-sleeved shirt, trousers and socks from around 30 minutes before dusk until you retire to bed, and applying a DEET-based insect repellent to any exposed flesh. It is best to sleep under a net, or in an air-conditioned room, though burning a mosquito coil and/or sleeping under a fan will also reduce (though not entirely eliminate) bites. Travel clinics usually sell a good range of nets and repellents, as well as Permethrin treatment kits, which will render even the tattiest net a lot more protective, and helps prevents mosquitoes from biting through a net when you roll against it. These measures will also do much to reduce exposure to other nocturnal biters. Bear in mind, too, that most flying insects are attracted to light: leaving a lamp standing near a tent opening or a light on in a poorly screened hotel room will greatly increase the insect presence in your sleeping quarters. It is also advisable to think about avoiding bites when walking in the countryside by day, especially in wetland habitats, which often teem with diurnal mosquitoes. Wear a long loose shirt and trousers, preferably 100% cotton, as well as proper walking or hiking shoes with heavy socks (the ankle is particularly vulnerable to bites), and apply a DEET-based insect repellent to any exposed skin.

Because this is a rare complaint, most doctors in the West are unfamiliar with it. If you think that you may have been infected, draw their attention to the possibility. Treatment is straightforward, once a correct diagnosis has been made.

RETURNING HOME Many tropical diseases have a long incubation period, and it is possible to develop symptoms weeks or months after returning home (so it is vital that you keep taking antimalaria prophylaxis for the prescribed duration after you leave a malarial zone). If you do get ill after your return, tell your doctor where you have been. Alert him/her to any diseases that you may have been exposed to. Several people die from malaria in the UK every year because victims do not seek medical help promptly or their doctors are not familiar with the symptoms and are slow to make a correct diagnosis. Milder forms of malaria may take up to a year to reveal themselves, but serious (falciparum) malaria will usually become apparent within four months. If problems persist, get a check-up at a hospital that specialises in tropical diseases.

SAFETY

WILD ANIMALS Don't confuse habituation with domestication. Most wildlife in Africa is genuinely wild, and widespread species such as hippo or hyena might attack a person given the right set of circumstances. Such attacks are rare, however, and they almost always stem from a combination of poor judgement and poorer luck. A few rules of thumb: never approach potentially dangerous wildlife on foot except in the company of a trustworthy guide; never swim in lakes or rivers without first seeking local advice about the presence of crocodiles or hippos; never get between a hippo and water; and never leave food (particularly meat or fruit) in the tent where you'll sleep.

SNAKE AND OTHER BITES Snakes are secretive and bites are a real rarity, but certain spiders and scorpions can also deliver nasty bites. In all cases, the risk is minimised by wearing closed shoes and trousers when walking in the bush, and watching where you put your hands and feet, especially in rocky areas or when gathering firewood. Only a fraction of snakebites deliver enough venom to be life-threatening, but it is important to keep the victim calm and inactive, and to seek urgent medical attention.

CAR ACCIDENTS Dangerous driving is probably the biggest threat to life and limb in most parts of Africa. On a self-drive visit, drive defensively, being especially wary of stray livestock, gaping pot-holes, and imbecilic or bullying overtaking manoeuvres. Many vehicles lack headlights and most local drivers are reluctant headlight users, so avoid driving at night and pull over in heavy storms. On a chauffeured tour, don't be afraid to tell the driver to slow or calm down if you think he is too fast or reckless.

CRIME Namibia is not a dangerous country, and is generally surprisingly crime-free. Outside of the main cities, crime against visitors, however minor, is exceedingly rare. Even if you are travelling on local transport on a low budget, you are likely to experience numerous acts of random kindness, but not crime. It is certainly no more dangerous for visitors than most of the UK, USA or Europe.

That said, there are increasing reports of theft and muggings, in particular from visitors to Windhoek, so here as in any other city it is important not to flaunt your possessions, and to take common-sense precautions against crime. A large rucksack, for example, is a prime target for thieves who may be expecting to find cameras, cash and credit cards tucked away in the pockets. Provided you are sensible, you are most unlikely to ever see any crime.

Most towns in Namibia have townships, often home to many of the poorer sections of society. Generally they are perfectly safe to visit during the day, but tourists should avoid wandering around with valuables. If you have friends or contacts who are local

SAFETY FOR WOMEN TRAVELLERS   *Janice Booth*

When attention becomes intrusive, it can help if you are wearing a wedding ring and have photos of 'your' husband and children, even if they are someone else's. A good reason to give for not being with them is that you have to travel in connection with your job – biology, zoology, geography or whatever. (But not journalism; that's risky.)

Pay attention to local etiquette, and to speaking, dressing and moving reasonably decorously. Look at how the local women dress, and try not to expose parts of the body that they keep covered. Think about body language. In much of southern Africa direct eye contact with a man will be seen as a 'come-on'; sunglasses are helpful here.

Don't be afraid to explain clearly – but pleasantly rather than as a put-down – that you aren't in the market for whatever distractions are on offer. Remember that you are probably as much of a novelty to the local people as they are to you; and the fact that you are travelling abroad alone gives them the message that you are free and adventurous. But don't imagine that a Lothario lurks under every bush: many approaches stem from genuine friendliness or curiosity, and a brush-off in such cases doesn't do much for the image of travellers in general.

Take sensible precautions against theft and attack – try to cover all the risks before you encounter them – and then relax and enjoy your trip. You'll meet far more kindness than villainy.

and know the area well, then take the opportunity to explore with them a little. Wander around during the day, or go off to a nightclub together. You'll find that they show you a very different facet of Namibian life from that seen in the more affluent areas. For women travellers, especially those travelling alone, it is important to learn the local attitudes about how to behave acceptably. This takes some practice, and a certain confidence. You will often be the centre of attention, but by developing conversational techniques to avert overenthusiastic male attention, you should be perfectly safe. Making friends of the local women is one way to help avoid such problems.

Theft Theft is rarely a problem in Namibia – which is surprising given the poverty levels among much of the population. However, there are a couple of exceptions to this rule. First, theft from unattended vehicles is common in Windhoek (especially), and other larger towns. If you leave your vehicle (for any length of time) with anything valuable on view or the doors unlocked, then you will probably return to find a window smashed and items stolen. Sadly, in recent years there has been an increase in opportunistic muggings, particularly in Windhoek. Take extra care with your valuables and personal belongings – driving in the city is usually fine, but don't get out of your car in quiet areas or areas with thick vegetation. Viewpoints around the city are a hotspot for this kind of opportunistic theft, and it is easily avoided – just admire the view from your car!

If you are the victim of a theft then report it to the police – they ought to know. Also try to get a copy of the report, or at least a reference number on an official-looking piece of paper, as this will help you to claim on your insurance policy when you return home. However, reporting anything in a police station can take a long time, and do not expect any speedy arrests for a small case of theft.

Arrest To get arrested in Namibia, a foreigner will normally have to try quite hard. However, even though most Namibians are not paranoid about spies, it is always wise to ask for permission to photograph near bridges or military installations. This simple courtesy costs you nothing, and may avoid a problem later.

One excellent way to get arrested in Namibia is to try to smuggle drugs across its borders, or to try to buy them from 'pushers'. Drug offences carry penalties at least as stiff as those you will find at home – and the jails are worse. Namibia's police are not forbidden to use entrapment techniques or 'sting' operations to catch criminals. Buying, selling or using drugs in Namibia is just not worth the risk.

Failing this, argue with a policeman or army official – and get angry into the bargain – and you may manage to be arrested. It is *essential* to control your temper; stay relaxed when dealing with officials. Not only will you gain respect, and hence help your cause, but you will avoid being forced to cool off for a night in the cells.

If you are careless enough to be arrested, you will often only be asked a few questions. If the police are suspicious of you, then how you handle the situation will determine whether you are kept for a matter of hours or days. Be patient, helpful, good-humoured and as truthful as possible. Avoid any hint of arrogance. If things are going badly after half a day or so, then start firmly, but politely, to insist on seeing someone in higher authority. As a last resort you do, at least in theory, have the right to contact your embassy or consulate, though the finer points of your civil liberties may end up being overlooked by an irate local police chief.

Bribery Bribery may be a fact of life in some parts of Africa, but in Namibia it is very rare. Certainly no normal visitor should ever be asked for, or offer, a bribe. It would be just as illegal as offering someone a bribe back home.

6

Getting Around Namibia

DRIVING

Driving yourself around Namibia is, for most visitors, by far the best way to see the country. It is generally much easier than driving around Europe or the USA: many of the roads are excellent, the traffic is light and the signposts are usually numerous, clear and unambiguous.

Driving yourself gives you freedom to explore and to stop where you wish across the country, but it doesn't restrict you to your car every day. When visiting private camps or concession areas, you can often leave your hire car for a few days, joining daily 4x4 excursions into more rugged country, led by resident safari guides.

If possible, I'd recommend hiring a vehicle for your whole time in Namibia, collecting it at the airport when you arrive, and returning it there when you depart. This also removes any worries that you may have about bringing too much luggage (whatever you bring is simply thrown in the boot on arrival).

However, if your budget is very tight then you may only be able to afford to take a vehicle for just a few days, perhaps from Windhoek to Swakopmund via the Sesriem area, or to drive around Etosha. However long you keep the vehicle, the type you choose and the company you hire from can make an enormous difference to your trip.

HIRING A VEHICLE Think carefully about what kind of vehicle to hire, and where to get it from, well before arriving in the country. It is almost always better to organise this in advance. Similarly, check out the deals offered by overseas operators *before* you buy your flights. Arranging flights, car and accommodation with one operator, based in your home country, will usually be cheaper and easier than making all the bookings separately.

The normal minimum age to hire a car is 21, though many operators will accept drivers between the ages of 18 and 20 for an additional young-driver surcharge.

If time is not in short supply but money is, then you could consider hiring for just a few days at a time to see specific sights – which would not be too expensive if you are planning on sitting by waterholes in Etosha all day.

Hiring a car in one city and dropping it off elsewhere is perfectly possible with the major car-hire companies; just factor the relevant drop-off fee into your budget. Although these vary widely, depending on the distance and location, you'll probably be looking at a figure of approximately N$1,100 from Windhoek to Swakopmund, rising to about N$4,000 from Windhoek to the far north or south.

No matter where you hire your vehicle, do give yourself plenty of time when collecting and dropping it off. On collection you need to ensure that it's all in good order, including the spare wheel and tool kit, and that any existing damage is recorded; then dropping it off, you need the car-hire company to sign off to confirm if there's any damage or not. Make sure that, if possible, you get the *final* invoice before you leave the vehicle, or you may return home to an unexpected credit-card bill.

Rates Typical current 'per day' on-the-road prices from the more reputable companies, based upon 7–13 days' rental in high season with unlimited mileage and their maximum insurance (see *Insurance, CDWs and gravel roads*, page 87), are:

Medium saloon	eg: Toyota Corolla 1.6 or similar	£40/US$65
High-clearance 2WD	eg: Nissan Qashqai or similar	£50/US$80
High-clearance 4x4	eg: Nissan 4x4 D/cab	£75/US$120

The cheapest deals are usually available from local firms. Typically these have smaller fleets, often of older vehicles, and they seldom have the back-up support of the big companies. That's fine if you don't have problems, but you'll find that good support makes a massive difference if you have an accident or breakdown in a remote location. You will pay more for an automatic.

There's usually a cost for adding in a second driver, typically around N$275 per rental, plus an extra surcharge for drivers under 21 of around N$300 per day.

2WD or 4x4? Whether you need to hire a 2WD or a 4x4 vehicle depends on where you want to go. For virtually all of the country's main sights and attractions, and many of the more offbeat ones, a normal saloon 2WD car is adequate.

The only real exception to this advice is if you're travelling during the rains, around January to March, when you might consider taking a 4x4, just in case you need to ford any shallow rivers that block the road. Additional advantages of a 4x4 vehicle are:

- You relax more on gravel roads, knowing the vehicle is sturdier.
- You may be higher up, giving a slightly better view in game parks.
- It's easier to cross shallow rivers or sand patches if you encounter them.

However, the main disadvantages are:

- The cost of hiring a 4x4 is much higher than hiring a 2WD.
- 4x4s can be heavier to handle, and more tiring to drive.
- A 4x4's fuel consumption is much higher.
- 4x4s have higher centres of gravity, and so tend to roll more easily.
- There's usually no secure boot (trunk), where luggage is not on view, so you can't safely leave bags in the 4x4 when you are not there.

Regardless of any disadvantages, if you want to explore the northern Kunene Region, further than Tsumkwe in Bushmanland, or any of the really offbeat areas in the Caprivi – then you'll *need* a high-clearance 4x4. The main point is that in most of these more remote areas, just one 4x4 vehicle simply isn't enough. Your party needs to have a *minimum* of two vehicles for safety, and you should have a couple of experienced bush drivers (eg: a minimum of two vehicles is a condition of entry for Khaudum National Park). These areas are very dangerous if you drive into them alone or ill-equipped.

What kind of 2WD? This is really a question of budget. A small 2WD vehicle – the most basic typically being something like a Toyota Corolla 1.3 – is adequate for two adults and most trips. If you've any flexibility in your budget, then it's usually worth stepping up to a larger saloon, to give you more power and comfort given the long drives involved in most trips. All but the most basic cars come with air conditioning and a radio/CD player, both of which are useful; larger saloons tend to also have power steering, which is not always helpful on gravel roads.

Consider a high-clearance 2WD, like the Nissan Qashqai or X-Trail (or similar) as their higher wheelbase can be particularly useful, giving you some of the advantages of 4x4s mentioned above, but without the full cost of a 4x4. If you have three or four people in your party, then these are probably a better choice than any 2WD vehicle.

For a larger group, consider either two small cars or a VW Kombi (which seats eight). Two cars will give more flexibility if the group wants to split up on occasions. Conversely, the combis have lots of space to move around, and six window seats for game viewing. Their main disadvantage is that they lack a secure, hidden boot, so – as with most 4x4s – you can't safely leave the vehicle alone with any luggage in it.

What kind of 4x4? In order of increasing cost, the choice normally boils down to a single-cab Nissan or Toyota Hilux, a double-cab Nissan or Toyota Hilux, or a Land Rover Defender. Occasionally you'll find Mazdas used instead of Toyotas, but their design and limits are very similar. The only relevant difference is that Toyotas are more common, and hence their spares are easier to obtain.

For two people, the single-cab Toyota Hilux or Nissan is fine. This has just two seats (sometimes a bench seat) in the front and a fibreglass canopy over the pick-up section at the back. This is good for keeping the rain off your luggage, but it will not deter thefts. That said, it's worth noting that a double-cab will afford you a lot more space to move around and enable you to store cameras and drinks within easy reach.

For three or four people, you'll need the double-cab or the Land Rover. The double-cabs are lighter vehicles, generally more comfortable and faster on tar. However, the Land Rovers (TDi or earlier models) are mechanically simpler, and easier to mend in the bush – *if* you know what you're doing. Further, your luggage is inside the main cab, and so slightly safer, easier to access, and will remain a little less dusty. Five or more people will need the flexibility of two vehicles – more than four people with luggage in either of these is really quite squashed.

Insurance, CDWs and gravel roads
Wherever you hire your vehicle, you must read the fine print of the hire agreement very carefully. The insurance and the collision damage waiver (CDW) clauses are worth studying closely. These spell out the 'excess' that you will pay in the event of an accident. The CDW excesses vary widely, and often explain the difference between cheap rental deals and better but more costly options.

Namibia has long proved to be a very bad country for accidents; paradoxically the problem is that the gravel roads are too *good*. If they were consistently poor and pot-holed, then people would go slowly. But instead they are often smooth, even and empty – tempting people to speed. This results in an enormous damage and write-off rate among the car-hire fleets. Generally this isn't due to collisions, but to drivers who are unfamiliar with the conditions going too fast on gravel roads and losing control on a bend, or losing concentration and falling asleep on a long, straight, tar road. This phenomenon affects 2WDs and 4x4s equally.

Because of this, car-hire companies will sometimes have high excesses. A maximum 80% CDW is not unknown – which would mean that you will always pay 20% of the cost of any damage. With this level of cover, the bill for a major accident, even in a small vehicle, can easily run into thousands of pounds or US dollars.

Always check the fine print of the rental agreement, as some will have quite extreme clauses, stating that you are liable for *all* of the damage if you have an accident where no other vehicles are involved and you are driving on a gravel road.

6

Driving over borders and one-way hire Few car-hire companies will allow vehicles to be driven into Angola, Zimbabwe or Zambia. However, if a car-hire company has offices in Botswana and South Africa, then you can *usually* take cars into these countries. Then you will need to advise the company in advance, as they need a few days to apply for the right permits and insurances – which is likely to cost an extra N$800–1,300 or so depending on the company. There's also usually an additional one-way fee; for example expect about N$5,000 (£275/US$450) from Namibia to South Africa. Note that such fees, as well as car-hire rates, are usually asymmetrical: your car hire may be much cheaper from South Africa to Namibia than vice versa.

If you are planning to drive into Botswana from Namibia, you will surrender your cross-border permit at the control post, then pay for a short-term permit and road safety levy fee. On your return, you will probably need to buy a new cross-border permit.

One-way hire is usually possible, and it's usually easier to arrange with the larger companies who have a more widespread network of depots, but expect fairly substantial amounts for larger distances from Windhoek. Similarly, for pick-ups/drop-offs that are not from/to an airport, there will usually be an additional delivery or collection charge, which often increases out of hours, over weekends and on public holidays.

Car-hire companies Most of the big car-hire companies, including Avis, Budget, Europcar and Hertz, have franchises in Namibia. Their prices tend to be similar, as do their conditions of hire, which leaves quality and availability as appropriate criteria for choosing between them. These vary in cycles depending on the competence of the general manager.

Aside from these large firms, there is a plethora of others, including smaller, local car-hire companies in Windhoek, some of which are good. Others have more dubious reputations, and even buy their cars from the big companies, which dispose of their vehicles after one or two years. This makes their rates cheaper, but compromising on the quality of your vehicle is crazy when you rely upon it so completely. Economise on accommodation or meals – but rent the best vehicle you can.

The following companies are based in Windhoek, though many also have offices in other Namibian towns. All the local companies, and international companies marked *, are members of the Car Rental Association of Namibia (CARAN; *PO Box 80368, Windhoek;* ✆ *081 417 3797;* e *caran@iway.na*), a voluntary grouping of the more responsible members of the trade. This lays down guidelines for standards and provides an informal arbitration service if things go wrong.

International companies

🚗 **Avis*** Hosea Kutako Airport ✆ 062 540271; Safari Hotel ✆ 061 233166; www.avis.co.za
🚗 **Britz** Hosea Kutako Airport ✆ 062 540 660/242; e bookings@britz.co.za; www.britz.co.za
🚗 **Budget*** Hosea Kutako Airport ✆ 062 540225; Eros Airport ✆ 061 228720; e res. namibia@budget.co.za; www.budget.co.za
🚗 **Europcar*** Hosea Kutako Airport ✆ 062 543700; Eros Airport ✆ 061 227103; 24 Bismarck St ✆ 061 385100; e info@europcar.co.za; www.europcar.co.za
🚗 **Hertz*** Hosea Kutako Airport ✆ 062 540116; cnr AB May & Garten Strasse ✆ 061 256274; e res@ hertz.co.za; www.hertz.co.za

🚗 **KEA Campers** Hosea Kutako Airport; ✆ 062 540 660; e bookings@keacampers.co.za; www. keacampers.co.za
🚗 **Thrifty** Hosea Kutako Airport ✆ 062 540004; cnr Stein St & Sam Nujoma Dr ✆ 061 220738; Hilton Hotel ✆ 061 221165; www. thrifty.co.za

Smaller local companies

🚗 **Advanced*** 20 Palladium St; ✆ 061 246832; e info@advancedcarhire.com; www. advancedcarhire.com
🚗 **African Tracks*** 10 Pettenkofer St; ✆ 061 245072; e info@africantracks.com, tracks@iafrica. com.na; www.africantracks.com

Asco* 195 Mandume Ndemufayo Av; ☎061 377200; e reservations@ascocarhire.com; www. ascocarhire.com

Camel* 38 Jasper St; ☎061 248818; e info@ camel-carhire.com; www.camel-carhire.com

Camping Car Hire* 36 Joule St; ☎061 237756; m 081 127 2020; e carhire@africaonline. com.na; www.camping-carhire.com

Caprivi* 135 Sam Nujoma Dr; ☎061 256323; e info@caprivicarhire.com; www.caprivicarhire. com

Odyssey* 12 Seder St; ☎061 223269; m 081 127 2222; e odyssey@iway.na; www. odysseycarhire.com

Okavango Car Hire* 124 Andimba Toivo Ya Toivo St; ☎061 306553; e info@windhoekcarhire. com; www.okavango-carhire.com

Pegasus* 81 Daan Bekker St; ☎061 251451; m 081 124 4375; e pegasus.carhire@gmail.com; www.pegasuscar-namibia.com

Savanna 80 Trift St; ☎061 229272; m 081 129 9978; e savanna.auto@iway.na; www. savannacarhire.com.na

A warning Before signing up for a car hire, see the section on insurance on page 87. There is often fine print in these agreements which may mislead the unwary.

ON THE ROAD Almost all of Namibia's major highways – usually 'B' roads – are tarred. They are usually wide and well signposted, and the small amount of traffic on them makes journeys easy. Less important roads are often gravel, but even these tend to be well maintained and easily passable. The most important of these are 'C' roads, with others usually classified as 'D' – but there is also an 'M' classification. Confusion arises because many gravel roads have two or even three numbers – which is why in this guide you will sometimes find more than one number given for a particular road.

Most sights, with the exception of Sandwich Harbour, are accessible with an ordinary saloon car (referred to as 2WD here). Only those going off the beaten track – into Khaudum, Bushmanland or parts of the Kaokoveld – need to join an organised group. The only safe alternative to such a group trip is a convoy of two 4x4s with at least as many experienced bush drivers. Don't be fooled into thinking that a 4x4 will get you everywhere and solve all your problems. Without extensive experience of using one on rough terrain, it will simply get you into dangerous situations which you have neither the skill nor the experience to cope with. See also *4x4 driving*, pages 91–4.

Some sources advise that you require an international driving permit in order to drive here, but a normal overseas driving licence with the requisite passport generally seems to be fine, if the licence is written in English. You'll be asked to produce documentation at roadblocks, so keep these to hand. British licence holders can obtain an international permit in the UK from post offices or the AA; the US counterpart is the AAA.

The speed limit in urban areas is generally 60km/h, and elsewhere120km/h (but see *Gravel roads*, below, for more on appropriate speeds). Driving is on the left.

EQUIPMENT AND PREPARATION Driving around Namibia is usually very easy; much easier than driving in most developed, industrialised countries. But because the distances are long, and some areas remote, a little more preparation is wise.

Fuel Petrol and diesel are available in all the major towns, and many more rural corners too. For most trips, you just need to remember to fill up when you have the opportunity. Prices will depend to a certain extent on where you are, but in September 2014 unleaded petrol in Walvis Bay (where fuel prices are the lowest in Namibia) cost around N$11.99 a litre, and diesel N$12.42. In a major emergency, many farms will be able to help you – but you shouldn't need such charity if you think ahead a little.

If you are taking a small expedition into the northern Kaokoveld, Bushmanland or the more obscure corners of the Caprivi, then you will need long-range fuel tanks and/

or a large stock of filled jerrycans. It is essential to plan your fuel requirements well in advance, and to carry more than you expect to need. Using a vehicle's 4x4 capability, especially in low ratio gears, will greatly increase your fuel consumption. Similarly, the cool comfort of a vehicle's air conditioning will burn your fuel reserves swiftly.

It's worth knowing that if you need to transfer petrol from a jerrycan to the petrol tank, and you haven't a proper funnel, an alternative is to roll up a piece of paper into a funnel shape – it will work just as well.

Spares and repairs Namibia's garages are generally very good, and most larger towns have a comprehensive stock of spares for most vehicles. (Expect to pay over £80/US$140 for a new tyre for a small 2WD saloon, or around £9/US$14.50 for a repair.) You'll often find several garages specialising in different makes of vehicle. In the bush you'll find that farm mechanics can effect the most amazing short-term repairs with remarkably basic tools and raw materials.

In an emergency, some of the better garages and tyre companies offer a call-out service based on a rate per kilometre. One such is Mariental Fitment Centre (see page 185) which has several affiliates nationwide.

Navigation The TASA map of the country, available from good tour operators, is among the best for driving – but there are others. Note that many of Namibia's road numbers have changed in recent years, and continue to change, with several D roads being upgraded to C roads with entirely different numbers. The current TASA map indicates some of these changes but local signposts may not match, so it's wise to take particular care in out-of-the-way places.

Those mounting expeditions may want to think about buying more detailed maps from the Surveyor General's office (see page 120). If you are heading to the sand tracks of Bushmanland or the wilds of eastern Caprivi, then consider taking a GPS system. See *Maps and navigation* (pages 63–4) for further comments.

DRIVING AT NIGHT Never drive at night unless you have to. Both wild and domestic animals frequently spend the night by the side of busy roads, and will actually sleep on quieter ones. Tar roads are especially bad as the surface absorbs all the sun's heat by day, and then radiates it at night – making it a warm bed for passing animals. A high-speed collision with any animal, even a small one like a goat, will not only kill the animal, but will cause very severe damage to a vehicle, and potentially fatal consequences to you.

2WD DRIVING

Tar roads The vast majority of Namibia's tar roads are excellent, and a programme of tarring is gradually extending these. Currently they extend to linking most of Namibia's larger towns. Most are single carriageways (one lane in either direction), and it's an effort to rein back the accelerator to remain within the speed limit of 120km/h.

Remember that even on these you will find hazards like animals crossing. These roads are not as insulated from the surrounding countryside as the motorways, freeways and autobahns back home, so don't be tempted to speed.

On main roads, regular picnic sites with a shaded table and benches give the opportunity to stop for a break on long journeys. However, care should always be exercised; there are reports of these being used as ambush places by thieves.

Strip roads Very occasionally there are roads where the sealed tar surface is wide enough for only one vehicle. When you meet another vehicle travelling in the opposite direction on the same stretch of tar, the local practice is to wait until the last possible moment before you steer left, driving with two wheels on the gravel adjacent to the tar, and two on the tar. Usually, the vehicle coming in the opposite direction will do the same, and after passing each other both vehicles veer back on to the tar. If you are unused to this, then slow right down before you steer on to the gravel.

Gravel roads Most roads in Namibia are gravel, and most of these are very good. Virtually all are fine for 2WD vehicles. They don't normally suffer from pot-holes, although there may be slight ruts where others have driven before you.

You will occasionally put the car into small skids, and with practice at slower speeds you will learn how to deal with them. Gravel is a less forgiving surface on which to drive than tar. The techniques for driving well are the same for both, but on tar you can get away with sloppy braking and cornering which would prove dangerous on gravel.

The main problem with Namibia's gravel roads is that they are too good. Drivers are lulled into a false sense of security; they believe that it is safe to go faster, and faster. Don't fall for this; it isn't safe at all. See the *Insurance, CDWs and gravel roads* section on page 87, and promise that you'll never drive faster than 80km/h on gravel. That way you'll return from a self-drive trip still believing how safe and good the roads are! A few hints for gravel driving in a 2WD vehicle may be helpful:

- **Slowing down** If in any doubt about what lies ahead, always slow down. Road surfaces can vary enormously, so keep a constant lookout for pot-holes, ruts or patches of soft sand which could put you into an unexpected slide.
- **Passing vehicles** When passing other vehicles travelling in the opposite direction, always slow down to minimise both the damage that stone chippings will do to your windscreen, and the danger in driving through the other vehicle's dust cloud. If the dust cloud is thick, don't return to the centre of the road too fast, as there may be another vehicle behind the first.
- **Using your gears** In normal driving, a lower gear will give you more control over the car – so keep out of high 'cruising' gears. Rather stick with third or fourth, and accept that your revs will be slightly higher than they might normally be.
- **Cornering and braking** Under ideal conditions, the brakes should only be applied when the car is travelling in a straight line. Braking while negotiating a corner is dangerous, so it is vital to slow down before you reach corners. Equally, it is better to slow down gradually, using a combination of gears and brakes, than to use the brakes alone. You are less likely to skid.

Salt roads For details of driving on salt roads, see page 322.

4X4 DRIVING Having a high-clearance 4x4 can extend your options considerably. However, no vehicle can make up for an inexperienced driver, so ensure that you are confident of your vehicle's capabilities before you venture into the wilds. You need lots of practice, guided by an expert, before you'll be able to handle the vehicle in difficult terrain. Driving in convoy is essential in the more remote areas, in case one vehicle gets stuck or breaks down. Some of the key techniques are outlined below.

Driving in sand If you start to lose traction in deep sand, then stop on the next piece of solid ground that you come to. Lower your tyre pressure until there is a distinct bulge in the tyre walls (having first made sure that you have the means to reinflate them when you reach solid roads again). A lower pressure will help your traction greatly, but it will also increase the wear on your tyres. Pump them up again before you drive on a hard surface at speed, or the tyres will be badly damaged.

Where there are clear, deep-rutted tracks in the sand, don't fight the steering wheel – just relax and let your vehicle steer itself. Driving in the cool of the morning is easier than later in the day because when sand is cool it compacts better and is firmer. (When hot, the pockets of air between the sand grains expand and the sand becomes looser.)

If you do get stuck, despite these precautions, don't panic. Don't just rev the engine and spin the wheels – you'll only dig deeper. Instead stop. Relax and assess the situation. Now dig shallow ramps in front of all the wheels, reinforcing them with pieces of wood, vegetation, stones, material or anything else which will give the wheels better traction. Lighten the vehicle load (passengers out) and push. Don't let the engine revs die as you engage your lowest ratio gear, and use the clutch to ensure that the wheels don't spin wildly and dig themselves further into the sand.

Sometimes rocking the vehicle backwards and forwards will build up momentum to break you free. This can be done by intermittently applying the clutch and/or by getting helpers who can push and pull the vehicle at the same frequency. Once the vehicle is moving, the golden rule of sand driving is to keep up the momentum: if you pause, you will sink and stop.

Driving in mud This is difficult, though the theory is the same as for sand: keep going and don't stop. That said, even the most experienced drivers get stuck. Some areas of Namibia (like the *omurambas* in Khaudum National Park) have very fine soil known as 'black-cotton' soil, which can become totally impassable when wet.

If you are unlucky enough to need to push-start your vehicle while it is stuck in sand or mud, then there is a remedy. Raise up the drive wheels, and take off one of the wheels. Then wrap a length of rope around the hub and treat it like a spinning top: one person (or more) pulls the rope to make the axle spin, while the driver lifts the clutch, turns the ignition on, and engages a low gear to turn the engine over. This is a difficult equivalent of a push-start, but it may be your only option.

Rocky terrain Have your tyre pressure higher than normal and move very slowly. If necessary passengers should get out and guide you along the track to avoid scraping the undercarriage on the ground. This can be a very slow business, and is often the case in the highlands of the northern Kaokoveld.

Crossing rivers The first thing to do is to stop and check the river. You must assess its depth, its substrate (type of river-bed) and its current flow; and determine the best route to drive across it. This is best done by wading across the river (while watching for hippos and crocodiles, if necessary). Beware of water that's too deep for your vehicle, or the very real possibility of being swept away by a fast current and a slippery substrate.

If everything is OK then select your lowest gear ratio and drive through the water at slowly but steadily. Your vehicle's air intake must be above the level of the water to avoid your engine filling with water. It's not worth taking risks, so remember that a flooded river will often subside to much safer levels by the next morning.

Overheating If the engine has overheated, the only option is to stop and turn it off. Stop and let it cool. Don't open the radiator cap to refill it until the radiator is no longer hot to the touch. Keep the engine running and the water circulating while you refill the radiator – otherwise you run the risk of cracking the hot metal by suddenly cooling it. Flicking droplets of water onto the outside of a running engine will cool it. When driving away, switch off the air-con (as it puts more strain on the engine). Open the windows and turn the heater and fan full on. This won't be pleasant in the midday heat, but it'll help to cool the engine. Keep watching the engine temperature gauge.

DRIVING NEAR ELEPHANTS: AVOIDING PROBLEMS

Elephants are the only animals that pose a real danger to vehicles. Everything else will get out of your way, or at least not actively go after you, but if you treat elephants wrongly there's a chance that you might have problems.

To put this in perspective, most drivers who are new to Africa will naturally (and wisely) treat elephants with enormous respect, keeping their distance – simply out of fear. Also, in the more popular areas of Etosha, where the elephants are habituated to vehicles, you'd have to really annoy an already grumpy elephant for it to give you trouble.

To give specific advice is difficult, as every elephant is different. Each is an individual, with real moods and feelings – and there's no substitute for years of experience to tell you what mood they're in. However, a few basics are worth noting.

First, keep your eyes open and don't drive too fast. Surprising an elephant on the road is utterly terrifying, and dangerous for both you and the elephant. Always drive slowly in the bush.

Secondly, think of each animal as having an invisible 'comfort zone' around it. (Some experts talk of three concentric zones: the fright, flight and fight zones – each with a smaller radius, and each more dangerous.) If you actively approach then you breach that zone, and will upset it. So don't approach too closely: keep your distance. How close depends entirely on the elephants and the area. More relaxed elephants having a good day will allow you to get within 25m of them; bad-tempered ones that aren't used to cars may charge at 250m! You can often approach more closely in open areas than in thick bush. That said, if your vehicle is stationary and a relaxed, peaceful elephant approaches you, then you should not have problems if you simply stay still.

Thirdly, never beep your horn or flash your lights at an elephant (and if at night, you shouldn't be driving yourself anyhow!). Either is guaranteed to annoy it. If there's an elephant in your way, just sit back, relax and wait; elephants always have right of way in Africa! The more sound and fury – like wheel spins and engine revving – the more likely that the elephant will assume that you are attacking it, and this is especially the case with a breeding herd.

Finally, look carefully at the elephant(s):

- Are there any small calves around in the herd? If so, expect the older females to be easily annoyed and very protective – keep your distance.
- Are there any males in 'musth' around? These are fairly easy to spot because of a heavy secretion from the penis and the temporal glands (on the sides of their heads), and a very musty smell. Generally these will be on their own, unless they are with a cow on heat. Such males will be excitable; you must spot them and give them a wide berth.
- Are there any elephants with a lot of seepage from their temporal glands? If so, expect them to be stressed and easily irritable – beware. This is likely to have a long-term cause – perhaps lack of good water, predator pressure or something as random as toothache – but whatever the cause that animal is under stress, and so should be given an extra-wide berth.

Grass stems and seeds will get caught in the radiator grill and block the flow of air, causing the engine to overheat and the grass to catch fire. You should stop and remove the grass seeds every few kilometres or so, depending on the conditions.

DRIVING NEAR BIG GAME The only animals which are likely to pose a threat to vehicles are elephants (see box *Driving near elephants: avoiding problems* on page 93 for details). So treat them with the greatest respect and don't 'push' them by trying to move ever closer. Letting them approach you is much safer, and they will feel far less threatened and more relaxed. Then, if the animals are calm, you can safely turn the engine off, sit quietly, and watch as they pass you by.

If you are unlucky, or foolish enough to unexpectedly drive into the middle of a herd, then don't panic. Keep your movements, and those of the vehicle, slow and measured. Back off steadily. Don't be panicked, or overly intimidated, by a mock charge – this is just their way of frightening you away.

SUGGESTED ITINERARIES If you're organising a small 4x4 expedition, then it is assumed that you know exactly what you're doing, and where you want to go, and hence no 4x4 itineraries have been included here.

The suggested itineraries here, for 2WDs, are intended as a framework only, and the time spent at places is the *minimum* which is reasonable – if you have less time, then cut places out rather than quicken the pace. With more time to spare, consider taking the same routes, and exploring each area in greater detail.

When planning your own itinerary, try to intersperse the longer drives between more restful days. Avoid spending each night in a new place, as shifting your base can become tiring. Try to book hire cars and accommodation as far in advance as you can; that way you'll get the places you want, exactly when you want them.

Included here are two very loose categories: 'budget' and 'indulgent'. These reflect the cost of the choices – although even our 'budget' suggestions are designed as places where a good experience is possible, at a good value rate, rather than being simply the cheapest places to sleep. Where campsites are suggested, it's because of the experience and location offered, not simply because they offer a good way to reduce costs.

Two weeks
Southern–central Namibia

Night		Budget	Indulgent
1	Fly overnight to Namibia		
2	In/near Windhoek	Rivendell	Eningu Clayhouse Lodge
3–4	Mariental area	Bastion Farmyard	Bagatelle Game Ranch
5–6	Fish River Canyon area	Canon Roadhouse	Fish River Lodge
7–8	Lüderitz	Kairos Cottage	The Nest
9	Helmeringhausen area	Hotel Helmeringhausen	Dabis Guestfarm
10–11	Namib-Naukluft area	Sesriem Campsite	Wolwedans Dune Lodge
12–13	Namib-Naukluft area	Tsauchab River Camp	Sossus Dune Lodge
14	Fly overnight out of Namibia		

This itinerary, focused on the southern part of Namibia, offers the chance to hike in the world's second-biggest canyon, explore the deserted mining town of Kolmanskop just outside Lüderitz, see the sun rise over the world's biggest sand dunes and enjoy walking among the stunning scenery of the Namib-Naukluft area.

Highlights of Namibia

Night		Budget	Indulgent
1	Overnight flight to Namibia		
2	In/near Windhoek	Vineyard Country B&B	Heinitzburg Hotel/Hilton
3–4	Namib-Naukluft area	Büllsport Guestfarm	Wolwedans Boulders Camp
5–6	Namib-Naukluft area	Desert Camp	Little Kulala
7–8	Swakopmund	Organic Square	Desert Breeze Lodge
9–10	Damaraland	!Gowati Lodge	Mowani Mountain Camp
11–12	Etosha	Taleni Etosha Village	Ongava Lodge
13–14	Etosha	Campsite at Etosha Safari Lodge	Onguma Tented Camp
15	*En route* south	Campsite at Okonjima	Okonjima Bush Camp
16	Fly overnight out of Namibia		

This kind of circular two-week trip from Windhoek, visiting the desert in the Sesriem area, the coast around Swakopmund, a glance at Damaraland and some serious game-viewing in Etosha in the north, is probably the most common route for self-driving around the main highlights of Namibia. There are endless options, but the key to success is to avoid trying to 'speed up' this route. Two-and-a-half weeks around this rough route, staying in some of these areas longer, would be a real improvement; but try to squash this driving into ten days and it would seem like an endurance test.

En route you can climb the stunning rusty red sand dunes at Sossusvlei, kayak with hundreds of Cape fur seals at Walvis Bay, or get the adrenalin pumping with some adventure activities in Swakopmund. Admire the ancient Bushman rock art in Damaraland, and of course, explore Namibia's famous Etosha National Park.

Three weeks
Southern–central–Etosha

Night		Budget	Indulgent
1	Overnight flight to Namibia		
2–3	Mariental area	Bastion Farmyard	Bagatelle Game Ranch
4–5	Fish River Canyon	Ai-Ais Restcamp	Fish River Lodge
6–7	Lüderitz	Hansa Haus	The Nest
8	Namib-Naukluft area	Hotel Helmeringhausen	Wolwedans
9	Namib-Naukluft area	Desert Homestead	Hoodia Desert Lodge
10–11	Namib-Naukluft area	Desert Homestead	Moon Mountain
12–13	Swakopmund	Villa Margherita	Beach Hotel
14–15	Damaraland	Twyfelfontein Lodge	Damaraland Camp
16–17	Etosha	Okaukuejo Restcamp	Ongava Tented Camp
18–19	Etosha	Halali Restcamp	Mushara Outpost
20	*En route* to Windhoek	Camping at Omandumba Farm	Erongo Wilderness Lodge
21	Fly overnight out of Namibia		

Three weeks allows you to combine the highlights of both northern and southern Namibia, as above. Okaukuejo Restcamp is a highlight of this itinerary, with one of the best floodlit waterholes in southern Africa.

Trans-Caprivi Strip

Night		Budget	Indulgent
1	Overnight flight to Victoria Falls or Livingstone		

2–3	Victoria Falls area	Zambezi Waterfront	Tongabezi Lodge
4–6	Chobe River area	Camping in Kasane	Impalila Island Lodge
7–8	Mudumu area	Mavunje Campsite	Nambwa Lodge
9–10	Popa Falls area	Shametu River Lodge camping	RiverDance Lodge
11	Rundu	N'Kwazi camping	Taranga Safari Lodge
12–13	Etosha	Onguma Tamboti Campsite	Onguma Tree Top Camp
14–15	Etosha	Okaukuejo Restcamp	Ongava Lodge
16–17	Damaraland	Hoada Campsite	Grootberg Lodge
18–19	Damaraland	Brandberg Restcamp	Camp Kipwe
20	North of Windhoek	Elegant Farmstead	Okonjima Bush Camp
21	Fly overnight out of Namibia		

This trans-Caprivi route is intrinsically more expensive than spending the same length of time just in Namibia. Victoria Falls and the Chobe/Kasane are both relatively costly, Botswana's national park fees are relatively high, and there would also be a one-way drop-off fee levied on the car hire. Such a trip is much better suited to a second or third visit to Namibia, rather than the first.

It offers a completely different experience from the rest of Namibia. Hear the roar of the famous Victoria Falls, cruise the waters of the Kwando and Kavango rivers keeping your eyes peeled for hippos and crocodiles. Keep a pair of binoculars handy – the birdlife here is fantastic!

BY AIR

Namibia's internal air links are good and reasonably priced, and internal flights can be a practical way to hop huge distances swiftly. The scheduled internals are sufficiently infrequent that you need to plan your trip around them, and not vice versa. This needs to be done far in advance to be sure of getting seats, but does run the risk of your trip being thrown into disarray if the airline's schedule changes. Sadly, this isn't as uncommon as you might hope. See *Chapter 8*, page 149, for the contact details of airline head offices in Windhoek.

Increasingly, light aircraft flights are being used for short camp-to-camp flights. These are pretty expensive compared with driving but are great if you are short on time or do not want to drive.

REGIONAL FLIGHTS The main regional airports (with their international city codes) are Cape Town (CPT), Johannesburg (JNB), Livingstone, Zambia (LVI), Luanda, Angola (LAD), Maun, Botswana (MUB), Victoria Falls, Zimbabwe (VFA) and Windhoek International (WDH).

Air Namibia (*www.airnamibia.com.na*) operates regular and reliable flights around the region. There are daily flights to Cape Town and Johannesburg, from about N$3,080 and N$2,200 respectively, one-way. Other destinations from Windhoek include Maun (with flights continuing to Victoria Falls; one-way tickets from N$3,877), Victoria Falls (from N$4,036) and Luanda (from N$4,299). There are also flights to Lusaka and Accra. In general, you will find these to be the same price if you buy them locally or overseas. However, if you travel between Europe and Namibia with Air Namibia, and book your regional flights at the same time, then these routes become much cheaper. Prices and timetables of internal flights change regularly.

South African Airways (*www.flysaa.com*) and **Comair** (a subsidiary of **British Airways**, *www.comair.co.za*) also link Windhoek with Johannesburg and Cape Town

DISTANCE CHART
Distances in kilometres

Distances between towns are only one part of the equation when calculating travelling times. More important are the type of road (tar, gravel, salt) and the terrain, both of which must be taken into consideration.

The chart is a lower‑triangular distance matrix. Each line lists the distances (in km) from the named town to the towns listed diagonally above it, in the order: Aus, Buitepos, Epupa, Gobabis, Grootfontein, Henties Bay, Kamanjab, Karasburg, Karibib, Katima Mulilo, Keetmanshoop, Khorixas, Lüderitz, Maltahöhe, Mariental, Namutoni, Noordoewer, Okahandja, Okaukuejo, Omaruru, Opuwo, Oshakati, Otavi, Otjiwarongo, Outjo, Rehoboth, Ruacana, Rundu, Sesfontein, Sesriem, Swakopmund, Tsumeb, Tsumkwe, Walvis Bay.

```
Aus
989  Buitepos
1544 1171  Epupa
898  115  1439  Gobabis
1145 777  729  657  Grootfontein
798  786  733  630  645  Henties Bay
1156 783  388  688  425  345  Kamanjab
346  1010 1541 895  1142 1115 1153  Karasburg
876  501  802  388  242  414  873  794  Karibib
1422 1533 1470 1418 767  1404 1156 1901 1252  Katima Mulilo
211  802  1261 687  934  907  945  208  665  1693  Keetmanshoop
1149 777  501  662  419  234  113  1147 317  1150 982   Khorixas
125  1136 1667 1021 1268 923  1279 471  999  2027 334  1273  Lüderitz
249  692  1223 498  824  549  835  540  555  1583 332  829  374  Maltahöhe
432  381  1112 466  713  686  724  429  221  1472 969  221  718  111  Mariental
1226 863  791  677  506  677  761  484  926  1015 500  1349 905  794  Namutoni
442  991  1637 991  1238 1211 1249 147  969  1997 304  1286 609  636  443  1319  Noordoewer
764  393  780  276  381  395  392  761  112  1140 553  430  889  332  487  857   Okahandja
937  562  741  339  342  254  353  934  167  677  506  395  761  555  123  1221  364  Okaukuejo
1368 995  176  1263 637  557  212  1365 626  1085 1157 325  1491 1047 173  325   Omaruru
1401 708  387  913  342  852  681  398  659  989  1190 675  1524 1080 245  1494 857  364  325  565   Opuwo
1174 683  732  568  87   507  336  1053 404  846  845  330  1179 735  170  598  253  548  345  320   Oshakati
938  565  606  450  207  389  218  935  197  966  727  212  1061 617  288  1031 368  174  190  430  135  345   Otavi
1011 638  533  523  280  462  145  1008 269  1011 800  139  1104 576  247  117  208  247  117  357  191  436  73   Otjiwarongo
606  407  938  292  539  512  550  603  270  1298 395  544  729  285  174  620  699  158  522  331  762  450  795  332  405  Outjo
1553 1180 235  1065 494  1143 272  1550 686  1253 1342 377  1676 1232 157  534  750  152  490  615  688  Rehoboth
1393 1020 977  905  248  893  645  390  741  511  1182 639  1516 1072 236  561  497  287  561  624  834  742  Ruacana
1389 1016 465  921  658  578  233  1386 647  1389 1178 346  1512 1068 289  495  586  289  569  834  489  500  787  Rundu
434  877  709  683  771  356  709  725  472  1530 517  615  559  185  296  852  821  390  754  533  992  682  878  Sesfontein
1051 676  800  563  67   412  175  1048 446  175  1337 840  318  482  619  659  731  482  619  834  1015  Sesriem
1237 746  670  631  60   570  399  1116 377  819  907  367  1242 798  687  107  241  355  345  316  261  63   282  297  Swakopmund
1401 1028 985  913  256  901  581  1398 659  974  1190 675  1524 1080 969  423  1494 653  598  899  563  343  316  552  Tsumeb
700  709  831  594  690  98   443  1079 206  1458 814  349  938  451  267  593  655  403  521  866  475  316  Tsumkwe
693  320  851  205  452  466  463  690  181  1211 482  816  372  261  533  786  71   435  242  675  708  946  Walvis Bay
389  389  389  Windhoek
```

INTERNAL FLIGHTS

Scheduled internal flights Namibia has a reasonable network of scheduled internal flights, run by Air Namibia from its hub at Windhoek's Eros Airport (ERS). The number of destinations has been cut significantly in recent years, and both prices and timetables change regularly. Generally, though, these flights are not too expensive. As an example, Katima Mulilo to Windhoek, a distance of 1,950km, costs on average N$2,401 (£131/US$216) one-way. Currently, regular flights link Windhoek with:

Katima Mulilo (M'Pacha; MPA) N$2,401
Lüderitz (LUD) N$1,931
Ondangwa (OND) N$2,436

Oranjemund (OMD) N$2,071
Walvis Bay (WVB) N$1,681

Chartered internal flights

✈ **Namibia Commercial Aviation** ✆061 223562; e fly@nca.com.na; www.nca.com.na. Runs private charters in resorted aircraft, including a superb DC-6 dating from 1958 (see box, opposite). ✈ **Wilderness Air** ✆061 255735; e info@wilderness-air.com; www.wilderness-air.com. They offer private charters as well as more economical seat-in-plane rates, where you share the cost with others travelling on the same scheduled route. ✈ **Wings over Africa** ✆061 255001/2; m 081 129 3673; e info@wings.na; www.flyinafrica.com

Flexible fly-in trips In the last few years, there have been an increasing number of light aircraft flights around Namibia, arranged by small companies using small four- and six-seater planes as well as larger 16-seater 'caravans'. These are particularly convenient for linking farms and lodges which have their own bush airstrips. If you have the money, and want to make the most of a short time in the country, then perhaps a fly-in trip would suit you. Now it's possible to visit Namibia in the same way that you'd see Botswana's Okavango Delta, by flying from camp to camp. This is still the only way to see one or two of the private concessions in the extreme northwest. Any good tailor-made specialist tour operator (see pages 56–8) could put together such a trip for you – but expect it to cost at least £460/US$740 per person per night.

One particularly popular option is to take one of the scheduled flights that link Windhoek and Swakopmund with the properties around Sesriem and Wolwedans. This is usually arranged as part of a package through a tour operator, or one of the lodges. It's not cheap, but is a fast way to get into the dunes if time is limited. One company organising such trips is DuneHopper (*www.dunehopper.com*), which offers scheduled packages ranging from two to five nights to the NamibRand and Sossusvlei, with daily departures from Windhoek and Swakopmund. As an indication of costs, a return three-day, two-night trip from Windhoek or Swakopmund to Wolwedans Dune Lodge currently costs N$21,170 per person, based on a minimum of two passengers, and including full board and activities.

Of course, if you've a private pilot's licence and an adventurous streak, then Namibia's skies are marvellously open and free of hassles – but you'll have to spend a day in Windhoek sorting out the paperwork and taking a test flight.

BY RAIL

Generally, Namibia's trains cater better for freight than visitors (*Desert Express* excepted). An extensive network of tracks connects most of the main towns, but many of these are freight only. There is no through service to South Africa – the only passenger train to cross the border terminates at Upington, where there is no through connection to the South African network (the next mainline station, De

CLASSIC AIR FLIGHTS

Walking over the tarmac in the late 1990s at Hosea Kutako Airport to board your flight to Victoria Falls, you may have been surprised to find a silver, black, white and turquoise *Fish Eagle* in front of you – a glistening old propeller-driven plane. Aviation enthusiasts would recognise this as a vintage Douglas DC-6B, powered by four Pratt & Whitney R-2800 engines. It is one of two classic DC-6Bs which belonged to the privately owned Namibia Commercial Aviation (NCA).

In fact these two were the very last aircraft to roll off the production line in 1958. Initially they had a little less than three years of European commercial operations with JAT, of Belgrade, before they were transferred to the Yugoslav Air Force. The *Fish Eagle* was then used exclusively as the personal transport of the Yugoslav leader, Marshall Tito. For this it was fitted out in style with wood and leather, extra soundproofing, a kitchen/galley, and even six beds.

Over a decade later, in 1975, both aircraft were donated to the Zambian Air Force, where Marshall Tito's plane became President Kaunda's personal transport for several years, before falling out of favour. Then it was left to languish on the ground in Lusaka for 15 years. Finally, in 1992, the Zambian Air Force decided to sell 40 tonnes of DC-6 spares, and a condition of sale was that the buyers would agree to take away and dispose of these two aircraft. NCA bought the spares and, after a week working on the first of the planes, the engineers had restored the *Fish Eagle* sufficiently for it to be flown out to Rundu, their base in Namibia. This has now been sold, but the second aircraft, the *Bateleur*, was restored during 1998 and is still in use for private charters all over Namibia.

Aar, is 415km away). Within Namibia, routes have been curtailed in recent years, and now no passenger trains run north of Otjiwarongo or east to Gobabis.

The Starline passenger rail service is run by TransNamib (*www.transnamib.com.na/ Starline.htm*), but this service has been cut considerably over the last decade. Trains that run are pleasant and rarely full, but they are slow and stop frequently. This is not for those in a hurry but, while most visitors without their own vehicle prefer long-distance coaches or hitchhiking, travelling by train affords the chance to meet local people. Unfortunately the faster *Omugulu Gwombashe Star* from Windhoek to Swakopmund/ Walvis Bay, and Windhoek north to Ondangwa, suffered from technical problems from its introduction in 2004, and in 2007 was withdrawn from service.

With the exception of the route from Keetmanshoop to Karasburg, all train journeys are overnight. This means that there's no chance of enjoying the view but, on the plus side, it allows travellers to get a night's sleep while in transit, saving on accommodation costs and perhaps 'gaining' a day at their destination. Carriages are divided into 'economy' and 'business' sections, some with sleeper compartments that convert to seating in the daytime, and tickets come with a numbered seat reservation. There are vending machines dispensing snacks and soft drinks on most (but not all) trains, which also have water fountains; videos are shown throughout the journey.

Passengers need to check in half an hour before the train departs. Only two pieces of luggage may be carried free of charge; bicycles are not allowed.

FARES Fares for TransNamib's trains or buses are low (the 1,050km journey between Swakopmund and Windhoek, for instance, costs N\$106 in economy class, one-way, or N\$139 in business class). All train prices quoted in this guide are for one-way fares.

Travellers over the age of 60 should receive a discount, while one child under the age of six is permitted to travel free; any more are charged at half price.

SCHEDULES

TransNamib services cover the following routes (for more details, see individual chapters):

Windhoek–Swakopmund & Walvis Bay via Okahandja, Karibib & Usakos (departs daily except Sat at 19.55)

Walvis Bay & Swakopmund–Windhoek via Usakos, Karibib & Okahandja (departs daily except Sat at 19.00)

Windhoek–Keetmanshoop via Rehoboth, Kalkrand, Mariental, Gibeon, Asab & Tses (departs daily except Sat at 19.40)

Keetmanshoop–Windhoek via Tses, Asab, Gibeon, Mariental, Kalkrand & Rehoboth (departs daily except Sat at 19.00)

Keetmanshoop–Karasburg via Grünau (departs Wed, Sat at 08.00)

Karasburg–Keetmanshoop via Grünau (departs Sun, Thu at 11.00)

BOOKING

Starline trains and buses may be booked at any station. Main station telephone numbers for passenger enquiries are as follows:

Karasburg ✆ 063 271 1202
Keetmanshoop ✆ 063 229 202
Mariental ✆ 063 249 202
Okahandja ✆ 062 503 315

Swakopmund ✆ 064 208 512
Walvis Bay ✆ 064 208 504
Windhoek ✆ 061 298 2175

A booking fee of N$12 is charged for ticket collection after 16.00 or on a Sunday.

THE *DESERT EXPRESS*

(✆ *061 298 2600;* e *dx@transnamib.com.na; www. transnamib.com.na/desert-express.html*) The result of years of planning and work, the *Desert Express* was introduced in 1998, having been designed, built and fitted for the journey between Windhoek and Swakopmund. It offers a luxurious overnight trip, stopping *en route* at different places in each direction. One-way tickets cost N$3,500 per person sharing a twin cabin, or N$4,500 single. You can also transport a vehicle for an additional N$1,200 one-way.

The train has just 24 air-conditioned cabins (making advance booking vital). Each is small but ingeniously fitted: beds that pull down from the walls, washbasins that move, and various switches hidden away. Each has its own en-suite facilities and will sleep up to three people, though two in a cabin is ideal. It's a unique way to be whisked between Windhoek and Swakopmund in comfort, ideally at the start or end of a trip.

Check-in is 30 minutes before departure; if you've free time around Windhoek station, it is worth taking advantage of the wait to visit the TransNamib Museum (see page 154).

Westbound, the train leaves Windhoek on Friday afternoon at noon in winter (first Sunday in April to first Sunday in September), or 13.00 in summer. After about 3 hours it reaches Okapuka Ranch, where travellers disembark for a short game drive. Continuing on the train, a sundowner drink and nibbles are served before an impressive dinner, after which the train stops in a siding for the night. It starts moving early in the morning, catching the spectacular sunrise over the desert and passing through the Khan Valley before stopping in the dunes between Swakopmund and Walvis Bay, for travellers to take a short walk in the desert. It arrives in Swakopmund at 10.00 after a good breakfast.

Eastbound, it departs from Swakopmund on Saturday afternoon at 15.00, winter and summer. After a few hours it stops at a siding from where passengers are taken for a late-afternoon sundowner drink before dinner at 19.00. The following morning, at 08.00, the train stops at Okapuka Ranch for an hour for a short activity, before continuing with breakfast and arriving at Windhoek station by 10.30.

There are also occasional seven-day all-inclusive trips between Swakopmund and Etosha (*N$32,500/21,700 sgl/pp sharing*). There is not a fixed schedule for the *Desert Express*; the best thing to do is contact them on the number above and enquire about when you'd like to travel. Bookings for all trips can be made through good overseas operators, local agents, or direct with *Desert Express*.

BY BUS

In comparison with Zimbabwe, east Africa or even South Africa, Namibia has few cheap local buses that are useful for travellers. That said, small Volkswagen **combis** (minibuses) do ferry people between towns, usually from townships, providing a good fast service, but they operate only on the busier routes between centres of population. Visitors usually want to see the more remote areas – where local people just hitch if they need transport. As an indication of fares, you could expect to pay around N$280 (£15.50/US$25) between Windhoek and Ondangwa, one-way.

COACHES

Intercape The South African coach company, Intercape (\ +27 21 380 4400; m 0861 287287; e info@intercape.co.za; www.intercape.co.za), operates its luxury Mainliner vehicles on long-distance routes covering many of the main towns. These are comfortable, with refreshments, as well as music, videos, toilets and air conditioning.

Reservations for all coaches should be made at least 72 hours in advance. Tickets may be bought online with a credit card, or through Intercape's reservations office at the Galilei Street depot in Windhoek, off Jan Jonker. They are also available at all money market outlets at Shoprite, and at a few selected branches of Spar. Alternatively, get in touch with one of their **booking agents**:

Gobabis Boekhou & Sekretariële; \ 062 562470
Grünau Grünau Country House; \ 063 262001
Katima Mulilo Tutwa Travel & Tourism; \ 064 404099
Keetmanshoop JJ's Supermarket; \ 063 225251

Lüderitz Lüderitz Safari & Tours; \ 063 202719
Swakopmund Sure Ritz Travel \ 064 405151; or Trip Travel \ 064 404031
Windhoek The Travel Professionals; \ 061 253528

Timings given in this guide for Intercape services are local summer time (September–March), which is 1 hour behind winter time. Schedules have changed little over the years, but they do vary slightly from year to year so it's as well to use the information in the individual chapters as a guide, and to check the latest timetables before planning a trip. Buses are run on the following routes:

Windhoek–Swakopmund & Walvis Bay via Okahandja, Karibib & Usakos (4 weekly, departing Mon, Wed, Fri, Sat, returning Mon, Wed, Fri, Sun)
Windhoek–Victoria Falls Border (Zambia side) via Okahandja, Otjiwarongo, Otavi, Tsumeb, Grootfontein, Rundu & Katima Mulilo (2 weekly, departing Mon, Fri, returning Wed, Sun)

Windhoek–Cape Town via Rehoboth, Mariental, Keetmanshoop, Grünau & Karasburg (4 weekly, departing Mon, Wed, Fri & Sun, returning Tue, Thu, Fri, Sun)
Windhoek–Upington via Rehoboth, Mariental, Keetmanshoop & Grünau (4 weekly, departing Mon, Wed, Fri, Sun, returning Tue, Thu, Fri, Sun)

Fares Intercape's fares, like airline fares, are no longer charged at a fixed rate. The figures quoted in this guide are based on the cost of a one-way 'Full Flexi' ticket on a weekday in 2014, but 'Flexi' and 'Saver' tickets are also on offer, and fares also vary significantly according to factors such as the date of travel, seat availability and, one assumes, profitability of the route. Note that booking agents usually charge a handling fee on each ticket of around N$10.

Up-to-date schedules and fares may be obtained online. The following gives an indication of one-way fares:

Windhoek to Rehoboth N$320
Windhoek to Okahandja N$220
Windhoek to Swakopmund N$410
Windhoek to Walvis Bay N$420
Windhoek to Otjiwarongo N$240
Windhoek to Grünau N$520

Windhoek to Rundu N$540
Windhoek to Cape Town N$950
Windhoek to Johannesburg (via Upington: Windhoek to Upington N$690, Upington to Johannesburg N$730) N$1,420
Windhoek to Victoria Falls Border N$760

Namib-Naukluft Lodge Shuttle African Extravaganza (✆ *061 372100;* e *afex@ afex.com.na; www.african-extravaganza.com*) runs a useful shuttle service linking Windhoek and Swakopmund with their Namib-Naukluft Lodge, near Solitaire (see page 267). Though in practical terms this limits you to staying at their lodge, it is a convenient way to see part of the desert if you don't want to drive.

The shuttle departs daily from Windhoek or Swakopmund at 14.00 (13.00 Apr–Sep), arriving at the lodge just before sunset. After an early morning trip to Sossusvlei, with breakfast in the dunes, guests return to the lodge via Sesriem, for lunch and a sundowner on the property. The return shuttle leaves the lodge early in the morning to reach Windhoek or Swakopmund at around 12.30. The round trip costs N$5,700 per person sharing, or N$6,000 single. If you want to start from Windhoek and end in Swakopmund, or vice versa, rates are N$6,950 per person sharing, N$7,250 single. This includes accommodation and meals, drinking water *en route* and park entrance fees.

LOCAL TRANSPORT

Private **taxis** operate in the larger towns, and are useful for getting around Windhoek, Swakopmund and Walvis Bay. They are normally summoned by phoning, rather than being hailed from the street.

Minibuses serve the routes between the townships and the centre, usually leaving only when (very!) full. Unless you know where you are going, and have detailed local advice about which ones to take, you're unlikely to find these very useful.

HITCHHIKING

Hitchhiking is still an essential mode of transport for many rural Namibians. For visitors from overseas, it's only feasible provided that they're patient and fairly hardy. It can be a great way to meet people, speedy and cheap – but I couldn't recommend it for female travellers, especially those travelling on their own. How fast you get lifts is determined by how much traffic goes your way, where you stand, and how you look. Some of the gravel roads have very little traffic, and you will wait days for even a single car to pass. So do set off with enough food and water to be able to wait for this long, and choose very carefully the lifts that you take, and where they leave you.

For the sake of courtesy, and those who come after you, don't abuse people's kindness: offer to help with the cost of fuel (most people will refuse anyhow) or pay for some cold drinks on the way. Listen patiently to your host's views and, if you differ, do so courteously – after all, you came to Namibia to learn about a different country.

7

Camping and Walking in the Bush

BUSH CAMPING

Many boy scout-type manuals have been written on survival in the bush, usually by military veterans. If you are stranded with a convenient multi-purpose knife, then these useful tomes will describe how you can build a shelter from branches, catch passing animals for food, and signal to the inevitable rescue planes which are combing the globe looking for you – all while avoiding the attentions of hostile forces.

In Namibia, bush camping is usually less about survival than about being comfortable. You're likely to have much more than the knife: probably at least a bulging backpack, if not a loaded 4x4. Thus the challenge is not to camp and survive, it is to camp and be as comfortable as possible. With practice you'll learn how, but a few hints might be useful for the less experienced African campers.

WHERE YOU CAN CAMP In national parks and areas that get frequent visitors, there are designated camping sites, usually at restcamps. Most people never need to use any sites other than these.

Outside the parks, there are a number of private campsites, as well as a smattering of community ones. In default of either of these, ask the local landowner or village head if they are happy for you to camp on their property. If you explain patiently and politely what you want, then you are unlikely to meet anything but warm hospitality from most rural Namibians. They will normally be as fascinated with your way of life as you are with theirs. Company by your camp fire is virtually assured.

CHOOSING A SITE Only experience will teach you how to choose a good site for pitching a tent, but a few general points, applicable to any wild areas of Africa, may help you avoid problems:

- Avoid camping on what looks like a path through the bush, however indistinct. It may be a well-used game trail.
- Beware of camping in dry river-beds: dangerous flash floods can arrive with little or no warning.
- Near the coast, and in marshy areas, camp on higher ground to avoid cold, damp mists in the morning and evening.
- Camp a reasonable distance from water: near enough to walk to it, but far enough to avoid animals which arrive to drink.
- Give yourself plenty of time before it gets dark to familiarise yourself with your surroundings.
- If a storm with lightning is likely, make sure that your tent is not the highest thing around.
- Finally, choose a site that is as flat as possible; it will make sleeping much easier.

CAMPFIRES Campfires can create a great atmosphere and warm you on a cold evening, but they can also be damaging to the environment and leave unsightly piles of ash and blackened stones. Deforestation is a cause for major concern in much of the developing world, including parts of Namibia, so if you do light a fire then use wood as the locals do: sparingly. If you have a vehicle, then consider buying firewood in advance from people who sell it at the roadside in the more verdant areas.

If you collect it yourself, then take only dead wood, nothing living. Never just pick up a log: always roll it over first, checking carefully for snakes or scorpions.

Experienced campers build small, highly efficient fires by using a few large stones to absorb, contain and reflect the heat, and gradually feeding just a few thick logs into the centre to burn. Cooking pots can be balanced on the stones, or the point where the logs meet and burn. Others will use a small trench, lined with rocks, to similar effect. Either technique takes practice, but is worth perfecting. Whichever you do, bury the ashes, take any rubbish with you when you leave, and make the site look as if you had never been there. (See *Appendix 3* for details of Christina Dodwell's excellent *Explorer's Handbook – Travel, Survival and Bush Cookery*.) Finally, a practical warning: cooking after dark, especially in the rainy season, by any form of artificial light poses its own hazards in the form of flying insects. Unless you want mopane moths in with the stir-fry, it's best avoided.

Don't expect an unattended fire to frighten away wild animals – that works in Hollywood, but not in Africa. A camp fire may help your feelings of insecurity, but lion and hyena will disregard it with stupefying nonchalance.

Finally, do be hospitable to any locals who appear – despite your efforts to seek permission for your camp, you may effectively be staying in their back gardens.

USING A TENT (OR NOT) Whether to use a tent or to sleep in the open is a personal choice, dependent upon where you are. In an area where there are predators around (specifically lion and hyena) then you should use a tent – and sleep *completely* inside it, as a protruding leg may seem like a tasty take-away to a hungry hyena. This is especially true at organised campsites, where the local animals have got so used to humans that they have lost much of their inherent fear of man. At least one person has been eaten while in a sleeping bag next to Okaukuejo's floodlit waterhole, so always use a tent in these restcamps.

Outside game areas, you will be fine sleeping in the open, or preferably under a mosquito net, with just the stars of the African sky above you. On the practical side, sleeping under a tree will reduce the morning dew that settles on your sleeping bag. If your vehicle has a large, flat roof then sleeping on this will provide you with peace of mind, and a star-filled outlook. Hiring a vehicle with a built-in roof tent would seem like a perfect solution, until you want to take a drive while leaving your camp intact.

CAMPING EQUIPMENT If you intend to camp in Namibia, then your choice of equipment will be affected by how you are travelling; you'll have more room in a vehicle than if you just carry a backpack. A few things to consider are:

Tent Mosquito-netting ventilation panels, allowing a good flow of air, are essential. Don't go for a tent that's small; it may feel cosy at home, but will be hot and claustrophobic in the desert. That said, strength and weatherproofing are not so important, unless you're visiting Namibia during the height of the rains.

Mat A ground mat of some sort is essential. It keeps you warm and comfortable, and it protects the tent's ground sheet from rough or stony ground (do put it underneath the tent!). Closed-cell foam mats are widely available outside Namibia, so buy one before you arrive. The better mats cost double or treble the cheaper ones, but are stronger, thicker and warmer – well worth the investment.

Therm-a-Rests, the combination air-mattress and foam mat, are strong, durable and also worth the investment – but take a puncture repair kit with you just in case of problems. Do watch carefully where you site your tent, and try to make camp before dark.

Sleeping bag For most purposes, a three-season down sleeping bag is ideal, being the smallest and lightest bag that is still warm enough for winter nights. Synthetic fillings are cheaper, but for the same warmth are heavier and bulkier. They do have the advantage that they keep their warmth when wet, unlike down, but clearly this is not so vital in Namibia's dry climate.

Sheet sleeping bag Thin pure-cotton or silk sleeping-bag liners are good protection for your main sleeping bag, keeping it cleaner. They can, of course, be used on their own when your main sleeping bag is too hot.

Stove 'Trangia'-type stoves, which burn methylated spirits, are simple to light and use, and cheap to run. They come complete with a set of light aluminium pans and a very useful all-purpose handle. Often you'll be able to cook on a fire with the pans, but it's nice to have the option of making a brew in a few minutes while you set up camp. Canisters for gas stoves are available in the main towns if you prefer to use these, but are expensive and bulky. Petrol- and kerosene-burning stoves are undoubtedly efficient on fuel and powerful – but invariably temperamental, messy and unreliable in the dusty desert. If you're going on a long hike then take a stove and fuel, as firewood may not always be available in the drier areas.

Torch (flashlight) This should be on every visitor's packing list – whether you're staying in upmarket camps or backpacking. Find one that's small and tough, and preferably water- and dust-proof. Head torches leave your hands free (useful when cooking or mending the car) and the latest designs are relatively light and comfortable to wear. Consider one of the new generation of superbright LED torches; the LED Lenser range is excellent.

Those with vehicles will find that a strong spotlight, powered by the car's battery (perhaps through the socket for the cigarette lighter), is invaluable for impromptu lighting.

Water containers For everyday use, a small two-litre water bottle is invaluable, however you are travelling. If you're thinking of camping, you should also consider a strong, collapsible water-bag – perhaps 5–10 litres in size – which will reduce the number of trips that you need to make from your camp to the water source (10 litres of water weighs 10kg). To be sure of safe drinking water, consider taking a bottle with a filter (see page 77).

Drivers will want to be self-sufficient for water when venturing into the bush, and so carry several large, sturdy containers of water. If you're driving a vehicle specially kitted out for camping, ensure that the water tank is full at the outset.

See *Chapter 4*, page 63, for a memory-jogging list of other useful items to pack.

DANGERS FROM WILDLIFE Camping in Africa is really very safe, though you may not think so from reading this. If you have a major problem while camping, it will probably be because you did something stupid, or because you forgot to take a few simple precautions. Here are a few general basics, applicable to anywhere in Africa and not just Namibia.

Large animals Big game will not bother you if you are in a tent – provided that you do not attract their attention or panic them. Elephants will gently tiptoe through your guy ropes while you sleep, without even nudging your tent. However, if you wake up and make a noise, startling them, they are far more likely to panic and step on your tent. Similarly, scavengers will quietly wander round, smelling your evening meal in the air, without any intention of harming you.

- Remember to use the toilet before going to bed, and avoid getting up in the night if possible.
- Scrupulously clean everything used for food that might smell good to scavengers. If possible, put these utensils in a vehicle; if not, suspend them from a tree, or pack them away in a rucksack inside the tent.
- Do not keep any smelly foodstuffs, like meat or citrus fruit, in your tent. Their smells may attract unwanted attention.
- Do not leave anything outside that could be picked up – like bags, pots, pans, etc. Hyenas, among others, will take anything. (They have been known to crunch a camera's lens, and eat it.)
- If you are likely to wake in the night, then leave the tent's zips a few centimetres open at the top, enabling you to take a quiet peek outside.

Creepy crawlies As you set up camp, clear stones or logs out of your way with extreme caution: underneath will be great hiding places for snakes and scorpions. Long, moist grass is ideal territory for snakes and Namibia's many dry, rocky places are classic sites for scorpions.

If you are sleeping in the open, note that it is not unknown to wake and find a snake lying next to you in the morning. Don't panic; it has just been attracted to you by your warmth. You will not be bitten if you gently edge away without making any sudden movements. (This is one good argument for using at least a mosquito net!)

Before you put on your shoes, shake them out. Similarly, check the back of your backpack before you slip it on. A spider, in either, could inflict a painful bite.

WALKING

Walking in the African bush is a totally different sensation from driving through it. You may start off a little unready – perhaps even sleepy for an early morning walk – but swiftly your mind will awake. There are no noises except the wildlife's, and your own. So every noise that isn't caused by you must be an animal; or a bird; or an insect. Every smell and every rustle has a story to tell, if you can understand it.

With time, patience and a good guide you can learn to smell the presence of elephants, and hear when impala are alarmed by a predator. You can use ox-peckers to lead you to buffalo, or vultures to help you locate a kill. Tracks will record the passage of animals in the sand, telling what passed by, how long ago, and in which direction.

Eventually your gaze becomes alert to the slightest movement, your ears aware of every sound. This is safari at its best. A live, sharp, spine-tingling experience that's hard to beat and very addictive. Be careful: watching animals from a vehicle will never be the same for you again.

WALKING TRAILS Namibia has several long hikes suited to those who are both fit and experienced in Africa. These include unaccompanied trails along the Fish River Canyon, in the Naukluft Mountains and on Waterberg Plateau, and guided trails on Waterberg, at Tok Tokkie Trails in the Namib, and in the private areas of Fish River Canyon, north of the national park.

There are also hundreds of shorter hikes, varying from half an hour's stroll to a few days, and many areas which cry out to be explored on foot. None involve much big game, though you may come across larger animals; all are more about spending time in the environments to increase your understanding of them.

SAFETY OF GUIDED WALKS In many areas where guided game walks are undertaken, your chances of being in a compromising situation with seriously dangerous game – namely lion, buffalo or elephant – are almost zero. There are many first-class guided walks in the desert and the mountains, showing you superb scenery and fascinating areas, which don't have these risks to contend with.

Generally Namibia isn't the place for a walking safari that concentrates on big game (as always, there are exceptions, such as Desert Rhino Camp and Ongava). Hence many guides don't need to carry a gun, or know how to use one. This is fine for most of Namibia.

However, in areas where you may meet lion, buffalo or elephant, you need extra vigilance. A few lodges will take chances, and send you out walking with a guide who doesn't have big game experience. Don't let them. If lion, buffalo or elephant are present, then you need a professional guide who carries a loaded gun and knows how to use it.

This applies especially in Mahango, Mamili and Mudumu, which have thick vegetation cover and healthy game populations. Don't accept the logic that 'experience and large stick' will be good enough. It will be for 99.9% of the time… but you don't want it to become the 0.1%. Don't walk in such areas unless your guide has experience of both big game and firearms.

Further east, in Zambia and Zimbabwe where walking safaris have been refined, the guides must pass stringent exams and practical tests before they are licensed to walk with clients.

GUIDED WALKING SAFARIS If you plan to do much walking, and want to blend in, try to avoid wearing any bright, unnatural colours, especially white. Muted shades are best; greens, browns and khaki are ideal. Hats are essential, as is sunblock. Even a short walk will last for 2 hours, and there's often no vehicle to which you can retreat if you get too hot.

Cameras and binoculars should be immediately accessible – ideally in dust-proof cases strapped to your belt. They are of much less use if buried at the bottom of a camera bag.

With regard to safety, your guide will always brief you in detail before you set off. S/he will outline possible dangers, and what to do if they materialise. Listen carefully: this is vital.

FACE TO FACE ANIMAL ENCOUNTERS Whether you are on an organised walking safari, on your own hike, or just walking from the car to your tent in the bush, it is possible that you will come across some of Africa's larger animals at close quarters. Invariably, the danger is much less than you imagine, and a few basic guidelines will enable you to cope effectively with most situations.

First, don't panic. Console yourself with the fact that animals are not normally interested in people. You are not their normal food, or their predator. If you do not annoy or threaten them, you will be left alone.

If you are walking to look for animals, then remember that this is their environment, not yours. Animals have been 'designed' for the bush, and their senses are far better attuned to it than yours are. To be on less unequal terms, remain alert and try to spot them from a distance. This gives you the option of approaching carefully, or staying well clear.

Finally, the advice of a good guide is more valuable than the simplistic comments noted here. Animals, like people, are all different. So while we can generalise here and say how the 'average' animal will behave – the one that's glaring over a small bush at you may have had a really bad day, and be feeling much more grumpy than average.

Below are a few general comments on how to deal with some potentially dangerous situations.

Buffalo This is probably the continent's most dangerous animal to hikers, but there is a difference between the old males, often encountered on their own or in small groups, and large breeding herds.

Lone male buffalo are easily surprised. If they hear or smell anything amiss, they will charge without provocation – motivated by a fear that something is sneaking up on them. Buffalo have an excellent sense of smell, but fortunately they are short-sighted. Avoid a charge by quickly climbing the nearest tree, or by side-stepping at the last minute. If adopting the latter, riskier, technique then stand motionless until the last possible moment, as the buffalo may well miss you anyhow.

The large breeding herds can be treated in a totally different manner. If you approach them in the open, they will often flee. Occasionally though, they will stand and watch, moving aside to allow you to pass through the middle of the herd. Neither encounter is for the faint-hearted or inexperienced, so steer clear of these dangerous animals wherever possible.

Black rhino The Kunene Region has one of the world's best populations of black rhino – a real success story for Namibian conservation. However, if you are lucky enough to find one, and then unlucky enough to be charged by it, use the same tactics as you would for a buffalo: tree-climbing or dodging at the last second. (It is amazing how fast even the least athletic walker will scale the nearest tree when faced with a charging rhino.) If there are no trees in the vicinity, you have a problem. Your best line of defence is probably to crouch very low, so you don't break the skyline, and remain motionless.

When tracking black rhino in Namibia, you'll almost always be in the company of two or three professional guides/trackers, usually staff of Save the Rhino Trust. I've often been out with them; and the experience can be amazing. On one occasion, we were joined by visitors sporting bright outdoor clothing, who proved disastrously poor at listening to instructions. Having been told to remain dead still because a rhino with a calf was close, one of the group ignored this, stood up and clicked a camera.

The rhino charged. It was so fast: this was a very dangerous situation. Seconds later, as it approached, the trackers all jumped up in unison, shouting and clapping. The rhino changed direction almost instantly, and carried on running into the distance with its calf for miles. It was a tense situation and we were lucky. The one most harmed was the rhino – running for its life, followed by its calf, in 35° heat. We'd put the calf's life in danger, because one visitor couldn't listen to his guide.

Elephant Normally elephants are only a problem if you disturb a mother with a calf, or approach a male in musth (state of arousal). So keep well away from these. However, after decades of persecution, Namibia's 'desert elephants' have a reputation for almost unprovoked aggression. Many people (mostly local villagers) are killed by them each year. The moral is to give these elephants a very wide berth, and to be extremely cautious when in areas where they are likely to be found.

Normally, if you get too close to an elephant, it will first scare you with a 'mock charge': head up, perhaps shaking; ears flapping; trumpeting. Lots of sound and fury. This is intended to be frightening, and it is. But it is just a warning and no cause for panic. Just freeze to assess the elephant's intentions, then back off slowly.

When elephants really mean business, they will put their ears back, their head down, and charge directly at you without stopping. This is known as a 'full charge'. There is no easy way to avoid the charge of an angry elephant, so take a hint from the warning and back off slowly as soon as you encounter a mock charge. Don't run. If you are the object of a full charge, then you have no choice but to run – preferably round an anthill, up a tall tree, or wherever.

Lion Tracking lion can be one of the most exhilarating parts of a good walking safari, although sadly they will normally flee before you get close to them. However, it can be a problem if you come across a large pride unexpectedly. Lion are well camouflaged; it is easy to find yourself next to one before you realise it. If you had been listening, you would probably have heard a warning growl about 20m ago. Now it is too late.

The best plan is to stop, and back off slowly, but confidently. If you are in a small group, then stick together. *Never* run from a big cat. First, they are always faster than you are. Secondly, running will just convince them that you are frightened prey worth chasing. As a last resort, if they seem too inquisitive and follow as you back off, then stop. Call their bluff. Pretend that you are not afraid and make loud, deep, confident noises: shout at them, bang something. But do not run.

John Coppinger, one of Africa's most experienced guides, adds that every single compromising experience that he has had with lion on foot has been either with a female with cubs, or with a mating pair, when the males can get very aggressive. You have been warned.

Leopard Leopard are very seldom seen, and would normally flee from the most timid of lone hikers. However, if injured or surprised, they are very powerful, dangerous cats. Conventional wisdom is scarce, but never stare straight into the leopard's eyes, or it will regard this as a threat display. (The same is said, by some, to be true with lion.) Better to look away slightly, at a nearby bush, or even at its tail. Then back off slowly, facing the direction of the cat and showing as little terror as you can. As with lion – loud, deep, confident noises are a last line of defence. Never run from a leopard.

Hippo Hippo are fabled to account for more deaths in Africa than any other animal (ignoring the mosquito). Having been attacked and capsized by a hippo while in a dugout canoe on the Okavango, I find this very easy to believe. Visitors are most likely to encounter hippo in the water, when paddling a canoe or fishing. However, as they spend half their time grazing ashore, you'll sometimes come across them on land. Out of their comforting lagoons, hippos are even more dangerous. If they see you, they will flee towards the deepest channel nearby – so the golden rule is never to get between a hippo and its escape route to deep water. Given that a hippo will outrun you on land, standing motionless is probably your best line of defence.

Snakes These are really not the great danger that people imagine. Most flee when they feel the vibrations of footsteps; only a few will stay still. The puff adder is responsible for more cases of snakebite than most other venomous snakes because, when approached, it will simply puff itself up and hiss as a warning, rather than slither away. This makes it essential always to watch where you place your feet when walking in the bush.

Similarly, there are a couple of arboreal (tree-dwelling) species which may be taken by surprise if you carelessly grab vegetation as you walk. So don't.

Spitting cobras are also encountered occasionally; they will aim for your eyes and spit with accuracy. If the spittle reaches your eyes, you must wash them out *immediately* and thoroughly with whatever liquid comes to hand: water, milk, even urine if that's the only liquid that can be quickly produced.

CANOEING

There is comparatively little canoeing done in Namibia, though operations do run on the country's borders: down the Orange River, on the eastern side of the Kunene, and occasionally on the Kwando, the Chobe and the Zambezi. The main dangers for canoeists are:

HIPPO Hippos are strictly vegetarians, and will attack a canoe only if they feel threatened. The technique for avoiding hippo problems is first of all to let them know that you are there. Bang your paddle on the side of the canoe a few times (most novice canoeists will do this constantly anyhow).

During the day, hippopotami congregate in the deeper areas of the river. The odd ones in shallow water, where they feel less secure, will head for the deeper places as soon as they are aware of a nearby canoe. Avoiding hippos then becomes a simple case of steering around the deeper areas. This is where experience and knowing the river become useful.

Trouble starts when canoes inadvertently stray over a pod of hippos, or when a canoe cuts a hippo off from its path of retreat. Either situation is dangerous, as hippos will overturn canoes without a second thought, biting them and their occupants.

CROCODILES Crocodiles may have sharp teeth and look prehistoric, but are of little danger to a canoeist… unless you are in the water. Then the more you struggle and the more waves you create, the more you will attract their unwelcome attentions. They become a major threat when canoes are overturned by hippos – making it essential to get out of the water as soon as possible, either into another canoe or on to the bank.

When a crocodile attacks an animal, it will try to disable it. It does this by getting a firm, biting grip, submerging and performing a long, fast barrel-roll. This disorients the prey, drowns it, and probably twists off the bitten limb. In this dire situation, your best line of defence is to stab the reptile in its eyes with anything sharp that you have. Alternatively, if you can lift up its tongue and let the water into its lungs while it is underwater, then a crocodile will start to drown and will release its prey.

There is one very reliable report of a man surviving an attack in the Zambezi. The crocodile first grabbed his arm and started to spin backwards into deep water. The man wrapped his legs around the crocodile, to spin with it and avoid having his arm twisted off. As it spun, he tried to poke his thumb into its eyes, but this had no effect. Finally he put his free arm into the crocodile's mouth, and opened up the beast's throat. This worked. The crocodile left him and he survived with only a damaged arm. Understandably, anecdotes about tried and tested methods of escape are rare.

MINIMUM IMPACT

When you visit, drive through, or camp in an area and have 'minimum impact', this means that the area is left in the same condition as – or better than – when you entered it. While most visitors view minimum impact as being desirable, spend time to consider the ways in which we contribute to environmental degradation, and how these can be avoided.

DRIVING Use your vehicle responsibly. If there's a road, or a track, then don't go off it – the environment will suffer. Driving off-road leaves unsightly tracks which detract from the 'wilderness' feeling for subsequent visitors. In the drier western areas these tracks can also crush fragile desert plants and scar the desert for decades.

HYGIENE Use toilets if they are provided, even if they are basic long-drop loos with questionable cleanliness. If there are no toilets, then human excrement should always be buried well away from paths, or groundwater, and any tissue used should be burnt and then buried.

If you use rivers or lakes to wash, then soap yourself near the bank, using a pan for scooping water from the river – making sure that no soap finds its way back into the water. Use biodegradable soap. Sand makes an excellent pan-scrub, even if you have no water to spare.

RUBBISH Biodegradable rubbish can be burnt and buried with the camp fire ashes. Don't just leave it lying around: it will look very unsightly and spoil the place for those who come after you.

Bring along some plastic bags in which to remove the rest of your rubbish, and dump it at the next town. Items which will not burn, like tin cans, are best cleaned and squashed for easy carrying. If there are bins, then use them, but also consider when they will next be emptied, and if local animals will rummage through them first. Carrying out all your own rubbish may still be the sensible option.

HOST COMMUNITIES While the rules for reducing impact on the environment have been understood and followed by responsible travellers for years, the effects of tourism on local people have only recently been considered. Many tourists believe it is their right, for example, to take intrusive photos of local people – and even become angry if the local people object. They refer to higher prices being charged to tourists as a rip-off, without considering the hand-to-mouth existence of those selling these products or services. They deplore child beggars, then hand out sweets or pens to local children with outstretched hands.

Our behaviour towards 'the locals' needs to be considered in terms of their culture, with the knowledge that we are the uninvited visitors. We visit to enjoy ourselves, but this should not be at the expense of local people. Read the box, *Cultural guidelines*, on pages 26–7, and aim to leave the local communities better off after your visit.

LOCAL PAYMENTS If you spend time with any of Namibia's poorer local people, perhaps staying at one of the community campsites, then take great care with any payments that you make.

First, note that most people like to spend their earnings on what *they* choose. This means that trying to pay for services with beads, food, old clothes or anything else instead of money isn't appreciated. Ask yourself how you'd like to be paid, and you'll understand this point.

Secondly, find out the normal cost of what you are buying. Most community campsites will have a standard price for a campsite, an hour's guided activity, or whatever. Find this out before you sleep there, or accept the offer of a walk. It is then important that you pay about that amount for the service rendered – no less, and not too much more.

As most people realise, if you try to pay less you'll get into trouble – as you would at home. However, many do not realise that if they generously pay a lot more, this can be equally damaging. Local rates of pay in rural areas can be very low, and a careless visitor can easily pay disproportionately large sums. Where this happens, local jobs can lose their value overnight. (Imagine working hard to become a game scout, only to learn that a tourist has given your friend the equivalent of your whole month's wages for just a few hours' guiding. What incentive is there for you to carry on with your regular job?)

If you want to give more – for good service, a super guide, or just because you want to help – then either buy some locally made produce (at the going rate), or donate money to one of the organisations working to improve the lot of Namibia's most disadvantaged. For suggestions, see *Travelling positively*, pages 73–4.

Part Two

THE GUIDE

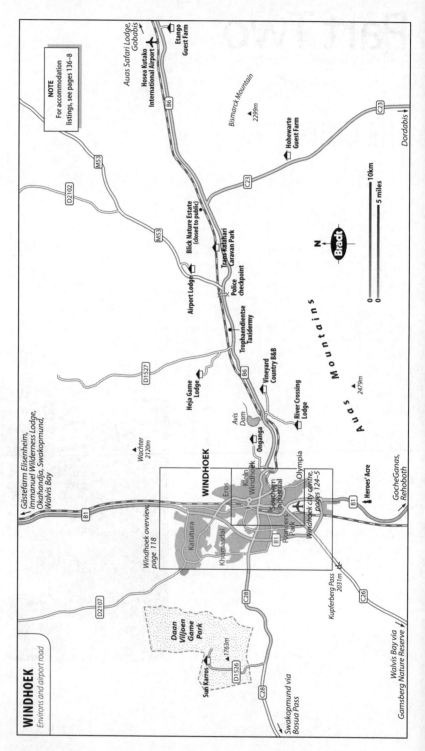

WINDHOEK
Environs and airport road

NOTE
For accommodation
listings, see pages 136–8

Auas Safari Lodge,
Gobabis

Hosea Kutako
International Airport

Etango
Guest Farm

B6

Bismarck Mountain
2299m

Hohewarte
Guest Farm

C23

Dordabis

M53

D2102

M53

Blick Nature Estate
(closed to public)

Trans Kalahari
Caravan Park

Police
checkpoint

Airport Lodge

Trophaendientse
Taxidermy

D1527

Heja Game
Lodge

B6

Vineyard
Country B&B

River Crossing
Lodge

Avis
Dam

Onganga

Auas Mountains

2479m

10km

5 miles

0
0

N

Bradt

Gästefarm Elisenheim,
Immanuel Wilderness Lodge,
Okahandja, Swakopmund,
Walvis Bay

B1

Wachter
2120m

Windhoek overview
page 118

WINDHOEK

Katutura

Eros

Klein
Windhoek

Southern
Industrial

Khomasdal

Pioneers'
Park

Olympia

Windhoek city centre,
pages 124–5

B1

Heroes' Acre

GocheGanas,
Rehoboth

B1

D2107

C28

Daan
Viljoen Game
Park

1763m

Sun Karros

D1526

C28

Swakopmund via
Bosua Pass

Kupferberg Pass
2031m

C26

Walvis Bay via
Gamsberg Nature Reserve

C23

114

8

Windhoek

Namibia's capital spreads out in a wide valley between bush-covered hills and appears, at first sight, to be quite small. Driving from the international airport, you pass quickly through the suburbs and, reaching the crest of a hill, find yourself suddenly descending into the city centre.

As you stroll through this centre, the pavement cafés and picturesque old German architecture conspire to give an airy, European feel, while street vendors remind you that this is Africa. Look upwards! The office blocks are tall, but not skyscraping. Around you the pace is busy, but seldom as frantic as Western capitals seem to be.

Leading off Independence Avenue, the city's main street, is the open-air Post Street Mall, centre of a modern shopping complex. Wandering through here, between the pastel-coloured buildings, you'll find shops selling everything from fast food to fashion. In front of these, street vendors crouch beside blankets spread with jewellery, crafts and curios for sale. Nearby, the city's more affluent residents step from their cars in shaded parking bays to shop in air-conditioned department stores. The atmosphere is relaxed, to the extent that visitors tend to forget that this is a capital city. As in any city, it is important to remember that tourists tend to stand out, and as such are potentially vulnerable to crime. So it makes sense to keep any valuables well hidden, and to keep a watchful eye on bags or rucksacks. Similarly, if you're in your own vehicle, keep the doors locked – even when you're just getting out to open a gate – and be aware of what's going on around you.

Like many capitals, Windhoek is full of contrasts, especially between the richer and poorer areas, even if it lacks any major attractions. For casual visitors the city is pleasant; many stop for a day or two, as they arrive or leave, though few stay much longer. It is worth noting that the city all but closes down on Saturday afternoons (although some shops open on a Sunday morning), so be aware of this if you plan to be in town over a weekend. Note, too, that during the holiday season, from Christmas to around 10 January, large numbers of locals head for the coast, leaving many shops, restaurants and tourist attractions closed. That said, this is the centre of Namibia's administration, and the hub of the country's roads, railways and communications. If you need an embassy, good communications or an efficient bank, then Windhoek is the right place for you. And to prepare for a trip into the bush, Windhoek is by far the best place in Namibia to get organised and buy supplies.

HISTORY

At an altitude of about 1,650m, in the middle of Namibia's central highlands, Windhoek stands at the head of the valley of one of the Swakop River's tributaries. The Nama people named this place Ai-gams ('fire-water') and the Herero called it

,omuise ('place of steam'), after the group of hot (23–27°C) springs, now situated in the suburb of Klein Windhoek.

The springs were long used by the original Khoisan hunter-gatherer inhabitants. However, the first recorded settlement here was that of the important chief Jonker Afrikaner and his followers, around 1840. (Jonker had gradually moved north from the Cape, establishing himself as the dominant power in the centre of the country, between Nama groups in the south and Herero to the north.) Many think that the name Windhoek was bestowed on the area by him, perhaps after Winterhoek, his birthplace in the Cape. Others suggest that Windhoek is simply a corruption of the German name for 'windy corner'. Jonker Afrikaner certainly used the name 'Wind Hoock' in a letter to the Wesleyan Mission Society in August 1844, and by 1850 the name 'Windhoek' was in general use.

By December 1842, Rhenish missionaries Hans Kleinschmidt and Carl Hahn had established a church and there were about 1,000 of Jonker's followers living in this valley. The settlement was trading with the coast, and launching occasional cattle-rustling raids on the Herero groups to the north. These raids eventually led to the death of Jonker, after which his followers dispersed and the settlement was abandoned.

The Germans arrived in 1890, under Major Curt von François. They completed the building of their fort, now known as the Alte Feste – Windhoek's oldest building. This became the headquarters of the Schutztruppe, the German colonial troops. Gradually German colonists arrived, and the growth of the settlement accelerated with the completion of the railway from Swakopmund in 1902.

In 1909 Windhoek became a municipality. The early years of the 20th century saw many beautiful buildings constructed, including the landmark Christus Kirche, constructed between 1907 and 1910. Development continued naturally until the late 1950s and 1960s, when the South African administration started implementing policies for racial separation: the townships began to develop, and many of Windhoek's black population were forced to move. This continued into the 1970s and 1980s, by which time rigid separation by skin colour had largely been implemented. The privileged 'whites' lived in the spacious leafy suburbs surrounding the centre; black residents in Katutura (see box, page 158); and those designated as 'coloured' in Khomasdal. Even today, these divisions are largely still in place.

The 1990s, following independence, saw the construction of new office buildings in the centre of town. More recently, impressive government buildings such as the Supreme Court building have been constructed on the east side of Independence Avenue, while the open spaces between the old townships and the inner suburbs are gradually being developed as modest, middle-income housing.

GETTING THERE AND AWAY

Most visitors passing through Windhoek are either driving themselves around or are members of a group trip. Relatively few will need to rely on the local bus, coach or train services detailed here, despite their efficiency.

BY AIR Windhoek has two small but modern airports: Hosea Kutako International Airport (*www.airports.com.na*), which is generally used for international flights, and Eros, which caters mostly for internal flights and a few international flights. Be sure to check which one is to be used for each of your flights. For international air links see page 60; for internal air travel see pages 96–8.

Hosea Kutako International Airport [Map, page 114] The international arrivals airport is located 42km east of the city, along the B6 towards Gobabis. The arrivals area has three small bureaux de change: American Express (⊕ *05.00–19.00 daily*) and the adjoining bank (⊕ *08.30–14.30 Mon–Fri, 08.30–11.30 Sat*); Thomas Cook (⊕ *daily for all incoming & outgoing flights*); and a Western Union. There's a useful ATM beside the men's toilets. The Omaandje Biltong shop doubles as a post office (⊕ *08.00–13.00 & 14.00–17.00 Mon–Fri, 08.00–noon Sat, 09.00–13.00 & 14.00–17.00 Sun*), where you can buy SIM cards (N$7/6 months), which can also be bought from the Mtc and Telecom Namibia outlets, also in the terminal. There are also a few gift shops, Ilamo, a coffee shop cum bar (⊕ *06.00–21.00 daily;* $$), and an office for Wilderness Safaris and their affiliates. Wi-Fi vouchers can be bought landside from Kidz Paradise and airside from Out of Africa (*both N$50/hr*).

Inside the departure lounge, beyond customs, there's plenty of seating, the Premium Bistro, a café-bar, a couple of souvenir shops, and a larger duty-free shop that also has a range of souvenirs, safari clothes and books. This last shop accepts Namibian dollars, credit cards and some foreign currency. You will probably get your change in South African rand, and the staff here will also exchange N$100 notes for the equivalent in rand, if asked. There is a business lounge, but it's rather shabby at the time of writing and perhaps not worth economy-class passengers paying for its use.

Airport transfers Hertz, Avis, Budget, Dollar/Thrifty and Europcar car-hire companies (see pages 88–9) all have their own offices at the airport, and others will meet you there on request, so picking up a hired car on arrival is straightforward.

If you don't plan to have your own vehicle, and have made no other arrangements, you can prebook one of the services run by local companies. Operators include:

Camelthorn Transfer & Tours 📞061 255490; www.camelthorntours.com
Dial a Driver 📞061 259677; m 081 124 4663
Shuttle Namibia 📞061 302007; m 081 1228888; www.shuttlenamibia.com

Transfer Excellence 📞061 244949; m 081 122 0584
Windhoek Airport Transfers, Tours & Rentals 📞061 258792; www.namibiatours.com.na

Alternatively, a taxi to/from the airport should cost from around N$350–400, depending on the number of passengers. If you've asked a porter to carry your bags to your car or taxi, a tip of around N$1–2 is about right.

Eros Airport [125 C7] Windhoek's second airport stands near the main B1 on the way south to Rehoboth, about 500m from the Safari Hotel. It is even smaller than the international airport – positively bijou. Eros is used for most of Air Namibia's internal flights, a few regional services (and sometimes Cape Town flights) and a steady stream of light aircraft traffic. It has a few car-rental desks, including Avis (but there is hardly ever anyone there), and a small café, and is usually refreshingly informal.

Airport transfers There's no public transport to/from here, but as it's relatively close (4km) to the centre of town, taxis are easily summoned by phone (see page 120). Failing that, the Safari Court Hotel and its cheaper partner, the Safari Hotel, are just a few minutes' walk away, and they can transport via Shuttle Namibia (see above).

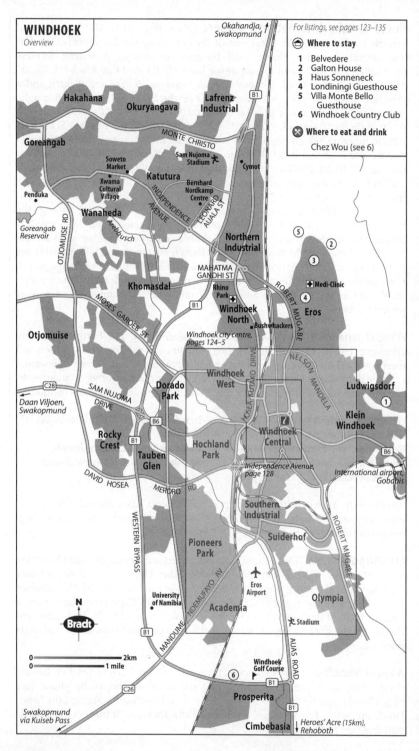

WINDHOEK
Overview

For listings, see pages 123–135

Where to stay
1 Belvedere
2 Galton House
3 Haus Sonneneck
4 Londiningi Guesthouse
5 Villa Monte Bello
  Guesthouse
6 Windhoek Country Club

Where to eat and drink
Chez Wou (see 6)

Okahandja,
Swakopmund

B1

Hakahana

Okuryangava

Lafrenz
Industrial

MONTE CHRISTO

Goreangab

Soweto
Market

Sam Nujoma
Stadium

Cymot

Katutura

Xwama
Cultural
Village

Bernhard
Nordkamp
Centre

Penduka

Wanaheda

INDEPENDENCE AVENUE

LEONARD AUALA ST

Arebbusch

Northern
Industrial

Goreangab
Reservoir

MAHATMA
GANDHI ST

ROBERT MUGABE

Khomasdal

Rhino
Park

Medi-Clinic

MOSES GAROEB ST

B1

Windhoek
North

Eros

Otjomuise

Bushwhackers

Windhoek city centre,
pages 124–5

NELSON MANDELA

C28

SAM NUJOMA DRIVE

Dorado
Park

HOSEA KUTAKO DRIVE

Windhoek
West

Ludwigsdorf

Daan Viljoen,
Swakopmund

B6

Belvedere 1

Rocky
Crest

B1

Hochland
Park

Windhoek
Central

Klein
Windhoek

Tauben
Glen

i

B6

DAVID HOSEA

MERORO RD

Independence Avenue,
page 128

International airport,
Gobabis

WESTERN BYPASS

Southern
Industrial

Suiderhof

MANDUME NDEMUFAYO AV

Pioneers
Park

ROBERT MUGABE

N

Bradt

University
of Namibia

Eros
Airport

Olympia

Academia

Stadium

0   2km
0   1 mile

AUAS ROAD

B1

Windhoek
Golf Course

6

C26

Prosperita

B1

Swakopmund
via Kuiseb Pass

Cimbebasia

Heroes' Acre (15km),
Rehoboth

118

BY BUS/COACH

Intercape Mainliner [128 D7] ✆061 227847; www.intercape.co.za. Coaches depart from opposite the Intercape office in Bahnhof St by Windhoek's TransNamib Station. These head south for Upington (with connections to Jo'burg) & Cape Town on Mon, Wed, Fri & Sun. Westbound coaches head to Walvis Bay via Okahandja, Karibib, Usakos & Swakopmund on Mon, Wed, Fri & Sat. There is also a service between Windhoek & Victoria Falls (Zambia) on Mon, Wed & Fri. See pages 101–2 for more details.

Townhoppers ✆064 407223; m 081 210 3062; www.namibiashuttle.com. Operate a daily shuttle service between Windhoek & Walvis Bay with stops in Okahandja, Wilhelmstal, Karibib, Usakos & Swakopmund. Buses leave daily from parking area near Hilton Hotel at 14.00 arriving in Walvis Bay at 19.30. Fares start at N$170.

BY TRAIN Windhoek is at the hub of TransNamib's (*www.transnamib.com.na*) relatively slow services around the country, with regular Starline services from the city's railway station (*off Bahnhof Street;* ✆ *061 298 2032/2175*). Departures to Keetmanshoop are daily (except Saturday) at 19.40 and to Swakopmund and Walvis Bay daily (except Saturday) at 19.55. See pages 98–100.

TransNamib also own and run the *Desert Express* – a luxury tourist train with lounge, bar and fine-dining restaurant – that departs from Windhoek station on Friday at midday and arrives in Swakopmund the following morning at 10.00. There are also occasional seven-day all-inclusive trips to Swakopmund and Etosha. For more details see page 100.

ORIENTATION

Under South African rule, Windhoek grew like most large South African cities, forming an 'atomic' structure. Its nucleus was the central business district and shopping areas, surrounded by leafy, spacious suburbs designed for whites with cars. Beyond these, the sprawling, high-density townships housed Windhoek's non-white population.

In modern Windhoek, two decades after independence, this basic structure is still in place, though the colour divisions have blurred. The leafy suburbs are still affluent, though are now more mixed, and new suburbs have sprung up in the southern parts of the city. Meanwhile, however, the districts of Khomasdal and Katutura remain crowded, poorer and with very few white residents.

The rapid growth in traffic within Windhoek has resulted in considerable development in the road infrastructure, with flyovers now carrying through traffic over the city's more congested areas. This can make orientation for the driver – particularly someone who has visited the city on a previous occasion – quite a challenge, so do get an up-to-date map and keep an eye on the signposts.

In common with other towns in Namibia, Windhoek undergoes occasional road name changes to reflect the prominence of local or international figures. Changes in the past decade include the following, though it is likely that both names will remain in use for a considerable period of time:

Bülow Street *now* Frans Indongo Street
Gloudina Street *now* Joseph Mukwayu Ithana Street
Hochland Road *now* David Hosea Meroro Road
Malcolm Spence Street *now* Mose Tjitendero Street
Mission Street and Gever Street *now* Dr Kwame Nkrumah Road
Omuramba Road *now* General Murtala Mohammed Road
Peter Müller Street *now* Fidel Castro Street

Stübel Street *now* Werner List Street
Uhland Street *now* Dr Kenneth David Kaunda Street

MAPS For most visitors, the TASA map available from several tour operators is one of the best around. Overall, it is good and reasonably accurate. Less detailed maps issued by the Namibia Tourism Board are available free from the tourist information offices (see opposite).

For detailed maps, head for the Surveyor General's office at 45 Robert Mugabe Avenue (✆ *061 296 5036; closed lunchtime*), between Dr May and Lazarett streets. Ordnance Survey maps are around N\$50 each. The 1:1,000,000 map of the whole country is wall-size and shows all commercial farms and their names. The 1:250,000 maps are good for vehicle navigation in the wilder areas, while the 1:50,000 series suits walkers. Most of the surveys were originally made in 1979, so despite being recently printed these maps are old. However, they are the best available.

GETTING AROUND

PRIVATE TAXIS In and around Windhoek it's usually best to walk, as everything is central and close together. It's not a good idea to hail a taxi on the street, particularly for women on their own, so prebook from a reliable source, or try one of those below. In general, agree the fare before you take the taxi.

🚗 **A Kasera Dial-a-Cab** ✆ 061 223531;
m 081 127 0557
🚗 **Dial a Driver** ✆ 061 259677; m 081 124 4663

🚗 **Shuttle & Taxi 2000** m 081 222 8294
🚗 **Taxi Express & Shuttle** ✆ 061 239739
🚗 **Transfer Excellence** ✆ 061 244949; m 081 122 0584

HIRED CAR Windhoek is fairly easy to navigate, with just a few main roads, good signposting and surprisingly little traffic, even at so-called 'peak' times of the day. Parking for a short period is straightforward, too: there are meters along Independence Avenue and some side roads, costing N\$0.50 for 20 minutes near the Thüringer Hof Hotel, rising to N\$0.50 for just 10 minutes as you get nearer to the post office. Parking is free after 18.00 Monday to Friday, or after 13.00 on Saturday and all day Sunday. Car guards – easily recognised by their orange or yellow vests – are regularly on duty on main roads. Ask them to keep an eye on your car in return for a tip of around N\$2–4 for half a day, or up to N\$5 in the evening. How vigilant they are is a matter for guesswork, of course, but their presence affords some sense of protection for your vehicle.

If you're shopping in the centre of town, secure and shaded parking is available in the multi-storey car park behind the Kalahari Sands Hotel (turn down Fidel Castro Street off Independence Avenue, then left again into Werner List Street; the entrance to the car park is on the left). For details of car-hire companies, see pages 88–9.

SHARED TAXIS AND MINIBUSES Shared minibuses and taxis do shuttle runs between the centre of town and both Katutura and Khomasdal. These are primarily for workers from the townships, and as such are mostly at the beginning and end of the working day, though some do run at other times. They are crowded and inflexible, but very cheap. If you want to take one, ask locally exactly where the taxi you need stops in town.

TOURIST INFORMATION

Namibia Tourism Board [128 B3] 1st Floor Channel Life Towers, 39 Post St Mall; ✆061 290 6000; e info@namibiatourism.com.na; www. namibiatourism.com.na; ☺ 08.00–17.00 Mon–Fri

Namibia Wildlife Resorts [128 C4] Erkraths Bldg, 189 Independence Av; ✆061 2857200; e reservations@nwr.com.na; www.nwr.com. na; ☺ 08.00–17.00 Mon–Fri. NWR is where you book accommodation in the national parks, & get (limited) information about them, either in person or by fax, email or phone. Credit cards are accepted. To book a campsite, you need to pay a deposit of 10%, with the balance payable 60 days before arrival. Alternatively, you can take a chance & turn up at campsites – if there's space, you can

pay direct. This is also the place for any dealings with the Ministry of Environment & Tourism (MET; *www.met.gov.na*), who have a desk in the same office.

Windhoek Tourist Information Office [128 B3] Post St Mall; ✆061 290 2690; www. cityofwindhoek.org.na, www.windhoek.my.na; ☺ 07.30–13.00 & 14.00–16.30 Mon–Fri. For information on Windhoek itself & the surrounding area, or to find a guide to take you off the beaten track, this is the place. The bureau also operates a temporary small pop-up information kiosk (✆*061 290 2596*) during the same hours on the corner of Fidel Castro St & Independence Av while the glitzy new Freedom Plaza is being constructed.

TRAVEL AGENTS AND TOUR OPERATORS

There is a list of Windhoek's travel agents in *Where to Stay: Namibia Travel Planner*, published annually by the tourist board, but it is unlikely to be comprehensive, with old ones ceasing to trade and new ones starting up with alarming regularity. Have a look, too, at *Namibia Holiday & Travel*, published by Venture Publications and widely available in Namibia. You could also pop into the Namibia Tourism Board or the tourist information centres for advice. For companies operating local excursions, see page 122.

Most arrangements are best made as far in advance as possible. Unless you are travelling independently and camping everywhere, this usually means booking with a good specialist operator before you leave (see pages 56–8), which will also give you added consumer protection, and recourse from home if things go wrong. However, if you are in Windhoek, and want to arrange something on the spot, then try one of the following:

UPMARKET

African Extravaganza 316 Sam Nujoma Av; ✆061 372100; e afex@afex.com.na; www. african-extravaganza.com. Good for guided lodge tours.

ATI Holiday ✆061 228717; e info@infotour-africa.com; www.infotour-africa.com. Tailor-made trips or group safaris to Namibia & neighbouring countries to suit all budgets.

Blue Sky Namibia Tours ✆061 229279; e info@ blueskynamibia.com; www.blueskynamibia.com. Tailor-made trips for small groups.

Chameleon Safaris 5–7 Voigt St N; ✆061 247668; e info@chameleon.com.na; www. chameleonsafaris.com. From budget trips to guided tailor-made & special-interest safaris. Scheduled camping & accommodated safaris

have weekly departures to Sossusvlei, Etosha & elsewhere.

Ondese Travel & Safaris ✆061 220876; e info@ondese.com; www.ondese.com. A well-established safari operator covering Namibia, Botswana, South Africa & the Victoria Falls.

Sense of Africa 41 Nickel St, Prosperita; ✆061 275300; e info@sense-of-africa.com.na; www. senseofafrica-namibia.com. Namibia specialist tour operator that offers everything from day tours to fly-in safaris.

SWA Safaris 43 Independence Av; ✆061 221193; e swasaf@swasafaris.com.na; www. swasafaris.com. A family-owned operator offering self-drive & guided tours of Namibia, Botswana & the Victoria Falls.

BUDGET

Cardboard Box Travel Shop 15 Bismarck St; \061 256580; e info@namibian.org; www. namibian.org. General agents, ideal for short-notice trips.

Uakii Wilderness \062 564743; e info@uakii. com; www.uakii.com. Culture tours of 3–5 days with the Bushmen & various day tours in the Windhoek & Gobabis areas.

Wild Dog Safaris (See ad, page 159) \061 257642; e info@wilddog-safaris.com; www. wilddog-safaris.com. Small-group guided trips – camping & accommodation. Quotes for privately

guided trips & self-drive tours on request. Online availability & booking.

SPECIALIST

DuneHopper \061 234793; e info@ dunehopper.com; www.dunehopper.com. 2–5-night fly-in trips from Eros Airport to Sossusvlei & the NamibRand Nature Reserve.

The Trail Hopper \061 264521; e hiking@ trailhopper.com; www.trailhopper.com. Specialises in hiking, including Brandberg & Naukluft Mountains & Fish River Canyon.

LOCAL TOURS Various small agencies offer tours of the city, some walking, some by vehicle. Often an afternoon tour will be combined with driving out on to some of the mountains overlooking Windhoek for a sundowner drink. It is also possible to visit the township of Katutura as part of a Windhoek city tour, though these aren't as popular as Johannesburg's tours of Soweto. Other alternatives include half- or full-day trips to one of the outlying game farms, or 4x4 trail driving.

If you prefer to drive yourself, and want to head off the beaten track, it is worth contacting the Windhoek tourist information office in Post Street Mall (page 121), who can arrange for a local community guide to accompany you. Guides are accredited by the City of Windhoek. The companies running day trips seem to change often. Current favourites are:

Be Local Tourism \061 305795; e aziza@ be-local.com; www.be-local.com. In addition to cultural tours of central Windhoek & Katutura, Be Local specialises in 4x4 trail drives, & runs helicopter, hot-air balloon & motorbike tours. They also hire satellite phones, radios or GPS units & there's a handy office at Hosea Kotako International Airport to collect these on arrival in Namibia.

Camelthorn Transfers & Tours 36 Bismarck St; \061 255490; e camelthorn@africaonline. com.na; www.camelthorntours.com. Dinah & Joseph Uanguta began offering transfers & some

of the best township & city tours about 6 years ago. They collect & drop off clients from/at their accommodation, with each 3hr tour departing daily at ☉ 09.00 & 14.00.

Windhoek City Tours 117 Independence Av; \061 275300; www.afrizim.com. Set up by Sense of Africa, a restored double-decker London bus operates a 2hr tour of Windhoek, taking in many of the city's historical buildings, the suburbs & the township of Katutura. Tours depart at ☉ 09.30 & 14.30 daily from their office.

WHERE TO STAY

Windhoek has accommodation to suit all budgets, from four-star hotels to backpackers' dorms, and hardly any are run down or seedy. Prices range upwards from about N$300 per person sharing a double room with en-suite toilet and bathroom. Single travellers will usually pay about 30–50% more. Dormitory beds at backpackers' lodges cost around N$140.

The dividing line between hotels and pensions/guesthouses used here is somewhat artificial: one of atmosphere rather than title or price. Hotels tend to be larger and more expensive, but often have more amenities: you can be more anonymous and blend into the scenery. Windhoek's pensions and guesthouses are smaller, often family-run, and usually friendlier and more personal. See also *Accommodation* on pages 67–9. The larger hotels invariably put on extensive spreads for their meals. Eat-as-much-as-you-can buffet meals, especially breakfasts, are the norm.

HOTELS IN WINDHOEK

Map, pages 124–5, unless otherwise indicated.

✳ 🏠 **Heinitzburg** [Map, page 128] (16 rooms) 22 Heinitzburg St; ☎061 249597; e heinitzburg@heinitzburg.com; www. heinitzburg.com. This distinctive white turreted fort was built in 1914 for German Count von Schwenn, who gave it to Countess Margarethe von Heinitz as a wedding gift. Both lived in separate parts of the fort before marriage, but legend has it that a secret tunnel connected their 2 bedchambers. The castle became a luxury hotel in 1996, is part of the Relais et Châteaux group & is owned by mother-&-son team Beate & Tibor Raith. Set high on a hill, it is elegant, quiet & secluded, & one of the most stylish places in town. The huge rooms are all individually decorated & have AC/heating, free Wi-Fi, DSTV, a safe, fridge/minibar & gilded bathrooms. Expect impressive furniture with expanses of beautiful, solid wood, dreamy white quilts & sumptuous fabrics; this is a truly romantic hideaway. Outside, a garden terrace commands super views of the city below – an attraction in its own right for non-residents who come for afternoon tea, cakes & cocktails – & there is a sheltered freshwater pool area with sun-loungers & elephant fountain. Spa treatments can be arranged on request. B/fast is served in the wood-panelled Knight's Room in the main castle, while delicious lunches are served on the terrace, & in the evening the sophisticated Leo's (see page 140) offers gourmet dinners. Room service available too. **$$$$$**

✳ 🏠 **Hilton** [Map, page 128] (150 rooms) Cnr Sam Nujoma & Rev Michael Scott St; ☎061 2962 929; e wdhhi.reservations@hilton.com; www. windhoek.hilton.com. This new 5-star is a modern interpretation of the world-famous hotel chain built on an elevated position overlooking central Windhoek. It's a bright, airy establishment with lots of glass & contemporary African artwork. There is a variety of rooms, but all are decorated in similar hues of creams, browns & golds & feature high padded headboards, Serenity mattresses, wired & wireless internet, in-room ironing board,

laptop safe, radio clock/iPod dock, room service, laundry, tea/coffee station, minibar, & a sleek modern bathroom that can be kept open-plan or closed off with sliding frosted-glass windows. There's a 24hr gym, the Breeze spa (⊕ 08.00–22.00), no less than 5 on-site eating & drinking establishments & the pièce de résistance: an 18m heated rooftop pool with Skybar (⊕ 10.00–midnight) that has stunning city views. A casino may be built in the basement in future. **$$$$$**

🏠 **Kalahari Sands** [Map, page 128] (173 rooms) Gustav Voigts Centre, 129 Independence Av; ☎061 280 0000; e kalahari.reservations@ suninternational.com; www.suninternational. com. Dominating the city's skyline in the centre of Independence Av, this hotel is accessed via escalators that whisk you through the shopping arcade below to its lobby, which is pretty much like that of any other 4-star hotel. The rooms are up again, reached by one of several slow lifts; most have good views of the city. All are carpeted & well furnished, with AC, safe, direct-dial phone, satellite TV, & either twin beds or a king-size dbl. Facilities include the Dunes restaurant (*lunch buffet N$125, dinner N$215, N$245 Fri*), Oasis bar, Sands Casino, a small gym & spa, & a rooftop pool. Now Windhoek's second-best hotel following the arrival of the Hilton (see opposite), it has a convenient central location. Reserved parking for guests is located on level 4 of the car park behind the mall on Werner List St; get your ticket stamped at reception so you can exit for free. Surprisingly for a large hotel, Wi-Fi isn't free – it costs N$90/2hr & tickets have to be bought from the business centre on the 1st floor. **$$$$$**

✳ 🏠 **Olive Exclusive** (7 suites) 22 Promenaden Weg, Klein Windhoek; ☎061 383890; e info@theolive-namibia.com; www. theolive-namibia.com. Next door to its sister guesthouse, the Olive Grove (see page 131), this beautiful boutique hotel is 10mins walk to the centre of town. With strong eco-friendly credentials, its elegant rooms are designed to represent different regions of Namibia with natural materials, stunning photographic works & individual furnishings & fittings. The 4 premier suites have private plunge pools on terraces

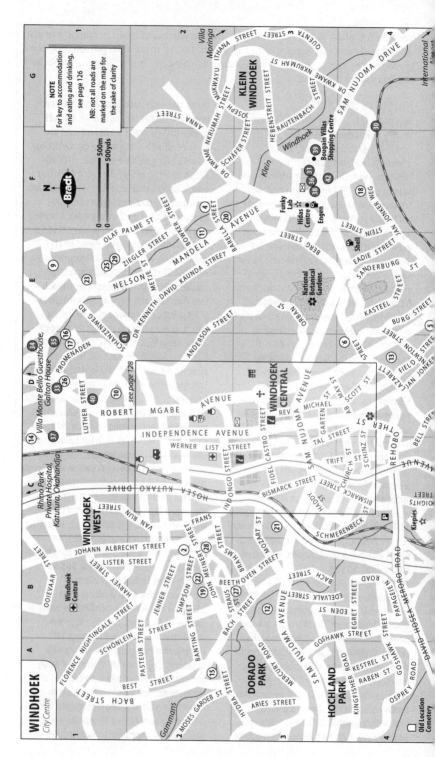

WINDHOEK
City Centre

NOTE
For key to accommodation and eating and drinking, see page 126

NB: not all roads are marked on the map for the sake of clarity

0   500m
0   500yds

Bradt

N

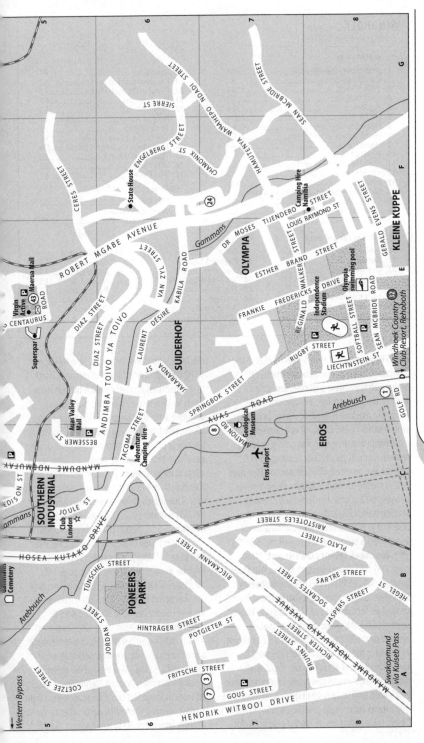

overlooking the olive grove & junior suites share a communal pool in the shade of olive trees. Indoors, all suites have a relaxing lounge area with TV, laptop & gas fire; a kitchenette with Nespresso machine & minibar; a huge bedroom with another TV, hairdryer, robes & slippers; & a bathroom with free-standing bath & separate shower-room. AC, underfloor heating, Wi-Fi & safe are also provided. Olive's restaurant (see page 140) is among the best in Windhoek, serving an imaginative à la carte lunch menu & 4-course set dinner (*N$350*), & the service throughout is second to none, an effortless combination of friendliness & efficiency. Secure parking. **$$$$$**

🏠 **Windhoek Country Club Resort** [Map, page 118] (152 rooms) Western Bypass, Windhoek South; 📞061 2055911/2055109; e windhoek@ legacyhotels.com; www.legacyhotels.co.za. You'd be forgiven for thinking you'd landed in Las Vegas upon entering this gaudy mega hotel that is situated on the B1 bypass that skirts the city almost right next to the industrial area of Prosperita & the residential area of Cimbebasia. Popular with gambling Angolans, its cavernous, vaulted entrance hall is lined with various small shops & an ATM. Opposite reception is the cavelike entrance to the Desert Jewel casino, where rows of people fill slot machines with money or gamble at tables from 10.00 through to 04.00 the next morning. (Note that casino dress is smart casual & the minimum age is 18.) The resort's rooms are plush & well designed, with AC, heating, DSTV, minibar/fridge, phone, hairdryer, safe (big enough for a laptop) & a balcony or patio. Some have a proper work desk & each has a bath & separate shower en suite; one is adapted for paraplegics. The main restaurant, the Kokerboom, overlooks the pool, a manmade circular river & manicured lawns, serves buffet lunch (*N$205*) & dinner (*N$215*), & has an à la carte menu as well (**$$$$**). Tappers bar is ideal for cocktails. There's also a good Chinese restaurant, Chez Wou (see page 141) that is independently owned. Beyond, an 18-hole golf course (see page 148) offers special rates for guests. The complimentary city shuttle bus that runs Mon–Sat is a bonus, but the Wi-Fi is only free up to 500MB. **$$$$$**

🏠 **Fürstenhof** [Map, page 128] (33 rooms) 4 Frans Indongo St; 📞061 237380; e furstenhof@ proteahotels.com.na; www.proteahotels.com/ furstenhof. Less than 1km west of the centre, the 4-star Fürstenhof is perched slightly above the city off Frans Indongo St. Central areas are light, bright & contemporary, the neutral décor offset by dashes of acidic lime green. Its spacious rooms all have AC, minibar/fridges, phones, Wi-Fi, satellite TV, digital safes, hairdryers & en-suite shower or bath.

The restaurant is good but expensive, & has changed little in recent years. Outside are a turquoise swimming pool & a few plastic sun-loungers, with a nearby spa that opens on to a small garden, sadly next to a noisy road. **$$$$**

🏠 **Hotel Safari & Safari Court Hotel** (450 rooms) Cnr Auas & Aviation Rd; ☎061 296 8000; e reservations@safarihotelsnamibia.com; www. safarihotelsnamibia.com. These 2 adjacent hotels are located about 3km from the city centre, just off the B1 to Rehoboth, & literally round the corner from Eros Airport. Although both share the same entrance & parking area, each is a separate building with its own reception & check-in areas. Rooms at each hotel have the same facilities: tea/coffee station, fridge with minibar, safe, direct-dial phone, satellite TV & Wi-Fi. All residents have the full use of the public areas of each hotel, including the swimming pools, gardens, restaurants & bars &, as an added bonus, use of the gym, sauna & steam rooms at the Safari Court is complimentary to guests at both hotels (but other spa services & treatments are charged separately). A complimentary all-day (⊕ 07.00–19.00) shuttle service operates hourly to the city & the shopping centre at Maerua Park, & transfers to & from Eros Airport are free of charge on request. (Transfers to the International Airport cost around N$250 pp.) Catering mainly to businesspeople, it all feels a little generic.

🏠 SAFARI COURT HOTEL (204 rooms) Classed as a 4-star, the Safari Court is the more luxurious of the 2 & has modern, elegant rooms of a high standard, with en-suite baths & powerful showers. Recent refurbishment includes upgraded Wi-Fi. Home to the elegant Acacia restaurant, serving an international à la carte menu (**$$$$**) including Namibian oysters, ostrich steak & seafood & a fixed-price buffet at lunch & dinner (N$160); the Palms Ladies Bar & Terrace Bar; the Oukolele Day Spa complete with its own juice bar & gym; and shady landscaped gardens with a large swimming pool. **$$$$**

🏠 HOTEL SAFARI (197 rooms) This 3-star is less smart & has 2 types of room: standard, laid out motel style, & slightly more expensive 'business class', housed in a separate 2-storey block. There is a lovely big grassy pool area with a café & bar serving snacks & drinks to sun worshippers, making this a popular venue for a mid-afternoon bite to eat. The Welwitschia & Steakhouse restaurants (**$$$–$$$$$**) are slightly cheaper than the

Acacia, while Coffee Corner serves cakes & ice creams & the Skeleton Coast screens sports events. **$$$**

🏠 **Hotel Thule** (25 rooms) 1 Gorges St; ☎061 371950; e reservations@hotelthule.com; www. hotelthule.com. Once an impressive private home, this striking hotel is situated in a prime spot high on the hill above Eros, with sweeping views across the city. To get here from the airport, follow Nelson Mandela Av to the traffic lights after the BP garage, then turn right into Metje St. Take the third left into Olaf Palme St, then left at the top of the hill into Gorges (later Gutsche) St. At the top of the next hill, turn left again, & the Thule is behind the imposing gates on the left. From its flag-festooned entrance past tall palms, the Thule oozes style. Airy, light & very modern, its carpeted rooms are a blend of whitewashed wood furniture complemented by darker, fairly opulent soft furnishings. Each room has AC/heating & a dbl or twin beds, with a safe, TV, phone, minibar/fridge, coffee/tea facilities, hairdryer & Wi-Fi. En suite are a bath & shower, with underfloor heating for maximum comfort. VIP rooms have a sofa & dressing room, & there is also a family unit & a room designed specifically for the disabled. Views come as standard, either across the mountains at the back, or over the central fountain to the city beyond.

In the main building, & the surrounding grounds, no expense has been spared to maximise the impact of the hotel's location: this is not a place for vertigo sufferers, or for families with young children. Varying levels feature a pool set in a small lawn, a terrace with elegant tables & chairs, a small formal courtyard & a sports bar. The restaurant, appropriately called On the Edge, with its wide curved expanse of glass & terrace beyond, plus sweeping views across the city, is open for b/fast & dinner (**$$$–$$$$$**). The bar (⊕ open to public 14.00–21.30 Mon–Fri, noon–21.30 Sat, 16.00–21.00 Sun) is a great place for a sundowner. And if you look over the edge of the hill at sunset, you may even spot guinea fowl in the trees below. **$$$$**

🏠 **Thüringer Hof** [Map, page 128] (26 rooms) Cnr Independence Av & Bahnhof St; ☎061 226031; e fom.thuringerhof@proteahotels.com. na; www.marriott.com. A member of the Protea chain, close to the centre of town, this hotel is popular with the German & local business markets & tends to be quite noisy. Dbl or twin rooms are clean & functional, if generally unremarkable: all have AC/heating, direct-dial phones, tea/coffee stations, a safe, Wi-Fi & DSTV – safe-deposit boxes

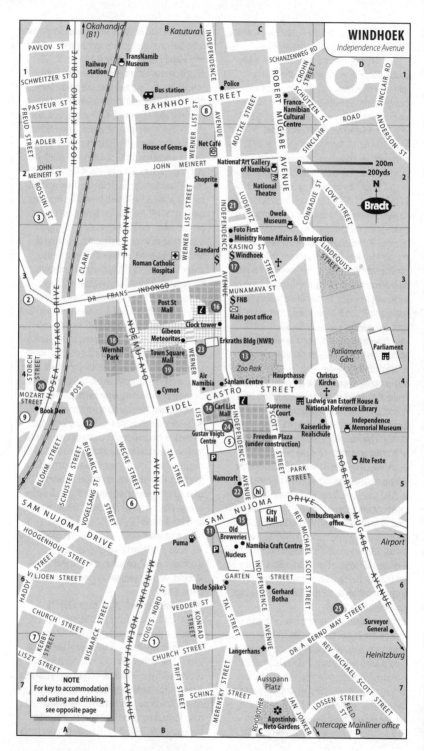

WINDHOEK
Independence Avenue

Bradt

N

0 ———— 200m
0 ———— 200yds

NOTE
For key to accommodation
and eating and drinking,
see opposite page

behind reception. One attraction of the hotel is its lively beer garden. Here you can order food as well as drinks, & choose from the pub-grub menu, with good-value daily specials. In the front is the popular Ivy Grill, with its traditional no-nonsense square tables, white tablecloths & à la carte lunch & dinner menus (**$$$**). If you want to stay somewhere that's straightforward & convenient, the Thüringer Hof might fit the bill. **$$$$**

🏠 **Roof of Africa** (27 rooms) 124 Nelson Mandela Av, Klein Windhoek; 📞 061 254708; 📱 081 124 4930; 📧 info@roofofafrica.com; www. roofofafrica.com. Clearly visible as you're entering Windhoek on Nelson Mandela Av, Roof of Africa has its main entrance in Gusinde St. This well-equipped hotel with a lively atmosphere & helpful staff has a popular bar & restaurant open to the public, serving freshly cooked buffets daily from around N$120 or a 3-course dinner from N$139. All rooms are en suite, with AC, phone, Wi-Fi, TV & safe, while additional luxuries are a solar-heated swimming pool & private sauna. The on-site travel office is a useful extra, as is

the shuttle service to the airport (*N$180 pp*) & the city centre (*N$20 pp*); prices are based on 2 people min. **$$$**

🏠 **Motown Hotel & Conference Centre** (37 rooms) Cnr Brandberg & Independence Av; 📞 061 234646; 📱 081 128 1871; 📧 motown@ namibnet.com. Located at the northern end of Independence Av, this hotel focuses primarily on the backpacker market & those looking for no-frills accommodation at a sensible price. Clean & comfortable, it offers good security – rooms are accessed with a swipe card, there is a security guard on duty round the clock, & there is secure parking. Some rooms share bathrooms, others are en suite, but all have AC, DSTV, a safe & tea/coffee station. There is a licensed restaurant serving basic 2-choice set menus (*around N$107 lunch, N$127 dinner*). A laundry service is available. **$$**

PENSIONS AND B&BS

Map, pages 124–5, unless otherwise indicated. There has been a proliferation of pensions & guesthouses in recent years. Most are situated in the suburban areas surrounding Windhoek, particularly in Eros, Klein Windhoek & the more affluent Ludwigsdorf, whose neighbourhoods also have plenty of restaurants & bars. In Olympia, to the southeast of the city, pensions are relatively scarce.

Central Windhoek and Windhoek West

🏠 **Villa Verdi** (18 rooms, 1 luxury suite) 4 Verdi St; 📞 061 221994; 📧 res1@leadinglodges.com; reservations 📞 061 375300; 📧 fovv@leadinglodges. com; www.leadinglodges.com. In many ways this place off John Meinert St set the standard for small hotels in Windhoek in 1994, when the stylish use of ethnic décor & African art broke the mould of the traditional German pensions. Each room has a dbl or twin beds, bath or shower, TV with Mnet, direct-dial phone, minibar/fridge & electric blankets for the winter; AC is available in some rooms. Despite its promising start, standards are not always up to the mark & some rooms smelled of stale smoke on our visit. **$$$$**

🏠 **Fig Tree** (6 rooms) 11 Robert Mugabe Av; 📞 061 400966; 📧 info@figtree.com.na; www. figtree.com.na. Super stylish B&B designed by well-known architect Claud Bosch, who used to live here. Equipped with business travellers in mind, each room has an HP printer, DSTV, free

Windhoek WHERE TO STAY

8

129

Wi-Fi, kitchenette & safe. A family suite features 1 dbl & 2 sgls. Out the back a smart wooden decking area surrounds a pristine pool, a lapa-style covered bar area & small gym, & the property has its own organic veg & herb garden. The professional chef, Cellia Gomachas, makes use of this produce when preparing her fantastic b/fast; lunch & dinner on request. Recommended. **$$$**

🏠 **Rivendell** (12 rooms, flat) 40 Beethoven St; 📞061 250006; e rivendell@infotour-africa. com; www.rivendellnamibia.com. This guesthouse offers a homely, comfortable, clean & relaxed place to stay to the west of the city, about 15–20mins' walk from the centre. Rooms overlooking the swimming pool are en suite, while those in the main house share bathrooms. Extra beds can be added if required. There is also a self-catering flat for up to 5 people with a bedroom, lounge & kitchenette. Facilities include a communal lounge with honesty bar, free Wi-Fi, TV, metered phone & laundry services. Rates include a full English b/fast, but guests are welcome to use the self-catering kitchen. **$$$**

🏠 **Steiner** [Map, page 128] (16 rooms) 11 Wecke St; 📞061 414400; e steiner@iafrica.com.na. This small, quiet pension, built on several levels, is a convenient short walk from the centre, squeezed into a cul-de-sac off Trift St, between Sam Nujoma Dr & Fidel Castro St. Its rooms have tiled floors, Mnet & German TV channels, phones, fridges & ceiling fans (with AC in some rooms). Behind the building is a thatched bar overlooking a deep swimming pool. Steiner is a popular & pleasant place to stay & its atmosphere is one of helpful efficiency. **$$$**

🏠 **Vondelhof** [Map, page 128] (8 rooms) 2 Puccini St; 📞061 248320; e reservations@ vondelhof.com; www.vondelhof.com. The friendly Vondelhof, with its tall turret, ochre-washed walls & large pool set in attractive gardens, is close to the centre of Windhoek. Each room is individual – with a private patio, or a desk, or interconnecting for families – but all have TV, phone, minibar, safe, fan & coffee/tea facilities. Light lunches are available, & there's Wi-Fi access for guests. **$$$**

🏠 **Handke** [Map, page 128] (13 rooms) 3 Rossini St; 📞061 234904; e pensionhandke@ iafrica.com.na; www.natron.net/handke. The inexpensive Handke is within about 5mins' walk of the centre of town – ideal if you've no car (though if you have, approach via John Meinert St & there's

convenient off-street parking in front). Even though it doesn't have a pool, & the rooms are small & simple, they offer good value, particularly those at the back which are quieter than the others. All have AC, fridges & direct-dial phone. There's little space around the rooms, but the tree-shaded garden is a pleasant place to sit, & the TV lounge & b/fast area offer real home comfort. Wi-Fi costs N$100 per stay. **$$**

🏠 **Kleines Heim** (14 rooms) 10 Volans St, Windhoek West; m 081 362 6207; e info@ kleinesheim.com, info@elonga-internship.com; www.kleinesheim.com. About 5mins' drive from the city centre, or a 15min walk, & with secure parking, Kleines Heim is a beautiful colonial building dating back to 1911 set in peaceful gardens with a swimming pool & impressive palm trees. Having been closed for 3 years & sadly neglected, it is now managed by the enthusiastic Gerda Schuler, who is passionately restoring it to its former glory. Still linked with the Polytechnic of Namibia as part of the hotel training school, its rooms are simple but comfortable & spacious, inc 2 6-bed dorms, free Wi-Fi & kitchens for self-catering. At the time of our research, facilities were limited with some rooms having fans & safes, but watch this space – Gerda's enthusiasm will undoubtedly lead to improvements. Communications can be problematic: contact via the mobile is the most reliable. *B/fast N$60. Dorm N$145.* **$$**

🏠 **Ol-ga** (4 rooms) 91 Bach St, Windhoek West; 📞061 235853; e olgaguest@iway.na; www.olga-namibia.de. Gesa Oldach claims that her home is one of the oldest B&Bs in Windhoek. Located about 2.5km west of the centre of the city, it will appeal particularly to birdwatchers, as numerous species are attracted to its mature trees & pretty gardens. Pine-furnished rooms (one with a private veranda & kitchenette) are small, & with local art adorning the walls. TV, kettle with tea & coffee, fridge & mosquito nets throughout. There is a BBQ available for guests. **$$**

🏠 **Pension Cori** (18 rooms) 8 Puccini St, Windhoek West; 📞061 228840; m 081 127 7397; e cori@iway.na; www.pension-cori-namibia.com. It's not difficult to spot this lilac pension near the corner of Hosea Kutako Dr & Puccini St, a 5min walk from the city centre. Owner Rini lives on the premises & has run her hospitable pension since the late 1990s. Rooms sleep 2–4 people with a private entrance from the garden, & feature a TV, coffee/tea-making facilities, fridge, safe, Wi-Fi & a fan or AC. The attractive garden offers plenty of shady trees, with a swimming pool & a thatched seating area. There are 2 well-equipped outdoor kitchens for guest use, as well as a braai. Airport collection can be arranged (*N$200 pp, less for a group*), or Rini will collect you from the airport shuttle stop in Windhoek. There is secure parking. **$$**

🏠 **Tamboti** [Map, page 128] (15 rooms) 9 Kerby St; 📞061 235515; e tamboti@mweb.com. na; www.guesthouse-tamboti.com. This friendly guesthouse, 15mins' walk from the centre of town, boasts 2 swimming pools, a patio where you can watch the sunset, & secure parking. Each of the varied rooms, including a family room with its own lounge area, has its own small shaded area with a bench or chairs & umbrella, & guests also benefit from tea/coffee stations & an honesty bar. A nominal charge is made for Wi-Fi. Facilities for the disabled are considered excellent. **$$**

🏠 **Tilla's Guesthouse** (9 rooms) 9 Strauss St, Windhoek West; 📞061 259799; m 081 262 4478; e borges@iway.na; www.tillasguesthouse. com. On the corner of Beethoven & Strauss sts & a 15min walk to the town centre, Tilla's is a new, good value, no-frills guesthouse with clean, simply furnished en-suite rooms offering AC, DSTV, fridge & tea/coffee facilities. Secure parking & laundry service available. **$$**

Eros, Klein Windhoek and Ludwigsdorf

🏠 **The Village Courtyard Suites** (7 suites) Cnr Lilliencron St & Robert Mugabe Av; 📞061 400510/232740; m 081 767 4254; e reservations@villagecourtyardsuites.com; www. villagecourtyardsuites.com. This collection of suites (2 accommodating 4 people), developed from once-derelict apartments, resembles a yuppie apartment complex. Vast, loft-style rooms fitted with designer furniture, large arty prints, DSTV, Wi-Fi, minibar & well-equipped kitchenette all overlook a central courtyard, where a fish-pond feature is surrounded by boutique shops. Accommodation includes a b/fast voucher to the value of N$75 for the Fresh 'n' Wild café – one of the best cafés currently available in Windhoek (see page 142). **$$$$–$$$$$**

🏠 **Olive Grove** (10 rooms, 1 suite) 20 Promenaden Weg, Klein Windhoek; 📞061

239199; e info@olivegrove-namibia.com; www. olivegrove-namibia.com. This smart guesthouse is located in a renovated old house about 10mins' walk from the centre of Windhoek. From the airport, turn right off the B6 into Nelson Mandela Av, then left into Schanzen St, & right near the end of the road into Promenaden Weg; the Olive Grove is on the right, on the corner of Ngami St. Friendly yet professional, it boasts excellent service & good food (*3-course dinner N$285 pp*), prepared in an open-plan kitchen that creates an air of informality. Stylish, minimalist décor throughout, including the lounge area, is softened by Moroccan lanterns & old wooden doors of Indonesian origin. Each of the rooms, with AC, minibar, TV, Wi-Fi & plenty of other mod cons, has twin beds set on grey cement plinths, with the same theme running through into large, well-appointed bathrooms (some with bath, others with shower, or even both). In one corner of the courtyard, a small raised terrace incorporates a pool shaded by the signature olive tree, while above, well away from prying eyes, lie a freshwater spa pool & lounging area. There's also a wellness room offering various massage & facial treatments. The luxurious garden suite offers all the mod cons, and was a prelude to Olive Exclusive, its boutique sister-hotel next door (see page 123), with 7 smart suites, similarly excellent service & great views. **$$$–$$$$$**

🏠 **Galton House** [Map, page 118] (8 rooms, inc 1 tpl & 1 family) 72 Amasoniet St, Eros; 📞061 230416; m 081 142 6300; e reservations@ galtonhouse.com; www.galtonhouse.com. Galton House is a contemporary & stylish offering about 10mins' drive to the centre of town. It's set high on a hill in leafy suburbia with a quiet, relaxed vibe. All rooms have slate floors & neutral, minimalist décor with striking aerial photos of African wildlife. Facilities include AC, TV, phone, safe & free Wi-Fi, with tea/coffee station available on request. The main house has a bright guest lounge, an open kitchen & dining area, with seating indoors & outdoors, serving a buffet b/fast, à la carte lunches & a set dinner menu (*N$220*) with excellent quality meals. Outside, the pool is surrounded by loungers & a small covered smoking area. Secure parking available. **$$$$**

🏠 **The Elegant Guesthouse** (6 rooms) 56 Ziegler & Von Eckenbrecher sts, Klein Windhoek; 📞061 301934; m 081 302 8255; e info@ the-elegant-collection.com; www.the-elegant-collection.com. Elegant by name & nature, this lovely guesthouse can be reached from the airport by following Nelson Mandela Av to the traffic lights after the BP garage, then turning right into Metje St & left into Ziegler St. Each of the airy, modern rooms combines neutral, earthy tones to create stylish quarters with twin beds, AC, DSTV, Wi-Fi, safe, phone & small courtyard. Central facilities include secure parking, a small pool & a b/fast room with an honesty bar. **$$$$**

⌂ **Palmquell** (16 rooms) 60 Jan Jonker Rd; ☏061 234374; m 081 127 1036; e hotel. palmquell@iafrica.com.na; www.palmquell.com. Owned by Austrians Trude & Fritz Pfaffenthaler, this upmarket pension offers a quiet setting among the palm trees that give it its name. If you're coming from the airport, it is clearly signposted to the left off Sam Nujoma Dr. Follow Jan Jonker Rd past the junction with Nelson Mandela Av, & you'll find it on the right. It's a bit too far to walk into Windhoek centre but Maerua Mall is nearby & it's a nice quiet location, with secure parking. Relax in the sauna, lounge by the pool or take a cool dip, perhaps followed by a drink at the bar. Dbl & family rooms are simply furnished, but very well equipped, with AC & underfloor heating, phone, TV & safe; paintings by Namibian artists provide an individual touch. A select dinner menu (*N$118*), but not lunch, is available daily except Sat. The tomato soup is recommended & there's a good range of South African wines. No on-site parking. **$$$$**

⌂ **Belvedere** [Map, page 118] (18 rooms) 76–8 Dr Kwame Nkrumah, Ludwigsdorf; ☏061 258867; e jdavin@psg.com.na; www.belvedere-boutiquehotel.com. The beautiful colonial-style family home of Herman & Jeanne Davin has been transformed into a guesthouse which sets out to attract both tourists & business travellers. As well as a heated swimming pool surrounded by a wooden deck & a few holes of minigolf, there is a floodlit tennis court, a small-but-smart on-site spa, & private areas within the manicured gardens for individual barbecues. Along with this, each of the tasteful & well-appointed rooms – available in standard or luxury – has all the facilities of a good hotel: DSTV, desk with phone & free Wi-Fi, AC & heating, bath or shower (rooms 14, 15 & 17 have baths), honesty minibar, coffee/tea facilities, hairdryer & safe. A further 9 rooms & a restaurant should be completed at the end of 2015. **$$$**

⌂ **Casa Piccolo** (16 rooms) 6 Barella St, Klein Windhoek; ☏061 221155; e casapiccolo@iafrica.com.na; www.natron.net/tour/casapiccolo. Further down the road on the opposite side to Pension BougainVilla, Casa Piccolo has recently expanded to include the neighbouring property. However, it still has the bright yellow walls giving the place a sunny atmosphere that permeates through the tiled floors & simple white décor of its twin-bed rooms. There is now also a family room sleeping 4. Claudia Horn has run this 2-star guesthouse since 2000, mostly catering for the South African business market, though holidaymakers would be just as much at home with the bright, clean facilities that include fan, AC/heater, fridge, minibar, coffee & tea facilities, phone, DSTV, Wi-Fi & a central pool. Off-street parking will add to peace of mind if you have a vehicle. **$$$**

⌂ **Haus Sonneneck** [Map, page 118] (8 rooms) 1 Robyn St, Eros; ☏061 225020; e haussonneneck@afol.com.na; www. haussonneneck.com. Located beyond the Medi-Clinic at Eros, on the corner of Eros Way & Robyn St (but with the main entrance on Eros Way), Haus Sonneneck is well established as one of Windhoek's best pensions. German owners Gisela & Rudolf, and their playful dachshund, ensure that all runs smoothly & are a good source of local knowledge. Spacious rooms line a long entrance drive amid an oasis of bougainvillea, bananas, palms & even a stunning white pepper tree. Although slightly clinical in feel, all rooms have bright, white tiled interiors & deep-pile rugs, AC, minibar/hot drinks, digital safe, satellite TV, Wi-Fi, phone & a small, private patio garden with table & chairs. 2 rooms also feature a small open-plan kitchenette, & for families there's a very large room with a dbl & a sgl bed, & a ¾-size futon (with a cot available on request). There's a large b/fast room (no other meals are served) & bar area & an inviting chemical-free swimming pool. Self-drivers will welcome the plentiful secure parking. Iron bird sculptures, a few trickling water features & plenty of resident birdlife make this a thoroughly pleasant & peaceful retreat, only a few mins' drive from downtown Windhoek. **$$$**

⌂ **Hotel Uhland** (24 rooms) 147 Dr Kenneth David Kaunda St; ☏061 389700; e info@hoteluhland.com; www.hoteluhland.com. Situated northeast of Windhoek, off Independence Av, this friendly, pink-painted pension stands on the side of a hill, making it an airy spot when it's hot. The city centre is a 10–15min walk, but Uhland has plenty of secure parking if you have a car. Cane furniture complements the carpeted rooms, which each have TV, clock/radio, phone, mosquito nets, ceiling fans, tea/coffee-making facilities & minibar. The Superior rooms also have AC & some have safes. 2 family rooms sleep 3–4 people. There's also separate internet access for the guests, with Wi-Fi available. A comfortable living room with TV & stereo adjoins the b/fast room, while outside is a patio with a pool & a thatched bar area. Coffee & homemade cake in the afternoon & a snack menu at dinner complete the package. **$$$**

⌂ **Klein Windhoek Guesthouse** (65 rooms) 2 Hofmeyer St, Klein Windhoek; ☎ 061 239401; e kwgh@iway.na; www.kleinwindhoekguesthouse. com. Situated in a quiet cul-de-sac next to the Klein Windhoek River, this guesthouse has grown tremendously over the past few years, almost taking over both sides of Hofmeyer St. Rooms vary in size ranging from budget to luxury to self-catering units sleeping up to 6 people with small kitchenettes. Each has AC, fridge, TV & tea/ coffee facilities, with some also having Wi-Fi access. Seating areas are dotted throughout the gardens there's a swimming pool that is very small considering the number of potential users. An Italian-influenced restaurant & bar complete the central facilities. If you prefer intimate B&Bs, this isn't the place for you, but it's good value & efficiently run. **$$$**

⌂ **Londiningi Guesthouse** [Map, page 118] (9 rooms) 11 Winterberg St, Eros Park; ☎ 061 242378; m 081 128 1017; e londiningi@afol. com.na; www.londiningi.com. French-speaking Nathalie & Alex have run this pretty suburban guesthouse for 10 years. Very relaxed, family-focused pension with spotless rooms with simple African fabrics, a minibar stocked with soft drinks & beer, DSTV, phone, free Wi-Fi & safe. Some rooms interconnect for family use. The open kitchen enhances the family home feel of the place, with b/fast served in a conservatory overlooking the swimming pool. Dinners & packed lunches available on request. They support a grass-roots preschool project called Peri Naua (*www.peri-naua.com*) and welcome enquiries from guests about bringing teaching aids or old clothes which they sell to benefit the project. **$$$**

⌂ **Pension BougainVilla** (16 rooms) 66 Barella St, Klein Windhoek; ☎ 061 252266; e bougainvilla@afol.com.na; www. pensionbougainvilla.com. On the corner of Nelson Mandela St, just after the turning into Barella St beyond the traffic lights as you approach Windhoek from the airport, this pension is the large olive-green building behind a wall draped in bougainvillea; it's not difficult to spot.

Dbl rooms with queen-size beds & opulent soft furnishings each have TV, AC, phone, Wi-Fi, minibar & hairdryer. Outside are 2 pools, 1 surrounded by tranquil, flower-decked gardens & shady pavilions with chairs & tables. There's secure parking (though the centre of town is just 15mins' walk away). Although it's a lovely guesthouse, lack of attention to detail sometimes lets it down. **$$$**

⌂ **Villa Monte Bello Guesthouse** [map, page 118] (11 rooms) 30 Akwamaryn St, Eros; ☎ 061 224045; m 081 298 2535; e info@ villa-moringa-montebello.com; www.villa-moringa-montebello.com. This contemporary B&B is owned by the same proprietors as Villa Moringa (see below). It might seem stark from the outside but it has a warm, stylish ambience in a quiet residential part of Windhoek. The 9 rooms on ground level, some of which open on to the pool area, have neutral décor with splashes of colour, cool tiled floors, AC, TV, free Wi-Fi, minibar, tea/ coffee stations, a safe & laundry service. The 2 rooms on the 1st floor of the main house are much more spacious & the whole floor can be made into a self-contained apartment with a well-appointed kitchenette & lounge area. On the ground floor, the airy b/fast room & lounge area overlook the small pool with sun-loungers & rattan chairs & tables. **$$$**

⌂ **Villa Moringa** (11 rooms) 111A Joseph Mukwayu Ithana St, Ludwigsdorf; ☎ 061 224472; m 081 124 0617; e info@villa-moringa.com; www.villa-moringa.com. Run by Portuguese Mrs Ru, this guesthouse lies east of the city & is a favourite with travelling businesspeople. From the airport, turn right from the B6 into Mission Rd soon after entering the first suburbs. After about 700m this joins Dr Kwame Nkrumah St; Joseph Mukwayu Ithana St is the 3rd right, & the guesthouse is on the first bend. Each of the modern rooms has a different colour theme running through the high-quality furnishings. AC, DSTV, free Wi-Fi, tea & coffee & a free minibar come as standard, while central facilities include a restaurant/b/fast room with licensed bar, a pool & sun terrace. Accommodates families & more rooms are being added. **$$$**

🏠 **Villa Violet** (6 rooms) Cnr Ziegler & König sts, Klein Windhoek; 📞061 256141; 📱 081 475 6379; 📧 villaviolet@iway.na; www.villaviolet. info. Formerly the Elegant Bed & Breakfast, Villa Violet is now owned by Heidi & Ben Dassac, who run a friendly & efficient B&B. The rooms, all well appointed with splashes of violet in the accessories, open out on to central lawns & a small pool. In a peaceful location, it has a relaxing ambience with open kitchen/b/fast room & a pleasant lounge with an honesty bar. All rooms have AC, TV, Wi-Fi & safe. **$$$**

Olympia and southeast Windhoek

🏠 **Moni** (17 rooms) 7 Rieks van der Walt St; 📞061 228350; 📧 reswhk@monihotel.com; www. monihotel.com. Within 20mins' walk of the city centre, & 10mins from Maerua Mall, this quiet, friendly pension run by Marita Schneider is easiest to reach from the Dr Agostinho Neto roundabout, at the south end of Independence Av. From there take Jan Jonker, then first left on to Lazarett, first right on to Feld, & then first left into Rieks van der Walt St. Everything is immaculately kept – from the gardens to the en-suite accommodation, which overlooks a central pool area. Rooms are bright & cheerful, with original paintings on the walls, & direct-dial phones, clock radio, fans, DSTV & tea/coffee-making facilities. Trpl & quad rooms make it a good option for families. Dinner is not automatically available, but can be prepared for groups, & sandwiches or snacks are available on request. Wi-Fi costs N$50/24hrs. **$$$**

🏠 **Terra Africa** (10 rooms) 6 Kenneth McArthur St, Olympia; 📞061 252100; 📧 info@ terra-africa.com; www.terra-africa.com. Terra Africa has 10 off-street parking places & is set in a residential road behind a gate adorned with pink bougainvillea. The rather utilitarian square building belies the care that has been lavished on the modern interior. Tastefully decorated rooms feature artwork by local artists which is for sale & have DSTV, a safe, stocked minibar, AC/heating, tea & coffee & free Wi-Fi. Ask for a south-facing room if possible: they're quieter than those overlooking the pool. There is also a computer terminal in the lounge that guests can use free of charge & a small

gift shop opposite reception. A spacious homely lounge with dining area & big picture windows overlook the landscaped, tree-shaded gardens. The pool deck & gardens are quiet & shady, & residents can braai their own food there if they wish. Light lunches (N$50) such as mini pizzas & toasted sandwiches are available noon–14.00 Mon–Fri. Families are welcome. **$$$**

Pioneers Park and southwest Windhoek

🏠 **Casa Blanca Hotel** (16 rooms) 2 Gous St/cnr Fritsche St, Pioneers Pk; 📞061 249623; 📧 casablanca@afol.com.na; www. casablancahotelnamibia.com. Just next to Etambi, the turreted Casa Blanca with wrought-iron finishing has a slightly classier atmosphere but remains geared to the business market, with a small conference room/bar. It is located on the main road so at busy periods rooms at the front can be quite noisy. Comfortable, stylish rooms, grouped round a small, Italian-style courtyard, have king or twin beds with minibar, DSTV & AC combi, & artwork adorning the walls. Room 17 is classed as luxury & features an open fire & corner bath, while rooms 14, 18 & 19 have pool views. Each also has its own desk with plug for a laptop computer. To the front is a mature garden with numerous indigenous plants & areas where guests can relax, while at the side are a small gym, small pool & 'Bedouin's Rest' lounge area with fire pit. B/fast is a hot-&-cold buffet, lunch is light meals & dinner à la carte. On-site parking & free Wi-Fi. **$$$**

🏠 **Hotel Etambi Garni** (11 rooms) 6 Gous St, Pioneers Pk; 📞061 241763; 📧 etambi@mweb. com.na; www.etambi.com. Now under the ownership of Namibian Michael Meyer, Etambi is 10mins' drive from the city centre, so you really need your own vehicle to stay here. To find it, take Marconi St westward, before turning on to Jordan St, following the signs for Pioneers Pk. The road sweeps around to the right, & after about 1km you take the 3rd left on to Hintrager St. After a further 1km, turn right on to Fritsche St, then left after the shopping centre on to Gous St; Etambi is on the right. Etambi caters a lot for independent businesspeople – so has phones, free Wi-Fi & DSTV in the rooms, each of which has its own entrance off the garden. It's a friendly & efficient little pension, its rooms large & comfortable with modern furnishings, a kettle, minibar/fridge &

safe. There is an honesty bar, outside braai for guests to use, & small pool. 9 secure parking places are available. Daily shuttles to the city cost N$80 pp. **$$$**

HOSTELS AND CAMPING

Map, pages 124–5, unless otherwise indicated. Windhoek has a handful of excellent backpackers' hostels. The city's only dedicated campsite, Arebbusch, is just south of town, so of benefit only to those with vehicles. Campers without transport can pitch a tent at some of the backpackers' hostels.

Arebbusch Travel Lodge (mixed) Auas Rd, Olympia; ☎061 252255; e reservations@ arebbusch.com; www.arebbusch.com. Less than 10km south of the centre, between the Safari Hotel & Windhoek Country Club, this is Windhoek's only dedicated campsite. In addition to the 18 camping/ caravanning sites with power, water, kitchen & washing facilities, it offers a host of other serviced options too: 2 luxury self-catering villas with 3 bedrooms; 1 luxury dbl-storey cottage also with 3 bedrooms & fireplace – both have 2 bathrooms (1 en suite), bedlinen, a fully equipped kitchen, lounge/dining area, DSTV, covered parking & braai facilities; 23 self-catering serviced chalets that can sleep up to 5 people; & 8 budget rooms with fans & bathrooms shared with camping. There's a spotless restaurant on site, with a good range of steaks & salads, some vegetarian options & a kids' menu. Added to this is a bar & a good pool with waiter service for snacks & drinks. The only real snag is that you need a car to get here. *Camping N$120.* **$$**

Cardboard Box (28 dorm beds, camping) 15 Johann Albrecht St; ☎061 228994; e info@ cardboardbox.com.na; www.cardboardbox.com. na. On the corner of John Meinert St, a short uphill walk from town, this is Windhoek's original backpackers' lodge where the emphasis remains on offering independent travellers a relaxed social atmosphere where they might meet potential travelling partners. The capital's favourite for many years thanks to its lively atmosphere, Cardboard Box has 4 6–8 bedded dorms & 3 private rooms with shared facilities, & a campsite at the rear of the property. Campers without a tent can book a colourful converted combi fitted with a double mattress. Friendly dogs are welcome to accompany their owners. A large, open-sided bar with booths,

ceiling fans & sports TV & a separate wooden deck both overlook an inviting pool area where braais are served on Mon &Thu. The bar serves b/fast, snacks, light lunches & evening meals for those who want a break from self-catering in the communal kitchen. A new restaurant is planned for 2015. Coin-operated washing machines & internet access are available & there is secure parking & free pick-up from the Intercape Bus Station on Bahnhof St. Free b/fast of pancakes & tea/coffee. *Dorm N$120; camping N$80.* **$$**

Chameleon Backpackers & Guesthouse [Map, page 128] (12 dorm beds, 17 rooms) 5–7 Voigt St; ☎061 244347; e chameleonbackpackers@iway.na; www. chameleonbackpackers.com. Relaxed & friendly, yet efficiently run, this lodge is also very central. A range of options is available: the basic backpacker rooms, en-suite guesthouse rooms in standard, luxury or honeymoon, & 3 flats for long-term accommodation. Bright, cheerful & clean, each 6-bed dormitory has lockers & its own bathroom. Dbl, twin & family rooms offer more privacy. It's a homely complex, with numerous communal 'rooms': a large lounge, various terrace areas with seating, a fully fitted kitchen, & a thatched bar by an inviting pool with sun-loungers. Other facilities include TVs & video, internet access, Wi-Fi & payphone, a BBQ area & a secure cage for luggage, not to mention a pool table & book exchange. Secure off-street parking is available, as are airport pick-ups/drop-offs (*N$280*). Trips can be booked too. *Dorm N$150; guesthouse N$400.* **$$**

Paradise Garden Backpackers (22 dorm beds, 2 en-suite rooms) 5 Roentgen St, Windhoek West; ☎061 303494; m 081 280 9208; e paradisegarden@iway.na; www.paradisegarden. iway.na. Every city has a homely, quirky, hard-to-find backpackers' lodge that has a vibe all of its own & Windhoek is no exception – with Paradise Garden fitting the bill. Although 'paradise' might be stretching it a bit for the garden, this small, friendly backpackers has a pool with hammocks, Wi-Fi & computer terminal, an airy TV room/ lounge with DSTV, an honesty bar & a laundry service. There is a pleasant outside area with table tennis & a braai & they will organise bookings for tours & shuttles. They even offer b/fast for N$50 & dinner by prior arrangement. Vanilla the dog, Yellow the cat & 2 turtles are part of the family. *Dorm N$130.* **$$**

JUST OUTSIDE TOWN

Map, page 114, unless otherwise indicated.
Lodges and guest farms have proliferated
around Windhoek, & many of these make good
alternatives to staying in the city, especially on the
way to or from the airport.

To the east (towards the airport)

There are quite a few places to stay between
Windhoek & Hosea Kutako International Airport.
The benefits of staying out of town in relatively
rural surroundings are self-evident, & there are
many different styles of accommodation from
which to choose. Those below are listed in order of
their distance from Windhoek.

🏠 **River Crossing Lodge** (20 chalets) ☎061
401494/061 246788; e reservations@rivercrossing.
com.na; www.rivercrossing.com.na. Smart lodge
with superb views designed to offer an alternative
to city accommodation, while being close to the
airport & town amenities. To find it, take the B6
east towards the airport for 6km, pass under the
old railway bridge & 200m further on the right is a
signpost. Follow the signs along a track for about
6km. Chalets are well spaced & all have a view over
the valley & the Moltkeblick Mountains. All are
fitted with AC/heating & have DSTV, tea & coffee,
free Wi-Fi & black-slate walk-in showers. The
central lodge area has a comfortable lounge, a bar,
a large balcony & pool with spectacular views, &
a restaurant offering set-menu lunch (*N$65–125*)
& 3-course dinner (*N$200*). Game drives (*N$600
pp/3hrs*) & horseriding on request (*from N$250
pp*; see page 157) are available in the mountains.
Airport transfer N$550 per car. **$$$$**

🏠 **Etango Guest Farm** (11 rooms) ☎062
540423/540451; m 081 129 3007/2569017;
e etangoranch@mweb.com.na; www.
etangoranch.com. This family-run cattle & sheep
ranch is only 3.5km from the international
airport; to get there, drive just 150m east of the
airport on the B6, then turn right through a gate
& continue 2km or so down a sandy track until
you come to the farm. Owned by Volker & Anke
Grellmann & managed by their son, Robert, it
is in the Namatanga Conservancy. There are 3
bungalows with 2 en-suite twin/dbl rooms with
their own veranda, spacious showers, & a tea/
coffee station; 6 AC simply furnished rondavels
ideal for hikers or riders; & the 'Nest' with 2 en-

suite dbl rooms (non-AC) with veranda, DSTV,
a pond & garden. A large lounge/dining room
allows for dining *en famille*, with set menu for
lunch & dinner & a wine list; vegetarians are
welcome. As well as a small pool, there are
excellent opportunities for birdwatching, 1–2hr
nature drives, & walks on the farm, which has a
range of endemic wildlife such as kudu, oryx &
hartebeest, & a group of mountain zebra. With its
rural location close to the airport, this is an ideal
spot for the beginning or end of a trip. **$$$**

🏠 **Hohewarte Guest Farm** (7 rooms)
m 081 426 1893/354 5290; e info@hohewarte.
com; www.hohewarte.com. Once a German
colonial police station & post office & still a
working cattle farm owned by Heike & Marcus,
Hohewarte stands in an area of some 10,000ha,
at the foot of the 2,299m Bismarck Mountain. To
get there, follow the B6 for about 28km, then turn
right towards Dordabis; after 15km, Hohewarte is
on the left. Basic rooms with a safe are either en
suite or with shared facilities. A further 2 rooms are
housed in a separate bungalow near the pool. Tea
& coffee are always available, & although there is
no internet or TV, there is a cell phone connection.
Meals are informal & with the family. The area is
beautiful with several self-guided walking trails,
including one to the top of the mountain. Nature
drives (*from N$150/2hrs*), horseriding (*from
N$350*) & guided walks (*from N$150*) are on offer.
Interested guests can also have a tour of the farm.
Finally, for N$360/month, you can store your car
with them. **$$$**

🏠 **Heja Game Lodge** (50 rooms) ☎061
257151/2; e info@hejalodge.com; www.
hejalodge.com. Signposted off the B6, 27km from
the airport, this all-singing all-dancing lodge
caters for tourists, weddings & conferences. To find
it, take the turning for Otjihase Mine & follow the
tarred road for 3km, then turn left & follow a heavy
gravel track – through land grazed by wildebeest,
springbok, blesbok, oryx, ostrich & warthog to
name a few – for a further 3km. Rooms 1–26 have
AC, rooms 27–50 have ceiling fans; all have DSTV,
free Wi-Fi & most also have a phone. 'Luxury' rooms
are just a bit larger. Activities include game drives
(*from N$175/1hr or N$300/3hrs*); 20min horse &
camel rides (*horses Sun only, camels Sat–Sun; both
N$20–30*) with a guide; & a new on-site snake
park. Archery, paintballing & 'dragon boat' trips can
also be arranged with nearby operators. There's a

bar (⏰ 20.00–late daily) & the plastic-tablecloth restaurant is open daily with an à la carte menu ($$$–$$$$); it's especially busy on Sun when there's a buffet lunch (⏰ noon–14.00; N$185), so you'll need to book. There's a swimming pool overlooking the dam & a trail around the dam that takes about 1hr to walk. For lovebirds, there are 2 private churches for wedding ceremonies & two hosting spaces – 'The View' & 'The Waterfront' – overlooking the dam. *Airport transfers N$150 pp.* **$$$**

🏠 **Onganga** (10 rooms, 1 family room) 11 Schuckmann St, Avis; ☎ 061 241701; **m** 081 127 3494; **e** onganga@mweb.com.na; www. onganga.com. This simple, modern pension near Avis Dam is signposted to the left off the B6 airport road, shortly after leaving Windhoek – turn on to Christa Davids St, the right on to Avisweg & then second left on to Schuckmann. Built on several levels, it has quiet twin & dbl rooms, each with AC, DSTV, phone, free Wi-Fi, minibar/fridge & tea/coffee-making facilities. Screened doors & windows mean that guests can take advantage of the breeze afforded by Onganga's hillside position. Under new Chinese ownership, plans are afoot to build a new Chinese restaurant for guests. The b/fast room is decorated with cane furniture. There's also a small craft shop. Outside, a small pool facing the mountains is surrounded by a grassy area set with umbrellas, overlooked by a rustic bar with a BBQ. There are several walking trails behind the pension, & access to Avis Dam. *Airport collection costs N$220 pp (2+) & 3–4hr city tours of Windhoek N$300 pp.* **$$$**

🏠 **Airport Lodge** (6 bungalows, 6 tents, camping) ☎ 061 231491; **m** 081 122 6101; **e** reservations@airportlodgenamibia.com; www.airportlodgenamibia.com. Run by Brian & Hermine Black, Airport Lodge is signposted from the B6, halfway between the international airport & the city; it lies 600m along the M53. Set well apart in extensive bush, each of the lodge's ethnic-décor thatched bungalows has 3 sgl beds (children will love the 3rd, set high up in its own 'loft' area), kitchenette, minibar, DSTV, direct-dial phone & mosquito nets, not to mention a small veranda. Some rooms have AC, others have fans; heaters are provided in winter & a 4th bed can be added. Camping pitches have electricity, water & clean ablution blocks with washing-up facilities, which are shared with the 6 new fixed tents that

sleep up to 6 & have a small wooden balcony & electric lights. There's a large swimming pool with outside & inside bars, a braai, an open fire for winter evenings & a conference room. Free Wi-Fi is available around reception, the swimming pool & bars. Dinner is served à la carte. With lovely mountain views & plenty of wildlife (oryx, ostrich & several bird species) living on the property this is a peaceful & convenient stop before or after a flight (*airport transfers N$295 for up to 6*). *B/fast N$75; camping N$95.* **$$**

🏠 **Trans Kalahari Caravan Park** (9 rooms, 9 camping) 65 Kappsfarm, B6; ☎ 061 222877; **e** info@transkalahari-inn.com; www. transkalahari-inn.com. Set back from the B6, just 21km from the airport, this is more than just a caravan park, with large, simply furnished, en-suite rooms (6 luxury and 3 standard), some with AC, catering mainly for the German market. Rooms 8 & 9 are very large & would suit families. Pitches at the campsite have electricity, water & a grill area, & a toilet block with hot-water showers. There is a solar-heated swimming pool & the main building features a rustic bar (⏰ 19.30–21.00 daily) with TV & restaurant (*mains N$90–140*) with lounge area & a good range of crafts for sale – ideal for last-minute souvenirs. The panoramic views across the surrounding Kappsberg Mountains are spectacular. The restaurant serves Namibian-German cuisine, with the emphasis on game. Some may be put off by the owner's 3 Labradors & 5 cats; others will appreciate the privacy. Also on site is Bobo Campers who rent & offer repairs. *Airport transfers N$135 pp; b/fast N$90; camping N$50 pp plus N$50 per pitch.* **$$**

🏠 **Vineyard Country B&B** (8 rooms, 1 self-catering cottage, 8 camping) ☎ 061 224144; **m** 081 124 3620; **e** info@vineyardcountrystay. com; www.vineyardcountrystay.com. Situated 1km along the same track as River Crossing Lodge (see opposite), this B&B caters mainly for conferences, but owners Colin & Noelene Bassingthwaighte have tried hard to inject charm into the converted century-old buildings of a vineyard. Some of the rooms are modern (room 8), some traditional (room 1) – all have a fridge, fans & heaters, safe, DSTV & walk-in en-suite shower. There is also a 4-bed cottage. New camping sites at the back of the property have braais, kitchen sinks & luxurious bathrooms with solar-heated water. The Wi-Fi is dodgy, but there are nice touches such as homemade rusk biscuits to go with in-room tea/coffee facilities & 2 free-of-use mountain bikes. B/fast is the whole hog, continental & full English combined. There's a small, cold pool & Avis Dam walks are close by. *Airport transfers N$280 pp; camping N$125.* **$$**

To the north and west

Additional options in this direction, but within relatively easy reach of Windhoek, are Okapuka (see page 168) & Düsternbrook (see page 167).

⌂ **Sun Karros** Daan Viljoen Nature Reserve; ☏061 232393; e reservations@sunkarros.com; www.sunkarros.com. Situated in the middle of the Daan Viljoen reserve, it offers 17 luxurious & modern en-suite chalets with private patio, as well as 12 smart, equipped camping sites located beside the Augeigas River & equipped Meru-style canvas tents. The on-site Kraal restaurant serves an à la carte menu & there's a well-stocked kiosk (ideal for self-drivers needing supplies for their journey), an internet café & large swimming pool. At the time of writing, no activities were on offer save for 2 marked hiking trails. Rates exclude park entrance fees (see page 156). *B&B chalet N$1,200 pp; B&B tent N$750 pp; camping N$160.* **LLL**

⌂ **Gästefarm Elisenheim** (9 rooms, hut, camping) ☏061 264429; e elisenheimgf@afol. com.na; www.natron/net/tour/elisenheim; ⊕ closed 15 Dec–15 Jan. Set in grounds of some 5,000ha at the foot of the mountains, Elisenheim offers German hospitality & a place to relax under the care of Andreas & Christina Werner. It is signposted to the left of the main B1 as it leaves the city, just 15km north of the centre. Cross over the highway & follow the track – & the signs – for a further 6km before turning right towards the farm. En-suite rooms are comfortable, & outside is a tree-shaded swimming pool surrounded by a grassy area. Weaver birds nest in the bamboo that shelters the house. Close by is a small campsite, with 5 pitches & its own pool. Campers need to be totally self-sufficient, as nothing is available here except firewood. Travellers with a 4x4 can book the self-catering mountain hut built into the rocks. Dinner & light lunches are available at extra cost. Visitors may explore the area, which is home to kudu, warthog, steenbok & plenty of baboons, independently or on a guided farm tour

(*N$120, min 4*). *B&B N$510/1,400 sgl/dbl; hut N$2,000; camping N$100 pp.* **LL**

⌂ **Immanuel Wilderness Lodge** (9 rooms) ☏061 260901; m 081 3248198; e office@immanuel-lodge.de; www.immanuel-lodge.de. Set in 10ha of land, Immanuel is on the D1474, a turning off the B1 about 20mins north of Windhoek. It's run by Stephan & Sabine Hock, who came to Namibia from Germany with their 2 children. Dogs, rabbits, parrots, ostriches & a vertically challenged springbok (caused by an ear infection in its infancy) are part of this delightful homestead where visitors are proclaimed to be 'part of the family'. Stephan produces a delicious b/fast, afternoon tea & 4-course dinner for guests at N$230. There's also a solar-heated slightly salty pool to cool off in, a nature trail & horseriding (*N$500/2hrs*) can be arranged via Equitrails (see page 157). Dbl & twin rooms are in 3 separate thatched bungalows, with elegant rustic furniture – some of it homemade. Each has a ceiling fan, tea/coffee facilities &, outside, a small patio with chairs. Don't come here expecting luxury, but for genuine hospitality & warmth, it would be hard to beat. *B&B N$670/1,060 sgl/dbl.* **LL**

⌂ **Penduka** [Map, page 118] (11 rooms) Goreangab Dam; ☏061 257210; e hospitality@penduka.org; www.penduka.com. 8km northwest of Windhoek city centre, this co-operative employs local women in a village setting to produce a range of crafts, including textiles & baskets sold in an on-site shop (see page 147), & can organise excursions to Windhoek townships & home visits to visit Katutura women's homes. To get there, follow Independence Av north through Katutura, cross over Otjomuise Rd, then bear left on to Green Mountain Dam. The centre is down a dirt track to the left. It offers 6 luxury rondavels & 5 backpacker units with a communal bathroom. The restaurant has a terrace overlooking the lake & serves b/fast, lunch & dinner. *Airport pick-up N$350/pp; Rondavel: luxury €27/50 sgl/dbl; standard €24/44 sgl/dbl; dorm N$140.* **L**

To the south

Other accommodation options south of Windhoek include: **Amani Lodge** (see page 162), a French-owned lodge 26km southwest of Windhoek on the C26; & **Eningu Clayhouse Lodge** (see page 177), a stylish option within 1hr of the airport.

🏠 **GocheGanas** (16 chalets) ☎ 061 224909; e info@gocheganas.com; www.gocheganas.com. Drive 20km south of Windhoek on the B1 then turn left on to the D1463; GocheGanas – which means 'Place of the Camelthorns' – is on the right after a further 9km. This self-styled 'wellness village' is set on a hill overlooking a private 6,000ha reserve. With both outdoor & heated indoor pools, cave sauna (open on request), gym & 3 treatment 'hives', there's all you could wish for in the pampering stakes (from crystal baths to massages), including a fruit & juice bar. Above the spa sits reception & gift shop, & at the top of the hill a fine-dining restaurant & the Toko bar – both with wall-to-wall glass windows. Complimentary tea & cake is served 16.00–17.00. Rooms – named after gemstones – are large & smart, with great views across the reserve; each is kitted out with AC, TV, safe, DVD/video, minibar, sunken bath & shower as well as outdoor shower. Twin beds are the norm, but 5 superior suites have dbls – as well as a private terrace & generally greater luxury. There's also a crown suite catering for up to 4 people, with a spacious master bedroom, as well as a living/dining room with sofa bed, & a kitchenette. The reserve boasts 24 large game species, affording the opportunity for relaxing game drives (*N$375 pp*), as well as guided walks (*N$150 pp*), mountain biking (*N$150 pp*), 2hrs stargazing (*N$375 pp*) & free 1½hr self-guided walk with map. Free Wi-Fi in public areas. *DBB N$2,354/4,066 sgl/dbl.* **LLLLL**

🏠 **Auas Safari Lodge** (16 rooms) ☎ 064 406236; e info@auas-safarilodge.com; www.auas-safarilodge.com. Auas is about 44km southeast of Windhoek into the Kalahari & is run by the team that operates Desert Breeze (see page 285) & The Stiltz (see page 282). To reach it, take the B1 or the C23 heading south, then turn left on to the gravel D1463 – the road may not be viable in a 2WD in the rainy season, so check in advance. The lodge is 22km from the B1, or 16km from the C23. Auas is on a game farm whose residents include black wildebeest, giraffe, & a leopard in a separate enclosure. The active will appreciate the swimming pool, game drives (*N$350 pp*) & guided nature walk (*N$250 pp*), while more sedentary guests can relax on their own veranda. *Dinner N$220; B&B N$1,000/1,400 sgl/dbl.* **LL**

GAME LODGES AND GUEST FARMS

Even if you're staying in Windhoek, you may like to spend half a day or so visiting a local game lodge or guest farm. Places within easy reach of the centre that welcome day visitors include Midgard (see page 167), Auas Safari Lodge (see above), Amani Lodge (see page 162) & Hohewarte Guest Farm (see page 136).

✕ WHERE TO EAT AND DRINK

Windhoek has lots of cafés and restaurants, though you'll often have more success searching for European cuisine than African specialities. Until the late 1990s, most served fairly similar fare, often with a German bias, but now Italian, Portuguese, Chinese and even Indian specialities have been added to the mix. Many reach a very high standard, and few are expensive in European or American terms.

Note that many places are closed on Sundays. Not surprisingly, as a spin-off from the burgeoning restaurant scene, there are plenty of fast-food places, particularly in the new shopping malls. Pies, burgers and the like are freely available at points right across the city, including Nando's on Independence Avenue, just up from the station, while in the shopping malls, particularly at Maerua Park, pizza parlours proliferate. It's often worth picking up a free copy of the monthly *Out & About in Windhoek* booklet from the tourist information office – it lists new bars and restaurants.

Eating at the very best, and without restricting your choices, you would have to try very hard to make a meal cost more than N$250 per person. Here's a selection of favourites.

RESTAURANTS

Maps, pages 124–5, 128 and 118, as indicated.

✕ **Bushbar** [Map, pages 124–5] 6347 Tennis St, Olympia; ☎ 061 304 480; ⊕ 16.00–midnight Tue–Thu, noon–midnight Fri–Sun. This trendy watering hole on the outskirts of town sums itself up with the slogan 'Beer, Beef, Bush.' Windhoek's hip crowd come here for the superb steaks &

led out vibe aided by its lovely ⎯ flaxen grasses. Has free Wi-Fi ⎯ ride. Not particularly smart, but ⎯ $$$

⚔ [⎯ page 128] Hilton Hotel (see page 123); ⏰ lunch: noon–14.30 Mon–Fri, 12.30–15.00 Sat–Sun, dinner: 18.00–22.30 daily. Upmarket dining room with state-of-the-art open kitchen inside the Hilton Hotel, which offers an extensive buffet or an à la carte menu featuring wood-fired pizzas, burgers, freshly grilled meats & Namibian specialities. Frequently hosts themed foodie nights, such as Indian. If you're in the mood for sushi, see listing for the hotel's Dvine bar on page 143. $$$$$

⚔ **Gathemann** [Map, page 128] 175 Independence Av; ☎ 061 223853; ⏰ noon–15.00 & 18.00–22.00 Mon–Sat. This grand old owner-run establishment has really stood the test of time, offering upmarket dining with friendly service & separate lunch & dinner menus. With one of the best positions of the capital's restaurants, on a 1st-floor balcony in the centre of town, it has commanding views over Zoo Park. The traditional German cuisine (with a bias towards game) remains a treat &, while prices are higher than average for Windhoek, they're not excessive. The wine list is extensive, & therefore good in parts. $$$$$

⚔ **Leo's at the Castle** [Map, page 128] 22 Heinitzburg St; ☎ 061 249597; ⏰ 18.30–22.00 daily. Small, modern & sophisticated, the Heinitzburg's stylish restaurant is one for special occasions. The carefully selected à la carte menu, masterminded by the hotel's owner/chef, is based on French international cuisine & is dominated by fish & game (but vegetarians are well catered for on request). Alternatively, try the 4-course gourmet menu. The wine cellar is the largest in Namibia with over 15,000 bottles, so be prepared to linger over the wine list. Leo's is expensive, but you get what you pay for – although the wine is a little overpriced. Bookings essential, guests prioritised. $$$$$

⚔ **Nice** [Map, page 128] 2 Mozart St; cnr Hosea Kotako Dr; ☎ 061 300710; www.nice.com.na; ⏰ noon–14.00 & 18.00–22.00 Mon–Fri, 18.00–22.00 Sat–Sun. One of Windhoek's most popular dining venues, the Namibian Institute of Culinary Education is a training restaurant for budding Namibian chefs. Situated in a huge old

house that has been renovated into a labyrinth of small dining areas, it has outside seating with small pools as a feature too, & open fires are lit for winter evenings. Dishes from the small but imaginative menu are created in a kitchen that is on full view behind a large glass window. Lunch menus change weekly & booking is recommended. Attached are the lively Theo's Bar & Sushi at Nice (see below). $$$$$

✳ ⚔ **Olive** [Map, pages 124–5] 22 Promenaden Weg, Klein Windhoek; ☎ 061 383890; www.theolive-namibia.com; ⏰ 07.00–21.30 daily. Part of Olive Exclusive, the luxury all-suite hotel near the centre of Windhoek (see page 123), the Olive restaurant gives priority bookings to its guests but it's well worth trying to get a table here, if only to get a glimpse of its stunning décor, with wall-size images of Himba people & clever use of natural resources like huge pieces of granite & wood. The food is exquisite too, with elegantly presented 4-course set dinners & light à la carte lunches served in a very relaxed atmosphere either indoors or out on the terrace overlooking the city. $$$$$

⚔ **Peppercorn** [Map, pages 124–5] Maerua Mall; ☎ 061 254154; ⏰ 11.00–late daily. Once called the Cattle Baron, this grill & steakhouse is relaxed & very family-friendly thanks to its separate kid's menu. It's pricey, but we've been told the chateaubriand is melt-in-the-mouth delicious. $$$$$

⚔ **Sardinia Blue Olive** [Map, pages 124–5] Cnr Sam Nujoma Dr & Nelson Mandela; ☎ 061 258183; ⏰ 09.30–22.30 Wed, Thu & Sun, 09.00–23.00 Fri–Sat, closed Mon–Tue. Upmarket Italian restaurant that, despite rumours of arrogant staff, is praised by locals for its vegetarian options, perfect pizzas & fresh fish, fast service & freshly baked bread. $$$$$

⚔ **Sushi at Nice** [Map, page 128] ☎ 061 300710; ⏰ 18.00–late Mon–Sat; lunch on request. On the roof above Nice, this excellent sushi restaurant with a view serves platters for 2 at N$250–500. Reservations essential. $$$$$

⚔ **O Portuga** [Map, pages 124–5] 312 Sam Nujoma Dr, Klein Windhoek; ☎ 061 272900; ⏰ noon–23.00 daily. This friendly & relaxed Portuguese/Angolan restaurant has a wide-ranging menu that is particularly strong on seafood, with huge portions. South African wines are fairly standard; Portuguese are very expensive. It's popular with a mixed clientele, but service can be very slow when the place is busy. $$$$-$$$$$

✗ **Primi Piatti** [Map, pages 124–5] Maerua Mall; ☎061 303050; ⊕ 08.00–22.00 daily. Along with good pasta & meat dishes, Primi Piatti serves a great range of cocktails. $$$$-$$$$$

✳ ✗ **The Stellenbosch** [Map, pages 124–5] 320 Sam Nujoma Dr; ☎061 309141; www.thestellenboschwinebar.com; ⊕ noon–15.00 & 18.00–22.00 Mon–Sat. Outstanding bistro with a finely honed menu featuring all manner of mouth-watering dishes such as risotto, pork belly, gourmet salads & prime flame-grilled steaks – all paired with top-notch yet affordable South African wines. $$$$-$$$$$

✳ ✗ **C/o Sixty2nd** [Map, page 128] 62 Bismark St corner of Fidel Castro and Bismark St; ☎061 246288; m 081 789 0811; www.cornerof62nd.com; ⊕ noon–22.00 Mon–Sat, kitchen closed 14.00–18.00. This newcomer is fast becoming one of Windhoek's must-visit restaurants. There's a pretty garden for alfresco dining or indoors, the setting is elegant & atmospheric. The emphasis is on fresh, imaginative dishes with strong flavours (the menu helpfully advises 'garlic alarms' on various items) & sometimes unusual combinations (think oryx carpaccio with tuna sashimi). Considering the quality of the food & the generous portions, prices are reasonable. $$$-$$$$$

✗ **Cordon Bleu** [Map, page 128] 16 Fidel Castro St; ☎061 221 293; www.cbnamibia.com; ⊕ 10.00–01.00 or later Mon–Sat, 10.00–22.00 Sun. This contemporary restaurant in the city centre has a bold décor of black, white & red with a varied international menu including burgers, pastas, grills & seafood dishes. There have been mixed reports about the service but it merits inclusion because, unusually for Windhoek, it's open until the early hours. $$$-$$$$$

✗ **Café Zoo/La Marmite Royale** [Map, page 128] 129 Independence Av; ☎061 235647; ⊕ 07.00–11.00 daily. Set at the bottom of Zoo Park, this elegant & central restaurant has a shaded terrace, making it a perfect lunchtime venue. The new owner poached Cameroonian chef, Martial, from the once-popular La Marmite restaurant, so fans of his cooking should now head here. His African/Western fusion dishes are served alongside pizzas & seafood. During the day it serves delicious cakes, coffee & light meals, & at night locals come

for the cocktails (*happy hour* ⊕ *18.00–20.00 daily*), Cuban music & a cigar. $$$$

✗ **Chez Wou** [Map, page 118] Windhoek Country Club; ☎061 205591; ⊕ 11.00–14.00 & 17.00–23.00 daily. The very good Chinese restaurant at the Windhoek Country Club attracts a busy trade from outside the hotel. $$$$

✗ **Wine Bar** [Map, page 128] 3 Garten St; ☎061 226514; www.windmill-wines.com; ⊕ 16.00–23.30 Mon–Thu, 15.00–midnight Fri, 17.00–22.30 Sat. From the top of one of Windhoek's many hills, the Wine Bar has great views over the city & is quite central. With seating inside & out & a covered balcony area, this is a local favourite for a sundowner on the way home from the office. Wine is their trade; the range is extensive & expert advice is available, with a wine shop on the premises too. The small but varied menu is good, with braais on Thu & Fri nights. $$$$

✗ **Joe's Beerhouse** [Map, pages 124–5] 160 Nelson Mandela Av; ☎061 232457; www.joesbeerhouse.com; ⊕ 16.30–late Mon–Thu, 11.00–late Fri–Sun. The cavernous thatched premises that houses Joe's Beerhouse seats over 400 people in a rustic environment set around a large bar area & is a stalwart of Windhoek's restaurant scene. Despite changing ownership in 2012, the cuisine remains good value. Although traditionally strictly for serious 'carnivores', with lots of game & huge portions, veggies are now getting a look in too with a limited choice of meals, along with some seafood options. Beers & spirits are excellent, but wines are mediocre. Service can be slow & lackadaisical, but there's always a lively vibe here. Joe's reputation goes before it: the place is almost always full & booking usually essential. A small craft shop sells postcards too. $$$-$$$$$

✗ **Paguel** [Map, pages 124–5] 416 Independence Av; ☎061 240786; www.paguelrestaurant.com; ⊕ noon–22.00 Mon–Wed, noon–23.00 Thu–Sat. This lively new restaurant serves a range of Angolan & Portuguese dishes, particularly seafood & fresh fish, along with local delights such as mopane worms & goat tripe. Downstairs, more basic meals (burgers, piri-piri chicken & the like) are served in the Tasca bar & restaurant which stays open until 02.00 Thu–Sat, & the affiliated Dragon Lounge cocktail bar simply stays open 'till late.' $$$-$$$$$

✗ **The Gourmet** [Map, page 128] Kaiserkrone Centre, off Post St Mall; ☎061 232360; ⊕ 09.00–21.00 Mon–Sat. On the left of Post St Mall as you walk from Independence Av, this established favourite has friendly staff & good international food served either indoors or in the pleasant, tree-shaded courtyard. Game & African dishes feature but the emphasis is on German dishes & pizzas/pasta. There's a car park for diners available from 18.00. $$$–$$$$$

✗ **Am Weinberg** [Map, pages 124–5] 13 Jan Jonker Rd, Klein Windhoek; ☎ 061 236050; www.amweinberg.com; ⊕ 11.30–23.00 daily. This smart, stylish restaurant in a renovated old house is one of the best in town. There's seating inside & out & a balcony area with good views over the suburbs, as well as an outside 'beach bar' for predinner cocktails & snacks. Am Weinberg serves consistently good food from a broad menu (the seafood platter will set you back N$250) with daily lunchtime specials (*around N$100*) & some oriental influence. $$–$$$$$

✗ **Grand Canyon Spur** [Map, page 128] 251 Independence Av & Maerua Mall; ☎ 061 231003; ⊕ 10.00–22.00 daily. Situated above street level, opposite the Bank Windhoek, the Wild West-style Spur offers mediocre American burgers, steaks & a host of side orders. It's all a bit sticky & cheap, but the atmosphere is lively & it's a godsend for parents because of the soft-play kids area. $$–$$$$$

✗ **Kubata** [Map, pages 124–5] 151 Nelson Mandela Av, Eros; ☎ 061 404944; www.kubata.com.na; ⊕ noon–22.00 Mon–Sat, noon–21.00 Sun. A cosy restaurant offering doner kebabs & a good variety of seafood alongside such as paella. $$–$$$$$

✗ **Yang Tze** [Map, pages 124–5] 351 Sam Nujoma Dr; ☎ 061 234779; ⊕ 11.30–14.30 & 17.30–22.00 daily. This large, efficient Chinese restaurant is situated on the upper level of a small shopping centre near the junction with Nelson Mandela Av. It also has a take-away service. $$–$$$$$

✗ **Andy's** [Map, pages 124–5] 318 Sam Nujoma Dr; ☎ 061 401 516; ⊕ 16.00–23.00 Tue–Thu, noon–23.00 Fri–Sun. German pub claiming to serve the 'best worse in the southern hemisphere', as well as gigantic pizzas, although service can be slow. See also opposite. $$$

CAFÉS

Maps, pages 124–5 and 128, as indicated.

☕ **Dulcé Café** [Map, pages 124–5] Upper Mall, Maerua Mall; ☎ 061 239966; ⊕ 07.30–18.30

Mon–Fri, 08.00–15.30 Sat, 08.00–13.30 Sun. Superb light, modern café serving Continental fare such as pizzas & wraps, as well as all-day b/fasts & gourmet burgers. Very popular with locals. $$$$

☕ **Wecke & Voights Kaffee Bar** [Map, page 128] Gustav Voight Centre, Independence Av; ☎ 061 377000; ⊕ 07.00–17.30 daily. Urban-chic coffee bar attached to the left-hand side of this upmarket interior design shop. Good sandwiches & 'build your own' b/fasts. $$$–$$$$

☕ **Fresh 'n' Wild** [Map, pages 124–5] Cnr Robert Mugabe Av & Liliencron St; ☎ 061 240346; ⊕ 07.00–17.00 Mon–Fri, 08.00–13.00 Sat–Sun. Set in a shady courtyard & overlooking a split-level fish-pond, this popular café serves delicious b/fasts, tasty open sandwiches & light lunches, & a variety of well-made coffees & juices. $$$

☕ **The Crafter's Kitchen** [Map, page 128] 117 Independence Av; ☎ 061 250342; ⊕ 08.30–18.00 Mon–Fri, 08.30–17.00 Sat–Sun. Inside the Namcraft shop, this little café makes the ideal refuelling station when exploring the main strip. Dishes up toasties, soups & burgers, as well as coffee & cakes. $$$

☕ **Mugg & Bean** [Map, pages 124–5] Town Sq Mall & Maerua Mall; ⊕ 06.45–18.45 Mon–Fri, 06.45–14.45 Sat–Sun. Chain coffee shop popular with shoppers & office workers who come for the muffins & mammoth slices of cake. The 1st-floor Town Sq store has a terrace overlooking the arcade. $$–$$$

☕ **Craft Café** [Map, page 128] 40 Tal St, Old Breweries; ☎ 061 249974; www.craftcafe-namibia.com; ⊕ 08.00–18.30 Mon–Fri, 08.00–15.00 Sat, 09.00–15.30 Sun. A popular café with open-air balcony, this is one of Windhoek's best eateries, even if the view isn't up to much. Frequented by locals & visitors, it serves a great range of homemade quiches, salads, cakes & puddings, not to mention fresh lemonade & all sorts of other goodies. It's on the same premises as the excellent Craft Centre – though open slightly longer hours (if the Craft Centre is closed, take the stairs to the left in what looks like a red steel tower). $$

☕ **Ins Wiener** [Map, page 128] Ground Floor, Wernhil Park; ☎ 061 231082; ⊕ 07.00–18.00 Mon–Fri, 07.00–14.00 Sat, 08.30–13.30 Sun. This traditional German coffee shop that has stood the test of time has a great selection of cakes. It also serves b/fasts, & light lunches such as Greek, tuna or chicken salad. $$

⌑ **Yaeli** [Map, pages 124–5] Lower Mall, Maerua Mall; ☎081 140 5506; ⏱ 08.00–21.00 Mon–Fri, 08.00–16.00 Sat. Named after its Israeli owner, this small café does a roaring trade in healthy salads, build-your-own shakes & smoothies, rustic sandwiches & (of course) felafel. There are a few tables, but most customers order to go. $$

⌑ **Caffe Brazza** [Map, pages 124–5] Upper Mall, Maerua Mall; ☎061 247 123; ⏱ 06.30–18.00 Mon–Fri, 08.00–14.00 Sat, 09.00–13.00 Sun. Serves light meals such as paninis, good coffee, smoothies & Italian-style snacks. $–$$

✳ ⌑ **Old Continental** [Map, page 128] Continental Passage; ☎061 307176; ⏱ 07.00–17.00 Mon–Fri. What a find! Tucked away in a quiet alleyway off Independence Av, this bustling café is run by Sebastiaan Broeders. Passport stamps from his epic 8-month Holland–Kenya journey in 1984 are framed on the walls & his filled sandwiches & pittas, burgers, salads, soup of the day, Illy-brand coffee & free Wi-Fi & newspapers attract Windhoek's well-heeled. $–$$

⌑ **Vintage** [Map, pages 124–5] Cnr Robert Mugabe Av & Luther St; ☎061 259295; ⏱ 09.00–15.00 Mon, 07.15–15.30 Tue–Fri, 07.30–13.00 Sat. A converted house with large terrace offering b/fasts & light lunches. It's a particularly good spot for families as there are child-size tables & a playground. $–$$

⌑ **Wilde Eend Coffee Shop** [Map, pages 124–5] 10 Dr Kenneth David Kaunda St, Klein Windhoek; ☎061 272632; ⏱ 08.00–17.00 Mon–Fri, 08.00–13.00 Sat, 09.00–13.00 Sun in summer, 10.00–13.00 Sun in winter. One of Windhoek's best-kept secrets, this delightful little coffee shop is set among the plants of Wilde Eend garden centre. Enjoy a tasty b/fast, salad, wrap or sandwich accompanied by a fresh juice, smoothie or coffee in tranquil surroundings. $–$$

BARS

Maps, pages 124–5 and 128, as indicated.

♀ **Andy's** [Map, pages 124–5] 318 Sam Nujoma Dr; ☎061 401 516; ⏱ 16.00–late Tue–Thu, 11.00–late Fri–Sun. German pub with Cheers-style square bar & walls decorated with car licence plates. It's owned by the larger-than-life bald Andy & draws a very loyal drinking crowd. Has a garden out the back, serves food (see page 142) & usually screens sports as well.

♀ **Boiler Room** [Map, page 128] 46 Tal Street; ⏱ 16.00–late Mon–Sat. Good for drinks prior to

events at the Warehouse Theatre (see page 144) located next door.

♀ **Bushbar** [Map, pages 124–5] 6347 Tennis St, Olympia; ☎061 304 480; ⏱ 16.00–midnight Tue–Thu, noon–midnight Fri–Sun. This cosmopolitan watering hole, situated on the outskirts of town, has a chilled-out vibe & a lovely terrace overlooking flaxen grasses. Has free Wi-Fi. See also page 139.

♀ **Dragon Lounge** [Map, pages 124–5] 416 Independence Av; ☎061 240786; www. paguelrestaurant.com; ⏱ noon–22.00 Mon–Wed, noon–23.00 Thu–Sat. Part of the Paguel restaurant (see page 141), this purple-walled cocktail bar lacks atmosphere, but will suit for a quick drink.

♀ **Dvine Wine & Sushi Bar** [Map, page 128] Hilton Hotel (see page 123); ⏱ 17.00–22.00 Mon–Sat. Sleek new wine bar inside the Hilton Hotel. Fine wines are displayed in glass-fronted fridges that line the room. These are served with first-rate sushi platters ($$$$$).

♀ **Hotel Heinitzburg** [Map, page 128] 22 Heinitzburg St; ☎061 249597; www.heinitzburg. com. For a special occasion or a treat, enjoy cocktails on the garden terrace of this upmarket boutique hotel (see page 123).

♀ **Joe's Beerhouse** [Map, pages 124–5] 160 Nelson Mandela Av; ☎061 232457; www. joesbeerhouse.com; ⏱ 16.30–late Mon–Thu, 11.00–late Fri–Sun. Best known for its carnivorous menu, Joe's is just as popular as a drinking hole thanks to its lively atmosphere & excellent beers & spirits.

♀ **Que Tapas** [Map, pages 124–5] Maerua Mall; ☎081 698 5313; ⏱ 09.00–02.00 Mon–Sat. Lively corner bar serving tapas & large selection of cocktails inside the shopping mall.

♀ **Skybar** [Map, page 128] Cnr Sam Nujoma & Rev Michael Scott St; ☎061 2962 929; ⏱ 10.00–midnight daily. The Hilton Hotel's rooftop bar is unquestionably the hippest place for drinks no matter the time of day. The views overlooking town are superb & the slimline pool just adds to the glamour.

♀ **Wine Bar** [Map, page 128] 3 Garten St; ☎061 226514; ⏱ 16.00–23.30 Mon–Thu, 15.00–midnight Fri, 17.00–22.30 Sat. A local favourite for a sundowner, it has great views over the city, with seating inside & out & a covered balcony area. As you'd expect from the name, wine is their trade; the range is extensive & expert advice is available.

ENTERTAINMENT AND NIGHTLIFE

Windhoek is not famous for its nightlife. Most visitors choose to go to a restaurant for a leisurely dinner and perhaps a drink, and then retire for an early start the next day. But if you feel livelier, there are a few cocktail bars (see page 143) and nightclubs, as well as the occasional concert. Friday is usually the best night. Similarly, weekends at the start/end of the month, when people have just been paid, are busier than those in the middle.

A word of note: in the poorer areas, especially in the old townships, there are some illegal *shebeens* (so-called *cuca shops*), geared purely to serious drinking. It's worth noting that here, as in most traditional cultures in southern Africa, respectable women are rarely seen in bars. Furthermore, if you get word of a local club in one of the townships, go with a local or get a reliable taxi that will take you and collect you.

To find out what's on, take a look at the online events calendar www.whatsonwindhoek.com and pick up a free copy of the monthly *Out & About in Windhoek* booklet from the tourist information office – it lists new bars and restaurants. Information is also advertised at the back of newspapers, especially the Friday editions of *The Namibian* and *Windhoek Observer*, which cover the weekend. Otherwise, keep an eye out for posters around the city, try the Windhoek city information office, or ask at your hotel or pension.

NIGHTCLUBS

☆ **Club London** [125 C5] 4 Nasmith St, Southern Industrial; ⊕ 20.30–02.00 Fri–Sat. Formerly La Dee Da's, this club puts on a wide range of parties from foam to hip hop every w/end. No under 18s.

☆ **El Cubano** [128 C5] Basement of Hilton (see page 123); ⊕ 21.00–late Fri–Sat. Accessed via a side entrance in the basement of the Hilton Hotel, this is the place to go if you like salsa. Can be expensive: drinks are bought with tokens that aren't refunded at the end of the night.

☆ **Funky Lab** [124 F3] Hidas Centre, Klein Windhoek; ⊕ 16.00–late Sun–Thu, 14.00–late Fri–Sat. Hip, sophisticated hangout where you can boogie to disco classics. There's usually cheap-drink offers midweek.

☆ **Kiepies** [124 C4] Marconi St, Southern Industrial; ☏ 061 256957; ⊕ Wed, Fri & Sat. Specialises in country & live Afrikaans music. Serves pizzas if you work up an appetite on the dance floor.

CINEMAS AND CASINOS

🎭 **Maerua Park Cinema** [125 E5] Maerua Mall; ☏ 061 215 912. Windhoek's only city centre cinema has been closed for renovation since Jun 2013 – it's scheduled to open at the end of 2014. Ticket prices are low compared with Europe or the US. Films shown are very much the latest Hollywood releases, and drinks and snacks are available too.

Casinos Windhoek's only two officially licensed casinos are located inside the Kalahari Sands Hotel (see page 123) & Windhoek Country Club Resort (see page 126). A third may open in the Hilton Hotel basement in future.

THEATRES AND CONCERTS

College of the Arts 41 Fidel Castro St; ☏ 061 225841. Occasionally hosts classical concerts in its auditorium.

Franco-Namibian Cultural Centre (FNCC) [128 C1] 118 Robert Mugabe Av; ☏ 061 387330; www.fncc.org.na. Showcases a variety of small concerts, exhibitions & cultural events, & screens art-house films in its cinema too.

National Theatre of Namibia [128 C2] 12 John Meinert St; ☏ 061 374400; www.ntn.org.na. Hosts concerts, opera, theatre, ballet & contemporary dance performances.

Warehouse Theatre [128 B5] 48 Tal St; ☏ 061 402 253; www.warehousetheatre.com.na; ⊕ 16.00–02.00 Mon–Sat. Jazz, reggae, *mbaganga* & pop bands perform on Thu & Fri at this relaxed & trendy venue housed in the Old Breweries Building; upcoming artists showcase their work on Wed. Cover charges vary with the band. Snacks are available, but dine elsewhere before you arrive; the Boiler Room bar is next door (see page 143).

SHOPPING

Shopping in Windhoek was revolutionised when the **Town Square** shopping mall (⊕ *daily; morning only at w/ends*) was opened right in the centre. It's a top-notch mall with plenty of choice and sets the standard for shops throughout the capital. Around this, most of the area is pedestrianised, incorporating **Post Street Mall**, Mutual Platz, Levinson Arcade and the **Wernhil Park** (*www.wernhilpark.com*). At weekends in particular it's a busy, bustling place.

Parking in the city centre is still relatively straightforward, with a couple of car parks clearly marked. Alternatively, if you want to stay for an hour at most, use one of the meters on Independence Avenue.

Beyond the centre is **Maerua Mall** with plenty of free parking. Then to the east of town, in Klein Windhoek, the relatively new **Bougain Villas Shopping Centre** houses various boutique shops focusing on arts and crafts alongside cafés, delis and salons. At the time of writing a third mall called **Freedom Plaza** is being constructed near the Hilton Hotel and plans for a fourth, called the Grove Mall, in the southern suburb of Klein Kuppe, are progressing.

BOOKS AND MUSIC Imported books are generally expensive in Namibia, and even those published locally are subject to a heavy sales tax. But if you want something specific on Namibia, then often you'll get titles here which are difficult to find abroad.

CNA [128 C5, 125 E5 & 128 A4] Gustav Voigts Centre, 129 Independence Av, Maerua Mall & Wernhil Park. A large South African book chain with a section on the latest titles. Very mainstream.
Der Neue Bücherkeller [128 C4] Carl List Mall, Fidel Castro St; ☎061 231615. Linked to Swakopmund Buchhandlung, the New Book Cellar has a good choice of travel books, field guides & natural history books in German & English, plus the usual novels & coffee-table books.
Musica [125 E5] Upper Floor, Maerua Mall. Sells a large range of CDs & DVDs – good for African music.
Onganda Y'Omambo Books [128 B3] North side of Post St Mall; ☎061 235796. A wide range of new & secondhand books, with a particularly good selection on Namibian history & culture, & by Namibian authors.

Orombonde Books Main entrance of Namibia Craft Centre, Tal St; ☎081 148 84 62; ⊕ 09.00–17.00 Mon–Fri, 10.00–14.00 Sat. Run by historian Wolfram Hartmann & his dog, this is one of the most diverse bookstores in town with a variety of titles in numerous languages.
The Book Den Gutenberg Platz, Werner List St; ☎061 239976; ⊕ 09.00–17.00 Mon–Fri, 09.00–13.00 Sat. Namibia's largest privately owned bookshop with friendly staff to boot.
Uncle Spike's Book Exchange [128 C6] Garten St, cnr Tal St; ☎061 226722; ⊕ 08.00–17.30 Mon–Fri, 08.00–13.00 Sat. Corner den with shelves stuffed with secondhand books, particularly guidebooks. Buzz to be let through the grid gate.

CAMERAS AND OPTICS Most popular cameras can be found here, though they are usually more expensive than they would be in Europe or the US. There are numerous places that will print your snaps – often within the hour – or sell you a film, but Windhoek's best specialists are:

Foto First [128 C3] Independence Av; ⊕ 08.00–17.00 Mon–Sat. Offers 1hr photo service.

Gerhard Botha [128 C6] 44 Independence Av; ☎061 235551
Nitzsche-Reiter Front of Sanlam Centre, Independence Av; ☎061 231116; ⊕ 08.00–17.00 Mon–Fri

CAMPING KIT

To rent It is easy to arrange the hire of camping kit in Windhoek, provided that you can return it at the end of your trip. Both the following companies have a comprehensive range, from tents and portable toilets to full 'kitchenboxes', gaslights and jerry cans. They are best contacted at least a month in advance, and can then arrange for a pack incorporating what you want to be ready when you arrive. The minimum rental period is three days. They usually request a 50% deposit to confirm the order, with full payment due on collection of equipment.

Adventure Camping Hire [125 C6] 33 Tacoma St; 061 242478; m 081 129 9135; e adventur@ iway.na; 08.00–13.00 & 14.00–17.00 Mon–Fri. Affordable outlet whose owner, Immo Kersten, is usually on hand to provide expert advice.

Camping Hire Namibia 78 Mose Tjitendero St, Olympia; 061 252995; m 081 124 4364; e camping@iafrica.com.na; www.orusovo.com/ camphire; 08.00–13.00 & 14.00–16.00 Mon–Fri; w/ends by appointment. Rents everything from tents to coffee mugs. Payment in cash only.

To buy If you need to buy camping kit in Namibia, then Windhoek has the best choice. Items from South Africa are widely available, but kit from Europe or the US is harder to find.

Bush Beat [125 E5] Upper Mall, Maerua Mall; 061 222 219; www.bush-beat.com; 09.00–17.30 Mon–Fri, 09.00–13.30 Sat. Split into 2 stores either side of the aisle: 1 sells safari clothes, the other brand-name surf clothing such as Quiksilver & Roxy.

Bushwhackers [map, page 118] 32 Rhino St, Rhino Park; 061 258760; 08.00–17.00 Mon–Fri, 08.00–noon Sat. One of the biggest & best outdoor shops, Bushwhackers is north of the city, & a good one-stop option before heading out into the wilds. Follow Hosea Kutako towards the Northern Industrial area, turn left on to Ooievaar St & then right to Rhino St; Bushwhackers is 200m along on the right. Along with a full range of camping/hiking gear, a huge fishing section & all the 4x4 gadgets & supplies, they also deal in caravans & boats, sales & spares.

Cape Union Mart [125 E5] Maerua Mall; 061 220424; 09.00–17.30 Mon–Fri, 09.00–14.00 Sat, 09.00–13.00 Sun. A wide range of camping equipment, safari clothes & shoes.

Cymot [Map, page 118] 60 Mandume Ndemufayo Av; 061 2957000; 08.00–17.00 Mon–Fri, 08.00–12.30 Sat; 342 Independence Av; 061 237759; 08.00–17.00 Mon–Fri, 08.00–noon Sat; www.cymot.com.na. With 1 central branch &

a 2nd a little way out in northern Windhoek, Cymot has the best range around: everything from tents & outdoor equipment to a good selection of cycles & spares, to spare parts for cars. There are smaller branches throughout the country.

Due South [125 E5] Lower Mall, Maerua Mall; 061 370445. South African store with selection of upmarket safari clothing, shoes & camping basics.

Safari Den [128 C5] 8 Bessemer St, Auas Valley Shopping Mall; 064 290 9294; 08.00–17.00 Mon–Fri, 08.00–13.00 Sat. A plush shop with binoculars, knives (including Swiss Army & Leatherman tools) & a useful range of tents, sleeping bags & other camping kit.

Safariland (Holtz) [128 C5] Gustav Voigts Centre; 061 235941; www.safarilandholtz. com; 08.00–17.30 Mon–Fri, 08.00–13.00 Sat, 09.00–12.30 Sun. Has a similar variety of safari & bush wear.

Trappers Trading Co [128 A4] Wernhil Park; 061 223136; 09.00–17.00 Mon–Fri. Good for practical bush wear – cotton clothes are cheaper here than in Europe, & the quality's reasonable though rarely excellent. Happy to accept emergency calls.

CRAFTS AND CURIOS The Post Street Mall [128 B3] normally hosts one of the capital's largest craft and curio displays, as street traders set out their wares on blankets in front of the shops.

Off the streets, if you visit only one place for curios and souvenirs, make sure it's the **Old Breweries Complex** on Tal Street. This attractive courtyard has a number of craft shops and cafés, as well as the excellent Namibia Craft Centre.

Bushman Art Gallery Erkraths Bldg, 187 Independence Av; ✆061 228828/229131; www. bushmanart-gallery.com; ⊕ 08.30–17.30 Mon–Fri, 08.30–13.00 Sat, 09.00–13.00 Sun. Despite the name, this is primarily a shop, albeit with an unusually large selection. At the front it is purely a curio/gift shop, with a good selection of books on Namibia (in German & English), as well as T-shirts, jewellery, gemstones, cards, hats & even socks. At the back, however, among artefacts on sale from all over Africa, are small displays of Bushman tools, clothing, etc, various African masks & Karakul carpets.

Casa Anin [125 F3] Bougain Villas Shopping Centre, 78 Sam Nujoma Dr; ✆061 256410; www.anin.com.na. Built up by Heidi von Hase from a small village embroidery group with the aim of empowering women whose only skill is sewing learned from missionaries, Casa Anin is now a sought-after brand & supplies many of Namibia's top lodges with their linen & soft furnishings. This is their only retail outlet, selling fine handmade bedlinen, embroidered textiles & interesting gifts.

House of Art [125 E5] Upper Mall, Maerua Mall; ✆061 251700. Almost a small gallery, there's a good selection of art for sale here alongside a few local artefacts & jewellery.

Namcraft [128 C5] 117 Independence Av; ✆061 250342; ⊕ 08.30–18.00 Mon–Fri, 08.30–17.00 Sat–Sun. Main store of this Namibian-owned chain which sells crafts & a wide array of jewellery made by Namibian & worldwide craftspeople – ideal for presents. There's an outlet in the Old Breweries complex too.

Namibia Craft Centre 40 Tal St; ✆061 242 2222; ⊕ 09.00–17.30 Mon–Fri, 09.00–13.30 Sat–Sun. At the heart of the Old Breweries complex, this remains the capital's best place for arts & crafts. Numerous stalls showcase the full range: paintings, sculptures, designs in copper, hand-painted fabrics, carvings, basketwork, jewellery & much else. Many of the exhibitors welcome visitors to their workshops located around the country. The centre also has an excellent café.

Penduka [map, page 118] Goreangab Dam; ✆061 257210; www.penduka.com; ⊕ 08.00–17.00 Mon–Sat. Out beyond Katutura, overlooking the Goreangab Dam 8km northwest of Windhoek city centre, this co-operative employs local women in a village setting to produce a range of crafts, including textiles & baskets. You can buy them in the on-site shop, have a cup of coffee & slice of cake & – with advance notice – book a workshop in basket braiding, batik or recycled-glass jewellery-making from €15. Overnight accommodation also available on site (see page 138). A selection of Penduka crafts is for sale in the Namibia Craft Centre.

GEMSTONES Given the incredible minerals and precious stones that are mined in Namibia, it's a wonder that there aren't better gemstones for sale as curios. Sadly, many of the agates and semi-precious stones seen in curio shops on Independence Avenue are imported from as far away as Brazil. The exceptions to the rule are:

House of Gems [128 B2] 131 Werner List St; ✆061 225202; www.namrocks.com; ⊕ 09.00–13.00 & 14.00–17.00 Mon–Fri, 09.00–noon Sat. Tucked away near John Meinert St, this was established in 1947 by Sid Peters, one of the country's leading gemmologists. It's a real collector's place, packed with original bits & pieces. Even if you're not buying, it is worth visiting, since here you can see the raw stones sorted, cut, faceted & polished on the premises.

The Diamond Works [128 C5] Unit 40, Old Breweries; ✆061 229049; www.thediamondworks. co.za; ⊕ 09.00–18.00 Mon–Fri, 09.00–14.00 Sat–Sun. Glossy shop selling predesigned diamond, Tanzanite & other gemstone jewellery, but you can also pick a rock & watch them cut it on site while sipping on a glass of bubbly.

LEATHERWORK AND TAXIDERMY Windhoek is a good place to buy leatherwork. You'll see lots of ostrich, game and karakul leathers. Don't expect any give-aways, but if you know what you want then there are good deals to be had. The standard varies greatly; highest-quality sources in the centre of town are:

Leder Chic [128 C4] Carl List Mall, Fidel Castro St (near Der Neue Bücherkeller); ☎061 234422; ⏰ 08.30–17.00 Mon–Fri, 08.30–13.00 Sat. For a selection of leather bags, wallets and belts. **Nakara** 165 Independence Av; ☎061 224209; www.nakara-namibia.com; ⏰ 09.00–18.00 Mon–Fri, 08.00–13.00 Sat. For Namibian ostrich & leather goods including zebra, springbok & kudu skins.

Trophäendienste Taxidermy [map, page 114] B6, towards International Airport; ☎061 232236; www.trophaendienste.com; ⏰ 06.30–18.00 Mon–Fri, 09.00–17.00 Sat–Sun. 10km from Windhoek on the main road to the airport – look out for the gaudily painted animals standing on each other by the roadside – it has a huge souvenirs showroom selling preserved African animals & a coffee shop. All a bit macabre, to be honest.

SUPERMARKETS

Checkers [128 C5] Gustav Voigts Centre, Independence Av & Maerua Mall; ☎061 237410; ⏰ 08.00–20.00 daily.
Food Lovers' Market Fruit & Veg City [128 C4] Sanlam Centre; ☎061 377150; ⏰ 08.30–18.00 Mon–Thu, 08.30–19.00 Fri, 07.00–17.00 Sat, 09.00–13.00 Sun. Healthy living supermarket. There's another bigger branch on Frankie Fredericks St in the southern suburb of Klein Kuppe.

Pick 'n' Pay [128 A4] Basement of Wernhil Park; ☎061 2964500; ⏰ 09.00–18.00 Mon–Fri, 09.00–14.00 Sat, 09.00–13.00 Sun.
Shoprite [128 C2] on Independence Av itself, towards the Thüringer Hof Hotel.
Superspar [125 E5] Maerua Mall; ☎061 377000; ⏰ 07.30–19.00 Mon–Fri, 07.30–19.30 Sat, 07.30–18.00 Sun.

SPORTS

Nucleus [128 C6] Old Breweries, Tal St; ☎061 225493; www.nucleushfc.com; ⏰ 05.00–21.00 Mon–Thu, 05.00–20.00 Fri, 09.00–17.00 Sat–Sun. This centrally located fitness gym has been operating since the early 1990s. It's at the top of several flights of stairs (getting there is a workout in itself) & offers full changing facilities, basic running/cycling machines & general fitness apparatus. There's another branch at Baines Shopping Centre, Pioneers Park. *N$150/day, N$300/wk.*
Olympia swimming pool [125 E8] Cnr Sean McBride & Frankie Fredericks sts, Olympia; ☎061 2903089; ⏰ daily. This aptly named pool has an Olympic-size main pool, children's paddling pool, kiosk & trained lifeguards. A second pool, the Western Suburbs Swimming Pool, also has a 50m pool.
Virgin Active [125 E5] Centaurus Rd, by Maerua Mall; ☎061 234399; ⏰ 05.00–21.00 Mon–Thu, 05.00–20.00 Fri, 06.00–19.00 Sat–Sun. The city's biggest gym has a large indoor pool, plus a large gym with lots of training machines, an

aerobics studio, several glass-backed squash courts, & steam & sauna rooms. Day membership as a casual visitor is N$170, so if you need to relax & have a shower in town before travelling, this is the perfect place. Although the car park is patrolled, don't leave your luggage unattended in your vehicle.
Windhoek Golf [map, page 118] Western Bypass; ☎061 2055223; e gm@wccgolf.com. na; www.wccgolf.com.na. Hotel residents N$130/260 9/18 holes; non-affiliated N$170/340 9/18 holes; driving range N$20/30 30/60 balls. This 18-hole golf course next to Windhoek Country Club (see page 126) offers upmarket facilities, including a resident professional, motorised caddies, a driving range & a well-equipped pro shop. The clubhouse has a bar area & a restaurant. Next door is the Windhoek Bowls Club, which has its own clubhouse, bar & swimming pool.

above   **Two young crocodiles (*Crocodylus niloticus*) on a sand bank beside the Zambezi River** (VS/DT) page 51

below left   **Giraffe (*Giraffa camelopardis*)** (MY) page 523

below right   **Black rhinoceros (*Diceros bicornis*)** (AVZ) page 522

bottom   **Elephant (*Loxodonta africana*)** (MY) pages 521–2

above   Leopard (*Panthera pardus*) (CM) pages 509–10

left   Bat-eared fox (*Otocyon megalotis*) (AVZ) page 511

below left   Lion (*Panthera leo*) (AVZ) page 509

below right   Caracal cub (*Felis caracal*) (CM) page 510

above left **Brown hyena (_Hyaena brunnea_)**
(CM) page 514

above right **African wild dog (_Lycaon pictus_)**
(TL) page 511

right **Black-backed jackals (_Canis mesomelas_)** (AVZ) page 511

below **Spotted hyena (_Crocuta crocuta_)**
(CM) page 514

top	**Red hartebeest (*Alcelaphus buselaphus*)** (AVZ) page 517
above left	**Kudu (*Tragelaphus strepsiceros*)** (EP/DT) page 518
above right	**Male black-faced impala (*Aepeceros melampus petersi*)** (AVZ) page 519
left	**Springbok (*Antidorcas marsupilis*)** (CM) page 520

above   **Zebras (*Equus quagga*) and ostriches (*Struthio camelus*) at Etosha Pan** (MY) pages 380–2

right   **Desert horses** (A/DT) page 219

below   **Oryx (*Oryx gazella*)** (MA/DT) page 516

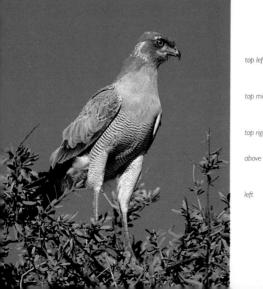

top left   **Northern black korhaan (*Eupodotis afraoides*)** (AVZ)

top middle   **Crowned lapwing or plover (*Vanellus coronatus*)** (AVZ)

top right   **Lilac-breasted roller (*Coracias caudatus*)** (AVZ)

above   **Great white pelicans (*Pelecanus onocrotalus*)** (AVZ)

left   **Pale chanting goshawk (*Melierax canorus*)** (CM)

above left	Double-banded courser (*Rhinoptilus africanus*) (AVZ)
above right	Yellow billed stork (*Mycteria ibis*) (TL)
right	Swallow-tailed bee-eater (*Merops hirundineus*) (TH)
below	Greater flamingos (*Phoenicopterus ruber*) (MTF/DT) page 316

above left	**Fog-basking beetle (*Onymacris ungularis*)** (SS)
above right	**Namib sidewinder (*Bitis peringueyi*), endemic to the Namib Desert** (AVZ)
below	**Palmato gecko (*Pachydactylis rangei*)** (B/DT)
bottom	**Rock hyrax (*Procavia capensis*)** (MA/DT) page 526

OTHER PRACTICALITIES

AIRLINES

✈ **Air Berlin** [128 A4] Middle Level, Wernhil Park; 061 302220; e wdh@sisatravel.com; www.airberlin.com; ⏰ 08.30–16.30 Mon–Fri.

✈ **Air Namibia** [128 B4] Cnr Werner List & Fidel Castro sts; 061 299 6333; e central.reservations@airnamibia.aero; www.airnamibia.com.na; ⏰ 08.00–17.00 Mon–Fri, 09.00–noon Sat. Eros International Airport 061 299 6508. Mostly domestic & regional flights. Hosea Kutako International Airport 061 299 6600. The main airport for international arrivals & departures.

✈ **British Airways** [128 C4] Sanlam Centre, 154 Independence Av; 061 248528; e bamnwdh@africaonline.com.na; www.britishairways.com; ⏰ 08.00–13.00 & 14.00–16.30 Mon–Fri. Comair, the South African regional carrier, is now owned by British Airways & shares the same premises & phone number.

✈ **South African Airways (SAA)** [128 C4] Sanlam Centre, Independence Av; 061 273340; www.flysaa.com; ⏰ 07.30–17.00 Mon–Fri, 08.00–noon Sat.

✈ **TAAG Angolan Airlines** [128 C4] Sanlam Centre, Independence Av; 061 226625/236266; www.taag.com; ⏰ 09.00–17.00 Mon–Fri.

BANKS AND MONEY The centre of town has all the major banks in the country. All have ATMs and are generally very efficient; there are also ATMs in the various shopping malls across the city and at many of the petrol stations. If you need anything complex, like an international money transfer, go to the largest branch possible. In any event, remember to take your passport with you.

Rates for exchanging money are the same at most of the banks, though you can expect to get considerably lower rates from a hotel. Outside of normal banking hours, the bureau de change at Nedbank is open on Saturdays and also accepts American Express cards, while the bureaux de change at the airport are opened for incoming flights. Money can also be changed at the main post office (see below).

$ **Bank Windhoek** [128 C3] 262 Independence Av; 061 299 1500; www.bankwindhoek.com.na

$ **FNB** 209–11 Independence Av; 061 299 2111; www.fnbnamibia.com.na; ⏰ 09.00–15.30 Mon–Fri, 08.30–noon Sat.

$ **Nedbank** Main branch: 12–20 Dr Frans Indongo St, 061 2952163; Central: Carl List House, 27 Independence Av, 061 295 2180; www.nedbank.com.na

$ **Standard Bank** [128 C3] 261 Independence Av; 061 2944111; www.standardbank.com.na; ⏰ 09.00–15.30 Mon–Fri, 08.30–11.00 Sat.

COMMUNICATIONS AND POST By far the most economical means of staying in touch while you're away is to buy a local SIM card on arrival. These are available at Hosea Kutako International Airport (see page 117), or from any of the numerous Mtc outlets around the city, including Post Street Mall and Maerua Park. With regards to internet, almost every hotel, pension, B&B and backpackers offers Wi-Fi services now.

✉ **Post office** [128 C3] Cnr Independence Av & Daniel Munamava St; 061 2013006; www.nampost.com.na; ⏰ 08.00–16.30 Mon, Tue, Thu & Fri, 08.30–16.30 Wed, 08.00–noon Sat. It's cheap & easy to send packages overseas from here, & it has an efficient poste restante facility; it also sells phonecards. Aside from this, the office has a foreign-exchange desk, a good philately counter, a place to make international phone calls or send faxes, plus access to the internet.

📧 **Net Café** [128 B2] Cnr Robert Mugabe & John Meinert St; 061 304165; ⏰ 08.00–21.00 daily. Charges N$10 per 30mins & sells drinks.

EMBASSIES AND HIGH COMMISSIONS Namibia's diplomatic missions abroad can be found on pages 59–60. For visa extensions or anything to do with immigration, you need the Ministry of Home Affairs and Immigration (*Cohen Bldg, cnr Kasino St & Independence Av;* ☎ *061 292 2111;* ⏱ *08.00–13.00 Mon–Fri).*

ⓔ Angola (embassy) 4th Floor, Angola Hse, 3 Dr Agostinho Neto St; ☎061 227535; ℯ embangola@mweb.com.na; www.angola.visahq.com; ⏱ 09.00–15.00 Mon–Fri

ⓔ Botswana (high commission) 101 Nelson Mandela Av, Klein Windhoek; ☎061 221941/2/7; ℯ botnam@gov.bw; ⏱ 08.00–13.00 & 14.00–16.30 Mon–Fri

ⓔ Brazil (embassy) 52 Bismarck St; ☎061 237368; ℯ brasemb@mweb.com.na

ⓔ Canada (consulate) 1st Floor, Office Tower, Maerua Mall; ☎061 251254; ℯ canada@mweb.com.na; ⏱ 08.00–13.00 & 14.00–16.00 Mon–Fri

ⓔ China (embassy) 28 Hebenstreit St, Ludwigsdorf; ☎061 402598; ℯ chinaemb-na@mfa.gov.cn; http://na.chineseembassy.org; ⏱ 08.30–noon & 14.30–17.00 Mon–Fri (office), 09.00–11.30 Mon, Wed & Fri (consular)

ⓔ Denmark (consulate) 11 Eland St, Finkenstein Estate; ☎085 1244219/081 2266838; ℯ cfnorgaard@gmail.com; www.namibia.um.dk; ⏱ 08.00–16.30 Mon–Thu, 08.00–15.00 Fri

ⓔ Egypt (embassy) 10 Berg St, Klein Windhoek; ☎061 221501; ℯ embassy.windhoek@mfa.gov.eg; ⏱ 08.30–15.00 Mon–Fri

ⓔ Finland (embassy) 2 Crohn St; ☎061 221355; ℯ sanomat.win@formin.fi; www.finland.org.na; ⏱ 09.00–noon Mon, Wed, Thu

ⓔ France (embassy) 1 Goethe St; ☎061 276700; www.ambafrance-na.org; ⏱ 09.00–noon Mon–Fri

ⓔ Germany (embassy) 6th Floor, Sanlam Centre, 145 Independence Av; ☎061 273100; ℯ info@windhoek.auswaertiges-amt.de; www.windhuk.diplo.de; ⏱ 09.00–noon Mon, Tue, Thu & Fri, 14.00–16.00 Wed

ⓔ Ghana (high commission) 5 Nelson Mandela Av, Klein Windhoek; ☎061 221341; ⏱ 09.00–15.00 Mon–Fri

ⓔ Italy (consulate) 41 Von Falkenhausen St, Pioneers Park; ☎081 147 1250; ℯ rosannareboldi@yahoo.com; ⏱ 09.00–noon Tue & Thu or by appointment

ⓔ Kenya (high commission) 5th Floor, Kenya Hse, 134 Robert Mugabe Av, PO Box 2889; ☎061 226836; ℯ kenyanet@mweb.com.na

ⓔ Nigeria (high commission) 4 General Murtala Mohammed Rd, Eros; ☎061 232103; ℯ enquiries@nhcwindhoek.org; www.nhcwindhoek.org; ⏱ 09.00–17.00 Mon–Fri, visas: 09.00–noon Mon–Fri

ⓔ Norway & Sweden (consulate) 39 Schanzen Weg; ☎061 258278; ℯ klaus@appih-endresen.com; ⏱ 09.00–noon Mon–Fri

ⓔ South Africa (high commission) RSA Hse, 48 Jan Jonker Rd, Klein Windhoek; ☎061 205 7111; ℯ windhoek.consular@dirco.gov.za; www.dirco.gov.za; ⏱ 08.00–16.30 Mon–Thu, 08.00–15.00 Fri, consular: 08.15–12.15 Mon–Fri

ⓔ Spain (embassy) 58 Bismarck St; ☎061 223066; ℯ embespna@mail.mae.es; www.exteriores.gob.es

ⓔ Switzerland (consulate) 175 Independence Av; ☎061 2238 53; ℯ windhoek@honrep.ch

ⓔ UK (high commission) 116 Robert Mugabe Av; ☎061 274800; ℯ general.windhoek@fco.gov.uk; www.gov.uk; ⏱ consular: 08.00–noon & 14.00–15.30 Mon–Thu, 08.00–11.00 Fri

ⓔ USA (embassy) 14 Lossen St; ☎061 2958500; ℯ consularwindho@state.gov; windhoek.usembassy.gov; ⏱ Mon & Wed mornings by appointment only.

ⓔ Zambia (high commission) 22 Mandume Ndemufayo St; ☎061 237610; ℯ zahico@iway.na; www.zahico.iway.na; ⏱ 09.00–13.00 &14.00–16.00 Mon–Fri

ⓔ Zimbabwe (high commission) Cnr Independence Av & Grimm St; ☎061 227738; ℯ info@zimwhk.com; www.zimwhk.com; ⏱ 08.00–16.30 Mon–Fri, consular: 08.00–noon Mon–Fri

HOSPITALS In an emergency, call ☎ 211111, or ☎ 112 from a mobile. You will be put through to an operator who can reach the ambulance or fire services. In case of difficulty getting through, phone ☎ 1199. For an ambulance from the private International SOS, call ☎ 0800 911911 toll free, or ☎ 061 230505. If you're calling from a mobile, the number is m 081 707. The police can be reached on ☎ 10111. If you've a serious problem outside Windhoek, then contact **International SOS** (see pages 76–7).

➕ **Windhoek Central Hospital** [124 B1] Oievaar St; ☏ 061 203 9111; ⏱ 24hrs. Windhoek's main hospital is good, but with huge demands from the local population it can become very busy. If you've a serious medical condition then it's better to use your medical travel insurance & contact one of the private hospitals (each of which is open 24hrs & has an accident & emergency department):
➕ **Medi-Clinic** [map, page 118] Heliodoor St, Eros; ☏ 061 4331000, emergency ☏ 061 222687;

www.mediclinic.co.za. Windhoek's most expensive clinic, reached via Nelson Mandela Av & then General Murtala Mohammed Rd.
➕ **Roman Catholic Hospital** [128 B3] 92 Karl Werner List St; ☏ 061 237237; www.rcchurch.na. More central, but not so plush.
➕ **Rhino Park Private Hospital** [map, page 118] Hosea Kutako Dr; ☏ 061 225434; www. hospital.com.na. Aims to provide affordable health care, but has no casualty department.

PHARMACIES There are numerous pharmacies throughout the city, most with a range of goods and drugs that is equal to anything in western Europe or the USA.

✚ **Kalahari Pharmacy** [128 C4] 1st Floor, Gustav Voigts; ☏ 061 252448; ⏱ 09.00–17.30 Mon–Fri, 09.00–13.00 Sat, closed Sun
✚ **Langerhans Pharmacy** [128 C7] 7 Independence Av; ☏ 061 222581;

⏱ 08.30–17.20 Mon–Fri, 08.30–12.50 Sat, closed Sun
✚ **MediSun** [128 A4] Ground Floor, Wernhil Park; ⏱ 08.30–18.00 Mon–Fri, 08.30–13.30 Sat, 10.00–13.00 Sun

WHAT TO SEE AND DO

Although Windhoek isn't the planet's liveliest capital, there are some beautiful old buildings, a number of museums – including the glitzy new Independence Memorial Museum – plus art galleries and some tours worth taking.

WINDHOEK'S HISTORICAL BUILDINGS: A WALKING TOUR (*Duration: 2/3hrs*) Most of Windhoek's historical buildings date from around the turn of the 20th century, and are close to the centre of town. Walking is the obvious way to see these. Starting in the Post Street Mall [128 B3], look for the **Gideon Meteorites** [128 B4] – a series of odd rock clumps displayed on plinths outside Town Square Mall. In fact, these reddish rocks freckled with holes are pieces of meteor that were discovered near Gibeon, a village some 60km south of Mariental, in 1838 by General J E Alexander. He took samples back to London and the iron-rich clumps were identified by renowned astronomer and chemist Sir John Herschal. They were part of what is thought to have been the world's heaviest meteorite shower, which occurred around 600 million years ago. About 150 meteorites – ranging in weight from 195 to 596kg – have been recovered so far; many of these are in museums around the globe.

At the junction of the mall with Independence Avenue is a replica of the **clocktower** [128 C3] that was once on the old Deutsche-Afrikabank. The original was constructed in 1908.

Now turn southeast, towards Christus Kirche, and cross Independence Avenue into Zoo Park. From here, you can get a good view of three fine buildings on the west side of Independence Avenue. They were designed by Willi Sander, a German who designed many of Windhoek's older landmarks. The right-hand one of the three, **Erkraths Building** [128 B4], was built in 1910: a business downstairs, and a place to live upstairs. **Gathemann House** [128 C3], the building in the middle, was designed for Heinrich Gathemann, who was then the mayor of Klein Windhoek, and built in 1913 to a basically European design, complete with a steep roof to prevent any accumulation of snow! Again, it originally had living quarters above the business. Next along is the old **Kronprinz Hotel**, designed and built by Sander in 1901 and 1902. It was extended in 1909, and refurbished and extended in 1920. It is now overshadowed by the Sanlam building, but a plan has been made to modernise the shops (one of which is Nakara, page 148) while preserving the façades.

Continuing into **Zoo Park** [128 C4], you will find two features of note on green lawns under the palm trees. A sculptured **Elephant Column** over a metre high marks the place where primitive tools and elephant remains, dated to about 5,000 years ago, were found. Scenes of an imagined elephant-hunt kill are depicted in bas-relief by Namibian sculptress Dörte Berner, and a fossilised elephant skull tops the column. On the south side of the elephant column is the **war memorial**, about a century old, crowned by an eagle and dedicated to German soldiers killed while fighting the Nama people. As yet there is no memorial here for the Nama people, led by Hendrik Witbooi, although they have been remembered as part of the new monument at Heroes' Acre (see pages 156–7).

Now head south on Independence Avenue a short way until your first left turn, up Fidel Castro Street. This junction is the site for the new **Freedom Plaza** [128 C5] currently under construction, causing Windhoek's best street-sellers for baskets to be moved to a temporary market near the Hilton Hotel. The tourist information kiosk is also in a temporary pop-up container on the corner of the junction.

On the left, on the far corner of Lüderitz Street, you will see the **Hauptkasse**. Once used as the house of the Receiver of Revenue, as well as officers' quarters and even a hostel, it is now used by the Ministry of Agriculture. Opposite the Hauptkasse, on the south side of Fidel Castro Street, **Ludwig Van Estorff House** [128 C4] was simply built in 1891, as a canteen, and is named after a commander of the Schutztruppe, the German colonial troops, who lived here in 1902–10. It is now the National Reference Library.

Nearby, in a commanding position on its own roundabout, is **Christus Kirche** [128 D4], a 'fairy-tale' Evangelical Lutheran church and Windhoek's most famous building. It was designed by Gottlieb Redecker in Art Nouveau and Neo-Gothic styles, and built between 1907 and 1910 of local sandstone. Kaiser Wilhelm II donated the stained-glass windows; his wife, Augusta, gave the altar Bible. Originally this church commemorated the peace at the end of various wars between the German colonists and the indigenous people of Namibia, and inside are plaques dedicated to the German soldiers who were killed. (As yet, there's no mention of the losses of the indigenous people.) The church is now normally locked, but if you wish to see inside it should still be possible to borrow the key during office hours (⊕ *07.30–13.00 Mon–Fri*) from the church offices, just down the hill at 12 Fidel Castro Street.

On the west side of Robert Mugabe Avenue, just near Christus Kirche, the **Kaiserliche Realschule** [128 D4] is now part of the National Museum. However, it was originally built in 1907–08 as a school, and became Windhoek's first German high school.

Walking further south along Robert Mugabe Avenue, you'll see the new Bank of Namibia building. On your right, just before crossing Sam Nujoma Drive, is the **Office of the Ombudsman** [128 D5]. Built as a dwelling for the chief justice and his first clerk, this was originally erected in 1906–07, and has much decorative work typical of the German 'Putz' style of architecture. The original stables are now a garage and outbuilding.

Now turn around and walk back towards Christus Kirche, on the right (east) side of Robert Mugabe Avenue. The large building on the right is the old fort, **Alte Feste**, built by the first Schutztruppe when they arrived here around 1890. It is strategically positioned overlooking the valley, though its battlements were never seriously besieged. A plaque on the front maintains the colonial view that it was built to 'preserve peace and order' between the local warring tribes – which is as poor a justification for colonialism as any. Inside, much of the main historical section of the National Museum has been moved to its new neighbour, the Independence Memorial Museum, but some displays remain (see page 154). In front of the building stands a new **statue of a man and woman representing the heroes of the struggle for independence**, with words from the Namibian National Anthem written below: 'Their blood waters our freedom.' This controversially replaced the large Equestrian Statue in December 2013 (see box, page 155), which commemorated the German soldiers killed during the wars to subdue the Nama and Herero groups, around 1903–07 (but with no mention of the Nama or Herero people who died).

To the left of the Alte Feste, on a hill towering over Christus Kirche, you can't help but notice the new **Independence Memorial Museum** [128 D4] (see page 154). The N$60 million triangular building looks like a high-spec glass-fronted office block gleaming in the sun. Inaugurated by President Pohamba on 20 March 2014, it tells the story of Namibia's struggle for independence with a towering statue of Sam Nujoma, the country's founding father, in front of it.

Once back at the Christus Kirche, turning right (east) leads you to what were originally the administrative offices of the German colonial government, the **Parliament** [128 D4]. The building became known as the Tintenpalast, or Ink Palace, for the amount of bureaucracy that went on there, and has housed successive governments since around 1912. The Germans occupied it for only about a year, before losing the colony to South Africa after World War I. Now this beautiful double-storey building is home to Namibia's parliament. Normally, 1-hour tours of the building are on offer (⊕ 09.00, 10.00 & 15.00 Mon–Fri; a/h ☏ 061 288 2583, 061 202 8097/8062; www.parliament.gov.na), but during research it was unclear whether this was still available (please notify us if so). Even if you don't take a tour, do make time for the lovely formal gardens and fountain that grace the area in front.

As you continue north along Robert Mugabe Avenue, on the left is the old **State House** [125 F6]. Built in 1958, on the site of the old German governor's residence, it was used by South Africa's administrator general until 1990, when it became the president's official residence. (A new State House has since been constructed.)

It is now a short walk left, down Daniel Munamava Street, back to join Independence Avenue by the main post office.

MUSEUMS, GALLERIES AND LIBRARIES Windhoek has, perhaps after Swakopmund, some of the country's best museums, galleries and libraries, though even these state collections are limited. The South African regime, which controlled the museums until 1990, had a polarised view of the country's history, understandably, and, undesirably, slanted towards their involvement in it. It remains difficult to find out much of the history of Namibia's indigenous peoples. However, the museums are gradually redressing the balance, particularly with the opening of the new Independence Memorial Museum.

Alte Feste and State Museum [128 C5] (*Robert Mugabe Av;* \ *061 276800;* ⊕ *09.00–17.00 Mon–Fri, 10.00–12.30 & 15.00–17.00 Sat–Sun; open till 18.00 in summer, Oct–Apr; admission free, but donations actively encouraged*) This is the capital's best museum, concentrating on Namibia's history over the last few centuries. A number of old wagons and even a steam engine adorn the terrace in front of the building. Inside the fort is an exhibition of historical photographs, and displays of household implements of the missionaries and the country's indigenous peoples. The exhibit on the independence process, and the transition to majority rule in 1990, has moved to the neighbouring Independence Memorial Museum. In a separate wing is an excellent display covering Namibia's rock art, with a smaller exhibition on bead-work. Whether or not you have time to visit one of the sites mentioned, it's well worth spending a bit of time here. Of particular interest is the visual explanation of how some of the paintings developed over time through layering and overpainting. Sadly, with the development of the Independence Memorial Museum, the infrastructure of the Alte Feste has been neglected and underresourced and the building itself is deteriorating.

Independence Memorial Museum [128 D4] (*Robert Mugabe Av;* \ *061 276800;* ⊕ *09.00–17.00 daily; open until 18.00 in summer, Oct–Apr; admission free*) Next to Alte Feste, this new museum finally opened on 20 March 2014 to coincide with the 24th anniversary of Namibia's independence. (It had originally been planned for 2010.) Using newspaper archives, military exhibits, personal records and vividly detailed paintings, the first floor depicts the years of colonial repression under the rule of Germany and South Africa, the second covers the Liberation War and the third recounts the events on the road to independence, culminating in a dramatic and enormous mural called the History Panorama. It's an interesting, thought-provoking museum focusing on a relatively little-known part of African history that was inextricably linked to yet overshadowed by events in neighbouring South Africa. The glass lifts on the exterior of the building are worth a visit too, providing great views of the city as you ascend. There is talk of a restaurant opening on the top two floors, but at the time of research the floors were locked and empty.

Owela Museum [128 C2] (*4 Robert Mugabe Av;* \ *061 276825;* ⊕ *09.00–18.00 Mon–Fri, 10.00–12.30 & 15.00–17.00 Sat–Sun; open until 18.00 in summer, Oct–Apr; admission free*) North of State House, almost opposite Conradie Road, Owela Museum houses the natural history sections of the State Museum, with a good section on cheetah conservation, and a little on the country's traditional cultures.

TransNamib Museum [128 B1] (*1st Floor Windhoek Station, Bahnhof St;* \ *061 298 2186;* ⊕ *08.00–13.00 & 14.00–17.00 Mon–Fri; admission N$5*) Housed upstairs in the old railway station building, this museum is run by the parastatal transport company, TransNamib. It shows the development of transport in the country over the last century, with particular emphasis on the rail network. Ring the bell when you arrive; the museum is probably open, even if the gate is locked!

National Art Gallery of Namibia [128 C2] (*Cnr Robert Mugabe Av & John Meinert St;* \ *061 231160; www.nagn.org.na;* ⊕ *08.00–17.00 Tue–Fri, 09.00–14.00 Sat; admission free, but donations encouraged*) Namibia's small National Gallery has a permanent exhibition of Namibian art – some historical, some contemporary – and also hosts a variety of visiting exhibitions. It's well worth checking out.

THE MYSTERY OF THE MISSING REITERDENKMAL   *Sue Watt*

Once one of Windhoek's best-known landmarks, the Reiterdenkmal (Equestrian Statue), disappeared under cover of darkness on Christmas Eve 2013. For years the subject of controversial debate, it stood proudly opposite Christus Kirche, commemorating German soldiers who fell during the Namibian war of resistance 1903–07. But with no equivalent memorial to the Herero and Nama – whose losses far outnumbered the colonialists – it represented to many a distorted and supremacist view of Namibian history.

In 2010, with the building of the new Independence Memorial Museum, the statue was moved to a plinth outside neighbouring Alte Feste. Government plans to declassify it as a national monument required a public consultation period of 60 days, and on 20 December 2013 notice was given to this effect. However, on the evening of 25 December, while the city centre was deserted, the Reiterdenkmal was surreptitiously removed by the authorities and squirrelled away to the yard in the Alte Feste. Its whereabouts were a mystery – even the receptionist at the Alte Feste knew nothing about its relocation until he saw the horse and rider the following morning, ignominiously propped up by scaffolding poles, peering into his office window. A media frenzy ensued, with fierce debate about the significance of the memorial in today's Namibia and the secretive nature of its removal.

Three German groups in Namibia started legal proceedings to reinstate the Reiterdenkmal, but eventually accepted they were fighting a losing battle. At the time of writing, it remains in the Alte Feste courtyard like a stateless refugee with rumours suggesting it might return to Germany.

Geological Museum [125 C7] (*1 Aviation Rd;* ☏ *061 2848111;* ⏱ *08.00–13.00 & 14.00–17.00 Mon–Fri, admission free*) Very few tourists know this museum exists or, if they do, bother to make the journey towards Eros airport to see it, which is a shame. Treasures include 750-year-old stromatolites, fossilised eggshells and reptiles, and the lower jaw of the first fossil ape found in the southern hemisphere that is over 13 million years old.

National Reference Library [128 C4] (*11 Fidel Castro St;* ☏ *061 293 4203*) Housed in Ludwig Van Estorff House (see page 152), this is really of more relevance to serious researchers than casual visitors.

Franco-Namibian Cultural Centre [128 C1] (see page 144) Many of the books and magazines in the centre's **library** are in French, but there is a good selection of French books that have been translated into English, books on Namibia and books by Namibians. The gallery in the building hosts various photography and art exhibitions.

Also of interest are the **John Muafangejo Art Centre**, which exhibits the work of young Namibian artists, and the **Centre for Visual and Performing Arts**.

NATIONAL BOTANICAL GARDENS [124 E3] (*8 Orban St;* ☏ *061 202 2014; www. nbri.org.na;* ⏱ *08.00–17.00 Mon–Fri, 08.00–11.00 1st Sat of month; admission free*) One of Windhoek's lesser-known attractions is this 12ha garden, in which 99% of the plants are indigenous species. Part of the gardens have been landscaped, with areas representing the different habitats found in Namibia, while the remainder is

...indhoek bush dotted with impressive aloes. It's an attractive spot for ... there are self-guided trails through the garden, with plant and bird ... from the reception. To find it, turn left on to Hügel Street from Sam ..., then right after about 200m into Orban Street. The gate into the ... ..e end of the street.

KATUTURA [map, page 118] Windhoek's northern township, Katutura (see box, page 158), is becoming more accessible to visitors, in a similar way to Johannesburg's Soweto.

For the visitor, streets in the township are very confusing and it's easy for an outsider to get lost, so it's best to stick to the main thoroughfares. Nevertheless, it's safe enough here in the daytime, though at night it is not advisable to come without a guide. Some of the city tours (see page 122) include Katutura on their itineraries.

There are two **markets** in Katutura: Soweto on Independence Avenue, and Kakukaze Mungunda Market on Mungunda Street. To find out about opening times, contact the Windhoek city information office in Post Street Mall (see page 121). Beyond the townships is the Penduka co-operative (see page 147).

Xwama Cultural Village [map, page 118] (*Cnr Independence Av & Omongo St;* ✆ *061 210270;* e *info@xwamacultural.com; www.xwamacultural.com; admission free*) In the heart of Katutura, Xwama cultural village has been set up to showcase Namibia's cultures, song, dance – and particularly its cuisine. There's a restaurant, take-away food outlet and craft shop. Visitors can also stay at the on-site bed and breakfast. To reach it, drive north along Independence Avenue. Cross the junction with the B1 and drive into Katutura for about 4.2km. Turn left into Omongo Street and the cultural village is immediately on your right.

EXCURSIONS OUTSIDE WINDHOEK

AVIS DAM [map, page 114] On the road to the international airport, there's Avis Dam. Paths around this manmade lake, which was created by a dam across the Klein Windhoek River, are mostly frequented by local dog walkers, but birders might like to know that morning guided walks can be arranged through the Namibia Bird Club (✆ *061 225727; www.namibiabirdclub.org*). The lake is also popular with locals for fishing, picnics, canoeing and bike rides, but there's little of any scenic interest to attract visitors.

A better option for visitors interested in **watersports** would be Lake Oanob (see page 180), about an hour's drive south of Windhoek.

DAAN VILJOEN NATURE RESERVE [map, page 114] (⊕ *daily sunrise–sunset; admission N\$40 pp, N\$10/vehicle*) Namibia's smallest game park, situated some 20km west of the city, is ideal for a 'close to the city' bush experience. Among others, it is home to klipspringer, zebra, giraffe, oryx, blue wildebeest and numerous bird species, including Rüppell's parrot. Happily, visitors are free to walk around the park and there are two marked hiking trails you can follow. Mountain biking is also possible and there's a short 6.5km self-drive game route as well. Inside the reserve is the Sun Karros lodge and camping (see page 138).

HEROES' ACRE [map, page 114] (*B1 towards Rehoboth, left exit; admission free*) About 15km south of the city, to the left of the B1 as you head south from Windhoek, Heroes' Acre scales up the hillside and is dedicated to 'the Namibian

BERNHARD NORDKAMP CENTRE, KATUTURA   *Hilary Bradt*

A visit to the Bernhard Nordkamp Centre in Katutura may rank as one of the highlights of your trip. It is run by MaryBeth Gallagher (*Hans Uirab St, Katutura;* m *081 228 5717; www.thebncnamibia.com*) and her team of volunteers who work with boundless energy and enthusiasm to improve the lives of children who work in the township.

Initially the centre's aim was to provide after-school facilities for deprived youngsters, but these days there are literacy and numeracy classes to help children who are failing at school. MaryBeth says, 'We are now looking for people who want to teach in the afternoons. You don't have to be an experienced teacher, but you must love kids and be willing to teach the basics to small groups. We have all the materials; we just need people to help. We also have our computer room, and the sports programme: soccer, basketball, tennis, badminton, ping-pong and swimming in the warm months.' Even if you can only spare an afternoon it is worth contacting MaryBeth to see if you can help – and she is always in need of stuff that's unavailable in Namibia.

When I first went there, my group of eight brought footballs, sports gear and much-needed felt-tipped pens ('sharpies'). We spent the afternoon with the children, talking, playing games, taking photos and generally learning about an aspect of Namibia that we would never have seen otherwise. We still talk about it, and follow MaryBeth's blog with admiration for what she is achieving.

peoples' struggle for independence and self-emancipation'. It was completed in 2002 for the annual Heroes' Day, 26 August – a public holiday.

Entering through the soaring square arches, the eye is drawn to the 170 graves that lead in stepped terraces up to a 34m-high obelisk meant to symbolise a sword and the bravery and strength of the fighters who fought for liberation. The enormous bronze mural behind it depicts the various struggles Namibians have faced throughout history; from left to right: the oppression under German rule (1884–1915), the 1960s fight for liberation from South Africa's occupation and apartheid policies, and the Unknown Soldier leading soldiers to victory and raising the flag for an independent Namibia in 1990.

In front of the obelisk stands an 8m-high bronze statue of Namibia's Unknown Soldier carrying rifle and a grenade. Beneath him, on a pedestal, is a replica of President Sam Nujoma's handwriting reading: 'Glory to the fallen heroes and heroines of the motherland Namibia!'

HORSERIDING Several game farms around the city offer horseriding to guests but you'll need to book well in advance.

Equitrails m 081 338 0743; e sam@equitrails. org; www.equitrails.org. Established by Sam McCartney, a qualified British Horse Society instructor with over 10yrs' experience of horse safaris in Africa, Equitrails is based at Elisenheim Guest Farm (see page 138). As well as rides by the hour (*N$380 pp/hr*), it offers 3hr sundowner rides (*N$650 pp*), 5hr champagne brunch rides in the mountains (*N$900 pp*), day rides with a picnic

(*N$900 pp*) & 1–5-night lodge-based trails (*from N$2,500 pp*). Return transfers from Windhoek can be arranged.

Hohewarte Guest Farm (See page 136) Hohewarte mostly offers sunrise/sunset rides for their guests but Heike Koehler will also quote on tailor-made horseback excursions.

River Crossing (See page 136) Set up by local horseriding personality Andrew Gillies, this

Since 1913, most black people in the city had lived in what is now known as the Old Location, to the west of Independence Avenue around Hochland Park. When, during the 1950s, the authorities decided to build a new location as part of the Union National Party's enforced apartheid, they were met with stiff resistance, culminating in riots on the night of 10 December 1959. The Old Location was duly abolished, and the people forcefully resettled to Katutura and the neighbouring townships of Khomasdal, Wanaheda and Okuryangava.

Although the line dividing the white areas of Windhoek from the black townships was effectively Hosea Kutako Avenue, the real division came earlier, at the point where Independence Avenue crosses the railway line. During the years of apartheid, workers heading into the centre of town needed to show a *kopf* (or 'head') card to be allowed over the bridge; in the evening, the gate was closed at 18.00, preventing further movement in and out of the centre of Windhoek by black Namibians.

In the early days, there was strict segregation in the townships by tribe, with houses labelled 'D' for Damara, 'H' for Herero, 'O' for Owambo, etc. Even now, house numbers indicate tribal affiliations, each in different areas. After the declaration of independence in 1990, the government invited Namibians from the north to come to the capital to work, with promises of a house, a garden, a job and even a car. Thousands of people accepted the invitation, and the population of the townships swelled – even if the reality did not necessarily match up to the promises. Today, the population of Katutura is officially around 40,000, but unofficial estimates place that figure far higher, at up to 200,000.

At first, long houses were built to meet the needs of large, extended families of farm workers. Later, small corrugated-iron 'box' houses formed the second phase of development. The third phase, with the best of intentions, was the construction by various NGOs of modern houses. Most of the people who moved into the area came from traditional kraals in the north of the country, and were ill-equipped to cope with the challenges of urban life. Where there were small houses, families of eight to 12 people would move in, and Western-style kitchens were left empty as the tradition of cooking in the open air was continued in the small yards.

It would be unsurprising if the streets of Katutura were strewn with litter, but by and large the reverse is the case. It is striking that, in spite of the sprawling nature of the township, and the density of housing, it is both orderly and clean. Water pipes are stationed every 300–400m. In some areas, bougainvillea lines the streets, and there are occasional sunflowers in the gardens. Maize, too, is grown, though this is almost exclusively for *tombo* – maize beer – not to eat. There is little in the way of cultivation of food, and malnutrition is rife.

Perhaps unexpectedly, there is no shortage of schools. These are government run, but most were built by donations from overseas charities and governments. Although, in theory, education is compulsory, the reality is not so straightforward. Aside from the cost of schooling, each child must have a uniform. As wages in the black community are significantly lower than those for white workers, many families cannot afford to provide this uniform, and their children remain on the streets. For the post-school generation, there are a number of training opportunities provided by churches, hospitals and schools, as well as the government, in fields that include nursing and waitressing.

operation organises 2½hr sundowner rides (*N$650 pp*) & 3–4hr rides with a champagne b/fast (*N$750*) in the nearby & spectacular Moltkeblick Mountains. Hourly rates (*N$350*) apply for longer or tailor-made rides.

OTHER POSSIBILITIES Within relatively easy reach of Windhoek are Okahandja (about 1½ hours by car), with its woodcarvers' markets, and the nearby Von Bach Recreational Resort and Gross Barmen Hot Springs (see page 169). Or if you just want to escape the city for a day, you could try some watersports at Lake Oanob Resort (see page 180).

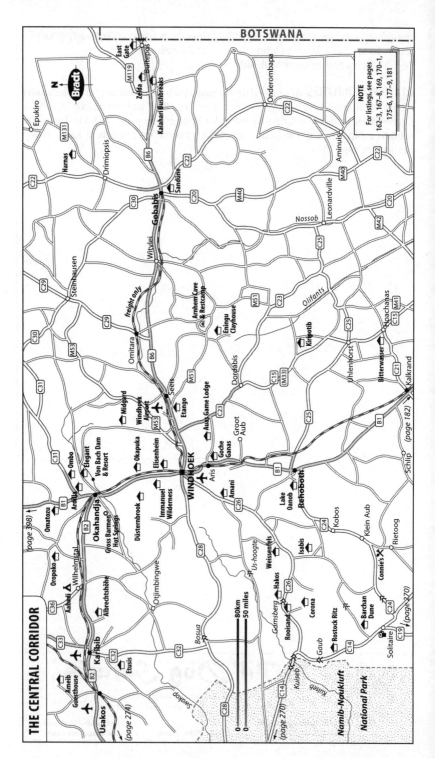

THE CENTRAL CORRIDOR

9

The Central Corridor

Despite Windhoek's dominance of the country's central region, it still occupies only a relatively small area. The city doesn't sprawl for miles. Drive just 10km from the centre and you will be on an open highway, whichever direction you choose. The completion of the Trans-Kalahari Highway means that you can drive directly from Walvis Bay right across this region to South Africa's northern heartland, without leaving tarmac. In time, this may have a major impact on the area.

This chapter concentrates on this central swathe of Namibia, working outwards from Windhoek – to the edges of the Namib-Naukluft National Park in the west, and to the border with Botswana in the east. Most of the towns in this region don't require more than a day's visit at most – they mainly serve as useful refuelling stops.

WEST FROM WINDHOEK: TO THE COAST

Travelling from Windhoek to the coast, there's a choice of three obvious roads: the main tarred B2, the C28 and the more southerly C26. If speed is important, then you must take the B2: about 4 hours of very easy driving. Both the 'C' roads are gravel, and will take at least 6 hours to drive. However, they are more scenic.

Note that some of the side roads off these three main roads are used very little. The D1412, for example, is a narrow, slow road whose crossing of the Kuiseb is wide and sandy. It would probably be impassable during the rainy season.

THE C28 The shortest of the gravel roads, the C28, goes through beautiful scenery, but is also tortuous, with numerous cattle grids along its route. Around halfway along, you drive (slowly!) through the steep gradients (20%) of the Bosua Pass – where the central Namibian Highlands start to give way to granite kopjes of rounded boulders before the low, flat Namib.

Between the C28 and the B2, Etusis Lodge (see page 170) makes a good stop when travelling north–south, as it is somewhat off-piste between Windhoek and Swakopmund.

THE C26 The C26 is much longer than the C28, but just as scenic. Just after its start, it drops steeply through the Khomas Hochland Mountains (the Kupferberg Pass), then later passes through the remarkable folded mountains of the Gamsberg Pass, which itself involves 20km of twists and turns, and 40 minutes' driving if you go gently (admiring the fine views). Further on still, the Kuiseb Pass sees the road wind down into the river's valley, cross on a small bridge, and then gradually climb back on to the desert plain (discussed in *Chapter 12*). Rooisand (see page 162), at the foot of the Gamsberg Pass, would make an excellent stop on the C26.

Guest farms and lodges along the C26 *Map, page 160.*

🏠 **Amani Lodge** (5 chalets) ☏ 061 239564; e info@amani-lodge-namibia.com; www.amani-lodge-namibia.com. Some 28km southwest of Windhoek on the C26, just over the Kupferberg Pass, Amani greets you with Namibian & French flags flying side-by-side over the entrance gate. At an altitude of 2,150m, the lodge is perhaps best known as the highest in Namibia. It is run by Alain, Shanaaz & Olivier Houlet, originally from France, & has been built to a high standard in neutral, earthy colours, with African influences mixed with touches of French style. Individual mountain chalets with twin beds & en-suite showers all have superb views. The main house includes a b/fast area, & there's also a communal bar & lounge/dining area, while outside is a pool. The lodge's major attraction lies in its cheetahs, including some orphans that were unable to survive in the wild, so some are tame & some wild. Other activities include hiking in the mountains & stargazing: the lodge has its own telescope. *B&B N$1,650/1,950 sgl/dbl.* **LLL**

🏠 **Weissenfels Guest Farm** (10 rooms, 4 pitches) ☏ 062 572112; e rowins@iafrica.com.na; http://weissenfels-volunteer-project.jimdo.com/. 120km west of Windhoek on the C26 – just west of the D1265, & east of the Gamsberg Pass – Weissenfels covers 40km² of rolling highlands. A guest farm since 1992, it is now run by Winston Retief & Rosi Rohr, who have refurbished it while retaining its fairly traditional feel. Accommodation is in dbl rooms: either 'budget', which share bathrooms, or en suite. There's also a larger family room. (Because of its location, Weissenfels does cater for occasional small tour groups.) Weissenfels makes a good stopover for a snack or lunch if you're travelling on the C26 (if you book in advance), but if you decide to stay for longer then there are some pleasant hiking trails (which you can follow with a guide, or on your own), & there's a fair amount of game around. Alternatively, 4x4 game drives & horseriding (*from N$250/hr*) are possible, as are picnics at the farm's various rock pools, & a scenic sunset drive into the mountains nearby. The lodge also offers a range of massage & therapy treatments, from N$80, & labyrinth walks. *B&B N$600/1,000 sgl/dbl; camping N$150 pp.* **LL**

🏠 **Rooisand Desert Ranch** (10 rooms) ☏ 062 572119; m 081 127 7629; e lifestyle@rooisand.com; www.rooisand.com. Situated at the foot of the Gamsberg Pass on the C26, Rooisand is about 30km from the junction of the C14 & C26. Once a traditional guest farm, it has been reinvented with a focus on family-orientated activities. Now, in addition to hiking & drives in the mountains, there is a large swimming pool, & even a floodlit tennis court. Of course, activities don't stop in the evening – that's when the opportunity to stargaze using the farm's telescope arises. Added interest comes from Bushman paintings to be seen on various rocks around Rooisand, as well as an old Schutztruppe camp, & a quarry that occasionally throws up some interesting semi-precious stones. More mundanely, the rooms are decorated in assorted designs & are all different sizes, with dbl & sgl rooms. *B&B N$990–1,265/1,660–2,190 sgl/dbl.* **LLL**

🏠 **Corona Guest Farm** (3 suites, 6 rooms, 4 tents) ☏ 061 681 045; e corona@iway.na; www.natron.net. Corona is about halfway between Windhoek & Walvis Bay, 20mins south of the C26. To reach it, take the exceedingly bumpy D1438 turn-off (which is about 31km east of the C14/C26 junction north of Solitaire) south for 18km. Corona boasts family-size suites, large dbl rooms all named after animals & safari tents – each with its own bathroom. There are also several verandas, small lounges (one upstairs with satellite TV), a bar, a reading corner, & an outdoor swimming pool with sundeck under some lovely jacarandas. Activities include various farm pursuits plus nature drives & hiking; it's possible for hikers to climb the Gamsberg Mountain, though this is unguided and not recommended during the warmer summer months. There are also a number of shelters containing rock art on the farm. *DBB N$1,000/2,000 sgl/dbl; tent N$700 pp.* **LLL**

🏠 **Hakos Guest Farm** (14 rooms, camping) ☏ 062 572111; e info@hakos-astrofarm.com; www.hakos-astrofarm.com. This small guest farm is signposted 7km to the left (if you're heading east) from the top of the Gamsberg Pass. Rooms are clean & simple with cool stone floors & there are also 4 private camp pitches. There are great views over the surrounding mountains, various hiking trails on the farm & a 4x4 route into the mountains. More unusual attractions include the indoor swimming pool & a small observatory with a 'roll-off roof' which has mirror & lens telescopes on a heavy mount with automatic tracking.

A second equally well-equipped observatory was added in 2007, & the farm is also home to the International Amateur Observatory. That said, Johann encourages amateur astronomers to bring their own equipment, & enthuses about the clarity of the night sky. *DBB N$975/1,600 sgl/dbl; camping N$120 pp.* **LLL**

Horseriding

Namibia Horse Safari m 081 470 3384; e info@namibiahorsesafari.com; www. namibiahorsesafari.com. Led by Sarah-Jane Gullick, who has a wealth of experience in African horseback safaris, this professional operation can organise adventurous trips on horseback, from the central highlands across the desert to Swakopmund, by the Fish River Canyon & through Damaraland. There are 5 established trails to choose from, lasting 5–10 days. Covering up to 70km a day, these usually include a few nights to get used to the horses, & one to relax at the end. Participants must be fit, have extensive experience of riding & horses, & be totally at ease on the back of a cantering horse. Riders camp throughout the trip & trucks transport the equipment ahead of the party. Dates for most trails are fixed ahead (see website for details), although shorter rides & trails incorporating luxury lodge accommodation can be arranged on request.

THE MAIN B2   The B1 heads north from Windhoek to Okahandja before turning west – as the B2 – towards the coast. Although the distance to Swakopmund is 358km, the road is flat and the tarred surface means that it is around 4 hours of very easy driving. Indeed, the section between Okahandja and Karibib was widened and resurfaced in 2010, further improving communications along this stretch.

Okahandja   This small town is 71km north of Windhoek, at the junction of the B1 and B2. It has some reasonable shops, a couple of banks, 24-hour fuel, and two of the country's best open markets for curios. Add to this a reputation for excellent biltong (dried meat), and quite a lot of old buildings and history, and it's worth breaking your journey here.

History   Okahandja is the administrative centre for the Herero people (see page 25), despite being considerably southwest of their main settlements. Missionaries first reached the area in the late 1820s, but it wasn't until 1849 that the first of them, Friedrich Kolbe, settled here. He remained for less than a year, driven away by the attacks of the Namas, under Jonker Afrikaner.

He fled with good reason as, on 23 August of the following year, about 700 men, women and children were killed by the Namas at the aptly named Blood Hill. It is said that after the massacre, the women's arms and legs were chopped off in order to take their copper bangles.

The small kopje of Blood Hill can be seen just to the east of the main Windhoek–Swakopmund road. Jonker Afrikaner lies peacefully in his grave, next to several Herero chiefs, opposite the church on Kerk Street.

Getting there and away   Most overseas visitors coming through Okahandja are driving, but the town is also served by both coach and train services. Those driving themselves should note that the main B2 bypasses the town, so to go into the centre you'll need to turn off the road at the signposts.

By bus   Intercape Mainliner's services from Windhoek to Walvis Bay stop at Okahandja's Engen and Wimpy Garage on the B1 Highway at 10.10 on Monday Wednesday, Friday and Saturday, returning at 13.40 on Monday, Wednesday, Friday and Sunday. Buses between Windhoek and Victoria Falls reach Okahandja at 13.00

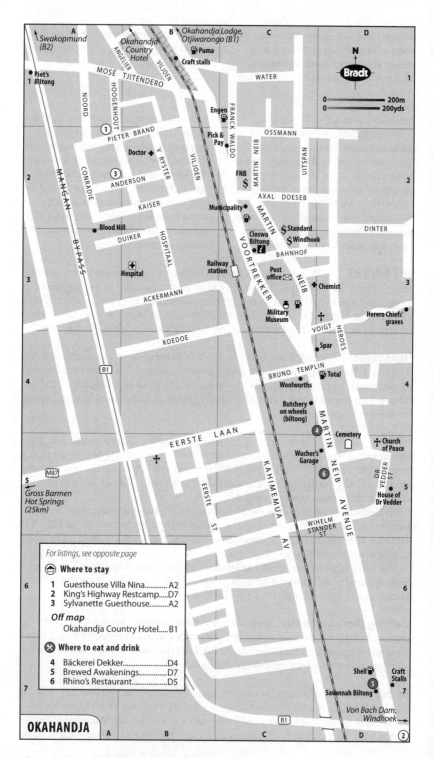

Where to stay

1 Guesthouse Villa Nina............ A2
2 King's Highway Restcamp.....D7
3 Sylvanette Guesthouse..........A2

Off map
  Okahandja Country Hotel.....B1

Where to eat and drink

4 Bäckerei Dekker....................D4
5 Brewed Awakenings.............D7
6 Rhino's Restaurant.................D5

For listings, see opposite page

OKAHANDJA

on Monday and Friday, with the return journey stopping in Okahandja at 04.20 on Monday and Thursday. Fares vary from N$160 to N$320 to Windhoek, and N$252 to N$280 to Walvis Bay. See pages 101–2 for more details.

By train Trains – very slow trains – depart from Okahandja for Windhoek at 05.00, daily except Saturday, and on the same days for Swakopmund and Walvis Bay at 21.50. For details, see pages 98–100.

Where to stay *Map, opposite.*
Most visitors opt to stay at one of the guest farms surrounding Okahandja (page 167), but there are a few options in town. For camping try **King's Highway Restcamp** (✆ *062 504086*) just south of town.

Okahandja Country Hotel (24 rooms, camping) ✆ 062 504299; e okalodge@africaonline. com.na; www.okahandjalodge.com. About 2km north of town, signposted to the east of the bypass. Its en-suite rooms, 2 for families, are in large, thatched blocks partially circling an open lawn with a nearby pool. They are pleasant inside, with AC & DSTV, if somewhat unoriginal. Wi-Fi is available in the reception area. The campsite has a lawn with 16 pitches, clean ablution facilities & 220V plug points. The restaurant offers a good range of meals. The indoor dining room is bland, but the dining area in the garden is pretty, under thatch & surrounded by ponds & fountains. *Camping N$100 pp.* **$$$**

Guesthouse Villa Nina 327 Conradie St; ✆ 062 502497; m 081 2683753; www.

namibiatouristik.de. Run-down pension – a last resort, or for those on a tight budget. Cash only. **$$**

Sylvanette Guesthouse (11 rooms) 311 Hoogenhout St; ✆ 062 501213/505550; m 081 127 3759; e sylvanette@iway.na; www.sylvanette. com. Sylvanette sits in a quiet street close to town with a landscaped garden that adds to the peaceful ambience. Each of the dbl en-suite rooms is decorated with individual touches including cute friezes & impressive animal photographs, & has AC, DSTV, fridge, coffee/tea station & Wi-Fi. There's an airy lounge where sundowners are served, & a cosy b/fast room adjacent to a fully equipped kitchen for self-caterers. Dinner can be arranged if requested in advance (*N$80 pp*). Outside, there's a swimming pool & secure parking. **$$**

Where to eat and drink *Map, opposite.*
Aside from the hotel, Okahandja has several good small coffee shops and cafés dotted along Martin Neib Avenue and Voortrekker Street.

Okahandja Country Hotel ✆ 062 504299; ⊕ 07.00–21.00 daily. Recommended by locals, this hotel has a bar & sizeable restaurant. You can sit on the terrace, overlooking the grounds. **$$$–$$$$**

Rhino's Restaurant 92 Martin Neib Av; ✆ 062 500866. ⊕ 09.00 until late Mon–Sat. This lively local sports bar has a varied menu including burgers, grills & pizzas. Outdoor seating on the pavement to the front. **$$–$$$$**

Steers 331 Martin Neib Av; ✆ 062 502662; ⊕ 09.00–20.00 Mon–Sat. Namibia's version of Burger King – with ribs, too. **$$**

Bäckerei Decker ✆ 062 501962; ⊕ 07.00–15.30 Mon–Fri, 07.00–noon Sat. Local bakery on the left as you drive into Okahandja. Outside seating with plastic tables under a shade-cloth. **$–$$**

Brewed Awakenings ✆ 062 500723; ⊕ 07.00–16.00 Mon–Sat, 08.00–14.00 Sun. Modern coffee shop with seating in an attractive garden, next to the Shell fuel station. **$–$$**

Other practicalities Okahandja has a scattering of **fuel stations** alongside its main roads. The town's **post office** is almost opposite its **pharmacy**, and if you need a **bank** you'll find branches of Standard Bank and FNB on the main Martin Neib Avenue, and Bank Windhoek on the corner of Bahnhof Street, all with ATMs.

For **food and provisions**, there's a large Spar supermarket by the junction of Martin Neib Avenue and Voortrekker Street, and Pick 'n' Pay and Shoprite supermarkets at the north end of Voortrekker Street. The town also has a reputation for excellent biltong, with several outlets including the renowned Closwa Biltong [164 C3] (*Voortrekker St;* \ *062 501123;* ⏲ *08.00–17.00 Mon–Fri, 08.00–13.00 Sat*), which doubles as a **tourist information kiosk**, the popular Piet's Biltong on the left of the B1 junction with Mosé Tjitendero Street and Savannah Biltong by the Shell fuel station south of the town. In an **emergency**, the police are reached on \ 062 10111, the ambulance on \ 062 503030, the hospital \ 062 503030, and the fire service \ 062 505100 (*a/h* **m** *081 284 9179*).

What to see and do At each end of the town is a large open-air **curio market with craft stalls** [164 B1 and D7], probably the two best places in the country for wooden carvings (see pages 30–1). These include some beautiful thin wooden giraffes (some 2m or more high), huge 'tribal' heads, cute flexible snakes, and wide selections of more ordinary carved hippos and bowls. Do stop for a wander around as you pass, especially if you're on the way to Windhoek airport to leave – this is the perfect spot for last-minute present shopping, and it's open on Sundays. A word of caution, though: the traders here have become quite aggressive in their sales tactics, and some of the prices quoted appear extortionate. If you're not prepared for the hassle, and to bargain fairly hard (it's not unusual to be 'quoted' a price that's more than ten times the market value), then a curio shop could be a better bet.

Historical sites The town has many historical sites, including the **graves** [164 D3] of a number of influential leaders, such as Jonker Afrikaner, the powerful Oorlam leader; Chief Hosea Kutako, an influential Herero leader who campaigned against South African rule in the 1950s; and Chief Clemens Kapuuo, once president of the DTA, who was assassinated in 1978. Note that casual visitors cannot access these graves.

Close by is the **Church of Peace**, a Lutheran-Evangelistic church built in 1952 and now enclosed by a high fence, and also the **house of Dr Vedder**, one of the oldest in town.

Just south of the post office, on Hoof Street, is a building known as **the old stronghold**, or the old fort. This was the town's old police station, started in 1894, though now it is empty and falling into disrepair. Meanwhile to the west, **Blood Hill** [164 A3], scene of the 1850 massacre, is found between Kaiser and Duiker streets, although there's little to see now. In 2004 a very smart **military museum** [164 C3] was built on Voortrekker Street, though it is still not open to the public.

HERERO PARADE

Okahandja still holds great cultural importance to the Herero, and each year thousands of women in traditional coloured dresses and men in military outfits parade through the town to commemorate their ancestral chiefs – in particular Chief Samuel Maharero, an important figure in the struggle against imperial Germany. The chief died in 1923 while in exile as a refugee of the British in Bechuanaland (present-day Botswana). His body was returned by steam train to Okahandja where he was laid to rest by his father, Chief Maharero, on 23 August 1923. Every year since, on the Sunday nearest that date, the Herero parade gathers to remember the chieftains, beginning at about 09.00 near the chiefs' graves.

Guest farms around Okahandja *Map, page 160.*

Around Okahandja lies some of the best farmland in the country. Some of the local farms accept guests, and some of those are good. The best include:

Omatozu Safari Camp (3 tents, 4 pitches) 081 643 7100; e info@omatozu.com; www. omatozu.com. Omatozu's large thatched main area has a bar on the deck, dining & lounge facilities. A braai area & campfire offer views over the farm dam. Three 'luxury' fixed tents boast en-suite bathrooms, AC, electric lights & power points, with a laundry service on request. About 200m from the main area is a very clean & well-maintained campsite with 4 pitches, equipped with lights, power points, WC & hot showers. Firewood is available to buy, & campers can make use of the bar facilities at the main camp, with b/fast & dinner available on request. Guided walks (*N$100 pp*) & farm drives (*N$150 pp*) are offered here; the more energetic may enjoy the pool & volleyball pitch. *DBB N$800/1,400 sgl/dbl; camping N$130.* **LL**

Ombo Restcamp (6 chalets, 3 rooms, camping) 062 502003; m 081 206 2791; e omborestcamp@africaonline.com.na; www. ombo-rest-camp.com. Owned by Ires Döring, this is a great option for campers & backpackers. There's a well set-up area with WC, showers, power points, tables, open kitchen, a kiddies' play area & a small shop. On a different part of the property, 6 chalets aren't much to look at from the outside but are very comfortable inside with AC & en-suite bathrooms. Each has a BBQ & kitchenette or fully equipped kitchen, & overlooks a small water point which attracts a variety of antelope. There's a central restaurant with an à la carte menu, & short tours introducing the farm ostriches & crocodiles are on offer. *B&B bungalow N$300 pp, camping N$110 pp.* **LL**

Elegant Farmstead (11 rooms) 062 500 872; e info@the-elegant-collection.com; www. the-elegant-collection.com. Originally Otjisazu, this guest farm was bought & refurbished in 2010 by the owners of the Elegant B&B & Guesthouse in Windhoek. An hour's drive from the capital, it is reached by taking the D2102 signposted to Von Bach Dam about 1km south of the bridge over the Okahandja River. After about 4.5km & again at about 16.5km there are very sharp bends, & the road crosses a number of dry river-beds. (This isn't a road to drive for the first time when it's dark.) It reaches the Farmstead on the left after about 27.5km. The area around is rolling acacia scrub/bush – typical of the central plateau around Windhoek.

The farm stands in pleasant, well-watered gardens with a variety of seating areas. There is also a separate outside boma dining area & bar, overlooking a good-size pool & nearby campfire. The main building was built as a mission in 1878, & outside retains its old look & feel. Inside, the en-suite rooms are modern & stylish & there is a trendy cigar lounge. Morning & afternoon nature drives (*N$200–320 pp inc drinks & snacks*), sundowners on Signal Hill (*N$150 pp*), champagne brunches in the river-bed & self-guided hiking trails are usually on offer on the 2,500ha farm. There are more activities in the local area, so do enquire about what else you may be able to do during your stay. With luck you'll spot a few of the farm's kudu, springbok, waterbuck, ostrich or giraffe. *DBB N$1,418/1,992 sgl/dbl.* **LLL**

Midgard Country Estate (46 rooms) 062 503888; e welcome-midgard@ol-leisure. com; www.midgardcountryestate.com. Midgard is about 85km from Windhoek on the D2102. It covers 65km^2, which includes a large swimming pool, tennis courts & hiking trails. Midgard is popular for an outing from town for Sunday lunch (*N$165 pp*), though it is better suited to conferences than casual visitors. This is reflected in the style & layout of its rooms, which have all the accoutrements of a good business hotel. *B&B N$1,150–1,570/1,560–2,200 sgl/dbl.* **LL–LLL**

Düsternbrook Guest Farm (8 rooms, 1 suite, 2 safari tents, 2 chalets, camping) 061 232572; m 081 864 3000; e info@ duesternbrook.net; www.duesternbrook.net. To reach Düsternbrook, turn west off the B1, about 30km north of Windhoek, opposite Okapuka Lodge & in the same entrance as Windhoek Greenbelt & Namib Poultry, on to the D1499, & then follow the clear signs for another 18km. Düsternbrook's venerable claim to fame is its leopards & cheetah, which are kept in several large enclosures, the smallest being 10 acres, & can be viewed from a vehicle. It also has a much larger area of land for game drives & 4 well-marked walks to view less dangerous game, including zebra, waterbuck, hartebeest, giraffe, eland, oryx, kudu, 4 hippo & smaller buck, not to mention a rich birdlife. Horseriding with game-viewing & an early morning mountain drive into the Khomas Mountains are added attractions; the big cat drive costs N$280 pp. The main building is a large old colonial farmhouse dating from 1908. Its walls are adorned with paintings & hunting trophies: limited & sustainable trophy hunting provides meat for the table. There's also a large pool, an information centre & a range of books on wildlife & natural history.

Düsternbrook was one of Namibia's first guest farms. The owner, Johann, is very into sustainable tourism & has received several Eco awards for his water, energy & waste management. *Rooms N$593/1,186 sgl/dbl; tents N$459; camping N$150.* **LL**

🏠 **Okapuka Ranch** (29 rooms, 1 suite) 📞061 257175/234607; e okapuka@iafrica.com. na; www.okapuka-ranch.com. Imposing gates to the east of the main B1, about 40km south of Okahandja & 30km north of Windhoek, herald this lodge. A 2.5km drive winds through 120km² of well-stocked land, protecting herds of sable,

giraffe & blue wildebeest, as well as gemsbok, kudu, ostrich & crocodile.

The lodge itself has been stylishly built on a rise, & lavishly equipped with a chic swimming pool, for the use of residents only. Accommodation is split across 2 sites: most of the thatched rooms are set together at the edge of the park, while an entirely separate mountain lodge has its own 4 rooms & broad views across the bush. Individual en-suite rooms are attractively designed, with karakul floor rugs & original artwork on the walls. Each boasts, a minibar, kettle & phone, as well as a private terrace, & some are equipped with AC/heating. The large, thatched bar/lounge area is beautiful, though more imposing than relaxing. Alongside, the restaurant caters for both residents & day visitors. Except on Sun, when there is a 3-course lunchtime buffet, the menu is à la carte, focusing on game. Okapuka encourages day visitors, offering daily 1½hr game drives & mountain drives. There are also 2 walking trails of 2 & 6hrs duration respectively. Note that the ranch sometimes accommodates guests from the *Desert Express* train (see page 100), which inevitably brings the occasional influx of visitors. *B&B N$819/1,932 sgl/dbl.* **LLL**

Von Bach Dam and Gross Barmen Hot Springs These two recreational resorts, close to Okahandja, have traditionally been used as weekend getaways by local urbanites – though travellers also use them for somewhere cheap to stay.

After being run by the NWR for many years, management of the **Von Bach Dam** resort (📞 *062 500162; reservations* e *reservations@tungeni.com; www. tungeni.com;* ⊕ *07.00–17.00 summer, 08.00–18.00 winter; admission N$40 pp per day, plus N$10 per car; under 16 free*) was taken over by Tungeni Serenity in 2009. Von Bach Dam supplies most of the capital's water, and is surrounded by a nature reserve. The environment here is thorn-scrub and particularly hilly, supporting game including kudu, warthog, baboon and leopard, as well as Hartmann's mountain zebra, springbok, eland and even ostrich. However, with only one road through the park they are all very difficult to spot, so don't come here just for the game.

Gross Barmen Hot Springs (📞 *062 501091;* ⊕ *6.30–18.00 all year; admission N$50 adult, N$25 child 6–12 per day for access to picnic area, N$100 per person per day for access to hot springs; under 5 free; see opposite*) was closed for most of 2014, but reopened after extensive renovations on 1 December 2014. It is run by Namibia Wildlife Resorts. The cheaper entrance fee gives access to the picnic area – where there are braai stands, a small pool and a bar. The entrance fee of N$100 gives access to the hot springs, the larger swimming pool, the gym and the sauna and steam room – note that on this entry basis you may not bring your own food or drink, but there are bar and restaurant facilities. Gross Barmen's main attraction is its mineral spring and swimming baths. The fountain here, clearly visible, wells up at about 65°C.

Getting there and away Von Bach Resort is signposted a few kilometres along the D2102 just south of Okahandja, and 1km south of the bridge over the Okahandja River.

Gross Barmen Resort is built around a dam about 25km southwest of Okahandja, on the banks of the Swakop River, and is easily reached from the town's southern side along the M87.

Where to stay, eat and drink Map, page 160.

🏠 **Von Bach Resort** (22 chalets, 12 pitches) Contact details as listed opposite. With a central restaurant & pool area, activities currently offered are canoeing, hiking & fishing, with plans for game drives, boat cruises & watersports to be available. At the time of research, 3 self-catering units were under construction, as well as a conference centre. The campsite facilities include WC, hot showers & a braai area, but no power. There are future plans for a wellness spa. *N$450–650/900–1,200 sgl/dbl.* **LL**

🏠 **Gross Barmen Resort** (39 chalets, camping) Contact details as listed opposite. Following extensive and expensive renovations,

Gross Barmen reopened, new and improved, in Dec 2014. Rooms are either premier or bush chalets, with family units also available. Premier chalets are modern & stylish, with a spacious bedroom & a separate lounge area, with a small seating area in-between. Bathrooms are large, with bathtubs & both inside & outside showers. Bush chalets are decorated in a similar style, with dbl or twin beds & a veranda with a view of the outdoor pool. Guests have access to all the spa facilities as listed opposite, & meals are taken at the restaurant close to this main area. *B&B bush chalet N$1,740 pp; premier chalet N$2,000 pp.* **LL**

Karibib

For over 90 years, this small town on the railway line from Windhoek to Swakopmund, 112km from Okahandja on the B2, has been known mainly for the very hard, very high-quality marble which comes from the Marmorwerke quarry nearby. This produces about 100 tonnes of finished stone per month – mainly kitchen/bathroom tiles and tombstones.

More recently, in the late 1980s, South Africa's Anglo-American Corporation opened the opencast Navachab Gold Mine on the south side of town, to mine low-grade ore. There's a lot of small-scale mining in the area, especially for gemstones. Amethyst, tourmaline, aquamarine, quartz, silver topaz, citrine and garnets are just some of the minerals found in the region around here. See the tumbled stones on the floor display of the information centre (see below) for an idea of what is around – they all come from the local area.

Trains between Windhoek and Walvis Bay call at Karibib – for details see pages 98–100.

Tourist information

Henckert Tourist Centre 38 Hidipo Hamutenya St; ☎ 064 550700; e bhenckert@henckert.com; ⏰ 08.00–17.00 Mon–Fri, closed Sat–Sun. This landmark is a first-class curio shop that doubles as a Namib I information centre. It began as a small gem shop in 1969, & now has a very large range of carvings & curios, including one of the country's best selections of Namibian semi-precious stones & gemstones. There's also a facility to change money if necessary, & a friendly café serving drinks & snacks. There's even a children's corner with eye-catching stones.

Where to stay

In town there's the choice of a backpackers' lodge and a country club, but there are also several guest farms nearby (see page 170).

🏠 **Angi's Self-Catering Guest House** (10 rooms) 315 Fracht Street; ☎ 064 550 126; e angis@iway.na. Offering self-catering or catered

accommodation in the centre of Karibib, en-suite rooms are equipped with AC, TV & a kitchenette with a fridge, microwave & kettle. There's a pool

& a restaurant (🕐 *for b/fast on request, lunch noon–14.00 & dinner 18.00–21.00*). **$$**

🏠 **Klippenberg Country Club & Guesthouse** \064 170693; 📱 081 124 8730. Near the mountainous outcrop known as Klippenberg, this is signposted on the main road. It has tennis courts, squash, a small golf course & a bar/restaurant that is popular with some of Karibib's residents. It's not really geared to tourists, but is hospitable enough if you drop by. **$$**

🏠 **Tommy's Lodge** (8 rooms, 16 dorm beds) 310 Hidipo Hamutenya St; \064 550081; e tommyslodge@gmail.com. At the eastern entrance to town on the B2, Tommy's is next to the Engen garage. With its painted walls & mature trees, it has a welcoming appearance, & is popular with backpackers. 3-bed rooms have en-suite facilities, while each of the 4 dorms sleeps 4 & shares facilities. It also has Wi-Fi, a pool, self-catering kitchen, BBQ area & secure parking. *Dorm bed N$160.* **$$**

✗ Where to eat and drink In addition to the hotels above, there's the OK minimarket bakery and café inside the OK supermarket, where you can sit and relax. If it's just a drink and a snack you're after, though, head for the simple café at the Henckert Tourist Centre (see page 169).

Other practicalities Karibib boasts an OK **supermarket** next to Tommy's Lodge, and an Engen fuel station with attached bakery and ATM, as well as a **post office** and a branch of the FNB bank. There's also a garage on the main road where staff can carry out vehicle repairs.

In an **emergency**, the police are reached on \064 10111, the ambulance on \064 530192, and the fire service on \064 550016.

What to see and do The town is dotted with several **historic buildings** dating from the early 1900s. Back then, Karibib was an important overnight stop on the railway between Windhoek and Swakopmund, as well as a trade centre. Ask at the information centre for their brief guide to the town.

There are a few **hiking trails** into the rolling landscapes south of town, behind the country club. In town itself, the Club Western Gambling and Entertainment Centre, and its adjacent Club Western Restaurant, seem to be the focus of local excitement although, as an alternative, the town's cemetery is beautifully lit at night!

The **gold mine** has occasional site tours, but requires a minimum of ten people for a tour. For these, enquire at the information centre (in advance, if possible).

🏠 **Around Karibib: guest farms** *Map, page 160.*

🏠 **Albrechtshöhe Guest Farm** (5 rooms) \062 503363; e meyer@iafrica.com.na; www. safariwest.de. Albrechtshöhe is off the D1988, about 2km south of the main B2, 92km west of Okahandja & 26km from Karibib. It's a traditional guest farm, run by Paul-Heinz & Ingrid Meyer, which started life as a railway station. Because of the natural springs of the area, the Schutztruppe completed Albrechtshöhe in 1906 to provide water for horses & steam trains. Today these historic, fortified buildings house the guest farm. Activities include bush walks & game drives as well as hikes to explore the local mountains; on site, there's a small swimming pool. Like many Namibian guest farms, this is also a hunting farm. *DBB N$680/1,360 sgl/dbl.* **LL**

🏠 **Etusis Lodge** (7 bungalows, 5 tents, camping) \064 550826; e lodge@etusis. com; www.etusis.com. The turning for Etusis is signposted from the C32, about 19km south of Karibib. The lodge itself is 16km from the road, standing at the foot of the Otjipatera Mountains: a range of white marble.

Solid, comfortable bungalows with exposed wooden beams & attractive thatch have en-suite WC & showers. Each sleeps up to 4 people, & has 220V electricity, solar-heated water, minibar, AC & a ceiling fan. Simple 'luxury' tents on a concrete base stand nearby; 3 are en suite & 2 share clean communal facilities. The campsite is 19km from the lodge; 5 pitches, each with a BBQ & shade-cloth covered area, share ablutions. Central to the lodge itself is a large thatched building with a bar & dining area, small curio shop & TV/lounge – all overlooking a small swimming pool. There are also limited conference facilities & free Wi-Fi Activities include scenic drives in search of impala, kudu, mountain zebra, leopard, jackal & blesbok, horseriding & the opportunity to hike unguided in the mountains behind the lodge. *DBB bungalow N$1,125–1,250; tent N$837–930; camping N$110 pp.* **LL**

Usakos This small town, 147km from Swakopmund, used to be the centre of the country's railway industry, though now it's little more than a stop on the line between Windhoek and Walvis Bay, with banks and fuel to tempt those who might otherwise pass right through. The Namib I information centre is useful if you're planning to do much exploration of the local area.

Where to stay, eat and drink

🏠 **Bahnhof Hotel** (14 rooms) Theo-Ben Gurirab St; 📞064 530444; e websmith@iway.na; www.erongominerals.com/bahnhof. The 2-star Bahnhof, located next to the post office, is fully licensed with an à la carte restaurant, bar, beer garden & undercover off-street parking. Each en-suite room has AC, satellite TV, Wi-Fi & a phone. Birdwatching & local Bushman art are on offer at the nearby Mansfield farm. At the time of writing, Bahnhof was closed for renovations with tentative plans to reopen sometime in 2015. **$$$**

🏠 **Jodo Tours & B&B** (4 rooms) 93 Victoria St; 📞064 530578; m 081 129 0611; e jodotours@ mweb.com.na, www.jodotours.com. Owned by Tina Weiwadel, this small company offers lodge safaris through Namibia geared towards mature travellers. They run operations from their base, a guesthouse in Usakos, clearly signposted from the main road. Overlooking a small, plain courtyard, each of the simple en-suite rooms has a small wardrobe, plus twin beds covered in colourful, big-print duvets. **$$**

✕ **Namib Oasis Farmstall and Deli** 1km west of Usakos on B2 to Swakopmund; 📞064 530283; e namiboasis.deli@iway.na; ⏲ 07.00–19.00 daily. On the outskirts of town, this surprising find is the best place to stop for a good meal. They serve farm-style meals, burgers, sandwiches & lunch specials with a free pint of beer, plus a collection of local crafts for sale. **$$$**

Other practicalities If you need **money** then there's a branch of FNB, and for **supplies** try the mini market at Engen, Lewis Stores or the Usakos Self-help (which is a shop, not a therapy group). These, like the **fuel stations**, are all on Theo-Ben Gurirab Street – the erstwhile Bahnhof Street.

In an **emergency**, the police are reached on 📞 064 10111, the ambulance and fire service on 📞 064 530023 (*a/h* m *081 485 4875*), and the hospital on 📞 064 530067.

Around Usakos: guest farms *Map, page 160.*

🏠 **Ameib Guesthouse** (7 rooms, 3 bungalows, 2 cabins, camping) m 081 857 4639; e ameib@erongosafaris.com; www.ameib.com/ site/guesthouse.html. Ameib has been accepting guests for years, & is quite idiosyncratic, but it does have superb rock formations & excellent rock art, so is worth a visit. Approaching from the east on the B2, turn right towards Swakopmund in the centre of town, then immediately right again, on to the D1935. This turning can be inconspicuous: there's a small sign to Ameib on your right as you turn, & a hospital on your left. (From Swakopmund, if you reach the main junction in the centre of town, you have missed the turning.) From here, follow the gravel D1935 for 12km to a signposted right turn on to the D1937. The landscape is beautiful: a little like Damaraland's vegetation, with sparse cover on the hillsides, & lush river valleys. About 5km further (on poor gravel) you reach Ameib's imposing gates. Another 11km brings you to the ranch, set among rounded granite boulders in the Erongo Mountains. Its rooms & bungalows are large & clean, with en-suite facilities, but uninspiring décor: they are functional, but not beautiful. The rooms & bungalows are very similar, except that the bungalows are separate from the house, although still very close. The campsite has a pool & braai area. En-suite cabins offer a self-catering option close to the campsite.

Visitors come here mainly for the excellent rock paintings. Many are within Phillip's Cave, a large eyelash-shaped cave made famous by Abbé Breuil's *Rock Paintings of Southern Africa* (see *Appendix 3*, page 532). It's a classic site for Bushman art, & the paintings here include a famous elephant, giraffe & red sticklike people. Getting there is a 1.8km drive from the ranch itself, followed by a 30min trail (15mins at a fast,

serious hiking pace). If possible, do this in the cool of the morning.

There are also unusual rock formations, like the Bull's Party – a group of large rounded boulders which (allegedly) look like a collection of bulls talking together. These are about 5.2km from the main ranch, & around them are lots of unusually shaped rocks, including mushroom-shaped & balancing boulders – worth exploring for an afternoon. *DBB rooms N$825/1,620 sgl/dbl; bungalows N$975/1,900 sgl/dbl; cabin N$450 pp B&B; camping N$138.* **LLL**

EAST FROM WINDHOEK

The main tarred B6, west to Windhoek and east into Botswana, is part of the Trans-Kalahari Highway that links Walvis Bay with South Africa's Gauteng Province (the area around Johannesburg and Pretoria). There's little of interest to visitors before Gobabis. Even the fuel station at **Witvlei** has closed, though there's still a post office – and perhaps one day the attractive restcamp, Ziegie's, will reopen.

GOBABIS This busy town, standing at the centre of an important cattle-farming area on the western edges of the Kalahari, forms Namibia's gateway into Botswana via the Buitepos border post, about 110km further east. The B6 bypasses the town, which lies on the C20. With its wide, tree-lined avenues and many shops and businesses, it's a prosperous-looking community. As such, it's an ideal place to use the banks, fill up with fuel or get supplies before heading east towards Ghanzi, where most goods aren't so easily available. However, it's less interesting as a stopover.

Getting there and away Most visitors to Gobabis are driving through on the main road. With trains between Windhoek and Gobabis no longer operating, this is the only realistic means of reaching the town.

Tourist information

Uakii Wilderness Survival/Gobabis Information Centre [173 C2] 62 Church St; 062 564743; m 081 252 1270; e contact@ gobabis.net; www.gobabis.net; ⊕ 08.00–17.00 summer, 07.30–16.30 winter. Something of a one-stop shop it offers tourist information, game drives & tours of the region & specialises in cultural, historical & community-based tourism, both locally & further afield. There is also a campsite (currently closed due to fire damage, see page 174) & a café (see page 174), with plans for a guesthouse, craft shop, cultural centre & even a swimming pool.

🏠 Where to stay *Map, opposite.*

If you want to stay in the area for a few days, then consider one of the guest farms in the vicinity (see pages 175–6). Nearer town are several possibilities, including:

🏠 **Horizons** (18 rooms, 11 flats) Mark St; 062 564878; e kalaharicc@iway.na. The restaurant offers a number of rooms with en-suite baths, TV & kettle. Outside is a long swimming pool & secure parking. **$$**

🏠 **Onze Rust** (5 rooms) 95 Rugby St; 062 562214, 081 128 4668; e onzerust@iafrica. na; www.natron.net/tour/onzerust. An attractive courtyard garden is the focus for a lounge/dining area & purpose-built rooms. These are en suite

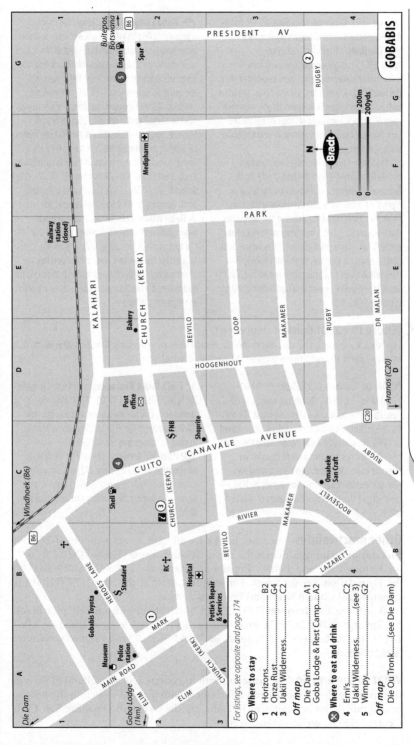

GOBABIS

For listings, see opposite and page 174

Where to stay
1 Horizons..................................B2
2 Onze Rust...............................G4
3 Uakii Wilderness....................C2

Off map
   Die Dam..................................A1
   Goba Lodge & Rest Camp......A2

Where to eat and drink
4 Erni's.......................................C2
   Uakii Wilderness..............(see 3)
5 Wimpy.....................................G2

Off map
   Die Ou Tronk.............(see Die Dam)

with sgl, dbl & family permutations, AC, TV, fridge & private braai facilities. Secure parking. **$$**

🏠 **Die Dam** (10 chalets, camping) \062 565656; e gobabisdam@mweb.com.na; www.transkalahariendresort.com. Located next to the small Tilda Viljoen Dam, Die Dam is an attractive spot just a short drive from town. As you approach from Windhoek, turn right off the C20 before the arch over the road, then right again, past the police station, following the signs.

Thatched, brick-built chalets are compact but well designed with a dbl bed, 2 sgls above, & a small kitchenette in each room. There's also a private terrace with BBQ overlooking the dam. As well as 7 tree-shaded pitches at the campsite, there are pre-erected 3-bed tents with electricity, kettle & fan. This is primarily a holiday venue, with paddle boats on the lake, freshwater fishing & minigolf, & there's an interesting restaurant, Die Ou Tronk (see below), as well as a bar. *B/fast N$60 pp; camping N$80.* **$$**

🏠 **Goba Lodge & Rest Camp** (28 rooms, 4 pitches) \062 564499; e goba@iway.na; www.goba.iway.na/. Signposted 1km west of town, this well-maintained site overlooks the Black Nossob River. Dbl & family rooms at the lodge have all the usual accoutrements – TV, AC, tea-making facilities, & some rooms have safes. The restcamp, next to a small enclosure with ostrich, oryx & blesbok, has both a campsite & simple twin rooms, all sharing an ablution block, kitchen & TV room. Guests can dine inside or out at the à la carte River Restaurant (⊕ *07.00–21.00 Mon–Fri, 07.00–noon & 16.00–21.00 Sat–Sun*). There's also a (fenced) pool. *Camping N$90 & N$30 per vehicle.* **$$**

⚊ **Uakii Wilderness** In the centre of town, a campsite with ablution facilities is located at the tourist office (see page 172), & is ideally located for backpackers, with secure parking, too. Unfortunately, at the time of research the campsite had suffered a fire & so was closed. There are plans to reopen in the future.

✘ **Where to eat and drink** *Map, page 173.*
For snacks during the day there are several take-aways along Church Street, and a Wimpy next to the Engen garage. More substantial are:

✘ **Die Ou Tronk** \062 565656; ⊕ 07.00– 22.00 Mon–Fri, 08.00–20.00 Sat, noon–14.00 Sun. The restaurant at Die Dam is a must, if only for the setting: an old German prison, abandoned in 1966. Thick walls & heavy doors keep the cells cool, but today's inmates benefit from views over the dam, albeit through barred windows. Alongside traditional Afrikaans dishes such as *afval* (tripe) there's a tempting range of pizzas & grills. **$–$$$**

✘ **Erni's Pub & Restaurant** 29 Cuito Canavale Av; \062 565222; ⊕ 07.00–21.00 Mon–Sat, closed Sun. Erni has long gone, but you can still have a sandwich lunch or bubblegum milkshake, or dine on 'carpet-bag steak'. **$–$$$**

⚊ **Uakii Wilderness** The café at the tourist information office (see page 172) is pleasantly located on a shady veranda & offers several local dishes – including the inviting-sounding 'Uakii's dish'. **$**

Other practicalities The main **banks** are all here, as are a couple of 24-hour **fuel stations**. **Garages** include the useful Gobabis Toyota [173 B1] (\062 562081) on Heroes Lane and Pottie's Repairs and Services [173 B3] (\062 563148) for Hyundai on Reivilo Street. For **supplies**, start at the Spar [173 G2] at the crossroads of Church Street and President Avenue.

There's a private **hospital** [173 B2] on Church Street with adjacent **pharmacy**, Medipharm (\062 563983). In an **emergency**, the police are reached on \062 10111, the ambulance and hospital on \062 566200, and the fire service on \062 566666.

What to see and do The **museum**, with its collection of agricultural tools, is in the process of being moved and refurbished, with plans to reopen in the not too near future. If you're interested in crafts, try the dedicated **Omaheke San Craft Centre** [173 C4] on Roosevelt Street.

Around Gobabis: guest farms and lodges *Map, page 160.*

There is an assortment of fairly offbeat guest farms and lodges within reach of Gobabis, and several places geared up to catch people taking overnight stops on the Trans-Kalahari Highway. Next to the border post itself there's also East Gate Rest Camp (see page 176).

Sandüne Lodge (14 rooms, 7 tents, villa) m 081 143 7923; e sandune@mweb.com.na. This 3,400ha reserve south of Gobabis is 7.4km off the C22, down a narrow, sandy track & is home to blue & black wildebeest, giraffe, zebra & kudu, among others. It's a relatively new lodge, popular with groups. Rectangular buildings & metal-framed windows aren't initially appealing, but staff are welcoming, the rooms are well appointed & the game is close by in an open Kalahari setting. As well as various hiking trails, there are game drives, Bushman walks & visits to a Bushman village (*each N$250 pp*). *B&B rooms N$725–945; tents N$645.* **LL**

Kalahari Bushbreaks (8 rooms, camping) ☏ 062 568936; reservations ☏ 064 464 144; e enquiries@kalaharibushbreaks.com; www. kalaharibushbreaks.com. About 87km east of Gobabis, & 26km west of the Botswanan border, Kalahari Bushbreaks is 3km south of the main B6, & clearly signposted. Owned & run by Ronnie & Elsabe Barnard, it's an established lodge on a working farm, with 40km² under game, including eland, oryx, giraffe, kudu, red hartebeest, warthog, zebra (both Burchell's & Hartmann's mountain) & blue & black wildebeest. Several species of antelope that wouldn't normally be found in the Kalahari are here, too, such as waterbuck & blesbok (both normal & albino). Predators include cheetah, leopard & caracal.

The main lodge building consists of a warm, enclosed lounge & bar area with high thatched ceiling. Above this are 3 cosy en-suite bedrooms under the eaves, with another 4 in purpose-built chalets close by, & 2 more, set slightly apart, sharing a huge private lounge/dining area that overlooks the bush. All are attractively decorated making good use of wood, reeds & leather. 2 campsites – one with power & the other more rustic – are close to the entrance, but campers are welcome (with advance notice) to take part in activities & meals at the lodge (*lunch N$110, dinner N$230*). The food is good, & there's an interesting choice of wines, personally selected from independent vineyards.

A large boma area, ringed with thatch but open to the stars, forms part of a spacious outdoor eating area, with a central fire & canvas 'walls' for cooler evenings. Reflecting Ronnie's profession of architecture, it's been carefully designed with solid wood on a large scale. Be aware that there are a few animal trophies on the walls, & that the farm is occasionally used for hunting – although hunting & photographic guests are kept separate.

Many visitors simply stop over here, but others try out the various walking trails or the 20km 4x4 trail, which visits interesting sites such as local rock engravings, & guided bush walks (*N$180 pp*) are also offered. *B&B N$760–1,050/1,680–2,250 sgl/ dbl. Camping N$60–100 pp.* **LLL**

Zelda Game & Guest Farm (16 rooms, 10 pitches) ☏ 062 560427; e bookings@ zeldaguestfarm.com; zeldaguestfarm@iway. na; www.zeldaguestfarm.com. About 90km east of Gobabis, & 20km west of the border, Zelda is 1.3km north of the B6. Half of the 100km² farm is dedicated to game, & the rest to cattle farming. Most people use the farm, with its 'Baboona' bar, restaurant (*dinner N$150*), souvenir stall & leafy, almost tropical garden, as a stopover. For action, there's a cool pool for those hot Kalahari days, or you can watch leopard being fed each afternoon. Rather more interesting are farm trails accompanied by a local Bushman tracker, or visits to the !Xhananga village on their 'Be Wild' programme to learn more about the traditions of these people – or indeed to stay overnight. At the farm itself, rooms with AC – some in the house & others in the grounds – are decidedly ornate in décor. There's a good campsite, too, with space for independents & overland groups. *B&B N$580/940 sgl/dbl; camping N$70 pp.* **LL**

Harnas Guest Farm (3 cottages, 3 'igloos', camping) ☏ 062 568828/38; m 081 140 3322; e bookings@harnas.org; www.harnas.org. Almost 100km northeast of Gobabis, Harnas probably has the highest profile of any guest farm in the region. To get here, take the B6 east from Gobabis & turn left after about 6km on to the C22. After 12.5km of tar, this reverts to a wide gravel road for about 30km until it reaches a Harnas sign at Drimiopsis, when you take a right. About 7.5km further on the road branches & you keep left. Continue for a further 38km & the entrance to Harnas is on the left.

Once a cattle farm, Harnas has evolved into a sanctuary for injured & orphaned animals – including several wild dogs – & now houses over 200 of them. The Harnas Wildlife Foundation has several projects, which include the rehabilitation & reintroduction of animals wherever possible. Another key element of the farm's activities is a medical outreach project focusing on AIDS prevention & bringing specialist services such as cataract operations to the local people. The foundation runs a volunteer scheme, too; for details, see their website.

Spread around quite a large grassy area are brick-built cottages, overlooking a waterhole, & stone igloo-style bungalows. All are en suite & equipped with AC, kitchenettes & braai areas. Backing this up is a campsite with 3 pitches, each with power, kitchen, braai areas & a central ablution block. Though many self cater, simple set menus (*b/fast N$60, lunch N$75, dinner N$150*) are available with advance notice. There's also a large swimming pool. Activities centre around morning & evening animal feeding tours (*N$165–275 pp*), sundowner drives (*N$275 pp*) & – by prior arrangement – horseriding (*N$150 pp/hr*). Note that any guest not taking part in an activity will be charged the day visitor's fee of N$165 pp. *DBB N$1,470–1,745/2,060–2,500 sgl/dbl; camping N$200 pp; day visitor N$165 pp.* **LLL**

CROSSING THE BORDER INTO BOTSWANA The Buitepos border (⊕ *06.00–23.00 winter; 07.00–midnight summer*) is suitable for 2WD vehicles. There's little on the other side apart from a border post until you reach the small Kalahari cattle-farming town of Ghanzi.

Gobabis is probably the best place for **hitching** from Namibia into Botswana, as many trucks pass this way. Don't accept anything that will stop short of the border at Buitepos, and do carry plenty of food and water. Please consider the risk you are taking by getting into a stranger's vehicle.

⌂ Where to stay, eat and drink *Map, page 160.*

⌂ East Gate Rest Camp (13 bungalows, 13 cabins, camping) ✆ 062 560405; e bookings. eastgate@iway.na; www.eastgate-namibia. com. This well-maintained site, with shady trees & neat paths, is a haven for travellers, offering fuel (⊕ *06.00–midnight*), a shop & a restaurant (*both* ⊕ *06.00–22.00*). Turquoise-&-cream-painted bungalows & cabins & a grassy campsite attract visitors to break a long journey. En-suite bungalows with AC vary in standard & size, from 1 bedroom with kitchen to 2 bedrooms with TV & phone, sleeping 6. Simple twin-bed cabins share facilities. The camp also has a swimming pool. *Bungalow N$600–1,200 (2–6 people); cabin N$180 pp; camping N$80 pp.* **LL**

DORDABIS The tiny town of Dordabis, at the end of the tarred C23 to the southeast of Windhoek, is closer to the capital than Gobabis. Set in a beautiful valley covered with tall acacia trees, and between rounded, bush-covered hills, it has a township just outside the centre.

In recent years the area has attracted attention as the base for several artists and craftspeople, especially weavers, although Dorka Teppiche was closed in 2008 and the equipment donated to the Dorkambo Co-operative near Ondangwa (✆ 065 248 155; m 081 211 0048), who continue to produce karakul rugs, among other items.

Other practicalities The town has few facilities aside from a police station, a fuel station (⊕ *08.00–19.00 daily*) and a shop selling a limited selection of food and drink (⊕ *08.00–13.00 & 15.00–18.00 Mon–Fri, 08.00–13.00 Sat, closed Sun*).

TO SAVE OR NOT TO SAVE

Several farms, often driven by kind individuals with the very best of motives, have set up 'orphanage' or 'rehabilitation' programmes in Namibia for injured/ unwanted animals. Before visiting, it's perhaps worth considering the logic of some of the arguments for this, and perhaps discussing the issues with your hosts while there.

Some aim just to keep alive damaged or orphaned animals, some of which can be rehabilitated and released, though others can't be. The problems of keeping, say, a small orphaned antelope like a bushbuck are minimal. However, the problems caused by big cats are more major. Keeping such carnivores is difficult, as they need to be in very secure pens. Further, animals need to be killed to feed them. If it's a kindness to keep an injured lion alive, what about the horses, cows or antelope that are slaughtered to feed it? Why is the lion's life more valuable than the herbivores'?

Demand for visitors to see big cats and other 'sexy' species close up makes keeping habituated big cats a potentially lucrative draw for a guest farm. (Note that I don't use the term 'tame' as neither lions nor leopards ever seem to become anything like truly tame.) So is this why it's done?

Cynics claim that it's far from pure compassion. They question why there's a paucity of rescue centres for, say, black-faced impala, a species that is seriously endangered and rare. They're very beautiful and well worth preserving – but are they sexy enough to attract guests? Probably not, the cynics observe.

Most pragmatic conservationists focus on preserving environments and species, believing that individual animals are much less important. They don't see the point in spending time and money keeping a lion alive when the same money could go towards preserving a whole ecosystem elsewhere.

One could argue, however, that when well run, such projects generate large incomes from visitors. This cash can then be used to fund serious, necessary (but perhaps less attractive) research programmes, or education programmes, which really do benefit Africa's wildlife on a much broader scale. That's a fine argument – but if it's the case, and this is their rationale for keeping caged animals as an attraction to raise money, then the cynics argue that it's time such organisations came clean.

🔲 Where to stay Map, page 160.

Many of the guest farms in the area around Dordabis and Gobabis promote hunting rather than just watching game, though there is a handful of exceptions. All are unusual, and worth a visit:

Eningu Clayhouse Lodge (9 chalets)
062 581880; e info@eningulodge.com; www. eningulodge.com. Just 1hr's drive (65km) south of the international airport, Eningu is 5km from the D1471, close to its junction with the M51. On the fringes of the Kalahari, surrounded by bush-covered dunes on the fringes, it's an environment of round eroded hills, beloved of masked weaver birds, with perhaps a little Kalahari sand when the grass dies down. It is one of Namibia's most original small

lodges, with a strong connection with the arts that owner Bettina Spoerndle is likely to maintain.

The semi-detached chalets & family chalet are constructed, as the name suggests, of Kalahari clay bricks, though the apricot adobe effect & boxy design give more than a hint of Mexico. Each has a cool, rustic interior, comfortably furnished with batik bedding, gourd lampshades & colourful cushions, while enchanting portrait photos add a touch of class. Painted floors are dotted with locally woven rugs, & smooth concrete bases ensure the beds are scorpion- & snake-free. There are fans for summer & gauze windows – even in the en-suite shower – are effective at catching the cool evening breeze. In winter, guests are given hot water bottles.

A small thatched veranda, mosquito nets, ceiling fans & a tea/coffee station add to the creature comforts.

Eningu's attention to detail stretches beyond the chalets to the kitchen, where innovative dishes are prepared from fresh ingredients & served in an intimate dining area. There's a comfy lounge, too, & an underground 'cellar' off the attractive boma stocking a range of wines. A bird hide makes a great venue for a sundowner, overlooking a waterhole that's floodlit after dark – when porcupines are fed daily.

Activities include 3 marked walking trails & a longer hiking trail, plus archery, volleyball & badminton, though lounging by the swimming pool & whirlpool-jacuzzi is equally popular. Visits to the local sculptor Dorte Berner, game drives on the adjacent farm & other local tours can be organised with at least 2 days' notice. This is a tranquil & well-run little lodge, perfect for a first/last night in Namibia. *DBB N$1,250/2,300 sgl/dbl.* **LLL**

🏠 **Arnhem Cave & Restcamp** (4 chalets, camping) ☎062 581885; 📱081 252 8777; 📧arnhem@mweb.com.na. Arnhem is on the D1808, about 4km south of its junction with the D1506. From the airport take the B6–M51–D1506–D1808; from Gobabis turn left at Witvlei on to the D1800–D1808.

The main attraction here is a cave system, claimed to be the longest in Namibia & the 6th-longest so far discovered in Africa, with about 4.5km of passages. It's thought to have been a home for bats for around 9,500 years, & still probably contains about 15,000 tonnes of bat guano, despite it being mined on & off for the last 70 years. Six species of bat have been identified here, including the giant leaf-nosed bat – the world's largest insectivorous bat. There are also shrews, spiders, beetles, water shrimps & various invertebrates, some of which are endemic to the cave.

Though very dusty, & not at all fun for claustrophobics, there are guided trails through the cave, departing daily at 09.00 & 15.00 & lasting around 2hrs (*N$150 pp*) or 2½hrs (*N$200 pp*). Dress in old clothes & bring a torch (or hire one).

The small restcamp has good, thatched chalets with twin beds, fridges & a couple of mattresses on a platform above, as well as grassy camping sites & a swimming pool. Wood is for sale & braai facilities are provided, but meals must be booked in advance. *Chalet self-catering N$325/576 sgl/dbl; camping N$150 pp.* **L**

🏠 **Kiripotib Guest Farm** (14 rooms, 2 chalets, 2 luxury tents) ☎062 581419; 📧info@kiripotib.com; www.kiripotib.com. The engaging Hans Georg & Claudia von Hase run this friendly guest farm on the D1448, just 12km from its junction with the M33 (C15) & about 2hrs' drive from Windhoek airport. It's also the base for several other ventures: a thriving little arts & crafts business (*day visitors welcome, ⊕ all day*), a gliding centre, an observatory, & African Kirikara Safaris, which offers mobile safaris around the region.

Kiripotib's spacious accommodation – all en suite with separate WC – is split between pleasant rooms laid out around an attractive garden & pool, & brick-built chalets with AC set in open grassland, with two luxury tents. Meals (*lunch N$105, dinner N$195*), including home-grown produce (& even freshly squeezed orange juice in season), are served in an extensive thatched lapa, or around the fire under the stars. For winter evenings, a cosy sitting room has a small library.

Perhaps the most interesting aspect of Kiripotib is its craftwork. You can visit the spinning workshop & weavery, where a variety of unique Namibian carpets are made from karakul wool & displayed – along with other arts & crafts – in the gallery. If you're planning to buy one, at around N$2,200 per m², bring colours & fabric samples to Kiripotib or one of their shops in Swakopmund or Windhoek, so the team can make up one of their designs to match your colours & sizes as closely as possible. (Obviously this takes time, but there is no extra charge, & they send regular shipments to Europe, so delivery is easily arranged.) Also on site, thanks to Claudia's training as a goldsmith, is a small jewellery workshop which, when in full production, makes fascinating viewing.

More traditional are farm & game drives (*from N$280 pp*) in this classic Kalahari landscape. There are walking trails, too, & it's possible to arrange a drive & ½-day walk in the Karubeams Mountains (*N$230 pp*), where it takes 1–2hrs to climb on to a lovely plateau, with a fair chance of seeing oryx, kudu & klipspringer. Expert pilots can take to the skies in a glider; for details, see the website. Finally, for the serious astronomer the lodge has its own small observatory with a sliding roof & a computer-controlled reflecting telescope. *B&B chalet N\$1,240/2,080 sgl/dbl; room N\$990/1,650 sgl/dbl; tent N\$790/1,340 sgl/dbl.* **LLL**

SOUTH FROM WINDHOEK

REHOBOTH Just north of the Tropic of Capricorn and 87km south of Windhoek on the tarred B1, Rehoboth is the centre of the country's Baster community (see pages 18–19), which is quite different from any of Namibia's other ethnic groups, and jealously guards its remaining autonomy. Sadly, it's little more than a scruffy bottle-shop town and there are few reasons to stop here; other than the museum, most people pass on through.

Getting there and away If you're without a vehicle and want to visit Rehoboth, it's possible to get there by train or coach.

By bus Intercape's coaches from Windhoek to Cape Town stop at the Shell service station on the corner of Springbok Street and the B1, at 18.00 on Monday, Wednesday, Friday and Sunday, and return at 05.10 on Tuesday, Thursday, Friday and Sunday. These cost around N\$845 to Cape Town and a very steep N\$380 from Windhoek. Note that seats on buses to Windhoek must now be prebooked. See pages 101–2 for more details.

By train Trains depart from Rehoboth for Windhoek at 04.00 daily except Saturday, and for Keetmanshoop at 21.40. However, not only are the trains very slow (see pages 98–100), but the station is too far north of the town to walk, so this is rarely a good option for visitors.

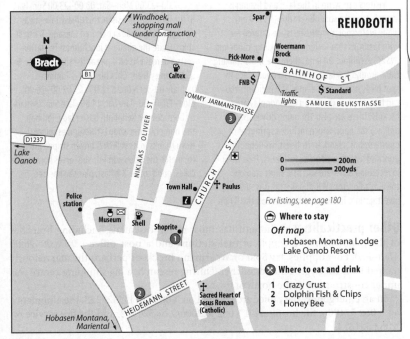

REHOBOTH

Windhoek, shopping mall (under construction)

Spar

Pick-More

Woermann Brock

BAHNHOF ST

N

Bradt

B1

Caltex

FNB

Standard

Traffic lights

SAMUEL BEUKSTRASSE

TOMMY JARMANSTRASSE

NIKLAAS OLIVIER ST

CHURCH ST

3

D1237

Lake Oanob

0 — 200m
0 — 200yds

Town Hall

Paulus

Police station

Museum   Shell   Shoprite

1

For listings, see page 180

Where to stay

Off map
　Hobasen Montana Lodge
　Lake Oanob Resort

Where to eat and drink
1　Crazy Crust
2　Dolphin Fish & Chips
3　Honey Bee

HEIDEMANN STREET

2

Sacred Heart of Jesus Roman (Catholic)

Hobasen Montana, Mariental

Tourist information There is a tourist information office on Church Street (✆ 081 2832526; ⏰ 08.00–13.00 & 14.00–17.00 Mon–Fri).

🏠 Where to stay, eat and drink *Map, page 179.*

🏠 **Lake Oanob Resort** (9 rooms, 13 chalets, camping) ✆062 522370; e reservations@ oanob.com.na; www.oanob.com.na. Created in 1990 following construction of the highest dam in Namibia, Lake Oanob Resort is now run by a Swiss-Namibian couple, Helena & Christie Bernade-Bruhin. En-suite dbl & family rooms have rustic furnishings, & each has a small veranda – ideal for checking out the night sky – while chalets, all overlooking the lake, are extremely well equipped for a longer stay. Campers have a choice of shady sites, priced according to facilities & location. The resort's à la carte restaurant & bar by the waterfront (⏰ 08.00–20.00 Sun–Thu, 08.00–22.00 Fri–Sat) is relaxed & friendly, and is open to both day visitors and overnight guests. Nearby, with lovely views over the dam, is the new Giraffe pool bar (⏰ 1 Sept–end Mar) with jacuzzi & heated pool where you can order drinks from the water; nonguests can use it for N$30 (towels & lockers provided). Beside this in an infinity pool & shallow kids' pool open all year.

Visitors can swim in the lake and fishing is available, as are speedboat trips (*N$150 pp*), while watersports enthusiasts are catered for with facilities that include waterskiing, canoeing (*N$20*) & tubing. On land, there are short walking trails around the lake, which is a good place to spot birds such as fish eagles and pelicans. You can hire a bike & there's an outdoor play area for kids. There are also 1hr game drives (*N$150 pp*) into the park, which includes springbok, giraffe, zebra, eland, hartebeest, wildebeest, oryx and ostrich among its residents. Free Wi-Fi in reception & restaurant. As a short stop on the way to or from Windhoek, this is well worth investigating. To reach it, turn west off the B1 on to the D1280 about 6km north of Rehoboth, and follow this for around 7km. From the south, take the D1237 as far as the crossroads, then turn left and continue for a further 3km. *Camping N$70– 130 pp; day visitor N$30 pp.* $$$–$$$$

🏠 **Hobasen Montana Lodge** (4 rooms) ✆062 525704; m 081 256 9962; e cloejp@iway. na. A grand name belies this simple stone-built lodge, perched above the B1 about 2km south of town. It's run by Vicky Cloete, her son & 4 small dogs. En-suite rooms have twin beds, a fridge, kettle & cups & tea/coffee, & there's now 2 new grass-surrounded swimming pools. A hot b/fast costs N$60 & other meals usually available on request. There's a small charge to use their Wi-Fi & they can provide a shuttle to town on request. $$

✗ **Crazy Crust** Church St; ✆062 522292; ⏰ 08.00–22.00 Mon–Thu, 08.00–midnight Fri–Sat, 08.00–20.00 Sun. Low-key fast-food joint serving pizzas & burgers, as well as ice cream & waffles. $–$$

✗ **Dolphin Fish and Chips** ✆062 524400; ⏰ 07.00–23.00 Mon–Sat, 08.00–23.00 Sun. Part of the local supplies shop, this greasy take-away does a roaring trade in battered sausage, & fish & chips. Quite the queue at lunchtimes! The latter costs a bargain N$14 – pay at the shop counter. $

🍽 **Honey Bee** Cnr Church St & Tommy Jarmanstrasse; ✆062 522777; ⏰ 07.00–20.00 Mon–Fri, 07.00–late Sat, 14.00–late Sun. Owned by born-&-bred Rehoboth Baster lady, Terlinah, this homely coffee shop is the sunniest place in town thanks to its yellow & brown striped interior (to match the café's name!). She serves homemade cakes, good coffee & b/fast, plus she has free Wi-Fi. $

Other practicalities Rehoboth has most of the essentials, including branches of the major **banks**, a couple of **fuel stations** and a **post office** (⏰ 08.00–16.00 Mon–Fri). For **supplies**, try Spar or Woermann Brock, or perhaps the marvellously named Pick-More grocer and butcher. During research, a big shopping centre was under construction in the north of town.

In an **emergency**, the police are reached on ✆062 10111/523223, the ambulance on ✆062 521900, the hospital on ✆062 522006/7 or 524502, and the fire service on ✆062 521814.

What to see and do Rehoboth's only real attraction for visitors is its small museum (◊ 062 522954; www.rehobothmuseum.com; ⏰ 09.00–noon & 14.00–16.00 Mon–Fri, 08.00–noon Sat, closed Sun, and Sat in winter; admission N$25/10 adult/child), which has good local history exhibits on the origins of the Baster community, and the flora and fauna in the surrounding area, as well as an unexpected but interesting section on banknotes.

SOUTH OF REHOBOTH South of Rehoboth on the B1, a fuel station with a take-away at the small town of **Kalkrand** is probably the only reason for most drivers to stop.

If you're heading **southwest** towards Sesriem along the C24 (MR47), after about 94km you'll come across a road sign showing a cup and saucer:

✗ **Connie's Restaurant** [Map, page 160] ◊ 062 539014; f 062 539018. Connie's warm welcome, larger-than-life personality & home-baked cookies make this the perfect place for a break when driving to Sossusvlei. With advance warning she offers B&B (**$$**) & will prepare lunch (but there's no electricity). Her place is well signposted, 1km off the road, about a ½hr drive from Klein Aub; you can't miss it. **$$$**

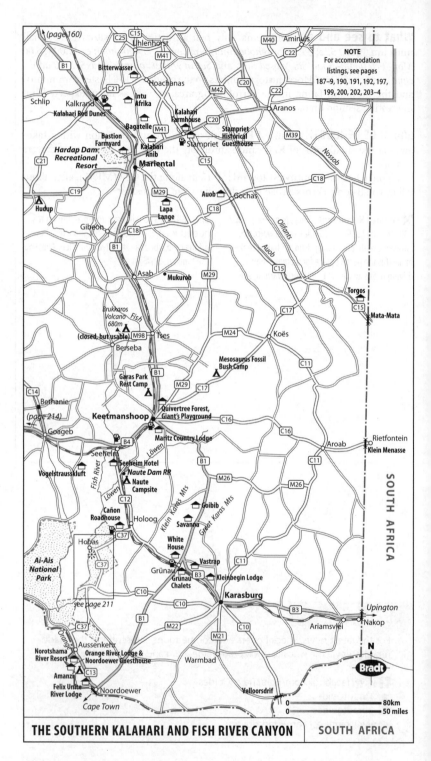

THE SOUTHERN KALAHARI AND FISH RIVER CANYON   SOUTH AFRICA

10

The Southern Kalahari and Fish River Canyon

If you have journeyed north from South Africa's vast parched plateau, the Karoo, or come out of the Kalahari from the east, then the arid landscapes and widely separated towns of southern Namibia will be no surprise. Like the towns, the region's main attractions are far apart: the Fish River Canyon, Brukkaros, the Quivertree Forest, and scattered lodges of the Kalahari.

Perhaps because of their separation, they receive fewer visitors than the attractions further north, so if you want to go hiking, or to sleep out in a volcano, or just to get off the common routes – then this southern side of the country is the perfect area to do it.

MARIENTAL

Despite being the administrative centre of the large Hardap Region, which stretches from the Atlantic coast to Botswana, Mariental still avoids being a centre of attention by having remarkably few attractions – and on Sundays it's a ghost town. It is central and has a sprinkling of efficient businesses, ranging from the Desert Optics optometrist to the Spar supermarket on the north side of town, serving the prosperous surrounding farmlands. By and large it contains very little of interest. Visitors view it as a place to go through, rather than to, often skirting around the town on the main B1 – stopping only for fuel and cold drinks, if they stop at all.

Standing on the edge of the Kalahari Desert, in an area which has long been a centre for the Nama people of Namibia, Mariental gained its name from the area's first colonial settler, Herman Brandt, who called it 'Marie's Valley', after his wife.

This area receives virtually no rain some years, so Namibia's successful commercial farmers have diversified in order to survive. The (welcome) current trend towards managing native game rather than farm animals, and earning income directly from tourism, are just two examples of this. Similarly, the shrinking trade in pelts of karakul sheep – once so important to southern Namibia – seems to be concentrating around the town, while an ostrich abattoir has established Mariental as an important centre for the country's ostrich farming.

GETTING THERE AND AWAY

By car Approaching by car you can't miss Mariental. It's set slightly back, adjacent to the main B1, and is very well signposted. There are two main turnings for the town centre: one south of the larger side roads to Stampriet and Hardap Dam, and the other just north of the tarred C19 to Maltahöhe. Between the two is the

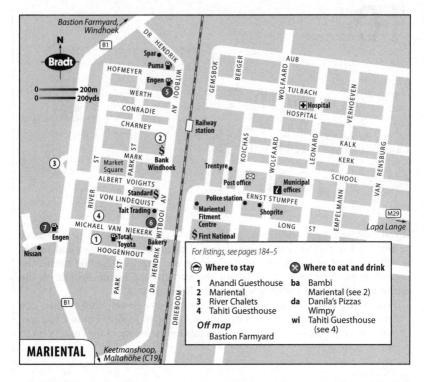

MARIENTAL | *Keetmanshoop,*
Maltahöhe (C19)

For listings, see pages 184–5

Where to stay

1 Anandi Guesthouse
2 Mariental
3 River Chalets
4 Tahiti Guesthouse

Off map
Bastion Farmyard

Where to eat and drink

ba Bambi
Mariental (see 2)
da Danila's Pizzas
Wimpy
wi Tahiti Guesthouse
(see 4)

modern, efficient Engen garage, which incorporates a Wimpy restaurant and small supermarket. The railway line from Windhoek south bisects the town, allowing only one crossing point (Michael van Niekerk Street).

By bus The Intercape service between Windhoek and Cape Town stops at Mariental, at the Engen station, at 21.25 on Monday, Wednesday, Friday and Sunday heading south, and then at 04.00 on Tuesday, Thursday, Friday and Sunday going north. Tickets cost around N$560 to Cape Town, N$230 to Keetmanshoop and N$250 to Windhoek, and must be booked in advance. See pages 101–2 for details.

Starline buses link Mariental with Gochas on Wednesday, leaving Mariental at 08.00 and returning at 15.30. There are also buses on Monday and Thursday to Maltahöhe, departing at 08.00 and returning at 15.00, and east to Aranos via Stampriet, leaving Mariental on Tuesday and Friday at 08.00, and returning at 16.30.

By train Mariental is linked to Windhoek and Keetmanshoop by a slow, overnight train service. It departs daily except Saturday for Keetmanshoop at 02.20 and for Windhoek at 00.20. See *Chapter 6*, pages 98–100, for details, or call TransNamib (✆ *063 249202*).

 WHERE TO STAY *Map, above.*

Anandi Guesthouse (9 rooms) 15 River St; ✆063 242220; m 081 241 1822; e anandi@iway.na; www.anandiguesthouse.com. The Anandi stands out with its lilac-painted block building behind high lilac walls. Both dbl & sgl rooms are en suite with DSTV,

AC or fan & a small walled balcony. 1 self-catering unit also available. B/fast (*N$50*) is served in a large, pleasant restaurant, with lunch on request. Has 10 parking places. The empty swimming pool can be filled on request. Free Wi-Fi, laundry on request. **$$**

Bastion Farmyard (5 rooms, camping) 063 240827; **m** 081 2745574; **e** bastion@iway. na; www.bastionfarmyard.com. Clearly signposted off the B1, this farmstay is 10km north of Mariental & offers an attractive alternative to in-town accommodation. Pleasant, light rooms are equipped with AC/heating & fans, kettles & hairdryers. B/fast is served in the farmhouse, & there's an excellent kitchen & courtyard braai area for those who are self-catering. A small shop (☼ *summer 08.00–13.00 & 14.00–18.00 Mon–Fri, 09.00–noon Sat, winter 08.00–13.00 & 14.00–17.00 Mon–Fri, 09.00–noon Sat*) sells homemade jams & preserves, drinks, braai packs & bread, as well as a few local crafts. Free Wi-Fi. *Camping N$120 pp*. **$$**

Mariental Hotel (28 rooms) Cnr Hendrik Witbooi Av & Charney Rd; 063 242466/7; **e** mrlhotel@iafrica.com.na; www.marientalhotel. com. The grey & dingy Mariental Hotel has sadly filled in its swimming pool & covered it with grass, & converted the gym into a conference room. Furthermore, the sports bar (☼ *14.00–23.00 Mon–Thu, 10.00–02.00 Fri–Sat*) & gambling house (☼ *10.00–23.00 Mon–Fri, 10.00–midnight Sat*) give the hotel a seedy feel despite the friendly service. All the rooms are en suite & equipped with AC, clock radio, coffee station & direct-dial phone. Caters mainly to businessmen. There is a reasonable restaurant (☼ *10.00–14.00 & 18.00–*

22.00 daily) serving grills & steaks, & a convenient car park at the back. Free Wi-Fi in main lounge. **$$**

River Chalets (4 rooms, 6 chalets, camping) 063 240515; **m** 081 128 2601; **e** garbers@iway.na; www.riverchalets.com. Run by South African Elrien Garbers, this well-priced option – located on the west side of the main B1 as it bypasses Mariental – has modern dbl or twin rooms with AC, DSTV, fridges & kettles, as well as 3-, 5- or 7-bed self-catering chalets with AC, DSTV, equipped kitchenette & BBQ facilities on patio. 10 camping plots also available. Aimed at families & small groups. Free 30min Wi-Fi in lounge, thereafter N$10/30mins. B/fast not served on site – take voucher (*N$65*) to Bambi café near petrol station. 20% discount when paying cash. *Camping N$140 pp*. **$$**

Tahiti Guesthouse (16 rooms) 66 Michael van Niekerk St; 063 240636; **e** Tahiti@iway. na. Looked after by smiley manager, Christa, this simple guesthouse has 6 dbls, the rest twin rooms set around a brick courtyard. Small, but clean, some are self-catering with TV, microwave, fridge, toaster & cutlery/pans. Wi-Fi stretches to rooms 1, 2, 4 & 5, & is available in the popular restaurant (☼ *07.00–21.00 Mon–Fri, 08.00–14.00 & 18.00–21.00 Sat, 10.00–14.00 Sun*) that serves good surf 'n' turf, pizzas, burgers & kids' options. B/fast N$65. Good budget option. **$$**

✘ **WHERE TO EAT AND DRINK** *Map, opposite.*

Options for dining are limited, but are listed below. For those just passing through, the main garages have facilities to bite-and-run: the Engen garage at the north end of town has the **Bambi** take-away, serving pies and simple meals, while the slick Engen garage on the B1 has a more extensive **Wimpy** with tables and menus. This serves what you'd find in any Wimpy across the world, and opens late into the evening.

✘ **Mariental Hotel** See above.
✘ **Tahiti Guesthouse** See above.
✘ **Danila's Pizzas** Dr Hendrik Witbooi Av; 081 3701 664; ☼ 07.30–21.00 Mon–Fri, 08.00–17.00 Sat, 10.00–18.00 Sun. Low-key pizza parlour. **$$$$**

✘ **Bakery** Cnr Dr Hendrik Witbooi Av & Hoogenhout; ☼ 07.30–15.30 Mon–Fri, 07.30–noon Sat. Local bakery that prepares sandwiches & sells soft drinks. **$**

OTHER PRACTICALITIES

$ Banks Bank Windhoek & Standard on Dr Hendrik Witbooi Av; FNB on Drieboom St. There's an additional ATM at the Engen fuel station on the B1.
✚ **Hospital** Hospital St; 063 242092
Mariental Fitment Centre Ernst Stumpfe Rd; 063 240840; a/h **m** 081 122 3080, 148

3441; ☼ 07.00–17.00 Mon–Fri, 08.00–noon Sat, closed Sun. This centre offers a call-out service for replacement tyres to anywhere in the country.
Police station Ernst Stumpfe St; 063 10111
✉ **Post office** Koichas St; 063 242000

Spar supermarket Dr Hendrik Witbooi Av;
⏰ 08.00–19.00 Mon–Fri, 08.00–15.00 Sat,
08.30–13.00 Sun
Tait Trading Dr Hendrik Witbooi Av; 📞063
240906; **m** 081 7963002; ⏰ 08.30–13.00 Mon–

Sat. Office supplies shop with photocopying &
internet facilities.
ℹ Tourist information office ⏰ Mon–Fri
only. Housed within the municipal offices.

HARDAP DAM RECREATIONAL RESORT

Sadly closed for renovations until further notice, Hardap Dam – situated less than
25km north of Mariental – dams the upper reaches of the Fish River, creating
Namibia's largest manmade lake and providing water for Mariental and various
irrigation projects.

The origin of Hardap's name is uncertain. It is probably derived from a Nama
name for a big pool that was flooded by the dam, although the word also means
'nipple' (or possibly 'wart') in the Nama language – and one of the rounded hills
around the dam is said to resemble a female breast.

The dam wall is 39.2m high and 865m long and was completed in 1963. It holds
a maximum of about 300 million cubic metres of water, and covers around 25km².
Occasionally, when the rains are exceptional, it fills. In 2006, February rains caused
the dam waters to rise so high that the authorities feared that the wall would burst.
The decision was taken to open the gates to ease the pressure, but too much water
was released, flooding the surrounding plain and leaving Mariental under about
1.7m of water, with massive consequential damage.

FLORA AND FAUNA Hardap stands in the central highlands of Namibia, and its
rolling hilly landscape is mostly covered in low-growing bushes and stunted trees.
Its river courses tend to be thickly vegetated, often having dense, taller stands of
camelthorn and buffalo-thorn trees.

The most interesting birds found here are often Cape species, at the northern
edge of their range, like the cinnamon-breasted warbler, the Karoo eremomela and
the uncommon Sclater's lark. Others are Namibian species towards the southern
edge of their ranges, like the delightful rosy-faced lovebirds. Among the waterbirds,
flocks of pelicans are a highlight.

Hardap's larger game includes Hartmann's mountain zebra, oryx, kudu,
springbok, eland and red hartebeest, most concentrated in the mountainous section
of the park. Cheetah used to occur, but they thrived and escaped on to neighbouring
farms, so now they have been excluded. This is classic leopard country, hilly and
thickly bushed – so these are the dominant predators, though they are seldom seen.
There are no lion, elephant or buffalo, but a handful of black rhino were relocated
here from Damaraland in 1990, and have settled towards the north of the park.

EAST OF MARIENTAL AND THE B1: THE KALAHARI

The Kalahari Desert often surprises people when they first see it. It is very different
from the Namib. First of all, remember that the Kalahari is not a true desert: it
receives more rain than a true desert should. The Kalahari is a *fossil* desert. The
box on page 36 gives a more complete explanation, but don't expect to find tall
Sossusvlei-style dunes devoid of greenery here. The Kalahari's dunes are very
different. They are often equally beautiful, but usually greener and less stark, and
with this vegetation comes the ability to support more flora and fauna – including
bat-eared foxes – than a true desert.

Thus a few days spent in a Kalahari environment adds another dimension to a trip to Namibia, and provides game-viewing away from the ever-popular Etosha, or the lush reserves of the Caprivi.

With the reopening of the Namibia–South Africa border at Mata-Mata (🕓 08.00–16.30), opportunities for tourism in the area southeast of Mariental are opening up as more people pass though. Mata-Mata links Namibia with the huge Kgalagadi Transfrontier Park, a truly integrated trans-national wildlife reserve between South Africa and Botswana that was Africa's first 'Peace Park' – although perhaps to the chagrin of the Kalahari Gemsbok's small band of existing devotees, who have always regarded this out-of-the-way corner as one of the best national parks on the subcontinent.

GUEST FARMS AND LODGES Map, page 182.

To the east of Mariental, on the Kalahari side, there are several excellent lodges/ guest farms. Of these, Bitterwasser (see page 189), and Kiripotib near Dordabis (see page 178), cater for accomplished glider pilots during the season, between November and February.

✳ 🏠 **Kalahari Red Dunes** (12 chalets)
📞 063 26 40 03; e info@redduneslodge.com; www.redduneslodge.com. Situated 8km south of Kalkrand & set against the stunning backdrop of the Kalahari's red sands & flaxen grasses, this lovely lodge is accessed via a 3km drive from the gate off the B1 along a smooth sand road. Its 12 chalets blend sympathetically into the surrounding landscape & are joined via a series of raised wooden walkways. All the spacious chalets – 10 dbls & 2 family rooms that sleep 4 – are named after animals & have their own shaded terrace with a couch & table with views across the quiet dunes. They're constructed from canvas tents attached to solid bathroom walls at the back & topped with a thatch roof. All have wooden floors & chunky dark wood furniture shipped over from Germany, & facilities include fridge/minibar with complimentary wine & drinks, tea/coffee station, hairdryer & combi AC/heat system; safes will be installed in future. Most rooms also have a real-wood fireplace for cold desert nights.

Note that all the beds are constructed from 2 single mattresses positioned on a single base – they can't be separated. The bathrooms have art built into the walls, huge walk-in showers & unique arty basins brought all the way from Germany.

The main chalet houses the reception, opposite which stands a cabinet selling a small selection of gifts. Moving towards the back of the tent, there's a circular bar, a central fireplace surrounded by Moroccan-style couches, & out the back a small pool with loungers. Free Wi-Fi is available here.

Activities include a choice of 4 self-guided walking or jogging trails ranging from 5km to 20km, sundowner drives (N$300 pp), morning game drives (N$200 pp), mountain bikes that are free to rent, as well as a 2-day, 3-night Trans-Kalahari Walk with a nature guide (N$5,100 pp). *DBB N$2,100/3,400 sgl/dbl.* **LLLL**

🏠 **Kalahari Anib Lodge** (55 rooms, camping) 📞 063 240529; e anib@iway.na; www. gondwana-collection.com. Set among the Kalahari dunes, 3km from the main gate, this large but well-ordered lodge attracts both tour groups & independent travellers. It is situated on an 10,000ha farm lining the C20 towards Stampriet, about 33km northeast of Mariental. The reception & a good shop occupy the original farmhouse, now extended to provide a capacious restaurant where light lunches (N$45–100) & dinner – a 4-course affair (N$230) – are served. There's a separate bar with free Wi-Fi, TV & plenty of space for a meal or drink outside, too. Arranged around shaded lawns with a large swimming pool are 36 en-suite AC rooms with private verandas, which include a variety of trpl & family rooms. The other 17 rooms are larger, geared more to independent travellers, & set further back with a separate, smaller pool with views over the open Kalahari savannah. Well away from the lodge are 3 exclusive pitches with private bathrooms & BBQs, for campers, who may use all lodge facilities. Both morning & sunset game drives (N$365 pp) allow guests to witness the attractions of the Kalahari on the reserve, home to giraffe, zebra, red hartebeest & oryx, among others, while for those bent on exploring on foot, there are 3 trail maps covering 5.8/7.3/9.3km. *N$1,257/2,010 sgl/dbl*. **LLL**

✳ 🏠 **Bagatelle Kalahari Game Ranch** (19 rooms, camping) 📞063 240982; e info@bagatelle-kalahari-gameranch.com; www.bagatelle-kalahari-gameranch.com; reservations 📞061 224712/224217; e reservations@resdes.com.na. New owners Angela & Etienne Carsten are making big changes to this 7,000ha former sheep & cattle farm. Set amid rolling, linear dunes 37km north of Mariental, it's a warm & welcoming stopover. The original farmhouse has been converted into a comfortable lounge, restaurant (serving superb food) & library area, with a hotel-style reception, free Wi-Fi, large curio shop & bar, & there is a pool (being enlarged) & boma for lazy afternoons & casual dining. Four wooden chalets are raised on stilts atop a russet sand ridge, while the others, built of brick & some insulated with bales of straw, line the inter-dune 'street'. Of these, garden rooms are closest to the heart of the lodge, suiting the less mobile. Interiors are similar: white walls with impala-print wallpaper, dark wood furniture, African objets d'art, wicker lampshades, comfortable beds, with modern bathrooms separated by a curtain (not door), & extras include bathrobes, mosi spray, digital photo frame, AC & fan, complimentary wine & an honesty bar. The only notable differences are that ridge rooms have baths as well as showers (& a view!). There is also a campsite with 5 pitches & hot water, but no electricity. The charm here is being totally immersed in nature: from the blue wildebeest & eland that wander through camp to the 10-year-old springbok called 'Skundy' that usually strolls into the lounge at dinnertime. Morning, sundowner & night nature drives (*N$275/295/200 pp*) offer the opportunity to see kudu, oryx, hartebeest, giraffe, eland, steenbok, wildebeest & ostrich, & as part of a Cheetah Conservation Fund project, 3 male cheetahs – Etosha, Rolf & Touno (Thunder) – are housed in a 12ha enclosure beside the main lodge, where guests can watch them being fed (*N$195 pp*). New tours include horseback safaris (*N$350*), stargazing & an early morning Bushman-walk tour (*N$280*). Plans are also in place to add a farm garden, build a spa offering couples massages using organic Kalahari products, & a carve out runway by 2016, so VIP

guests staying at a new luxury chalet, tentatively called 'Little Bagatelle', can fly in. *DBB Garden: N$1,263/1,900 sgl/dbl; Dune: N$2,061/3,100 sgl/dbl; camping N$145 pp*. **LLLL**

🏠 **Intu Afrika Kalahari Game Reserve**
📞063 683218; e info@leadinglodges.com; www.intu-afrika.com. The small (10,000ha) private reserve of Intu Afrika is located on the D1268, 86km north of Mariental & just 19km south of the C21, & is clearly signposted from the B1 in both directions. The landscape is classic Kalahari: deep red longitudinal dunes, usually vegetated, separated by lighter clay inter-dune valleys covered in grass, trees & shrubs. The reserve's larger game includes giraffe, oryx, ostrich, blue & black wildebeest, Burchell's zebra & springbok – but it is the smaller bat-eared foxes that are the stars. These social creatures seem to thrive here, yet are not generally common.

Each of the 3 accommodation options is run individually, with its own facilities, though activities – game drives, guided Bushman walks & quad bikes – are common to all.

🏠 **ZEBRA KALAHARI LODGE & SPA** (13 rooms) 📞063 240855. Despite being completely rebuilt in 2009, Zebra Lodge – situated 5km from the main Intu Africa gate – feels a bit drab & soulless. Large en-suite rooms with outside showers & AC flank its substantial main building, where a semi-open-air bar, lounge with free Wi-Fi & fireplace, & dining area are furnished with dark wood & leather chairs. The rooms themselves are functional with a minimum of clutter, AC, minibar & tea/coffee, & overlook an unheated L-shaped pool. A short distance away are a further 5 split-level rooms, each boasting a sitting area & bedroom. The 'spa' is a simple room only offering massages (*N$400/1hr*). Babysitting is available on request. Activities include quad bikes (*N$187/1hr*), game drive (*N$350*) & Bushman walks (*N$200*). *DBB N$2,420/3,740 sgl/dbl*. **LLLLL**

🏠 **CAMELTHORN KALAHARI LODGE** (11 chalets) Undergoing renovations at the time of writing, this rustic lodge is dotted among camelthorn trees in natural bush. At its heart is a central lapa with comfortable restaurant, bar area & small swimming pool. It will probably be the best of the 3 when it's finished. *DBB N$1,870/2,860 sgl/dbl*. **LLLL**

🏠 **SURICATE TENTED LODGE** (12 tents) 📞063 240846. Accessed from a separate entrance some 6km further south on the D1268, Suricate, too, has been fully refurbished to a high but unfussy standard. The wow factor here comes from the lodge's location atop a low red sand dune, overlooking a grassy pan that's popular with wildlife. A large, airy, tented lapa looks out on to an infinity pool, flanked by a gazebo & fire pit, & beyond to the pan. Canvas-tented rooms lined up on each side come with wooden decks & plenty of creature comforts, from fans & small plug-in heaters to a safe, minibar, kettle, walk-in mosi nets & phone. Room 9 has the best views of the plains & a watering hole that attracts wildebeest & springbok, while the honeymoon suite has its own private plunge pool with sun-loungers. Free Wi-Fi in the main areas. *DBB N$1,980/3,080 sgl/dbl.* **LLLL**

🏠 **Bitterwasser Lodge & Flying Centre** (22 bungalows, 13 rondavels) 📞063 265300; e info@ bitterwasser.com; www.bitterwasser.com. South of Uhlenhorst on the C15, about 59km from the B1, this specialist lodge caters to glider pilots up to world-class level. Note that this is not a school for gliding – it is a place for those who know how. Pilots often stay for weeks, & have broken so many records that there's an avenue of palm trees lining the way to the airfield, where each palm was planted to commemorate a record. Every year the avenue grows.

Bitterwasser has a range of gliders available for hire, but most pilots prefer to ship out their own craft by container for the season, which runs late Oct–Feb. If you're a serious glider, email them for details of their facilities & prices, or check out their website. Gliding aside, the action is limited to swimming, & sundowner & nature drives. Out of season, the lodge caters primarily for groups. The extensive restaurant & bar feel rather corporate, but there's a more intimate lounge area. Comfortable accommodation comprises en-suite bungalows, both twin & sleeping up to 4, & all with AC. More basic rondavels share 3 ablution blocks. *DBB bungalows N$1,818–2,556/2,554–3,638 sgl/dbl; rondavel N$1,319/2,222 sgl/dbl.* **LLL**

🏠 **Lapa Lange** (5 chalets, 14 suites, camping) 📞063 241801; e lapalange@iway.na; www. gamelodgenamibia.com. Located on the M29 towards Gochas, 32km southeast of Mariental, Lapa Lange seems to be trying to attract all comers. But while the stuffed lion, leopard & other animals that stalk the walls of the lavish lapa will appeal to some, they'll be a turn-off for others. That said, Sky TV above the extensive bar has its aficionados, there's Wi-Fi in the main building, & day visitors are welcome for lunch. Chalets (4 superior, 1 honeymoon with jacuzzi) packed with several beds & 2 bathrooms have AC, mosi nets & fans, while tasteful luxury suites with AC, TV, fridge & private patio are set round a lawn with central pond. The campsite has space for 6 plots with water, power & ablution facilities. *Chalet N$403 pp; camping N$92 pp & N$92 per vehicle.* **LL**

UHLENHORST North of Mariental, this dot on the map seems little more than a large farm. It marks a fuel station (⏱ *07.00–19.00 daily*) and a general farm store, even if the latter is often closed. However, you might be surprised to learn that in the 1930s and 1940s there were two hotels, several shops, a post office and a bank here. Uhlenhorst is typical of many small Namibian towns that were once important, but faded with the advent of communications and good roads into mere shadows of themselves.

STAMPRIET TO GOCHAS Stampriet itself has little of intrinsic interest to drivers except a bank and a small fuel station – useful should you be running low – and Gochas likewise, but there are a couple of interesting accommodation options. As an added bonus, the C15 between the two small towns makes a pleasant drive, passing through a fertile stretch of farmland parallel to the Auob River. Ground squirrels inhabit the banks lining the road, so it's a great place to observe them as they go about their daily routines. From Gochas, it is a straight drive on the C18, a good, empty road, to rejoin the B1 near Gibeon.

For those without a vehicle who are tempted in this direction, Starline runs a bus from Mariental to Gochas via Stampriet every Wednesday, arriving in Stampriet at 09.30 and Gochas at 11.00, and departing at 12.30 and 14.30 respectively. A second service links Mariental with Stampriet and then further east to Aranos on Tuesday and Friday, again arriving in Stampriet at 09.30, but leaving at 15.30.

Guesthouses and lodges *Map, page 182.*

Kalahari Farmhouse (11 rooms) ☏ 063 260259; e farmhouse@gondwana-collection.com; www.gondwana-collection.com. Just off the C20, close to the sports stadium in Stampriet, & 61km from Mariental, this small, intimate lodge is a sister to Kalahari Anib – & at the heart of Gondwana's self-sufficiency project. Central to the lodge is a lovely 1950s farmhouse, incorporating the original kitchen as a dining area. To one side is a large bar & lounge area, leading on to a patio with good-size pool. To the front, a broad, shaded terrace looks over individual en-suite rooms which are whitewashed inside & out to blend with the farmhouse, with AC/heating for all extremes of temperature, & patchwork quilts adding splashes of colour. Guests may explore the farm, including the Self Sufficiency Centre where they grow all the produce for the Namibia Gondwana properties, from veg to milk & cheese, or do a nature drive at Kalahari Anib. Free Wi-Fi around reception. *B&B N$1,257/2,010 sgl/dbl.* **LLL**

Auob Country Lodge (25 rooms, camping) ☏ 063 250101; reservations ☏ 061 374750; e auob@ncl.com.na. Situated on the C15, about 6km north of Gochas & around 190km from the Mata-Mata border post, Auob Lodge stands in the Kalahari, close to the dry Auob River, within 80km² of its own land. It also has its own airstrip. Despite the name, the place has the atmosphere of a European hotel, with heavy furniture, a bar, pool room, lounge & separate restaurant. The rooms, located around a swimming pool, are comfortable, with AC, ceiling fans & en-suite shower & toilet, but don't expect much in the way of frills. For campers, there are 17 pitches with water & electricity. The lodge offers stargazing, guided hikes & unguided walking trails, & game drives among typical Kalahari game species, including giraffe, eland, oryx & blue wildebeest. *B&B N$895/1,404 sgl/dbl.* **LL**

Stampriet Historical Guesthouse (10 rooms) ☏ 063 260013; e reservations@ travel-weaver.com; www.stamprietguesthouse. com. Neighbours with Kalahari Farmhouse, this characterful guesthouse – located just before the entrance to Stampriet village – is run by Petro & Kobus Hayman & sits on a hill offering lovely views. Rooms are homely & the honeymoon suite has a claw-foot bath. Perks include free Wi-Fi, a pool table, swimming pool, jungle gym for kids, free tea/coffee throughout the day, a lovely arts & crafts souvenirs table, & superb restaurant. *DDB N$880/1,560 sgl/dbl.* **LL**

THE B1 FROM MARIENTAL TO KEETMANSHOOP

Between Mariental and Keetmanshoop is a 221km stretch of tar road that most visitors see at speed. However, a few places are worth knowing about as you hurry past, and Brukkaros is worth a detour for those keen on walking. If you're heading this way by train from Windhoek, you'll find that it stops every day except Saturday at Gibeon, Asab and Tses, *en route* to Keetmanshoop.

GIBEON About 6km west of the B1, this sprawling community lies in a valley. Its sole claim to fame is as the site of what is thought to be the world's heaviest shower of meteorites some 600 million years ago. Many of these are now displayed outside Windhoek's Town Square Mall (see page 151), while a smaller specimen may be seen at the museum in Rehoboth.

Just off the main B1 itself, opposite the bright red station building, is a small cemetery maintained by the Commonwealth War Graves Commission, commemorating both German and South African troops who fell during the Battle of Gibeon on 27 April 1915. The battle itself proved to be decisive in the South African campaign against German colonial occupation of what was then South West Africa.

MUKUROB Known as 'the Finger of God', Mukurob was once an immense rock pinnacle, which balanced on a narrow neck of rock and towered 34m above the surrounding plains. It collapsed around 8 December 1988, leaving a sizeable pile of rubble. Its demise caused much speculation at the time, as the finger's existence was linked to divine approval – and the country was in the process of becoming independent. Initially it was claimed that God was displeased with contemporary developments in this independence process. Later, right-wing extremists were blamed rather than God. Eventually, though, theories linked its fall firmly with the shock waves from the large Armenian earthquake of 7 December. To drive to where it stood, turn east off the B1 on to the D3919, just south of Asab, and follow the road for about 23km. To see it as it once was, drop into the museum in Keetmanshoop and have a look at the replica.

TSES Two-thirds of the way towards Keetmanshoop, almost opposite the turning to Berseba and Brukkaros, Tses is a small township to the east of the B1, and a stop on the line for both Intercape buses and the Starline train between Windhoek and Keetmanshoop. As in any small, poor country township, visitors passing through are treated as something of a curiosity, but made welcome. Across the railway there's a post office, a small trading store, a Catholic school and a fuel station – which occasionally runs out, so don't let your fuel supply run too low in this area.

BRUKKAROS Rising to 650m, the volcanic crater of Brukkaros – or Bruckaros – towers over the expanse of bare, flat plains that surround it. It's a classic volcano shape, clearly visible west of the B1. In the 1900s the Germans used the eastern side of the crater as the base for a heliograph. Then in the early 1930s, the Smithsonian Institute built a solar observatory on the western side, taking advantage of the clear air and lack of artificial lights nearby. Both the Germans and the observatory have now gone, and the skies are as clear as ever – so it's a great place to explore and possibly camp.

Getting there and away About 80km north of Keetmanshoop, and just south of the turning to Tses, turn west on to the M98 (signposted simply 'Berseba'). The road crosses the Fish River after about 19km, and it's worth a short stop to check out the waterbirds, including sacred ibis, that congregate here. In late afternoon you may even spot a family of baboons crossing the river. After a further 19km, just before you reach Berseba, turn north towards the volcano on to the D3904. Though this looks like a short distance, it'll be 9km or so on a flat road before you reach the gates and start to climb the volcano.

Where to stay *Map, page 182.*

Å **Brukkaros Campsite** In theory it's still possible to use this discontinued community campsite. There are 2 camping spots at the base with drop toilets & bucket showers. Above this, you need a 4x4 to reach the second camping area, with just 3 pitches. Neither fuel, firewood nor water are available so come fully equipped; there's a small store in Berseba if you're out of the basics.

What to see and do From the 4x4 campsite, a footpath leads to the eroded edge of the crater's southern lip. The path here was made while the observatory was being constructed, and it goes over the lip and into the crater, taking about 40 minutes, then continues up to the old observatory just below the western rim after an hour or so. The rim itself is a very short scramble away.

You can hike around here, or just sit and watch the dust-devils twist their way for miles around as the sun goes down. It is a superb place to sleep out under the stars, which you will probably never see more clearly.

BERSEBA The nearest town to Brukkaros, Berseba is one of the region's oldest settlements – notable for having had a Rhenish missionary, Samuel Hahn, based here as early as 1850. Now it remains a large though poor settlement, surviving by subsistence farming. This area often receives very little rain, and agriculture of any kind is difficult. There are a couple of shops for essentials and a fuel pump at the end of the road, though don't rely on the latter.

Continuing south on the B1, the road remains level and straight. If you're camping and hoping to stop before Keetmanshoop, it may be worth considering:

 Where to stay *Map, page 182.*

Ⓧ Garas Park Rest Camp ✆063 223217; m 081 4913863; e marian.hulme.z@gmail. com. 20km north of Keetmanshoop, & just west of the B1, this makes a pleasant stop for passing motorists. The campsite is owned by artist Marian Hulme & her sculptures are dotted along the road. Facilities are basic but clean. However, the real appeal is the small stand of quivertrees dotted among giant boulders like a child's building bricks. A rather eclectic mix of traditional huts & other artefacts are displayed around the place. Wood & water are available, but otherwise campers need to be entirely self-sufficient. *Camping N$95 pp.* **L**

KEETMANSHOOP

Pronounced 'Keet-mans-verp', which is often shortened in slang to just 'Keetmans', Keetmanshoop lies about 480km south of Windhoek at an altitude of 1,000m. It's a bustling little town, and the administrative centre of this region.

Originally there was a Nama settlement on the banks of the seasonal Swartmodder River here, also known as just Swartmodder. Then, in 1866, the Rhenish Missionary Society sent Johan Schröder here from their established station at Berseba. He organised the building of a church and named it Keetmanshoop (which means 'Keetman's hope'), after Johan Keetman, one of the rich benefactors who had paid for the building.

In 1890 that church was swept away by a freak flood, but a new one, built on higher ground, was completed five years later. This was disused for years, but restored and declared a monument in 1978. Now it shelters the town's museum, so at least visit this, even if you see nothing else here.

GETTING THERE AND AWAY
By car Keetmanshoop is situated at the hub of the road network in southern Namibia, linked to Windhoek, Lüderitz and South Africa by good tar roads.

By bus Intercape runs a good service linking Windhoek and Cape Town, via Keetmanshoop. Buses leave the local office at the Engen garage on Lafenis Avenue at 00.05 on Monday, Wednesday, Friday and Sunday heading south, and at 01.10 on Tuesday, Thursday, Friday and Sunday going north. For further details see pages 98–100).

The Starline bus that once connected Keetmanshoop with towns throughout the south is no longer operational, but occasional minibuses run between here and Lüderitz (see page 223).

By train Keetmanshoop's 1928 train station (*ticket desk ⊕ 07.15–18.30 Mon–Fri, 07.15–10.00 Sat, 16.15–18.30 Sun, 14.15–18.30 public hols*) is linked to Windhoek. Trains leave the capital every day except Saturday at 19.40, arriving at 07.00 the next morning. In the other direction, from Keetmanshoop to Windhoek, trains depart

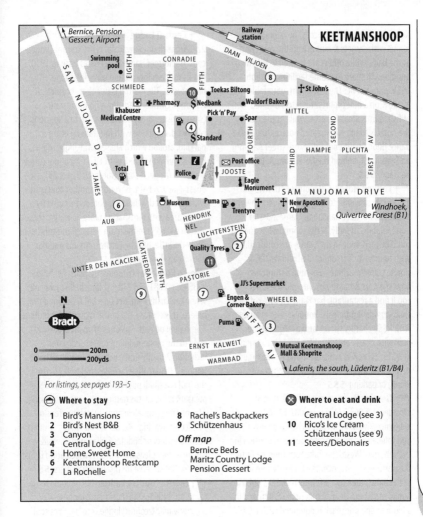

KEETMANSHOOP

Bernice, Pension
Gessert, Airport

Railway station

Swimming pool

CONRADIE

DAAN VILJOEN

EIGHTH

SIXTH

FIFTH

SCHMIEDE

Toekas Biltong

St John's

Khabuser Medical Centre

Pharmacy

Nedbank

Waldorf Bakery

Pick 'n' Pay

Spar

MITTEL

SAM NUJOMA DR

ST JAMES

Total

LTL

Standard

FOURTH

THIRD

HAMPIE   PLICHTA

SECOND

FIRST   AV

Police

Post office

JOOSTE

Eagle Monument

SAM   NUJOMA   DRIVE

Museum

Puma

Trentyre

New Apostolic Church

Windhoek, Quivertree Forest (B1)

HENDRIK NEL

LUCHTENSTEIN

AUB

(CATHEDRAL)

SEVENTH

Quality Tyres

UNTER DEN ACACIEN

PASTORIE

JJ's Supermarket

Engen & Corner Bakery

WHEELER

Puma

FIFTH   AV

ERNST KALWEIT

WARMBAD

Mutual Keetmanshoop Mall & Shoprite

Lafenis, the south, Lüderitz (B1/B4)

N

 Bradt

0 ———— 200m
0 ———— 200yds

For listings, see pages 193–5

🛏 **Where to stay**

1   Bird's Mansions
2   Bird's Nest B&B
3   Canyon
4   Central Lodge
5   Home Sweet Home
6   Keetmanshoop Restcamp
7   La Rochelle
8   Rachel's Backpackers
9   Schützenhaus

Off map
Bernice Beds
Maritz Country Lodge
Pension Gessert

❌ **Where to eat and drink**

Central Lodge (see 3)
10   Rico's Ice Cream
Schützenhaus (see 9)
11   Steers/Debonairs

10

at 18.50 and arrive in Windhoek at 07.00. There's a railroad café to the left of the station, before entering, for last-minute snacks.

TOURIST INFORMATION

ℹ **Tourist office** Cnr Hampie Plichta & Fifth Av; ☎063 221266; e stfkeet@iway.na; ⏱ 07.30–12.30 & 13.30–16.30 Mon–Fri, but closed 16.00 Fri. The tourist office resides in perhaps the town's most historic building, the

Kaiserliches Postamt – or imperial post office – built in 1910, & is now a national monument. It aims to promote the whole region & will help book accommodation.

WHERE TO STAY   *Map, above.*

A new B&B called **Home Sweet Home** (*Luchtenstein St;* ☎*081 127 5397*) seemed to be on the verge of opening up during research – guest experiences welcomed.

🏠 **Bird's Mansions Hotel** (23 rooms) 90 Sixth Av; ☎063 221711; e hotel@birdsaccommodation.

com; www.birdsaccommodation.com. In the centre of town, Bird's Mansions is linked to Bird's

Nest B&B, & friendly service is the hallmark. Large rooms with carpets & fans are off the courtyard at the back, while others are located in the main building. All share the same facilities, though: DSTV, phone & AC. The restaurant, with tables inside & on a quiet courtyard, offers a varied menu of fish, game, steak & pasta, while at the rear of the hotel is a lapa with heated pool, eating area & dance floor. An internet café & off-street parking on Seventh St, behind the hotel, complete the package. **$$$**

🏠 **Canyon Hotel** (70 rooms) Fifth Av; 📞063 223361; e canyonhotel@iway.na; www.canyon-namibia.com. Keetmanshoop's largest 3-star hotel remains friendly, & the rooms, while they could be anywhere in the world, are comfortable, with twin beds, TVs, direct-dial phones, AC & simple coffee machines. En-suite bathrooms have showers & hairdryers. Around the hotel you'll find a restaurant, bar & the Erokwe coffee shop serving light meals. Room service available with N$50 charge. There's also a large outdoor pool with grassy area & tables. Wi-Fi is charged at N$15/21hrs & is available in the lounge, plus there's a handy postbox outside for postcards. Plenty of parking. **$$$**

🏠 **Bernice Beds** (5 rooms) 129 10th St, Westdene; 📞063 224851; m 081 124 6278; e bernice@iway.na. Stef & Christi Coetzee & their dog Jolena run this pleasant, peaceful pension in the suburb of Westdene. Take Sam Nujoma Dr to the northwest, cross over the bridge & turn left at the lights, then first left into 10th St. 3 dbl & 2 family rooms are clean & functional & situated in a block at one side; each is equipped with TV, AC/heating & fridge, & there's 5 safe parking places. It all adds up to good-value accommodation, although they don't provide lunch/dinner & there's no Wi-Fi. **$$**

🏠 **Bird's Nest B&B** (10 rooms) 16 Pastorie St; 📞063 222906; e birdnest@iafrica.com.na; www.birdsaccommodation.com. This good little B&B close to the centre of Keet is under the same ownership as Bird's Mansions. Rooms, arranged around a quiet courtyard, are fairly small, but light & modern, with attractive fabrics, AC/heating, ceiling fans, DSTV, phone & facilities for making hot drinks. One is suitable for families. Outside, the gardens are well tended, underlying the care that goes into this place. There's a small bar but no Wi-Fi. **$$**

🏠 **Central Lodge** (24 rooms) Fifth Av; 📞063 225850; e clodge@iway.na; www.central-lodge. com. The former Hansa Hotel dates back to 1910, but its modern incarnation owes little to its predecessor. The Central is just that – central. A reception corridor leads through the restaurant (see opposite) & cupboard-like bar, to a spacious courtyard, complete with fountain & secure parking, around which are set large, light rooms. Each is well appointed, with TV, AC/heating, coffee station & fridge, & some (rooms 2, 3, 4 & 23) also boast a jacuzzi bath. Beyond is another courtyard with a secluded swimming pool surrounded by a grassy area with ramshackle tables & chairs. There's also Wi-Fi access in the main areas. Standards have slipped a little, but the Central remains popular with locals & visitors. **$$**

🏠 **La Rochelle** (7 rooms) 12 Sixth Av; 📞063 223845; m 081 278 2383; e larochelle@iway.na; www.keetmans.com. Set on a hill & catching the breeze, this century-old house is owned by Joubert & Annalein de Witt. Splashes of vivid colour add style to the modern dining room. Bedrooms, including 2 family units, vary in size, but all have remote TV, tea/coffee facilities, fridge & AC. On the roof is a small pool with views over town & a pleasant rocky cactus garden, plus secure parking. Also on site is Annalein's beauty salon offering manicures, waxing, etc, but no massages. Joubert keeps a variety of budgies & diamond doves & you can hear their pleasant chirrups while eating b/fast (N$60). Not suitable for disabled travellers. **$$**

🏠 **Maritz Country Lodge** (19 bungalows, camping) 📞063 224316; e maritzlodge@iway. na; www.maritzcountrylodge.com.na. 5km south of Keetmanshoop on the B1, about 2km from the junction with the B4 for Lüderitz, this upmarket restcamp offers a mixture of luxury & standard bungalows decorated in soft greys & greens with white linen & equipped with AC, DSTV, tea/coffee, fridge & very smart en-suite bathrooms; luxury rooms have flat-screen TVs. There's a campsite with electric hook-ups, a figure-of-8 swimming pool with shaded thatched area & bar, & a small à la carte restaurant. Campsites have power, smart wash blocks & toilets, & simple cooking/braai areas. Currently, there's no Wi-Fi. Game drives also available. Note that the entrance is through the Engen garage – do not attempt the signposted track further south. *Camping N$80 pp, plus N$120 per site*. **$$**

🏠 **Pension Gessert** (7 rooms) 138 13th St, Westdene; ☎ 063 223892; e gesserts@iafrica.com.na; www.natron.net/gessert. This welcoming B&B is a homely place, decked out with crafts made by the owner Hendrik's previous wife. Today, he & his new spouse Zelna Knouwds offer attractive country-style rooms – with AC, & some with fridges or TVs – set around a pretty floral garden that is candlelit by night. 2 of the rooms link to make a family unit. To reach it, head northwest on Sam Nujoma Dr, across the railway line. Turn left at the lights into Westdene, then right into 19th Av; 13th St is the third turning on the left. There's a sunny b/fast room with free Wi-Fi, an honesty bar & a resident grey parrot; other meals are available on request. Outside is a small shaded pool & gazebo with tables. There's secure off-street parking. **$$**

🏠 **Schützenhaus** (19 rooms) Cnr Pastorie St & Cathedral Av; ☎ 063 223400; e schuetzenhaus@iway.na; http://schutzenhausguesthouse.wheretostay.na. Built in 1899, the old German Club at the edge of town has been transformed into a guesthouse & backpackers. Relics of the past remain: in the colonial architecture; in the large high-ceilinged rooms; in the restaurant (see below); in the bar. Spread around the complex are en-suite rooms – some with kitchens, some for families – & 2 4-bed backpacker dorms, with shared bathrooms & kitchen. Rooms 11, 14 & 20 have baths. Free Wi-Fi in restaurant & reception. Laundry service available. *Dorm N$175/150 with/without bedding.* **$$**

🏠 **Rachel's Backpackers** (12 rooms, 30 dorm beds) Schmiede St; ☎ 063 225177; m 081 148 1145. Rachel's is central, very simple & cheap – so fine for a night if those are your priorities. However, the dorms – which have 5 beds & share bathrooms – smell of smoke. Dbl rooms are en suite, but beware friends travelling together: even if you book a dbl (N$250) you'll each be charged the higher price of a dorm bed – bit bizarre. There's a large, equipped kitchen & a few gated parking spots. *Dorm N$135.* **$**

🏕 **Keetmanshoop Restcamp** (16 camping) Eighth Av; ☎ 063 221265. This has long been one of Namibia's best municipal sites. Inside protective coils of razor wire lie clean ablution blocks with hot water surrounded by grass lawns (easily pierced by tent-pegs), with lots of space for cars & caravans on the gravel drives. It's a very good site, if you are happy to camp in town. *Adult N$67.80, child N$27.10, N$27.10 per vehicle.* **$**

✕ WHERE TO EAT AND DRINK   Map, page 193.

There's a dearth of places to eat in Keetmanshoop. The best bets are the hotels which have their own restaurants, and some of the garages have a café attached serving pies, burgers and cold drinks – useful if you're pushed for time.

✕ **Schützenhaus** Cnr Pastorie St & Cathedral Av; ☎ 063 223400; ⏲ lunch & dinner Mon–Fri, dinner only Sat–Sun. Old German trophies displayed in the large, rather formal, very quiet, restaurant hint at the history of the former German Club. At lunch, come for a toasted sandwich, but in the evenings it's a place for committed carnivores, with an à la carte menu offering *eisbein* & schnitzel among others. **$$$–$$$$**

✕ **Central Lodge** Fifth Av; ☎ 063 225850; ⏲ 11.00–16.00 & 18.30–21.30 daily. Although the Central is widely considered Keetmanshoop's best restaurant, don't raise your hopes too high: the plastic tablecloths set the tone. We're told the steak, stew & burgers are good, but it's best to steer clear of the pizzas. A kids' menu is also available. There's a cupboard-like bar alongside with a sad-looking stuffed oryx head & a few cursory bar stools. The wine list isn't up to much either. **$$–$$$$**

✕ **Steers/Debonairs** Cnr Fifth Av & Pastorie; ☎ 063 226763; ⏲ 09.00–22.00 daily. The South African equivalent of McDonald's, this fast-food take-away chain offers pizzas, burgers & chips. **$$**

🍦 **Rico's Ice Cream** Schmiede St; ☎ 081 1272669; ⏲ 09.00–17.00 Mon–Fri, 09.00–13.00 Sat. Treat the kids or yourself to a scoop of soft-whip ice cream from the little sweet shop. **$**

OTHER PRACTICALITIES Keetmanshoop could well be vying for the record for the greatest number of **fuel stations** per head of population; there are plenty. If you're after **biltong**, try Toekas Biltong on Fifth Avenue and, for **souvenirs**, it may be worth checking out the craft stalls by the side of the B1, near the junction with the

C16. In an **emergency**, the main hospital (✆ *063 220 9000*) is on the main road as you're heading out of town, while the ambulance is on ✆ 063 223388 and the police on ✆ 063 10111.

$ Banks Standard: Hampie Plichta St; Nedbank: Mittel St
Camping supplies & vehicle repairs LTL: Hampie Plichta St; ✆ 063 223351
⊞ **Khabuser Medical Centre** ✆ 063 225687/8; a/h m 081 202 2313

✚ **Pharmacy** Mittel St; ✆ 063 223300/9; a/h m 081 124 9369; ◷ 08.00–17.00 Mon–Fri, 08.00–12.30 Sat
Supermarkets JJ's: Fifth Av; ◷ 06.00–22.00 daily; Shoprite: Mutual Keetmanshoop Mall
Tyres Trentyre: ✆ 063 223357; Quality Tyres: ✆ 063 224413

WHAT TO SEE AND DO Like many of Namibia's provincial towns, Keetmanshoop doesn't have a wealth of attractions, but you can while away a couple of lazy hours visiting the museum.

Keetmanshoop Museum (*Sam Nujoma Dr;* ✆ *063 221256;* ◷ *07.30–12.30 & 13.30–16.30 Mon–Thu, 07.30–11.30 & 13.30–16.00 Fri; admission free, but donations welcome*) This centrally located old Rhenish Mission Church was built in 1895 to replace the original one that the floods destroyed. Now it is surrounded by rockeries and used as the town's museum. Don't ignore these rockeries, however, as they are dotted with native plants, as well as old wagons, machinery and even a Nama hut. If you're not visiting the Quivertree Forest, then take a close look at the small trees in the museum's garden.

Inside the church is a beautiful pulpit and an interesting collection of local memorabilia, including an elephant's skull, fossils, gemstones, early cameras, photographs, and various implements that were used by past townspeople. Upstairs is a replica of Mukurob, the Finger of God (see pages 190–1).

AROUND KEETMANSHOOP If you prefer to base yourself in a town, then both Fish River Canyon and Brukkaros could be day trips from Keetmanshoop. However, each is a destination in its own right and so they are covered separately. The two obvious excursions from town, the Quivertree Forest and the Giant's Playground, are almost adjacent. A little further afield, on the way to the Fish River Canyon via Seeheim (see pages 215–16), is Naute Dam Recreational Resort.

Quivertree Forest and Giant's Playground (◷ *sunrise–sunset, outside these hours by arrangement only; admission N$55 pp*) Also known as the 'Kokerboomwoud', the Quivertree Forest is a dense stand of *Aloe dichotoma* tree aloes, just 14km from Keetmanshoop on the privately owned Gariganus Farm. To find it, take the B1 north for about 1km, then turn right on to the C16 towards Koës, then left on to the M29 shortly after.

These trees are found all over southern Namibia and the northern Cape, but in few places are so many seen together. (A second is a few kilometres south of Kenhardt, on the R27 in South Africa.) Ideally drop in close to sunset or sunrise, when the light is at its best. These skeletal 'trees' make particularly striking photographs when the lighting of a fill-in flash is balanced against a flaming sunset behind.

Just 5km further down the M29 are some marvellous balancing basalt rocks known as the Giant's Playground. Reminiscent of formations in Zimbabwe's Matobo Hills, these are more limited but still interesting.

QUIVERTREES

The quivertree or kokerboom, *Aloe dichotoma*, occurs sporadically over a large area of southern Namibia and the northern Cape, usually on steep rocky slopes. Its name refers to its supposed use by the Bushmen for making the quivers for their arrows – the inside of a dead branch consists of only a light, fibrous heart which is easily gouged out to leave a hollow tube.

The quivertree is specially adapted to survive in extremely arid conditions: its fibrous branches and trunk are used for water storage, as are its thick, succulent leaves, while water lost through transpiration is reduced by waxy coatings on the tree's outside surfaces. Roots, though, are shallow, making the tree vulnerable to high winds and, in common with most desert-adapted flora, its growth rate is very slow. Its beautiful yellow flowers bloom in winter.

Where to stay   *Map, page 182.*

Quivertree Forest Restcamp (8 rooms, 8 igloos, camping) ☏063 683421; e quiver@iafrica.com.na; www.quivertreeforest.com. From Keetmanshoop veer left on to the C16, look for signs, & drive 13km along a dirt track: the camp is on the left. Run by Coenie & Ingrid Nolte, plus an assortment of 12 dogs, they offer a number of guesthouses each with their own lounge & minibar, & one with a kitchen. They also have 8 en-suite Star Wars-style 'igloos' with a kitchen, AC & minibar, but they are a bit gloomy inside due to the blacked-out windows. There is also a tree-shaded campsite adjacent to the Quivertree Forest, with BBQ facilities & electricity. Free Wi-Fi in the main areas. It's a great place for children, with a swimming pool & a trampoline. Don't be put off by the cages to the left of, & behind, the farm buildings; this is a holding area for 5 orphaned cheetahs, which are permanently housed in separate enclosures of 15ha & 37ha respectively; guests can watch them being fed at 16.00 (winter) and 17.00 (summer). Staying here is a good alternative to Keetmanshoop, & makes it easier to see the forest & the rocks around dawn & dusk, when the light is at its best for photography. *DBB N$720/1,200 sgl/dbl; camping N$100 pp.* **LL**

Mesosaurus Fossil Site   Located some 42km from Keetmanshoop on the C17 towards Koës, this is the place to see the fossils of the huge mesosaurus that inhabited the freshwater lakes of Gondwanaland 270 million years ago. Stands of quivertrees are also a feature of the landscape, as are the giant dolorite rock formations. It's also possible to visit the graves of two German Schutztruppers who died in a 1904 battle between the Germans and the Namas. For visitors, there are guided tours of the site (*N$100 pp*), as well as – for overnight guests – 3–10km hiking trails and a 16km off-road trail for high-clearance vehicles.

Where to stay   *Map, page 182.*

Mesosaurus Fossil Bush Camp (4 chalets, camping) ☏063 683641; e mesosaurus.camp@gmail.com; www.mesosaurus.com. This simple camp has (3 twin-bed & 1 family) rustic, en-suite chalets, pitches for camping, & an isolated bush camp in the river-bed. Each pitch has a table, hot water & braai, with ablution blocks close by & wood available on site, though you will need to bring all other provisions with you. Cash only. *Chalet N$220 pp; camping N$70 pp.* **L**

Naute Dam Recreational Resort (☏063 173681; m 081 237 7867; ☉ 07.00–17.00 daily; *viewpoint visitor N$4, day visitor N$7*) Surrounded by low hills, and overlooked by the Klein Karas Mountains, the muddy-coloured lake created by Naute Dam is about 26km long and, at its widest, some 7km. The 470m-long dam was opened in

1972. Standing 37m above the river-bed, it holds back the water from the Löwen River as it feeds into the Fish River to the southwest. From the main entrance, where there are picnic tables and a small snack kiosk, there is a good vantage point over both the dam itself and the lake beyond with its cluster of small islands.

Despite its obvious attractions, investment in tourist facilities has been relatively limited. Instead, efforts have been concentrated on an irrigation project fed by water from the dam, leading to the production of dates, grapes, prickly pears and pomegranates for export (you can see the date palms just west of the causeway as you drive to the viewpoint).

Flora and fauna The lake has become a focus for numerous birds. There are opportunities for birdwatching from the viewpoint, but it is the reed-fringed sandy lakeshore to the south of the main entrance (follow the signs for 'camping') that is the real haven for waterbirds, with pelicans, herons, kingfishers, cormorants, African darters and sacred ibis all in evidence. Walking, fishing and boating are also permitted in this area. The 23,000ha game park protects springbok, klipspringer, oryx, kudu and ostrich, but is not open to the public.

Getting there and away From Keetmanshoop, take the B4 west to Seeheim, then turn south on to the C12. The resort is signposted to the left on the D545, about 25km from Seeheim after crossing the Löwen River. After a further 13km, a turning right by a farm, signposted 'camping area', will take you to the southern part of the dam. Continue along the D545 for another 2km and the road leads across a causeway which is often flooded in the early months of the year. Even in summer it may still be covered with water, though if you drive carefully it can usually be crossed in a 2WD. The road goes sharply to the right and the entrance to the viewpoint and campsite is signposted on the right. Alternatively you can drive along the B4 for 31km, then turn left on to the D545 (some 12km before the Seeheim turn-off). After about 18km the resort is signposted on your left. Again, this will eventually meet the causeway, so you may have to retrace your steps after looking at the dam unless a detour is marked.

 Where to stay *Map, page 182.*

Ⓧ **Naute Campsite** ☎ 063 250533. The area by the lake is no longer designated for camping, despite the signs to the contrary. Instead, campers now have a level, purpose-built site that looks over the lake. Though it feels a bit like a car park, there are toilets & piped drinking water, but no showers or hot water. Stock up before arriving. *N$70 per pitch.* **L**

THE DEEP SOUTH

South and east of Keetmanshoop, Namibia's central highlands start to flatten out towards South Africa's Karoo, and the great sand sheet of the Kalahari to the east. Many of the roads here are spectacular: vast and empty with enormous vistas. The C10 between Karasburg and the B1, and the D608, are particular favourites.

The towns here seem to have changed little in years. They vary from small to minute, and remind the outsider of a typical South African *dorp* (a small town). Expect some of them to be on the conservative side.

KOËS This small outpost lies about 124km northeast of Keetmanshoop, deep in the Kalahari Desert. It is the centre for the local Afrikaans farming community, and has a few small shops and a basic hotel.

Where to stay *Map, page 182.*

🏠 **Torgos Safari Camp** (8 tents, 2 chalets)
📞063 260106; e torgos@iway.na; www.
torgoslodgenam.com. Bordering the Kgalagadi
Transfrontier Park (🕐 08.00–16.30 daily), Torgos
is well located for those crossing using the newly
opened Mata-Mata Gate into South Africa, just
7km to the east. The 11,000ha wildlife-rich plot
has both chalets & tents with en-suite facilities;
chalets have AC, tents have fans. A high-ceilinged
thatched lapa incorporates a bar, restaurant &
lounge, with a boma for evening BBQs. Plus, there's
a pool. Dawn & sundowner drives offered. *Tent
N$780; chalet N$780–840.* **LL**

🏠 **Hotel Koës** (8 rooms, 1 chalet) 2 Fontein
St;📞063 252716. Some of the rooms at this small,
basic hotel are en suite; others share facilities.
It's perhaps not going to be the highlight of your
holiday, but it might be useful in an emergency. **L**

BETWEEN KEETMANSHOOP AND GRÜNAU The long straight B1 between the two
towns is characterised by farmland, backed to the east by the Karas Mountains. In
recent years, a number of guest farms along this road have opened their doors to
visitors. The most established of these is the White House, but others are worth
considering. The following are listed in order of distance from Keetmanshoop.

Where to stay *Map, page 182.*

🏠 **Goibib Mountain Lodge** (8 rooms,
camping) 📞063 683131; e goibib@mweb.com.
na; www.goibibmountainlodge.com. Located west
of the B1 & close to the road, some 112km south
of Keetmanshoop & 48km north of Grünau. This
working farm sits at the base of the Great Karas
Mountains & offers 8 traditional but tasteful en-suite
rooms, all with AC, radio, minibar, Wi-Fi, tea/coffee
facilities & safe. In the lounge, there's a big-screen TV
& a range of reference books, while the linked dining
area also has tables outside on a shaded veranda.
Outside, backed by hills, there's an attractive walled
pool area, & behind this a campsite with 5 pitches,
each with its own braai, plus a central wood stove &
ablution block; campers can use the swimming pool.
As well as hiking on the surrounding 8,400ha farm,
guests can hire a mountain bike, go stargazing, or
take a 2hr game drive (*N$180*). While it lacks the
personality of a guest farm, Goibib is comfortable &
efficiently run. *DBB N$660/1,320 sgl/dbl; camping
N$115 pppn.*

🏠 **Savanna Guest Farm** (5 rooms) 📞063
683127; m 081 1245269; e savannaf@gmail.
com; www.savanna-guestfarm.com. This 22,000ha
farm at the foot of the Great Karas Mountains is
just off the B1, 42km north of Grünau, opposite the
D203. In the 1900s the German army billeted their
troops here, with a kraal for the horses, rooms for
their officers & a watchtower – which is now part
of the farmhouse – to keep an eye on heliograph
communications from stations in the mountains.
Today it is a working sheep farm owned & run by
Erich von Schauroth, who is also involved in training
Arab horses for endurance racing. En-suite rooms
with AC are comfortable, though not luxurious; 3
have self-catering facilities & some are suitable for
families. Don't come expecting to be entertained,
but for walkers or those interested in the farm, this
could be a good location, with a heated pool for
added relaxation & a 4x4 trail. There's an honesty
bar in the b/fast room, where a 3-course dinner with
traditional farm cooking is available by arrangement
(*N$120*). *N$350/1,100 sgl/dbl; b/fast N$60.* **LL**

🏠 **White House Guest Farm** (5 rooms, 3
chalets, camping) 📞063 262061; m 081 2856484;
e withuis@iway.na; www.withuis.iway.na. On a
working 15,000ha sheep farm which stretches to the
distant mountains, the White House is off the B1,
about 11km north of Grünau, & some 4km from the
main road. The stunning old farmhouse has Oregon
pine floors, high wooden ceilings, wide verandas, a
huge kitchen & even an old radiogram. It was built
in 1912 for £2,500, & bought by the present owner's
grandfather in 1926 for £3,500. After use as a school,
among other things, it fell into disuse until bought
by Dolf & Kinna De Wet, who began to renovate it
in 1995. They have done a superb job. Just sit down
quietly to soak up the atmosphere & journey back
to the early 20th century. The self-catering chalets
dotted around the grounds are very well equipped
& come with AC, heaters, bedding, towels, a stocked
fridge, cutlery, toaster & kettle with tea/coffee. Braai
packs (*N$90 pp*) can be ordered with 2 weeks' notice,
but an excellent dinner (*N$100*) may be ordered in
advance: come with a good appetite! In the main
house are 4 beautiful old family rooms with en-suite

facilities. The kitchen, with a large fridge, stove, crockery & utensils, isn't luxurious (though it would have been 70 years ago), but it is comfortable & very authentic with a stocked drinks fridge. At the back is a separate 1-room studio with its own fridge & dining table, & little shower-toilet adjacent. For campers, there are 4 pitches, & birders have the choice of 2 hides close to the house. The White House is a beautiful old place which is excellent value & well worth a visit (though the historical aspect will pass you by if you're not in the main house). Those with an interest in geology should visit the rose-quartz mine on the farm, & there are also game drives (min 3) that should be booked in advance. *Room N$250/300 sgl/dbl; chalet N$500/620 2/4 people; camping N$80 pp; b/fast N$50.* **L**

GRÜNAU

Grünau is a crossroads, where the railway from Upington in South Africa crosses the main B1. It has a petrol station but no shops. The little town also, more or less, marks the spot where the main tarred B3 from the central and eastern parts of South Africa meets with the B1 coming from the Cape. Thus it is strategically positioned for overnight stops between South Africa and Namibia – but isn't a destination of note in its own right.

Getting there and away Trains stop on Sundays and Thursdays at 12.25 *en route* to Keetmanshoop, and on Wednesdays and Saturdays at 13.10 as the train returns to Upington. The Intercape bus between Upington and Windhoek departs from the Shell truck stop in Grünau on Tuesday, Thursday, Friday and Saturday at 22.50, returning from Windhoek at 01.55 on Monday, Tuesday, Thursday and Saturday. Fares between Grünau and Windhoek are around N$385 one-way, and from Grünau to Upington about N$480.

Where to stay *Map, page 182.*

Grünau Country House (10 rooms, 4 bungalows, camping) Old Main Rd; 063 262001; e grunauch@iway.na; www.grunauch.iway.na. When Altus & Izane took over the former Grünau Hotel following a fire, they set about rebuilding, renovating & refurbishing. The result is a well-run, traditional hotel, with a 'ladies' bar' (no swearing allowed) & an à la carte restaurant (⊕ b/fast (N$80) & dinner (N$130) daily). It is signposted to the west off the B3, just south of the junction with the B1.

All rooms are en suite, with 3 of them, & the main building, having wheelchair access. Bungalows share an ablution block with the campsite, where there are electricity & water points, & trees for shade are slowly growing. The lodge is an agent for Intercape Mainliner, & runs a shuttle between here & the bus stop. *N$330/530/575–640 sgl/dbl/family; bungalow N$175 pp; camping N$80 pp.* **L**

Grünau Chalets (6 chalets, camping) 063 262026; e willa@iafrica.com.na; www.grunaulodge.com. Just north of Grünau is a Shell fuel station (with ATM), with a simple restcamp. The surroundings are flat & characterless, but the small 1–8-bed bungalows are clean & well appointed, with AC, en-suite bathroom, TV, kitchenette & secure parking. 4 camping pitches have their own private ablution facilities, plus power point, & there are 2 larger self-catering houses in town. The shop sells snacks & basic foodstuffs, & has a simple restaurant (⊕ closes 19.00, 18.00 on Mon), & there's also a kiosk. Animals welcome for N$30. *N$370/550 sgl/dbl; camping N$120 per pitch, plus N$25 pp.* **L**

Vastrap Guest Farm (6 rooms, 2 chalets) 063 262063; e vastrap@afol.com.na; www.vastrapguestfarm.com. Around 5km southeast of Grünau on the B3 is a sign to the attractive & welcoming Vastrap Guest Farm, which is about 2km from the road, on a farm belonging to Rean & Hettie Steenkamp. GPS users please note that this is the only road in! The design is unusual, as these are rooms within old farmstead buildings that have been linked together, rather than in separate bungalows. Rooms are simple but cheerful, with en-suite showers & AC. Self-catering chalets are en suite. There is also a dining room where home-cooked meals are served on request, & guests can make use of both braai & freezer facilities. Outside is a swimming pool, & there's the opportunity for day trips on the farm & guided hunting safaris. *N$430/550 sgl/dbl; family up to N$890; b/fast N$80; dinner N$130.* **L**

KARASBURG Karasburg is really just a bigger version of Grünau – a busy but convenient overnight stop on a long journey.

Getting there and away Trains, too, stop here between Upington in South Africa and Keetmanshoop on Sunday and Thursday at 11.20, and on the return journey on Wednesday and Saturday at 14.30. Intercape buses between Upington and Windhoek head north from the BP garage (XL Motors) next to Spar at 21.15 on Tuesday, Thursday, Friday and Sunday, returning south at 01.30 on Monday, Wednesday, Friday and Sunday.

Where to stay, eat and drink The one hotel in town – Kalkfontein Hotel – is closed until further notice, so you'll have to pick from the meagre handful of B&Bs. For dining, you could try the Pizza Den Seafood Restaurant, opposite the Engen garage on Main Street. Alternatively, there are several take-aways. There's even an ice cream parlour, Rico's, near Engen.

Karas Cottages (6 rooms) 88 Kalkfontein St; 063 270349; e jswartz@iway.na. Has 4 en-suite rooms in the main house with tea/coffee facilities, DSTV & 2 self-catering 1-bedroom cottages with lounge & kitchen with fridge, 2-plate stove, cutlery & crockery. Outside is a small pool, & a BBQ area under lots of shady trees. A restaurant & supermarket are located nearby. **$–$$**

Kleinbegin Lodge (7 rooms) 063 269315; e kleinbeginlodge@webmail.co.za. This homely guesthouse, located on the northern outskirts of Karasburg on the B3, is run by Otto & Martie Cloete. They have 7 traditional dbl en-suite rooms with minibars & guests can use the swimming pool, pool table and table tennis, & kids the small playground. Provide b/fast & dinner. **$$**

Other practicalities The town has several 24-hour **fuel stations**, while for **supermarkets** there is Spar next to the Total garage and USave next to BP. Robb's Motors (063 270189) could be handy if you're in need of tyres or **vehicle repairs**. There's a **post office** on Park Street, and a couple of **banks**: Bank Windhoek on 9th Avenue and FNB on Main Street – so if Namibia's dollar ever floats free from South Africa's rand, you can expect these to be busy. The **hospital** can be contacted on 063 270167. Signposts to Lordsville and Westerville point the way to Karasburg's old-style satellite townships.

WARMBAD About 48km south of Karasburg, sleepy Warmbad (the name means 'hot bath' in German) is known for its hot springs, a small but fascinating museum, and a lovely old stone church, built in 1877. The town was the location of the first Christian mission in 1806, and the centre of the Nama-German war in the early 19th century.

Sadly, it's a bit of a depressing place. The discovery of uranium deposits in 2009 brought hope that investment would improve the area, but changes appear to be slow. We weren't able to visit on our last research trip, but visitors have reported that the springs – which had been smartened up in 2006 – are not looked after, a bit unsanitary and unswimmable in winter. There's also a lack of accommodation, with one community campsite reported to still be open (we'd welcome details). For now, we suggest just stopping by to visit the museum.

What to see and do
Warmbad Museum (09.00–13.00 & 14.00–17.00 Mon–Fri, 09.00–13.00 Sat, or collect key from lodge; admission N$10/5 adult/child) Warmbad's old German prison makes a thought-provoking base for this small museum, which encapsulates the history of the Bondelswarts. A group of mixed origin, they fell foul of the German

colonisers, who in 1906 stripped them of their lands and forced their leader, Abraham Morris, into exile. After World War I, far from redressing the situation, the new South African occupiers placed added restrictions on the people. When Morris attempted to return across the Orange River in 1922, a warrant was issued for his arrest, but the Bondelswarts refused to hand him over. In retaliation, the full might of the South African military was mobilised, crushing the Bondelswarts with the loss of over 100 men, women and children, and resulting in the death of their leader. Surrender was inevitable. The remaining guerrillas were taken prisoner and marched to Warmbad, where they were imprisoned – in the building that now houses the museum.

NOORDOEWER This small settlement on the Orange River stands about 3.5km from the main crossing point for Namibia–Cape traffic at Vioolsdrif. If you're crossing into Namibia from that point, you're advised to get there early; the border post is open 24 hours but tends to get busy after about 10.00.

Noordoewer is just 43km from the edge of the Ai-Ais Richtersveld Transfrontier Park. It is also one of the embarkation points for canoeing and rafting trips down the Orange (see page 204). A final point of interest is that, thanks to a ready supply of water, there are several large-scale irrigation projects in the area, some producing table-quality grapes like those on the Orange further east in South Africa.

Tourist information

🛈 Tourist office Die Mielie Padstal; ☎063 297566; ⏱ 08.00–18.00 Mon–Fri, 08.00–noon Sat. This farm shop – looked after by the owners of Noordoewer Guesthouse (see below) – sells produce & handmade crafts & doubles as an information centre stocked with a variety of maps & brochures.

Where to stay, eat and drink *Map, page 182.*

🏠 Noordoewer Guesthouse (8 rooms) ☎063 297108; m 081 231 7271; e nikos@iway. na; www.noordoewerguesthouse.com. On the C13 close to the Engen garage, this pleasant guesthouse has modern en-suite rooms with AC, kettle & fridge. Tables are set out on a terrace, and there's a small pool. Dinner is available on request. **$$**

🏠 Orange River Lodge (12 rooms) ☎063 297012; e orlodge@iway.na; www.orlodge.iway.

na. About 3km from the border, next to the petrol station, this small lodge is set in attractive grounds. Dbl, twin & family rooms, 3 of them self-catering, are set around well-watered lawns with a small pool. Each has a private bathroom, AC, TV & tea/coffee facilities. It's a good place for an overnight stop, with à la carte meals served in a thatched lapa, where there's a TV & bar, or on an umbrella-shaded terrace. Activities include fishing & canoeing. *B/fast N$45.* **$$**

Other practicalities The town itself has a couple of 24-hour **fuel** stations, a supermarket and a branch of **Bank** Windhoek, which could be useful for changing Namibian dollars before crossing into South Africa.

ALONG THE ORANGE RIVER Forming the border between Namibia and South Africa, the Orange River tends to be overlooked by visitors. However, with South Africa's wild Richtersveld National Park (now amalgamated with Ai-Ais National Park as one of the first 'Peace Parks' in the region) on its southern side, and very little access to its northern banks, it makes a perfect wilderness destination.

Against this backdrop, the largely seasonal settlement at **Aussenkehr**, whose population fluctuates from 5,000 or so to 21,000 in tune with the pruning and harvesting of grapes in the reserve, comes as quite a surprise. From a practical point of view, it supports a branch of the Standard Bank, a couple of ATMs, a post office, and a large Spar with separate Tops off-licence.

Flora and fauna The flora in this area of the Namib is particularly unusual, because its proximity to the Cape leads it to receive some winter rainfall. This seems to promote the growth of succulents, including various *Lithops* and *Mesembryanthemum* species, several of which are endemic to this area. Visit in July, August or September and you may find whole areas in bloom, like Namaqualand just over the border to the south.

There are some fascinating larger plants here too, including *Aloe pillansii*, a close relative of the quivertree, which grows to 6–7m in the shape of a candelabra, and the rare, protected *Pachypodium namaquanum*, or halfman, a curious succulent which grows to 2m tall with a great girth. Its head always faces north.

With the presence of permanent water, expect to see several kingfishers among the birds, including the tiny but beautiful malachite. Look out, too, for the locally common Orange River white-eye – aptly named for its white eye ring.

Where to stay *Map, page 182.*

In addition to the places to stay in Noordoewer itself, there are a few more attractive options along the river – listed below from east to west. All are accessed from the C13/D212, which is tarred until just west of Norotshama, and all except Norotshama are linked to one of the canoeing operators. As well as being popular with canoeists, these lodges make excellent spots for birdwatching or fishing – if you have your own equipment.

Felix Unite River Lodge (20 chalets, tents) +27 87 3540578; www.felixunite.com. The old Provenance Camp has been renamed. With a beautiful setting on a bend in the river looking towards the Geelkrans cliffs, this attractive, well-run camp is geared largely to canoeists & overlanders, though others are welcome. There are 10 'cabanas' beside the river & 7 higher up on a hill overlooking the river. All have a kettle, fridge & AC – crucial in the summer months when the mercury tops 40°C – as well as sliding doors leading on to a veranda with a view. There's also a large honeymoon suite on the river. If – & only if – the cabanas are fully booked there is a group of green canvas tents sleeping 1–2 people with shared ablution facilities, towels & sheets. High above the river is an extensive restaurant with an à la carte menu for b/fast, lunch & dinner, overlooking a pool & the river below. There's laundry, Wi-Fi throughout & an internet café in the shop, which also has an ATM & stocks everything from snacks to camping equipment & clothes. Although many guests are booked on longer trips, there is the option of full-day canoeing too. *Bed-only 'cabana' N$945; family 'cabana' & suite N$1,595; tents N$595/1,300 sgl/dbl.* **LL**

Amanzi Trails River Camp (1 chalet, camping) 063 297255; www.amanzitrails.co.za. This grassy, level campsite, just 3km off the C13, is 16km downstream from the Noordoewer border post & has views on to the lovely Goelkrans cliffs. With reed shelters, screens & braai areas, the pitches are shaded by trees & have good ablution blocks. Tucked away in a private corner is a self-catering chalet that can sleep 4, has lovely views & has steps leading to the river. Bedlinen can be hired (*N$20 pp*). There's also a thatched lapa and separate bar, & electricity, wood & ice are available. *DBB chalet N$350 1st person, N$80 for each additional; camping N$90/60/50 adult/child/car.* **L**

Norotshama River Resort (30 rooms, camping) Aussenkehr; 063 297215; e norotshama@africaonline.com.na; www. norotshamaresort.com. The 2km avenue of grapevines that leads from the C13, 50km west of Noordoewer, heralds something a little different. In the heart of the Aussenkehr Reserve, the lodge is making a stab at being all things to all people, with 4 well-equipped luxury chalets, 2 stone self-catering chalets, 4 family chalets & 10 river-edge rooms. Facing the river itself is a cavernous restaurant, with outside seating on a vine-shaded terrace, & an à la carte menu that majors on steaks. Wi-Fi across the resort is a plus, as are a pool set among lawns, a curio shop & a friendly bar with TV. A nail & beauty salon is on the way. Activities include canyon trips, canoeing, fishing, rock climbing & a village trip to Aussenkehr.

Alternatively hire a fishing rod or mountain bike, follow one of the 4x4 trails or try a spot of rock climbing & abseiling when the nearby 'adventure camp' is complete – though you'll need your own kit for these. *B&B N$670/1,234 sgl/dbl; camping N$170/90 adult/child, inc parks entry fees.* **LL**.

Canoeing

Several companies run canoeing and/or river-rafting trips along the Orange River, most of them based around Cape Town. Many are geared towards South African visitors, and work well for those driving across the border who want to stop for a few days' canoeing. Unlike the Victoria Falls, this isn't a white-water experience, and neither is it a game experience, though you may catch glimpses of game as you paddle. Instead, it is a gentle trip through a stunningly beautiful wilderness area that is notable for its scenery and lack of people.

Prices vary, but for a four-day trip you can expect to pay from N$3,000 per person (minimum six people), including meals, or less for those who are self-catering. For a trip of this length, you'll cover around 65km as far as Aussenkehr, spending about 6 hours each day on the river and camping on the riverbank at night. A six-day trip reaches the Fish River. Such trips can also cater for those with limited mobility.

Rafting companies

Amanzi Trails ☏ Namibia 063 297 255; SA +27 21 559 1573; e info@amanzitrails.co.za; www. amanzitrails.co.za

Aquatrails ☏ +27 21 782 7982; e info@ aquatrails.co.za; www.aquatrails.co.za

Felix Unite ☏ +087 354 0578; e reservations@ felixunite.co.za; www.felixunite.com. The most experienced & probably the largest of the companies currently running this river.

The River Rafters ☏ +27 21 975 9727; e info@ riverrafters.co.za; www.riverrafters.co.za

What to take The arrangements with each canoeing company are different, but most will supply two-person Mohawk canoes, paddles, life jackets, all meals and cool boxes for your own drinks (soft, alcoholic and bottled water – but note that glass bottles are not allowed on the river, so you'll need to decant liquids beforehand). They will also have watertight containers to keep limited luggage dry.

As well as drinks, you must bring a sleeping bag, personal toiletries (preferably biodegradable), a set of clothes for the river and one for when you're away from the water. A hat, long cotton trousers and long-sleeved cotton blouse/shirt, as well as a bathing costume, are fine for the river, plus trainers and warm tracksuit (the temperatures can drop!) for wearing off the river.

Some companies advise that you will also need your own knife, fork, spoon, mug, plate, torch, toilet paper and sleeping mat. Participants sometimes take small tents and even folding chairs along, and often you'll be requested to bring large, strong plastic bin liners. The better companies, like Felix Unite, have stocks of all this kit available to hire for their trips.

FISH RIVER CANYON

At 161km long, up to 27km wide, and almost 550m at its deepest, the Fish River Canyon is arguably second in size only to Arizona's Grand Canyon – and is certainly one of Africa's least-visited wonders. This means that, as you sit dangling your legs over the edge, drinking in the spectacle, you're unlikely to have your visit spoiled by a coachload of tourists – at least, as long as you walk away from the main viewpoint. In fact, away from the busier seasons you may not see anyone around here at all!

The canyon itself starts about 7km south of Seeheim, winding its way south to Ai-Ais. From Hobas through to Ai-Ais it is protected within the Ai-Ais National

Park, while immediately to the north, protection continues through private reserves on both sides of the river.

GEOLOGY The base rocks of the Fish River Canyon, now at the bottom nearest the river, are shales, sandstones and lavas which were deposited about 1,800 million years ago. Later, from 1,300 to 1,000 million years ago, these were heated and strongly compressed, forming a metamorphic rock complex, which includes intrusive granites and, later, the dolorite dykes which appear as clear, dark streaks on the canyon.

A period of erosion then followed, removing the overlying rocks and levelling this complex to be the floor of a vast shallow sea, covering most of what is now southern Namibia. From about 650 to 500 million years ago various sediments, limestones and conglomerates were deposited by the sea on to this floor, building up into what is now referred to as the Nama Group of rocks.

About 500 million years ago, the beginnings of the canyon started when a fracture in this crust formed a broad valley, running north–south. Southward-moving glaciers deepened this during the Dwyka Ice Age, around 300 million years ago. Later faults and more erosion added to the effect, creating canyons within each other, until a mere 50 million years ago, when the Fish River started to cut its meandering way along the floor of the most recent valley.

HISTORY Situated in a very arid region of Namibia, the Fish River is the only river within the country that usually has pools of water in its middle reaches during the dry season. Because of this, it was known to the peoples of the area during the early, middle and late Stone Ages. Numerous sites dating from as early as 50,000 years ago have been found within the canyon – mostly beside bends in the river.

Around the beginning of this century, the Ai-Ais area was used as a base by the Germans in their war against the Namas. It was finally declared a national monument in 1962. Ai-Ais Restcamp was opened in 1971, though it has been refurbished since then.

FLORA AND FAUNA Driving around you will probably see few larger animals, though there are many if you look hard. These include herds of Hartmann's mountain zebra, small groups of kudu and the smaller klipspringer antelope, which are usually seen in pairs. Baboon make no secret of their presence if around, and dassies (alias rock rabbits) are common, but leopard, though certainly present, are very rarely seen. It's not unusual to drive for a few hours and see no mammals at all.

Birds, too, are around but often not obvious. This isn't a centre for birdwatching, as only about 60 species are thought to live here, but look out for the majestic black eagle, as well as the rock kestrel and rock pigeon, and especially for the localised yellow-rumped eremomela which occur near Ai-Ais. Karoo bustards and ostrich are the highlights of the open plains above the canyon. In the canyon itself, herons, cormorants and kingfishers take advantage of the river's bounty, while both martins and mountain wheatear keep the hiker company from above.

Vegetation is sparse. Both on the top and on the canyon's slopes, the larger species are mostly euphorbias, with the odd quivertree and occasional deep red aloe, *Aloe gariepensis*. However, parts of the canyon's base where there is water are quite lush – like the Sulphur Springs with its palm trees and further south towards Ai-Ais. There you can expect camelthorn, wild tamarisk and ebony trees, among others.

GETTING THERE AND AWAY Detailed routes to the various lodges and camps are given below. Note that you can't drive between the west and the east sides of the canyon quickly. If you are approaching the east side from the north during the rainy season, and the C12 is blocked by flooding, then try taking a short cut from the B4, on to the D545 and then the C12. If the water pouring over the retaining wall is too fast to cross, then a detour to your left will bring you to a crossing on top of a dam wall – avoiding the need to ford the torrent. Alternatively, take the longer and more secure tar route on the B1 and C10.

 WHERE TO STAY   Seeing the canyon as a day trip from a base some way off is practical, particularly as the diagonal rays of early morning or late evening light do little for photographers' hopes of capturing the depths of the canyon. Thus Keetmanshoop is one possibility, while for a less urban setting you could opt for somewhere around Karasburg or Grünau to the east, or Seeheim to the north. However, if only to minimise your driving, stay closer if you can – at Hobas Campsite or Ai-Ais Hot Springs Spa within the national park, or at one of the private lodges on either side of the canyon.

Private lodges
East of the Fish River   Map, page 211.

Gondwana Cañon Park \061 427000; a/h **m** 081 129 2424; **e** info@gondwana-collection.com; www.gondwana-collection. com. Several accommodation options lie within the 1,260km² Gondwana Cañon Park, which borders Ai-Ais National Park. It was established by Manni Goldbeck in 1996 from 7 commercial sheep farms, with the aim of reclaiming the land from overgrazing & returning it to its natural state. Today it is grazed by springbok, oryx, red hartebeest, blue wildebeest, ostrich & Burchell's & mountain zebra, as well as newly released black rhino. A hallmark of Gondwana is its self-sufficiency project, for a hefty proportion of fresh food served comes from its own farms, both here & further north at Stampriet. Provisions such as bacon, milk, eggs & salad vegetables & herbs, not to mention homemade bread, salamis & cheeses, add considerably to the meals enjoyed by guests, who are welcome to visit the farm near Cañon Lodge. Apart from Cañon Roadhouse, the other accommodation options are clustered close

together, just 2km off the C37 & 7km south of the turn-off to the canyon's main viewpoint. The properties share & host a variety of activities, such as a free sundowner walk (🕐 16.30; just pay for drinks), a sundowner drive (🕐 15.30; 2hrs; N$365 pp), a guided morning hike (🕐 08.00; 6km; 3hrs; N$255 pp), a day hike (🕐 09.00; 1½hrs; 3km; N$125 pp) or a drive around the reserve (🕐 09.00 dep; 3hrs; N$650 pp).

CAÑON ROADHOUSE (22 rooms, camping) \063 683111; **e** roadhouse@iway.na. North of Cañon Lodge, the Roadhouse is signposted about 17km off the C12 near Holoog, along the C37. Don't be deterred by the name: this quirky outback-style inn with its red roof & sense of fun never fails to charm. A popular stop for overland adventure-travel trucks & visitors who are drawn to its reliable fuel station (🕐 07.00–22.00) & tyre repairs, this oasis is famous for its interior littered with rusting old vehicles displayed in the garden & – more ostentatiously – in the restaurant, where an old truck becomes a reception desk & others are commissioned as offbeat fireplaces, while a huge central *pompstasie* (filling station) serves as the bar. Look out for the saucy paintings of 'Jongelolo' & 'Pandora's Box' in the female & male toilets, respectively – if curiosity gets the better of you, a bell will ring & you'll owe a round of drinks to everyone the bar! The à la carte lunch menu features toasties or fish & chips in the N$50–80 range, or more substantial fare, including game, in the evening. Next door is an information centre with internet terminal, rock displays & boards explaining history & conservation of both Fish River Canyon & the wider environment. A new licensed quivertree (see box, page 197) nursery is also in development, but only African residents can buy them. There's also free Wi-Fi. At the back around a couple of courtyards are attractive en-suite rooms, their décor picking out the rich reds & yellows of the surrounding landscape. All are thoughtfully kitted out with AC/heating & international plugs. Further back, over a wooden bridge leading from the pool (towels available at reception), is a campsite with 12 pitches. *B&B N$1,257/2,010 sgl/dbl; camping N$165 pp.* **LLL**

🏠 **CAÑON VILLAGE** (42 rooms) ✆ 063 693 025. Just 2km before Cañon Lodge, at the foot of the surrounding mountains, the 'village' is mainly used for groups. Thatched, en-suite cottages of stone, each with AC, fan & mosquito nets, form a semicircle overlooking the plains. Original artwork on the walls of both the rooms & the long, thatched lapa gives a glimpse of the history of the Nama people in the area. Meals are served buffet-style in the restaurant, where there's a central fireplace, & there's a large separate bar, as well as a large swimming pool & terrace. *B&B N$1,257/2,010 sgl/dbl; dinner N$230.* **LLL**

🏠 **CAÑON LODGE** (30 chalets) ✆ 063 693 014; e c-lodge@iway.na. NB: On the approach to the lodge, watch out for the steep sleeping policemen. The lodge centres on an old farmhouse, built in 1904, which has been restored & now functions as the reception, with a well-stocked gift shop, a bar with free Wi-Fi & papered with old smoking adverts, & adjoining restaurant area. Ingeniously spaced among the surrounding kopjes – small hills of bare stone boulders – are innovative chalets, rustic in concept but comfortably appointed. Dbl or twin beds, umbrellas in case of rain, mosquito nets, AC/heating & fans, safe, a terrace overlooking the rocks & en-suite showers sit within raw-stone walls under a thatched roof; rooms 21 & 28 have corner baths. Both guests & day visitors are catered for in the large but intimate restaurant (*b/fast* ⏰ *06.30–09.00; lunch* ⏰ *noon–14.00; dinner* ⏰ *18.00–20.30*), which in summer spills out on to the terrace with a minigolf course below, but on chilly winter evenings is warmed by blazing open fires. Buffet meals are substantial & tasty, with considerable choice, largely due to the self-sufficiency project. In addition to the obvious attractions of the canyon itself, there is plenty to do while here; there's even a small swimming pool with an honesty bar set 100m from the lodge itself, where you can relax in complete privacy. *B&B N$1,715/2,743 sgl/dbl sharing; dinner N$230.* **LLLL**

🏠 **CAÑON MOUNTAIN CAMP** (8 rooms) This simple converted green & white farmhouse is 6km beyond Cañon Lodge, where visitors should book in. Accommodation is ideal for small groups or families who are self-catering (although dinner can be taken at the lodge, N$230 pp). Basic but comfortable en-suite rooms enclose a stone-paved courtyard with an equipped communal kitchen with fireplace & a large braai area overlooking the plains. This is a secluded spot with few mod cons (though there's now electricity, but still no phone reception), offering the opportunity to explore independently for a day or two. *N$310 pp.* **L**

West of the Fish River *Map, page 211.*

Access to the private lodges along the western side of the river is via the D463, a turning off the B4 that is signposted 'Canyon Nature Park' and 'Feldschuhorn'. It's a scenic drive, taking in pans, rolling red dunes and rocks eroded into sometimes extraordinary shapes and formations. Be careful, though, as patches of soft sand can make driving hazardous, and note that the more westerly D462 crosses several river-beds with thick patches of sand, so is not recommended as an alternative.

🏠 **Vogelstrausskluft Lodge** (24 rooms, camping) ☎ 063 683086; e info@ vogelstrausskluft.com; www.vogelstrausskluft. com. Built overlooking a dry river-bed, Vogelstrausskluft is 2.5km from the D463, about 22km from its junction with the B4. The 27,000ha reserve includes a 54km stretch of the Löwen River, where it flows into the Fish. Although the rivers flow in a canyon at this stage, it is not comparable with the spectacle further south. The imposing thatched lapa leads straight into a smart dining area. Food is taken seriously here, with buffet dinners (*N$210*) lit by candelabra & lovely wicker-shaded lamps. Dark wood furniture intensifies the rather grand atmosphere, alleviated by squashy leather sofas looking out to a pool & surrounding deck, & beyond to the river-bed. Against this, most of the en-suite twin rooms, built in pairs under thatch, seem relatively small & slightly austere, albeit with AC & a balcony. Nicer are 4 'luxury suites' with a dbl & sgl bed, plus a comfy chair & sofa, & a kettle. And perhaps campers have the best: a secluded campsite with just 4 pitches under camelthorn shade, backed by dunes & overlooking the pan. The lodge offers 2hr nature drives (🕐 *09.00 or 16.30; N$240 pp*) or a full-day excursion to Fish River Canyon (*N$1,220 pp*), but of real appeal is the 2-day canyon excursion, which includes a couple of hikes & open-sky braai dinner (*N$4,220 pp*). B&B room N$1,374/1,822 sgl/dbl; suite N$1,679/2,260 sgl/dbl; camping N$130 pp; b/fast N$95. **LLL**

🏠 **Fish River Lodge** (20 chalets) ☎ 063 683005, reservations ☎ 061 228104; e reservations@fishriverlodge.com.na; www. fishriverlodge-namibia.com. The only lodge right on the rim of Fish River Canyon & set in the 45,000ha private Canyon Nature Park, this is one of Namibia's most spectacularly sited lodges. Sparsley dotted with quivertrees & strewn with irregular chunks of rock, this undulating terrain above the canyon boasts considerable clumps of *Euphorbia gregaria*, & is home to dassies, oryx, klipspringer & ostrich. From a distance, a row of military pillboxes appears to line the ridge, but closer inspection reveals a series of spacious,

ultra-modern, stone-clad chalets on either side of a large central area of similar design. It's all minimalist in concept, some would say stark, with high ceilings, cool grey paintwork, white bathroom fittings & wide metal-framed French windows, yet designed both to blend into the environment & to cope with soaring summer temperatures. By contrast, 2 central fires in the main lodge don't entirely take the edge off the chill when the mercury plummets, so bring warm clothes. Yet what transcends all is the breathtaking view across the canyon, shared by the central building, the infinity pool & individual chalets. (A word of warning: children are welcome, but with sheer cliffs & few barriers, the lodge is definitely not child-friendly.) The large main area has a bar – with an inventive cocktail list – on one side, a central lounge area adorned with zebra rugs, & the dining area on the far left. Leading off this is the reception, which displays a small selection of high-end souvenirs. There's intermittent Wi-Fi. B/fast is served as a buffet, optional afternoon tea & cake is available 15.00–15.30 & dinner is 3 courses chosen from an à la carte menu; lunch is normally included in the price of activities. Sometimes the staff serenade the guests with a series of traditional songs after dinner. There are 2hr self-guided walking trails along the rim (track to right takes 1½hrs; left track 2½hrs), as well as guided walks (*N$275*) & scenic drives (*N$300*). Most popular, though, is the canyon excursion (*7hrs; N$1,000*) – combining bathing in a rock pool & champagne lunch – or a drive to the sundowner point with a descent either on foot or by vehicle into the canyon. A further attraction is the possibility of organising flexible, catered hikes into the canyon, with all your gear (including camping equipment) transported ahead. For details, see page 213. Spa treatments also available.

To find it, follow the D463 – nice & firm despite its 'D' classification – from the B4 for 84km, then turn left & continue for a further 19km to the lodge; if you're in a 2WD allow about an hour. Pass through the gate belonging to a goat farm. *DBB N$1,760/2,695 sgl/dbl*. **LLLL**

Inside the national park   *Map, page 211.*

The two options below are the only places to stay within the national park. Camping is not permitted anywhere else.

Ai-Ais Hot Springs (☉ *sunrise–sunset*) Ai-Ais is best reached from Keetmanshoop by driving south on the main B1, and then turning west on to the C10. (Try to avoid this in the late afternoon, as the sun is directly in your face.)

Alternatively, from Lüderitz, reach Seeheim on the B4 and take the gravel C12 south. Then turn right on to the C37 towards Hobas and the C10. Coming from the south, you can turn left off the B1 on to the D316 – though this road is quieter and perhaps less well graded than the C10.

However you reach it, the final few kilometres of the C10 spiral down, cut into the rock layers of the canyon's side, until it reaches the bed of the Fish River. It's a marvellous road, though steep in parts, with some sharp corners – so drive carefully. You can arrive at any time, so do not fear being locked out if you are late.

🏠 **Ai-Ais Hot Springs Spa** (36 rooms, 7 chalets, camping) ✆063 262045; reservations ✆061 285 7200; e reservations@nwr.com.na; www. nwr.com.na. Sitting at the bottom of the canyon at the end of the C10, towards the southern end of the conservation area, this lodge also marks the finishing point for the 5-day hiking trail. '/Ai/Ais', which means 'burning water' in the Nama language, is a reference to the hot, sulphurous springs that well up here at a fairly constant 65°C. These feed both a large outdoor pool & a classy indoor spa, with several pools & a wellness centre offering massages, facials & the like. En-suite dbl rooms lead off from the indoor spa: some facing the river; others – smaller & less expensive – at the back (though the 'mountain view' isn't much of a draw). Clustered around a courtyard are 2-bedroom chalets with kitchens. For campers, some 70 level, sandy pitches share 3 ablution blocks & 3 kitchens – so in high season don't come expecting peace & quiet. Campers are free to make use of the main facilities. The restcamp has a basic shop & fuel station, as well as a restaurant that serves b/fast 06.00–08.30, lunch noon–13.30 & dinner 18.00–20.30. Despite the face-lift, standards of catering remain in the category of school dinners. The more active might bring tennis rackets to play on the courts here, or wander off up the canyon, which is beautiful. Guests can use the spa free of charge; day visitors are charged N$30 & should bring their own towels; hikes along the Fish River trail cost N$275 pp & guided ½- & full-day excursions cost from N$330 pp. *B&B room N$660–770/1,100–1,320 sgl/dbl; chalet N$743 pp; camping N$143 pp (max 8); park fees extra.* **LL**

Hobas Visitors to Fish River Canyon pass through the gate at Hobas, where park fees are payable before continuing on to the viewpoint.

⛺ **Hobas Campsite** (14 pitches) ✆063 683469; reservations as for Ai-Ais above. This busy campsite near the main viewpoint of the canyon has sandy sites spread out under shady, willowy trees. For extra shelter during the intense midday sun there are thatched sunshades, as well as tables & chairs for picnics, & a small pool.

As the only convenient base in the area for overland groups, this site gets many large trucks stopping here, so it can become festive at times; competition for the quieter sites is high. Those tackling the 5-day hike often camp here the night before they set off, too. Security guards the gate at night. Recycling bins are by reception, which doubles as a shop selling drinks, postcards, clothes & basic food supplies. Power is available (☉ *05.00–13.00 & 16.00–22.00 daily*). There are plans to add bungalows & a restaurant in the near future. *Camping N$120 pp.* **L**

AI-AIS NATIONAL PARK (☉ *sunrise–sunset; entry N$175/85 adult/child per day; additional fee payable at Hobas Campsite only, for admission to viewpoint & surrounding area*) The area around the southern part of Fish River Canyon was proclaimed a conservation area in 1969. The land was as poor in potential for agriculture as it is rich in potential for tourism, and this was a way of protecting the area from uncontrolled development. The 345,000ha national park now encompasses Ai-Ais and Hobas. A more recent initiative has seen the park linked with the environmentally similar Richtersveld in South Africa, to form Namibia's first transfrontier or peace park: Ai-Ais Richtersveld Transfrontier Park.

Those wishing to cross the Orange River that forms the border between the two parks can now do so at the Sendelingsdrift border post (⊕ *08.00–16.00*) where a pontoon on cables takes a couple of vehicles and passengers (*N$150 per vehicle one-way, N$250 return*). Note, however, that operation of the pontoon is often suspended during the rainy season due to the high levels of the river, so it's best to phone ahead to check (☏ *063 274760, South Africa +27 27 831 1506*).

The park's borders are well marked along the main access roads. Other than at the control post south of Rosh Pinah (where you sign in or out), most are simply signboards. Access to the park itself is largely free of charge, with the exception of Fish River Canyon.

What to see and do Once in the area, a day is enough to see the canyon properly, unless you've arranged (in advance) to do the five-day hike (see *Hiking the Fish River Canyon*, below). Note that no other visitors are allowed to descend into the canyon from the lip at any time of year.

Start the morning by driving past Hobas for 10km to the **Main Viewpoint**. This is *the* classic view of Hell's Bend, featured in most of the photographs – and probably the only view that you'll see if you're on a bus tour. A visitors' centre features toilets and information boards about the canyon's geology, as well as a raised, shaded platform from which to look down on the canyon.

To the right, a 3km track leads to the **Hikers' Viewpoint**, which lends a different perspective and is worth the wander if it is cool. This is also the starting point for the five-day hike.

Then take the road that leads to the left of the Main Viewpoint. This is a continuation of the D324, which doubles back to run roughly parallel to the canyon, generally keeping within a few hundred yards. There are several stops for viewpoints along its length, perhaps the best being the **Sulphur Springs Viewpoint** (Palm Springs), which has a picnic table and a stunning view of another tight switchback in the river's course.

This road is little used and graded less, so it's bumpy in parts but suitable for a 2WD car driven slowly and carefully. The scenery is so spectacular that you won't want to rush. If you have a 4x4, you can continue past the Sulphur Springs Viewpoint to the southernmost viewpoint at Eagle's Rock – a further 12km of very rough, stony road, but offering a good view of the canyon further south. Either way, you'll eventually have to retrace your tracks to return on the D324, back past the Hobas gate and south.

At the southern end of the canyon, **Ai-Ais** makes a great afternoon stop, giving you time to relax in a mineral pool or to take a gentle walk up the canyon for a taste of what the hikers experience near the end of the route.

HIKING THE FISH RIVER CANYON
Within the national park For fit, experienced and self-sufficient backpackers, the Fish River Canyon is the venue for one of southern Africa's greatest hikes: a chance to follow the river within the national park where vehicles never venture, about 80–90km from Hikers' Viewpoint to Ai-Ais. However, numbers are limited to a maximum of 30 hikers per day, and hikes must be prearranged with the NWR (see pages 56 and 121) months in advance, so you need to work out your logistics carefully long before you get here.

Regulations and costs Hiking trips within the national park are allowed from 1 May to 15 September, and limited to a maximum of 30 hikers per day. The NWR

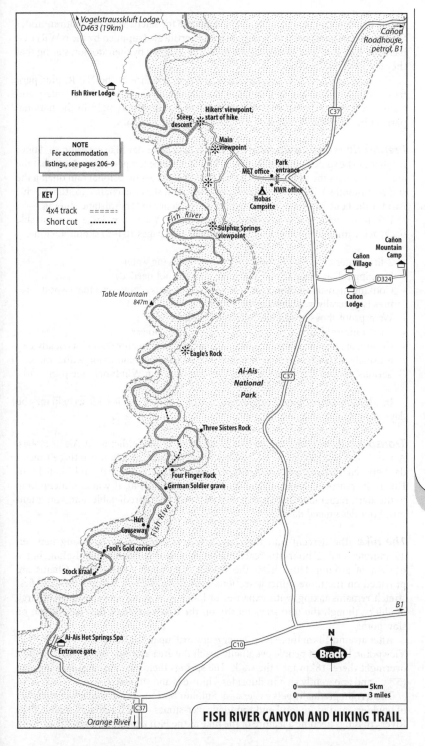

Vogelstrausskluft Lodge,
D463 (19km)

Cañon
Roadhouse,
petrol, B1

C37

Fish River Lodge

Hikers' viewpoint,
start of hike
Steep
descent
Main
viewpoint
Park
entrance
MET office
NWR office
Hobas
Campsite

NOTE
For accommodation
listings, see pages 206–9

KEY
4x4 track ======
Short cut ··········

Fish River

Sulphur Springs
viewpoint

Cañon
Mountain
Camp
Cañon
Village
D324
Cañon
Lodge

Table Mountain
847m

Eagle's Rock

Ai-Ais
National
Park

C37

Three Sisters Rock

Four Finger Rock
German Soldier grave

Hut
Causeway

Fish River

Fool's Gold corner

Stock kraal

B1

Ai-Ais Hot Springs Spa
Entrance gate

N

Bradt

C10

0   5km
0   3 miles

FISH RIVER CANYON AND HIKING TRAIL

C37
Orange River

insists on each group being at least three people for safety, with no children under the age of 12. Hikers need to bring a medical certificate (supplied by the NWR) that has been issued within 40 days of the hike and is signed by their doctor, stating that they are fit to do the hike.

The hike costs N$275 per person, paid for in advance at the NWR, plus park fees of N$80. Hikers are responsible for all their own food, equipment, safety and transport to/from the canyon. Hikers must stay at least one night in the national park, either at Hobas Campsite or at Ai-Ais Hot Spring Spa.

Preparations and equipment This is a four- or five-day hike covering 80–90km in what can be some of the subcontinent's most extreme temperatures. (Note that the area experiences the same climate as the Cape, so can get occasional rain during the summer months.) There's no easy way out once you start; no chance to stop. So this isn't for the faint-hearted, or those without experience of long-distance hiking.

For those who come prepared, it's excellent. Your own large, comfortable backpack with your normal hiking equipment (see pages 104–5) should include:

- 2-litre water bottle, with some method of purifying water
- Sleeping roll and bag to –8°C (though a tent is not needed)
- Cooking utensils and food for at least six days, plus a stove and fuel (wood for fires is generally available on the second half of the hike)
- Waterproof shoes or sandals for river crossings
- Light rainproof jacket, in the unlikely event of a shower
- Good map. One rough route-plan with pretty colour pictures and lots of advice is usually available at Hobas, though it is best used in conjunction with a more 'serious' version from the Surveyor General's office in Windhoek (see page 120).

In addition, each group should have a comprehensive medical kit, as help may be days away if there is an accident.

Transport If you're driving yourself, leave your vehicle either at Ai-Ais or Hobas. A shuttle bus (*N$150 pp one-way, min 3 people*) covers the 62km trip three times a day between the two points, officially leaving Ai-Ais at 06.00, 10.00 and 14.00. From Hobas, it transports hikers to the start for a further N$40. If you are hitchhiking to the start, remember that your arrival date will be unpredictable, and you might miss your designated date.

The hike The descent into the canyon is very steep in parts, taking between 45 minutes and 2 hours to reach the river – a distance of just 1.5km, but a descent of around 430m from the Hikers' Viewpoint to the river. Chains are provided on the more difficult sections near the top. Even beyond this, the first stretch remains taxing, with expanses of loose river-sand between areas of large boulders, though the trail stays mostly on the eastern side of the river. It can be slow going.

After around 14km there is an 'emergency exit' up to the Sulphur (Palm) Springs Viewpoint, but most people eventually reach the area around Sulphur Springs and overnight there, 18km into the walk. The springs themselves are fast-flowing, hot (57°C) and apparently rich in fluorides, chlorides and sulphates.

The terrain gradually gets easier after Sulphur Springs, traversing fewer stretches of boulders, and more sand and rounded river-stones – but it remains challenging. River crossings become a feature of the hike as the Fish zigzags through the canyon.

As the canyon widens out, the vegetation increases and landmarks appear in the canyon walls: Table Mountain, Three Sisters and Four Fingers Rock. Towards the end, the route options increase, some heading away from the river across the mountains, and it's surprisingly easy to get lost. Finally, 80–90km from the start (depending on how many times you cross the river and if you cut corners) you arrive at Ai-Ais.

Trail etiquette Trail etiquette here is the same as sensible rules for responsible hiking anywhere in the bush (see pages 111–12). However, as groups cover the same trail regularly here, these guidelines are all the more vital. In particular:

- There are no 'official' fireplaces; use existing ones if possible. Use only dead wood for fires.
- Leave no litter in the canyon – even fruit peel looks unsightly and takes a long time to biodegrade.
- Use only biodegradable soap, and wash away from the main river from which people will be drinking.
- Never feed animals; baboons in particular can be a problem.
- There are no toilets, so burn all toilet paper and bury it with the excrement, in a shallow hole far from the river.

Outside the national park
North of the national park, in the areas of the canyon that are bordered by private reserves, hiking is less restricted than in the park itself. Here, there are various options for hikers, both from the western side of the Fish River and from the east.

Fish River Lodge (See page 208) The lodge offers a range of two- to five-day hikes ranging from N\$5,000–13,000 per person between April and September. Your overnight kit is transported from one camp to the other, leaving you to carry just a light daypack containing personal items such as hat, sunglasses, suncream and camera, plus a light lunch. Bush dinners and breakfasts are prepared by a private chef.

Gondwana Collection (✎ 061 230066; m 081 129 2424; e info@gondwana-collection.com; www.gondwana-collection.com) Like their counterpart Fish River Lodge, Gondwana offers guided or unguided hikes of flexible length, lasting two to five days. Here, however, you will be carrying all your equipment and, if you choose to go unaccompanied, all provisions as well. As for the national park trail, groups must comprise a minimum of three participants, each of whom should have a medical certificate stating that they are physically fit.

Mule Trails Also operated by the Gondwana Collection (see above), the mule trails are designed so that you do the walking and mules carry the packs. Typically the mules set off after their human counterparts, overtaking them at some stage during the day and going ahead with their drivers to set up camp.

There are two options: the three-day Fish Eagle Trail costing N\$6,500 per person, or the two-day Klipspringer Trail costing N\$5,500 per person. Both operate between April and September. The hikes themselves start at either the Mule Station or Cañon Outpost. However, although both are signposted from the C12, the meeting point for all hikers is at Cañon Roadhouse (see page 206), where participants can spend the night before and after their hike.

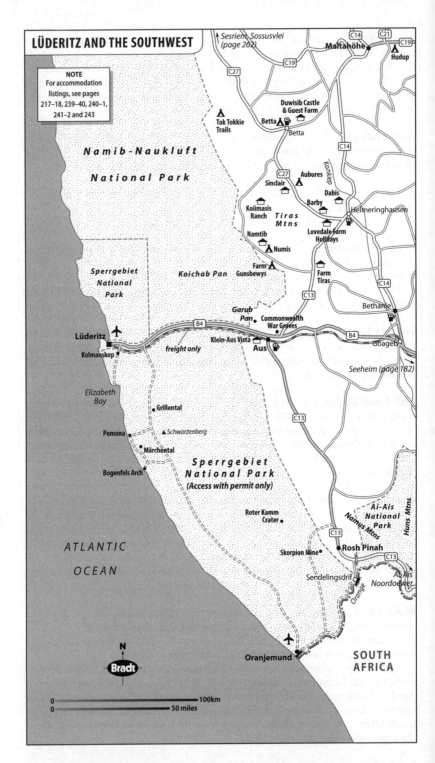

LÜDERITZ AND THE SOUTHWEST

NOTE
For accommodation
listings, see pages
217–18, 239–40, 240–1,
241–2 and 243

*Sesriem, Sossusvlei
(page 262)*

Maltahöhe

Hudup

C14 C21 C19

C19

C27

C19

Namib-Naukluft

National Park

Tok Tokkie
Trails

Duwisib Castle
& Guest Farm

Betta

Betta

C14

Konkiep

Aubures

C27

Sinclair

Dabis

Koiimasis
Ranch

Barby

Helmeringhausen

*Tiras
Mtns*

Namtib

Lovedale Farm
Holidays

*Sperrgebiet
National
Park*

Numis

Koichab Pan

Farm
Gunsbewys

Farm
Tiras

C14

C13

Bethanie

*Garub
Pan*

Commonwealth
War Graves

B4

B4

Lüderitz

Klein-Aus Vista

Goageb

Kolmanskop

freight only

Aus

Seeheim (page 182)

*Elizabeth
Bay*

Grillental

C13

Pomona

▲ *Schwarzenberg*

Märchental

Bogenfels Arch

*Sperrgebiet
National Park*
(Access with permit only)

Roter Kamm
Crater

*Ai-Ais
National
Park*

Namus Mtns

Huns Mtns

C13

ATLANTIC

OCEAN

Skorpion Mine

Rosh Pinah

C13

Sendelingsdrif

*Ai-Ais
Noordoewer*

Orange

N

Bradt

Oranjemund

**SOUTH
AFRICA**

0 ————— 100km
0 ————— 50 miles

214

11

Lüderitz and the Southwest

Though the European colonisation of Namibia started in this southwestern corner, it remains perhaps the country's least-known area for visitors. At the end of a long road, Lüderitz is now being rediscovered, with its wonderful turn-of-the-20th-century architecture, desolate beaches, and position as the springboard for trips into the once-forbidden area that is now the Sperrgebiet National Park.

But there is more than Lüderitz in this region. Early historical sites from the 1900s are dotted throughout the area – and though places to stay are often far apart, most of the hotels and guest farms are excellent value. Best of all are the amazing landscapes. Rugged mountains and flowing desert sands make the empty roads spectacular – with the D707, the southern sections of the C13, and even the main B4 across the Koichab Pan ranking among the country's more dramatic drives.

THE ROADS TO LÜDERITZ

FROM KEETMANSHOOP As you drive east from Keetmanshoop to Lüderitz, the main B4 is now all tarred. After about 44km the C12 turns off left to the Fish River Canyon. A kilometre or so afterwards the B4 crosses the Fish River itself, which meanders down a broad, shallow, vegetated valley with few hints of the amazing canyon to the south.

To the north of the road are some spectacular flat-topped hills, capped by hard dolorite which erodes slowly. One of these has been named Kaiserkrone, the 'Kaiser's crown', as it is an unusual conical shape capped by a symmetrical dolorite crown.

There are several small towns along this road, outlined below. Most can supply fuel and essentials, but none is comparable in size to Lüderitz or Keetmanshoop, so – except increasingly at Aus – few visitors stop at any for long.

Seeheim About 45km from Keetmanshoop just south of the modern B4, Seeheim offers straightforward access along the C12 to the Fish River Canyon, passing Naute Dam on the way. In its heyday, in the late 19th century, the town was on the old east–west road and was larger than Keetmanshoop, supporting three hotels. Now, marooned by the side of the railway, just one hotel remains.

Where to stay

Seeheim Hotel (32 rooms, camping)
\063 683643; m 081 128 0349; e seeheim@iway. na; www.seeheimhotel.com. Dating back to 1896, the stone-built Seeheim is hidden away in a quarry of sorts. It's one of those quirky finds that defies categorisation. Owned & run by Zirkie Kloppers & family, it is something of a one-stop shop, with an emergency fuel supply (they'll only sell 20/25 litres at a time), a shop selling souvenirs & safari clothes, meat & other basics, a publike bar (selling grapes in summer; oranges in winter), a games room with table tennis, darts & a pool table, a simple

restaurant & outside à la carte dining area (☉ *all day*, $$$) overlooking a swimming pool (*non-residents N$10*) – & a thriving furniture business (not to mention a taxidermy practice, evidenced by the bizarre optics which will alienate some). All the non-AC en-suite rooms – some in the original building, others added at various levels around the complex – are different & individually furnished with pieces the Kloppers have designed & made themselves from 'kiaat' wood. Rooms 19–32 are newer/more modern with open-plan bathrooms & zebra-print cushions. Around the buildings are 20 camping pitches. Guests can hike around the lodge, visit the kudu & chickens kept in a pen to the right of the entrance, while Zirkie's organic garden & farm, 50km away, offers the opportunity for game drives (*N$900 pp, min 4*) if booked in advance. There are always offers on, so email for rates. *DBB N$1,059/1,725 sgl/dbl; camping N$100 pp.* **LLL**

Goageb

Goageb Once a stop on the railway, this tiny town still appears on maps but today is totally derelict – a ghost town. It sits to the left of a new white bridge, just past the exit for Bethanie.

A more uplifting spot is **Kuibis Restaurant** (✆ *081 335 3523;* ☉ *07.00–17.00 Mon–Sat (18.30 in summer), 09.00/10.00–17.00 Sun;* $), some 55km to the west, run by Mrs Greef. It serves light meals such as toasted sandwiches and has a small shop selling kudu and oryx biltong.

Bethanie

Bethanie About 30km north of Goageb, Bethanie (or Bethanien) is a centre for local administration. The main road into town from the B4 is the tarred C14, but if you're coming from Lüderitz turn on to the D435 about 20km further west. There is no longer any public transport here.

The town is dominated by the apparently modern Lutheran church, which was actually one of the first churches in Namibia. Originally built in 1859, it was restored by American evangelists in 1998.

🏠 ***Where to stay, eat and drink***

🏠 **Bethanie Guesthouse** (10 rooms, camping) Keetmanshoop St; ✆ 063 283013; 📱 081 2948730; e bestbed@iway.na. One of the country's oldest hotels, built around 1880, the Bethanie is located on the right as you enter town & owned by the rather serious Wessel Esterhuysen. Character remains in the form of a huge lapa at the rear encompassing dining, seating, TV, swimming pool & BBQ areas, all under thatch with a fire pit & outside heaters for added comfort. En-suite rooms – 4 with AC & others with fans – are off to the side, while campers have fenced pitches & an ablution block being upgraded. Lunch (*N$65*) & dinner (*N$100*) also available. *Camping N$100 pp.* $$

🍴 **Coffee Shop** Beside the Puma petrol station; ☉ 07.00–16.00 Mon–Fri, 07.00–13.00 Sat. Cheery café with a pleasant terrace decorated with cacti & a few tables. They sell sausage rolls, pies, pastries, chips, sandwiches, crisps, penny sweets & super slices of cake. They also have a Windhoek Bank ATM & very clean toilets – ask for the key at the till. $

Other practicalities There's a **post office** (☉ *08.00–13.00 & 14.00–16.30 Mon–Fri*) selling mobile phone top-up cards and internet facilities, a rather empty **grocery store** (☉ *08.00–17.00 Mon–Fri, 08.00–13.00 Sat, closed every third Sat*), an agency for **Standard Bank** (☉ *09.00–13.00 Mon–Fri*), a basic restaurant, (☉ *08.00–17.00 Mon–Fri*) and a **fuel station** (☉ *08.00–18.00 daily*).

Aus About 211km west of Keetmanshoop a slip road turns left off the B4 to Aus, notable for its unpredictable weather and its history as a POW camp. Just after turning off the B4, you'll see a smart **tourist information centre**, but don't get your hopes up – after opening in 2006, it sadly closed a few years ago due to 'funding issues'. Today, this small hillside town is mostly used as a stopover by truckers and motorcyclists who come to refuel at the 24-hour **fuel station**, which stands in the heart of the village. Just down the road from the tourist centre, on the left, is a **police post** (☏ *063 258005*), and near the petrol station is the **post office** (⊕ *08.00–16.30 Mon–Fri, 08.00–11.30 Sat*).

Weather and flora Aus's weather can be extreme, very cold in winter and hot in the summer. It is also unpredictable – which stems from its proximity to the Cape – although the winter rain, and its associated flora, is more pronounced in the area around Rosh Pinah. (The Cape has a different weather pattern from anywhere else in southern Africa, with winter rainfall from May to September, and gloriously warm, dry summer weather from November to February.)

Sometimes Aus's weather will follow a typically Namibian pattern; at others it will have the Cape's weather, with showers in winter, and occasionally even snow. If heavy or prolonged, this rain can cause a sudden flush of sprouting plants and blooms, rather like the 'flower season' in Namaqualand, south of the border. Many unusual plants have been catalogued here, including a rather magnificent species of bulb whose flowers form a large globe, the size of a football. When these seed, the globe breaks off and rolls about like tumbleweed. Endemic to this small area is the yellow-flowered Aus daisy (*Arctotis fastiosa*), which grows only within a 30km radius of the town (a slightly more orange subspecies is found at Rosh Pinah). In winter, the yellow *kuibi* or butterflower (*Papia capensis*) brightens up the plains at the foot of the mountains, interspersed with the blue sporry (*Felicia namaquana*) and the bright purple fig bush. Higher up, the mountain butterflower holds sway, the western slopes are scented by wild rosemary, and the Bushman's candle is to be found – although here it is yellow or, rarely, white, unlike its bushier pink cousin in the desert to the west.

History When the German colonial troops surrendered to the South African forces in 1915, a camp for the prisoners of war was set up a few kilometres outside what is now Aus, just off the C13 about 1km south of the B4. At one point 1,552 German POWs were held by 600 guards. It seems that the German prisoners worked hard to make their conditions more comfortable by manufacturing bricks, building houses and stoves, and cultivating gardens. They eventually even sold bricks to their South African guards. The camp closed shortly after the end of the war, and little remains of the buildings bar a few ruined huts, although a memorial marks the spot. On a hill 1.3km to the east of town, however, behind the local cemetery, is a small **cemetery** maintained by the Commonwealth War Graves Commission. Here lie 61 prisoners of war, and a further 60 members of the garrison, most of them victims of a flu epidemic in 1918. If you're driving up here, keep to the right-hand track.

Getting there and away Nowadays, visitors to Aus have little choice but to arrive by car. The railway through town is being upgraded for freight traffic, but it is unlikely to be reopened for passenger trains.

Where to stay, eat and drink

✳ 🏠 **Klein-Aus Vista** [Map, page 214] (30 rooms, 8 chalets, hikers' cabin, camping) ☏ *063 258116*; ✉ info@klein-aus-vista.com; www. klein-aus-vista.com. Nestled against the Aus Mountains, 1,400m above sea level, Klein-Aus

Vista is 3km west of Aus to the south of the main B4. It's a family business, owned & run by brothers Piet & Willem Swiegers, who grew up here & have amalgamated 5 farms to form the privately owned 51,000ha Gondwana Sperrgebiet Rand Park. This is an evocative landscape, defined by granite outcrops & mountains, dry river-beds scattered with rocks & vast rose-hued desert plains. After winter rain, from Jul to Sep, the plains explode into an expansive carpet of yellow & violet flowers. To the north, the park borders the Namib-Naukluft Park, home of the Namib desert horses.

Hiking is a major attraction, with a number of very well-marked circular trails of varying levels of difficulty & covering 4–20km (*1.5–5hrs*). Alternatively, there is plenty of scope for striking out on your own to seek out wild flowers or choose a vantage point to watch the sunset. Guided trips include sunset drives (*N$290 pp*) in the reserve. Piet is also a keen mountain-biker (he organises the annual 2-day MTB Challenge (*www.klein-aus-vista-mtb-challenge.com*) at the start of May), so 5 bikes & helmets are available for intermediate & advanced riders (*N$250 pp/day*) who can follow a series of trails marked in the booklet (*N$30*) sold at reception; the price includes a park permit.

Sundecks, a horseshoe-shaped pool & braai facilities are planned for the end of 2014. This is a super spot to spend a day or three unwinding during a long trip, with good service & diverse accommodation, & is highly recommended.

🏠 **DESERT HORSE INN** (30 rooms) The Desert Horse Inn incorporates the original 4 stylish rooms & the main reception, bar & restaurant – where an excellent 3-course dinner (*N$250*) is served, with a reasonable selection of wines. A further 20 rooms have been built in pairs on a nearby hill, with 6 more added near the main building – these can be chilly, but come with fan heaters & hot water bottles. Leading off from reception is a superb little gift shop kept by Piet's wife, & a cosy lounge with fast free Wi-Fi, TV, bar & fireplace sits beneath the restaurant. *B&B N$1,125/1,820 sgl/dbl.* **LLL**

🏠 **EAGLE'S NEST** (7 chalets) Those seeking to enjoy the solitude & beauty of the mountains may be better served by these highly individual en-suite chalets, some 7km from the main reception. Built around gigantic granite boulders, with private verandas, these combine the best of rustic design – stone walls, heavy wooden furniture & a traditional fireplace – with electricity, modern bathroom fittings & a well-equipped kitchenette, minibar stocked with wine & beer, & dining table. Guests can arrange take-away BBQ packs & b/fast platters, or eat in the main restaurant. Detailed information books on the history, flora & fauna of the area are to be found in the rooms. *B&B N$1,550/2,450 sgl/dbl.* **LLL**

🏠 **GEISTERSCHLUCHT** (hikers' cabin) Small groups can take advantage of this self-catering cabin, named 'Ghost Gully' after a group of diamond thieves who were shot by detectives trying to escape in a Hudson Terraplane in 1934, & are said to return for their lost treasure at full moon. Inside are a kitchen/bar & living area, & 2 rooms with bunks & sgl beds for up to 18 visitors. *From N$200 pp; for groups under 3 N$600 pp.* **L**

⛺ **CAMPSITE** (10 pitches) Well-spaced pitches are situated in a peaceful, narrow valley with shade from camelthorn trees, & good ablution blocks with hot water. Braai, tables & benches are available, but pitches don't have power. *N$100 pp.* **L**

🏠 **Bahnhof Hotel** (21 rooms) 📞063 258091; 📱081 235 6737; e kaikoro@iway.na; www.hotel-aus.com. Modern hotel on a hill, which has large, twin rooms with en-suite showers (1 with wheelchair access) & a further 8 new rooms built to the side with fans, small radiators & African art above the beds. Between them is a courtyard with a beer garden & fountain. À la carte meals with freshly baked bread are available to guests & non-residents alike – while those on the move can order b/fast & lunch packs. A raised wooden terrace at the front makes a pleasant place to eat, or to while away an hour with a cool drink. Gated parking is available at the back of the property & there's free Wi-Fi for guests (*N$10/30min for nonguests*). They offer a number of tours, including half- or full-day tours of Huib Park (*N$895 pp*), a 1½hr history tour of Aus (*N$200 pp*) & sundowner tours (*N$210 pp*). **$$$**

🏠 **Namib Garage** (15 rooms, camping) 📞063 258029; e namibaus@afol.com.na; www.ausnamibia.com. Run by Henriette, Aus's fuel station owner, who has self-catering rooms – some more luxurious than others – divided between 2 separate houses. All are simple & clean, ideal for longer stays. Opposite the garage itself, a wall encloses the campsite, with its 7 pitches with hot water in the ablution blocks. Accommodation enquiries should be made at the garage (🕐 *fuel 24hrs*), which also has a well-stocked mini supermarket (🕐 *07.00–19.00 Mon–Sat*). *Camping N$75 pp.* **$$**

THE DESERT HORSES

On the edge of the Koichab Pan, around Garub, perhaps the world's only desert-dwelling horses are thriving. On average, the numbers fluctuate between 90 and 300 at any one time, depending on the annual rainfall. In 1996, for example, there were about 134 horses, and the following year at least ten new foals were born, but 1999 saw a sharp drop to just 89 animals. The current number stands at over 200.

Their origins have fuelled considerable controversy over the years. Some considered that they were descended from farm animals that had escaped, or horses that the German Schutztruppe abandoned at the start of World War I. Others, that they came from Duwisib Castle, near Maltahöhe. By October 1908 Captain Von Wolf, Duwisib's owner, had assembled a herd of about 33 animals, namely '2 imported stallions, 17 imported mares, 8 Afrikaner mares, 6 year-old fillies'. He was a fanatical horseman, and by November 1909 he had expanded this collection to '72 horses. Mares: 15 Australians, 23 others, 9 thoroughbreds. Rest: Afrikaners and foals. 2 imported thoroughbred stallions'. Von Wolf left Duwisib in 1914 and was later killed at the battle of the Somme. Yet there were reports of wild horses near Garub in the 1920s, ten years before Von Wolf's farm manager reported the loss of any horses.

New research conducted by biologist Telané Greyling in 2005, with the support of the MET, as well as Klein-Aus Vista and the Gondwana Desert Collection, suggests that the herd was drawn together from all of these sources, as well as those of the South African Army. As a result of this research, plans have been drawn up to protect the welfare of these animals that are neither domestic nor natural game, with resources to be raised in part by improving tourist options. For more information, see www.wild-horses-namibia.com.

Observe the horses in March, surrounded by a wavy sea of fine green grass, and their situation seems idyllic. But see them on the same desolate gravel plains on an October afternoon, and you'll appreciate their remarkable survival.

What to see and do

Feral horses at Garub At the foot of the Aus Mountains, about 20km west of Aus, a sign 'feral horses' points north off the road. Follow the track for 1.5km and you'll come to Garub 'pan', an artificial waterhole that sustains the desert horses and is popular with the local oryx and ostrich as well.

A wooden observation shelter is a good spot to watch the horses and take photographs, with the added bonus of an information panel about their origins.

Koichab Pan to Lüderitz
Driving west from Garub, you enter the flat, gravel plains of the huge Koichab Pan, ringed by mountains in the distance. It's a vast and spectacular place where you'll be able to see any oncoming traffic on the straight road for perhaps 20km before you pass it.

As you draw nearer to Lüderitz, the last 20km or so of the road cross a coastal dune-belt of marching barchan dunes – which are constantly being blown across the road from south to north. Ever-present bulldozers battle to clear these, but sometimes you will still encounter low ramps of sand on the tar. Drive very slowly for this last section, as hitting even a small mound of sand can easily wreck a vehicle's suspension.

11

FROM AI-AIS OR NOORDOEWER VIA ROSH PINAH Noordoewer (see page 202) is one of the main access points into Namibia from South Africa. But while most drivers head north on the fast B1 towards Keetmanshoop, there is a second road, the C13, that travels northwest, running along the boundary of the Ai-Ais Richtersveld Transfrontier Park then on to Rosh Pinah, along the border of the Sperrgebiet National Park. Much of the road runs through spectacular mountain scenery, often alongside the Orange River, offering some excellent picnic spots and opportunities for birdwatching. (For details of accommodation and canoeing expeditions along the river, see pages 202–4.) There are few settlements along the C13 – except at Aussenkehr – so you should take more than the usual 'emergency rations' of food and water.

For those coming from Ai-Ais, it is well worth considering taking this southerly route to Lüderitz, too. The erstwhile 4x4 track to the southwest has now been upgraded to the C37/D207, joining up with the C13 along the Orange River, and on to Aus via Rosh Pinah. Note, however, that west of the C37 there are some sharp twists and turns, and hidden inclines that may be unexpectedly steep, so exercise considerable caution on this stretch. And a final word of warning: after heavy rain, usually in the early months of the year, the Fish River can flood. Even with a 4x4 the road is often impassable, so do check this before you set out.

ROSH PINAH About 165km south of Aus, and a similar distance from Ai-Ais (165km) or Noordoewer (154km), the mining town of Rosh Pinah lies in a very remote corner of Namibia, almost on the eastern border of the Sperrgebiet National Park. Yet the combination of a tarred toad through to Aus, and the border post at Sendelingsdrift (⊕ *08.00–16.30 when river not flooded*), has already led to an increased trickle of visitors. If – or perhaps when – access to the new national park is improved, the town's importance for visitors is likely to grow significantly.

For now, there is a palpable air of prosperity about the town, a reflection of the success of the new Skorpion mine. The road between Rosh Pinah and Aus has been tarred to facilitate the heavy goods vehicles that trundle regularly between here and the port at Lüderitz, cutting the drive from Ai-Ais to Aus from around 6 hours to just 4 hours or so.

History A deposit of copper was discovered just south of here by a Prussian Jew, Mose Eli Kahan, who had fled Europe to escape persecution. By the 1920s this was being worked, but was abandoned when the price slumped in the 1930s. Thirty years later, in 1968, Kahan found a zinc deposit in the mountains, which he named Rosh Pinah. Though he died soon afterwards, his son eventually joined forces with the large South African mining company Iscor to develop it.

Production began in 1969, and by the end of the century the mine was producing around 72,000 tonnes of zinc per year, as well as a lead concentrate, and also a little silver. More recently, the discovery of better-quality zinc led to the development of the nearby Skorpion mine, which opened in 2003 at a cost of U$54 million, representing the largest investment in Namibia since independence, and expected to have a life of around 15 years.

Where to stay, eat and drink

Amica Guesthouse (10 rooms) 306 Mukarob Close; ☏063 274 043; http://amicaguesthouse.wheretostay.na. We haven't visited this one yet, but it receives glowing reviews from travellers. The 10 en-suite rooms have DSTV, AC, safe, laundry service & phone. There's a swimming pool in the courtyard, a cocktail bar, coffee shop & internet. Food is described as 'gourmet'. **$$$**

🏠 **Four Seasons Lodge** (28 rooms) 📞063 274416; **m** 081 270 6040; **e** fourseasons@iway. na; www.roshpinahinfo.co.za. The smart, white-painted buildings of this lodge, with green roofs & canopied carports, are clearly visible next to the fuel station. All rooms have AC, fridge & TV, with the carports belonging to self-catering chalets. In the centre, surrounded by a low wall, are a good pool, a large bar & a restaurant serving the usual steaks & grills. Safe on-site parking. **$$$**

🏕 **Namuskluft Rest Camp** 📞063 274282; **m** 081 122 3543. Signposted from the C13 about 1km north of Rosh Pinah and a further 14km to the east, this campsite offers a swimming pool, walking trails & self-drive 4x4 trips. Cash only. *Camping N$60 pp, plus N$20 car.* **$**

Other practicalities Branches of FNB and Standard **banks**, a couple of **supermarkets**, a **post office** and a 24-hour **fuel** station smack of a town on the up. There are also a couple of **tyre-repair** places and a branch of Cymot.

LÜDERITZ

'A small drinking town with a fishing problem' is the motto emblazoned across T-shirts worn by the locals. This sleepy and laid-back town is famed for its seafood brought in by the freezing waters of the South Atlantic Benguela Current that sweeps up the coast. Lüderitz is a fascinating old German town, full of character, with relaxed locals who often have time to talk, but the recession has bitten hard here, with high unemployment and ensuing social problems.

Around the centre of town, houses are painted in improbable pastel shades, which makes Lüderitz feel like a delightful toy town at times.

The air here is tangibly clean, even on the foggiest of mornings. Local Namibians say that Lüderitz can have all four seasons in a day, as the weather can change in hours from bright, hot and sunny, to strong winds, to dark, cold and foggy – and then back to sunshine again. This variation, together with a cold sea and the prevailing southwest wind, rule out Lüderitz as a beach destination, though brave souls still take brief dips from the beach near the Nest Hotel or round on the peninsula.

In the evenings, there are a few lively bars, and a handful of quiet restaurants, notable for their seafood. But the entertainment here pales in comparison with Swakopmund. Because of its location, Lüderitz is not somewhere to 'drop in on' as you need to make a special journey to come here – but it's worth visiting for its architecture, its peninsula, and to see a part of Namibia which seems almost unaware of the outside world.

If you choose to visit the area, allow a minimum of two nights to appreciate it, and to see its surrounds properly. Try to avoid Sundays and public holidays, though, when almost everything closes down and the town is empty.

Tourism is having an impact here, but only gradually. Although several new hotels and guesthouses opened their doors in the years following independence, there's been a marked downturn in the town's economy, offset only partly by visiting cruise ships. Even the trendy new waterfront development near the harbour is looking a little tired. On the plus side, use of the harbour as the export base for the Skorpion zinc mine near Rosh Pinah has brought considerable new business into the town. Investment in the town's infrastructure is also ongoing: the conversion of the 1909 power station (built in Germany, dismantled and rebuilt on site), near the Nest Hotel, into a space housing a new maritime museum (it'll be Africa's largest, supposedly), craft market and 350-seat auditorium for the local university, is under way.

A lively time to coincide your visit is during the annual Crayfish Festival held at the end of May. Stalls offering taste testing and lots of music make it the highlight of their social calendar. Also starting to draw big crowds is the annual Lüderitz Speed Challenge, where world-class windsurfers come to compete at the end of September.

HISTORY Stone Age tools and artefacts found in the region confirm that Khoisan people knew the area centuries before any Europeans arrived. The first recorded visit by a European was that of Bartolomeu Dias, the great Portuguese explorer, who sheltered here in 1487. He returned the following year and erected a limestone cross at the spot now known as Diaz Point, naming the place Angra Pequena, or 'Little Bay'.

Passing mariners recognised it as one of the best natural harbours on the southwest coast of Africa – even if the land around the harbour was desolate, forbidding and totally lacking in fresh water. The Dutch East India Company sent an emissary to start trading with Nama groups in the region. This failed. In 1793 the area was annexed by the Dutch authorities in the Cape – who proceeded to do nothing with it.

By the mid-1800s, whalers, sealers, fishermen and guano collectors were exploiting the area's rich marine life and there are reports of hundreds of ships around the harbour area. By 1862 some had set up shore bases here.

In March 1883 a German trader, Adolf Lüderitz, with help from Heinrich Vogelsang, a merchant from the Cape, bought a small ship, the *Tilly*, and surreptitiously set sail northward from the Cape. They arrived at Angra Pequena on 10 April, landed their supplies, and Vogelsang set off to Bethanie in the interior. By 1 May he had bought the bay (and 8km around it) from the Nama *kaptein* Josef Frederiks for £100 and 200 rifles.

On 12 May the German flag was hoisted in Angra Pequena, and in August Vogelsang returned to Kaptein Josef, buying a 32km-wide coastal belt from the Orange River to the 26th degree of latitude south for a further £100 and 60 rifles. He named the area Lüderitzland.

While Vogelsang cultivated a business selling guns throughout the region, Lüderitz returned to the Cape in September to find his land rights challenged. Negotiations ensued, by which time Germany was waking up to the scramble for Africa, and sent a gunboat, the *Nautilus*, to what they called Lüderitz Bay. By August 1884 the British had agreed that Germany could found its first colony here – their first foothold which led to the eventual annexation of South West Africa.

Lüderitz himself made little money out of the venture, and disappeared a few years later while out prospecting. The town grew slowly, and was an important supply base for the German Schutztruppe during the war with the Nama people in 1904–07. The construction of a railway line to Keetmanshoop, between 1906 and 1908, promised more trade, but was overshadowed by the diamond boom that began as the railway was finished (see box, *The diamond boom*, page 236).

From then the town exploded as the centre of supplies and operations of the diamond-mining company, Consolidated Diamond Mines (CDM) – the forerunner of today's NAMDEB Diamond Corporation, a partnership between South Africa's huge De Beers and the Namibian government. Gradually the town's fishing industries developed, and an important export trade of rock lobster was established. However, the CDM headquarters moved to Oranjemund in 1943, precipitating the start of the town's slow decline.

Only in the last few years, through tourism and fishing, has Lüderitz's economy started to look up again. There is still some diamond diving here, too (see box, page 224), and the diamond company NAMDEB continues to have a considerable stake in the town. Ironically tourism has been helped by the lack of development between the 1940s and the 1990s, which preserved many of the beautiful buildings of the early 20th century.

GETTING THERE AND AWAY Most visitors drive to Lüderitz between visiting the Namib-Naukluft National Park and the Fish River Canyon. The town is out on a limb, and the drive, across an empty sandy plain punctuated by telephone poles, takes time. Although the town is bisected by a railway, passenger trains have not run for several years, and slow ongoing work on upgrading the track is geared only to freight.

By car See *The roads to Lüderitz* (pages 215–21) for comments on the whole journey, but note that for the last 20km there is a 60km/h speed limit. This is because the fast tarmac road cuts through a field of shifting barchan dunes, which constantly march across it. Go slowly. Even a small pile of sand is hard when hit at speed.

By air Air Namibia operates direct flights from Windhoek to Lüderitz departing on Mondays, Wednesdays, Fridays and Sundays; the return route from Lüderitz to Windhoek flies via Oranjemund on the same days. The airport is about 11km east of the town, opposite Kolmanskop.

By bus There are currently no bus services linking Lüderitz with the rest of Namibia, increasing the town's isolation. However, local minibus operator 'Aunty Anna' (\ *081 390 9210*) runs transfers to Keetmanshoop (*N$170 pp*) and sometimes to Windhoek; rates vary. Book through Lüderitz Safaris and Tours (see below), who also acts as booking agents for Intercape, so you can plan onward journeys here even though the coaches don't operate in this area.

Hitchhiking Compared with many of Namibia's attractions, Lüderitz is relatively easy to reach by hitching. The tar road from Keetmanshoop has a steady trickle of traffic along it, and intrepid hitchhikers have even made it from Walvis Bay along the C14 via Sesriem – though taking food and water with you is essential on this route.

By sea There are no regular passenger boats calling at Lüderitz, but the town is a port of call for a number of cruise ships throughout the year.

GETTING AROUND If you don't have your own car, there are two options – hire a car or use the service of one of the town's tour operators (see page 224). Transport from the airport or to Kolmanskop with one of the tour operators costs at least N$140 for two people, and a further N$70 for each additional passenger. Again, arrange through Lüderitz Safaris and Tours (see below).

Car hire Two of the big car-hire companies have offices in Lüderitz – but be aware that you should book ahead in order to ensure availability.

Avis \ 063 203968; m 081 124 1829   Budget \ 063 202777; m 081 251 5835

TOURIST INFORMATION AND TOUR OPERATORS

Lüderitz Safaris & Tours [226 B4] Bismarck St; \ 063 202719; m 081 129 7236; ludsaf@ africaonline.com.na; ⊕ winter 08.00–12.30 & 13.30–17.00 Mon–Fri, 08.00–noon Sat, 08.30–10.00 Sun; summer ½hr later. Owned & run by the all-knowing Marion Schelkle, this convenient & very efficient tour operator doubles as an excellent tourist information office & is also the booking agent for Intercape buses (though there is no service to Lüderitz). They issue permits & book tours for Kolmanskop & Zeepaard boat trips, & run a range of day excursions to ensure that the visitor can make the most of a limited stay in the town. A large selection of books & crafts is on sale in the office, & owner also organises trips around southern Namibia. **MET** [226 B4] Schinz St; \ 063 202 8111; ⊕ Mon–Fri. Next door to the NWR office (see page 224), is the Ministry of Environment & Tourism.

DIVING FOR DIAMONDS

The wealth of southwestern Namibia may have been built on diamonds from the Sperrgebiet, but today the greatest proportion of the diamonds found in the area around Lüderitz are mined from under the sea rather than in the Sperrgebiet itself. These alluvial diamonds are found all along the Orange River and at its mouth, but over the years many have been swept farther north by the Benguela Current, with significant deposits now to be found in the seas around Lüderitz harbour.

The leading company in this field is Namibian Minerals Corporation (NAMCO), which has been operational since 1994. Following the company's estimates that around 2.6 million carats of diamonds were to be found in these waters, large-scale operations went live in 1998, with some 650,000 carats now produced each year. Boats put out to sea regularly from the harbour in Lüderitz. On the larger diamond boats, robotic machines trawl in waters up to 150m deep, digging a trench in the sea bed then sucking up the material from depths of 10–16m, up to 25m, ready for processing on board. While the first bags collected contain little except sand, beneath this layer is gravel; it is among the gravel that diamonds are most likely to be found. NAMDEB, too, has considerable resources devoted to this sector within an area that extends 200km out into the Atlantic.

Smaller boats are owned and operated under licence to NAMDEB by diamond divers. Each boat is allocated a specific area, not more than 5km from the coast, in which to search. Theirs is a dangerous job, in unforgiving conditions, but the potential rewards are traditionally high: in 1999, 60,000 carats of diamonds were collected in this way. That said, hauls are decreasing – and most boats have ceased operating since the recession, and the attendant fall in the value of diamonds.

When the boats return to port, the sacks are taken by officials from NAMDEB to their processing plant, where the contents are classified. All boats, including any personal luggage on board, are thoroughly checked and inspected for any gravel that may have been overlooked before they are declared 'clean'.

NWR [226 B4] Schinz St; 063 202752; e reservations@nwr.com.na; www.nwr.com.na; ⏲ Mon–Fri. Housed in the old post office building dating back to 1907, the Namibia Wildlife Resort office is the place to book the campsite at Shark Island & pick up permits for Dorob National Park (see page 318).

TOUR OPERATORS

Coastways Tours [226 C7] Bay Rd; 063 202002; m 081 122 9336; e lewiscwt@iway. na; www.coastways.com.na. Operators of self-drive 4x4 trips to Walvis Bay, & Saddle Hill & Spencer Bay in the Namib-Naukluft Park, north of Lüderitz (*N$980 pp, min 4*), Coastways also runs trips to Bogenfels in the Sperrgebiet (see page 237).

Ghost Town Tours [226 A3] Lüderitz Boatyard; 063 204030; e kolmans@iafrica.com.na; www.ghosttowntours.com. The company that, at the time of writing, administers Kolmanskop & the oyster farm sells tickets for these attractions. **Mukorob Tours** m 081 275 5440; e mukorob-mta@mbweb.com.na. Mukorob operates ½-day trips into the Sperrgebiet, visiting Elizabeth Bay & Kolmanskop. See page 237.

Lüderitz has several hotels varying from the upmarket Nest and slightly less corporate Zum Sperrgebiet to several more personal establishments. A proliferation of self-catering guesthouses reflects the long-term nature of many visitors to the town, but there's also a backpackers' lodge and a windswept campsite (complete with super lighthouse). It is best to book most of them in advance, as the town's rooms quickly fill up during the busier times of year (see *When to visit*, pages 49–51).

Nest Hotel (73 rooms) 820 Diaz St; ☎063 204000; e info@nesthotel.com; www.nesthotel.com. Set on its own right on the sea to the southwest of town, with its own beach, the 4-star Nest is Lüderitz's largest hotel. Rooms are built around a sheltered courtyard enclosing a good-size swimming pool, & each has a sea view. Rooms have en-suite shower or bath, twin or dbl beds, flatscreen TV, phone, new AC/central heating, coffee/tea-making facilities & hairdryer. 3 are adapted for disabled: 1 with shower, 2 with bath. There is a large reception area, the lovely waterfront Penguin restaurant where the excellent buffet b/fast is served, as well as the chic new Crayfish Bar (page 229) & a play area for kids on the beach. There's free Wi-Fi & an internet café too (*N$1/ min*). Outside is a guarded parking area. Staff can arrange airport transfers & book tours for you. **$$$$**

Protea Sea-View Zum Sperrgebiet (22 rooms) Cnr Woermann & Stettiner sts; ☎063 203411; e rec.sperrgebiet@proteahotels.com. na; www.proteahotels.com.na. Part of the Protea Hotels group, this modern hotel is efficient & comfortable, & sits on a low hill above the harbour. Each of the compact rooms, however, is a bit faded & dark, but comes with TV, safe, coffee/tea-maker, hairdryer, en-suite facilities that include a good shower (some also have baths), & a small balcony with a view over either the harbour or the courtyard.The restaurant is rather soulless, but there are balcony tables above a small (but impressive) unheated indoor swimming pool that's surrounded by banana trees & shaded glass walls, & overlooking the harbour in the distance. A small sauna in the basement can be heated on request. Free Wi-Fi everywhere. **$$$$**

Bay View (22 rooms) Diaz St; ☎063 202288; e bayview@iway.na; www.luderitzhotels.com. If you're looking for a hotel with a feel for the old town, this family-run option is a good choice: clean, comfortable & friendly, albeit rather dated. Rooms – dbl, twin & family – are built around a swimming pool, each with TV, phone, radio, tea/ coffee & Wi-Fi. There are computers in reception

for guests' use, & off-street parking at the back. A small, cosy restaurant with adjoining bar is open to all comers. Wheelchair friendly. **$$$**

Haus Sandrose (2 rooms, flat) 15 Bismarck St; ☎063 202630; m 081 241 5544; e haussandrose@iway.na; www.haussandrose. com. Linda & Erich Looser's central accommodation is guaranteed to make visitors feel individual. Entirely distinct styles mark out their 3 self-catering units, each with private facilities: the roomy Grosse Bucht flat (which has a connecting door with Klein Bucht & is ideal for family of 4) & the twin Bogenfels & Halifax rooms all have their own kitchens. Outside, there's a quiet, shady courtyard with braai facilities. **$$**

Island Cottage (3 rooms) Kreplin St, Shark Island; ☎063 203626; m 081 292 2984; e retha.c@mweb.com.na. Small red-walled B&B situated on the windswept Shark Island peninsula. En-suite rooms are modern, classy & well equipped, 2 with twin beds & a couch, & a 3rd with a dbl. A kitchen area, TV, phone & – optimistically – fan are standard, & there's an outside braai area, but the big plus of the 2 larger rooms is a superb west-facing sea view from the veranda. The owner, Retha, also runs a nail salon on site. **$$**

✳ **Kairos Cottage** (5 rooms) Kreplin St, Shark Island; ☎063 203080; e christo.b@iway.na. Lüderitz's newest B&B is smart & family-owned. 3 dbl & 2 twin en-suite rooms all have ocean views, kitchenette with fridge & coffee station, heaters, flat-screen TV & free Wi-Fi. It also doubles as a coffee shop serving homemade cakes; in summer the wraparound terrace has stunning uninterrupted sea views. Superb value for money. **$$**

Kratzplatz (12 rooms) 5 Nachtigal St; ☎063 202458; m 081 129 2458; e kratzmr@iway. na; www.kratzplatz.info. On the right side of Barrels (see page 228), this friendly & comfortable B&B run by Manfred & Monica Kratz is painted bright red, so you can't miss it! The main building, a converted church, features whitewashed, high-ceilinged rooms, all of which are now en suite, with TVs,

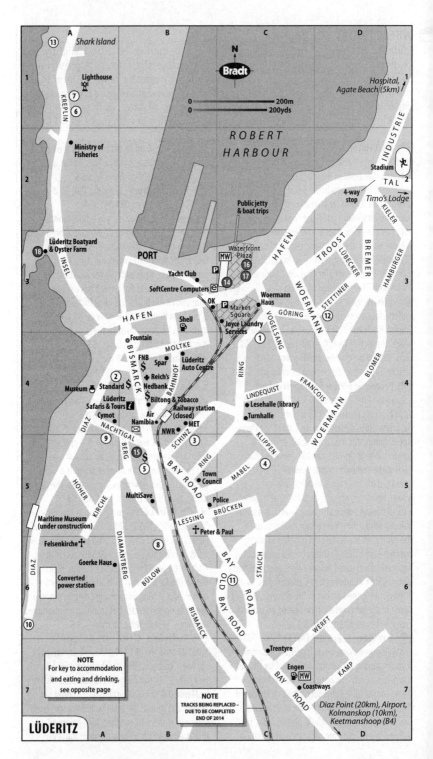

LÜDERITZ

coffee facilities & fridges. The style & furnishings are modern & simple: this is a pleasant place, with secure parking & free Wi-Fi throughout. **$$**

🏠 **Obelix Village Guesthouse** (15 rooms) 🝏 063 203456; m 081 128 3667; e obelixvillage@ iway.na. Named after the comic strip, this quirky guesthouse has dbl (twin beds pushed together) & family en-suite rooms arranged around a central courtyard. Where they are simple, the central lapa is ostentatiously over the top: lined with animal skins, trophies & stuffed wild animals. Guests may use the kitchen & braai facilities, & there's a bar, but the only meal served is b/fast. Free Wi-Fi & safe parking. **$$**

🏠 **Timo's Lodge** (17 rooms) Tal St, Township; 🝏 081 124 5812; e timoslodge@iway.na; www. timoslodge.com.na. Superb budget option run by local township resident, Timo. Full of smiles, he offers homely, very clean, en-suite, self-catering rooms of varying sizes arranged around a gated courtyard; there's a security guard on post at night, so it's very safe. The entrance is round the back, in front of the yellow Rotary Club. Ideal for families. **$$**

🏠 **Backpackers Lodge** (5 rooms, camping) 2 Ring St; 🝏 063 202000; m 081 261 2174; e luderitzbackpackers@hotmail.com. Lüderitz's

original backpackers offers very simple twin or family rooms that share facilities with the dormitories. Its large main room with TV has lots of space for playing table tennis, too – albeit surrounded by beds, as it doubles as an overflow dormitory for overland groups. There's also an equipped kitchen with free Wi-Fi, laundry service & a yard at the back for braais & 3 or 4 camping cars – it's too undulating for tents. *Dorm bed N\$110; camping N\$80 pp; dbl N\$270 pp.* **$**

🏠 **Element Riders** (4 rooms) 7 Schinz St; 🝏 081 8734860; e info@element-riders.com; www. element-riders.com. Look out for the surfboard sign posted outside this budget option, which is slightly better than Backpackers Lodge. They have one dorm room, a shedlike family room that can sleep 5 & dbl rooms dotted around a concrete courtyard sharing communal showers. There's a self-catering bright, sunny kitchen with hotplates (no ovens), free Wi-Fi, laundry for N\$15/bundle; they also rent bikes & can organise numerous sports activities from surfing to land-boarding. *Dorm N\$90 pp.* **$**

☀ 🏠 **Hansa Haus** (4 rooms) Mabel St; 🝏 063 202134; m 081 128 4336; e hansahaus@iway.na; www.luderitznamibia.com/hansa-house.htm. Right at the top of Mabel St, this imposing blue house was built in 1909 with a commanding view of the town. Run by Cicely Burgers (who also owns the Oyster Bar, page 228), it accommodates self-catering guests (no b/fast available) in a mix of 4 dbl & twin-bed rooms – some (rooms 1, 2, 3) with sea views – with lovely wooden floors & high ceilings. Except for family room 4 with a bath, they share a shower-room, separate lounge with flat-screen TV & free Wi-Fi, & a modern, well-equipped kitchen. There's also a balcony at the front with harbour views. The only snag is they're all located up steep steps on the 2nd floor of the building & therefore not suitable for disabled travellers or families with very young children. *N\$250 pp/night.* **$**

🏠 **Krabbenhöft & Lampe** (2 flats, 5 rooms) 25 Bismarck St; 🝏 063 202466; m 081 206 4682; e cishas@yahoo.com. This imposing place at the top of the town houses some unexpected guest accommodation. Constructed in 1910, & proclaimed a national monument in 1992, the building used to be home to a carpet-weaving factory but is now simply a shop. Upstairs, however, the large, spotless rooms retain many architectural features with high ceilings & old wooden floors, albeit now with modern kitchens, bathrooms &

beds. 2 flats on the 1st floor are fully self-catering, while one flight further up ('Oberdeck') are 5 twin rooms sharing 2 bathrooms, kitchen facilities & a TV. Free Wi-Fi. It's certainly distinctive, & represents good value for money. The entrance is the brown gate on the right of the main building; if no-one is there ask for Katrina, the supervisor of the premises, inside the shop or in the courtyard at the back. *Oberdeck N$200 pp.* **$**

⚓ Shark Island Resort (26 pitches, lighthouse, 2 bungalows) Kreplin St. Book via NWR, page 224. The campsite here has a superb location, with power, functional wash blocks & toilets, & braai facilities, but it is amazingly windy; make sure your tent is well anchored. If there's nobody on the gate then just pitch your tents – but try to find a site sheltered by the rocks; the attendants will come over to collect money. The sites are overlooked by a sparsely furnished lighthouse, with 2 twin bedrooms, kitchen, DSTV, 2 bathrooms & living area, which must be Lüderitz's most imposing place to stay. The nearby self-catering en-suite bungalows in turquoise & cream livery sleep up to 6, are good value, & warmer than the campsites! *Camping N$100 pp; lighthouse N$250 pp; bungalow N$200 pp.* **$**

✕ WHERE TO EAT AND DRINK *Map, page 226.*

There's not an endless choice of cuisine in Lüderitz, but seafood (and particularly crayfish in season (Nov–Apr) is a speciality. If seafood is above your budget (you can expect to pay around N$300 for a seafood platter) then fish, steaks and more usual Namibian fare are also available, while some good smaller take-aways serve burgers and bar food, which can be excellent value.

Lüderitz doesn't major on nightlife, but locals congregate frequently at Barrels (see below).

✕ Pelican 820 Diaz St; ☎063 204000; ⏰ b/fast 07.00–10.00, light meals 11.00–18.00, lunch 12.30–14.00, dinner 18.30–22.00, all daily. The Nest Hotel's smart restaurant serves up lovely sea views & has the best crayfish in town. Their buffet b/fast & 3-course set-menu lunch (*N$129*) & an à la carte dinner are all open to nonguests as well. For dessert, the house speciality is crêpe Suzette, prepared & flambéed at your table – quite a show! Reservations advised. **$$$$$**

✳ ✕ Barrels 5 Nachtigal St; ☎063 202458; ⏰ 18.00–21.30 Mon–Fri. With a lapa-style roof above the bar, walls festooned with candles dripping wax, & barrels serving as tables, this lively joint at Kratzplatz (see page 225) is hugely popular with the backpacking fraternity & beyond, & hosts occasional live music. Alongside its pizza menu (*N$60–90*) is a substantial dinner buffet (*N$120*) – usually either *eisbein* (pork knuckle) or chicken, served with salad & vegetables – served informally around the fire & sideboards. **$$$$**

✕ Bay View Diaz St; ☎063 202288; ⏰ noon–14.00 & 18.00–22.00 daily. The small, cosy restaurant at the Bay View Hotel is renowned for its seafood platters (*N$350/2 people*). Certainly the prawns are excellent, & the menu offers plenty of choice including steaks, grills & vegetarian options. Reservations are essential. **$$$–$$$$**

✕ Ritzi's Waterfront; ☎063 202818; ⏰ 08.00–22.00 Mon–Sat. Friendly staff & generally good food are the hallmarks of this popular eatery, though service can be slow & the stark modern building on the Waterfront lacks atmosphere. If it's warm enough, ask for a table on the veranda. The menu majors on seafood, but alternatives include a range of pizzas & several specials. Prices come as a pleasant surprise, including a seafood platter at N$195, & the wine list is unusually good value. Booking is advisable in the evenings. **$$$–$$$$**

☕ Diaz Coffee Shop Cnr Bismarck St & Nachtigal Rd; ☎063 203147; ⏰ 07.30–17.30 Mon–Fri, 08.00–14.00 Sat–Sun. This well-positioned & relaxed café has free Wi-Fi (ask for access code) & is a good place to take the chill off a Lüderitz morning, with b/fast, snacks & delicious cakes, as well as daily lunch specials. **$–$$**

☕ Sea Breeze Coffee Shop Waterfront; ☎063 204235; ⏰ 07.20–19.00 Mon–Fri, 08.00–21.00 Sat, 10.00–21.00 Sun. A pleasant small café overlooking the harbour, serving b/fast, light meals, coffee & cake. **$**

✕ Shearwater Oyster Bar Lüderitz Boatyard, Insel St; ☎063 204031; m 081 128 4336; ⏰ 11.00–18.00 Mon–Thu, 11.00–19.00 Fri. Above the oyster-processing plant (an interesting diversion in itself), this is the place for oysters at N$5–8 each, fresh or grilled. Add a glass of bubbly for N$22, or if you're not in the mood there's a tapas menu too. $

✕ **Captain Macarena** Waterfront; ✆063 203958; ⊕ 09.00–18.00 Mon–Fri, 09.00–13.00 Sat. Serves fish & chips, & good calamari to take away from premises in the modern Waterfront development. $

♀ **Crayfish Bar** Nest Hotel, page 225; ⊕ noon–22.00 daily. The Nest Hotel's renovated bar is the ideal spot for a coffee mid-morning, or a sundowner thanks to its superb sea views, chic décor with surfer photographs & underlit bar. They serve a selection of tapas, oysters & seafood platters ($$$) if you get peckish while sampling their large choice of cocktails.

SHOPPING

Biltong & Tobacco [226 B4] Bismarck St; ✆063 203776; ⊕ 07.30–17.30 Mon–Fri, 09.00–13.00 Sat. Stock up on biltong nibbles at this small store with lime-green front entrance.

Cymot [226 A4] 4 Nachtigal St; ✆063 203855; ⊕ 08.00–13.00 & 14.00–17.00 Mon–Fri, 08.00–noon Sat. Handy in case you need any camping equipment before heading north into the Namib-Naukluft.

OK Grocer [226 B3] Hafen St; ⊕ 08.00–18.00 Mon–Fri, 08.00–13.00 Sat–Sun.

Spar [226 B4] Cnr Bahnhof & Moltke St; ⊕ 07.30–17.30 Mon–Fri, 08.00–13.00 Sat, 09.00–13.00 Sun.

OTHER PRACTICALITIES All the major Namibian banks – Standard, FNB, Bank Windhoek and Nedbank – have branches and ATM facilities in Lüderitz. The **post office** is on Bismarck Street and it's worth looking for the town's monthly **newspaper**, *Buchter News* (*www.buchternews.com*) with event listings.

🖃 **Alltronics** Waterfront; ✆060 7038007; ⊕ 08.30–13.00 & 14.00–16.30 Mon, Tue, Thu & Fri, 09.30–13.00 & 14.00–16.00 Wed. Only offers Wi-Fi.

Emergencies Police ✆063 202255; ambulance & hospital ✆063 202446; fire service ✆063 202255.

Joyce Laundry Services [226 C3] Hafen St; ✆081 291 1306; ⊕ 07.00–18.00 Mon–Fri, 08.00–14.00 Sat–Sun.

✚ **Reich's pharmacy** [226 B4] Bismarck St; ✆063 202806; ⊕ 08.00–17.30 Mon–Fri, 08.00–13.00 Sat.

🖃 **Softcentre Computers** [226 B3] Waterfront; ⊕ 08.00–17.00 Mon–Fri, 08.00–13.00 Sat. Charges 50 cents/min & can do photocopying.

Fuel and vehicle repairs There's a Engen fuel station ([226 C7] ⊕ *06.00–21.00 Mon–Fri, 06.00–18.00 Sat–Sun*) on the edge of town, and Shell in the centre ([226 B3]). For tyres, there's Trentyre ([226 C7] ✆*063 202137*; m *081 122 3482*) on Bay Road, but for more serious vehicle repairs try Lüderitz Auto Centre ([226 B4] *Bahnhof St*; ✆*063 204051*; m *081 366 8635*; ⊕ *07.30–17.00 Mon–Fri, 07.30–12.30 Sat*).

WHAT TO SEE AND DO Even visitors with a limited attention span find enough to occupy themselves around Lüderitz for a day, while those who enjoy a more leisurely pace will take three or four to see the area's main attractions.

For many visitors, the focus of the town is the new Waterfront [226 C3]. With a small tower that affords a good overview of the town, and a public jetty, it is a pleasant place to while away an hour or so watching the boats in the harbour. There is a good seafood restaurant, a café and public toilets (with a nominal charge – if they're open).

Walking tour The best way to explore Lüderitz is on foot. The following suggested route takes in a selection of the highlights, but if you'd like to know more, including about the town's architectural heritage, ask at Lüderitz Safaris and Tours.

Start at the **fountain** [226 B4] opposite the port, at the junction of Diaz and Bismarck streets. This was built in 1967 to mark the advent of a permanent water supply from the Koichab Pan. Continue up Bismarck Street, cross over the currently used railway tracks on Bay Road and turn left into Schinz Street. On the left you'll pass the **old post office**, built close enough to the railway station to transfer mailbags to and from the train, but now housing the offices of the NWR and MET. At the end of this road, on the corner, are the brightly painted **Lesehalle** [226 C4] or library, and the adjacent **Turnhalle**, or gymnastics hall, which dates to 1909 and is still used for public functions – though no longer as a gym. From here, turn right along Ring Street, then left on Bay Road to find the **Town Council** [226 B5] on your left. Built as a school in 1908, its function was soon switched to that of town hall, a purpose which it still fulfils. On the wall in front, the large **blue-and-white tiled mural** was presented to the town by the Portuguese community in 1988 to celebrate the landing of Bartolomeu Dias in 1488. A short detour to the left from here takes you up **Mabel Street** [226 C5], where the houses on the right were built in 1908 for the Imperial German Railway commissioners. Now in private hands, these represent some of Lüderitz's most attractive buildings, and include the Hansa Haus guesthouse (see page 227). Back on Bay Road, continue a little way before turning right across the railway – currently being restored. Almost in front of you is the **Krabbenhöft und Lampe** building [226 B6], constructed in 1910 as a fashionable store trading everything from fancy foodstuffs to fashion. Guesthouse accommodation is now offered on the upper floors (see page 227).

Leaving the best until almost last, turn left here up Zeppelin Street and on to Diamantberg to the **Goerke Haus** [226 A6] (see below), undoubtedly one of the town's architectural highlights and well worth a visit in its own right. From here, walk downhill then back up to another Lüderitz landmark, **Felsenkirche** [226 A6] (see below), built high on **Diamantberg** and with views across the bay. Finally, make your way back down Berg and Nachtigal streets, passing the striking **bright red building** that started life as a greengrocery before becoming a church, and is now Barrels restaurant. At the end, turn right into Diaz Street, where you'll find the **museum** [226 A4] (see below). If you've timed it right, and you're here during the afternoon, you may be able to visit at least one of these last three attractions – though opening hours are very limited.

If you've still time (and energy) you could continue to **Shark Island** [226 A1], now joined to the mainland by a causeway and the newly built harbour development. Most people visit only if they're staying here, but it's a pleasant – if windy – walk past the harbour and boatyard, and gives a hint of the town's maritime heritage.

Felsenkirche [226 A6] (❨ 081 228 7317; ⊕ Apr–Aug 16.00–17.00 Mon–Fri; Sept–Mar 17.00–18.00 Mon–Fri; donations welcome)
From almost every angle on land and sea, this small, rather stark Lutheran church, whose name translates as 'Church of the Rock', is clearly visible. Located close to the Goerke Haus, it was built in 1912 and has some stunning stained-glass windows – the altar window was a gift from German Chancellor Bismarck.

Museum [226 A4] (❨ 063 202532; ⊕ 15.30–17.00 Mon–Fri except hols; admission N$15 pp)
Built by German schoolchildren in 1968, this small museum opposite the Bay View Hotel on Diaz Street has exhibits on the diamond-mining industry (including fake diamonds), an egg collection, a good section on the Bushmen, a variety of small exhibits on other indigenous cultures, and assorted cases of local flora and fauna.

Goerke Haus [226 A6] (⊕ Zeppelin St; 14.00–16.00 Mon–Fri, 16.00–17.00 Sat–Sun, closed public hols; admission N$25 pp)
High up on Diamantberg, Goerke Haus

is the beautiful cream building with a blue roof that is built into the rocks above the level of the road. The town's best-preserved historical building, visible from afar, it is one of Lüderitz's so-called 'diamond palaces', thought to have been designed by a German architect, Otto Ertl.

The original owner, Hans Goerke, was born in Germany in 1874 and arrived in German South West Africa with the Schutztruppe in 1904. In 1907 he became provisions inspector for the German forces – just before diamonds were discovered near Kolmanskop. By the end of 1909 he had resigned from the army and was making a fortune in the diamond rush, which enabled him to have this house built. When completed in 1910, it was valued at 70,000 Deutschmarks (£3,500/US$5,250).

Goerke himself returned to Germany in 1912. In 1920 the house was bought by CDM, but in 1944 they sold it back to the government of South West Africa for £2,404 (US$3,606), and the house became the residence of the local magistrate. When, in 1981, the magistrate was recalled to Keetmanshoop – Lüderitz just didn't have enough crime – the CDM repurchased the house and restored it for use by their visitors.

Although the house was built during the Art Nouveau period (Jugendstil in German), it isn't typical of that style. Nevertheless, an informative leaflet notes some of the relevant details to look out for, including the flamingo motifs used on the stained-glass windows and the decorative detail on either side of the hat-and-coat stand in the hall, resembling Egyptian papyrus bells. Typical of Art Nouveau, too, is the mix of artistic styles, seen in the Roman arches over the stairwell, supported by an Egyptian lotus column, and capped by a Grecian Doric capital, while the posts at the foot of the stairs resemble dentilled Gothic spires.

The house retains many original features, and others – such as the carpets, curtains and friezes – have been restored or replicated. Although there have been moves to have the house's original furniture returned from South Africa, the current furniture is beautiful, from the piano with ivory keys to marble-topped dressing tables in the bedrooms and oak furniture around the lounge. Don't miss it.

Diamantberg [226 B6] Behind Goerke Haus, Diamantberg is the highest land around town. With a pair of stout shoes you can easily scramble up for a good view of the town and harbour beyond. Standing in the cool sea breeze, under desert sun, much about the landscape seems extreme. There is little vegetation to soften the parched land, while the sea beyond seems cold and uninviting. However, as if to compensate, the townspeople have painted many of their buildings in soft pastel shades. Quaintly shaped wooden buildings, just a few storeys high and painted baby-blue, pink and green, all give Lüderitz the air of a pleasant, gentle town.

EXCURSIONS FROM LÜDERITZ

If you have your own transport then Lüderitz Peninsula, Agate Beach and Kolmanskop are well worth visiting. To see some of the area to the south of Lüderitz, in the Sperrgebiet – the restricted diamond area – you must join an organised tour. There is also an excellent boat trip from the harbour.

BOAT TRIPS Weather permitting, boat trips leave the harbour [226 C2] at around 08.00 for a 2-hour trip (*N$350 pp*) – under sail if you're lucky – past the whaling station at Sturmvogel Bucht, around Diaz Point and on to Halifax Island in search of African penguins, seals and the endemic heavyside dolphin. While visitors are almost guaranteed to see these creatures, keep your eyes open and you'll spot plenty of birds as well, from scoters and various species of cormorant to oystercatchers and flamingos. The traditional schooner, *Sedina*, is now out of service, but you can still sail in the more comfortable motorised catamaran called *Zeepaard*, run by Heiko Metzger (☎ *063 202173;* m *081 604 2805;* e *zeepaardboattours@gmail.com*). He also offers – weather depending – a 2½-hour sunset cruise (*N$350 pp*), oyster trips (*N$350 pp/3hrs*), and fishing trips.

Trips can be booked through Lüderitz Safaris and Tours (see page 223) or direct with the operators.

OYSTER TOURS ([226 A3] ☎ *063 204031;* m *081 128 4336; tours start 15.00 Mon–Fri; N$50 pp/45mins*) Oysters are an important part of the fishing industry in Lüderitz, and now visitors can find out about what happens before they reach the table. Tours are at Lüderitz Boatyard, starting in the oyster-processing factory and ending at the Oyster Bar – where there's the option of oyster tasting with a glass of wine for a further N$30 pp. Book in advance.

AGATE BEACH This windswept beach is a 5km drive north of Lüderitz, alongside fenced-off areas of the Sperrgebiet National Park that add to the air of desolation, particularly in winter. To get there, follow the signs out of Lüderitz along the coast road from the corner of Tal and Hamburger streets, past Lüderitz Secondary School on the right and the town sewerage works and then just keep going. *En route*, a pond to the right of the road attracts small numbers of flamingos and other waterbirds, while nearby the odd springbok or oryx takes advantage of a patch of green around the water treatment plant. The beach stretches a long way and is fun for beachcombers. The sand is sprinkled with fragments of shining mica – and the occasional agate. The occurrence of agates depends on the winds and the swell: sometimes you will find nothing, at others – especially at low tide – you can pick up a handful in a few hours. The beach's braai spots and picnic tables make it a popular place at weekends, and swimming, too, is an (albeit chilly) option.

LÜDERITZ PENINSULA To the southwest of the town lies the Lüderitz Peninsula, bordered by the sea on three sides yet a rocky desert within. Here, the lower slopes are dotted with a surprising variety of salt-tolerant succulent plants. In winter, if there's been some good rain, many of these are in flower, affording scope for hours of plant spotting. Around the coast there are some rocky beaches and some sandy ones; all are worth exploring. Note that while the roads here are fine for 2WD cars, don't be tempted to follow tracks across soft sand made by local 4x4 enthusiasts, or you'll need their help to pull your vehicle out. Note, too, that the pans in this area are favourite nesting spots for the rare Damara tern, which is another important reason to stay on the tracks. Easier to spot are flamingos, swift terns and the occasional African black oystercatcher.

To reach the peninsula, simply follow the B4 out of town for about 2km where there's a turning clearly signposted to the right. If you'd prefer a tour, this can be arranged through Lüderitz Safaris and Tours (see page 223) from around N$500 for 2 hours. Aside from at Diaz Point, there are no facilities except a few old toilet blocks.

The most interesting parts of the peninsula are:

Radford Bay This is reached shortly after leaving the town, and is often home to a flock of flamingos.

Second Lagoon Also a popular spot with visiting flamingos, and sometimes the odd stranded motorist. Continuing to the right, you'll come to…

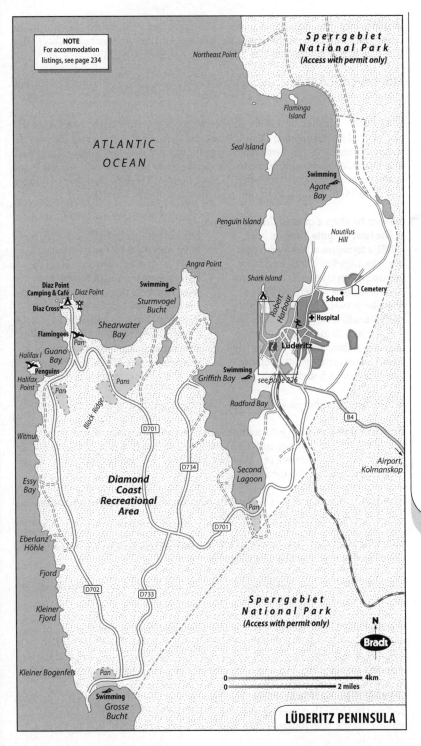

NOTE
For accommodation
listings, see page 234

Sperrgebiet
National Park
(Access with permit only)

Northeast Point

Flamingo
Island

ATLANTIC
OCEAN

Seal Island

Swimming
Agate
Bay

Penguin Island

Nautilus
Hill

Angra Point

Shark Island

Cemetery

Diaz Point
Camping & Café *Diaz Point*

School

Swimming

Diaz Cross

Sturmvogel
Bucht

Robert
Harbour

Hospital

Flamingoes

Shearwater
Bay

Pan

Lüderitz

Halifax I

Guano
Bay

see page 226

Penguins

Pans

Swimming
Griffith Bay

Halifax
Point

Pan

Radford Bay

Black Ridge

Witmut

D701

B4

Diamond
Coast
Recreational
Area

D734

Essy
Bay

Airport,
Kolmanskop

Eberlanz
Höhle

Second
Lagoon

Fjord

Pan

D701

D702

D733

Kleiner
Fjord

Sperrgebiet
National Park
(Access with permit only)

N

Kleiner Bogenfels

Pan

Bradt

Swimming
Grosse
Bucht

0 ——————— 4km
0 ——————— 2 miles

LÜDERITZ PENINSULA

Griffith Bay Excellent views of the town across the cold, misty sea, plus a few crystal-clear rocks pools to dabble in. It is named after an American officer who sheltered here and was then killed during the American Civil War.

Sturmvogel Bucht The whaling station here can no longer be visited by boat, but is visible from the sea as part of a boat trip.

Diaz Point Reached by a short wooden bridge is a granite cross, a replica of the one erected by Bartolomeu Dias, the first European explorer to enter the bay. He sheltered here on 25 July 1488, referring to the bay as Angra Pequena, or 'Little Bay'. There are often seals sunning themselves on the rocks here. Just south of Diaz Point is a grave bearing a stark reminder: 'George Pond of London, died here of hunger and thirst 1906'. Today a small café saves visitors from the same fate.

Where to stay, eat and drink *Map, page 233.*

⚊ Diaz Point Campsite (camping) ☎ 063 202288; ✉ bayview@iway.na; www.diaz-point. com. A 20km drive from Lüderitz across a lunar landscape, it's easy to feel you've got lost on the way to this campsite situated at the tip of the peninsula – just keep going! Looked after by the elderly Regina Korff, this windswept beach has a simple café (🕒 *08.00–sunset daily*) – serving cake & toasted sandwiches – & a campsite. There's minigolf & a tyre swing to entertain kids while parents have a coffee. To spend the night, you can pitch your tent in the shelter of a reed screen, head for the safety of a 10-bed house with bedding & cutlery, or – more fun – sleep in one of two old boats marooned on the beach: the white boat sleeps 3 people, the old blue diamond boat 4 people – all in narrow bunk-beds. Gas-heated hot water (driven from town) in the ablution block is a big plus & there's a covered braai & solar lights in the toilets. There are plans to add electricity. Book through Bay View Hotel (see page 225). *Camping N$85 per site plus N$55 pp (max 4); house N$200 pp.* **L**

Guano Bay Another good place to spot flamingos, either from land or from the sea.

Halifax Island The large African penguin colony here can be viewed with a good pair of binoculars from the cliffs and beaches on the western side of Guano Bay, or – closer up – from the deck of a boat (see page 231). The empty houses you can see belonged to guano collectors.

Essy Bay A number of very rocky little bays, each with a place for a braai. All are linked by a network of good sand roads.

Eberlanz Höhle A cave cut deeply into the rock, about 10 minutes' walk from the road; there's a path marked over the rocks.

Kleiner Fjord A small sandy beach with deep water and lots of kelp, so unsuitable for swimming.

Grosse Bucht A wide sandy beach with dark sand, long stranded pieces of kelp, plenty of kelp flies, and several turn-off points for stopping. The sand is dotted with mounds of salt-tolerant succulent plants in beautiful greens and reds, and the bay is perfect for accomplished windsurfers and kiteboarders, with very strong winds.

SPERRGEBIET NATIONAL PARK The Sperrgebiet, or 'forbidden zone', was first declared in 1908. Then mining was confined to within a few kilometres of the coast, while a coastal belt 100km wide was declared 'out of bounds' as a precaution to prevent unauthorised people from reaching the diamond fields. At the height of restrictions there were two diamond areas: No. 1 from the Orange River to 26°S, and No. 2 from 26°S northward to the Kuiseb, incorporating most of Namibia's great dune sea. Over the years these areas have shrunk, leaving – until recently – only parts of No. 1 as forbidden. Then, in 2009, the whole area, as far south as the Orange River and north to Lüderitz and beyond, was designated a national park. Covering 26,000km², the new park is in its infancy and it will take some time before NAMDEB has restored much of the damage caused by mining. In the meantime, security remains tight. Signs by the roadside threatening fines or imprisonment for entering these areas unaccompanied remain serious.

History and archaeology Archaeologists estimate that early Stone Age people inhabited the area around the Orange River at least 300,000 years ago, while the presence of rock art indicates that their descendants made their way inland. It wasn't until the 15th century that the first Europeans – Portuguese sailors – arrived here. As trading in international waters increased, so did the value of the ships' cargo – borne out by the discovery in 2008 of a 16th-century Portuguese ship beneath the sands. Carrying a cargo of over 2,000 heavy gold coins, as well as ivory, astrolabes and a veritable arsenal of weapons, the *Bom Jesus* was part of a fleet that left Lisbon in early 1533 in search of fortune. That it sank in foul weather off a coast where diamonds were for the taking is a cruel irony.

Later sailors, the whalers and sealers of the 19th century, sought less glamorous bounty, trading with the small Khoi communities they found along the coast. The discovery in the 20th century of diamonds – riches beyond the wildest dreams of the early traders and prospectors – was almost by chance.

Flora and fauna Lack of human intervention within most of the Sperrgebiet for almost a century has left a remarkable diversity of wildlife. Plants, in particular, have thrived, with over a thousand species identified: almost a quarter of Namibia's total, qualifying the Sperrgebiet as one of the world's top 34 biodiversity hotspots. Many of these are succulents that bring bursts of colour to the desert during the rainy season.

A total of 215 bird species have been identified within the park as a whole, many of them congregating at its southern edge, in the wetlands at the mouth of the Orange River. The authorities claim that 80 mammals live within the park confines, including the solitary brown hyena, and a further 38 marine mammals off shore.

Getting there and permits The most readily accessible area within the new national park is Kolmanskop, which you can visit in your own car, provided that you buy a permit in advance (see page 224). Trips to Elizabeth Bay or Bogenfels, however, must be booked well in advance. In order to obtain a permit, you will need to give a copy of your passport with your full name, ID number and nationality to the relevant tour operator (see page 224) *at least* two working days before the trip. Note that visitors may not take anything out of the area, including rock samples – take note, all amateur geologists. Vehicles coming from the Sperrgebiet remain subject to random searches by NAMDEB officials.

Kolmanskop (\ *063 204031;* ⊕ *08.00–13.00 daily, or longer with photographic pass; admission N$75/40 adult/child; photographer's pass N$200*) In truth most travellers come to Lüderitz just to visit this now-famous ghost town. Once the principal town of the local diamond industry, it was abandoned in 1956 – with the

Kolmanskop, or 'Kolman's hill', was originally a small hill named after a delivery rider, Kolman, who used to rest his horses there.

In April 1908, Zacharias Lewala was working nearby when he picked a rough diamond from the ground. He took this to his German foreman, August Stauch, who posted a claim to the area, and then got the backing of several of the railway's directors to start prospecting. Stauch exhibited some of his finds in June 1908, prompting an immediate response: virtually everybody who could rushed into the desert to look for diamonds. Famously, in some places they could be picked up by the handful in the moonlight.

T V Bulpin (see *Appendix 3*) records the story of one resident, Dr Scheibe, going prospecting:

> While he plotted his position on a map, he told his servants to look for diamonds. One of them simply went down on his knees, filled both hands with diamonds, and even stuffed some into his mouth. Dr Scheibe stared at the scene in amazement, repeating over and over again, '*Ein Märchen, ein Märchen*' ('A fairy tale, a fairy tale').

This first large deposit at Kolmanskop lay in the gravel of a dry river-bed, so soon a mine and a boom town developed there. Deposits were found all over the coastal region, all around Lüderitz. Quickly, in September 1908, the German colonial government proclaimed a Sperrgebiet – a forbidden zone – to restrict further prospecting, and to license what was already happening.

Between 1908 and the start of World War I over 5 million carats of diamonds were found, but the war disrupted production badly. At the end of it Sir Ernest Oppenheimer obtained options on many of the German mining companies for South Africa's huge Anglo-American Corporation, joining ten of them into Consolidated Diamond Mines (CDM) of South West Africa. In 1922–23, CDM obtained exclusive diamond rights for 50 years over a coastal belt 95km wide, stretching 350km north of the Orange River, from the new South African administrators of South West Africa. These were later extended to the year 2010, allowing NAMDEB to control the country's diamond production for 20 years following independence. Although these rights have now theoretically lapsed, the government is a 50% shareholder in the business, and little has changed.

Meanwhile many small towns like Kolmanskop were flush with money. It had a butcher's, a baker's and a general shop; a large theatre, community hall and school; factories for furniture, ice, lemonade and soda water; a hospital with the region's first X-ray machine; comfortable staff quarters, elaborate homes for the managers – and a seawater pool fed by water pumped from 35km away. Yet Kolmanskop was fortunate: it was next to the main railway line. Often deposits were less accessible, far from water or transport – and many such early mines still lie half-buried in the Namib.

final three families admitting defeat in 1959 – and now gives a fascinating insight into the area's great diamond boom. In its heyday, the town was home to over 300 adults and 44 children, and luxuries included a bowling alley, iced refrigerators and even a swimming pool. A few of the buildings, including the imposing concert hall, have been restored, but many are left exactly as they were deserted, and now the surrounding dunes are gradually burying them.

In a room adjacent to the concert hall, there is a simple café-style restaurant (⊕ *09.00–14.00 Mon–Sat*). Do make time to look at the photographs that adorn the walls, from early mining pictures to some chilling reminders of the far-reaching effects of Nazi Germany.

A century since diamonds were first discovered here, it's now possible to buy diamonds in the 'Diamond Room', with prices upwards from N$500. There's also a display charting the history of the diamond boom and the people with whom it is inextricably linked.

Getting there and other practicalities Kolmanskop is just beside the main B4 road, 9km east of Lüderitz. You can buy a permit in advance from Lüderitz Safaris and Tours, or Ghost Town Tours in Lüderitz (see pages 223 and 224); or, if you're travelling from Aus along the B4, permits can now be bought directly at the entrance gate. NB: these rules may change when the ownership of the concession changes in January 2015 – write and let us know. The N$70 permit includes a 45-minute guided tour departing from the main hall at 09.30 and 11.00; travellers are split into English- and German-speaking groups. If you'd like to be there earlier or later, buy a photographer's pass. This also includes a guided tour, but allows you to park outside the gate and visit at any time between sunrise and sunset, for as long as you like, giving the chance to absorb the eerie atmosphere without other visitors. Because the town faces east, the best photographs are taken in the morning. Arrive early, take your photographs without other visitors around, and have a quick snack in the on-site café before joining the first guided tour. And note that all visitors are permitted to take photographs; a photographer's pass simply buys you more time.

Elizabeth Bay This south-facing bay, 40km south of Lüderitz, has a band of diamond-bearing coarse grits and sands measuring about 3km by 5km. It was mined from 1911 to 1948, and then reopened in about 1991, with a projected minimum lifespan of ten years.

Guided tours pass into the Sperrgebiet through the Kolmanskop gate, and from there to Elizabeth Bay. The scenery on the way is mostly flat gravel plains, with some dunes as you approach the coast. This is a chance to see the working diamond mine, albeit from a distance.

Getting there and away Mukorob Tours (see page 224) run half-day trips from 08.30 to about 13.00, Monday–Friday, for four to eight people. These cost N$500 per person based on four people, including a light snack. No children under 14 are permitted. Book in advance.

Pomona/Bogenfels A day trip into the Sperrgebiet as far as Bogenfels covers some 265km on mostly good gravel roads, passing through areas of considerable historical, geological and botanical interest. *En route* you'll visit the ghost town of Pomona and the Idatel or Märchental ('fairy-tale') valley, famous for the diamonds that were collected in the moonlight here.

Where it has been untouched by diamond mining, much of the environment is pristine, but many of the diamond areas have been ravaged by the industry, leaving behind expanses of bare rock devoid of sand and without a hint of vegetation. In some areas there is shining dolomite rock, its colours varying in the sun from blue or pink to pure white. In the occasional winter, if there has been some rain, other areas are alight with colour from numerous plants, many of them seen only once every ten years or so, taking advantage of nature's brief bounty. Here, in among grey scrubby plants, are the soft green of new grasses, the bright pink Bushman's candle, and the milk bush, favoured by oryx; here too are the so-called 'window' plants, whose leaf tips feature tiny windows that allow light through to the main plant buried below, so that photosynthesis can take place inside the plant.

Pomona itself once housed over a thousand people, of whom some 300–400 were German, and the rest black Namibian workers, these latter living in huts that accommodated up to 50 people. While the black workers were on fixed-term contracts, away from their families, whole clans of Germans lived here, with their own school, church, hotel and even a bowling alley. Water was brought in by narrow-gauge railway from Grillen Tal, several kilometres away, where the crumbling ruins of the main pump station can still be explored.

In the early years, a claim could be bought for 60 Deutschmarks, rising to a staggering 6,000DM by 1917–18. Diamonds were not mined, but were sifted by hand with great trommel sieves, their rusting frames now good only for photographers.

The third mining town in the area was at Bogenfels, where a small desalination plant is still to be seen right on the beach. The main attraction for visitors, though, is the spectacular rock arch that stands about 55m high beside the sea. Despite its inaccessibility, photographs have made it one of the south's better-known landmarks.

Getting there and away Full-day guided tours are run by Coastways Tours (see page 224), departing from Lüderitz at around 08.30 and returning around 17.00. Costs are N$1,400 per person, including national park fees and lunch, based on a minimum of four people. Book in advance.

Future possibilities Several options for opening more of the park to visitors are under consideration, along with the establishment of some basic restcamps. Guided hiking trails and drives are strong contenders, as are visits to various fossil and archaeological sites, diamond mines, shipwrecks and seal and seabird colonies. One significant attraction in its own right is the **Roter Kamm Crater**, west of Rosh Pinah. Said to be the fourth-largest meteorite crater in the world, it can be viewed from the Aurusberg Mountain, which itself has a botanical hiking trail.

Oranjemund This prosperous mining town in the far southwest corner of Namibia is the headquarters of NAMDEB, who for many years have owned all the property – hence daily Air Namibia flights linking the town with Windhoek. Without an invitation from a resident, and the permission of NAMDEB, visitors have usually been forbidden entrance. Even then, those leaving the mining area have had to pass strict X-ray checks, which search for hidden diamonds. According to the MET, the town will 'soon' be open to visitors, with opportunities for exploring the new national park, and the mouth of the Orange River, from its southern boundary. However, this has been the case for nigh on a decade, so don't hold your breath.

NORTH OF THE B4

HELMERINGHAUSEN Despite being a large dot on the map, this is just a farm that has grown into a village, in the middle of some very scenic roads. Just to the north are flat plains with little hills of balancing rocks – rather like the cairns found on Scottish mountains, only somewhat bigger.

Heading southwest on the C13 towards Lüderitz, the road winds down and opens out into an immense valley – a huge plain lined by mountains with a clear escarpment on the east, and a more ragged array – the Tiras Mountains – to the west. It is most spectacular, especially at sunset.

Helmeringhausen itself feels like an oasis. There is the well-stocked **Helmringwinkel shop** (◷ *07.30–16.30 Mon–Fri, 07.30–13.00 Sat, 09.00–13.00 Sun*) for basics and a vital **fuel** station (◷ *07.00–17.30 daily*) beside it.

Where to stay, eat and drink

🏠 **Helmeringhausen Hotel** (22 rooms, camping) 📞063 283307; e info@helmeringhausen. com; www.helmeringhausen.com. This super little place, started in 1938, is a classic example of a well-maintained local hotel. Expanded considerably in recent years, it continues to offer simple yet attractive en-suite rooms with twin beds & pristine bed nets. There is safe parking at the back (though it's difficult to imagine a crime problem here), & a few tables & chairs around a small pool with a braai area. For those winter evenings, there's a separate lounge with a fireplace & even a piano, while for the more energetic hikes or farm drives can be arranged.

Lunch & a set 3-course dinner (*N$180*) are available in the hotel's restaurant, which is open for afternoon tea & snacks too. The adjacent coffee shop is a magnet for passing drivers, drawn to light lunches or fresh apple crumble in a shady garden with lawns & picnic tables. A row of vines separates this from a campsite with 6 neat pitches, & opposite is a self-catering house for up to 6 people. There have been reports of the owners behaving very rudely, so bear this in mind – and report back to Bradt! *B&B N$580/1,020 sgl/dbl; camping N$220 pp.* **LL**

Nearby guest farms Map, page 214.
There are a handful of excellent small guest farms around here. Dabis makes a natural overnight stop when driving between the Fish River Canyon and the Sesriem area, while Namtib (and others in the Tiras Mountains; see page 240) is also a candidate if you are travelling between Lüderitz or Aus and Sesriem. It seems like a large area, but the community is, in fact, very close-knit and most of the owners below socialise together regularly.

🏠 **Dabis Guest Farm** (11 rooms) 📞063 283 3003; e gaugler@farmdabis.com; www. farmdabis.com. Owned by the Gaugler family for 4 generations, since 1926, Dabis is currently run by Jörg & Michelle Gaugler (& their 4 children!). From its entrance on the C14, 10km north of Helmeringhausen, it's a further 7km down a track with some steep dips & humps (still manageable in a 2WD) to the old farmhouse, in a valley surrounded by hills.

Dabis has achieved an effective balance between welcoming guests – including day visitors with advance notice – & operating as a farm. It's a personal place, & near to self-sufficiency, with home-grown vegetables & fruits, homemade jam (which you can buy), & farm-reared sheep bred for lamb production & leather, using advanced rotation techniques to survive on the meagre rainfall. Be sure to sample their homemade smoked meats.

Accommodation is in comfortable en-suite twin rooms (room 5 has a bath instead of shower); although 2 have outside bathrooms. Outside, guests benefit from a swimming pool & tennis court in very good condition (rackets available). One of the main attractions of staying here, however, is learning about the farm. Most guests arrive in time for coffee & cake at 16.00, then go out on a complimentary farm drive for an hour or two, when Jörg will explain his techniques in depth, as well as ecology & sustainability issues, considerably enriching a visit. If you're lucky, you may spot one of the small animals on the farm, such as bat-eared foxes. *DBB N$1,500/2,520/3,600 sgl/dbl/trpl.* **LLLL**

🏠 **Lovedale Farm Holidays** (4 self-catering units, camping) 14km along C27 from Helmeringhausen, just off road; m 081 281 9074; e stay@lovedale-namibia.com; www.lovedale-namibia.com. Malcolm & Louisa Campbell run this Jersey stud & Swakara sheep farm, which offers

11

4 fully equipped self-catering units sleeping 2–7 people, each with their own braai area (braai packs available N$25, as well as eggs, butter & cream). Furnishings are simple & rustic. The soft-sand shady campsite has hot showers, electricity & toilets. Kids will be delighted by the wooden trip-trap bridge that leads across a duck pond to the reception. Activities include a self-guided 45min 2km walking trail, swimming in a nearby reservoir & joining farm work. *Units N$450–740; camping N$250 pp for first 2 people, then N$35 pp.* **L**

🏠 **Barby** (4 chalets, 1 hunter's hut, 3 campsites) 32km along C27 from Helmeringhausen, 500m off road on right; ☎081 612 8359; e barbyguestfarm@gmail.com.

Run by the ebullient David & Penny Schutte, this basic Swakara sheep farm has 4 en-suite chalets with wood-fired hot water on request & solar lighting, 1 secluded self-catering hunter's hut & 3 campsites with braai areas & ablution blocks, but no electricity. In the main house, they serve meals which previous guests have said are delicious. *DBB chalets N$410 pp; camping N$85/50 adult/child.* **L**

🏠 **Farm Aubures** 51km up C27 from Helmeringhausen, with 5km driveway; ☎063 683314; e amiller@iway.na. This working sheep farm is run by Adrienne & Jörn Miller who offer 6 camping sites 1km from their farmhouse with no electricity, but flushing toilets & geyzer hot water. *Camping N$90/60 adult/child.* **L**

TIRAS MOUNTAINS Dominating the skyline southwest of Helmeringhausen, and fringing the Namib's red dunes, the jagged Tiras Mountains are increasingly attracting visitors. Between the two runs the scenic D707, linking the C13 in the south to the C27/D407, a detour that takes in the beauty of both mountains and dunes.

 Where to stay *Map, page 214.*

The pick of the accommodation options here is Namtib Biosphere Reserve. Others fall within an area of 125,000ha that has been loosely designated by a group of local farmers as the Tiras Berge Conservancy. Accommodation below is roughly clockwise from the south.

🏠 **Farm Tiras** (chalet, hut, camping) ☎063 683048. Just off the main C13, 42km south of Helmeringhausen. An oasis of green among flaxen grasses, this cattle farm is run by Anita Koch (her husband, Klaus, sadly died in Jun 2014). As well as a smart self-catering house on the farm itself, across the road are a campsite, & a 1-room hut with outdoor bathroom & good views. You're welcome to charge your phone at the house, but there's no internet. *Self-catering guesthouse N$760 dbl; hut N$253pppn; camping N$135 pp.* **LL**

🏠 **Farm Gunsbewys** (2 rooms, guesthouse, camping) ☎063 683053; www.tirasmountains.com. Bordering the Namib-Naukluft National Park, & clearly signposted from the D707 just 24km from its junction with the C13, Gunsbewys is owned & run by Peter Gräbner. The 3km approach track is sandy, but usually navigable in a 2WD with care. Small, simple & idiosyncratic, with solar panels for power & absolutely no frills, it's an unlikely spot for a small museum, but a large room is crammed with posters & exhibits of the local flora & fauna. Come for the walking: guided early morning walks in the dunes (*N$100 pp*), or 2–3-day hiking trails

(*N$1,000 pp/day inc camping equipment & meals*); just bring good shoes & a hat. Note that the website is currently only in German. *Guesthouse N$140 pp; self-catering N$250 pp; camping N$80 pp.* **L**

✳ 🏠 **Namtib Biosphere Reserve** ☎063 683055; e contact@namtib.net; www.namtib. net. Nestled in an isolated valley surrounded by mountains, & overlooking the edge of the desert plain, Namtib lies 12km east of the scenic D707. It is clearly signposted (as Namtib Desert Lodge) from the C27/D407 (*76km*) & the C13 (*47km*).

Don't be put off by the name – this is not a scientific project, but a welcoming lodge & campsite with a personal feel, run on strongly ecological lines by Thorsten & Linn Theile. Theirs is a working farm, with klipspringer, oryx & springbok roaming the plains. It is also favoured by Rüppell's korhaan & the rare endemic dune lark. The evasive kudu inhabits the gorges & mountains, where black eagles nest & leopard, cheetah & lynx are hidden. There are some rock hyraxes around as well, not to mention bat-eared fox, aardwolf & porcupine. Visitors can explore on foot, perhaps on the waymarked botanical trail in the kopjes, which are also suitable for mountain bikes (bring your own), or go on guided nature drives (N$250/3hrs) to gain a deeper insight into life at the edge of the desert. 3–4 day horseback riding will be added soon. It all adds up to a good en route stopover, or a place to spend several days relaxing.

🏠 NAMTIB DESERT LODGE (8 rooms) The original simple chalets are unusually designed, comfortable & clean with twin or dbl beds, & separated from a private bathroom by a small open-air quadrangle, where many guests choose to sleep in the heat of the summer. A further 3 rooms (2 sgls, 1 family) are in a separate building. Electricity is provided by generator & lights are battery powered but, for those who have long appreciated the simplicity at Namtib, candles are still provided in the rooms. Candlelight plays a part in the extensive lounge & dining area, too, where guests can relax in front of the fire or drink a cool beer, & where delicious home-cooked 3-course meals are served en famille (lunch N$90; dinner N$190). There's a small book exchange & Wi-Fi costs N$10 for your whole stay. B&B N$916/1,446 sgl/dbl; camping N$100 pp. **LL**

Å LITTLE HUNTER'S REST (5 pitches) About 2.5km from the lodge is a separate campsite, in a beautiful location backed by mountains & overlooking the plains & the desert beyond. Pitches are widely spread under camelthorn trees & there's a central ablution block, but no electricity. Provisions such as firewood & meat are available; alternatively, campers may have dinner at the lodge, space permitting. N$100 pp. **L**

🏠 **Koiimasis Ranch** ✆063 683052; e koiimasis@yahoo.com; www.namibia-farm-lodge.com. Located along a 20km 4x4 track east of the D707, this ranch is run by Wolf & Anke Izko who offer 4 self-catering chalets & camping. **LL**

MALTAHÖHE This small town is an important crossroads, as it is linked by the tarred C19 to the main north–south B1. Although it is sometimes used by budget travellers as a base to visit Sossusvlei, the round trip distance of over 340km is off-putting. For most visitors, the town and its immediate environs are too far from the desert to be of major interest. The most interesting attraction locally is virtually unknown. About 30km north of here, on the farm Sandfeld, is a fascinating valley which, when the rains are good, fills with water to a depth of about 30cm. This doesn't happen every year, but when it does – normally between mid-February and mid-March – the shallow lake quickly becomes covered in a spectacular bloom of red, pink and white lilies, *Crinum crinum paludosum*. These last about a week, and are said to be endemic to the valley, which is known as the 'lily-veld'.

Where to stay, eat and drink Map, page 214.

There's accommodation in Maltahöhe itself, and Duwisib Castle is within easy reach. Those going west from the B1 along the C19 might be interested in Hudup Campsite.

🏠 **Maltahöhe Hotel** (27 rooms, 18 dorm beds) ✆063 293013; e info@maltahoehe-hotel.com; www.maltahoehe-hotel.com. Smart option with glass veranda where the predominantly German clientele sit at tables adorned with fresh flowers & sip filter coffee. There is a well-stocked bar, an à la carte restaurant serving lunch & dinner, a pool at the rear & a small internet café. The en-suite dbl & family rooms are clean & cool: tiled floors, good walk-in showers, & fans. There is also an 18-bed dormitory across the road for backpackers & budget travellers. If you're not staying, it's worth popping in for a drink if only to study the large old map mounted in the bar: it shows the allocation of Namibia's farmland. B&B N$475/750 sgl/dbl; dorm bed N$150. **L**

🏠 **Ôa Hera** (5 rooms, camping) ✆063 293028; m 081 215 2595; e oaheraa@iway.na; www.oaheraart.com. Ôa Hera, meaning 'that which is sought after', started life as a warehouse-style art gallery & craft centre (🕐 08.00–17.00 daily). Affiliated to the Red Stone restaurant, & located at the western end of town, it is now increasingly popular with backpackers. Affordable accommodation is in small rooms with a dbl or bunk-beds, sharing a bathroom. There's free (slow) Wi-Fi.

In the funky, semicircular restaurant, orange poles support swathes of hessian, affording shade, while succulent plants in terracotta pots, unusual sculptures & brightly painted concrete tables & benches rest on the gravel floor. It's a cool, pleasant place for a good bite to eat – from toasted sandwiches to more

substantial fare such as game goulash – most of the veg come from their own garden. *Dorm N$160 pp excluding b/fast; camping N$70 pp.* **L**
⋏ Hudup Campsite ✆063 293512; e ottohunt@mweb.com.na. Signposted around 300m from the C19, this rustic site is idyllically sited on a tributary of the Fish River about 13km east of Maltahöhe. There are BBQ areas & clean ablution facilities, but often you'll have just ground squirrels, lizards & the wind in the trees for company. In theory, hiking trails & game drives can be organised. *N$160 per vehicle (2–4 people).* **L**

Other practicalities The town has a fuel station (with an ATM), a post office, a Standard Bank (⊕ *Mon & Fri only*), and a useful information office at the Maltahöhe Hotel. There are also a few shops, including Pappot (✆063 293 397; e *pappot@mweb. com.na;* ⊕ *06.00–19.00 Mon–Sat;* **L**), which stocks most of the essentials, including bread, meat and eggs, and has a small campsite with 5 rooms to let.

DUWISIB CASTLE (✆061 285 7333; ⊕ *08.00–13.00 & 14.00–17.00 daily; admission N$66 pp*) Standing solidly amid the rolling hills 72km southwest of Maltahöhe, beside the D826, the sandstone fortress of Duwisib Castle is another of those anachronisms in which Namibia seems to specialise. Look from a distance and you won't believe it: a small, square castle with fortified battlements and high turrets in the middle of the African bush. Now under NWR ownership, it's apparently pretty run down. Nonetheless, the castle itself is built around an open central quadrangle, where there is now a small lawn and fountain, shaded by a couple of beautiful jacaranda trees. Its rooms are sparsely furnished, though there are some excellent original pieces dating back to around the turn of the 20th century, and interesting paintings and prints on the walls – many equestrian in theme. Above the entrance hall is a steep set of stairs (easily missed) up to a small gallery overlooking the entrance, and there is also a cellar, which now seems to be a storeroom.

You can park around the back, where you will find a café (⊕ *09.00–17.00 daily*) – part of Duwisib Guest Farm – selling coffee and homemade apple pie, as well as other drinks and snacks.

History The castle's history has been documented in an excellent booklet by Dr N Mossolow (see *Appendix 3*), available at the castle. It tells how Hansheinrich von Wolf was born in 1873 into a military family in Saxony and served with the Royal Saxon Artillery near Dresden. He came to South West Africa as a captain in the Schutztruppe, when he volunteered after the outbreak of the Herero War. He was decorated in 1905, and returned to Germany where he married Miss Jayta Humphrey in 1907.

Later that year he and his wife returned to German South West Africa, and over the next few years bought up farming land in the area. By October 1908 he had '33 horses, 68 head of large stock and 35 head of small stock' on his farm, and two wells. An 'extravagant residence of undressed stone, with 22 rooms and a cellar' had reached 2m above its foundations. He bought up more farmland, up to 50,000ha, and by 1909 the castle was complete, with furnishings and paintings imported from Germany.

Von Wolf proceeded to enlarge the area under his control by buying more land. A fanatical horseman and breeder of horses, he spent much time and energy developing his stable (see box, *The desert horses*, page 219).

In 1914 he set off with his wife to England, to purchase another thoroughbred stallion, but on the way war broke out. The ship diverted to South America, where they were briefly interned before he arranged a secret passage back to Europe. Eventually they arrived back in Germany where von Wolf reported for duty as an officer. On 4 September 1916 he was killed at the battle of the Somme.

Where to stay *Map, page 214.*

Duwisib Guest Farm (5 rooms, 2 bungalows, camping) 063 293344; e duwisib@ iway.na; www.farmduwisib.com. On the D826 within walking distance of Duwisib Castle, this working cattle & goat farm is owned & run by Christian Frank-Schultz. Choose from castle-view en-suite rooms; a fully equipped self-catering family unit; & the twin-bed self-catering Springbok bungalow. There are also 5 camping pitches nestling in a picturesque valley below, & sharing ablutions. Excellent farmhouse cooking makes it worth prebooking meals (*b/fast N$110,* *dinner N$160*), & wood is available. The reception/ shop/dining area doubles as a café during the day for visitors to the castle. *DBB N$800/1420 sgl/ dbl; 2-bed self-catering bungalow N$650 pp/night; camping N$95 pp.* **LL**

Duwisib Campsite (10 pitches) 066 385303; reservations 061 236975–7; e reservations@nwr.com.na; www.nwr.com.na. This friendly site offers pleasant pitches (no. 3 is a favourite, under a great tree) – though camping is cheaper at the adjacent farm, where hot water is more reliable, too. *N$110 pp (max 8 people).* **L**

BETTA The small settlement of Betta, 20km west of Duwisib Castle at the crossroads of the D826 and C27, is a veritable oasis for those travelling between Sesriem and Aus. Notable for the presence of a cash-only fuel station (⏲ *07.00–17.30 daily*) that carries out tyre repairs, boasts a campsite and a small restaurant with a well-stocked shop that usually sells fresh vegetables and fruit, ice creams, wine, firewood, gifts – and homemade cakes.

Where to stay *Map, page 214.*

Betta Camp (6 rooms, camping) m 081 128 4419, 081 477 3992; e info@bettacamp.net; www. bettacamp.net. Surrounded by mountains, this spacious level, sandy site is ideal for individuals or groups. Pitches have electricity, a sink area with lockable cupboard stocked with plates, pots, etc & their own shelter for a car, with the option of sleeping on the roof above if you're after a snake-free zone. If you don't fancy camping, there are fully equipped self-catering chalets with 2 or 4 beds & lovely private bathrooms, all modern & cool with walled verandas – & a welcome lollipop! The restaurant serves cold drinks, toasted sandwiches, burgers & pies, as well as dinner (*N$120*) available on request. No Wi-Fi. *Room N$275 pp; camping N$80 pp; b/fast N$60.* **L**

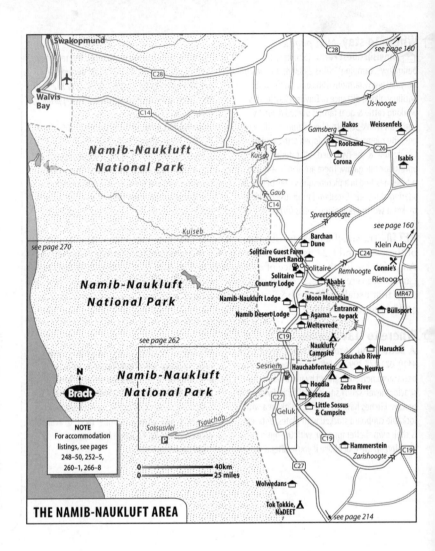

THE NAMIB-NAUKLUFT AREA

NOTE
For accommodation listings, see pages 248–50, 252–5, 260–1, 266–8

0 ——— 40km
0 ——— 25 miles

N
Bradt

12

The Namib-Naukluft National Park

People have different reactions when they encounter a desert for the first time. A few find it threatening, too arid and empty, so they rush from city to city, through the desert, to avoid spending any time there at all. Some try hard to like it for those same reasons, but ultimately find little which holds their attention. Finally there are those who stop and give the place their time, delighting in the stillness, strange beauty and sheer uniqueness of the environment. The desert's changing patterns and subtly adapted life forms fascinate them, drawing them back time after time.

Covering almost 50,000km², the Namib-Naukluft National Park is one of the largest national parks in Africa, protecting the oldest deserts in the world. The Namib Desert's scenery is stunning, and its wildlife fascinating; you just need to make the time to stop and observe it.

The sections in this chapter run roughly south to north. Note that the NamibRand, Sesriem, the Naukluft and Solitaire are very close together.

HISTORY

The park has grown gradually to its present size. In 1907 the area between the Kuiseb and Swakop rivers was proclaimed as 'Game Reserve No. 3'. It was augmented by the addition of Sandwich Harbour in 1941.

In 1956 the Kuiseb Canyon and Swakop River Valley were added, along with the Welwitschia Plains, and in 1968 the park was renamed the Namib Desert Park. In 1979 a large area of what was the protected 'Diamond Area No. 2' was added, including Sesriem and Sossusvlei, and the park was officially joined to the Naukluft Park, creating the Namib-Naukluft National Park.

Most recently, in 1986, the rest of 'Diamond Area No. 2' was added, taking the park's southern boundary as far south as the main road to Lüderitz, and increasing its area to its present size of 49,768km² – larger than Switzerland, or about the same as Maryland and New Jersey combined.

FLORA AND FAUNA

With a wide variety of fascinating species and unique adaptations, the Namib's community of animals and plants may not be as obviously appealing as those on Africa's grasslands, but it is equally impressive to the informed and observant visitor.

Though the Naukluft's wildlife is discussed separately, the flora and fauna elsewhere in the Namib-Naukluft are similar, dependent more on the landscape than on precise location. (Dr Mary Seely's book, *The Namib*, is a superb and simple guide to this area, widely available in Windhoek and Swakopmund. See *Appendix 3*, page 531.) The four basic types of environment found here, and some of their highlights are:

'Desert' is an arbitrary term whose meaning is widely disputed, even among experts. Some refer to Noy-Meir's definition of a 'water-controlled ecosystem with infrequent, discrete and largely unpredictable water inputs'. Others are quantitative, defining a desert as receiving an average of less than 100mm of rain per annum. In practice, any arid habitat can be called a desert – and the Namib is certainly very arid.

Antarctica has close to zero precipitation, and most of the water there is frozen, so, strictly speaking, the whole continent is a desert. However, the normal usage of 'desert' refers to dry places which are also hot. These cover 5% of the land on Earth, and are to be found in two neat rings around the globe, straddling the lines of the tropics of Capricorn and Cancer.

The uniform distribution of deserts is due to the pattern of sunlight landing on the planet. Sunlight intensity is highest at the Equator, which is directly underneath the sun for most of the year. With all this light energy, water evaporates more vigorously at this latitude. As the water rises in the atmosphere, it condenses and falls on to the equatorial rainforests. The dry air remaining in the upper atmosphere journeys away from the Equator towards the tropics. Here it descends to ground level, waterless. What water there is at ground level is then picked up and exported by low-altitude winds travelling back towards the Equator to complete the cycle – hence the desert.

This desiccating climate creates a habitat that challenges life. Levels of solar radiation are enormous; air temperatures can soar during the day and, without insulating cloud cover, plunge below freezing at night; the ground is almost too hot to touch; strong winds are common and, where there is sand, sandstorms scour the land. Worst of all, water becomes a luxury. Since all living things are built from water-packed cells, there could hardly be a more uninhabitable environment on Earth. It is a credit to evolution that deserts are often inhabited by a wealth of organisms with sophisticated adaptations to survive in these conditions.

SAND DUNES Dunes are everybody's idea of a desert, and generally thought of as being bare and lifeless. While this is not inaccurate for many deserts, the Namib is sufficiently old for endemic species to have evolved.

Various grasses grow on some of the more stable dunes, but most of the vegetable matter comes from wind-blown detritus. This collects at the bottom of the dunes, to be eaten by fish-moths (silverfish), crickets and the many tenebrionid beetles – or *tok tokkies*, as they are known – near the base of the food chain. Particular tenebrionid species occur in specific environments, with those in the coastal fog belt adapting in ingenious ways in order to harness the available moisture.

These then provide food for spiders, geckos, lizards and chameleons which, in turn, fall prey to sidewinder snakes. Rare Grant's golden moles eat any small beetles or larvae that they can catch, and birds are mobile enough to move in and out of the dunes in search of the smaller animals. Endemic to this region is the dune lark, which is seldom found outside the dune areas.

RIVER VALLEYS AND PANS The river valleys that run through the Namib are linear oases. Though dry on the surface, their permanent underground water sustains trees and bushes, like the camelthorn (*Acacia erioloba*) and nara melon (*Acanthosicyos horrida*), found in the middle of the great dune sea at Sossusvlei.

Other common river-valley trees include the ana tree (*Acacia albida*); the shepherd's tree (*Boscia albitrunca*), easily identified by its white trunk; the wild green-hair tree (*Parkinsonia africana*) and the marvellously weeping false ebony (*Euclea pseudebenus*).

The lush vegetation found in these valleys makes them a favourite for numerous insects and birds, as well as larger mammals like oryx, kudu and springbok. These are the most likely areas to find nocturnal cats from leopard to caracal, especially where the rivers cut through mountains rather than dunes.

GRAVEL PLAINS Throughout the desert, and especially north of the Kuiseb River, the Namib has many expansive, flat plains of rock and stone. These come alive during the rains, when they will quickly be covered with tall thin grass and creeping yellow flowers, attracting herds of oryx, springbok and even Hartmann's mountain zebra. During drier times there are fewer large mammals around, but still at night black-backed jackal, aardwolf and the occasional aardvark forage for termites, while bat-eared and Cape foxes scavenge for insects, reptiles, and anything else edible.

Spotted hyena and even the rare brown hyena are sometimes recorded here. Both leave distinctive white droppings, but only the sociable spotted hyenas make such eerie, mournful calls.

Resident larger birds include ostrich, secretary birds, Rüppell's korhaan and Ludwig's bustard, while enthusiastic 'twitchers' will seek the pale, apparently insignificant Gray's lark (among other larks), which is endemic to the gravel plains of the Namib.

INSELBERGS AND MOUNTAIN OUTCROPS Throughout the Namib there are mountains, often of granite or limestone. Some, like many between Sesriem and Sossusvlei, have become submerged beneath the great dune sea. Others, especially north of the Kuiseb River, jut up through the flat desert floor like giant worm casts on a well-kept lawn. These isolated mountains surrounded by gravel plains are inselbergs (from the German for 'island-mountain') – and they have their own flora and fauna. Euphorbia, acacia, commiphora, zygophyllum and aloe species are common, while the succulent lithops (often called living rocks, for their pebble-like shape) occur here, though less frequently.

Many inselbergs are high enough to collect moisture from morning fogs, which sustain succulents and aloes, and with them whole communities of invertebrates. Temporary pools in crevices can be particularly interesting, and there's a whole microcosm of small water creatures that lay drought-resistant eggs. These survive years of desiccation, to hatch when the pools do finally fill.

Being open land, these make perfect perches for raptors: lappet-faced vultures, greater kestrels and red-necked falcons are typical of this environment. Also watch for sandgrouse, which congregate at water around dusk and dawn, and other well-camouflaged foraging birds.

NAMIBRAND NATURE RESERVE

Covering about 2,100km², an area equivalent to about half the size of Belgium, the NamibRand Nature Reserve is one of the largest private reserves in Africa. Lying south of Sesriem, it borders on to the main Namib-Naukluft National Park in the west, a boundary of about 100km, and in the east its extent is generally defined by the Nubib Mountains.

There is a wide variety of different desert landscapes and environments within this, from huge red sand dunes to vegetated inter-dune valleys, sand and gravel plains, and some particularly imposing mountains. It's a spectacular area of desert.

There are several ways to visit this, all utilising small lodges and camps as bases for expert-led guided trips. If you want a detailed look at the central Namib, with guides who understand it, this is an excellent complement to a day or two of driving yourself around Sesriem and Sossusvlei.

HISTORY The reserve was formed from a number of separate farms established in the 1950s to eke out an existence farming in the desert. Several severe drought years in the 1980s demonstrated that farming domestic stock here just wasn't viable. There were allegations of farmers opening their fences to game from the Namib-Naukluft National Park, only to kill the animals for their meat once they left the park.

Game was the only option, and this survived well on the farm Gorrasis, owned by Albi Brückner (a businessman, rather than a farmer, who'd bought the farm for its landscapes).

In 1988 Brückner bought out two neighbouring farms, Die Duine and Stellarine, and gradually the reserve was broadened from that base. Now various shareholders have contributed money to the reserve, and different operators hold 'concession' areas which they utilise for tourism.

FLORA AND FAUNA The NamibRand's flora and fauna are the same as that in the western areas of the Namib-Naukluft. However, there are also red hartebeest, which aren't usually found in the national park, and blesbok which have been introduced from South Africa.

WHERE TO STAY/WHAT TO SEE AND DO *Maps, pages 244 and 262.*
What you see and do here depends entirely on where you stay, as many of the camps in the concession have a different emphasis.

Wolwedans \061 230616; e info@wolwedans.com; www.wolwedans.com. Wolwedans now comprises 4 separate accommodation choices, each a considerable distance from the others across the reserve. While all cater for the top end of the market, they have a range of styles to suit different visitors. Particularly special is the possibility of arranging a wedding, from a religious service to a civil ceremony.

The turning to the main farmhouse, west off the C27, is about 32km of bumpy road to the north of the junction of the D827 & C27. Coming from the north, it is 50km south of the C27/D845 junction. If you are approaching from Sesriem, that's about 40km south of the first NamibRand signboard south of Sesriem on the C27. The camp has its own airstrip as well. Once on the 'drive' to Wolwedans, ignore the small house on the left & continue about 20km from the gate to the Wolwedans farmhouse, from where transfers into the various camps are arranged. Beware of turning off this track, as you may become stuck in the sand. All rates below include the NamibRand entrance fee; pilot and guide fees for each camp aren't included and cost an extra N$975.

WOLWEDANS DUNE CAMP (6 tents) The flagship of the reserve since it opened, the Dune Camp is built on wooden decks raised above the sand. Each tent includes an en-suite hot shower & toilet, has twin beds & solar-powered lights, with a veranda set to the side for uninterrupted views of the landscape. The lodge's central open dining area & sundeck are furnished with soft leather-seat chairs so you can sit enjoying the views with a glass of wine. An open kitchen allows you to chat to the chef while your meal is being prepared (the standard of food is excellent). Activities usually consist of afternoon & full-day drives, including a picnic lunch, into the reserve with a professional guide & guided walks. Scenic flights to the Diamond Coast & Sossusvlei can be arranged. This camp is more suited to the adventurous traveller who will appreciate its quiet atmosphere & old-style feel. *Min 2-night stay. FBA*

N$6,945/10,050 sgl/dbl, inc sgl supplement. **LLLLL**

🏠 **WOLWEDANS DUNE LODGE** (8 chalets, 1 suite) Since 1998, the Dune Lodge has been run with all the courtesy & attention to detail of a country house, with an atmosphere of relaxed gentility. More luxurious than the Dune Camp, it sits atop one of the red dunes. Purpose-built wooden chalets are built on stilts with their own secluded verandas & en-suite showers & toilets. The real coup is the bedrooms. Solid wooden twin beds, draped with nets that give all the allure of a dreamy 4-poster, face directly east through a canvas 'wall' that, when rolled up, affords unparalleled stargazing & a front-row view of sunrise over the mountains.

Simple walkways over the dunes lead to the hub of the camp, where a comfortable bar with leather armchairs, a separate library & 2 lounges all share the view. There are also 2 dining rooms where meals are taken at individual tables or around a large table, depending on individual preference. Dinner is a relatively formal affair, with some of the best food to be had in Namibia, & good wines to match from a chilled wine cellar. And after dinner, what better than to while away the evening around the campfire on the deck? This is a place to relax, unwind & get a real feel for the surroundings. Guided activities follow the same pattern as those of the camp, usually returning in time for a civilised afternoon tea, or perhaps a leisurely dip in the pool before lounging on the surrounding deck. *FBA N$6,525/9,450 sgl/dbl, inc sgl supplement.* **LLLLL**

🏠 **WOLWEDANS PRIVATE CAMP** (suite) Tucked away in a secluded valley, the Private Camp caters for just 6 guests: ideal for honeymooners or anyone seeking the ultimate in privacy. It has 3 spacious bedrooms with verandas & en-suite bathrooms, while an adjoining sala with a day bed makes an inspired place for children to sleep. The camp boasts its own lounge, dining area, library & a fully equipped kitchen. But forget the washing up – all this comes with a dedicated chef & housekeeper, so total relaxation is the order of the day. *FBA N$5,525 pp based on min 3 people, inc private drives.* **LLLLL**

🏠 **BOULDERS SAFARI CAMP** (4 chalets) ⊕ Closed 1 Dec–28 Feb. Set 40km south of the base camp, this latest addition to the Wolwedans collection is nestled among the massive granite boulders that give it its name & is reached by a leisurely 2hr scenic drive through the reserve. Staying here gives a true feeling of peace & isolation, with only the sound of the wind to break the silence. The canvas-

&-wood chalets, each with its own bathroom, are decorated in natural tones, with 4-poster beds draped in flowing white nets. The canvas sides can be rolled up for seemingly endless views over the plains & the distant mountains, or for watching the sunrise from the comfort of your bed.

The lounge & dining area is tastefully decorated with dark wooden furniture & old German bookcases full of leather-bound books. Meals can be eaten around the large wooden dining table or, for a more personal touch, private dinners can be arranged on the veranda by lantern-light. But wherever you eat, you cannot fail to be impressed by the skilfully created food & quality wines. Activities are similar to the other camps, but also include hikes up the kopjes & sundowners on top of the boulders. *Min 2-night stay. FBA N$8,345/12,050 sgl/dbl.* **LLLLL**

🏠 **Sossusvlei Desert Lodge** (10 chalets) ☎+27 11 809 4300; e contactus@andbeyond.com; www.andbeyond.com. In the north of the NamibRand Reserve, about 97km from Betta & 40km south of Sesriem & 4km from the C27 down a rather rocky driveway, this is one of Namibia's most stylish modern lodges.

Spacious split-level chalets, made largely of stone & glass, are built into the rocks overlooking a desert plain. Their graceful interiors use a mix of bright chrome & earthy, desert colours; these personal cocoons have minibars, CD systems & AC. Most of their glass walls slide or fold away to open up the room to the desert, & at night a skylight can slide back above your bed allowing you to stargaze: telescopes provided!

The main lodge is similarly luxurious, with a lovely terrace with sweeping views, an upstairs lounge with AC, satellite TV & a small observatory with computer-controlled telescope. The food is excellent; the wine cellar impressive – & there's a slightly surreal pool outside. Activities focus on Sossusvlei walking & driving trips, while hot-air balloon trips are an unusual & fun addition to the normal trips. *FBA N$5,250 pp sharing low season, N$8,430 pp sharing high season.* **LLLLL**

🏠 **Le Mirage Desert Lodge & Spa** (30 rooms) ☎063 683019; reservations ☎061 224712; e info@mirage-lodge.com; www.mirage-lodge.com. Forget hazy images in the desert heat: Le Mirage is a collection of sizeable buildings merging little with the desert surroundings. It's a curious fusion of a grand Arthurian castle – cathedral-style windows, trefoil turrets, monogrammed linen – & a Moroccan riad, with inner courtyards, palm trees, antique chests & sapphire-blue mosaic bathrooms. Accommodation is divided between 2 buildings: the smaller (7 rooms) characterised by its cool, galleried courtyard, complete with gushing waterfall & cascading bougainvillea. Rooms in both locations are spacious & tastefully furnished with antiques & good quality, modern amenities: AC, safe, minibar & coffee/tea station. Stone walls, sand-blasted room dividers, high, beamed ceilings & 4-poster beds add to the interior of grandeur. In the new building each room boasts a small balcony, & 2 of the rooms have access to 'star decks' where guests can sleep under the night sky on top of the turret. At ground level, a decadent spa offers all types of massage, facials & aromatherapy baths in 5 treatment rooms. There's also an outdoor pool & a colonial style, open-sided bar & lounge. The last of the buildings contains the restaurant & wine cellar. Here, heavy wooden tables are interspersed with gas patio heaters, as the central atrium can make this a chilly dining option. Activities include ½-day Sossusvlei drive (N$925 pp), 2hrs quad biking (N$475 pp), sundowner (N$500 pp) & night game drive (N$300 pp). DBB N$2,095/3,150 sgl/dbl. **LLLL**

🏠 **Nubib Mountain Guest Farm** (5 rooms) ✆063 293 240; **m** 081 129 3573; **e** hbaumann@ nubibmountain.com; www.nubibmountain.com. A little gem discovered 10km along D845, with a 5km driveway, it's a quiet oasis set amid a 30,000ha farm run by Germans Horst & Irmelien Baumann, who inherited the land from her parents. There are just 5 dbl rooms: 2 classic rooms in the main house & 3 modern ones in a separate block at the back of the main house, with French doors overlooking a watering hole & the Tiras Mountains. These outer rooms have solar-heated hot water. The house is surrounded by luscious cacti gardens & there's a circular pool with astounding views. Meals are taken

under a covered open-air porch with your hosts. DBB N$880/1,560 sgl/dbl. **LLL**

🥾 **Tok Tokkie Trails** ✆061 264521; **e** toktokkie@toktokkietrails.com; www. toktokkietrails.com. As the name suggests, this place is about walking. It is signposted 400m or so north of the C27/D827 junction, from where it's a further 11km to the base, through a couple of gates.

The Tok Tokkie Trail, named for the specially adapted beetles that are found in the Namib, is designed to offer a really close-up look at the Namib Desert environment, concentrating not only on the flora & fauna but also on how the whole desert ecosystem works. The landscape is beautiful: small vegetated sand dunes, mountains, dry rivers, open plains & the huge African sky. The 22km trail is run over 2 nights & 3 days, starting at around 14.00 on day 1, & finishing at about 11.00 on day 3. If you'd like lunch beforehand, you'll need to book it in advance & arrive by midday.

The walk is accompanied by a specialist desert guide. While you need to be reasonably fit, the group travels at the pace of the slowest; this is no route march. You carry only a daypack with water, picnic lunch & personal items; your luggage is delivered to the camp by a support crew, who prepare a 3-course dinner under the stars. At night, you'll sleep out on comfortable stretcher beds with mattress, duvet & pillow, laid out in separate dbl or twin 'dune bedrooms'. There are long-drop toilets & a hot-water bucket shower is available.

A sunhat, sunscreen & sunglasses are essential, but water bottles & all bedding are provided. Hiking boots are a good idea but comfortable closed walking shoes are fine. In the winter, Jun–Sep, the desert nights can be cold, & warm clothing, including a woolly hat, is recommended. FBA N$2,799 pp low season; N$3,034 pp high season; min age 8. **LLLLL**

Driver's note If you're heading south of the NamibRand, you'll come across some of the most scenic routes in the country: the D826, C27 and D707 (see *Chapter 11*). Sand dunes line the west of these roads, and mountains overlook the east – spectacular stuff. However, they do tend to be quite slow-going, and the gravel is sometimes not as good or as wide as the faster C19 or C14, so allow plenty of time for your journey (an average of about 50km/h is realistic).

NAUKLUFT MOUNTAINS

An hour's drive northeast of Sesriem, the main escarpment juts out into the desert forming a range known as the Naukluft Mountains. In 1968 these were protected within the Naukluft Mountain Zebra Park – to conserve a rare breeding population of Hartmann's mountain zebra. Shortly afterwards, land was bought to the west of the mountains and added to the park, forming a corridor linking these mountains into the Namib National Park. This allowed oryx, zebra and other game to migrate between the two, and in 1979 the parks were formally combined into the Namib-Naukluft National Park.

GEOLOGY The uniqueness of the area stems from its geology as much as its geographical position. Separated from the rest of the highlands by steep, spectacular cliffs, the Naukluft Mountains form a plateau. Underneath this, to a height of about 1,100m, is mostly granite. Above this base are alternating layers of dolomites and shales, with extensive deposits of dark limestone, rising to about 1,995m. Over the millennia, rainwater has gradually cut into this massif, dissolving the rock and forming steep kloofs, or ravines, and a network of watercourses and reservoirs – many of which are subterranean. The name Naukluft, which means 'narrow ravine', is apt for the landscape.

Where these waters surface, in the deeper valleys, there are crystal-clear springs and pools – ideal for cooling dips. Often these are decorated by impressive formations of smooth tufa – limestone that has been redeposited by the water over waterfalls.

FLORA AND FAUNA Receiving occasional heavy rainstorms in summer that feed its network of springs and streams in its deeper kloofs, the Naukluft supports a surprisingly varied flora and fauna.

The high plateau and mountainsides tend to be rocky with poor, if any, soil. Here are distinctive euphorbia, acacia, commiphora and aloe plants (including quivertrees, which are found in a dense stand in Quivertree Gorge). Most are low, slow-growing

SUSTAINABLE LIVING IN THE NAMIB DESERT

Many people wonder how anything survives in the Namib Desert which, at 55 million years old, is the oldest desert in the world, and one of the driest. Enter NaDEET (the Namib Desert Environmental Education Trust), which from its base in the NamibRand Nature Reserve teaches Namibia's youth about this harsh environment, and how it is possible not only to survive here, but also to live in a sustainable manner.

NaDEET has hosted thousands of youngsters on its sustainable living programme, which focuses on energy, water, waste and biodiversity, while also encouraging teamwork and co-operation. Practical, experimental learning allows participants, many of whom have never visited the desert before, to see first hand the importance of looking after their environment and the benefits to themselves and Namibia of sustainable living. The children are expected to look after their own living space, do their own cleaning and cook their own food using fuel-efficient stoves, self-constructed solar ovens and handmade fire bricks of recycled paper.

Guests at Wolwedans, or even passers-by, can arrange a visit (*between 08.00 and 17.00*) to find out more and perhaps to join in with the activities. For those willing to make a greater contribution, NaDEET occasionally accepts short-term volunteers for a minimum of three months. To arrange this, contact their new office in Swakopmund (3 *Antonius Garden, Nathaniel Maxuilili St, Swakopmund;* 081 367 5310; e admin@nadeet.org; www.nadeet.org).

species, adapted to conserving water during the dry season. The variations of slope and situation result in many different niches suiting a wide variety of species.

Down in the deeper kloofs, where there are permanent springs, the vegetation is totally different, with many more lush, broad-leaf species. Wild, cluster and sycamore figs are particularly prevalent, while you should also be able to spot camelthorn, buffalo-thorn, wild olive and shepherd's trees.

The Naukluft has many animals, including large mammals, though all are elusive and difficult to spot. Hartmann's mountain zebra, oryx, kudu and klipspringer are occasionally seen fleeing over the horizon (usually in the far distance). Steenbok and the odd sunbathing dassie are equally common, and springbok, warthog and ostrich occur, but are more often found on the plains around the mountains. The mountains should be a classic place for leopard, and the smaller cats – as there are many small mammals found here – though these are almost never seen.

Over 200 species of birds have been recorded here, and a useful annotated checklist is available from the park office. The Naukluft Mountains are at the southern limit of the range of many species of the northern Namib – Rüppell's parrot, rosy-faced lovebirds and Monteiro's hornbill all occur here, as do species typical of the south like the Karoo robin and chat. In the wetter kloofs, watch for species that you wouldn't find in the drier parts of the park, like the water-loving hamerkop, brubru and even African black ducks. Raptors are usually seen soaring above. Black eagles, lanner falcons, augur buzzards and pale chanting goshawks are common.

GETTING THERE AND AWAY The national park's entrance is on the D854, about 10km southwest of the C14, which links Solitaire and Maltahöhe. Approaching from Windhoek, pass Büllsport and take the D854 towards Sesriem.

Alternatively, Büllsport Guest Farm owns a section of the Naukluft Mountains, accessible from the farm without going into the national park, and Ababis borders on to the mountains.

 WHERE TO STAY *Map, page 244.*
The options are to camp at the basic national park's site, or to use one of these guest farms as a base. The mountains are also within a few hours' drive from most of the lodges in the Solitaire and Sesriem areas.

Büllsport Guest Farm (14 rooms, 2 campsites) 063 693371; e info@buellsport. com; www.buellsport.com. Run by Johanna & Ernst Sauber, this is one of the best traditional guest farms in the country, attracting a wide range of nationalities to stay. You can expect excellent food & wonderful 3-course dinners with wine. The 8 standard rooms are en suite, while the 6 luxury rooms behind the main house all have toilets separated from the bathroom, underfloor heating & cooling, & spacious patios where guests can relax after a hard day's hiking. There is an indoor dining area with a large sliding glass door that opens on to a patio with views of the garden, while the lovely swimming pool has picturesque views of the surrounding mountains.

Alternatively, there are 2 campsites, both tucked away in the mountains 3km from the farm.

1 is for private use, the other for general use. Both have 2 flush toilets, 2 sinks, a shaded lapa & 2 showers – you'll have to buy wood from the farm shop & burn it in the 'donkey' water heater. The general campsite doesn't have electricity.

Many visitors use this as a base for visiting the Naukluft Mountains, as Büllsport owns a section of them. There are a number of trails varying in length & difficulty, & Johanna also offers short horseriding trails into the mountains. For 2 or more experienced riders, she can arrange a 2-day trail, including meals & an overnight bushcamp in the Naukluft. A short drive from the farmhouse is an old German Schutztruppe post, & a few hrs' walk from that is a large natural rock arch – dubbed the 'Bogenfels of the Naukluft', after the original in the Sperrgebiet. Alternatively, the farm is just under 2hrs' drive (*115km*) from Sesriem, so makes a practical base for day trips there if closer accommodation is full. 4x4 excursions to Sossusvlei are available by arrangement. *DBB standard N$1,185/2,065 sgl/dbl, luxury N$1,350/2,370 sgl/dbl; private campsite N$924 per group; general campsite N$185 pp.* **LLL**

🏠 **Zebra River Lodge** (13 rooms) ✆063 693265; e zebrariverlodge@gmail.com; www.zebra-river-lodge.com. A renovated farmhouse set in 12,500ha in its own canyon in the Tsaris Mountains & reached by turning south from the D850 (between the D854 & the D855). Note that their driveway is several kilometres long & crosses a sand river, which – in exceptional years – flows across the road. Owned by Louis & Geraldine Fourie, some of the guest rooms lead off a wide veranda around a fish-pond, while the quieter rooms are located further away from the main building for extra privacy. All are en suite with plenty of space & lovely old-fashioned German furniture – & the 'honeymoon' suite has a large stand-alone bath, a king-size bed, & even more space.

The lodge's main area also includes a swimming pool surrounded by green lawns. Home-cooked 3-course dinners are served every evening on the terrace, or in the dining room in cooler weather.

ZRL can be used as a base for driving yourself to Sesriem or the Naukluft, but don't ignore the lodge's own area – it's home to the world's oldest examples of stromatolite fossils; a tour costs N$200 pp. Other activities include a sundowner drive (*N$200 pp*), guided walk to natural spring (*N$200 pp*), ½-day Sossusvlei excursion (*N$1,200 pp*) & various guided walking trails (*N$100 pp*). *DBB standard room N$1,360/1,865 sgl/dbl; chalet N$1,560/2,100 sgl/dbl.* **LLL**

🔺 **Tsauchab River Camp** (6 bungalows, 6 chalets, camping) ✆063 293416; reservations ✆064 464144; e reservations@logufa.com; www.tsauchab.com. Johan & Nicky Steyn offer a very warm welcome & well-priced accommodation across their quirky & highly original camps. The entrance is on the D850, very close to the junction with the D854. They operate 10 different campsites, each very individual in feel, and accommodating approx 2–50 guests. In addition there are 6 en-suite twin-bed bungalows at Tsabi-Tsabi (with 12v power, water & BBQ) & 6 dbl chalets at the Eagle Hide Out.

Facilities are spread across this huge farm. Walking in the wild fig forest (detailed trail maps available), tackling the 4x4 drives, chilling out in the springs & water pools, & taking time to admire Johan's inspired, homemade metal sculptures that line the entrance are all great pastimes. There is no formal restaurant menu but Nicky will do any meals on request, from picnic lunches to tasty braais, or there's a wide selection of fresh food & cold drinks available in the farm shop. *B&B N$760/1,300 sgl/dbl; camping N$100 pp, plus N$150 per pitch.* **LL**

🔺 **Hauchabfontein Camping** (camping) ✆063 293433; e irmi@mweb.com.na; www.hauchabfontein.com. Part of Immo & Irmi Foerster's farm, this neat, scenic campsite lies beside the Tsauchab river-bed & close to a lovely quivertree forest. It's located on the D854, between the D850 & C19, about 5km southwest of the Naukluft View, 59km from Sesriem & 44km from Naukluft. Facilities are clean & reliable with stone-built hot-water showers & toilets, & peaceful acacia-shaded pitches. Occasionally fresh fruit & vegetables are available from the farm, as are trips to the nearby natural springs & sundowner trips. *N$120 pp, children under 10 free.* **L**

🏠 **Betesda Lodge & Camping** (22 rooms, camping) ✆063 693253; e betesda@iway.na; www.betesdalodge.com. Created by Tony & Leny Rust in 1998, Betesda is a Christian retreat at the junction of the C19 & D854 which has opened its doors to wider tourism; as you'd expect, it's a calm, friendly place. 18 twin & 4 family rooms are built in a row with a long, shaded veranda running along one side & small private terraces along the other. Inside, each is cool & clean with a crazy-paving-style stone floor, pine furniture, large tiled en-suite shower, mosi net, free-standing fan & solar heating. Family rooms are huge with a half-height partition wall separating the dbl & 2 sgl beds. The main stone & thatch building is very lodgelike, with a wide check-in area, & a huge dining area (*dinner N$160 pp*) with large leaded patio doors & a long buffet counter. Shaded loungers surround a lovely stone pool, & there's a stepped-down rectangular boma with fixed tables, chairs & a built-in BBQ & bar. The campsite, set a little distance away, has 15 pitches around a large tree, 5 showers & toilets with electric lights, a fire pit & running water. Wood can be bought at the lodge, or campers can eat in the restaurant with advance notice. Free Wi-Fi in reception. If prebooked,

12

the following activities are available: 1hr sundowner (*N$150 pp*), 1hr quad biking (*N$370 pp*) & Sossusvlei (*N$2,000 for 6 people max*). *DBB N$995/1590 sgl/dbl; camping N$80 pp.* **LLL**

⌂ **Ababis Guest Farm** (5 dbl rooms, 2 houses) ✆063 683080; e info@ababis-gaestefarm.de; www.ababis-gaestefarm.de. Ababis stands on the west side of the C14, opposite the junction with the C24, on the northern edge of the Naukluft Mountains. The 160-year-old colonial farmhouse, owned by Kathrin & Uwe Schulze Neuhoff, has been a guest farm since 1993, offering large en-suite rooms that are simply furnished, with a desert-inspired colour scheme. Former interior designer Kathrin has added her own touches to the main areas, with a strange mixture of colonial artefacts, modern art & sculptured lighting in the lounge & dining room. There's also a stone-clad swimming pool & tanning deck. In addition to the rooms at the main house, guests can rent a twin-bed 'river house' & the 1940s 'Berghouse' that sleeps up to 4 has an outdoor toilet, solar-heated shower & small kitchen; you can buy supplies at their farm shop.

The farm has around 160 cattle & a few ostriches, as well as areas devoted purely to wildlife including oryx, springbok, blesbok, occasional zebra, a few kudu & some bat-eared foxes. It is a good base for long hikes, but there's also a gentle walking trail down to a (usually) dry river, which takes a few hours, & a more energetic 1½hr hike to the summit of a nearby mountain for panoramic views over the farm. If you reserve 3 days in advance, they can arrange a 4x4 trip to Sesriem Canyon & Sossusvlei; trips costs about N$2,915 per vehicle. Uwe also offers training courses for off-road drivers. *DBB standard/comfort room N$1,200–1,400 sgl/2,000–2,400 dbl; camping N$150 pppn.* **LLL**

⌂ **Hammerstein Lodge & Camp**
(5 bungalows, 51 rooms, camping) ✆063 693111; e hammerst@hammerstein.com.na; www.hammerstein.com.na. Situated on the C19, the turn-off north to Hammerstein has a clear signpost between the D845 (which goes past the Naukluft Mountains) & the D827. Run by the same people as Hoodia Desert Lodge, & yet poles apart, this is a well-established private restcamp catering predominantly to large German groups. As well as en-suite twin rooms in staggered rows, there are self-catering bungalows, each with 2–4 beds. Rooms are clean & bright, & feature pine furniture.

Each has an outside bench overlooking a wide gravel pathway, or there's a more pleasant grassy area beside the pool where garden tables are shaded by lovely camelthorn trees. Buffet meals are served in either the cavernous restaurant or at a long banqueting table, & there's a bar, complete with wall-mounted animal skins, for after-dinner drinks. There is some game kept here (including caracal, cheetah & 'Lisa' the leopard in unimpressive 1ha enclosures), & you're encouraged to join their Wild Cat Walk. *B&B standard room N$680/1160 sgl/dbl; bungalow N$290 pp; camping N$140 pp.* **LL**

⌂ **Haruchas Guest Farm** (6 rooms) ✆063 683071; e haruchas@iway.na; www.haruchas-namibia.de. Situated on the D855, between Büllsport & the D850, Haruchas is a typical farm (it covers 20,000ha!) set high up on the Tsaris Mountains.

The farm buildings themselves sit in an established oasis of palms, eucalyptus & flowering shrubs. The 1907 outhouse, with thick walls to ensure good insulation, has been converted into a family unit with 2 twin rooms. Each has its own entrance, a shared en suite, & is kitted out with simple pine furniture & clean patterned bedding. The other, much newer rooms are in neat, purpose-built, semi-detached buildings beside the swimming pool & an intriguing stone garden created from local rocks & cacti. Painted white with cheerful, red doors & borders around the windows, these rooms are uniformly spacious & clean, with verandas, en-suite toilet & bath (with shower attachment) & pine furniture. Communal meals are served in the main house, where you're free to relax in the lounge, or peruse the impressive wall of curios. There are 3 hiking trails from the farm, ranging from 1.5 to 4hrs, detailed in books in the rooms, & nature drives are available on request (*N$180 pp*). This place would make a good writer's or artist's retreat. *DBB N$850/1,500 sgl/dbl.* **LL**

⋀ **Naukluft Campsite** (15 pitches) ✆063 293245; reservations ✆061 285 7200; e reservations@nwr.com.na; www.nwr.com.na. About 8km southwest of Büllsport, on the D854, is the ornate entrance to the Naukluft section of the Namib-Naukluft National Park. Through the gates, a road winds up northwest into the Naukluft for about 12km before the campsite.

The site has no bungalows, but beautifully situated camping spots, surrounded by mountains & trees. Of these, 5 are about 100m away from the others, in a peaceful area by the river-bed. Only water, firewood & toilets/showers are provided, so bring all your supplies. It can get busy, so it's w to book in advance. *N$132 pp.* **L**

WHAT TO SEE AND DO
Animals are seldom seen in this mountainous area, so hiking is the main activity. A recent addition is a 4x4 off-road driving trail, which takes two days and is aimed at local enthusiasts testing their vehicles to the limits.

Hiking
Naukluft has two circular day hikes, the Waterkloof and Olive trails. Both can be started from the Naukluft Campsite, and neither needs booking ahead, or any special equipment. That said, at least a day's water, snacks and a medical kit should be taken along, as rescue would be difficult if there was an accident. Walkers should be fit and acclimatised, and strong hiking boots are essential as the terrain is very rocky.

There is also one long eight-day Naukluft Trail, rated as one of Africa's toughest hikes – though it can be shortened to four days. Like the others, this is unguided, but simple diagrammatic maps are available from the park warden's office.

Waterkloof Trail
The Waterkloof is 17km long and starts near the campsite. It takes 6–7 hours to walk comfortably, and is marked by yellow-painted footprints on the rocks. At first the trail follows the Naukluft River upstream, through some beautiful gorges, and in the early months of the year you'll often find pools here, complete with tadpoles and frogs.

After a gentle 2 hours you reach a painted rock marking the last water point (though bring water, don't rely on this), beyond which the canyon opens out. After about 2 hours more there's a marked halfway point, from where a steep climb leads you to the trail's highest point: a 600m peak with fine views all around.

From there the trail winds down through a stand of euphorbia into a large valley, to follow the course of the (usually dry) river. It cuts off several of the bends, and keeps left to avoid some steep shelves, which form waterfalls in the rainy season. In this area some large cairns mark the route of the old German cannon road, which also follows the river valley for a while, before climbing steeply up to the main southern ridge of the plateau. Below those waterfalls, you meet the Naukluft River, and turn left to follow the trail for a few kilometres back to camp.

Olive Trail
This starts about 4km from the park office – clearly signposted off the track from the entrance gate. You can walk here, or drive and park in a small parking area.

The Olive Trail is 10km long and takes about 4 hours to complete. From the parking area it gradually climbs to the top of a small plateau, before descending through a series of river valleys and gorges (using chains in places), to meet a rough 4x4 track which leads back to the parking area.

Naukluft Trail
(⊕ *1 Mar–31 Oct; hikes start every Tue, Thu & Sat for first 3 weeks of each month; book in advance at the NWR in Windhoek; group limit 3–12 people; N$135 pp, inc space at Hiker's Haven for nights before & after trail, excluding park fees, paid separately; medical certificate required*) This 120km, circular seven- to eight-day trail starts from the park office, where there's a bunkhouse known as Hiker's Haven. Hikers can use this on their first and last nights. Initially it follows the (usually dry) Naukluft River south for a while, as it flows out of the mountains, before climbing up to the edge of the escarpment, with excellent views to the left over the plains. The Putte shelter is reached about 14km (6 hours) after starting.

id day the route covers 15km (6 hours), crossing a rolling plateau
junction, before dropping down the narrow Ubusis Kloof to reach
y three starts by retracing your steps to Bergpos, and turning left
au to Alderhost shelter (12km, taking 6 hours).

the trail is level, before dropping down to a shelter at Tsams Ost for
the evening – 17km later (6 hours). There's a rough 4x4 track from here down and
west to the main C19, and hikers doing only a four-day trip can be collected here.

Day five is steep and then undulating, though it levels out towards the end where
it follows a tributary of the Die Valle River, to reach the Die Valle shelter about
17km (6 hours) later. Day six is a tough one, climbing up a narrow gorge to reach a
high point called Quartz Valley, before dropping down the Arbeid Adelt Valley to
the Tufa shelter, 16km and about 6 hours later.

On day seven the trail climbs steeply, using chains in places, back up to the
plateau and some excellent views, to reach Kapokvlakte shelter after 14km (5
hours). Finally, on the last day, the trail descends gradually, then steeply, to meet
the Waterkloof Trail and follow the Naukluft River back to camp. Energetic hikers
could combine the last two days into a 30km walk which would take about 11 hours
to complete. An early start from Tufa shelter is essential, and if there are less than 5
hours of daylight, then you should stop at Kapokvlakte shelter.

4x4 trail (⊕ *all year, weather permitting; book in advance at the NWR in Windhoek;
groups of 1–4 vehicles, with max 4 people per vehicle; N$290 per vehicle, excluding
park fees, which are paid separately*) This is a 73km two-day trail for those with a
4x4 and the experience to use it properly. After the first 28km there is an overnight
camp, where four stone-walled, partially open, A-frame shelters have built-in
bunk-beds. There are toilets here, water, a solar-heated shower and a braai area.
Bring your own firewood, camping kit and supplies.

Neuras Winery (✆ *063 293417;* e *neuras@naankuse.com; www.neuraswines.com;
⊕ all year; wine tour N$285/185 with/without wine-tasting*) In a delightful setting
surrounded by trees and inviting blue pools, this organic winery is on a 14,400ha
farm just off the D850 between Tsauchab River Camp and Zebra River Lodge.
Although you might not expect to find wine-producing vineyards in a country as
dry as Namibia, Neuras offers 1-hour tours (with advance notice) of the winery,
including the historic garden which dates back to the 1890s. Crystal-clear natural
springs irrigate the vines, which produce a high-quality grape due to the unique
microclimate. The farm is also home to mountain zebra, springbok, oryx, ostrich
and a wide variety of birds.

Wine and food are the passion of British-born owner Allan Walkden-Davis, who
offers lunch (*N$110*) to day visitors and dinner to guests staying overnight in the
rustic chalets (*DBB N$900 pp*), tented camp (*FBA N$650 pp*) with shared washing
facilities, or luxury self-catering family units (*FBA N$1,350 pp*). Guests can also
join the Honey Canyon tour (*N$285 pp*) that explains how the San survive in this
environment, a visit to Namibia's 14th-longest cave and opportunities to spot the
rare Elephant's Foot plant.

SESRIEM AND SOSSUSVLEI AREA

When people speak of visiting the Namib Desert, this is often the area they mean. The
classic desert scenery around Sesriem and Sossusvlei is the stuff that postcards are
made of – enormous apricot dunes with gracefully curving ridges, invariably pictured

in the sharp light of dawn with a photogenic oryx or feathery acacia adjacent.

Sesriem and Sossusvlei lie on the Tsauchab River, one of two large rivers (the other being the Tsondab, further north) that flow westward into the great dune field of the central Namib, but never reach the ocean. Both end by forming flat white pans dotted with green trees, surrounded by spectacular dunes – islands of life within a sea of sand.

GETTING THERE AND AWAY Sesriem is clearly signposted 12km southwest along the C27 from its junction with the C19. The best, easiest and cheapest way to see the area is with your own car – so the vast majority of visitors drive. There is no public transport, and while hitching is possible it is difficult, as there are many possible routes here. (This also makes it easier to get away than to arrive.)

If you don't have your own transport, you have several choices. Various tour groups run trips to Sossusvlei from both Windhoek and Swakopmund (see *Tour operators*, pages 121–2 and 309–10). Alternatively, there's a private shuttle bus that links Namib-Naukluft Lodge with Windhoek and Swakopmund (see page 102). This lodge runs day trips into Sesriem and Sossusvlei which cost about N$900 per person. The third option is to fly in by light aircraft with one of the pleasure flight companies (see page 312). These drop visitors at either Sossusvlei Lodge or Wolwedans, from which there are guided tours around the area – though neither is a cheap option.

Best routes
Quickest The quickest route from Windhoek is normally south on the B1, then west on the C47 just after Rehoboth to Rietoog, right on to the D1206 to Büllsport (where the guest farm makes a good overnight stop if you're just off a plane). Then continue on the D854, almost in the shadow of the Naukluft Mountains, right on to the C19 and then left for 12km to Sesriem. This takes about 4½ hours.

Most spectacular The most spectacular route from Windhoek is via the C26, followed by the steep Spreetshoogte Pass on the D1275 – easily be a 6-hour drive.

From Keetmanshoop Approaching from Keetmanshoop, taking the main tar road to Maltahöhe is best, followed by the obvious C19.

From Lüderitz From here Sesriem is really too far for comfort in one day, and a stopover would be wise. This approach does allow you to take the D707 and the C27, which can both be slow going, but are certainly among the most spectacular roads in the subcontinent – with desert sands to their west, and mountain ranges to the east.

From Swakopmund From Swako it is quickest to drive south to Walvis Bay and then take the C14, via the Kuiseb River canyon. Allow at least 4 hours for this – more if you want to drive at a leisurely pace and stop for a picnic.

Rainy season access For a few days each year, rain causes rivers to wash across certain roads – making them difficult, or impossible, to cross. (See advice on crossing rivers, page 92.)

The D854 is often badly affected, having three or more rivers flowing across it, fed by rains that fall on the Naukluft Mountains. The third of these, nearest Sesriem, usually seems the deepest – though this does depend on where the rain falls in the mountains.

Similarly, the Tsauchab River (which flows through Sesriem Canyon, and on to Sossusvlei) crosses the C19 between its junctions with the D854 and C27. It also

7 south of Sesriem (but north of the turn-off to Kulala). Both these
look very wide, but are usually shallow and can be crossed with care
WD.

cipate problems, then approaching from Maltahöhe, on the C19, is
safest route – though it's a long way around from Windhoek. It is vital
to ask reliable local advice before you set off.

Other practicalities There is a reliable Engen **fuel station,** the Sossus Oasis
(⏰ *05.30–18.00 daily*), at the junction along the C27, opposite Sesriem Campsite. It
sells almost anything you could possibly need for your journey, including fuel, fresh
sandwiches, cold drinks, car parts and tyre repairs, hot and cold food, souvenirs and
clothes, plus an ATM and attached Outback internet café (*N$30/30mins, N$50/1hr;
ask for code from shop*) – and it now has its own luxury campsite (see opposite).

WHERE TO STAY *Map, page 262, unless otherwise noted.*
Sossus Dune Lodge (see below) is the only accommodation option inside the gates,
and the only one that allows visitors to access the park before sunrise. However,
Sesriem campsite (see below), which sits just outside the gate, has its one entrance
which opens 1 hour before the main gates (see times on map on page 262).

Alternatively, you can broaden your choice and stay at one of the nearby lodges. None
of these is cheap, but if you're prepared to travel 35km, then the Desert Homestead is
probably the least expensive. Realistically, though, anywhere in the Naukluft, Solitaire
or even northern NamibRand also makes a practical base for visits to the Sossusvlei
area, provided that you don't insist on being at Sesriem for sunrise. In fact, as tourism
to this corner of the desert increases, brighter visitors are starting to move away from
the busy Sesriem and Sossusvlei area, to find superb desert experiences in the private
areas of desert that lie to the north and south – like Wolwedans. For the present,
however, this remains an area where you must book well in advance in order to have
any hope of finding good accommodation when you arrive.

✳ 🏠 Sossus Dune Lodge (25 chalets)
☎063 693 258, reservations ☎061 285 7200;
✉ reservations@nwr.com.na; www.nwr.com.na. Run
by the NWR, Sossus Dune has a great location just
4km inside the Sesriem Gate, so visitors can access
the park before sunrise & after sunset. This is a good
choice for photographers who wish to capture the
sunrise or Sossusvlei without the crowds. Identical
rondavel-style chalets in yellow canvas & thatch are
lined up in a row, linked by wooden walkways – a
quick tip: room numbers are posted on the floor of
the walkway entrance to your chalet. They're large &
bright, with floor-to-ceiling glass panels so you can
take in the mountain views while lying in bed, or
from the curved sun-loungers in front of the window.
Dark wood furniture contrasts with brightly coloured
mosquito nets, & there are fans instead of AC, plus
wooden chairs on a private veranda which offers
superb stargazing at night. Bathrooms have open-
plan showers & his 'n' hers sinks. Room 13 has the
best view of the watering hole.

The central chalet has a large open-plan bar
& separate dining room looking out over the
mountains. Next to this is a glittering pool with a
shady sunbathing area where you can cool off from
the afternoon heat. Currently, there's no Wi-Fi,
but there are plans for it to be installed. Guests
can drive themselves to Sossusvlei as long as they
return by 1hr after sunset, or if they plan to set off
before sunrise before b/fast (which starts at 06.30
in winter, 07.00 in summer) they can arrange for
b/fast bags at no extra cost. To reach the dunes,
turn right out of the car park, then left when you
reach the tar road. Guests can also take advantage
of the lodge's guided sunset & nature drives
(*N$330 pp*), & trips to Sesriem Canyon (*N$175 pp*)
& Elim Dune (*N$330 pp*). DBB N$2,500/4,600 sgl/
dbl inc park fees. **LLLLL**

Ⲗ Sesriem Campsite (24 pitches, overflow
field) ☎063 293 3652; central reservations ☎061
285 7200; ✉ reservations@nwr.com.na; www.nwr.
com.na. In 1989, Sesriem campsite had just 10

pitches, & was the only place in the area. Each was shaded by an old camelthorn tree, which boasted a tap sprouting beside its trunk, & was protected by a low, circular wall. It was stunning. Times have changed, but the bonus is the gates into the park from the campsite open 1hr earlier than the main gates, giving you a head start to reach Sossusvlei.

Today there are 24 pitches, an overflow field (on the left) – which is often busy – & 4 ablution blocks, which can be none too clean. But it's still a marvellous place to camp, especially if you get one of the original pitches, on the edge of the campground. Fuel & wood are available & the campsite shop has a large selection of basic foods, drinks & souvenirs, as well as useful items such as matches – though it's better to bring food with you. The Sossus Dune Lodge welcomes campers to dinner, provided they book a table before midday. There's no Wi-Fi, but free tea/coffee are available in the bar & there's a swimming pool.

To guarantee camping space, especially in the high season, you should book at the NWR in Windhoek before arriving, although it's always worth checking on arrival to see if there's a space available. *N$154 pp & park fees (N$80 pp & N$10 per vehicle).* **L**

🏠 **Sossus Oasis** 📞 063 293 6332; e reservations@sossus-oasis.com; www.sossus-oasis. com. Owned by the same people as Sossusvlei Lodge & Desert Camp, the Sossus Oasis sits at the entrance gate to Sesriem & Sossusvlei. It offers 2 options for campers: simple sites with shared washing & cooking facilities, or private shaded sites with extended tin roofs, en-suite bathroom area inside log cabin with solar-heated showers, & electricity. There's also a swimming pool. *Camping simple N$120 pp; luxury N$166 pp, plus N$120 for site.* **L**

🏠 **Sossusvlei Lodge** (51 rooms) 📞 063 293 636; reservations 📞 +27 21 930 4564; e reservations@sossusvleilodge.com; www. sossusvleilodge.com. Immediately on the right of the national park entrance at Sesriem, Sossusvlei Lodge has a convenient location for anyone wanting to drive to Sossusvlei at first light, or leave the park late in the day. Its construction is an innovative mix of materials & colours: concrete, ironwork, canvas & leather; reds, apricots, greens & whites.

The twin 'tents' are elaborate, permanent constructions; each has an en-suite shower, toilet & basin built as part of the solid base, which supports the canvas walls of the bedrooms. Inside is fairly spacious, with adjoining large sgl beds,

bedside tables, lamps, easy chairs, a dressing table, etc – so banish any thoughts of camping when you read of 'tents' here.

The shaded bar & beer garden have views of the plains & sit near a walled swimming pool surrounded by grass & sun-loungers. The 2 restaurants – one small, one large – serve help-yourself b/fasts & light, modern, à la carte lunches. Dinner is buffet-style, with various meats (often including unusual game) cooked to order.

The sky at Sesriem is clear for about 300 days per year. Why not climb their central water tower to see the stars at their best or for aerial photos?

The reception has a book exchange, 24hr coffee station with juice & cookies, & the Wi-Fi signal is strongest here. There's also a big curio shop. The atmosphere is that of a hotel, as you will be left to organise yourself, though morning & afternoon trips into the park can be organised through the on-site Adventure Lodge (e *adventure@ sossusvleilodge.com*) – the area's main operator for helicopter, hot air balloon & scenic flights over the dunes, as well as quad biking & archery. It also has a reasonably reliable ATM. It's best to prebook your activities at the same time as your accommodation. Sossusvlei Lodge is not cheap, but is very comfortable & perfect for early starts into the Sossusvlei area of the national park. *DBB N$2,741/3,886 sgl/dbl.* **LLLLL**

🏠 **Desert Camp** (20 tents) 📞 063 683205; e info@desertcamp.com; www.desertcamp. com. 8km from C19 & D826 junction, with a 2km driveway, Desert Camp is owned by the same team behind Sossus Oasis & Sossusvlei Lodge. Here, somewhat smart safari tents of light brown canvas have exterior wooden pole frames on an orange base, blending into the surrounding desert scenery with views across to the mountains. Inside, each has twin beds, en-suite bathroom & granite tiled floors. The surprise is on the outside, where a compact lock-up kitchen compartment, complete with 2-plate stove, fridge/freezer & washing facilities, sits to one side of the porch, fronted by a picnic table. Guests can rent boxes of cooking utensils from reception but those who prefer to let someone else do the cooking can eat dinner & b/fast at Sossusvlei Lodge or, for real pampering, have a private chef from the lodge come & cook a private braai for them; each tent has its own BBQ & a shaded parking spot. For groups, two central bomas with self-catering facilities are available

12

on request, with a fully stocked & serviced bar with a flat-screen TV showing whatever sporting event is on at the time. There's also a small pool that is very tempting in the heat; collect towels from reception. Free Wi-Fi can be picked up in the central bomas & in the first, closest, rooms. *DBB (meals at Sossusvlei Lodge) N$1,413/2,032; room-only rate N$1,088/1,382 sgl/dbl.* **LLL**

✱ 🏠 **Hoodia Desert Lodge** [Map, page 244] (12 rooms) ☎ 063 683321; reservations ☎ 061 237 294; e hoodia@hammerstein.com.na; www.hoodiadesertlodge.com. Run by Thomas & Henreza Becker, Hoodia is located halfway between the junction with the C27 & the D854 along the C19, 22km from Sesriem; it has a 7km driveway. The setting is stunning – on the banks of the dry Tsauchab River, with mountains in all directions – & the lodge itself is equally attractive. The spaced out, lovingly looked-after thatched bungalows all have AC, an empty fridge for your own supplies & en-suite terracotta-coloured bathrooms, with an outside bath & shower for lingering under the stars. Rooms are clean & bright with cool cream curtains, white bedlinen & lots of windows, & a terrace that looks out over the mountains. Handily, guests are also provided with battery-operated mini lanterns to guide them between their room & the main lodge after dark.

In the main lodge, modern portraits of African women painted by a local artist hang in the lounge decorated with deep sofas, a coffee table littered with nature books, a chessboard & other games, a TV quietly playing & a small cupboard selling T-shirts & fleeces. Leading off from this, on a lower level, is the round dining room, which has floor-to-ceiling windows on 3 sides & a central fireplace used as a braai in good weather. Food is delicious, influenced by dishes from all over the world, & is complemented by a range of South African wines; complimentary tea/coffee & rusk biscuits are available all day in the dining room. The wooden deck over the river is a good spot to watch birds & appreciate the peace & quiet with a sundowner. The mountain views are also visible from the small, raised turquoise swimming pool off to the right-hand side. Sundowner drives *(N$275 pp; book before 15.30 on day)* & excursions to Sossusvlei *(N$1,250 pp; min 2 people, inc entrance fee & food)* are available. A stay here is topped off by great service from attentive hosts. *DBB N$2,130/3,330 sgl/dbl.* **LLLL**

🏠 **Kulala Desert Lodge** (23 chalets) ☎ 063 683 024, reservations: ☎ +27 11 257 5111;

e kulala@iway.na; www.wilderness-safaris.com. Signposted off the C27, some 13km south of Sesriem (but north of the junction with the D845), & then about 14km from the road, Kulala sits against the red glow of the dunes, overlooking the national park from the southern banks of the Tsauchab River. It has a private entrance into the park, so guests on trips organised by the lodge can beat the crowds (& the heat) by reaching the dunes earlier than those who enter through the main gate. However, if you are self-driving, access to the vlei remains limited to the C27, & the park entrance at Sesriem, thus Sossus Dune Lodge, the Sesriem campsite & Sossusvlei Lodge are effectively a shorter drive from the vlei.

Inside, Kulala's light & airy décor is refreshingly cool, while inspiration for its cool clay construction came from North African designs. Brightly coloured sofas with fluffy cushions sit at heavy wooden tables, light pine furniture & yet more cushions in the lounge area encourage relaxation, earthy-toned sofas surround a blazing fire, & rich mahogany-leather footstools all add to the cosy charm of the place. A wraparound deck provides lovely views across the dunes, while a large pool & shaded loungers are welcome relief from the midday heat.

The chalets, or *kulalas*, are large tents built on wooden platforms overlooking the river-bed, topped with thatched roofs – they were all recently extended in size so are now very spacious. Each incorporates an en-suite stone-tiled bathroom, complete with shower & toilet. (A tip: use the bucket provided to collect cold water that runs off until the hot water comes through the pipes.) Gnarled & polished wood furniture is lovely, & the colourful green bed-covers are both unusual & tasteful, adding a dash of colour to each room's natural tones. A handful of the rooms have interconnecting doors or walkways for families. Outdoors enthusiasts can have their mattresses placed on the solid roof of the room's rear for a night under the stars – a fun & free option, if chilly in winter. There's no Wi-Fi, but there's a free internet terminal next to the office.

Sandwiched between the national park to the northwest, & the private NamibRand Nature Reserve to the south, Kulala has 32,000ha of its own land on which it operates nature drives & balloon safaris (see page 265), a truly wondrous experience which is well worth the cost. Sossusvlei excursions & eco quad biking are offered or, alternatively, many guests drive themselves around the area using Kulala as merely a stylish base. *FBA, inc local drinks N$5,062 pp.* **LLLLL**

✳ 🏠 **Little Kulala** (11 kulalas) 🗐063 683 022, reservations: 🗐061 274500; e lkc@iway.na; www.wilderness-safaris.com. Little Kulala is unlike any other property in Namibia: a stunning, über-chic, modernist take on a safari lodge. Its striking interior design is characterised by bleached timber decks, architectural objets d'art & textured fabrics in muted desert tones.

There are 11 *kulalas* (meaning 'to sleep' in the Oshivambo language), inc 1 family room that sleeps 4. These are light, bright & airy, with 2 sides being entirely glassed to ensure maximum views across to the dunes. Shaggy rugs, felt pebble cushions, fabulous beds & candles aplenty make them a great place to retreat to, while the large private deck, curved wicker loungers & plunge pool make the space beyond the room equally appealing. Bathrooms are en suite with an indoor power shower & an equally lovely, pebble-strewn outdoor shower. All rooms have AC, fully stocked fridge, tea/coffee station & a digital safe. Roof-top 'skybeds' (waterproof covered duvet & mattress) can also be arranged for romantic stargazing, but be aware of the cold night air when selecting this option.

The central dining area offers excellent cuisine under dramatic makuti thatch. There are suspended swinging chairs on the deck for casual daydreaming; a library & wine cellar for connoisseurs; a pool for a cooling dip & a friendly bar for fireside drinks at the end of the evening. Early morning guided game drives to the dunes use the reserve's private access, & local walks, sunset drives & ballooning can be arranged. *FBA N$8,966 pp.* **LLLLL**

🏠 **Little Sossus Lodge & Campsite** [Map, page 244] (20 rooms, camping) 🗐064 464 144; m 081 155 5512; e littlesossus@live.com; www.littlesossus.com.na. 20 spaced out chalets – 12 with twin beds, 4 4-bed family units – all have cool stone walls, polished wood furniture, mosquito nets, & a large en-suite shower, & all the cottages overlook the waterhole with sweeping views of the distant Nubib Mountains. The main lodge area offers outside dining on the veranda, a curved bar, a long dining room (*dinner N$230 pp*) with two fires built into the stone walls for colder winter evenings & a small pool area with sun-loungers. Wi-Fi costs N$40 per stay. Sundowner trips (*N$350 pp, max 4 people*) & guided Sossusvlei trips (*N$895*

pp) can be arranged, plus you can drive to a nearby natural springs to swim in 3m-deep rock pools.

Opposite the lodge is a campsite with 10 pitches – 7 dbl pitches & 3 family pitches – built on concrete bases with brick walls & high tin roofs, designed to take a roof tent. Each has its own basic 'en-suite' bathroom with a shower, sink, hot & cold water & flush toilet. (Family pitches have 2 bathrooms & a simple kitchenette.) In the centre is a small lounge & a large seating area. The shop (ring the bell) stocks most camping essentials including wood, food, ice & cold drinks, a wide range of foodstuffs, & produce from the vegetable garden. This is a peaceful place to camp, with mountain views on all sides & the occasional springbok & oryx wandering past. *B&B N$1,260/2,050/2,200–2,400 sgl/dbl/family; camping N$100 pp.* **LLL**

🏠 **The Desert Homestead & Horse Trails** (20 bungalows) 🗐063 683103, reservations: 🗐061 246788; e reservations@homestead.com.na; www.deserthomestead-namibia.com. Well signposted from the C19, 3km northwest of the D854 junction, Desert Homestead sits in a wide grassy valley, sheltered by the Nubib, Tsaris & Naukluft Mountains. It has sensational views shared by both the elevated central area & the sweeping curve of well-spaced bungalows. The large terrace, between the thatched entrance & the rock garden & crystal-clear swimming pool, is an idyllic spot for lunch or sundowners. Thatched, whitewashed pole bungalows are set below the main area & make for excellent retreats in the midday sun. The interiors are simple but stylish with elegant dark wood furniture, crisp white linen, mosquito net, a few interesting objets d'art and a long shower-room, with rustic brass pipes & a pleasing lack of general clutter. The only snag is there are no plugs in the rooms – these should be installed in the near future. Ceiling fans keep the rooms cool by day & thick fur blankets do the opposite in winter. Outside, a pair of wooden chairs on the concrete terrace make a great spot for solitary reading or simply admiring the view & watching the sunset.

Horseriding, for both beginners & experienced riders, is a core activity with well-trained horses for trips lasting from 1hr to a 2-night sleep-out ride (*N$3,500 pp*); the champagne b/fast ride (*N$800*) & sunset ride (*N$650*) come particularly recommended. Free Wi-Fi in main areas. *Dinner N$200 pp; lunch N$85 pp. B&B N$1,100/1,850 sgl/dbl.* **LLL**

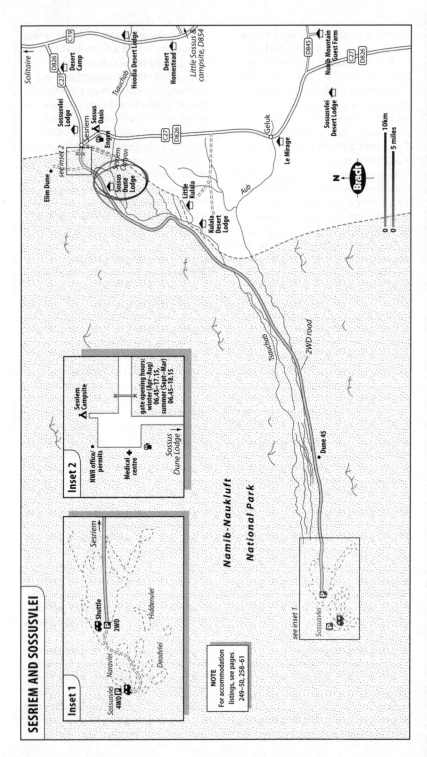

SESRIEM AND SOSSUSVLEI

Solitaire →

Desert Camp

Hoodia Desert Lodge

Little Sossus & campsite, D854

Desert Homestead

Nubib Mountain Guest Farm

Sossusvlei Lodge

Sossusvlei Lodge

Sossus Oasis

Sesriem

Engen

see inset 2

Elim Dune

Sesriem Canyon

Sossus Dune Lodge

Little Kulala

Geluk

Le Mirage

Kulala Desert Lodge

Tsauchab

Aub

N

Bradt

0 ——— 10km
0 ——— 5 miles

C19
D826
C27
C27
D826
C27
D826
D845
D826

Namib-Naukluft National Park

Tsauchab

2WD road

Dune 45

see inset 1

Inset 2

Sesriem Campsite

NWR office/ permits

Medical centre

Sossus Dune Lodge

gate opening hours: winter (Apr–Aug) 06.45–17.15; summer (Sept–Mar) 06.45–18.15

Inset 1

Sossusvlei

Sesriem

Shuttle

2WD

4WD

Naravlei

Hiddenvlei

Deadvlei

Sossusvlei

NOTE
For accommodation listings, see pages 249–50, 258–61

WHAT TO SEE AND DO Sesriem is the gateway to this part of the park, of the area. In summer (September–March) it's open ⊕ 05.45–18.15, a (April–August) it's open ⊕ 06.45–17.15. The NWR office, where everyl buy their entry permits – is located here and you can fill up with fuel of cold drinks at Sossus Oasis (see page 259). From here a short road leads left to Sesriem Canyon, and another heads straight on, through a second gate, towards Elim Dune, Sesriem's small airfield, and Sossusvlei.

Sesriem Canyon About 4km from Sesriem, following the signs left as you enter the gates, is Sesriem Canyon. This is a narrow fissure in the sandstone, 30m deep in places, carved by the Tsauchab River. It was used by the early settlers, who drew water from it by knotting together six lengths of hide rope (called *riems*). Hence it became known as *ses riems*.

For some of the year, the river's bed is marked by pools of blissfully cool water, reached via an easy path of steps cut into the rock. It's a place to swim and relax – perfect for the heat of the day. At other times, though, the water can be almost stagnant and definitely not a place to bathe – except for the large frogs that are marooned in these pools. It's also worth following the watercourse 500m upriver from the steps, where you'll find it before it descends into the canyon – another great place to bathe at times.

Beware of flash floods in the canyon itself. Heavy rain in the Naukluft Mountains occasionally causes these, trapping and drowning visitors.

Sossusvlei area The road from Sesriem to Sossusvlei is soon confined into a corridor, flanked by huge dunes. Gradually this narrows, becoming a few kilometres wide. This unique parting of the southern Namib's great sand sea has probably been maintained over the millennia by the action of the Tsauchab River and the wind.

Although the river seldom flows, note the green camelthorn (*Acacia erioloba*) which thrives here, clearly indicating permanent underground water. Continuing westward, the present course of the river is easy to spot parallel with the road. Look around for the many dead acacia trees that mark old courses of the river, now dried up. Some of these have been dated at over 500 years old.

For an overview of the natural history of the dunes, see *Sand dunes*, page 246.

Access (⊕ *sunrise–sunset; admission N$80, under 16s free, N$20 per car*) To protect the area, entry permits for Sossusvlei are limited. In theory, only a certain number of vehicles are allowed to start along the road during each of three periods in each day. The first is from sunrise, the second in the middle of the day, and the third in the afternoon. Until now, the number of visitors arriving has rarely exceeded the quota, but this may change as the area becomes increasingly popular.

After paying for your permit at the Sesriem Gate, continue southwest past Sesriem along a 60km tarred road. It's important to drive carefully: this stretch takes a lot of traffic and in the searing heat the condition of the road can deteriorate rapidly.

About 24km after leaving Sesriem, you cross the Tsauchab River and then, after a further 36km, low sand dunes apparently form a final barrier to the progress of the river or the road. Nowadays, this is as far as you can drive yourself, and is where you park – currently free of charge. A large group of acacias shades a couple of picnic tables. Nearby are a few toilets of dubious cleanliness.

From the parking area to Sossusvlei itself, you must either walk or take the shuttle bus. The exception is if you are staying at a nearby lodge and taking a guided excursion, in which case your guide will usually be able to drive closer.

The first pan is only about 500m over the sandbar, but it'll take an hour or more to cover the 5km to the farthest pan, Sossusvlei itself, on foot. Around five shuttle 4x4s are run by NWR from 06.00 until 16.00 (*N$50 pp one-way, N$100 return*). The driver will collect you from Sossusvlei or Dead Vlei at a prearranged time; if you don't want to be rushed, allow around 2–3 hours. Most visitors choose a leisurely walk into the pan when it's relatively cool, returning by bus as the heat intensifies.

Elim Dune As you drive towards Sossusvlei, Elim Dune is about 5km from Sesriem. The turning off to the right is shortly after the entrance into the park, leading to a shady parking spot. It is the nearest sand dune to Sesriem, and if you arrive late in the afternoon, then you might, like me, mistake it for a mountain.

From the parking spot you can climb it, though this takes longer than you might expect – allow at least an hour to get to the top. The views over plains towards the Naukluft Mountains on the east, and dune crests to the west, are remarkable. It is especially worth the long climb at sunset, and conveniently close to the gate at Sesriem.

Numbered dunes Along the final stretch of road towards the parking area are a few side-tracks leading to the feet of some of the dunes, numbered according to their distance along the road from the office. **Dune 45**, on the south side, is particularly photogenic. It is also closest to the road, with a small parking area, and makes a popular climb; you'll often see a black line of human ants slogging up in the early morning sun to catch the views.

Hidden Vlei On the left of the parking area, you'll see signs to Hidden Vlei – which is reached by climbing over the dunes for about 2km. As at Dead Vlei, here you'll find old, dead acacia trees, which were deprived of water when the river changed course, but still stand to tell the tale.

Dead Vlei Like Hidden Vlei, but perhaps more accessible, Dead Vlei is an old pan with merely the skeletons of trees left – some over 500 years old. Many consider it to be more starkly beautiful than Sossusvlei and, if time is short, we suggest that you spend your time here.

From the parking area, walk 1km over the sandbar following the track that will lead you into the large main pan. Keep to the left-hand side, and you'll soon find the old parking area for Dead Vlei. From here, it's a 500m hike over the dunes into Dead Vlei.

Sossusvlei and Nara Vlei After about 4–5km the track bends round to the right, and ends in front of Sossusvlei. This is as far as the pans extend. Beyond here, only tall sand dunes separate you from the Atlantic Ocean.

Most years, the ground here is a flat silvery-white pan of fine mud that has dried into a crazy-paving pattern. Upon this are huge sand mounds collected by nara bushes, and periodic feathery camelthorn trees drooping gracefully. All around the sinuous shapes of the Namib's (and some claim the world's) largest sand dunes stretch up to 300m high. It's a stunning, surreal environment.

Perhaps once every decade, Namibia receives really torrential rain. Storms deluge the Naukluft's ravines and the Tsauchab sweeps out towards the Atlantic in a flash flood, surging into the desert and pausing only briefly to fill its canyon.

Floods so powerful are rare, and Sossusvlei can fill overnight. Though the Tsauchab will subside quickly, the vlei remains full. Miraculous lilies emerge to bloom, and the bright yellow devil thorn flowers (*Tribulus* species) carpet the water's edge. Surreal scenes reflect in the lake, as dragonflies hover above its polished surface. Birds arrive and luxuriant growth flourishes, making this ephemeral treat.

These waters recede from most of the pan rapidly, concentrating in where they can remain for months. While they are there, the area's bir radically, as waterbirds and waders will often arrive, along with opportunist insectivores. Meanwhile, less than a kilometre east, over a dune, the main pan is as dry as dust, and looks as if it hasn't seen water in decades.

Individual dunes afford superb views across this landscape, with some of the best from 'Big Daddy'. It's a strenuous climb to the top, looking out across to 'Big Mama', but the climb, followed by a long walk, is rewarded by the spectacle of Dead Vlei laid out below – and the fun of running down the slip-face to reach it.

Ballooning Namib Sky Balloon Safaris (✆ *063 683188;* m *081 304 2205;* e *info@ namibsky.com; www.namibsky.com*) run early morning balloon trips over the desert – which are expensive but superb. You start from Sossusvlei Lodge, Kulala or Sossusvlei Desert Lodge before dawn, and are driven to a take-off site, which varies with the winds and conditions – though if it's too windy, the flight may be cancelled.

The crew gradually unfurl the balloon, and inflate it with propane burners. When ready, everybody climbs into the basket, and it is inflated to take off. Gradually, the balloon sails higher over a rolling vision of mountains, plains and iridescent sand dunes, observing the silent dawn as it rises over one of the earth's most beautiful landscapes. Floating at wind speed is travelling in still air – with only the occasional burst of gas interrupting the silence while you sip on champagne. It's an eerie experience, and an excellent platform for landscape photography.

Beneath the balloon a support vehicle follows as best it can, carrying a table, chairs and full supplies for a champagne breakfast – which is set up wherever the balloon lands. Eventually, everything is loaded on to the support vehicle and its trailer, and guests are returned to where they started, usually a little before midday.

Though a morning's ballooning costs N\$4,950 per passenger for a flight lasting between 45 minutes and 1¼ hours, it is such an unusual and exhilarating experience that it is not only highly recommended, but also (arguably) quite good value.

SOLITAIRE AREA ✨

North of the Sesriem area, the C19 leads into the equally beautiful, but pot-holed C14, often with dunes on one side and mountains on the other. These are the main routes from Sesriem to Swakopmund, so are relatively busy (typically a few cars per hour).

SOLITAIRE Solitaire is a large dot on the map, but it is just a few buildings, run by the helpful, if idiosyncratic, Moose. Yet it is so atmospheric, so typical of a middle-of-nowhere stop in the desert, that it's been the location for several film and advert scenes.

There is a fuel station here that is pretty reliable, and it is still the best place for miles to have punctures mended. The Solitaire General Dealer behind the garage opens all hours, selling quite a wide range of supplies (the best around, though that's no great praise). Shopping here, with the wooden counters, old-fashioned weighing scales and jars of sweets, feels like stepping back in time. Buy anything from tinned food and cold drinks to ostrich egg necklaces, kudu leather shoes, cold beer, firewood and basic medicines. They even offer reasonably accurate tourist information. Opposite the General Dealer is a newly opened bakery, selling superb fresh bread as well as a wide range of muffins, cakes and pastries and their legendary apple pie, all baked on the premises. Most people stop for a drink and a snack either here or at the neighbouring Café Van Der Lee (☉ *noon–15.00*), which serves a selection of sausages, steaks and chips for N$35–55.

🏠 Where to stay *Map, page 244, unless otherwise noted.*

Around Solitaire are several good places to stay while visiting the desert, several of them frequented by group trips. Many of these establishments can be used as bases from which to explore the Sesriem area, while those further north have spectacular mountainous scenery of their own worth seeing, and are useful stopovers on the way to/from Sesriem.

🏠 **Moon Mountain Lodge** (17 rooms) \063 293 352; m 081 681 7271, 081 681 3363; e bookings@moonmountain.biz; www. moonmountain.biz. Along the C19, about 50km north of Sesriem, with a 3km driveway, this impressively situated privately owned lodge has 11 luxury & 6 executive suites – all have private plunge pools & the suites come with espresso machines, mini kitchenette, bathrobes & particularly palatial bathrooms. Camping mattresses & cots available for kids. Alexia, one of the camp managers, designs the menu for their on-mountain Nebula restaurant – it should be good because her dad owns Joe's Beerhouse in Windhoek (see page 141)! There's also a TV lounge, bar & reading room. Excursions to Sossusvlei (*N$1,032 pp*) are the main attraction, but sunset drives (*N$290 pp*), nature drives & walks & stargazing are also on offer; they can also book ballooning (*N$4,400 pp*) & scenic flights. Free airport pick-up from Naukluft. The last section of the driveway is very steep; best to park at the bottom in the shaded area & be collected by the camp managers. *DBB luxury N$2,210/4,000 sgl/dbl; executive N$2,441/3,420 sgl/dbl.* **LLLLL**

🏠 **Agama River Camp** (10 chalets, 8 pitches) \063 683245; e bookings@agamarivercamp.com; www.agamarivercamp.com. This peaceful camp is located 50km north of Sesriem on the C19 – look out for the international flags blowing outside the gate. It has added 10 russet-coloured chalets with ladders leading up to white-painted roofs so travellers can sleep & stargaze on warm nights. Inside they're cool & spacious with AC, towels for the swimming pools, polished concrete floors, rustic en-suite bathrooms with copper piping & a small terrace.

The campsite has its own larger & deeper pool, while pitches have their own washing-up facilities & braai. There's the added bonus of a soft sand base, while the arty ablution facilities are open-

topped with stone walls & donkey boilers to heat the water in the evenings.

The communal space has a restaurant, viewing deck & a bar with Wi-Fi. There's shaded parking for cars &, with a 10-day warning, prearranged meals & b/fast packs are available. If you have no tent then tents, bedding, crockery & cutlery can be rented (*N$280 pp*). It has certainly upped its game, & is a super stop off on the way to or from Sossusvlei, There are a few walks in the area for those who wish to linger. *DBB N$962/1,924 sgl/ dbl; camping N130 pp.* **LLL**

🏠 **KuanguKuangu** contact via Barchan Dune, page 268; e filanciu@kuangukuangu.com; www. kuangukuangu.com. For those seeking the ultimate in privacy, this could be the answer: a hideaway cabin built of natural materials (with kitchen & bathroom, hot water, electricity & – for those who simply can't escape – mobile phone coverage) for just 2 people in an isolated setting to the northeast of Solitaire. The answer to every romantic city-dweller's dream lies on the farm owned by Willem & Hannetjie, who also run Barchan Dune Retreat. This place is easy to miss – follow the directions to Barchan Dune, but as you approach the farm building, turn left away from the farm towards the grazing horses. Down a winding sandy track you will find KuanguKuangu. If total solitude palls, help is at hand: meals or a braai pack are available at the farm, & a farm drive (€13) can also be organised. *€120 or N$1,669/night; dinner €23 pp; b/fast €7 pp; braai pack €7 pp.* **LLL**

🏠 **Namib Desert Lodge** (72 rooms) \063 293 665; m 081 129 2424; e info@gondwana-collection.com; www.gondwana-collection.com. Directly opposite Moon Mountain (see above), this large lodge sits at the foot of a red sandstone cliff – the 'fossilised' dunes of the protomorphic Namib – within the private Gondwana Namib Park. The 10,000ha reserve incorporates a range of these petrified dunes, & is frequented by oryx, springbok & ostrich. With its location just 60km north of Sesriem, & a mere 5km from the main C19, the lodge is a good starting point for an excursion to Sossusvlei. Expect a warm welcome at reception, which is also an enormous souvenir shop, selling everything from postcards to fluffy toys, including unique handmade Matukondjo dolls made by local unemployed women, & it has free – albeit slow – Wi-Fi in the evenings. Set among trees & palms are en-suite rooms (including 3 family rooms) with AC: neat & functional if a little uninspired. The main area is decorated with attractive murals, cow-skin rugs & a raised, hexagonal fireplace. As well as the large central dining area, with several long tables to accommodate the many bus groups that stay here, there's a well-stocked wine cellar & a bar with a long cocktail list. Outside, 2 swimming pools are fronted by an illuminated waterhole. Beyond this, visitors may take drives through the park to experience the magnificent scenery. Recommended are the 2hr sunset drives (N$365 pp), which explain the fossilisation & fairy circles (see box, page 269) occurring the desert. They can also arrange guided hikes customised to travellers' requests. B&B N$1,257/2,010 sgl/dbl. **LLL**

🏠 **Namib-Naukluft Lodge** (16 rooms) 📞061 372100; e trixim@afex.com.na; www. namib-naukluft-lodge.com. On the C19, south of Solitaire & 60km from Sesriem Gate, this is outwardly rather uninspiring, despite being designed by a well-known Namibian architect. Inside, though, it is plush, with 'normal' modern rooms built in a row. If these, rather than trendy tents, appeal, perhaps this is the place for you.

Through sliding glass doors, leading on to a veranda, the rooms face a huge desert plain. Each has adjacent twin beds, en-suite toilet & (powerful) shower. By reception are a large lounge bar & a dining room, though meals are often eaten on the veranda, where you can watch the antics of ground squirrels while looking out over the desert.

Behind the lodge, in the shade of a large kopje, is a braai area for sociable moonlit dining, while at the far end of the row of rooms is a small (popular) & sparklingly clean swimming pool & a shaded area for relaxing. There's even a 9-hole golf course – best in the winter months. You can take short walks on the lodge's own land, & – if you don't have a car – reserve a seat on their daily 4x4 trips to Sossusvlei (N$1,250 pp). B&B N$1,175/1,960 sgl/dbl. **LLL**

🏠 **Rostock Ritz** [Map, page 270] (20 'igloos', camping) 📞064 694000; reservations 📞061 258 5722; e reservations@rostock-ritz-desert-lodge.com; www.rostock-ritz-desert-lodge.com. Run by Kücki, of Kücki's in Swakopmund, this unusual lodge is about 5km off the C14, around 20mins' drive south of the C26, passing through the Tropic of Capricorn. Low, stone-built individual 'igloos' with en-suite facilities are designed to keep cool. Each sleeps 2 people & has magnificent views of the surrounding desert. 2 units are suitable for wheelchairs & 2 are luxury. The main area continues the igloo style, with 3 of them linked to create a restaurant, bar & reception area. Outside, the pool has its own commanding views from the unusual hanging sun-loungers. Day visitors are welcome to take advantage of the lodge's à la carte restaurant (🕐 lunch noon–15.00, dinner 18.00–late), which is a good spot to break for lunch on a long drive. 7km from the lodge is their campsite with 4 spots, epic views, electric lights, kitchen & solar-heated hot water showers. Wood can be bought at the lodge. Check-in at the lodge. Campers can dine at the lodge, but aren't allowed to use the pool. Attractions include 10 self-guided hiking trails, ranging from the easy to moderately difficult, leading through dunes, canyons & mountains, while for the less energetic there are dune drives, scenic flights & 4x4 trips to see Bushman cave paintings. B&B N$1,380/2,208 sgl/dbl; camping N$128 pp. **LLL**

🏠 **Solitaire Guest Farm Desert Ranch** (16 rooms, camping) 📞062 572024, reservations; 📞061 305 173; e reservations@solitaireguestfarm. com; www.solitaireguestfarm.com. Off the C14 500m east of the fuel station at Solitaire, this small guest farm on 5,000ha has been beautifully renovated while retaining its original charm. The en-suite dbl rooms & self-catering house are decorated with wooden carvings & African art, with bright animal-print bedspreads & elephant-print curtains adding a unique touch. In the large dining room, with a fireplace in the corner for winter evenings, owner Walter often eats with the guests around dining tables fashioned from tree trunks. The 2 pools at the front of the main building are a favourite with children. With rabbits, chickens, dogs, cats, ducks & even a few meerkats, this is a place for those who share Walter's love of animals. Walking, hiking & game drives, including sunset drives & night drives, ensure that the visitor can see something of the area, returning to the option of farm-cooked meals. DBB N$950/1,700/2,200 sgl/dbl/ trpl; camping N$120 pp. **LLL**

Barchan Dune Retreat (3 bungalows, 2 rooms) ☎ 062 682031; e barchan@iway.na; www.barchandunes.com. This friendly little guest farm, owned by Willem & Hannetjie, is about 3km off the D1275; coming from Rehoboth, take the C24 to Nauchas, turn right on to the D1275, then about 20km beyond the Spreetshoogte Pass you'll reach a sign on the left to the farm. Well-camouflaged bungalows, built into the hillside & barely visible from the main house, are bright & airy. Each has 3 beds, a sofa, fresh flowers & a huge en-suite bathroom which bizarrely contains a desk. Dbl rooms are smaller with AC & a shower. At the foot of a kopje, the main area has a lovely carved table for indoor dining, or, in warmer weather, home-cooked meals are served on the porch. It's a peaceful setting with gorgeous views & attracts numerous birds, which you can watch while relaxing on the terrace. For those who want to see something of the area, hiking trails & scenic drives are available. Cash only. *DBB N$975 pp.* **LL**

Solitaire Country Lodge (25 rooms, camping) ☎ 063 293 621, reservations ☎ 061 305 173; e reservations@solitairecountrylodge.com; www.solitairecountrylodge.com. Immediately next to the bustling petrol station, bakery & general store, behind a pole fence neatly planted with aloes & cacti, Solitaire Country Lodge has 23 twins & 2 family rooms; all are very clean & spacious with free-standing fans, wrought-iron beds, clean linen & en-suite, tiled shower-rooms (hot water all day). A glass-fronted restaurant overlooks a lush central quad of grass & a large swimming pool make this a pleasant outpost. The single-storey buildings are painted apricot & have flat roofs & a wide, inward-looking veranda area which continues around the quad. A

campsite sits behind the lodge, where there's a hot & cold water ablution block & electricity at all plots. Meals are served at set times (*b/fast 07.00–09.00, dinner 19.00–21.00*), with a choice of a 4-course set menu or a buffet at dinner. Next door is the famous Solitaire Moose McGregor Bakery famed for its apple pie, but there is quite a lot of noise from the petrol station traffic & nearby airstrip. For walkers, the 8km Sunset Hill trail is signposted from the lodge. *DBB N$880/1,560 sgl/dbl; camping N$100 pp.* **LL**

Weltevrede Guest Farm (15 rooms, camping) ☎ 063 293 208; m 081 685 3433; e info@weltevredeguestfarm.com; www.weltevredeguestfarm.com. Signposted east of the C14, Weltevrede is about 47km from Sesriem, 37km from Solitaire, with a 1.5km driveway. Next to the farm's main buildings, en-suite rooms are motel-style, simple structures with 24hr electricity, a good-size private terrace & parking. They are furnished with a wardrobe, carved table, cream linens, have a small patio for sunsets, & are clean & spacious – bathrooms are being modernised at the time of writing. Rooms 1–12 have views of the plains & a small watering hole. A small bridge beside the papyrus-filled pond leads to the large thatched dining area, where meals are served, an honesty bar operates & there's free tea & coffee. Weltevrede also has 4 tent pitches under shady trees, best booked in advance. Pitches have water but electricity costs N$50/day, & there are showers, flush toilets & a fire pit (wood & ice can be bought). Both campers & farm guests can use the circular swimming pool. The reception area doubles as a curio shop selling postcards & souvenirs. Wi-Fi, available in the bar, costs N$20/day. *DBB N$995/1,570 sgl/dbl; camping N$120 pp.* **LL**

THE PARK'S NORTHERN SECTION

Between the normally dry beds of the Swakop and Kuiseb rivers, the desert is largely rock and stone. Though the area has few classic desert scenes of shifting dunes, the landscapes are still striking and certainly no less memorable. They range from the deeply incised canyons of the Swakop River Valley to the open plains around Ganab, flat and featureless but for the occasional isolated inselberg.

WHEN TO VISIT The prime time to visit this section of the park is towards the end of the rains, when the vegetation is at its most lush and, if you are lucky, you'll find scattered herds of oryx, springbok and zebra. During this time the best campsites to go to are the more open ones, like Ganab, on the plains.

For the rest of the year it is still spectacular, but you'll find fewer animals around. Then perhaps it's better to visit Homeb, or one of the inselbergs, as the flora and

FAIRY CIRCLES
Emma Thomson

For years strange, circular, bare patches of sand have been appearing in a narrow band that stretches from northwest South Africa, through the eastern outskirts of the Namib Desert, to mid-Angola. Nicknamed 'fairy circles', dozens of theories abounded – including UFOs – as to their cause, but it wasn't until recently that the truth was unearthed. One Professor Juergens has determined that sand termites (*Psammotermes allocerus generates*) create them to retain a high moisture level within the circles, so it's easier for them to build tunnels through the soil, which doesn't collapse as easily as dry soil.

fauna there remain a little more constant than on the plains – not shrivelling up so much in the dryness of winter.

ACCESS TO THE PARK (*N$80 per adult, plus N$10 per vehicle, under 16s free*) To drive off the main roads in this area (that is anywhere *except* the C14, C28, D1982 and D198), you need a permit, which must be obtained in advance from the NWR in Windhoek (see page 121) or the park office at Sesriem. These permits allow you to venture on to the park's smaller roads and to camp in any of the area's sites for an additional fee. Most of the roads are navigable by 2WD, with only a few around Oryxwater and Groot Tinkas classed as 4x4. Even these are probably negotiable with a high-clearance 2WD and a skilled driver, though you'd be waiting a very long time indeed for anyone to pass by if you became stuck.

Few of the maps of Namibia show these roads clearly, with the notable exception of the Globetrotter map, published by Struik.

WHERE TO STAY *Map, page 270.*

Namib-Naukluft campsites (*No advance reservations: permits available from the MET, who have an office in Swakopmund; N$80 per site plus N$20/10 adult/child, excluding park fees*) Basic campsites are situated at Kuiseb Bridge, Homeb, Mirabib, Groot Tinkas, Kriess-se-Rus, Vogelfederberg, Bloedkoppie, Ganab and Swakop River. They have no facilities to speak of, except for communal ablution facilities, but there is plenty of variety for you to choose from. To spend a night or two camping here – which is the only way to do this part of the desert justice – you must be fully independent in terms of fuel, food, water and firewood.

⋀ Bloedkoppie (or Blutkopje) Literally 'blood hill', for its colour in the light of sunset, this large, smooth granite inselberg rises out of the Tinkas Flats near the Swakop River. It can provide some challenging scrambles if the heat has not drained your energy. Do not approach any birds' nests, as some of the raptors in the park are very sensitive to disturbance; they may even abandon them if you go too close. Look out for the temporary pools after the rains, filled with life. Sadly, there have been reports that facilities here are not maintained as well as they could be, & that the bins are not changed often enough.

⋀ Ganab Right next to a dry watercourse, which winds like a thin green snake through the middle of a large gravel plain, this open site has a wind-powered water pump nearby. Around March, if the rains have been good, then it can be an excellent spot for herds of springbok & oryx – & you can see for miles.

⋀ Groot Tinkas Hidden away in a valley amid a maze of small kopjes, there is a small dam with sheer walls of rock & some fairly challenging rough driving too. Look out for frogs in the pool, & turn over a few stones to find scorpions & their harmless mimics, pseudo-scorpions.

⋀ Homeb This excellent site is in the Kuiseb River valley, where perennial vegetation includes camelthorn (*Acacia erioloba*), false ebony (*Euclea pseudebenus*), wild tamarisk (*Tamarix usneoides*)

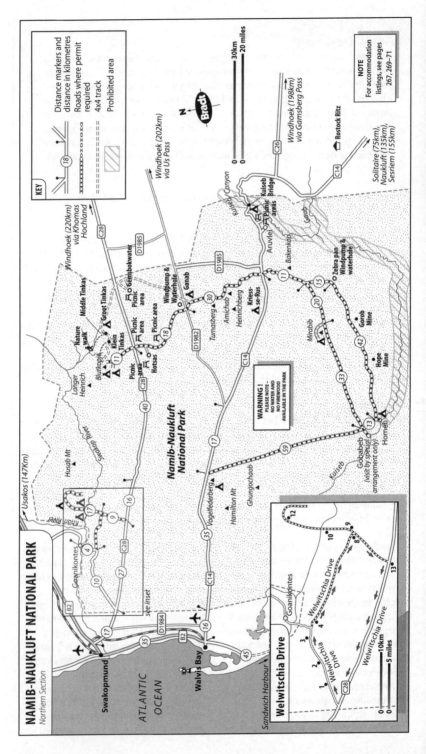

NAMIB-NAUKLUFT NATIONAL PARK
Northern Section

KEY

Distance markers and distance in kilometres

Roads where permit required

4x4 track

Prohibited area

NOTE
For accommodation listings, see pages 267, 269–71

WARNING !
PLEASE NOTE –
NO WATER AND
NO FIREWOOD
AVAILABLE IN THE PARK

Namib-Naukluft
National Park

ATLANTIC
OCEAN

Swakopmund

Walvis Bay

Sandwich Harbour

Usakos (147Km)

Windhoek (220km)
via Khomas
Hochland

Windhoek (202km)
via Us Pass

Windhoek (198km)
via Gamsberg Pass

Solitaire (75km), Naukluft (135km),
Sesriem (155km)

Rostock Ritz

Kuiseb
Bridge

Kuiseb Canyon

Picnic areas

Aruvlei

Bakenkop

Zebra pan
Windpump &
waterhole

Goob
Mine

Hope
Mine

Mirabib

Homeb

Gobabeb
(visit by special
arrangement only)

Kuiseb

Ghungchaob

Hamilton Mt

Vogelfederberg

Kriess-
se-Rus

Heinrichberg

Amichab

Tumaberg

Windpump &
Waterhole

Ganab

Picnic
area

Gemsbokwater

Picnic
area

Picnic area

Middle Tinkas

Groot Tinkas

Klein
Tinkas

Nature
walk

Blutkoppe

Picnic
area

Hotsas

Langer Heinrich.

Husab Mt

Swakop River

Khan River

Goanikontes

see inset

Welwitschia Drive

Goanikontes

Welwitschia Drive

Welwitschia Drive

Welwitschia Drive

Welwitschia Drive

270

& several species of wild fig. The Kuiseb forms the northern boundary of the great southern dune field, so observe the dunes on the south side of the river as they creep northward. Only the periodic floods of the river prevent the park to the north from being covered in shifting sands. The site is adjacent to a small village.

Homeb's well-placed location gives you the opportunity to cross the river-bed & climb among the dunes, as well as to explore the river valley itself. The proximity of 3 different environments is why Namibia's Desert Research Centre is located at Gobabeb, on the Kuiseb to the west of Homeb.

⋏ Kriess-se-Rus Again in a dry river-bed, Kriess-se-Rus lies below a bank of exposed schist. The layers of rock are clear to see, providing an interesting contrast to the flat calcrete plains nearby. You'll find quivertrees (*Aloe dichotoma*), many camelthorns, & some euphorbia & commiphora bushes.

⋏ Kuiseb Bridge Just off the main C14 route, west of the Gamsberg Pass, this can be very bare during the dry season, but is pleasant after the rains. The river is said to have less underground water stored here than further down its course, though it is more prone to flash floods. Make it your picnic stop if you are travelling between the Swakopmund & Sesriem areas (& be sure to take your rubbish away with you).

⋏ Mirabib Another large grey inselberg, but even quieter than the others. It has great views from the top. Around it, where any rainwater runs off, are small trees & bushes. There are always a few lizards to be found around here, & even the odd snake.

⋏ Swakop River Being beacon number 10 on the Welwitschia Drive (see below) means that this beautiful dry river-bed can get rather busy at times with day trippers from Swakopmund.

⋏ Vogelfederberg This rounded granite outcrop is the closest site to the ocean, & gets more moisture from the fog than the others. Its shape helps form a number of fascinating temporary pools. Polaroid glasses will help you to see past the reflections & into the pools; if you've a pair, take them.

WELWITSCHIA DRIVE (*N$40 pp, plus N$10 per vehicle; permits must be bought in advance from the MET office in Swakopmund – see page 278*) In the northern corner of the Namib-Naukluft National Park, the Welwitschia Drive is perhaps best treated as a half-day excursion from Swakopmund. It is essential to get a permit from the MET office in Swakopmund first, and note that the condition of the road is pretty poor, so think carefully before taking a 2WD along here.

This is a route through the desert along which are 13 numbered stone beacons at points of particular interest. It culminates at one of the country's largest, and hence oldest, welwitschia plants (see also page 354, and take a look at www.plantzafrica.com, a website run by the South African Biodiversity Institute). To find the drive, leave Swakopmund on the B2 towards Windhoek, then turn right shortly on to the C28. Follow this road for around 16km when you'll come to a junction with the D1991 – you could follow this north for 4.5km to have coffee or lunch at the Goanikontes Oasis Rest Camp. Turn left here for the start of the circuit (see map, page 270). You'll need to allow about 4 hours so that you can stop at each place and explore.

The recent discovery of uranium in this area means that the drive route will shortly be changed. It is best to check the latest information at the MET office in Swakopmund before attempting the trip. However, here is a brief outline of the different points of interest at the beacons:

1   **Lichen field** Look carefully at the ground to see these small 'plants', the result of a symbiotic relationship (ie: a mutually beneficial relationship between two organisms, each depending on the other for its survival) between an alga, producing food by photosynthesis, and a fungus, providing a physical structure. Look closely, and you'll see many different types of lichen. Some are thought to be hundreds of years old, and all are exceedingly fragile and vulnerable.

2   **Drought-resistant bushes** Two types of bush found all over the Namib are the dollar bush, so called because its leaves are the size of a dollar coin, and the ink bush. Both can survive without rain for years. Despite the sign here, there are few drought-resistant bushes to be seen!

3 **Tracks of ox wagons** Although made decades ago, these are still visible, showing the damage that can so easily be done to the lichen fields by driving over them.

4 **The moonscape** This is an unusual and spectacular view, usually called the moonscape, looking over a landscape formed by the valleys of the Swakop River. It is best seen in the slanting light of early morning or late afternoon.

5 **More lichen fields** These remarkable plants can extract all their moisture requirements from the air. To simulate the dramatic effect of a morning fog, simply sprinkle a little water on one and watch carefully for a few minutes.

6 This is another impressive view of the endless moonscape.

7 **Old South African camp** This is the site of an old military camp, occupied for just a few days during World War I.

8 Turn left at this marker to visit the next few beacons.

9 **A dolorite dyke** These dark strips of rock, common in this part of the Namib, were formed when molten lava welled up through cracks in the existing grey granite. After cooling it formed dark bands of rock which resisted erosion more than the granite – and thus has formed the spine of many ridges in the area.

10 **The Swakop River Valley** Picnicking in the river-bed, with a profusion of tall trees around, you might find it difficult to believe that you are in a desert. It could be said that you're not – after all, this rich vegetation is not made up of desert-adapted species. It includes wild tamarisk (*Tamarix usurious*) and anaboom (*Acacia albida*), better known for its occurrence in the humid Zambezi Valley almost 1,600km east – sustained by underground water percolating through the sands beneath your feet.

11 **Welwitschia Flats** This open expanse of gravel and sand is home to the Namib's most celebrated plant, the endemic *Welwitschia mirabilis*. These are found only in the Namib, and at just a few locations which suit their highly adapted biology.

12 **The big welwitschia** This beacon marks the end of the trail, and one of the largest *Welwitschia mirabilis* known – estimated at over 1,500 years old. Visitors are asked not to walk inside the ring of stones placed here to protect the plant.

13 **Old mine workings** On the way back to Swakopmund, continue straight past beacon 8, without turning right. Where the road joins route C28 to Swakopmund, marked by this final beacon, is one of the desert's old mine workings. In the 1950s, iron ore was mined by hand here. Now it is just another reminder of the park's chequered past.

Swakopmund and Walvis Bay Area

Flying low over Namibia's coastline is probably the best way to get a sense of perspective about it. You see how it divides the South Atlantic Ocean from the baking desert. Both seem harsh and unforgiving.

Clinging to the boundary, often under a blanket of morning fog, are Swakopmund and Walvis Bay. Politically, Walvis Bay has always been vital. It has the only deepwater harbour between Lüderitz and Angola. Historically, Swakopmund is probably the more interesting, with old German architecture to rival that in Lüderitz.

Most visitors stay in Swakopmund, which tends to be the livelier of the two, though birders may prefer Walvis Bay. Both have a good choice of small hotels and restaurants, making them obvious stops when driving between the Namib-Naukluft National Park and the Skeleton Coast or Damaraland.

HISTORY

In 1884, the whole of present-day Namibia was declared a protectorate of Germany – except the region's only large natural harbour, Walvis Bay, which remained under British control. Thus, in order to develop their interests in the area, the German authorities decided to make their own harbour on the northern banks of the Swakop River, and beacons were planted in 1892 to mark the spot, where the Mole is today (see page 293). Following this, the German authorities made several (largely unsuccessful) attempts to develop landing facilities. A quay was built, although it subsequently silted up, followed by a wooden, and later an iron, jetty. Finally in 1915, when Germany's control of the country was surrendered to South Africa, all maritime trade reverted to Walvis Bay.

During the South African administration of Namibia, before independence, there was a deliberate policy of developing no other ports to compete with Walvis Bay – as South Africa anticipated keeping hold of the Walvis Bay enclave, even if it was forced into giving most of Namibia independence.

As planned, South Africa kept the Walvis Bay enclave as part of the Cape Colony even after Namibian independence in 1990, though it agreed to a joint administration in 1992, and finally relented in February 1994, when Walvis Bay officially became part of Namibia.

SWAKOPMUND

Considered by most Namibians to be the country's only real holiday resort, this old German town spreads from the mouth of the Swakop River out into the surrounding desert plain and is instantly and immensely likeable. Climatically more temperate than the interior, the palm-lined streets, immaculate old buildings

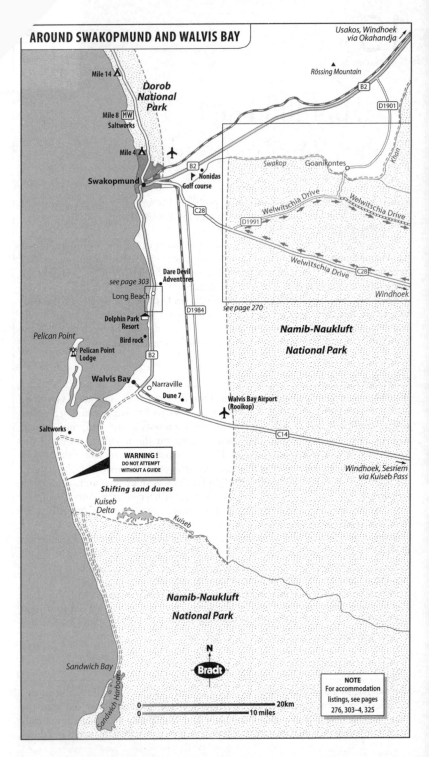

AROUND SWAKOPMUND AND WALVIS BAY

Usakos, Windhoek
via Okahandja

Rössing Mountain

B2

D1901

Mile 14

Dorob
National
Park

Mile 8 MW
Saltworks

Khan

Mile 4

B2

Swakop

Goanikontes

Swakopmund

Nonidas
Golf course

C28

Welwitschia Drive

Welwitschia Drive

D1991

Welwitschia Drive

see page 303

C28

Dare Devil
Adventures

Long Beach

D1984

see page 270

Windhoek

Dolphin Park
Resort

Pelican Point

Bird rock

B2

Pelican Point
Lodge

Namib-Naukluft

National Park

Walvis Bay

Narraville

Dune 7

Saltworks

Walvis Bay Airport
(Rooikop)

C14

WARNING !
DO NOT ATTEMPT
WITHOUT A GUIDE

Shifting sand dunes

Windhoek, Sesriem
via Kuiseb Pass

Kuiseb
Delta

Kuiseb

Namib-Naukluft

National Park

Sandwich Bay

N

Bradt

0   20km
0   10 miles

NOTE
For accommodation
listings, see pages
276, 303–4, 325

and well-kept gardens give Swakop (as the locals call it) a unique atmosphere, and make it a hugely pleasant oasis in which to spend a few days.

Unlike much of Namibia, Swakopmund is used to tourists, and has a wide choice of places to stay and eat, and many things to do. The town has also established a name for itself as a centre for adventure travel, and attracting adventurous visitors seeking 'adrenalin' trips, with numerous new and highly original options from free-fall parachuting to dune-bike riding and sandboarding. This is still too small to change the town's character, but is enough to ensure that you'll never be bored. On the other hand, visit on a Monday during one of the quieter months, and you could be forgiven for thinking that the town had partially closed down!

To a certain extent, Swakopmund is a victim of its own success, with more and more people seeking to buy property on the coast, which in turn has put pressure on its infrastructure. While the increasing diversity of shops is for some a positive result, it also means that you'll have to book a table at the town's most popular restaurants, even out of season. Rather more importantly, there is now enormous pressure on the already overstretched water supply, which is currently piped in from elsewhere in Namibia. Talk of building desalination plants so that the town can be self-sufficient has been partially realised, with one completed and another under construction. This, however, has only been triggered by the massive water demand made by new uranium mines in the coastal desert: uranium has provided the cash and therefore uranium gets the water. But there is light at the end of the tunnel. Uranium mines have a lifespan of around 10–15 years and thereafter the water should become available to the public. It is hoped that this will eventually become a lasting and positive legacy of the current, highly controversial mining policy.

GETTING THERE AND AWAY

By air Air Namibia currently has no scheduled flights into Swakopmund, so visitors need to fly to Walvis Bay (see page 296). A transfer from Walvis Bay Airport into Swakopmund costs around N$320 per person. Air Namibia on Sam Nujoma Avenue ([280 D4]; ☎ 064 405123; ⊕ 08.00–13.00 & 14.00–17.00 Mon–Fri) is a useful office for reconfirming onward flights and other airline business.

By train Swakopmund is linked to Windhoek and Walvis Bay by the normal, slow TransNamib train services. These run from and to Windhoek every day except Saturday, arriving Swakopmund at 05.20, and thence to Walvis Bay for 07.15. Trains depart from Walvis Bay at 19.15, arriving in Swakopmund at 20.30, and Windhoek at 07.00 the next day. See *Chapter 6*, pages 98–100, for details, or call the station in Swakopmund (☎ 064 463187).

The *Desert Express* is a completely different service, aimed primarily at tourists. It departs from Swakopmund on Saturday, arriving back in Windhoek on Sunday morning, with stops *en route* for a sundowner or short walk. All the cabins have air conditioning and en-suite facilities. Ticket prices include excursions, dinner and breakfast. For details, see page 100. However, be aware that sometimes this service won't run if the train has been booked for private excursions.

By bus Several bus services link Swakopmund and Windhoek, with stops at Usakos, Karibib and Okahandja. Note that times for all buses will be an hour earlier between April and October.

The Intercape Mainliner service between Windhoek and Walvis Bay stops in Swakopmund behind the Pick 'n' Pay supermarket on Hendrik Witbooi Street [280 E4]. Buses depart from Windhoek at 06.00 on Monday, Wednesday, Friday and Saturday, and leave Swakopmund for the return journey at 12.45 on Monday, Wednesday, Friday and Sunday. Tickets cost N$160–200 one-way and must be booked in advance. To book, contact Intercape (↳ *061 227847; www.intercape.co.za*) or Sure Ritz Travel (see below). For more details, see *Chapter 6*, pages 101–2. For details of the Ekonolux bus, see page 296.

Two additional options are the Welwitschia Shuttle (↳ *064 405105/2721*) and Townhoppers (↳ *064 407223;* m *081 210 3062;* e *townhoppers@iway.na*). Both of these companies offer a daily service between Windhoek and Swakopmund, departing Swakopmund early morning and departing Windhoek in the early afternoon. The journey time is about 5 hours, with tickets around N$260, and the service includes door-to-door collection and drop off. It is also possible to arrange airport transfers with either company. Tickets can be booked directly or through Namib I (see page 278), for no extra cost.

Sure Ritz Travel (*4 Hewepa Arcade, Sam Nujoma Avenue;* ↳ *064 405151; www. sureritztravel.com*) handles all Intercape bus tickets. Note that they charge a ticket-handling fee of N$25 per person.

By car For comments on the choice of roads from Windhoek to Swakopmund, see *Chapter 9, West from Windhoek: to the coast*, pages 161–72. If you're taking the C28 or C26 then also see comments on the northern section of the Namib-Naukluft National Park, pages 268–72. The long coastal road to the north is covered in *Chapter 14, The Skeleton Coast*.

ORIENTATION Viewed from above the Atlantic, Swakopmund has a simple layout. One tar road, Sam Nujoma Avenue (the B2), enters the town from the interior; another heads off left, northward, to Henties Bay (C34). A third crosses the mouth of the Swakop, southward towards Walvis Bay. Where they meet is the centre of town, a raised area about four blocks from the Promenade – the palm-lined road that skirts the seashore.

Most of the hotels are near the compact centre, as are the shops and restaurants, so it's an easy town to walk around. In recent years, though, an explosion of development has hit this small resort, obliterating sea views almost overnight in the scramble to build ever closer to the shore. Whereas once the campsite at 'Mile 4' was quite literally four miles from Swakopmund, today the town's suburban sprawl has crept up to meet it. While this has had little impact on the centre of town in itself, it has certainly changed the picture from above.

Street name changes A number of street name changes have recently been introduced in Swakopmund, replacing the familiar German names with others to honour local and national dignitaries. Inevitably, many of the former names are still used, as follows:

Bahnhof Street *is now* Theo-Ben Gurirab Avenue
Breite Street *is now* Nathaniel Maxuilili Street
Brücken Street *is now* Libertina Amathila Avenue
Kaiser Wilhelm Street *is now* Sam Nujoma Avenue
Knobloch/Kolonnen *is now* Rakotoka
Lazarett Street *is now* Anton Lubowski Avenue
Moltke Street *is now* Tobias Hainyeko Street
Nordring/Sudring *is now* Moses Garoëb Street
Post Street *is now* Daniel Tjongarero Avenue

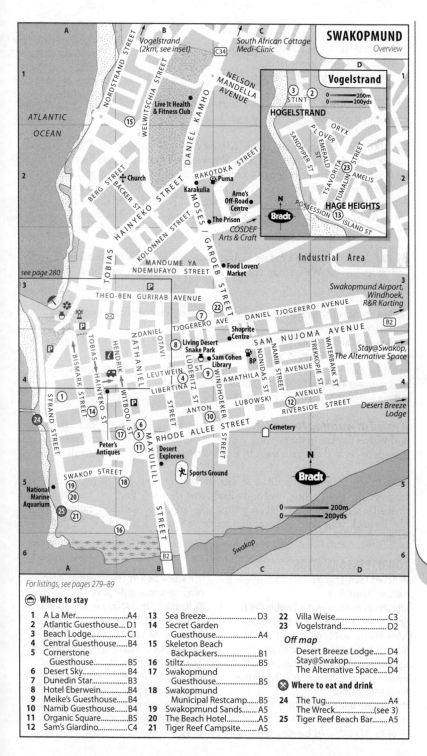

SWAKOPMUND
Overview

Vogelstrand

ATLANTIC OCEAN

Industrial Area

Swakopmund and Walvis Bay Area   SWAKOPMUND

13

Promenade *is now* Molen Street
Roon Street *is now* Hendrik Witbooi
Schlacter *is now* Welwitschia
Woermann St *is now* Leutwein Street

GETTING AROUND Swakopmund's centre is so small that most visitors walk around it, although obviously you'll need a car to get out of the centre.

By bike The Cycle Clinic ([280 E3] *10 Hendrik Witbooi St;* ✆ *064 402530*), between the Hansa Hotel and Sam Nujoma Avenue, hires out bicycles (*N$20/ hr, N$100/day*). These range from mountain bikes to touring models, and come complete with (compulsory) cycle helmets. A deposit of N$200 is required. Alternatively, Swakop Cycle Tours (see page 310) can drop off rental bikes at your hotel. Another option is to hire a scooter from Scooter Rentals (*Sam Nujoma Av;* m *085 581 0570*).

By car If you're hiring a car on arrival, then any of the local **car-hire** companies will meet you at Walvis Bay Airport (there are currently no direct flights into Swakopmund):

🚗 **Avis** Swakopmund Hotel & Entertainment Centre; ✆ 064 402527
🚗 **Bonanza Car & 4x4 Hire** ✆ 064 404503
🚗 **Budget** 3 Moses Garoëb St; ✆ 061 463380; m 081 127 2560
🚗 **Crossroads 4x4 Hire** Cnr Theo-Ben Gurirab & Moses Garöeb sts; ✆ 064 403777; e crossroads@

iway.na; www.crossroads4x4hire.com. 4x4 specialist.
🚗 **Europcar** Tobias Hainyeko & Mandume Ya Ndemufayo sts; ✆ 064 463812
🚗 **Hertz** Sam Nujoma Av; ✆ 064 461826; e walvis@hertz.co.za

A word of warning for drivers It is not advisable to drive between Swakopmund and Walvis Bay late in the evening. Although the distance is short and the road good, it tends to be used as a race track by drink-drivers, and there are frequent accidents.

Taxis There is no organised taxi service in Swakopmund, but during the day taxis frequent the town centre, where it's likely that they will find you before you find them. Do exercise caution when getting into any unbooked taxi; rather, organise one through your hotel or pension. One reliable option is Skolla Cabs (✆ *081 255 5148*).

TOURIST INFORMATION

Henckert Tourist Centre Cnr Sam Nujoma Av & Nathaniel Maxuilili Av
Ministry of Environment & Tourism (MET) [280 D4] Cnr Sam Nujoma Av & Bismarck St; ✆ 064 404 576; ⊕ 08.00–13.00 & 14.00–17.00 Mon–Fri, 08.00–13.00 Sat–Sun & public hols. Upstairs from NWR you can obtain permits for entry to national parks here, including the new Dorob National Park.
Namibia Wildlife Resorts (NWR) Cnr Sam Nujoma Av & Bismarck St; ✆ 064 402 172; ⊕ 08.00–17.00 Mon–Fri. Travellers make

reservations for NWR accommodation, including campsites in some of the parks.
🛈 **Namib I** [280 E3] Cnr Sam Nujoma Av & Hendrik Witbooi St; ✆ 064 404827; e namibi@ iway.na; ⊕ 08.30–13.00 &14.00–17.00 Mon–Fri (opens & closes ½hr earlier in winter), 09.00–13.00 Sat–Sun. The superb tourist information bureau in the centre of town has an extensive selection of pamphlets & information on Namibia, with a special emphasis on the local area, & it sells postcards & stamps – don't miss it.

WHERE TO STAY When thinking about visiting Swakopmund, note that, from about mid-December to mid-January, the whole population of Windhoek seems to decamp to the relative cool of Swakopmund for their 'summer break'. This means that the hotels and guesthouses are fully booked, and the town is filled to bursting. Reservations are essential. At other times, Swakopmund is not so frantic, though the better (and better value) hotels usually need reserving before you arrive. As the town is well used to families, many establishments offer a special rate for children, so it's well worth asking.

Because of Swakopmund's cooling morning fogs, and the moderating maritime influence on its temperatures, air conditioning is seldom needed here and few of the hotels provide it, though several do have heating. For the same reason, camping on the large, open sites by the sea can be very cold and uncomfortable, while the cheaper bed and breakfasts and guesthouses are very reasonably priced. So even if you're camping for most of your trip, this may be a good place to treat yourself to a bed for the night. Below, the various establishments are divided into hotels, pensions and bed and breakfasts, backpackers' lodges, restcamps and camping.

Hotels

Map, page 280, unless otherwise indicated.
The large Hotel & Entertainment Centre and the more intimate Hansa are Swakopmund's only international-standard hotels, though there are many other small hotels full of character, & a few gems.

Hansa (58 rooms) 3 Hendrik Witbooi St; 064 414200; e reservations@hansahotel. com.na; www.hansahotel.com.na. The Hansa is privately owned, & probably the best hotel in Swakopmund. It is fairly large, though has a private residents' lounge with a small library & a separate wood-panelled bar with a fireplace for the winter. Light lunches (*about N$120*) can be eaten on the terrace next to a lush tropical garden, as well as in the award-winning restaurant (see page 287). Good-size rooms with solid furnishings feel old but well maintained & cared for. All are heated, have AC, direct-dial phones, digital safes, well-stocked minibars & 15-channel TVs with CNN, BBC & Mnet. Rooms 5 & 6 are adapted for guests in wheelchairs. There's free Wi-Fi & 2 terminals for guests. The Hansa's management is sharp & the service good: they provide courtesy transport around town. **$$$$$**

Swakopmund Hotel & Entertainment Centre (90 rooms) 2 Theo-Ben Gurirab Av; 064 410 5200; e swakopmund@legacyhotels. co.za; www.legacyhotels.co.za. Built from the shell of Swakopmund's late 19th-century yellow railway station, this leisure complex includes the Mermaid Casino, a gym, a hair salon & a reflexologist, the privately owned Atlanta

cinema, & is the base for Avis car hire (see opposite).

Entering the huge lobby, passing the Caboose gift shop & reception, you emerge into a central grassy quadrangle, dominated by a pool. This is surrounded by palm trees & easy chairs, & surmounted by fountains. Overlooking the courtyard are brightly furnished & well-equipped rooms, 1 with disabled access; try to book a pool-facing room, as they're quieter. All come with a black-&-white photograph of the old railway above the bed, tea/coffee-maker, phone, Mnet TV, minibar/fridge (filled on request), AC, free Wi-Fi & digital safe. The safe may come in useful for your winnings at the casino, which has some 184 slot machines & 8 gaming tables. Fortunately, as this is often busy, it is a few hundred yards away – the hotel is having more success attracting local clientele than high-rolling foreign gamblers. Close by is an 18-hole golf course.

The centre's main restaurant, Platform One (☺ *b/fast 06.30–10.00, lunch 12.30–14.30, dinner 18.30–22.00*), offers a varied à la carte menu Mon–Sat & a popular buffet lunch on Sun (**$$$$$**). Alternatively, you can make use of 24hr room service or visit the on-site Chinese restaurant Chez Wou (☺ *13.00–14.30 & 17.30–22.00 daily*; **$$$$$**). Airport transfers can be arranged. **$$$$$**

Hotel Zum Kaiser (21 rooms) 4 Sam Nujoma Av; 064 417100, reservations +27 21 930 4564; e reservations@hotelzumkaiser. com; www.hotelzumkaiser.com. Formerly the Swakopmund Boutique Hotel, this stylish option is painted from top to toe in white & neutral

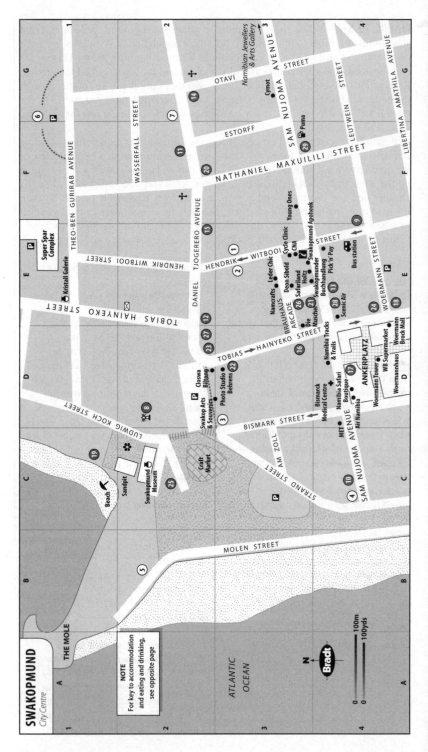

SWAKOPMUND
City Centre

NOTE
For key to accommodation and eating and drinking, see opposite page

ATLANTIC OCEAN

THE MOLE

Beach

Sandpit

Swakopmund Museum

Craft Market

Super Spar Complex

Kristall Galerie

Swakop Arts & Souvenirs

Photo Studio Behrens

Closwa Biltong

Nancrafts

BRAUHAUS ARCADE

Leder Chic

Dean Sibold

Holtz

Safariland

Die Muschel

Swakopmunder Buchhandlung

Namibia Tracks & Trails

Bismarck Medical Centre

Namibia Safari

MET Boutique

Air Namibia

W8 Supermarket

Woermann Brock Mall

Woermannhaus

Woermann Tower

ANKERPLATZ

Scenic Air

Pick 'n' Pay

CNA

Swakopmund Apoheek

Eye Clinic

Young Ones

Cymot

Puma

Bus station

Namibian Jewellers & Arts Gallery

MOLEN STREET

STRAND STREET

AM ZOLL

SAM NUJOMA AVENUE

BISMARK STREET

TOBIAS HAINYEKO STREET

TOBIAS HAINYEKO STREET

LUDWIG KOCH STREET

DANIEL TJOGERERO AVENUE

HENDRIK WITBOOI STREET

THEO-BEN GURIRAB AVENUE

WASSERFALL STREET

ESTORFF STREET

OTAVI STREET

NATHANIEL MAXUILILI STREET

SAM NUJOMA AVENUE

WOERMANN STREET

LEUTWEIN STREET

LIBERTINA AMATHILA AVENUE

Atlantic Ocean

0   100m
0   100yds

Bradt

N

280

tones. On entering the airy lobby you are bathed in light from the skylight above. The white theme is continued in the rooms, with the only colour coming from bright cushions scattered on the sofas & beds. All are en suite with a corner bath & separate shower, phone, hairdryer, DSTV, minibar (filled on request), digital safe, as well as tea & coffee, & all have balconies with a mixture of street/neighbouring apartment views. For a better view head to the private rooftop terrace, looking out over the sea & Woermann Tower, where there's also a bar in summer (*Dec–Jan*) for cocktails. There's a lounge opposite reception with a TV & free Wi-Fi everywhere. There's an activity desk behind reception & you can book a massage at the 2nd-floor spa room. B/fast is served in the next-door Bistro Zum Kaiser (see page 288). **$$$$**

🏠 **Kempinski Hotel** (125 rooms) The Mole; www.kempinski.com. Occupying the seafront site left by the demolition of the Strand Hotel, the Kempinski has been under construction for years, but is on track to be completed in 2015. The new 4-star hotel is expected to have all the usual facilities, including 3 restaurants, a bar/lounge, a health club & a pool. Several shops are planned within the complex, too. **$$$$**

🏠 **The Beach Hotel** [Map, page 277] (33 rooms) 1 Südstrand/The Strand; ☎ 064 41 77 00; e info@beach.na; www.beach.na. A new 3-star privately owned hotel located at the southern end of Swakopmund, just yards from the beach. The bedrooms are crisp & modern & decorated in white & dark wood with a splash of colour lent by blue bedspreads. All come equipped with DSTV, combi heat/AC system, hairdryer, tea/coffee station, digital safe & a stocked minibar. Upgrading from a standard to a comfort room buys sea views; family rooms have limited sea views. Comfort & luxury apts with a lounge, open-plan kitchen & 2 en-suite bathrooms are also available. None of the bathrooms feature a bath – a water-saving move – but the finish is high quality.

The main area, for relaxing, is restricted to a lounge on the 4th floor with a small, unofficial-looking bar for sundowners & a balcony with pleasant sea views. However, they do offer a same-day laundry service (pay per item), free hotel parking & free Wi-Fi everywhere, as well as an internet terminal by reception. There's a wraparound roof terrace with a small corner pool with superlative 360° views. On-site massages available too (*N$315/hr*).

Buffet b/fast is served in the ground floor restaurant Anchor Point, which is also open for lunch (🕑 *noon–14.00*) & dinner (🕑 *18.00–21.30*) & is decorated in smart dark woods & cream linen tablecloths. Out the front, there is a covered terrace overlooking the street with flaming patio heaters that look very inviting on cold misty evenings. **$$$$**

🏠 **Hotel Eberwein** (17 rooms) Sam Nujoma Av (cnr Otavi St); ☎ 064 414450; e eberwein@ iafrica.com.na; www.hotel-eberwein.com. This former family house, built in 1909 & close to the centre of town, has been a privately owned hotel since 1999. Its rooms (*16 dbl, 1 sgl*) all have en-suite shower, flat-screen TV, minibar, tea/coffee, phone & underfloor heating. They are clean & bright & some have Victorian-style high ceilings & sculpted drapes. It is very German in character, efficiently run & with friendly staff. There's a cosy bar & b/fast area, but no restaurant. Secure parking is available

e Wi-Fi can be picked up in the
, plus 1 laptop & a fixed computer
est use. **$$$**

Hotel Schweizerhaus (24 rooms)
1 Bismarck St; 064 400331–3; e schweizerhaus@
mweb.com.na; www.schweizerhaus.net. Above
the genteel & popular Café Anton (see page 288),
the 2-star Schweizerhaus is the grandfather of
Swakopmund's hotels, having been around since
1965. Its ocean views still make it popular & en-
suite rooms have been updated in recent years &
come with TV & direct-dial phone. Most rooms also
have a balcony, including all of the luxury rooms
which face the sea. Others overlook a courtyard
at the back. The staff are normally very friendly,
& there's a night porter on duty should you arrive
late. **$$$**

Swakopmund Sands [Map, page 277]
(21 rooms) 3 The Strand; 064 405 045;
e swakopsands@iway.na; www.swakopsandshotel.
com. Formerly the Hotel Garni Adler, this beachside
hotel has been given a face-lift & now offers very
smart variety of luxury, sgl, dbl & family rooms
with high padded headboards, DSTV, fridge, tea/
coffee & small digital safe; some come with corner
baths, others with rain showers. The only public
areas are a lounge with deep sofas & fireplace
behind reception, & the b/fast room. There's a large
open car park off to the side. It caters mainly to
businesspeople, but is attractive & you can't fault
the standard of furnishings & the beach location.
$$$

Bundu N See (20 rooms) 6 Hendrik Witlooi
St; 064 402 360; e res@bundunsee.com; www.
bundunsee.com. This hotel's winning card is its
incredibly central location – the rooms are clean &
unspectacular, but they come with free Wi-Fi, DSTV
& are cheap as chips. **$$**

Lodges, pensions and B&Bs
Swakopmund excels at the B&B &, if you don't
need the facilities of a larger hotel, there are
numerous high-quality options offering more
personalised service & local insights. Almost all are
within walking distance of the town centre.

Close to the centre
Maps, page 277, unless otherwise indicated.
Swakopmund Guesthouse (12 rooms)
35 Hendrik Witbooi St; 064 462008;
e reservations@swakopmundguesthouse.com;

www.swakopmundguesthouse.com. Fresh, light
& modern, this guesthouse is directly opposite
Cornerstone, just 5mins from the beach &
shopping area. The seaside theme running through
the décor is highlighted by scattered beach pebbles
& seashells, crisp white linen, & bright turquoise
waves painted carefully on the walls. All rooms are
en suite with a minibar, fridge, TV, safe, hairdryer
& Wi-Fi, with 7 luxury rooms being slightly more
spacious than the others, & a suite. The outside
courtyard makes a pleasant place to sit, in unusual
hanging pod chairs. **$$$$**

The Stiltz (9 rooms, 2 villas) Strand St;
064 400771; e info@thestiltz.com; www.
thestiltz.com. In an entirely new departure
for Swakopmund, The Stiltz combines a great
location at the edge of town, within easy reach
of restaurants & shops, with a flair for design,
resulting in a place that defies conventional
categorisation. Accommodation consists of a
series of rustic wooden chalets, built (as the name
suggests) high on stilts, & linked by wooden
walkways. Zany colours adorn the insides, giving
the place a bright feel on the days when the sun
shines, & compensating for those when the sea is
shrouded in mist. Views from the chalet balconies
vary – some look out over the dunes, some out to
sea (rooms 4, 6, 7 & 8), & others over the Swakop
River bed & its resident birdlife or the lagoon at its
mouth. Typically, each has twin beds or a large dbl,
en-suite bathroom, an honesty minibar, heating,
& the odd idiosyncratic design feature that serves
to accentuate the individuality of the place. The
only niggle is a distinct lack of plugs in the rooms,
but the free Wi-Fi connection is very good. The
superb b/fast is served in a large purpose-built
chalet set on its own with panoramic views. No
lunch or dinner offered. It's definitely a place to
linger. There's a small car park off the road which is
guarded overnight. **$$$–$$$$**

A La Mer (24 rooms) 4 Libertina Amathila
Av; 064 404130; e alamer@iway.na; www.
pension-a-la-mer.com. Just across the road
from the Tug (see page 287) & 50m from the
promenade, the hard-to-miss orange exterior of
A La Mer makes it look more like a motel than a
hotel. However, things are in a state of flux & some
of the newer rooms are really quite stylish, with
white linens set against red walls, & chunky stone
basins, copper towel rails & underfloor heating in
the bathrooms. Rooms 25–27 have sea views from

their balconies, while rooms 28–30 overlook the gated car park. Other rooms have pine furniture & look a little tired. Downstairs, there's small bar for guests & the high-ceilinged restaurant serves b/fast, which can also be eaten outside. The changes have made it into a very good budget option – visit the website to see any further changes that have been taking place. **$$$**

🏠 **Central Guesthouse** (8 rooms) Cnr Leutwein & Lüderitz sts; ☎ 064 407189; e info@ guesthouse.com.na; www.guesthouse.com.na. Monica & Jockle Grüttemeyer run this boutique guesthouse, whose bright & comfortable en-suite rooms are equipped with mahogany furniture, contrasting with clean white linen. Little touches in the rooms such as extra-length beds, hairdryers & sewing kits, are in addition to flat-screen TVs & safes. Well-stocked minibars with tea/coffee facilities & snacks are shared between rooms. The lounge has free Wi-Fi, cosy deep sofas, board games & a bookcase with lots of books on Namibia. The b/fast area has an open fire in winter. There's a covered area with braai & secure parking outside with guard. This is a lovely, friendly place to stay. **$$$**

🏠 **Cornerstone Guesthouse** (7 rooms) 40 Hendrik Witbooi St; ☎ 064 462468; m 081 129 90026; e info@cornerstoneguesthouse. com; www.cornerstoneguesthouse.com. Peter & Margo Bassingthwaighte are on hand to look after you at this charming & intimate guesthouse, which is within walking distance of the town centre; you can't fail to spot the yellow building, surrounded by pretty gardens. Rooms are bright, clean & comfortable with whitewashed bedsteads & wooden floors. All are en suite with their own patio, as well as satellite TV, fridge, safe, hairdryer, international wall sockets & free Wi-Fi, with details such as sprigs of lavender & personal toiletries. A delicious b/fast is served to a background of classical music, & laundry & off-street parking add to the facilities. Margo & Peter also own 2 luxury self-catering apts by the beach & 1 in town (*N$1,500–2,550*). The most special is **An der Mole**, an immaculate, fully furnished & extremely homely 3-bedroom apt, with fully equipped kitchen & laundry, a large balcony with ocean views, a BBQ, dbl underground garage & DSTV – you'll want to stay forever.

With personal attention & homely extras, this place is good value for money. **$$$**

🏠 **Namib Guesthouse** (8 rooms) 61 Anton Lubowski St; ☎ 064 40 71 71; e info@ namibguesthouse.com; www.namibguesthouse. com. A serene, privately owned guesthouse about 15mins' walk from Swakopmund centre & beach. Run by Nicoletta Betts, the compound sits behind a large electric gate & rooms are arranged around a small astroturf-laden 'garden' with a few palm trees. Rooms 1 & 2 are designated 'luxury' & decked out with red imitation-leather headboards, black cushions & white linens, while the black-&-white tiled en-suite bathroom is fitted with a bath & roomy walk-in shower. Standard rooms are spacious with cool blue walls stencilled with gold floral patterns, high-up panoramic windows on the back wall & a large window at the front looking on to the courtyard. All the rooms are equipped with a laptop safe, flat-screen TV with DSTV, tea/coffee station, hairdryer & free Wi-Fi. A laundry service is available.

Rooms 1–4 are wheelchair friendly; there are no rails, but they're open plan & spacious. Rooms 4 & 5 can function as family rooms. There's no gated parking, but a security guard is posted at night. The main area is made up of the reception & b/fast room; the b/fast buffet receives many compliments from guests. Artworks by local artists hang on the walls & are for sale. The owner arranges all manner of Swakopmund-based activities for guests, from fishing to desert tours. **$$$**

✳ 🏠 **Organic Square Guesthouse** (8 rooms) 29 Rhode Allee; ☎ 064 463 979; e info@ guesthouse-swakopmund.com; www.guesthouse-swakopmund.com. A new, privately owned, luxury guesthouse in central Swakopmund. This corner property is decorated with a vibrant mix of rustic wood, modern artworks, polished concrete floors & cool grey walls interspersed with bright pops of lime paint. The colour scheme continues in the spotless, open-plan bedrooms where the walk-though bathrooms are positioned behind a wall behind the bed. Most have showers; room 4 has a bath. All rooms face on to the inner courtyard, which has a trickling fountain & planters filled with lavender. There's 1 family room that can sleep 4. All are equipped with flat-screen TV with DSTV, hairdryer, minibar, & a tea/coffee station. There's no AC to save energy. Nice touches include complimentary snacks, including welcome Ferrero Rocher chocolates.

There's free Wi-Fi everywhere, but it's slower in the rooms. A laundry service is available. The b/fast is organic continental. No lunch or dinner is provided, but complimentary tea & coffee are available all day – there's an espresso machine in b/fast room. Lovely. **$$$**

🏠 **Sam's Giardino** (9 rooms) 89 Anton Lubowski Av, Kramersdorf; 📞064 403210; e reservation@giardinonamibia.com: www. giardinonamibia.com. If you want somewhere quiet with personalised service, this kooky Swiss-run B&B is just 10–15mins' walk east of the town centre. Sam Eggar, the owner, doesn't accept groups & loves to chat with guests. The rooms are simple & airy, with pine-clad ceilings & wicker furniture to match, plus en-suite shower, phone & hairdryer. Almost all the rooms overlook the well-kept garden that gives the pension its name, which has sun-loungers & a mini bridge spanning a carp pond. There's secure parking & a security guard on duty at night; laundry is available & there's free Wi-Fi in the main areas.

At b/fast expect candles & Wagner, with real Swiss muesli & the warmth of an open fire to offset Swakopmund's famed morning mists. There are books aplenty, & a TV lounge with a selection of natural history videos. In the evenings, Sam will lay on a 5-course set meal (*N$250 pp*) at 19.30 – you can choose to have fewer courses, if you want – with the help of local staff whom he has trained in European cuisine & service; the small restaurant makes a surprisingly romantic setting for dinner. But his real passion is for wine – he offers tastings if you book ahead (*min 2 people*). This is a highly individual pension that is a little tired around the edges, but would appeal to anyone seeking privacy. **$$$**

🏠 **Villa Margherita** [Map, page 280] (8 rooms) 34 Daniel Tjongarero St; 📞064 402 991; m 081 332 429; e info@villamargherita.com.na; www. villamargherita.com.na. Dubbed 'the charming house' by its Italian owners, Villa Margherita lives up to its name: a beautiful colonial house built in 1913 & lovingly looked after. Its stylish en-suite rooms are all slightly different, with 3 upstairs in the main house itself, & 5 others in a newer wing outside. Large block-colour paintings adorn the walls, with a mix of antique & contemporary artwork. Rooms have king- or queen-size beds, a flat-screen DSTV, safe, hairdryer & free Wi-Fi, with personal laptops to be provided. Most rooms have a private lounge area, too, or you can curl up in the communal living room, with a large fireplace & a selection of books. There's also the Il Tulipano apt out the back with living room & modern kitchen. There's also a small leafy garden

with fountain where b/fast is served in the summer. The intimate b/fast/dining room is also used for lunch (🕐 *12.30–14.00*) & dinner (🕐 *18.00–20.00*) with an organic à la carte menu (**$$$$**). Massages are available at the on-site spa room. A stay here will give you quality & professional service in a beautifully designed setting. **$$$**

🏠 **Meike's Guesthouse** (8 rooms, 1 apt) 23 Windhoeker St; 📞064 405863; e meike@ africaonline.com.na; www.meikes-guesthouse. net. It's easy to spot this eco-friendly guesthouse thanks to the guinea fowl painted on the outer wall – Meike is a fan of the bird & you'll see her devotion stretches all the way to the napkin rings! This bright, modern guesthouse is about 5mins' walk from the centre of town & has 5 dbls & 3 family rooms. All are simple & tastefully decorated, with en-suite shower, flat-screen TV, fridge & a small terrace in front. There's also a seaside-themed self-catering apt sleeping 4. B/fast is a generous German buffet. This is very much a personal B&B run on traditional lines. Free Wi-Fi & 1 computer terminal for guest use. **$$$**

🏠 **Secret Garden Guesthouse** (11 rooms) 36 Bismarck St; 📞064 404037; e sgg@iway.na; www.secretgarden.com.na. Just 500m from the beach, & close to the centre of town, this attractive, terracotta-painted guesthouse is run by the slow-to-warm-up Peter Odendall & has en-suite rooms – 6 standard dbls & 2 suites – that look over the lush palm-shaded garden courtyard that gives the guesthouse its name; a further 3 'comfort' rooms are located in a private garden. Modern & well appointed, with soft blue-&-white furnishings reminiscent of the seaside, each has tiled or wooden flooring, coffee/tea facilities & hairdryer, & underfloor heating in the bathroom. Suites have a kitchenette, 4 beds, TV, free Wi-Fi & AC. In addition to a spacious lounge with DSTV, there's a b/fast room with honesty bar. Laundry costs N$70/5kg. The adjacent bistro serves guests with a huge choice of wood-fired pizzas in the evenings (🕐 *17.00–22.00 Mon–Sat*; **$$$**). 9 secure parking spaces are available & transfers to & from the airport & station are offered free of charge. **$$**

North and east of town
Map, page 277.

☀ 🏠 **Beach Lodge** (19 rooms) 1 Stint St; 📞064 414500; e reservations@beachlodge.com. na; www.beachlodge.com.na. The architects have excelled themselves here! Each room forms part of a boat-shaped building that occupies a stunning site right on the beach 5km from town in the Vogelstrand neighbourhood. Rooms are named after shipwrecks on the Namibian coast & are light, airy & stylish with en-suite shower &/or bath, floor-to-ceiling sliding doors on to a patio or a private balcony area with sweeping sea views, desk with glass strip filled with sand & shells, DSTV & direct-dial phone. Fireplaces are found in 9 of the rooms, but all have heaters (very useful in winter) & 5 family rooms have small kitchenettes. Luxury rooms have free-standing baths. The b/fast room doubles as the Wreck restaurant (see page 288). The atmosphere is one of shipshape efficiency rather than personal care, so it's well suited to those seeking absolute privacy & relaxation. Gated parking spaces are allocated to your room name. Free Wi-Fi. **$$$$**

🏠 **Desert Breeze Lodge** (13 rooms) Riverside Av; 📞064 406 236; e info@ desertbreezeswakopmund.com; www. desertbreezeswakopmund.com. Owned by the creators of The Stiltz (see page 282), Desert Breeze is a collection of eco-chalets spread along the granite cliffs, overlooking the dunes, on an (as yet) unnamed road in the eastern suburbs of Swakopmund. The town centre feels a million miles away as you enter the grounds that are dotted with cacti & carved statues. The earth-coloured walls of the chalets are almost camouflaged against the sandy backdrop of the desert save for one blue, orange or lime-green wall to set them apart. The standard rooms feature dbl or twin beds that are positioned on a slightly raised level & angled to look out over the dunes through a large corner window – the views sitting up in bed are stunning. On a lower level is a sofa, rustic wooden coffee table & wood-burning stove, & the en-suite walk-in glass-block shower with open-plan toilet & sink. Each chalet also has a small, private terrace & comes equipped with a minibar, tea/coffee station, fan, digital safe, a solar-heated water reserve on the roof & an in-room Wi-Fi booster. There is 1 villa that features a large open-plan dining room & lounge with wood-burning stove & L-shaped wicker sofa. Leading off from this central area are the 2 rooms, 1 en suite.

The main area features a spacious reception area, & – up a flight of stairs – the open-plan lounge & b/fast room whose pièce de résistance

is panoramic windows overlooking the dunes & a viewing deck with stove for colder nights. A waterhole is due to be built & the cliffs up-lit at night, so guests can watch the wildlife. Reception can organise activities via Living Desert (see page 310) & airport transfers. **$$$$**

🏠 **Sea Breeze** (7 rooms, 4 self-catering flats) 48 Turmalin St; 📞064 463348; e seabre@iafrica. com.na; www.seabreeze.com.na. Sadly, the sea views that gave this guesthouse its name originally have been obscured by construction of a few properties. However, the warm welcome offered by owners Bennie & Charlot more than compensate. Lovingly looked-after en-suite rooms are named after precious stones & decorated tastefully & smartly with corresponding colour schemes. Flats have a bedroom, lounge/kitchenette with TV, international-style plugs, bathroom & balcony; some have up to 5 beds, & all have heating. Paintings by local artists adorn the walls, & if you feel like splashing out, a champagne b/fast is available on request.

Outside is secure parking & garage spaces for up to 11 vehicles at no extra charge. There's free Wi-Fi throughout & Charlot runs a small curio shop supporting the Tsumkwe Bushmen community.

To get here, follow the beach road north towards Veneta along the Strand. The road becomes First Av, then eventually Fischreier; turn left into Turmalin St & Sea Breeze is on the left by the beach. It's about 4.5km from the centre of town, which represents a 45min stroll along the beach, or a 10min N$30 taxi ride. **$$$**

🏠 **Stay @ Swakop** (12 rooms) 173 Anton Lubowski St; 📞064 403 138; m 081 634 5212; e info@stay-at-swakop.com; www.stay-at-swakop.com. This large house is a new option in the peaceful eastern suburbs, a 3min drive from town, that offers clean, functional rooms in a mixture of sgl, dbl & trpl with flat-screen TV, tea/coffee, safe, but no AC. There's a roof terrace, but the views aren't very inspiring & b/fast costs N$65 pp. **$$$**

🏠 **The Alternative Space** (4 rooms) 167 Anton Lubowski Av (cnr Alfons Weber St); 📞064 402713; m 081 300 9352; e nam00352@mweb. com.na; www.thealternativespace.com. One of a kind, this Greek-style boutique guesthouse is owned (& was built) by your hosts Sibylle & Frenus & is located in a quiet neighbourhood 15mins' walk due east of the town centre. Having started life as an 'off-the-wall' backpackers' lodge, it now has 4 luxury rooms with off-street parking. An architectural gem, the rooms are minimalist, simple & clean with exposed wooden beams, lots of white, en-suite shower & toilet, & 3 feature romantic antique free-standing baths, including 1 that sits outside beneath the bougainvillea. Complimentary wine & chocolate bars are a nice touch. B/fast is semi-self-service (you can boil your own eggs to perfection) & guests can use the kitchen to prepare other meals. Above the kitchen is a library. The atmosphere remains as relaxed as ever, Namibian art adorns the walls, braais in the central courtyard are a regular occurrence &, in the evening, you can gather in the communal lounge for a game of chess beside the open fire while reclining on one of the large Moroccan-style sofa beds or swaying in the hammock. The TV only plays 1 channel & the free Wi-Fi only works in the main areas, so the focus here is on enjoying the simple things in life: good conversation, a drink from the ice-box honesty bar, & access to a wide-ranging music collection. It's certainly one of the quirkiest & coolest locations in Swakopmund. $$$

🏠 **Vogelstrand** (6 rooms) 33 Tsavorite St; 📞064 403 287; m 081 611 4662; e info@ vogelstrand-guesthouse.com; www.vogelstrand-guesthouse.com. This friendly, simple-yet-elegant guesthouse, run by Stephen & Annalie Turner, is on the outskirts of Swakopmund. From the town centre pick up Moses Garoëb St & drive north, turning left into Dr Schwietering St, left into Rose Quartz St & left again into Tsavorite St. Vogelstrand will be on your left. It has small but clean rooms including a larger dedicated family unit. Facilities include DSTV, a fridge, tea & coffee, & in-room snacks. The outside areas are large & pleasant, with picnic tables. Security is good with off-street parking & rooms all have individual alarms. Dinner is available on request (guests can ask for a braai), as are lunch or lunch packs. $$$

Backpackers' lodges
Map, page 277.

🏠 **Dunedin Star** (27 rooms) 50 Daniel Tjongarero St (cnr Windhoeker St); 📞064 403437; e bookings@dunedinstar.com; www.dunedinstar. com. Named after the ship involved in the Skeleton Coast's most famous wreck in 1942 – & the same rust red colour – the Dunedin Star is just 5mins' walk from the centre of town. It has simple, no-frills

en-suite sgl, dbl & trpl rooms with safes on the wall. There is a small garden, a bar & a laundry service (N$80/bag), & massages on request at reasonable prices. Given the main road location, it's fortunate that most rooms are at the back, so reasonably quiet, & that there's secure parking. There's free Wi-Fi in the main areas & a book exchange in the b/fast room. N$420/570 sgl/dbl. $$

🏠 **Skeleton Beach Backpackers** (9 rooms, camping) 14 Moses Garoëb St; 📞061 259 485; m 081 287 7420; e magicbus@iafrica.com.na. Newest backpackers with 6 dbls & 3 dorm rooms (1 8-bed, 1 6-bed) with fresh décor, low beds & lovely en-suite showers with stone tiles. There's a small communal kitchen, a lounge with big flat-screen TV & free Wi-Fi that looks on to a garden with a brick-built braai & a few plastic tables & chairs, & lots of gated parking. There are 4 shaded camping spots for small tents. Laundry N$50/kg; dorm N$120; camping N$80 pp. $$

🏠 **Desert Sky** (10 dorm beds, 5 dbl rooms, 2 family rooms, camping) 35 Anton Lubowski Av; 📞064 402339; m 081 210 6779; e info@ desertskylodging.com; www.desertskylodging. com. This centrally located backpackers' hostel not far from the beach is one of the most popular in town, & it is easy to see why. It's welcoming & helpful, the atmosphere is friendly, & facilities are good. In addition to 3 clean, cheerful 3-, 4- & 8-bed dormitories & private rooms, are a fully equipped kitchen, storage lockers & safe, plus central coffee & tea area & TV lounge. A laundry service is available. Outside is safe parking & a small grassed area for 2/3 tents. If you're after action, this is also a pretty good place to come for advice. Phonecards are sold at reception, unlimited Wi-Fi costs N$30, & laundry costs N$25/kg. Dorm bed N$150; camping N$220 pp. $

🏠 **Villa Wiese** (36 dorm beds, 8 rooms) Cnr Theo-Ben Gurirab Av & Windhoeker St (entrance on Windhoeker St); 📞064 407105; e bookings@ villawiese.com; www.villawiese.com. This colourful old building on the outskirts of town is named after the German who built it in 1905. A friendly option with plenty of atmosphere, its facilities include a lounge with white piano & a book exchange, a rather dirty & dark self-catering kitchen (⏰ 11.00–23.00), a large & lively upstairs bar (⏰ 15.00–23.00) with free Wi-Fi & board games, laundry service (N$80/bag) & lockers in the rooms. Each dormitory has 4–5 beds (with bedding but no towels) on 2 levels, & its own passably clean shower & separate toilet, while dbl rooms (fully equipped) are all en suite. Outside there's a BBQ in a pleasant courtyard, & secure parking. They can arrange trips. A bacon & eggs b/fast costs N$50. *Dorm bed N$160.* **$**

Restcamps and campsites

Map, page 277.

⌂ Swakopmund Municipal Restcamp (200 chalets) ☎064 401 4618; e restcamp@ swkmun.com.na; www.swakopmund-restcamp. com;
⊕ office 07.30–22.00 daily. On the north side of the road that crosses the Swakop River to Walvis Bay, this huge old restcamp is quite an institution. Packed closely together inside a large electric fence, its chalets & bungalows vary from tiny fishermen's cabins, whose cramped beds in minute rooms have changed little in the last decade, to luxury VIP flats with modern décor & bright pastel colours.

There's a rolling programme of modernising the restcamp, which at present supplies linen but not towels; pans & cutlery can be borrowed from the storage hut (⊕ 07.30–16.30 Mon–Fri, 08.00–11.00 Sat–Sun) for free. The flats are fine & simple, with the luxury flats being larger, but otherwise similar.

The A-frame chalets have a much more interesting design, & their wooden construction is warmer in the winter than the others – though all the beds in these are sgls. All are good value, provided you don't mind getting lost in the maze of other identical chalets while you search for your own. The camp has its own restaurant serving dinner from 16.00 to 22.00. Room safes can be hired from reception for N$10/day. No Wi-Fi. Credit cards accepted. *2-bed N$387–468; 4-bed N$691; 'A' frame to resthouses N$805–1,002; key deposit N$150–300.* **$–$$**

Å Tiger Reef Campsite (23 sites) Strand; ☎064 400 935; m 081 791 0133; e campsite@ lighthousegroup.com.na; www.goingwhere. co.za/tiger-reef. In the south of town, close to the beach, this revitalised campsite has 23 lapa-style covered camping areas each with their own private ablution block & arranged around a circular green lawn with a greenery-lined brick pathway running the circumference. There's a pool, free Wi-Fi picked up by the chalets closest to reception & lots of other plans in store. The popular Tiger Reef Beach Bar (see page 290) is a great place to while away afternoons & evenings. Alternatively, C J Horn, the manager, can arrange a host of activities from skydiving & paragliding to sandboarding & fishing. *N$90 pp + N$220 site, N$70/car.* **$**

✗ WHERE TO EAT AND DRINK *Map, page 280, unless otherwise indicated.*

Swakopmund's café culture has exploded in recent years. There are plenty of innovative, high-quality options acting as fuel stops during sightseeing.

✳ ✗ 22 Degrees South 111 The Strand; ☎064 400 380; ⊕ 11.30–15.00 & 18.00–21.00 Tue–Sun. This is one of the few restaurants in the world housed inside a lighthouse – one dating from 1904, no less. It's run by Italian Silvio & his Namibian wife Esbi who prepare some of the best food – let alone Italian – in town, because everything is homemade. There's a narrow dark wood bar for cocktails & then guests are escorted to one of 2 intimate dining rooms either side of the main entrance. You can't make a wrong choice from the menu, but recommended is the handmade ravioli, any of the wood-fired pizzas & the gorgeous gelato. $$$$$
✗ Cosmopolitan 37 Daniel Tjongarero Av; ☎064 400 133; ⊕ 16.00–late Mon–Sat. We didn't have a chance to try it, but this luxury restaurant/ lounge bar claims to have the best sushi in town, plus a very good cocktail bar (see page 289). $$$$$

✗ Erich's 21 Daniel Tjongarero Av; ☎064 405141. ⊕ 18.00–late Mon–Sat. Despite various changes in management, Erich's has stood here for nearly 30 years thanks to its reputation for well-presented fish & Namibian game dishes, & a generally innovative menu. $$$$$
✗ Hansa 3 Hendrik Witbooi St; ☎064 414200; ⊕ noon–14.00 daily, 18.30–21.00 winter, 19.00–21.30 summer. The award-winning European restaurant at the Hansa serves stylish, elaborate & quite heavy cuisine – using lots of sauces – in quite formal surroundings. It majors on seafood, though has a good range of steaks & a couple of vegetarian dishes. Its selection of South African wines is impressive, with bottles averaging around N$150–180 each, from some good vineyards. Reservations essential. $$$$$
✗ The Tug [Map, page 277] The Strand; ☎064 402356; ⊕ dinner 18.00–22.00 (sundowners from

17.00) daily, lunch noon–15.00 Sat–Sun only. Without doubt the most interesting place to eat in Swakopmund, The Tug is just that – an old tug raised up above the seafront next to the old jetty. The terrace is a great place to watch the surf as the sun goes down. The menu is among the best in town & majors in seafood, in a style that's lighter & less traditional than the Hansa's restaurant. The wines are undistinguished & a little expensive, but the place is always full & booking is essential. $$$$$

✖ **The Wreck** [Map, page 277] 1 Stint St; ☎064 414 500; www.the-wreck.com; ⏰ 18.00–21.30 Mon–Sat, noon–15.00 Sun. The restaurant at Beach Lodge (see page 284) continues the ship theme that defines the lodge, with floor-to-ceiling windows looking out to sea, from which you can spot the occasional surfer. With excellent, friendly service & candlelit tables, the atmosphere is suited to couples, but families & groups eat here too. The reasonably priced menu has a range of delicious game, seafood, pasta & curry dishes, plus a children's menu. Beautifully presented food features quality ingredients with interesting flavour combinations. It may be a short drive from the town centre, but this place is worth it – it's one of Swakopmund's best. $$$$$

✖ **Bistro Zum Kaiser** 4 Sam Nujoma Av; ☎064 416 136; ⏰ 06.30–20.00 Mon–Sat, 06.30–14.00 Sun. The restaurant of the Hotel Zum Kaiser (see page 279) sits beside it as a separate building. Decked out in calming dark woods & with a portrait of the Kaiser above the fireplace, it serves a continental & English buffet b/fast until 10.00 that's open to nonguests as well. After that, it's posh pub fare such as gourmet sandwiches, game steaks, seafood & salads – be sure to try their Malva pudding for dessert. $$$$

✖ **Bits 'n' Pizzas** 30 Daniel Tjongarero Av; m 081 726 3126; ⏰ 11.00–14.00 & 16.00–21.00 Tue–Thu, 11.00–14.00 & 16.00–22.00 Fri–Sat, 16.00–21.00 Sun. Take-away or sit-in pizzeria with very good wood-fired pizzas (with the option of gluten-free bases when the flour is available), pastas, salads & a few meat & fish dishes. $$$$

✖ **Kücki's Pub** 22 Tobias Hainyeko St; ☎064 402407; www.kuckispub.com; ⏰ 18.00–late daily. A bit of an institution, this spit & sawdust-style pub has a lively atmosphere & serves very good food despite the motto: 'Hot beer, lousy food, bad service – welcome'. The shellfish is excellent & the service friendly, & there are kids' options. It

is German in character, though there are always visitors around. Tables are situated both on the ground floor & upstairs. Do book in advance, as it's often full. $$$$

✖ **Swakopmund Brauhaus** The Arcade; ☎064 402 214; ⏰ 10.00–15.00 & 17.00–21.30 Mon–Fri, 10.00–15.00 & 18.00–21.30 Sat, 18.00–21.30 Sun & public hols. Authentic German tavern-style bar & restaurant dishing up German classics. $$$$

✖ **Lighthouse Pub & Restaurant** The Mole; ☎064 400894; ⏰ 11.00–23.00 daily. Good for sundowners overlooking the sea, the large restaurant here adjoins an equally large bar. You can eat outside on the wooden terrace with magnificent sea views, or there are tables inside for cooler periods. With everything from a seafood platter to charcoal grills & burgers, prices vary considerably, but one reader found standards were slipping & the service lackadaisical. $$–$$$$

✖ **N'Amigos** Cnr Nathaniel Maxuilili St & Daniel Tjongarero Av; ☎064 406 711; ⏰ 17.00–late Mon–Sat. Cheap & cheerful Mexican offering nachos, burritos, chimichangas & steaks. $$$

✖ **Pizzeria & Western Saloon** 8 Tobias Hainyeko St; ☎064 403925; ⏰ 17.00–late Mon–Sat, 17.00–21.00 Sun. With 2 separate shopfronts, but run by the same team. Despite the name, the Western Saloon serves neither burgers or hotdogs, but classic German fare. $$

Cafés and light meals
Map, page 280, unless otherwise indicated.

⌨ **Café Anton** Schweizerhaus Hotel, 1 Bismarck St; ☎064 400 331; ⏰ 06.30–19.00 daily. In comparison with Swakopmund's trendy slew of new cafés, this classic is looking a little dated. However, the views of the Mole & the ocean, genteel atmosphere & excellent range of cakes & pastries – the cheesecake is delectable – make this a pleasant place for morning coffee or afternoon tea. There are also tables outside, under the palm trees. $$$$

✳ ⌨ **Stadmitte Café** Cnr Woermann St & Tobias Hainyeko St; ☎064 400 893; ⏰ 07.30–17.30 Mon–Fri, 08.00–14.30 Sat & public hols. Parodying the green Starbucks logo, this chic & popular café has an unusual ordering system: order at the till, pay, take a number, find a table & they'll bring it to you. The open-plan kitchen does all-day b/fasts, burgers, toasties & has a separate sushi counter. At the back are a trio of computers where you can surf the internet for free. $$$$

Strand Café The Strand; ☎064 400 935; ⏰ 10.00–16.00 Tue–Fri, 09.00–16.00 Sat–Sun. Next door to the Kempinski (see page 281) – which has slightly obscured the view – this cosmopolitan open-air café has a large wooden terrace & a please-all menu of salads, steaks, fish, toasties & cake. $$$$

✳ **Bojo's** 13 Daniel Tongarero Av; ☎064 400771; ⏰ 07.00–17.00 Mon–Fri, 08.00–16.00 Sat, 09.00–15.00 Sun. Friendly eco-friendly café whose walls are festooned with black-&-white photos, paintings, quotes & coffee-related sayings. Locals come for the delicious cakes made with organic stoneground flour, very good coffee & filled bagels, pancakes & croissants. There's free Wi-Fi, but a donation to their sponsored charities is the decent thing to do. Some gluten-free options. $$$

Garden Café 11 Tobias Hainyeko St; ☎064 403 444; ⏰ 08.00–18.00 Mon–Fri, 08.00–15.00 Sat–Sun & public hols. Grassy knoll – albeit astroturf – tucked away behind the Art Africa shop with palm trees, a sandpit for kids & a lovely light menu of all-day b/fasts, salads, ciabatta sandwiches & Italian coffee – try their 'Red Cappuccino' made from Rooibos tea, cinnamon & honey. To access it walk through the shop, or go down the graffitied alleyway to the left-hand side, where local artists display their work. Great for families. $$$

Ice & Spice 11 Sam Nujoma Av; ☎ 081 360 7588; ⏰ 07.30–17.30 Mon–Fri, 07.30–14.30 Sat, Sun in summer. We visited the day before this new candy-coloured café's grand opening. German owners Friedrich & Liesl offer homemade ice creams & light lunches. A bougainvillea-covered outdoor terrace sits to the left-hand side & has patio heaters; they offer cocktails here in the evening. Free Wi-Fi. $$$

✳ **Wild Rocket** 37 Sam Nujoma Av; ☎064 461 046; ⏰ 07.00–17.00 Tue–Fri, 07.00–14.00 Sat, 09.00–13.00 Sun. Tucked behind the Autohaus Swakopmund, to the right of the Puma petrol station, this oasis is decorated in lavenders & greens. It specialises in healthy wraps, sandwiches & the only veggie b/fast in town – using organic products whenever possible. Homemade wholewheat breads, freshly squeezed juices & smoothies feature too. They also sell farmers' cheese, juices & jams, & every Wed from noon you can buy freshly delivered farm vegetables too. There are a few tables outside. Free Wi-Fi. Cash only. $$$

The Village Café 23 Sam Nujoma Av; ☎064 404723; ⏰ 07.00–17.00 Mon–Fri, 07.00–13.30 Sat. Next door to Café Treff, this popular & chilled-out place states that 'we open when we get here & we close when we go home'. Frequented by locals & with garden seating, it offers a range of coffees, sandwiches, milkshakes, cakes, waffles & pancakes to the sounds of Bob Marley. Free Wi-Fi. $$$

Café Treff Sam Nujoma Av; ☎064 402034; ⏰ 06.30–17.00 Mon–Fri, 07.00–13.00 Sat. Opposite the Nedbank, this bakery & take-away cake shop serves toasties, sandwiches & light meals, plus a good selection of ice creams, smoothies & teas. $$

Raith's Gelateria Tobias Hainyeko St; ☎064 404454; ⏰ 07.00–21.00 Mon–Thu & Sat, 07.00–14.00 Fri & Sun. Handy for a coffee, light lunch &/or ice cream after visiting the Swakopmund Museum (see page 293). $$

Slow Town 9 Altona Haus, Daniel Tjongarero Av; ☎081 127 7681; www.slowtowncoffee.com; ⏰ 08.00–17.00 Mon–Fri, 09.00–13.00 Sat. If you're in need of a caffeine fix, this place serves the best in town. It roasts its own beans in a warehouse in Swakopmund & offers varieties from Costa Rica, Ethiopia & Guatemala, as well as its own house blend, with a selection of cakes. The rustic interior is ideal for chillaxing thanks to the laid-back music, free newspapers & chessboard. Free Wi-Fi on the way. $$

Tea Time 9 Tobias Hainyeko St; ☎064 406 769; ⏰ 10.00–17.00 Mon–Sat. This classy, tiny teahouse has over 85 varieties from across the globe. Owner Brigitte Hartz makes cakes & soup to serve with them & you can browse the shelves lined with books. On the 1st Fri of the month she hosts screenings of French movies with English subtitles; tickets cost N$35 & include wine & snacks. $$

Beryl's Cnr Hendrik Witbooi St & Woermann; ☎064 403 963; ⏰ 06.30–18.00 Mon–Thu, 06.30–18.30 Fri, 06.30–17.00 Sat, 07.30–15.00 Sun. Need a fast food fix? This greasy spoon is frequented by local office workers who come for the cheap burgers. $

Bars

Map, page 280, unless otherwise indicated.

Cosmopolitan 37 Daniel Tjongarero Av; ☎064 400 133; ⏰ 16.00–late Mon–Sat. Upmarket cocktail bar also serving fine wines & cigars. On w/ends they have live music. They also have a good restaurant (see page 287).

♀ **Tiger Reef Beach Bar** [Map, page 277] Strand St; ⊕ 13.00–midnight Tue–Fri, 11.00–midnight Sat–Sun. On the beach, just beyond the aquarium, this is a popular spot for sundowners. Attracting a predominantly younger crowd, this still makes a great place to sit with your toes in the sand & watch the sunset.

ENTERTAINMENT AND NIGHTLIFE Swakopmund has a surprisingly lively nightlife, especially in the summer holiday season, although many travellers just have a few drinks in their hotel bar before retiring to bed. Then, around Christmas and New Year, many of Windhoek's more affluent residents arrive at their cool seaside cottages, intent on fishing by day and partying by night. For listings of all events, check the Namib I information board (see page 278) posted outside the entrance.

The 2-screen city cinema, **Atlanta** (⚲ *064 402743*) shows the latest Hollywood films, including those in 3D, and is based inside the Swakopmund Hotel and Entertainment Centre (see page 279). It has a shop selling sweets and hot and cold drinks in the foyer.

The annual 'Kuska' **carnival** is held on the last weekend of June with a parade of flotillas and lots of parties.

SHOPPING
Food and drink
Closwa Biltong [280 D2] 2 Tobias Hainyeko St; ⚲ 064 407 273; ⊕ 09.00–17.00 Mon–Fri, 09.00–13.00 Sat. Specialist biltong shop selling a huge variety from chilli beef to eland & oryx.
Pick 'n' Pay supermarket [280 E4] Sam Nujoma Av, opposite the tourist information office.
Shoprite Centre [277 C4] On the main B2 out of town, at its intersection with Windhoeker Street, this houses an FNB ATM, a fast-food take-away & Shoprite supermarket.

Super Spar Complex [280 E1] Cnr Tobias Hainyeko & Mandume ya Ndemufayo streets; ⊕ 07.00–20.00 Mon–Sat, 08.00–20.00 Sun & public hols. One of the town's most recent shopping complexes, it has a large Spar supermarket & a range of other shops offering everything from mobile phones to shoes.
WB supermarket [280 D4] Woermann Brock Mall on Sam Nujoma Av, near Bismarck St.

Clothes and equipment
Cymot [280 G3] 43 Sam Nujoma Av; ⚲ 064 400318; www.cymot.com.na; ⊕ 08.00–17.00 Mon–Fri, 08.00–noon Sat. Sells camping equipment, car spares & cycling gear.
Namibia Safari Boutique [280 D4] Sam Nujoma Av; ⚲ 064 403 391; ⊕ 08.00–13.00 & 14.00–17.00 Mon–Fri, 08.30–13.00 Sat. Sells all manner of safari clothing & accessories, including binoculars, knives, flasks, torches, etc.

Photo Studio Behrens [280 D3] 7 Tobias Hainyeko St; ⚲ 064 404711. 280 D3 batteries, does 1hr photo processing & will also carry out minor camera repairs. They stock a range of binoculars, too.
Safariland Holtz [280 E3] 21 Sam Nujoma Av; ⚲ 064 402 387; ⊕ summer 08.00–18.00 Mon–Fri, 08.00–13.00 Sat, 09.00–13.00 Sun, winter 08.30–17.30 Mon–Fri, 08.30–13.00 Sat, 09.00–13.00 Sun. Safari clothes & equipment.

Books and music
Die Muschel [280 E3] Brauhaus Arcade; ⚲ 064 402874; www.muschel.iway.na; ⊕ 08.30–18.00 Mon–Fri, 08.30–13.00 & 16.00–18.00 Sat, 10.00–18.00 Sun. A good selection of books & fine art, as well as the on-site Art Café offering coffee & cakes.
CNA [280 E3] Hendrik Witbooi St, next to Namib I. A branch of the South African chain; more mainstream than Swakopmunder Buchhandlung.

Swakopmunder Buchhandlung [280 E3] 22 Sam Nujoma Av; ⚲ 064 402613; ⊕ 08.00–17.30 Mon–Fri, 08.00–13.00 Sat, 09.30–12.30 Sun. Open since 1900, this oasis of peace has a reasonable selection of English-language books on Namibia, & some novels too, as well as stationery.
Young Ones [280 F3] 32 Sam Nujoma Av; ⚲ 064 405795. African music specialist.

Arts, crafts and souvenirs Swakopmund is filled with commercial art galleries and curio shops, particularly in the centre of town around Brauhaus Arcade [280 E3] off Sam Nujoma Avenue, and in the attractive Ankerplatz complex [280 D4] further down the road near the sea. Some of the best of these include The Art Gallery (064 404312) in Brauhaus Arcade, which specialises in Namibian (as against African) art, and in the same complex, African Curiotique (064 462 732) and Okaporo Curio Shop (064 405795; ⊕ *daily*). There is also a **curio market** around the lighthouse area [280 D2], with a good range of crafts on sale, though some are more authentic than others.

African Kirikara Arts & Crafts [280 D4] Ankerplatz, Sam Nujoma Av & Brahaus Arcade; 064 463146; www.kirikara.com; ⊕ 09.00–13.00 & 14.30–18.00 Mon–Fri, 09.00–13.00 & 16.00–18.00 Sat, 10.00–noon Sun (Brahaus Arcade 13.00–16.00 Sat–Sun). This is a first-class place to look for hand-woven rugs, made on the owner's farm Kiripotib (see page 178). It also has a range of crafts & gemstones, & makes jewellery.

Amber Moon [280 E3] Inside Namib I tourist office (see page 278). An independent craft shop which supports local industries & various nonprofit organisations by providing a platform for local people to sell their own handmade crafts.

COSDEF Arts & Craft [277 C2] New Industrial Area, cnr Einstein & Newton; 064 406122; www. cosdef.org.na. This non-profit organisation has a brand new centre (opened Nov 2014) where community members sell their crafts, such as beaded jewellery, leather purses & crochet. There's a restaurant, small Namibia food stalls, live shows on the stage & amphitheatre, & production units where you can see the crafts being made.

Deon Sibold [280 E3] Brauhaus Arcade; 064 404790; ⊕ 08.00–18.00 Mon–Fri, 08.00–13.00 Sat. Specialises in shoes, bags & belts.

Karakulia [277 B2] 2 Rakotoka St; 064 461415; www.karakulia.com.na. Karakulia has a shop in Brauhaus Arcade, off Sam Nujoma Av, but its workshop is just off the main road as you head north from Swakopmund, opposite the junction of

Tobias Hainyeko & Moses Garoëb streets. It's a very long walk, so transport would be useful! Here you can watch the whole art of spinning & weaving karakul wool (see box, page 32) into carpets & wall-hangings, as well as buy the finished products. You can even have designs made to order & then reliably shipped home for you. Karakulia has grown considerably since its inception in 1979 & now has around 50 employees, who also benefit from a programme of adult education.

Leder Chic [280 E3] Brauhaus Arcade; 064 404 778; ⊕ 08.30–13.00 & 14.00–17.30 Mon–Fri, 08.30–13.00 Sat. Leather suitcases & bags.

Namcrafts [280 E3] Brauhaus Arcade; 064 405910; www.namcrafts.com; ⊕ 08.00–18.00 Mon–Fri, 08.30–14.00 Sat–Sun. Beautifully crafted wooden carvings sold here come from local sources.

Namibian Jewellers & Arts Gallery [280 G3] 55 Sam Nujoma Av; 064 404525; www. namibian.jewellers.online.ms; ⊕ 08.00–13.00 & 14.30–17.30 Mon–Fri, 09.00–13.00 Sat. To the east of the centre, Michael Engelhard's modern shop & gallery features contemporary Namibian art & jewellery, with exhibitions changing every 6 weeks or so.

Swakop Arts & Souvenirs [280 D2] Next to Café Anton (see page 288); 064 402 942; ⊕ 10.00–18.00 daily. Fairly cheap & cheerful souvenir shop selling carvings, postcards, batik, magnets & jewellery.

Semi-precious stones are much in evidence in this part of Namibia, but two places stand out: **Kristall Galerie** (see page 295) and **Stonetique** (*27 Libertina Amathila Av;* 064 405403).

Antiques

Peter's Antiques [277 A4] 24 Tobias Hainyeko St; 064 405624; e petersantiques@yahoo. com; ⊕ 09.00–13.00 & 15.00–18.00 Mon–Fri, 09.00–13.00 & 17.00–18.00 Sat, 17.00–18.00

Sun. Perhaps the best antique shop in Africa, Peter's is a most comprehensive & eclectic collection. The owner, an intense Namibian of German origin, started the shop in the early extension of his hobby, & since ———ection, his reputation & the shop ————lly grown. Now he has a network of ————— all over sub-Saharan Africa, who buy & ship old African artefacts to Swakopmund. (Purchasers should carefully consider the ethics of such a collection before even considering making a purchase.) He also sells some new, cheaper arts & crafts that are produced specifically for tourists.

The shop is now quite large, & densely packed with all sorts of things. The smells of wood, skins & dyes that go to make the pieces pervade the place, making it instantly fascinating & slightly revolting. As well as tribal artefacts, Peter's has an extensive collection of antique books, many in German, concerned with Namibia's history. In recent years he has been involved with commissioning & distributing facsimile reprints of old books & maps, reproducing these manuscripts for future generations.

SPORTS

Swimming The city's municipal swimming pool near The Mole has closed and now all the action takes place at **Live It Health and Fitness Club** [277 B1] (*Welwitschia St*; ☏ *064 401 085*; *www.liveit.com.na*; ⊕ *05.00–21.00 Mon–Thu, 05.00–20.00 Fri, 06.00–19.00 Sat–Sun*), north of the city centre. Facilities include a heated swimming pool and saunas, gym, two squash courts, and a number of fitness classes. There's also the Fusion Health Café on site with free Wi-Fi.

Golf About 7km west of Swakopmund, on the main B2 road from Windhoek, Rossmund golf course (☏ *064 405644*; e *rossmund@iafrica.com.na*) is set on the northern banks of the Swakop River, backed by the dunes. The 18-hole, par 72 course is open to day members, who occasionally find themselves playing alongside the local springboks. The club has its own restaurant overlooking the greens, and the unremarkable **Rossmund Lodge** (☏ *064 414600*; e *roslodge@mweb.com.na*; **$$**), that's mainly aimed towards the business crowd, but it does have an inviting sculpted swimming pool.

OTHER PRACTICALITIES

Banks There are plenty of banks in the centre of town, many with ATMs. These include the Nedbank on Sam Nujoma Avenue, close to the tourist information office.

Communications With the advent of Wi-Fi, most of Swakopmund's **internet cafés** have closed down, but a few terminals remain inside Stadmitte Café (see page 288), or you could try **IT Solutions** at the Super Spar Complex [280 B1] (☏ *064 404 338*; ⊕ *08.00–18.00 Mon–Fri, 08.00–13.00 Sat; N$30/1hr*). If you want a local SIM card, or indeed a whole handset, try Coastal Cellular at the Super Spar Complex (☏ *064 405936*; m *081 128 3283*), or their other branch in Woermann Brock Mall.

The **Nampost post office** is on the corner of Tobias Hainyeko Street [280 D2] (⊕ *08.00–16.30 Mon, Tue, Thu & Fri, 08.30–16.30 Wed, 08.00–noon Sat*).

Emergency and health The police can be reached on ☏ 064 10111, the ambulance and Cottage hospital on ☏ 064 412200, and the fire service on ☏ 064 410411. For sea rescue services, call ☏ 064 404213 or the police – which is also the emergency number to use if you can't get through anywhere else.

✚ **South African Cottage Medi-Clinic** [277 C1] Cnr Haupt Av & Franziska van Neel St; ☏ 064 412200; www.mediclinic.co.za. Located north of the town, this is probably the 1st port of call for overseas visitors who are in need of urgent health care.

⊞ **Bismarck Medical Centre** [280 D4] 17 Sam Nujoma Av; 📞 064 405894; ⊕ 08.00–noon & 17.00–18.00 Sat, 10.00–11.00 & 17.00–18.00 Sun. For less serious illnesses. Has a pharmacy that's also open at w/ends.

✚ **Swakopmund Apoheek** [280 E3] Sam Nujoma Av; 📞 064 402825, a/h 📞 064 463610; ⊕ 08.00–18.00 Mon–Fri, 08.00–13.00 & 17.00–18.00 Sat, 10.00–noon & 17.00–18.00 Sun, 09.00–13.00 & 17.00–19.00 public hols.

Fuel and vehicle repair 24-hour fuel stations abound in Swakopmund. The best garage is Arno's Off-Road Centre on Hidipo Hamutenya Street ([277 C2] 📞 064 400300).

WHAT TO SEE AND DO Unlike most Namibian towns, there's plenty to do in Swakopmund. Below are a few attractions in town, but see also *Activities around the towns*, pages 309–18, for ideas in the areas surrounding Swakopmund and Walvis Bay.

The Mole [280 A1] If you only have a little time to spare, then wander down to the Mole. This was to be a harbour wall when first built, but the ocean currents continually shifted the sandbanks and effectively blocked the harbour before it was even completed. A similar 'longshore drift' effect can be seen all along the coast, at inlets like Sandwich Harbour. Partially because of this sandbank's protection, the beach by the Mole is pleasant (though watch out for jellyfish) and generally safe to swim from, if small and surprisingly busy at times.

Historical buildings As you might expect, Swakopmund is full of amazing old German architecture in perfect condition, some of the buildings now housing museums, art galleries or libraries.

Pre-eminent among these is the beautiful **Woermannhaus Building** [280 D4], in the centre of town just off Sam Nujoma Avenue, dating from 1894. For an overview of the town and its setting, you could do worse than climb the 93 steps up the **Woermann Tower** [280 D4]. The door to the tower is labelled as 'No Unauthorised Access', but from Monday to Saturday lawyer Percy Mushaninga looks after the building, so the door should still be open – climb the dusty stairs to the top for 360° views over town.

Also of note are the old **railway station** [280 G2], completed in 1901 and now the home of Swakopmund Hotel and Entertainment Centre, and the **old prison** [277 B2], on Moses Garoëb Street as it heads north out of town.

Guided 2½-hour walking tours of the individual buildings can be arranged in English and German with Frau Angelika Flamm-Schneeweiss (📞 064 461647; m 081 272 6693); prebook one at the Namib I tourist office (see page 278).

Alternatively, both the handout from the municipality itself, and the short book entitled *Swakopmund – A Chronicle of the Town's People, Places and Progress*, available at the museum, give descriptions and brief histories for some of the buildings.

For a guided historical tour of the city, see page 295.

Museums, galleries and libraries Swakopmund Museum ([280 C2] *Strand St*; 📞 *064 402046; www.scientificsocietyswakopmund.com;* ⊕ *10.00–17.00 daily, inc public hols; admission adult/child N$25/10, student N$20*) Situated in the old customs building, the museum was founded by Dr Alfons Weber in 1951. Something of a British Museum of yesteryear, it has exhibits on life in the Namib Desert and the South Atlantic, huge collections of insects and birds' eggs, an excellent section on rocks and minerals, and lots of information on the colonial German history in the region.

The main hall is dominated by a long row of taxidermy animals, such as zebra, cheetah, hyena and ostrich, with elephant and hippo skulls sitting to the side. Also in the entrance, on the left, is a section showing the history of the Hansa Brewery.

In the museum's newest wing, the 'People of Namibia' exhibition covers Namibia's indigenous cultures and, in the same section, there's a new permanent exhibition about Devil's Claw – a plant with anti-inflammatory healing properties used by the San Bushmen – with interactive video screens. There's also a re-creation of what old doctors' and dentists' surgeries must have been like. Frightening stuff.

Upstairs are archaeology exhibits, including a plaster cast of the skull of Otjisewa Man, thought to be 100,000 years old; the original sits in Windhoek's State Museum (see page 154).

Attached is Raith's Museum Café (⊕ 09.30–Mon–Fri, 09.00–18.00 Sat–Sun) selling ice creams and overlooking the beach.

Finally, on the first Friday of the month the museum arranges tours of **Rössing Mine** – the largest opencast uranium mine in the world. It costs N$40/30 adult/child and the proceeds go to the museum.

Sam Cohen Library ([277 B4] Cnr Sam Nujoma Av & Windhoeker St; ☏ 061 402695; ⊕ 09.00–13.00 & 15.00–17.00 Mon–Fri, 09.00–13.30 2nd Sat of month; admission free, research N$75/hr) Built in the 1970s to accommodate over 2,000 volumes of the Africana collection belonging to the estate of Ferdinand Stich, a local bookshop owner and collector, this private and peaceful library also houses a further 8,000-plus volumes encompassing most of the literature on Swakopmund, and has a huge archive of newspapers from 1898 to the present day (some in German, some in English). There's also a collection of old photographs and maps. It used be the case you could pop in for free, but they feel quite strongly nowadays that you should offer a donation. The entrance is on the left-hand side of the building.

Living Desert Snake Park ([277 B4] Sam Nujoma Av; ☏ 064 405100; ⊕ 09.00–17.00 Mon–Fri, 09.00–13.00 Sat; admission N$60/30 adult/4–6yrs) This privately owned snake park has been open more than 20 years and belongs to Stuart Hebbard. It boasts more than 25 types of Namibian snakes, lizards, chameleons, scorpions and other creatures, which is enough to satisfy even the most inquisitive child – or adult. The animals are kept under glass in two small rooms, where snake feeding takes place on Saturdays from 10.00 to 13.00 and, for N$60, you can have your photo take with 'Dodo' the python draped around your neck.

National Marine Aquarium ([277 A5] Strand St; ☏ 064 410 1214; ⊕ 10.00–16.00 Tue–Sun & hols; admission N$30/15 adult/child, student or pensioner) It's a cold fish indeed that isn't impressed by Swakopmund's gleaming new aquarium. Everything centres around the main tank that holds a staggering 320,000 litres of water pumped directly from the ocean and housing fish found in Namibia waters. The highlight is a walk-through tunnel with perspex ceiling, so you can watch massive dusky kobs, garrick, spotted gulley sharks and Atlantic spotted grunter swim overhead. Raised cabins with portholes, where kids – big and small – can lounge while watching the fish are inventive too. Feeding time at the main tank takes place daily at 15.00, and on Tuesdays, Saturdays and Sundays a diver goes into the tank to hand-feed the fish. On the upper floor there's open views of the top of the main tank and a small games area for kids featuring giant fish they can sit in and answer quizzes on embedded computer screens.

Kristall Galerie ([280 E1] *Cnr Tobias Hainyeko St & Theo-Ben Gurirab Av;* 📞 *064 406080; www.namibiangemstones.com;* 🕘 *09.00–17.00 Mon–Sat; admission N$20/12 adult/child*) This ultra-modern building houses what is claimed to be the largest-known crystal cluster in the world, estimated to be around 520 million years old and weighing over 14 tonnes. Displays include a 'scratch pit' (a fake outdoor rockery) where visitors – mainly children – can rummage among the piles of semi-precious stones and pick their favourites to take home (parents, you'll need to collect an empty bag from reception; small ones cost N$20, medium N$40 and large N$60), an exact replica of the original Otjua tourmaline mine – where the huge crystal was discovered – and a craft area with windows where you can watch jewellery makers at work: from sorting and drilling to designing and beading. And there's a shop, of course, selling expensive and glittering semi-precious stones in various guises. It's fun for kids and mums, and well worth a visit for anyone fascinated by geology.

Activities
Birding Tours Batis Birding (see page 309) offer half- or full-day tours; their qualified guides can help with special requests. Rates start from N$650 per person.

Camel rides See page 318.

Guided city tours
Historical Walk around Swakopmund The walk starts at the Swakopmund Museum at a prearranged time and lasts 2 hours. The guide will enlighten you on the early days on the Namibian Coast, with plenty of anecdotes. It costs between N$250 and N$300 depending on the number of people.
Operators: Historische Stadtfuehrungen, Panorama Cycle Tours – see page 310.

Tour of Swakopmund Yesterday, Today and Tomorrow A 1½-hour guided tour by car. It needs to be prebooked and requires at least two people. N$300 per person.
Operators: Charly's Tours, Kallisto Tours – see pages 309–10.

Township tours If you'd like to visit the townships of Mondesa and DRC, you'll be picked up at 09.00 or 15.00 from your accommodation to visit the market, traditional elders and the kindergarten. You will then take tea at a private DRC home, and have lunch at a *shebeen* with traditional foods including *mahangu*, mopane worms and wild spinach. It's a 4-hour tour and costs N$420 per person including snacks and drinks.
Operators: Hafeni Tours, Hata Angu Tours, Panorama Cycle Tours – see pages 309–10.

WALVIS BAY

Walvis Bay (meaning 'whale bay') seems larger and more spaced out than Swakopmund, although it's also quieter and slightly lacking in character. Perhaps Afrikaans was the dominant influence here, whereas German was clearly the driving force in shaping Swakopmund's architecture and style.

Most visitors still stay in Swakopmund, where they eat and relax, and venture down to Walvis Bay to go birdwatching, as there are a number of sites attracting huge flocks of seabirds and migrant waders, including the famous flamingos and pelicans. Even if you haven't much time, the drive on the Trans-Kalahari Highway between the two towns is an excursion in itself, for here is nature at its most elemental, as white rollers from the sea crash right into the **sand dunes** from the Namib Desert.

Although a small-town feel still prevails, Walvis Bay has changed fast in recent years, reflecting the town's expanding population and its increasing popularity with visitors keen to stay near the lagoon. Alongside lots of new development, both industrial and commercial, several new hotels, restaurants and bed and breakfasts have sprung up.

HISTORY The first Europeans at Walvis Bay came with the Portuguese navigator Bartolomeu Dias on the ship *São Cristóvã* in 1487, although at that time no formal Portuguese claim was made. Over the ensuing years, the territory passed through Dutch, British and South African hands until it finally became part of Namibia.

Although Namibia became independent in 1990, from 1990 until 1994 the port of Walvis Bay, and the enclave that surrounds it, remained part of South Africa – despite being surrounded by the newly independent country of Namibia. However, at midnight on 28 February 1994 the South African flag was taken down, and 5 minutes later the Namibian flag was raised here. This transferred the enclave to Namibian control and ended a point of contention between the two countries. Walvis Bay is strategically important as the coast's only deepwater port, and ceding control of it to Windhoek was a very significant step for South African politicians to make.

GETTING THERE AND AWAY

By air Air Namibia has daily flights between Windhoek and Walvis Bay; there's a 14.55 departure from Windhoek on Mondays and Wednesdays, with the return flight to Windhoek departing 16.05; and an 11.10 departure the rest of the week, with returns to Windhoek only departing on Tuesdays, Thursdays and Saturdays at 14.20. There are no flights between Walvis Bay and Swakopmund. The airport is located 11km to the east of town on the northern edge of the desert. A shuttle from the airport into the centre of Walvis Bay can be prebooked through the tourist information office in Swakopmund (see page 278) for around N$165 per person.

By train Walvis Bay is linked to Windhoek via Swakopmund and Karibib by the normal, slow train services. These run to and from Windhoek every day except Saturday, arriving in Walvis Bay at 07.15 and departing at 19.00. An economy ticket costs N$86. See *Chapter 6*, pages 98–100 for details, or call TransNamib in Walvis Bay (✆ 064 208505).

By bus Intercape Mainliner (✆ 061 227847) runs a good service linking Windhoek and Walvis Bay, which stops outside the Hickory Creek Spur restaurant on Theo-Ben Gurirab Street, close to 12th Road [299 F3]. This arrives from Windhoek at 13.55 on Monday, Wednesday, Friday and Saturday, and returns Monday, Wednesday, Friday and Sunday at 10.00, arriving in Windhoek at 14.45. Tickets cost N$230–300 one-way, and must be booked in advance. See *Chapter 6*, pages 101–2 for more details.

There is also a weekly Ekonolux bus (✆ 061 258961; e *ekonolux@iway.na; www. ekonolux.com.na*; N$695 sgl, N$1,390 return) between Cape Town and Walvis Bay, via Windhoek and Swakopmund. Timetables vary with the seasons, but typically buses run two or three times a week in both directions. In winter, buses depart around 10.30 from Theo-Ben Gurirab Street, arriving in Swakopmund at the Spar shopping complex at around 11.05, and in Windhoek at 16.00, before reaching Cape Town at 14.30 the following day. The return trip leaves Cape Town at 09.30, arriving in Swakopmund at around 11.30, and Walvis Bay at noon.

For reservations, contact Intercape or Ekonolux direct, or one of their agents (you'll need to go to their office in person). See also the Welwitschia Shuttle and Townhoppers (see page 276).

ORIENTATION Without Swakopmund's beautiful architecture or its buzz, Walvis Bay seems to have no real focus or centre for visitors. However, if you're a keen birdwatcher you'll probably base yourself here just for the lagoon.

Walvis Bay was built for its harbour, and its streets were originally numbered from there: 1st Street nearest the harbour, parallel to the sea, and 16th Street furthest from it. Similarly its roads are perpendicular to the harbour, starting with 1st Road in the south and continuing to 18th Road in the north.

These somewhat unexciting thoroughfares form a grid that is the city, and are easily navigable. Or at least would have been easily navigable if the planners had had a little imagination. Instead they stuck zealously to numerical names and, where roads were split, they coined names like 3rd Street North, 3rd Street West and 3rd Street East for completely separate roads. Now, to compound the problem, several of the street numbers have been changed to names. To add to the entertainment, Tom Swemmer Street and Civic Centre Street were both at one time called 12th Street. And 13th Street, 14th Street, Simon Luanda Street and Piet //Heibeb Street were all, at one time, called Hidipo Hamutenya Avenue. (Even with four sections of this street now renamed, there is still one section of Hidipo Hamutenya Avenue remaining!)

Since many people still refer to the original street names, the following may be useful:

6th Road *is now* Robert Forbes Street
10th Road *is now* Cyril Fernandez Street
12th Road *is now* Sport Road
13th Road *is now* Rikumbi Kandanga Street
18th Road *is now* Ana Mupentami Road
6th Street is now Peter Dixon Street
7th Street *is now* Sam Nujoma Avenue
8th Street *is now* Hage G Geingob Street
9th Street *is now* Theo-Ben Gurirab Street
10th Street *is now* Nangolo Mbumba Drive
11th Street *is now* John Muafangejo Street
15th Street *is now* Peter Mueshihange Street
Kuiseb Street *is now* Nathaniel Maxuilili Avenue
Oceana Street *is now* Ben Amathila Drive
2nd Street West *is now* JJ Cleverly Street
4th Street West *is now* Paul Vincent Street
5th Street West *is now* Frank Guthrie Street
8th Street West *is now* Fritz Lange Street
9th Street West *is now* Thomas Morris Street

GETTING AROUND Most visitors to Walvis Bay have their own transport, as the city's quite spread out and there's little in the way of local public transport. If you've no vehicle then walking is usually pleasant, and hitching is occasionally successful, even in town. Local boys, often wearing reflective vests, will offer to watch your car for you – you should tip them N$3–5 during the day and N$5+ at night when returning to your vehicle.

If you're hiring a car on arrival, or dropping one here, then try:

🚗 **Avis** Airport: 📞064 207527; town centre: 89 Hage Geingob St: 📞064 209633; ⏱ 08.00–17.00 Mon–Fri, noon–16.00 Sun

🚗 **Budget** Airport: 📞064 204 128; ⏱ 10.00–17.00 Mon, Wed, Fri–Sat, 10.00–15.00 Tue & Thu, 11.00–17.00 Sun; Pelican Bay Hotel; 📞064 204128

🚗 **Europcar** Pelican Bay Hotel; 📞064 207407

🚗 **Hertz** 📞064 209 450; m 081 127 9200; ⏱ 08.30–17.00 Mon–Fri

TOURIST INFORMATION

ℹ️ **Tourist office** [299 D4] Cnr Union St & 5th Rd; 📞064 200 606; m 081 868 8520; e booking@ walvis-info.com; ⏱ 09.30–17.00 Mon–Fri, 09.00–noon Sat–Sun & public hols. Has a variety of leaflets, free maps, souvenirs & can book accommodation. They also have a laptop under the stairs where you can surf the internet for N$20/30min or N$40/hr. Out the back, they have 3 self-catering dune chalets with kitchenette (*N$450 pp*); book through the mobile number above.

TRAVEL AGENTS AND TOUR OPERATORS

Chamore Travel Agency [299 D4] Cnr of Union St & 5th Rd; 📞064 206 003; e chamore2@iway.na; ⏱ 08.00–17.00 Mon–Fri. Books accommodation, flights, transfers & visas.

Ultra Travel [299 G3] 199 Nangolo Mbumba Dr; 📞064 207997; m 081 129 7997; e res@ ultratravel.net; www.ultratravel.net; ⏱ 08.00–17.00 Mon–Fri, 08.30–12.30 Sat. Can arrange dolphin tours, air tickets, cruises & act as Intercape bus ticket agents.

Sure Ritz Travel Swakopmund; see page 276

Loubser's Tours 📞064 203 034; m 081 128 7347; www.loubsertours.com. Offers multiday camping tours all over Namibia, Sandwich Harbour day tours & ½-day Welwitschia visit.

 WHERE TO STAY Walvis Bay doesn't have the variety of places to stay, or to eat, found in Swakopmund, although options have widened considerably in the last decade. There is the odd gem and, if you're looking for large, family self-catering units for a longer stay, then something here may be perfect for you.

In Walvis Bay
Map, opposite, unless otherwise indicated.

Hotels

🏠 **Pelican Bay Hotel** (48 rooms, 2 suites) The Esplanade; 📞064 214000; reservations 📞+27 21 430 5300; e res.pelicanbay@proteahotels.com.na; www. proteahotels.com. This imposing hotel right by the lagoon was opened in 2003. The light, lofty lobby, with fountains either side of the entrance, reinforces the architect's vision of sun, sea & sand. Rooms are sea-facing, furnished using a light lime-washed wood but somewhat lacking in individuality. All have en-suite bathroom/showers with AC, TV, phone, Wi-Fi & coffee-making facilities; some are interconnecting to make family suites, & there's one with disabled access. The elegant blue-themed Aquarius restaurant looks out across the bay. The Neptune coffee shop provides light snacks throughout the day & night. There's also a new Angelz Beauty parlour on site & free Wi-Fi throughout. **$$$**

🏠 **Protea Hotel** (58 rooms) Cnr Sam Nujoma Av & 10th Rd; 📞064 213700; e info@ proteawalvis.com.na; www.proteahotels. com. The original Protea has been significantly enlarged over the years, but still caters more to businesspeople than tourists. Its rooms follow the standard Protea formula: modern, carpeted twin-bed rooms with DSTV, facilities to make tea & coffee, direct-dial phones, AC, & en-suite toilet & bath with a powerful overhead shower. There are 4 wheelchair-adapted rooms, the Oasis restaurant which serves both buffet & à la carte meals, a lounge & an enormous car park round the back. In short, this is an efficient & comfortable if rather soulless hotel, in the centre of Walvis Bay. Free Wi-Fi. **$$$**

🏠 **Hotel Courtyard** (15 rooms, 3 family) Cnr 16 3rd Rd & J J Cleverly St; 📞064 213600; www. thecourtyardhotelwb.com. In a residential road just a few blocks from the harbour, the Courtyard is run by Kallie & Bernd & has a large & lively bar area with braai facilities inside & out. Everything is set around 2 grassy courtyards, shaded by a couple of sturdy palm trees. En-suite sgl, dbl & family rooms have direct-dial phone, satellite TV & radio-alarm

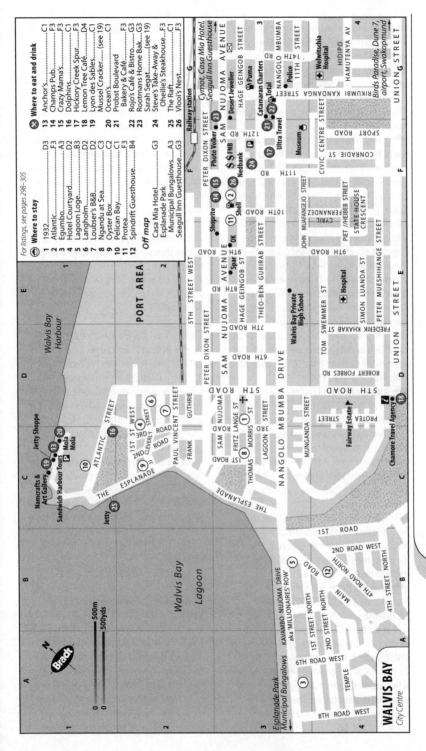

WALVIS BAY

WALVIS BAY
City Centre

PORT AREA

For listings, see pages 298–305

Where to stay
1 1932.................................D3
2 Atlantic..............................F3
3 Egumbo...............................A3
4 Hotel Courtyard..................D2
5 Lagoon Loge.......................B3
6 Langholm...........................D2
7 Loubser's B&B....................D2
8 Ngandu at Sea....................C3
9 Oyster Box..........................C2
10 Pelican Bay........................C1
11 Protea................................F3
12 Spindrift Guesthouse..........B4

Off map
Casa Mia Hotel....................G3
Esplanade Park....................A3
Municipal Bungalows...........A3
Seagull Inn Guesthouse.......G3

Where to eat and drink
13 Anchor's.............................C1
14 Champs Pub.......................F3
15 Crazy Mama's.....................C1
16 Dolphins.............................D2
17 Hickory Creek Spur.............F3
18 Lemon Tree Café................D4
19 Lyon des Sables.................C1
      Mussel Cracker........(see 19)
20 Ocean's..............................C1
21 Probst Boulevard
      Bakery & Café...................F3
22 Rojo's Café & Bistro............G3
23 Rootmans Home Bak...........G3
      Sarah Segat................(see 19)
24 Steve's Take-Away &
      Oheilie's Steakhouse.........F3
25 The Raft..............................C1
26 Vlooi's Nest........................F3

clock. Some have a microwave, coffee machine, kettle, cutlery & minibar/fridge (stocked if you wish). The furniture is sturdy & stylish, but kept to a minimum. It is certainly one of the better places in Walvis Bay, good value for money & close to the Raft restaurant – or dinner is available on request. There's secure parking, & dogs are welcome with advance notice. **$$$**

🏠 **Langholm Hotel** (13 rooms, 3 suites) 24 2nd St W; 📞 064 209230; e desk@langholmhotel. com; www.langholmhotel.com. This friendly, green-&-white-painted 2-star hotel with secure parking is owned by the welcoming Nic Adams, & is very near to the lagoon. Lime-green dbl & twin rooms are all en suite with white linens, a fridge (stocked on request), safe, tea/coffee station, direct-dial phone & DSTV, & free Wi-Fi is also available. Rooms 1–4 & 15 have baths instead of corner showers. The 2 luxury suites are lovely & one of them is suitable for a wheelchair user. There's a relaxing lounge with a bar (🕐 *until 22.00 every evening*), the ceiling of which is festooned with a huge assortment of hats (1,300 at the last count!) left by visitors. Don't sleep in so late that you miss the extensive b/fast. An à la carte dinner is available Mon–Sat. **$$$**

🏠 **Atlantic Hotel** (32 rooms) 128 Sam Nujoma Av; 📞 064 213000; m 081 128 4501; e reservations@atlantichotel.com.na. At the time of writing, major works were taking place in front of this newly renovated central option, which is just finding its feet. A light, tiled lobby leads through to the whitewashed restaurant with dark wood furnishings; there's also a separate bar area. Rooms have been enlarged throughout & feature DSTV, a large oval bath & shower, fridge, ceiling fans, tiled floors & new beds. The fittings are stylish & the large rooms give a feeling of space; if a proper hotel is what you are looking for, this might be the place for you. **$$**

🏠 **Casa Mia Hotel** (23 rooms) 224–228 Sam Nujoma Av; 📞 064 205975; e info@ casamiahotel.com. Behind the garish airbrick wall at the front, Casa Mia has smallish but modern en-suite rooms with DSTV, phone, tea/ coffee-maker & AC. The restaurant (🕐 *07.00– 21.30 daily*) has a good reputation but the menu is limited (*mains around N$90*), so don't come expecting modern cuisine. The Nautilus bar has a pool table & TV & there is a casino. Free Wi-Fi in the main areas. **$$**

🏠 **Ngandu at Sea** (20 rooms, 1 apt) Cnr 1st Rd & Thomas Morris St; 📞 064 207327; e theart@ iafrica.com.na. Although owner Oswald Theart is normally in residence at Ngandu Safari Lodge in Rundu, he views the Ngandu as his seaside home. Just a stone's throw from the lagoon, it takes as its theme the coastal location, with colourful murals & paintings by local artists.

Every room – dbl, twin, sgl & family – has an en-suite shower, & some have views of the lagoon. Dbls have DSTV, phone, tea/coffee-making facilities, fridge & fan. One room is self-catering, & a self-catering apt is a short walk from the main building. Free Wi-Fi in the main areas.

Lunch & dinner (on request) are served in the large, angular dining area complete with bar. Outside there is a pleasant courtyard festooned with pot plants. Run with Germanic efficiency & with 2 conference rooms for up to 40, this is a place that would suit businesspeople as well as holidaymakers. **$$**

Pensions, B&Bs and restcamps

✳ 🏠 **Pelican Point Lodge** [Map, page 274] (9 rooms) Pelican Point Peninsula; 📞 064 22 1281; e info@pelicanpointlodge.com; www. pelicanpointlodge.com. Marooned on Pelican Point Peninsula, a 45min drive by 4x4 from Walvis Bay town, this converted 1915 German lighthouse offers one of the most unique accommodation options in Namibia.

On the drive out, guests will pass the flamingo-laden lagoon & crashing waves popular with surfers, & on to the sandy spit, where the driver attempts to follow existing tyre tracks. It's almost impossible (& unsafe) to drive after dark due to the afternoon mists rolling in, but it feels like a real adventure.

The approach to the lighthouse is jaw-dropping as the full extent of your isolation hits home.

The staff ferry your bags inside & up to your room, while you're given a tour of the beach-chic interior, which is a contemporary & calming combination of teak wood, white polished concrete floors & cool blue-&-green walls. Each of the rooms is named after sea-themed items: Seal, Pelican, Dolphin & Lighthouse are situated on the 3rd floor & have superior views compared with Jetty, Lagoon, Ocean & Oyster, which are situated on the ground floor. Each is decorated with a panoramic photograph – taken locally – that corresponds to the room name. All feature crisp white linens, floor-to-ceiling windows looking out on the ocean, free-standing bio-fuel fires (not working at time of visit), a digital safe, laundry, tea/coffee facilities, complimentary bottled water & snacks. All have en-suite open-plan bathrooms with his 'n' hers sinks. A steel bucket is supplied beside the rainfall shower so guests can collect the cold water that runs out initially, so it can be reused. Fluffy bathrobes & toiletries are supplied. Rooms Ocean (*a dbl & 2 sgl beds*) & Oyster (*2 dbls*) can be used as family rooms. The 4th floor is dedicated to the breathtaking Captain's Cove which boasts 360° views & a wraparound deck with a spacious terrace decorated with wicker sun-loungers. It features a free-standing 2-person oval bath with nearby candelabra for romantic nights, a walk-in shower, a dbl bed & lounge situated on a lower mezzanine level.

The main area consists of a spacious open-plan lounge/restaurant/bar. On one side the all-glass window overlooks the beach, while the other is built up slightly so you don't feel completely exposed while snuggling on the sofas with the fire blazing. There's almost always relaxing music playing quietly, & there's a selection of board games & DVDs to play. High-speed Wi-Fi is available here when the generator is on (2hrs in the morning & 5hrs at night).

Considering the logistics, dining here is a real treat. B/fast, lunch & dinner are all served in the restaurant – a collection of 9 tables that share the same space as the lounge, so the vibe is very relaxed. B/fast is a smart buffet, a light lunch can be prepared on request, while dinner is always 3 courses with friendly & attentive silver service. You're offered a concise but sumptuous menu, usually with a choice of meat or fish, & there's a small but refined selection of wines – which must be ordered by the bottle. The bar is a homely wooden drinks cabinet in the lounge with a select offering – the waiter will mix anything he can for you. High-quality espresso machines are situated in the hall of the 1st & ground floors, so free coffee is available throughout the day. Nonguests can visit for lunch (not dinner), but it requires 3 days' notice at least.

Activities centre around going for long, windy walks along the peninsula to visit the numerous seal colonies & see sea birds, jackals & shipwrecks. A watering hole will be constructed in future to attract the jackals, so guests can view them at night. **$$$$$**

Egumbo (9 rooms) 42 Kovambo Nujoma Dr; 064 20 77 00; e info@egumbolodge.com; www. egumbolodge.com. An upmarket, privately owned B&B located on 'Millionaire's Row', an exclusive street of Walvis Bay town overlooking the lagoon & its resident flock of flamingos. Each of the rooms is named after wine farms in South Africa &, although each is individually designed, they all follow a similar colonial theme of dark woods, white walls & natural fabrics such as hessian carpet. They are all equipped with extra-length queen-size beds, espresso machine, flat-screen TV & free Wi-Fi. Rooms of note include room 1, 'Warwick', in the main house, featuring twin beds beneath a thatch roof, a free-standing claw-foot bath, a small balcony with a view of the lagoon, & an antique writing desk; room 9, 'Columella', with a 4-poster bed, writing desk, views of the pool from its terrace & large bathroom with a claw-foot bath & walk-in glass-screen shower; & room 8, 'Saxenburg', whose sunken shower/bath takes up the ground floor; the upper mezzanine level has a dbl sleigh bed & small balcony with a view of the pool.

The intimate main area has a lounge/ b/fast room with an open fire & old photos of Swakopmund hanging on the walls.

There's an outdoor rectangular swimming pool surrounded by smart sun-loungers & grass.

The manager, Katryn Smidt, is also the chef. Currently only b/fast is on offer, but she has plans to offer a Mediterranean-style dinner menu too. Until then, lunch & dinner are only available on request. **$$$$**

Lagoon Loge (8 rooms) 88 Nangolo Mbumba Dr; 064 200850; m 081 129 7953; e french@lagoonloge.com.na; www.lagoonloge. com.na. Using the French spelling of 'lodge', much to the puzzlement of the locals, this distinctive yellow building decked with flowers is owned & run by Helen & Wilfred Meiller. A must for bird lovers, it is situated right opposite the lagoon, with daily entertainment provided by flocks of flamingos & other waterbirds.

Wilfred's skills as a wood-turner are evident in the individually decorated rooms, each with a different theme. If you're into the seaside, then a large mural of Walvis Bay may suit your style, & if birds are your passion, ask for their bird room. There's also a family room. All are en suite, with TV, phone, & a balcony or terrace facing the lagoon. Facilities also include an unheated swimming pool in the secluded rear garden, & a roof terrace with deck-chairs & sweeping views of the bay. For dinner, consider a table at the excellent Lyon des Sables restaurant (see page 304), which is run by the Meillers' son, maître d' Virgile. There is the possibility of the Meillers selling up at the end of 2014/15 – so call beforehand & let Bradt know of any changes. **$$$$**

☀ ⌂ Oyster Box (12 rooms) Cnr The Esplanade & J J Cleverly St/2nd St West; ℑ 064 202 247; **e** info@oysterboxguesthouse.com; www. oysterboxguesthouse.com. Owned by Beate & Tibor Raith, the proprietors of Hotel Heinitzburg in Windhoek (see page 123), this intimate guesthouse replaces the Free Air Guesthouse that stood here formerly. It's situated just across the street from Walvis Bay lagoon & a short walk from the popular Raft restaurant (see page 304). The entire property follows a beach-chic theme, with lots of whites & photographs of shells hanging on the walls.

Bedrooms are modest in size, but feel luxurious thanks to soft grey walls & crisp white linens. White wooden headboards with built-in cubbyholes for books surround the very comfortable beds, & there's a white wooden wardrobe & a small desk. Other amenities include a flat-screen TV, AC & combi international & Namibia plug sockets. The stone-floored bathrooms are again all white, except for a bright red mirror above the sink. Room 5 is recommended for honeymooners; rooms 4, 5, 6 and 9 have a large corner bath & lagoon views.

The main areas are comprised of an open-plan lounge – situated to the right of reception – with a few tables & chairs & wicker sofas, & the b/fast room on the 2nd floor. It has large double windows overlooking the lagoon & is furnished with white wooden tables & black-&-white canvas deck-chairs. B/fast items are arranged attractively on a country-style dresser. A small lunch/dinner menu featuring quiches, steaks, etc, is available all day until 20.30 & there's also a small bar serving sundowners until 21.00. There's a wraparound terrace so guests can dine outside on warmer mornings. Secure gate parking is available for 4 cars at the back of the property & there's free Wi-Fi throughout. All Swakopmund-based activities can be booked through reception. **$$$**

⌂ 1932 (7 rooms) 26 8th St West; ℑ 064 274 850; **e** info@1932house.com.na; www.1932house. com.na. This original 1930s house was renovated by South Africans Peter Kroon & Michael Birch in

2010 & it opened a year later. In truth, apart from the parquet floors & dark wood antiques, there's little to give away its age. En-suite rooms – 3 dbl, 2 sgl, 1 trpl & 1 family – are light & airy & there are 2 self-catering apts attached for longer stays. Both have access to the cactus-studded garden with small swimming/splash pool, outdoor bar & braai area. Lunch & dinner can be prepared on request, but there's a spacious kitchen in the main house for guest use. Free Wi-Fi. **$$$**

⌂ Loubser's B&B (6 rooms) 11 3rd St W; ℑ 064 203 034; **m** 081 237 2339; **e** falou@iway. na; www.loubseraccommodation.com. This family home is rather shabby around the edges, but its rooms – 3 dbl, 2 dorms, 1 family room – are clean. Dorm rooms in the courtyard are equipped with a hotplate, fridge, DSTV, kettle, sink & en-suite shower; en-suite dbls have fridge, TV & lockers. Sometimes b/fast is included in the room price for dorms, it depends if smoky matron of the house, Lala, is in the mood! Otherwise she'll charge you N$25 for eggs & cereal. Her husband, François, runs activity-based tours (see page 298). Only for those on a strict budget. *Dorm N$130 pp.* **$$**

⌂ Seagull Inn Guesthouse (8 rooms) 199 Sam Nujoma Av; ℑ 064 202775. Despite the garish blue walls at the entrance, the Seagull has modern, light, en-suite rooms arranged around an inner courtyard studded with palms. They come with DSTV & wicker dressing table & chair. It's not terribly well organised when owner Andreas Soldan is not there, but the staff are friendly & it's good value, so perhaps worth checking out. Note that it's not to be confused with the excellent B&B of the same name in Swakopmund. *B/fast N$30 pp.* **$$**

⌂ Spindrift Guesthouse (8 rooms) 22 Main Rd; ℑ 064 206 723; **m** 081 625 3453; **e** spindrift@ iway.na. Run by Kim Jansen van Rensburg, this home-from-home option makes a lovely first impression thanks to its lush gardens, mature palms & the small wooden bridge, spanning a carp pond, that you have to cross to get to the property. The colourful rooms – 4 dbls, 1 twin, 3 family rooms – all have DSTV, tea/coffee & are decorated with paintings by Kim's mother – whose work is also on display at the Art Gallery on the Waterfront (see page 306). Rooms 1, 2, 3 & 7 have baths (some of them claw-foot). Communal b/fast table; lunch & dinner provided on request. There's free Wi-Fi, an L-shaped swimming pool & a couple of secure parking spots at the back of the property too. **$$**

Esplanade Park Municipal

Bungalows (27 bungalows) Esplanade;
064 206145; e esplanadepark@iway.na; www.
walvisbaycc.org.na; ⏰ office 08.00–13.00 &
14.00–17.00 daily. Situated past Hesko St on the
left, on the way south towards Sandwich Harbour,
this complex of quite smart, cream-coloured,
well-equipped bungalows faces the lagoon. Each
of the 1- & 2-bedroom bungalows (sleeping 3 or
5 people respectively), & the VIP one (sleeping
6) has a living room, toilet & separate bathroom,
& a proper kitchen with stove, fridge/freezer,
kettle, toaster, cutlery, crockery & glasses. They
also have outside braais, sinks & a private garage.
Bedding is provided, but towels & soap are not. It's
good-value accommodation, though it feels like a
restcamp & is not at all cosy. *1-bed N$450, 2-bed
N$700, VIP N$1,000.* **$–$$**

At Long Beach (Langstrand)

Some 19km north of Walvis Bay, on the B2 from
Swakopmund, is the area known as Long Beach,
or Langstrand. Once scarcely more than a handful
of houses, Long Beach has become the focus of
property developers, with houses of all styles joining
up the once-isolated resorts that flank the beach.
It remains very quiet out of season, but expect the
whole atmosphere to go up a few notches in the
main holiday periods, especially around Christmas
& New Year. With the development have come a
couple of places to eat, with a choice of The Burning
Shore or the more down-to-earth cuisine of the
restaurants at Long Beach Leisure Park.
Map, opposite, unless otherwise noted.

Protea Burning Shore (9 rooms, 1 suite)

4 4th St, Long Beach; 064 220 695;
e reservations.burningshore@protea.com.na;
www.burningshore.com. Don't be deterred by
it being part of the Protea hotel group – this
beachfront lodge is lovely. All the rooms are
named, not numbered, & beautifully decorated;
rooms Shiloh, Burning Shore, Wave Crest, Restless
Wave, Beach Camper, Peninsula & The Bay have a
sea view – Shiloh is a suite with jacuzzi & fireplace.
En-suite bathrooms all have shower, bath or
both, & one has its own fireplace & jacuzzi. Other
facilities include DSTV, safe, phone, coffee station &
free Wi-Fi, & there is a laundry service. Downstairs,
the lounge oozes colonial-style elegance,
overlooking an expanse of lawn & beyond to the

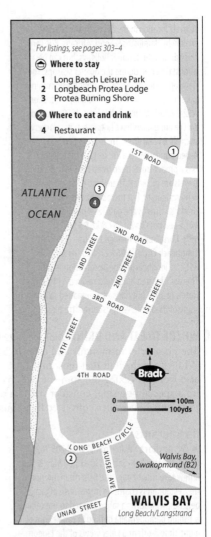

For listings, see pages 303–4

Where to stay
1 Long Beach Leisure Park
2 Longbeach Protea Lodge
3 Protea Burning Shore

Where to eat and drink
4 Restaurant

WALVIS BAY
Long Beach/Langstrand

13

sandy beach. The lodge also has a formal seafood
restaurant, Crayfish Creek (⏰ 07.00–21.30 daily;
$$$$$**), located next door. **$$$$

Dolphin Park [Map, page 274] (21

bungalows, house) 064 204343; m 081 143 1291;
e dolphinpark@iway.na; ⏰ office 08.00–17.00
daily (if no-one in, ring bell to left). Dolphin Park is
being expanded into a new housing development
right next to Long Beach. Although only a few
houses have so far been built, you can expect more
over the coming years. The original purpose-built
resort, with self-catering 2- & 4-person brick
bungalows with rounded black roofs, is located at
the extreme northern end of the development.

A lovely location in the desert by the sea, it is used mainly by Namibians & South Africans, & is very busy during the summer holidays, but can be almost deserted during the quieter seasons. The development was designed around a swimming pool complex (⏰ 10.00–17.00 daily; admission N$24/12 adult/child; 3 slide rides N$10) and slide. All the bungalows have hotplate, pots, crockery & utensils & braai drum. There are 2-bed bungalows, 4-bed bungalows & a VIP cottage that sleeps 6 & has a proper stove, deep freezer & DSTV. Bedding & towels are provided. There is no camping available & no restaurant, but there's a kiosk selling sweets, drinks & crisps by the gate. 2–4 people N$400–800; VIP 3-bedroom house N$1,800. **$$$**

🏠 **Longbeach Protea Lodge** (17 rooms) Longbeach Circle; 📞064 218820; m 081 738 8567; e longbeachlodge@proteahotels.com.na. This well-located lodge was taken over by Protea Hotels in 2007 but has so far managed to retain some of its charm. With its terracotta tiles & ochre-

patterned fabrics, it reflects the warmth & setting of the surrounding desert. Downstairs, a large lounge with veranda overlooks the beach, while above, dbl or twin en-suite rooms each have an all-important sea-view balcony too. Otherwise they vary: some have bath, some just a shower, & a few have both. TV, fridge, AC, coffee machine & direct-dial phone are all standard. There is free Wi-Fi, a small pool & braai area for guests' use, & lunch & dinner are available on request. **$$$**

⛺ **Long Beach Leisure Park** (120 campsites) 📞064 200163; m 081 124 3537; e bfernandez@walvisbaycc.org.na. Located at the far northern end of the Long Beach development, this campsite has spaces for both caravans & tents with electricity & water taps. Squeezed in between the desert dunes & the Atlantic, the location is lovely but the whole place is shabby & in desperate need of smartening up – a last resort, really. There's a play park & braai area on the beach, as well as yellow-&-blue picnic tables. **$**

✖ WHERE TO EAT AND DRINK *Map, page 299, unless otherwise indicated.*

The number of restaurants and cafés in Walvis Bay has burgeoned in recent years. While it's to the Raft that most first-time and regular visitors are drawn initially, it's also worth checking out some of the smaller or less well-known establishments. If it's a special occasion, consider making a reservation at Pelican Point Lodge (see page 300), housed in a converted lighthouse marooned on a sand spit across the bay.

Restaurants

✱ ✖ **Anchor's** Waterfront; 📞064 205 762; ⏰ 07.30–late Tue–Sat, 07.30–15.00 Mon & Sun. A new favourite of ours, the fisherman interior of this restaurant is charming mish-mash of picnic benches, windsurfing sails strapped to the ceiling, & fishing paraphernalia bathed in candlelight at night-time & offering killer views of the lagoon & jetty during the day. Its calamari come highly rated, there are excellent oysters & the chef's specials are certainly 'something to write home about', as the menu claims. They also do a b/fast menu (⏰ 07.00–11.00). **$$$$$**

✱ ✖ **Lyon des Sables** Waterfront; 📞064 221220; ⏰ noon–14.30 & 18.30–21.30 Mon–Sat. Relocated from an old church to the Waterfront, this is Walvis Bay's most respected restaurant. French chef David Thomas has been voted Namibia's best chef in 2010, 2011 & 2013 thanks to his high-quality & imaginative French cuisine. The dishes come beautifully arranged on the plate & taste as good as they look, if not better. Be sure

to leave room for the to-die-for desserts. Highly recommended – make a reservation. There's also an adjoining cocktail/wine bar for drinks before dining; wines around N$140/bottle. **$$$$$**

✖ **The Raft** Esplanade; 📞064 204877; www.theraftrestaurant.com; ⏰ noon–14.30 & 18.00–21.30 daily, except Sun low season. Built by the same team as the Tug in Swakopmund, this even more adventurous construction is a raft built on stilts in the middle of Walvis Bay lagoon, near the new Pelican Hotel. Food is very good, if relatively expensive, with seafood, salads & steaks making up most of the menu. If the house steenbras speciality is on the menu when you visit, it's strongly recommended, & vegetarian options are well worth trying, too. For a really sweet tooth, try the 'Absolutely Fabulous Chocolate Brownie'! At lunchtime, bring your binoculars & ask for a window table – the opportunities for birdwatching are such that you may just forget about your meal. Later on, the bar (⏰ 11.00–22.00 daily) is a great place to watch the sun sink into the waves, & is still the most stylish place in town. Free Wi-Fi. $$$–$$$$$

✕ Ocean's   Waterfront; ✆064 21 13 81; ⊕ 08.00–21.30 daily. Slightly rougher around the edges compared with Anchor's (see opposite), this place has a similar décor of fishing nets hanging from the ceiling, ropes coiled around supporting poles & a brick-pavement floor. The menu features a similar offering of oysters, fresh fish & light lunches, but it's worth consulting the specials menu scribbled on blackboards. Their Sunday buffet (*N$165 pp*), with lamb spit, is particularly popular. $$$$

✕ Crazy Mama's   138 Sam Nujoma Av; ✆064 207364. ⊕ noon–15.00 & 18.00–23.00 Tue–Fri & Sun, 18.00–23.00 Sat. Opposite the Shell garage, Crazy Mama's has an enthusiastic fan club of locals & travellers. It serves what some claim are the best pizza & pasta dishes in Namibia, & does a reasonable line in seafood, too. Second only to the Raft in appeal, but much lighter & less serious, it's good value with good service & very popular – so book in advance. $$$–$$$$$

✕ Mussel Cracker   Waterfront; m 081 494 6923; ⊕ 07.00–17.00 Sun–Tue, 07.00–21.00 Wed–Sat. Informal restaurant/coffee emporium that has rustic wooden tables, chairs made from whole slivers of wood & a book exchange. Their handwritten menu features a larger selection of b/fast options, seafood baskets, pizza, toasties, salads & tapas. There's a wine bar station, of sorts, & if you're just after a drink you can order there, instead of via a waitress. Great vibe. $$$

✕ Hickory Creek Spur   Theo-Ben Gurirab St, close to 12th Rd; ✆064 207990/1; ⊕ 11.00–23.00 Sun–Fri, 09.00–23.00 Sat. This lively upstairs chain outlet serves good American burgers, steaks & a host of side orders together with a salad bar, & children's menu. There's also a children's play area. $$–$$$$$

Cafés, light meals & take-aways

✳ ✕ Lemon Tree Café   Cnr Union St & 5th Rd; ✆064 206 959; ⊕ 10.00–19.00 Mon, Tue & Thu, 10.00–22.00 Wed & Fri, 09.00–15.00 Sat. Above the Pro-Shoppe golf store, it's easy to spot this lovely café thanks to its colourful blue/green exterior. Inside it's no less charming thanks to its surfer-esque vibe. It has free Wi-Fi & serves fresh juices, healthy wraps, gourmet burgers, good b/fasts & – best of all – plates of freshly made sushi: N$164 for 14 pieces. $$$$

✕ Steve's Take-away & Oheilie's Steakhouse 89 Theo-Ben Gurirab St; ✆064 205384; ⊕ 08.00–22.00 Mon–Sat. A locals' hangout with a surprisingly varied menu, from pies to T-bone steak. $$$

⌂ Probst Boulevard Bakery & Café   148 Theo-Ben Gurirab St (near 12th Rd); ✆064 202744; ⊕ 06.30–17.45 Mon–Fri, 06.30–14.00 Sat. Open since 1957, this licensed café & bakery is very popular with the locals, with seating inside & out, & a reasonably priced menu for b/fast & lunch. $$–$$$

✕ Dolphins   Cnr Atlantis & Esplanade; ✆064 205 454; ⊕ 07.00–15.00 Tue–Fri, 07.00–14.00 Sat–Mon. Popular beach-themed locals' coffee shop with seagulls hanging from the ceiling & a whale tail disappearing into the wall. They serve toasties, gourmet sandwiches, salads, cakes, good coffee & milkshakes. There's no Wi-Fi, but a few outdoor tables for when the weather is good. $$

⌂ Rojo's Café & Bistro   199 Nangolo Mbumba Dr (next door to Ultra Travel); ✆064 221739; ⊕ 07.00–15.00 Mon, Tue & Thu, 07.00–21.00 Wed & Fri. Busy, boisterous café serving burgers, toasties & the like. $$

⌂ Rootmans Home Bak   Sam Nujoma Av; ✆064 207916; ⊕ 07.00–17.00 Mon–Fri, 07.00–13.00 Sat. A simple, friendly place with outside seating & a wide menu featuring cakes, pastries, soft drinks & a selection of homemade jams & biscuits. $$

✕ Vlooi's Nest   Hage G Geingob St; ✆064 220157; ⊕ 07.00–17.00 Mon–Fri, 08.00–14.00 Sat. A smart, spacious venue with pine furniture, a carp pond & a broad menu, this friendly restaurant is tucked away in a small arcade, but worth finding for b/fast, lunch specials, good grills, & their popular salads. Eat inside or out under umbrella shade & try the genuine Italian ice cream for dessert. $$

Bars

🍷 Champs Pub   Cnr 6th St & 10th Rd; ✆064 209884; ⊕ Mon–Sat. DJ on Wed, Fri & Sat. Champs is a sports bar with a dance floor & there is strong local following. Popular both early evening & post-dinner.

🍷 Sarah Segat   Waterfront; ✆081 122 0181; ⊕ 10.00–02.00 Mon–Sat, 10.00–18.00 Sun. Best bar in town for sundowners, sold at locals' prices. Right down by the Waterfront, its porch has 360° views of the lagoon, there's live bands most Fri & Sat nights playing a mixture of rock, 80s & 60s music, & their Cheers-style square bar offers cocktail specials. If you get peckish they're happy for you to order in food from Mussel Cracker (see page 305) – just keep buying beers! There's a roof terrace in summer.

NIGHTLIFE AND ENTERTAINMENT Walvis Bay is quieter than Swakopmund. Try the bars listed on page 305 or ask local advice as to what's good, and take care if you're thinking of a club in one of the townships. Along Sam Nujoma Avenue, numerous seedy gambling houses feature banks of slot machines and little else.

SHOPPING With your own car, you are close enough to drive easily to Swakopmund, where the choice of shops is usually greater. However, there are a number of shops and services within Walvis itself.

Equipment

Cymot [299 G3] 136 Hage G Geingob St; ☎ 064 202241; www.cymot.com.na; ⏰ 08.00–17.00 Mon–Fri, 08.00–noon Sat. For camping equipment, car spares & cycling gear.
Anglers Kiosk Behind Caltex petrol station, cnr 8th St & 13th St; ☎ 064 206373. Fishing equipment galore.
Photo Volker [299 F3] 141 Sam Nujoma Av & Waterfront; ☎ 064 203015; ⏰ 08.00–13.00 & 14.00–17.00 Mon–Fri, 08.00–12.30 Sat. Has some camera equipment & can print digital images as well as processing film.

Food and provisions

Shoprite [299 E3] Sam Nujoma Av; ⏰ 08.00–18.00 Mon–Thu
OK Grocer [299 E3] Sam Nujoma Av; ⏰ 07.30–21.30 daily
Spar [299 E3] ⏰ 08.00–21.00 daily

Souvenirs

On the main street, Sam Nujoma Avenue, there are a couple of shops catering for the tourist market.

Art Gallery [299 C1] Waterfront; m 085 625 5791; ⏰ 14.30–17.00 Mon, 09.30–17.00 Tue–Fri, 11.00–14.00 Sat–Sun. Pick up something for the walls back home. It's located on the top floor, above Namcraft.
Desert Jeweller & Curios [299 G3] Sam Nujoma Av; ☎ 064 206 750; ⏰ 09.00–13.00 & 14.00–17.00 Mon–Fri, 09.00–13.00 Sat. Has an upmarket range of gifts & souvenirs, including woodcarvings.
Jetty Shoppe [299 C1] Waterfront; m 081 147 3633; ⏰ 07.45–17.00 Mon–Sat, 07.45–15.00 Sun. Sells sea-themed hats, fleeces & bags.
Namcraft Waterfront; ☎ 064 221 390; ⏰ 08.00–18.00 Mon–Fri, 08.00–17.00 Sat–Sun. Store of the famous chain selling lovely jewellery & other shiny knick-knacks.

SPORTS FACILITIES There is a 9-hole Fairways Estate **golf course** on the left of 18th Street before the lagoon. For details of fees for visitors, contact them on m 081 271 6950.

OTHER PRACTICALITIES Although there's a state hospital in Walvis Bay ([299 E4] ☎ 064 216300), visitors in need of treatment would be better advised to contact the private Welwitschia Hospital ([299 G4] ☎ 064 218911), which brought Namibia to worldwide attention following the birth of Angelina Jolie and Brad Pitt's baby, Shiloh, in 2006. Should you need a pharmacy, try Walvis Bay Pharmacy (*Sam Nujoma Av;* ☎ 064 202117) or the ABC Chemist at the Welwitschia Centre (☎ 064 202271).

In an **emergency**, the police are reached on ☎ 064 10111, the fire service on m 081 122 0833/0888 or m 081 922 from a mobile phone, and the ambulance on m 081 924 from a mobile. If you need any sea rescue services then call Namport control, ☎ 064 208 2221/2265, or contact the police – which is also the emergency number to use if you can't get through anywhere else.

The **post office** ([299 G3] ⊕ *08.00–17.00 Mon–Fri, 09.00–noon Sat*) is on the corner of Sam Nujoma Avenue and 14th Road.

WHAT TO SEE AND DO Most of the town's activities centre around the lagoon. There are some superb birdwatching opportunities both here and in the surrounding area (see box, pages 314–15), and a couple of highly recommended kayak trips in the lagoon and out to Pelican Point (see page 300). Boat trips from the yacht club take visitors out to see dolphins in the lagoon and beyond (see page 316). Alternatively, if you have a 4x4 you can also drive out towards Pelican Point around the lagoon, past the salt-works: a desolate track lined with salt ponds that have been reclaimed from the sea, inhabited only by seabirds and the occasional brown hyena.

Off the water, options are more limited. At the office of the Municipality of Walvis Bay, where local people make their utilities payments, the walls are covered in an intricate **bas-relief** of wooden carvings, showing, among other things, the mating dance of flamingos, desert life, sea life and human fishing.

WALVIS BAY LAGOON: A BLEAK FUTURE

Walvis Bay lagoon dates back some 5,000 years, making it the oldest lagoon on the Namibian coast. A safe haven for over 150,000 birds, it also acts as a feeding station for a further 200,000 shorebirds and terns on their biannual migration to and from the Arctic. Up to 90% of all South African flamingos spend the winter here, while 70% of the world's chestnut-banded plovers depend on the lagoon for their survival.

Pressure on the lagoon in recent years has built up from a number of areas: construction of housing to the southeast, salt-pans to the south and west, and a road dyke to the east and south. All these factors have served to reduce flooding, which would naturally keep up the water levels. Added to this is the knock-on effect of the diversion of the Kuiseb River in 1967, since when the dunes have effectively 'marched round' and headed straight for Walvis Bay. The sand blown from the desert contributes significantly to the silting up of the lagoon.

The salt-works that surround the edge of the lagoon in Walvis Bay are South African-owned; salt is exported raw from Namibia, then processed in South Africa for industrial use (as against that from Swakopmund, which is for human consumption). The salt-pans in Walvis Bay are entirely manmade, with the company now owning as far as Pelican Point. As salt extraction increases, it is forecast that the entrance to the lagoon will eventually close up and the lagoon itself will dry up. Initiatives to re-establish the natural flow of water include the construction of culverts under the road leading to the salt-works.

On the basis of current information, the lagoon could in the future disappear completely. Nevertheless, it has been protected as a wetland of international importance under the Ramsar Convention since 1995, and other agencies are on the case. The Coastal Environmental Trust of Namibia (☎ *064 205057; www.nnf.org.na/CETN/index.htm*) has a three-phase 'lagoon integrated environmental management plan' in place, and protection of the lagoon is also part of the Walvis Bay Local Agenda 21 Project, based at the municipality.

Impressive, and all done by the local artist Peter Downing. Otherwise, there is little to see in the town itself, although the small **museum** ([299 F3] ⊕ *09.00–12.30 & 15.00–16.30 Mon–Fri*) next to the Civic Centre has a collection that includes photographs and maps.

Birds Paradise [299 G4] (✆ *064 403 905;* m *081 218 8325;* e *nacomatemp@gmail.com; www.birdsparadise.net; nature walk N$150–300*) If you follow an extension of 18th Road (the C14 towards Sesriem and the airport) inland from Walvis Bay and over the roundabout, heading for Dune 7, then on your right you will shortly see a series of freshwater pools, albeit often close to dried up. Sit here with binoculars for a few minutes and you'll often be able to spot some of the pelicans, flamingos, avocets and other assorted waders that attract birdwatchers to Walvis Bay. The Karel !Naibab staff manning the post can provide 2-hour guided nature walks.

Boat trips A few companies run excellent boat trips from the harbour around the lagoon and out to Pelican Point and Bird Island, with catamaran trips an additional option. Trips usually start from the yacht club at around 08.30, and vary from short cruises in the lagoon to longer cruises round the harbour and out to Pelican Point, or birdwatching trips further out to sea. Many operators include elaborate snacks that may include oysters or a seafood platter, with sparkling wine. Typically, a half-day trip to see dolphins will cost from around N$450 per person, with lagoon cruises slightly cheaper.

In October and November, whales frequent these waters, with possible sightings of humpback, southern right, Minke and even killer whales, while from then until April there is the chance of seeing the leatherback turtle. Dolphins – both the bottlenose and the endemic Benguela (heavysides) – are present all year round, as are Cape fur seals, which may often cavort around the boats.

For details of fishing trips, see page 313.

Boat operators

Catamaran Charters [299 G3] Main office: 12th Rd (next to Probst Bakery); ⊕ 09.15–14.00 Mon–Fri; & at Waterfront ⊕ 08.30–21.00 daily; ✆ 064 200798; m 081 129 5393; e seawolf@iway.na; www.namibiancharters.com. A sail aboard one of these splendid 15m catamarans to view the marine life & birds of Walvis Bay makes a winning combination, with plenty of space on deck to enjoy the boat trip in itself & high-class snacks. Their 3 yachts, *Silverwind*, *Silversand* & *Silvermoon*, are motorised but when conditions are suitable the sails are hoisted for a more exhilarating ride. A 3½hr cruise costs N$600 inc sparkling wine & snacks. Private charters are available, & they offer seafood beach braais too.

Laramon Tours ✆ 064 402359; m 081 124 0635, 081 128 0635; e laramontours@iway.na. ½-day dolphin & sightseeing cruises by motorised catamaran. Most trips operate from Walvis Bay, but in Dec they also depart from Swakopmund. From N$450 pp for 3–4hrs.

Levo Tours Cnr 5th Rd & Union St; ✆ 064 207555; m 081 29 6270; e bookings@levotours.com; www.levotours.com; ⊕ 08.00–17.00 Mon–Fri. Trips in one of 6 ski-boats to do seal & dolphin cruises (*depart 08.30, return 12.30*), combine cruise with a dune excursion, & add on a visit to Sandwich Harbour, returning at 17.30. Departs from the Tanker Jetty.

Mola Mola (See ad, page 318) [299 C1] Waterfront; ✆ 064 205511; m 081 127 2522; e info@mola-namibia.com; www.mola-namibia.com. The well-respected Mola Mola organises 3½hr bird- and dolphin-watching cruises & a combo including a dune excursion.

Ocean Adventures ✆ 064 402377; m 081 240 6290/081 672 1440; e info@swakopadventures.com; www.swakopadventures.com

Sun Sail Namibia m 081 978 6786, 081 124 5045; e fun@mweb.com.na; www.sailnamibia.com. Offers excellent 3–4hr cruises (*N$450/350 adult/child*) aboard one of their luxury catamarans:

Fairweather 1, Manatee or *Que Sera*. Setting off (usually under sail) from the yacht club, cruises include superior snacks & some complimentary drinks. Sunset cruises are also available.

Sunrise Tours & Safaris 17 Dunen St, Swakopmund; 064 404561; m 081 294 4825; e sunrisetours@iafrica.com.na; www.sunrisetours. com.na. Boat trips, fishing excursions & desert tours.

Kayak trips Jeanne Meintjes runs Eco Marine Kayak Tours (see ad, page 272; 064 203144; m 081 129 3144; e emkayak@iway.na; www.emkayak.iway.na). This guided excursion involves a Land Rover trip to Pelican Point, where visitors kayak around Pelican Point and out to the seal colonies (*N$650 for a 5hr trip*), where there is also the possibility of seeing dolphins. Trips are run in the mornings only, when winds are light and the sea is generally calm. Warm jackets, waterproof shoes and dry bags for cameras are provided, and participants have a choice between a single or double kayak. A light snack is served afterwards. This tour can be combined with an afternoon trip to Sandwich Harbour with Sandwich Harbour 4x4 (*Waterfront, Walvis Bay*; 064 207663; m 081 147 3933; e info@sandwich-harbour.com; www. sandwich-harbour.com).

ACTIVITIES AROUND THE TOWNS

Because the towns of Swakopmund and Walvis Bay are just 30km apart (about 25 minutes' drive, on a super tar road), this section covers attractions in the areas outside both of the towns.

There are numerous activities on offer, from sandboarding to nature tours, and because there's a lot of crossover between tour operators and the tours they run, we've listed all the tour operators together and then made it clear at the end of which activity entry who you can book with.

TOUR OPERATORS

African Adventure Balloons 064 403455; m 081 242 9481; e flylo@iway.na; www. africanballoons.com

African Eagle 064 403866; m 081 147 5336; e daytours@iway.na

Alter-Action Ltd 064 402737; m 081 128 2737; e alteraxn@iafrica.com.na; www.alter-action. info/web. The original sandboarding company.

Aquanaut Tours 064 405 969; e info@ aquanauttours.com; www.aquanauttours.com

Batis Birding 064 406 741; m 081 639 1775; www.batisbirdingsafaris.com

Charly's Desert Tours 064 404341; e info@ charlysdeserttours.com; www.charlysdeserttours. com. One of Swakopmund's longest-running operators, established in 1966. ½-day trips include sightseeing tours of Swakopmund & Walvis Bay, plus trips into the desert & to Cape Cross; full days go further into the desert, to Spitzkoppe or down to the Kuiseb Delta.

Close-Up Africa Safaris 064 404207; m 081 200 4073; e info@close-up-africa.com; www.close-up-africa.com

Dare Devil Adventures 064 220158; m 081 755 3589, 081 149 1261; e daredev@iway.na; www.daredeviladventures.com. Based opposite Long Beach. Offer quad biking (*1hr; N$350 pp*) sandboarding (*1hr; N$250 pp*), or combos of the two.

Desert Adventure Safaris 064 403274; e info@dastours.com.na. Full- & ½-day excursions around Swakopmund & to Cape Cross, Spitzkoppe or the Namib Desert, plus longer trips, including Damaraland & Kaokoland.

Desert Explorers Adventure Centre [277 B5] Nathaniel Maxuilili St, Swakopmund; 064 406096; m 081 124 1386; e info@namibiadesertexplorers. com. The booking office for the Desert Explorers quad bike trips. Acts as agent for most, but not all, of Swakopmund's small adventure operators, with activities like dune-boarding, skydiving & kayaking.

Dune 7 Adventures m 081 626 1714, 081 624 9665; e dune7adventures@mweb.com.na; www. dune7adventures.com

Eco Marine Kayak Tours (See ad, page 272) 064 203144; m 081 129 3144; e emkayak@iway.na; www.emkayak.iway.na

Element Riders m 081 666 6599; e info@element-riders.com; www.element-riders.com

Ground Rush Adventures m 081 124 5167; e info@skydiveswakop.com.na; www.skydiveswakop.com.na

Hafeni 064 400 731; m 081 146 6222, 081 277 3074; ⏰ 10.00–13.00 & 15.00–18.00. Runs tours of the Mondesa township, the local craft market, historical walking tours & home visits to Damara, Namas & Oshiwambo people. Portions of the proceeds go to supporting Hope Orphanage & Hanganeni Primary School. Recommended.

Hata Angu Cultural Tours m 081 124 6111; e info@culturalactivities-namibia.com; www.culturalactivities-namibia.com. Also offer 4hr tours of the township departing at 10.00 & 15.00; visits to local herbalists, lessons in the Damara click language & prearranged visits to HIV centre & orphanage.

Kallisto Tours & Services 064 402473; m 081 269 5630; e info@kallistotours.com.na; www.kallistotours.com.na. A full range of town tours, excursions & longer trips, as well as transfers.

Kuiseb Delta Adventures 064 202550; m 081 128 2580; e fanie@kuisebonline.com; www.kuisebonline.com. Historical & educational desert tours.

Laramon See page 308.

Living Desert Adventures 064 405070; m 081 127 5070; e nature@iafrica.com.na; www.livingdesertnamibia.com. A highly respected company offering superb 4–5hr trips (N$650) into the desert departing at 08.00 that both locals & travellers rave about. The desert tour can also be booked in combination with the rocky canyon tour. Tailor-made options are also available.

Namibia Tracks & Trails 14A Sam Nujoma Av, Swakopmund; 064 416820; m 081 269 7271; e sales@namibia-tracks-and-trails.com; www.namibia-tracks-and-trails.com. An efficient one-stop shop that acts as agent for many of Swakopmund's adventure operators.

Ocean Adventures Angling Tours 064 404281; m 081 124 0208/081 128 5523; e info@fishingtoursnamibia.com; www.fishingtoursnamibia.com

Okakambe Trails 064 402799; e okakambe@iway.na; www.okakambe.iway.na

Panorama Cycle Tours Contact tourist information centre Namib I (see page 278).

Photo Ventures m 081 426 1200; e info@photoventures-namibia.com; www.photoventures-namibia.com. Offer seal & dolphin tours, Sandwich Harbour & kayaking, as well as special photographic tours around Namibia.

Pleasure Flights & Safaris 064 404500; m 081 129 4545; e redbaron@iafrica.com.na; www.pleasureflights.com.na

Sandwich Harbour 4x4 064 207 663; m 081 147 3933; e info@sandwich-harbour.com; www.sandwich-harbour.com

Scenic Air 061 248 268; e windhoek@scenic-air.com; www.scenic-air.com

Swakop Cycle Tours m 081 251 5916, 081 222 1667; e panoromatours@gmail.com. Run 3½hr biking tours around the township (N$380 pp), with departures at 09.00 & 14.00; 2½hr walking tours of the city (N$285 pp), with departures at 09.30 & 14.30. They also rent bikes & will deliver them to your hotel at no extra cost (½ day N$195 pp, full day N$255 pp).

Swakop Tour Company Daniel Tjongarero St; 064 404088; m 081 124 2906; e proverb@mweb.com.na. This well-recommended company, run by Georg Erb, offers set tours for small groups that are of particular appeal for geologists & botanists. These include a 5hr klipspringer tour into the desert (N$650) & a shorter 'dunes of the Namib' tour around sunset (N$450). Customised itineraries can be arranged focusing on individual interests.

Swakopmund City Tour m 081 129 9076; e Gerald@dtnamibia.com. 1½hr tours of historical Swakopmund departing at 08.30 & 14.00 with a minimum of 2 people (N$300 pp). They also offer 4hr desert ecosystem tours.

Swakopmund Sky Diving Club 064 405 671; m 081 343 1843; e info@skydiveswakopmund.com; www.skydiveswakopmund.com

Tommy's Living Desert Tours m 081 128 1038; e tommys@iway.na; www.livingdeserttours.com.na. Tommy Collard's expertly guided 5–6hr tours (N$650, under 12s half price) departing at 08.00 that offer a comprehensive insight into the desert & dunes, & the creatures that live there.

Turnstone Tours 064 403123; e turn@iafrica.com.na; www.turnstone-tours.com. If you're interested in an informative day in the desert with a first-rate guide who is also excellent company, try Bruno Nebe at Turnstone Tours. You might pay a bit more than you will for a normal tour, but you often get the Land Rover to yourselves, &, if you're lucky, the owner Bruno Nebe, one of Namibia's best guides. Turnstone's day trips (*N$1,250 pp for 2 people, N$1,150 pp for 4 people or more*) come with a picnic hamper full of hot, home-cooked food & a selection of hot & cold drinks, & visit destinations like Sandwich Harbour & the Namib Desert (½-day tours also available at N$750 pp, min 3 people), as well as others on request. For those with more time, there are short camping tours into Damaraland, the Erongo Mountains & the Namib Desert, as well as from Bruno's own farm, Mundulea, to the east of Etosha. Private tours are available on request.

Ultimate Sandboarding m 081 421 6021; e ultimateboarding@gmail.com; www. ultimatesandboarding.com

Wings over Africa 064 403720; m 081 129 1554; e wings@mail.na; www.flyinafrica.com

DESERT-BASED TOURS New activities in the dunes are constantly being dreamed up to add to the existing range. Some, such as quad biking, skydiving and sandboarding, may be combined in one trip. Current options include:

Sandboarding (*About NS$300 pp lying down, NS$400 for stand-up boarding*) Typically, trips leave from Swakopmund in the morning around 09.30, collecting you from your accommodation and returning around 13.30. The idea is to push off the top of a dune and lie on the board as it slides down. Speeds easily reach 70km/h or more, though at first you'll do a few training rides on lower dunes, where you won't go much faster than 40km/h. Finally, they take you to a couple of the larger dunes, for longer, faster runs, before lunch in the desert, and the return drive to Swakopmund. As a spin-off from sandboarding, offered by all operators, stand-up boarding, also known as dune-boarding, uses a modified snowboard. Participants stand on a small surfboard which shoots down the side of dunes – rather like skiing, only on sand. It may have more finesse, and certainly requires more skill.
Operators: Alter-Action, Dare Devil, Dune 7, Ultimate Sandboarding

Quad biking (*Around N$550 pp for 2hrs; longer & shorter trips available, departing through the day*) Ride four-wheel motorcycles through the dunes. Manual, semi-automatic and automatic bikes are available, with helmets, goggles and gloves provided.

If you're setting off on your own, please consider the harmful effect on the environment (see box, page 317). Note that quad bikes are not allowed into the Namib-Naukluft National Park.

Historical quad bike tour Drive through the dunes and Kuiseb Delta (see box, pages 314–15), to see fauna, flora, fossils and petrified elephant footprints. Starts 08.30 from Lagoon Chalets in Walvis Bay and returns at 12.30. Costs N$750 per person including cold drinks.
Operators: Kuiseb Delta, Photo Ventures

Quad bike tours through the dunes Guided 1-hour tour from N$350, 90-minute tour from N$450, 2-hour tour from N$550, 90-minute sundowner tours at N$500 (all prices per person). Participants should be over 16, younger children can accompany parents on their quad, although there might be an additional charge.
Operators: Dare Devil, Desert Explorers, Dune 7, Element Riders

Power kiting Level 1 for beginners from N$400 per person including kite and gear.
Operator: Element Riders

Desert ecosystem tours While many local companies offer half-day or even full-day tours covering a relatively well-beaten trail that includes the Welwitschia Drive, a really attractive alternative is to discover less well-known areas of the desert in the company of a specialist, such as Turnstone Tours. One such trip might take you inland near the old railway, then over rolling dune fields towards the moonscape, from where you can see Rössing Mountain in the distance. Down below, mining claims have been staked out here and there on the gravel plains. While most of the material mined is granite, many other minerals are to be found, including small quantities of yellowish-green uranium oxide, or purpurite; this is the raw material that is processed into yellowcake, and eventually refined into plutonium and other substances. Look out, too, for the cellophane-like hornblend, or the pinky-orange of titanium.

There's a lot more to this apparently barren plain than minerals, however. Individual welwitschia plants and quivertrees form an integral part of the landscape, as do the tiny stone plants (*Lithops karasmontana*) that may be found hidden beneath a quartz outcrop. Lichens cling to the rocks, small holes tell of hairy-footed gerbils, and day geckos scurry past. Across the plain is the linear oasis of Goanikontes on the Khan River. Built by the Germans, Goanikontes was once used as a staging post for horse-carts from Swakopmund, since food for horses and cattle could be grown. Here and along the huge plain of the Swakop River numerous plants can be identified clinging to life, and klipspringers eke out a precarious existence along the rocks.

Dune 7 Past the Bird Sanctuary in Walvis Bay, just off the C14 on the way to the airport and Sesriem, this is one of the highest dunes in the area and has a small picnic site near its base, among a few shady palms. It's a popular spot for both energetic dune-climbers and sundowners.
No operator required; self visit

Little Five Desert Tour Highly recommended, this guided 4x4 drive into the dunes explores the incredible landscape and its living creatures. Starts at 08.00 from Swakopmund and returns by 13.30. The cost is N$650 per person including cold drinks. Pick-up from your accommodation.
Operators: Batis Birding, Close up Africa, Living Desert Adventures, Tommy's Tours

Welwitschia Tours (see box opposite) Offered on a half-day, ¾-day or full-day basis with some departing at 09.00, others at 14.00. Rates vary and usually include pick-up within Swakopmund and drinks from N$600 per person half-day, and N$700 per person for the full-day tour.
Operators: Batis Birding, Charly's Desert Tours, Kallisto Tours, Swakop Tour Company

AIR-BASED TOURS
Hot Air Ballooning Start at 05.30 in the early morning from Swakopmund and travel leisurely over the desert. A 1-hour flight at sunrise with champagne breakfast for a minimum of two participants costs N$3,300 per person including breakfast and drinks. You'll return to Swakopmund by roughly 11.00.
Operator: African Adventure Balloons

Scenic flights Offered from Swakopmund, with the most popular being the 2¼-hour Sossusvlei flight and the 1½-hour Concepcion Bay flight. You fly via the Kuiseb and down south of the dune landscape, returning over the coastline where you can see shipwrecks and Sandwich Harbour (see box, page 314). Rates per person on the assumption of five participants per plane start from N$2,320 for the Concepcion Bay and N$3,125 for the Sossusvlei flight.
Operators: Pleasure Flights, Scenic Flights, Wings over Africa

WELWITSCHIA DRIVE

N$40 pp, plus N$10 per vehicle; permits must be bought in advance from the MET in Swakopmund, page 278.

In the northern corner of the Namib-Naukluft National Park, an afternoon's excursion from Swakopmund or Walvis Bay, the Welwitschia Drive (see *Chapter 12*, pages 271–2 for a full description) is a route through the desert with numbered beacons at points of interest, culminating in one of the country's oldest welwitschia plants. Part of the drive is the 'moon landscape', or 'moonscape' – a rolling, barren area of rocky desert formed by the valleys around the course of the Swakop River. It's a spectacular sight, often spoken of, and best viewed by the slanting light of mid-morning or late afternoon. However, be warned that the recent discovery of uranium close to the route means that the MET are in the process of changing it, so check with them when you buy your permit, and before attempting the drive.

Skydiving With clear air and a starkly beautiful coastline, Swakopmund is a natural space to learn to fly or even skydive. Jumps can normally only be booked at short notice because they're weather-dependent. After a basic safety chat and a scenic flight over Swakopmund and the surrounding area, you are strapped to an experienced instructor to throw yourselves out of a plane at 10,000ft. Your free fall lasts for about half a minute before, hopefully, your parachute opens and there's a further 5-minute 'canopy ride' before landing. There is no age limit, but participants are limited to those who are large enough to fit the equipment. It costs from N$2,000 per person for a tandem jump, and it takes about 3 hours. Also available are static line jumps from N$700 per person. *Operators: Ground Rush, Swakopmund Sky Diving Club*

WATER-BASED TOURS
Boat trips/kayaking For details of trips run from Walvis Bay, see pages 308–9.

Fishing Long popular all along this coastline with South African visitors, fishing is good all year round, although the best times are October to April. The turn of the year is particularly busy, with anglers arriving in search of big-game fish such as copper sharks and other similar species, which can weigh as much as 180kg. Other species that may be caught include kabeljou, steenbras, barber, galjoen and garrick.

The area is good for crayfish, too, although the catch is limited to a maximum of seven per person, or 14 per vehicle. Permits are required for all types of fishing.

Fishing trips aboard a boat or on shore are offered from Swakopmund daily, on a full-day basis only. You depart at 08.00 and return by 16.00. Rates from N$1,250 per person include tackle and bait, equipment, fishing licence, lunch and drinks. *Operators: Aquanaut Tours, Ocean Adventures Angling Tours*

Intertidal Drive at Wavis Bay 2½-hour trip at low tide with expert guide to discover molluscs, anemones, seaweeds, crustaceans interacting with birdlife, and remnants of shipwrecks. Costs N$480/350 adult/child. *Operator: Aquanaut Tours*

Kayaking on the Walvis Bay Lagoon Start at 07.30 from the lagoon with a 4x4 ride towards Pelican Point. Enter the water with kayaks close to the Point, paddle between seals and dolphins, and return to Walvis Bay by noon. It costs N$600 per

There is some excellent birdlife in the vicinity. Just take a walk on the southwest side of Walvis Bay, around the lagoon. The flock of feeding flamingos and pelicans that I often find there usually allows me to get much closer than others that I come across in the area. Birdwatchers might also want to stop at one of the guano platforms in the sea between Walvis and Swakopmund.

SWAKOP RIVER DELTA Here small tidal lagoons surrounded by reeds are very good for birding. Expect whimbrels, curlews, the odd flamingo and pelican, white-breasted cormorants, Cape cormorants, black-winged stilts, avocets and more.

The remains of the old railway bridge lie here, washed down in 1934 when the Swakop River performed its flood-of-the-century stunt. On the pillars there are often crowned and bank cormorants, while along the river-bed, between the tamarisk trees, kestrels swoop around catching mice.

The local Wildlife Society has laid out a pleasant 4km trail starting next to the cemetery. This takes you downstream into the river mouth, and back to the beach. Walkers should beware of quad bikes that move pretty fast through this area.

KUISEB DELTA This area is criss-crossed by a labyrinth of tracks in which even experienced guides can get lost. Unmarked archaeological sites dot the area, where pottery shards, beads, shell middens and stone tools can be seen. Wildlife includes springbok, ostrich, jackal and brown hyena, and birds such as the endemic dune lark.

Look out for the nara bushes (*Acanthosicyos horrida*) – their spiky green (and hence photosynthesising) stems have allowed them to dispense with leaves completely. This is an advantage given the propensity of leaves to lose water. Naras are perhaps not truly desert plants, as their roots go down many metres to reach underground water, which they need in order to survive. From February to April and August to September the local Topnaar people harvest nara melons here.

The area is accessible only by 4x4 and you'll only appreciate it with a good guide. To approach on your own, take the Esplanade by the lagoon southwest from Walvis Bay, and after about 4km ignore the sign to Paaltjies (where the road divides) and keep left. The track splits and you take the left fork marked Rooibank via Wortels.

 SANDWICH HARBOUR This small area about 45km south of Walvis Bay has a large saltwater lagoon, extensive tidal mudflats and a band of reed-lined pools fed by freshwater springs, together forming one of the most important birdlife refuges in southern Africa. Typically you'll find about 30 species of birds at Sandwich. It offers food and shelter to thousands of migrants every year and some of Namibia's most spectacular scenery – for those lucky enough to see it. Where else can you walk along a pelican-covered beach while pink flamingos glide above the sand dunes?

Getting there – and a warning Several operators offer half-day trips to the harbour, but it deserves a full day tour, so pick your operator accordingly. If you're travelling independently, getting to Sandwich Harbour requires a high-clearance 4x4 and an experienced driver. As several vehicles have been lost to the sea in recent years, many of the area's guides have stopped coming. Despite this, Sandwich Harbour is still the best place for birding in the area, so don't believe rumours that it's silted up or devoid of birdlife. It isn't – it's superb. That said, occasionally there may be access problems due to fog or flooding, which can lead even the experts to cancel or curtail a trip.

The most experienced operator doing regular trips here is Turnstone Tours (see pages 310–11). These are best booked far in advance, and are highly recommended. Other operators include Mola Mola Tours and Sandwich Harbour 4x4 – see *Boat operators* and *Tour operators*, pages 308–11. Trips include lunch and soft drinks.

Driving yourself The reluctance of most guides to come here should be a warning to you: even experienced desert drivers get stuck here if they don't know the place, so it's dangerous to go without a local expert. If you do try to drive yourself, check the fine print of your vehicle's insurance and buy a permit in advance from the MET office in Swakopmund, or the Omega or other filling stations in Walvis Bay.

Then, from Walvis Bay, take the Esplanade by the lagoon southwest out of town, towards the Kuiseb Delta. After about 4km ignore the sign to Paaltjies (where the road divides) and keep to your left. The track then splits and you take the right fork, ignoring the road marked Rooibank via Wortels. From here, cross the salt flats and continue until you reach a fence which marks the boundary of the Namib-Naukluft National Park. Turn right and drive along the fence towards the beach, crossing into the park where the fence stops. You'll be turned away if you don't have a permit.

From here it's about 20km of sandy terrain to Sandwich Harbour. You can drive all the way on the beach, following the tyre tracks of the fishermen, although the going can get rough. Beware: if the tide is high and catches you, expect serious problems.

It's better to take an immediate left after passing the control post, and follow these tracks. After some 200m, they turn parallel to the sea and are considerably firmer than the ones on the beach. Leaving these tracks to cross the apparently dry pans, where there are none, is foolhardy.

What to see and do Once you reach the bird sanctuary, vehicles must be left and you have to proceed on foot. The northern part consists of a number of almost enclosed reed-lined pools at the top of the beach, which back directly on to huge dunes. These are fed partly by the sea via narrow channels which fill at high tide, and partly with fresh water which seeps from a subterranean watercourse under the dunes and enables reeds (albeit salt-tolerant ones) to grow. These in turn provide food and nesting sites for a number of the resident waterbirds found here. On my last visit I managed to spot dabchicks, moorhens, shelducks, common and marsh sandpipers, several species of tern (Caspian, swift, white-winged and whiskered all visit) and even avocets and African spoonbills – as well as the pelicans and flamingos.

As you continue along the beach, the 'harbour' itself comes into view. During the early 18th century it was used by whalers for its deep, sheltered anchorage and ready supply of fresh water. Subsequently a small station was established there to trade in seal pelts, fish and guano. Later, in the early part of the 20th century, it was used as a source of guano but, after the mouth of the harbour silted up, this ground to a halt in 1947, leaving only a few bits of rusting machinery to be seen today.

It's worth climbing up one of the dunes, as from there you can see the deep lagoon, protected from the ocean's pounding by a sand spit, and the extensive mudflats to the south, which are often covered by the tide.

This is a trip to make a whole day of, so when you start walking from your vehicle, take some windproof clothes and a little to eat and drink, as well as your binoculars, camera and lots of memory card space/film. Even if you're not an avid ornithologist, the scenery is so spectacular that you're bound to take endless photos.

Of the world's half-dozen or so species of flamingo, two are found within southern Africa: the greater (*Phoenicopterus ruber*) and the lesser (*P. minor*). Both species have wide distributions – from southern Africa north into east Africa and the Red Sea – and are highly nomadic. The best way to tell the two species apart is by their beaks: that of the greater flamingo is almost white, while the lesser flamingo has a uniformly dark beak. Looking from further away, the body of the greater flamingo appears white, while that of the lesser looks smaller and pinker.

Flamingos are usually found wading in large areas of shallow saline water, where they filter-feed by holding their specially adapted beaks upside down. The lesser flamingo walks or swims while swinging its head from side to side, mainly taking blue-green algae from the surface. The larger, greater flamingo holds its head submerged while filtering out small organisms (detritus and algae), even stirring the mud with its feet to help the process. Both species are gregarious; flocks can number millions of birds, although hundreds are more common.

Only occasionally do flamingos breed in southern Africa, choosing Etosha Pan or perhaps Botswana's Makgadikgadi Pans. When the conditions are right (usually March to June, following heavy rains) both species build low mud cones in the water and lay one or (rarely) two eggs in a small hollow on the top. These are then incubated by both parents for about a month until they hatch, and after a further week the young birds flock together and start to forage with their parents. Some ten weeks later the young can fly and fend for themselves.

During their first few months, the young are very susceptible to the shallow water drying out. In 1969, a rescue operation was mounted when Etosha Pan dried out. Thousands of chicks were moved to nearby Fischer's Pan, which was still covered in water.

Namibia's best places for flamingos are usually the lagoons at Walvis Bay and Sandwich Harbour – unless you hear that Etosha or Nyae Nyae are full of water. Then, by the time you arrive, the flamingos will probably have beaten you there.

person and includes a light breakfast, coffee and all equipment. See also page 309.
Operators: Eco Marine Kayak Tours, Sandwich Harbour 4x4

Dolphin and seal cruise on Walvis Bay Lagoon This tour starts at 09.00 from Walvis Bay, but pick-up can be arranged at your accommodation in Swakopmund for free from 08.00 Cruise through the harbour, visiting the guano islands and Pelican Point (home to more than 60,000 seals), with the chance of seeing dolphins. Champagne brunch, including Walvis Bay oysters. From N$500 per person. Return to Walvis Bay Harbour at 13.00; return transport to Swakopmund departing 14.00. See also page 308.
Operators: Catamaran Charters, Laramon Tours, Levo Tours, Mola Mola, Ocean Adventures, Sun Sail Namibia

Surfing This activity is dependent on weather and swells, but surfboards and wetsuits can be rented from N$100 per person per day.
Operator: Element Riders

Kitesurfing Courses for individuals or beginners are available, with rates from N$700 per person, up to N$4,700 for full training, including all gear and equipment.
Operator: Element Riders

✖ Sandwich Harbour Tour (See box, pages 314–15) Departs Swakopmund with a 4x4 via the salt-pans and lower Kuiseb Delta to the lagoon. Encounter fau.. flora, quicksand and hummock dunes. Full-day returning at 17.00. Includes a delicious lunch of homemade pâtés, bread, salad, fruit and cake. Costs from N$1,290 per person.

This tour is also available as a combo including a half-day boat cruise and half-day Sandwich Harbour tour, rates on enquiry.
Operators: Photo Ventures, Sandwich Harbour 4x4, Turnstone Tours

Cape Cross Tours Departs Swakopmund at 09.00; includes a tour of the salt-pans, lichen fields and Henties Bay. Return by 14.00. N$940 per person including drinks.
Operators: Charly's Tours, Kallisto Tours

RIDING
Horseriding Through the Swakop Valley from N$550 per person per hour, with a minimum of two participants, singles pay more. Rides are planned to suit the experience of the participants. A late-afternoon ride costs N$590 for a 1½-hour trip per person. Weight limitation: 80kg for inexperienced riders; 90kg for experienced riders. Transfer from Swakopmund and back included.
Operator: Okakambe Trails

Camel riding The Camel Farm (*east of Swakopmund, down the D1901;* ☏ 064 400 363; e *erbelke@mweb.com.na*) offers a 20-minute ride costing N$150/75 adult/child Monday to Saturday between 14.00 and 17.00.

PROTECTION OF THE DESERT

Many companies around Swakopmund have taken advantage of the unique environment to introduce adventure sports. Quad biking, sandboarding, sand-skiing and other activities are growing in popularity, but they could have serious consequences for the sand dunes and other desert areas on which they depend.

While most operators take this issue seriously, confining their sports to a specific area and spelling out to participants the harm that can be caused by thoughtless manoeuvres, individuals may not be so careful. Even then, sandboarding and sand-skiing have a weight-to-surface relationship that is unlikely to cause significant damage. Sadly, though, serious harm is being caused by individuals on privately owned bikes setting off across the dunes and gravel plains without any understanding of the nature of the area.

Broadly, the low-impact part of the dunes is the area on the top, with the greatest potential for danger to the habitat being on the lee side. Most of the life in the dunes is found in the top 10cm, so a thoughtless biker can cause untold damage in just a few seconds. Beyond the dunes, slow-growing lichens form an integral part of the region's ecology, but they are very fragile. Trample them underfoot or ride over them and they are unlikely to survive, depriving many forms of wildlife of food and shelter. The gravel plains of the Namib Desert are the nesting area of the endemic Damara tern, one of the rarest terns in the world, yet – with a quick twist of the handlebars – a nest can be crushed in seconds.

The creation of the Dorob National Park (see page 318) should go a long way to protecting the ecosystem.

⬦EXCURSIONS BEYOND THE TOWNS

Dorob National Park (*Permit required from MET office, page 278*) Namibia's newest national park stretches from the Swakop River to the Ugab River bordering the Skeleton Coast Park. It was created on 1 December 2010 to protect the fragile desert ecosystem – which acts as a breeding ground for Damara terns and other sea birds – from quad bikers that have been tearing across the landscape. Within its perimeter is a 'dead sea' salt-pan litter with old mining equipment and tracks, and the Messum Crater, the result of a volcano implosion slowly filled in with sand – the crater impression can be seen in the sand. Permits are required to enter the area with your own car; they can be collected from the MET office, are free, and valid for three months.

Rössing Mine (🕐 *First Fri of month; tickets via Swakopmund Museum, page 293; N$25/15 adult/student or child*) Rössing is remarkable, particularly if you're interested in engineering, mining or geology. It's a vast open cast uranium mine. For children (especially the sort that never grow up) there are the biggest lorries in the world.

The opencast mine is awesome, so deep that the same vehicles working at the bottom of the pit look like Dinky toys. You certainly get an alternative view of the desert, and the viewpoints Rössing has set up (with information plaques) provide interesting photo opportunities. There's a video charting the mines and the uranium production process, with the requisite emphasis on safety, and a tour of the whole site.

Visiting Rössing is probably the sort of thing that I would have done when I was a child, on holiday with my family, to fill in a rainy day. Then I'd look back on it, and be glad that I'd done it. It certainly appeals to those already interested, but many will feel they see enough of this kind of industrial development at home. Trips leave from outside Café Anton on Bismarck Street in Swakopmund on the first and third Fridays of each month. Reservations should be made at Swakopmund Museum.

Minerals Tours These are offered either to the Rössing Mountain (4 hours; N$650 per person), or including the canyons (7 hours; N$900 per person). Pick-up in Swakopmund. Prices include drinks. Fewer participants are quoted on enquiry. *Operators: Charly's Tours, Kallisto Tours*

Spitzkoppe Day Tour Guided tour to Namibian Matterhorn with explanations of fauna/flora, Bushman paintings and geology. Pick-up in Swakopmund at 09.00 and return at 18.00. It requires a minimum of three participants and costs N$1,100 per person including cold drinks. Tours can be done for two people, but at a higher rate. *Operator: Kallisto Tours*

14

The Skeleton Coast

By the end of the 17th century, the long stretch of coast north of Swakopmund had attracted the attention of the Dutch East India Company. They sent several exploratory missions, but after finding only barren shores and impenetrable fogs, their journeys ceased. Later, in the 19th century, British and American whalers operated out of Lüderitz, but they gave this northern coast a wide berth – it was gaining a formidable reputation.

Today, driving north from Swakopmund, it's easy to see how this coast earned its names of the Coast of Skulls or the Skeleton Coast. Treacherous fogs and strong currents forced many ships on to the uncharted sandbanks that shift underwater like the desert's sands. Even if the sailors survived the shipwreck, their problems had only just begun. The coast here is a barren line between an icy, pounding ocean and the Namib Desert. The present road, the C34, runs parallel to the ocean, and often feels like a drive along an enormous beach – with the sea on one side, and the sand – or gravel – continuing forever on the other. It's a tribute to the power of the ocean that, despite the havoc wreaked on passing ships, very few wrecks remain visible.

This fragile coast is divided into three narrow, protected areas. North of Swakopmund up to the Ugab River, covering about 200km of coast, is Dorob National Park. Beyond this lies the Skeleton Coast Park, the southern part of which – as far as Terrace Bay – is freely accessible to the public, while access to the northern section is restricted to fly-in visitors.

For the first 250km or so, from Swakopmund to about Torra Bay, there are almost no dunes. This is desert of gravel and rock. Then, around Torra Bay, the northern dune sea of the Namib starts, with an increasingly wide belt of coastal dunes stretching north to the Kunene River. But nowhere are these as tall, or continuous, as the Namib's great southern dune sea, south of the Kuiseb River.

At first sight it all seems very barren, but watch the amazing wildlife documentaries made by the famous film-makers of the Skeleton Coast, Des and Jen Bartlett, to realise that some of the most remarkable wildlife on earth has evolved here. Better still, drive yourself up the coast road, through this fascinating stretch of the world's oldest desert. You won't see a fraction of the action that they have filmed, but with careful observation you will spot plenty to captivate you.

FLORA AND FAUNA

SAND RIVERS A shipwrecked sailor's only hope on this coast would have been to find one of the desert's linear oases – sand rivers that wind through the desert to reach the coast. The Omaruru, the Ugab, the Huab, the Koichab, the Uniab and the Hoanib are the main ones. They are few and far between. Each starts in the highlands, far inland, and, although normally dry, they flood briefly in years of good rains. For most

THE SKELETON COAST

ANGOLA

Serra Cafema
Kunene River Camp
Kunene

Skeleton Coast Park

Hartmann's Valley

Kaiu Maru

Cape Frio

ATLANTIC OCEAN

Khumib

Opuwo

Rocky Point
Plane wreck
Purros
Hoarusib
C43

Möwe Bay

Hoanib   Sesfontein

Cold Benguela current

Hoanib Skeleton Coast Camp

Etendeka Mountain Camp

Terrace Bay

Palmwag Lodge

Uniab

Torra Bay

Desert Rhino Camp   C40

Springbokwasser Gate   C39   C43

Koigab

Damaraland Camp

C34

Skeleton Coast Park   Kuidas Camp

Toscanini

Huab

Doros Crater   Twyfelfontein   C39

South West Sea

Ugab

Ugab River Gate

Winston

Mile 108

Brandberg Massif

Messum Crater   C34   C35

Cape Cross Lodge   National West Coast Tourist Recreation Area   Uis   C36

Cape Cross Seal Reserve   C35

Mile 72

Omdel Dam   Omaruru

Gross Spitzkoppe 1728m

Henties Bay
Jakkalsputz
Zeila   C34

Wlotzkasbaken

Mile 14

NOTE
For accommodation listings, see pages 328–9, 330–1, 339, 376

Swakopmund
B2   C28

0   80km
0   50 miles

Brack

N

---

of the time their waters filter westward to the sea through their sandy beds. Shrubs and trees thrive, supporting whole ecosystems: green ribbons which snake across seemingly lifeless plains.

Even in the driest times, if an impervious layer of rock forces the water to surface, then the river will flow overland for a few hundred metres, only to vanish into the sand again as swiftly as it appeared. Such watering places are rare, but of vital importance to the inhabitants of the area. They have allowed isolated groups of Himba people to stay in these parts, while also sustaining the famous desert populations of elephant and – in the past – black rhino.

In many of these river valleys there are thriving populations of oryx, kudu, springbok, steenbok, jackals, genets, small wild cats and even giraffe. The shy and secretive brown hyena is common, though seldom seen. Zebra are scarce residents, and even lion or cheetah will sometimes appear, using the sand rivers as alleys for hunting forays. Desert-adapted elephants, although seasonal, are surviving well along the perennial river systems into the Skeleton Coast. Lion used to penetrate the desert right to the coast to prey on seals. Although it is many years since the last such coastal lion was seen, rising game populations in the interior are encouraging a greater population of lion in the region, so perhaps we'll see individuals on the beaches again before too long.

BESIDE THE SEA Outside the river valleys, the scenery changes dramatically, with an outstanding variety of colours and forms. The gravel plains – in all hues of brown and red – are bases for occasional coloured mountains, and belts of shifting barchan sand dunes.

Yet despite their barren appearance, even the flattest of the gravel plains here is full of life. Immediately next to the sea, high levels of humidity sustain highly specialised vegetation, succulents like lithops, and the famous lichens – which are, in fact, not plants at all but a symbiotic partnership of algae and fungi, the fungi providing the physical structure, while the algae photosynthesise to produce the food. They use the moisture in humid air, without needing either rain or even fog. That said, frequent coastal fogs and relatively undisturbed plains account for their conspicuous success here.

In some places lichens carpet the gravel desert. Take a close look at one of these gardens of lichen, and you'll find many different species, varying in colour from bright reds and oranges, through vivid greens to darker browns, greys and black. Most cling to the rocks or the crust of the gypsum soil, but a few species stand up like the skeletons of small leafless bushes, and one species, *Xanthomaculina convoluta*, is even wind-blown, a minute version of the tumbleweed famous in old Western films.

All come alive, looking their best, early on damp, foggy mornings. Sections appear like green fields of wispy vegetation. But if you pass on a hot, dry afternoon, they will seem less interesting. Then stop and leave your car. Walk to the edge of a field with a bottle of water, pour a little on to a small patch of lichens, and stay to watch. Within just a few minutes you'll see them brighten and unfurl.

Less obvious is their age: lichens grow exceedingly slowly. Once disturbed, they take decades and even centuries to regenerate. On some lichen fields you will see vehicle tracks. These are sometimes 40 or 50 years old – and still the lichens briefly crushed by one set of wheels have not regrown. This is one of the main reasons why you should *never* drive off the roads on the Skeleton Coast.

Next to the sea, small flocks of sanderlings may descend on beachfront lagoons, along with white-fronted plovers, while higher up, lappet-faced vultures circle in search of carrion. You may even spot Ludwig's bustard as it rises up, an untidy bundle of white and yellow.

FURTHER INLAND East of the coastal strip, between about 30km and 60km inland, the nights can be very cold, and many mornings are cool and foggy. However, after about midday the temperatures rocket and the humidity disappears. This is the harshest of the Namib's climatic zones, but even here an ecosystem has evolved, relying on occasional early morning fogs for moisture.

This is home to various scorpions, lizards and tenebrionid beetles, living from wind-blown detritus and vegetation including dune-creating dollar bushes (*Zygophyllum stapffii*) and perhaps the Namib's most fascinating plant, the remarkable *Welwitschia mirabilis*.

This is the terrain favoured by Rüppell's korhaan. Several species of lark are at home here, too, though few – except perhaps the red-capped – are easy to distinguish. Birds of prey include the lanner falcon and brown snake eagle, while smaller species include the familiar chat.

GETTING THERE AND AWAY

It is even more vital here than in the rest of Namibia: you need a vehicle to see the Skeleton Coast – at least as far north as Terrace Bay. Although hitchhiking is not restricted, vehicles are few and far between, and – with often bitterly cold mornings and desiccating afternoons – heat exhaustion would be a real danger. An alternative is to join an organised tour. A few tour companies in Swakopmund run excursions to Cape Cross, about 120km or 1½ hours' drive to the north, stopping at one of the lichen fields and some of the more obvious sites of interest on the way. Tours can also be arranged from Henties Bay.

By far the best option is to drive yourself, equipped with plenty of water and a picnic lunch, and stop where and when you wish to explore. Set off north as early

WHERE TO FIND LIFE? The Namib Desert receives its stingy allotment of water in two ways. Its eastern edges, near the escarpment, get rare showers of rain. There you will find inselbergs (see page 247), which can store the water for a time and support permanent communities of perennial plants and resident animals. At the coast, the desert's western edge, the annual rainfall is even lower (less than 5mm at Walvis Bay), and there most organisms rely on the fogs which regularly roll in from the sea. However, in the middle of the desert where neither the rain nor fog reach, there is very little life indeed.

SURVIVING IN THE NAMIB: BY ESCAPING Many of the Namib's species can only survive at all if they either escape or retreat from the extremes. An 'escape' is an extended period of absence from the desert community, such as a suspension of the life cycle, aestivation (the desert equivalent of hibernation) or by actually migrating out of the desert.

Many of the Namib's plants stop their life cycle for particularly harsh periods, leaving behind dormant seeds able to withstand temperatures of up to 100°C and remain viable for years. Growth is eventually triggered by a threshold amount of rainfall, leading to the phenomenon of the 'desert bloom', where a carpet of flowers covers the ground. These plants, called ephemerals, must then complete their life cycles in a matter of days before the water disappears. A blooming desert obviously requires its pollinators, so various insect species also conduct ephemeral life cycles, switching them on and off as rainfall dictates.

On the great plains of the Namib, a different community waits for rain in any slight depression. When it arrives, and the depression fills, an explosion of activity occurs and pond life comes to the desert. Algae, shrimps and tadpoles fill the ponds for their short lives, employing rapid development techniques to mature swiftly to adulthood.

Large-scale migrations are not common in the Namib, but springbok do trek between arid regions, following any rain, and the Namib's largest mammal, the oryx, also moves in a predictable pattern. After rainfall, they move into the Namib's dune sea, looking for the ephemeral grasses. When these vanish, they travel to the dry Kuiseb River bed to compete with the resident baboons for acacia pods and water. Here they excavate waterholes, which they maintain from year to year.

SURVIVING IN THE NAMIB: BY RETREATING A 'retreat' is a short term escape, typically a matter of hours. This has a serious disadvantage: it results in what ecologists call a 'time crunch', where time for foraging and social activity is greatly reduced. It follows that retreating animals must be very efficient at foraging.

Most species retreat to some extent. The Namib's beetles, reptiles, birds and mammals disappear into burrows and nests during the hottest periods of the

as possible, catching the southern sections of the road in the fog, and prebook overnight accommodation if you plan to go as far north as Terrace Bay. The drive here takes about 5 hours, though most people stop to explore and have refreshments, and so make a whole day of it.

Up until the entrance to the national park, the main C34 is what is known locally as a salt road. Made of salt, gypsum and gravel compacted hard over the years, it has no loose surface, so is almost as solid and safe as tar. That said, it gets very slippery in the early morning mists, and sometimes gets bumpy – so while you can day. One of the most visible is the social weaver bird, which builds enormous communal nests that insulate the birds during cold nights, and provide a handy retreat during the heat of the day.

In order to extend the time spent on the surface, and minimise this time crunch, one Namib resident, the sand-diving lizard, has developed the remarkable behaviour of 'dancing' on the surface. By lifting its legs at intervals (never all at once!), it manages to reduce its body temperature and stay out for a few extra minutes of activity.

SPECIALISED PLANTS Although some form of escape or retreat is practical for most animal species, plants do not have the same luxury. They cannot move quickly and therefore have to become tolerant.

Most of the Namib's plants have very deep root systems, to acquire what little ground water is available, and adaptations to reduce water loss. Their leaves are usually small and often covered in hairs or a waxy coating. These designs all reduce water loss by evaporation. Smaller leaves mean less surface area, hairs trap still air adjacent to the leaf and waxy coatings don't allow moisture to pass through. The swollen, waxy leaves of succulents are filled with water, and hence must be protected from thirsty grazers. They usually employ toxins, or spines, but in the Namib there are also the extraordinary geophytes, plants – such as lithops – which camouflage themselves as stones.

Added to the problem of desiccation is that of overheating. Most desert plants are orientated to minimise heating, by having their narrowest edge facing the sun. Some geophytes go one better by growing almost entirely underground.

ANIMAL ADAPTATIONS Water, the ultimate limitation of the desert, is of key importance to the Namib's animals. Without exception, all of the animal species here tolerate extreme levels of desiccation, and some employ interesting techniques. The male namaqua sandgrouse travels miles to find water each day. When successful, he paddles in it, allowing his breast feathers to absorb water like a sponge. Laden with this cargo he travels back to the nest to feed the thirsty young and his partner. Springbok and oryx have kidneys that are so efficient at absorbing water that a pellet form of urine is produced.

The African ground squirrel faces away from the sun at all times, and uses its tail as a parasol while it forages. Perhaps most peculiar to the Namib are the dune beetles, which inhabit the crests of the desert's taller sand dunes. They are early risers when there is fog about, and sit motionless for hours in order to allow it to condense on their bodies. Periodically they perform a spectacular dance to move the precious water along their bodies and into their mouths.

drive faster on this than you would on normal gravel, there's no leeway for lack of concentration. Inside the national park, the road reverts primarily to the more normal gravel.

North of Terrace Bay, visitor access to the national park is restricted to those on fly-in safaris. For details, see pages 335–9.

Note Beware of driving on the salt-pans anywhere along this coast, as they can be very treacherous.

Permits are required to drive through this southernmost section of the Skeleton Coast, which has long been popular with fishing parties –they're free and can be obtained from the MET office in Swakopmund (see page 278). Several access points line the road, and campsites, some of them seasonal, dot the coastline. This area is also home to Cape Cross Seal Reserve, and the rapidly growing town of Henties Bay.

SWAKOPMUND TO HENTIES BAY

Sea ponds About 7km north of Swakopmund lie a number of large, shallow ponds. These are mostly natural ponds used for salt production by the Salt Company. Some are filled with sea water, which is then left to evaporate, while others are used for farming oysters. Sometimes you'll see one coloured bright red or green by algae, or pink by a flock of feeding flamingos!

Nobody lives here, but workers from Swakopmund manage the site. Both the salt and the oysters are sold within Namibia, and most restaurants in Swakopmund will offer you both.

Wlotzkasbaken This small settlement, about 31km north of Swakopmund, looks like a colony on the moon. Its houses spread out along the desert coast, each overshadowed by its own long-legged water tower (which rely on tankers driving the water from inland). It was named after Paul Wlotzke, a keen Swakopmund fisherman who first built a hut here, and guided visitors to this rich area for fishing.

Like the ghost towns near Lüderitz, nobody lives here permanently. Wlotzkasbaken is simply a collection of holiday homes, used mainly by those Namibians who love sea fishing and come here for their annual summer breaks around December and January.

To the east are a few apparently barren hills and boulders. Get out of the car to take a closer look, and you'll find many small plants and shrubs there. The Namib's fogs are densest (and so deliver more moisture) at higher elevations, so even these relatively small hills catch much more water from the fog than the flat plains.

Among the boulders there are also small land snails, beetles and small vertebrates. These include what is thought to be the world's only lizard that actually mimics an invertebrate for protection. The juveniles of the *Eremias lugubris* species have the same coloration and style of movement as a beetle known locally as the 'oogpister' – which protects itself like a skunk by expelling a foul-smelling liquid.

⌂ Where to stay   Map, page 320.

Government-owned campsites are positioned regularly along this coastline, used mainly in high summer when Namibian and South African families and those on fishing trips descend for the holidays. Otherwise, you can expect these sites to be totally empty.

Pitches are spread along the beach at intervals of 100m or so, each with toilets and running water. Central ablution blocks are perfectly adequate, with showers and fresh water available. There is usually also a basic shop selling soft drinks and tinned goods, and – more importantly – fuel, though as supplies rely on generator power, it's not wise to bank on availability. Each campsite also has a freezer available for campers to freeze the day's catch.

Bookings have traditionally been made through the **NWR** (❄ *061 285 7200;* e *reservations@nwr.com.na; www.nwr.com.na*), but in 2009 management of Jakkalsputz, Mile 72 (see page 328) and Mile 108 (see page 329) was taken over by the privately owned **Tungeni Serenity** (*47 Nelson Mandela Av, Windhoek;* 061 220081; *www.tungeni.com/tungeni_serenity.html*), who are working on a programme of improvement. In high season it's advisable to book in advance, but out of season it's possible just to turn up.

Ⓐ Jakkalsputz Campsite (67 pitches) Book via Tungeni Serenity, (see above). This is about 9km south of Henties Bay – small plots of desert beside the beach, with pitches marked off as campsites & shared ablution blocks.

Ⓐ Mile 14 Campsite [Map, page 274] Now under the management of NWR, at the time of writing Mile 14 was closed, with no indication of when it may reopen.

HENTIES BAY About 76km from Swakopmund, this windswept town is set immediately above the shore, around a stream (normally dry and sandy) of the Omaruru Delta. A surge in property development in recent years reflects the town's increasing popularity with Namibians and South Africans, who flock here during their annual holidays in December and January to escape the interior's heat and to go fishing. Brightly coloured bungalows penetrate the morning mists, while down in the river-bed surreal patches of green herald the local golf club. Perhaps the pair who erected the town's gallows in 1978 – as an appeal to residents to keep the place clean – are winning the battle.

Tourist information The Tourist office (*SME Centre, Nickey Iyambo Av;* 064 501143; e *info@hentiesbaytourism.com; www.hentiesbaytourism.com;* ⏰ 08.00– 13.00 & 14.00–17.00 Mon–Fri) offers plenty of helpful leaflets and maps, and staff who really know the area well. They have a café, Giggling Coffee Pot, and a visitors' WC. Arts and curios are for sale, along with homemade goods and biltong, and a small bookshop should materialise too. More adventurous are plans for interpretive displays about the surrounding desert, so that visitors will leave with a greater understanding of the environment.

Where to stay *Map, page 326.*
Along with the property boom in Henties Bay goes a rise in tourist accommodation. None is luxurious, but there's plenty of choice.

🏠 Desert Rendezvous (4 rooms) 238 Strandloper St; 064 500281; m 081 454 5546; e desertrendezvous@iway.na; www.desertrendezvous.co.za. Opened at the end of 2009, this modern guesthouse stands behind a rather stark brick wall. On the other side, though, is a smart terrace with seating area, while inside are 2 en-suite dbl rooms, plus a further dbl & a sgl, sharing a bathroom. Each is individually decorated, & comes with TV, fridge & tea/coffee facilities, & there's free Wi-Fi access. Apart from b/fast no food is served here, but the owners will be more than happy to recommend somewhere in town. **$$$**

🏠 Fisherman's Guest House (9 rooms) Cnr Brukkaros & Auas sts; 064 501111; e Louis.fenaux@huntandfishnamibia.com; www.fishermansguesthouse.com. Painted bright yellow, Fisherman's lies just 200m from the beach.

Popular with anglers, & with a strong nautical theme, it has a large lounge, bar & restaurant area, with meals available by arrangement (*3-course dinner N$195*). Dbl/twin rooms are all en suite, with minibar, TV & phone; there's also an attractive family room. Public rooms & 3 of the bedrooms are accessible by wheelchair. Outside, a sheltered garden overlooks the sea, & there's secure parking. Deep-sea fishing, rock & surf angling, & dolphin- & seal-viewing trips can be organised, as can hunting trips and various other shore-based activities. **$$$**

🏠 De Duine Hotel (20 rooms) 34 Duine Rd; 064 500001; e reservation@deduinehotel.com. Originally owned by Namibia Country Lodges, and then Protea, De Duine is now privately owned. Its staff are friendly & helpful, & its en-suite rooms comfortable, with TV, fridge, kettle & safe. Old newspapers adorn the walls of the restaurant

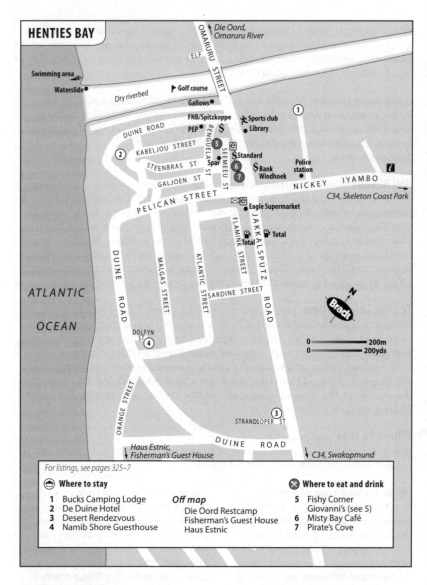

HENTIES BAY

Die Oord, Omaruru River

OMARURU STREET

ELF STREET

Swimming area

Waterslide

Dry riverbed

► Golf course

Gallows●

FNB/Spitzkoppe

DUINE ROAD

PEP ●

$

①

✦ Sports club

● Library

②

KABELJOU STREET

BENGUELA ST

SEEMEEU ST

⑤ e

$ Standard

STEENBRAS ST

Spar

⑥

Police station

SARDINE ST

⑦

$ Bank Windhoek

GALJOEN ST

NICKEY IYAMBO

C34, Skeleton Coast Park

PELICAN STREET

✉ e Eagle Supermarket

ATLANTIC

OCEAN

DUINE ROAD

MALGAS STREET

ATLANTIC STREET

FLAMINK STREET

JAKKALSPUTZ ROAD

Total

⊙ Total

SARDINE STREET

N

Bradt

0 _____ 200m
0 _____ 200yds

DOLFYN ST

④

ORANGE STREET

③

STRANDLOPER ST

DUINE   ROAD

Haus Estnic,
Fisherman's Guest House

↓ C34, Swakopmund

For listings, see pages 325–7

🛏 **Where to stay**

1 Bucks Camping Lodge
2 De Duine Hotel
3 Desert Rendezvous
4 Namib Shore Guesthouse

Off map
Die Oord Restcamp
Fisherman's Guest House
Haus Estnic

✕ **Where to eat and drink**

5 Fishy Corner
   Giovanni's (see 5)
6 Misty Bay Café
7 Pirate's Cove

(⊙ *07.00–22.00*) which serves everything from burgers to fish & pasta: simple but good. A separate bar has a cosy wood-burning stove. **$$**

🛏 **Die Oord Restcamp** (15 chalets) Rob St; ☏ 064 500239. This small, pleasant restcamp with neat gardens has fully equipped, self-catering chalets for 3–6 people, each with a garage. Don't expect luxury, but as a place to sleep it's fine. *3-bed N$420; 5-bed N$590; 6-bed N$680.* **$$**

🛏 **Haus Estnic** (3 rooms) 1417 Omatako St; ☏ 064 501902; m 081 201 2381; e hausestnic@

iway.na; www.hentiesbaytourism.com. This small, German-owned B&B offers well-appointed dbl rooms around a small, flower-decked courtyard with braai facilities. Each en-suite room has Wi-Fi, TV, fridge, hairdryer, kettle & cafetière. **$$**

🛏 **Namib Shore Guesthouse** (4 rooms) 303 Dolfyn St; ☏ 064 500182; m 081 127 5663; e namshore@iway.na; www.namshore.iway. na. This simple guesthouse has secure & quiet accommodation in en-suite dbl rooms, within walking distance of the beach. Also on offer are shore-based fishing & desert tours. **$$**

⚑ Bucks Camping Lodge (camping, 2 chalets) ☏064 501039; e buckcamp@mweb.com.na. Conveniently located for shops, restaurants, pubs & sports facilities, this immaculately maintained campsite with 24hr security offers 45 compact pitches, each with its own shower, WC, washing-up facilities & power points. There are also 1-bedroom chalets sleeping 4 people. *Camping N$250 per pitch (max 4 people), extra person N$40; chalet N$180 pp.* **$**

✗ Where to eat and drink *Map, opposite.*

Some claim that Henties Bay has the world's best crayfish, so this might be the opportunity to try them out. Close to the supermarket and fuel stations are a number of simple restaurants, and there's a café at the tourist information office. It's also possible to get take-away pizzas at the petrol station.

⊑ Misty Bay Café Jakkalsputz Rd (nr Pirate's Cove); ☏064 501336; ⊕ 08.00–16.00. B/fast, light lunches, as well as a range of food from the grill, fish & chips, & hamburgers. **$$$**

✗ Pirate's Cove Jakkalsputz Rd; ☏064 500960; ⊕ 11.00–22.00 daily, bar until 02.00. For burgers & 'divine' pizza in a range of guises, look no further than this popular sports bar. **$–$$$**

✗ Fishy Corner Benguela St; ☏064 501059;

⊕ 10.00–22.00 Mon–Sat, 11.30–15.30 & 18.00–22.00 Sun. The place for fish & chips (& other fish dishes). Eat in or take away. **$$**

⊑ Giovanni's Coffee Shop Benguela St; m 081 250 1740. ⊕ 07.00–16.00 Mon–Fri, 07.00–13.00 Sat. B/fast & light lunches, with burgers & a large range of open sandwiches. **$**

Shopping The town has two reasonable **supermarkets**, a couple of bottle stores, and a few general shops. Some are centred on the Eagle complex, in the middle of town, but carry on up the road and bear left, and you'll come to a branch of Spar. For fresh fruit and vegetables, there's also the National Youth Service Garden Project (drive straight past the welcome to Henties Bay sign, turn right in the direction of Spitzkoppe, and the Garden Project is immediately on your right).

For **curios**, try the tourist information office, or Henties Bay Arts and Crafts – by Pirate's Cove sports bar.

Other practicalities Do fill up with **fuel** in Henties Bay if you're heading north or east. Fuel stations are rare in either direction, but there are several here, including one on the main road that slightly bypasses town, and two in the town itself. For **vehicle repairs**, try Grobler Motors (☏*064 501211*), next to the restcamp. There are several **banks** with ATMs.

There's free Wi-Fi during office hours at the tourist information office, and more facilities at the Namtel office, next to the **post office**.

Should you need a **doctor**, make your way to the Benguela Health Centre in the Spar complex, which also has a **pharmacy** (☏ *064 500599;* m *081 127 0599*).

What to see and do

Fishing If you'd like to join the locals fishing, you'll need a permit (*N$25 for a month*) from one of the tour operators. Sought-after fish include kabeljou (carp), the rather oily galjoen (blackfish), steenbras and stompneus, as well as the now-scarce dassie, or – when the waters are very warm – shad. Angling equipment is available from various outlets, including the Spar supermarket.

Access to fishing spots by 4x4 is designated at regular intervals along the coast north of Henties Bay. Alternatively, contact one of the operators specialising in angling tours, who include:

Henties Angling Tours m 081 251 1489
Rock & Surf Angling m 081 240 3219

Sea Ace Fishing Adventures 064 500545;
m 081 233 9242; e info@seaace.com.na; www.
seaace.com.na. Options include deep-sea fishing.

Other sports While keen fishermen delight in declaring their catches, ardent **golfers** can have a game at the Henties Bay Golf Course (m *081 124 1251*). This resides in a section of the original Omaruru Delta, and doesn't suffer from a shortage of sandy bunkers. If that doesn't appeal, there are **tennis** courts (*064 500751*), or even **horseriding** at Erum Stables (m *081 611 4672, 081 696 8139*).

Hiking and birding Non-fishing visitors might like to take a short wander up the Omaruru's course, while fit, acclimatised hikers can choose from three circular but unmarked trails, taking in some of the desert scenery around the town. The 20km Omaruru River Walking Trail takes you north along the coast, then inland along the river-bed, returning to the centre of town, or there's a significantly longer option – at 70km – leading inland to the Omdel Dam on the Omaruru River. There's also the 18km Jakkalsputz Walking Trail, which runs south along the coast to Jakkalsputz Campsite, returning on a parallel track just inland. Maps are available from the tourist board.

Omdel Dam itself attracts numerous bird species when it's holding water, and makes a good picnic spot. To get there, take the C35 towards Uis for about 27km, then turn right for a further 14km before reaching the dam wall.

4x4 trails The tourist board has route maps with GPS co-ordinates, route descriptions and pictures (*N$100 each*) for a series of 4x4 trails from the town. The routes vary in length from 246km to 312km, and take in some of the region's most spectacular scenery, including the Omaruru and Ugab rivers, and Messum Crater (see page 348).

Quad biking While quad biking is strictly limited in order to prevent environmental damage, it is permitted up to 10km into the bed of the Omaruru River, and to the south of town as far as Swakopmund (except in front of the campsites). Ask for about this at the tourist information centre.

HENTIES BAY TO SKELETON COAST PARK

The C34 continues north along the coast from Henties Bay as far as the national park entrance gate – and beyond. Near Henties Bay, two roads break away to the right. The D1918 heads almost due east for about 121km, passing within 30km of Spitzkoppe (see page 343) before joining the main tarred B2 about 23km west of Usakos. The more popular C35 heads northeast across an amazingly flat, barren plain: certainly one of the country's most desolate roads, although enlivened on each side by views of Brandberg to the north, and Spitzkoppe to the south. This is the main route to Uis, the Brandberg and Khorixas, as well as to southern Damaraland – although if you are planning to stop for the night somewhere like Terrace Bay, Damaraland is best accessed along the C39 further north.

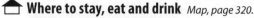

Where to stay, eat and drink *Map, page 320.*

Å Mile 72 Campsite (5 chalets, camping)
Book via Tungeni Serenity; for rates & facilities see page 325. Some 35km north of Henties Bay along the C34 is yet another desolate row of ablution blocks – desolate, that is, unless you're here in the summer. Chalets offer 2 sgl beds & a sleeper couch, with an en-suite shower & WC. An on-site kiosk sells snacks & cool drinks. **L**

⚤ Mile 108 (5 chalets, camping) Book via Tungeni Serenity (see page 325). 64km north of Mile 72, could this be more desolate? Even so, it still has a kiosk selling snacks & cool drinks. **L**

✗ Fisherman's Inn (3 rooms, 2 self-catering apts) m 081 129 8162. East of the road, some 3km north of Mile 72, this bar/restaurant has all the finesse of a transport café – but its simple rooms could be a good bet if it's too w to camp. Expect it to get rowdy at w/ the fishing season (*Dec–Apr*), with a sports TV to add to the entertainment. The menus straightforward: fish or steak & chips, & light snacks served throughout the day. *B&B N$250 pp; self-catering N$750 for 6 people.* **L**

Omaruru River

Driving north past Henties Bay, note all the vegetated depressions (indicating watercourses) that you pass through, spread out along 10–15km around the town. These are all part of the Omaruru River delta. Because of the high rainfall in its catchment area, in the mountains around Omaruru, this flows regularly and the sandy river-bed usually supports quite a luxurious growth of vegetation.

The vegetation includes a variety of desert flora, native to the Namib's many river-beds, as well as some exotics like wild tobacco (*Nicotiana glauca*), jimson weed (*Datura stramonium*) and the castor oil plant (*Ricinus communis*). These are found both here and in many of the other river valleys further north. Dr Mary Seely, in her excellent book *The Namib* (see *Appendix 3*), suggests that the seeds for the first such plants might have been imported with fodder for horses during the South African War. As they are hardy plants, eaten by few animals, they have been very successful.

Gemstones

With so little precipitation, even unobservant visitors notice that the basic geology of the Namib often lies right on its surface, just waiting to be discovered. Don't miss the chance to stop somewhere on the C34 or C35 around here. Wander a few hundred metres from it, and do some gem hunting. Even if you're not an expert, you should find some beautiful crystals.

It was while staying at Mile 72 in 1972 that a Namibian mineralogist, Sid Peters (founder of the House of Gems in Windhoek, page 147), went hunting for minerals. He found several aquamarines and then a long light-blue crystal that he couldn't identify. Eventually the Smithsonian Institute in Washington DC confirmed that this was jeremejebite, a very rare, hard mineral containing boron, first discovered in its white form over 80 years ago in Siberia.

✳ Cape Cross

The Portuguese captain and navigator Diego Cão landed in 1485. He was the first European of his time to reach this far south down the coast of Africa, and to mark the achievement he erected a stone cross on the bleak headland, inscribed in Latin and Portuguese with:

> Since the creation of the world 6684 years have passed and since the birth of Christ 1484 years and so the illustrious King John has ordered this pillar to be erected here by Diego Cão, his knight.

Diego Cão died for his daring, and was buried on a rock outcrop nearby, which they called Serra Parda. His cross remained in place until the 1890s, when it was taken to the Oceanographical Museum in Berlin. In 1974 the whole area was landscaped and a replica cross erected, which stands there today.

David Coulson, in his book *Namib* (see *Appendix 3*), relates that an old slate was found half-buried in the sand around here, with a message dated 1860 reading:

In mid- to late October the large males, or bulls, arrive, their massive body weight of around 360kg far exceeding that of the 75kg females. They stake their territorial claims and try to defend them from other males. Shortly afterwards, in late November or early December, each of the pregnant females gives birth to a single pup. These will remain in and around the colony, and continue suckling for the next ten or 11 months.

Shortly after giving birth, the females mate with the males who control their harems, and the cycle continues, with the pups born about a year later. When the females have all given birth, and mated, most of the males will leave to break their fast and replenish the enormous amounts of body fat burned while defending their territories. In the last few months of the year, the scene can be quite disturbing, with many pups squashed by the weighty adults, or killed by the area's resident populations of jackal and brown hyena.

I am proceeding to a river sixty miles north, and should anyone find this and follow me, God will help him.

It is not known who wrote the message, or what became of them.

Cape Cross Seal Reserve (⏲ *Jul–mid-Nov 10.00–17.00 daily, mid-Nov–Jun 08.00–17.00 daily; admission N\$80, plus N\$10 per car; no motorcycles*) All along the Namibian coast there are colonies of Cape fur seals (*Arctocephalus pusillus pusillus*), though the one at Cape Cross is one of the easiest to access. Occupied all year round, it numbers up to 100,000 animals. The amazing sight of tens of thousands of heads bobbing on land and in the water is matched only by the overpowering stench of the colony that greets you. The noise, too, is unexpected – a positive cacophony of sound that resembles an entire farmyard of animals at full volume. Today's visitors can watch the seals from boardwalks, which is a plus for the seals – if not for photographers. Other facilities include WCs and a picnic area.

Where to stay, eat and drink *Map, page 320.*

Cape Cross Lodge (20 rooms, 21 pitches) ✆ 064 694012/7; e frontoffice@capecross.org; www.capecross.org. Just 4km from the seal colony, this modern lodge – now more of a small hotel – is a beacon for visitors. This is where the desert meets the sea, the vast, open spaces reflected in light, airy rooms, with panoramic sea views from individual balconies or verandas. Solid, limed-wood furniture & pastel décor complement the maritime setting. 3 of the rooms are suitable for families, & 2 others are larger suites.

Downstairs is a cavernous restaurant, split by a central fire from a small lounge area & a bar. The restaurant (⏲ *07.00–10.00, noon–15.00 & 18.00–20.30*), serves both light meals such as pizzas & sandwiches, & main meals (*set lunch N\$175*), but non-residents must book for dinner,

either à la carte, or a 4-course set menu (*N\$235*); a candlelit meal on the beach can be organised on request. A rather quirky wine cellar affords a good selection of wines, & doubles as a cosy dining area for those seeking privacy, although this must be prebooked & may incur a small fee.

Aside from the seal colony itself, visitors are attracted by the sheer beauty of the setting. Just to sit on the screened terrace & watch baby seals cavorting in the waves can occupy half the afternoon, though for the more energetic there are plenty of walks & opportunities for birdwatching. Those planning to discover 'some of the best surfing in Namibia' should bring their own equipment. A word of warning though: don't even think of swimming without taking local advice; the water is cold, currents are very strong & riptides can be extremely dangerous. Advance notice is required for various tours: to Messum Crater (*from about N$1,200 pp, min 2 people*), the wreck of the *Winston*, & the 'Dead Sea' – a saline lake south of the lodge, with shorter excursions to the seal reserve. Advance notice is required for fishing trips (*N$1,800 pp, min 2 people*), & the price includes soft drinks, lunch packs, some fishing equipment, your licence & your permit (documents must be forwarded in advance for these).

Cape Cross Lodge also has a comfortable & fairly well-equipped campsite. High wooden fences protect your tent from the elements, while also allowing some privacy. Each pitch has a light,

power points, braai area & a sink with water. A central ablutions block provid WC & a hot shower. There is also a com for campers with a pool table & DSTV. *. ..op* sells basic foodstuffs, as well as some angling bits & pieces, & there's a separate bar close to the campsite. *DBB N$1,460–2,095/2,230–3,080 sgl/ dbl*. **LLL–LLLL**

Å Cape Cross Campsite There is a small, simple campsite at the seal reserve, with 5 pitches & basic ablutions. Although it provides some shelter from the cold winds, note that the campsite at Cape Cross Lodge is more comfortable & sheltered, albeit not nearly as wild & exciting. **L**

🦈 Wreck of the *Winston*

Just 12km south of the Ugab River Gate to the Skeleton Coast Park is a signpost west to the first of the coast's wrecks that remains visible: the *Winston*, a fishing boat that grounded here in 1970. Normally visited only by seals, terns and Cape gulls, it lies increasingly buried by the sands a couple of kilometres from the road, along a rutted track. Don't be tempted to drive on the salt-pans here (or anywhere else on this coast); they can be very treacherous.

⚓ SKELETON COAST PARK: THE SOUTH

(*Admission N$80 per adult, under 16s free, plus N$10 per car*) From the Ugab to the Kunene, the Skeleton Coast Park protects about a third of the country's coastline. The southern part of this, as far as Terrace Bay, is easily accessible to anyone with a car and some forward planning. It's a fascinating area and, surprisingly, is often omitted from scheduled tours and safaris – perhaps because the accommodation is relatively basic. This is a shame, though it does mean that from July to September – when some of the rest of the country is busy with overseas visitors – it is still blissfully quiet.

PARK ACCESS Access to the park is via one of two gates: the Ugab River Gate on the C34, to the south, or the Springbokwasser Gate on the D3245, to the east. Because the climate here is harsh, and the area quite remote, the Ministry of Environment and Tourism has fairly strict regulations about entry, which must be followed.

Entry permits may be bought at either gate, though note that you must reach your gate of entry before it closes to be allowed into the park – otherwise you will simply be turned away. If you're planning to stay at Torra Bay or Terrace Bay, it is strongly advised to book well in advance through the NWR (see page 56), and bring your confirmation slip with you. If you've left it too late, try calling ahead (📞 064 694007) to see if there's space. You cannot just turn up without any form of reservation.

The coast road inside the Skeleton Coast Park is mostly just normal gravel, so keep your speed below 80km/h to be safe. No driving is permitted within the park boundary after 19.00.

Ugab River (Ugabmund) Gate

(🕐 *07.00–15.00 daily; last exit 19.00*) Some 126km from Henties Bay, or 166km from Terrace Bay, this is the park entrance for those driving along the coast road. Inside, dusty displays of *Onymacris* spp beetles and other insects are rather more interesting than the rather macabre collection of animal skulls that adorn the building.

Springbokwasser Gate (⏲ *07.00–15.00 daily, last exit 19.00*) There's a small, privately owned **campsite** just outside the gate catering to those who arrive too late to access the park.

THE UGAB RIVER The catchment area for the Ugab (or Uchab) River stretches as far as Otavi, making this is a long and important river for the Namib. It flows at least once most years, and you drive across its bed just after the southern gate into the park. Although much of the visible vegetation is the exotic wild tobacco (*Nicotiana glauca*), there are still some stunted acacia trees and other indigenous plants, like the nara bushes (*Acanthosicyos horridus*) with their (almost leafless) spiky green stems, and improbably large melons.

Shortly after crossing the Ugab, look east to see the view becoming more majestic, as the escarpment looms into view above the mirages, which play on the gravel plains. Near the mouth of the Ugab is the wreck of the *Girdleness*, though it is difficult to see.

WRECK OF THE *SOUTH WEST SEA* Near the road, about 15km north of the Ugab River, this is clearly signposted (though not by name) and very easy to visit. It is one of the coast's most convenient wrecks (for the visitors, not the sailors), so if you're looking for a picnic stop, it is ideal. The *South West Sea* itself was a small vessel that ran aground in 1976.

Imagining the Skeleton Coast, most people think that it's littered with dozens of picturesque wrecks – but that's really no longer the case. Shipwrecks do gradually disintegrate. They're pounded by the waves, corroded by the salt water, and eventually what's left of them washes out to sea or vanishes into the sands. Further, modern navigation techniques, using accurate charts and most recently GPS receivers, have greatly reduced the accident rate on this coast. Thus while a few decades ago the coast probably was littered with wrecks, now they're few and far between – so take the opportunity to wander down to this one while you can!

THE HUAB RIVER North of the Ugab, the next river crossed is the Huab. This rises in the escarpment around Kamanjab, and is one of the coast's most important corridors for desert-adapted elephants and rhinos – though you're highly unlikely to see either so far from the mountains.

Immediately north of the river, if you look to the east of the road, you can see the beginnings of barchan dunes standing on the gravel plains. Here sand is blowing out of the bed of the Huab, and actually forming a dune field (see pages 37–8 for the origins of barchan dunes).

It's much easier to spot the rusting hulk of an old oil rig, c1960, with a turn-off to a small parking area adjacent. This was originally part of a grand scheme to extract oil from the coast, organised by a prospector called Ben du Preez, which ran up huge debts before his banks foreclosed. Amy Schoeman's superb coffee-table book, *The Skeleton Coast* (see *Appendix 3*), relates this story in detail. As a postscript, she notes that some of Terrace Bay was originally built by du Preez as his base.

Now the old framework provides a perfect breeding spot for Cape cormorants, so be careful not to disturb the birds by getting out of your car between around September and March.

TOSCANINI For such a significant dot on the map, this minute outpost ⟨is⟩ a great disappointment, especially if you miss it! Despite sounding like ⟨a⟩ campsite, it is in fact the site of a disused old diamond mine. More rusti⟨ng⟩ and decaying buildings.

Elsewhere this kind of dereliction would be bulldozed, landscaped and erased in the name of conserving the scenery, but here it's preserved for posterity, and the visiting seabirds.

North of Toscanini, before the Koigab River, you pass the wrecks of the *Atlantic Pride*, the *Luanda* (1969) and the *Montrose* (1973), though they're not easy to spot, and the road is far enough from the sea for what's left of them to be obscured.

THE KOIGAB RIVER Squeezed between the larger Huab and Uniab rivers, the Koigab (or Koichab – not to be confused with Koichab Pan near Lüderitz) has quite a small catchment area and floods relatively rarely. Thus it seems more of a depression than a major river-bed. For fishing visitors, the Koigab is the southern boundary of the Torra Bay fishing area.

TORRA BAY Shortly before Torra Bay, the C39 splits off from the main coastal C34 and heads east, leaving the park (39km later) at the Springbokwasser Gate and proceeding into Damaraland. Watch the vegetation change quite quickly on this route, as the road passes the distinctive Sugar Loaf Hill on the right, through ecosystems that are increasingly less arid, before finally entering Damaraland's distinctive flat-topped mountains dotted with huge *Euphorbia damarana* bushes.

Just north of this C34/C39 junction is a section of road that stands in the path of barchan dunes that are marching *across* it. Stop here to take a close look at how these dunes gradually move, grain by grain, in the prevailing southwest wind. Then turn your attention to the build-up of detritus on the leeward side of the dunes, and you may be lucky enough to spot some of the area's residents. Look carefully for the famous white beetles (*Onymacris bicolor*) which are endemic to the area and have been the subject of much study. White beetles are very uncommon, and here it is thought they have evolved their coloration to keep cool, enabling them to forage for longer in the heat.

Many of the plants on this gravel plain around the barchan dunes build up their own small sand dunes. The dollar bushes (*Zygophyllum stapffii*), with their succulent dollar-shaped leaves, and the coastal ganna (*Salsola aphylla*) are obvious examples. Big enough to act as small windbreaks, these bushes tend to collect wind-blown sand. These small mounds of sand, being raised a little off the desert's floor, tend to have more fog condense on them than the surrounding ground. Thus the plant gets a little more moisture. You will normally see a few beetles, too, which survive on the detritus that collects, and add their own faeces to fertilise the plant.

Just inland from Torra Bay is a fascinating area of grey-white rocks, sculpted into interesting curves by the wind and the sand grains.

⌐ Where to stay

⚡ Torra Bay Campsite Book via the NWR; for details, see page 56; 🕐 07.30–19.30 1 Dec–31 Jan only. The seasonal campsite at Torra Bay comes to life in Dec & Jan, when it plays host to a plethora of fishing parties. It's absolutely no frills, with small, square pitches marked out by rows of stone, & no shade, yet it's hugely popular – & booked up months ahead. Facilities include 5 ablution blocks with WC & 1 with a shower, a shop & a filling station. *Camping N$165 pp.* **L**

THE UNIAB RIVER Perhaps the most accessible river for the passing visitor is the Uniab Delta, between Torra Bay and Terrace Bay. If you stop in only one river for a good look around, stop here. Not only is it quite scenic, but its headwaters come from around the huge Palmwag concession, home to many of the region's larger mammals, so it offers your best chance of spotting the park's scarce bigger game.

In ancient times, the river formed a wide delta by the sea, but that has been raised up, and cut into by about five different channels of water. When the river floods now, the water comes down the fourth channel reached from the south, though the old channels still support much vegetation.

Throughout this delta you'll find dense thickets of reeds and sedges and small streams flowing over the ground towards the sea. Some 10km from Torra Bay (✹ *20°12.953'S, 13°12.603'E*) there's a pond just 5 minutes' walk east of the road, then 5km further north there's another by the road itself. Sometimes these will attract large numbers of birds – plovers, turnstones and various sandpipers are very common, as are ducks such as the Hottentot teal and Cape shoveller. Palaearctic migrants make up the bulk of the species.

Close to the first pond, a clear path leads east to the remains of an ancient 6th-century nomadic pastoral settlement. Several ruined stone structures hint at a small, Himba-style community, but little else is visible, although there is an interpretive signboard. A further 3km beyond this (✹ *20°11.358'S, 13°12.025'E*), between the two ponds, there is a small waterfall about 1.5km west of the road. Here a gentle trickle of water (supplemented by an occasional rainy-season torrent) has eroded a narrow canyon into the sandstone and calcrete layers of the river-bed, before trickling to the sea. If you go down as far as the beach, then look out for the wreck of the *Atlantic*, which ran aground here in 1977.

Keep quiet while you are walking and you should also manage to spot at least some springbok, oryx and jackal, which are all common here. Elephant, lion and cheetah have also been spotted, but very rarely. Slightly elusive are the brown hyena, whose presence can be confirmed by the existence of their distinctive white droppings (coloured white, as they will crunch and eat bones). Their local name, *strandwolf*, is an indication that they often scavenge on the beaches for carrion, especially near seal colonies. While these animals look fearsome, with their powerful forequarters and a thick, shaggy coat, they are solitary scavengers posing no danger to walkers unless cornered or deliberately harassed.

TERRACE BAY About 287km from Henties Bay, 8km beyond the sign to Dekka Bay, Terrace Bay is the furthest north that visitors can drive on the coast. It's a desolate spot, slightly surreal with its neat street-lighting and lone palm tree looming out of the mist. Originally built as a mining venture, it now functions solely as a restcamp for visitors. It makes an excellent short stop between Swakopmund and Damaraland, offering the opportunity to extend your time in the park, and thus get to know the desert better.

Fishermen, though, come here all year, and even the former president, Sam Nujoma, often took his holidays at Terrace Bay. His phalanx of bodyguards used to make fun company for the unsuspecting visitors he met there, though in later years he booked the whole place for himself and his entourage.

In the evening, take a look at the big shed behind the beach. On it you'll see (and smell) hundreds of cormorants which roost there every night – attracted by the warmth from the generator within. Though rarely seen, the occasional brown hyena patrols this area at night, looking for hapless cormorants that have fallen from the roof, or along the waterfront, where the day's catch is gutted.

The only supplies are limited to a small shop in the restcamp offering drinks and souvenirs, and a vital fuel station/garage (⊕ *07.30–19.30 daily*) tucked rather obscurely behind the beach.

Where to stay

🏠 **Terrace Bay Camp** (20 rooms, 2 chalets) Book via the NWR, page 56; www.nwr.com. na/index.php/resorts/terrace-bay-resort#. The restcamp at Terrace Bay is the resort's *raison d'être*, built originally for the mine staff, & inherited by the government in 1977 when that failed. Now there's nothing here apart from this small camp & its staff accommodation. Although you can in theory just turn up, almost everybody books ahead; space is limited, there's no campsite, & it's a long way to come only to be turned away.

While the bungalows are functional in construction, & include twin beds, a fridge, a new, enlarged shower & WC, & double-glazed windows, recent reports suggest they are due an upgrade & are looking a little tired. It's by no means luxurious, but it feels so isolated that it can be fun for a day or two. For groups, the VIP suite, with its own kitchen & lounge with TV, now hosts less imposing guests than the president, sleeping up to 8 people in 4 bedrooms. A surprising bonus is the bar & restaurant, with friendly service, good food (try the catch of the day, at around N$95) & walls that serve as a large-scale visitors' book completed by enthusiastic guests.

Fishing permits can be obtained from the lodge, as can hooks, line & bait. If time allows, one of the staff might be persuaded to take you fishing. Note that because they are government employees, they are forbidden from charging for such fishing expeditions – but they do appreciate a reasonable 'tip' for their time and help. *B&B N$750/1,340–1,700 sgl/dbl; self-catering suite N$495–770 pp (min 3 people); credit cards accepted, but slow.* **LL**

MÖWE BAY Around 80km north of Terrace Bay, this is the administrative centre for the national park and acts as a base for a few researchers who are allowed to work here. It is not open to the general public.

SKELETON COAST PARK: THE NORTH

Unlike the southern section of the Skeleton Coast Park, access to the north – formerly the 'wilderness area' – is restricted to visitors on a fly-in safari. No self-drivers are permitted into this area.

The visitor looking to see this remarkable northern area of the park currently has two choices. Both are fairly costly and packed full of activities, but they're very different in style. Both rank among the best trips on the subcontinent.

The only caveat to this eulogy is that, while this region appears harsh and 'in your face', it actually offers some of Africa's most subtle attractions. Endless savannah covered with wildebeest is enthralling; gravel plains dotted with welwitschia may seem less so. Most appreciate leopards, but the lichens' appeal is less obvious. Hence in some ways these trips are better suited to visitors who have been on safari to Africa before. Often it seems that the trips are praised most highly by the most experienced safari-goers. Much of the credit here is due to the calibre of the guides: the area's subtle attractions require top guiding skills to bring them to life – and both operations have this.

SKELETON COAST FLY-IN SAFARIS (📞 *061 224248*; e *info@skeletoncoastsafaris.com; www.skeletoncoastsafaris.com*) Even from the outset, the original fly-in safaris to the Skeleton Coast spent much time outside the concession – in the adjacent Kaokoveld, for example, and visiting Purros and the Kunene – as well as time in it. Thus although being excluded from the concession in 1992 was a blow, they were able to adapt their trips to use similar, adjacent areas and offer trips which were just as good, if not better, than the original ones. The flying and guiding ability of the Schoemans is such that they could organise a fly-in safari to an industrial wasteland… and end up making it one of the most fascinating places you've ever been.

14

To understand the current situation in these northern concessions, it's helpful to know the history of the park, as well as some of the politics.

The Skeleton Coast Park was initially part of Etosha National Park, proclaimed in 1906. Then in 1967, South Africa's Odendal Commission cut Etosha down to 25% of its original size, making in the process several 'homelands' for the existing communities. Included among these were parts of what became known as Damaraland and Kaokoland, and also the Skeleton Coast.

During the late 1950s and 1960s various private companies, including the Sarusas Mining Corporation, were granted the rights for mining and fishing on the Skeleton Coast. In the late 1960s, the corporation assembled a project team to build a brand new harbour at Cape Frio. They did all the research and got backing from investors, but at the last moment the South African government pulled the plug on the project. After all, a new Namibian port would reduce the stranglehold on the country held by Walvis Bay, which had historically belonged to South Africa even before it took over the administration of German South West Africa.

The corporation took the case to court and, as part of an out-of-court settlement, the South African government agreed that the Skeleton Coast should be reproclaimed as a national park, a status that was confirmed in 1971. Instrumental in this case was the young lawyer on the corporation's team, Louw Schoeman.

In order to preserve part of the area in totally pristine condition, the northern part was designated as a 'wilderness area' – to be conserved and remain largely untouched. Strictly controlled rights to bring tourists into one part of this area were given to just one operator. Rules were laid down to minimise the operator's impact, including a complete ban on any permanent structures, a maximum number of visitors per year, and stipulations that *all* rubbish must be removed (no easy task) and that visitors must be flown in.

During the course of his research into the case, Louw had fallen in love with the amazing scenery and solitude of the area. He had already started to bring friends up to the area for short exploratory safaris; as word spread, he started taking paying passengers too. When he won the tender for this concession, giving him the sole right to operate in one section of the area, he started to put his new company, Skeleton Coast Fly-in Safaris, on a more commercial footing. The logistics of such a remote operation were difficult and it remained a very exclusive operation. Its camps took a maximum of 12 visitors, with much of the travel by light aircraft. The whole operation was 'minimum impact' by any standard. Louw was one of the first operators to support Namibia's pioneering Community Game Guard schemes (see page 45), and he maintained a very ecologically sensitive approach long before it was fashionable.

I travelled to the coast with Louw in 1990. It was spellbinding: one of the most fascinating four days that I've spent anywhere. Partly this was the area's magic, but much was down to Louw's enthusiasm, and the sheer professionalism of his operation. Gradually, Skeleton Coast Fly-in Safaris had become a textbook example of an environmentally friendly operation, as well as one of the best safari operations in Africa. Louw's wife, Amy, added to this with the stunning photographs in her book, *The Skeleton Coast* (still the definitive work on the area; see *Appendix 3*), and his sons, André and Bertus, joined as pilot/guides, making it a family operation. In many ways, it put the area, and even the country, on the map as a top-class destination for visitors. Largely due to Louw's passion for the area, fly-in safaris to the Skeleton Coast had become one of Africa's ultimate trips.

POST-INDEPENDENCE POLITICS In 1992, the new government put the wilderness area concession up for tender, to maximise its revenue from the area. No Namibian operator bid against Louw; it was clear that he was conducting an excellent, efficient operation in a very difficult area. However, a competing bid was entered by a German company, Olympia Reisen, which has extensive political connections in Namibia and Germany. They offered significantly more money, and won the concession.

Local operators were uniformly aghast, and Louw, somewhat inevitably given his legal background, started legal proceedings to challenge the bid. Tragically, the stress of the situation took its toll and he died of a heart attack before the case was heard. Although his challenge succeeded, the decision was overturned by the cabinet, and Olympia Reisen was awarded the concession for an unprecedented ten years.

The monthly 'rent' that Skeleton Coast Safaris had paid was abolished. In its place, Olympia Reisen paid the government N$1,000 for every visitor taken into the concession. However, with no 'rent' and no minimum number of visitors, the government's income from the concession dropped drastically.

By the mid-1990s it was clear that Olympia Reisen was never going to make a commercial success of the operation. Finally, in 1999, Wilderness Safaris – a major player in southern Africa with a good reputation for sensitive development and responsible operations – made a deal with Olympia Reisen to take control of tourism in the area. They ripped down the poor structures that Olympia Reisen had erected, removed from the area truckloads of accumulated rubbish, and set about a series of ecological impact assessments prior to opening a totally new camp in 2000. As part of their ecological management, Wilderness continued to monitor the area, providing a base for a number of wildlife researchers.

They won the long-term concession here in 2003, but when this came up for renewal in 2010, it was extended for only a year. The same happened the following year. In December 2011, disaster struck: a fire burned down the kitchen and main area of Wilderness's Skeleton Coast Camp. For the following year, 2012, we understand that Wilderness were again offered the option to extend their lease by 12 months. However, this proved too short-term for them to invest in rebuilding, so they declined, and in early 2012 they broke down what was left of the camp and pulled out of the concession completely. In mid-2014 they opened the carefully named Hoanib Skeleton Coast Camp (see page 339), in the northwest corner of the Palmwag concession just outside the Skeleton Coast National Park, which promises some of the same kind of experiences that their old Skeleton Coast Camp used to offer.

While researching this, we asked the MET what was happening to this amazing area and when a tender would be offered. Despite corresponding with a number of MET officials, and pressing this question over a number of weeks, no reply has been forthcoming.

Meanwhile, the Schoeman family continued to operate their own fly-in safaris by using remote areas of the Skeleton Coast just south of the wilderness area, and parts of western Kaokoland and Damaraland just east of the park's boundary. Although these are slightly different areas of the coast and its hinterland, their style and guiding skills remained as strong as ever – and their trips remained superb. On several occasions I've spoken with travellers whom I've sent on these trips who have been full of praise and described them as 'life-changing experiences'.

Getting there and away Skeleton Coast Safaris use light aircraft (typically six-seater Cessnas) like most safaris use Land Rovers: exploring areas from the sky, flying low-level over dune fields, and periodically turning back for better views. So there's a lot of flying in small aircraft – generally short 30–40-minute hops which most people find fascinating.

Trips and accommodation Currently they concentrate on four main trips, Safaris A, B, C and D respectively, though these are really variations around the main theme of their core trip: Safari A. Trips operate all year, and normally require a minimum of two people. Prices include all meals, drinks and activities. As with most upmarket options in Africa, you should find it slightly cheaper to book this through an overseas tour operator who specialises in the region.

Safari A: Skeleton Coast (*4 days/3 nights; US$7,046 pp*) This starts at 10.00 at Eros Airport in Windhoek, before flying west over the escarpment to Conception Bay, south of Sandwich Harbour, and north to refuel at Swakopmund. It stops again for a beach picnic lunch and a visit to a seal colony, before flying north and inland to the first of their three main camps, **Kuidas Camp**. This is in the Huab River valley, west of Damaraland Camp and east of the park's boundary. It's positioned in a dry, rocky landscape that's typical of western Damaraland, and there are some rock engravings within walking distance of the camp. Like all these camps, Kuidas has small but comfortable igloo tents containing twin beds separated by a bedside table, an en-suite bucket shower and a chemical loo (so you don't need to go outside your tent to use the WC at night). There are also flush WCs in the camp. Kuidas Camp is the base for the next morning's exploration of the Huab River valley and huge gravel plains dotted with *Welwitschia mirabilis*.

After lunch you'll hop to Terrace Bay for a short Land Rover trip to explore the beach and nearby roaring dunes (one of the highlights of the trip for me; totally surreal), before flying out to **Leylandsdrift Camp**, in the heart of the Kaokoveld near the Himba community at Purros (see page 374). Camp is under a broken canopy of camelthorns (*Acacia erioloba*) and makalani palms (*Hyphaene petersiana*), near the (almost invariably dry) Hoarusib River. From here the early morning is spent exploring the river valley, which has a thriving population of desert-adapted elephants, among other game, and visiting some of the local Himba people.

Continuing up the coast there are the remains of the *Kaiu Maru* shipwreck to be seen before the northwestern corner of Namibia is reached: the mouth of the Kunene River. Further inland, east of the dunes (which cover most of the park in this northern area), you'll land at the north end of Hartmann's Valley. The afternoon is spent exploring this beautiful and very remote area, before finally reaching the last camp, **Kunene Camp**, which overlooks the river at the north end of Hartmann's Valley (see page 375). The last morning of the trip is usually spent on a boat trip on the Kunene, before lunch and a long scenic flight to arrive back in Windhoek, in the late afternoon.

Safari B (*4 days/3 nights; US$7,640 pp*) This starts earlier, and includes a stop at Sesriem, a drive into Sossusvlei, and a scenic flight over the vlei before flying on to Conception Bay, and continuing with Safari A.

Safari C (*5 days/4 nights; US$9,250 pp*) Starts off like Safari B, but then after Kunene Camp includes a final night beside Etosha National Park, at one of the lodges on the eastern side, and time spent exploring the park by private 4x4.

Safari D (*6 days/5 nights; US$13,062 pp*) Starts off at 07.00, with a flight to Sesriem and a trip into Sossusvlei, before flying on to Wolwedans Dune Camp (see page 248) for two nights. An afternoon exploring the NamibRand Reserve is followed the next day by a flying day trip south to Lüderitz for a 4x4 excursion into the Sperrgebiet, ending up at Elizabeth Bay (see page 237). This has big advantages over doing the same excursion on your own from Lüderitz, as you'll have one of Skeleton Coast Safaris' excellent guides with you, who will bring this amazing area to life. After your second night at Wolwedans, this trip continues as Safari A.

WILDERNESS SAFARIS (061 274500; *www.wilderness-safaris.com*) With just 18 beds, the Hoanib Skeleton Coast Camp is one of Wilderness Safaris newest camps. Note that they normally prefer travellers to make arrangements through a good overseas tour operator (see pages 56–8) in their own country, rather than directly with them in Namibia.

Getting there and away
Flights up to the camp, and back, are with Wilderness Air from Windhoek's International Airport in a comfortable twin-engine 13-seater Cessna 'caravan' (a type that's increasingly common in southern Africa), or similar. Flights are daily, and require a straightforward change of plane *en route* at Doro !Nawas.

The trips
Flights to Hoanib operate daily, usually leaving Windhoek in the morning and arriving at the Skeleton Coast in time for lunch. The return journey usually departs mid-morning from Hoanib and will have you back in Windhoek in the early afternoon. A four-night five-day trip costs around N$43,000/36,500 single/double and includes flights from Windhoek, all meals, drinks, activities and park fees. A shorter trip of three nights/four days costs around N$36,000/31,000 single/double. Opt for the longer trip if funds allow – you'll still leave feeling that you've only scratched the surface – or consider combining a trip here with Serra Cafema Camp (see page 376), on the northern edge of Hartmann's Valley, northeast of the Hoanib Skeleton Coast Camp.

Where to stay *Map, page 342.*
Hoanib Skeleton Coast Camp (8 tented chalets) 061 247500; e info@wilderness.com. na; www.wilderness-safaris.com. Opened in Aug 2014, Hoanib is Wilderness Safaris' newest camp, & viewed as a successor to the now-closed Skeleton Coast Camp. Located in the Hoanib River bed, Hoanib offers an exclusive & very comfortable stay in an extremely remote location. There are 8 tents (1 family unit), with en-suite bathrooms & shaded decks. Accessible only by light aircraft; activities at the camp will focus around exploring on foot, by 4x4 & by air (weather permitting); with chances of seeing desert-adapted elephant & some of the elusive predators found in the area. *FBA N$7,223–10,764/11,112–16,560 sgl/dbl.* **LLLLL**

The sights
While you'll be based at camp for breakfast and dinner, you'll usually spend the whole of each day on a 4x4 safari exploring some of the area's many attractions. These can be long days, but are always varied – and punctuated by stops for regular drinks and picnics. Although there are some specific 'sights' to see, these are almost incidental. Visiting this whole region is about experiencing the solitude and the beauty of a variety of landscapes, each with its own fragile ecosystem, existing side-by-side. While on safari, you'll frequently stop to study the plants and smaller animals, or perhaps to capture landscapes on film. A few of the better-known places in the area include:

The coast Along the coast's misty, desolate beaches there is always something of interest to take a closer look at, or to photograph. Ghost crabs scuttle among the flotsam and jetsam of the centuries, while rare Damara terns fly overhead. Tree skeletons dot the sands, weathered by wind and sea, and bleached whale bones testify to a once-profitable whaling industry in these waters.

Inland
Strandloper rock circles These rock circles are found in several areas of higher moisture near the coast. Probably made by Khoisan people, some of these are simply circles, the remains of shelters used by hunter-gatherers (Strandlopers, or beachcombers) who lived near the shore. Others are more elaborate, covering larger areas and laid out in lines, and it's speculated that perhaps they were hunting blinds – which suggests that the area had a denser population of game in relatively recent (in geological terms) times.

Lichen fields and welwitschia plants Such plants are widespread on gravel plains throughout the Namib. However, here they are at their most extensive and usually in pristine condition. In several places there are clearly visible vehicle tracks which have left a lasting impression on the lichens. These can be precisely dated by historical records.

The roaring dunes These dunes are one of the most amazing experiences on the coast. If you slide down one of the steep lee sides, these large sand dunes make an amazing and unexpected loud noise which reverberates through the whole dune. It really has to be felt to be believed, and gets even louder when you slide a whole vehicle down the dune! One theory links the 'roar' with electrostatic discharges between the individual grains of sand when they are caused to rub against each other. Why some dunes 'roar' and others don't remains a mystery – but there are other roaring dunes: some in the Namib south of the Hoanib River, and in Witsand Nature Reserve in South Africa's northern Cape.

above   A kayaking trip offers a unique chance for a close encounter with the seals in Walvis Bay (JM) page 316

right   Horseriding is possible at many lodges all over Namibia (ET) page 91

below   Get a bird's eye view of the desert on a hot-air balloon ride (CM) page 265

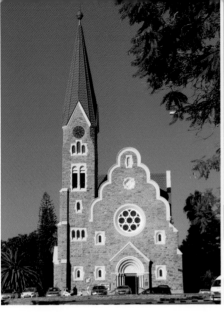

above left Built between 1907 and 1910, Christus Kirche is Windhoek's most famous building and a landmark within the city (WW) page 152

above right The monument in front of the Independence Memorial Museum in Windhoek commemorates the heroes of the struggle for independence (WW) page 153

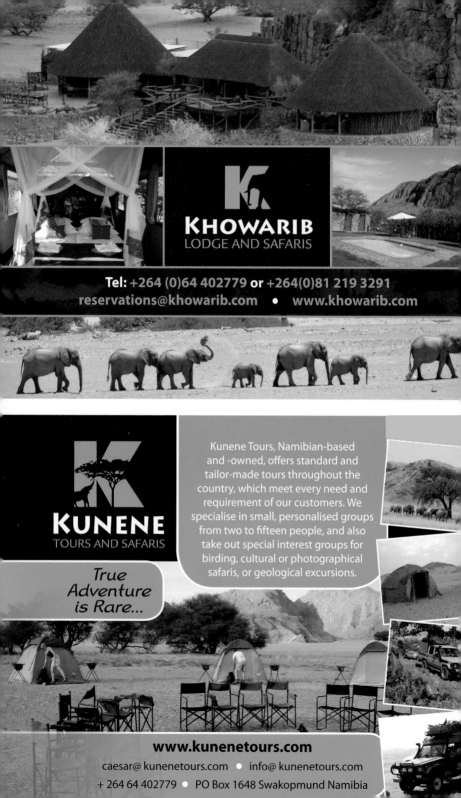

15

The Kunene Region

The Kunene Region incorporates one of Africa's last wildernesses. Namibia's least-inhabited area, it stretches from the coastal desert plain in the northwest and rises slowly into a wild and rugged landscape. Here slow-growing trees cling to rocky mountains, while wild grass seeds wait dormant on the dust plains for showers of rain.

Because of the low population in the northern parts of this region, and the spectacularly successful Community Game Guard scheme (see box, page 45), there are relatively good populations of game here, living beyond the boundaries of any national park. This is one of the last refuges for the black rhino, which still survive (and thrive) here by ranging wide and knowing where the seasonal plants grow.

It is also home to the famous desert elephants. Some naturalists have cited their apparently long legs and proven ability to withstand drought as evidence that they are actually a subspecies of the African elephant. Though this is not now thought to be the case, these remarkable animals are certainly adept at surviving in the driest of areas, using their amazing knowledge of the few water sources that do exist.

Historically the region has been split into two areas: Damaraland in the south, and Kaokoland in the north. Together these were always known as the Kaokoveld. However, more recently usage of the term 'Kaokoveld' has become blurred and is now sometimes used to mean Kaokoland. Though the area is all now officially known as the Kunene Region, this book has retained the old names as they are still widely in use. Further, this chapter subdivides Damaraland because, for the visitor, its north is very different from its south.

Southern Damaraland's most interesting places are easily accessible in your own 2WD vehicle. It is an area to explore for yourself, based at one of the camps or lodges. Its main attractions are the mountains of Spitzkoppe and Brandberg, the wealth of Bushman rock art at Twyfelfontein, the Petrified Forest, and various rock formations.

Northern Damaraland attracts people to its scenery, landscapes and populations of game – and is best visited by driving yourself to one of the three huge private concession areas: Palmwag, Etendeka and the Damaraland Camp. From there you can join the guided 4x4 trips run by these lodges, which is the best way to appreciate the area.

Kaokoland is different. North of Sesfontein and the Hoanib River, there are few campsites and only a handful of very remote lodges. This is the land of the Himba (see *Chapter 2*, pages 25–6), a traditional, pastoral people, relying upon herds of drought-resistant cattle for their livelihood. Their villages are situated by springs that gush out from dry river-beds.

Most of Kaokoland's remote 'roads' need high-clearance 4x4 vehicles and are dangerous for the unprepared. Although the main C43 to Epupa, and the D3701, which links this to the Kunene River, are now graded, they should still be treated with respect. Independent drivers planning to explore further afield will need

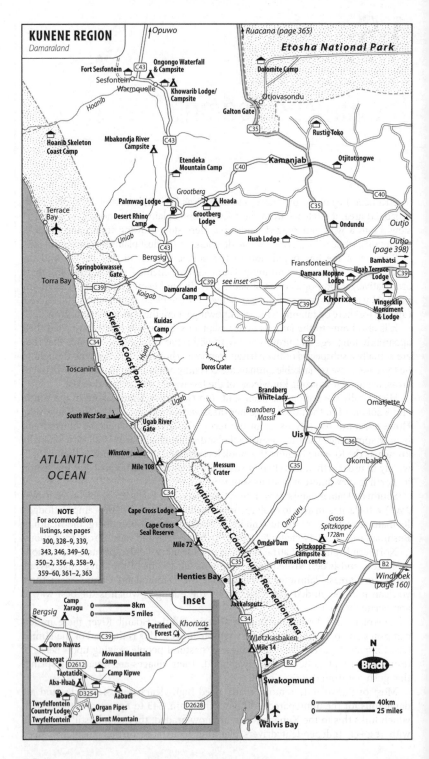

KUNENE REGION
Damaraland

Opuwo

Ruacana (page 365)

Etosha National Park

Fort Sesfontein
Sesfontein
Warmquelle
C43

Ongongo Waterfall
& Campsite

Dolomite Camp

Khowarib Lodge/
Campsite

Otjovasondu

Galton Gate

C35

Hoanib

Hoanib Skeleton
Coast Camp

Mbakondja River
Campsite

C43

Rustig Toko

Kamanjab

Otjitotongwe

Etendeka
Mountain Camp

C40

Grootberg

Terrace
Bay

Palmwag Lodge

Hoada

C40

Desert Rhino
Camp

Grootberg
Lodge

C35

Ondundu

Outjo

Uniab

Huab Lodge

Outjo
(page 398)

C43

Bergsig

Fransfontein

Bambatsi

Springbokwasser
Gate

C39

Damara Mopane
Lodge

Ugab Terrace
Lodge

C39

Torra Bay

C39

Koigab

see inset

C39

Khorixas

Damaraland
Camp

Vingerklip
Monument
& Lodge

C34

Kuidas
Camp

C35

Huab

Doros Crater

Toscanini

Ugab

Brandberg
White Lady

South West Sea

Ugab River
Gate

Brandberg
Massif

Omatjette

Winston

Uis

C36

Mile 108

C34

Messum
Crater

Okombahe

C35

**ATLANTIC
OCEAN**

NOTE
For accommodation
listings, see pages
300, 328–9, 339,
343, 346, 349–50,
350–2, 356–8, 358–9,
359–60, 361–2, 363

Cape Cross Lodge

Cape Cross
Seal Reserve

Omaruru

Gross
Spitzkoppe
1728m

Mile 72

Omdel Dam

Spitzkoppe
Campsite &
information centre

B2

Henties Bay

C35

Windhoek
(page 160)

Jakkalsputz

C34

Wlotzkasbaken

N

Bradt

Mile 14

B2

Inset

Bergsig

Camp
Xaragu

0   8km
0   5 miles

Petrified
Forest

Khorixas

C39

Doro Nawas

Wondergat

D2612

Mowani Mountain
Camp

Taotatide
Aba-Huab

Camp Kipwe

D3254

Aabadi

Twyfelfontein
Country Lodge
Twyfelfontein

D3214

Organ Pipes

D2628

Burnt Mountain

Swakopmund

0   40km
0   25 miles

Walvis Bay

their own expedition: two or more equipped 4x4s, with experienced drivers and enough fuel and supplies for a week or more. This isn't a place for the casual or inexperienced visitor.

For the less intrepid, the best way to visit is by air, or with one of the more experienced local operators who know the area and understand the dangers.

Throughout the area, if you're driving yourself and see local people hitching, bear in mind that there is no public transport here. In such a rural area, Namibians will often stop to help if there is a hope of cramming a further person into their car. It is up to you whether you give a lift to hitchhikers, but your insurance will not cover anyone you give a lift to – make sure you consider the risk you're taking.

SOUTHERN DAMARALAND

With several very accessible attractions, including the World Heritage Site at Twyfelfontein, this is an easy area to visit yourself. Because of the region's sparse population, it's wise to travel with at least basic supplies of food and water. If you plan to explore the area's great mountains – Brandberg and Spitzkoppe – then coming fully equipped to camp and fend for yourself will give you greater flexibility.

SPITZKOPPE (*Day visit N$30 pp, plus N$50 per vehicle*) At the far southern end of the Kunene Region lies a small cluster of mountains, rising from the flat gravel plains that make up the desert floor. These include Spitzkoppe, Klein Spitzkoppe and the Pondok Mountains. Of these the highest is Spitzkoppe, which at 1,728m towers 600m above the surrounding plains: a demanding technical climb. Its resemblance to the famous Swiss mountain earned it the name of the Matterhorn of Africa, while the extreme conditions found on its faces ensured that it remained unclimbed until 1946.

Despite rumours of a new uranium mine around Klein Spitzkoppe in recent years, this has not yet come to fruition. Two (of many) reasons for this are: first, that Spitzkoppe was declared a conservation area; and secondly, that the price of uranium has fallen – and so the mine is of less potential value. At the time of research, Spitzkoppe is still considered safe to visit, although you should always be vigilant with your valuables.

Getting there and away Spitzkoppe – and the restcamp – is reached on the D3716; a 4x4 is advisable. From Henties Bay take the D1918 eastward for 103km, then turn left on to the D3716. Coming from Usakos, take the Henties Bay turn-off after 23km on the B2 and follow it for about 18km before taking a right turn on to the D3716. From Uis, leave on the C36 to Omaruru, but turn right on to the D1930 after only 1km. It's then about 75km to the right turn on to the D3716.

↑ Where to stay *Map, page 342.*

⚊ Spitzkoppe Campsite (3 rooms, 31 pitches) 📞064 464144; e reservations@logufa.com; www. spitzkoppe.com. The local community runs a very quiet campsite with pitches dotted around at the foot of the rocks, as well as simple chalets with bedding, towels & outside showers/toilets. At the entrance to the site is an ablution block with hot showers & a reception area where you can also purchase water, beer & soft drinks, a few provisions such as firewood, a few souvenirs, & (prebooked only) basic hot meals. Otherwise you will need to bring all your own requirements. With a strong emphasis on sustainability, & all proceeds going back into the local community, this campsite is well worth supporting. *Camping N$120 pp; chalet N$370 pppn.* **L**

What to see and do Aside from being a spectacular place to camp, Spitzkoppe's lower slopes provide some difficult scrambles. Nowadays, to explore the mountains you must have a guide, who can be organised from the campsite. A guided tour (*N$50 pp/hr for up to 4 people, then N$35 pp/hr*) takes in some of the rock-art sites that litter the mountains – although some, such as those in the verdant valley known as Bushman's Paradise at the extreme eastern end of the hills, have been vandalised (even here!). There are also several guided hiking trails, taking from half an hour to a full day, or you could take a short ride in a donkey cart. Experienced climbers with their own gear can tackle the Pondoks or Gross Spitzkoppe, but must take a guide for either of these routes – book this at reception on arrival.

Because of their height and proximity to the ocean, these mountains receive more fog and precipitation than most, much of which runs off their smooth granite sides to form small pools. These are ideal places to search for the shrimps and invertebrates that have adapted to the environment's extremes by laying drought-resistant eggs.

UIS Once known as Uis Mine, this small town was almost an extension of the tin mine which dominated it until 1990. When the mine closed, much of the town's population left, but for those who remained, tourism has become an important source of income.

The smart tourist information office at the eastern entrance to the village comes courtesy of a government grant. While information of a practical nature is in short supply, more rewarding are display panels about the mine and local rock art, as well as the adjacent coffee shop, some clean toilets, and a small selection of curios. For something more individual, try the UIDAGO Weaving centre.

Where to stay, eat and drink

In addition to the following, there's also Brandberg White Lady Lodge (see page 346), nearer the Brandberg Massif.

Brandberg Restcamp (5 flats, 11 rooms, camping) 064 504038; e brandberg@ africaonline.com.na; www.brandbergrestcamp. com. Under the management of the enthusiastic, if somewhat eccentric, Basil Calitz, the Brandberg is an unusual, no-frills complex. It was once the recreation area for the mines – which explains the badminton court, snooker room (fully refurbished), table tennis & 25m swimming pool. Spilling out from the restaurant & bar is a shaded poolside terrace with tables for open-air dining. B/fast, a light lunch (served à la carte), & dinner (*3-course set menu N$150*) are open to non-residents, as is the Old Prospectors' Pub – complete with dartboard & an unusual Namibian L-shaped pool table. If you're still bored, there's live music when it's busy, free Wi-Fi access, & even a TV room.

Guests choose from en-suite twin or backpackers' rooms (both with fans & the latter with 2 sets of bunks), 2-bedroom flats (each sleeping 6, with en-suite bathrooms, living area & kitchenette), poolside twin rooms where b/fast is included & a campsite with electric points & ablution block.

Basil's enthusiasm for the region & its geology makes him a fascinating guide. A sundowner tour (*N$100 pp*), especially to the old Uis tin mine, is a must. Other trips (*all min 2 people*) include desert elephant tracking (*May onward*), 360° around the Brandberg & an excursion to Spitzkoppe. Geological tours of 1–2 days with a qualified geologist need to be organised well in advance. Oh, & if you do pitch up here, take a bottle of beer or a beer mat to add to Basil's collection! *Self-catering N$300/200 adult/child (max 6); B&B poolside room N$600/900 sgl/dbl; backpacker N$200 pp; camping N$100/60 adult/child.* **LL**

Uis White Lady B&B & Camping (13 rooms, camping) 064 504102; m 081 128 0876; e whitelady@iway.na; www.namibweb.com/ whiteladyuis.htm. Clearly signposted from the entrance to the town, this is the original White

The discovery of tin deposits in the Uis area was made early in the 20th century, but it was not until 1924 that even small-scale extraction was carried out. This continued for over three decades, until the end of the 1950s, when the South African state-owned company, ISCOR, set out to realise the commercial potential of the mine.

Full-scale production started in the early 1960s. This was an opencast mine, for several years the world's largest hard-rock tin-mining operation. Materials were transported from the pits by truck and the waste dumped in huge white heaps, which continue to dominate the town. Some 84,000 tonnes of tin were extracted over the years, much of it low-grade ore. This, however, was expensive to process, and by 1990 the business was rapidly losing money. The cost of production, together with a downward spiral in the market price of tin, finally led to the closure of the mine in 1990. Around 2,000 jobs were lost, and the small town that had grown up to support the workers was left destitute.

Lady guesthouse, built in 2001 & restored in 2006 by the Namibian-born owner, Analene Van Dyk. Tile-floored rooms with high, thatched roofs & ceiling fans/AC are designed to keep cool; each has dbl or twin beds, a fridge & coffee/tea facilities. Alongside is a grassy area & pool, with b/fast served in the new thatched lapa with its own kitchen. The shaded campsite is spotlessly clean with neatly separated pitches, electrical points & a separate braai area. Wi-Fi is available on site. *B&B N$702/936 sgl/dbl; camping N$100 pp.* **LL**

🏠 **Montes Usti Restaurant & Guesthouse** (6 self-catering flats, 5 rooms) Cnr Uis & Sports sts; 📞081 257 1307. Named after the *Acacia montis-usti*, which is endemic to the Brandberg area, Montes Usti is owned & managed by Wilma De Klerk, whose sister owns the White Lady B&B. It's primarily a restaurant, lofty & barnlike in design, with whitewashed walls, serving b/fast, light lunches & steaks in the evening (*N$150*). There's a separate take-away area next door & a small terrace with BBQ at the back. At the time of research, Montes Usti was undergoing extensive renovations, & was not offering accommodation. However, the restaurant is still open for business & they hope to reopen bigger & better in early 2015. **$$$**

Other practicalities Uis has one fuel station, which also handles basic repairs – almost opposite the Brandberg Restcamp (🕐 *06.00–21.00 daily*). Adjacent to this is the Brandberg supermarket (🕐 *07.30–17.30 Mon–Fri, 08.00–16.00 Sat–Sun*), selling basic foodstuffs.

What to see and do Although many visitors to Uis are *en route* to somewhere else, the area still has two strong draws. For most people, the nearby Brandberg Massif (see page 346), now a national monument in recognition of the importance of the wealth of Bushman art secreted among its rocks, is the greatest attraction. Rather less obvious, though, are the mines themselves. There are no organised tours as such, but Basil Calitz at Brandberg Restcamp regularly takes visitors up in the evening for a sundowner. With its air of desolation and stunning scenery, the place would make a great film set. Should you visit alone, don't attempt to swim in – or drink – the water, however tempting. Its mineral content makes it toxic, and the depth, as well as the near impossibility of access, makes it unsafe for swimming.

For those interested in **geology**, Uis and the surrounding area is something of a Mecca, with even the shortest walk in the hills likely to throw up something of interest. It's straightforward enough to set out on foot from the village, but for guided tours contact Basil at Brandberg Restcamp.

If a **hot air balloon trip** holds more appeal, these can be taken from most Uis accommodation at N$3,450 per person, including transfers from your accommodation and a champagne breakfast (✆ *081 129 9565*).

BRANDBERG
Measuring about 30km by 23km at its base and 2,573m at its highest point, this ravine-split massif of granite – Namibia's highest mountain – totally dominates the surrounding desert plains. Designated a national monument in 1951, and now under consideration for World Heritage Site status, the mountains contain one of the world's richest galleries of rock art, dating from 1,000 to 6,000 years ago. Of these, the most famous – and fortunately for visitors among the most accessible – is the White Lady.

Getting there and away Though you cannot miss seeing it while driving in the vicinity, getting to Brandberg without driving over the fragile lichen plains needs thought. Its eastern side, around the Tsisab Ravine, is easily reached in an ordinary car via the D2359, a turning west off the C35 about 14km after Uis on the way to Khorixas. This is the location of a ranger post where guides are on hand to take visitors into the hills, and it is from this point that visitors can see the White Lady (Witvrou in Afrikaans), the famous rock painting.

Those with 4x4 vehicles can also use the extensive network of rough tracks which turn towards the massif from the north, west and south, off the D2342, starting some 14km southwest of Uis on the Henties Bay road.

If you are heading out to the coast, then the D2342 and D2303 are passable in a 2WD. The D2342 has some sharp turns, though the spectacular scenery and profusion of welwitschia plants make it worth the journey. In the past these roads, particularly the D2303 as it approaches the Ugab River, have been in poor shape, but they are now graded a couple of times a year, so should usually be more accessible.

Where to stay   *Map, page 342.*
In addition to several places to stay in nearby Uis, the Ugab Valley has its own lodge and campsite (also known as the Ugab Campsite), close to the mountains.

Brandberg White Lady Lodge (15 rooms, 8 chalets, 6 tents, camping) ✆ 064 684004; e ugab@iway.na; www.brandbergwllodge.com. Beautifully situated at the foot of the mountains, the lodge is clearly signposted from the D2359, from where it's a further 11km down a sandy but easily navigable track. It's a joint venture with the Tsiseb Conservancy, & staff are largely drawn from the local community. Its central garden with pond is overlooked by a terrace with chairs & tables, shaded by passion fruit & an Angolan bean climber. Behind lie a thatched, brick-built dining area, a separate bar & a lounge with squashy sofas, all decked out in dark wood. The two swimming pools provide a welcome chance to cool off, almost a necessity in the intense desert heat.

Guest accommodation lies some way from the hub, so is very quiet. There are 2 blocks of rather small en-suite twin or family rooms, decorated in ochres & browns with bamboo ceilings, & with roof fans to help with the summer heat. Well-spaced individual stone-built chalets are potentially cooler & offer greater privacy at the same price. Dotted further out across a huge site are pre-erected 'Sahara Delux' tents on stone platforms with 2 beds, open-air facilities & BBQ area. Finally, there's self-camping on a level, sandy site under camelthorn shade with six shared, simple but clean ablutions; each pitch has water, BBQ & a bin, with firewood available. Overlanders have a separate site & their own ablutions & bar.

While for many visitors this is a base from which to explore the mountain, various drives are on offer: sundowner (*N$200 pp*), scenic drive

(N$350 pp) & 'elephant' drive (N$400 pp). All activities are for a minimum of 5 people. DBB

N$925/1,550 sgl/dbl; tent N$715/1,17 camping N$100, plus vehicle N$30. LL

What to see and do Two attractions – the area's rock art, and the opp for climbing in the mountains – are drawing increasing numbers of visitors. Walking alone into the mountains is no longer permitted, so you'll need to take a guide from the Dâureb Mountain Guide Centre (✆ 081 203 0537) – contact on the day is fine for guided day trips, but for excursions on the Brandberg you will need to plan much further in advance, and obtain a permit from the National Heritage Council (see page 348).

Rock paintings This area has been occupied by Bushmen for several thousands of years and still holds a wealth of their artefacts and rock paintings, of which only a fraction have been studied in detail, and some are undoubtedly still to be found. The richest section for art has so far been the Tsisab Ravine, on the northeastern side of the massif. Here one painting in particular has been the subject of much scientific debate, ever since its discovery by the outside world in 1918: the famous White Lady of Brandberg (see box, below). Further up the Tsisab Ravine there are many other sites, including the friezes within the Girls' School, Pyramid and Ostrich shelters.

Guided walks to see the paintings (*2hr White Lady N$50 pp, N$20 per vehicle*) are organised at the Dâureb Mountain Guide Centre. Initially these follow the river-bed, taking in some of the area's flora and fauna on the way, including the tall

THE WHITE LADY OF BRANDBERG

The figure of the 'white lady' stands about 40cm tall and is central to a large frieze which apparently depicts some sort of procession, in which one or two of the figures have animal features. In her right hand is a flower, or perhaps an ostrich egg-cup, while in her left she holds a bow and some arrows. Unlike the other figures, this has been painted white from below the chest. The colouration and form of the figure are reminiscent of some early Mediterranean styles and, together with points gleaned from a more detailed analysis of the pictures, this led early scholars to credit the painters as having links with Europe. Among the site's first visitors was the Abbé Henri Breuil, a world authority on rock art who studied these paintings and others nearby in the late 1940s, and subsequently published four classic volumes entitled *The Rock Paintings of Southern Africa* (see page 532). He concluded that the lady had elements of ancient Mediterranean origin.

More recent scholars consider that the people represented are indigenous, with no European links, and they regard the white lady as being a boy, covered with white clay while undergoing an initiation ceremony. Yet others suggest that the painting is of a medicine man. Whichever school of thought you prefer, the white lady is well signposted and – though somewhat faded – worth the 40-minute walk needed to reach it.

If you wish to get more out of the rock art, then Breuil's books cannot be recommended too highly – though as beautifully illustrated antique Africana they are difficult to find, and expensive to buy. More accessible, but well worth a visit, is the exhibition on rock paintings at the Alte Feste and State Museum in Windhoek.

endemic Brandberg acacia (*Acacia montis-usti*) with its red trunk, and the khori or mustard bush (*Salvadora persica*). Families of dassies make their homes among the rocks, while colourful lizards dart in and out of the shrubby vegetation. The walk to the White Lady is relatively flat and not particularly challenging, with just a few rocky areas and a short climb at the end, but even in the early morning the heat is intense, so go prepared with a hat and plenty of water. The site itself is fenced, and to prevent further damage to the painting flash photography is not permitted.

Climbing With the highest point in Namibia and some good technical routes in a very demanding environment, the massif attracts serious mountaineers as well as those in search of a few days' interesting scrambling. Prior to your climb you need to get a hiking permit, and regardless of your climbing experience an official guide must accompany you on your excursion. Permits (*N$150*) in theory take one or two days to prepare, but allow plenty of time for these to avoid disappointment. You can obtain a permit two ways – first, in person at the National Heritage Council offices in Windhoek (*52 Robert Mugabe Av;* \ *061 244 375;* ⊕ *08.00–17.00 Mon–Fri*). Alternatively email Bertold (e *bkaripi@nhc-nam.org*) to organise the permit by email – thus avoiding waiting around in Windhoek. After your permit is issued, a guide will be organised for you at the Brandberg and you'll be supplied with contact details for them. The costs of a typical Brandberg climb will be N$600 for your climb and guide, as well as the N$150 that you will have already paid for your permit. You'll need to be fully self-sufficient with tents, sleeping bags and all your own food supplies and drinks. It's very important to remember to take adequate safety precautions, however, as the temperatures can be extreme and the mountain is very isolated. If you'd prefer to let someone else do the organising, contact Basil at Brandberg Restcamp in Uis, but please note that it is essential Basil is contacted at least one month in advance, to allow time for organising a permit for the trip.

TWO CRATERS In the remote west of southern Damaraland, these two craters are close to accessible areas, and yet themselves very remote. The only practical way to get in here is with a guide who knows the area – as for safety's sake you need back-up in case of problems.

Messum Crater Southwest of Brandberg, straddling the boundary of the National West Coast Tourist Recreation Area, Messum Crater is an amphitheatre of desert where once there was an ancient volcano, over 22km across. Now two concentric circles of mountains ring the gravel plains here. It's possible to climb down to the salt-pan at the bottom of the crater, where there are also rock engravings.

Messum was named after Captain W Messum, who explored the coast of southwest Africa from the sea, around 1846–48, venturing as far inland as Brandberg – which at that time he modestly named after himself. Only later did it become known as Brandberg.

Doros Crater Northwest of Brandberg, and south of Twyfelfontein, in southern Damaraland, is the remote Doros Crater (or Doros Craters, as it is sometimes called). The geology's interesting here, and there's evidence of early human habitation. You'll need a full 4x4 expedition to get into this concession area.

KHORIXAS Khorixas used to be the administrative capital of the old 'homeland' of Damaraland. Now it is less important – but it is conveniently placed for the visitor between Swakopmund and Etosha. Because of this, and its accessibility by tarred road from the east, it makes a good base for visiting southern Damaraland's attractions, with several good lodges within striking distance. As an aside, in August 2009 the town was the site of a mild earthquake, which at 5.6 on the Richter scale was the largest ever recorded in Namibia.

The construction of a modern football stadium on the outskirts of town, and some development in the centre, seem to have diminished the level of hassle experienced by visitors. Nevertheless, if you do stop, keep a careful eye on your belongings, and be prepared to stand firm if you're offered a craft item – such as a key ring with your name on – that you don't want.

Where to stay

There are a couple of accommodation options in Khorixas itself, and several others in the surrounding area (see pages 349–52), all with their advantages.

iGowati Country Hotel (29 rooms, camping) 067 331592; e igowati@afol.com. na; www.igowatilodge.com. Right in the centre of Khorixas, opposite the fuel station, iGowati Country Hotel is something of a peaceful oasis, with its well-kept grounds & cool fountains, & it makes a good overnight or lunch stop. Efficient & welcoming, it has a comfortable restaurant (⊕ all day), with more tables by the pool, serving b/fast (N$75), lunch (N$100) & dinner (N$190). There's also a bar & curio shop. Uncluttered en-suite rooms run in a curved thatched block overlooking a central lawn. Each has twin beds, or a dbl bed with twin loft room. Camping is at the back, with power & braai facilities, & some pitches with private ablutions. Rooms N$440 pp; camping N$100/50 adult/child. **L**

Khorixas Restcamp (28 chalets, 10 rooms, 20 pitches) Reservations 061 285 7200; e reservations@nwr.com.na; www.nwr.com. na/index.php/resorts/khorixas-restcamp. In a convenient position, just 1km west of town along the D2625, this old restcamp was significantly upgraded in 2009. En-suite chalets built in pairs come as sgl, bush (twin) or family (4 beds); they're modern, light & airy, with AC, linen, kitchenette & BBQ. The campsite has 20 pitches with electricity, BBQ & tables under thatch. The restaurant with bar offers an à la carte menu of grills & steaks with tables both inside & around a large pool. A shop in the reception area sells the basics. B&B chalets N$616/1,056 sgl/dbl; rooms N$330; camping N$110. **LL**

Other practicalities The town has a reliable 24-hour Engen fuel station, and several shops – including a pharmacy, an outlet for Camping Gaz, and a branch of OK Value (⊕ daily) with an ATM. A second ATM is located at the Standard Bank across the road. On weekdays there's a craft shop opposite the fuel station, close to iGowati Country Hotel, where a sign proclaims 'Crafts for Conservation' (⊕ 08.00–17.00 Mon–Fri).

EAST OF KHORIXAS This area of Damaraland is home to the Vingerklip, and some striking scenery, but is quite a way from the main attractions of southern Damaraland. For most visitors, it is best considered as a stopover en route between Etosha and the Twyfelfontein area, rather than as a destination in its own right.

Where to stay Map, page 342.

Damara Mopane Lodge (55 chalets) 061 230066; m 081 129 2424; e info@ gondwana-collection.com; www.gondwana-collection.com. Situated on the C39, 20km east of Khorixas, Damara Mopane opened in 2010. Designed to resemble an African village, its clay chalets are fanned out along sandy paths beneath mopane trees. Each of these has AC & mosquito nets & is set in its own walled vegetable & herb garden, which is harvested for the guests' dinner. Alongside the main buildings in the central area is a pool. B&B chalets N$1,258/2,012 sgl/dbl. **LLL**

Ugab Terrace Lodge (16 bungalows) 081 140 0179; e info@ugabterracelodge.com;

celodge.com. Situated on the
km south of the main Khorixas–
Terrace is perched on a ridge,
stunning scenery of flat-topped
mountains. Its main thatched dining area/lounge
boasts stunning views, with a large patio on 2
sides with tables & chairs, & umbrellas for shade.
The chain of 3 swimming pools (2 baby pools & 1
large) are built into the stone surrounding, with
great views down the valley.

There are 16 comfortable, if a little dated,
bungalows, spaced out along the edge of the
terrace hill. Each has twin beds, an en-suite
bathroom with a shower, ceiling fans & a small
balcony. Activities focus on walking, as well as
nature drives & stargazing. *DBB N$1,500/2,200 sgl/
dbl*. **LLL**

★ ⌂ Vingerklip Lodge (25 bungalows)
\067 290 319; reservations \061 255344;
e reservations@vingerklip.com.na; www.
vingerklip.com.na. Just 1km from the Vingerklip
itself, on the D2743 southeast of Khorixas, this
lodge has been designed to take advantage of the
scenery. From the top, a thatched seating area with
360° views looks down over a bewildering series of
terraces, where pools, a jacuzzi, bars, a braai area &
sun-loungers share the equally breathtaking views,
many of them overlooking the lodge's waterholes.

Despite the name, Vingerklip is more hotel than
lodge. Its small bungalows, spread out in pairs
along an adjacent hillside, are modern & stylish,
but not luxurious. Each has twin or dbl beds &
en-suite facilities, with a safe & private terrace, & 5
have lofts sleeping 2 children. Their strongest point
is a stunning view – though for the best you'll have
to climb up to the Ugab Terrace plateau behind
the lodge, where the Heaven's Gate bungalow
has unbeatable views across the plains – shared
with the adjacent Eagle's Nest restaurant. Back at
ground level, the main lounge/dining area is large,
& the food is buffet-style, so don't leave dinner
too late, or you may find little left. Vingerklip
makes a useful overnight stop, with some excellent
waymarked & guided walks in the immediate area.
It's also possible to organise a range of day trips,
including a sundowner drive (*N$220 pp*). *DBB
N$1,603/2,290 sgl/dbl; suite N$2,520/3,600 sgl/
dbl*. **LLL**

⌂ Bambatsi Guest Farm (8 chalets,
camping) \081 245 8803; e bambatsi@iway.
na; www.bambatsi.com. Bambatsi is off the C39
about 58km east of Khorixas, & 75km from Outjo.
A 5km bumpy track leads to a plateau overlooking
mopane woodlands. Each chalet has an en-suite
shower & toilet, with a private terrace at the back
overlooking the plains. Meals are served on a
broad terrace (*dinner N$180*), & facilities include
a large, sparkling pool. *B&B N$800 pp; camping
N$130 pp*. **L**

✱ Vingerklip (⏰ *09.00–17.00; admission N$10 pp, free to lodge guests*) For years now
the Vingerklip, or 'rock finger', has been a well-known landmark in this area, some
61km to the east of Khorixas. Around it are flat-topped mountains, reminiscent of
Monument Valley (in Arizona), which are so typical of much of Damaraland. They
are the remains of an ancient lava flow which has largely now been eroded way.

Amid this beautiful scenery, Vingerklip is a striking pinnacle of rock, a natural
obelisk balancing vertically on its own. It's an impressive sight, and similar to the
(now collapsed) Finger of God near Asab.

WEST OF KHORIXAS With stunning scenery and attractions that include both
the world-renowned Twyfelfontein rock engravings and the opportunity to see
desert-adapted elephants, this is arguably the most popular part of Damaraland
for visitors. There's little in the way of facilities in the area, but a small kiosk at the
junction of the C39 and the D2612 offers snacks, cold drinks and basic dried foods.

⌂ Where to stay *Map, page 342.*
Options below are listed broadly from east to west.

⋏ Aabadi Mountain Camp (5 tents, camping)
m 081 3412875; e aabadi.mountaincamp@gmail.
com; www.aabadi-mountaincamp.com. Run by
Dutch owners Tamara & Jeroen Verhoef, Aabadi is

a friendly, no-frills place, eschewing the luxuries of many of Namibia's camps. Located 300m south of the D2612, almost 8km east of the turn-off to Twyfelfontein, it was relaunched in May 2009 following storms in 2008. Well spaced around the grassy site, which is dotted with mopane trees, are plain safari tents erected on concrete plinths with a couple of chairs in front. Inside are twin beds, with a battery cum wind-up torch for light. A zipped door leads to an open-air shower & flush toilet, with a donkey boiler for hot water. Campers (max 8 per group) have 12 pitches well away from the tents, sharing bucket showers & flush toilets. At the heart of the camp is a bar & dining area under canvas, where a traditional African dinner (*N$190*) is a welcome extra & the fire pit is the focus of conversation under the stars. During May–Oct, elephants are frequent visitors to camp. *B&B N$908/1,550 sgl/dbl; camping N$80 pp.* **LL**

🏠 **Camp Kipwe** (9 rooms, 1 suite) reservations ✆ 061 232009; e kipwe@ visionsofafrica.com.na; www.kipwe.com. Taken over by the owners of Mowani in 2009, Camp Kipwe is signposted from the D2612, almost opposite the approach to Mowani.

It's a tribute to Francesca Mattei & the late Wolfgang Rapp, who initially built the camp, that the design of their airy, igloo-shaped *epondoks* – Oshivambo for 'rooms' – has been retained. Set among the kopjes with stunning views west across the surrounding plains, each is constructed of stone with a private veranda shaded by rustic poles. Interiors are simple & modern, with twin beds & rush matting enlivened by splashes of lime green. A door leads to an open-air shower, WC & basin, artfully arranged among the rocks. A family room incorporates a children's tent with camp beds, ideal for the over 3s, & there's a suite with private lounge.

The harmonious circular theme continues into the linked lounge & dining areas, with umbrellas on a wooden deck & a fire pit to the side. Altogether more laid-back than its sister camp, & a little less expensive too, Kipwe appeals to a slightly younger clientele & families, & has a greater sense of freedom. Climb to the top of a well-placed kopje for a sundowner, cool off in the small pool tucked among the rocks, or stretch your legs on the plains. Longer, guided walks can sometimes be organised, as with other activities as at Mowani. *DBB N$2,800–3,400/4,100–5,100 sgl/dbl; FBA*

(2-night package) N$3,193–3,793/4,886–5,686 sgl/dbl. **LLLLL**

🏠 **Mowani Mountain Camp** (13 tented rooms, 2 suites), reservations ✆ 061 232009; e mowani@visionsofafrica.com.na; www.mowani. com. Well signposted on the D2612, about 3km south of its junction with the D3214, Mowani is a further 3km along a sandy track. The rounded, thatched domes of its main buildings, with views across to the surrounding mountains, give the impression of a grand African village, blending beautifully with the giant granite boulders that surround them. There's a pool hidden among the rocks, & a stunning sundowner bar to make the most of the view. Then, in the evening, the candlelit restaurant takes on a special-occasion feel, backed up by an extensive wine list – with coffee served in the lounge or around the fire pit.

Dotted among the boulders are large thatch & canvas tented rooms; from their private verandas, 6 of them share the views, & the others face east. The tents are comfortable though not large, with dbl or twin beds, table fans, tea/coffee stations, safes & en-suite showers & toilets. Of the suites, the honeymoon suite is truly special, combining African colonial design with a high standard of 21st-century luxury, including a lounge area with DSTV, indoor/outdoor bath & shower, & a private pool set into the rocks.

Activities include nature drives in search of desert elephants (*N$620 pp*), guided walks & excursions to the attractions around Twyfelfontein – although, as elsewhere in this area, many people use this as a base for driving themselves around. Mowani is far from cheap, but you do get both good service & good design for your money! *DBB tented rooms N$3,090–4,040/5,900–6,380 sgl/dbl; FBA N$3,483–4,433/5,466–7,166 sgl/dbl.* **LLLLL**

🏕 **Aba-Huab Community Campsite** ✆ 081 129 0410; e abahuabreservation@iway.na. Aba-Huab is owned & managed by the entrepreneurial Elias Xoagub. Well signposted on the D3254, about 11km before Twyfelfontein, it stands on a large site beside a (usually) dry river-bed. Shady pitches for independent travellers & groups have water, BBQ & electricity points. If you don't have your own tent, there are simple pre-erected tents – but bring your own sleeping bag & mat. Aba-Huab also rents out tents equipped with bedding kits for N$250 pp per night. The site spans the road, with the much quieter 'exclusive' site on the left. As well as 3 ablution blocks with solar-heated showers & flushing toilets, there's a communal fire pit, a pool table & a bar where meals (*including traditional dishes; dinner N$120*) can be prepared with advance warning. Firewood & ice are available too. *Camping with own equipment N$120 pp, with hired equipment N$260 pp.* **L**

🏠 **Twyfelfontein Country Lodge** (56 rooms, 1 suite) ☏061 374750; e twyfelfontein@ncl.com.na; www.namibialodges.com. This well-staffed 3-star lodge is set in a rock-strewn valley near the Aba-Huab River, 10km from the world-renowned rock art site of Twyfelfontein along the D3214. Indeed, close to the lodge entrance it has its own 2,000-year-old rock engravings. The en-suite thatched rooms are built in blocks of 8, with 4 that will convert into family units. They're quite small inside – in contrast to the completely over-the-top VIP suite. Expect twin beds, a ceiling fan, & fairly traditional, even heavy, décor with dark wood & African-print fabrics. A very large thatched open-plan central area, built on 2 storeys with open sides, backs on to a rocky hillside with a good-size, curved pool to one side. Upstairs are a dining room (*dinner N$130–215*) & bar, with reception & a curio shop below.

While most people use the lodge as a base to drive themselves around the area, or as a stopover that's conveniently close to Twyfelfontein, walks can be arranged, as can nature drives (in quite large, trucklike 4x4s) down the Huab River in search of elephants & other wildlife. Stargazing is another option. Twyfelfontein Lodge opened a small petrol station in Mar 2015 selling 95 petrol & 50ppm diesel. There's also a workshop for minor & tyre reparis. Cash payments only. *B&B N$1,530/2,240 sgl/dbl.* **LLL**

🏠 **Doro Nawas** (17 chalets) ☏061 274 500; e info@wilderness.com.na; www.wilderness-safaris.com. Brooding on the crest of a low hill, like a dark Moorish castle, Doro Nawas sits between the Etendeka Mountains in the north & Twyfelfontein in the south, with 360° panoramic views of the Damaraland Plains. It is a joint venture between Wilderness Safaris & the local community, & is clearly signposted almost 5km from the C39. Guest chalets are huge, individually spaced around the foot of the hill, their thatch merging into the surrounding landscape; 2 combine to form a family unit. A moody darkness prevails in the natural stone walls, dark wood for the roof & heavy, stone-effect bedhead, though the cavelike effect is lightened by sliding doors leading out to a wide, secluded veranda, which – courtesy of beds that can be rolled out – makes a great place to spend a night under the stars. A roomy ablutions area incorporates 2 washbasins, separate toilet, & inside & outside showers.

Up in the castle, the dining room cum bar dominates the whole of one side, while stairs lead up to an open-air rooftop area that lends itself to sundowners or taking in the majesty of the heavens. There's a pool with a view, too, ensuring that you're never divorced from the beauty of the location. Attentive & well-trained staff, 90% from the local area, set out to ensure that your visit is enjoyable – even on the rare occasions when activities are on hold & lashing rain serves to intensify the brooding atmosphere.

In addition to trips in search of desert elephants, which are regularly spotted quite close to the lodge, there are guided walks, & visits to Twyfelfontein, the Organ Pipes, Burnt Mountain & the Petrified Forest, although many guests drive themselves to these attractions. *DBB N$4,198–6,094/5,070–8,844 sgl/dbl; FBA N$8,002–10,540/10,414–15,460 sgl/dbl.* **LLLLL**

What to see and do

🔖 **Twyfelfontein rock engravings** (⏲ *08.00–17.00 daily (last booking at 15.30 in winter); admission N$50/25 per adult/child inc. guide, N$10 per vehicle*) Twyfelfontein was named 'doubtful spring' by the first European farmer to occupy the land – a reference to the failings of a perennial spring of water which wells up near the base of the valley. The valley was once known as Uri-Ais, and seems to have been occupied for thousands of years. Then its spring, on the desert's margins, would have attracted huge herds of game from the sparse plains around, making this uninviting valley an excellent base for early hunters. This probably explains why the slopes of Twyfelfontein, amid flat-topped mountains typical of Damaraland, conceal one of Africa's greatest concentrations of rock art. At first glance, these just seem like rock-strewn hillsides. But the boulders that litter these slopes are dotted with thousands of paintings and ancient engravings, only a fraction of which have been recorded.

Declared a World Heritage Site in 2007, Twyfelfontein was unusual among African rock art sites in having both engravings and paintings, though today only engravings can be seen. Many are of animals and their spoor, or geometric motifs – which have been suggested as maps to water sources. Why they were made, nobody knows. Perhaps they were part of the people's spiritual ceremonies, perhaps it was an ancient nursery to teach their children, or perhaps they were simply doodling.

All visitors must be accompanied by a guide along one of two demarcated trails, taking around 30 minutes and 45 minutes respectively. The paths are quite uneven, so you'll need stout shoes, as well as a hat and some water. The best time to visit is first thing in the morning or – especially for photographs – in the early evening, but this last is also the most popular, so try to get there before the tour buses descend. A modern visitor centre provides comprehensive information, and is well worth a half-hour or so of your time. There's also a shaded picnic area with cold drinks for sale.

Getting there and away To reach the valley, which is well signposted, take the C39 west from Khorixas for 73km. From here, turn left on to the D2612 for almost 15km, then right on the D3214 for a further 11km (ignoring the left fork to the D3254 after 6km).

Organ Pipes and Burnt Mountain Retracing your tracks from Twyfelfontein, turn right at the junction on to the D3254, signposted to Burnt Mountain. After 4.5km there's a flat area above a small gorge. Park here and take one of the paths down, where you'll find hundreds of tall, angular columns of dolorite in a most unusual formation: these are the **Organ Pipes**. They were thought to have formed about 120 million years ago when the dolorite shrank as it cooled, forming these marvellous angular columns up to 5m high in the process.

Continuing just 1km beyond the Organ Pipes, you'll see what is known locally as the **Burnt Mountain**. Seen in the midday sun this can be a real disappointment, little more than a heap of black shale amid the dominant sandstone, but when the rocks catch the early morning or late afternoon light, the mountainside glows with a startling rainbow of colours, as if it's on fire.

The Living Museum of the Damara (e *contact@lcfn.info*; ⊕ *daily; admission: village experience N\$80 pp, bushwalk N\$70 pp*) North of the Aba-Huab River, the local Damara villagers have constructed a small village to showcase their culture. Opened at the end of 2009, it is clearly signposted to the east of the D3254, just short of the D2612. From the neatly demarcated parking area, two huge boulders mark the entrance to the compound, which incorporates traditional Damara houses for both the chief and his wife. Visitors may have the opportunity to see weapons, tools, jewellery and crafts are made, as well as enjoying dancing, singing and traditional games. Bushwalks offer the chance to see how the Damara people foraged and hunted in the past.

Wondergat Off the D2612, north of the turn-off to Twyfelfontein, there's a track heading south to Wondergat. After about 500m this comes to a huge hole in the ground – thought to be the remnants of a subterranean cave whose roof collapsed long ago. There are no signposts or safety barriers, so be careful near the edge.

Petrified Forest (⊕ *08.00–16.00 daily; admission N\$80 pp inc. guide, plus N\$20 per vehicle*) Signposted beside the C39, about 44km west of Khorixas, lie a number of petrified trees on a bed of sandstone. Some are partially buried, while others lie completely exposed because the sandstone surrounding them has eroded away. It is thought that they were carried here as logs by a river some 260 million years ago, and became stranded on a sandbank. Subsequently sand was deposited around them, creating ideal conditions for the cells of the wood to be replaced by silica, and thus become petrified.

Now there is a small office here with good crafts for sale, toilets and a car park. Demarcated paths lead around the site, with helpful guides to point out some of the highlights of the forest, including some ancient welwitschia plants.

It's worth noting that there are several 'petrified forests' signposted from the C39, all claiming the presence of welwitschia plants, too. This site, however, is the one that has been declared a national monument. It is staffed by trained guides and is well worth your support.

Desert elephants Most of the lodges in the area run nature drives in search of desert-adapted elephants which are regularly seen between May and October. (It's worth noting that once the rains start, the elephants retreat up the Huab River, so at each end of the season drives from some of the lodges can be very long, with significant stretches along the road.) Fortunately the river itself, lined with tamarisk and reeds, is an attraction in its own right. Pools attract birds from the hamerkop to the blue-cheeked bee-eater, while away from the river, keep an eye out on the

WELWITSCHIA MIRABILIS

Welwitschia, perhaps Namibia's most famous species of plant, are usually found growing in groups on the harsh gravel plains of the central Namib and western Kunene Region. Each plant has only two, long, shredded leaves and is separated from other welwitschia plants by some distance. They appear as a tangle of foliage (some green, but mostly desiccated grey) which emerges from a stubby wooden base.

They were first described in the West by Friedrich Welwitsch, an Austrian botanist who found them in 1859. Since then scientists have been fascinated by welwitschia, earning the plant the scientific name of *mirabilis* – Latin for 'marvellous'!

Research suggests that welwitschia can live for over 1,000 years and are members of the conifer family (some sources still class them with the succulents). Though their leaves can spread for several metres across and their roots over a metre down, it is still a mystery how they obtain water. One theory suggests that dew condenses on the leaves, and then drips to be absorbed by fine roots near the surface of the ground.

Welwitschia rely on the wind to distribute their seeds, but young plants are rare. They germinate only when the conditions are perfect, in years of exceptional rain. I was shown one on the Skeleton Coast that was eight years old. It was minute: consisting of just two seedling leaves and no more than 2cm tall.

Their ability to thrive in such a harsh environment is amazing, and their adaptations are still being studied. There has even been a recent suggestion that the older welwitschia plants may change the chemical constitution of the soil around them, making it harder for young plants to establish themselves nearby and compete for water and space.

plains for Rüppell's korhaan, birds of prey such as black-breasted snake eagles, and lappet-faced vultures.

NORTHERN DAMARALAND

Approaching from the west, along the C39, is perhaps the most interesting way to enter this area north of the Huab River. After the flat coast, you soon find the gravel plains dotted first with inselbergs, then with low chains of weathered hills. The land begins to rise rapidly: you are coming on to the escarpment, around 50km from the coast, which is the edge of one of the largest sheets of ancient lava in the world. Sheets of molten lava poured over the land here in successive layers, about 300 million years ago. Now these Etendeka lavas dominate the scenery, with huge flat-topped mountains of a characteristic red-brown-purplish colour.

The rainfall here is still low, and the sparse covering of grasses is dotted with large *Euphorbia damarana* bushes. These grow into spiky, round clumps, perhaps 3m in diameter and over 1m tall, and are endemic to this region. Break a stem to reveal poisonous milky-white latex, which protects the bushes from most herbivores, except black rhino and kudu, which are both said to eat them. (A tale is told of a group of local people who roasted meat over a fire of dead euphorbia stems – only to die as a result.)

If you could continue as a bird, flying northeast towards Etosha, then the land below you would become progressively less dry. Flying over the Hobatere area, you'd notice that the higher rainfall promotes richer vegetation. In the northern areas of that concession you would see an undulating patchwork of mopane scrub and open grassy plains, dotted with various trees, including the distinctive flat-topped umbrella thorn (*Acacia tortilis*). You would have left the desert.

FAUNA Generally the amount of game increases as the vegetation becomes lusher in the east. In the mountains around Palmwag, Etendeka and Damaraland Camp there are resident steenbok, baboon, kudu, porcupine and the occasional klipspringer and warthog, joined by wide-ranging herds of Hartmann's mountain zebra, gemsbok and springbok. Equally nomadic but less common are the giraffe and desert-adapted elephant.

An enduring memory from here is the sight of a herd of giraffe. We watched them for almost an hour, as they skittishly grazed their way across a rocky hillside beside what is now the main C43. Their height seemed so out of place in the landscape of rocks and low trees.

Black rhino are present throughout the region, but spend most of their days sleeping under shady bushes, and so are rarely seen, even by those who live here. (Strenuous rhino-tracking trips are run by Desert Rhino Camp, as well as – with advance notice – by Grootberg Lodge, Khowarib Lodge and sometimes Damaraland Camp.)

Leopard occur, and both cheetah and lion have been seen – but it is thought that only small numbers of big cats are left in the region, and they range over huge areas in search of suitable prey.

The birdlife is interesting, as several of the Kaokoveld's ten endemic species are found here. Perhaps the most obvious, and certainly the most vocal, are Rüppell's korhaan – whose early morning duets will wake the soundest sleeper. The ground-feeding Monteiro's hornbill is another endemic, though not to be confused with the local red-billed hornbills. There is also an endemic chat, the Herero chat, which occurs along with its more common cousins, the ant-eating tractrac and familiar chats. Though not endemic, black eagles are often seen around the rockier hillsides: surely one of Africa's most majestic raptors.

Looking further east, to Hobatere and Huab, there is more vegetation, making a classic environment for big game animals. These areas can support more game, and it shows. Elephants are certainly more common, and more easily spotted. The desert-adapted species seen to the west are joined in Hobatere by eland, black-faced impala and Damara dik-dik – both of the latter are subspecies endemic to the region. Similarly, the variety of birds becomes wider as you move east, with species that occur in Etosha often overlapping into Hobatere.

 WHERE TO STAY *Map, page 342.*

North of the Huab River lie a number of large concession areas, which are set aside for tourism. These are chunks of land that the government has allocated to one operator, who has the sole use of the land for tourism purposes. Local people can live and even keep animals within some of these tourism concessions, but development is limited. With Namibia's increasing emphasis on community conservancies, considerable change is afoot in this area. Yet, while this is very significant for local people, the impact on visitors is likely to be less noticeable, not least because all the operators in this area have long worked closely with their local communities and to the benefit of the environment.

Several areas are used by operators to give visitors an insight into the area's ecosystems. Both Damaraland Camp and Grootberg are within community-owned conservancies. Palmwag and Etendeka are still concessions. Finally, there is Huab Lodge, which is in a private reserve rather than a concession area, but is similar in style. Although each of the areas is totally different, Damaraland Camp, Palmwag and Etendeka occupy broadly similar environments, unlike Huab Lodge.

These aren't places that you can drop into for a day and expect to fully appreciate, and a visit to any is best arranged in advance. The lodges listed below follow a rough clockwise circle as far as Huab, followed by Palmwag, Etendeka and the areas north to Sesfontein.

Damaraland Camp (10 chalets) Contact via Wilderness Safaris ☏ 061 247500; e info@wilderness.com.na; www.wilderness-safaris.com. Damaraland Camp was originally modelled on Etendeka (see page 359), & initially seemed very similar: both were remote tented camps on a rocky hill, nestling amid the stunning red-purple mountain scenery that is typical of the Etendeka lava flows. While it has always been much more luxurious than Etendeka, it has also always had a stronger community involvement.

Physically, the camp lies close to the Huab River, along a 13km track southwest of the C39. The turning (⊕ *20°19.464'S, 14°04.969'E*) is next to a smallholding, some 42km west of the D2612 to Twyfelfontein. Although an experienced driver going slowly could negotiate the track in a normal 2WD that's not overloaded, a rendezvous is normally arranged at the junction. From here you'll be taken to the camp by 4x4, leaving your

vehicle under the watchful eyes of a local family. Reservations are essential; it's not a camp that you can just drop into.

Damaraland Camp was completely rebuilt in 2009, though still on firm environmental principles. In place of the green tents, set facing west at the foot of rolling hills, are thatched square chalets on wooden platforms: some on high stilts to ensure a view; others lower down. Creative use of wooden poles, canvas walls, zip-up doors & reed screening combines with plenty of space to realise light, airy & cool accommodation. Floors are of natural wood; lighting is subtle but effective; & there are plenty of thoughtful touches: a sensible desk with chair; tea & coffee (with water on request); ceiling fans; & a roll-down door to the bathroom for privacy. Batteries can be charged in the office.

Décor, a mix of creams & soft browns, continues into the extensive main area, where a 22-seater dining table lines one side & a large pool with umbrella-shaded chairs the other, with decking at the front. With simple, almost minimalist seating, the effect is soft & uncluttered.

The area around the camp is dry & vegetation is sparse; even *Euphorbia damarana* is not present to any great extent except along the river-bed. However, there are some good examples of welwitschia on the way to the Huab River valley, which makes a good venue for drives in search of desert elephant & other game. A couple of 3km trails, the Damarana & the Shepherd's, afford the chance to explore the mountains on foot, while closer at hand guests can visit a local village. For longer stays, rhino tracking may be possible on request. However, there is no guarantee of finding rhino, as they move freely in a truly vast, unfenced area.

Damaraland Camp's brand of community involvement has attracted numerous accolades. These aside, it is one of Namibia's best camps, now 40% owned & largely run by the local community. Visitors often comment on how positive & happy the atmosphere is, so it is well worth stopping for 2–3 nights (just 1 night is too short). *DBB N$4,198–6,094/5,070–8,844 sgl/dbl; FBA N$8,002–10,540/10,414–15,460 sgl/dbl.* **LLLLL**

C40 east of Palmwag

⌂ **Grootberg Lodge** (14 twin & 2 family chalets) ⛌067 333 212; reservations ⛌061 228 104; e reservations@grootberg.com; www. grootberg.com. Perched at the top of the Grootberg Pass, between Palmwag & Kamanjab, this lodge in the /Khoadi//Hôas Conservancy was opened in 2005. Under the watchful management of Isabel & Lloyd, local staff are being trained to run the lodge, with the aim of running it themselves by 2020.

To get there, simply follow the C40 from Palmwag towards Kamanjab; the lodge is at the very top of the Grootberg Pass, at a commanding 1,645m. Unless you have a good 4x4, & are very confident in your driving ability, don't attempt the extremely steep, narrow track up to the lodge. Just park at the bottom & the warden will arrange for you to be collected.

The lodge's primary attraction is its stunning location, with breathtaking views sweeping south down the valley towards the Brandberg Mountains. The buildings, clad in the local 'lava' stone, are whitewashed inside, with an uncluttered décor that is both cool & relaxing –

think comfy, neutral sofas with casual throws, classic wooden tables & chairs in the dining area, classy photographs on the walls, & a small range of well-chosen books. Outside, a wide veranda with tables & umbrellas makes the most of the view, though the vertiginous drop makes this less than relaxing for parents with young children. Each of the twin or dbl chalets faces south, with sliding doors leading to en-suite bedrooms whose handmade furniture is of unpolished pine. Power is supplied from a generator, there are no sockets in the rooms but guests are welcome to charge electrical appliances in the main area.

In addition to guided walks (*from N$295*) & scenic sundowner drives (*N$565*), guests can visit a Himba village (*N$1,180*), or track elephants (*N$1,180*) or rhinos (*N$1,440*) – all pp for 2 people min. *DBB N$1,845/2,714 sgl/dbl.* **LLLL**

⛺ **Hoada Campsite** (6 pitches) ⛌067 333 212; e reservations@grootberg.com. Under the same management as Grootberg Lodge (25km east of Grootberg Lodge on the C40), this small community campsite lies at the foot of a kopje about 200m from the road. This beautiful & secluded spot offers shady & private camping areas, & a small swimming pool cleverly built into the boulders. Each spacious campsite has its own kitchen area with running water & BBQ facilities, as well as its own outside shower with warm water & a flush toilet. Note that the campsites have no electricity or power points. Guests here are welcome to participate in activities offered at Grootberg Lodge, but must drive themselves to the lodge for these. *Camping N$180 pp.* **L**

⌂ **Huab Lodge** (8 bungalows) ⛌067 312070; e info@huab.com; www.huab.com; reservations ⛌061 224712; e reservations@resdes.com.na; ⊕ all year round. A private concession area in spirit, Huab is owned & run by Jan & Suzi van de Reep, who have worked in tourism in Namibia for years. Together with friends, they bought up a number of adjacent farms in a hilly area, around the headwaters of the Huab River. Although this land was of significance as a refuge for some of the Huab River's desert-adapted elephants, farmers had fenced the land, & didn't enjoy the elephants' feeding forays on to their farms, causing much tension for both men & beasts. With the fences down, antelope have returned, the ecosystem has reverted to its natural state & elephants are seen around the lodge more. This is a textbook demonstration of how tourism can be used to finance conservation initiatives, & is a compelling argument for encouraging ecotourism to Namibia.

The lodge is situated on the banks of the Huab (beware: if the rivers are in flood, reaching here can be difficult). It is along the D2670, well signposted from the C35 between Kamanjab & Khorixas. The approach road is some 30km long, with 4 farm gates, & becomes increasingly scenic, so don't expect a quick arrival.

Huab boasts classic thatch-on-brick design, tasteful décor, a little landscaping, & lots of quality. Light, spacious bungalows, with a wide frontage & private veranda, all have 2 queen-size beds & en-suite rooms for the toilet & separate shower. Electricity & hot water are mostly solar. Solid, handmade Rhodesian teak furniture is offset by soft furnishings that are made up at the lodge from locally designed fabrics, which are also on sale in the curio shop.

Jan, who, if you're lucky will guide you for an activity, is one of the country's best guides, so even if there's no game around (& that's unusual now that the animals have repopulated the land), you'll still find the drives & walks fascinating, or plenty to spot from the bird hide. Similarly, Huab's hospitality is excellent, with meals served for everyone together – relaxed, social occasions in a thatched central hub where it's easy to feel completely at home. For total relaxation, you can bathe away the day's aches under thatch in natural hot springs, alongside a cooler tub for contrast, or treat yourself to a wellness therapy (the only extra cost). To keep in touch, there's Wi-Fi in the rooms & central area. *DBB N$1,749–2,674/3,498–4,020 sgl/dbl.* **LLLLL**

Palmwag to Sesfontein

A veterinary fence on the C43 marks the road north towards the Palmwag and Etendeka concessions, and on to Sesfontein. Just before the fence is a small fuel station (⊕ *24hrs daily*). Everybody seems to fill up here (but remember that payment for fuel is accepted only in cash). The small shop opposite is a welcome place for a cold drink or a packet of crisps. This is also the location of the airstrip.

You may come across people selling carved vegetable ivory trinkets near here, but it's as well to be suspicious of those offering you tours. They are very unlikely to be licensed guides.

Beyond the vet fence, the grading is rougher than to the south, so it's even more important than usual to watch your speed. There are also several steep descents into river-beds, which make this road especially challenging during the rains.

Palmwag Concession (*Admission N$50 pp per day, N$100 pp overnight, plus N$100 per vehicle*) The huge Palmwag (pronounced 'Palumvag') Concession occupies an area of 4,500km² to the north of the junction of the C43 and the C40, immediately after the veterinary fence, and stretches west as far as the Skeleton Coast. It is bordered by three conservancies and, on the eastern side of the C43, the Etendeka Concession.

You can buy a day permit around the Palmwag Concession from Palmwag Lodge itself, and Twee Palms Gate (5km north of the vet fence) or the Aub Gate, further north also on the C43. However, unless you are an experienced 4x4 enthusiast, used to the terrain, and with good navigational skills (and preferably a GPS), this is not practical. (One trainee guide based at Palmwag got lost in his vehicle, became disoriented, and was found severely dehydrated in the Skeleton Coast Park. It is a difficult area.) The best way to see the area is to leave your car at the lodge (see below) and take one of the guided game drives. The area's ecosystem is too fragile to withstand the impact of many vehicles, and the animals are still wary of people. They have enough problems without being frightened from waterholes by tourists seeking pictures.

🏠 **Palmwag Lodge** [Map, page 342] (15 tented chalets, 15 rooms, camping) ☎ 067 333 214; reservations: ☎ 061 234 342; e eden@africaonline. com.na; www.palmwaglodge.com. Palmwag is the oldest lodge in the area, beautifully situated on the edge of the concession, 500m north of the veterinary fence on the left, & next to a palm-lined tributary of the Uniab River. This often flows overground &, as water is very scarce in this area, its presence regularly draws elephants close to camp. Now privately owned, at the time of research the lodge was undergoing huge renovations, as well as upgrading systems & giving staff further training.

Something of a crossroads for travellers in the area, it attracts all sorts, from South African families camping to shady mineral prospectors, & from upmarket visitors on fly-in safaris to local game guards back from the bush, who are staying at the adjacent base of the excellent Save the Rhino Trust (see box, page 360). The resultant holiday atmosphere indicates that most people are here to relax & unwind.

This fairly large lodge has a wide range of accommodation, & a licensed restaurant with an à la carte menu. The sparkling swimming pool has some shaded areas & its own pool bar, open for drinks & snacks all day. All rooms are en suite, & all campsites have lights, power points & water. In addition to guided game drives (*N$500 pp; max 6 people*), there are excursions to the Himba (*N$1,150 pp; min 3 people*), guided walks (*N$140 pp*), & an under-canvas sleep-out (*N$2,940 pp, min 2 people*). Concession fees are extra. *DBB N$1,705/2,690 sgl/dbl; camping N$255.* **LLLL**

🏠 **Desert Rhino Camp** [Map, page 342] (8 tents) Contact via Wilderness Safaris; 📞 061 274500; e info@ wilderness.com.na; www.wilderness-safaris.com. A smart tented camp in the Palmwag Concession. It takes up to 16 guests in large, Meru-style tents. Each is built on a low wooden platform, with large mesh windows (& velcro canvas flaps) & a good measure of style. Expect very comfortable twin beds with high-quality linen, & an en-suite bathroom with flush toilet, twin washbasins & a good hot shower.

The food is good, & activities major on rhino-tracking – usually with a guide from camp & trackers from Save the Rhino Trust. Typically you're likely to drive around looking for tracks from the vehicle. Then, when a promising set is found, you'll get out to follow them on foot, led by the trackers. It's an excellent option if you are moderately fit & want to try to get close to one of these amazing beasts.

However, note that the dangers inherent in approaching big game at close quarters can be thrown into sharp contrast on such a trip. No trip to Africa (or indeed anywhere) can be guaranteed as totally safe; this is no different. If you don't follow your guide's instructions precisely, then you're likely to have 1,000kg of nimble-footed, sharp-horned rhino heading at you very rapidly. These activities are not for the faint-hearted, so don't book in here unless you fully accept that you may be placing yourself far out of your comfort zone – & potentially in some danger. *FBA N$7,550–9,938/9,824–14,576 sgl/dbl.* **LLLLL**

In addition to the lodges, there are six **campsites** dotted along the main 'track' within the concession. These are very basic areas, with a tree for shade, and no toilet or shower facilities. It really is wild camping. Details of these, together with a map and GPS co-ordinates, are available from the lodge or the staff at each gate. For those looking to camp outside the concession, there are several campsites close to the road between the vet fence and Sesfontein (see pages 361–2).

Etendeka Concession This private concession shared by two conservancies is home to the established Etendeka Mountain Camp. There are plans under consideration to build a second lodge on the concession, nearer to the road and with a more upmarket approach. However, these plans have been in place, with little movement, for several years. So, while researching for this edition I was assured the wheels are still in motion, I'm not expecting any fast developments here.

🏠 **Etendeka Mountain Camp** [Map, page 342] (10 tents) 📞 061 239199; e info@etendeka-namibia.com; www.etendeka-namibia.com. Etendeka is an excellent tented camp about 18km east of Palmwag, on the open, rolling Etendeka lava plains. A model of sustainability, it was

established & is still run by Dennis Liebenberg, who takes a no-frills approach to giving his guests a real experience of the Kaokoveld.

Etendeka doesn't aim at luxury, but what it does, it does very well. Guests are accommodated in twin-bed tents, each of them with their own

This excellent local charity (064 403829; e srt@rhino-trust.org.na; www.savetherhinotrust.org), founded by the late Blythe and Rudi Loutit in 1982, grew out of the slaughter of the region's wildlife that was taking place during the 1970s and 1980s, when some 95% of all rhino in Africa were lost to poaching. As these rhino numbers shrank to near extinction, Blythe and Rudi started a pressure group to stop indiscriminate hunting in the area.

Once the worst of the hunting was stopped, SRT continued and pioneered conservation and protection in the area, even employing convicted poachers as game scouts. Who would know better the habits of rhino, and the tricks of the hunters? Eventually, they were able to reverse the extermination of the rhino from the communal areas of the Kaokoveld – a process that has been enthusiastically supported by the chiefs and headmen, as well as the neighbouring farming community. In many ways it's work like this so long ago that laid the foundations for the successful community conservation programmes that now operate in the region.

Working closely with the government and many local communities has gradually brought more benefits to these communities, through revenues generated by tourism, as well as providing security for the rhino. SRT's work is undertaken to support the rhino conservation efforts of the Ministry of Environment and Tourism (MET), and is carried out through a Memorandum of Understanding. SRT continues to operate many daily rhino patrols, monitoring and protecting the rhino. These include patrols from Desert Rhino Camp, which guests can join, with prior arrangement. The income from these trips funds some of the trust's patrols and rhino-monitoring programmes, and in the last three decades the population of black rhino has significantly increased.

bathroom, just outside the tent. Bathrooms are equipped with a washbasin, bush shower with hot & cold water, flush toilet & electric light. The main dining & bar areas are under canvas, & meals are a social occasion when everybody, including Dennis & the guides, normally eats together around the fire (it gets very chilly in winter), upon which much of the food is cooked. Such bush-cooking has been refined to an art form, so the cuisine from the embers is impressive. A small, sparkly blue swimming pool was added in 2013, next to the main area, complete with sun-loungers.

Activities – guided walks & scenic & game drives – are tailored to guests' interests & abilities. After an early b/fast, a normal day might include a 2–4hr walk, lunch, a few hours to relax, & perhaps a long afternoon game drive, incorporating a short hike on to one of the area's mountains for a sundowner. This is a great place to come walking, though walks are usually at a fairly gentle pace & so not exclusively for those who are very fit.

The concession's game includes good populations of giraffe, Hartmann's mountain zebra, oryx & springbok, as well as desert-adapted elephant, & very occasionally black rhino. The striking *Euphorbia damarana* are the predominant shrubs all around this area, & Etendeka's guides are excellent on their plants & birds, as well as animal identification.

Etendeka is remote & you cannot 'drop in' as you can at Palmwag; it must be prebooked. Most visitors drive themselves to Palmwag Lodge, where you can leave your car safely & are met for a 4x4 transfer to the camp (normally 16.00 in summer, 15.30 in winter – but check when you book).

The lodge is closely involved with the region's Community Game Guard scheme, & gives a proportion of its revenue to the local communities, so that they too can benefit from the income generated by visitors, & have an incentive to help preserve the region's wild game. *FBA inc transfer to camp N$3,058/4,872 sgl/dbl.* **LLLLL**

Anabeb Conservancy Bordering the Palmwag Concession to the east, this narrow conservancy straddles the C43 north to Sesfontein, with game such as giraffe, springbok, kudu and ostrich frequently seen from the road. There's a good campsite along this road between the vet fence and Khowarib:

⚲ Mbakondja River Campsite [Map, page 342] (8 pitches) There are 2 access tracks signposted from the C43 to this private campsite. The first, a distance of 6km, is 47km from the vet fence; the second, 8km further north, is 10km from the road. Both are rocky, with a high-clearance vehicle strongly advisable on the southern route. The site has very little shade, but each neatly demarcated pitch has its own traditionally built block housing a flush toilet & shower, supplied with water heated in an old oil drum, & firewood (N$20) is available.

This is a place to come for the people more than the location. It's owned & run by a welcoming Damara family, who will take visitors by donkey cart to see game such as ostrich, zebra, oryx, kudu & springbok, in return for a donation. *Day visits N$20 pp; camping N$80 pp*. **L**

Khowarib and Warmquelle

Little more than a handful of homesteads and boasting a couple of tyre-repair places, Khowarib lies on the perennial Hoanib River, some 73km north of Palmwag vet fence, and 31km from Sesfontein.

About 10km further north is the small settlement of Warmquelle, situated on the site of a spring. In the early years of the 20th century the spring was used in an irrigation project, for which an aqueduct was constructed. Now only a few parts of the old aqueduct remain, together with a small Damara settlement which supports a basic shop, a baker and a tyre-repair outlet.

The main attraction at Warmquelle is the **Ongongo Waterfall** (*day visit N$20 pp*), where a deep, clear pool is sheltered by an overhang of rock. Few can resist the temptation to strip off and swim here, which isn't surprising given the temperature, although it's considerably less inviting when the water is low. Access is as for Ongongo Campsite (see page 362).

The opening of a new lodge at Khowarib in 2009, and a sprinkling of campsites in the vicinity, increases the options for those heading north. Of the campsites, some are just a patch of ground where camping is shared with donkeys, cattle and the odd rusting vehicle, but two are worth a mention: Khowarib and Ongongo. Both were originally set up with the help of the Save the Rhino Trust and the Endangered Wildlife Society, and both channel most of their income back into the local communities. If these are full, basic camping is also possible at Anmire Cultural Village, signposted just 300m to the south of Khowarib, at Okondju Herero Traditional Village, 8.5km to the north, and at Red Rocks Campsite at the junction in Warmquelle. There are also a couple of good choices in Sesfontein itself.

⌂ Khowarib Lodge (See ad, 3rd colour section) (14 chalets, 8 pitches) ☎ 064 402779; m 081 219 3291; e reservations@khowarib.com; www. khowarib.com. After a long, dusty drive, there are plenty of surprises at this scenic lodge, 75km north of the Palmwag vet fence, or 25km from Sesfontein. Set 1km east of the C43, it's in an enviable location on the river, framed by the craggy mountains of the Khowarib Gorge – managed by Zané Oosthuizen.

Giant metal masks guard the entrance to a trio of thatched buildings comprising the reception, bar & dining area. While meals are often served alfresco under the starlit sky, by attentive & friendly staff from the nearby village, this last is screened for windy evenings or the occasional burst of rain.

Steps & a slope lead to a row of individual chalets on stilts. Nestling among mopane trees, each has a private balcony in a canopy of acacia, leadwood & jackalberry trees, where cicadas fail to drown out the soft gurgle of the river some 3m below. The chalets themselves are simple, rustic affairs, built of solid poles & canvas, with wooden doors, gauze-panelled windows & – another surprise – mains electricity (a mini-fridge is a welcome feature). Behind each, &

open to the stars, is a large, stone-walled enclosure with toilet, shower & twin basins. Black eagles nest in the surrounding rocks, & the rare short-toed thrush is occasionally spotted, but few visitors will have anticipated such common waterbirds as the blacksmith plover or Egyptian goose.

Full-day elephant (N$1,200) & rhino-tracking trips (N$1,320 pp) must be organised in advance. Other activities include ½-day visits to a Himba village (N$450 pp) or to see Bushman paintings (N$660 pp), birding & nature walks (N$250 pp) & nature drives (N$450–660 pp).

There is a pool, enclosed with a mopane structure surrounded by a well-kept lawn. There is shading with sun-loungers, as well as a shower & separate toilet.

A campsite just 500m to the east provides 4 pitches along the river, & 4 behind, each with electric points, braai & water. Khowarib has an enviable location, & makes the most of the wild terrain, though it's a shame that their campsite competes with the established community campsite nearby. While chalet balconies are not suitable for children, there are 2 family chalets (one sleeping 3 & one sleeping 4), but steps to & within the chalets make the lodge unsuitable for the less mobile. *DBB N$1,730–2,150/2,788–3,460 sgl/dbl; camping N$150 pp.* **LLLL**

Å Khowarib Campsite (4 pitches) ✆081 407 9539; e maxi@nasco.org.na; www.nacso.org.na. 1km past the lodge along the same track, which is suitable for 2WD vehicles, this established campsite is set on the edge of the cliff overlooking

a bend in the river. It's a spotless site, run by the local community, with private hot & cold showers, flush toilets, dining shelters & braai facilities. One of the pitches, with pre-erected tents, is designed for groups – so be aware of that if you're in search of peace & quiet. Aside from water, beer & soft drinks, you'll need to come fully equipped (although with sufficient notice, simple local meals can be arranged). Guides are sometimes available for walks around the area. *Camping N$80 pp.* **L**

Å Ongongo Campsite (30 pitches) ✆061 230 888; e maxi@nasco.org.na; www.nacso.org.na. About 11km north of Khowarib along the C43 is the turn-off for another community campsite, signposted from Warmquelle itself. The track follows a water pipeline for about 6km, heading roughly northward. The road is rough & very rocky in parts, sandy in others, & at one point you cross the dry bed of the river, before turning right to reach the site's office. 2WD's are not recommended; it is more sensible to park in a designated area at the top & carry equipment down to the campsite. It's a sprawling site, administered by the Ongongo community, with some shelters to camp under, BBQ areas, & a few blocks with flush toilet & hot shower. Bring all your food & equipment as only soft drinks, ice & firewood (N$20/bundle) are available.

The site's main attraction is the Ongongo Waterfall, which is open to day visitors (N$20 pp) as well as campers, but keep an eye out, too, for rosy-faced lovebirds chattering in the trees. *N$80 pp.* **L**

SESFONTEIN Named after the 'six springs' that surface nearby, the small town of Sesfontein marks the northern edge of Damaraland – and the gateway to Kaokoland. It is a dusty but photogenic spot, set between mountains in the Hoanib Valley.

The local vegetation is dominated by umbrella thorns (*Acacia tortilis*), the adaptable mopane (*Colophospermum mopane*), recognised by its butterfly-shaped leaves, and the beautiful, feathery real fan palms (*Hyphaene petersiana*). You will often be offered the 'vegetable ivory' seeds of these palms, carved into various designs, as souvenirs by the local people. These are highly recommended, as often the sellers are the carvers, and it is far less destructive than buying woodcarvings – though note that sellers can occasionally be quite pushy.

In the early 20th century, the German administrators made Sesfontein into an important military outpost. Following the severe rinderpest epidemic in 1896, they wanted to control movement of stock around the country, so in 1901 they built a fort here, complete with running water and extensive gardens to grow their own supplies. However, by the start of World War I this had been abandoned, and it was only much later that it was renovated into a picturesque lodge.

Sesfontein still feels like an outpost in many ways, despite being an important centre for the local people, who live by farming goats and the occasional field of maize. The efficiency of the foraging goats is shown by the lack of vegetation lower than the trees, and hence the clouds of fine dust which often hang in the valley's air. A jumble of signs offering everything from Himba tours and desert excursions to tyre repairs and internet cafés suggests that tourism is on the rise, but so far it's all very low key.

Sesfontein still offers the adventurous an interesting view of a real small town, not sanitised by the colonial designs of townships. It is spread out and very relaxed, home largely to Himba and Herero people. If you're staying here, then try to rise early to watch the village come to life. Sometimes the national anthem will drift across the cool air, beautifully sung by the school within earshot of the fort. Watch as farmers drive their cattle to water, and smartly dressed workers head for town. In the afternoon there are always a few people about, and there's no better way to watch village life than sitting with a cold drink on the steps of one of the shops – though you may attract a crowd of playful children, or the odd sideways glance from the local youth who hang out here at weekends to listen to music.

Getting there and away The C43 from Palmwag makes an interesting drive in a normal 2WD vehicle, passing through a narrow gap in the mountains just east of the town. Whereas continuing north to Opuwo is relatively straightforward, the going gets much tougher northwest of Sesfontein.

Where to stay *Map, page 342.*
Fort Sesfontein remains the only lodge in town, but Sesfontein's increasing popularity as a springboard for Kaokoland is reflected in a proliferation of campsites. In addition to those listed here, you could try Zebra or Para campsites, just to the west.

Fort Sesfontein (22 rooms) 065 685034; e fort.sesfontein@mweb.com.na; www. fort-sesfontein.com. When it opened in 1995, Fort Sesfontein was one of the most original & imaginative places to appear following independence. Rebuilt more or less to the old plans, it is set around a lush central courtyard full of palm trees alive with masked weaver birds. The rooms, including 2 for families, are mostly in the old fort, but 3 family rooms are upstairs, with one in the tower. They're large & rustically furnished, with en-suite facilities & fans that are as essential as the large swimming pool: Sesfontein can get very hot. If you need a TV, though, you are in the wrong place.

The old officers' mess is now an extensive bar/ lounge with dining tables that spill out by the pool, with lunch (N$120) available to all comers, & a set dinner menu (N$250).

Guided 4x4 day trips can be organised to see local Himba villages, desert elephants or rock paintings, & they'll provide a guide, lunch & drinks for a self-drive safari. If you're arriving by air, the lodge will collect you at Sesfontein's airstrip. **$$$$$**

Camel Top Campsite (6 pitches) m 081 8808550. With large pitches, private toilets, hot showers & firewood available, this is a perfectly acceptable site, if nothing special. It lies west of the town, just over 1km off the D3707 along one of 2 clearly signposted tracks, & accessible in a 2WD. **$**

Sesfontein Conservancy Campsite (4 pitches) 065 275502. South of the D3707, this small, well-maintained site is next to the church & school. Pitches are separated from one another with reed screens, & have private hot & cold showers, flush toilets & sinks, with some tree shade. If there's no-one in the office when you arrive, just take a pitch & they will be around later. **$**

Other practicalities That the number of outlets offering **tours** is matched only by the number of **tyre-repair** outlets is an indication of the increasing popularity of this isolated spot – and the severity of the roads further west. For tours, drop in to Sesfontein Conservancy (⊕ 08.00–17.00 Mon–Fri; 065 275502), which organises

15

full-day trips to a Himba village or in search of desert-adapted elephants. They can also arrange village visits within Sesfontein in return for a donation. Do note, however, that when we were researching this book the conservancy was almost impossible to contact – visiting the office in person is likely to be more successful than trying to get in touch by phone.

If you are just passing through then you'll find the supplies in the small **shops** useful, and there is a convenient **fuel** station here (⏰ *06.30–17.00 winter; 07.30–18.00 summer*). There is little other fuel available between Sesfontein and the Kunene, except at Opuwo.

What to see and do Aside from relaxing in town, to explore further into Kaokoland is difficult (see below). For most people, the best way to see the area is on an organised trip: either one prearranged with a specialist before you arrive, or a day trip arranged locally.

KAOKOLAND

This vast tract of land is Namibia at its most enticing – and yet most inhospitable. Kaokoland appeals to the adventurer and explorer in us, keeping quiet about the dangers involved. On the eastern side, hilly tracks become mudslides as they get washed away by the rains, while the baking desert in the west affords no comfort for those who get stranded. Even dry river-beds hide soft traps of deep sand, while the few which seem damp and hard may turn to quicksand within metres. Having struggled to free a Land Rover with just one wheel stuck in quicksand, it is easy to believe tales of vehicles vanishing within an hour.

One road on the eastern side was particularly memorable for me – it started favourably as a good gravel track. After 20km, it had deteriorated into a series of rocky ruts, shaking us to our bones and forcing us to slow down to 10km/h. After a while, when we'd come too far to think of returning, the track descended into a sandy river-bed, strewn with boulders and enclosed by walls of rock. The only way was for passengers to walk and guide the driver, watching as the tyres lurched from boulder to boulder.

Hours later we emerged – on to another difficult track. Gradually it flattened and the driving eased: we were happy to be travelling faster. Then the pace was interrupted. Streams crossed the road. Someone would wade across to check the depth, and then the 4x4 would swiftly follow, its momentum carrying it across the muddy bed. The third stream stopped us: more than thigh-high, fast flowing – a river in flood. We slept dry in our tents, thankful that the floods hadn't reached that first rocky river-bed while we were there.

In recent years, the region's main arteries have been improved, making it more accessible to independent drivers. Two newly graded roads – specifically the C43 and the D3701 – are generally safe enough in the dry season, though even then it's important to stay alert as some river-bed crossings are both steep and occasionally rocky. The rest of the D roads, however, are another matter. For these you should ideally still have a two-vehicle 4x4 expedition, all your supplies, an experienced navigator, detailed maps and good local advice on routes. Even then you'll probably get lost a few times. This is not a trip to undertake lightly: if things go wrong you will be hundreds of kilometres from help, and days from a hospital.

If you can get an expedition together then, in contrast to Damaraland's regulated concession areas, you'll find that Kaokoland has yet to adopt any formal system of

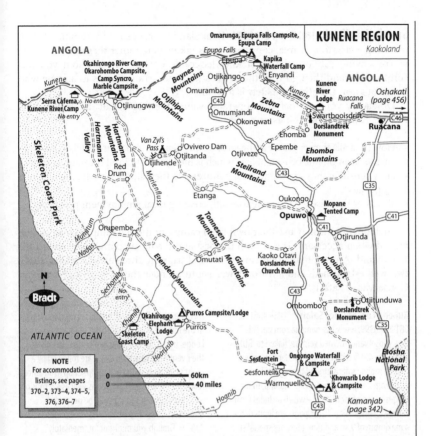

control, and you are free to travel where you can. However, this freedom is causing lasting damage to the region. The drier areas, especially to the west, have a very fragile ecosystem: simply driving a vehicle off the tracks and 'across country' can cause permanent damage – killing plants and animals, and leaving marks that last for centuries. Vehicle trails made 40 years ago can still be seen, as the crushed plants and lichens haven't yet recovered. So you must be responsible and treat the environment with care – and never drive off the tracks.

In addition to a handful of upmarket lodges, there are several demarcated campsites, some run directly by the community. These cater for self-sufficient expeditions in 4x4s, and travellers are urged to support them. Where there is no such provision, you can choose your own site, provided that you obtain permission from the head of the local village, and show due respect to the area's inhabitants (see *Where you can camp*, page 103). Here, more than anywhere else, there is a need to be responsible.

HOW TO VISIT KAOKOLAND Although the main arteries through Kaokoland have opened up in recent years, much of it remains remote; touring this area independently is not an option for most people. The few camps here tend to be either very basic or very organised. The basic ones are simple campsites, often run by the local communities with the backing of one of the conservation/development organisations. The organised camps are expensive, most linked with small, specialist, fly-in operators.

Specialist Kaokoland operators Kaokoland is rugged and remote. When planning a visit to this area, consider who is taking you, rather than exactly where you're staying. Choose the most knowledgeable operator with whom you feel comfortable, and then go with them. Trusting your arrangements to anyone who does not know the area intimately is foolish.

Do satisfy yourself that your operator values the fragility of the area and its culture. Among other things, consider:

- How (if at all) they ensure that the local people benefit from your visit. Do they charge an automatic bed-night levy which is then paid into local community funds?
- How sensitive they are to the local cultures. Do their staff speak the local languages?
- Whether they use local people for staff, creating local employment prospects.

Such operations may use their own fixed camps, or mobile camps, which can be moved when necessary. This is both the best and the most comfortable way to see Kaokoland. Among many that run occasional trips are three excellent specialists: two well established, and a third, newer venture under the auspices of Namibian Conservancy Safaris.

Kunene Conservancy Safaris ☏ 064 406136, 081 149 0399; www.kcs-namibia.com.na. This new conservancy-owned venture, linked to IRDNC (see page 45) & with excellent credentials, offers guided mobile safaris around the region. Tours start from 2 nights/3 days in Damaraland, to the longest – 9 nights/10 days – which includes Etosha & the Kunene Region. Participants are limited to a maximum of 9. In addition, there are specialist safaris led by acknowledged experts in their fields, covering topics from desert lions to conservation & culture. Not surprisingly, these trips aren't cheap – but then they're far removed from the norm, & all profits go to a group of 5 conservancies in the far northwest, which host the safaris.

Kunene Tours & Safaris (See ad, 3rd colour section) ☏ 064 402779; e info@kunenetours.com; www.kunenetours.com. Run by Caesar Zandberg, this established specialist organises overland trips in the Kunene Region, based out of Khowarib Lodge. In the interim, days exploring – in either their vehicle or your own 4x4 – are followed by a night's camping, with each camp set up in advance, ready for the arrival of guests. As well as set trips of 3–8 days, customised trips can be organised.

Skeleton Coast Fly-in Safaris See pages 335–9. Though you might not immediately associate the experts on the Skeleton Coast with the Kaokoveld, most of their trip to the Skeleton Coast is, in fact, spent just inland in the Kaokoveld. They normally visit the Purros area, & the region around the Kunene River, at the north end of the Hartmann's Mountains.

Wilderness Safaris See page 339. Wilderness trips to this area head to Serra Cafema, & Hoanib Skeleton Coast Camp, which opened in Aug 2014.

Also worth considering in this region is the more general operator **Namibia Tours and Safaris** (☏ 064 406038; e enquiries@namibia-tours-safaris.com; www. namibia-tours-safaris.com).

OPUWO This rough-and-ready frontier town is the hub of Kaokoland and – with improved access from the north and south – it's becoming increasingly important for visitors too. Most come to learn more about the Himba people who inhabit the surrounding area, but some are *en route* to Epupa Falls.

While the town is the Himba 'capital', it does not provide the photographic opportunities to match the visitor's image of 'primitive tribespeople', and it isn't an attractive place in its own right; the proliferation of bars tells its own tale. It does, however, attract an eclectic mix of people. Even if you're just waiting to fill up, take a look around. Herero women in their Victorian-style dresses contrast with traditional rural Himba, who come into town to trade or buy supplies, with their decorated goatskin dress and ochre-stained skins. Strong, powerful faces speak clearly of people who have yet to trade their own culture for what little is being offered to them here. As with any frontier post, the place abounds with shady local traders. These mix with occasional businessmen, and the eccentric characters who emerge from the bush to replenish supplies, and then disappear again with equal speed.

Getting there and away Opuwo is at the junction of the tarred C41 and the gravel C43, some 54km west of the main C35 between Kamanjab and Ruacana. As you approach, large, irrigated maize fields give way to the dry, dusty town, sprawling over a low hillside with no apparent centre. Its buildings are functional rather than attractive, and the outskirts fade into ramshackle groups of Himba and Herero huts.

Where to stay *Map, opposite.*
Despite its frontier-town appearance, Opuwo has a fair range of accommodation, topped by Opuwo Country Lodge.

Opuwo Country Lodge (40 rooms, 12 pitches) 065 273461; e reservations@ opuwolodge.com; www.opuwolodge.com. Situated on a hilltop overlooking the valleys & mountains, this privately owned hotel was opened on a 30ha site in 2005. The impressive main building incorporates the reception, lounge & dining areas (*3-course dinner N$270*), a curio shop, wine cellar & bar. Running the whole length of the building is an extensive terrace-with-a-view, fronted by an infinity pool. Rooms (including 3 family units) have AC, a balcony & plenty of mod cons, but only the larger 'luxury' ones have a scenic view. The campsite is located well away from the main hotel.

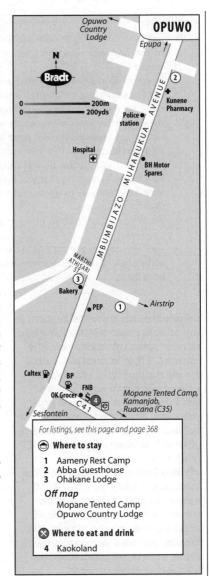

For listings, see this page and page 368

Where to stay
1 Aameny Rest Camp
2 Abba Guesthouse
3 Ohakane Lodge
Off map
   Mopane Tented Camp
   Opuwo Country Lodge

Where to eat and drink
4 Kaokoland

Excursions include a 3hr Himba village trip (*N$535 pp*), which can feel rather commercialised, & day trips to Epupa Falls (*weather permitting; N$1,423 pp*). Closer to home, a good 2.5km self-guided walking trail leads down into the valley, with the potential to spot some of the area's flora & birdlife. *Camping N$140.* **$$$$**

Ohakane Lodge (13 rooms) Marthi Athisari St; 065 273031; e ohakane@iway.na. This small lodge, named after the local word for 'wild dog', is

Read the camping advice in *Chapter 7*, pages 103–6, and remember the following:

- Never camp in a river-bed; flash floods often claim lives.
- Never camp close to a water point. Desert-adapted animals will often travel for days to get to one of these. They may die of thirst if you keep them from the water with your presence.
- Gather any firewood you will need in the highlands before you get to this area, and keep its use to a minimum.
- In such a dry landscape be very careful not to cause bush fires.
- Take home everything that you bring in. No rubbish should be buried: it may take centuries to decay, and will almost certainly be dug up before then by scavengers.
- Water is very limited, so bring in all you need. Use sparingly any that you find.
- The few streams and springs in the area are used for drinking by animals and people. Do not contaminate them, and be sure to wash well away from them.

well signposted just behind the Shell fuel station. An unprepossessing entrance belies an attractive lodge, with secure parking. Light, spacious rooms, all en suite with AC & TV, are set around lawns & a small pool with a bar. Lunch (*N$75*) & dinner (*N$130*) are served under thatch or outside beneath the trees, & there's a small selection of curios for sale. Unfortunately, the proximity to a local bar can mean loud music over the w/ends. Both Himba village trips (*N$495 pp, ½-day*) & trips to Epupa Falls (*N$5,525 per vehicle*) can be organised. **$$$**

Abba Guesthouse (15 rooms) Mbumbijazo Muharukua Av; 065 273155; m 081 234 6810; e abbaguest@gmail.com, abba@iway.na. This unexpected find has a strong Christian ethos – & the bonus of internet access (*N$10/30mins*). Dbl & twin rooms, all en suite & some with microwave, are pleasant, & there's a small garden but, other than b/fast (*N$45 pp*), no food is served. **$$**

Aameny Lodge (8 bungalows, 10 rooms, camping) 065 273572; m 081 275 0156; e westerntjiposa@yahoo.com, aamenylodge@ yahoo.com. Taken over by Western Tjiposa, a Himba man, in 2009, Aameny is quietly situated just off the main road, with secure parking. The well-maintained site with plenty of trees boasts small, grassy pitches with picnic tables & electric light, & 2 ablution blocks (with hot water). Traditional-style twin rooms offer accommodation under thatch, from simple rondavels with electric light & fan to others that are en suite with kettle & TV. Meals (*b/fast N$60, dinner N$120 pp*), including local dishes on request, are served in a simple dining area, where internet & Wi-Fi is also available. Western also offers visits to Himba villages, but he alternates them to spread tourist money & minimise impact. *Camping N$80.* **$$**

Where to eat and drink *Map, page 367.*

As in many Namibian towns, most tourists eat in their hotels, but the **Kaokoland Restaurant** (⊕ *08.00–21.00 daily*) is good for those passing through. This rather grandly named coffee shop next to OK Grocer is unexpectedly pleasant, and has Wi-Fi. Stop here for breakfast, light meals, grills and burgers, and a range of drinks.

Shopping For supplies go to the large and well-stocked OK Grocer, complete with its own bakery (⊕ *08.00–18.30 Mon–Sat, 8.30–13.00 Sun*), next to the BP garage. If you're planning to visit a Himba village, that is probably the best place to buy

curios. Otherwise, have a browse through the wares displayed on the pavement in front of the supermarket. Here and elsewhere in town you can usually find someone selling little piles of ochre, used by the Himba women to colour their skin.

Other practicalities Approaching from the C41, the town's main facilities are on the right, just before the T-junction. In Opuwo, fuel is available at the 24-hour BP station, as well as at a second garage, Caltex, just right of the T-junction. From a logistical point of view, this is the only fuel north of Sesfontein and west of Ruacana, so it's an important place to top up. Another option for fuel is the Shell garage.

In the complex adjacent to the BP garage is a branch of FNB bank, with an ATM and a foreign-exchange bureau, making Opuwo more traveller-friendly than in previous years, and the internet café here should ease any communication problems while in the vicinity. If you're in need of tyres or vehicle repairs, try B H Motor Spares (✆ *065 273101*) or Wesstech Autorepairs (✆ *065 273494*).

In an **emergency**, the police can be contacted on ✆ 065 273148, and the ambulance or hospital on ✆ 065 272800. For minor medical needs, try the Kunene Pharmacy (✆ *065 273221;* **m** *081 128 5140;* ⏰ *08.00–17.00 Mon–Fri, 08.00–noon Sat*), next to Abba Guesthouse.

KUNENE RIVER From the hydro-electric dam near Ruacana, the Kunene River threads west through the Baynes Mountains to the Atlantic, meandering between arid hills and wild, rough-looking mountains on both sides. Angola lies to its north, Namibia to its south; both look identical. Along its way, photogenic, feathery fronds of green makalani palms line its path. This narrow strip extends for perhaps only 30m from the river itself. Further from the water than that, the land reverts to its parched, dry state: the preserve of Kaokoland's semi-desert flora and fauna.

Note that water levels in the river itself are largely controlled by the dam rather than the seasons, and can vary considerably.

Flora and fauna The flora and fauna along the Kunene are representative of the ecosystem found in the palm forest which lines the river for most of its length.

Hippos have been exterminated from much of the river, although some have been reintroduced upstream. Crocodiles are still common, though (bathing is safe only immediately beside the falls at Epupa), and small mammals are a feature of the palm forest. Few large wild mammals are regularly seen around here, although spotted impala and kudu are resident, and both mountain zebra and giraffe have been reintroduced into the Kunene River Conservancy.

Away from the river, mopane scrub reclaims the land, spotting the arid landscape with patches of dusty green. To relieve the monotony, you're rarely out of sight of the mountains, layered against the horizon in darkening shades of grey.

Birdlife Ornithologists will find a fascinating variety of birds, including various bee-eaters, kingfishers ranging from the giant to the tiny malachite kingfisher, louries, bulbuls and hornbills, as well as rollers (purple, lilac breasted and European), golden and lesser masked weavers, scarlet-breasted sunbirds, and perhaps the odd, lost, great white egret. The rare rufous-tailed palm thrush and the Cinderella waxbill also occur in this riverine palm forest, which is typical of their highly restricted habitat; both are resident around Epupa Falls and close to Kunene River Lodge. Equally unusual is the yellow-breasted shrike, a morph of the more common crimson-breasted shrike. Easier to see, though, are the colonies of rosy-faced lovebirds that colonise the trees along the river, and Rüppell's parrot, with its flashy yellow shoulder stripe. Distinctive among the birds of prey are Verreaux's eagle, the bateleur and the gymnogene, as well as the inevitable fish eagles.

Getting there and away From the south, access to the Kunene River has been dramatically improved following the grading of the C43 (also signposted as the D3700) north of Opuwo. While you should still exercise considerable care along this road, it's perfectly passable during the dry season, although a high-clearance vehicle is essential to negotiate the steepest river-bed crossings.

Driving from the east is more challenging. The D3700 runs directly from Ruacana along the Kunene for about 145km as far as Epupa Falls. However, although the first 65km or so, as far as Kunene River Lodge, is reasonable driving (though a high-clearance 4x4 is strongly advised), the latter stages remain very rough – taking me three days of painstaking driving on one occasion – and should not be taken lightly. Thus the best – and by far the quickest – route is to follow the road along the river between Ruacana and Swartbooisdrift, then to cut inland along the D3701, graded in 2009 to a smooth roller-coaster of a ride, before joining the C43 near Epembe. From here, it's a further 103km to Epupa. Ideally, nothing west of the lodge along the river should be attempted without a self-sufficient two-vehicle party of rugged 4x4s.

Some 40km north of Opuwo, on the C43, there's a signpost for the pretty and quiet **Omungunda Campsite** (m *081 838 2556; N$100 pp*). The campsite is very simple and rustic, but provides hot showers and flush toilets.

Epupa Falls Though visitors go to Kaokoland more for the whole experience than any individual sight, Epupa Falls is one of its highlights.

Here at Epupa the river widens to accommodate a few small islands, before plunging into a geological fault. This is 35m deep in places and, as the river is sizeable – at least in the early months of the year – it makes a lot of noise and some spray. The falls don't compare with Victoria Falls in scale, but they are all the more beautiful for occurring in such an arid region. Add to the scene a phalanx of watchful baobabs, many balancing improbably on precarious rocks above the chasms, or standing forlornly on the small islands in the stream. It's a magical spot.

Central to the small community around the falls is a Himba settlement with a shop from which music emanates for much of the day. The increase in the number of visitors has led to the establishment of a small craft stall near the falls, but most Himba visits concentrate on more traditional communities a short distance away.

With generally dry vegetation, and strong winds, the area is particularly susceptible to bush fires. One of these, in 2009, jumped the river from Angola, blackening the trees, destroying one of the campsites, and leaving a general trail of destruction in its wake.

Where to stay *Map, page 365.*

⌂ **Epupa Camp** (9 tents, 6 pitches) ☎061 237294; e reservations@epupa.com.na; www. epupa.com.na. On the palm-fringed banks of the Kunene, 700m east of the main falls, this established camp occupies a tranquil, compact site opposite a small island. Accommodation is in safari tents with a shaded balcony, mosquito-netted doors & windows, camp-style beds & a simple en-suite shower & toilet at the back. 7 of the tents face the river, as do the dining area & terrace, a fire pit & a tiny swimming pool. Behind sits the reception area with a small library. Lights are powered by a generator or batteries.

For several years the Namibian and Angolan governments have been considering the construction of a hydro-electric dam across the Kunene. It's a highly controversial project, and after considerable opposition the original site, at Epupa, has been discounted in favour of one 40km downstream, in the Baynes Mountains. Here, it is proposed to construct a 200m-high dam, flooding some 57km² of Himba tribal lands.

Advocates of the scheme have pointed to Namibia's rising power consumption, the apparent 'waste' of the Kunene's huge potential, and the lack of employment opportunities in the northern Kunene Region; critics regard it as a 'prestige project' for the government, arguing that its power will be expensive and unnecessary, and that it will do immense damage to the Kunene's ecosystems and the culture of the Himba people who live near the river. That the Epupa site has been taken out of the equation is thanks to considerable efforts from local and international groups since the project's inception in 1998. On the environmental side, the California-based International Rivers (*www.internationalrivers.org*) concluded that the original report was 'riddled with incorrect conclusions, false assumptions and missing data', and continues to campaign against a dam at the Baynes site. Socially, several organisations, including Namibia's nonprofit law firm Legal Assistance Centre (LAC; *www.lac.org.na*) and the London-based Survival (*www.survival-international.org*), have helped the Himba communities to put their case forward, and to campaign against the dam. In 1998, leaders in the Kunene Region submitted 11 major objections to the proposed site at Epupa, many of which will pertain to the new site. These include loss of land and riverine resources (the narrow palm forest beside the river is a vital source of food for both people and livestock); disappearance of wildlife; inundation of ancestral grave sites; health threats brought about by a large lake; overcrowding through the construction period; increased crime; loss of ecotourism potential; and the creation of a barrier, putting a stop to regular river crossings by Himba communities on opposite sides of the river.

The status of the project has not changed for several years, and it doesn't look like there will be much movement in the near future. A further feasibility report was completed, but never really saw the light of day. The main 'energy drive' at the moment is focused around the development of the Kudu gas fields near Oranjemund, and so this dam project is on the back burner for now.

Key to the success of this camp is a welcoming & attentive team of staff, largely drawn from the local community. Activities include sundowner trips to the hills & falls (*N$170 pp*), guided visits to a local Himba village (*N$420 pp*), & gentle ½-day rafting trips on the Kunene (*N$420 pp*). The falls themselves are an easy walk away. *DBB N$1,785/2,646 sgl/dbl; camping N$120 pp.* **LLLL**

🏠 **Omarunga Camp** (14 chalets; 9 camping pitches) 📞 064 403096; e camtrav@iafrica.com. na; www.natron.net/omarunga-camp. This immaculately maintained lodge is spread out along the river, with a riverside bar & restaurant. Tented chalets (1 suitable for a family) under light thatch are set on stone plinths interspersed with patches of grass; 5 directly face the river, & a further 5 have a river view. Gauzed windows allow the circulation of air, while inside are tiled floors, smart mosi nets & stone bathrooms with flush toilets. Camping chairs on a narrow veranda complete the picture. To one side, adjacent to Epupa Falls Campsite, is a spotless campsite with 9 pitches & central ablution blocks; campers can use the bar & have dinner (*3 courses for N$250*) by prior reservation.

The Kunene Region   KAOKOLAND

15

Activities range from Himba tours with a local guide (*N$510 pp*) to guided walking trails (*N$140*), crocodile walks (*N$180*) & sunset excursions (*N$180 pp*). Day trips to include flights, transfers, lunch & excursions can be arranged. *DBB N$1,705/2,690 sgl/dbl; FBA N$2,730/4,740 sgl/dbl; camping N$120 pp; airstrip transfer N$600 per vehicle.* **LLLL**

🏠 **Epupa Falls Lodge & Campsite** (5 chalets, camping) 📞 lodge 081 393 0244, campsite 081 149 2840; 🇪 bookings@ epupafallslodge.com; http://epupafallslodge. com. As Epupa became more of a Mecca for visitors to Kaokoland, a site next to the falls was set up to benefit from these visitors, & in order to protect the fragile palm forest from being ruined by those in search of virgin camping sites. Owned by Koos Verwey, who used to operate the highly respected Kaokohimba Safaris, it's got an excellent location on the banks of the river, right above the falls. There are en-suite 5 chalets, built on stilts & boasting excellent views, & a rustic but spotlessly clean campsite, its stone-built ablution blocks with flush toilets & water heated by donkey boilers. High up on stilts is a kitchen (*dinner N$250*) & bar, with tables overlooking the rapids. Campers can often buy vegetables & even a few crafts from the local villagers, & there's a small curio shop on site, with firewood, fresh boerewors & chicken & ice when available.

In the river just upstream of the camp are hot springs. When the water is low, these are accessible.

Koos himself now specialises in taking small-groups hiking, cycling & on guided tours of the Kunene Region. These are not scheduled & are worked out to cater for the individual. *DBB chalets N$1,250–1,550/2,100–2,400 sgl/dbl; camping N$110 pp.* **LLL**

🏠 **Kapika Waterfall Camp** (10 chalets) 📞 065 685111; reservations 🇪 ansonet@iway.na; www.kapikafalls.com. Kapika offers en-suite twin chalets overlooking the river. There is a restaurant (*b/fast N$110; lunch N$100; dinner 3-course set menu N$255*), bar & pool. Scenic drives, nature walks, Himba village tours (*N$450 pp*), sundowners (*N$160 pp*) & rafting (*N$400 ½-day*). *B&B N$1,300/2,000 sgl/dbl.* **LLL**

Other attractions Sunrise bathes the nearby hills in clear red light, and this is a good time to explore. The hills have an uneven surface of loose rock, so wear a stout pair of shoes and watch out for snakes. Temperatures are cold at first, but it warms up very rapidly, so take water, a sunhat and suncream. As with exploring anywhere near this border, seek local advice. Some areas were mined during the liberation struggle, and injuries still occur, albeit not in the last ten years or so.

Most lodges and campsites in the area can arrange trips to visit a Himba village. For comments on these, see box opposite.

Gemmologists should keep their eyes on the ground for the rose quartz crystals that abound. You may also find the chipped stone implements of past inhabitants.

Canoeing Several of the lodges along the river have canoes available for their guests, usually offering a haul upstream followed by a gentle drift back with the current. For those in search of more exciting waters, the specialist operator Felix Unite (see page 204) offers 10-day itineraries for groups of at least 16, incorporating a couple of days in Etosha, and six days paddling the Kunene from Hippo Pools to Epupa. Although there is some white water along this stretch, the appeal is more in the environment, with plenty of birdlife and a diversity of habitats. This is a participation-based expedition, but a back-up crew carries the heavy kit by vehicle. The best time to go is in the winter months, between late June and August.

East of Epupa: Swartbooisdrift With little in the way of tourist infrastructure, this isolated spot retains much of the magic of the Kunene River, its water levels regulated by the dam some 50km upstream at Ruacana. When river levels are high, rafting through the canyon upstream can be arranged at Kunene River Lodge.

Just west of the lodge is the Dorslandtrek Monument, which marks the spot where in 1928 a group of the original Dorslandtrekkers from South Africa crossed back over the border from Angola into what was then South West Africa.

Where to stay Map, page 365.

There are a few simple campsites along the river in the area around Swartbooisdrift. Of these, **Ondoozu Himba Community Restcamp** and **Okapupa Camp** lie beside each other about 12km east of Kunene River Lodge. A third, **Swartbooisdrift Rivercamp**, is about 6km in the other direction. All are basic, and you can expect to pay around N$80 per person to camp. If you're after something more comfortable, the lodge has its own camping area. For campsites near Ruacana Falls, see *Chapter 19, page 466*.

Kunene River Lodge (8 rooms, 4 chalets, 12 pitches) 065 685016, 065 274300; e info@ kuneneriverlodge.com; www.kuneneriverlodge. com; ✆ 17°21.410'S, 13°52.988'E. This private lodge within the Kunene River Conservancy is owned & run by Peter & Hillary Morgan. It lies on the D3700, about 65km west of Ruacana, just east of the junction with the D3701. During the rainy season, a 4x4 is essential.

It's a well-vegetated spot, with mature leadwood & jackalberry trees, one entwined with an increasingly rare snake vine. At one end of the site, an attractive pool is screened by banana trees, beloved of the local monkeys, while at the other, a bar & restaurant overlook the river.

Set along the river are 12 grassy, tree-shaded camping pitches, with flush toilets & hot water in a stone ablution block. Sharing this, & set behind the campsite, are small, rustic chalets, while further back is a row of 8 bungalows which are more upmarket, one suitable for families & all en suite. There is mains power available.

This is a great place for water-based activities, including white-water rafting through the Onduroso Gorge (*N$450 ½-day*), canoeing (*N$200/ day, 2 people*) & fishing – with rods available at N$105/day. Note, however, that these are subject to water levels, which fluctuate according to flow levels determined at Ruacana. Motorboat trips are on offer, too (*sundowner N$310 pp*). Peter is

HIMBA VILLAGES

Because Opuwo, Epupa and the surrounding area are situated in a traditional Himba area, you may get the opportunity to visit a typical local family. Go with a guide who speaks the local language, and try to learn a few words yourself – *Perivi* ('Hello, how are you?') and *Okuhepa* ('Thank you') make a good start. Make sure, too, that the village receives some real benefit from your visit. Buying craftwork made by the villagers is one very good way of doing this, but simply taking along some mielie-meal – which may well be organised by your guide – would also be a positive gesture. With patience, and a good interpreter/guide, you should be able to glimpse a little of the Himba lifestyle.

Of all the Namibians that you encounter, the Himba require some of the greatest cultural sensitivity. While many are becoming accustomed to – and benefit from – tourist interest in their lifestyle, their culture is adapting to centuries of changes within a matter of years. Until the late 1980s there were people living in the area who relied entirely on a hunter-gatherer existence, using only stone implements – a reminder of how remote this area was until very recently.

And now a word of advice. If you offer a lift to a Himba lady in traditional costume, be careful to cover your vehicle's seats with an old towel or rug. The ochre with which the women adorn their bodies may be both practical and beautiful, but it isn't easy to get off the upholstery!

an enthusiastic & knowledgeable birder, happy to lead guests along a usually dry tributary in search of rarities such as the Cinderella waxbill (*N$300 pp*) & also to find the newly discovered Angola Cave Chat located in the Zebra Mountains (*N$650 pp*) – just two of the 285 species recorded here.

There are also trips to a Himba village (*N$280 pp*). With this range of options, Kunene River Lodge suits adventurous travellers as well as those in search of more leisurely activities – &, of course, keen birders. *B&B N$695–895 pp sharing; camping N$150 pp*. **LLL**

THE WESTERN VALLEYS

THE WESTERN VALLEYS In the west, Hartmann's Valley and the Marienfluss are often visited by the Kaokoveld's specialists. Both valleys run north–south, bounded in the north by the Kunene, which flows all year. The main approach road is the D3707, a 4x4 track heading northwest from Sesfontein.

Purros

Purros Some 106km west of Sesfontein (and a similar distance from Orupembe), you'll come to the village of Purros, located on the Hoarusib River. Largely a Himba area, Purros is increasingly popular with visitors to its traditional Himba village, as well as to see the wildlife that congregates along the river.

Getting there and away Purros has its own airstrip, used by most of the visitors to the new lodge; the flight from Windhoek takes 2¼ hours. Those planning to drive in should do so only with a fully equipped 4x4 vehicle – and preferably two. The D3707 from Sesfontein may be deceptively good for the first few kilometres, but then deteriorates significantly as it crosses increasingly hostile terrain with no shade. Boneshaking surfaces do nothing for even the hardiest of tyres, and numerous river crossings make losing the road altogether a real possibility. This is not a trip to be taken lightly.

 Where to stay *Map, page 365.*
The village's community campsite also has a separate 'bush lodge', both of which are worth visiting. These options have recently been extended with the opening of a new upmarket lodge, just across the river from the village.

Okahirongo Elephant Lodge (8 chalets) \065 685018/20; e info@okahirongo.com; www.okahirongolodge.com; ✆ 18°46.557'S, 12°55.953'E. From a distance the collection of dark-brown boxes lined up on a ridge against the hills is a bit of an anticlimax, but appearances can be deceptive: contemporary style at this joint Italian-South African venture is serious business.

Between each pair of 'boxes', heavy pole doors pivot on a central axis to reveal a day bed on a shaded platform looking across to the mountains. To one side is a spacious bathroom with twin basins, large clay bath, showers inside & out, & a separate toilet; to the other, dark wood chairs & desk complement a rather grand dbl bed with 4-poster mosi nets. At one end, 2 units combine to give a family suite.

In the centre of the ridge, a Himba-style domed entrance leads to more boxes – a reception area, 2 lounges, 2 dining areas, curio shop, a library & even a sun-lounger cube – all decorated in rich earthy tones & grouped around an azure infinity pool. It's open & airy to make the most of any breeze, but curtains & blinds are there for colder nights, as is a welcoming fire pit. Food – claimed as a fusion of Italian & African cuisine – is generally a cut above the average, well prepared & well presented.

For all its luxury, the lodge's greatest draw is a truly panoramic view of the mountains across the plains. Activities focus on nature drives along the Hoarusib River in search of elephant & lion, & trips to a Himba village near Purros. Other possibilities are scenic drives to the Skeleton Coast, fly-in fishing trips, & scenic flights. Rather bizarrely, there's also a golf driving range, with clubs available, & cookery classes are under consideration.

Although some guests drive themselves in, most arrive at the airstrip, a 5min drive away. A 2-night stay is ideal, & if you're after a spot of R&R, a 3rd wouldn't go amiss. *DBB N$3,898–4,419/6,144–6,946 sgl/dbl*. **LLLLL**

Å Purros Campsite (6 pitches) Reservations ☏ 081 716 2066; e robbinuatokuja@hotmail.com. Managed by the charismatic Robbin Uatokuja, the community-run Ngatutunge Pamue site, meaning 'We build together', is 2km north of Purros, on the D3707. The approach road has patches of sand, so drive with care. Large pitches, set on a sandy, wooded site on the bank of the Hoarusib River, each have their own flush toilet, hot & cold shower, fireplace (no grid), sink with tap, & bin. Firewood (*N$30 bundle*) is available (though use sparingly; it's in short supply), but in all other respects you'll need to be entirely self-sufficient.

A major purpose of the camp, & its sister lodge, is to provide employment for the local Himba from Purros village. Full/½-day walks (*N$600/350 per group*) & drives (*N$350 full day per group*), & 3–4hr expeditions to see the Himba people (*N$350 per group*) & local elephants (*N$450 per group*) can be arranged with a local guide, & this is an effective way to put some money directly into the local economy. Note that elephants occur frequently in the area & around the campsite, & should not be harassed in any way; they are dangerous & unpredictable animals, & have killed people. *Camping N$100 pp.* **L**

🏠 Purros Bush Lodge (7 rooms) Contact as for the campsite, see above. Close to the campsite, but signposted along a separate track, this community option opened in Apr 2009. It offers self-catering accommodation in thatched, stone-built rooms, including 1 for families. All are en suite & nicely laid out, with cream curtains at screened windows & solar-powered lights, though there's no fan. Outside each is a washing-up area & a parking shelter. Commanding views across the landscape are to be had from a lookout tower. Activities can be arranged as at the campsite, & here, too, you'll need to be entirely self-sufficient except for firewood. *N$300 pp.* **L**

What to see and do Close to Purros is a traditional **Himba village** where visitors are welcome (*N$30 pp*). While the village is used to visitors, it's worth remembering that it is their home; this is in no way a show village. It may be possible to visit the village on foot, which is a more leisurely and satisfying way to meet these pastoral people, allowing plenty of time for an exchange of views and questions through your guide. After all, how would you like it if a group of strangers drove up to your house, came in and took pictures of your family and then departed within just a few minutes? So do greet the villagers, and spend time talking with them, and learning a little of how they live. Many now are helped by the income made from selling jewellery, or guiding visitors around their local area – they deserve your support.

The area's other attraction is the **Hoarusib River**, whose pools of permanent water attract both desert-adapted elephant and a small pride of desert-adapted lion. Baboons cavort along the edge, and high in the rocks are the tell-tale white marks of rock dassies. Birds, too, are drawn to the river. Vivid flashes of colour signal the Madagascar bee-eater, the dusky sunbird or the common waxbill, while at the water's edge congregate plovers, lapwings, Egyptian geese and the occasional hamerkop.

Hartmann's Valley As you enter the valley, a small weather-worn sign stresses the ecologically important things you must do, and includes a diagram of how to turn a vehicle around to minimise damage to the environment. Take time to read and memorise it.

Hartmann's Valley itself is very arid, though its weather can vary dramatically. As well as searing heat, the valley receives sea mists which creep up from the coast, making it an eerie place to visit.

It is 70km from end to end, a minimum of 2½ hours' drive one-way, and the condition of the track along it varies. In the south, the road starts by crossing a number of steep-sided river valleys. It soon changes to compacted, corrugated sand, which shakes your vehicle violently. Finally, this becomes soft before high dunes prevent you reaching the Kunene by vehicle. Despite the harsh conditions, it is very beautiful. Drive through at sunrise if possible; then it's cooler than later and shows off the surrounding hills at their finest.

 Where to stay *Map, pages 320 and 365.*

There are two private camps at the end of the valley:

Serra Cafema Camp (8 chalets) Contact via Wilderness Safaris; 061 274500; e info@ wilderness.com.na; www.wilderness-safaris.com. This exclusive camp beside the Kunene has been reinvented several times over the last decade, each time on a grander scale. It's now luxurious & spacious; a haven on the edge of the harsh Kaokoveld & Skeleton Coast. You'll find a pool, sunken bar & lounge, & a palpable air of remote relaxation.

Large elevated chalets linked by decking are spread out in a fringe of riverine vegetation. Each has canvas walls & a thatched roof, but any similarity to a tent stops there. One long side of each chalet is a series of glass doors which concertina open on to a vast wooden deck, complete with tempting hammock. Inside are a bedroom with canopied bed, writing table & several fans; a small lounge area, with sofa & coffee tables; & a large dressing area cum bathroom, with bath, shower & double sinks. Soft lighting & natural wood aplenty are offset by cream-coloured fabrics.

While some just relax at camp, it is a great place from which to explore this remote area – home to springbok, ostrich & oryx, but very few people. Guests can walk in the mountains & along the river valley, but most prefer the guided quad bike excursions among the dunes & to visit local villages. A full day outing to the Marienfluss Valley, complete with a delicious picnic lunch, is also offered here. Boat trips promise relative cool in the afternoons. The cost of flying in & the high quality of the camp itself make this one of Namibia's most expensive camps. *FBA N$10,514–14,100/14,586–21,720 sgl/dbl.* **LLLLL**

Kunene River Camp Run by Skeleton Coast Safaris, this very small & simple camp is usually used for a final night as part of their fly-in trips to the Skeleton Coast & the Kaokoveld. See pages 335–9 for more details on this operation, including costs for the various itineraries on offer. Please note that this is always booked as part of a fly-in trip; they do not accept people who try to just drop in.

The Marienfluss
The next valley inland from Hartmann's is the Marienfluss. If you are driving, this is reached via the Himba settlement at Red Drum – a crossroads marked by a red oil can.

The Marienfluss has more soft sand and is greener than Hartmann's Valley. It is covered with light scrub and the odd tree marks an underground river. A most noticeable feature of the Marienfluss is its 'fairy circles' (see box, page 269), although they are also found, to a lesser extent, in Hartmann's Valley.

 Where to stay *Map, page 365.*

At the northern end of the Marienfluss there is a nice selection of simple campsites, and one very luxury lodge. Campsites are set mainly under the shade of camelthorn trees (*Acacia erioloba*) on the banks of the Kunene River. There are also a couple of community-run campsites further south.

Okahirongo River Camp (6 chalets) 065 685018/20; e info@okahirongo.com; www. okahirongolodge.com. Set up by the team behind Okahirongo Elephant Lodge, this small camp in the Marienfluss Conservancy opened in Mar 2010. From its vantage point on a low hill overlooking the Otupambua rapids, it looks across the Kunene River to dramatic mountain scenery in Angola. For birders, this is a potential place to spot the

Cinderella waxbill or the grey kestrel, while limited game includes oryx, giraffe, springbok & ostrich.

Standards here are as high as at its sister lodge, although here the chalets are large safari tents with inside & outside showers; 1 is suitable for a family. Activities, too, are similar, focusing on Himba trips, river trips, fishing & guided walks. Most visitors to the camp fly in to the nearby airstrip. *DBB N$3,898–4,419/6,144–6,946 sgl/dbl.* **LLLLL**

Ⓧ Marble Campsite ☎061 230 888; e maxi@nasco.org.na; www.nacso.org.na. Private pitches at this site between Orupembe & Red Drum have their own sinks & braai areas, but share ablution blocks with solar-heated water. Both beer & soft drinks are available, & a freezer is a rare bonus. *N$60/30 adult/child.* **L**

⌂ Camp Syncro (3 bungalows, 4 pitches); e campsyncro@gmail.com. Under the ownership of Ryan & Sarah Christinger since Feb 2014, Camp Syncro occupies a lovely spot overlooking the Kunene from the end of the Marienfluss. At the time of research, 3 basic bungalows were being rebuilt, as was a bar/kitchen & a small pool. The campsite is already open, with 4 pitches each with their own fireplace, table & sink. The shared ablution block provides hot showers & flushing toilets. Cool drinks, ice & firewood are available here, as is Wi-Fi. *Camping N$100 pp; other rates on request.* **L**

Ⓧ Okarohombo Campsite (4 pitches) ☎065 658 993; e maxi@nasco.org.na; www.nacso.org.na. This simple, remote campsite under ana trees is run by the local Himba community, who speak little English. Contact the Marienfluss Conservancy Office (see above) for reservations. It offers 4 private sites, each with private shower, toilet & kitchen area, & a further 5 sharing ablution & cooking facilities. Hot water is supplied by solar panels. Like most community campsites, it is worth your support. *N$60 pp.* **L**

Ⓧ Van Zyl's Pass Campsite (6 pitches) ☎081 211 6291; e maxi@nasco.org.na; www.nacso.org.na. On the banks of a sandy river-bed, this community campsite is 20km east of Van Zyl's Pass. 3 pitches have private flush toilets, hot showers, basins, braais & sinks, & there's a 4th 'overflow' pitch. *N$120 pp.* **L**

What to see and do The track that goes past these camps leads after about 3km to three options. The left fork goes to an excellent viewing point, over some rapids in the river. The centre and right turns are both blocked to vehicles. If you walk up the middle track, you'll find a small beach on the Kunene. The right track leads off to some trees, which may have been a campsite once.

In the morning and evening you'll see many Himba people going about their business, often with their cattle. There is also some wildlife around, including springbok, ostrich, bat-eared fox, bustards, korhaans and many other birds.

UPDATES WEBSITE

You can post your comments and recommendations, and read the latest feedback and updates from other readers, online at www.bradtupdates.com/namibia.

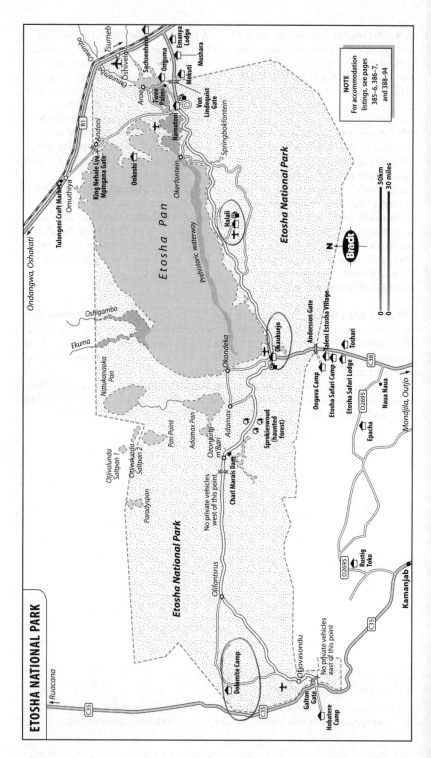

ETOSHA NATIONAL PARK

NOTE
For accommodation
listings, see pages
385–6, 386–7,
and 388–94

Etosha Pan

Prehistoric waterway

Etosha National Park

Etosha National Park

Ruacana

Tsumeb

Omuthiya

Ondangwa, Oshakati

Tulongeni Craft Market

Omuthiya

Oshigambo

Ekuma

Natukanaoka Pan

Otjivalunda Saltpan 1

Otjivakuada Saltpan 2

Paradyspan

Pan Point

Adamax Pan

Adamax

Ozonjuitji m'Bari

Sprokieswoud (haunted forest)

Charl Marais Dam

No private vehicles west of this point

Olifantsrus

Ojovasondu

Dolomite Camp

Galton Gate

Hobatere Camp

No private vehicles east of this point

Rustig Toko

Kamanjab

Naua Naua

Epacha

Mondjila, Outjo

Toshari

Etosha Safari Lodge

Etosha Safari Camp

Taleni Etosha Village

Ongava Camp

Andersson Gate

Okaukuejo

Okondeka

Okerfontein

Onkoshi

King Nehale lya Mpingana Gate

Andoni

Namutoni

Springbokfontein

Von Lindequist Gate

Twee Palms

Aroe

Sachsenheim

Onguma

Mokuti

Mushara

Emanya Lodge

Oshivelo

Omundaungilo

Omuramba Omuthiya

B1

C35

C35

C38

D2695

D2695

Halali

N

Bradt

50km

30 miles

0

0

16

Etosha National Park

Translated as the 'Place of Mirages', 'Land of Dry Water' or the 'Great White Place', Etosha is an apparently endless pan of silvery-white sand, upon which dust-devils play and mirages blur the horizon. As a game park, it excels during the dry season when huge herds of animals can be seen amid some of the most startling and photogenic scenery in Africa.

The roads are all navigable in a normal 2WD car, and the park was designed for visitors to drive themselves around. If you insist on guided trips – or want an introductory guided tour in a safari vehicle – these can be organised both at restcamps and lodges within the park, and by the private lodges just outside (or consider instead one of the concession areas in Damaraland).

For most people, though, Etosha is a park to explore by yourself. Put a few drinks, a camera, a couple of memory cards and a pair of binoculars in your own car and go for a slow drive, stopping at the waterholes – it's amazing.

There are three restcamps within the park, and two lodges, as well as an increasing number of lodges outside its boundaries.

BACKGROUND INFORMATION

HISTORY Europeans first knew Etosha in the early 1850s when Charles Andersson and Francis Galton visited it. They recorded their early impressions:

> … we traversed an immense hollow, called Etosha, covered with saline encrustations, and having wooded and well-defined borders. Such places are in Africa designated 'salt pans'… In some rainy seasons, the Ovambo informed us, the locality was flooded and had all the appearance of a lake; but now it was quite dry, and the soil strongly impregnated with salt. Indeed, close in shore, the commodity was to be had of a very pure quality.

They were among the first explorers and traders who relentlessly hunted the area's huge herds of game. In 1876 an American trader, McKiernan, came through the area and wrote of a visit to Etosha:

> All the menageries in the world turned loose would not compare to the sight that I saw that day.

The slaughter became worse as time progressed and more Europeans came until, in 1907, Dr F von Lindequist, the governor of German South West Africa (as Namibia was then), proclaimed three reserves. These covered all of the current park and most of Kaokoland – between the Kunene and Hoarusib rivers. The aim was to stem the rapid depletion of the animals in the area, and protect all of the land through which the seasonal migrations passed. It was an excellent plan for conserving the wildlife – though perhaps not so perfect for the people who lived in these areas.

This protected area remained largely intact until the 1950s and 1960s. Then, just as a nature conservation unit and several tourist camps were set up, the reserves were redefined and Etosha shrank to its present size.

In recent years, there has been persistent and increasing talk of developing a 'people's park' – designed to link Etosha with the Skeleton Coast. If this were to come to fruition, it would cross the concessions currently held by Hobatere, Etendeka and Palmwag, creating a 20km-wide corridor to allow free movement of wildlife between the two national parks.

GEOGRAPHY, LANDSCAPE AND FLORA The defining feature of the national park is the huge Etosha Pan, which appears to be the remnant of a large inland lake that was fed by rivers from the north and east. One of these was probably the Kunene, which flowed southeast from the Angolan highlands and into the pan. However, some 12 million years ago continental uplift changed the slope of the land and the course of these tributaries. The Kunene now flows west from the Ruacana Falls and into the Atlantic. Thus deprived, the lake slowly vanished in the scorching sun, leaving behind only a salty residue. Few plants can grow on this and so wind erosion is easy, allowing the pan to be gradually hollowed out.

The pan has probably changed little over time. It is roughly 110km from east to west and 60km from north to south, covering an area of 6,133km² (around a quarter of the park's surface) with flat, silvery sand and shimmering heat. If the rains to the north and east have been good, then the pan will hold water for a few months at the start of the year, thanks mainly to the Ekuma River and the Omuramba Ovambo. Only very rarely does it fill completely.

In the rest of the park, beyond the sides of the pan, the terrain is generally flat with a variety of habitats ranging from mopane woodland to wide, open, virtually treeless plains. In the east of the park, around Namutoni, the attractive makalani palms (*Hyphaene ventricosa*) are found, often in picturesque groups around waterholes. The small, round fruit of these palms, a favourite food of elephants, is sometimes called vegetable ivory because of its hard white kernel. In the west, one of the more unusual areas is the Haunted Forest, Sprokieswoud in Afrikaans, where the contorted forms of strange moringa trees (*Moringa ovalifolia*) form a weird woodland scene. Further west still, the environment becomes hillier, with mopane woodlands dotting the open savannah: very pretty but with few obvious centres for the game to congregate.

Etosha is so special because of the concentration of waterholes that occur around the southern edges of the pan. As the dry season progresses, these increasingly draw the game. In fact, the best way to watch animals in Etosha is often just to sit in your vehicle by a waterhole and wait.

Three types of spring create these waterholes, which differ in both appearance and geology:

Contact springs These occur in situations where two adjacent layers of rock have very different permeabilities. There are many to be seen just on the edge of the pan. Here the water-bearing calcrete comes to an end and the water flows out on to the surface because the underlying layers of clay are impermeable. Okerfontein is the best example of this type of spring, which is generally weak in water supply.

Water-level springs These are found in hollows where the surface of the ground actually cuts below the level of the water table, often in large depressions in the limestone formations. They are inevitably dependent on the level of the water table, and hence vary greatly from year to year. Typical of this type are Ngobib, Groot Okevi and Klein Okevi.

Artesian springs Formed when pressure from overlying rocks forces water up to the surface from deeper aquifers (water-bearing rocks), these normally occur on limestone hillocks, forming deep pools that often have clumps of reeds in the centre. These springs are usually very reliable and include Namutoni, Klein Namutoni and Chudob.

MAMMALS The game and birds found here are typical of the savannah plains of southern Africa, but include several species endemic to this western side of the continent, adjacent to the Namib Desert.

The more common herbivores include elephant, giraffe, eland, blue wildebeest, kudu, gemsbok, springbok, impala, steenbok and zebra. The most numerous of these are the springbok, which can often be seen in herds numbering thousands, spread out over the most barren of plains. These finely marked antelope have a marvellous habit of pronking, either (it appears) for fun or to avoid predators. It has been suggested that pronking is intended to put predators off in the first place by showing the animal's strength and stamina; the weakest pronkers are the ones predators are seen to go for. The early explorer Andersson described these elegant leaps:

> This animal bounds without an effort to a height of 10 or 12 feet at one spring, clearing from 12 to 14 feet of ground. It appears to soar, to be suspended for a moment in the air, then, touching the ground, to make another dart, or another flight, aloft, without the aid of wings, by the elastic springiness of its legs.

Elephant are very common, though digging for water below the sand wears down their tusks, so big tuskers are very rare. Often large family groups are seen trooping down to waterholes to drink, wallow and bathe. The park's population has been under scientific scrutiny for the infrasonic noises (below the range of human hearing) which they make. It is thought that groups communicate over long distances in this way.

Among the rarer species, black rhino continue to thrive here, and the floodlit waterholes at Okaukuejo and Halali provide two of the continent's best chances to observe this aggressive and secretive species. On one visit here, I watched as a herd of 20 or so elephants, silently drinking in the cool of the night, were frightened away from the water, and kept at bay, by the arrival of a single black rhino. It returned several times in the space of an hour or so, each time causing the larger elephants to flee, before settling down to enjoy a drink from the pool on its own.

Your best chance of seeing white rhino is in the east of the park, around Aus, Springbokfontein, Batia or Okerfontein, either early or late in the day.

Black-faced impala are restricted to Namibia and southern Angola, occurring here as well as in parts of the Kunene Region to the west. With only isolated populations, numbering under a thousand or so, they are one of the rarest animals in the region. The Damara dik-dik is the park's smallest antelope. Endemic to Namibia, it is common here in areas of dense bush.

Roan antelope and red hartebeest occur all over the subcontinent, though they are common nowhere. This is definitely one of the better parks in which to look for roan, especially in the mopane areas around Aus and Olifantsbad.

16

All of the larger felines are found in Etosha, with good numbers of lion, leopard, cheetah and caracal. The lion tend to prey mainly upon zebra and wildebeest, while the cheetah rely largely upon springbok. The seldom-seen leopard take a varied diet, including antelope and small mammals, while the equally elusive caracal go for similar but smaller prey.

There have been several attempts to introduce wild dog here, but so far with no success. The usual problem has been that the dogs don't know to avoid lion, which have subsequently killed them for no apparent reason.

Also found in the park are both spotted and brown hyenas, together with silver jackal (or Cape fox), and the more common black-backed jackal – many of which can be seen in the late evening, skulking around the camps in search of scraps of food.

BIRDS Some 340 species of birds have been recorded in Etosha, including many uncommon members of the hawk and vulture families.

Among the birds of prey, bateleur, martial, tawny and Wahlberg's eagles are fairly common, as are black-breasted and brown snake eagles. Pale chanting goshawks are more often seen than the similar Gabar or the smaller little banded goshawk. The list of harriers, falcons and kestrels occurring here is even longer, and worthy of a special mention are the very common rock kestrels, and the unusual red-necked and particularly cute pygmy falcons, which are less readily seen. The impressive peregrine falcon and Montagu's harrier are two of the rarer summer migrants.

Lappet-faced and white-backed vultures are common here, outnumbering the odd pair of white-headed or hooded vultures. Palmnut vultures are occasionally seen in the east of the park.

The number of large birds stalking around the plains can strike visitors as unusual: invariably during the day you will see groups of ostriches or pairs of secretary birds. Equally, it is easy to drive within metres of many kori bustards and black korhaans, which will just sit by the roadside and watch the vehicles pass. In the wet season, blue cranes, both beautiful and endangered, are common here: Etosha is worth visiting in January and February for them alone. Other specialities of the park include violet wood hoopoe, white-tailed shrike, bare-cheeked and black-faced babblers, short-toed rock thrush, and a pale race of the pink-bellied lark.

PRACTICAL INFORMATION

WHEN TO VISIT To decide when to visit, think about the weather, consider the number of other visitors around, and work out if your main reason for coming is to see the animals or the birds.

Weather Etosha's weather is typical of Namibia, so see *Weather* in *Chapter 3*, pages 36–7, for a general overview. At the beginning of the year, it's hot and fairly damp with average temperatures around 27°C and cloud cover for some of the time. If the rains have been good, then the pan will have some standing water in it.

The clouds gradually disperse as the rains cease, around March–April. Many of Etosha's plants are bright green during this time but, with some cloud cover, the park's stark beauty isn't at its most photogenic.

From April to July the park dries out, and nights become cooler. Nights in August are normally above freezing, and by the end of September they are warm again. October is hot, and it gets hotter as the month progresses, but the humidity remains very low.

Even the game seems to await the coming of the rains – traditionally in late November, or perhaps December – but becoming earlier. When these do arrive, the tropical downpours last only for a few hours each afternoon, but they clear the air, revive the vegetation, and give everything a new lease of life.

Photography From a photographic point of view, Etosha can be stunning in any month. A personal favourite is late April to June, when the vegetation is green, yet the skies are clear blue and there's little dust in the rain-washed air.

Other visitors Etosha can get very busy, particularly around Easter and in high season (July–October). Then advanced bookings are *essential*; you may not even get a camping site without a prior reservation. The accommodation inside the park during August can be full up to a year in advance.

The dates of the South African school holidays seem to be less relevant than they used to be, as Namibia is no longer the only foreign country where South African passport holders are welcomed. However, ideally try to avoid Namibian school holidays. February to mid-April, late May to July, and November are probably the quietest months.

Game viewing Etosha's dry season is certainly the best time to see big game. Then, as the small bush pools dry up and the green vegetation shrivels, the animals move closer to the springs on the pan's edge. Before the game fences were erected (these now surround the park completely) many of the larger animals would have migrated between Etosha and the Kaokoveld – returning here during the dry season to the region's best permanent waterholes. Now most are forced to stay within the park and only bull elephants commonly break out of their confines to cause problems for the surrounding farmers.

Hence the months between July and late October are the best for game. Though the idea of sitting in a car at 40°C may seem unpleasant, October is normally the best month for game and the heat is very dry. Park under a shady tree and be grateful that the humidity is so low. During and after the rains, you won't see much game, partly because the lush vegetation hides the animals, and partly because most of them will have moved away from the waterholes (where most of the roads are) and gone deeper into the bush. However, often the animals you see will have young, as food (animal or vegetable) is at its most plentiful then.

Birdwatching The start of the rainy season witnesses the arrival of the summer migrants and, if the rains have been good, the aquatic species that come for the water in the pan itself. In exceptional years thousands of flamingos will come to breed, building their nests on the eastern side of the main Etosha Pan, or in Fischer's Pan. This is an amazing spectacle (see box on *Flamingos*, page 316). However, bear in mind that Etosha's ordinary feathered residents can be seen more easily during the dry season, when there is less vegetation to hide them.

GETTING THERE AND AWAY

By road Hiring your own vehicle is best done in Windhoek (see *Hiring a vehicle*, pages 85–9). However, if you are travelling through, and hiring a car just for Etosha, then consider doing so from Tsumeb. This is normally best organised in advance, through a tour operator (see pages 56–8) or a car-hire company in Windhoek (see pages 88–9), some of which will let you pick up and drop off cars at Mokuti or Ongava.

Many operators organise guided trips around Namibia, including a few days in Etosha, often staying in the national park's accommodation. However, you only need to see one air-conditioned 75-seater coach driving through the park to convince you that this is not the best way to visit either Etosha or Namibia. Most have their bases in Windhoek; see pages 56–8 for details.

By air Wilderness Air runs daily flights between Windhoek and the Ongava airstrip (*about 1½hrs; from N$7,100*), just south of the parks' Andersson Gate. Scenic Air also run flights from Windhoek to either Ongava/Mokuti (*1½–2hrs; from N$6,610/7,720*), though there is no fixed schedule for these.

PARK ACCESS (⊕ *sunrise– sunset; admission N$80 per adult, plus N$10 per vehicle, under 16s free*) There are four gates into the national park, although the majority of visitors use either the Von Lindequist Gate, near Namutoni, which is 106km from Tsumeb, or the Andersson Gate, south of Okaukuejo, 120km from Outjo. A less well-known option, introduced in 2003, glories in the name of King Nehale Lya Mpingana Gate. This is in the northeast corner of the park, near Andoni, with access 17km from the B1 north of Tsumeb. The fourth access point, the Galton Gate, lies at the western end of the park. Previously, this whole western region was closed to the public, and only accessible to guests of Dolomite Camp. However, as of March 2014 the Galton Gate is now open for general public access.

Entry permits are issued at the gates. From there, you must proceed to the nearest camp office (usually a restcamp) and settle the costs of your permit and any accommodation within the park. With the exception of Onkoshi Camp, rates for accommodation within the park exclude entrance fees, so be aware that even if you are staying overnight, fees are still payable.

If you go out of the park for lunch, then strictly you should pay two park entry fees, but this rule *might* be relaxed if you politely tell the gatekeeper that you intend to return later in the day.

The gates open around sunrise and close about 20 minutes before sunset. For the precise times on any given day, see the notice next to the entry gates of each camp. Driving through the park in the dark is not allowed, and the gates do close on time.

GETTING AROUND To see Etosha you need to drive around the park. There is no way to walk within it, or to fly just above it. If you do not have your own vehicle then you must either hire one (see *Getting there and away*, page 383), or book an organised trip.

Etosha was designed for visitors to drive themselves around. The roads are good; a normal 2WD car is fine for all of them. The landscapes are generally open, as the vegetation is sparse, so you don't need eyes like a hawk to spot most of the larger animals. Thus very few people use organised tours to visit the park.

Organising your own safari Most of Etosha's roads are made of calcrete and gravel, which gives a good driving surface without tar's unnatural appearance, although they can be slippery when wet. The speed limit within the park is 60km/h. Be warned that most of the park's accidents occur near sunset, as people try to dash back to camp before the gates close.

An excellent map of the park and the more colourful 'Honeyguide' publication, with colour sketches of most of the common birds and animals, are normally for sale in the restcamp shops.

For details of planning your day, and the main waterholes to visit, see pages 395–7.

Organised tour Some visitors really don't want to drive thems~~~
Others appreciate the benefit of a local guide or the height of a s~~~
though a higher viewpoint isn't necessarily better for photographs, w~~~
best at eye level for realism.

Many organised trips to the park emanate from the surrounding p~~~ ~~~ ~~~.
See *Accommodation near Etosha* (pages 387–94) for ideas about what is possible
from each. Alternatively, you could try one of the tour operators in Windhoek.

WHERE TO STAY, EAT AND DRINK
Inside Etosha *Map, page 378.*
In addition to the three long-established national park restcamps inside Etosha,
there is the more upmarket Onkoshi Camp, and the relatively new Dolomite Camp
which opened in 2011 in the previously private western side of the park. All the
accommodation options within the national park are operated by Namibia Wildlife
Resorts (NWR; see page 56).

Aim to spend a minimum of two nights at any camp you visit. Remember that, with
a speed limit of 60km/h, it will take you at least 2 hours to drive between Namutoni
and Halali, or Halali and Okaukuejo. To get to Onkoshi, you'll need to allow around
1½ hours from Namutoni, and Dolomite Camp is around 180km from Okaukuejo,
taking around 4–5 hours once you've factored in some game viewing *en route*.

Reservations Booking accommodation in advance at the NWR (✆ *061 285 7200;*
e *reservations@nwr.com.na; www.nwr.com.na*) is wise, but you need to be organised
and stick to your itinerary. The alternative is to plan on camping, while hoping for
spaces or cancellations in the chalets and bungalows. For this you'll need to ask at
the camp office just before it closes at sunset. This is often successful outside the
main holiday months, but you need a tent in case it is not.

Note that during the main holiday seasons, around Easter and August, even
Etosha's campsites are fully booked in advance. If you haven't a reservation, you
must stay outside the park and drive in for day trips.

Lodges
Onkoshi Camp (15 tents) Opened in 2008, this was envisaged as the jewel in the crown of NWR's Etosha resorts. It lies 42km north of Namutoni in an area closed to all but lodge guests, who can either leave their vehicles at Namutoni & be taken on a 1½hr game drive to the lodge, or drive directly to the lodge in their own vehicles.

Approached down a wooden walkway, the stone-&-thatch central building has a comfortable lounge & bar area with modern furniture in earth colours & just a touch of 'Africa'. This, together with a restaurant & terrace, a small pool & loungers, & luxury tents, gaze over the vast open space of Etosha Pan.

Spread out on either side of the main areas along the walkway, the tents are beautifully designed with folding glass doors opening on 2 sides & the twin beds (or 1 dbl), inside their mosquito net, positioned so that you could feel you were sleeping outside.

Complete the picture with mock leather headboard & bedside tables, a sleeper couch, bath tub, inside & outside showers & separate WC.

Cocktails are served on the terrace at sunset & there is a telescope for stargazing after dinner. Although not a game-rich area, morning & evening drives are offered (*N$500 pp*) but the beauty here is the pan: between Jul & Oct you may be lucky enough to see flamingos that come here to nest. On the downside, as the pan dries out prolific insect life may occur; while this affects the whole park, the camp's proximity to the pan makes it particularly susceptible. B&B *N$2,200/4,000 sgl/dbl*. **LLLLL**

Dolomite Camp (20 rooms) The newest of the NWR properties in Etosha, opened in 2011, brings the previously off-limits area of western Etosha into the public domain, with public access through the Galton Gate. The land in this part of

. park is hilly with much bush: very pretty but with few obvious centres for game to congregate. Set among dolomite outcrops, the camp has views to east & west over the surrounding savannah from the reception, lounge, bar, infinity pool & restaurants. The chalets on both sides are private & widely spaced, accessed by wooden walkways & stone pathways. Note that there are many steps & some of the paths are long & uneven, & so unsuitable for the less agile. Constructed of thatch & canvas with wooden decking, each chalet is comfortable & stylish, if a little cramped. Morning & afternoon game drives (*N$500 pp*) are offered in the surrounding areas of the park, & at the time of research a licence for night driving was in the pipeline. *B&B N$1,550–1,800/2,700–3,200 sgl/ dbl.* **LLLL**

Restcamps The reception office at each restcamp (⊕ *dawn–dusk*) is where you pay for your stay, as well as any park fees due. Don't forget to pay all your park fees before you try to leave the park. You can't pay them at the gate.

Facilities Each camp has a range of accommodation, including bungalows and a campsite (see below) and a restaurant where most visitors take at least one of their meals. At the time of research, meal prices (*b/fast N$120, lunch N$130, dinner N$180*) were common to all camps, but this is likely to change before long. Outside prescribed mealtimes, there's usually a kiosk that sells drinks and snacks (⊕ *10.00– 17.00 daily*). After dinner, the bar normally stays open until about midnight.

The camp shops (⊕ *06.00–19.00 daily*) sell a remarkable assortment of foodstuffs: frozen meat, sausages and firewood (with braais in mind), as well as tinned and packet foods and often bread, eggs and cheese. Beer, lots of cold drinks, and a limited selection of wine are also found here. Take your own cooking equipment. Aside from food, there is also the usual mix of tourist needs, from curios, T-shirts, print film (occasionally slide, but nothing too unusual) and wildlife books to postcards and even stamps. You can normally buy phonecards at the shop for the payphone.

Each camp also has a swimming pool and – importantly – a fuel station (⊕ *sunrise to sunset*), but don't run it too close; diesel wasn't available at Halali when we visited.

🏠 **Okaukuejo Camp** [Map, page 391] (40 rooms, 62 chalets, camping) ☎067 229800. Etosha's oldest restcamp is the administrative hub of the park & the centre of the Etosha Ecological Institute. It occupies a level, grassy site at the western end of the pan, about 120km north of Outjo. We found the waiting staff very friendly, but note that standards of service & cleanliness are highly variable, & we understand that the US State Department warns of credit card theft, so be on your guard.

Okaukuejo's big attraction is that it overlooks a permanent waterhole which is floodlit like a stage at night, giving you a chance to see some of the shy, nocturnal animals that come to drink – oblivious to the noise, the bright lights & the people sitting on benches just behind a low stone wall. The light doesn't penetrate into the dark surrounding bush, but it illuminates the waterhole like a stage – focusing all attention on the animals. During the dry season you would be unlucky not to spot something of interest by just sitting here for a few hours in the evening, so bring a couple of drinks, binoculars & some warm clothes to settle down & watch. You are virtually guaranteed to see elephant & jackal, while lion & black rhino are very regular visitors. The main annoyance is noise from the bungalows beside the waterhole, or from the many people sitting around. Accommodation is in well-spaced standard & luxury dbl rooms, including 2 for families & 2 suitable for the disabled. Smartly fitted out but with a rustic feel, these are in various configurations, but all are en suite, with AC & seating areas, plus fridge & kettle; 20 bush chalets have kitchenettes. Next to the waterhole are 35 chalets, some with kitchenettes & braai areas, & 5 on 2 storeys, with a large bedroom & terrace above, & a combined sitting room & 2nd bedroom below. The campsite's 46 pitches have BBQ facilities & power points, but no grass & little shade. Good food (it's a buffet in season) is served at reasonable prices in the modern restaurant, which has AC. Sweets & drinks are available from the kiosk by the large circular swimming pools. A launderette (*N$50*) is operated by a coin from reception.

Okaukuejo's shop is well stocked, while opposite reception is the park's only post office (⏰ *08.30–13.00 & 14.00–16.30 Mon–Fri, 08.00–11.00 Sat*), as well as a tourist information office & a curio shop (⏰ *08.00–17.00 daily*). Nearby, a spiral staircase inside a small round tower can be climbed for a good view of the surrounding area.
Game drive N$450/550 pp day/night; B&B room N$1,188/2,156 sgl/dbl; bush chalet N$1,210/2,200 sgl/dbl; waterhole chalet N$1,500/2,800 sgl/dbl; camping N$220/pitch, plus N$120 pp (max 8). **LLL**

Halali Camp [Map, page 391] (39 rooms, 22 chalets, camping) ☎067 229400. Located 75km from Namutoni, 70km from Okaukuejo, Halali is just northwest of the landmark Tweekoppies. There's a small dolomite kopje within the camp's boundary, accessible on a short self-guided trail signposted as 'Tsumasa'.

Halali is the smallest, & usually the quietest, of the restcamps. In 1992, the Moringa waterhole was built on its boundary, & can be viewed from a natural rock seating area a few hundred metres beyond the campsite. This regularly attracts elephant, black rhino & other game. It isn't as busy as Okaukuejo's waterhole, but it is set apart from the camp, so usually has fewer disturbances & a more natural ambience.

As you enter the camp, the shop & restaurant are either side of the office & reception, with a kiosk by the large pool. Meals are served buffet style in season, or à la carte the rest of the year. Accommodation, less extensively refurbished than at the other camps, is smaller and simpler. Twin or dbl en-suite rooms come with AC, fridge & kettle; bush chalets have a kitchenette in the living room; & larger family chalets have a separate kitchen, lounge & big braai area with terrace. There are also honeymoon suites & 2 chalets with disabled access. The 40 camping pitches are very close together but usually with reasonable tree shade.

Game drive N$450/550 pp day/ni... N$946/1,672 sgl/dbl; chalets N$9... 2,530 sgl/dbl; camping N$220/pit... (max 8). **LLL**

Namutoni Camp [Map, pag... (24 rooms, 20 chalets, camping) ☎067 229300. Situated on the eastern edge of the pan, Namutoni is based around a beautiful old 'Beau Geste' type fort, in an area dotted with graceful makalani palms (*Hyphaene petersiana*). It dates back to a German police post, built before the turn of the 20th century. Later it was used as an army base & then for English prisoners during World War I, before being restored in 1957. At the time of research, Namutoni was looking a little tired. However, we hear that it is currently undergoing renovations, due to finish in late 2014. As far as we understand, the plan is to move all of the accommodation back into the fort where it was originally, & the main areas, including the shop, bar & restaurant, which are currently within the fort, will now be outside it. Opposite reception, a museum gives the history of the park, its flora, fauna & people. For some downtime, there's a shady thatched viewing area for the waterhole, & a swimming pool. Rooms, at the time of writing, are contemporary in style with twin or dbl leather beds. Each has a private entrance patio enclosed by a pole fence, & a luxurious bathroom with sunken bath & shower, 2 basins & outside shower. Chalets are more spacious but similarly appointed. At the time of research, guests leave their vehicles in the secure car park, & are taken to the rooms via a drop-off area at the end of the walkway, although we understand this may change following the renovations. None of the rooms has braai or cooking facilities. For these you'll need to camp on one of 25 grassy & well shaded pitches, each with power, & sharing good ablutions.

The morning drive starts 1hr before the gates open; the evening one ends 1hr after they close.
Game drive N$450/550 pp day/night; B&B room N$1,001/1,782 sgl/dbl; chalet N$1,188/2,156 sgl/dbl; camping N$220/pitch, plus N$120 pp (max 8). **LLL**

Accommodation near Etosha *Map, page 378, unless otherwise noted.*

Several private lodges are clustered around each of Etosha's entrance gates. Notable among these are Mokuti, Onguma and Mushara on the eastern side, near Namutoni, with Ongava, Etosha Safari Camp and Lodge and Taleni Etosha Village south of Okaukuejo. Other options lie within 30–45 minutes' drive of the gates in each direction.

Traditionally such lodges have cost more than the public camps and lodges within the park but, following significant investment by the park's authorities, the gap in terms of both rates and facilities is closing. Many have their own vehicles and guides, but note that all vehicles in the park are subject to the park's strict opening and closing times, and none is allowed off the roads while inside Etosha. Places listed below start with those closest to the park gates. For additional accommodation south of Etosha, but within easy distance of the park, see *Chapter 17, Highlands south of Etosha*, pages 399–423.

South of Etosha (Andersson Gate)

🏠 **Ongava Reserve** ✆061 274500; e enquiry@wilderness.co.za; www.wilderness-safaris.com. Down a long drive just by the Andersson Gate, the private Ongava reserve, abutting Etosha's southern side, covers 30,000ha, & is the base for 4 discrete camps. For costly but quick transfers, you can use small aircraft, operated by Wilderness Air.

The environment & wildlife are similar to those near Okaukuejo, although without the huge salt-pan its scenery is less spectacular. Nevertheless, Ongava offers a greater choice of activities than is possible in the national park. The reserve has over 25 lions & in excess of 2,500 head of game, & is one of the few remaining places in Africa where visitors have a fairly reliable chance of encountering both black & white rhino. Don't try to walk without a guide.

Activities at each of the camps are conducted independently. They feature escorted walks/drives on Ongava's own reserve (although Andersson's Camp does not run afternoon drives here), & longer game drives into the national park. In summer there is normally a long (around 5hrs) activity in the morning. This is followed by lunch & time at leisure before dinner, after which there is a night drive. In winter the morning activities are shorter, about 3–4hrs long, & lunch is normally followed by a late-afternoon game drive which often continues after dark by floodlight.

🏠 **ONGAVA LODGE** (14 chalets) ✆067 229602/3. This is the original focus of the reserve, set on a hill 10km from the entrance gate. Centred around a 3-level thatched boma that covers the lounge, bar & restaurant (serving excellent food), it overlooks 2 waterholes from a well-designed viewing area. There's plenty of space for relaxing & a swimming pool to cool off. The original thatched, stone-built chalets stand on the hillside, each surrounded by eco-friendly vegetation with a view over the reserve from its own enlarged wooden deck, with comfy chairs. Rooms are large & luxurious, with AC, twin queen-size beds (& 1 family unit), 24hr mains electricity, a kettle with tea/coffee, & lots of other mod cons. En-suite bathrooms have showers inside & out, as well as twin basins & a WC. At the entrance, a large curio shop also stocks safari clothes & camera film. *DBB N$3,656–5,714/4,448–8,334 sgl/dbl; FBA N$6,974–9,888/9,134–14,564 sgl/dbl.* **LLLLL**

🏠 **LITTLE ONGAVA** (3 luxury suites) This exclusive hideaway, set on the crest of the hill above Ongava Lodge, operates as an entirely self-contained camp, with dedicated & exceptionally well-trained staff. Wooden walkways link the suites, with spectacular views across the reserve, views that are shared by the central living area & accentuated by an eternity pool on the veranda. If that's not enough, contemplation of the view from a luxurious shaded day bed is another option.

Each suite boasts all the mod cons of a 5-star establishment but manages to combine style with comfort & – crucially – a strong sense of place. A series of sliding doors separate the bedroom from a huge bathroom, & further sliding doors lead outside. All is tastefully furnished, with solid wood & neutral colours bringing an intimacy that is all too often lacking in similar upmarket establishments. *FBA N$11,282–16,652/14,024–26,240 sgl/dbl.* **LLLLL**

🏠 **ONGAVA TENTED CAMP** (10 tents) ✆067 687041. Very large Meru-style tents, under shade nets, form the basis of this small, relaxed camp, located some 10km north of Ongava Lodge. The tents, erected on timber decks, have twin beds (or 1 family unit), chairs & mosquito nets, plus an en-suite bathroom with both indoor & outdoor showers, & a veranda. B/fast & lunch are taken at individual tables, & dinner is eaten as a group in the central boma, set just 20m from the busy waterhole, with a small pool alongside. *FBA N$6,974–9,888/9,134–14,564 sgl/dbl.* **LLLLL**

🏠 **ANDERSSON'S CAMP** (20 tents) 📞 067 687 181. Some 8km from the entrance, Andersson's is set around an old farmhouse, & is almost entirely built of reclaimed materials. The tents, erected on timber decks, have glazed door & windows, a fan & a safe, while quirky en-suite bathrooms feature a tin tub, shower & WC. Meals are taken close to the house, under a large veranda where there is also a comfortable lounge area overlooking both a waterhole & a mudhole. The underground hide giving eye-level views of the waterhole is excellent for photographers. There are 2 swimming pools: the first, a farm-style dam, & the second a larger pool surrounded by grass. *DBB N$2,506–3,364/3,580–5,182 sgl/dbl; FBA N$4,726–5,834/8,022–10,124 sgl/dbl.* **LLLLL**

🏠 **Taleni Etosha Village** (40 chalets) 📞 067 333 413; ✉ reservations@etosha-village.com; www.etosha-village.com. Just 2km from the Andersson Gate, this lodge opened in Oct 2008. Styled loosely on a traditional village, its tented chalets on timber decks are well spaced among mopane trees. Bedrooms have AC, a sleeper couch, a safe & sockets for charging. There's an en-suite bathroom & shower, plus a kitchen comprising a fridge, 2-ring cooker & kettle. Pots, pans, crockery & cutlery can be hired from the shop, which also stocks a wide range of goods. Alternatively, there are 3 separate dining areas serving good buffet-style meals, & 3 pools, all in attractive gardens. Activities include ½/full-day game drives (*N$475/695*) into Etosha & sundowner drives (*N$195*), & stargazing (*N$170*) on the property. *DBB N$1,259–1,415/1,910–2,116 sgl/dbl.* **LLL**

🏠 **Etosha Safari Camp** (50 chalets, camping) 📞 067 333 404; ✉ info@gondwana-collection. com; www.gondwana-collection.com. Part of the Gondwana Group, this lodge brings the spirit of a township to life, with a funky 'village' feel. There's a *shebeen*, a shop in a railway carriage, a games room & a central courtyard with 'wheelbarrow' & 'bathtub' chairs, & the whole place is decorated with 1950s memorabilia. The swimming pool is on a raised deck area nearby, & at the time of research was soon to be renovated. Scattered across the hillside are brick-built chalets, 4 for families, 3 trpls, all with AC, safes & a fun shower enclosure. There's also a large, open campsite. Popular with small groups, the camp is right by the C38, & just 9km south of Etosha. *B&B chalet N$1,067/1,706 sgl/dbl; camping N$150 pp.* **LLL**

🏠 **Etosha Safari Lodge** (65 rooms) 📞 067 333 411; ✉ info@gondwana-collection.com; www. gondwana-collection.com. This large lodge has a spacious dining area, bar & lounge in a central thatched building with a wraparound terrace & long sunset deck making the best of its spectacular view. Well-appointed individual chalets stretch out along the ridge in either direction (there is a shuttle service for those at the far ends!). Each has twin beds, AC, kettle, internal phone, open shower area & separate WC, & a small terrace taking in that view; 5 are family units. Dinner (*N$250*) is either buffet or a set menu, with sunset cocktails & occasional drumming sessions. Activities include a 1½hr walking trail to the sister property, Etosha Safari Camp, & back & guided game drives (*N$650/950 ½/full day*) into Etosha. Back at the lodge, 3 swimming pools offer further options. *B&B N$1,462/2,338 sgl/dbl.* **LLL**

🏠 **Toshari Lodge** (38 rooms, camping) 📞 067 333418/333440; ✉ toshari@iway.na; www. etoshagateway-toshari.com. About 27km from the Andersson Gate, & 71km north of Outjo, Toshari has a large thatched central building housing a reception area with comfy sofas & internet access, a bar & a restaurant with tasteful artwork, & a pool with grassy surrounds. All rooms have AC, mosi nets, tea/coffee facilities & deck-chairs on the terrace; the 4 luxury rooms also have glass sliding doors overlooking the wilderness plus a minibar. 3 grassy camping pitches have their own bathrooms, power points & braai area. Game drives into the park (*min 5 people*) cost N$640/840 pp ½/full day. *Lunch N$165; dinner N$250; B&B standard N$990/1,450 sgl/dbl; luxury N$1,120/1,720 sgl/dbl; camping N$135 pp.* **LL**

🏠 **Epacha Reserve** [Map, page 378] Reservations 📞 061 375300; ✉ res@leadinglodges. com; www.epacha.com. The private Epacha reserve covers 21,000ha of the wonderfully named Ondundozonandandana Valley, & is home to 2 exclusive camps owned by Leading Lodges of Africa. The reserve is stocked with game that includes 21 species of antelope, as well as black rhino. Aside from day & night game drives, guests can take part in clay-pigeon shooting. The entrance to the reserve is situated 27km along the D2695, although a new entrance road under construction will lead direct from the C38. Both Epacha & its sister camp, Eagle Tented Lodge, are set on a gentle slope in surrounding bush.

EPACHA GAME LODGE & SPA (18 chalets, presidential suite) 067 333 423; e epacha@ leadinglodges.com; www.epacha.com. The emphasis here is on luxury, with colonial-style solid wood furniture, large en-suite bathrooms & open-air showers, private balconies & all the trappings of a smart hotel, including Wi-Fi access. There's a 5-room presidential suite, complete with a private chef, ranger, butler & a vehicle for your own private use. Within the faded grandeur of the central area are several lounges overlooking a waterhole, while guests wanting more than the environment alone can seek out the smoking lounge, library or billiard room, or cool off in the pool. For further indulgence, there's a health spa with sauna, jacuzzi, steam room & splash pool, as well as a range of treatments. *DBB N$2,920–3,440/4,180–5,240 sgl/dbl*. **LLLLL**

EAGLE TENTED LODGE & SPA (16 tents) 067 333 463 e eagle@leadinglodges.com; www. eagletentedlodge.com. This lodge offers 2 styles of en-suite accommodation. Each of the 8 safari-style 'standard' tents, built on a 4m-high wooden platform, has an open view with glazed wooden doors leading out to a private balcony & splash pool. 8 'de luxe' tents, with open-air bath tubs, have been built away from the main areas at ground level under 'carport'-style shade-netting canopies. The main building is constructed of rustic-looking stone, carefully designed to incorporate a restaurant, where tables are laid with sparkling glasses & starched napery, a bar & a wine cellar. Outside, a pool with its own bar fits seamlessly into the whole. Even the boma is surrounded by stone columns & immaculate lawns. To complete the picture, a health spa offers massages, body wraps & scrubs to ease away the day's troubles. *DBB N$1,820– 2,400/2,640–3,800 sgl/dbl*. **LLLL**

Mondjila Safari Camp (11 tents, camping) 067 333446, reservations 061 237294; e reservations@exclusive.com.na; www. mondjilasafaricamp.com. Situated 47km south of Okaukuejo, just 3km from the C38 along the D2779. Walk-in Meru tents with twin beds & en-suite showers are set on a hillside with quite steep slopes. The restaurant, bar & pool have fabulous views, & the campsite, with 8 pitches, has braai areas, power & light. *Dinner N$210; B&B N$585– 615/990–1,080 sgl/dbl; camping N$110 pp*. **LL**

West of Etosha (Galton Gate)

Hobatere Lodge (14 rooms) reservations 061 228 104; e hobatere@journeysnamibia. com, reservations@journeysnamibia.com; www2. journeysnamibia.com. After a period of closure, Hobatere is due to reopen in mid-2015 under the management of Journeys Namibia. It's located about 65km north of Kamanjab, set on the banks of the small Otjovasondu River, just west of Etosha's Galton Gate (which opened to the public in 2014). Activities on offer will be full-day excursions into Etosha, as well as morning, afternoon & evening game drives, & guided walks on the Hobatere concession. The main area will have a restaurant, lounge, bar & outside veranda for viewing game at the waterhole. Facilities will include a swimming pool & curio shop. Although at the time of writing this lodge was not yet open, we have high hopes for it: Journeys Namibia currently manages Fish River Lodge in Fish River Canyon (see page 208) and Grootberg Lodge in Northern Damaraland (see page 357). Grootberg has particularly impressive levels of community involvement and staff hired from the local area, a style of management that probably helped them win this concession and will hopefully be repeated at Hobatere. *DBB N$1,800/3,000 sgl/dbl*. **LLLL**

East of Etosha (Von Lindequist Gate)

Mokuti Etosha Lodge (106 rooms) 067 229 084, reservations 061 207 5360; e reservations@ol-leisure.com; www. mokutietoshalodge.com. Situated on the C38, 25km west of the B1, Mokuti is set in its own 4,300ha reserve, immediately next to Etosha's Von Lindequist Gate. More of a hotel than a lodge, it's traditional in design, yet spread out & with up-to-date facilities. In addition to the recently refurbished bar & boma restaurant, there's a 24hr gym, & a spa offers massages, manicures & aromatherapy. Rather less indulgent are the conference facilities, business centre for guest use & Wi-Fi access in the main building, free to residents.

Most of the twin rooms, with their AC, high thatched ceilings & en-suite facilities, are dotted across the lawns. A few more luxurious units boast dbl beds & separate lounges. There are also 8 'luxury family rooms' for 2 adults & 3 children, & 2 twin units for people with disabilities, modified

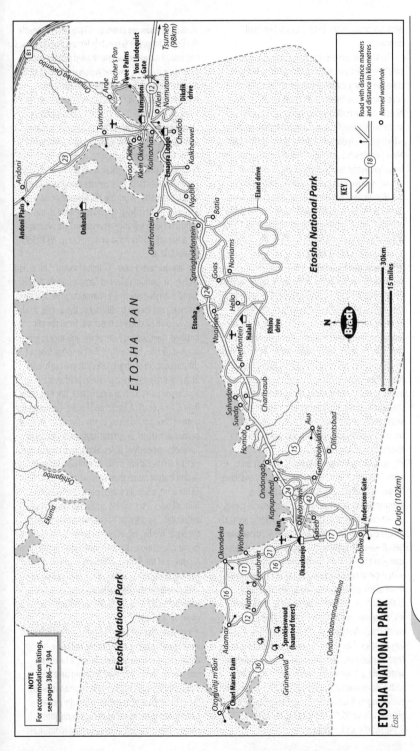

ETOSHA NATIONAL PARK
East

NOTE
For accommodation listings,
see pages 386–7, 394

KEY

⫻⫻ Road with distance markers
     and distance in kilometres

○ Named waterhole

Etosha National Park

Etosha National Park

ETOSHA PAN

391

with handrails in the bathrooms & widened doorways.

Mokuti's reserve is fenced & so it is generally safe to wander around. A couple of short walking trails are clearly marked, though it is equally easy to spot wandering antelope from the poolside; more elusive on the trails are the snakes that can be seen in the hotel's reptile park. Look out for the bontebok, which are not indigenous, but come from the Cape. Most people who stay here have their own cars (the hotel has useful fuel pumps for diesel & unleaded petrol), & drive themselves around eastern Etosha, but Mokuti does run game drives into Etosha with its own vehicles & guides (*N$550 pp, or N$4,180 for a private vehicle seating 9*), from sunrise until 11.00, & 14.00 until sunset. DBB *N$1,465–2,365/2,346–4,006 sgl/dbl.* **LLL–LLLLL**

🏠 **Onguma Reserve** ✆061 237005; e reservations@onguma.com; www.onguma.com. Right next to Etosha's eastern gate, & accessed through an impressive fortified gate, Onguma Reserve boasts more than 34,000ha of protected land, bordering Fischer's Pan. The easy 9km drive through the reserve feels like eastern Etosha, with its mix of pans, woodland & open plains. Game found here includes lion, leopard & rhino, as well as the widely seen impala, oryx, wildebeest & springbok; some 300 species of bird have been spotted. There are 6 separate accommodation options, whose activities include game drives in the reserve & into Etosha.

🏠 ONGUMA BUSH CAMP (14 rooms, 3 family units, 1 suite) This fully fenced camp is, technically speaking, Onguma's budget option, geared to families, although its stylish main area & comfortable rooms do not come across as 'budget' at all. Rooms are fairly simple but well furnished, & all have AC, mosquito nets & en-suite bathrooms. 6 waterhole/pool-view rooms are bigger than the others, & notably the waterhole view rooms are outside of the perimeter fence of the camp, giving you a feeling of being in the bush, with plains game such as black-faced impala often seen at the waterhole. These are comfortable & stylish, & also have en suites. A cool & airy multilevel lounge & dining area is the highlight here. Partially on stilts overlooking the crystal clear waterhole, it's open, spacious & stylish; complete with a downstairs playroom for children. A pool with sun-loungers & umbrellas for shade complete the picture. *Dinner N$325; B&B N$1,620–2,200/1,980–3,140 sgl/dbl.* **LLL–LLLL**

⛺ ONGUMA LEADWOOD CAMPSITE (6 pitches) Alongside the Bush Camp, but separately fenced, lies Onguma's Leadwood campsite, whose shaded pitches each have their own WC, shower & power point. Campers can use the pool & restaurant (with advance reservation) at Bush Camp, but otherwise need to bring all their own food. *N$190/95 adult/child.* **L**

⛺ ONGUMA TAMBOTI CAMPSITE (15 pitches) Situated 3km from the Onguma entrance gate, Tamboti is a new luxury fenced campsite, complete with a restaurant, pool, waterhole & supply store selling camping essentials. Each private campsite has its own kitchenette, & private WC & showers, as well as power points. Deep verandas provide shade. Campers (with advance reservation) are welcome for meals at Etosha Aoba or Bush Camp. *N$190/95 adult/child.* **L**

🏠 ONGUMA TENTED CAMP (7 tented rooms) Some 2km further on, Onguma's Tented Camp reinvents the term 'tents', with its modern & minimalistic style. It is most definitely not for the traditionalist; think style, think chic, & you'll be closer to the mark. From the tall, brushed-steel, woven vases at the entrance to lime-washed giraffes by the door, the camp has more of the atmosphere of an art gallery than a bush lodge. In the central area, creamy canvas held aloft by solid light wood poles hints at a circus tent, but here with light & air aplenty. A backdrop of stone-clad walls & a cement floor are balanced by squashy sofas, unusual beaded armchairs, & director-style chairs featuring luminous-green dyed hides. Skin rugs complete the picture. In the corner, a tiny infinity pool suggests a design feature rather than somewhere to cool off. To the front, a floodlit waterhole that is overlooked from all sides is set among indigenous vegetation; fortunately, no attempt has been made to beautify the bush. The big-top effect continues to each of the rooms where more skin rugs soften the chrome, stone & cement of the fixtures & fittings – visitors lack for nothing (except AC). Sliding doors lead to a private deck where comfy chairs afford a great view of the waterhole. *DBB N$3,360/5,040 sgl/dbl; no children under 12.* **LLLLL**

🏠 ONGUMA TREE TOP CAMP (4 tree houses) Reached via a drawbridge up to a timber walkway, this entire camp is built on stilts facing a beautiful waterhole. The bar, lounge & dining area are alongside an open kitchen where you can watch the chef prepare your meals. Carefully chosen furnishings use natural materials: hide, jute & canvas. The thatched, canvas-walled rooms have basin, WC & outdoor shower. There is a real feeling of being in the bush at this camp, with guided walks an option; it would be ideal for a single group or family. *N$2,310/3,360 sgl/dbl; no children under 10.* **LLLL**

🏠 **ONGUMA PLAINS: THE FORT** (12 suites) This unique spot is pure fantasy. The Moorish feel of the fort, with its grand tower, is mirrored by separate suites. The terracotta-mud finish to the 60cm-thick walls, the timber ceilings & pierced bronze lights would not disgrace a riad in Marrakech, but here your large room opens on to timber decking overlooking Fischer's Pan & the national park beyond. There are few places where you can watch passing wildlife at the waterhole from the comfort of your bed! A bathroom is set in the tower of each suite with a shower, 2 basins & WC, & a separate shower outside on the deck. All have an air-cooling system, minibar, fridge & kettle, & the 'fort' suite in the tower of the main building also boasts a bath & flat-screen TV.

Stepping stones across cooling streams lead to the open dining area & terraces, overlooking the waterhole & serving superb meals. You can view the sunset from a shallow pool set with tables & chairs, so you can cool your feet, or from the adjacent swimming pool. The area is not fenced, so animals roam free & close to your suite. For safety, guests are taken to the main areas from their suites by golf buggy. *DBB N$3,790/5,690 sgl/dbl; Sultan suite from N$3,470 pp. No children under 7.* **LLLLL**

🏠 **ONGUMA ETOSHA AOBA** (11 bungalows) Located in a tamboti forest on the private Onguma Reserve, Etosha Aoba is a friendly lodge in a pretty location. Thatched bungalows are well designed, with plenty of natural light. From a small veranda, a large patio door, which interchanges with a gauze screen, leads to a room with twin beds under a mosquito net & ceiling fan, a kettle & safe, & a door leading to a tiled WC & shower. 4 renovated luxury bungalows have AC & a secluded outside area with loungers & outdoor shower, while 3 Bush Suites (family units) also have a private veranda with seating, a 'bush' minibar as well as the same amenities as the bungalows.

The main oval lodge consists of a large thatched area with bar & tables for b/fast & dinner, & a small office that doubles as a curio shop. Free Wi-Fi is available in the rooms & the main area. Close by is a pool surrounded by sun-loungers for the foolhardy. A 2hr guided bush walk into the reserve is offered in the mornings. Morning game drives into Etosha can be organised, & there's a sundowner drive on the Onguma Reserve (*N$350 pp*), but most guests drive themselves into the park from here. Etosha Aoba lacks the camaraderie of an all-inclusive lodge, but it's comfortable, pleasantly run & with good food (*3-course set dinner N$270*), making it an excellent base for driving around eastern Etosha. *B&B N$1,570–1,990/2,500–3,340 sgl/dbl; DBB N$1,840–2,260/3,040–3,880 sgl/dbl.* **LLLL–LLLLL**

🏠 **The Mushara Collection** ✆ 067 229106; e reservations@mushara-lodge.com; www.mushara-lodge.com. The only privately family-run lodge on the eastern side of Etosha occupies a 2,500ha reserve, with nature walks & game drives (*N$540 pp*) available. Marc & Mariza Pampe offer 4 choices of accommodation:

🏠 **MUSHARA LODGE** (13 rooms, 1 family house) Located 8km from the eastern entrance of the national park, Mushara is close to a private airstrip, just 500m from the main road. Despite the name, its style is more that of a hotel, albeit one with a high standard of service & attention to detail.

A cavernous entrance leads through to a split-level bar & smart lounge where ostrich-egg chandeliers, zebra hides & solid wood are complemented by modern, comfortable chairs & metal tables arranged into intimate seating areas. Outside, more seating surrounds a large pool backed by lawns. Rooms are very attractive & built in pairs in spacious terracotta-painted bungalows. Each is slightly different, but all are decorated in neutral colours, airy & light, with a porch overlooking the pool. Expect AC, all-round mosquito nets, an en-suite bath or shower, fridge, hairdryer & phone. The family house has 2 en-suite dbl rooms, a lounge, a kitchenette & a terrace & a climbing frame in a small fenced garden. Lunch N$110; lunch pack N$80 pp. Internet access is available. *DBB room N$1,450–1,840/2,900–3,040/4,350–4,560 sgl/dbl/trpl; family house N$5,800–6,080.* **LLLL**

🏠 **VILLA MUSHARA** (2 villas) Top-of-the-range accommodation is in luxury villas, whose thatched roofs contrast with the glass & monochrome décor of their beautifully kitted out spacious interiors, each with all the accoutrements you could possibly wish for, & a mini patio & square pool that could grace Chelsea Flower Show. *Lunch N$110; lunch pack N$80 pp; DBB villa N$3,300/5,600 sgl/dbl; FBA N$5,500/8,400 sgl/dbl.* **LLLLL**

BUSH CAMP (16 tents) With a separate
3km further down the road, this is a
idly, comfortable & affordable base
from which to explore Etosha. From the gravel
pathways to the central lounge & dining area, the
feeling is of light & space. The canvas walls of the
main building are open on 3 sides, & whitewashed
safari chairs, silvered tables & splashes of vibrant
colour suggest a stylish boutique hotel rather than
a traditional lodge. Large secluded tents have
twin beds, with side ledges as bedside tables,
colour co-ordinated mosquito net, basin & open
shower with separate WC, & deck-chairs on the
veranda. 4 tents have a sleeper couch that can take
2 children. The lodge is very child-friendly, with a
separate play area (complete with tractor, sandpit
& slide), toy boxes & even kiddie-size dining tables.
A circular swimming pool is set in newly seeded
gardens, & a computer at reception, next to the
curio shop, offers internet access (*N$1.50/min*),
though there is also free Wi-Fi access in the main
areas. *Lunch N$110 pp; lunch pack N$80 pp; DBB
N$1,400–1,460/2,200–2,320 sgl/dbl.* **LLL**

 MUSHARA OUTPOST (8 tents) The luxurious
Outpost has discreet tents on raised decks with
glass sliding doors & windows looking out into
the trees. Beautifully furnished, each has AC, a
small safe, kettle & cafetière, & a shower that is
glazed all round to give an indoor/outdoor feel.
The main stone building, housing the reception,
lounge & communal dining table, has squashy
settees & chairs spilling out on to a large terrace,
& 2 fireplaces to ensure warmth on cold winter
evenings. Adjacent are a pool & curio shop, &
brick pathways lead to a waterhole & viewing

hide. *Lunch N$110 pp; lunch pack N$80 pp; DBB
N$2,300/3,700 sgl/dbl; FBA N$3,750/6,400 sgl/
dbl.* **LLLLL**

🏠 **Emanya Lodge** (20 chalets) ☏061 222
954; e bookings@emanya.com. Off the C38,
about a 20min drive from the eastern gate of
Etosha, Emanya is a privately owned, chic 'luxury'
lodge. Offering accommodation in chalets; there's
a tea/coffee station, AC, TV, electric safe & en-
suite bathroom. The main area includes a large,
sparkling blue pool, stylish lounge & dining area,
viewing deck, a wine cellar, internet facilities &
relaxing foot spa treatments. *Dinner N$205; DBB
from N$1,730/3,068 sgl/dbl; FBA N$2,461/4,528
sgl/dbl.* **LLLL**

🏠 **Sachsenheim Guest Farm** [Map, page
424] (22 chalets, camping) ☏067 230011;
e sachse@iway.na. Off the B1, 3km north of the
C38 turning towards Namutoni, & across the
railway line, Sachsenheim is an old-style game
farm turned restcamp. Owned by the Sachse
family since 1946, it's an oasis of green & colour
– with bottlebrush & jacaranda trees, & is the
most affordable place in the area. A wide range of
spotlessly clean accommodation options brings to
mind a model village: neat individual chalets, plus
a small central campsite under trees, where new
pitches have individual ablutions, shade, power &
light. Rooms – all en suite – are nicely appointed
with fridge, kettle, fan & mosquito nets. A
restaurant, bar & large pool have been added, with
a lovely garden with sitting areas. There is a floodlit
waterhole, & Wi-Fi is available. *B/fast N$90; dinner
N$200; B&B from N$665/1,100 sgl/dbl; camping
N$120 pp, plus N$50 per vehicle.* **LL**

WHAT TO SEE AND DO

If you are staying at one of the private lodges then you may have the choice of walking
trips on their land. Otherwise, although some will opt for a guided drive (see page
385), most visitors come to Etosha to explore the park for themselves by car.

PLANNING YOUR DAY The best times for spotting animals are in the early morning
and the late afternoon, when they are at their most active. So, if you can, leave your
camp as the gates open at sunrise, for a few hours' drive before breakfast. Before you
leave, check the book of recent sightings in the park office, as animals are creatures of
habit. This record may help you to choose the best areas to visit for that particular day.

Use the middle of the day for either travelling or relaxing back at camp. Dedicated
enthusiasts may park beside one of the more remote waterholes. Excellent sightings
are occasionally reported in the midday heat – though photographs taken in the
glare of day are disappointing.

Finally, check when the gate to your camp closes, and then leave for a late afternoon drive. Aim to spend the last few hours before sunset at one of the waterholes near your restcamp, or the entrance gate if you're staying outside the park. Leave this in time for a leisurely drive back.

THE WATERHOLES The excellent map of Etosha available at the park shows the roads open to visitors, and the names of the waterholes. Obviously the game seen at each varies enormously. One day you can sit for hours watching huge herds; the next day the same place will be deserted. However, some waterholes are usually better, or at least more photogenic, than others. Here are a few personal notes on some of the main ones:

Adamax A dry waterhole in acacia thickets, notable more for adjacent social weaver nests than for its game.

Andoni As far north as you can go, through some elephant-damaged mopane woodlands, this isolated spot is a manmade waterhole in the middle of an open vlei. I've never seen much game up here.

Aus A natural water-level spring here is supplemented by a solar pump, in the middle of woodlands of stunted mopane. As you look from the parking area, the sun rises directly over the pan. It is said to be a good, busy spot for animals – though I've never had much luck here.

Batia Away from the side of the pan, near Springbokfontein, the road to Batia is often better than the waterhole itself, which is a very flat and almost marshlike collection of reeds with puddles dotted over a large area.

Charitsaub Away from the pan, Charitsaub is in the middle of a huge area of grassy plains. It has a small spring below and close to the parking area. Likely game includes zebra, wildebeest and springbok.

Chudop An excellent artesian waterhole, which usually hosts good concentrations of game. There's lots of open space around the water, and I've spent many hours here on several occasions. Don't miss it.

Dolomietpunt The nearest waterhole to Dolomite Camp but, unfortunately, not visible from the most of the camp itself. However, you can drive down, and there's a circle fairly close to the waterhole, which is frequented by elephants and other plains game.

Etosha Just north of Halali, this is not a waterhole, but a most spectacular lookout place. There's a short drive across the pan, joining a circle where you can stop and admire the flatness. It is often closed when wet.

Fischer's Pan The road from Namutoni skirts the edges of this small pan, and when there's standing water in the pan it is *the* area for waterbirds. Take care of the road across the pan, between Aroe and Twee Palms, which often floods. When dry there will be fewer birds around, though the palm trees remain picturesque.

Gemsbokvlakte In the middle of a grassy plain, dotted with the odd stand of acacia, combretum and mopane bushveld, this permanent (with a solar-powered pump) waterhole attracts plains game species like springbok, gemsbok, zebra, giraffe and ostrich.

Goas This is a large, flat, natural waterhole and cars can view it from several sides, which is good as there's often a lot of game here. Elephants drinking here can be spectacular, and it is big enough to attract a constant buzz of bird activity.

Groot Okevi The parking area is a super vantage point, overlooking the waterhole which is about 25m away. There is some thick bush around the water. This is a known haunt of black rhino and conveniently close to Namutoni.

Helio A small, flat, manmade waterhole near Halali, just a few hundred metres from one of the kopjes. Its position is marked incorrectly on the national park map, and I've rarely seen any game there.

Homob A small spring in a deep depression, quite far from the viewing area. Just a few springbok and oryx were present when last visited. There is also a long-drop WC here; bring your own WC paper.

Kalkheuwel A super waterhole which often has lots of game. There's a permanently filled water trough, and usually also a good pan, which is close to the car park.

Kapupuhedi On the edge of the pan, with the parking area above it, this is often dry.

Klein Namutoni A pretty waterhole, close to Namutoni. It's good for game viewing and the wildlife is relaxed and used to traffic.

Koinachas A very picturesque artesian spring, perhaps 100m in diameter, with a large thicket of reeds in the centre. It's an excellent birding spot, but seldom seems crowded with game.

Nebrowni A small waterhole on the edge of a side channel to the main pan. This is just 200m from the main road, but often omitted from maps. With bush to one side, and grassy plains to the other, it can attract a wide variety of game, though is often deserted.

Noniams Though it's convenient for Halali, I've never had much luck seeing any game here.

Nuamses A very deep water-level spring with a large clump of tall reeds in the centre. Quite photogenic with lots of rocks around – though the foreground is obscured by a lip of rock in front of the waterhole. Not known for its prolific game.

Okerfontein Right on the edge of the pan. The viewpoint is slightly elevated, and the nearer parts of the water are hidden from view by a lip of rocks.

Okondeka This waterhole often attracts large numbers of wildebeest, zebra, oryx, springbok and ostrich. On the edge of the pan, Okondeka often has streams of game arriving and leaving it, which stretch for miles across the surrounding grasslands. The water is a little far from the car-parking area for close-up photos, but shots taken from the road just before the parking area, with vistas of the main pan in the background, can be spectacular.

Olifantsbad Literally 'elephant's bath', this is another natural water-level spring helped by a solar pump – making two good waterholes in a large arena for wildlife. It is notable for elephant, kudu, red hartebeest and black-faced impala.

Ombika Despite its proximity to the Andersson Gate, Ombika shouldn't be underestimated as it is often a busy waterhole. Unfortunately for photographers, this water-level spring is far from the viewing area, inside a deep natural rock cavern, allowing even zebra to almost disappear from view when drinking.

Ondongab Like Kapupuhedi, this is on the edge of the pan but recently dry. Its view is spectacular.

Ozonjuitji m'Bari This is a small waterhole filled by a solar pump. Flat, grassy plains surround it, and the game varies greatly. Sometimes it is deserted, and on other occasions you'll find one of the park's largest gatherings of gemsbok. In the dry season, likely sights include ostrich, wildebeest, zebra, springbok, perhaps the odd giraffe and lots of dancing dust-devils in the background. (One correspondent even spotted a black rhino here during the day.)

Pan On the edge of the pan, the waterhole is not obvious, and there is often little game. This road becomes a mess of sludge in the wet season.

Rietfontein A large, busy, water-level spring, with quite a large area of reeds in the water, surrounded by much open ground. There's a wide parking area with plenty of space, and at the waterhole giraffe, zebra and springbok were drinking when last visited.

Salvadora On the edge of the pan, Salvadora attracts columns of zebra, wildebeest and springbok. The viewpoint is higher than the spring, and close to it – so is perfect for photographs, with the main pan stretching off forever behind it.

Springbokfontein A shallow collection of reeds to one side of the road, which often has little game at it. However, look to your right as you drive to nearby Batia, as there is often game at a spring there.

Sueda Away from the pan, and just west of Salvadora and Charitsaub, Sueda has a large area of reeds, and rocklike clay outcrops, around a spring on the edge of the pan. Again, parking is above the level of the spring.

Wolfnes A location where you can appreciate the vast expanse of the pan. Just switch your motor off, and listen to the silence.

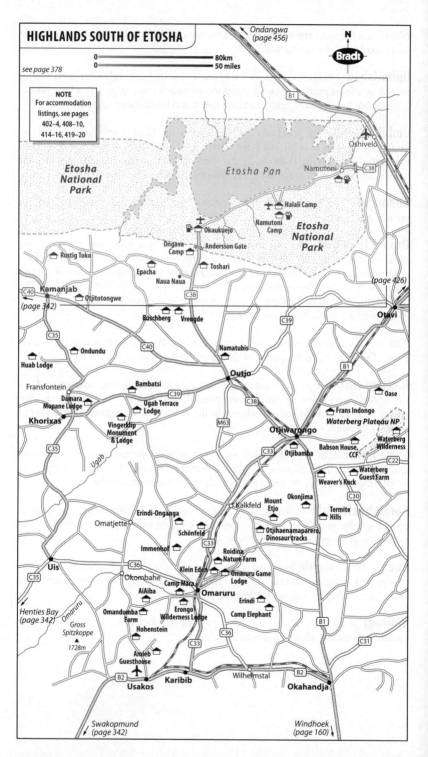

0   80km
0   50 miles

N

Bradt

Ondangwa
(page 456)

NOTE
For accommodation
listings, see pages
402–4, 408–10,
414–16, 419–20

Etosha National Park

Oshivelo

Etosha Pan

Namutoni

C38

Halali Camp

Okaukuejo

Namutoni Camp

Etosha National Park

Ongava Camp

Andersson Gate

Rustig Toko

Epacha

Toshari

Naua Naua

C38

(page 426)

C40 Kamanjab

Otjitotongwe

(page 342)

Buschberg

Vreugde

C39

Otavi

C35

Ondundu

C40

Namatubis

Huab Lodge

Fransfontein

Bambatsi

Outjo

C39

B1

Oase

Damara Mopane Lodge

Ugab Terrace Lodge

C38

Frans Indongo

Waterberg Plateau NP

Khorixas

Vingerklip Monument & Lodge

M63

Otjiwarongo

C35

Ugab

Waterberg Wilderness

Babson House, CCF

C22

C33

Otjibamba

Weaver's Rock

Waterberg Guest Farm

Erindi-Onganga

Kalkfeld

Mount Etjo

Okonjima

C30

Omatjette

Schönfeld

Termite Hills

C33

Otjihaenamaparero, Dinosaur tracks

Immenhof

Roidina Nature Farm

Uis

C36

Okombahe

Klein Eden

Omaruru Game Lodge

AiAiba

Camp Mara

Omaruru

Erindi

Henties Bay
(page 342)

Omaruru

Gross Spitzkoppe
1728m

Omandumba Farm

Erongo Wilderness Lodge

Camp Elephant

B1

Hohenstein

C33

C36

C31

Amieb Guesthouse

B2

Usakos

Karibib

Wilhelmstal

B2

Okahandja

Swakopmund
(page 342)

Windhoek
(page 160)

17

Highlands South of Etosha

While Etosha is the main attraction in the north of Namibia, the region south of it has much of interest. Large farms dominate these hilly, well-watered highlands, and many have forsaken cattle in favour of game to become guest farms that welcome tourists. Okonjima was one of the first of these, and remains a major draw for visitors. Many of the others are less famous, but they still offer visitors insights into a farmer's view of the land, and opportunities to relax. On the eastern side of this area, the Waterberg Plateau is superb, though more for its hiking trails and scenery, and feeling of wilderness, than for its game viewing.

OMARURU

At a crossroads on the tarred C33 and the less-frequented C36, about 60km north of Karibib, Omaruru is a green and picturesque town astride the (usually dry) river of the same name, in a gently hilly area. Many of the farms around it have turned to tourism, which is on the increase, so there is no shortage of lodges or guest farms in the area. The town has also acquired something of a reputation for the creative arts, with many artists settling here to work.

GETTING THERE AND AWAY The demise of the TransNamib train service from Windhoek means that most visitors have no alternative but to reach Omaruru by road.

WHERE TO STAY *Map, page 400.*

🏠 **Villa Oleandra** (2 rooms) 22 Spoorweg St, cnr River St; m 081 332 4293, e info@ villamargherita.com.na; www.villamargherita. com.na. This stylish villa is the sister property to the charming Villa Margherita in Swakopmund (see page 284). It's a fully equipped house with large en-suite bedrooms, a living area & kitchen, all kitted out in classy furniture, designer fittings & contemporary artwork. Indoor mod cons include AC, coffee machine, TV/DVD, stereo system & laptop with Wi-Fi, while outside are a veranda, BBQ, mature garden & large heated pool. Better suited for visitors spending more than a night in Omaruru, the villa is within walking distance of cafés, craft stores & antique shops. **$$$**

🏠 **Central Hotel** (11 rooms) Wilhelm Zeraua Rd; ☏ 064 570030; e alexma@iway.na; http:// centralhotelomaruru.wordpress.com. On the main street north of the river, this small, traditional hotel had been sadly neglected in recent years but is now being sensitively restored by its new owners Alexander & Alma Steyn. Think dark slate floors, original wooden beams & hand-carved doors in the main building, with an attractive bar & bright b/fast room. It has modern rooms with AC, TV, fridges, coffee/tea facilities & private patios in individual rondavels or set in line in a whitewashed block, softened by thatch. It also has a pool, a popular beer garden & restaurant, & secure parking. **$$**

🏠 **Evening Shade** (5 rooms) 116 Wilhelm Zeraua Rd; ☏ 064 570303; m 081

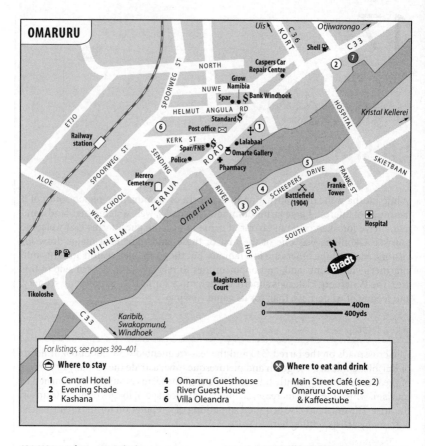

OMARURU

For listings, see pages 399–401

⌂ Where to stay
1. Central Hotel
2. Evening Shade
3. Kashana
4. Omaruru Guesthouse
5. River Guest House
6. Villa Oleandra

✕ Where to eat and drink
Main Street Café (see 2)
7. Omaruru Souvenirs & Kaffeestube

124 6184; e info@evening-shade.com; www.
omaruruselfcatering.com. Tucked behind the
brightly coloured façade of Main Street Café (see
opposite) are 5 new self-catering units sleeping
between 2 & 6 people, each simply but stylishly
decorated with exposed brickwork, ceramic
ceilings & well-equipped kitchens, along with free
Wi-Fi, DSTV & a safe. They surround a huge acacia
tree in a shady garden where vegetables for the
café are grown. Laundry service & secure parking
available. **$$**

⌂ **Kashana** (17 rooms) Dr Ian Scheepers Dr;
☎064 571434; e info@kashana-namibia.com;
www.kashana-namibia.com. Built in 2007, just
south of the Omaruru River, Kashana is a small
shopping centre with accommodation attached,
& is clearly marked. The complex offers a large
restaurant (**$$$–$$$$**) with terrace area, a
lively bar & a small parade of craft & jewellery
shops. The main reception building dates back to
1907 & has been carefully restored. Behind this are

large thatch-&-brick chalets & a block of smaller
rooms. These vary in size & price with family
rooms on 2 levels, but each is spacious & stylish
with African-print linen, crafted dark furniture,
locally made metal sculptures & mosaic floor tiling.
Rooms have AC, DSTV, fridges, safes & Wi-Fi. There's
also an L-shaped pool & secure parking. **$$**

⌂ **Omaruru Guesthouse** (20 rooms) 305
Dr Ian Scheepers Dr; ☎064 570035; e hello@
omaruru-guesthouse.com; www.omaruru-
guesthouse.com. Given a fresh lease of life in 2012
by new owner Christian Hafner, this long-standing
B&B is excellent value with bedrooms (inc 2 family
rooms) in a separate block from the main building.
All have fridge, fan, DSTV, Wi-Fi & hairdryer. The
older main building has a bright dining room & TV
lounge, while outside is a small pool, pretty garden
and secure parking. **$$**

⌂ **River Guest House** (6 rooms, camping) Dr
Ian Scheepers Dr; ☎064 570274, 081 124 5365;
e eckmitt@iway.na; www.river-guesthouse.

com. Opposite Franke Tower lies a family home transformed into a quirky little owner-run guesthouse, cheerfully painted outside & originally decorated inside. Set around a central courtyard, almost overgrown by a jungle of palm & banana trees, are 4 dbl & 2 family rooms, all en suite & with fans & coffee/tea facilities, & fridges in some, along with a b/fast room, a small bar & a boma. There's also a pool surrounded by hammocks & snooker table. A nearby campsite offers 6 pitches, 2 sets of ablutions, plug points & BBQ areas. *Camping N$90 pp; no credit cards.* **$$**

✕ WHERE TO EAT AND DRINK *Map, opposite.*

In addition to restaurants at Kashana and Central Hotel, there are the following options:

✕ Main Street Café 116 Wilhelm Zeraua Rd; ☏ 064 570544; m 081 124 6187; e chris@johnstonenamibia.com; ⊕ 08.00–15.00 Tue–Sun. Formerly a derelict bakery, this popular new café serves homemade, natural food from its own garden & local suppliers wherever possible. Try the cheesecake – they even make their own cheese for it. The café also sells locally made preserves & pickles. Check out the impressive photo gallery & studio next door of owner Chris Johnston. **$$–$$$$**

☕ Omaruru Souvenirs & Kaffeestube 122 Wilhelm Zeraua Rd; ☏ 064 570230; ⊕ 07.30–17.00 Mon–Sat, 08.30–17.00 Sun. The historical & handsome Wronsky House contains a well-stocked souvenir shop & a charming coffee house with a terrace overlooking a small plant nursery. Built as a general trading store by Wilhelm Wronsky after he settled here from Brazil in the 1890s, the building was completed in 1907. Today many of the original tiles, ceiling wood & fittings remain, all transported by boat from Germany & then by ox wagon from the coast. It also doubles as a small information centre. **$–$$**

OTHER PRACTICALITIES There are branches of FNB, Bank Windhoek and Standard **banks** and a **post office** on the main Wilhelm Zeraua Road, as well as several **fuel stations** and **garages** and Omaruru's **pharmacy** (☏ *064 571262;* m *081 234 1270;* e *ongwari@iway.na*). For **vehicle repairs**, Caspers Car Repair Centre (☏ *064 571464;* e *vmcaspers@gmx.de*) is probably the best option in town.

For **food and provisions**, there's a huge Spar supermarket (⊕ *08.00–18.00 Mon–Sat, 09.00–13.00 & 16.00–18.00 Sun*) with an ATM on Helmut Angula Road.

In an **emergency**, the police are reached on ☏ 064 10111 or 064 570010, the ambulance and hospital on ☏ 064 570037, and the fire brigade on ☏ 064 570029/570046 or m 081 351 0502.

WHAT TO SEE AND DO The town's main attraction is **Franke Tower**, a monument to Captain Victor Franke, who is said to have heroically relieved the garrison here after they were besieged by the Herero in 1904. The achievement earned him Germany's highest military honour and this monument built by grateful German settlers in 1908. It's normally locked, but to climb up it ask at your hotel if they have the keys.

Mineralogists should drop in to see Karen and Christopher Johnston at Main Street Café (see above), who have a fascinating selection of very specialist local minerals which they even send abroad on a mail-order basis.

Omaruru has become the arts and crafts centre of Namibia, with new shops opening regularly. In addition to those noted above, take time to visit **Omarte Gallery** (☏ *064 570017;* e *omarte@rocketmail.com*), a lovely, community-based antiques and craft gallery, as well as **Lalabaai** (☏ *064 570679/807;* m *081 128 2859*), both on the main road, and **Grow Namibia** (m *081 147 5077;* e *grow@omaruru.na*), on Helmut Angula Street. The latter is a project empowering disadvantaged people in the area to earn a living by creating fun crafts from recycled glass, recycled paper fortified with dung, flowers and herbs.

Don't miss a visit to **Tikoloshe** (☏ *064 570582/571215; www.tikoloshe.iway.na, www.tikolosheafrika.com*), on the western side of town, where craftsmen carve imaginative animals from roots.

Finally, if you're visiting Omaruru on the second-last weekend of September, look out for the Artist Trail, a series of events and exhibitions to celebrate the work of local artists.

AROUND OMARURU: LODGES AND GUEST FARMS *Map, page 398.*

✳ ⌂ **Erongo Wilderness Lodge** (10 tents) ☏ 061 239199, 064 570537; e info@ erongowilderness-namibia.com; www. erongowilderness-namibia.com. The Erongo Conservancy encompasses 30 farms & their lodges over which fences have been taken down in order to create a protected area. As proof of its success, white rhino were released here in 2009 & the first calf born in 2010, although they are rarely spotted. From Omaruru, take the C33 south for 2km & turn right on to the D2315. You'll soon enter an area of many kopjes – huge piles of rounded rocks which make up hills that look like piles of giant pebbles: these are the Erongo Mountains. 10km from the junction & soon after passing through the manned gate to the 2,000km² Erongo Mountain Nature Conservancy, you'll find the lodge to the south of the road. Unless you have a 4x4 & are confident using it, leave your vehicle in the parking area at the bottom from where you & your luggage will be transferred the 800m to the lodge.

Accommodation has recently been upgraded with spacious new tents (inc 1 family room) & large terraces built high on wooden stilts among the foothills. The rustic feel is deliberate, but with a minibar, kettle, fan & toiletries, guests won't be deprived of mod cons. The honeymoon tent has a plunge pool & outdoor shower too. Various wooden walkways & paths connect these to the main lounge & dining room area, which has a large new terrace overlooking a stunning vista of the mountains. Look out for the rosy-faced lovebirds that hang around at b/fast. Food here is excellent, accompanied by an extensive wine list. Nearby, a small swimming pool has been built into the rocks alongside a playground for active children.

It's a lovely spot to spend a few days, but Erongo's real attraction is as a base for walking. Guides are on hand for both short walks in the late afternoon (usually to the top of the nearby kopje for a G&T while the sun sets), & longer walks: on the flat, or around the base of the

hills, or on steeper routes where short scrambles may be needed. For those wishing to set out unaccompanied, there are 4 marked walking trails of 1½–4½hrs. Even so, a GPS would be useful – it's easy to get disoriented or lost in these hills. The rough rock generally grips rubber soles well. There are also nature drives & guided visits to local rock paintings (*N$440*), described by Hilary Bradt as 'wonderfully lively, and the location in a cave with terrific views is superb'.

Pause for a while wherever you are & you'll realise that there's game around, from leopards & klipspringers to dassies & brightly coloured rock agamas, but you'll have to look for it. For birders, this is also a good spot to see some of Namibia's endemic species including Hartlaub's francolin, Damara hornbill & Damara rockrunner. *DBB N$1,590 pp sharing low season; N$1,945 pp sharing high season; N$295 sgl supplement high season only.* **LLLLL**

⌂ **AiAiba** (20 rooms) ☏ 064 570330; e info@ aiaiba.com, aiaiba@africaonline.com.na; www. aiaiba.com. Self-styled 'the Rock-painting lodge', AiAiba is under the same ownership as Okapuka Ranch, north of Windhoek. It is situated about 45km west of Omaruru, just off the D2315, & within the Erongo Mountain Nature Conservancy. From Damaraland, turn south on to the D2306, 56km east of Uis & after 33km turn on to the D2315; AiAiba is shortly on the left. Nestling in the shelter of giant granite boulders, each of its attractive thatched bungalows houses 2 en-suite rooms, their cool tiled floors offset by solid rustic furniture & neutral fabrics. The matching central building, its open beams giving it the feeling of a large barn, overlooks a small pool flanked by palms. Guided walks, 4x4 drives to visit rock paintings & a 6hr picnic tour are the main draws (at additional cost). *Dinner N$215; B&B N$967/1,730 sgl/dbl.* **LLL**

⌂ **Erindi-Onganga Guest Farm** (5 rooms, camping) ☏ 067 290112; e fnolte@iway.na; www. natron.net/erindi-onganga (in German). This traditional, working guest farm with a German atmosphere is about 62km from Omaruru. To reach it take the C36 towards Uis for about 6km before branching right on to the D2344 towards Omatjete. Follow this for about 25km before turning right on to the D2351 towards Epupa (note this Epupa is closer than the one on the River Kunene!). After about 25km, Erindi-Onganga is signposted off to the right, about 6km along a farm road.

Accommodation is carpeted throughout, & rooms are clean, with en-suite facilities. The main farmhouse, Fritz & Petra Nolte's home, has a dining room (where traditional farm-cooked meals are served), a lounge area with large fire for cool evenings, & even a sauna. About 800m from the farmhouse is a campsite overlooking a large reservoir. Pitch your own tent or stay in one of 3 pre-erected, equipped tents. Outside are a swimming pool, some marked hiking trails & the working farm which most visitors come to see. Nature & sunset drives (*N$150 pp*) on the farm offer the chance to see a variety of antelope & other small game. *DBB N$580 pp sharing, inc farm drive if staying 2 nights; camping N$80/150 own tent/pre-erected tent.* **LLL**

🏠 **Omaruru Game Lodge** (20 bungalows)
📞 064 570044; e omlodge@iafrica.com.na; www.omaruru-game-lodge.com. Northeast of Omaruru, about 15km along the D2329, this lodge is owned by a Swiss architect, which explains the impressive design of its bungalows. All are beautifully built of stone, with thatched roofs that reach almost to the ground, AC, heating, & en-suite shower & toilet. Some, designated 'superior', are simply bigger.

The lounge/bar/dining area is equally impressive, & overlooks a dam on one side of the lodge's fenced 'small game park' (150ha in size), which is regularly visited by game, including giraffe, hartebeest, wildebeest, eland, sable & roan antelope. This is separate from the lodge's 'large game park' which covers a more respectable 3,500ha, & is home to the same range of antelope plus a small family of elephants.

Paths wind around the camp & the figure-of-8 pool among well-watered lawns under beautiful apple-ring acacias (*Acacia albida*), which the elephants would relish if only they could get to them. Walk at night, when the paths are lit, & it's hard to escape the feeling that this is Africa at its neatest & tidiest, but not its wildest.

A few hundred metres away are 5 more basic self-catering bungalows, each with a useful kitchenette (but no cutlery, crockery or pans) & an outside fireplace. They share a separate swimming pool. *DBB standard N$1,200/1,900 sgl/dbl; superior N$1,350/2,300, sgl/dbl; self-catering N$450 pp sharing.* **LLL**

🏠 **Roidina Nature Farm** (6 rooms)
📞 064 571188; m 081 366 9818; e bookings@ roidinanaturefarm.com; www.roidinanaturefarm. com. Roidina is situated on a 50km² farm & signposted off the C33, 19km north of Omaruru. From there it is a 5km drive on a good gravel road. New owners Corne & Francois Kotze took over this guest farm in Feb 2014. It has 5 attractive thatched bungalows & a honeymoon suite. A central restaurant & bar lapa overlooks a pool & landscaped cacti gardens & waterhole. Bush walks & nature drives are possible but various horseriding trails, from short rides to all-day events with a bush b/fast or a picnic lunch, are the real highlight (*from N$300/hr*). *DBB N$950 pppn.* **LLL**

🏠 **Omandumba Farm** (8 rooms, camping)
📞 064 571086; m 081 245 3713; e omandumba@ iway.na; www.omandumba.de. About 45km from Omaruru on the D2315, just after the turn-off to AiAiba lodge, the farm is marked by a sign with figures of an African family walking above a board noting the owner's names: Harald & Deike Rust. Omandumba was about to undergo major refurbishment at the time of research, with 8 new rooms planned to be completed by Jan 2015, each with private terrace & car port. Rather than being a guest farm or lodge, the emphasis here is on 'normal' Namibian farm life, where the owners dine with their guests. They also have a fully equipped self-catering house 8km from the farm, sleeping 6 in 3 bedrooms. 5 private camping pitches with showers and toilets are also available. The key attractions here are walking trails in the Erongo Mountains, excellent rock art drives guided by the owners who have detailed knowledge of the area's rock paintings & engravings (*N$200*), & a new Living Museum of the San People where guests learn about their culture in what was believed to be an outpost of the San communities (*N$100*). *FB N$950 pp; self-catering N$380 pp; camping N$120 pp.* **LLL**

🏠 **Hohenstein Lodge** (14 rooms) 📞 064 530900; e info@hohensteinlodge.de; www. hohensteinlodge.de. To the southwest of the Erongo Mountains, Hohenstein is about 25km north of Usakos on the D1935. It's a community venture, set on the edge of Damaraland within the Erongo Mountain Nature Conservancy, & named after the highest mountain in the Erongo chain. The lodge has been carefully built to take advantage of the panoramic views from both the bungalows & the central area, where dinner (N$195) is taken inside or out on the veranda, overlooking a waterhole. Simply decorated rooms have twin beds with bright animal-print covers. Visitors may opt for a guided walk to the Boulder Forest & small gemstone miner claims, nature drives, or a sundowner drive. Hohenstein also offers a new, exclusive 2-day package (N$2,390/1,990 sgl/pp sharing) called Absolut Erongo, inc 1 night at the luxury Etemba Wilderness Camp with walking tours to see Etemba's renowned Bushmen paintings. To reach Etemba, you will need to drive to AiAiba farm (see page 402), turning left at the entrance gate – don't even attempt the drive to camp without a 4x4. *Lunch N$90; B&B N$850/1,300 sgl/dbl, inc sundowner drive.* **LL**

🏠 **Camp Mara** (3 rooms) ☎ 064 571190; m 081 128 1203; e campmara@iway.na; www.

campmara.com. Opposite the entrance to Erongo Wilderness Lodge (see page 402), this quirky self-catering farm is in a beautiful location in the Erongo Mountains. The thatch rooms are all different, with simple, rustic interiors & private terraces, & a plunge pool in the garden. 5 individual camping pitches are to be found near the banks of the Omaruru River, with ablution blocks, fireplaces & braais. B/fast & dinner available on request (N$80/120). *N$800 dbl; camping N$120.* **L**

🏠 **Klein Eden Guest Farm**
(7 chalets) ☎ 064 570620; m 081 384 6772; e kleinedengasteplaas@iway.na. To reach this new self-catering guest farm, take Hospital Rd east from Omaruru, then left on to the D2328 for 28km & left again on to the D2330 for 500m. Each of the 7 chalets has a different layout & furnishings but all are modern & shiny, with indoor braais & well-equipped kitchens, AC, fans, DSTV, safe & Wi-Fi. Facilities include a swimming pool & children's playground on the lawns. The rather bland communal hall/lapa area has cooking facilities & pool tables but no restaurant, bar or shop, so bring all food & drink with you. *N$585 dbl.* **L**

OTJIWARONGO

Originally a staging post on the railway from Tsumeb to Swakopmund, which was completed in 1906, Otjiwarongo is conveniently situated at a crossroads for the road network in an area dominated by commercial cattle ranching. Once a small market town with a mix of people that includes many Herero women in traditional dress, Otjiwarongo is experiencing something of a boom just now due to new industries nearby, including a gold mine due to open at the end of 2014 and a new cement factory claimed to be the most modern in the world. Although it has few intrinsic attractions, and most visitors just pass through, there are some decent new hotels that are aiming beyond the local business market, and plenty of shops for provisions.

GETTING THERE AND AWAY Somewhat ironically, given the town's history, there are no longer any passenger trains to Otjiwarongo.

By bus The Intercape Mainliner bus service linking Windhoek with Victoria Falls drops into Otjiwarongo, stopping at Engen Service Station on Hage Geingob Street. Going northbound, it stops at 16.45 on Monday and Friday. Heading south, it stops at 02.35 on Monday and Thursday and 03.00 daily except Thursday and Sunday. One-way fares are around N$250–380 to Windhoek, and N$390–440 to Victoria Falls. See *Chapter 6*, pages 98–100, for more details.

Hitching Hitching from central Otjiwarongo is difficult. First start walking out in the direction you want to go, and then hitch from there.

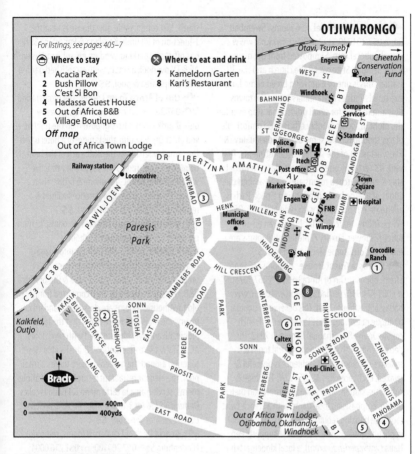

For listings, see pages 405–7

⊝ Where to stay

1　Acacia Park
2　Bush Pillow
3　C'est Si Bon
4　Hadassa Guest House
5　Out of Africa B&B
6　Village Boutique

　　Off map
　　Out of Africa Town Lodge

✕ Where to eat and drink

7　Kameldorn Garten
8　Kari's Restaurant

TOURIST INFORMATION At 5 St George's Street, **Omaue Namibia** (↳ *067 303830; ⏱ 08.00–13.00 & 14.00–17.00 Mon–Fri, 08.00–13.00 Sat*) doubles as a friendly and useful information centre.

WHERE TO STAY *Map, above.*

Most visitors in the area stay at one of the guest farms (see pages 408–10). However, some of the establishments in town are also worth considering for a stopover.

🏠 **Bush Pillow** (7 rooms) 47 Sonn Rd; ↳ 067 303 885; m 081 128 5323; e reservations@ bushpillow.hypermart.net; www.bushpillow. hypermart.net. This good, trendy guesthouse is just over 1km from the main Hage Geingob St; turn left into Sonn Rd at the first Caltex fuel station, & it's on the corner of Hoog St. It has safe parking & a pleasant garden (with pool) behind secure walls, where there's also space for a BBQ. The rooms, each named after a famous (or infamous!) elephant, are clean & bright, with en-suite bathrooms & satellite TV; decorated in rich, warm colours, many

also have fun artistic touches. Some have AC. The communal areas include pleasant indoor & outdoor lounges, a dining area (*dinner N$170 with advance notice*) & a well-stocked bar. Laundry & Wi-Fi are also available.

　　Day trips to the Cheetah Conservation Foundation, 40km away, & shorter excursions to nearby Whale Rock for a sundowner, are worth considering, & longer, multiday trips to Etosha & other areas of Namibia can be arranged, as well as trips to Zambia, Victoria Falls & Chobe National Park in Botswana. **$$**

C'est Si Bon Hotel (56 rooms) Swembad Rd; ☏067 301240; e cestsibon@iway.na; www. cestsibonhotel.com. Signposted from the main Hage Geingob St between the church and the BP station, this is one of a growing breed of medium-size hotels/lodges in Namibia's provincial towns that aim to cater for small groups that stop over for the night. It's a thoroughly efficient & comfortable place, though it lacks some of the individuality (& idiosyncrasies) of the smaller establishments. That said, it's certainly one of the best places in town to stay & eat. Thatched rooms are spread around the edges of a large lawn, overlooking a pool. Each is adequate but not huge, with twin beds, AC, DSTV, Wi-Fi, fridge, tea/coffee facilities, & an en-suite toilet & shower. Luxury & presidential rooms are more spacious, some sleeping up to 4. **$$**

Hadassa Guest House (9 rooms) 36 Lang Street, opposite Out of Africa Lodge; ☏067 307505; m 081 774 9382; e hadassa@otjiweb.com; www. hadassaguesthouse.com. This deservedly popular boutique guesthouse was taken over by French couple Orlane & Emmanuel Bonnin in 2012. The décor is chic, with dark wood, neutral tones & splashes of colour, & the ambience is peaceful & relaxed. Each room has AC, DSTV, Wi-Fi, fridge & coffee/tea station. They pride themselves on their dining, emphasising local game with a French twist (advance booking required) & there's a lovely pool in pristine gardens. The guesthouse supports Peri Naua (www.peri-naua.com), a local kindergarten project for underprivileged children & guests are encouraged to bring school materials or old clothes, which they pass on. Guests are also entitled to 10% discount on activities at the Cheetah Conservation Fund (see box, page 417). **$$**

Out of Africa B&B (30 rooms) Rikumbi Kandaga St; ☏067 303397; e levaneck@iway.na; www.out-of-afrika.com. Signposted on the right almost as soon as you enter Otjiwarongo from the south, this comfortable guesthouse is near the T-junction of Rikumbi Kandaga & Panorama St & has off-street parking. Modern en-suite rooms with AC & TV overlook a small, well-established garden with a lapa area & pool. **$$**

Out of Africa Town Lodge (44 rooms) Long St; ☏067 302230; e oatlodge@iway.na; www. out-of-afrika.com. Also signposted on the right as you enter Otjiwarongo, this is more of a hotel under the same ownership as the B&B. Each of the brightly painted en-suite rooms housed in this attractive white building has AC, TV, phone & fridge. There is secure parking, a pool, conference facilities & a restaurant with an à la carte menu. **$$**

Village Boutique Hotel (28 rooms, 12 more planned) Cnr Hage Geingob & School St; ☏067 306679; m 085 600 0911; e infovillage@ iway.na; www.villageboutiquehotel.com. Sister property to Out of Africa Town Lodge & Out of Africa B&B, this smart hotel has been converted from 2 old townhouses. Rooms are classed as standard or luxury, the main difference being that the latter are bigger. All are stylishly furnished with tiled floors, AC, DSTV & tea/coffee stations, & are located close together around the gardens, where there's a small pool. The elegant restaurant is spread across various rooms, serving an à la carte menu & fabulous cakes (around N$150 for 3-course meal, booking preferred, closed evenings Sat–Sun). **$$**

Acacia Park (2 chalets, 8 rooms, camping) Hindenburg St; ☏067 303100; m 081 216 0004; e caciapa@mweb.com.na. Although there are several reasonable B&Bs in Otjiwarongo, travellers on a shoestring budget might consider Acacia Park. It is a large, fairly noisy restcamp with a pool, pub & restaurant offering camping pitches with BBQ, tap & power point, plus simple, functional en-suite chalets, 3 en-suite rooms & 5 rooms with shared ablutions. A large perimeter fence with manned gate offers reasonable security. Camping N$65 pp. **$**

✖ WHERE TO EAT AND DRINK *Map, page 405.*

Most visitors dine at their hotels or at the C'est Si Bon Hotel. The restaurant at the Crocodile Ranch serves a substantial sit-down lunch, but for something lighter, or a coffee stop, try:

✖ **Kari's Restaurant** Corner of Hindenburg & Hage Geingob sts; ☏067 304310; ⏱ 08.00–21.00 Mon–Fri, 08.00–17.00 Sat. This thatched restaurant has an upstairs terrace & tables scattered around the gardens. Its varied menu includes pizzas, salads, sandwiches & steaks. **$$–$$$$**

🍴 **Kameldorn Garten** 17 Hindenburg St; m 081 244 5967; ⏱ 07.00–17.00 Mon & Thu, noon–21.00 Wed & Sun, 07.00–15.00 &18.00–

21.00 Fri, 08.00–15.00 Sat. Just off Hage Geingob St & under the arched entrance on the left (there's parking round the back), this coffee shop & bistro is recommended. Run by chefs Eleini & Dieter Radeck, it offers sandwiches, daily specials & the 'biggest burgers in Namibia'. Adjacent is a small craft shop with secondhand books. $–$$$$

OTHER PRACTICALITIES The new shopping mall called Town Square (*on the corner of Rikumbi Kandaga St and Dr Libertina Amathila Av*) is a good illustration of how the town is growing, full of smart clothes shops, a pharmacy, ATM, a large Shoprite and fast-food outlets. There's also a large car park with car guards.

There are several **fuel stations** around town (some open 24 hours), and Standard, Bank Windhoek and FNB **banks** are all in the centre. For **food and supplies**, seek out the shops on the main Hage Geingob and St George's streets, including both Spar and Pick 'n' Pay. If you're in need of **vehicle repairs**, there's a Nissan/Toyota dealer (*38 Hage Geingob St;* ✆ *067 302903*) here, too.

Otjiwarongo has various **internet cafés** including CompuNet Services on the corner of West and Hage Geingob streets, and Itech around the corner from the information shop (*Hage Geingob St;* ⊕ *08.00–13.00 & 14.00–17.00 Mon–Fri*).

In an **emergency**, your first port of call should be the excellent private hospital, **Medi-Clinic Otjiwarongo** (*Sonn Rd;* ✆ *067 303734; www.mediclinic.co.za*), which handles serious cases for much of northern Namibia. A friend of mine needed some serious emergency surgery here, and on returning to London her private consultant told her that the operation had been performed to the highest standards. Otherwise the ambulance service is on ✆ 067 302411, the fire brigade on ✆ 067 304444, and the main government hospital on ✆ 067 300900. The police are reached on ✆ 067 10111/300600.

WHAT TO SEE AND DO One of the locomotives that first served Otjiwarongo has been preserved and stands in front of the railway station building. It is worth a quick look even if you're not a steam enthusiast.

A visit to the **Crocodile Ranch** (✆ *067 302121;* ⊕ *09.00–16.00 daily; admission N$40*) makes for an interesting hour or so. The ranch has been going for over 20 years, and has established a small export business for crocodile skins, while the meat is sold locally. It is one of just a few captive breeding programmes for the Nile crocodile (*Crocodylus niloticus*), which has been registered with CITES. Under new ownership since 2009, the property has received a bit of a face-lift and there's a restaurant on site serving light lunches, which include toasted sandwiches, burgers and steaks.

Further afield, the **dinosaur footprints** at Otjihaenamaparero (see page 411) and the **Cheetah Conservation Fund** (CCF; see box, page 417) are the only excursions suitable from Otjiwarongo. **Waterberg Plateau** (see pages 412–14) is a destination in its own right, as is **Okonjima and the AfriCat Foundation** (see box, page 411), although if you're short of time, the new **AfriCat Day Centre** (✆ *067 687032; www. africat.org;* ⊕ *09.00–15.00 daily; admission free*) is well worth a visit and reachable from Otjiwarongo. Visitors can go on hiking trails, take the excellent AfriCat tour (*N$385*) and use the swimming pool at Omboroko campsite in Okonjima's grounds. There's a bar and café where light lunches are available, as well as showers, useful if you're heading back to Windhoek for a late flight.

En route to Okonjima is the **Rare and Endangered Species Trust (REST)** (✆ *081 367 9425; www.restafrica.org;* ⊕ *10.00–15.00 Mon–Sat; nominal admission fee*), which focuses primarily on the protection of the Cape vulture, with 500–1,000 wild vultures feeding at its 'restaurant' every week.

Highlands South of Etosha   OTJIWARONGO

17

AROUND OTJIWARONGO
Nearby guest farms *Map, page 398.*

There are several guest farms in the area. Okonjima is well known for its excellent work with big cats, and Mount Etjo has much interesting publicity material, though seems to appeal more to Afrikaans-speaking visitors than those who rely on English. Frans Indongo makes a good base for visits to the CCF.

Frans Indongo Lodge (6 rooms, 8 chalets, camping) ☎ 067 687012; e indongo@afol.com.na; www.indongolodge.com. This attractive lodge, situated 43km northeast of Otjiwarongo on the D2433, is owned by businessman Dr Frans Indongo. It is designed to reflect his roots as a farmer's son in northern Namibia, with the tall wooden stakes that typically enclose an Ovambo homestead used to separate & define areas of the lodge.

Rooms & chalets, one with wheelchair access, are cool & modern in design. All are en suite, with all the extras that you would expect in a good quality lodge: AC, phone, Wi-Fi, TV, hairdryer, fridge & kettle. The central area has a pleasant pool, bar & restaurant, & is fronted by a large wooden deck which looks out over the 17,000ha farm. This & an observation tower provide plenty of opportunities for checking out animals at the illuminated waterhole, or birds attracted to the artificial stream. The bush campsite has 4 pitches (1 for small private groups, the others for groups of up to 20) with hot showers, toilets & fire pits but no power.

Guests can take part in game drives on the farm (N$230 pp) or 3 hiking trails, while excursions include visits to the Waterberg Plateau & the CCF information centre. *Dinner N$230; B&B N$1,008/1,811 sgl/dbl; camping N$120 pp.* **LLL**

Otjibamba Lodge (20 rooms) ☎ 067 303133; e bamba@iway.na; www.otjibamba.com. Situated just 1km off the main B1, about 3km south of Otjiwarongo, Otjibamba is a useful overnight stop on the way from Windhoek to Etosha. It's more like a modern hotel set in the country than a guest farm, with a large, comfortable lounge & restaurant, well-stocked curio shop & a pool outside, along with a children's playground & pool.

The rooms are purpose-built bungalows, set out in rows separated by lawns. They looked tired on our last visit but renovations are planned, including new tiled floors & bathrooms. They are like hotel rooms in style, & quite close together. Each has 2 dbl beds, AC, DSTV, safe, phone, tea/

coffee facilities & medium-size en-suite bathroom, with separate bath & shower cubicles. It's efficient but anonymous, although if you've been forced to be sociable at lots of guest farms, then dinner from room service may be just what you need. The rooms overlook a waterhole frequented by a variety of game.

The lodge stands in its own small game park stocked with giraffe, black & blue wildebeest, red hartebeest, blesbok, gemsbok, kudu, eland, nyala, springbok, impala, zebra, ostrich & waterbuck. There are 3 hiking routes in the grounds. *B&B N$830/1,220 sgl/dbl.* **LL**

Termite Hills (4 rooms) ☎ 067 306222; m 081 148 5076; e reservation@termitehills.com; www.termitehills.com. In Apr 2010, Werner & Lotte Dedig opened their farmhouse to visitors, offering simple, cosy en-suite rooms, each with a private sitting area outside. Translated from the Afrikaans name for the farm, Miershoop, Termite Hills is situated 55km south of Otjiwarongo, east of the B1, along a 13km sand & gravel road. The main focus is on introducing visitors to life on an 8,000ha Namibian cattle farm, & the Dedigs enjoy imparting their knowledge over afternoon tea & homemade cake. Activities include scenic, sundowner & farm drives, & self-guided walking trails. There's also a pool. *DBB N$860/900 sgl/dbl.* **LL**

Okonjima ☎ 067 687032; m 081 127 6233; e reservations@okonjimalodge.com; www.okonjima.com. Set amid the rolling Omboroko Mountains & overlooking the plains, Okonjima is best reached from the B1, about 130km north of Okahandja (7km south of Otjiwarongo). From the turn-off, take the private road that is clearly signposted 'Okonjima 10km', & follow the signs to the main gate for a further 14km drive to the lodge.

Run by the Hanssen family for 3 generations, this relaxed place has, over the years, been one of Namibia's most popular & successful draws for visitors. Much of its appeal has been because this is the base for the AfriCat Foundation (see box, page 411). Income from the lodge helps to support the foundation, as well as funding a critical environmental education programme & the running of the 220km² park which is home to released cheetah & leopards. Visitors are virtually guaranteed to get close to at least some of the big cats. That said, levels of hospitality have always been well above the norm, too. (The team is particularly adept at dealing with film crews & the press, so their exposure in the media is second to none in southern Africa.)

All the camps here operate independently, with their own dining facilities. Meals, served plated or buffet-style, are consistently good, with quality wines at good prices. Children under 12 can stay only at Plains Camp, the Bush Suite and the campsite.

While each of the camps has separate activities in the early morning and late afternoon, they essentially offer the same ones, taking a maximum of 9–12 visitors at Plains Camp, or 6 at Bush Camp. Alternatively, a private guide & vehicle is available at extra cost. Tracking the radio-collared leopards from a 4x4 takes in the rocky Etjo sandstone outcrops & the reserve's natural wildlife – from wildebeest & giraffe to kudu, eland & Hartmann's mountain zebra, as well as birding 'specials' such as Carp's tit & the Damara rock runner. Leopard tracking can yield superb photographs; if you look closely, many winners of photo competitions have taken their shots at Okonjima! There is also the opportunity to track cheetah, wild dog & hyena on foot. Tours of the AfriCat Centre provide a fascinating overview of their conservation, cheetah welfare & education projects. And during 'Bushman Trail' a guide explains how the Bushmen live & the uses of some of the plants. There are also several self-guided trails of 3–8km. After dinner, scraps are put out at a floodlit hide to attract porcupines & honey badgers; if you can drag yourself away from the bar for an hour's watching & waiting, this can be fun. Night drives are also available. Okonjima no longer allows guests into close contact with the animals, or to touch the cheetahs.

With so much going on, Okonjima has become a destination in itself rather than simply a stopover at the end of a trip – to get the best out of it, you should spend at least 2 nights here. It's usually best to arrive around 16.00 (15.00 in winter), in time for tea & the afternoon activities. If you're short of time, visitors can now call in at the new Day Centre complete with a café, showers and use of the camping site pool, & can join the AfriCat tour. There's nowhere else quite like it & for some visitors it's a 'must-see'.

🏠 **PLAINS CAMP** (28 rooms) This is the hub of Okonjima, previously called Main Camp but substantially rebuilt in 2014. It has 14 'standard' rooms ideal for families & more budget-orientated visitors & 14 new 'view' rooms, bigger than the standard ones with a more modern feel. All furnishings have been made on site, with the décor cool & fresh rather than rustic bush. Each has a desk, fridge & sliding doors opening to a veranda shielded by big bamboo poles. A new central lapa lies between the standard & view rooms, designed like a traditional barn with huge glass windows to make the most of the views, & a new pool called the Waterhole with a windmill to the side. Plains Camp isn't inclusive, with additional charges for activities & lunch. 1 standard room & 1 view room are wheelchair accessible with convertible rails in bathrooms. *DBB standard/view rooms N$1,630/2,500 pppn; sgl supplement N$750; activities N$540 pp per activity*. **LLLL**

🏠 **BUSH CAMP** (8 chalets, junior suite) Large, thatched rondavels at this more traditional camp, 3km from Plains Camp, are well separated & more luxurious. Due to undergo renovation at the time of research, each will have 2 dbl beds, Hemingway-style furnishings & sliding glass doors opening on to a veranda to reveal views over the bush – or the night sky. A (wheelchair accessible) junior suite boasts sliding glass doors, a lounge with fireplace, & a bath & outside shower too. The curved theme continues to the central lapa & restaurant (serving excellent food), overlooking a fire pit, a small pool & a waterhole. *DBB N$3,520 pppn; FBA N$4,700 pppn; sgl supplement N$750*. **LLLLL**

🏠 **OKONJIMA VILLA** (2 rooms & 2 suites) & **BUSH SUITE** (2 rooms). Up there with the best accommodation in Namibia, each of these exclusive & secluded options has its own game-drive vehicle & is staffed by a private chef & guide. The villa is located in the actual park rather than in the Okonjima camp zone so, with leopards roaming freely, children under 12 are not permitted. Tasteful & über-comfortable bedrooms & living rooms under deep thatch are fronted by an extensive veranda with a large pool overlooking a waterhole. In each, there's the option to roll beds out under the stars. This is serious if understated luxury in an open bush setting, ideal for well-heeled families or groups of friends. For those who can't escape reality, there's Wi-Fi internet & mobile phone reception. *FBA N$6,000 pppn*. **LLLLL**

🏕 **OMBOROKO CAMPSITE** At the other end of the scale, the campsite up in the hills features 4

uded – & exclusive – pitches. Each
ty, private hot showers, flush toilets,
ai, & there's a pool just for campers,
but other than firewood you'll need to be entirely
self-sufficient. Booking is essential. *AfriCat tours &
Bushman Trail N$385 each pp. N$250 pp.* **L**

🏠 **Mount Etjo Safari Lodge** (15 rooms,
camping) 📞 067 290173/4; e mount.etjo@iway.na;
www.mount-etjo.com. The name *etjo*, meaning
'a place of refuge', describes this lodge founded
in the early 1970s by Jan Oelofse, now well
known in local political circles. (The 'Mount Etjo
Declaration' was signed here on the way to political
independence in 1989.) To find it, turn west from
the main B1 on to the D2483, about 63km south
of Otjiwarongo. From here, continue for 40km on
a gravel & sand road as it heads towards the huge,
flat-topped sandstone massif of Mount Etjo, which
is often a deep shade of burgundy. The road surface
colour changes from white to red in the distance,
but watch how it differs from the deeper soil, made
into tall termitaria. Approaching from the west,
the lodge is about 28km from Kalkfeld: 14km on
the D2414 then another 14km on the D2483.

Accommodation is luxurious & there's no shortage
of animal prints for that safari feel. All rooms are en
suite, some with a jacuzzi. Most have dbl beds, but
2 suites have king-size beds, private sitting rooms
& private gardens. Dinner is served in a lapa around
a campfire. A beautifully spacious private villa has
recently opened with a private garden, pool &
waterhole. With terracotta flooring & thatch ceiling,
it blends rustic & luxury with leather sofas, vast
bathrooms & bedrooms, & private kitchen.

There are usually 2 activities per day, & there's
no lack of game on the ranch, brought in to attract
visitors. As well as elephant, black & white rhino,
zebra & giraffe, there are hippo & nyala, which
don't naturally occur in the area. A pride of lion
kept in an enclosure are fed regularly & can be
observed by guests (*N$150 pp*). About 3km from
the lodge, Camp Dinosaur offers 6 individual pitches
for 4 people, each with private toilet/shower, 220V
sockets & shared BBQ facilities. Campers can join
any of the activities offered by the lodge. *DBB rooms
from N$1,650 pp; junior suite from N$1,785 pp;
villa from N$3,150 pp; camping N$400 per site for 4
people; game drive N$300 pp.* **LLLL**

🏠 **Erindi** (47 rooms) 📞 064 570800; m 081 145
0000; e reservations@erindi.com; www.erindi.com.
Owned by Gert Joubert & opened in late 2008, Erindi

is a 710km² private game reserve boasting the only
free-roaming lion pride on private land in Namibia.
Other species introduced to attract tourists include
wild dog, elephant & rhino, all viewed on morning
& evening game drives in open 4x4 safari vehicles.
There are 4 gates into the reserve, reached from
Omaruru (D2328) to the west, Kalkfeld (D2414) to
the north & Otjiwarongo (D2187) or Okahandja to
the east. Coming from Okahandja, take the B1 north
for about 45km, then turn west on to the D2414 &,
after 40km, fork left on to the D2328. 4km further
on, turn left & follow signs for 20km to the reserve.

At additional cost, a whole raft of activities
are available here, including special game drives
for children, night & full-day drives, telemetry
tracking drives, cheetah & leopard project walks &
visits to a San village on the reserve.

Accommodation, at the Old Traders Lodge in the
southern part of the reserve, overlooks a waterhole.
The 36 rooms & 11 suites are luxurious with teak &
leather furniture, AC, DSTV, fridge, safe & en-suite
bathrooms with shower & bath. Buffet meals are
served in a large thatched dining area with adjacent
lounge & fireplace, or on the terrace. There's also a
pool & children's play area. *DBB from N$2,259/3,718
sgl/dbl; FBA lodge from N$3,304/5,808 sgl/dbl, inc 2
game drives daily.* **LLLLL**

🏠 **Camp Elephant** (14 2-bed self-catering
chalets & 30 camping pitches) About 30km away
from the main lodge but still very much part of
Erindi, opened in Nov 2013. Private ablution blocks
& kitchens. There's no restaurant or bar here, but
there is a shop for provisions. *Chalets from N$1,500
per night for 2 people plus additional charge for
more guests; camping from N$700 per night for 4
adults plus 2 children.* **LL**

🏠 **Babson House, CCF** (3 rooms) 📞 061
237294; e visit@ccfnamibia.org; http://cheetah.
org/you-can-help/visit/. Located at the Cheetah
Conservation Fund's (CCF) research centre & helping
to generate funds for the cause, the house offers
luxurious accommodation overlooking the orphan
cheetah pen. The décor is Africa meets English manor
house: large 4-poster beds, rich fabrics & leather
furniture. There are 2 spacious en-suite dbl rooms
upstairs & a smaller, less extravagant room with small
en suite downstairs. A private lounge & dining room
comes with DSTV, Wi-Fi & binoculars for guests to sit
on the veranda watching cheetah while the house
chef prepares meals. *FBA N$9,000/12,000
sgl/dbl.* **LLLLL**

What to see and do

Dinosaur footprints (☉ *sunrise–sunset daily; admission N$20/10 adult/under 12*) Several fossilised animal tracks are preserved in the area's distinctive Etjo sandstone on the farm with the unforgettable name, Otjihaenamaparero. All date from about 150–200 million years ago. The most spectacular is a series of prints about 25m in length, which were made by a large, three-toed, two-legged dinosaur. Just imagine yourself in Jurassic Park.

To get here take the C33 south for over 60km from Otjiwarongo until Kalkfeld is signposted left, on to the D2414. The farm is 29km from there, signposted 'Dinosaur's Tracks'. Follow the signs which will take you down the D2467, a road not recommended for 2WD vehicles, and then through a farm gate (but note that signs for 'Dinosaur Camp Site' lead to Mount Etjo Safari Lodge, not to Otjihaenamaparero.

Where to stay *Map, page 398.*

Otjihaenamaparero (3 rooms, camping)
\ 067 290153; e dinotracks@afol.com.na, service-team-dino@web.de; www.dinosaurstracks.com.

Otjihaenamaparero Farm began with a campsite, to which owners Adele & Reinhold Strobel added a small whitewashed guesthouse in 2003. Alongside

AFRICAT FOUNDATION

Based out of Okonjima, the nonprofit AfriCat Foundation (e *info@africat. com*) is focused on the long-term conservation of large carnivores in Namibia. Initially, the foundation aimed to rescue, relocate and even rehabilitate both problem and unwanted big cats. Today their priority is to raise awareness of the issues involved in cheetah conservation and living with predators, focusing on environmental education, habitat preservation and animal welfare.

Claimed as the largest rescue-and-release programme in the world, the foundation has rescued over 1,000 big cats in the last 20 years, representing a cheetah-to-leopard ratio of around 2:1. Of these, over 90% of the leopards and nearly 80% of the cheetahs have been released into the wild.

Animals being rehabilitated at Okonjima have for many years been protected within a 4,500ha area, but in 2010 fencing was completed around a further 16,000ha with its own existing leopard population. In May of that year, the first cheetahs, and later hyena and wild dog, were released into this area, learning to hunt for themselves while being closely monitored. Their aim now is for the big cats to roam freely in this extended park rather than be kept in captivity, and this involves clearing thousands of hectares of encroached bush to create the open spaces that cheetah need. Those animals that cannot hunt for themselves, including several cheetah, are cared for within a smaller reserve dedicated to welfare rather than conservation. Some can occasionally be seen on the excellent AfriCat tour, which includes a visit to the information centre and clinic and explanations on how the animals are looked after.

Central to the foundation's work is environmental education for all members of the community. This is now the priority for the AfriCat Foundation, with a new Environmental Education Centre for children from schools across Namibia as well as for farmers and teachers.

Guests interested in AfriCat stay at Okonjima, and learn more about the foundation's work from there, or can visit the new Day Centre. AfriCat no longer offers their volunteer programme, PAWS.

17

ooms, there's a living area with
for self-catering – though
s are available on request. The
te has 5 pitches, each with
place, 2 toilets/showers & a

central sink for dishwashing. Aside from visiting
the dinosaur tracks, guests can take nature drives,
& guided walking tours can be arranged. *B&B from
N$385/660/825 sgl/dbl/family; camping N$80 pp;
no credit cards.* **L**

WATERBERG PLATEAU PARK

(\ *067 305001;* ☉ *sunrise–sunset daily; admission N$80 pp, plus N$10 per vehicle
(2WD access), under 16 free; day visitors must phone ahead*) Historically important
during the war between the German forces and the Hereros, the plateau was first
envisaged as a reserve for eland, Africa's largest species of antelope. In 1972 it was
proclaimed a reserve and has since become a sanctuary for several rare animals,
including eland and (introduced) white rhino.

GEOGRAPHY The park centres on a plateau of compacted Etjo sandstone, some 250m
high. This lump of rock, formed about 180–200 million years ago, is the remnant of a
much larger plateau that once covered the whole area. It is highly permeable (surface
water flows through it like a sieve), but the mudstones below it are impermeable. This
results in the emergence of several springs at the base of the southern cliffs.

FLORA AND FAUNA For a fairly small park, there are a large number of different
environments. The top of the plateau supports a patchwork of wooded areas (mostly
broad-leaved deciduous) and open grasslands, while the foothills and flats at the
base of the escarpment are dominated by acacia bush, but dotted with evergreen
trees and lush undergrowth where the springs well up on the southern side. This
diversity gives the park its ability to support a large variety of animals.

Waterberg has become an integral part of a number of conservation projects,
seeing the relocation of several endangered species (including white rhino, roan
and sable antelope) in an attempt to start viable breeding herds. These have added
to the game already found here, which ranges from giraffe and kudu to leopard,
brown hyena, cheetah and (reports claim) wild dog.

The birdlife is no less impressive, with more than 200 species on record. Most
memorable are the spectacular Verreaux's (black) eagles, and Namibia's only
breeding colony of Cape vultures. Although REST is working to conserve these
imposing raptors, numbers have sharply declined in recent years due to both the
changing environment and the increasing use of farm poisons (both intentional
poisons, and the chemicals in fertilisers and pesticides). One innovation encourages
them to eat at a vulture restaurant (open once a week, on Wednesday morning)
where carcasses are prepared and left out for them.

GETTING THERE AND AWAY Waterberg is very clearly signposted, 91km to the east
of Otjiwarongo: follow the B1, the C22 and finally the D2512, this last for about
24km. Note that although the park is accessible in a 2WD, the road from the B1 can
be very rutted, so allow yourself plenty of time. On the plus side, that gives you a
better chance to watch out for wildlife.

WHERE TO STAY *Map, opposite.*

🏠 **Waterberg Camp** (34 rooms, 35 chalets)
Reservations via NWR, Windhoek (see page 56) or at
the park office (☉ *06.00–18.00 daily*). Established

in 1989, the camp is beautifully landscaped over the
escarpment's wooded slopes. In 1910 the Germans
built a police station on a plantation here: now

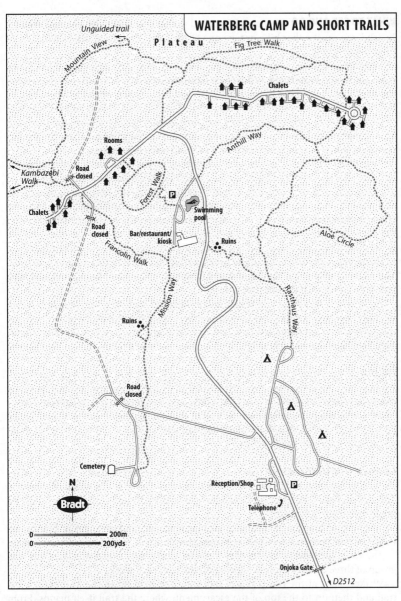

Unguided trail

P l a t e a u

Mountain View

Fig Tree Walk

Chalets

Anthill Way

Rooms

Kambazebi Walk

Road closed

Forest Walk

P

Swimming pool

Chalets

Road closed

Bar/restaurant/ kiosk

Ruins

Aloe Circle

Francolin Walk

Mission Way

Ruins

Resthaus Way

Road closed

Cemetery

N

Bradt

Reception/Shop

P

Telephone

0 — 200m
0 — 200yds

Onjoka Gate

D2512

it's a restaurant – & the prison cell has become a wine cellar! Much of the original building remains, its history captured in fascinating photographs & memorabilia on the walls. The plantation itself has regenerated into bush, but it is said that the occasional orange tree can still be found. Other amenities include a poorly stocked kiosk (⏲ 06.00– 18.00 daily), large swimming pool & conference facilities.

Accommodation ranges from dbl rooms & 'luxury' dbl chalets, to 'standard' 2-room chalets with 4 beds. The campsite is well shaded, with chairs, lights & good ablutions, but watch out for dawn raids from baboons & ground squirrel burrows pock-marking the road. There's also a fuel station, but note that they don't have diesel. *B&B room N$660/1,100 sgl/dbl; chalet N$770–902/660–792 sgl/pp sharing; camping N$110 per site plus N$121 pp (max 8 people).* **LL**

WHAT TO SEE AND DO This park is unusual in that you can't drive yourself around. Instead you must either hike or take one of the park's organised drives with one of their driver/guides.

Waterberg had been gaining a reputation for its excellent long guided hikes, particularly the **Waterberg Wilderness Trail,** a three-day, 42km hike to the west of the park, but at the time of research these had been closed until further notice by the Ministry of Environment and Tourism. If resurrected, this is an excellent way to enjoy the best of Waterberg. There are some good marked trails around the camp area, however, and even up on to a lookout point on the plateau. These are perfect if you are bored sitting in a vehicle and yearn to stretch your legs.

Organised drives lasting about 3 hours (*N$330 pp*) take place in the morning and late afternoon, and are best booked with the park office as soon as you arrive. They tour around the plateau in search of game, visiting the permanent waterholes and some of the hides. However, although the guiding is usually good, and there are chances of seeing uncommon sable and roan antelope, the bush here is thicker and the game densities appear much lower than, say, Etosha, so many visitors find the game disappointing. One possibility for the dedicated is to take the morning trip on to the plateau, get off at one of the hides, and spend the day there game-watching. You need to take some food and water (and perhaps a good book), but can then return to camp with the afternoon drive.

Between the reception and restaurant, a side road leads to a war cemetery where intricate headstones remember German soldiers killed in the Waterberg battle during the 1904 Herero uprising led by Chief Samuel Maharero (see box, *Herero Parade*, page 166). Perhaps unsurprisingly, there are no equivalent memorials to the Herero.

Hiking If you come to Waterberg for the walking, then you won't be disappointed. All year round there are nine short trails that you can take around the vicinity of the camp, described in booklets from the office, and designed to give visitors a flavour of the park. The panorama from the end of the trail up to Mountain View (*N$100 pp with guide; book through the office*) is definitely worth the effort and time (about 45 minutes) that it takes to get there.

Longer unguided trail (*N$340 pp*) During the dry season, from April to November, an unguided four-day 50km trail can be done in the south of the park. There is no better way to experience this game park, though reservations must be made months in advance.

You need to bring your own sleeping bag, food and cooking utensils. During the walk, you will sleep in stone shelters, provided with simple long-drop toilets and water.

The trail starts every Wednesday at 09.00, and returns on Saturday. Only one group of three to ten people is allowed on the trail each week.

Walkers start at the resort office, following the road up to the Mountain View trail and then on to the top of the escarpment, where the trail itself begins. From here it is a relatively short 42km. The first night is spent at the Otjozongombe shelter, and the second and third nights at the Otjomapenda shelter, allowing you to make a circular day-walk of about 8km. This all takes place around the spectacular sandstone kopjes on the southern edge of the plateau.

 AROUND WATERBERG: NEARBY LODGES AND GUEST FARMS *Map, page 398.*

Waterberg Wilderness Farm Otjosongombe; 067 687018; m 081 284 9630; e info@waterberg-wilderness.com; www. waterberg-wilderness.com. Waterberg Wilderness is situated 280km north of Windhoek: turn off the B1 on to the C22 (28km south of Otjiwarongo), turn left on to the D2512, & drive past Waterberg Camp & Resort; at Otjosongombe turn left (clearly signposted) towards a small gorge in the plateau, & drive for a further 4km to the reception.

The farm includes part of the Waterberg Plateau itself, as well as some of the flatter farmland around. A stay here includes the option of joining guided hikes of around 3hrs on to & around the plateau in the morning or afternoon (N$100 pp). The scenery is stunning, & although getting on to the plateau can be steep at times, walking around the top is relatively flat. You'll see plenty of signs of game although, like walking safaris anywhere, the animals will usually flee before you get too close. Given that both buffalo & rhino live on the property, it's wise to keep your wits about you. There's a series of self-guided walking trails, too, with a map provided to identify the plants along the way. Nature drives (N$350 pp) on the flat land below the plateau are more productive for game, & the owners are gradually restocking the property, having converted it from a cattle farm to a game area. It's a good place to spot Damara dik-dik, & along with the usual antelope there are also small numbers of giraffe & rhino. Finally, there's the option (with a day's notice) of spending half a day visiting a local Herero community with a guide.

In short, Waterberg Wilderness is an excellent & good-value spot for a little relaxed walking; it's perfect for a 2/3-night stay.

WATERBERG WILDERNESS LODGE (12 rooms) 2.2km from the main reception, the original farm building has been converted into a lovely lodge by owners Joachim & Caroline Rust. Built from Waterberg's red sandstone & set in a green oasis, surrounded by cliffs, it has 3 family & 9 dbl rooms. All are en suite & are spotlessly clean, fairly spacious & designed traditionally though with an eye for touches of stylish minimalism. B/fast is usually buffet, often mixing traditional German fare with other European styles. If you arrive by 15.30 on your first afternoon then you'll be in time for tea & cakes on the terrace (also included); later dinner is served & everyone eats together. There's a fire for winter evenings, while 2 spring-water pools offer a refreshing dip in the hotter months. *DBB N$1,160 pp.* **LLL**

WATERBERG PLATEAU LODGE (8 chalets, camping) Up a steep drive, nestled among the rocks along the edge of the plateau, are en-suite chalets, each with a wood-burning fire, private plunge pool & spectacular views. Afternoon tea is served in

the restaurant atop a rocky outcrop offering 180° views. *DBB N$1,413 pp.* **LLL**

WATERBERG VALLEY LODGE (5 tents) Opened in Aug 2014 as a halfway house between chalets & camping, this is a tented camp with its own pool & lapa, & beautiful views over the valley. *DBB N$967 pp.* **LLL**

In the valley below, 2 campsites each have pitches with private BBQ & tap. There are clean ablution facilities & a shared swimming pool, & wood/BBQ meat can be purchased at the office. *Camping N$170 pp.* **L**

Oase Guest Farm (5 rooms) 067 309010; e farm-oase@gmail.com; www.farm-oase.com. At the northeastern end of the Waterberg Plateau, on the D2804 about 50km from the B1, Oase offers guests the chance to experience life on a traditional cattle farm, as well as to take guided hikes in the surrounding hills, or a sundowner to finish off the day. Guest rooms are built alongside the farmhouse around a courtyard with a pool. Each is en suite, with a private veranda & views over the farm to the hills. Meals, served *en famille*, are based on farm-grown produce, including beef & game; special diets can be catered for. *DBB N$900 pppn; no credit cards.* **LLL**

Waterberg Guest Farm (4 rooms, 6 bungalows) 061 237294; e info@ waterbergnamibia.com; www.waterbergnamibia. com. Situated on the south side of the tarred C22, 32km east of the main B1, this guest farm is run by Harry & Sonja Schneider-Waterberg, whose family have owned the 40,000ha farm for over 100 years. It lies at the centre of the much larger Waterberg Conservancy, which also incorporates the Cheetah Conservation Fund (CCF) & much of the Waterberg Plateau. Its location, a little distance from Waterberg, allows great views of sunrise over the plateau, an experience missing from many of the lodges situated immediately below the plateau.

En-suite, sparsely furnished rooms are either in the original farm buildings, which have been converted with care & quality, or in bungalows just 200m from the main house. All are simply furnished, & a 'family unit' consists of linked dbl & twin rooms, each with a small sitting area. Bungalows are built to a traditional Herero design, but with no shortage of mod cons, including indoor & outdoor showers. A further 2 bungalows are family units. Outside is a small splash pool &, beside it, a thatched bar. B/fast & dinner are served in the dining room with guests seated together, & the lounge houses an impressive wine collection.

The main activities here are ½-day trips to the CCF. There are also opportunities for hiking in the mountains behind the farm, which are of a very similar geology & form to the Waterberg. Harry's a good birder, & knows his way around the bush very well, so is a good man to guide you if he's there. NB: if you're not a fan of dogs, this place probably isn't for you – Harry has 5. A key deposit of N$100 is requested. *Dinner N$220 pp; B&B room N$805 pp; bungalow N$1,192 pp.* **LLL**

 Weaver's Rock Guest Farm (6 rooms, camping) 067 304885; e wrgf@iway.na; www. weaversrock.com. The guest farm is situated on Hohenfels ('high rock') Farm which was purchased from the German colony in 1903 by Duke zu Bentheim Tecklenburg-Rheda after completing his service in Sumatra. Six generations later it is still in the family, run by the lovely Sabine & Alex.

After turning on to the C22 towards Waterberg Plateau & driving for 5km, it is signposted up the hill on a farm road for another 5km. Guests are accommodated in 4 en-suite bungalows with great views across the valley, & 2 rooms with shared bathrooms. There are also 2 very simple bush chalets, built of stone & wood, with tin roofs & outdoor shower-rooms. 11 grassy camping sites with BBQ, water & electricity border a well-established garden. Fresh home-grown produce is part of the fare with b/fast & dinner served in the thatched lapa overlooking a swimming pool; campers can join farm meals on request.

Activities include farm drives, pony rides for children or horseriding for adults, full moon drives, bush dinners, a wellness salon & self-guided hikes, including a great 20min walk to a small lake for a refreshing swim. *Dinner N$150; B&B from N$542/1,016 sgl/dbl; bush chalet N$285/270 sgl/pp sharing; camping N$100 pp.* **LL**

OUTJO

This small ranching town of about 5,000 people is some 65km from Otjiwarongo and 115km south of Etosha's Okaukuejo camp. It stands on a limestone formation in fertile grasslands, dotted with livestock ranches and the odd fruit farm. The name 'Outjo' is variously translated as 'place on the rocks' or 'little hills' – referring to the area's hilly topography. This territory had long belonged to the Herero people when the first Europeans arrived to stay. The adventurer Tom Lambert settled here with his family in 1880, and few others followed until the Schutztruppe established a control post here in 1897. The following year the first 'stand' of town land was officially given out.

In 1901 the town water tower was completed, and is still easily seen today. Development ground to a halt during the Herero war around 1904–05, and again just before independence, but in the last two decades or so the town seems to have had a new lease of life thanks to tourists *en route* to Etosha. That said, the town is still small, and keep an eye out for minor hassle in the form of curio sellers who won't take 'no' for an answer.

Outjo is a useful pit stop on the way to or from Etosha, Khorixas or the northern Kaokoveld, but not usually a destination in itself.

TOURIST INFORMATION The town's tourist information office (08.00–17.30 *daily*) can be found inside Namibia Gemstones shop, in the corner almost opposite the Outjo Bäckerei. The curio shop opposite the Caltex also has helpful local tourist information.

WHERE TO STAY *Map, page 418.*

 The Farmhouse (6 rooms) m 067 313 444; e bookings@thefarmhouse-outjo.com; www.thefarmhouse-outjo.com. Above the new & trendy Farmhouse café is a small guesthouse. Each of its stylish en-suite rooms has Wi-Fi & TV,

and some have AC. It's a good option for a small group or family & there is safe parking. **$$$**

Buschfeld Park Restcamp (5 rooms, camping) 067 313665; m 081 148 2636; e buschfeldpark@iway.na. Almost 2km north of

The Cheetah Conservation Fund (\ *067 306225;* e *ccfinfo@iway.na; www. cheetah.org*) was started by Laurie Marker in 1990 to develop a permanent conservation research centre for cheetah. Today they are based on a 15km² farm northwest of Waterberg Plateau, 44km east of Otjiwarongo (turn right as you head north out of Otjiwarongo, just before the bridge over the railway line). Their aim is to 'secure habitats for the long term survival of cheetah and their ecosystem through multi-disciplined and integrated programs of conservation, research and education'.

The foundation has a thriving Visitor and Education Centre (⊕ *08.00–17.00 daily except Christmas day, last admission 16.00; N$180/90 adult/child*). To get there, take the B1 north from Otjiwarongo; as you leave the town, the D2440 is on the right, with a brown sign to CCF. Take this road and follow it for about 45 minutes.

Visitors may just turn up during opening hours, but if you time your visit for around 14.00 you should be there for feeding time (though it's as well to phone first to check). With advance booking it's also possible to watch the cheetahs on their morning exercise. This takes place at around 07.30 each morning, when a group is taken out for a run, following a coloured lure that is dragged in front of them around a 'track' (*N$480*). Note, however, that only adults aged 16 and over are allowed in the run area. At all times, you can expect to see some of the orphaned cheetahs living at the centre, and to visit the interactive museum that covers everything from the history of the cheetah to its behaviour and habitat. Conservation issues are prominently covered in the centre, too. There's also a small, well-stocked shop that sells drinks and souvenirs. For those wishing to stay longer, the new Visitor Centre sells light lunches and breakfasts can be pre-ordered for those going on the cheetah run.

The museum provides visitors and students with the opportunity to learn more about the behaviour and biology of the cheetah, and the Namibian ecosystem that supports Africa's most endangered cat species. Excellent graphics and interactive displays chart the history of the cheetah from prehistory to modern times, and explain how their range and numbers have diminished. Other exhibits show where the cheetah fits into the cat species family tree, how it differs from the 36 other cat species, how it is adapted for a high-speed sprint and its specialised hunting techniques, and finally its life cycle from cub to adult. A life-size 'playtree' shows the importance of these trees in a cheetah's territory.

The CCF's research programmes include radio-tracking research to understand more about cheetah distribution and ecology; bio-medical research to learn more about overall health, diseases and genetic make-up; habitat and ecosystem research; wildlife and livestock management to reduce predator conflicts; and non-lethal predator control methods. In addition to supporting extensive environmental education programmes, both on site and in schools, CCF also sells 'bushblok': excellent burning firewood made from encroaching bush, which is otherwise a menace to wildlife and especially to a hunting cheetah.

Visitors to the centre can stay at the luxurious Babson House (see page 410) but most stay in Waterberg Plateau Park, or at one of the surrounding lodges, and spend half a day visiting the centre from there.

Highlands South of Etosha   OUTJO

17

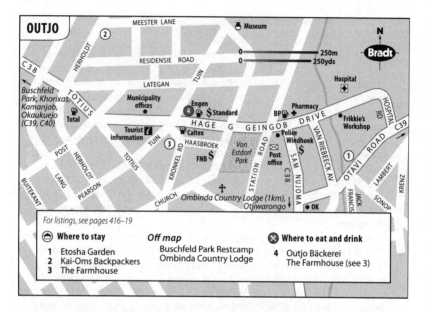

OUTJO

MEESTER LANE

Museum

N

RESIDENSIE ROAD

0 — 250m
0 — 250yds

Bradt

C38

HERHOLDT

TOTIUS

LATEGAN

TUIN

Hospital

Buschfeld
Park, Khorixas,
Kamanjab,
Okaukuejo
(C39, C40)

Total

Municipality
offices

Engen

Standard

Pharmacy

BP

Frikkie's
Workshop

HOSPITAL RD

Tourist
information

Caltex

HAGE G GEINGOB DRIVE

Police
Windhoek

VAN RIEBEECK AV

C39

POST

HERHOLDT

TUIN

HAASBROEK

KRONKEL RD

FNB

Von
Estdorf
Park

STATION ROAD

Post
office

SAM NUJOMA

OTAVI ROAD

LAMBERT

KRENZ

TOTIUS

C38

LANG

PEARSON

BUITEKANT

CHURCH

Ombinda Country Lodge (1km),
Otjiwarongo

OK

JACK FRANCIS

SONOP

For listings, see pages 416–19

🏠 **Where to stay**

1 Etosha Garden
2 Kai-Oms Backpackers
3 The Farmhouse

Off map

Buschfeld Park Restcamp
Ombinda Country Lodge

❌ **Where to eat and drink**

4 Outjo Bäckerei
The Farmhouse (see 3)

Outjo, just across the Storm River on the left, this relaxed restcamp set in 95ha feels more like a small guest farm than a restcamp, & makes a pleasant stopover. Lush grounds with mature citrus trees offset cream-painted buildings with simple but clean rooms. 3 twins have bathroom, lounge area, fridge & kettle, & a further 2 are set up for families with adjoining bedrooms. The sloping campsite has level pitches with power & some shade, & a BBQ area. For entertainment, there's a lovely pool with grassy surrounds, or 2 self-guided walking trails into the mountains, offering good birding & game such as kudu, Damara dik-dik & duiker. *Camping N$110 pp.* **$$**

🏠 **Etosha Garden Hotel** (20 rooms) 6 Otavi St; ☎067 313130; e etoshahotel@iway.na; www.etosha-garden-hotel.com. This is a lovely hotel & the town's top accommodation. The rooms are large, normally with twin beds, simple wooden furniture, & rugs scattered on cool, waxed concrete or tiled floors. Each has a large bathroom with shower. All overlook an open courtyard, shaded by jacaranda, palm trees & lush greenery. There is also a small swimming pool. Adjacent is an à la carte restaurant where you can enjoy lunch, tea or coffee with apple strudel, or dinner. The restaurant (**$$–$$$$**) is well known for its game specialities. Popular with groups, this is a good option for a 1-night stop, or even just an extended lunch, on the way to/from Etosha. **$$**

🏠 **Ombinda Country Lodge** (16 chalets, 9 rooms, camping) ☎067 313181; e ombindagerald@iway.na; www.ombindalodge.com. Ombinda rose from the remnants of Outjo's old municipal restcamp in 1995, & has been thriving ever since. It lies about 1km southeast of town, signposted off the main C38 towards Windhoek. Chalets & rooms – 4 individual & 5 in a block – are all thatched, built around a grassy central area with large pool, thatched bar/restaurant with TV & alfresco dining area. Lunch & dinner are à la carte. Each room is clean & well kept with twin or trpl beds & en-suite shower. There's also a small, tree-shaded campsite that's popular with overlanders. Ombinda is pleasant, safe & secure, ideal for families with children, but its chalets are close together so this may not be the place to get away from it all. *Camping N$120 pp.* **$$**

🏠 **Kai-Oms Backpackers Lodge** (6 rooms, dorms, camping) Meester Ln; ☎067 313597; m 081 346 3644, 081 375 0152; e info@kai-oms.com, vzyl.deon@yahoo.com; www.kai-oms.com. Situated in a quiet Outjo suburb & well signposted off the main street, this backpackers' lodge is full of character considering it's in a small, rural town. The rooms are built around a central courtyard split into various shaded sitting & BBQ areas & decorated with fun murals, antiques, carvings & plant pots. There's a small camping area, off-street parking, a self-catering kitchen & dining room. *Dorm bed from N$160; camping N$120 pp; b/fast not inc.* **$**

✗ WHERE TO EAT AND DRINK *Map, opposite.*

In addition to the restaurants at the hotels, lodges and campsites, Outjo boasts a couple of cafés that would make a good stop; both are on the main Hage Geingob Drive.

✗ **Outjo Bäckerei** ☏067 313055; e imagesofafrica@iway.na. ⏰ 06.30–17.00 Mon–Fri, 07.00–14.00 Sat. Directly opposite the Caltex garage on the north side of town, this popular bakery recently expanded &, in addition to a small seating area inside, now has a welcoming, partly thatched garden restaurant. There's a selection of burgers, some excellent pies & a good range of confectionery & German-style pastries. Picnic lunch packs can be arranged on request & there is free Wi-Fi internet available, although the connection is quite slow. If you don't have your own device you can use the internet on the computer there, which costs N$20 for 30mins. $–$$$

✗ **The Farmhouse** Cnr Hage Geingob Dr & Tuin St; m 067 313 444; e bookings@thefarmhouse-outjo.com; ⏰ summer 07.00–22.00, winter 06.30–21.00. Part of a relatively new & trendy complex, this is a friendly café with a cosy interior & a new but well-laid-out beer garden – which will improve as vegetation grows. It's a good option for a cooked b/fast, sandwich, wrap, burger or light lunch & offers internet (*N$30 for 30mins*) & good coffee. There is also a small guesthouse (see page 416). $–$$$

OTHER PRACTICALITIES Outjo is a good place to get organised. In the centre is an open area, like a village green, near which can be found most of the town's facilities, including fuel stations, supermarkets, several curio shops, a couple of cafés and a post office. (The last was memorable for having an old-style public phone as late as 1994, which accepted 10c or 20c pieces and needed cranking into action.) For **banks**: the FNB is beside the green, with the Standard Bank (and ATM) almost opposite and Bank Windhoek close to the OK supermarket on Sam Nujoma Drive.

For **fuel** there are the BP station opposite the police station, the Engen garage (with workshop) next to the Standard Bank, and the Total station on the way northwest out of town. All are (in theory) open 24 hours. Frikkie's Workshop (☏ *067 313561*) offers **vehicle repairs** and is almost opposite the hospital.

The best places to access the **internet** are Outjo Bäckerei and The Farmhouse.

In an **emergency**, the police are reached on ☏ 067 10111 or 067 313005, the ambulance on ☏067 313250 and m 081 421 3000, the hospital on ☏067 313250 and the fire brigade on ☏ 067 313404 and m 081 2550060. The Outjo **pharmacy** (☏ *067 313216*) is on the main street.

WHAT TO SEE AND DO The town's **museum** (☏*067 313402*; ⏰ 07.30–13.00 & 14.30–17.00 Mon–Fri; admission N$10 pp) is well worth a visit, with displays of local history and a variety of animal horns, skins and bones, minerals and gemstones. There's also a unique sheep-shearing machine that works with a bicycle chain. If you can't get to it during normal opening hours, it's worth phoning to see if they will open specially.

AROUND OUTJO
⌂ Nearby guest farms *Map, page 398.*

In addition to the following, take a look at the accommodation around Etosha's Andersson Gate (see pages 388–90).

⌂ **Vreugde** (7 rooms) ☏067 687132; m 081 210 7693; e info@vreugdeguestfarm.com; www. vreugdeguestfarm.com. Since the delightful Elsie & Danie Brand opened the 3,400ha family farm to guests in 2001, they have offered a remarkably warm welcome that reflects their name for the farm: *vreugde* means 'joy'. The farm is signposted 9km along the D2710, a turning to the west off the C38 about halfway between Outjo & Etosha's Andersson Gate. Accommodation is in traditionally decorated rooms or in chalets (1 for families) looking over a carefully tended lawn & flower-beds. These are individually & tastefully decorated in shades of creams & terracotta, with ceiling fans & cool stone floors. Allergy sufferers who struggle with thatch will appreciate the metal roofing of all but 2 of the rooms. Outside, mature trees provide plenty of shade & attract numerous birds, while in the centre, additional shade is afforded by a lapa that feels like an English summerhouse, albeit thatched & open to the breeze. There is a pool to one side & a braai area. Meals are served around a large table, giving guests the chance to find out about the farm, & drives or walks are also on offer. Longer guided day trips into Etosha can be arranged.

With its location just 40km/½hr from Etosha, the award-winning Vreugde is a well-recommended place to stop *en route* from Kaokoland, or for day trips into the national park. *DBB N$950–1,025/1,700–1,850 sgl/dbl.* **LLL**

 Buschberg Guest Farm (7 rooms, 1 pitch) \ 067 312143; m 081 279 5667; e info@buschberg.com; www.buschberg.com. Run by close friends of the Brands at Vreugde, this small guest farm lies 10km further west along the D2710, & on occasion takes the overspill from Vreugde. The farmhouse here is also surrounded by well-maintained gardens & there is a campsite. *DBB N$750/1,400 sgl/dbl; camping N$150 pp.* **LL**

Nearby mountains The hills of the Ugab Terrace, west of the town, deserve special mention for their unusual shapes. A particularly interesting section, signposted 'Ugab terraces', can be found near the Vingerklip, west of Outjo, about 9km south from the C39. There, some of the formations have been likened to castles from the Middle Ages. These are made of conglomerate, and stand on the edge of a plateau that stretches for more than 80km and eventually forms the northern boundary of the Ugab River valley. Because of differential erosion, only the harder section now remains – often sculpted rather spectacularly.

KAMANJAB

Just to the east of Damaraland, Kamanjab is a tiny town at the junction of the main C40 and C35. Its all-important 24-hour Shell garage is the last certain fuel stop before Ruacana if you're heading north – and comes as a relief to those driving south. The adjacent Kamanjab Stores is far better stocked than MultiSave across the road, though both have ATMs. Sadly, the Women's Craft Centre, Khâimaseni, opposite the fuel station was closed when we visited, and looked very unloved. Most people are just passing through, but the rock engravings at Peet Albert's Kopje could be worth a stop.

WHERE TO STAY, EAT AND DRINK

Oase Garni Guest House (19 rooms) \ 067 330032, reservations \ 061 237294; e oaseguesthouse@iway.na; www.exclusive. com.na. This small hotel right in the centre of town is popular both with local businesspeople and tourists wanting an overnight stop. Its rooms are at the back: clean & comfortable, with fans, mosi nets, a kettle for hot drinks, & en-suite shower & toilet. Dark wood lends a cosy atmosphere to the bar & restaurant (⊕ *daily*), where meals – from steaks & pizza to occasional African dishes – are available to all comers. If you're not in a hurry, you can visit a Himba village (*N$250 pp*) or Peet Albert's rock engravings. Back at base, relax in the beer garden by the swimming pool or indulge in a massage with the resident beautician. **$$**

Kamanjab Rest Camp & Game Park Lodge (4 chalets, 8 pitches) \ 067 330290; m 081 323 8370; e kamanjabrestcamp@iway.na; www.kamanjab-camp-namibia.com. 3km west of Kamanjab off the C40, this well-run restcamp is privately owned & very welcoming. Spotless twin-bed rooms are en suite, while campers share ablutions in the large, well-designed campsite. Here, 3 pitches each have power, & all have a water tap & a BBQ area. Guests can visit the small game park, home to antelope species including oryx, kudu & springbok, or dip in the small pool. This also makes an excellent lunch stop with, unusually for Namibia, home-grown salad. *Camping N$80 pp; no credit cards.* **$$**

Oppi Koppi (17 bungalows, camping) 067 330040; e info@oppi-koppi-kamanjab.com; www.oppi-koppi-kamanjab.com. Up a side road from the guesthouse, this Belgian-Dutch-owned spot was being redeveloped when last visited. At the time of writing, the campsite & about half of the bungalows were open. It now has a bar, pool & restaurant. *Camping N$90 pp.* **$$**

PEET ALBERT'S KOPJE Set among the granite hills, some 5km east of Kamanjab off the C40 to the left, this is the site of a large number of 2,000-year-old rock engravings. Many of these, including those depicting animals, were created by the San people, while the more geometric designs were the work of the Khoi. A further attraction is the 'gong rock', a granite boulder which resounds when struck, thus gaining the name.

Although designated a national monument, the site is quite overgrown. To visit independently, you'll need to pick up the key from Oppi Koppi in Kamanjab (⊕ 07.00–22.00 daily). This is also where you pay the admission fee (N$60 pp). From the gate to the entrance is a further 1.5km. There's a pamphlet entitled *The Rock-engravings at the Peet Alberts Koppie near Kamanjab*, but unfortunately getting hold of a copy is exceptionally difficult.

GUEST FARMS AROUND KAMANJAB

There are several guest farms around Kamanjab, especially to the south. Also nearby is a large private reserve, which in style is more like the private concession areas of southern Damaraland: **Huab Lodge** (see page 357).

AFRICAT NORTH (FORMERLY AFRI-LEO FOUNDATION)

Led by Tammy Hoth-Hanssen, the former Afri-Leo Foundation (*www.africat. org/about/africat-north*) was renamed AfriCat North in 2010, a reflection of many years of working closely with AfriCat (see box, page 411). Since 1997, the foundation has focused on 'the protection and conservation of wild lion populations in Namibia… in order to ensure the long-term survival of the species'. Central to this is encouraging communities to reinstate herdsmen and improve livestock kraals in order to reduce the number of livestock killed, leading to a greater tolerance of these animals among the farming community. AfriCat North monitors the movement of lions across the boundaries of Etosha National Park and the Hobatere Concession area, establishing lion numbers and movement patterns, and thereby offering an early warning system via GPS-satellite collars, and working to ensure that farmers adopt modern livestock management and protection methods.

Alongside this is a series of educational projects for schoolchildren across the region where they spend a couple of days learning through experiments on communal farmland – how to build a kraal, for example – about sustainability. If the highlight for many is the meals, the visits also provide hours of fun and interest for each child. It is Tammy's belief that if children understand the value of conservation, they will in turn spread the word among their own communities, and thus offer a greater chance to the lion – and to the environment as a whole.

Toko Lodge & Safaris (14 rooms, camping) ☎ 067 687095; e rustig@iway.na; www.tokolodgesafaris.com. Run by Karola & Nico Potgeiter, Toko is a traditional lodge, set in attractive gardens on a game farm of some 60km². It isn't for those in search of the glittery or fake, & you'll find no recently arranged attractions to tempt you, but the hospitality is warm & spontaneous, the birding good, & numerous activities are available. To find it, take the C35 8km north of Kamanjab, then follow the signs along the D2763 & D2695 for about 19km; it's then a further 6km to the gate along a reasonably well-maintained track. From the lodge, it takes about 2½hrs across the back roads to Etosha's Andersson Gate, & the interesting Peet Albert's Kopje is just around the corner for visitors to explore by themselves.

Each of the large, stone-floored rooms – some in the old farmhouse, others higher up with their own verandas overlooking the plains – has terracotta-painted walls, twin beds with mosquito nets, & a table & chairs; a stone-clad wall screens the en-suite facilities. A veranda runs along the outside of the old farmhouse, & there is a small pool with a good view. A lapa forms an extension to the original farmhouse, with a cool dining & lounge area, & bar. Toko also has a few good campsites in an area of mopane bush, a little way from the lodge. These are well set up with hot showers, flush toilets & a place to cook, or meals can be arranged in advance at the farmhouse.

Excursions, usually for 4 people, range from game drives around the farm (*N$150 pp, night N$200*), & tours of the farm's own Himba village (*N$180 pp*). *B&B from N$830/1,460 sgl/dbl; camping N$80 pp.* **LL**

Otjitotongwe Cheetah Guest Farm (6 rooms, camping) ☎ 067 687056; m 081 233 8802; e cheetahs@iway.na, www.cheetahparknamibia.com. Clearly named for its main attraction, Cheetah Guest Farm is a 7,000ha farm about 24km southeast of Kamanjab on the C40. Turn left on to the P2683 & 8km further you will find the reception; the lodge is another 2km from here. The farm has 4 tame cheetahs, as well as 15 wild ones within a 250ha area. There is game, too, including giraffe, oryx, kudu, mountain zebra & some smaller buck, & game drives or walks are an option. Day visitors are welcome by arrangement from 15.00/16.00 winter/summer, but not during the busy months of Jul, Aug & Sept.

Elaborate chalets are faced in local stone, & nearby is a camping area where overlanders have their own separate sector of the site. There is a bar/ dining area for lodge guests, & and a communal lapa with a vending machine selling drinks & snacks for campers. In the evening, atmospheric paraffin lanterns are used throughout, adding to the impression that this is neither a lodge nor a guest farm, but something in-between. *DBB N$800 pp, inc cheetah tour; camping N$300 pp, inc cheetah tour.* **LLL**

NORTH OF KAMANJAB The 291km stretch of road from Kamanjab north to Ruacana (see page 465) is tarred as far as the C41, then on good gravel. Initially it passes through ranch country, and then between the game areas of Hobatere and Etosha (note the high game fences here). After a checkpoint on the veterinary cordon fence, the land reverts to subsistence farms – so watch for domestic animals straying on to the road. From here the bush is bare: only mopane bushes and acacia survive the relentless onslaught of the local goats.

18

The Triangle and Bushmanland

The triangle of Otavi, Tsumeb and Grootfontein has long been one of the most prosperous areas of Namibia, rich both minerally and agriculturally. Geologists will find it particularly fascinating because of its interesting underground caverns and the famous Tsumeb mine, while the rolling farmland has a lush, well-watered feel that is seldom found south of here.

From the highlands, the old homelands of Hereroland and Bushmanland extend east to the Botswana border, sloping down from the agricultural plains of the central plateau into the endless, gently undulating Kalahari. This 'desert' is very different from the Namib, in landscape and people, although its population density is almost as low. This northeastern corner of the country is time-consuming, and even difficult, to visit, but offers a fascinating wilderness experience for those who are well prepared and make the time to reach it. It's also the home of many groups of San people: a draw for a small, but increasing, number of visitors.

OTAVI

Situated in a fertile farming area near one of the country's biggest irrigation schemes, this small town has the 24-hour Fourways Total service station on the main road that skirts around it to the east. Although the region's new gold and copper mines are equidistant between Otjiwarongo and Otavi, the latter has seen little benefit economically compared with Otjiwarongo and it remains quiet and sleepy. Some of the streets are tar, others are gravel.

Near Otavi are several interesting **cave systems** (see page 428), though visits to these need to be carefully organised in advance. Just 3km out of town, and exceedingly well signposted, is the **Khorab Memorial**, which marks the spot where the German colonial troops surrendered to the South African forces on 9 July 1915.

GETTING THERE AND AWAY
By train Passenger trains to Otavi are no longer operational.

By bus Intercape Mainliner's services from Windhoek to Livingstone and Victoria Falls stop at the Fourways Total service station in Otavi at 17.50 on Monday and Friday, and in the opposite direction at 01.20 on Monday and Thursday, with additional coaches to Windhoek at 01.30 daily except Thursday and Sunday. The one-way trip costs around N$260 to Windhoek, and N$430 to Victoria Falls. See pages 98–100 for more details.

The small local minibuses (normally VW combis) that link Otavi with Tsumeb and Grootfontein usually stop at the main Fourways service station, too, and this is probably also the best place from which to hitchhike.

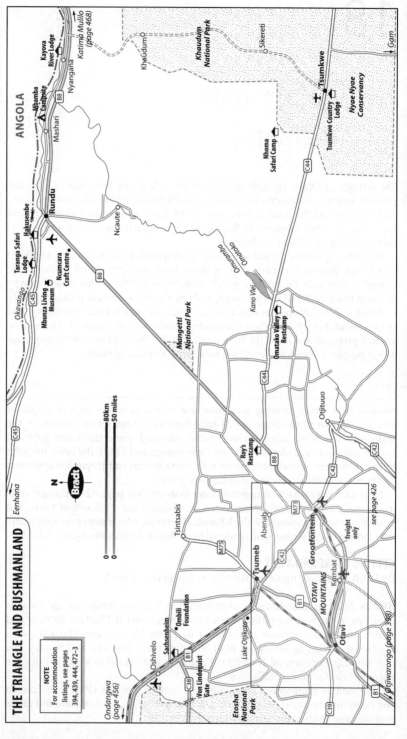

THE TRIANGLE AND BUSHMANLAND

NOTE
For accommodation listings, see pages 394, 439, 444, 472–3

Ondangwa (page 456)

Eenhana

ANGOLA

Katima Mulilo (page 468)

Kayova River Lodge

Mbamba Campsite

Nyangana

Mashari

Khaudum

Khaudum National Park

Sikereti

Gam

Nhoma Safari Camp

Tsumkwe

Tsumkwe Country Lodge

Nyae Nyae Conservancy

Rundu

Hakusembe

Taranga Safari Lodge

Mbunza Living Museum

Ncumcara Craft Centre

Ncaute

Okavango

Omuramba

Kano Vlei

Mangetti National Park

Omatako Valley Restcamp

Roy's Restcamp

Otjituuo

Tsintsabis

Otjiwarongo (page 398)

Tsumeb

Grootfontein

see page 426

Abenab

Kombat

freight only

Otavi

OTAVI MOUNTAINS

Oshivelo

Sachsenheim

Ombili Foundation

Von Lindequist Gate

Lake Otjikoto

Etosha National Park

80km
50 miles

N

Bradt

424

WHERE TO STAY

In town

Hotel Otavi & Grasdak Restaurant
(16 rooms, 3 chalets, 8 new rooms being built in 2014) 6 Park St; 067 234334; m 081 127 4913, 081 285 4388. The busy bar at the former Otavi Gardens Hotel seems also to act as reception & restaurant, & is a focal point for some of the town in the evening. All rooms are en suite with fans & tea/coffee-making facilities. En-suite chalets have AC & TV with dbl & twin beds. **$$$**

Palmenecke Guest House (7 rooms)
96 Hertzog Av; 067 234199; m 081 285 8400; e susan@africaonline.com.na; www.palmenecke.co.za. Alexander & Susan du Toit's immaculate & cheery B&B is set among pretty gardens under the palms. Bright, airy rooms are all en suite, with AC, Wi-Fi & DSTV. Guest facilities include a lapa & braai, a bar & restaurant (with a huge fireplace for chilly winter nights), a swimming pool, & secure parking. *B/fast N$60; dinner N$85.* **$$$**

Near Otavi
Map, page 426.

Khorab Lodge (14 chalets, 2 houses, camping) 067 234352; m 081 149 2670; e reservations@khorablodge.com; www.khorablodge.com. About 3km south of Otavi, Khorab is set back just off the main B1 to Otjiwarongo, & is a beautiful place to stop. The main building has a large, plush bar area, relaxing couches & a restaurant with a varied à la carte menu, all under high thatched ceilings. At the back, set around green lawns, herbaceous borders & even a small artificial stream, are 10 standard chalets, with tiled floors dotted with rugs, twin or dbl beds & airy thatched ceilings. They are large

& well built, using colourful fabrics, with fans & en-suite showers & WC. New luxury chalets, built further back facing the bush, are decorated in a very modern style with a leather day bed, & have AC, DSTV, fridge, microwave, iron & even a dinky folding ironing board. Set apart, each within its own walled garden, are 3-bed family houses with fully fitted kitchen, laundry & flat-screen TV. Wi-Fi is available in the central area. There is also a well-equipped campsite, & a large pool with fitness area. Note that some rooms can be noisy at night with traffic on the B1. *B&B N$510 pp; camping N$100 pp.* **LL**

Zum Potjie Restcamp (5 bungalows, camping) 067 234300; e info@zumpotjie.com; www.zumpotjie.com. Signposted from the B1 to Tsumeb, 6km north of Otavi, Zum Potjie is 2km off the main road. In a lovely, unpretentious smallholding, home to Friedrich & Erika Diemer, each of the twin-bed bungalows is clean & simple with a basic, prefabricated design & en-suite shower & WC, while camping pitches have braais, excellent ablution blocks, power & water. A small swimming pool is set in the well-tended garden, food is available in the small restaurant & bar, which is decorated with an amazing collection of African artefacts, & laundry can be arranged.

There is a botanic walking trail, & a quirky & rather fascinating farm museum full of the owners' family memorabilia over the generations. Guests can take short trips guided by Friedrich, & Erika's homemade jams, served at b/fast, are also for sale, as is game for braais. Dinner N$140; B&B *N$420/760 sgl/dbl; camping N$80 pp, plus electricity N$35 per pitch.* **L**

WHERE TO EAT AND DRINK You'll find fish and chips at the Fruit Store, and drinks at Ot-Quell Bottle Stall or the supermarkets. Alternatively, there's Grasdak Restaurant at Hotel Otavi or the Camel Inn Restaurant at the Fourways service station, where you can stop for steaks and ribs and a drink. Or 3km south of town is Khorab Lodge restaurant, with its à la carte menu including steaks, fish, pasta and salads.

OTHER PRACTICALITIES There are two **fuel** stations – Fourways next to the main road and Circle in the centre of town – and very good Spar and OK **supermarkets**. Cymot (067 221161) has a branch on Rheinhold Shilongo Street.

There are branches of Standard, Bank Windhoek and First National **banks**, and the small post office offers **internet** facilities, albeit on the slow side.

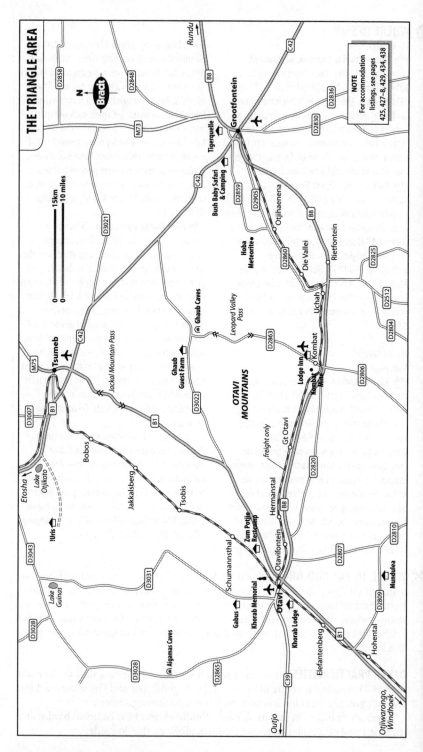

THE TRIANGLE AREA

NOTE
For accommodation
listings, see pages
425, 427–8, 429, 434, 438

N

0   15km
0   10 miles

Rundu

C42

D2858

D2848

D2836

D2830

B8

Grootfontein ✈

Tigerquelle

Bush Baby Safari
& Camping

D2859   D2905

Otjihaenena

Hoba
Meteorite   D2860   Die Vallei   Rietfontein   D2825

D2823

D3021

C42

Ghaub Caves

Leopard Valley
Pass   D2863   Uchab   D2512

D2804

D2806

Ghaub
Guest Farm

OTAVI
MOUNTAINS   Lodge Inn ✈   Kombat   Kombat
Mine

Tsumeb ✈

M75

Jackal Mountain Pass

D3022

D3007

B1

B1

freight only   Gt Otavi   D2820

D2810

Bobos

Jakkalsberg

Tsobis

Hermanstal   B8   D2807

Etosha   Lake
Otjikoto

!Uris   Schumannsthal

Zum Potjie
Restcamp

Otavifontein   D2809

Mundulea

Lake
Guinas   D3031   Gabus   Otavi ✈   Mundulea

D3043   Khorab Memorial

Khorab Lodge

D3028   Algamas Caves   D2865   Elefantenberg   B1   Hohental

C39

D3028   Outjo   Otjiwarongo,
Windhoek

AROUND OTAVI

Nearby guest farms *Map, opposite.*

✴ 🏠 **Ghaub Guest Farm** (10 rooms) ✆067 240188; ℯ info@ghaub.com, ghaub@iway.na; www.ghaub.com. Situated in the Otavi Mountains, in the heart of the Triangle, Ghaub was originally founded as a mission station in 1895. It lies some 60km northeast of Otavi, & 50km from Tsumeb, on the south side of the D3022, about 3km west of its junction with the D2863. The 11,800ha reserve is today owned by former guest Andrew Compion. As a guest farm, it has successfully retained a lot of character, with high ceilings & plenty of space, especially in the recently upgraded rooms. Each is en suite, clean & well cared for, with twin beds & a large veranda with impressive views of the surrounding land & hills; these include 3 family units sleeping 4. There are also 3 lovely campsite pitches with private ablutions, kitchens, braai, electricity & water, & campers can use the pool & restaurant if the bungalows aren't busy. There's Wi-Fi access in reception. Tours of the Ghaub Caves (see page 428), 3.5km away, are organised from here. Other activities include farm drives, nature drives & walking trails. The atmosphere is informal & friendly, thanks to the engaging manager Mika Shapwanale, who has been here for 16 years.

Ghaub is recommended for a few nights if you want somewhere to relax by the pool, & perhaps do a little gentle walking – provided that you don't mind a lack of must-see attractions in the vicinity. *Dinner N$220; B&B low season N$900/1,300 sgl/dbl, high season N$1,100/1,800; camping N$200 pp.* **LLL**

🏠 **Mundulea** (4 walk-in tents) ✆064 403123; ℯ turn@iafrica.com.na; www.turnstone-tours. com. Biodiversity is the watchword for one of the most intriguing & fulfilling back-to-nature experiences in Namibia's fast-expanding repertoire: Mundulea. A private reserve established in 2001, it covers 120km² of prime bush & mountain savannah in the ancient Otavi karstveldt. This lime & marble landscape spans dolomite ridges, steep gorges & underground caverns. Deep subterranean water feeds spreading trees & the rich soil provides fertile ground for a huge diversity of animal, bird & plant life.

The reserve is surprisingly easy to find. Driving southwest from Otavi, keep to the main B1 for 20km. Just before the railway bridge, turn left on to the D2809 & drive a further 10km on good gravel road. As it bears round to the left, you'll see Mundulea's entrance gate on your right; it will be open if you are expected (booking is essential). Follow the farm road for about 15mins to reach the old lime-and-clay farmhouse at the top of the hill. Here you'll be met by Mundulea's owner, Bruno Nebe, who personally takes guests out for 4 days on walking trails, developed to give visitors a chance to get out into the natural environment at the end of a long, round-Namibia journey. Numbers are kept small – maybe 2 or 3 couples – & walks can be gentle rambles or more serious hikes, according to the interests & pace of individual guests. But they always revolve around what occurs naturally, giving a real sense of exploration & minimising disturbance.

Bruno has set out to restore the area to its former importance as the heartland of Namibia's game populations. With everything in its favour in terms of natural habitat, high rainfall & low human impact, Mundulea has made a gradual transition from a heavily fenced cattle ranch to a low-profile but very successful wildlife sanctuary.

There are good numbers of eland, which thrive in the privacy of the hills & valleys. Kudu, oryx, hartebeest, wildebeest, duiker, steenbok, dik-dik & warthog are common sights, while newly introduced species such as giraffe, tsessebe, mountain zebra & roan are becoming easier to spot as their numbers increase. There are also leopard, cheetah, & brown & spotted hyena, as well as rarities like pangolin, aardvark & bushbabies. Doing particularly well is a group of indigenous black-faced impala. Having veered dangerously towards extinction, this essentially Namibian subspecies was the initial *raison d'être* for Mundulea, which Bruno envisaged as a safe haven for Namibia's critically endangered endemic game species. Working closely with the Ministry of Environment & Tourism & international researchers, Mundulea is also proud custodian of several black rhino, including the last of the subspecies *Bicornis chobiensis*. A successful breeding programme to keep this bloodline flowing is in operation, & you'll hear more of this project during your visit.

For birders, Mundulea has notched up some 230 species, while for the more geologically inclined, the reserve offers a fascinating array of rock formations, with the chance to explore caves & caverns. There are fossils dating back to key periods in African palaeontology.

Accommodation has been recently upgraded, with as little disturbance as possible to the natural surroundings. Each of the large tented rooms has a private, covered *stoep*, or porch, & an en-suite bathroom, with hot & cold running water. Wooded footpaths connect the tents with the dining area, with protected hides looking over a well-frequented waterhole.

Delicious meals – natural, wholesome food with a stylish twist – are prepared on an open fire in a bushcamp kitchen: Thai calamari with coconut or pan-fried kudu fillet vie with the traditional braai for supper. A light b/fast before a short morning wander is followed by a hearty brunch & the main walk of the day – which varies each day – to explore Mundulea's contrasting landscapes, diverse habitat & wildlife.

Getting acquainted with this place, with Bruno & the project is seriously worthwhile for visitors who want to look a little deeper into Namibia's environmental issues. Mundulea is an ideal 'last stop' on the way back to Windhoek, an opportunity to explore the bush properly in the company of an outstanding guide. But be warned, guests tend to find themselves drawn back to Mundulea & the ideas it embodies time & time again.

4 days/3 nights N$11,900 pp sharing (4–5 people), N$13,900 pp sharing (2–3 people). **LLLLL**

🏠 **Gabus Game Ranch** (9 rooms, cottage, camping) 📞 067 234291; m 081 127 9278; e office@gabusnamibia.com; www.gabusnamibia.com. Gabus Farm, north of Otavi, has been in the Kuehl family for 4 generations, & has been developed into a comfortable guest farm by its current owners, Heidi & Heinz Kuehl. To get here, take the C39 towards Outjo for 2km, then turn right on to the D3031 for a further 8km. Accommodation is well thought out for everyone from couples & honeymooners to families. All rooms are fresh & spacious, with en-suite bath & WC, AC, tea/coffee facilities & hairdryers. These – & all of the areas open to guests – overlook a waterhole which is the focus of kudu, eland, waterbuck, impala, springbok & hartebeest, among other wildlife. Activities include game drives & guided hikes with Heinz. They also offer an adventurous day trip to some stunning caves on a neighbouring farm – but be warned, it's not for the faint-hearted. A new campsite has been built close to the lodge with ablution blocks, power & water. *Dinner N$220; game drive N$300; B&B N$1,018/1,628 sgl/dbl; camping N$100 pp.* **LLL**

Cave systems

The area around Otavi doesn't have a wealth of big attractions, unless your passion is caves. In that case, plan to spend quite a lot of time here, as there are many systems to explore – although for some you'll need to plan in advance.

Ghaub Caves

(*Guided tour N$180/2hrs*) On the Ghaub Farm, 50km northeast of Otavi, are some caves famous for their stalactites (but no Bushman paintings, as the farm owners are at pains to point out). Designated a national monument, they are signposted from the D2863, from where you can drive to the entrance – and a locked gate. This must be booked in advance by phoning the farm (see page 427) to organise a guide and a heavy-duty torch; you cannot visit independently, and the place is not suitable for a casual visit. From the entrance, after some steep steps for around 20m, it's a scramble over rocks, which get very slippery when wet. The reward, however, is a network of caves extending for some 2.5km, of which around 2km are accessible.

Aigamas Caves

Some 33km northwest of Otavi, on a tectonic fault-line, this cave system is about 5km long. It has aroused particular interest as the home of *Clarias cavernicola*, a species of catfish that appears to be endemic to this cave system, although it is now threatened by falling water levels. These fish are a translucent light pink in colour and totally blind, having evolved for life in the perpetual darkness of these caves. Interestingly, their breeding habits are still unknown and no young fish have ever been found.

To visit the cave, make arrangements at the municipal offices in Otavi, next to the restcamp. This may take several days.

Uiseb Caves   More extensive than Ghaub, these caves have chambers and passages containing some impressive stalactites With no facilities at all, they are described as 'unspoilt' and arr these, too, must be made at the municipal offices in Otavi.

Kombat   Memorable largely for its name, Kombat is just off the halfway between Otavi and Grootfontein, and is known in Namibia for its mine. This accounts for a thriving little centre, where you'll find the Tierkloof Butchery and General Dealers, and a small post office. Turn off here for the Leopard Valley Pass.

Where to stay *Map, page 426.*
 Lodge Inn (5 rooms) ☎ 067 231149; m 081 124 0714; e kombatlodge@iway.na. Has 5 clean | & simple rooms, a pool & restaurant in a thatch & brick building. **L**

✳TSUMEB

The attractive town of Tsumeb stands in the north of the central plateau, an area of rich farmland and great mineral wealth. Its wide streets are lined with bougainvillea and jacaranda trees, and in the centre of town is a large, green park, a favourite for the townspeople during their lunch break.

Economically the town was dominated by the Tsumeb Corporation which, in the early 1990s, mined a rich ore pipe here for copper, zinc, lead, silver, germanium, cadmium and the variety of unusual crystals for which Tsumeb is world famous. Tsumeb's one pipe has produced about 217 different minerals and gemstones, 40 of which have been found nowhere else on earth. However, in the late 1990s this closed, badly affecting the town. Although the mine has since been reopened for specimen mining, this isn't on a fraction of the scale of the original operation.

Fortunately, Tsumeb still retains some light industries, and is close enough to Etosha to benefit from a steady flow of tourists. It remains a pleasant place to visit, and doesn't have any of the air of depression that you might expect given the erstwhile importance of the mine.

GETTING THERE AND AWAY   The largest of the Triangle's towns, Tsumeb once had the best connections. Today, though, although the town has its own airstrip, it is rarely used by visitors, and there are no scheduled flights into the region.

As in the rest of northern Namibia, there are no longer any passenger **trains** to Tsumeb.

By bus   Intercape Mainliner's services from Windhoek arrive in Tsumeb at the Engen/Wimpy Gateway on Omeg Allee on Monday and Friday at 18.35, and daily excluding Tuesday and Saturday at 23.35. The return journey is on Monday and Thursday, departing from Tsumeb at 00.35, and daily excluding Thursday and Sunday at 00.45. A one-way ticket costs from N$320.

On Sunday and Wednesday, buses leave Victoria Falls for Tsumeb at 10.00, arriving at 00.30 the next morning; they return on Mondays and Fridays, leaving Tsumeb at 18.40, and arriving at 10.30 the following day. One-way fares start at N$500; see *Chapter 6*, pages 98–100, for details. For tickets, contact Travel North Namibia (see page 431), who also run their own shuttle services to Windhoek three times a week.

For more local transport, keep a lookout for the small minibuses (normally VW combis) that link the Triangle towns. Both south- and northbound combis arrive and depart at the old Caltex garage on Hage G Geingob Drive.

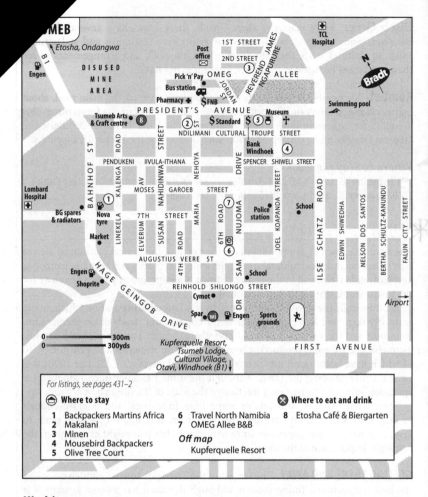

For listings, see pages 431–2

Where to stay

1. Backpackers Martins Africa
2. Makalani
3. Minen
4. Mousebird Backpackers
5. Olive Tree Court

6. Travel North Namibia
7. OMEG Allee B&B

Off map
Kupferquelle Resort

Where to eat and drink

8. Etosha Café & Biergarten

Hitching Hitching from central Tsumeb is difficult. You must first get yourself to the main junction of the B1 and the C42 (see *By bus*, page 429). If you're going south, then hitch on Dr Sam Nujoma Drive, about 500m after leaving town, before the caravan park.

ORIENTATION
Street name changes Various street names have been changed in Tsumeb in the last few years. Although in theory these are now in place, many people still refer to the original names, so the following may be useful:

2nd Road *is now* Elverum Avenue
3rd Road *is now* Susan Nahidinwa Street
10th Road *is now* Edwin Shiwedha
11th Road *is now* Nelson dos Santos
12th Road *is now* Bertha Schultz-Kanundu
13th Road *is now* Falun City Street
3rd Street *is now* Ndilimani Cultural Troupe Street

4th Street *is now* Pendukeni Iivula-Ithana Street
5th Street *is now* Maria Nehoya Street
6th Street *is now* Moses Garoëb Street
8th Road *is now* Joel Koapanda Street
Hospital Street *is now* Rev James Ngapurure Street
Main Street *is now* President's Avenue
Omeg Allee *is now* Dr Sam Nujoma Drive
Post Street *is now* Omeg Allee

TOURIST INFORMATION

Travel North Namibia Dr Sam Nujoma Dr; 067 220728; m 081 299 4214; e info@travelnorthguesthouse.com; www. travelnorthguesthouse.com. Tsumeb's unofficial tourist information centre is about 300m from the main traffic lights. Here you'll find an extensive range of leaflets & information from around the country, an internet café, & helpful, efficient staff who can sort out travel problems. They are agents for Intercape & Europcar in the north, run their own transfer service to & from Windhoek & offer comfortable guesthouse accommodation (see page 432). They also have a hair & beauty salon on the premises, & delicious homemade cakes.

WHERE TO STAY, EAT AND DRINK *Map, opposite.*

With established hotels, guesthouses, a restcamp and a couple of places for backpackers, Tsumeb has something for everyone. Most visitors eat in their hotels, with the restaurants at the Makalani and the Minen being the most popular.

Kupferquelle Resort (40 rooms, camping) 067 220139; m 081 148 6895; e booking@ kupferquelle.com; www.kupferquelle.com. Occupying a tree-shaded site about halfway between the town & the main road intersection, some 1km from each, this large resort boasts a range of chalet accommodation as well as a campsite with 27 pitches. With a popular Dros Steakhouse restaurant & swimming pool on site, too, this could be a good option for those just passing through. *Camping N$115 per site per day, plus N$57.50 pp.* **$$$**

Minen Hotel (49 rooms) Omeg Allee; 067 221071/2; e contact@minen-hotel.com; www.minen-hotel.com. The friendly Minen is in an attractive spot opposite the park. Its more modern twin rooms are set round a courtyard with a swimming pool & a beautiful lush garden, while older but refurbished dbls overlook a 2nd courtyard. All have AC/heating & fan, en-suite WC & shower or bath, TV & fridge. Rooms are almost out of earshot of the busy bar at the front, which can become quite lively at w/ends, especially at the end of the month when people are paid.

To the side of the hotel is a pleasant outdoor veranda with umbrella-shaded tables & chairs: a popular spot for lunch or drinks. Inside is a more formal restaurant (⊕ *18.00–21.30 daily).* **$$$**

Makalani Hotel (28 rooms) Ndilimani Cultural Troupe St; 067 221051; e reservation@ makalanihotel.com; www.makalanihotel.com. This smart & efficient hotel, distinctively painted in yellow with green windows, is right in the centre of town. Rooms are comfortable with (firm!) twin beds, direct-dial phones, AC & satellite TV. The restaurant is small & friendly, with a reasonable if not adventurous à la carte menu; alternatively, meals may be taken by the pool or in the rustic bar. Other facilities include a private bar & gambling. **$$**

Mousebird Backpackers (4 rooms, 6 dorm beds) Cnr Pendukeni Iivula-Ithana & Joel Koapanda sts; 067 221777; m 081 272 2650; e info@mousebird-namibia.com; www.namibweb. com/mousebird.htm. In the centre of town, near the museum, the colourful Mousebird is aimed squarely at backpackers, with private twin or dbl rooms (1 en suite), dorm accommodation & camping on the lawn. There's a fully equipped kitchen & dining room, with free tea & coffee. The small bar area is usually busy &, for those who miss electronic home comforts, there is a satellite TV, a collection of videos & a PlayStation, with internet access at extra cost. Outside are a braai area & secure parking. *Dorm bed N$120; camping N$90 pp.* **$$**

Olive Tree Court (2 self-catering apts) President's Av, next to Tsumeb Museum; m 081 272

9852; e mandypas@iway.na. These new 1-bedroom flats opened in Apr 2014 in an excellent location opposite the park. With a fresh, modern décor, they have an open-plan, fully equipped kitchenette/lounge with sleeper couch, bedroom with 2 twin beds & shower-room. Facilities include AC, DSTV, DVD player & Wi-Fi, with free tea & coffee & homemade muffins to welcome guests. Secure parking. **$$**

🏠 **OMEG Allee B&B** (9 rooms) Dr Sam Nujoma Dr; 📞067 220631; e omegalle@gmail.com. This immaculate B&B, named after both a railway company & the town's first mine (Otavi Minen Eisenbahn Gesellschaft), has 7 dbl & 2 sgl rooms, all with AC, en-suite showers, satellite TV, fridge, kettle, hairdryer & safe. **$$**

🏠 **Travel North Namibia** (8 rooms) Dr Sam Nujoma Dr; 📞067 220728; m 081 299 4214; e info@travelnorthguesthouse.com; www.travelnorthguesthouse.com. Although Travel North is not an official tourist information office, staff here are particularly helpful (see page 431) & also run a friendly guesthouse with en-suite dbl & twin rooms (& 1 with a private bathroom across the corridor), each with AC, Wi-Fi, DSTV, fridge, tea/coffee facilities & braai. There's a pleasant garden

& play area for children with an excellent coffee shop, a hair & beauty salon, & a launderette. It also has 24hr reception, useful for those arriving on the Intercape services. **$$**

🏠 **Backpackers Martins Africa** (16 rooms, 11 dorm beds) Linekela Kalenga; 📞067 220310; f 067 222964. While still operating some rooms, this classic backpackers' place was undergoing extensive refurbishment at the time of research & will be changing to a more upmarket guesthouse in due course. Currently, its en-suite rooms have AC, TV, fridge & kettle, as do 2 family rooms (4 beds & sleeper couch). Standard rooms have ceiling fan & share several showers & WCs with the 4 dorm rooms. The central areas have chairs & tables, & TV, as well as a fully equipped self-catering kitchen & laundry facilities, a BBQ area, pool & children's playground. No meals are served here. *Dorm bed N$200.* **$**

🍴 **Etosha Café & Biergarten** (5 rooms) President's Av; 📞067 221207; m 081 127 3855; ⏰ 07.00–17.00 Mon–Fri, 08.00–14.00 Sat. This pleasant café with a relaxing garden at the back offers light lunches, as well as coffee & cake. It also sells a range of local books & postcards, & has basic rooms. **$$**

OTHER PRACTICALITIES There are several **fuel stations** around town, many of them open 24 hours. President's Avenue has branches of FNB, Standard and Bank Windhoek **banks**. Travel North Namibia offers **internet** access at N$30/hr.

The mine has made Tsumeb relatively rich, and its main shopping street is often bustling, with various clothes shops, take-aways and curio outlets. With a branch of Shoprite in the new Le Platz Shopping Centre on Hage G Geingob Drive, as well as the Pick 'n' Pay supermarket at one end of Omeg Allee (opposite the post office), and Spar in 9th Street, food shopping is not a problem either. Barry Jacobs Apteek (📞 067 222190, a/h 📞 067 220508) is the place to call if you're in need of medication.

The police are reached on 📞067 10111, the hospital and ambulance service on 📞067 224300/221082, and the fire service on 📞067 221004 (a/h m 081 124 8677). There is also a private hospital (📞067 221001) serving the mine, which may be able to help in an emergency.

WHAT TO SEE AND DO With parts of the old De Wet Mine, whose entrance was in the centre of town, to be opened to visitors, Tsumeb's mining heritage is set to become a focus for tourism with the opening to visitors of the De Wet shaft and other areas of the mine, including the smelter. Other attractions include:

Tsumeb Museum (*President's Av;* ⏰ *09.00–noon & 14.00–17.00 Mon–Fri, 09.00–noon Sat, other times by special arrangement; admission N$25*) Facing the park, next to a beautiful Lutheran church, is one of Namibia's best little museums. It has an excellent section on the region's geology and exhibits many of the rare minerals collected from the mine. It also has displays on the German colonial forces, and a small section on

THE GREATEST CRYSTAL-PRODUCING MINE ON EARTH

Mining was started in the place now known as Tsumeb well before historical records were kept. Then it's thought that the San, who were known to have settlements at Lake Otjikoto, 24km away, were probably attracted by the hill's green colour, and perhaps mined malachite here. This they probably then traded with Ovambo people who would smelt it to extract the copper. Perhaps the earliest records of this are from the writings of Francis Galton who, in 1851, met both Bushmen and Ovambos transporting copper near Otjikoto.

In 1893, Matthew Rogers came to the Green Hill here for about a year, sinking test mine shafts and concluding that there was a major deposit of copper and lead, along with quantities of other commodities including gold and silver. Similar tests in 1893 and 1900 quantified this further; all suggested a very rich area for minerals and ore.

To exploit this deposit, a railway was built in 1905 and 1906, linking Tsumeb with Walvis Bay. By 1907 the mine was producing high-grade copper and lead ores. Despite halting production during World War I and World War II, mining expanded steadily. By 1947 the mine extended to 576m below the surface, and most of the higher levels of the mine had been exhausted. Further investigations showed the existence of more reserves.

Various changes in ownership of the mine occurred after the wars. By 1966 the mine had produced over nine million tonnes of ore; its reserves were estimated at eight million tonnes. However, in May 1996 mining ceased in some of the deeper levels (which, by then, were around 1,650m below the surface) because the cost of pumping out water from these levels had finally outweighed the cost of the ore recovered. This was the beginning of the end. In June one of the main shafts was flooded after its pumps were switched off, and a large strike (July/August 1996) finally stopped mining operations, and the mine closed.

As well as producing huge quantities of ore, Tsumeb was described as 'the greatest crystal-producing mine on earth' for its amazing variety of geological specimens, crystals and minerals. Numerous rare minerals had been found here, some completely unique to Tsumeb. Unfortunately, a specialist mining company that started mining the upper levels of the complex in 2000, looking for one-off 'specimens', ceased operations just two years later. Other operations, albeit on a larger scale, have so far met with a similar fate, and now it looks as though tourism will be the latest seam to be mined.

the lifestyle of the Bushmen, Ovambo, Herero, Kavango and Himba people. Train buffs will be drawn to the gleaming steam engines outside the museum, as well as to exhibitions covering the construction of the Otavi railway line from Swakopmund to Otavi – though Otavi itself is no longer served by passenger trains.

The Khorab Room contains old German weaponry, recovered from Lake Otjikoto, which was dumped there by the retreating German forces in 1915 to prevent the rapidly advancing Union troops from capturing it. Since that time, pieces have been recovered periodically, the most recent being the Sandfontein cannon on display here. Also on display is the uniform of the German Schutztruppe (colonial troops), along with the photo album of one of them, General von Trotha, which makes fascinating reading if your German is good. Appropriately, the museum is located in a historic German school dating from 1915, now a national monument.

ɔingana Kondombolo Cultural Village \ *067 220787;* ⊕ *08.00–*
ɔn–Fri, 08.00–13.00 Sat–Sun & hols by arrangement; admission N$55/17
ɔd, although at the time of research there were suggestions that this might be
reduced) Facing the park, between the old municipal campsite (now Kupferquelle)
and the centre of town, is a relatively new building which was constructed with
Norwegian funds and modelled on the fort at Namutoni. Open-air displays on
most of the country's main ethnic groupings and their traditional housing make for
a worthwhile visit. There's also a small curio shop.

Tsumeb Arts and Crafts Centre (*TACC; 18 President's Av;* \ *067 220257;*
⊕ *08.30–13.00 & 14.30–17.00 Mon–Fri, 08.30–13.00 Sat*) Next to the Etosha Café
and Biergarten, the TACC is a charitable trust set up to help develop the skills
of Namibian artists and craftspeople. It provides them with a base, training and
some help in marketing their produce – including this shop selling their work at a
reasonable price, with no haggling or pressure to buy. It's well worth a visit.

AROUND TSUMEB
Nearby lodges
Map, page 426.

!Uris Safari Lodge (14 rooms, camping)
\ 067 221818/220248; e reservations@uris-
safari-lodge-namibia.com; www.uris-safari-
lodge-namibia.com. Access to this lodge is from
the B1, 10km west of Tsumeb, from where it's a
further 12km through a private 17,000ha game
reserve. Dbl & family rooms are laid out in pairs in
renovated mine cottages, with these & the central
building alike under steep thatch. A Moroccan
twist prevails, with coloured glass lanterns,
silvered chairs, traditional rugs & deep cushions,
while in the en-suite rooms, following the theme,
are tasselled mosquito net 'tents', as well as AC,
kettle, hairdryer, safe & phone. Family rooms have
a loft area for children aged 6–12.

There's an attractive swimming pool with in-
water loungers, set in luscious gardens; a function
area known as 'the chapel' that is available for
weddings; & a conference room. Check out the
underground wine cellar, which is flooded every
couple of days to keep the humidity balanced for the
cigars also stored there. Wi-Fi is available in reception.

At the campsite in the hills, about 5km from
the lodge, only ablutions & water are provided,
so campers must take everything they need.
However, new pitches next to the lodge have
private ablutions, power & light, & are very
convenient for the restaurant (*b/fast N$85; lunch
N$95; dinner N$165*).

Walking trails lead visitors in the footsteps
of the 19th-century miners, who scoured the
landscape for signs of valuable minerals for
export – copper was first mined in Namibia here
– while guided tours take you underground into
a derelict mine with its machinery still in place.
Various drives in game-viewing vehicles take in
the reserve's wildlife, including eland & kudu. *B&B
N$1,245/1,904 sgl/dbl; camping N$150.* **LLL**

Lake Otjikoto About 20km north of Tsumeb, just west of the B1, this lake (once
thought to be bottomless) was formed when the roof of a huge subterranean cave
collapsed, leaving an enormous sinkhole with steep sides. Together with Lake
Guinas, the lake is home to a highly coloured population of fish: the southern
mouthbrooder (*Pseudocrenilabrus philander*). These have attracted much scientific
interest for changes in their colour and behaviour as a result of this restricted
environment. Now the lake is also home to some *Tilapia guinasana*, which are
endemic to Lake Guinas but have been introduced here to aid their conservation.

Sub-aqua enthusiasts regularly dive in the lake's green waters and have recovered
a lot of weaponry that was dumped in 1915 by the retreating German forces. Much
is now on display in Tsumeb Museum (see pages 432–3), though some is still at the
bottom of the lake.

Andersson and Galton passed this way in May 1851, and noted:

> After a day and a half travel, we suddenly found ourselves on the brink of Otjikoto, the most extraordinary chasm it was ever my fortune to see. It is scooped, so to say, out of the solid limestone rock... The form of Otjikoto is cylindrical; its diameter upwards of four hundred feet, and its depths, as we ascertained by the lead-line, two hundred and fifteen... To about thirty feet of the brink, it is filled with water.

After commenting that the local residents could remember no variation in its height, and musing on where its supply of water came from, Andersson described how he and Galton:

> standing in need of a bath, plunged head-foremost into the profound abyss. The natives were utterly astounded. Before reaching Otjikoto, they had told us, that if a man or beast was so unfortunate as to fall into the pool, he would inevitably perish.
>
> We attributed this to superstitious notions; but the mystery was now explained. The art of swimming was totally unknown in these regions. The water was very cold, and, from its great depth, the temperature is likely to be the same throughout the year.
>
> We swam into the cavern to which the allusion has just been made. The transparency of the water, which was of the deepest sea-green, was remarkable; and the effect produced in the watery mirror by the reflection of the crystallized walls and roof of the cavern, appeared very striking and beautiful...
>
> Otjikoto contained an abundance of fish, somewhat resembling perch; but those that we caught were not much larger than one's finger. We had several scores of these little creatures for dinner, and very palatable they proved.

The lake has changed little since then, except perhaps for its water level, which has lowered as a reflection of the area's water table: the gradual diminution of the groundwater around here is a threat to the lake's future. For most visitors, though, it represents something of an anticlimax – although experienced divers relish the challenge of exploring the lake's depths.

In terms of practicalities, there's a N$50 entrance fee. Drinks and curios are available from dawn until dusk, and there's a craft shop on site, but camping is no longer permitted. A small enclosure houses eland, ostrich and warthog, and there's also an aviary and a croc pool.

Lake Guinas On a private farm with access for visitors, 32km west of Tsumeb, Lake Guinas, with its blue waters, is deeper and more attractive than Otjikoto, though there are no facilities at all. To get there, take the B1 towards Ondangwa, turn left on to the D3043, and then left again after 19km on to the D3031. The lake is about 5km along, near the road. It is home to a colourful species of cichlid fish, *Tilapia guinasana*, which is endemic here. In recent years these fish have been introduced into Otjikoto and several reservoirs to safeguard their future.

Ombili Foundation (⚲ 067 230050; e info@ombili.de; www.ombili.de) Established in 1989 by a group of farmers, the Ombili Foundation aims to help the San people to adapt to the demands of the 21st century. It is based on a farm north of Tsumeb, on which areas have been set aside for both foraging and gardening, as well as cattle. The foundation has its own nursery and primary schools, as well as a community centre, workshop and shop for the essentials. Aside from being an interesting project in its own right, Bushman crafts are on sale.

Visitors are welcome to visit by appointment (⊕ *07.00–noon Mon–Fri*). To get there, take the B1 northwest from Tsumeb for around 55km, then turn off right on to the D3004 for a further 20km. The farm is off that road to the right.

GROOTFONTEIN

This small, bustling town is found at the northern end of the central plateau, amid rich farmland. For the visitor, Grootfontein has few intrinsic attractions, but it is the gateway to both Bushmanland and the Caprivi Strip. If you are heading to either, then resting here or in the environs for a night will allow you to tackle the long drive ahead in the cool of the morning.

There have been incidents of theft from tourist vehicles in the town, so stay on your guard. Typically a gang will approach a vehicle with open windows; some will distract the driver, while others steal from the other side of the vehicle. (As far as I know, there has never been any violence reported.)

GETTING THERE AND AWAY

By bus Intercape Mainliner's services between Windhoek and Victoria Falls stop on the main road at Maroela Motors. For Victoria Falls, these depart on Monday and Friday at 19.15. Southbound they depart on Sunday and Wednesday at 23.50. One-way tickets cost around N$387 to Windhoek, and N$420 to Victoria Falls. See *Chapter 6*, pages 98–100, for details.

Hitching Hitching from Grootfontein is relatively easy with a clear sign, as most traffic passes through town. Alternatively, talk to drivers at the fuel stations.

🏠 **WHERE TO STAY** Grootfontein does not have any really impressive places to stay, but both the hotel and guesthouses are adequate for brief stops, and there are a couple more options just a short distance from the town.

In town
Map, opposite.

🏠 **The Courtyard** (8 rooms) 2 Gauss St (top of Hidipo Hamutenya); ✆067 240215; e kenl@iway. na. This popular guesthouse is centred on a small courtyard, with a pool under palms & a sausage tree, with airy en-suite rooms having AC, DSTV, ceiling fan, fridge, kettle & hairdryer. Older-style rooms feature the kiaat-wood furniture typical of the Grootfontein region. There's an atmospheric bar in the thatched lapa & courtyard, & a restaurant serving a huge range of pizzas (inc take-away service) along with an à la carte menu. Wi-Fi access payable by voucher. **$$$**

🏠 **Meteor Travel Inn** (13 rooms) Cnr Okavango Rd & Hage Geingob St; ✆067 242078/9; e meteor@ iway.na. The Meteor's rooms are laid out around a courtyard at the back. Each has AC or fan, those with AC costing more, & free Wi-Fi. It isn't luxurious, but neither is it at all dingy, as small-town hotels often are. Lunch, dinner & drinks are served in a thatched lapa beneath banana trees, or in the

main restaurant. On Friday evenings pizzas are the speciality, from purpose-built brick ovens. **$$**

🏠 **OLEA Town Lodge & Caravan Park** (24 rooms, camping) ✆067 243040; e oleatownlodge@iway.na. This small camp is close to the centre of town, near the museum. It was being renovated at the time of our visit, with some rooms closed, but has 9 camp pitches & en-suite rooms in 4 accommodation blocks. The mosquitoes are bad in the rainy season &, being so close to town, you should always take precautions to avoid theft; it has secure fencing & a security gate. There is a small bar, & steaks can be ordered in advance. *Camping N$100 pp, plus electricity.* **$$**

🏠 **Stone House** (4 rooms) 10 Toenessen St; ✆067 242842; e boet@iway.na; www.stonehouse. iway.na. As the name suggests, this small guesthouse on a quiet residential street is clad in stone. It's an attractive place, its stylish rooms featuring large en-suite bathrooms, plus AC, DSTV, Wi-Fi, minibar & coffee/tea facilities, while outside is a small pool. **$$**

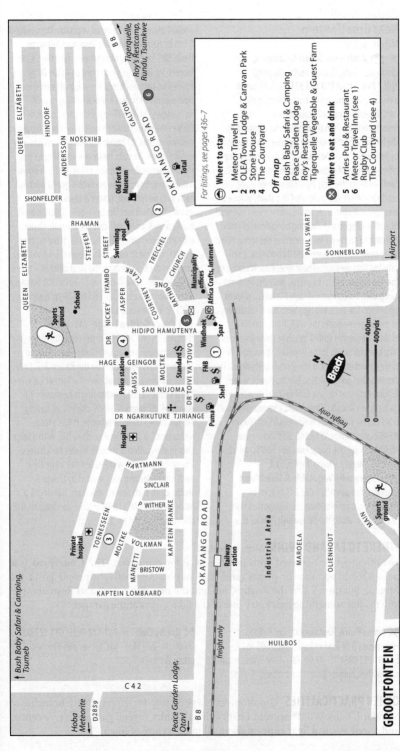

For listings, see pages 436–7

Where to stay
1 Meteor Travel Inn
2 OLEA Town Lodge & Caravan Park
3 Stone House
4 The Courtyard

Off map
Bush Baby Safari & Camping
Peace Garden Lodge
Roy's Restcamp
Tigerquelle Vegetable & Guest Farm

Where to eat and drink
5 Arries Pub & Restaurant
6 Meteor Travel Inn (see 1)
Rugby Club
The Courtyard (see 4)

Near Grootfontein

Map, page 426.

✳ 🏠 **Bush Baby Safari & Camping**
(5 rooms, 5 bungalows, 3 tents, camping)
📞067 243391; **m** 081 829 3711; **e** info@bush-babycamping.com; www.bush-babycamping.com. To reach Bush Baby take the C42 west of Grootfontein for 7km then follow the signpost on the left for a further 4km on a gravel drive. Owned by Jan Jensen from Denmark, this delightful camp offers a variety of accommodation from 'tree tents' (walk-in tents sleeping 2 people with en-suite outdoor shower-rooms located in a shady wooded area, but not up in trees as the name might suggest), to well-equipped self-catering bungalows of stone & thatch to pretty en-suite rooms at the lodge 900m away overlooking a waterhole. In addition, 2 self-catering flats are located near reception. It's not over-the-top luxury, but it is a pretty, well-thought-out camp with simple rustic design & a lovely, relaxed ambience. The thatched lapa with bar & restaurant at the lodge overlooks the waterhole, floodlit at night & frequently visited by white rhino & various antelopes including kudu, impala & springbok, & there's another lapa near the tents & bungalows. The campsite has good ablution blocks, power, water & light. Activities include fishing (catch & release), game drives & walks. There's also a swimming pool & Wi-Fi. Day visitors are welcome (*N$30*). *Dinner N$160; game drives N$180 pp; B&B lodge room N$500/850 sgl/dbl, bungalows N$450/750 sgl/dbl; tents N$200 pp; camping N$90 pp.* **LL**

🏠 **Tigerquelle Vegetable & Guestfarm**
(6 rooms, camping) 📞/**f** 067 243143; **m** 081 2621098; **e** tigerveg@iway.na. Signposted from Grootfontein along the B8 towards Rundu, this oddball place is a commercial vegetable farm owned & run by Herr Wander. After 2km, turn left on to the D2885 for 1.8km; alternatively, take the C42 to Tsumeb for 2km, then turn right on to the D2905 (there's no signpost here). The original farmhouse, built around 1904, has a superb dining room & an 'orangery'-style hallway, with later additions such as the sunset tower housing the bar. A large swimming pool set beside ancient fig trees has only natural water. En-suite rooms are very simple, but the real gem is the campsite, set in the bush down a track away from the house with 6 grassy pitches, each with water point, power & braai – & 1 with its own thatched loo! The brick-built ablution block is adjacent, & a new self-catering en-suite chalet is nearby. Food can be purchased from the farm or meals – cooked to order using vegetables from the farm & meat & game from the local butcher – taken at the house. Coffee & cake at 15.30 (*N$30*). Advance reservations are essential. *DBB N$680 pp; camping N$85 pp inc firewood.* **LL**

🏠 **Peace Garden Lodge** (48 chalets, camping) 📞067 243648; **e** peacegardenlodge@iway.na; www.peacegardenlodge.info. Around 5km west of Grootfontein on the B8 towards Otavi, Peace Garden Lodge took over the former Lala Panzi Lodge in 2011, extending it to include 13 standard, 20 luxury & 15 VIP chalets, all having AC, tea/coffee stations & fridge. It has a large restaurant & a somewhat soulless bar, with a large pool in the garden & another nearer the chalets. The campsite has few trees, but the 10 pitches each have a seating area shaded by thatch & shade-cloth with power, ablutions, lighting & a braai area. *B&B N$630/945/1056 standard/lux/VIP dbl; camping N$65 pp.* **LL**

✗ WHERE TO EAT AND DRINK *Map, page 437.*

Grootfontein isn't blessed with much choice for eating out. **The Courtyard** (see page 436) is popular for pizzas (and take-aways). Alternatively, people go to the Meteor, but there's also the Rugby Club and the new Arries Pub and Restaurant. If you're after something quick, try one of the take-aways at the garages.

✗ **Arries Pub & Restaurant** Cnr Hidipo Hamutenya & Dr Toivo va Toivo; 📞060 803 6513; **m** 081 233 6863; ⏰ 07.00–late daily. B/fast, toasted sandwiches, burgers & steaks/schnitzels. **$–$$$$**

✗ **Rugby Club** **m** 081 128 9825, 081 127 0074; ⏰ 09.00–late Mon–Sat. Serves pub lunches, pizzas & steaks. **$$$**

OTHER PRACTICALITIES Grootfontein is a good stop for supplies, with branches of Standard, Bank Windhoek and First National **banks**, several **garages**, a tyre centre, and a well-stocked Spar **supermarket**, all in the centre of town.

The **post office** is on the triangle of green just behind the municipal between the main Okavango Road and Rathbone Street.

In an **emergency**, the police are reached on ☎ 067 10111, the ambulance and hospital on ☎ 067 240064 and 067 242141/2, and the fire service on ☎ 067 243101/242321.

WHAT TO SEE AND DO There's not much to do in the town itself, with the museum the only real attraction during the day. Even the outdoor pool by the restcamp has been closed for some years (though should it reopen, that's likely to be between October and May).

In the evenings things are even more limited, although the bars at the Courtyard guesthouse, Meteor Travel Inn and the Rugby Club are open all week, except Sunday. For excursions from Grootfontein, see below.

Old Fort Museum (*Eriksson St* ☎ *067 242456;* ⏰ *09.00–12.30 & 14.00–16.30 Mon–Fri; admission N$15*) This small, privately run museum close to the centre of town was originally a Schutztruppe fortress. It was built in 1896 and a tower added eight years later. At its heart is the original forge of a local blacksmith, featuring a range of tools and wagon wheels. There are also significant displays focusing on the Himba people, with photos and artefacts.

AROUND GROOTFONTEIN
Where to stay *Map, page 424.*

🏠 **Roy's Rest Camp** (8 rustic chalets inc 1 disabled access, camping) ☎ 067 240302; e royscamp@iway.na; www.roysrestcamp.com. Situated on the main B8 to Rundu, 55km north of Grootfontein & just past the C44 turn-off to Tsumkwe, Roy's is a super little lodge built in an artistic & very rustic style. It was opened on the established Elandslaagte farm in 1995 by Wimple & Marietjie Otto, whose ancestors were some of the first European settlers in Namibia. The camp is named after Wimple's father, Royal; when the authorities didn't approve of 'Royal Restcamp', it was cut to Roy's Rest Camp.

Bungalows – including 2 family units & 3 budget rooms – are wonderfully rustic to the point of being quite offbeat, even down to the en-suite showers & private braai area. All have AC & are serviced by electricity, although paraffin lamps light the way to the bungalows & campsite. Good

home-cooked meals (best arranged in advance) are served in the bar/dining area next to the swimming pool.

15 green, well-watered camp pitches, complete with electricity, braai sites (for which braai packs are available), tree shade, & ablutions with hot & cold water, are available to campers, plus a bush kitchen with stove, fridge, etc. All of this is set in 28km^2 of natural bush, which has been stocked with blue wildebeest, eland, kudu, zebra, duiker, steenbok & warthog. Through this are 2 marked walking trails, of 1.5km & 2.5km respectively, on which many of the trees are labelled. Day visitors are welcome 10.00–17.00 (*N$30*). Light lunch/ buffet dinner N$105/175 pp.

Assuming that you're happy with the rustic environment, this is an ideal spot to spend a night *en route* between the Triangle & the Caprivi. *B&B N$510 pppn; camping N$95 pp.* **LL**

Excursions from Grootfontein There are a couple of attractions in the area that are accessible only if you have a vehicle, although Dragon's Breath Cave is not open to the general public.

✦ *Hoba Meteorite* This famous lump of rock is about 20km west of Grootfontein, clearly signposted from the C42 approach road from Tsumeb. Here, in 1920, the farm's owner discovered the world's heaviest metallic meteorite. It weighs about 50 tonnes, and analysis suggests it is mostly iron (about 80%) and nickel.

It was declared a national monument in 1955 and has since received the protection of a permanent tourist officer because it was suffering badly at the hands of souvenir hunters. The locals became particularly irate when even the UN's Transition Assistance Group (UNTAG) personnel were found to be chipping bits off for souvenirs as they supervised the country's transition to democracy. Now the site is open full time, with a picnic area, a campsite and a small kiosk selling souvenirs, sweets and soft drinks. There's an entrance fee of around N$10 pp.

Dragon's Breath Cave and Lake This cave is claimed to contain the world's largest-known underground lake. It is 46km northwest of Grootfontein, just off the C42 to Tsumeb, on the farm Harasib. Although it is not open to casual visitors, it is sometimes visited by specialist cave divers.

The lake has crystal clear, drinkable water with a surface area of almost 2ha, and lies beneath a dome-shaped roof of solid rock. The water is about 60m below ground level and to get to it currently requires the use of ropes and caving equipment, with a final vertical abseil descent of 25m from the roof down to the surface of the water. This perhaps explains why it is not open to the public.

Mangetti National Park Proclaimed as a national park in September 2008, this relatively unknown area lies on community land to the east of the B8, roughly halfway between Grootfontein and Rundu. Covering just 41,990ha, it has been fenced as a game park since 1973.

Wildlife includes large antelope, especially eland, which are at home in the woodlands and bush that characterise the park, as well as the much rarer sable. Elephant and giraffe are also resident, along with leopard, hyena and wild dog. It is hoped that designation as a national park will bring benefits not just to wildlife and the environment but also to the local community.

BUSHMANLAND

To the east of Grootfontein lies the area known as Bushmanland. (This is an old name, but I'll use it here for clarity; it is still what most people call the area.) This almost rectangular region borders on Botswana and stretches 90km from north to south and about 200km from east to west.

Drive east towards Tsumkwe, and you're driving straight into the Kalahari. However, on their first trip here, people are often struck by just how green and vegetated it is, generally in contrast to their mental image of a 'desert'. In fact, the Kalahari isn't a classic desert at all; it's a *fossil* desert. It is an immense sand sheet which was once a desert, but now gets far too much rainfall to be classed as a desert.

Look around you and you'll realise that most of the Kalahari is covered in a thin, mixed bush with a fairly low canopy height, dotted with occasional larger trees. Beneath this is a fairly sparse ground-covering of smaller bushes, grasses and herbs. There are no spectacular sand dunes; you need to return west to the Namib for those!

This is very poor agricultural land, but in the east of the region, especially south of Tsumkwe, there is a sprinkling of seasonal pans. Straddling the border itself are the Aha Hills (see page 452), which rise abruptly from the gently rolling desert. This region, and especially the eastern side of it, is home to a large number of scattered Bushman villages of the Ju/'hoansi !Kung.

he wildlife is a major attraction. During the late dry season, around nd October, game gathers in small herds around the pans. During and ns, from January to March, the place comes alive with greenery and and noisy bullfrogs abound, and travel becomes even more difficult

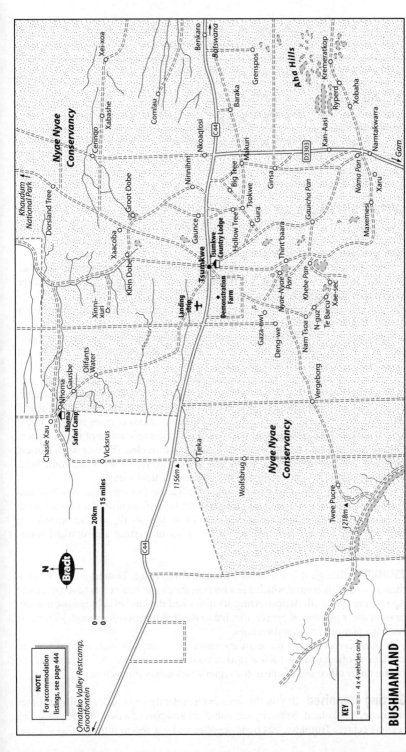

NOTE
For accommodation
listings, see page 444

Omatako Valley Restcamp,
Grootfontein

Nyae Nyae Conservancy

Khaudum National Park

Dorsland Tree

Chasie Xau
Nhoma
Gausbe
Nhoma Safari Camp
Olifants Water

Vicksrus

Xaacoba
Klein Dobe
Xinni-xuri

Groot Dobe

Cenngo
Xabashe
Xei-xoa

Comtau

Ninnihihi
Gaunce

Benkaro
Botswana

Grenspos

Baraka

Nkoaqlosi

C44

Big Tree
Makuri
Tsokwe
Gura

Hollow Tree

Tsumkwe
Country Lodge

Tsumkwe
Landing strip
Demonstration Farm

Gaza-nwi

Deng-we

Thint'baara

Nyae-Nyae Pan
Khebe Pan

Nam Tsoa
N-guz
Te Barcu
Xae-sec

Ginsa
Goucha Pan

Maxemesi

D303
Kan-Aasi
Namtakwarra
Xaru

Nama Pan

Xobaha
Ryperd
Kremeratkop
Aha Hills

↓ Gam.

Vergeborg

Tjeka
1156m ▲

Wolfsbrug

Twee Pucre
1218m ▲

Nyae Nyae Conservancy

C44

N
Bradt

0   20km
0   15 miles

KEY
==== : 4 x 4 vehicles only

than usual, as whole areas turn into impassable floodplains. From April the land begins to dry, and during July and August the daytime temperatures are at their most moderate and the nights cold. But whenever you come, don't expect to see vast herds like those in Etosha or you will be disappointed.

CULTURE The other reason for visiting is to see the Bushman people. The conventional view is that less than a century ago these people's ancestors were a traditional hunter-gatherer society using Stone Age technology. Yet they possessed a knowledge of their environment that we are only just beginning to understand. Tourism is increasingly seen as a vital source of revenue for these people. In placing a high value on traditional skills and knowledge, it is hoped that it will help to stem the erosion of their cultural heritage.

GETTING THERE AND AWAY The C44 through to Tsumkwe is the main access route into the area. This is long, a total of about 226km to Tsumkwe, before continuing a further 50km east to the new border post with Botswana at Dobe ($\oplus$ *06.00–16.30 daily in summer, 06.00–15.30 daily in winter*).

From there it's another 150km (a 3-hour drive) of patchy gravel road to the small Botswanan town of Nokaneng, on the main tar road that runs down the western side of the Okavango Delta.

Tsumkwe feels remote, but it is easily reached from Grootfontein by ordinary 2WD vehicle. From Nokaneng, an experienced driver should be able to get a high-clearance 2WD through to Tsumkwe, but doing this journey in a 4x4 is recommended. Virtually all the other roads in Bushmanland require a sturdy 4x4 and a good guide, or a GPS, or preferably both.

Along the C44, about 31km from the B8, is a police station on the south side of the road. Beyond this, about 88km from the tar, is Omatako Valley Restcamp. Then around 89km before Tsumkwe, one of the turnings to the right is signposted 'Mangetti Duin', marking the way to one of the best stands of mangetti trees in the area – notable because mangetti nuts are one of the staple foods of the Bushmen. Otherwise there are a few turnings to villages, but little else. The area is not densely populated, and travellers coming this way should carry both water and some food, as only a handful of vehicles use the road on any particular day.

One good way to visit is by combining it with a trip through Khaudum National Park, thus making a roundabout journey from Grootfontein to the Caprivi Strip. Alternatively, approaching Bushmanland from the south, via Summerdown, Otjinene and the old Hereroland, would be an interesting and unusual route. Expect the going to get tough.

TSUMKWE Though it is the area's administrative centre, Tsumkwe is little more than a crossroads around which a few houses, shops and businesses have grown up. Apart from the South African Army, it's never had the kind of colonial population, or even sheer number of people, that led to the building of (for example) Tsumeb's carefully planned tree-lined avenues.

It is an essential stop for most travellers in the area though, even if only to stock up on fuel, or to get a few cans of cool drinks. It is also the location of the conservancy office and of one of the region's two lodges for visitors.

Getting organised To visit this area independently you must, as with the outer reaches of Kaokoland, be totally self-sufficient and part of a two-vehicle party. The region's centre, Tsumkwe, has basic supplies and – a recent introduction – a fuel

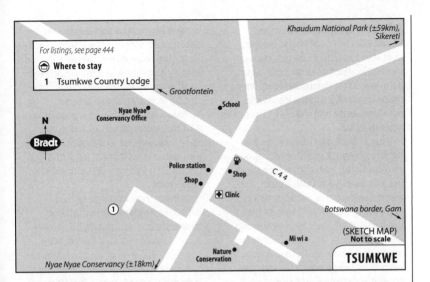

For listings, see page 444

⌂ **Where to stay**

1 Tsumkwe Country Lodge

Grootfontein

School

Nyae Nyae
Conservancy Office

N

Bradt

Police station

Shop

Shop

Clinic

①

Nyae Nyae Conservancy (±18km)

Nature
Conservation

Mi wi a

Khaudum National Park (±59km),
Sikereti

C 44

Botswana border, Gam

(SKETCH MAP)
Not to scale

TSUMKWE

station. That said, if there is any problem here, the nearest fuel station is either in Grootfontein, or at Divundu in the Caprivi. So while you can get fuel and basic foodstuffs here, it makes sense to set off for this area with supplies and fuel for your complete trip, relying only on getting water locally.

Before embarking on such a trip, obtain maps from Windhoek and resolve to navigate carefully. Travel in this sandy terrain is very slow. You will stay in second gear for miles, which will double your fuel consumption. Directions can be difficult; if you get them wrong then retracing your steps will take a lot of fuel. As a guide, you'll need a minimum of about 100 litres of fuel to get from Tsumkwe to Rundu or Divundu, or at least 150 litres to travel from Grootfontein via Bushmanland and Khaudum to Rundu or Divundu. You'll need more if you plan to do much driving around the area while here. So do plan ahead – even if you top up in Tsumkwe, you'll need to consider your fuel requirements very carefully.

If you're venturing into the bush, it's a good idea to tell someone where you are planning to go, and when you'll be back. Then at least someone will know if you go missing.

Nyae Nyae Conservancy Office (`\` 067 244011; www.nacso.org.na; ⊕ 08.00–17.00 Mon–Fri; admission N$30 pp/day) The office of the Nyae Nyae Conservancy (see page 445) is on the right side of the road when travelling east from Grootfontein, just before you reach the main Tsumkwe crossroads. This is the place to find out about campsites within the conservancy and to arrange a local guide (usually about N$250 per day). If you're planning on camping in the area for a few days and exploring a little, then a guide is highly recommended. He or she can help you get a lot more out of the area – and you will actively be giving a little more back to the local community. For details of the Nyae Nyae headquarters in Windhoek, see box, page 446, but note that it's not possible to make reservations through that office.

⬐ **Where to stay in and around Tsumkwe** Map, page 424, above, and page 468.
As well as the following, there are several basic campsites within the Nyae Nyae Conservancy (see page 445).

⌂ Omatako Valley Restcamp www.
omatakovalley.com. On the way to Tsumkwe,
about 88km east of the B8, is a restcamp run by
one of the local Bushman communities as part
of the Omatako San Community Project. Driving
into Bushmanland, it is hard to miss, in a dip
immediately on the right of the C44, 13km past the
veterinary control.

If you are heading for Tsumkwe then stop
here for cool drinks. A small shop sells a good
selection of locally made crafts including beads,
necklaces, spears, various tools & baskets. For
overnight visitors there is a campsite with a
good shower & flush WC, BBQ areas & a few
basic mud-&-thatch rondavels (bring your own
bedding & mosquito net). There's firewood for
sale (N$20), lamps for hire (but no electricity),
& sometimes a whole variety of things to do,
including guided bush walks & cultural events
(N$80 pp). Such events might include the
opportunity to try bush food or attend a dance
evening, but they are dependent on which of
the villagers are around when you are, so none is
guaranteed. *Camping N$50 pp.* **L**

⌂ Tsumkwe Country Lodge [Maps, pages 443
and 468] (25 rooms, camping) ☎ 067 687055;
e tsumkwecl@iway.na. The lodge is well signposted
a kilometre or so from the centre of Tsumkwe: just
turn right at the crossroads, then right again opposite
Nature Conservation. Twin rooms constructed of
canvas & metal are all en suite, with twin beds & a
private veranda. A small campsite has just 6 pitches,
each with electricity & BBQ, & sharing an ablution
block. Meals (*lunch and dinner N$130 each*) are
available in the deeply thatched lapa, where there's
also a bar, & outside is a small pool. Visitors can
take drives to Khaudum National Park & Nyae Nyae
Pan, or visit one of the local Bushman villages. *B&B
N$631/886 sgl/dbl; camping N$95 pp.* **LL**

⌂ Nhoma Safari Camp [Map, page 468] (10
tents, camping) m 081 273 4606; e tsumkwel@
iway.na; www.tsumkwel.iway.na. This remote
& fairly simple camp stands beside the Ju/'hoan

village of Nhoma, 80km from Tsumkwe. The turn-
off to the camp from the C44 is 185km east of the
B8, or 41km before you reach Tsumkwe. The road is
normally good enough for a 2WD but, before you
set off, phone ahead to find out the state of the
road & if necessary to arrange to be met.

Walk-in tents with en-suite or private showers
& WC have twin or dbl beds, or an extra sgl.
There's a campsite, too, with campers welcome to
participate in meals (*b/fast N$120; lunch N$165;
dinner N$275*) & activities (*N$1,650 pp/day*) by
arrangement.

Activities centre around the Ju/'hoan
community: hunting & veld food gathering,
traditional games, ancient crafts & the healing
dances – though each day is different. In the
winter (Jul–Oct), there are day trips to Khaudum
National Park, with the possibility to overnight
in the park in a mobile camp, & from May to Jan
a full-day trip to visit Nyae Nyae Pan is a further
option. Advance bookings are essential.

Nhoma's origins lie in the mid-1990s, when
Arno & Estelle Oosthuysen built Tsumkwe Lodge.
They knew the local people well, had a sensitive
attitude to working with them & soon started
introducing them to tourists. By 2007, when they
sold Tsumkwe Lodge, they'd been working so
closely with the Ju/'hoan community at Nhoma
that they built this small camp.

At its best, the Ju/'hoan cultural experience at
Nhoma can be insightful & truly amazing. It's as
interesting for children as for adults, because the
local youngsters will relax & start playing with
the young visitors very quickly – integrating far
more easily than the adults. So if your children are
active & not shy, expect to have difficulty dragging
them away from Nhoma when it's time to leave.
That said, as I write in 2014 there is uncertainty
about the future. Nhoma may be changing hands,
& Arno & Estelle may leave – so things may be
different when you visit. *FBA N$3,500/5,750 sgl/
dbl; additional day N$2,800/2,300; camping N$200
pp; discounts for groups of 6 or more.* **LLLLL**

Mi wi a (☎ *081 311 7621; ngtsumke@iway.na*) One place you shouldn't miss is Mi
wi a, which means 'thank you'. A shop selling Bushman crafts, it has been taken
over from Reverend Hendrik van Zyl, minister of the local Dutch Reform Church
Congregation, and his wife, Elize, by a local family: Gerrie Cwi, Leviet Kxao and
Gerrie's son, Cwi. Crafts are sourced from Bushman villages throughout the region,
regardless of their commercial value or otherwise, thus encouraging the full range
of traditional skills, and not just the artefacts in vogue with that year's visitors.

It's a trade that has built up over 12 years or so, and virtually all of the region's villages are now involved in regularly supplying crafts for the centre. If the sellers earned cash, they would have to walk 10–50km to Tsumkwe just to buy food; instead, food is taken out to the villages and exchanged for crafts. Given the loss of the large areas used for traditional hunting and gathering, many people are now dependent upon this food source for the more difficult parts of the year. So this scheme provides much-needed food relief to many of the poorest villages, and at the same time encourages the people to value their traditional crafts and skills.

It's well worth supporting, not only because it directly benefits the villages, but also because you won't find a larger range of authentic Bushman crafts for sale anywhere. These include axes that also function as adzes (woodcarving utensils), various children's games, bags made from birds' nests woven with wild cotton, hunting bags (containing a dry powder from fungus as kindling), dry grass, flint, wooden sticks, acacia gum, poisons, a 'string bag' made from giraffe tendons (for carrying things home), love bows, witchcraft bows, hunting bows and arrows, necklaces, bracelets and containers for poison pupae. It's fascinating.

So if you're one of the many visitors who see great poverty in Africa, and wring your hands saying: 'What can I do?', now you have an answer. You can come here and buy as much craftwork as you can afford – if you're being honest with yourself, that really is a lot of crafts! – thus appeasing your conscience with a valuable donation, while finding endless fascinating curios to give to friends when you return.

Currently, the main problem is the limited distribution channels for these crafts. Only a few visitors pass through Tsumkwe, and overseas mail order arrangements are only small scale. Shame – as they would sell superbly at small craft markets overseas.

NYAE NYAE CONSERVANCY Stretching 9,000km² around Tsumkwe is the Nyae Nyae Conservancy area, first gazetted in 1998. Here the communities have been given the right to manage their wildlife and tourism in a sustainable way, for their own benefit. While they have always hunted the wildlife here using traditional methods, now they can also derive income from trophy hunting in the area.

The Nyae Nyae Conservancy has an office in Tsumkwe (see page 443). This should be your first stop in the region and is where you pay conservancy fees, organise guides and sort out campsites (you should pay any camping fees to the village nearest the campsite).

Some of the villages are more accessible than others, with cleared campsites underneath baobab trees and a greater likelihood of finding an English-speaking member of the community to act as guide. //Xa/hoba village, 23km north of Tsumkwe, is now a Living Hunters Museum, offering authentic tourist activities on a daily basis. Almost all are accessible only by 4x4 but, depending on the season, some can be reached with a 2WD with good clearance. There are no vehicles for hire in the area.

Where to stay In the past, campers have set up their sites randomly in Bushmanland, with no permits necessary. Many left litter behind them and caused problems for the local people and the wildlife. They often used to camp close to water, frightening the area's already skittish animals, and even go swimming in reservoirs meant for drinking. Visitors were unaware that they were staying in an area used for hunting or gathering, and didn't realise the effect that their presence was having on the wildlife. This 'free camping' has now been banned. Instead, head for one of the (increasing number of) village sites, where you'll find a place to camp for which you pay the nearby community directly.

In the first edition of this book – in 1998 – I listed three such sites. Now many more villages have simple adjacent sites and welcome visitors. Ask at the Conservancy Office in Tsumkwe and they'll give you a map of these, or better still, a local guide, and advise you of their costs.

Wherever you camp, you must take great care not to offend local people by your behaviour. It is customary to go first to the village and ask for permission to stay from the traditional leader, but first read the guidelines on cultural etiquette on pages 26–7.

Remember that you are in a wilderness area, where hyena, lion and leopard are not uncommon, so always sleep within a tent. Try not to scare the wildlife, or damage the place in any way. Keep fires to a minimum, and when collecting fuel use only dead wood that is far from any village.

Some local people have been designated as community rangers, with a brief to check on poaching and look out for the wildlife. They may ask what you are doing, and check that you have paid your camping fees.

NYAE NYAE DEVELOPMENT FOUNDATION

Based just east of Tsumkwe, the Nyae Nyae Farmers Co-operative was established in 1986 with a charter to support and encourage the Ju/'hoansi of Eastern Otjozondjupa to return to their historical lands known as Nyae Nyae.

Historically, this group of Bushmen has been in a difficult position. The South African Army (SADF) moved into what was Eastern Bushmanland in 1960, to occupy the region as part of its war against SWAPO and the destabilisation of Angola. It formed a battalion of Bushmen to track down guerrilla fighters – using the Bushmen's tracking ability to lethal effect. Many of these people moved to Tsumkwe; whole families were dependent on the SADF.

This social upheaval, with lifestyles changing from nomadic hunter-gathering to dependence on an army wage, led to social problems among the people, including crime, alcohol and prostitution. Towards the end of the war, it was decided to improve their quality of life by taking them back to the ground they had come from, a move initiated by the Nyae Nyae Development Foundation (*PO Box 9026, Windhoek;* 061 236327; e *nndfn@iafrica.com.na*) and its founder, John Marshall.

So in the late 1980s and early 1990s, the Nyae Nyae Farmers Co-operative focused on grass-roots self-help projects, encouraging the Bushmen to start farming, rearing cattle and growing their own food. Boreholes were provided, but few made a success of these projects. The Bushmen are not natural farmers or pastoralists. They seem to have a different approach to survival from most other ethnic groups in Africa.

The Nyae Nyae Development Foundation continues to run various development programmes such as training conservancy staff, water development in villages and traditional gardens. A craft programme is well established, providing workers with training in production, and buying their products to sell in Tsumkwe and Windhoek.

However, perhaps the most interesting project was initiated by the WWF in 1994. This has aimed to set up a conservancy for sustainable utilisation and management of the wildlife in the eastern area of Bushmanland – which was finally put into place in 1997. This is being administered by the Nyae Nyae Development Foundation.

Guiding and camping fees Payment to the communities should be fair. The camping fee is likely to be around N$60 per day per person, depending on the village. Each of the guides will expect around N$250 per day plus food if staying out overnight. This must be discussed and agreed beforehand. The Living Hunter's Museum provides a range of activities such as tracking (*N$250 pp/day*), bushwalks (*N$150 pp*) and dancing (*N$120 pp*). For more details, see their website (*www.lcfn. info/en/ju-hoansi/ju-hoansi-home*).

Guidelines for visiting villages The traditional leader (*n!ore kxao*) or headman is usually one of the older men of the village, who will normally make himself known to visitors. Never enter someone's shelter, as this is very rude. Often the headman will be assisted by someone who speaks Afrikaans or even English, and if he's not around then somebody else will normally come forward to help you. Unless you have a basic grasp of Afrikaans, you may have to rely upon sign language.

Taking photographs of the people or place is normally fine, provided that you ask in advance, and pay for the privilege.

If you wish to buy crafts from the village, then do not try to barter unless specifically asked for things; most people will expect to be paid with money. Similarly, if one of the villagers has been your guide, pay for this with money. Remember that alcohol has been a problem in the past, and do not give any away.

Water is essential for everybody, and in limited supply for most of the year, so be very careful when using the local waterholes or water pumps. Often there will be someone around who can help you. Never go swimming in a waterhole or reservoir.

Cultural sensitivity and language Cultural sensitivity isn't something that a guidebook can teach you, though reading the box on cultural guidelines in *Chapter 2*, pages 26–7, may help. Being sensitive to the results of your actions and attitudes on others is especially important in this area.

The Bushmen are often a humble people, who regard arrogance as a vice. It is normal for them to be self-deprecating among themselves, to make sure that everyone is valued and nobody becomes too proud. So the less you are perceived as a loud, arrogant foreigner, the better.

Very few foreigners can pick up much of the local Ju/'hoansi language without living here for a long time. (Readers note that spellings of the same word can vary from text to text, especially on maps.) However, if you want to try to pronounce the words then there are four main clicks to master:

/	is a sucking sound behind the teeth
//	is a sucking sound at the side of the mouth, used to urge a horse
!	a popping sound, like a cork coming out of a bottle
≠	a sharper popping sound (this is the hardest)

Cultural questions When you see the Bushmen, it's tempting to lament their passing from noble savage to poor, rural underclass: witness the lack of dignified 'traditional' skins and the prevalence of ragged Western clothes, or see the PVC quivers that the occasional hunter now uses for his arrows.

While they clearly need help in the present, part of the problem has been our blinkered view of their past. This view has been propagated by the romantic writings of people like Laurens van der Post and a host of TV documentaries. However, modern ethnographers now challenge many long-cherished beliefs about these 'noble savages'.

Essential reading in this respect is *The Bushman Myth: The Making of a Namibian Underclass*, by Robert J Gordon (see *Appendix 3*). It stands out as an excellent, scholarly attempt to place the Bushmen in an accurate historical context, and to explain and deconstruct many of the myths that we hold about them. In partial summary of some of his themes, he comments:

> The old notion of these people as passive victims of European invasion and Bantu expansion is challenged. Bushmen emerge as one of the many indigenous people operating in a mobile landscape, forming and shifting their political and economic alliances to take advantage of circumstances as they perceived them. Instead of toppling helplessly from foraging to begging, they emerge as hotshot traders in the mercantile world market for ivory and skins. They were brokers between competing forces and hired guns in the game business. Rather than being victims of pastoralists and traders who depleted the game, they appear as one of many willing agents of this commercial depletion. Instead of being ignorant of metals, true men of the Stone Age, who knew nothing of iron, they were fierce defenders of rich copper mines that they worked for export and profit. If this selection has a central theme, it is to show how ignorance of archival sources helped to create the Bushmen image that we, as anthropologists, wanted to have and how knowledge of these sources makes sense of the Bushmen we observe today.

Gordon's book isn't a light or swift read, but it will make you think. See also my comments on the wider context, including the modern media's portrayal of the San, in *Chapter 2*, pages 19–24.

What to see and do
Nyae Nyae Pan Aside from coming here out of a general curiosity about the area's wildlife and culture, one area stands out: the Nyae Nyae Pan. This is a large complex of beautiful salt-pans, about 18km south of Tsumkwe. During good rains it fills with water and attracts flamingos to breed, as well as dozens of other waterbirds including avocets, pygmy geese, grebes, various pipers and numerous plovers. Forty-six different species of waterbirds have been recorded here when the pan was full.

Towards the end of the dry season you can normally expect game to be drinking here, and the regulars include kudu, gemsbok, steenbok, duiker and elephant. Meanwhile black-backed jackals patrol, and the grass grows to 60cm tall around the pan, with a belt of tall trees beyond that.

Cultural activities It's worth being realistic from the outset of your visit: if you're looking for 'wild Bushmen' clad in loincloths and spending all day making poison arrows or pursuing antelope, you will be disappointed.

The people in this area have been exposed to the modern world, and often mistreated by it, for decades. None now live a traditional hunter-gatherer lifestyle. Walk into any village and its inhabitants are more likely to be dressed in jeans and T-shirts than loincloths, and their water is more likely to be from a solar-powered borehole pump than a sip-well.

However, many of the older people have maintained their traditional skills and crafts, and often their knowledge of the bush and wildlife is simply breathtaking.

Those that I met appeared friendly and interested to show visitors how they live, including how they hunt and gather food in the bush – provided that visitors are polite and ask permission for what they want to do, and pay the right price.

This kind of experience is difficult to arrange without a local guide who is involved in tourism and speaks both your language and theirs. Without such a guide, you won't get very much out of a visit to a local village. So even if you have your own 4x4 transport, start by dropping into Nhoma Safari Camp or, if it is open, the conservancy office in Tsumkwe. Ask for a local guide to help you, who can travel around with you. You can pay them directly, and this will open up many possibilities at the villages.

None of the village activities is artificially staged. They are just normal activities that would probably take place anyhow, though their timings are arranged to fit in with your available time. However, because they are not staged, they will take little account of you. As a visitor you will just tag along, watching as the villagers go about their normal activities. All are relaxed. You can stop and ask questions of the guide and of the villagers when you wish. Most of the local villagers are completely used to photographers and unperturbed by being filmed – provided, of course, that you have agreed a fee for this in advance.

Ideally, for a detailed insight, spend a few days with a guide and stay beside just one village. If they are happy about it, see the same people for an evening or two as well as during the days. This way, you get to know the villagers as individuals, not simply members of an ethnic group. Both you and they will learn more from such an encounter, and so enjoy it a lot more. Typical activities might include:

Food-collecting/hunting trips These trips normally last about 3–4 hours in the bush. You'll go out with a guide and some villagers and gather, or hunt, whatever they come across. The Bushmen know their landscape, and its flora and fauna, so well that they'll often stop to show you how this plant can be eaten, or that one produces water, or how another fruits in season.

Even Arno (an expert on the area who currently runs Nhoma Safari Camp) comments that after years of going out with the Bushmen, they will still often find something new that he's never seen before. It's an ethno-botanist's dream.

The hunting tends to be for the smaller animals, and in season the Bushmen set up trap-lines of snares to catch the smaller bucks, which need checking regularly and setting or clearing. Spring hares are also a favourite quarry, hunted from their burrows using long (typically 5m), flexible poles with a hook on the end.

Don't expect to go tracking eland with bows and arrows in half a day, though do expect to track anything interesting that crosses your path. These trips aren't intended as forced marches, and the pace is generally fairly slow. However, if there's some good food to be had, or promising game to be tracked, then these walks through the bush can last for hours. Bring some water and don't forget your hat.

It's usually best to discuss payment in advance, and agree a cost. However, bear in mind that working with money is relatively new to many of these people, so don't expect any sophisticated bargaining techniques. As a quid pro quo, don't use any such ruses yourself, or try to screw the people into a hard bargain; just aim for a fair price (which you learned when you stopped and asked at the conservancy office!).

Traditional craft demonstrations As part of a half-day trip into the bush, you'll often stop for a while at the village, and there the people can show you how they make their traditional crafts. The Bushmen have a particularly rich tradition of storytelling, and it shows clearly here if they also demonstrate how snares are made and set, and give animated re-enactments of how animals are caught. This would normally be included in a half-day bush trip.

Irene Jessop

'I hope someone in the village remembers me from last year.'

'Ja, ja.' Arno, my guide, was certain they would. 'You should have seen the excitement when they shared out the beads you sent. You remembered them: they won't have forgotten you.'

I walked through the circle of yellow, beehive-shaped huts to where the headman was sitting, the only one on a chair, a concession to his age. As he clasped my hand my translator, Steve, explained, 'My father says he is very pleased you have come back to see us.' From across the village Javid stared at me briefly and then dashed across to shake my hand. People smiled spontaneously as they recognised me: I didn't know who to say hello to first.

My stay at Nhoma the previous year had been brief. A Ju/'hoan village in remote northeast Namibia, it is one of about 30 villages at the edge of the Nyae Nyae Conservancy. I was persuaded that visitors provided vital revenue to the villagers, but had also read about marginalised people with problems of poverty, unemployment and ill health. I anticipated that a visit would be at best a glum affair, and perhaps even a voyeuristic intrusion on a suffering people. Instead I found fun. Women sat by small fires in front of their huts with tall wooden mortars and pounded protein-rich mangettis that tasted pleasantly nutty, if a little gritty. Some boiled vivid scarlet beans: after the flesh is eaten, the kernel is roasted. Waste nothing: sometimes there is only nothing. While the women prepared food the men made hunting necessities. With his chop-chop, the Bushman's axe, Sao scraped fibres from mother-in-law's-tongue; these are twisted to make rope for a bird trap. Abel cleaned a dried steenbok skin to make a kit bag for the hunt. With great concentration Joseph squeezed the grub of a beetle cocoon to put poison on some arrows. Care is needed, as there is no known antidote and to avoid an accidental scratch it is not put on the tip. Even with all this work going on, it was never quiet: all around was talking and laughter.

The previous year N!hunkxa made ostrich-egg beads, painstakingly filing them to the same size with a stone. These, along with pieces of leather, wood and porcupine quills, were threaded into necklaces and bracelets, all brown and white. But what the women really wanted, they told me, were small glass beads, especially red and yellow ones. A few of them already had brightly coloured glass-bead necklaces and bracelets. Some, mainly the older ones, had bead medallions fixed through their hair so that they hung down on to their foreheads. The beads I had sent had all been used. Not only were the women wearing more necklaces and bracelets than last year, but also rings. Some of the men too wore ornate beaded belts or had circles of beads embroidered on their shonas, leather loincloths.

This time I had brought more beads and I was going to learn how to make something. As N!hunkxa unwrapped the beads a dozen or so women stopped work to see what I had brought. We sat on the sand in a circle under the shade of

Evening singing and dancing In the evenings, you can arrange (in advance, with payment agreed first) to visit a local village, and join an evening of traditional dancing. This probably means driving to just outside a village, where those who want to take part will meet you. They will build a fire, around which the women and children will gradually gather. Eventually those sitting will start the singing and clapping, and men will start dancing around the circle sitting in the firelight. They will often have percussion instruments, like shakers, strapped to their ankles.

a large tree. Pleasantly warm now; it would soon be too hot to be in the sun. In the middle of the group was a large canvas sheet and we made indentations in it to stop the beads rolling away. N!hunkxa chose an easy style for me to make, two parallel lines which crossed over at intervals. Other women made elaborately decorated coils or wide headbands with zigzag patterns. Steve kept my pattern correct by calling out the numbers and colours of beads, 'Two blue, one red...'. Jewellery-making was obviously the chance for a good gossip. Though I couldn't understand the words I could absorb the rhythms of the conversation, quick one-line repartee, and long stories with a punchline.

Everyone was generous in praise of my necklace when it was finished. As I tried it on I thought 'When I get home this will always remind me of Nhoma.' This was followed by the realisation that I had brought the beads because the women liked them: it seemed pointless to take them away. Did I really need an object to remind me of that morning? It was better if N!hunkxa had it.

'Steve, please can you tell N!hunkxa that I would like her to have this so that she always remembers me.'

'Kaja' ('Good'), several of the women said, knowing this was one of the words I understood. The approval in their expressions too told me that inadvertently or instinctively I had done just the right thing. I was later to find out that in Ju/'hoan society, gift exchange, xaro, is important in bonding people together. What is significant is the act of exchanging of gifts, not their value: bead-work is often a preferred offering for exchange.

N!hunkxa disappeared, to return a few moments later with an ostrich-bead necklace with a leather medallion, which she fastened round my neck.

'N!hunkxa would like to give you a name,' Steve said.

'What is it?' I wondered, knowing that visitors are often very accurately if not always flatteringly likened to animals, for example 'Elephant man' for someone with a big nose.

'No, no, you don't understand. She wants to give you her name.'

'Mi wi a (thank you),' I said, sensing that an honour had been conferred, but not quite understanding.

I now know that by taking N!hunkxa's name I had essentially taken on her relationships and obligations. Any customs governing her behaviour towards other Ju/'hoan would apply to me also: thus I would have obligations of care towards those she did. Those who would look after her would look after me too. I had become one of her kin. However, we live so many miles apart that it is difficult to nurture this relationship, to help in difficult times or take pleasure at the good things. So I send beads because I know how much pleasure they give, because beads to me represent the connections made that morning.

The singing is beautiful, essentially African, and it comes as no surprise that everybody becomes engrossed in the rhythm and the dancing. On rare occasions, such concentration among the dancers can induce states of trance – the famous 'trance dances' – which are traditionally used as dances to heal, or prevent illness.

As an observer, expect to sit on the ground on the edge of the firelight, outside of the dancers' circle. You will mostly be ignored while the villagers have a good time. They will have been asked to dance for your benefit, for which they will be paid, but everything else about the evening is in their control. This is the kind of dancing that they do for themselves, with nothing added and nothing taken away.

Note that they're used to most visitors just sitting and watching while they dance. If you want to join in it's often not a problem... but expect to be the source of a lot of amusement for the resident professionals.

Further information For more information about the area and its people, contact either Nhoma Safari Camp (see page 444) or the Nyae Nyae Development Foundation (see box, page 446); both are closely involved with the welfare of the Bushmen.

AHA HILLS Look southeast of Tsumkwe on the maps and you'll find an isolated group of hills straddling the border between Botswana and Namibia: the Aha Hills. Named, it's claimed, after the onomatopoeic call of the barking geckos that are so common in the area, these are remote enough to have a certain mystique about them – like their counterparts in Botswana, the Tsodilo Hills.

However, there the similarity ends. The Aha Hills are much lower and more flattened. Their rock structure is totally different: a series of sharp, angular boulders quite unlike the smooth, solid massifs of Tsodilo. So they are quite tricky to climb, and have no known rock art or convenient natural springs. All of this means that though they're interesting, and worth a visit if you're in the area – they do not have the attraction of Botswana's Tsodilo Hills.

With a guide, the track past Xobaha village does lead on to the hills, and it's possible to climb up Kremetartkop (which has some lovely baobabs on the top) in an hour or so. The view from the top – across into Botswana and 360° around – is pure Africa.

Do leave at least a whole afternoon for this trip, though. I didn't, and ended up driving back to Tsumkwe in the half-light, which wasn't ideal. However, I caught a rare glimpse of a caracal bounding through the long grass in the headlights.

KHAUDUM NATIONAL PARK (*Min 2 4x4 vehicles per party; entry N$50 pp per day, plus N$10 per vehicle*) Situated next to Botswana and immediately north of Bushmanland, Khaudum is a wild, seldom-visited area of dry woodland savannah growing on old stabilised Kalahari sand dunes. These are interspersed with flat clay pans and the whole area is laced with a life-giving network of *omurambas*.

Omuramba is a Herero word meaning 'vague river-bed', which is used to describe a drainage line that rarely, if ever, actually flows above ground but often gives rise to a number of waterholes along its course. In Khaudum, the *omurambas* generally lie along east–west lines and ultimately link into the Okavango's river system, flowing underground into the delta when the rains come. However, during the dry season the flood in the Okavango Delta helps to raise the level of the water table in these *omurambas* – ensuring that the waterholes don't dry up, and do attract game into Khaudum. The vegetation here can be thick in comparison with Namibia's drier parks to the west. Zambezi teak and wild syringa dominate the dunes, while acacias and leadwoods are found in the clay pans.

Flora and fauna The bush in and around Khaudum is quite complex. Different areas have totally different types of vegetation; biologists say that there are nine different 'biotypes' in Bushmanland.

Towards the southern end of the park, and between Tsumkwe and Sikereti, the bush is thick. Umbrella thorn, leadwood and cluster-leafed terminalia (also known as silver-leaf terminalia) are the dominant vegetation. The dune crests often have stands of

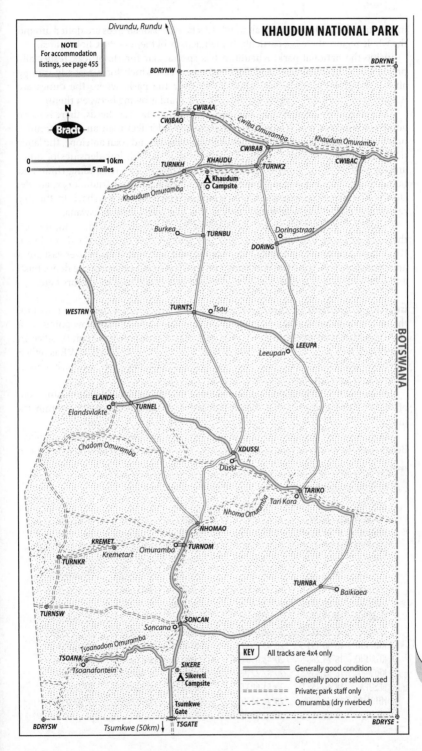

KHAUDUM NATIONAL PARK

NOTE
For accommodation listings, see page 455

Divundu, Rundu

N

Bradt

0 ——————10km
0 ——————5 miles

BDRYNW

BDRYNE

CWIBAA
CWIBAO

Gwiba Omuramba

Khaudum Omuramba

CWIBAB

CWIBAC

TURNKH   KHAUDU   TURNK2

Khaudum Campsite

Khaudum Omuramba

Burkea   TURNBU

Doringstraat

DORING

WESTRN   TURNTS   Tsau

LEEUPA

Leeupan

BOTSWANA

ELANDS   TURNEL
Elandsvlakte

Chadom Omuramba

XDUSSI

Dussi

TARIKO

Tari Kora

Nhoma Omuramba

NHOMAO

KREMET.   TURNOM
Kremetart   Omuramba

TURNKR

TURNBA   Baikiaea

TURNSW

SONCAN

Soncana

Tsoanadom Omuramba

TSOANA   SIKERE
Tsoanafontein   Sikereti Campsite

Tsumkwe Gate

BDRYSW   TSGATE   BDRYSE

Tsumkwe (50km)

KEY All tracks are 4x4 only

————— Generally good condition

————— Generally poor or seldom used

========= Private; park staff only

- - - - - Omuramba (dry riverbed)

The Triangle and Bushmanland   BUSHMANLAND

18

453

mangetti and marula trees and, although spectacular baobab trees are dotted around the whole region, there is a particularly high density of them in the Chokwe area.

Inside the national park, Khaudum has spectacular forests of teak (especially prevalent in the southeast) and false mopane trees, which form a shady canopy above low-growing herbs and grasses. All over the park, where the dunes are wooded you'll often find open expanses of grassland growing between them.

Though seldom occurring in numbers to rival Etosha's vast herds, there is some good wildlife here and Khaudum has a much wilder feel than any of Namibia's other parks. Its game includes the uncommon tsessebe and roan antelope, the latter noted for their penchant for lots of space, and areas with low densities of other antelope. Most of the subcontinent's usual big-game species (excluding rhino and buffalo) are also represented – blue wildebeest, red hartebeest, kudu, oryx, giraffe, steenbok, duiker – as well as smaller animals typical of the Kalahari. In the dry season there are often large herds of elephants that travel from Botswana.

Leopard, lion, cheetah and spotted hyena are the main predators and, though there are good populations of these, they are seldom seen through the dense bush. Khaudum is certainly Namibia's best park for wild dog, which range over vast areas and probably criss-cross the Botswana border. That said, because of the dense bush and relative lack of game-drive loops, they are very rarely seen by visitors here.

Getting organised Within the reserve, tracks either follow *omurambas* or link the dozen or so waterholes together. Even the distinct tracks are slow going, so a good detailed map of the area is invaluable. Try the Surveyor General's office in Windhoek (see page 120) before you arrive. Map number 1820 MUKWE is only a 1:250,000 scale, but it is the best available and worth having – especially when used in conjunction with the one here.

The map with GPS locations is included here by kind courtesy of Estelle Oosthuysen, of Nhoma Safari Camp, who personally mapped it out and noted the GPS co-ordinates in late 2002 (in UTM format – so any translation errors are entirely mine!).

Water is available but nothing else, so come self-sufficient in fuel and supplies. Because of the reserve's remote nature, entry is limited to parties with two or more

GPS REFERENCES FOR KHAUDUM NATIONAL PARK

BDRYNE	18°22.961'S	21°00.015'E	SONCAN	19°03.211'S	20°43.010'E
BDRYNW	18°23.289'S	20°43.050'E	TARIKO	18°53.661'S	20°52.332'E
BDRYSE	19°09.833'S	21°00.016'E	TSGATE	19°09.903'S	20°42.310'E
BDRYSW	19°09.922'S	20°32.244'E	TSOANA	19°05.648'S	20°35.583'E
CWIBAA	18°26.320'S	20°44.118'E	TURNBA	19°00.440'S	20°53.954'E
CWIBAB	18°28.740'S	20°49.967'E	TURNBU	18°35.032'S	20°44.909'E
CWIBAC	18°29.555'S	20°57.510'E	TURNEL	18°47.192'S	20°39.125'E
CWIBAO	18°26.331'S	20°42.964'E	TURNK2	18°30.143'S	20°49.099'E
DORING	18°35.705'S	20°50.677'E	TURNKH	18°30.479'S	20°43.618'E
ELANDS	18°47.212'S	20°38.052'E	TURNKR	18°57.932'S	20°33.451'E
KHAUDU	18°30.131'S	20°45.253'E	TURNOM	18°57.342'S	20°43.314'E
KHAUNO	18°23.289'S	20°43.050'E	TURNSW	19°01.720'S	20°32.222'E
KREMET	18°57.459'S	20°37.721'E	TURNTS	18°40.630'S	20°44.159'E
LEEUPA	18°43.157'S	20°51.693'E	WESTRN	18°40.484'S	20°36.094'E
NHOMAO	18°55.898'S	20°44.347'E	XDUSSI	18°50.825'S	20°47.092'E
SIKERE	19°06.157'S	20°42.399'E			

4x4 vehicles and each needs about 120 litres of fuel simply to get through the park from Tsumkwe to the fuel station at Mukwe, on the Rundu–Bagani road. This doesn't include any diversions while there. You'll need to use 4x4 almost constantly, even in the dry season, making travel slow and heavy on fuel. In the wet, wheel chains might be useful, though black-cotton soil, especially towards the south of the park, can be totally impassable.

Game-viewing is better here during the dry season, although most of the classic Kalahari game species found here are not strictly dependent on the presence of waterholes. Elephants are a notable exception to this rule, and they usually migrate away from sources of permanent water when it rains.

Getting there and away

From the north Turn off the main road 115km east of Rundu at Katere, where the park is signposted. Then Khaudum Camp is about 75km of slow, soft sand away.

From the south Khaudum is easily reached via Tsumkwe and Klein Dobe. Entering Tsumkwe, turn left at the crossroads just beyond the schoolhouse. This rapidly becomes a small track, and splits after about 400m. Take the right fork to Sikereti, which is about 60km from Tsumkwe and 77km south of the camp at Khaudum.

If you have a GPS with you, then Sikereti has co-ordinates ✪ 19°6.318'S, 20°42.325'E, while the crossroads at Tsumkwe is found at ✪ 19°35.514'S, 20°30.199'E.

Where to stay *Map, page 453.*

In theory, Khaudum National Park has two camps: Sikereti in the south, and Khaudum in the north. Both of these campsites are 'unserviced' (seemingly a euphemism for neglected and poorly maintained), but apparently still usable. I'm told there's running water, a WC and shower facilities – but little else. Be aware, too, that neither camp is fenced, so leave nothing outside that can be picked up or eaten, and beware of things that go bump in the night. In an emergency, the park staff at Sikereti and Khaudum may have radios. If you can find them, they can usually help you. A far more attractive alternative would be to organise a trip into the national park through Nhoma Safari Camp or Tsumkwe Country Lodge (see page 444).

At the time of writing, a new community lodge was under construction in Khaudum National Park, with a planned upgrade of the Khaudum campsite on completion of the lodge. I was also told that after these two projects are finished, the concession in the area will possibly be up for tender, exclusively for tourism, so there is likely to be some development here over the next few years. For now, camping is free, you only have to pay park fees, and you'll need to arrive with an absolute minimum of three days' food and water. For the sake of completeness:

⋀ Khaudum Restcamp Located in a lovely spot atop a dune, overlooking an *omuramba*. It is great for sunsets. The waterhole that used to be here has been shifted a few km away because of elephants in camp.

⋀ Sikereti Restcamp Sikereti stands in a grove of purple-pod terminalia trees, one of several such dense stands in the park.

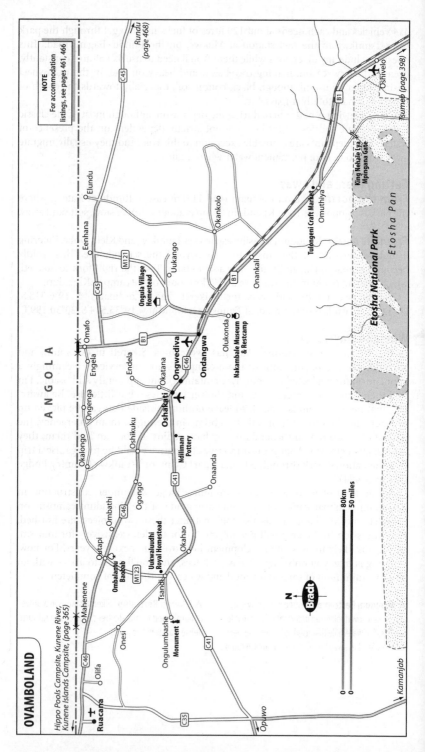

OVAMBOLAND

Hippo Pools Campsite, Kunene River,
Kunene Islands Campsite, (page 365)

ANGOLA

Etosha National Park

Etosha Pan

NOTE
For accommodation
listings, see pages 461, 466

Rundu
(page 468)

Tsumeb (page 398)

Oshivelo

King Nehale Lya
Mpingana Gate

Omuthiya

Tulongeni Craft Market

Okankolo

Onankali

Onaanda

B1

C45

M121

Elundu

Eenhana

Uukango

Uukango

Ongula Village Homestead

Omafo

Omafo

Engela

Ongenga

Endela

Okatana

Okalongo

Oshikuku

Ndilimani Pottery

Ongwediva

Ondangwa

Oshakati

Olukonda

Nakambale Museum & Restcamp

B1

C46

C46

C41

Ogongo

Ombathi

Otapi

Oukwaluudhi
Royal Homestead

Ombalantu Baobab

Tsandi

Okahao

M123

Onesi

Ongulumbashe Monument

Olifa

Ruacana

Mahenene

Opuwo

Opuwo

Kamanjab

C46

C46

C41

C35

N

80km

50 miles

Bradt

456

19

Ovamboland

This verdant strip of land between Etosha and the Kunene and Okavango rivers is largely blank on Namibia's normal tourist map. However, it is highly populated and home to the Ovambo people, who formed the backbone of SWAPO's support during the struggle for independence. The region was something of a battleground before 1990, and now the map's blank spaces hide a high concentration of rural people practising subsistence farming of maize, sorghum and millet.

Before independence this area was known as Ovamboland, but since then it has been split into four regions: Omusati, Oshana, Ohangwena and Oshikoto. Here, for simplicity, I will refer to the whole area as Ovamboland. During the summer Ovamboland appears quite unlike the rest of Namibia. It receives over 500mm of rain annually, and supports a thick cover of vegetation and extensive arable farming.

The Ovambo people are Namibia's most numerous ethnic group, and since independence and free elections their party, SWAPO, has dominated the government. Much effort continues to go into the improvement of services here.

There are two main arteries through Ovamboland: the B1/C46, and the more northerly C45, which links the region to Rundu and is being tarred throughout. The small towns that line these roads, like trading posts along a Wild West railroad, are growing rapidly.

You always see people hitching between the rural towns, and the small, tightly packed combi vans which stop for them: the local bus service. If you want to offer a lift to a hitchhiker who has waved you down, it is up to you, but make sure you consider the risk that you're taking – your insurance will not cover anyone you give a lift to.

Ovamboland has three major towns – Ondangwa, Ongwediva and Oshakati, while further west is the very different town of Ruacana, which was built solely to service the big hydro-electric power station there. Other, smaller towns vary surprisingly little and have a very similar atmosphere. There is usually a petrol station, a take-away or two, a few basic food shops, a couple of bottle stalls (alias bars) and maybe a beer hall. The fuel is cheaper at the larger 24-hour stations, in the bigger towns, and you can also stock up on cold drinks there. The take-aways and bars trade under some marvellous names, such as Never Return Bar and Gangsters' Paradise. They can be lively, friendly places to share a beer, but a word of warning: they are not recommended for lone women visitors.

Away from the towns, the land seems to go on forever. There are no mountains or hills or even kopjes; only isolated clumps of feathery palm trees and the odd baobab break the even horizon. After a year of good rains, the wide flat fields are full of water, like Far Eastern rice paddies, complete with cattle wading like water buffalo. Locally known as *oshanas*, these shallow lakes are also desirable fishing spots, drying out towards the end of the year into extensive flat pans beneath which African bullfrogs and small catfish live out the dry season in the mud.

The main B1 is a fast, tar road, running through several villages as it eats up the miles to the larger towns further north. Here and elsewhere in this area, watch out for cattle, goats and donkeys, as well as children, wandering across the road, and note that the speed limit in residential areas can be as slow as 40km/h.

Travelling north from Tsumeb, notice how the population density increases as the land becomes wetter, and the dominant maize crop gradually gives way to open fields where cattle graze. Where the land is not in agricultural use, greener mopane bushes gradually replace the acacia scrub by the roadside. Keep your eyes open for raptors – especially the distinctive bateleur eagles that are common in this southern area.

Some 110km north of Tsumeb, or 169km from Ondangwa, there's a turning west on to the C38 towards Etosha's Von Lindequist Gate, then a further 19km brings you to **Oshivelo**, where you must stop to pass through a police post and veterinary cordon fence. The small town is just a kilometre north of the bed of the Omuramba Ovambo, which feeds into Etosha Pan, but for most visitors it's more notable as a source of fuel. There's also an ATM at the garage, as well as a small supermarket.

After a further 65km, you'll come to a turning west clearly signposted to Etosha's northeastern King Nehale Lya Mpingana Gate (formerly the Andoni Gate), which is just 17km from the B1. The opening of this gate, in 2003, has broadened the options for those wishing to combine a visit to Etosha (see *Chapter 16*) with a trip along the country's northern border.

North of here, along the B1, are two of the region's small **craft projects** (see box, below), but if you miss these, don't despair: alongside the road are stallholders selling handmade baskets, varying in size up to the huge and highly decorative

CRAFT PROJECTS

Several small community craft projects have been set up in the north-central region, which broadly encompasses the area of Ovamboland. Such projects add an extra dimension for visitors into a region that has hitherto seen little of Namibia's tourist boom, and in the process bring much-needed income to small, rural communities.

Coming from Tsumeb, the first of these outlets, on the right-hand side of the road at Omuthiya, is the small **Tulongeni Craft Market,** where you'll find a selection of locally made baskets, pottery and woodcarvings. Some 28km further north, on the left of the B1 and 55km from Ondangwa, is the **Onankali Mahangu Paper Project** (\ *081 2916 235;* ⊕ *08.00–17.00 Mon–Fri, 09.00–noon Sat–Sun*). As the name suggests, it specialises in handmade paper and paper products, made from the stalks and leaves of *mahangu* – the millet staple grown throughout the area.

Closer to the heart of Ovamboland is the **Ndilimani Pottery**, poorly signposted on the C41, about 18km west of Oshakati, while north of Ondangwa, at Engela village, a group of basket-weavers around a Lutheran mission make baskets and hats under the name **Nghuoyepongo**. If you can't get to the individual projects themselves, then many of the crafts are available at the **Ombalantu Baobab Tree and Heritage Centre** in Outapi, where specialist wire-makers ply their trade, as well as at **Nakambale Museum** and **Uukwaluudhi Royal Homestead**, and in Windhoek at the Namibia Craft Centre.

grain-storage containers. From a practical standpoint, the rapidly growing linear town of **Omuthiya**, just 6km from the turning to Etosha, or 83km from Ondangwa, boasts a Standard Bank and a post office, as well as a fuel station.

ONDANGWA

Spread out along the main B1, Ondangwa is the first main town you come to in Ovamboland if approaching from Tsumeb, and is just 91km from Etosha's northern gate. Typical of the region, it is largely linear, spanning a distance of over 4km to the junction with the C46. Despite its proximity to the Angolan border (⊕ 08.00–18.00), the town itself is relatively hassle free. A lack of tourist attractions is balanced by the proximity of Nakambale Museum, just a few kilometres to the south.

GETTING THERE AND AWAY
By air The airport is on the C46, 3km west of the B1 turning north to Angola. Air Namibia (✆ 061 299 6600; www.airnamibia.com.na) operates three flights a day on Tuesdays and Thursdays, two a day on Sunday, Monday, Wednesday and Friday, and one on Saturday, between here and Windhoek's Eros Airport (*from N$1,840 one-way*).

By road Long-distance combis connect Ondangwa (as well as Ongwediva and Oshakati) with Windhoek (*around N$280 one-way*). More locally, you'll find numerous local combi vans, or taxis, stopping along the main roads to pick up and drop passengers. Expect to pay around N$35 between Ondangwa and Oshakati. Note that these prices will fluctuate with supply and demand – holiday periods will be particularly costly!

Car hire
🚗 **Avis** ✆ 065 241281
🚗 **Budget** ✆ 064 204128
🚗 **Europcar** ✆ 065 240249

By train TransNamib's passenger service between Windhoek and Ondangwa hasn't run for many years, and there is no sign of this being reinstated.

🏠 WHERE TO STAY *Map, page 460.*
Ondangwa's hotels are geared primarily to businesspeople, mostly aid workers and visiting government employees, although a trickle of tourists is making its way up here. If you're after somewhere more traditional, try Nakambale (see page 461). Either way, you shouldn't need to sample the none-too-inviting 'day and night accommodation' offered to the south of town.

🏠 **Protea** (90 rooms) Main St; ✆ 065 241900; e res.ondangwa@proteahotels.com.na; www.proteahotels.com/ondangwa. This 4-star hotel, typical of business hotels throughout the world, was upgraded in 2009. It sits on the corner where the B1 turns off towards Angola; follow the signs for Protea Hotel. En-suite twin or dbl rooms, which include 2 adapted for the disabled, have AC, kettle & satellite TV, & some rooms have a fridge. Facilities include a large swimming pool, restaurant with intercontinental menu, & bar, business centre & casino. There's free Wi-Fi throughout & airport transfers (*N$50 pp each way*). **$$$**

🏠 **Fantasia Guesthouse** (8 rooms) off Brian Simataa St; ✆ 065 240437; e eddublessis@gmail. com. North of the B1, this simple guesthouse offers immaculate twin or dbl en-suite rooms & secure parking. Outside is a bar with covered terrace.

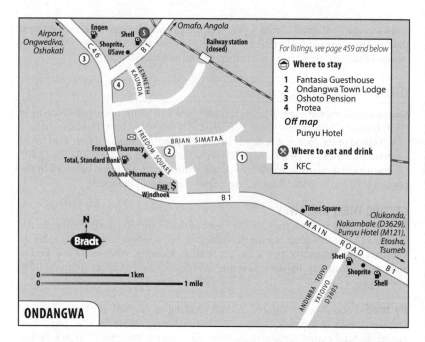

For listings, see page 459 and below

Where to stay
1 Fantasia Guesthouse
2 Ondangwa Town Lodge
3 Oshoto Pension
4 Protea
Off map
  Punyu Hotel

Where to eat and drink
5 KFC

ONDANGWA

At the time of research, a restaurant was soon to open to both guests & the public. **$$**

Ondangwa Town Lodge (26 rooms) Brian Simataa St; \065 241715/6; e ondangwatl@iway. na. Signposted north of the B1, the distinctive apricot walls & lilac trim of this modern hotel are clearly visible from the road. En-suite rooms – some with a 3rd bed – have AC, fan, TV & kettle, some also have a fridge. The restaurant is separate from the bar, which has a thatched seating area in front. There's also a small pool & secure parking. **$$**

Oshoto Pension Hotel (15 rooms) Main Rd; \065 240157; e oshotoht@iway.na. On the C46 just beyond the traffic lights towards Oshakati. Imposing

twin staircases lead up to the larger 'luxury' rooms, while others are in a block outside. All are en suite with AC, TV, kettle & fridge. There's a restaurant with a separate bar, & outside seating under thatch, while lawned gardens shelter a pool. **$$**

Punyu Hotel (30 rooms) \065 240556; f 065 240660. One of the oldest hotels in the area, the Punyu is 200m along the M121 towards Eenhana. It's a rather congested complex, but clean. Dotted around are a large restaurant, bar, swimming pool & thatched gazebos for outdoor drinks, while a casino opposite the car park was being renovated. Elaborately decorated rooms have TV, phone, AC & bath with shower. **$$**

WHERE TO EAT AND DRINK *Map, page 460.*

The modern restaurant at the Protea (see page 459) serves a broad international menu, with everything from pizzas to steaks. If you're passing through and in a hurry, there's a branch of **KFC** on the B1, just after the turning towards the Angolan border.

OTHER PRACTICALITIES There are 24-hour BP, Shell, Caltex and Engen **fuel** stations, a couple of big **supermarkets** and even an outdoor market. Try the latter for fresh vegetables, and perhaps a cob of maize to snack on.

On Main Road are branches of the major **banks** with ATMs, and a **post office**. Here you'll also find BZ Truck Repairs (\ *064 241324*). There are several **pharmacies**, including two on Freedom Square Street, behind FNB.

In an **emergency**, contact the police on \ 065 242663, or the ambulance or hospital on \ 065 240111.

WHAT TO SEE AND DO There's little to delay visitors in Ondangwa itself, but if you'd like to visit a local Ovambo homestead, ask at your hotel if this can be arranged (it should be possible from the Protea). More organised is the old Finnish mission at **Olukonda**, which has been restored as a museum and restcamp. (As an aside, Finland seems to have maintained its links with Namibia, forming a significant contingent of the United Nations' UNTAG force that supervised the country's transition to democracy in 1990.)

Nakambale Museum & Restcamp

(\ 065 245668; e *olukondamuseum@iway. na;* ⊕ *08.00–13.00 & 14.00–17.00 Mon–Fri, 08.00–noon Sat, noon–17.00 Sun; admission N\$20; guided tour N\$40*) Founded in the 1870s by Martti Rautanen – locally known as Nakambale – this former mission boasts some of the oldest buildings in northern Namibia. Today, the Rautanens' home and the original church form a museum that traces the development of missionary work in this area and gives an indication of daily life for those involved. It also acts as a showcase for Ovambo culture, with local guides on hand to explain various traditional skills and practices, and the option of a visit to a homestead (*N\$40 pp*). With advance notice, visitors can also sample traditional Ovambo food (*N\$100 pp*) or during the school holidays enjoy a musical performance (*N\$20 pp*). A small shop offers drinks and locally made crafts, including baskets.

Getting there and away To get here, turn southwest off the B1 on to the D3629, signposted 'Olukonda Mission'; it's just after the Shell garage and some 20km south of Ondangwa. Follow this road for about 5.5km to a new church on your left, where you turn towards the museum.

Where to stay Map, page 456.

⛺ Nakambale Restcamp (4 huts, 5 tented huts, camping) Accommodation is in closely grouped traditional huts with floor mats, mosquito nets & a lamp, or fixed twin tents under thatch – the latter with full bedding.

There is also a campsite. All share toilets & showers, & there's a kitchen with gas stove. *Traditional hut N\$200 pp; tent N\$100 pp; camping N\$50 pp.* **L**

AROUND ONDANGWA
Where to stay Map, page 456.

🏠 Ongula Village Homestead Lodge (5 huts) \085 625 6551; e hilya@ongula.com, reservations \061 250 725; e ongula@resdest. com; www.ongula.com. Turning off the B1 on to the M121 8km before Ondangwa, follow this road to the end of the tar, continue another 6km on the dirt road & the homestead is signposted from Oshigambo. 5 luxury rondavels offer a

comfortable stay in a secure compound, opposite a working Owambo homestead. During the day, guests can join in with the traditional chores at the homestead such as pounding *mahangu*, basket-weaving & clay-pot making. Day trips to nearby attractions are offered. *DBB N\$1,062/1,602 sgl/ dbl pp.* **LL**

ONGWEDIVA

Just 22km west of Ondangwa, the small town of Ongwediva is, with Oshakati, home to the northern campus of the University of Namibia, and – at least on the surface – displays an air of relative affluence. It's probably only a matter of time before it merges with the larger town of Oshakati, just a few kilometres further along the C46.

WHERE TO STAY, EAT AND DRINK

 Etuna Guest House (22 rooms) 5544 Valley of the Leopard St; \065 231177; e etunaent@ iway.na; www.etunaguesthouse.iway.na. To get here, turn right off the C46 as you head towards Oshakati, just before Shoprite; Etuna is 100m down on the left. Simply furnished rooms in chalets or rondavels are en suite with AC & fridges, & meals are available on request. **$$$**

 Afrika Stadt Haus (45 rooms) Marula St; \065 233600; e afrikastadt@mweb.com. na, jschmidt@mweb.com.na. Despite the clear signpost from the C46 opposite the Engen garage, this hotel isn't obvious – until you know that it's the striking red & yellow building to the left of the street. Red glass panels in the dining area & colourful wall paintings continue the theme, but the barnlike beer garden & bar, complete with big-screen TV, is decidedly functional. Rooms – in standard & luxury categories – are all en suite, AC, TV & free Wi-Fi. Outside there's a small pool. **$$**

 Bennie's Entertainment Park & Lodge (100 rooms) Cnr Auguste Tanyanda & Mandume Ndemufayo sts; \065 231100; e benniesparkreception@gmail.com. The eponymous owner of Bennie's has certainly made his mark on the area with this highly popular complex (see below). The lodge is set behind the entertainment park, just off the C46 by the Shell garage. En-suite dbl rooms are thoughtfully decorated with dark wood furniture, all with AC & DSTV. Some are in neat rows, their wooden balconies lining narrow walkways; others are larger with tiled verandas; & suites overlook the park. Guests have their own pool & the use of computers in the lobby; there's also Wi-Fi access. Other facilities are in the park (see below), which is open to guests. **$$**

OTHER PRACTICALITIES Aside from the usual run of **fuel** stations and **banks**, there are a couple of **supermarkets**: Spar next to the Engen garage, and Shoprite, as well as an open-air market. There is also a Pick 'n' Pay in the Oshana Regional Mall.

For medical matters, the private **Ongwediva Medipark hospital** (*Auguste Tanyanda St*; \065 232911) is close to Bennie's, with its own **pharmacy** and another nearby.

WHAT TO SEE AND DO Many visitors to Ongwediva are here because of the university, but **Bennie's Entertainment Park** (see above; ⊕ *07.00–late daily; admission N$20 pp, children N$10*) draws all comers looking for a spot of R&R. Peacocks patrol the landscaped gardens and springbok graze on the lawns. A rather formal restaurant serves salads, grills, pizzas and Portuguese dishes, and there's an upstairs bar and a casino. Outside, sun-loungers surround a large swimming pool, while a separate pool has a water slide. An ice cream kiosk and bar, individual braai areas, a children's playground, minigolf and an aviary add to the package.

OSHAKATI

By Namibian standards, this is a large, sprawling town, more commercialised than Ondangwa yet similar in character. That said, finding your way around is not as straightforward as in the more linear Ondangwa, and it's surprisingly easy to get lost in the streets off the main C46. There are no tourist attractions, but the town acts as the centre for several government departments.

GETTING THERE AND AWAY The town is located some 40km northwest of Ondangwa along the C46. The small airport was being upgraded in 2010, but there are as yet no commercial flights operating here.

 WHERE TO STAY *Map, opposite.*
Oshakati's hotels, as those in Ondangwa, cater mainly for businesspeople, although the choice here is wider.

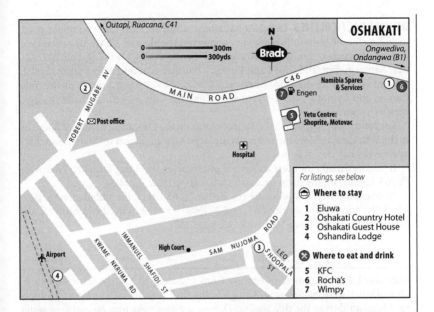

For listings, see below

Where to stay

1 Eluwa
2 Oshakati Country Hotel
3 Oshakati Guest House
4 Oshandira Lodge

Where to eat and drink

5 KFC
6 Rocha's
7 Wimpy

Oshakati Country Hotel (46 rooms) Robert Mugabe Av; ☏065 222380; e res.och@united.com.na. Great carved doors open into a thatched lobby where giant masks & tall wooden giraffes ooze a sense of Africa. Here you'll find a substantial sports bar, a restaurant (with tables outside on the terrace too) & a conference centre. Normally meals are à la carte, but a buffet dinner is served when it's busy. Rooms, set at the back around lawns & a pool, are spacious if uninspiring. All have AC, TV & phone. At the time of research, reports were sadly rather negative, mentioning poor service, & the cleanliness of the hotel has been called into question. **$$$**

Oshakati Guest House (22 rooms) Cnr Sam Nujoma Rd & Leo Shoopala St; ☏065 224659; e reservations@oshakatiguesthouse.com, www.oshakatiguesthouse.com. Opened in 2008, this pleasant guesthouse has cool en-suite dbl rooms with TV, AC, fridge & kettle. Set at the back of a brick-paved yard, they're well cushioned from any noise from the large sports bar & restaurant, where you can order dinner à la carte. **$$$**

Eluwa Hotel (38 rooms) Main Rd; ☏065 222038; e rochas@rochasbiscas.com. Next to Rocha's restaurant, this is the simplest of the bunch, its rooms built in a block around a central courtyard, garden & pool. The main draw is the restaurant. **$$**

Oshandira Lodge (23 rooms) ☏065 220443; e oshandira@iway.na. Close to the airport, with secure parking, Oshandira is convenient for business users. Since being taken over in 2008, it has seen the addition of an upstairs restaurant & a sundowner area. Rooms come with AC, DSTV, a phone & some have fridges. The restaurant is one of the best in town, so often gets busy; its menu incorporates traditional Ovambo food, with Portuguese dishes on request. Alongside the swimming pool is a popular sports bar with large-screen TV (⏱ 10.00–23.00). **$$**

WHERE TO EAT AND DRINK *Map, above.*

Rocha's is a favourite, and Oshandira Lodge offers a good menu, too. Fast food comes courtesy of KFC in the Yetu Centre, and a Wimpy at the Engen garage.

For an evening out, Oshakati can be excellent – provided that you enjoy joining in with the locals and don't demand anything too posh. Venues come and go so ask around for the current 'in' places.

By all means drop in for a burger or a beer at **Rocha's** (*Main Rd;* ☏ *065 222038;* ⏱ *06.00–midnight daily*), a relaxed bar/restaurant, but it's the Portuguese specialities that are highly rated (**$$–$$$$**).

OTHER PRACTICALITIES Oshakati has all the major services that you might need, including lots of 24-hour **fuel** stations, and several **banks** and ATMs. It's well served for **vehicle spares**, too, with a Nissan and Toyota dealer, Ozzy's (📞 *065 222132*), near Santorini Inn, and – for Land Rovers – Northern Auto Repairs (📞 *065 221802*) beyond Spar along the C46. Motovac (📞 *065 225672*) has a branch in the Yetu Centre, and Cymot (📞 *065 220916*) west along the C46, as well as smaller garages such as Trentyre.

For **food** shopping, there's the Spar complex on the C46, and a branch of Shoprite in the Yetu Centre. More interesting is the large African market on Main Road that's open every day except Sunday.

If you need medicine there are several **pharmacies**, including Oshakati Pharmacy (📞 *065 220964*) on the main road, which has good basic supplies.

In an **emergency**, the police are reached on 📞 065 10111, the ambulance on 📞 065 223 3222, and the fire service on 📞 065 229500. If you're in need of a hospital, the best option is Ongwediva Medipark (see page 462).

OSHAKATI TO RUACANA

The tarred C46 continues northwest from Oshakati to Outapi (also known as Ombalantu), some 86km away. Alongside the road is a canal – a vital water supply for Oshakati during the dry season. Driving by, you pass women carrying water back to their houses, while others wash and children splash around to cool off. Along the banks, piles of clay bricks lie drying in the sun. Occasionally there are groups meeting in the shade of canalside trees, and boys fishing in the murky water. Some have just a string tied to the end of a long stick, but others use tall conical traps, perhaps a metre high, made of sticks. The successful will spend their afternoon by the roadside, selling fresh fish from the shade of small stalls.

If you're not in a hurry, consider taking the C41 west to Okahao and Tsandi, before continuing north on the gravel M123 to Outapi. Some 18km from Oshakati, you'll pass a roadside sign indicating **Ndilimani Pottery** (see box, page 458) to the left.

OKAHAO While the small town of Okahao has all the essentials – a couple of fuel stations, a market, various shops including a pharmacy, a police station and even a hospital – it's not a place where you'd particularly want to linger.

Where to stay Should you need somewhere to stop for the night, there are a few guesthouses that could fit the bill, including Mika Ilonga Guesthouse next to the church, and King Uushona B&B a few kilometres to the west. Just east of town, the fairly large **Ongozi Guesthouse** looks promising, with rooms built in a semicircle at the back overlooking a huge baobab, but it was deserted when we visited.

TSANDI Some 25km from Okahao you'll come to Tsandi, a rural town with a fuel station but where donkey carts are still in regular use. It's worth stopping at the **Uukwaluudhi Royal Homestead** (📞 *065 258025;* ⊕ *08.00–17.00 Mon–Fri; admission N$40 pp*), on your right just east of the town. Built in 1960 for the royal family of Uukwaluudhi, one of seven traditional kingdoms in the region, it was home to King Taapoopi and his family. Although clearly designed with a view to protecting royalty, the reception areas, kitchens and bedrooms are similar to those of more humble Ovambo homesteads. Helpful guides explain what each room is for, and the uses of the various household items displayed, but to see traditional dancing, try the local food, or be presented to the king, you'll need to book in advance. For the visitor, there are toilets, a kiosk selling curios, cold drinks and an interesting – if overpriced – book: *A Journey Through Uukwaluudhi History*. It's worth mentioning that when researching this book it was exceedingly difficult to get in touch with the Royal Homestead, and we've heard that they can be unreliable in terms of their opening.

This area of northern Namibia is the heartland of SWAPO. A monument at **Ongulumbashe**, a 15-minute drive from the Royal Homestead, marks the spot where in 1966 the guerrillas first clashed with South African police, thus effectively launching Namibia's struggle for independence. To find it, take the left turning just 2km from the homestead, and follow the road. Ask at the homestead if you'd like a guide.

OUTAPI Approaching Outapi from the south, about a kilometre before the town behind the open market, is the **Ombalantu Baobab Tree and Heritage Centre** (*admission N$20*). A locally renowned hollow tree, it has served variously as a church, a post office and – in the war years – a hideaway, but is today the site of a community-run venture that incorporates a campsite, heritage centre and craft market.

From Outapi, it's an easy 70km of tar road to Ruacana. West of the border post with Angola, the flat plains give way to a more undulating landscape dotted with scrubby vegetation, culminating in views across to a large dam on the Angolan side of the border.

Where to stay, eat and drink

Outapi Town Hotel (29 rooms) \065 251029; e outapith@iway.na; www.outapith. iway.na. This brick-built hotel on the main C46 is traditional in style & deceptively spacious. Brown walls are enlivened by occasional murals, & rooms – complete with frilly bedding – have AC, TV, kettle & phone. There's a formal restaurant, serving local and international dishes, & separate

bar, while outside is a pool set in grassy surrounds. Secure parking. **$$**

Ombalantu Baobab Tree (4 pitches) \065 251 005; e obthc@iway.na. Part of the Heritage Centre, this campsite has an ablution block with WC & showers with warm water, & braai facilities. Each campsite has its own power & water points. *Camping N$50/20 adult/child; day visit N$20/5 adult/child.* **$**

Other practicalities Outapi is a good source of **supplies**, with a branch of Shoprite as well as a market. There are **banks** and a **pharmacy** here, too, and the town is also the location of the district **hospital**. Most of these facilities are located on the M123, but the **fuel** stations are on the main C46.

RUACANA

The small town of Ruacana perches on the border with Angola, about 291km north of Kamanjab and about 200km west of Oshakati. It owes its existence to the big hydro-electric dam that is built at a narrow gorge in the river some 20km downstream, and supplies over half of the country's electric power. This is of major economic and strategic importance, so the road from Tsumeb via Ondangwa has long been good tar all the way, and that from Kamanjab is now also tarred. The town itself is located 4km south of the C46 along the D3618.

Few visitors stop in Ruacana, and facilities – aside from the lodge – are limited to the supermarket, a large school and a BP fuel station with its own minimarket. This is the only source of fuel for miles, so do stock up if you're heading west.

WHERE TO STAY

Ruacana Eha Lodge (21 rooms, 5 huts, camping) 065 271500; e info@ ruacanaehalodge.com.na; www.ruacanaehalodge. com.na. This unexpected find was originally built for those working on the dam, which explains the presence of a squash court, gym & volleyball, as well as a good swimming pool. Set in attractive gardens, it has en-suite twin rooms that are slightly institutional in layout, but are modern & nicely appointed with AC, TV, phone, kettle, fridge & a private veranda. More fun – if more basic (albeit with AC & kettles!) – are traditional Himba-style huts with twin beds. A tree-shaded campsite has 15 pitches with individual braais, water & electricity. Both share the ablution block, with hot water, which also has facilities for people with disabilities. There's a spacious restaurant (*b/fast N$80; lunch N$170; dinner N$170*) & separate bar. Excursions to the falls & a Himba village can be arranged with 48hrs' notice; you must take your own transport but the lodge will arrange a guide for you. *B&B N$820/575 sgl/dbl.* **L**

RUACANA FALLS Just 20km west of Ruacana, the falls used to be an attraction for visitors, but now the water flows over them only when the dam upstream in Angola allows it to, and even then much is diverted through a series of sluices to the hydro-electric station on the border. Between June and December, they are usually dry.

The falls are well signposted from the C46, 2.5km east of Hippo Pools. The viewpoint is in no man's land, so technically you have to exit the country to see them. However, at the large and underused border post (⊕ 08.00–19.00) you can do so temporarily, without going through the full emigration procedures; at most you'll be asked to sign a book. Be careful when taking photographs: ask permission and don't take pictures of anything apart from the falls. This border area is still very sensitive.

Where to stay *Map, page 456.*

Hippo Pools Campsite (10 pitches) No contact details available, but we're assured it's still open. Located on the Kunene River just west of the falls, at the junction of the D3700 & the C46, this community campsite is also known as Otjipahuriro Campsite, & is a great place for birdwatchers. It's an attractive site at the foot of the valley, with pitches set out under trees overlooking the river, each with its own fireplace & water tap. The central eco-friendly ablution block has WC & showers, but there's no electricity or generator. You'll need to be totally self-sufficient except for firewood. Various trips can be arranged (*from N$25 pp*), including guided walks to the falls & visits to local villages. *N$50 pp.* **L**

Kunene Islands Campsite (3 tents, camping) m 081 127 3931, 081 129 3931; e unicorn@iway. na. Just 10km west of Hippo Pools, this attractive campsite with 21 pitches occupies an idyllic spot on the Kunene River, overlooking small islands & the hills of Angola. A variety of birds & the occasional monkey share the site with campers, who have pitches with braai facilities, taps & solar lighting. If you don't have your own tent, there are both sgl & twin ones here. A stone ablution block incorporates flush WC & hot/cold showers. The camp is kept as close to nature as possible: lighting is provided by solar lamps, but no further electricity is available. Water is pumped directly from the Kunene; we're told that it's drinkable, but can be discoloured in the rainy season. There's a pool on site & visits to river springs 4km upstream can be arranged. The site is within the Uukolonkadhi Ruacana Conservancy. *Tent N$100 pp; camping N$80 pp, plus N$10 per vehicle.* **L**

WEST OF RUACANA West of Ruacana is the Kunene Region, covered in *Chapter 15*. The road in this direction, as far as Kunene River Lodge, is relatively accessible (though a 4x4 is essential during the rains), but beyond that requires considerable care at all times; for details, see page 369.

20

Rundu and the Kavango/Zambezi Regions (The Caprivi Strip)

The north of Namibia is generally very lush, watered by a generous annual rainfall. East of Ovamboland – which means northeast of Grootfontein – lie the regions of Kavango East and West and Zambezi (formerly called the Caprivi Strip).

These support a large population, and a surprising amount of wildlife. The wildlife has visibly increased in the national parks here in the last few years, helped enormously by various successful community-based game-guard and conservation/development programmes (see *Chapter 3*).

The main B8 road across the strip, or Golden Highway as it has sometimes been called, is destined to become an increasingly important artery for trade with Zimbabwe and Zambia, and hence a busier road. Now fully tarred, it has come a long way since the dusty gravel road that I first crossed in 1989, when many viewed it as *terra incognita*.

Unlike much of the rest of Namibia, the Kavango and Zambezi regions feel like most Westerners' image of Africa. You'll see lots of circular huts, small kraals, animals, and people carrying water on their heads. These areas are probably what you imagined Africa to be like before you first arrived. By the roadside you'll find stalls selling vegetables, fruit or woodcarvings, and in the parks you'll find buffalo hiding in the thick vegetation. This area is much more like Botswana, Zimbabwe or Zambia than it is like the rest of Namibia. This is only what you'd expect if you look at a map of the subcontinent, or read the history of the area: it really is very different from the rest of the country.

THE KAVANGO REGIONS

Sandwiched between Ovamboland to the west, and Zambezi to the east, the Kavango Regions broadly correspond to the old region of Kavangoland. Divided into Kavango East and West for administrative purposes in August 2013, the split has little impact on travel. Within both regions, Rundu is the main town. It is a useful stopover for most visitors, but an end in itself for few. Further east is Popa Falls, a set of rapids on the Okavango River. These mark an important geological fault, where the Okavango starts to spread out across the Kalahari's sands to form its remarkable delta in Botswana. Popa Falls has only a small waterfall, but a lovely little restcamp.

Just downstream from Popa, tucked into a corner of the country on the border with Botswana, is Mahango National Park, theoretically part of the bigger Bwabwata National Park but often referred to as a park in its own right. Bounded on one side by the broadening Okavango, it encompasses a very wide range of environments in its

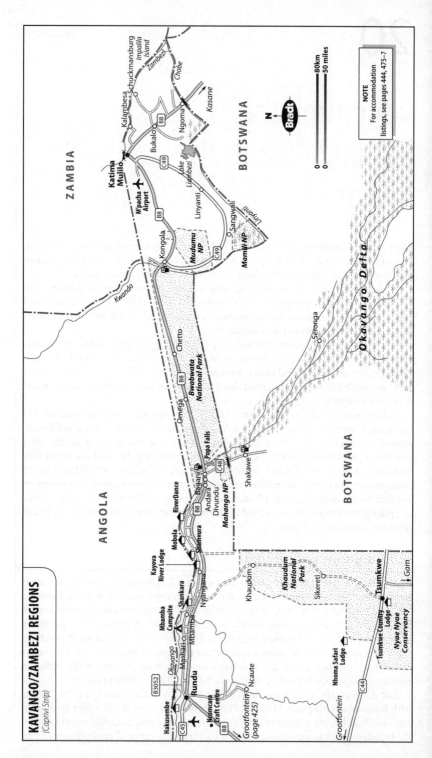

KAVANGO/ZAMBEZI REGIONS
(Caprivi Strip)

ZAMBIA

ANGOLA

BOTSWANA

Zambezi

Chobe

Kasane

Kalambesa

Schuckmansburg

Impalila Island

Ngoma

Bukalo

B8

Katima Mulilo

M'pacha Airport

B8

Kongola

Kwando

Lake Liambezi

C49

Linyanti

Sangwali

Mamili NP

Mudumu NP

C49

Chetto

Bwabwata National Park

Omega

B8

Popa Falls

Bagani

Andara

Divundu

Mahango NP

C48

Shakawe

Seronga

Okavango Delta

RiverDance

Mohembo

Shamvura

Kayova River Lodge

Mobola

Shankara

Nyangana

Mbamba Campsite

Mbamba

Mashari

Ncaute

Rundu

Hakusembe

Namkata Craft Centre

B3052

C45

Okavango

Grootfontein (page 425)

B8

Khaudum

Khaudum National Park

Sikereti

Tsumkwe

Tsumkwe Country Lodge

Nhoma Safari Lodge

Nyae Nyae Conservancy

Gam

Grootfontein

C44

BOTSWANA

N

Bradt

0   80km
0   50 miles

NOTE
For accommodation listings, see pages 444, 475–7

468

small area, and its game has improved vastly since the 1990s. With its expansive reed-beds, tall trees and lush vegetation, Mahango is typical of the game parks further east.

DRIVING FROM GROOTFONTEIN TO RUNDU The road between Grootfontein and Rundu is about 250km of good tar. Initially the only variation in the tree and bush thorn-scrub is an occasional picnic site by the roadside, or band of feathery makalani palms towering above the bush. About halfway to Rundu, however, you stop at a veterinary control post: a gap in the veterinary fence now known as the Mururani Gate. This is the line where land-use changes drastically: from large commercial ranches to small subsistence farms. The fence is put there to stop the movement of cattle, and the transmission of foot-and-mouth and rinderpest disease. The difference is striking; the landscape changes drastically, becoming more like the stereotypical Western view of poor, rural Africa. Drivers should take care, as with more settlements there are now many more animals and people wandering across the road.

Gradually shops and bottle stalls appear, and eventually stalls selling woodcarvings, wooden aeroplanes and pots. About 30km before Rundu, to the west of the road, is the **Ncumcara/Mile 20 Community Craft Centre** (m *081 294 7986, 081 285 6594*) selling Hambera products (the trademark of goods from the Kavango Regions): woodcarvings, baskets, jewellery, and jams made from indigenous fruits, all at very reasonable prices. All products originate solely from community forests and are harvested, processed and produced under controlled conditions by local people in the villages.

Closer to the town, especially during the wet season, kiosks appear piled high with pyramids of tomatoes and exotic fruits – evidence of the agricultural potential in the rich alluvial soils and heavy rainfall.

Where to stay For a good place to stop along this road, try Roy's Rest Camp, some 55km north of Grootfontein (see page 439).

RUNDU Northeast of Grootfontein and about 520km west of Katima Mulilo, Rundu sits just above the beautiful Okavango floodplain and comes as a pleasant relief after the long, hot journey to reach it. Perhaps because of this distance, it feels like an outpost; it certainly has few specific attractions although it has seen something of a boom in recent years, with many bright new shopping malls and businesses. But these distances also make it a prudent stopover, and most of the lodges expect visitors to spend just one night with them. Indicative of its proximity to Angola, just across the river, Rundu has a relaxed, slightly Portuguese atmosphere.

While the river itself is a powerful draw, with boat trips offered by many of the lodges, it is often so low from September to December that anything except, possibly, a shallow canoe will constantly ground on the sandbanks.

Getting there and away

By bus The Intercape Mainliner coach service linking Windhoek with Livingstone and Victoria Falls, stops at the Engen garage, B8 Highway on Monday and Friday at 22.20. On the way back to Windhoek, it stops on Sunday and Wednesday at 20.50. Fares are around N$400 to Victoria Falls, one-way, and N$450 to Windhoek. See pages 98–100 for details or, better, check the latest timetable on www.intercape.co.za.

Hitchhiking The best place for lifts is the Shell garage on the B8, as most people passing this will stop to fill up, or get a drink or food. Watch for thieves in the crowds here, as several problems have been reported in the past.

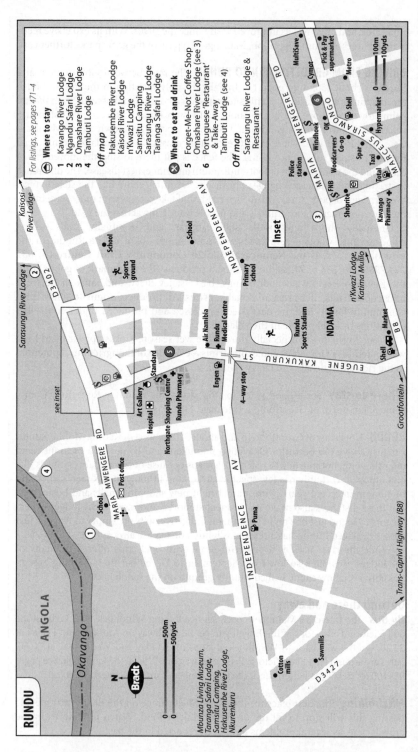

RUNDU

For listings, see pages 471–4

Where to stay
1 Kavango River Lodge
2 Ngandu Safari Lodge
3 Omashare River Lodge
4 Tambuti Lodge

Off map
Hakusembe River Lodge
Kaisosi River Lodge
n'Kwazi Lodge
Samsitu Camping
Sarasungu River Lodge
Taranga Safari Lodge

Where to eat and drink
5 Forget-Me-Not Coffee Shop
Omashare River Lodge (see 3)
6 Portuguese 'Restaurant'
& Take-Away
Tambuti Lodge (see 4)

Off map
Sarasungu River Lodge &
Restaurant

Inset

Police station
MultiSave
Cymot
Pick & Pay supermarket
Metro
Shell
OK Windhoek
Hypermarket
Woodcarvers' Co-op
Spar
FNB
Taxi
Total
Shoprite
Kavango Pharmacy

MARIA
MWENGERE RD
OMACEUS SIRANGO
MARCEUS SIRANGO

ANGOLA
Okavango

School
Sports ground
School
D 3402
Sarasungu River Lodge
Kaisosi River Lodge

INDEPENDENCE AV
Primary school
Air Namibia
Rundu Medical Centre
Rundu Sports Stadium
NDAMA
Shell
Market
n'Kwazi Lodge,
Katima Mulilo
EUGENE KAKUKURU ST
B 8
4-way stop
Engen
MARIA MWENGERE RD
Post office
School
Art Gallery
Hospital
Northgate Shopping Centre
Rundu Pharmacy
Standard
see inset
INDEPENDENCE AV
Puma

Mbunza Living Museum,
Taranga Safari Lodge,
Samsitu Camping,
Hakusembe River Lodge,
Nkurenkuru

Cotton mills
Sawmills
D 3427
Grootfontein
Trans-Caprivi Highway (B8)

Bradt
N

0   500m
0   500yds

0   100m
0   100yds

470

By air The 'airport' – little more than a military airstrip – is signposted off the main road to Grootfontein, to the west of the town, but no longer sees any regular, scheduled internal flights.

Orientation The B8 is the main artery on which people arrive and depart, though it actually skirts the town. To get into Rundu itself, turn off at the buzzing Shell fuel station. This brings you past the sports stadium on your right and to a four-way stop junction, marked by an Engen garage. Continue straight on, and you eventually meet the old river road – now the D3402 – at a T-junction, opposite Omashare River Lodge. This road used to be the main gravel road east to Katima. Now it runs between the river and the newer B8 all the way to Divundu, with occasional access roads between the two.

Getting around Rundu has no public transport network, but taxis congregate near the various supermarkets in town and may also be hailed on the streets.

Where to stay *Map, opposite, unless otherwise noted.*
Rundu has boomed in the last few years. The Zambezi region has opened up more to tourism, and visitors need to stop over on their way there and back. Now there is a wide choice of places to stay, some in town, but most dotted along 30km of riverfront and clearly signposted from the road.

In town

Kavango River Lodge (18 chalets) \066 255244; e kavlodge@namibnet.com. Situated on a secure 3ha site on the western edge of Rundu, with superb views across the Okavango River, the long-established Kavango River Lodge is owned by Jackie Parreira. There are dbl & family en-suite chalets, each with AC/ceiling fan, direct-dial phone, Wi-Fi, TV & small kitchen.

There's a small pool by the Riverview restaurant, set on a hill with stunning west-facing views. It is open to non-residents for b/fast & à la carte dinner (*N$80–150*). River trips, including fishing (for tigerfish & bream) & sundowner cruises can be organised when there's enough water in the river. The tennis courts next door can usually be used by arrangement but lack the net because it kept getting stolen. **$$$**

Ngandu Safari Lodge (41 rooms, 4 houses, camping) Usivi Rd; \066 256723; e ngandu@iafrica.com.na. Just off the main road by the river, beside the turn-off to Sarasungu, Ngandu is an efficiently run complex originally intended as an affordable alternative for holidaymakers, but well suited to the business community. To its whitewashed A-frame chalets with thatched roofs, reminiscent of Cape Dutch style, have been added a range of smaller rooms in various configurations, clustered close together.

Both 'luxury' rooms & 2 family units have AC, DSTV, direct-dial phone, fridge & kettle. 'Semi-luxury' rooms are slightly smaller, while standard have no TV. Wi-Fi is available in central areas. There's also a campsite.

The lodge has a separate restaurant, a curio shop, a laundry, a swimming pool, shaded parking spots, braai facilities, a conference room & 24hr security. New management was due to take over shortly after our visit so the above info may well change. *Camping N$60 pp.* **$$$**

Omashare River Lodge (20 rooms) \066 266600; e reception@omasharehotel.com; www.omasharehotel.com. In the very centre of town, this is in a convenient location & popular with business travellers. Inside the main building are carpeted lounges, soft chairs, a restaurant with à la carte menu (*dinner N$60–150*), the Back Stage bar (the liveliest in town; ⊕ 11.00 into early hours Fri–Sat, until 23.00 Mon–Thu), & casino with slot machines, as well as a conference room. Outside there's a large pool with banana trees planted to provide shade.

The recently renovated rooms are built in a line facing sloping lawns, which overlook the Okavango to Angola beyond. They are small but comfortable, with AC, direct-dial phone, tea/coffee-maker, fridge, safe, flask with water, en-suite shower or bath & WC, & TV; most are twin, but there are some family rooms. Wi-Fi in central areas. **$$$**

✳ 🏠 **Tambuti Lodge** (8 bungalows) ☏066 255711; e tambuti@iway.na; www.tambuti.com. na. This small, eco-friendly Luxembourg/locally owned guesthouse on the western edge of Rundu is perched above the river about 300m from the road leading down to the river, yet near the centre of town. Its whitewashed bungalows with tin roofs are scattered around lush gardens & have been substantially upgraded, are clean, light & airy, with minibar, DSTV, stone floors, roll-top baths &/ or en-suite showers. At the back is a tree-shaded pool, & guests can make use of a braai area & a bar overlooking the river. With a strong emphasis on supporting local businesses, the new restaurant specialises in traditional food, & the lodge arranges village visits and river activities, the latter through Samsitu Camp (see below). *Camping N$60 pp.* **$$**

Further out along the river

🏠 **Hakusembe River Lodge** [Map, page 424] (20 chalets, camping) ☏066 257010; e info@ gondwana-collection.com; www.gondwana-collection.com. On the opposite side of town to most other lodges, Hakusembe is about 14km west of Rundu – off the main road to Nkurenkuru. To reach it, turn northwest off the main B8 on to the B10 about 4km southwest of Rundu. Follow this towards Nkurenkuru for about 10km, until the lodge is signposted towards the river. Now part of the Gondwana Collection, the lodge has recently been renovated.

Hakusembe's riverside location is enhanced by a beautiful flower garden, complete with carefully tended roses, lovingly restored following recent flooding. Each of the en-suite chalets has AC & mosquito nets. They are set amid green lawns leading on to the river. Behind these are 4 camp pitches taking 8 people each, with private ablution blocks, power points & water. A 2-storey family house has a lounge, bathroom & kitchen, & upstairs a loft bedroom opens on to a terrace – ideal for sunset watching. There is also a swimming pool, & nearby, under thatch, a newly renovated popular bar & dining area – though meals are often served on the terrace.

Boat trips (prices vary depending on numbers) are available Jan–Oct; options include fishing, birdwatching (with an excellent guide when we visited) & sightseeing trips, as well as waterskiing, parasailing & kneeboarding. Sunset champagne cruises (*N$195 pp*) are also popular, as well as full-

day tigerfishing trips (*N$120 pp/hr, min 2 people*). *Dinner N$250; B&B N$1,462/1,169 sgl/pp sharing; camping N$150 pp.* **LLL**

🛆 **Samsitu Camping** (5 pitches) ☏066 257023/255602; m 081 129 3290; e kavpharm@ iafrica.com.na. Right next door to Hakusembe River Lodge, Andrew Fudge's campsite can accommodate 10–30 campers with lovely pitches right on the river, each with BBQ & fireplace, water, power & light. The central area has a bar & pool under deep thatch with a kiosk selling snacks. There are several boating options, from morning safaris & sunset cruises (*N$160*) to unguided canoeing (*no charge*). This is a relaxed place with lots of opportunities for activities, but it is not really suitable for small children. *N$80 pp.* **L**

✳ 🏠 **Taranga Safari Lodge** [Map, page 424] (6 rooms, camping) ☏066 257236; e info@ taranganamibia.com; www.taranganamibia. com. This elegant new bush camp is 35km west of Rundu, just off the B10. Its 2 de luxe & 4 luxury tents overlook the river with private decks & are beautifully designed, all dark wood furniture & flooring, with leather & cream interiors. The de luxe tents are much bigger, open plan with roll-top baths & his 'n' hers sinks. All have fans, fridges & tea/coffee facilities. Walkways lead to the tented dining room/ bar area, similarly styled to the rooms, past a small pool & the lovely Kingfisher Bar on a small pontoon over the river. Activities include walks around the 12ha grounds where steenbok & springboks have been reintroduced, fishing (*N$150/hr*), birding walks (*N$120/hr*) & sunrise/sunset cruises (*N$180/250*). The 8 campsites have power, water, braai & tented camp-style ablution blocks. *DBB N$1,265/1,595 pppn lux/de luxe; camping N$120.* **LLLL**

🏠 **Sarasungu River Lodge** (26 bungalows, camping) ☏066 255161; m 081 367 9141/9132; e sarasungu@nawa.com.na; www. sarasunguriverlodge.com. One of the oldest lodges around Rundu, Sarasungu is by the river, just outside town. The well-signposted turn-off from the main road leads down a hill, passing Ngandu on your left, before reaching the lodge a kilometre or so down a rutted, sandy track.

Local fabrics & African artefacts bring an individual touch to large, comfortable en-suite bungalows spread out on green lawns. Brick-built bungalows with AC, a veranda & river view, have twin beds beneath mosquito nets, & showers under thatch. Most also have a small sitting area with chairs & coffee table, while 5 'luxury' rooms have DSTV, fridge & kettle. There are 26 camp pitches in 3 separate areas: the original shady site by the river, further along the river, or in the centre of the lodge grounds; each has its own ablution block.

The Fish Trap restaurant & bar, with its TV loft area & rustic décor, is the focal point of the lodge, & its menu extensive. Alongside pizzas, pastas & more traditional grills, African dishes are added to buffet selections to tempt you to try, with the most popular dishes featuring on the regular menu. Excursions include boat trips (*around N$120*), fishing trips & sunset cruises with champagne (*both N$150 pp/hr*). Wi-Fi is available at reception. *B&B N$600 dbl; camping N$60 pp*. **L**

🏠 **Kaisosi River Lodge** (16 rooms, camping) 📞 066 267125; e kaisosi@iway.na; www. kaisosiriverlodge.com; ✪ 17°52.477'S, 19°49.954'E. Right on the river to the east of Rundu (take the first turning to the left as you head east out of town), Kaisosi is a pleasant, well-maintained hotel. Rooms, all with AC, are housed in deep red, 2-storey chalets, & either have a fan & shower, or are larger, with combined bath & shower. Sound-proofing isn't great, so ask for an upstairs room if you're averse to noisy neighbours. Furnishings are slightly dated. Each room is carpeted, with twin or dbl beds, direct-dial phone, & sliding doors opening on to a patio or balcony with river views. There's also an excellent campsite with private showers. The brick-built main building includes the reception, bar & dining area (*b/fast N$85; lunch & dinner à la carte*), all under a grand thatched roof. Just outside are a couple of pools overlooking the river, & a large area of wooden decking. Activities range from a champagne b/fast (*N$250*) or sunset cruise (*N$150 excluding drinks*), to fishing (*N$1,600/hr*). It's a comfortable place for a stopover, if somewhat lacking in atmosphere. *B&B N$865 dbl; camping N$100 pp*. **LL**

🏠 **n'Kwazi Lodge** (18 chalets, camping) m 081 242 4897, 081 718 5371; e nkwazi@iway. na; www.nkwazilodge.com; ✪ 17°52.063'S, 19°54.502'E. About 22km east of Rundu, n'Kwazi is well signposted (with fish eagle logos) from the main Rundu–Katima road. Take the tar road for 10km, then the 3rd turning left (✪ *18°03.308'S, 19°52.071'E*); 5km later, turn right on to the D3402, the old gravel Rundu–Katima road, then left after a further 3km. The lodge is about 4km along this dirt road.

N'Kwazi was built in 1995 by Wynand & Valerie Peypers, & their son, Pieter, is now the manager. It's a relaxed, friendly place, with families particularly welcome. A couple of large thatched areas – one the main dining room, the other a bar, with ample comfortable seating & a central fire – are the focus of the lodge, overlooking the river beyond. A small pool lies in the gardens behind the bar. Good, home-cooked meals are available, with excellent, fresh buffets in the evenings (*lunch on request only, dinner N$195*).

The bungalows are large, comfortable, wood & stone structures, with high thatched ceilings, large meshed windows & warm fabrics. They are lit by paraffin lamps when the generator stops at 22.00. The adjacent campsite has ample space, showers & power.

Since the unrest in the Caprivi Strip, the Peypers have supported the local community through the villages, schools & churches. As part of this, they run a scholarship project to enable children to progress to high school, & 2 have completed university & a further 3 are attending as a direct result. They have also set up their own preschool supported by guest donations. Visitors to the lodge can visit the local school, kindergarten & churches on request (*N$150–200*), & local dancers perform at the lodge (*N$50 pp*). There are also sunset cruises (*N$130 pp*). *B&B N$390–480 pp; camping N$70 pp*. **L**

✖ **Where to eat and drink** *Map, page 470.*
Rundu has few choices for eating out, and most people eat at their hotel or lodge. Of these, **Tambuti Lodge** (see opposite) is by far the most interesting, with its emphasis on local foods – think Kalahari truffles, baobab ice cream and marula oil – in a charming setting under a shady acacia tree. **Omashare** (see page 471) is the most central, while **Sarasungu** is also fairly close; both serve pizzas or more substantial mains from around N$50. Further afield, Hakusembe, n'Kwazi and Kaisosi also have good tables.

Forget-Me-Not Coffee Shop (📞 066 267283) is a pleasant café on Eugene Kakakuru Street. Close to the centre there's the **Portuguese 'Restaurant' and Take-**

away (☏ *066 255240/255792*), which is actually just a take-away; it's almost opposite the Shell fuel station in the centre of town, near the Woodcarving Co-op.

Shopping **Northgate Shopping Centre** on Eugene Kakakuru Street has plenty of shops for provisions, clothes and IT requirements. For **food and supplies**, try the Pick 'n' Pay, Spar or large new Shoprite supermarkets, which all have a good selection of produce. Close to the Shell garage, stallholders sell a range of fresh fruit and vegetables. Out of town, heading east on the old gravel road, 2km past the turning to Kaisosi River Lodge is the **Vungu Vungu Farm Development** (☏ *066 255162*). For those with a sophisticated line in camp cooking, this is a useful source of juices and fresh dairy produce like milk, butter and cream.

For medical needs, Rundu Pharmacy (☏ *066 255849*) is on the road into town from the B8, and the new Rundu Medical Centre at 3 Eugene Kakakuru Street houses a medical practice (☏ *066 267 233*) and a dentist (☏ *066 255376*).

If you're after **crafts or curios**, there are several options:

The Art Gallery & Tea Garden Eugene Kakukuru St; ☏ 066 256140. Next door to Rundu Pharmacy, this gallery sells paintings by members of the Sikhosana family, as well as other curios, with the aim of raising money for their education. Tea, coffee and cake are served among the plants of the garden nursery.
Mbangura Woodcarvers' Co-op ☏ 066 256170. With a retail outlet in the centre of town, this large,

thriving co-operative supplies many of the curio markets further south, including in Okahandja. It is worth a visit, although most of the carvings on display are larger items such as tables and chairs.
Ncumcara/Mile 20 Community Craft Centre m 081 294 7986, 081 285 6594. 30km south of Rundu; see *Driving from Grootfontein to Rundu*, page 469.

Other practicalities There are several 24-hour **fuel stations** in town, including the main Shell and Engen stations, both of which have shops, and a number of **garages**, including Gabus Garage (☏ *066 255641/255541*), Auto Body Works in the industrial area (☏ *066 256841*) and Dunlop Tyre Services (☏ *066 255445*). There's also a branch of cycle/outdoor specialists Cymot (☏ *066 255668*). For **banks**, there are branches of Bank Windhoek, Standard and FNB.

Sparks Enterprise (☏ *066 255752*) in the centre of town, close to the supermarkets, offers internet facilities.

The hospital and ambulance services are on ☏ *066 265500*, and the police on ☏ *066 10111*.

What to see and do Many lodges in the area support the new **Mbunza Living Museum** (m *081 215 2496*; ☉ *08.00–17.00 daily; www.lcfn.info/mbunza*), on the road to Hakusembe Lodge (see page 472). Its interactive programmes show visitors traditional Kavango culture, from arts and crafts to fishing, bushwalking and singing and dancing, and has received excellent feedback (*N$120–250 pp*)

While Rundu itself lacks any obvious attraction, the Okavango River more than makes up for it, so if the water is high enough (usually January to October), it's worth making time for a river trip.

On the Angolan bank, which at this point is generally steeper and more densely vegetated than its Namibian counterpart, numerous small villages line the river, with men, women and children constantly up and down the tracks to bathe and wash clothes. Tall reeds line the banks on the Namibian side, with villagers crossing between the two countries in *mokoros*.

In excess of 400 species of birds have been recorded along this part of the river, making it a haven for birders. The African fish eagle, no longer hunted now that the

Angolan war is over, has returned to the river to breed. From its vantage point in the tall trees overlooking the river, it looks down on a domain that boasts several species of kingfisher (including the pied, giant, malachite and woodland), and two of jacana, as well as the swamp oboe, the wire-tailed swallow and a range of colourful bee-eaters. During one evening trip here in March, all of these were seen, as well as Senegal coucal, black-crowned night heron, common sandpiper, wagtails, black-headed heron, little bittern and pygmy geese.

Hippos, too, are returning, though are less welcome to the villagers than to visitors seeking out the region's wildlife.

Sunset cruises are run by several of the lodges, with birdwatching trips a speciality of some. Typically, a trip will involve a slow meander against the current, then a leisurely drift back. For the more active, fishing for tigerfish or bream draws plenty of hopeful anglers and, when the water is sufficiently high, the river is also popular for watersports (see *Hakusembe River Lodge*, page 472, for details).

RUNDU TO DIVUNDU: 204KM While the tarred B8 lacks any real diversion, it is straight and even, allowing a consistent speed. The equivalent section of the old road makes a pleasant if considerably slower drive, much of it surrounded by green, irrigated fields with the Okavango River as a backdrop. Do watch out for goats straying on to the road, though, even away from the villages.

Where to stay *Map, page 468.*
Should you wish to break the journey, there are a few places not far from the main road, listed here from west to east.

⚠ Mbamba Campsite (4 pitches) 📞061 255977. This immaculately kept community campsite about 35km east of Rundu was opened in 2006 in the Joseph Mbambangandu Conservancy. It occupies a deeply wooded, tranquil site close to the Shamange River, a tributary of the Okavango. At the time of research, this campsite was closed due to flooding & there was talk that it might not reopen. To find it, follow the signposts for Shambyu off the B8 on to the D3402. After 3km on a tarred road, turn left, then at the fork over the river, bear left & follow the wooden poles. Firewood is available, with hot water & flush WC an unexpected bonus. If you fancy a turn on the river, there's a 1hr *mokoro* trail (*N$50 pp*). *N$100 pp*. **L**

🏠 Shankara Lodge (6 bungalows, camping) 📞/f 066 258616; **m** 085 554 8051; **e** shankara@ gmail.com. About 85km east of Rundu, this would make a reasonable stopover to break a journey. To get there, turn left off the B8 at ✤ 17°59.791'S, 20°30.202'E (there is no sign), follow the tarred road about 3km to the T-junction, then turn left again on to the D3402; the entrance is about 1km on your right. Simple but clean self-catering 6-bed bungalows set in well-kept grounds each have fridge/freezer & braai facilities, or meals are

available at the lodge (prior booking required). Newer 2-bed bungalows are closer to the river, & there's space for camping with ablutions & power. There is a large pool, & a small boat with outboard engine can be hired for N$300/hr. *Bungalow N$500/900 (2/6 people); camping N$90 pp.* **LL**

🏠 Kayova River Lodge (8 rooms, camping) 📞066 258212; **m** 081 786 6058; **e** kayovariverlodge@iway.na; www. kayovariverlodge.com. This pleasant new lodge owned by the Kayova Community Development Foundation lies 110km east of Rundu following the signposts on to the D3411 & the D3024. The 8 chalets are spread in a row in simple gardens & river views. With wood floors & high thatch ceilings, they all have DSTV, fridges, tea/coffee facilities & mosquito nets. The bar & restaurant, with à la carte menu & Wi-Fi access, are near the small pool. 12 campsites are in a large open space with power, water & braai, & shared ablution blocks. *B&B N$830 dbl.* **LL**

🏠 Shamvura Camp (1 cottage, 4 tents, 6 campsites) 📞066 264007; **e** shamvura@iway.na; www.shamvura.com. Set high above the river, this lodge is 120km from Rundu. From the B8, turn left on to the D3411 opposite the Khardoum

Although, administratively, the boundary between the Kavango and Zambezi (formerly Caprivi) regions lies halfway across Bwabwata National Park (formerly the Caprivi National Park), the term 'Caprivi Strip' refers to the entire 450km strip of land that thrusts east between Angola and Botswana from Namibia's northeast corner, and continues to the Zambian border to the east of Katima Mulilo. While the Zambezi region, lying at the eastern half of the Strip, changed names in August 2013 in a continuing drive to reclaim places evoking an unhappy colonial history, it's likely that the Caprivi Strip itself will be known as such for some time yet.

HISTORY OF THE STRIP On the map, the Caprivi Strip appears to be a strange appendage of Namibia rather than a part of it. It forms a strategic corridor of land linking Namibia to Zimbabwe and Zambia, but seems somehow detached from the rest of the country. The region's history explains why.

When Germany annexed South West Africa (now Namibia) in 1884, it prompted British fears that they might try to link up with the Boers, in the Transvaal, thus driving a wedge between these territories and cutting off the Cape from Rhodesia. Out of fear, the British negotiated an alliance with Khama, a powerful Tswana king, and proclaimed the Protectorate of Bechuanaland – the forerunner of modern Botswana. At that time, this included the present-day Caprivi Strip. Geographically this made sense if the main reason for Britain's claim was to block Germany's expansion into central Africa.

Meanwhile, off Africa's east coast, Germany laid claim to Zanzibar. This was the end game of the colonial 'scramble for Africa', which set the stage for the Berlin Conference of July 1890. Then these two colonial powers sat down in Europe to reorganise their African possessions with strokes of a pen.

turn-off (✪ *18°03.152'S, 20°46.346'E*), or – if coming from Divundu – turn right after 80km on to the D3438 (✪ *18°03.305'S, 20°53.518'E*), then follow the signs for 12km. The central bar & pool are home to both a goat & occasionally orphan otters, as well as owners Mark & Charlie Paxton. Accommodation is in either a timber & reed family cottage on a raised platform sleeping up to 6, with fridge/freezer, small cooker, crockery & cutlery, or in well-spaced 2–4-bed Meru tents, each named for its own private area under a tree with WC/shower & braai; 1 also has a freezer/stove, etc, like the cottage. Meals are available at the lodge. Campers have 6 pitches with a double ablution block. Free firewood & water provided, along with free Wi-Fi by reception. Activities include guided walks & birding (412 species recorded to date), small-boat fishing (*from N$400/hr*), canoeing & *makoro* trips in high water only. Day drives with a specialist guide can be organised to Mahango (*from N$4,000*) & occasionally Khaudum (*from*

N$2,400) national parks. *Cottage from N$500 pp; tent from N$400 pp; camping N$120 pp.* **LL**

☀ 🏠 **Mobola Lodge** (5 bungalows, camping) **m** 081 230 3281; **e** mobolalodge@gmail.com; www.mobola-lodge.com. This lovely self-catering lodge lies 175km east of Rundu. From the B8, turn left on the D3415 for 4km then right at the T-junction on to the D3402 for a further 11km. The 3 dbl & 2 family bungalows are well equipped, with kitchenette & outdoor braai. Each has a terrace overlooking the Okavango River & beautiful gardens full of bougainvillea. The pretty pool has a waterfall pumped from the river & there's an island bar reached by a small bridge, perfect for sundowners. There's no restaurant, but pre-ordered b/fasts (*N$90 pp*) can be brought to your rooms & braai packs & game are available. There are 6 camping pitches with shared ablutions, power, water & light. Boat trips, fishing & village visits can be arranged. *N$550/460 sgl/pp sharing per night for 2 nights; single-night stays incur an additional N$50 pp; camping N$90 pp.* **LL**

Britain agreed to sever the Caprivi from Bechuanaland and give control of it to Germany, to add to their province of South West Africa. Germany hoped to use it to access the Zambezi's trade routes to the east, and named it after the German Chancellor of the time, Count George Leo von Caprivi, who apparently never set foot in Namibia (making the later name change even more understandable). In return for this (and also the territory of Heligoland in the North Sea), Germany ceded control of Zanzibar to Britain, and agreed to redefine South West Africa's eastern border with Britain's Bechuanaland.

At the end of World War I the Caprivi was reincorporated into Bechuanaland, but in 1929 it was again returned to South West Africa, then under South African rule. Hence it became part of Namibia.

More recently, during the late 1990s, cross-border skirmishes between Angolans and Namibians destabilised this whole area. Problems arose when Namibia's ruling SWAPO party went to the aid of Angola's MPLA (Popular Movement for the Liberation of Angola), in their civil conflict against the rebel UNITA party. An agreement between the Namibian government and the MPLA allowed Angolan troops to attack their rivals from Namibian soil, thus bringing the conflict over the border into Namibia. In 1999, the situation came to a head when members of a French family travelling through the Caprivi Region unwittingly became caught up in the conflict and were killed. As a result, the decision was taken that any traffic crossing the Caprivi Strip could proceed only in armed convoy. Thus, for the next few years, two armed convoys a day escorted all vehicles travelling between Kongola and Rundu.

Although the road across the Caprivi Strip is now safe, travellers are still advised to stick to well-travelled routes and not to venure off-road to the north where, in certain areas that are barred to public access, unexploded ordnance is still being cleared.

※ 🏠 **RiverDance** (5 rooms, camping)
☏ 066 686086; m 081 124 3255; e reservations@ riverdance.com.na; www.riverdance.com.na. Opened in Feb 2013, RiverDance is 180km east of Rundu, 4km further along the D3402 from Mobola. Stylishly elegant & relaxing, this lodge is owned & managed by Namibians Tino & Karin Punzul, who are committed to ensuring that the local people benefit from their success. All staff are from the nearby village of Mamono & 20% of lodge profits go to community projects. The bar & restaurant area is located on decking high above the river, with vast cream sofas for lounging & a small pool nearby. Most rooms are on stilts above the river, all different, with wood panelling & glass interiors, & private decked terraces. Imaginatively designed, 2 can be converted to family rooms & 3 have separate private bathrooms on the decking with free-standing baths & showers. The 5 grass campsites all have private facilities including kitchenettes & bathrooms. Braai packs are available, pizzas can be ordered & campers (& non-residents) can book meals in the restaurant (which has had excellent feedback), although lodge guests have priority. Activities include game drives to Bwabwata National Park (N$450), sunrise & sunset cruises, *mokoro* trips (*all N$300*), fishing (N$350/ hr for 2 people), island walks (N$250) & village visits (N$150) that give a real insight into local life. *B/fast N$85; lunch N$95; 3-course dinner N$245; DBB N$2,116 dbl; camping N$120 pp (max 4 per site).* **LLL**

DIVUNDU/BAGANI As the main B8 approaches Divundu and Bagani, which are really little more than road junctions, it passes through several villages before reaching a 24-hour Engen garage, which also has a surprisingly well-stocked supermarket that sells made-up rolls and cold drinks. The local bakery is just around the corner. The Intercape bus between Windhoek and Victoria Falls stops here.

The main B8 from Rundu to Katima is a good tarred road that runs parallel to the old gravel highway. While the old road is scenic in parts, it is pot-holed and dusty: not for those in a hurry. A word of warning about the tar road, though. Do not underestimate the distances on the Caprivi: they are deceptively long. Driving in one day from Rundu to Mudumu, or from Popa Falls to Katima Mulilo, or Mudumu to Kasane or Victoria Falls, are the maximum distances that you should attempt as part of a normal holiday trip:

Rundu to Divundu: 204km (see pages 475)
Divundu to Kongola and the Kwando River: 198km (see pages 489–90)
Kongola to Katima Mulilo: 110km (see page 499)

The South African initiative Open Africa has established almost 70 routes across the continent to encourage tourism and development in rural regions. Two of these are located in the Kavango/Zambezi regions. Member lodges, businesses and conservancies work together on common conservation and development aims, and all have a strong ethos of responsible, sustainable tourism. First, KOAR (the Kavango Open Africa Route) runs from Katwitwi in Ovamboland to the Popa Falls area and was launched in 2010. An excellent map of the route, with information on its members and the area, is available in local lodges, or contact Mark Paxton (owner of Shamvura Camp – see pages 475–6) on e mw.paxton@gmail.com. The second route, the Caprivi Wetlands Paradise Route, isn't marketed as well as KOAR but check www.openafrica. org for information. It stretches from the eastern end of Bwabwata National Park to the tip of the Strip. Niqui Bosch (m *081 124 4274*) is the Route Manager and Katy Sharpe at Tutwa Travel in Katima (see pages 500–1) is particularly knowledgeable and helpful.

DIVUNDU TO POPA FALLS AND THE BOTSWANA BORDER A few hundred yards before the bridge over the Okavango, where the new road meets the old, there's a junction. The road to the right – the C48/D3430 – leads to Botswana, via Popa Falls and Mahango National Park. Note that the only fuel in this area is on the east side of the bridge.

Popa Falls Reserve (⊕ *sunrise–sunset; 2WD access; admission N$11 pp if not dining at the restaurant, otherwise free*) Popa Falls lie at a point where the Okavango River breaks up and drops 2.5m over a rocky section, caused by the first of five geological faults. Essentially they are a series of rapids, pretty rather than spectacular; even the warden at the entrance admits that many visitors are disappointed. Beyond the falls, the Okavango begins gradually to spread out across the Kalahari's sands until eventually, in Botswana, it forms its remarkable inland delta.

The area by the riverside at Popa Falls is thickly vegetated with tall riverine trees and lush green shrubs, which encourage waterbirds and a variety of small reptiles. Footbridges have been built between some of the islands, and it's worth spending a morning island-hopping among the rushing channels, or walking upstream a little where there's a good view of the river before it plunges over the rapids. In a few hours you can see all of this tiny reserve, and have a good chance of spotting a leguvaan (water monitor), a snake or two, and many different frogs. The various birds include cormorants with a captivating technique of underwater fishing.

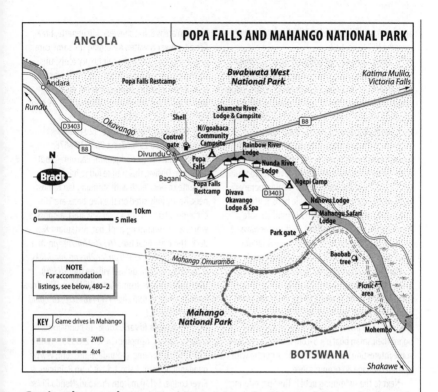

POPA FALLS AND MAHANGO NATIONAL PARK

ANGOLA

Bwabwata West
National Park

Katima Mulilo,
Victoria Falls

Andara

Popa Falls Restcamp

Rundu

D3403

Okavango

Shell

Shametu River
Lodge & Campsite

B8

Control
gate

N//goabaca
Community
Campsite

Divundu

B8

Popa
Falls

Rainbow River
Lodge

Nunda River
Lodge

Bagani

Popa Falls
Restcamp

Divava
Okavango
Lodge & Spa

D3403

Ngepi Camp

Ndhovu Lodge

Mahangu Safari
Lodge

N

Bradt

0   10km
0   5 miles

Park gate

Mahango Omuramba

Baobab
tree

NOTE
For accommodation
listings, see below, 480–2

Picnic
area

KEY   Game drives in Mahango

========= 2WD
━━━━━━━ 4x4

Mahango
National Park

Mohembo

BOTSWANA

Shakawe

Rundu and the Kavango / Zambezi Regions (The Caprivi Strip)

Getting there and away The falls are right on the Okavango's western bank, south of the Divundu Bridge, near Bagani. From the main B8, take the road signposted to Botswana just west of the Bwabwata National Park; the reserve is on the left after about 3.5km, immediately beside the road. Note that the gates usually close at sunset, so if you're planning on staying the night make sure you arrive before dark.

Where to stay, eat and drink *Map, pages 479–82.*
The restcamp at the falls is right on the spot. There are several alternative options, though, so there's plenty to choose from. They are listed below from north to south, and all are clearly signposted:

Popa Falls Restcamp (16 cabins, camping)
Book via the NWR (see page 56), or take pot luck. This neat, organised restcamp that lies right next to the falls has been substantially refurbished, costing some N$40 million. Now part of NWR's Eco Collection, it reopened in Dec 2013, taking on a very different character, quite modern & minimalist in style. The à la carte restaurant & bar (⏱ 07.00–09.00, noon–14.00 & 18.00–21.00) looks contemporary & stylish close to the river & swimming pool. At the time of research, feedback suggested that the service & food didn't quite live up to the ambience of the restaurant & that some teething issues were still to be resolved. There's also a stylish Jetty Bar on stilts right by the falls

but quite a walk from the main camp, although its opening times are vague.

Popa's excellent 2-bed river cabins & 6 family chalets are of a similar contemporary style, with a further 4 chalets due to open on an island. They include AC, TV, safe, fridge, tea/coffee facilities, minibar & Wi-Fi under thatch roofs, with kitchenettes and private terraces. There are 7 individual campsites with power, light, water & shared ablutions, & separate, larger camping areas for overlanders a healthy distance away. Activities include boat trips to the rapids (*from N$220*), fishing & game drives to Mahango National Park (*both N$330 pp ½ day or N$770 full day*). Beware of the mosquitoes, which

THE KAVANGO REGIONS

20

479

are numerous. *Cabin N$1,221/1,155 sgl/pp sharing; camping N$110 pp.* **LLL**.

🏠 **Divava Okavango Lodge & Spa** (20 chalets) 📞 066 259005; e info@divava.com; www.divava. com. Under new management from 2014, this lodge stands on the site of the former Suclabo Lodge. It's a stunning location, high on the bank of a bend in the river, some 2km downstream of Popa Falls.

Each of the thatched chalets, some built high in the trees close to the river, & others further back with open river views, has a split-level bedroom with a large terrace. Furnished in contemporary style with extremely comfortable beds & luxurious linen, they are equipped with AC, minibar, safe & tea/coffee-making facilities. Bathrooms have both a free-standing bath with a view & indoor & outdoor showers. Direct-dial phones, mobile coverage & Wi-Fi to some of the rooms ensures access to the outside world, & there is a computer for guest use in reception. The bar & restaurant are further down the bank, on a long terrace in the trees (or a private meal can be arranged on board their safari boat). A 5-course dinner features some interesting combinations: think quiche with braised cabbage & coconut sauce…

Next to the swimming pool is The Spa, offering facials, massages & manicures: the treatment rondavels, sauna & steam room probably have the best views at the lodge. Activities include boat trips, fishing, game drives in Mahango National Park & a traditional village tour. Staff are friendly & professional, but the many steps at this lodge may make it difficult for those with wobbly legs. *DBB N$2,926/2,200 sgl/pp sharing; FB N$3,153/2,370 sgl/pp sharing.* **LLLLL**

🏠 **Shametu River Lodge & Campsite** (5 tents, camping) 📞 066 259035; m 081 653 1901; e shameturiverlodge@iway.na; www. shameturiverlodge.com. This new lodge & campsite is next door to Divava Lodge (see above), 7km from Divundu off the C48/D3403. Still being built at the time of research were 5 en-suite tents on stilts on the river edge overlooking Popa Falls, promised to be in the luxury category complete with private jacuzzis. There will also be a floating bar, swimming pool & restaurant, & a coffee shop open to passers-by. Owners Mel & Cheryl Barry grow their own organic vegetables for use in their restaurant. Their 7 campsites, already operational when we visited, are immaculate with private, pretty thatch & cane

ablution areas & hot showers, kitchenette, braai, fire pit, power & water. Assuming the same care & attention are given to their luxury tents, this should be a great place to stay. Activities include boat & *mokoro* trips, fishing, birding walks, village visits & game drives. *DBB tent N$1,093 pp; camping N$125 pp.* **LLL**

🏠 **Rainbow River Lodge** (20 chalets, camping) 📞 066 259067; m 081 210 6678; e info@rainbowriverlodgenamibia.com. About 1km from Divava, this simple lodge has basic en-suite chalets, each with standing fan & mosi nets. Beautifully sited on the riverbank are 10 camping pitches (with power & water), alongside which are a swimming pool, bar, restaurant & deck. There are boat trips (*N$200 for 2hrs pp, min 6*), booze cruises (*N$350 pp for 2hrs pp, inc drinks & snacks*) & a 1½hr guided village tour (*N$80*). Overlanders are welcome here. Wi-Fi available for a nominal charge. *B&B chalet N$410–520; camping N$90–140 pp.* **LL**

✳ 🏠 **Nunda River Lodge** (8 bungalows, 4 chalets, 7 tents, camping) 📞 066 259093; m 081 310 1730; e bookings@nundaonline.com; www. nundaonline.com. A short drive from Rainbow River Lodge, & 1.4km from the road, Nunda River Lodge (*nunda* is the fruit of the jackalberry tree) is a lovely owner-run camp right on the river. The lounge & bar are housed in an airy thatched stone building with comfortable sofas, scattered rugs & a large terrace on the river. A pretty swimming pool is set among colourful gardens.

Comfortably furnished bungalows (thatched with brick, canvas & glass) & large Meru tents are scattered along 1km of river frontage, with individual terraces, en-suite bathrooms, 24hr power, fan, room safe & mosquito nets. A further 4 chalets are not river-facing & are slightly smaller. They include 1 family unit for 4. Wi-Fi access is available & there are points of purified drinking water around the site. Activities include a boat cruise (*N$200–220*), fishing (*N$275*), game drives & village walks. Traditional dancing, *mokoro* trips & bird walks can be arranged. *DBB bungalow N$1,491/882 sgl/pp sharing; tent N$1,259/1,033 sgl/pp sharing; camping N$120 pp.* **LLL**

✳ 🏠 **Ngepi Camp** (12 tree houses, 3 bush huts, 2 tents, camping) 📞 066 259903; m 081 202 8200; e bookings@ngepicamp.com; www. ngepicamp.com. Ngepi is 4km off the road, signposted between Divava & Ndhovu. From its inception as a sprawling, green, grassy campsite by the river under some shady trees, Ngepi seems to have grown in line with the enthusiasm of its owner Mark Adcock, its managers & staff, with some quirky touches that add colour & humour to the place. It's fun & lively, with something of a party atmosphere. Aside from the campsite, with 21 pitches & various ablution blocks, there are en-suite bush huts with their own braai areas, simply kitted out tents on high platforms, 3 family units & colourful dbl or twin tree houses with reed walls, mosi nets & open-air showers with great river views. It's all very eco-friendly – simple, but well thought out; & don't miss the throne room with its bathtub overlooking the river! The kitchen is open 07.30–17.00 (later dinners must be prebooked).

For the active, there's volleyball, frisbee-golf, & an innovative 'pool' in the form of an enclosure tied up alongside the riverbank, but a cool beer at the riverside bar is equally attractive. Guided *mokoro* trips are from N$200 pp/2½hrs, & further options range from boat cruises & fishing to game drives, guided walks, & dragon river rafting trips (*N$700/1,300 pp day/overnight*). B&B tree house N$790–880, hut N$690–770, both pp sharing; camping N$120–140 pp. **L**

Ndhovu Lodge (10 tents inc 1 floating, houseboat, camping) ☎066 259901; e ndhovu@iway.na; reservations ☎061 224712; e reservations@resdes.com.na. This long-established riverside lodge (the name means 'elephant') is clearly signposted 20km along the road between the bridge at Divundu & Popa Falls. Owner Horst Kock has a farm in the mountains around Windhoek, & brings his knowledge of the land to this very different part of Namibia. Indeed, the lodge has something of a guest-farm atmosphere, with home-cooked meals served *en famille* in the large, dark lapa. The attractive hand-painted crockery used for meals is also on sale in the curio shop.

Simple Meru-style walk-in tents are set on either side, facing the river, with twin or dbl beds, & a bath or shower & WC under thatch at the back. Rather different is a tent on a floating pontoon, its large dbl bed encased in a lace mosquito net, & the shower & chemical loo en suite. Mains electricity is backed up by solar power. Camping, limited to one group at a time (*max 10 people*), must be prebooked. There's a small pool shaded by trees, while a wooden deck over the river is a good place to chill. A houseboat is also available, sleeping 4, for all-inclusive cruises (*N$6,674/4,920 pp for 3/2 nights*).

Activities include boat trips (*N$195 pp*), fishing & 4x4 excursions into the nearby Mahango National Park or to Bwabwata West National Park (*N$375 plus park fees*). DBB N$1,420/1,060 sgl/pp sharing; camping N$125 pp. **LLL**

Mahangu Safari Lodge (13 bungalows, 6 tents, camping) ☎066 259037; e mahangulodge@iway.na; www.mahangu.com.na; reservations Eden Travel, ☎061 234342; e eden@mweb.com.na. The approach across a neat grassy lawn gives a slightly suburban feel to this thatched lodge, with its lime-green walls & reed fences. Situated adjacent to Ndhovu (bear right rather than left at the entrance), it was opened at the end of the 1990s, with German owner Ralf Walter aiming to make even the most nervous visitor feel entirely secure. Green-painted brick-built bungalows – including 3 for families – face the river; each is en suite, with animal-print fabrics, AC, fridge, safe & 24hr electricity. Camping is on the riverfront, with power, water & shared ablution blocks. Meru-style tents are backed by brick-built bathrooms with solid doors to keep out creepy crawlies.

Inside, photos & game trophies adorn the walls, so it's not to everyone's taste, but most meals are served outside beneath mature jackalberry trees & a riverside bar has draught beer on tap. Wi-Fi is available in central areas but is charged for. Nearby, a high tower affords views across the river, while below, a couple of decks shelter under thatch, & the pool is shaded by a marula tree. Activities include game drives to Mahango & Bwabwata national parks (*N$400–420 pp*), boat trips (*N$180 pp*), fishing (*N$280/hr up to 3*) & guided traditional walks of 2–2½hrs (*N$70 pp/hr*). DBB bungalow N$1,025/885 sgl/pp sharing; tent N$885/780 sgl pp sharing; camping N$90 pp. **LLL**

Ⓐ N//goabaca Community Campsite ☎061 255977; m 081 211 6291; e info@spitzkoppereservations.com. The turn-off for N//goabaca (see page 447 for explanation of obliques) is 1km east of the bridge, & the campsite is 4km from the road – the last 500m along a sandy track. There is talk of a new lodge being built here for 2015 in a joint venture with the community, but at the time of research there were few specific details on timescales. While the campsite was up & running, it was run down & in need of attention. Each of the 4 private pitches has flush WC, hot shower & a water tap; 2 have viewing decks, & all overlook the falls from the eastern bank. The site is run by Kxoe Bushmen, many of whom worked as trackers & scouts for the South African Army during the war, but have subsequently been economically & politically marginalised. Tourism can not only pay them, but also encourages them to put a higher value on their traditional skills & bushcraft, so support them if you can. *N$80 pp.* **L**

MAHANGO NATIONAL PARK (⊕ *sunrise–sunset; 2WD/4x4; N$40 pp, plus N$10 per vehicle, but no charge if you're driving straight through on the main road*) This small reserve, part of Bwabwata National Park, is tucked away in a corner of the Caprivi Strip, bounded by the Botswana border. It is bisected by one of the main roads between Namibia and Botswana, a wide gravel artery from which two game drives explore the area.

Though forming its eastern boundary, the Okavango River is also the focus of this reserve. The eastern loop road passes beside the river and is normally the better one for game. Here the river forms channels between huge, permanent papyrus reed-beds. Adjacent are extensive floodplain areas, where you're quite likely to spot red lechwe or sable, a relatively scarce but beautiful antelope which seems to thrive here.

Beside these, on the higher and drier land of the bank, are wide belts of wild date palm-forest, as well as the lush riverine vegetation that you'd expect. Further from the river are dry woodlands and acacia thickets, dotted with a few large baobabs. This rich variety of greenery attracts an impressive range of animals, including the water-loving buffalo, elephant, sable, reedbuck, bushbuck and waterbuck, and the more specialist red lechwe and sitatunga. Good numbers of hippo and crocodile are also present.

Mahango is a great favourite with birdwatchers; more species can be found here than in any other park in Namibia. This variation should come as no surprise, as the reserve has one of Namibia's few wetland habitats, adjacent to large stretches of pristine Kalahari sandveld. Thus many water-loving ducks, geese, herons, plovers, egrets, kingfishers and various waders occur here, along with the dry-country birds that you'll find in the rest of Namibia. Okavango specialities like the slaty egret can sometimes be spotted, and for many birds – including the lesser jacana, coppery-tailed coucal and racket-tailed roller – Mahango marks the western limit of their distributions.

Among the larger species, the uncommon western banded snake eagles occur, though black-breasted and brown snake eagles are more frequently seen. Similarly, the park's Pel's fishing owls are rare compared with its marsh, giant eagle and spotted owls.

When to visit As with most parks, the game varies with the season. The dry season, July to October, tends to be better as the riverfront is at its busiest with animals drinking. Sometimes the park is inundated with elephants and buffalo. During the summer rains (from November to April) the big game here can be disappointing. When visiting in early March one year, the highlight of my day's game viewing was a distant kudu, and a snatched glimpse of fleeing sable. While game densities have improved since then, the vegetation is still thick and the animals elusive. However, summer migrants like the exquisite carmine bee-eaters are then in residence, making this the perfect time for birdwatching here.

Where to stay There are no facilities in Mahango itself, so most people stay in one of the lodges or restcamps between the park and Popa Falls (see pages 479–82).

Game drives There are two game drives to explore, both branching from the main road about 800m south of the northern entrance to the park. The better, eastern road, which is good gravel, soon overlooks the floodplain, passing a picnic spot before returning to the main road farther south. The western course, suitable for high-clearance 4x4s only, follows a sandy *omuramba* away from the river, before splitting after about 10.7km. The right fork continues along the *omuramba*, terminating at a waterhole, while the left rejoins the main road again 19km later.

EXCURSIONS INTO BOTSWANA

As you drive across the Caprivi Strip, Botswana's Okavango Delta can feel so near, and yet so far. However, just south of Mahango, within Botswana, are several small camps which are close enough to reach while crossing the Caprivi Strip. They offer a taste of the Okavango Delta, within easy reach of Namibia.

At the southern end of Mahango lies Namibia's Mohembo border post (⏰ *06.00–18.00 daily*), followed by a new Botswana customs and immigration post. These are generally quiet posts, and staff on both sides seem pleasant and efficient, but you'll still need to allow around half an hour to clear the formalities in each direction. There are various forms to be filled out on both sides, so it's worth collecting these as you drive into Botswana, to save time on the return trip. In addition to the standard information required at border posts (passport details, vehicle registration, etc), you'll need to know your vehicle engine and chassis numbers, which are usually shown on the tax disk on the front windscreen; if it's not clear, the top number is probably the chassis number. The same information is required separately by the police, who rather unexpectedly may not be in uniform. On the Botswanan side, there's a charge of N$140 to 'import' a vehicle. When returning to Namibia, you'll be charged for a CBC (cross-border charges) permit, currently N$180 for a private car.

Note that prices within this section are in pula (£1 = P14.61; US$1 = P9.79; €1 = P10.73).

MOHEMBO BORDER AND FERRY From the border, the road leads shortly to a T-junction, about 13km north of Shakawe. A left turn takes you to the (free) Mohembo ferry, which usually takes a few vehicles at a time across the river, including the occasional small truck. Expect to find a lot of people waiting around here – some to cross, others to meet those who have crossed, or to buy and sell things here. To continue to Shakawe, turn right at the junction.

SHAKAWE This very large fishing village stands east of the main road on the northern banks of the Panhandle of the delta, some 281km north of Sehithwa and 13km south of the Mohembo border post on the Caprivi Strip. Driving into the village always used to feel like entering a maze of reed walls, each surrounding a small kraal, as the track split countless ways between the houses. The odd trap of deep sand was enough to stop you for an hour, and thus serve up excellent entertainment to numerous amused locals.

Today, however, Shakawe is a bustling little place. Just a stone's throw from the tar road you'll find a significant base for the Botswana Defence Force, as you'd expect in one of the country's more sensitive border areas, and a major police station. If you're going to be doing anything unusual here, then stopping to ask at the police station if it is OK to proceed is always a good idea. If you've the time, take a walk

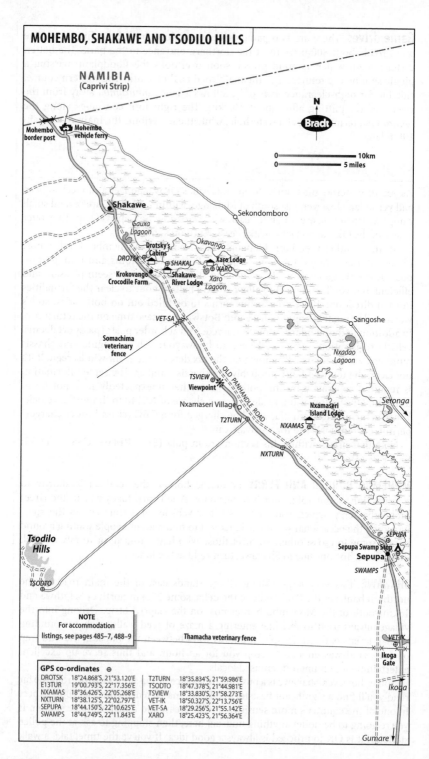

MOHEMBO, SHAKAWE AND TSODILO HILLS

NAMIBIA
(Caprivi Strip)

Mohembo border post
Mohembo vehicle ferry

Shakawe

Sekondomboro

Gauxa Lagoon

Drotsky's Cabins

DROTSK

SHAKAL

Okavango

Xaro Lodge

XARO

Krokovango Crocodile Farm

Shakawe River Lodge

Xaro Lagoon

VET-SA

Somachima veterinary fence

Sangoshe

Nxadao Lagoon

TSVIEW
Viewpoint

OLD PANHANDLE ROAD

Nxamaseri Village

Nxamaseri Island Lodge

T2TURN

NXAMAS

Seronga

NXTURN

Tsodilo Hills

SEPUPA

Sepupa Swamp Stop

Sepupa

TSODTO

SWAMPS

NOTE
For accommodation listings, see pages 485–7, 488–9

Thamacha veterinary fence

VET-IK

Ikoga Gate

Ikoga

GPS co-ordinates ⊕

DROTSK	18°24.868'S, 21°53.120'E	T2TURN	18°35.834'S, 21°59.986'E
E13TUR	19°00.793'S, 22°17.356'E	TSODTO	18°47.378'S, 21°44.981'E
NXAMAS	18°36.426'S, 22°05.268'E	TSVIEW	18°33.830'S, 21°58.273'E
NXTURN	18°38.125'S, 22°02.797'E	VET-IK	18°50.327'S, 22°13.756'E
SEPUPA	18°44.150'S, 22°10.625'E	VET-SA	18°29.256'S, 21°55.142'E
SWAMPS	18°44.749'S, 22°11.843'E	XARO	18°25.423'S, 21°56.364'E

Gumare ▼

along the river that is just behind the police station. Sometimes there's a *mokoro* ferry shuttling local people to and from the eastern side of the river, full with their wares to sell or recent purchases to take back home.

Of particular importance to drivers is the filling station, close to the entrance to the village when heading north. There are also a few shops and a post office, many concentrated within the small shopping centre around the bus stop. And if you can't leave the modern world behind, then Shakawe has mobile phone coverage which usually extends to Drotsky's, but not much further.

If you fancy a break before driving on, you could try a guided tour of **Krokovango Crocodile Farm** (⊕ *KROKO 18°25.817'S, 21°53.682'E;* **m** *+267 7230 6200;* ⊕ *08.00–17.00 Mon–Sat; admission P25/15 adult/child*), about 10km south of Shakawe. The farm is in an attractive woodland setting, with crocs at all stages of growth from hatchling to adult. They're at their most active at feeding time, usually at 11.00 on Tuesday and Friday – though the adults are not fed at all between May and July, so the first feed in August could be quite a spectacle!

Getting there and away There are good daily bus services to Maun via the rest of the western Panhandle from the centre of town. Of these, the fastest is the Golden Bridge Express (*P89 one-way*), which leaves at around 08.00 each morning, taking about 4½ hours to reach Maun. Another service leaves a little later in the day. Minibuses are cheaper but very cramped and take an hour longer; they also depart only when full. Alternatively, hitchhiking is relatively easy along this road.

Self-drivers will need to allow around 4 hours to reach Shakawe from Maun. And for fly-in guests, there's the option of charter flights taking about an hour. The airstrip is to the west of the main road, just 400m off the tarmac.

Where to stay *Map, page 484.*

In Shakawe itself, there's only one real option, but there are several water-based camps on the river about 10km south of town that cater mainly for fishing and birdwatching, while houseboats add further variety. With the increase in the number of travellers along the Caprivi Strip, trade here has picked up, so you will often need to book. The options here are listed from north to south, followed by the houseboats.

Hawk Guesthouse (10 rooms) Shakawe; ☏+267 687 5227. Some 5mins' walk from the river, this uninspiring guesthouse lies north of Shakawe. To find it, take the tar road north through the centre of town, following the line of the river as it turns west. Continue past the large Furniture Mart &, after 0.5km, look for the guesthouse on the left; if you reach the Brigade Vocational Training Centre, you've gone too far. En-suite sgl & dbl rooms are arranged on 3 sides of a small courtyard with a walled enclosure. It's hardly picturesque, but they're clean & come with AC, satellite TV & a fridge. You can pitch a tent here if you have to (though there's no designated site), & there's also a restaurant. *Camping N$100.* **$$**

Drotsky's Cabins (3 family chalets, camping) ☏+ 267 683 0226, +267 687 5035; e drotsky@botsnet.bw, drotskys@info.bw;

⊕ DROTSK *18°24.868'S, 21°53.120'E.* Almost 8km south of Shakawe you'll find a left turn off the tar road. This sandy track will lead you east, crossing the old road up the Panhandle for about 3km to reach Drotsky's Cabins – though note that there are now two Drotsky's Cabins (see also page 486). You should be able to drive this track in a normal 2WD car, though the sand can be very thick so some driving skill is needed.

The good news for many fans is that the original & long-established Drotsky's is still going strong, & still run by Jan & Eileen Drotsky & their family, who have seen Shakawe change from a remote outpost to a thriving little town. Central to the lodge are a thatched bar & a very large dining area, built on a high bank out over the river, & decorated with carvings, masks & local maps. (Look out for the rather beautiful wooden top to the bar, too!) The river at this point is several kilometres wide, a network of deepwater channels & large beds of papyrus. It's excellent for birdwatching or fishing – with several boats with a driver/guide for hire by the hour or day, & fishing tackle available too – but there's little game around except for hippos & crocodiles.

Drotsky's simple A-frame chalets are set among well-watered lawns under a canopy of thick riverside trees. Colourful shrubs & banana trees have been planted between them, creating the welcoming impression of a green & tropical haven. Built on 2 levels, the chalets have brick walls supporting a tall, steeply angled thatched roof, & sleep 5 people: there's an en-suite dbl room downstairs, with steps up to 3 sgl beds above. Expect mesh on the window, rugs on the tiled floor & a table-top electric fan. Campers enjoy a shaded but sandy campsite with 17 pitches, each with lights, electric points & a fire pit – but watch out for the local monkey population! Meals can be arranged with advance notice.

Drotsky's is a genuine old camp, where hospitality hasn't been learned from a manual. If you are willing to take it on its own terms, then it can be a super lodge, & offer you fascinating insights into the area, its history & its ecosystems. *B/fast P130; lunch P170; dinner P180; chalets P340–680 pp; camping P150 pp, inc firewood; boat hire P240–500/hr plus fuel, depending on size of boat; rod hire P100/day; Shakawe airport transfer P65 pp one-way*.

🏠 **'New' Drotsky's Cabins** (10 chalets) Contact via Drotsky's Cabins, page 485; ✪ DROTSK 18°24.868'S, 21°53.120'E. Under the same ownership as Drotsky's Cabins, & technically under the same name, the 'new' Drotsky's also has the same access point from the main road. However, to avoid confusion with its older sibling, we have listed it separately.

Built in 2010 by the Drotsky family, the 'new' Drotsky's is designed like a vast log cabin on high stilts, under a thatched roof, & is approached by an almost palatial series of steps & walkways. Adorned with wrought-iron chandeliers & wood carvings, & with a separate bar under whirling fans, it may sound rather grand, but the effect is homely rather than ostentatious. The log-cabin theme continues in the large, twin-bed en-suite chalets, also raised up on stilts; space is clearly not an issue here! AC, fans & flat-screen TVs are

standard, while old-fashioned armchairs add a touch of traditional comfort, & we loved the ornate ceramic basins. Outside, perfectly manicured lawns sweep around a pool to the river beyond. The main area is entirely wheelchair accessible, as is one of the chalets. For activities and prices, see Drotsky's Cabins, above.

🏠 **Shakawe River Lodge** (10 chalets, 4 dome tents, camping) ☎+267 684 0403; m +267 7230 6822; e info@shakawelodge.com; www. shakawelodge.com; ✪ SHAKAL 18°26.059'S, 21°54.326'E. Known for decades as Shakawe Fishing Camp, this entirely new lodge – opened in 2013 – has risen from humble surroundings. Gone is the simple fishing camp of yore, its expansive river frontage now hosting a stylish yet very open lodge that's all toning neutral colours beneath a topping of smart thatch. From the entrance, you're greeted by a riverside vista of palm trees & papyrus, where basket chairs hang enticingly in the breeze. Sun-loungers on a raised pool deck catch the river view, too, as do the smart restaurant & lounge. Most of the twin & king-size dbl en-suite chalets with sliding glass doors are lined up along a rather reedy section of the river, their contemporary décor enhanced by AC, TV & a bar fridge.

Downstream, the shady old riverside campsite has had a make-over, but remains relaxed & unpretentious, with 10 clearly demarcated pitches, its own bar, & spotless if well-worn showers & WC. Campers are welcome to dine at the lodge, where an à la carte menu features a good selection of pizzas. Beside the slipway, look out for the rusting hulk of an old houseboat, a relic of the Angolan war from the late 1970s. Apparently it was used by 32 Battalion of the South African forces, who were stationed in the Caprivi Strip, but it broke loose & drifted south, & has been gently rusting in Botswana ever since!

The lodge is clearly signposted some 2.5km east of the main road, about 5.5km north of the Somachima Veterinary Fence (✪ VET-SA 18°29.256'S, 21°55.142'E), or 11km south of Shakawe, & is accessible by 2WD. Guests have always come here to fish, especially during the peak season of Jun–Aug, & certainly fishing is still a focus; boats can be hired by the hour or day (*from P250/1,200 excluding fuel*), but birdwatching, as well as day trips to the Tsodilo Hills & Mahango Game Reserve (*P800 pp/day, min 4 people*) add another dimension. *B/fast P140; lunch P140; dinner P200; DBB chalet P1,840–2,510/1,140–1,160 sgl/ dbl; camping P125 pp.*

🏠 **Xaro Lodge** (8 Meru tents) Book via Drotsky's Cabins, page 485; ✪ XARO 18°25.423'S, 21°56.364'E. Xaro is about 8.5km downstream from Drotsky's Cabins, its parent camp, & is usually reached from there by a 15min boat trip. It is set in 30ha on an outcrop from the mainland, amid an old, established grove of knobthorn (*Acacia nigrescens*), mangosteen (*Garcinia livingstonei*) & jackalberry (*Diospyros mespiliformis*) trees, while in the garden you'll find a host of succulents & cacti, banana trees & even a small baobab tree (*Adansonia digitata*). Originally built in the mid-1980s by Hartley's Safaris, Xaro passed through several hands until it was acquired by Jan Drotsky, whose son, Donovan, now runs the camp with his wife, Yolande. Royal, one of the marvellous staff who has been with the family for years, recalls that the lodge has always been used for fishing & birdwatching from motorboats, never from *mekoro* – & that's still the situation.

The origins of a beautiful, old-style Okavango camp still remain in the thatched, stone dining area with a large table in the centre & various old books on shelves in the walls, but a new bar has been introduced, & the Meru-style tents replaced. With en-suite facilities & sliding doors leading to wooden decks, 2 of these can be accessed with a wheelchair. Activities are as at Drotsky's. *P600 pp sharing, inc transfer from Drotsky's; meals, boat hire & transfers as Drotsky's, above; fishing tackle P100/day.*

🏠 **Samochima Lodge** Contact Wilmot Safaris ☎+267 686 2615; e lloyd@wilmotsafaris.com; www.wilmotsafaris.com. This new lodge next to Shakawe River Lodge is still in the planning stages, but may come to fruition in the lifetime of this guide.

Houseboats

Moored on the river near Shakawe, several houseboats offer the opportunity to explore the western fringes of the delta while based on the river itself. It's an entirely different approach, & may well appeal to those seeking a more relaxing trip with less of an emphasis on fishing (although fishing is still an option!). For a general overview, contact Okavango Houseboats (*www.okavangohouseboats.com*), or consider one of the following:

🛥 **Kabbo Houseboat** (8 cabins) Contact Wilderness Dawning ☎+267 686 2962; e reservations@wildernessdawning.com; www.wildernessdawning.com; ☉ Apr–Oct. This 2-storey 'floating lodge', moored on the river near Hawk Guesthouse (see page 485), is designed to make the most of its location. On the lower deck, each en-suite cabin has sliding glass doors just above water level, while above are the dining area, bar & – for those who want to brave the African sun – sundecks. Boating & fishing trips (catch & release) are available or – if you tire of the water – there are visits to the Tsodilo Hills, all at US$75 pp (*min 2*). *US$1,680 up to 8 people, inc FB & 1 water-based activity per day; excluding transfers, most drinks.*

🛥 **Kubu Queen** (2 cabins) m +267 7230 6821/2; e oldafricasafaris@ngami.net; www.kubuqueen.com; ☉ all year. From its base at Shakawe, the *Kubu Queen* is moored at a different spot each night, with tender boats so that guests can explore the river & its channels, & go fishing (except in the closed season, Jan–Feb). Nature walks on some of the larger islands are a further option. Inside, there's a lounge, bar & dining area. Both cabins have a dbl bed, while a further 2 guests can sleep under the stars on the upper deck, where simple twin beds are set up under mosquito nets. The shower & WC are shared, but groups are not mixed, so you won't be sharing with strangers. Another alternative for up to 12 people is to camp on one of the islands. The boat is owned by Greg & Kate Thompson, who have worked in the safari industry in the Okavango for a decade; Greg is a professional guide. *P2,580 pp, excluding VAT.*

NXAMASERI Though the small village of Nxamaseri is not a stop for most visitors, I've included it in this section because the surrounding area is very interesting, offering an insight into the attractions of the delta that put it on a par with most of the reserves further east. Like Guma Lagoon, further south, it's also fairly easily accessible due to the presence of a lodge.

The Nxamaseri Channel is a side channel of the main Okavango River. When water levels are high, there are plenty of open marshy floodplains covered with an apparently unblemished carpet of grass, and dotted with tiny palm islands. It's very like the Jao Flats, and is one of the Okavango's most beautiful corners.

If you want a real delta experience in the Panhandle, then this should be high on your list of places to visit – though getting here requires either your own vehicle or a flight.

Flora and fauna highlights   The Nxamaseri Channel is north of the point where the main Okavango River divides at the base of the Panhandle, and is a stretch of open, clear water up to about 30m wide in places. Beside the edges you'll find stands of papyrus and common reeds, while its quieter edges are lined by patches of waterlilies, including many night lilies (*Nymphaea lotus*; aka lotus lilies), as well as the more common day lilies (*N. nouchali caerulea*). Look out also for the heart-shaped floating leaves, and star-shaped white or yellow flowers, of the water gentian (*Nymphoides indica*).

As with the rest of the Panhandle, this isn't a prime area for game viewing. You may catch glimpses of the odd lechwe or the shy sitatunga, and you're almost bound to see hippo and crocodile, but big game is scarce. However, the channel is a super waterway for birdwatching; home to a tremendous variety of waterbirds. Without trying too hard, my sightings included many pygmy geese, greater and lesser jacanas, lesser galinules, colonies of reed cormorants, darters, several species of bee-eater and kingfisher, green-backed herons, a relaxed black crake, numerous red-shouldered widows and even (on a cloudy morning in February) a pair of Pel's fishing owls. Beside the channel are pockets of tall riverine trees and various real fan and wild date palms, whose overhanging branches house colonies of weavers (masked, spotted-backed and brown-throated). Upstream of the lodge, on the main Okavango River, there's a colony of carmine bee-eaters at a location known locally as 'the red cliffs'. This is occupied from around early September to the end of December, but is probably at its best in late September/early October (the best time for most migrant species here). While watching for birds, keep an eye out for the elusive spotted-necked otter (*Lutra maculicollis*) which also frequents these waters.

Getting there and away   Nxamaseri village lies about 37km south of Shakawe, or 19km north of Sepupa. From the north, follow the tar road to the Somachima Veterinary Fence (✪ *VET-SA 18°29.256'S, 21°55.142'E*), then after 10km you'll pass a slight rise marked by a sign as 'Tsodilo View' (✪ *TSVIEW 18°33.830'S, 21°58.273'E*). From here, on a clear day you should be able to see the Tsodilo Hills to the southwest, but thick vegetation has obscured the view, and sand sprinkled with broken glass makes it a far from attractive place for a break. Less than 3km south of this viewpoint you'll pass a sign to Nxamaseri, which leads to the village of the same name. The turning to Nxamaseri Island Lodge (✪ *NXTURN 18°38.125'S, 22°2.797'E*) is clearly signposted almost 9km south of the village turn-off. Advanced reservations are essential; this is not a place to try to drop into unannounced. Most visitors are transferred to the lodge (✪ *NXAMAS 18°36.426'S, 22°5.268'E*) from the airstrip, but self-drivers leave their vehicle in the guarded parking spot by the turning, and are transferred by 4x4 vehicle and boat for the final few kilometres.

 Where to stay   *Map, page 484.*

Nxamaseri Island Lodge   (8 chalets)
m +267 713 26619; e info@nxamaseri.com;
www.nxamaseri.com. Started as a fishing
camp in about 1980, Nxamaseri is now back in
the hands of the original owners, P J & Barney
Bestelink, & remains a wonderful all-round lodge
justifying a stay of at least 2 days. It has been
built within a thick & tropical patch of riverine

vegetation. All around are knobthorn (*Acacia nigrescens*), waterberry (*Syzygium cordatum*), sycamore fig (*Ficus sycomorus*), mangosteen (*Garcinia livingstonei*), jackalberries (*Diospyros mespiliformis*), sausage trees (*Kigelia africana*) & some of the most wonderfully contorting python vines (*Cocculus hirsutus*) that you'll see anywhere.

Sensitive refurbishment in 2011 means that the strong sense of place has been retained, but with higher standards of accommodation & food. Its wide, thatched lounge/dining area is built around a couple of lofty old jackalberry trees, with an open frontage to the river: it's comfortable & well thought out, but not ornate. Wooden walkways lead to large chalets, & an open 'tree house'. Most are built of brick beneath high thatched roofs, but both the tree house & a trpl room are predominantly canvas structures. Each chalet has 4-poster-style mosi nets, bedside lights powered by a generator or batteries, an en-suite shower & WC, & a wooden deck above the river.

It is claimed that fly-fishing in the delta was pioneered at Nxamaseri, & certainly it remains an attraction for people who fish seriously, but to this have now been added first-class boat trips for birdwatching, visits to a local village to watch basket-making, & day trips to the Tsodilo Hills. There tends to be less emphasis on *mokoro* excursions, but these are also possible (& magical) when the water levels are high & there are suitable areas of shallow water nearby. Fly-fishing & lure/spinning fishing with top-quality equipment under expert guidance are possible throughout the year. That said, the very best tigerfishing months are Aug–Nov, while the best times for bream are Mar–Jun. During the first 3 months of the year the rain & new floodwaters are said to disturb the fish, which move out to the floodplains, so fishing in the channels can be more difficult. Nxamaseri's record tigerfish catch is about 10kg, though in a normal season they'd expect to have 10–15 catches over the 6kg mark. Like most Okavango lodges, Nxamaseri operates a 'catch & release' system, except for the occasional bream that has been damaged. They have a large, flat, bargelike boat which provides a particularly stable platform for several people fishing, & is also ideal for photography, plus a fleet of aluminium-hulled craft. *US$805/567.50 sgl/dbl Jul–Oct, US$450 pp rest of year, inc FB, most activities, fishing tackle, transfers from airstrip/road; excluding alcoholic drinks, lost tackle; day trip to Tsodilo Hills & full-day fishing US$160 pp.*

ZAMBEZI (CAPRIVI) REGION

The Zambezi (formerly called Caprivi) Region's nerve centre, Katima Mulilo, is closer to Lusaka, Harare or Gaborone than it is to Windhoek, and in many ways this region is more like the countries that surround it than like the rest of Namibia. For example, note the different designs of the rondavels and villages as you travel through. Some are identical to those in eastern Zimbabwe, while others resemble the fenced-in kraals in Botswana. Even the local language used in the schools, the region's lingua franca, is the Lozi language – as spoken by the Lozi people in Zambia.

Situated on the banks of the Zambezi, Katima Mulilo is a very lively, pleasant town with a bustling market and most of the facilities that you are likely to need. Away from the main town, the region has two established national parks, Nkasa Rupara (previously called Mamili) and Mudumu. These are both lush, riverside reserves with increasing numbers of animals. Bwabwata National Park (formerly Caprivi Game Park) is also seeing a boom in wildlife, having been badly abused during the war of independence, and it is now benefiting from the restocking of animals and closer involvement of communal conservancies. Right on the area's eastern tip, relying mainly on the riverside attractions of Botswana's Chobe National Park, several new lodges are now springing up, as indeed they are throughout the region.

For a history of the Caprivi Strip, see box on pages 476–7.

DIVUNDU TO KONGOLA AND THE KWANDO RIVER: 198KM Because it borders on Angola, this area was very sensitive and controlled by the military for many years

Communal conservancies such as those in Kunene are becoming the linchpin of sustainable tourism in the Zambezi region. Of 79 conservancies across the country, around a dozen can be found on this relatively tiny strip of land. Many are involved in joint ventures with lodges listed on the following pages (including Lianshulu, Nambwa, Nkasa Lupala and Mavunje) and/or have their own campsites (like Salambala and Rupara). Essentially, conservancies give local people ownership of their land, its natural resources and crucially its revenue, ensuring that they see a tangible benefit from tourism. Consequently, conservation becomes increasingly important, wildlife thrives and local economies improve, while tourists get more interesting and often more authentic travel opportunities. It's a win–win situation and the Namibian model is gaining worldwide recognition, informing development in destinations as varied as Nepal and Mexico. For further information, visit www. namibiawildlifesafaris.com and www.nacso.org.na

(see page 478). Now only two control posts remain to remind you of Caprivi's past troubles: one at Divundu and another at Kongola. You do not need any permits to cross the strip and the people staffing the control posts will usually just ask where you are going and wave you on with a smile; alternatively, you may be asked to provide information about you and your trip, including your vehicle's engine and chassis number.

Bwabwata National Park A large chunk of the Caprivi Strip is taken up by the Bwabwata National Park (frequently pronounced 'Babatwa'). It is bordered to east and west by the Okavango and Kwando rivers, and is divided into two – Bwabwata West and Bwabwata East – with the boundary between them falling 40km west of the Susuwe information point (see page 492). The B8 bisects this currently undeveloped park which, while it is home to much wildlife, has few facilities and little in the way of marked game-viewing side roads. This is changing, however, with considerable development planned over the next few years to include new gravel roads, improved infrastructure and new lodges and camps opening on the riverbanks. All that you can usually see from the main road are a few raptors aloft and the occasional elephant dropping on the road – but drive carefully in case something does appear unexpectedly.

Bwabwata has three 'core conservation' areas: Mahango and Buffalo (both to the west) and Kwando in the east (these are sometimes referred to as parks in their own right but they are in fact all part of Bwabwata). In-between is a 'multiple-use' area with villages and farming land. New measures aimed at helping these communities to coexist with wildlife include benefiting from a share of tourism profits and compensation payments for crops or livestock lost to elephants and predators. There are also, of course, new employment opportunities through tourism and most of the new lodges work hand in hand with their local communal conservancies.

The western entry point to the park is technically at the checkpoint on the bridge at Divundu, just before the fuel station which is the only reliable source of fuel for hundreds of kilometres in each direction. For visitors who are simply driving through the park in transit across the strip, there is no charge. Those planning to explore further, however, must purchase a permit. For Bwabwata West, permits are obtainable at Buffalo (stressed on the 'a', as Buff*a*lo), a few kilometres east of the bridge at Divundu.

There is nowhere to stay, but there is a map of the game drives in the vicinity. For permits for the eastern end of the park, visitors must go to Susuwe (see page 492).

The park is very sparsely populated by humans, with only a few larger settlements: Omega, 70km from Divundu, then Chetto, 40km further on, and Omega III, 60km to the east. Few visitors stop at any of these but they might be helpful in an emergency.

Kwando River area The southern border of the eastern Zambezi Region is defined rather indistinctly along the line of the Kwando, the Linyanti and the Chobe rivers. These are actually the same river in different stages. The Kwando comes south from Angola, meets the Kalahari's sands, and forms a swampy region of reed-beds and waterways called the Linyanti swamps. (To confuse names further, locals refer to sections of the Kwando above Lianshulu as 'the Mashi'.)

These swamps form the core of Nkasa Rupara National Park. In good years a river emerges from here, called the Linyanti, and flows northeast into Lake Liambezi. It starts again from the eastern side of Lake Liambezi, renamed the Chobe. This beautiful river has a short course before it is swallowed into the mighty Zambezi, which continues over the Victoria Falls, through Lake Kariba, and eventually discharges into the Indian Ocean in Mozambique.

To explore any of these areas on your own, ensure that you have the relevant 1:250,000 maps from the Surveyor General (numbers 1723, 1724, 1823 and 1824), plus a compass and a good road map of Namibia. Combine these with local guidance and you will find some interesting areas. If you are heading off into Nkasa Rupara, then you should have some back-up (eg: a second 4x4 vehicle) and a GPS might be very useful.

Kongola and environs Though a large dot on most maps, Kongola is just a small settlement, about 7km east of the impressive new bridge that carries the B8 over the Kwando – tangible proof, in tar and concrete, that the Caprivi Strip is regarded as a major trade artery of the future. Its centre, at the main road's junction with the C49 (confusingly marked on the ground as the MR125, but also labelled on maps as the D3501 or the D3511), is a fuel station. Fuel here, particularly unleaded, isn't entirely reliable, so do fill up earlier if you have a chance. There's also a shop on site selling freshly made bread, and a separate post office. On the opposite corner is **Mashi Crafts** (⊕ *Feb–Dec Mon–Fri; rest of year Sun only*), a community craft centre selling curios made by the local Kxoe community. It specialises in traditional baskets, bead-work and East Caprivian reed mats and carvings, each clearly labelled with the name of the maker, and his or her village.

Getting there and around The Intercape Mainliner bus between Windhoek and Victoria Falls stops at Kongola on Saturday and Tuesday, at 03.45, with southbound buses stopping at 17.15 on Wednesday and Sunday. One-way tickets cost N$456 to Victoria Falls, or N$490 to Windhoek.

Orientation From Kongola, the main B8 continues straight to Katima Mulilo. Heading south, the MR125 (also called the C49, D3501 or D3511) heads south towards Linyanti and eventually loops round to come out near Katima Mulilo. Initially, it passes a number of lodges that line the eastern banks of the Kwando River, before going deep inside Mudumu National Park, and skirting Nkasa Rupara. At the time of writing, this road was being upgraded and should eventually be completely asphalt, but allow yourself plenty of time in the meantime if you're using it all the way to Katima. About 126km from the B8 turn-off is the village of Linyanti, where there may be fuel available; it is then a further 90km or so to Katima.

20

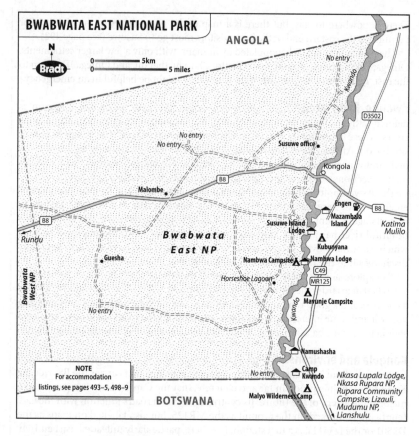

BWABWATA EAST NATIONAL PARK

ANGOLA

N

0 ————— 5km
0 ————— 5 miles

No entry

Kwando

D3502

No entry
No entry
No entry

Susuwe office

Kongola

B8

Malombe

Engen

B8

Mazambala
Island

Susuwe Island
Lodge

Katima
Mulilo

**Bwabwata
East NP**

Kubunyana

Nambwa Campsite

Nambwa Lodge

C49

Rundu

B8

Guesha

MR125

Horseshoe Lagoon

Mayunje Campsite

Bwabwata
West NP

No entry

Kwando

Namushasha

No entry

Camp
Kwando

Nkasa Lupala Lodge,
Nkasa Rupara NP,
Rupara Community
Campsite, Lizauli,
Mudumu NP,
Lianshulu

NOTE
For accommodation
listings, see pages 493–5, 498–9

Malyo Wilderness Camp

BOTSWANA

Bradt

About 4km west of the fuel station in Kongola, between the river and the MR125, is a turn-off south to Mazambala Island Lodge.

Susuwe Triangle To the west of the Kwando River, inside Bwabwata East National Park, is a narrow tract of land that is wide in the north, but becomes narrower towards the Botswana border. Known variously as 'the Triangle', 'the Susuwe Triangle' or 'the Golden Triangle', it is rich in game.

To explore this area you'll need a 4x4 and some detailed maps; you'll also need a permit from the MET rangers' station (⊕ *17°51.703'S, 23°19.159'E;* ⊕ *06.00–18.00 daily; N$40 pp per day, plus N$10 per vehicle*). To find this, turn south from the western end of the Kongola Bridge, ignoring the 'i' sign to the north saying 'Information at Susuwe' – the rangers' station was moved in 2013 but, confusingly, the signpost remains. The new Susuwe Gate station is just off the main road. Here you can buy your permit and will be given a useful map; it's also wise to ask their advice on what you plan to do.

Well worth visiting is Horseshoe Lagoon, about 5km south of Nambwa Lodge and Campsite. This stunning oxbow lake set in riverine woodland attracts excellent game and numerous birds. Elephant are in abundance near here, their presence evident both in the damage to trees and in the cleared sandy area lining the shore: even if you see nothing, you can't miss the prints of various animals in the sand. The overhanging trees have been colonised by a large family of baboons, which makes for entertaining viewing. A word of caution, though: driving alone in this area during or just after the rainy season is ill advised. It's all too easy to get bogged down in the black-cotton soil, and there are few people around to help out should you get stuck.

Tourist information Based at Camp Kwando (see page 495), **Caprivi Adventures** (m *081 206 1515; www.capriviadventures.com*) is a useful company to contact for exploring this region. They arrange tailor-made trips, including private photography, birding or fishing trips, and even excursions in search of Pel's fishing owls.

Where to stay There are several places to stay on the eastern bank of the Kwando River. Some are just campsites; others are much more comfortable. This area looks destined to develop with increased investment in the region, and there is much talk of new lodges being planned. There were also two community campsites on the western bank, within the national park. Nambwa Campsite has now become part of the new Nambwa Lodge (see below) and a second community campsite, Bum Hill, was burnt down in 2013. Rumours suggest that a new lodge will be built there in the near future. If you're driving yourself, be aware that the road south from Kongola is variously marked on the ground and on maps as the C49, the D3501 and the MR125.

In the park
Map, opposite.

✳ 🏠 **Nambwa Lodge** (10 rooms) ☏061 400510 (this may change so check the website); e reservations@africanmonarchlodges.com; www. africanmonarchlodges.com. Nambwa is south of the B8; the turn-off (⊕ *17°47.039'S, 23°20.141'E*) is the same as the new Susuwe Gate and rangers' station. Follow the track parallel to the river until you reach a fork; here you bear right, following the signposts to the camp. Note that the last 14km is through thick sand: a 4x4 is essential & it can take up to 45mins. Alternatively, a complimentary transfer is available from the park gate. This new lodge is on the site of the former community campsite. We visited when it wasn't quite the finished product but what we saw looked good, in a beautiful location on an island in the park. Still very much involved with the local Mayuni Conservancy, who own a share of the lodge & will benefit from a percentage of its turnover, Nambwa will have 10 huge, individually styled luxury tents raised (some up to 5m high) into the trees with views on to the river or waterhole. The tents are roomy and relaxing with pale wood & cream interiors, a comfortable lounge area & en-suite bathroom with free-standing bath. The décor will be opulent but the impact on the environment minimal, with the main lapa built around marula & sausage trees. Their chef hails from the 5-star Heinitzburg Hotel (see

page 123) in Windhoek, so all bodes well on the dining front. Viewing decks overlook a waterhole & plain well-frequented by wildlife (including Matthew, the resident hippo). As well as game drives, planned activities include *mokoro* trips on the river, fishing, bush walks with armed rangers, night drives (currently the only lodge that's allowed to do this), visits to a cultural centre, time with researchers on local lion & hyena projects & with birding experts. *FBA N$4,842–7,104 pp sharing, inc drinks, park fees & laundry*. **LLLLL**

⚊ **Nambwa Campsite** (4 campsites) m 081 428 0512; e juan@africanmonarchlodges.com. Near to the lodge, the site has 2 ablution blocks, with showers & hot water all day & a braai area, but no power. This will be upgraded once the lodge is completed & plans include a swimming pool, café & laundry. *N$80 pp*. **L**

East of the park
Map, opposite.

⚊ **Mazambala Island Lodge** (18 chalets, camping) ☏066 686041; m 081 219 4884; e reservations@mazambala.com; www. mazambala.com. Owned & managed by André Visser, this is the closest lodge to the main road. To get there, turn south off the B8 a few kilometres east of the Kongola Bridge, & follow this dirt road for about 2km to the campsite. Leave your car there & you'll be taken to the lodge by boat. The lodge is carefully sited about 100m from the river – away from the mosquitoes & on slightly higher ground to avoid flooding. The location comes into its own when viewed from the large, open-sided bar & dining area, built high on stilts & with a 12m viewing deck (possibly the highest structure in Caprivi) looking across the Kwando floodplain; there's also a river view from the 15m swimming pool.

At the heart of the lodge is a magnificent sausage tree, around 500 years old, near which small thatched chalets form a tight circle. Constructed of brick & reeds, these are simply appointed with twin beds (or 3 family units), netting windows & ceiling fans, & en-suite facilities at the back. Electricity is available 24hrs. The campsite is on the river at the boat station with its own ablution blocks & hot water. Activities comprise ½-day game drives (*N$380 pp*), boat trips (*N$340 pp*), fishing trips (*price on request*), & guided nature walks (*N$170 pp*). B/fast N$100; lunch N$130; dinner N$210; B&B N$890/1,420/620/550 pp sgl/dbl/trpl/family excluding bed levy; camping N$95 pp; no credit cards. **LL**

🏠 **Susuwe Island Lodge** (6 suites) 📞061 224420; ℯ reservations@caprivicollection.com; www.caprivicollection.com. Refurbished in 2012 to 5-star standard & one of the best lodges in the area, Susuwe is set on an island in the Kwando River, with a strong design focus & the emphasis on service & flexibility. Built, owned & run by the team responsible for Impalila Island Lodge (see page 507), it was constructed with impressive faith at a time of great uncertainty over the Caprivi's future for tourism.

Many fly in to Susuwe; if you're driving yourself you'll normally be met at the checkpoint 13km north of the lodge. To drive direct, take the road west of the river towards Nambwa Lodge & Campsite (see page 493) & follow the signs. After 10km of sandy track, you'll have to leave your vehicle & transfer by boat to the lodge.

Constructed around mature jackalberry & mangosteen trees on the banks of the Kwando River, Susuwe's attractive open central area is decorated with local artefacts & is deceptively spacious. Cool in summer & – courtesy of a welcoming central fire pit – warm in winter, it's fronted by thickly intertwined vines that filter the sunlight but allow the occasional elephant to come right up to the wooden railing. No dining tables inhibit the sense of space; instead, squashy sofas

create individual areas for relaxing, chairs surround the fire pit, & tables are set up for meals according to the number & make-up of guests. Up in the trees, a high 3-tier platform makes a great place for a relaxing lunch, or to spend time with a pair of binoculars – the top tier looks over the tree canopy.

Susuwe's impressive & beautifully designed chalets are entirely private, hidden among thick vegetation along the river. Each comes complete with a lounge area, leading out to a tiny private plunge pool set in a wooden veranda overlooking the river. The canopied bedrooms have king-size beds, mosquito nets, ceiling fans & even hairdryers, while huge bathrooms host twin basins, a large bath & separate shower. Intricate inlay details in doors & floors add a creative touch without losing the essence of space & of the environment.

Relaxed & attentive staff ensure that activities – which include game drives, night drives, boating trips, walks around the island & picnics in the bush – are tailored to individual requirements. This is a lodge to savour – & a place to linger. *FBA N$4,080–4,795 pp sharing, inc drinks, laundry & park fees; 30% sgl supplement.* **LLLLL**

✳ ⚐ **Mavunje Campsite** (3 tents, camping) 📱 081 461 9608; ℯ mashiriversafaris@gmail.com; www.mashiriversafaris.com. Signposted off the C49, 12km south of Kongola. A joint venture between Mashi communal conservancy & Dan Stephens from the UK, the emphasis here is on private river-based safaris & walking safaris with bush camping in undisturbed locations. It's not luxury: Dan provides everything you need but nothing you don't & you're expected to muck in with setting up camp, etc. But it is a great adventure for people who want to get that bit closer to the bush. Mavunje is the main base, located opposite the Horseshoe Lagoon, near the release boma for relocated animals & on an elephant corridor, so there's plenty of wildlife around! It has a small, private tented camp of 3 tents for exclusive use only, rustic & simple in design but well thought out. Each has 2 sgl beds, linen is provided, & there's a shared fully equipped kitchen with dining area & bathroom made of cane & thatch. Meals can be provided with advance notice. There are 3 individual campsites, well spaced out with private kitchen, dining area & ablutions. Dan has an excellent knowledge of the area & its wildlife, he guides & cooks on the river safaris & has exclusive use of campsites on islands where you'll stay. Safaris can be 1–3 nights or tailored to your plans with activities including walking, birding & swimming. Day trips on the river are also available. All staff are local & the community benefits from a percentage of the income received. *Day river safari N$850–1,000, inc lunch, drinks & activities; 1–2 night river safaris N$1,700/3,050 pp sharing, inc all meals, drinks & activities; tented camp N$300 pp; camping N$135 pp.* **L**

Ⅹ **Namushasha Lodge** (27 chalets, camping) ☎066 686024; e namu@iway.na, info@gondwana-collection.com; www.gondwana-collection.com. Standing above the Kwando River, overlooking Bwabwata National Park, all the chalets at Namushasha were totally refurbished in 2014. To get there, take the MR125 off the B8, then turn west at the signpost for a further 4km along the lodge's well-maintained drive. (The final kilometre of this is over a sandy ridge; 2WD vehicles need to be driven carefully.)

A baobab tree stands by the arched entrance, leading to solid, brick & thatch chalets with cream-painted walls & toning fabrics. Some are adjacent, others detached; all are very private. Twin or dbl beds have 4-poster mosquito nets, & each room has a private balcony, of which most look over the river. There's also a classy VIP suite with dbl bedroom, a modern living/dining room, & a huge shower & basin set into solid wood.

The central building features a lofty bar/lounge area under thatch, & a separate dining room (*dinner N$182 pp*) with netting to protect from mosquitoes, all overlooking the river & park beyond. Steps lead down to a deck fronting the water, with a fire pit for chilly winter evenings. Nearby is a swimming pool, with dugout canoes modified into poolside seats, surrounded by green lawns. A small curio shop has basic toiletries.

Activities include boat trips & game drives. There's also a 2.5km self-guided walking trail that circles the riverbank near camp. Namushasha is a good camp, professional & welcoming. The lodge is open to day visitors for lunch & activities; *dinner N$250. B&B N$1,462/1,169 sgl/pp sharing; camping N$150 pp.* **LLL**

Ⅹ **Camp Kwando** (6 tree houses, 14 chalets, camping) m 081 358 2260/206 1514;

e reservations@campkwando.com; www.campkwando.com. Camp Kwando lies 26km south of Kongola, along the C49/D3501, & then a further 3km west from that, past the 'traditional village' of Kwando, where visitors are welcome. Right by the river, the camp makes good use of traditional design, its central area comprising a series of rondavels interlinked in circles that include the lounge, dining & bar areas, plus a deck & fire pit. Furnished in solid wood & cream canvas, & decorated with local artefacts, it's stylish & comfortable, but not at all grand. Simple tented chalets on low stilts with a small veranda sit above the marshes; each has twin beds, mosi nets & 24hr solar-powered electricity, with en-suite WC & shower. Spacious tree houses, with wide staircase access & a higher specification that includes solid wood furniture & floors, overlook the river across to Botswana. The circular campsite has 4 pitches with private ablutions and power, benefiting from tree shade, & there's a nearby pool. Activities include boat trips (*N$310–330 pp*), fishing trips, visits to a traditional village & school, game drives to Mudumu & Bwabwata & guided walks. Unusually, Camp Kwando offers activities designed specifically with children in mind that include traditional fishing & basket-weaving (*N$150 each*). Caprivi Adventures is also based here (see page 493), & can arrange tailor-made activities such as a private tour in search of Pel's fishing owls. *B/fast N$120; lunch pack N$80; 3-course dinner N$240; B&B tented chalet N$790/680 sgl/pp sharing; tree house N$1,440/1,090 sgl/pp sharing; camping N$140/190 pp standard/private.* **LL**

Ⅹ **Malyo Wilderness Camp** (6 self-catering tents, camping) ☎081 124 1436; e deon@karambareservations.com; www.caprivi.biz/malyo.html. Approx 3km after the turning for Camp Kwando is the turn for this campsite at ⊕ 18°02.157'S, 23°21.048'E. It has 6 permanent self-catering tents (just bring food & bedding) & a large communal area for camping with your own equipment, right on the river. Three ablution blocks each have 4 WC & showers. Be warned, it's only accessible with a 4x4 because of thick sand en route. *Self-catering tents N$250 pp; camping N$110 pp.* **L**

Mudumu National Park (*Admission N$40 pp, plus N$10 per vehicle; permits from the NWR in Windhoek or at the Nakatwa Camp in the park*) The more northerly of the region's two reserves, Mudumu, covers 850km² of riverine forest south of

Kongola, either side of the C49. Bordered by the Kwando River on the west, the reserve has good populations of a large variety of animals. Together with Nkasa Rupara and the Triangle, Mudumu is notable for its buffalo (otherwise uncommon in Namibia), roan and sable antelope (both generally uncommon species), the water-loving lechwe and sitatunga, and often large herds of elephant.

Mudumu can be explored on foot or by 4x4, though don't expect much organisation or many clearly marked game drives.

🏠 **Where to stay** To stay in the park, the choice is either an unfenced campsite with river water and basic sanitation, Nakatwa Nature Conservation Camp, or Lianshulu Lodge, by the river. If you opt to camp, then follow the signs to the camp and note that the reserve, which is not fenced or clearly demarcated, borders on to hunting areas. Ask the scouts exactly where the boundaries are. Some of the camps beside the Susuwe Triangle also run trips into Mudumu.

🏠 **Lianshulu Lodge** (8 chalets, 3 suites) ✆ 066 686073/4; reservations ✆ 061 224420; e reservations@caprivicollection.com; www. caprivicollection.com. Lianshulu was one of the first private lodges to be built inside a Namibian national park in 1989 &, in common with all other Caprivi Collection properties, it is owner-run. The 4-star lodge stands on the banks of a backwater of the Kwando River, about 5km down a good bush track off the C49, & 40km from the B8 turn-off. It's usually accessible with care in a 2WD vehicle, but there is also a private airstrip.

The lodge is set on a 404ha private concession beneath a canopy of mature jackalberry & mangosteen trees, giving an air of seclusion & ensuring that it blends into the surrounding bush. Wildlife can come & go freely (daily visits to the lodge are made by Nandi, a large crocodile). An imposing entrance leads into a huge central area with an integral viewing platform looking west over the Lianshulu Lagoon, complete with fire pit, & a second fire right at the back, well away from chilly night breezes. Despite the size, the layout of solid wood furniture & ethnic fabrics combines to create a more intimate series of 'rooms', with lounge, bar & dining areas, & various brunch spots are available including on islands on the lagoon. Painted chalets (with en-suite shower) & suites (with bath, & capacious open-air shower) are well spaced along the river, affording a high standard of accommodation & privacy. Each is under thatch, with 2 dbl beds, mosquito nets, rugs on a tiled floor, a safe, a veranda overlooking the river, & lots of space. One room is designed for families, & is also wheelchair-adapted.

Under the eye of a team of 6 guides, visitors explore the river's channels afloat, go on game drives (including at night) & take guided bush walks through Mudumu, these last in an area that is exclusive to the lodge. Fishing & fly-fishing trips are also available. For guests seeking to appreciate both the aquatic attractions of the Okavango Delta & the wildlife of Mudumu, Lianshulu offers packages with Kwando Lagoon Camp in Botswana, & even has a border post on the concession to ensure a minimum of bureaucratic hassle during transfers.

Lianshulu is an efficiently run operation that maintains close links with the community, & is heavily involved with education at several levels. They are closely linked with the primary school at Lianshulu, having built WCs, repainted school buildings & installed power & solar pumps. *DBB N$3,070–3,685/2,360–2,975 sgl/pp sharing; FBA N$4,725–5,360/3,630–4,265 sgl/pp sharing, inc laundry.* **LLLLL**

🏠 **Bush Lodge** (8 chalets) Some 3km downstream from the main lodge, this is essentially a slightly smaller version of the main lodge, of 3-star quality & suited to more budget-conscious travellers. *DBB N$1,785–2,105/1,515–1,835 sgl/pp sharing; FBA N$2,595–2,915/2,325–2,645 sgl/pp sharing.* **LLLL**

Lizauli Traditional Village

This small village is well signposted on the C49, just to the north of Lianshulu, and is an important attraction for visitors. N$28 is charged as an entrance fee, and visitors are guided around the village where traditional arts and crafts are being practised. Aside from the fascination of the actual attractions

– an iron forge, a grain store, and various carvers and basket-weavers – a visit here gives a good opportunity to sit down and talk to some local people about their way of life. This is just one of several important community projects in this area.

Sangwali Museum In 1999, Stella Kilby, a distant relative of some British missionaries, founded a small museum at Sangwali in memory of her ancestors. To find the museum, continue along the C49 (D3511) from Lianshulu until you reach a sign indicating Sangwali, then a second pointing to Sangwali Health Clinic (this is about 50km south of the turning to Namushasha). Take this road for about 5km, passing the clinic, and continuing towards Mamili as indicated by some rough handmade signs. About 500m before the log bridge, you'll see the museum on the left. Inside, large wall maps trace the route of Livingstone's travels from South Africa through the Botswanan desert until he reached the Linyanti River at Sangwali in 1855. Here, he persuaded the London Mission Society to open a mission station. But four years later when two missionaries, Holloway Hellmore and Roger Price, arrived with their families, the local Makololo tribe weren't overjoyed. When eight of the travellers died after eating meat that had apparently been poisoned, the survivors turned their backs on the nascent mission and trekked all the way back to South Africa. The story is recorded in Stella's book, *No Cross Marks the Spot* (Galamena Press, Southend on Sea, 2001).

Nkasa Rupara (formerly Mamili) National Park (*N$40 pp, plus N$10 per vehicle*) This unfenced swampland reserve of about 350km^2 was created shortly before independence and consists largely of marshland, veined by a network of reed-lined channels. It includes two large islands: Nkasa and Lupala, also called Rupara, hence the new name for the park in 2013. Together with Mudumu National Park, it has the vast majority of Namibia's population of sitatunga, red lechwe and puku, as well as large herds of buffalo and a recorded 430 bird species.

Nkasa Rupara is located in the southwest corner of the eastern Caprivi Strip, where the Kwando sharply changes direction to become the Linyanti. Driving here is challenging, to say the least. Even during the normal rains, most of the park is flooded, but some roads have improved, with bridges to ease access. One remote lodge has been built along with a community campsite, both worth the bumpy road to reach them.

KAZA

In a bold new initiative, the Kavango-Zambezi Transfrontier Conservation Area (TFCA), the world's largest conservation area, was officially launched in Katima on 15 March 2012. Known locally as KAZA, the new 'peace park' (*www.peaceparks.org*) covers around 287,132km^2, a total of 26 protected areas in five countries, connecting the national parks of the Caprivi Strip and Khaudum with those in neighbouring Botswana, Zambia, Zimbabwe and Angola – and notably including the Okavango Delta and Victoria Falls. As with all the peace parks, the primary aim is to create corridors to allow migratory animals, in this case elephants, zebra and buffalo, to move freely between the various reserves, unencumbered by manmade boundaries. It focuses on sustainable development, in particular relating to tourism, to ensure that local communities themselves get value from protecting their wildlife. KAZA's website (*www.kavangozambezi.org*) is full of information on the project.

The conservation policy at Lianshulu is simple: to link the success of the lodge and the national park with direct economic benefits for the local community, and thus to promote conservation of the local wildlife.

The problem with many national parks in Africa has been that the surrounding local communities feel little benefit from the tourists. However, they are affected by the park's animals, which raid their crops and kill their livestock. Thus the game animals are regarded as pests, and killed for their meat and skins whenever possible.

In the area around Mudumu and Nkasa Rupara, the need to involve the communities in conservation is being directly addressed through at least four projects: the community game guard scheme and antipoaching project, the bed-night levy, the Lizauli Traditional Village, and the thatching grass project.

Under the first, game guards are employed from the local villages by the local conservancy offices to carry out regular antipoaching patrols.

Second, there is a nominal charge to visitors for each night stayed on the reserve (already included in Lianshulu's prices), which goes directly to the communities most affected by the park. It aims to compensate for any loss of crops or stock caused by wild animals, and to show that the wildlife can be of direct financial benefit to the local people.

The third project focuses on Lizauli Traditional Village, an attraction by which the local people themselves can earn money directly from visitors. This inevitably depends upon the flow of visitors through the reserve. Since more animals should mean more visitors and hence more income for the village, the local people benefit financially if the area's wildlife is preserved.

Finally, over the years Lianshulu has been involved in the commercial production of thatching grass, which remains important locally. It is, of course, a truly sustainable resource, which can only be produced if the local communities continue to conserve the environment.

Approaching along the D3501, the turn-off to Nkasa Rupara National Park is at Sangwali village. This community, together with the nearby villages of Samudono and Nongozi, has set up a conservancy in the area just outside the park, where they have a simple campsite. There is a small craft stall, Sheshe Crafts, about 4km from the D3501 as you head into Nkasa Rupara. This sells locally produced baskets, carvings, reed mats and some very authentic fishing traps.

Where to stay

Nkasa Lupala Tented Lodge (10 rooms)
m 081 147 7798; e info@nkasalupalalodge.com; www.nkasalupalalodge.com. Just outside Nkasa Rupara National Park, the lodge is 75km from Kongola. To reach it, take the C49 then the D3518 to Sangwali village then either leave your car there (safe parking is available) & be picked up by the lodge, or follow the road signposted to Nkasa Rupara/Mamili National Park for 11km. At Shisintze rangers' station, turn east for 1km. The route is well signposted but don't attempt it without a

4x4. Opened in 2011 by Italian Simone Micheletti, the lodge has 10 stylish en-suite tents on stilts overlooking a channel of the Linyanti swamps. It runs on solar power & is very eco-friendly – even the roof is made of recycled tin drums (it looks a lot better than it sounds!). The central lapa is on 3 floors, with great views from the relaxing lounge & bar. Despite its many comforts (inc Wi-Fi), you know you're deep in the bush, with no other lodges around. Birdlife is prolific here, with over 430 species, & elephants are frequent visitors to camp. Activities include game drives, walks, village visits & boat trips, or a combination of them. This is another lodge that works closely with its local communal conservancy, Wuparo, with local staff & a proportion of income going to community projects. *Activities N$350–800 pp; lunch N$160; DBB N$1,485 pppn sharing, min 2 nights.* **LLLL**

⋀ Rupara Community Campsite
(4 campsites) m 081 469 2558/081 406 7579. Owned & run by the Wuparo Communal Conservancy, this is located *en route* to Nkasa Lupala lodge above. It's a basic but pretty campsite with 4 pitches, with individual water taps & fire pit, shared ablutions with hot showers & a small bar. *N$80 pp.* **L**

Aside from staying in Nkasa Lupala Lodge, the other option for exploring Nkasa Rupara is to stop on the other side of the river in one of several exclusive camps in Botswana. Selinda, Linyanti, DumaTau and King's Pool are all in this area, overlooking the park from Botswana. For details of these, see my companion guide, *Botswana – Okavango Delta, Chobe, Northern Kalahari: The Bradt Safari Guide.*

KATIMA MULILO Established originally by the British in 1935, Katima is the regional capital of the eastern Caprivi. It replaced what is today called Luhonono, the old German centre of Schuckmannsburg, which now consists of just a police post, a clinic and a few huts. Another name change from August 2013, Luhonono was in fact the original name of the town, after a tree prevalent in the area, having been called Schuckmannsburg after the then governor of German South West Africa. Collectors of trivia note that the taking of Schuckmannsburg, on 22 September 1914, was the first Allied occupation of German territory during World War I.

Katima is a large town, beautifully placed on the banks of the Zambezi. Leafy outskirts lead to an open central square, from where it's a short stroll to the town's main street. Recently, as western Zambia has started to open up, Katima has taken on the role of frontier town: a base for supplies and communication for the new camps on the Upper Zambezi River in Zambia. It has just a little of the Wild West air that Maun used to have a decade ago, when it was remote and the hub of the Okavango's safari industry.

Getting there and away

By air Katima's M'Pacha Airport lies about 18km west of town, towards Rundu, and doubles as the military airbase. There are four Air Namibia services a week between Windhoek and Katima Mulilo, on Monday, Wednesday, Friday and Sunday, returning the same day. A one-way ticket costs around N$2,400.

Otherwise, aside from the odd private flight for Lianshulu or Namushasha, the airport is deserted, with no facilities whatsoever apart from WCs. The ever-helpful Tutwa Tourism and Travel (see page 500) runs a shuttle service to and from the airport on request. The **Air Namibia** office (✆ 066 253191; ⏰ 08.00–17.00 Mon–Fri) is on Hage Geingob Road.

By road Katima is about 69km from the Ngoma border post with Botswana, and with only one road through the Caprivi Strip, **hitching**, at least as far as Grootfontein or Kasane in Botswana, is relatively easy. Lifts to Victoria Falls and Etosha have also been reported.

The Intercape Mainliner **bus** from Victoria Falls and Livingstone to Windhoek stops at the Shell Garage on Hage Geingob Road. Buses for Windhoek leave Katima on Sunday and Wednesday at 15.30, arriving back on Monday and Thursday at 06.00. Victoria Falls-bound buses leave Katima on Tuesday and Saturday at 06.30. Tickets cost N$640 through to Windhoek, and around N$352 to Livingstone. Departure times are subject to change so check the website at www.intercapeco.za.

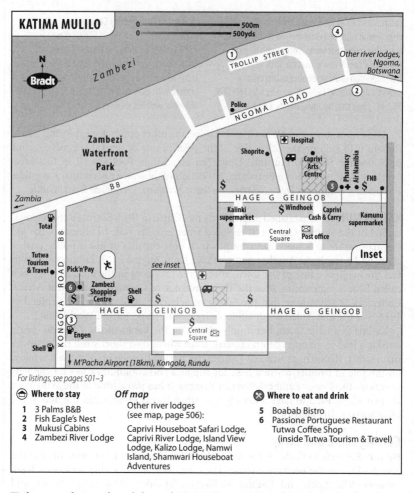

KATIMA MULILO

Zambezi

TROLLIP STREET

Other river lodges, Ngoma, Botswana

Police

NGOMA ROAD

Zambezi Waterfront Park

B8

Zambia

Total

Tutwa Tourism & Travel

Pick'n'Pay

Zambezi Shopping Centre

Shell

Shell

Engen

KONGOLA ROAD

HAGE G GEINGOB

see inset

Central Square

M'Pacha Airport (18km), Kongola, Rundu

Inset

Hospital

Shoprite

Caprivi Arts Centre

Pharmacy

Air Namibia

FNB

HAGE G GEINGOB

Kalinki supermarket

Windhoek

Caprivi Cash & Carry

Kamunu supermarket

Central Square

Post office

HAGE G GEINGOB

Central Square

For listings, see pages 501–3

Where to stay
1 3 Palms B&B
2 Fish Eagle's Nest
3 Mukusi Cabins
4 Zambezi River Lodge

Off map
Other river lodges
(see map, page 506):

Caprivi Houseboat Safari Lodge,
Caprivi River Lodge, Island View
Lodge, Kalizo Lodge, Namwi
Island, Shamwari Houseboat
Adventures

Where to eat and drink
5 Boabab Bistro
6 Passione Portuguese Restaurant
  Tutwa Coffee Shop
  (inside Tutwa Tourism & Travel)

Tickets may be purchased through Tutwa Tourism Travel (see below), who charge a handling fee of N$10.

In addition, **minibuses** ply between Katima Mulilo and Windhoek, via Rundu, while others go to Livingstone or into Botswana.

To and from Zambia To reach the Zambian border, drive west past Zambezi River Lodge until the tarred B8 turns left towards Rundu. Instead of following it, continue straight on to a gravel road for about 4km, passing the (unpleasant) rubbish dump. The border post here at Wenela opens 06.00–18.00 every day.

Sesheke, the small Zambian settlement near the border, is split in half by the Zambezi. Either side makes Katima look like a thriving metropolis in comparison. Namibian dollars can usually be changed into Zambian kwacha here, before continuing on the long gravel road north to Ngonye Falls and ultimately to Mongu.

Tourist information
Tutwa Tourism & Travel ☎ 066 252739; m 081
128 1927; e tutwa@tutwatourism.com; www.
tutwatourism.com. Just before the Zambia–Ndola
T-junction on the B8, this is a mine of useful

information, organising local trips, safaris, birding walks, activities & road transfers. It also sells postcards & souvenirs, acts as agent for Intercape Mainliner, & offers free Wi-Fi for customers at its coffee shop (see page 503).

Keep an eye out for the *Caprivi* magazine, which is an excellent resource for local news and developments. Sadly, the last edition is dated 2010 but there is talk of reviving the magazine in due course.

Where to stay *Map, opposite.*
In town

🏠 **3 Palms B&B** (6 rooms, inc 1 wheelchair accessible) 📞066 252850; **m** 081 279 3762; **e** info@3palms.com.na; www.3palms.com.na. This delightful, boutique guesthouse opened in 2013 & is the best place to stay in Katima town. Owners Michael & Mariana Erdtelt have paid tremendous attention to detail in its design. Rooms are individually decorated in neutral tones with splashes of colour & mosquito screens, AC, DSTV, fridge, tea/coffee facilities, safe, Wi-Fi access & private terraces. Of the 2 family rooms, 1 has been designed specifically for wheelchair users, with plenty of space & rails, & all areas of the guesthouse are wheelchair accessible. The gardens are immaculate with a swimming pool, a raised deck overlooking the river, a pretty lapa with an honesty bar, & masses of birds. The b/fast menu changes daily. Passione Restaurant (see page 503) will deliver dinner for guests. **$$$**

🏠 **Zambezi River Lodge** (38 standard, 4 luxury rooms, camping) 📞066 251500; **e** gm-zambezi@proteahotels.com.na; www. proteahotels.com. Just a few hundred metres off the main road as it enters Katima from Ngoma, this hotel caters mainly for business visitors & tourists who stop for a night. Though the service at its restaurant is attentive, service from the kitchen can be slow & its chefs seem too used to mass catering to produce anything outstanding, but there's always a swim in the pool to make you feel better.

Large, comfortable, en-suite rooms have dark wood furniture, carpets, AC, satellite TV, direct-dial phone, hairdryer & tea/coffee facilities. Set in a row along the river, these have wide patio doors with a view – but with a footpath right along the river, there's little privacy. Campers can stay on the west side of the lodge, on a small site with ablution block, fire pits & electricity. Wi-Fi is available in public areas & luxury rooms.

Zambezi River Lodge is pleasant, generally efficient & fine for a one-night stop. However, its activities are limited to fishing trips & 1½hr cruises on the river through Caprivi Houseboat Safaris, & it lacks the character or activities to entice visitors to stay longer. *Camping N$90 pp, plus N$40 per car.* **$$$**

🏠 **Fish Eagle's Nest** (14 rooms) 📞066 254287; **m** 081 291 7791; **e** fisheaglesnest@ afol.com.na; www.caprivi.biz. This pleasant B&B, opened in Feb 2009 by Martmarie Strauss, is situated just opposite the turning for Zambezi River Lodge. Its 12 en-suite dbl/twin rooms & 2 self-catering options are set around the pool in a peaceful garden with secure courtyard parking. All have AC, 4-channel DSTV, free Wi-Fi, fridge & kettle. A set-menu dinner is served Mon–Thu (N$70–100). **$$**

🏠 **Mukusi Cabins** (40 rooms) corner Hage Geingob/Kongola rds; 📞066 253255; **e** mukusi@ mweb.com.na. The entrance is on the left of the Engen garage forecourt. A cheap & cheerful place popular with local businessmen & backpackers, this has individual, no-frills rondavels positioned close to each other, some of wood & some of brick & tin roofs. It has helpful reception staff, a large bar & restaurant seating 80. Wi-Fi is free to residents. **$$**

Out of town *Map, page 506.*
Several lodges of different styles lie along the river east of town. They are listed here broadly in order of distance from Katima Mulilo.

🏠 **Namwi Island** (16 chalets, camping) 📞066 252243; **m** 081 284 7676; **e** namwiisl@iway.na; www.caprivi.biz/namwiisl.html. Some 5km east of town towards Ngoma, follow the signs to turn on to the gravel road for about 4km to where Lizelle Booysen has created a very smart site in beautiful gardens with 36 camping pitches. Each has its own paved parking area, grass tent pitch & power. The central ablution block has 5 WC & showers for each sex along with scullery & laundry facilities. 4 budget chalets of brick & thatch, containing just 2 beds, desk & light with a braai area, use the campsite ablutions. 1 fully equipped self-catering chalet sleeps 6 people, with 2 further chalets sleeping 2 & 8 luxury chalets with AC, bathroom & kitchen. There is a large pool. *Luxury N$500/750 sgl/dbl; budget N$220/340 sgl/dbl; self-catering N$380–1,000 (2–6 people); camping N$100 pp.* **L**

🏠 **Caprivi River Lodge** (8 chalets) Ngoma Rd; 📞 066 252288/252295; **e** hakumata@iway. na; www.capriviriverlodge.com; ✪ 17°29.280'S, 24°18.575'E. Some 5km east of town, & about 800m down a wide sandy track, this lodge has literally blossomed in recent years under the ownership of Mary Rooken-Smith & her ex-army husband, Keith. Compact, spotlessly clean chalets including 1 luxury family unit, are fronted by lush riverside gardens shared by a family of guinea fowl. Each of the chalets has its own patio, with sliding doors leading through to a room with stone-tiled floor, & beds whose intricately carved headboards, mostly of kiaat wood, are an attraction in their own right. 4 have AC, the rest have a ceiling fan, & fridge, kettle, phone & en-suite shower (or bath in the 'luxury' chalets) complete the picture. At the back of the site are some self-catering wooden cabins with AC & braai area: one is en suite with dbl bed, TV & sofa, while 'backpacker' cabins have a separate ablution block.

Lunch & dinner are served as a set menu in a large dining/bar area with high thatched ceiling; non-residents are welcome with a reservation. Wi-Fi is available here & there's a cosy fire for the evenings, & a cool pool for hotter days. Arranged trips include bird walks, sundowner cruises, guided kayaking & fishing tours. *B/fast N$90; lunch N$120; dinner N$180–230; B&B standard chalet N$950/1,426 sgl/dbl; luxury N$1,300/1,740 sgl/dbl; cabin N$796/1,177 sgl/dbl en suite, N$435/651 sgl/dbl sharing ablutions.* **LL**

🏠 **Caprivi Houseboat Safari Lodge** (5 chalets, 2 houseboats) 📞 066 252287; **m** 081 129 2811; **e** chs@iway.na; www. caprivihouseboatsafaris.com. Situated to the east of town, just after the turn for Caprivi River Lodge, this charming lodge is run by Silke Kauert & Curt Sagell, who took it over in 2011. The lounge areas & bar are on a deck high over the river, with the restaurant alongside. The stone & reed chalets have open-air showers at the rear and a canvas curtain at the front on to a terrace with river view. The 2 houseboats are of aluminium, with kitchen, shower & WC, & 2 roof tents on top: more like

'caravans' than houseboats! A further 2 people can be accommodated by collapsing the dining table to form a bed. Tailor-made itineraries would allow a fun excursion for 2–4 nights into Chobe inc 1–2 nights at the lodge (*from N$5,200–8,760 per boat per night self-catering, plus fuel – estimated at 150 litres*). More local are boat cruises (*sunset N$170–320; ½-day N$300–750; ½/full-day fishing with boat skipper N$1,000–1,700 inc tackle*). *B/fast N$110; light lunch N$100; dinner N$120–180; from N$580/810 sgl/dbl.* **LL**

🏠 **Island View Lodge** (14 chalets, camping) 📞 066 252801; **e** tiger@islandvl.com; www. islandvl.com. Owned & run by Marisa & Riaan Van Niekerk, Island View is primarily a fishing lodge, although the birding is considered to be an attraction, too. To get there, drive 12km from Katima towards Ngoma (about 56km from Ngoma), until the lodge is signposted off left on the D3508 (✪ 17°33.692'S, 24°30.923'E). Continue 17km down a gravel road, then follow the signs to the lodge (✪ 17°32.598'S, 24°31.368'E) for a further 2km; the road is passable all year in a 4x4, & accessible – if bumpy – by 2WD vehicle in the dry season. Transfers can be arranged from Livingstone, Victoria Falls & Kasane.

It's a pleasant site, with rustic, black-painted, reed & thatch chalets on concrete plinths right by the river. All are en suite, with twin beds, fully equipped kitchens, fan & mosi nets, & some have AC. The tree-shaded campsite has its own ablutions, braai area & electricity. There's a pool set amid lawns & the central bar area has a pool table; there's also a small shop selling fishing tackle. *Fishing N$660–1,450 depending on the boat, plus fuel; FB from N$900/800 sgl/pp sharing; self-catering N$600/420 sgl/pp sharing; camping N$115 pp; all excluding 2% levy.* **LLL**

🚤 **Shamwari Houseboat Adventures** (5 cabins) **m** 081 128 5637, 081 147 4253; **e** shamwari@mweb.com.na; www. shamwarihouseboat.com. To reach Shamwari, head towards Island View Lodge (see above), taking a right turn at the signpost for Kalambezi Rest Camp & Rice Project. Renovated in 2014, Shamwari has 2 twin cabins (only 1 en suite), with AC & large glass-panelled sliding doors. A spacious lounge/dining area leads to an open-air braai deck with jacuzzi, & DSTV is on board for those who can't leave it behind. Tender boats accompany the Shamwari for fishing, birding or game viewing – with trips to Chobe National Park possible via the Kasai Channel. Meals are provided but all drinks – beer, wine, bottled water, juices, etc – are extra; guests can provide their own or advise their requirements & they will be prepurchased accordingly. *FB self-catering from N$1,500/950 pp, inc tender boats but excluding fuel.* **LLL**

🏠 **Kalizo Lodge** (6 luxury tents, 2 chalets, 4 houses, camping) ☏ 066 686802/3; **m** 081 814 8861; **e** info@kalizolodge.com; www.kalizolodge. com. The family-run Kalizo stands on the banks of the Zambezi, downstream from Katima. To reach it, drive 12km from Katima towards Ngoma (about 56km from Ngoma), until Kalizo is clearly signposted off left on the D3508 (⊕ *17°34.219'S, 24°32.167'E*). Continue for 20km down a gravel road, then turn left at the sign indicating 5km & follow the arrows to the lodge (⊕ *17°32.419'S, 24°33.989'E*).

Cherie & Johann Griffioen took over Kalizo in Dec 2012 & have been busy transforming it into an elegant, relaxing camp. Set along the river, its luxury tents are stylish (think crisp white linen &

dark wood floor), many have bathrooms & even kitchenettes alongside that were part of the former chalets, & all have fans, fridges, mosquito nets, tea/coffee facilities & plenty of space. Both chalets are wheelchair friendly, & together with the large 3-bedroomed house, have been recently refurbished. They have plans to replace the other houses with 4-bed luxury tents. A large outdoor bar overlooks the river, there's an indoor restaurant under thatch & a pretty pool on a lawn surrounded by decking & loungers. The shady campsite (18 pitches), also on the river, has power, water points, braai & ablution blocks.

Much of the restcamp's original *raison d'être* was tigerfishing, & this is still a feature; boats & equipment can be hired with a guide on a ½- or full-day basis. It's now also popular with photographers, birders (especially for the massive carmine bee-eater colony that migrates here in Sep), with added interest provided by nature walks & the swimming pool. Trips further afield, to Chobe & Victoria Falls, can be organised too. *B/fast N$100; lunch N$125; dinner N$180; DBB N$800–860 pp; self-catering N$520–580 pp sharing; camping N$125 pp.* **LLL**

✖ Where to eat and drink   Map, page 500.

If you are staying in Katima Mulilo, then you'll probably eat at your lodge. Alternative options are at present limited to just:

✖ **Passione Portuguese Restaurant** Kongole Rd, upstairs above Windhoek Bank in the Zambezi Shopping Centre; ☏ 066 252282; **m** 081 221 2906; ⊕ 08.30–22.00 Mon–Sat, 10.00–22.00 Sun. A popular restaurant serving pizzas, fish & grills, it also serves take-aways. $$$

✖ **Boabab Bistro** Hage Geingob Rd; ☏ 066 252620; **m** 081 127 8632; ⊕ 07.00–17.00 Mon–Fri, 08.00–13.00 Sat. Centrally located café with b/fast & snack menus, pizzas, burgers & daily specials. $$
🍵 **Tutwa Coffee Shop** ⊕ 08.00–17.00 Mon–Fri. Inside Tutwa Tourism & Travel (see page 500) is a coffee shop serving b/fast & light meals. $$

Other practicalities There are branches of Bank Windhoek, FNB, Nedbank and Standard **banks**, all with ATMs. Note that changing Zambian currency in Katima is likely to be a problem, so if you have kwacha you may need to cross the border and exchange currency with local traders on the Zambian side.

For **food and provisions**, start just behind the square at the new Zambezi Shopping Centre. Supermarkets are well covered with the local Kalinki, Shoprite and Pick 'n' Pay all in the central area. If you're after something more colourful, there's a busy market in the centre of town, near the craft centre.

On the main parade on Hage Geingob Road is the practical Caprivi Cash and Carry, which carries all sorts of useful goods, including fishing equipment.

Should you be in need of **car repairs**, try Tractor and Truck Repairs on the main road in from Rundu. **Car hire** is available from the Budget Rent-a-Car office at the Engen Garage on Hage Geingob/Kongola Road.

Emergency and health The police can be contacted on ☏ 066 10111. Should you be in need of medical treatment, the number for the ambulance/hospital is ☏ 066 251400, but you'd be better advised to contact one of the town's doctors, Dr Ward (☏ 066 252418; m 081 128 0985) at Katima Medical Centre, next to the Caprivi Pharmacy (see below), or Dr Sitengu (☏ 066 252083), whose office is next to Shoprite. **Katima Dental Practice** (☏ 066 252083; ⊕ 08.00–17.00 Mon–Fri, 08.00–noon Sat) is next to the Air Namibia offices on Hage Geingob Road.

Caprivi Pharmacy also sits on Hage Geingob Road (☏ 066 253446; ⊕ 08.00–13.00 & 14.00–17.00 Mon–Fri, 08.30–11.00 Sat).

What to see and do Katima has few intrinsic attractions, although the lodges along the Zambezi are very pleasant places to stay. For those interested in local crafts, the **Caprivi Arts Centre** on Olifant Street is a good outlet and is well worth a visit.

If you have more time, then use it for trips on the river, or as a base for longer expeditions into Mudumu, Nkasa Rupara, the upper Zambezi and Lake Liambezi.

Zambezi Waterfront Tourism Park A new development in Katima is likely to have a considerable impact on the local economy and tourist infrastructure, if and when it finally opens. Located on a 21.66ha site along the B8 Ngoma Road, just past the T-junction, it is an ambitious public–private partnership which, when complete, will have various levels of accommodation, a campsite, restaurants and conferencing, plus an aquarium, museum and theatre, and even water-based sports and activities. Despite an original completion date of December 2009, by summer 2014 the place was still not open, although it looked complete, and there was no indication of an opening date.

LAKE LIAMBEZI This large, shallow lake is located between the Linyanti and Chobe rivers, about 60km south of Katima Mulilo. When full it covers some 10,000ha, although it has been largely dry, and frequently something of a dust bowl, since 1985. For most of the year, people and cattle now populate its bed.

Lake Liambezi's main source of water used to be the River Linyanti, but after this has filtered through the swamps it has for some time seemed unable to fill the lake, even in years of good rain. However, in 2009, for the first time in many years, Lake Liambezi had a few inches of water, due to good rains and possibly some flow-back from the Chobe River. It was still full in 2014, and has become a popular fishing area for local fishermen.

🏠 **Where to stay** A community campsite has been established in the nearby Salambala Conservancy (see page 508).

ZAMBEZI–CHOBE CONFLUENCE Two rivers bound the eastern end of the Caprivi Strip: the Chobe to the south, and the Zambezi to the north. Their confluence is at the end of Impalila Island, at the eastern tip of Namibia. The Zambezi flows relentlessly to the sea but, depending on their relative heights, the Chobe either contributes to that, or may even reverse its flow and draw water from the Zambezi. Between the two rivers is a triangle of land, of about 700km², which is a mixture of floodplains, islands and channels that link the two rivers.

This swampy, riverine area is home to several thousand local people, mostly members of Zambia's Lozi tribe. (The main local languages here are Lozi and Sobia.) Most have a seasonal lifestyle, living next to the river channels, fishing, keeping cattle, and farming maize, sorghum and pumpkins. They move with the water levels, transferring on to higher, drier ground as the waters rise.

Flora and fauna The area's ecosystems are similar to those in the upper reaches of the Okavango Delta: deepwater channels lined by wide reed-beds and rafts of papyrus. Some of the larger islands are still forested with baobabs, water figs, knobthorn, umbrella thorn, mopane, pod mahogany, star chestnut and sickle-leafed albizia, while jackalberry and Chobe waterberry overhang the rivers, festooned with creepers and vines.

Because of hunting by the local population, large mammals are scarce. Most that do occur come over from Botswana's Chobe National Park. Elephants and buffalo sometimes swim over, and even lion have been known to swim across into Namibia in search of the tasty domestic cattle kept there.

Even when there are no large mammals here, the birdlife is spectacular. Large flocks of white-faced ducks congregate on islands in the rivers, African skimmers nest on exposed sandbanks, and both reed cormorants and darters are seen fishing or perching while they dry their feathers. Kingfishers are numerous, from the giant to the tiny pygmy, as are herons and egrets. However, the area's most unusual bird is the unassuming rock pratincole with its black, white and grey body, which perches on the rocks of rapids, between hawking for insects in the spray.

Where to stay Map, page 506.

The largest island in this area, Impalila Island, is at the very tip of Namibia. It gained notoriety during the 1980s as a military base for the SADF (South African Defence Forces), as it was strategically positioned within sight of Botswana, Zambia and Zimbabwe. It still boasts a 1,300m-long runway of smooth tar, but now its barracks are a secondary school, serving most of the older children in the area.

The lodges here are usually reached by a short boat transfer from Kasane in Botswana, and use the customs and immigration post on Impalila (✆ 07.00–17.00).

Ichingo Chobe River Lodge (8 Meru tents) m +267 7130 2439 (on island), +267 7130 2439 (on island), +27 79 871 7603 (reservations); e info@ichobezi.co.za; www.ichobezi.co.za. Ichingo was the brainchild of Dawn & Ralph Oxenham, who have run the lodge since 1996, although Ralph sadly died in 2014. Occupying a secluded site on the south side of Impalila Island, it overlooks the quiet backwaters of some of the Chobe River's rapids, a world away from busy Kasane just across the water. It makes a super base for river trips & game viewing from boats along the Chobe River, & offers some excellent birdwatching too.

Guests stay in walk-in Meru tents, each set high above the flood levels – important in a location where the rise & fall of water is up to 2m. En-suite showers are at the back under thatch, & there's a balcony at the front, with views of the water through thick vegetation, dominated by the water-tolerant waterberry trees, *Syzygium guineese*, & the orange-fruited mangosteen, *Garcinia livingstonei*. In the evening a generator ensures a steady power supply, backed up by battery lights in each tent. Meals are around a large, solid wooden table in the thatched dining area/bar/lounge that fronts on to the river.

Activities are run individually, with a guide allocated to each tent for the duration of the guests' stay. Not surprisingly, the river is the main focus, with game viewing, birdwatching & fishing from motorboats, & fly-fishing in the rapids, as well as island walks through local villages to a giant baobab. Unusually for a bush lodge, the camp actively welcomes children of all ages, even when not accompanied by adults, as craft activities can usually be organised for them. *N$2,850–4,000 pp sharing, inc FB, most drinks, activities & boat transfer from Kasane Immigration Post.*

'Safari' boats m +267 7130 2439; e info@ichobezi.co.za; www.ichobezi.co.za. For those seeking to spend longer on the river, Ichingo (see above) has 3 luxury 'safari' boats: the 8-berth Ichobezi Moli & Ichobezi Mukwae, & the relatively newly acquired 10-berth Pride of the Zambezi, which cruise on the Zambezi & Chobe rivers, as well as into the contiguous wetlands of the Caprivi Strip. As Namibian registered vessels, they are permitted to cruise the waters of the Chobe when the national park is closed & all Botswanan vessels must leave,

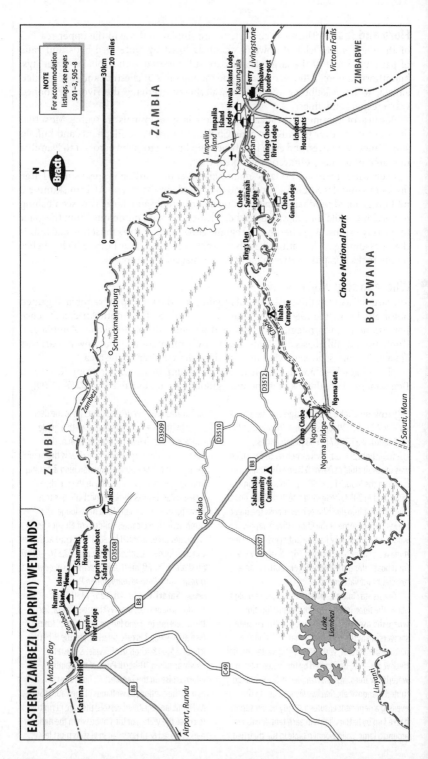

EASTERN ZAMBEZI (CAPRIVI) WETLANDS

NOTE
For accommodation
listings, see pages
501–3, 505–8

ZAMBIA

ZAMBIA

Schuckmannsburg

Kalize

Shamwati Houseboat

Namwi Island

Island View

Caprivi Houseboat
Safari Lodge

Caprivi
River Lodge

Maziba Bay

Katima Mulilo

Airport, Rundu

Bukalo

Salambala
Community
Campsite

Camp Chobe

Ngoma
Ngoma Bridge

Ngoma Gate

Lake
Liambezi

Linyanti

Savuti, Maun

Chobe National Park

BOTSWANA

Ihaha
Campsite

King's Den

Chobe
Savannah
Lodge

Chobe
Game Lodge

Kasane

Ichingo Chobe
River Lodge

Ichobezi
Houseboats

Impalila
Island
Lodge

Impalila
Island

Ntwala Island Lodge

Kazungula

Ferry
Zimbabwe
border post

Victoria Falls

Livingstone

ZIMBABWE

N

Bradt

0   30km

0   20 miles

so offer a unique opportunity to watch game & experience the tranquillity of the river after dark & at sunrise. With its crew of 5, each boat is considered an extension of the lodge, with small groups & personal attention. Each en-suite cabin has huge picture windows, so guests can sit & watch wildlife from their rooms or up on deck. This is the chance for total relaxation with a drink, or in the on-board plunge pool, but for more involvement tender boats are available for fishing or birdwatching with an experienced guide. *N\$3,000–4,700 pp sharing, inc FB, most drinks, activites, boat transfer from Kasane Immigration Post. Open all year.*

🏠 **Impalila Island Lodge** (8 chalets) An African Anthology, South Africa; \ +27 11 781 1661; e sales@anthology.co.za; www.anthology. co.za. Situated on the northwest side of Impalila Island, overlooking the Zambezi's Mambova Rapids, Impalila Island Lodge has in many ways brought the island to people's attention.

Accommodation is in raised wooden chalets, each with twin beds or a king-size dbl. It is fairly luxurious, with much made of polished local mukwa wood, with its natural variegated yellow & brown colours. The chalets have a square design, enclosing a bathroom in one corner, giving blissfully warm showers from instant water heaters. Below the high thatch ceilings are fans for warmer days, & mosquito nets. Large dbl doors open 1 corner of the room on to a wide wooden veranda, overlooking the rapids. These doors have an optional mosquito-net screen for when it's hot, though being next to the river can be quite cold on winter mornings.

The main part of the lodge is a large thatched bar/dining area & comfortable lounge built around a huge baobab. This is open to the breeze, though can be sheltered when cold. The wooden pool deck has reclining loungers, umbrellas & a great view of the river. Impalila's food is excellent & candlelit 3-course meals around the baobab make a memorable scene.

Activities include guided motorboat trips on the Zambezi & Chobe: the Zambezi mainly for birdwatching & fishing, while longer boat trips on the Chobe offer remarkable game-viewing on the edge of the national park. There are nature walks on the island, & superb fishing (especially for tigerfish, best caught on a fly-rod) with guides who are experienced enough to take both experts & beginners out to try their luck.

Since the design stage, the team at Impalila has worked in a low-key but positive way to involve the local community. Currently the lodge pays into a 'community development fund' that is utilised by the community for various projects – the clinic, the school, measures to encourage preservation of wildlife & to conserve the local environment – & administered jointly with the local chief. The lodge has been actively involved in setting up the Impalila conservancy, which protects local wildlife. The lodge also makes a US\$40 per guest donation to a community development fund.

Because of their excellent approach, don't miss the visits that the lodge organises to local villages, as they can be very rewarding. (Note that Impalila has a super sister lodge, Susuwe Island Lodge (page 494), in the Caprivi Strip, with an equally progressive approach to community involvement.

This is a stylish, well-run lodge ideal for fishing, birding, walking or just relaxing, with the added bonus of game viewing from the river in Chobe. *US\$355–395 pp sharing, inc FB, most drinks, laundry & activities; 30% sgl supplement. Open all year.*

🏠 **Ntwala Island Lodge** (4 suites) Ntwala Island; m 081 673 5652; reservations as for Impalila (see opposite). The secluded & ultra-exclusive camp operated by Impalila is situated on a cluster of islands within the Mambova Rapids, linked together by floating walkways. Each chalet has all that you would expect – & more – in the way of luxury, & comes complete with indoor & outdoor showers, complimentary minibar, its own sand-fringed plunge pool & deck, & a private sala extending over the water. Facing the rapids, the central building continues the theme, with guests coming together for evening meals. Guests in each suite are allocated a personal guide & their own boat, ready to explore the quiet backwaters, indulge in a spot of tigerfishing, or take in a sunset cruise on the Chobe River. *FB US\$415–595 pp sharing, inc most drinks, laundry, activities; 30% sgl supplement. Open all year.*

🏠 **Chobe Water Villas** (formerly King's Den) www.chobewatervillas.com. Overlooking Chobe National Park from Kasikili (Sedudu) Island, this lodge is currently being rebuilt, apparently to a very high standard. Note that it is nearer to the park than any of Impalila Island's lodges. It will have 16 'luxury' villas, built on stilts by the river - all with AC, Wi-Fi, minibar & safe. The main area will include a lounge, bar, restaurant, pool & deck. Chobe Water Villas is due to open in Jul 2015.

⚓ *Zambezi Queen* (14 suites) \ +27 21 438 0032; e info@zambeziqueen.com; www.

zambeziqueen.com. Formerly owned by King's Den, this prestigious 45m riverboat has had a serious makeover to emerge in late 2009 polished and kitted out in 5-star luxury. Up on deck there's a pool & various areas for relaxing in the shade or soaking up the sun, & at night a telescope beckons guests to explore the heavens. In the lounge areas, AC assures cool comfort, while from the adjacent restaurant you can spot animals at dusk as they approach the water. A well-stocked bar is popular, too. There's mosquito screening throughout, including in the individual suites which feature sliding doors to private balconies.

Cruises last either 2 or 3 nights, departing from Kasane on Mon, Wed & Fri. During the trip, expect to watch game or birds on the Chobe River from deck or from smaller boats, or – for rather a lot of effort – from a 4x4 within Chobe National Park.

Fishing (in season) for tigerfish or bream, and visiting a local village, are further options.

2 nights (dep Mon & Wed N$8,900–13,000 pp sharing; 3 nights (dep Fri) N$13,350–19,500. Open all year.

🏠 **Zambezi Voyager** (5 cabins) +27 83 726 4091; e info@zambezivoyager.com; www. zambezivoyager.com. A smaller houseboat, the *Zambezi Voyager* is made up of 3 decks. Accommodation is all on the bottom deck, where there are only 5 en-suite twin/dbl cabins. The middle & top deck are the 'entertainment' decks. The lounges, small library & dining area are all on the middle deck. The top deck is wholly focused on relaxation; there are sun loungers, & it's a great spot on the boat for birding & game viewing, & perfect for star-gazing at night. *N$3,250–4,950 pp sharing FB, inc most drinks, activities 50% sgl supplement.*

Ngoma border
The road from Katima to Ngoma is now fully tarred. At Ngoma itself there's little apart from the border post, a smart office next to the bridge by the Chobe River. About 2km further on, over the river, Botswana's border post is a newer building perched high above the water. Both seem efficient, pleasant and generally quiet. This crossing (⊕ 07.00–18.00) is fine for 2WD vehicles.

Beyond is fully tarred road to Kasane, which cuts through the Chobe National Park, or a choice of much slower, but more scenic routes. One leads to Kasane, for game-viewing along the Chobe riverfront; the other heads through forested and communal lands towards Savuti and Maun. Both the scenic options require park permits and a 4x4 vehicle.

🏠 ***Where to stay*** Map, page 506.

🏠 **Camp Chobe** (20 tents, camping) m 081 800 0762; e res@campchobe.com; www.campchobe. com. Sister property to Camp Kwando (see page 495), Camp Chobe is located off the B8 just 4km from the Ngoma border post. In the rainy season, guests park at the police station in Ngoma & are picked up by boat. The road is bumpy & rough, although improvements are planned – in the meantime, 2WDs should proceed with caution. Opened in Nov 2012, its 20 stylish tents on stilts (6 are family units, 1 has wheelchair access) look over the river to Chobe National Park in Botswana. The tents are solar powered & elegantly furnished with neutral décor & en-suite bathrooms. The central lapa has a raised bar with large leather sofas & dining area below, again making the most of river views, with a swimming pool on the lawn nearby. Wi-Fi is available in central areas. Activities include sunset cruises, Canadian canoe trips, nature walks & game drives. The 3

campsites each have their own ablutions & water, but no power. *B/fast N$120; lunch N$110; dinner N$250 (lunch & dinner must be prebooked); B&B N$800/700 sgl/pp sharing; camping N$130 pp; N$30 community levy pp per stay (not applicable to campers).* **LL**

🅰 **Salambala Community Campsite** (4 pitches) 066 252108; e salambala@ africasafaricamps.com; www.salambala.com. The turn-off for Salambala from the main B8 is about 15km north of Ngoma or 46km south of Katima Mulilo. Another of the Caprivi's excellent community campsites (see pages 46–7), it has 3 separate pitches for tents & a 4th better suited to larger groups. Each has a kitchen area, fire pit, private flush WC & a shower with hot water. A small waterhole attracts local game, & guided walks, fishing, game drives & village visits can be arranged. All profits from the camp go back to the community. *N$85 pp.* **L**

Appendix 1

WILDLIFE GUIDE

This wildlife guide is designed in a manner that should allow you to name most large mammals that you see in Namibia. Less common species are featured under the heading *Similar species* beneath the animal to which they are most closely allied, or bear the strongest resemblance.

CATS AND DOGS

Lion *Panthera leo* Shoulder height 100–120cm. Weight 150–220kg.

Africa's largest predator, the lion is the animal that everybody hopes to see on safari. It is a sociable creature, living in prides of five to ten animals and defending a territory of 20–200km². Lions often hunt at night, and their favoured prey is large or medium antelope such as wildebeest and impala. Most of the hunting is done by females, but dominant males normally feed first after a kill. Rivalry between males is intense and takeover battles are frequently fought to the death, so two or more males often form a coalition. Young males are forced out of their home pride at three years of age, and male cubs are usually killed after a successful takeover.

When not feeding or fighting, lions are remarkably indolent – they spend up to 23 hours of any given day at rest – so the anticipation of a lion sighting is often more exciting than the real thing. Lions naturally occur in any habitat, except desert or rainforest. They once ranged across much of the Old World, but these days they are all but restricted to the larger conservation areas in sub-Saharan Africa (one remnant population exists in India).

In Namibia, lions are increasingly visible in the Kaokoveld, even venturing down river valleys as far as the Skeleton Coast; in the Caprivi, where they often commute from Botswana; and in the central highlands, on a few specific game farms. However, Etosha is certainly the most reliable place to see them in the wild.

Leopard *Panthera pardus* Shoulder height 70cm. Weight 60–80kg.

The powerful leopard is the most solitary and secretive of Africa's big cats. It hunts at night, using stealth and power, often getting to within 5m of its intended prey before pouncing. If there are hyenas and lions around then leopards habitually move their kills up into trees to safeguard them. The leopard can be distinguished from the cheetah by its rosette-like spots, lack of black 'tear marks' and more compact, low-slung, powerful build.

The leopard is the most common of Africa's large felines, yet a good sighting in the wild is extremely unusual – in fact there are many records of individuals living for years undetected in close proximity to humans. They occur everywhere apart from the desert, though they favour habitats with plenty of cover, like riverine woodlands and rocky kopjes. Namibia's central highlands are perfect for leopard, where they are common on almost all

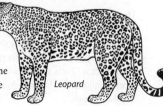

Leopard

the farms. At some lodges, like Okonjima, the leopard are radio collared, allowing them to be tracked by vehicle. Others encourage sightings by offering them food.

Cheetah *Acynonix jubatus* Shoulder height 70–80cm. Weight 50–60kg.

This remarkable spotted cat has a greyhound-like build, and is capable of running at 70km/hr in bursts, making it the world's fastest land animal. Despite superficial similarities, you can easily tell a cheetah from a leopard by the former's simple spots, disproportionately small head, streamlined build, diagnostic black tearmarks, and preference for relatively open habitats. It is often seen pacing the plains restlessly, either on its own or in a small family group consisting of a mother and her offspring. A diurnal hunter, cheetah favour the cooler hours of the day to hunt smaller antelope, like steenbok and duiker, and small mammals like scrub hares. Namibia probably has Africa's highest cheetah population – estimated at around 2,500–3,000, or 25% of the world's population. This is largely due to the eradication of lion and spotted hyena from large areas of commercial farmland, where cheetah are not usually regarded (by enlightened farmers) as a threat to cattle.

Cheetah

Cheetah are found in all of Namibia's major parks. Etosha is the best of these, although there's probably a higher density of them on many farms in the central highlands and the east side of the country. Cheetah can be domesticated to some extent, and in the past it wasn't uncommon to find guest farms with caged animals. Now this is thankfully rare, although rescued cheetah can be readily seen at Okonjima, where those that cannot be released are cared for and others prepared for release back into the wild.

Similar species The **serval** (*Felis serval*) is smaller than a cheetah (shoulder height 55cm) but has a similar build and black-on-gold spots giving way to streaking near the head. Seldom seen, it is widespread and quite common in moist grassland, reed-beds and riverine habitats throughout Africa, including Owamboland, Etosha, Bushmanland and the Caprivi Strip. It preys on mice, rats and small mammals, but will sometimes take the young of small antelope.

Caracal *Felis caracal* Shoulder height 40cm. Weight 15–20kg.

The caracal resembles the European lynx with its uniform tan coat and tufted ears. It is a solitary hunter, feeding on birds, small antelope and young livestock. Found throughout the subcontinent, it thrives in Namibia's relatively arid savannah habitats, and occurs everywhere except the far western coastal strip of the Namib. It is nocturnal and rarely seen.

Caracal

Similar species The smaller **African wild cat** (*F. sylvestris*) ranges from the Mediterranean to the Cape of Good Hope, and is similar in appearance to the domestic tabby cat. I once saw a wild cat in Sossusvlei, during the day, but they are more commonly seen on spotlit night drives. The African wild cat has an unspotted torso, which should preclude confusion with the even smaller **small spotted cat** (*F. nigripes*), a relatively rare resident of southeastern Namibia which has a more distinctively marked coat. Both species are generally solitary and nocturnal, often utilising burrows or termite mounds as daytime shelters. They prey upon reptiles, amphibians and birds as well as small mammals.

African wild dog *Lycaon pictus* Shoulder height 70cm. Weight 25kg.

African wild dog

Also known as the painted hunting dog, the wild dog is distinguished from other African dogs by its large size and mottled black, brown and cream coat. Highly sociable, living in packs of up to 20 animals, wild dogs are ferocious hunters that literally tear apart their prey on the run. The most endangered of Africa's great predators, they are now threatened with extinction. This is the result of relentless persecution by farmers, who often view the dogs as dangerous vermin, and their susceptibility to diseases spread by domestic dogs. Wild dogs are now extinct in many areas, and they are common nowhere. The global population is estimated to be just 3,000–5,500, and is concentrated in Tanzania, Zambia, Zimbabwe, Botswana, South Africa and Namibia.

Wild dogs prefer open savannah with only sparse tree cover, if any, and packs have enormous territories, typically covering 400km² or more. They travel huge distances in search of prey and so few parks are large enough to contain them. In Namibia, wild dogs are sometimes seen in Khaudum or on the Caprivi Strip. Botswana's nearby parks of Chobe and Moremi are one of their main strongholds, and so they certainly move across the border. Attempts to reintroduce them to Etosha have so far failed.

Black-backed jackal *Canis mesomelas* Shoulder height 35–45cm. Weight 8–12kg.

The black-backed jackal is an opportunistic feeder capable of adapting to most habitats. Most often seen singly or in pairs at dusk or dawn, it is ochre in colour with a prominent black saddle flecked by a varying amount of white or gold. It is probably the most frequently observed small predator in Africa south of the Zambezi, and its eerie call is a characteristic sound of the bush at night. It is found throughout Namibia, excluding the Caprivi Strip, and is particularly common in Etosha, where it is frequently seen inside the restcamps at night, scavenging for scraps.

Black-backed jackal

Similar species The similar **side-striped jackal** (*C. adustus*) is more cryptic in colour, and has an indistinct pale vertical stripe on each flank and a white-tipped tail. Nowhere very common, in Namibia it is found in the Caprivi Strip and occasionally Khaudum or Owamboland.

Bat-eared fox *Otocyon megalotis* Shoulder height 30–35cm. Weight 3–5kg.

This endearing small, silvery-grey insectivore is unmistakable with its huge ears and black eye-mask. It is mostly nocturnal, but can sometimes be seen in pairs or small family groups during the cooler hours of the day, usually in dry open country. It digs well, and if seen foraging then it will often 'listen' to the ground (its ears operating like a radio dish) while wandering around, before stopping to dig with its forepaws. As well as termites, bat-eared foxes will eat lizards, gerbils, small birds, scorpions and beetle larvae. They are relatively common throughout Namibia, anywhere that the harvester termite is found, although they are most frequently seen in the southern Kalahari. Intu Africa Kalahari Game Reserve seems to have a particularly high density of them.

Bat-eared fox

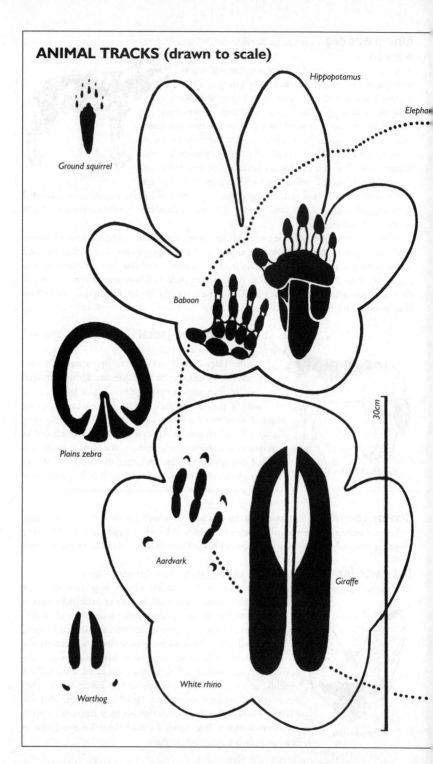

ANIMAL TRACKS (drawn to scale)

Ground squirrel

Hippopotamus

Elephant

Baboon

Plains zebra

Aardvark

Giraffe

White rhino

Warthog

30cm

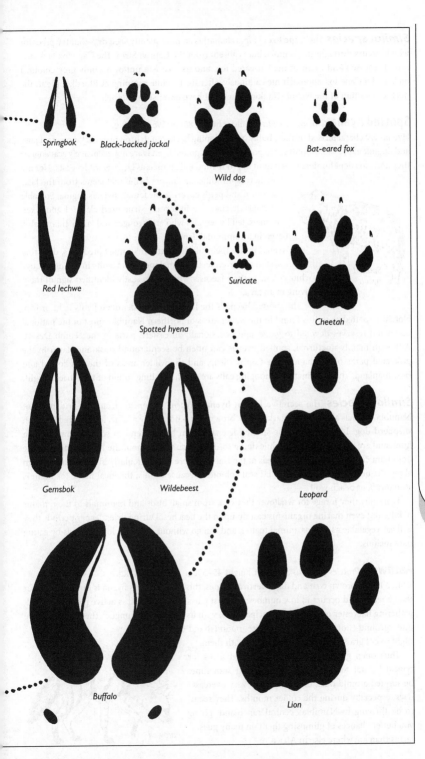

Springbok

Black-backed jackal

Wild dog

Bat-eared fox

Red lechwe

Spotted hyena

Suricate

Cheetah

Gemsbok

Wildebeest

Leopard

Buffalo

Lion

Similar species The **Cape fox** (*Vulpes chama*) is an infrequently seen dry-country predator which occurs throughout Namibia, but is absent from the Caprivi Strip. The Cape fox lacks the prominent ears and mask of the bat-eared fox, and its coat is a uniform sandy grey colour. I once had a Cape fox approach me cautiously, after dusk, while camping at Bloedkoppie in the northern section of the Namib-Naukluft Park, but have never seen another.

Spotted hyena *Crocuta crocuta* Shoulder height 85cm. Weight 70kg.

Hyenas are characterised by their bulky build, sloping back, rough brownish coat, powerful jaws and doglike expression. Contrary to popular myth, spotted hyenas are not exclusively scavengers; they are also adept hunters which hunt in groups and kill animals as large as wildebeests. Nor are they hermaphroditic, an ancient belief that stems from the false scrotum and penis covering the female hyena's vagina. Sociable animals, hyenas live in loosely structured clans of about ten animals, led by females who are stronger and larger than males, based in a communal den.

Hyenas utilise their kills far better than most predators, digesting the bones, skin and even teeth of antelope. This results in the distinctive white colour of their faeces – which is an easily identified sign of them living in an area.

Spotted hyena

The spotted hyena is the largest hyena, identified by its light brown, blotchily spotted coat. It is found in the wetter areas of northern Namibia, most of the national parks and reserves devoted to game, and occasionally in eastern parts of the Namib Desert. Although mainly nocturnal, spotted hyenas can often be seen around dusk and dawn in the protected parks of Etosha and the Caprivi Strip, and the wilder areas of the Kaokoveld and Bushmanland. Their distinctive, whooping calls are a spine-chilling sound of the African night.

Similar species The secretive **brown hyena** (*Hyaena brunnea*) occurs in arid parts of Namibia, and has a shaggy, unmarked dark brown coat – not unlike a large, long-haired German shepherd dog. In contrast to the spotted hyena, brown hyenas tend to scavenge rather than hunt, and are generally solitary while doing so. They occur throughout the Kalahari and are the dominant carnivore in the drier areas of the Namib. There is a particularly high density of them along the beaches, especially around seal colonies. Because of this, the local name for them is *strandwolf*, or beach wolf.

Normally they forage for whatever they can, from small birds and mammals to the remains of kills and even marine organisms cast up upon the beaches. During drier, leaner periods they will eat vegetable as well as animal matter, and can go without water for long periods by eating nara melons.

Aardwolf *Proteles cristatus* Shoulder height 45–50cm. Weight 7–11kg.

With a tawny brown coat and dark, vertical stripes, this insectivorous hyena is not much bigger than a jackal and occurs in low numbers in most parts of Namibia. It is active mainly at night, gathering harvester termites, its principal food, with its wide, sticky tongue. These termites live underground (not in castle-like termite mounds) and come out at night to cut grass, and drag it back down with them.

Thus open grassland or lightly wooded areas forr typical habitat for aardwolves, which can sometimes be spotted around dusk or dawn, or on very overcast days, especially during the colder months. They seem to be thriving in Namibia's central ranchland, giving you better chances of glimpsing them on many guest farms than anywhere else in Africa.

Aardwolf

PRIMATES
Chacma baboon

Papio cynocaphalus ursinus Shoulder height 50–75cm. Weight 25–45kg.

This powerful terrestrial primate, distinguished from any other monkey by its much larger

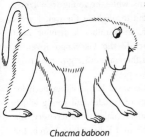

size, inverted U-shaped tail and distinctive doglike head, is fascinating to watch from a behavioural perspective. It lives in large troops which boast a complex, rigid social structure characterised by a matriarchal lineage and plenty of inter-troop movement by males seeking social dominance. Omnivorous and at home in almost any habitat, the baboon is the most widespread primate in Africa, frequently seen in most game reserves.

There are three African races, of which the chacma baboon is the only one occurring in Namibia. With a highly organised defence system, the only predator that seriously affects them is

Chacma baboon

the leopard, which will try to pick them off at night, while they are roosting in trees or cliffs. Look for them in less populated areas across the country.

Vervet monkey *Cercopithecus aethiops* Length (excluding tail) 40–55cm. Weight 4–6kg.

Also known as the green or grivet monkey, the vervet is probably the world's most numerous monkey and certainly the most common and widespread representative of the *Cercopithecus* guenons, a taxonomically controversial genus associated with African forests. An atypical guenon in that it inhabits savannah and woodland rather than true forest, the vervet spends a high proportion of its time on the ground. In Namibia, it is found only around the narrow belts of woodland beside the Orange and Kunene rivers, and in the lush areas of Mahango and the Caprivi Strip.

The vervet's light grey coat, black face and white forehead band are distinctive – as are the male's garish blue genitals. The only animal that is even remotely similar is the baboon, which is much larger and heavier.

Vervet monkey

Vervets live in troops averaging about 25 animals. They are active during the day and roost in trees at night. They eat mainly fruit and vegetables, though are opportunistic and will take insects and young birds, and even raid tents at campsites (usually where ill-informed visitors have previously tempted them into human contact by offering food).

Lesser bushbaby *Galago senegalensis* Length (without tail) 17cm. Weight 150g.

The lesser bushbaby is the most widespread and common member of a group of small and generally indistinguishable nocturnal primates, distantly related to the lemurs of Madagascar. In Namibia they occur throughout the north, from northern Kaokoland and Etosha to Khaudum and the Caprivi Strip.

More often heard than seen, the lesser bushbaby is nocturnal but can sometimes be picked out by tracing a cry to a tree and shining a torch into the branches; its eyes reflect as two red dots. These eyes are designed to function in what we would describe as total darkness, and they feed on insects – some of which are caught in the air by jumping – and also eating sap from trees, especially acacia gum.

Bushbaby

They inhabit wooded areas, and prefer acacia trees or riverine forests. I remember being startled while lighting a braai at Halali restcamp, in Etosha, by a small family of bushbabies. They raced through the trees above us, bouncing from branch to branch while chattering and screaming out of all proportion to their size.

LARGE ANTELOPE

Sable antelope *Hippotragus niger* Shoulder height 135cm. Weight 230kg.

The striking male sable is jet black with a distinct white face, underbelly and rump, and long decurved horns – a strong contender for the title of Africa's most beautiful antelope. The female is chestnut brown and has shorter horns, while the young are a lighter red-brown colour. Sable are found throughout the wetter areas of southern and east Africa. In Namibia, a thriving herd frequents the floodplain beside the Okavango River in Mahango National Park, and there are other groups further east in the Caprivi Strip's other parks.

Sable antelope

Sable are normally seen in small herds: either bachelor herds of males, or breeding herds of females and young which are often accompanied by the dominant male in that territory. The breeding females drop their calves around February or March, the calf remaining hidden away from the herd for its first few weeks. Sable are mostly grazers though will browse, especially when food is scarce. They need to drink at least every other day, and seem especially fond of low-lying dewy vleis in wetter areas.

Roan antelope *Hippotragus equinus* Shoulder height 120–150cm. Weight 250–300kg.

This handsome horselike antelope is uniform fawn-grey with a pale belly, short decurved horns and a light mane. It could be mistaken for the female sable antelope, but this has a well-defined white belly and lacks the roan's distinctive black-and-white facial markings. The roan is a relatively rare antelope; common almost nowhere in Africa (Malawi's Nyika Plateau being one obvious exception). In Namibia, small groups of roan are found in Etosha, Waterberg, Khaudum and the Caprivi.

Roan antelope

Roan need lots of space if they are to thrive and breed; they don't generally do well where game densities are high. Game farms prize them as one of the most valuable antelope (hence expensive to buy). They need access to drinking water, but are adapted to subsist on relatively high plateaux with poor soils.

Oryx or gemsbok *Oryx gazella* Shoulder height 120cm. Weight 230kg.

This is the quintessential desert antelope; unmistakable with its ash-grey coat, bold black facial marks and flank strip, and unique long, straight horns. Of the three races of oryx in Africa, the gemsbok is the largest and most striking. It occurs throughout the Kalahari and Namib and is widespread all over Namibia, from the coast to the interior highlands.

As you might expect, gemsbok are very adaptable. They range widely and are found in areas of dunes, alkaline pans, open savannah and even woodlands. Along with the much smaller springbok, they can sometimes even be seen tracking across flat desert plains with only dust-devils and mirages for company. Gemsbok can endure extremes of temperature, helped by specially adapted blood capillaries in their nasal passages which can cool their blood before it reaches their brains. Thus although their body temperature can rise by up to 6°C, their brains remain cool and they survive. They do not need drinking water and will eat wild melons and dig for roots, bulbs and tubers when grazing or browsing becomes difficult.

Oryx

Waterbuck

Waterbuck *Kobus ellipsiprymnus* Shoulder height 130cm. Weight 250–270kg.

The waterbuck is easily recognised by its shaggy brown coat and the male's large lyre-shaped horns. The common race of southern Africa and areas east of the Rift Valley has a distinctive white ring around its rump, while the defassa race of the Rift Valley and areas further west has a full white rump. In Namibia, waterbuck are very uncommon, only occasionally seen on the eastern fringes of the Caprivi Strip – or the occasional game farm to which they have been introduced. They need to drink very regularly, so usually stay within a few kilometres of water, where they like to graze on short, nutritious grasses. At night they may take cover in adjacent woodlands. It is often asserted that waterbuck flesh is oily and smelly, which may discourage predators.

Blue wildebeest *Connochaetes taurinus* Shoulder height 130–150cm. Weight 180–250kg.

This ungainly antelope, also called the brindled gnu, is easily identified by its dark coat and bovine appearance. The superficially similar buffalo is far more heavily built. When they have enough space, blue wildebeest can form immense herds – as perhaps a million do for their annual migration from Tanzania's Serengeti Plains into Kenya's Masai Mara. In Namibia they naturally occur in the north of the country, including Etosha, and east into the Caprivi Strip. They are also found in the Kalahari, Khaudum and the far eastern borders of Namibia. They are adaptable grazers, but prefer short grass plains and need access to drinking water. They have been introduced on to several game ranches.

Blue wildebeest

Similar species The **black wildebeest** *C. gnou*, endemic to South Africa's central highveld, now numbers a mere 4,000. It is seen most easily in South Africa's Golden Gate National Park, though has also been introduced into several private game areas in Namibia. It differs from the blue wildebeest in having a white tail, a defined black-on-white mane, and horns that slope sharply down then rise to form a 'U' when seen from the side.

Hartebeest *Alcelaphus buselaphus* Shoulder height 125cm. Weight 120–150kg.

Hartebeests are ungainly antelopes, readily identified by the combination of large shoulders, a sloping back, a glossy, red-brown coat and smallish horns in both sexes. Numerous subspecies are recognised, all of which are generally seen in small family groups in reasonably open country. Though once hartebeest were found from the Mediterranean to the Cape, only isolated populations still survive.

Hartebeest

The only one native to Namibia is the red hartebeest, which is found throughout the arid eastern side of the country, and north into Etosha and Owamboland. They have been introduced on to the NamibRand Nature Reserve but are absent from the Caprivi Strip, and common nowhere. Hartebeests are almost exclusively grazers; they like access to water though will eat melons, tubers and rhizomes when it is scarce. Etosha's waterholes, especially those in areas of mopane sparse woodland, probably offer your best chance to see hartebeest in Namibia.

Similar species The **tsessebe** (*Damaliscus lunatus*) is basically a darker version of the hartebeest with striking yellow lower legs. (Related subspecies are known as *topi* in east Africa.) Widespread but thinly and patchily distributed, the tsessebe occurs occasionally in the Caprivi Strip (though it is common in Botswana's Okavango Delta). Its favourite habitat is open grassland, where it is a selective grazer, eating the newer, more nutritious grasses. The tsessebe is one of the fastest antelope species, and jumps very well.

Bontebok *Damaliscus dorcas dorcas* Shoulder height 85–95cm. Weight 60–70kg.

Bontebok

Though endemic to the fynbos areas of the Western Cape in South Africa, bontebok have been introduced into many private reserves in Namibia. They look like particularly striking small hartebeest, with a distinctive white face, chestnut back, black flanks and white belly and rump. Bontebok were hunted close to extinction in the early 20th century, and now they are largely found in private protected areas, such as the grounds of Mokuti Lodge or the NamibRand Nature Reserve.

Similar species The duller but more common **blesbok** (*D. d. phillipsi*) is, in essence, the highveld race of bontebok native to eastern South Africa. That, too, has occasionally been introduced on to the odd private reserve in Namibia.

Kudu *Tragelaphus strepsiceros* Shoulder height 140–155cm. Weight 180–250kg.

The kudu (or, more properly, the greater kudu) is the most frequently observed member of the genus *Tragelaphus*. These medium-size to large antelopes are characterised by the male's large spiralling horns and dark coat, which is generally marked with several vertical white stripes. They are normally associated with well-wooded habitats.

The kudu is very large, with a grey-brown coat and up to ten stripes on each side. The male has magnificent double-spiralled corkscrew horns. Occurring throughout Mozambique, Zimbabwe, Zambia, Botswana and Namibia, kudu are widespread and common, though not in dense forests or open grasslands. In Namibia they are absent only from the Namib Desert – though they are found in the river valleys and are very common on farmland, where their selective browsing does not compete with the indiscriminate grazing of the cattle.

Kudu

Sitatunga *Tragelaphus spekei* Shoulder height 85–90cm. Weight 105–115kg.

The semi-aquatic antelope is a widespread but infrequently observed inhabitant of west and central African swamps from the Okavango in Botswana to the Sudd in Sudan. In Namibia it occurs in the Okavango River beside Mahango, and in protected areas of the Kwando–Linyanti–Chobe–Zambezi river system where there are extensive papyrus reed-beds. Because of its preferred habitat, the sitatunga is very elusive and seldom seen, even in areas where it is relatively common.

Sitatunga

Eland *Taurotragus oryx* Shoulder height 150–175cm. Weight 450–900kg.

Africa's largest antelope, the eland is light brown in colour, sometimes with a few faint white vertical stripes. Its somewhat bovine appearance is accentuated by relatively short horns and

Eland

a large dewlap. It was once widely distributed in east and southern Africa, but in Namibia is now found only in isolated Kalahari areas, Etosha and Waterberg. There is a particularly good population of eland on Mundulea Reserve. Small herds of eland frequent grasslands and light woodlands, often fleeing at the slightest provocation. (They have long been hunted for their excellent meat, so perhaps this is not surprising.)

Eland are opportunist browsers and grazers, eating fruit, berries, seed pods and leaves as well as green grass after the rains, and roots and tubers when times are lean. They run slowly, though can trot for great distances and jump exceedingly well.

MEDIUM AND SMALL ANTELOPE

Bushbuck *Tragelaphus scriptus* Shoulder height 70–80cm. Weight 30–45kg.

This attractive antelope, a member of the same genus as the kudu, is widespread throughout Africa and shows great regional variation in its colouring. It occurs in forest and riverine woodland, where it is normally seen singly or in pairs. The male is dark brown or chestnut, while the much smaller female is generally a pale reddish brown. The male has relatively small, straight horns and both sexes are marked with white spots and sometimes stripes, though the stripes are often indistinct.

Bushbuck

Bushbuck tend to be secretive and very skittish, except when used to people. They depend on cover and camouflage to avoid predators, and are often found in the thick, herby vegetation around rivers. They will freeze if disturbed, before dashing off into the undergrowth. Bushbuck are both browsers and grazers, choosing the more succulent grass shoots, fruit and flowers. In Namibia they have a very limited distribution around the Okavango River in Mahango National Park, and beside the Chobe and Kwando rivers on the eastern side of the Caprivi Strip.

Impala *Aepeceros melampus* Shoulder height 90cm. Weight 45kg.

This slender, handsome antelope is superficially similar to the springbok, but in fact belongs to its own separate family. Chestnut in colour, and lighter underneath than above, the impala has diagnostic black-and-white stripes running down its rump and tail, and the male has large lyre-shaped horns. One of the most widespread and successful antelope species in east and southern Africa, the impala is normally seen in large herds in wooded savannah habitats. It is the most common antelope in the Caprivi Strip, and throughout much of the country further east, although it is absent from much of Namibia.

However, a separate subspecies, the **black-faced impala** (*A. m. petersi*), occurs in Etosha, the Kaokoveld and southern Angola. This is almost identical to the normal impala, and distinguished only by extra black stripes on its face, including a prominent one down the front of its nose. The total population of black-faced impalas is about a thousand individuals, but with a few days spent in Etosha you have a surprisingly good chance of spotting some. (Sadly, the presence of both the common impala and the black-faced impala within Etosha has led to hybridising and thus the dilution of the gene pool for the black-faced subspecies.)

Impala

As expected of such a successful species, it both grazes and browses, depending on what fodder is available.

Springbok *Antidorcas marsupilis* Shoulder height 60cm. Weight 20–25kg.

Springbok are graceful, relatively small antelope – members of the gazelle family – which generally occur in large herds. They have finely marked short coats: fawn-brown upper parts and a white belly, separated by a dark brown band. Springbok occur throughout Namibia; they are often the most common small antelope. They occur by the thousand in Etosha – and I've also seen them from the Kalahari to the dunes at Sossusvlei.

They favour dry, open country, preferring open plains or savannah, and avoiding thick woodlands and mountains. They can subsist without water for long periods, if there is moisture in the plants they graze or browse.

Springbok

Reedbuck *Redunca arundinum* Shoulder height 80–90cm. Weight 45–65kg.

Sometimes referred to as the southern reedbuck (as distinct from mountain and Bohor reedbucks, found further east), these delicate antelope are uniformly fawn or grey in colour, and lighter below than above. They are generally found in reed-beds and tall grasslands, often beside rivers, and are easily identified by their loud, whistling alarm call and distinctive bounding running style. In Namibia they occur only on the Caprivi Strip and a few riverine areas in the far north.

Reedbuck

Klipspringer *Oreotragus oreotragus* Shoulder height 60cm. Weight 13kg.

The klipspringer is a strongly built little antelope, normally seen in pairs, and easily identified by its dark, bristly grey-yellow coat, slightly speckled appearance and unique habitat preference. Klipspringer means 'rockjumper' in Afrikaans and it is an apt name for an antelope that occurs exclusively in mountainous areas and rocky outcrops from Cape Town to the Red Sea.

They are common throughout Namibia, wherever rocky hills or kopjes are found – which means most of the central highlands and western escarpment, but not in the far north or the Caprivi Strip. Klipspringers are mainly browsers, though they do eat a little new grass. When spotted they will freeze, or bound at great speed across the steepest of slopes.

Klipspringer

Lechwe *Kobus leche* Shoulder height 90–100cm. Weight 80–100kg.

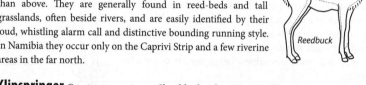

Lechwe

Otherwise known as the red lechwe, this sturdy, shaggy antelope has a reddish coat and beautiful lyre-shaped horns. They are usually found only in moist, open environments, and in Namibia they are found only beside the great rivers of the Caprivi Strip.

Lechwe need dry land on which to rest, but otherwise will spend much of their time grazing on grasses and sedges, standing in water if necessary. Their hooves are splayed, adapted to bounding through their muddy environment when fleeing from the lion, hyena and wild dog that hunt them.

Steenbok *Raphicerus cempestris* Shoulder height 50cm. Weight 11kg.

This rather nondescript small antelope has red-brown upper parts and clear white underparts, and the male has short straight horns. It is probably the most commonly observed small antelope; if you see a small antelope fleeing from you across farmland in Namibia, it is likely to be a

Steenbok

steenbok. Like most other small antelopes, the steenbok is normally encountered singly or in pairs and tends to 'freeze' when disturbed, before taking flight.

Similar species Sharpe's grysbok (*R. sharpei*) is similar in size and appearance, though it has a distinctive white-flecked coat. It occurs alongside the steenbok in the far eastern reaches of the Caprivi Strip, but is almost entirely nocturnal in its habits and so very seldom seen. The **oribi** (*Ourebia ourebi*) is a widespread but very uncommon antelope, which is usually found only in large, open stretches of grassland. It looks much like a steenbok but stands about 10cm higher at the shoulder and has an altogether more upright bearing. In Namibia you have a chance of seeing these only on the Caprivi Strip, and you'll need to look hard.

The **Damara dik-dik** (*Madoqua kirki*) occurs in central-north Namibia, Etosha and Kaokoland, as well as parts of east Africa where it is known as Kirk's dik-dik. It is Namibia's smallest antelope; easily identified from steenbok by its much smaller size. It is adapted to arid areas and prefers a mixture of bushes and spare grassland cover. Damara dik-diks are common in Etosha, and will often sit motionless beside the road while they are passed by without ever being seen. They are active during the cooler hours of the day as well as the night and are almost exclusively browsers.

Common duiker *Sylvicapra grimmia* Shoulder height
50cm. Weight 20kg.
This anomalous duiker holds itself more like a steenbok or grysbok and is the only member of its (large) family to occur outside of forests. Generally grey in colour, the common duiker can most easily be separated from other small antelopes by the black tuft of hair that sticks up between its horns. It occurs throughout Namibia, everywhere except the Namib Desert. Common duikers tolerate most habitats except for true forest and very open country, and are tolerant of nearby human settlements. They are opportunist feeders, taking fruit, seeds and leaves, as well as crops, small reptiles and amphibians.

Common duiker

OTHER LARGE HERBIVORES
African elephant *Loxodonta africana* Shoulder height 2.3–3.4m. Weight up to 6,000kg.
The world's largest land animal, the African elephant is intelligent, social and often very entertaining to watch. Female elephants live in close-knit clans in which the eldest female plays matriarch over her sisters, daughters and granddaughters. Mother–daughter bonds are strong and may last for up to 50 years. Males generally leave the family group at around 12 years to roam singly or form bachelor herds. Under normal circumstances, elephants range widely in search of food and water, but when concentrated populations are forced to live in conservation areas their habit of uprooting trees can cause serious environmental damage. Elephants are widespread and common in habitats ranging from desert to rainforest. In Namibia they are common in the Caprivi Strip and Etosha, and in Kalahari areas around Khaudum.

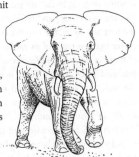

African elephant

Read about the history of Etosha, and you'll realise that the park used to cover much of the present Kaokoveld. Until about 50 years ago Etosha's elephants used to migrate, spending the wetter parts of the year in the Kaokoveld and the drier months nearer to Etosha's permanent waterholes. Etosha's boundary fence has stopped that. However, the herds still tend to head to the hills of western Etosha during the rains, returning to the pan several months later as the bush dries out. Every year a few break out of the park's fences.

The population which frequents the river valleys of the Kaokoveld are commonly known as 'desert elephants' – though desert-adapted might be a more accurate term. These family groups have learnt where the rivers and waterholes are, probably from their elders, and can navigate through the Kaokoveld's mountains and dunes to find water. The area's various conservation schemes have helped to rescue this population from the edge of oblivion; it is thriving to the point of conflict with the area's human population. After several decades of persecution by humans, these elephants are now (understandably) noted for their aggression. Even visitors in sturdy vehicles should treat them with exceptional respect (see *Driving near elephants*, page 93).

Black rhinoceros
Diceros bicornis Shoulder height 160cm. Weight 1,000kg.

This is the more widespread of Africa's two rhino species, an imposing and rather temperamental creature. It has been poached to extinction in most of its former range, but still occurs in *very* low numbers in many southern African reserves; Namibia offers its best chance of long-term survival – thanks in no small measure to the work of Namibia's Save the Rhino Trust.

Black rhinos exploit a wide range of habitats from dense woodlands and bush, through to the very open hillsides of the Kaokoveld. Often (and descriptively) referred to as the hook-lipped rhino, the black rhino is adapted to browse. Over its range it utilises hundreds of different plants, though local populations are often more specific in their diet: in the Kaokoveld, for example, *Euphorbia damarana* is a great favourite.

Black rhinoceros

Black rhinos are generally solitary animals and can survive without drinking for 4–5 days. However, they will drink daily if they can, and individuals often meet at waterholes – as visitors to the floodlit waterholes at Okaukuejo and Halali will usually see to their delight. They are often territorial and have very regular patterns of movement, which make them an easy target for poachers. Black rhinos can be very aggressive when disturbed and will charge with minimal provocation. Their hearing and sense of smell is acute, while their eyesight is poor (so they often miss if you keep a low profile and don't move). Rhino-tracking trips are possible in several areas of the Kaokoveld, most easily at Desert Rhino Camp.

White rhinoceros
Ceratotherium simum Shoulder height 180cm. Weight 1,500–2,000kg.

The white rhino is in fact no paler in colour than the black rhino: the 'white' derives from the Afrikaans *weit* (wide) and refers to its flattened mouth, an ideal shape for cropping grass. This is the best way to tell the two rhino species apart, since the mouth of the black rhino, a browser in most parts of its range, is more rounded with a hooked upper lip. (Note that there is *no colour difference at all* between these two species of rhino; 'white' and 'black' are not literal descriptions.)

In fact, the white rhino can be split into two subspecies (or possibly species, according to the latest research.) 'Northern white rhino' occur naturally in Uganda, southern Chad, southwestern Sudan, the eastern part of Central African Republic, and northeastern Democratic Republic of the Congo. However, these have sadly been hunted to extinction in the wild. There are fewer than ten individuals left in the world, of which seven were returned from captivity to Kenya in 2009, in an effort to save the species.

White rhinoceros

The Southern white rhino naturally occurred in a band across southern Africa, but was similarly poached to the verge of extinction in the 1970s and 1980s. By protecting populations in Umfolozi and Hluhluwe parks in South Africa, they effectively saved the species, and have since helped to repopulate many of southern Africa's parks. They were reintroduced to Waterberg and back into Etosha – where they seem to frequent the areas between Namutoni and Springbokfontein waterhole. Unlike their smaller cousins, white rhino are generally placid grazing animals which are very rarely aggressive. They prefer open grassy plains and are often seen in small groups.

Hippopotamus *Hippopotamus amphibius* Shoulder height 150cm. Weight 2,000kg.
Characteristic of Africa's large rivers and lakes, this large, lumbering animal spends most of the day submerged but emerges at night to graze. Strongly territorial, herds of ten or more animals are presided over by a dominant male who will readily defend his patriarchy to the death. Hippos are abundant in most protected rivers and water bodies, and they are still quite common outside of reserves, where they are widely credited with killing more people than any other African mammal.

In Namibia they occur only in the great rivers of the Caprivi Strip, and occasionally in the Kunene River, at the north end of the Kaokoveld. Otherwise you won't generally see them.

Cape buffalo *Syncerus caffer* Shoulder height 140cm. Weight 700kg.
Frequently and erroneously referred to as a water buffalo (an Asian species), the Cape, or African, buffalo is a distinctive, highly social oxlike animal that lives as part of a herd. It prefers well-watered savannah, though also occurs in forested areas. Common and widespread in sub-Saharan Africa, in Namibia it is limited to the Caprivi Strip, largely by the absence of sufficient water in the rest of the country. Buffalo are primarily grazers and need regular access to water, where they swim readily. They smell and hear well, and old bulls have a reputation for charging at the slightest provocation. Lion often follow herds of buffalo, their favourite prey.

Cape buffalo

Giraffe *Giraffa camelopardis* Shoulder height 250–350cm. Weight 1,000–1,400kg.
The world's tallest and longest-necked land animal, a fully grown giraffe can measure up to 5.5m high. Quite unmistakable, the giraffe lives in loosely structured herds of up to 15, though herd members often disperse and then they are seen singly or in smaller groups. Formerly distributed throughout east and southern Africa, the 'southern' subspecies of these great browsers (*G. c. giraffa*) are found in the north of Namibia, from northern Damaraland and Kaokoland to the Caprivi. Etosha has a thriving population, many of which are very relaxed with cars and allow visitors in vehicles to approach very closely.

Common zebra *Equus burchelli* Shoulder height 130cm. Weight 300–340kg.
Also known as Burchell's or plains zebra, this attractive striped horse is common and widespread throughout most of east and southern Africa, where it is often seen in large herds alongside wildebeest. It is common in most conservation areas from northern South Africa, Namibia and Botswana all the way up to the southeast of Ethiopia. Southern races, including those in Namibia, have paler brownish 'shadow stripes' between the bold black stripes that are present in all races.

Plains zebra

Similar species The **Hartmann's mountain zebra** (*E. grevyi hartmannae*), is confined to Namibia's western escarpment and the plains nearby. It is very closely related to the Cape mountain zebra which occurs in South Africa. Mountain zebra have a slightly lighter frame than the Burchell's, their underparts are not striped, the striping on their legs extends all the way to their hooves, and they have a dewlap which the Burchell's lack.

They occur from the conservation area around the Fish River Canyon to the Hartmann Valley in the Kaokoveld, and have been introduced on to several private reserves away from the escarpment area.

Warthog *Phacochoreus africanus* Shoulder height 60–70cm. Weight up to 100kg.

Warthog

This widespread and often conspicuously abundant resident of the African savannah is grey in colour with a thin covering of hairs, wartlike bumps on its face, and rather large upward curving tusks. Africa's only diurnal swine, the warthog is often seen in family groups, trotting around with its tail raised stiffly (a diagnostic trait) and a determinedly nonchalant air. They occur everywhere in Namibia apart from the far south and the western desert areas, although I have often seen them grazing, on bended knee, where the C36 cuts through the Namib-Naukluft National Park.

Similar species Bulkier, hairier and more brown, the **bushpig** (*Potomochoerus larvatus*) is only known to occur in Namibia in the Caprivi Strip. It is very rarely seen due to its nocturnal habits and preference for dense vegetation.

SMALL MAMMALS
African civet *Civettictis civetta* Shoulder height 40cm. Weight 10–15kg.
This bulky, long-haired, rather feline creature of the African night is primarily carnivorous,

African civet

feeding on small animals and carrion, but will also eat fruit. It has a similarly coloured coat to a leopard, which is densely blotched with large black spots becoming stripes towards the head. Civets are widespread and common in many habitats, but very rarely seen. In Namibia, it is restricted to the far north.

Similar species The **small-spotted genet** (*Genetta genetta*) and **large-spotted genet** (*G. tigrina*) are the most widespread members of a group of similar small predators. All of these are slender and rather feline in appearance (though they are *not* cats), with a grey to gold-brown coat marked with black spots and a long ringed tail. Most likely to be seen on nocturnal game drives or scavenging around game-reserve lodges, the large-spotted genet is gold-brown with very large spots and a black-tipped tail, whereas the small-spotted genet is greyer with rather small spots and a pale-tipped tail. Exact identification is a job for experts. The small-spotted genet is found all over Namibia, while the large-spotted genet is restricted to the Caprivi Strip and the area adjacent to the Okavango River.

Banded mongoose *Mungos mungo* Shoulder height 20cm. Weight around 1kg.
The banded mongoose is probably the most commonly observed member of a group of small, slender, terrestrial carnivores. Uniform dark grey-brown except for a dozen black stripes across its back, it is a diurnal mongoose occurring in playful family groups, or troops, in most habitats north and east of Okahandja. They feed on insects, scorpions, amphibians, reptiles and even carrion and bird's eggs, and can move across the veld at quite a pace.

Banded mongoose

Similar species Another eight or so mongoose species occur in Namibia; some are social and gather in troops, others solitary. Several are too scarce and nocturnal to be seen by casual visitors. Of the rest, the water or **marsh mongoose** (*Atilax paludinosus*) is large, normally solitary and has a very scruffy brown coat; it's widespread along the Caprivi Strip, the Kunene and the Orange. The **white-tailed ichneumon** (*Ichneumia albicauda*) is another mongoose that is widespread in the Caprivi. It is a solitary, large brown mongoose, easily identified by its bushy white tail.

The **slender mongoose** (*Galerella sanguinea*) is as widespread and also solitary, but it is very much smaller (shoulder height 10cm) and has a uniform brown or reddish coat and blackish tail tip. It is replaced in the far south of Namibia by the **small grey mongoose** (*G. pulveruntela*), similar in size but grey with white flecks on its coat.

The **yellow mongoose** (*Cynitis penicillata*) is a small, sociable mongoose with a tawny or yellow coat, and is commonly found across most of Namibia. It normally forages alone and is easily identified by the white tip on the end of its tail.

Finally, **the dwarf mongoose** (*Helogate parvula*) is a diminutive (shoulder height 7cm), highly sociable light brown mongoose often seen in the vicinity of the termite mounds where it nests.

Meerkat or suricate *Suricata suricatta* Shoulder height 25–35cm. Weight 650–950g.

Found throughout the Kaokoveld and southern Namibia, meerkats are only absent from the driest western areas of the Namib (although I have had one confirmed report of them being seen on the Skelton Coast) and the wetter parts of northeast Namibia. These small animals are sandy-to silvery-grey in colour, with dark bands running across their backs. They are exclusively diurnal and have a distinctive habit of sitting upright on their hind legs. They do this when they first emerge in the morning, to sun themselves, and throughout the day.

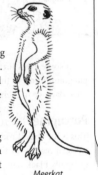

Living in complex social groups, meerkats usually seen scratching around for insects, beetles and small reptiles in dry, open, grassy areas. While the rest forage, one or two of the group will use the highest mound around as a sentry post – looking out for predators using their remarkable eyesight. Meerkats' social behaviour is very complex: they squeak constantly to communicate and even use different alarm calls for different types of predators. Because of their photogenic poses and fascinating social behaviour, they have been the subject of several successful television documentaries filmed in the southern Kalahari. Good sightings of meerkat are often made from Bagatelle in the Kalahari.

Meerkat

Honey badger *Mellivora capensis* Shoulder height 30cm. Weight 12kg.

Also known as the ratel, the honey badger is black with a puppyish face and grey-white back. It is an opportunistic feeder best known for its symbiotic relationship with a bird called the honeyguide which leads it to a beehive, waits for it to tear it open, then feeds on the scraps. The honey badger is among the most widespread of African carnivores, and also among the most powerful for its size; it occurs all over Namibia. However, it is thinly distributed and rarely seen, except *Honey badger* when it has been tamed enough to turn up on cue to artificial feedings at safari camps (Okonjima's nightly feeding session used to get occasional visits from honey badgers).

Similar species Several other mustelids occur in the region, including the **striped polecat** (*Ictonyx striatus*), a common but rarely seen nocturnal creature with black underparts and a bushy white back, and the similar but much scarcer striped weasel (*Poecilogale albincha*). The **Cape clawless otter** (*Aonyx capensis*) is a brown freshwater mustelid with a white collar, which is found in the Caprivi area, the Kunene and the Orange River. The smaller **spotted-necked otter** (*Lutra maculicollis*) is darker with light white spots on its throat, and is restricted to the Caprivi and Okavango River.

Aardvark (*Orycteropus afer*) Shoulder height 60cm. Weight up to 70kg.

This singularly bizarre nocturnal insectivore is unmistakable with its long snout, huge ears and powerful legs, adapted to dig up the nests of termites, on which it feeds. Aardvarks occur throughout southern Africa, except the driest western areas of the Namib. Though their distinctive three-toed tracks are often seen, and they are not uncommon animals, sightings of them are rare.

Aardvark

Aardvarks prefer areas of grassland and sparse scrub, rather than dense woodlands, and Namibia's ranchland suits them well – although their excavations into roads and dam walls are not appreciated by farmers.

Pangolin *Manis temmincki* Total length 70–100cm. Weight 8–15kg.

Sharing the aardvaak's diet of termites and ants, pangolins are another very unusual nocturnal insectivore – with distinctive armour plating and a tendency to roll up in a ball when disturbed. Sometimes known as Temminck's pangolin, or scaly anteaters, these strange animals walk on their hind legs, using their tail and front legs for balance. They occur in eastern and northern Namibia, but not in the Namib Desert, and are both nocturnal and rare – so sightings are exceedingly unusual.

Pangolin

In some areas further east, particularly Zimbabwe, local custom is to make a present of any pangolin found to the paramount chief (often taken to mean the president), which has caused great damage to their population.

Porcupine *Hystrix africaeaustralis* Total length 80–100cm. Weight 15–25kg.

This is the largest rodent found in the region, and occurs all over southern Africa, except for the western reaches of the Namib Desert. It easily identified by its black-and-white striped quills, generally black hair, and shambling gait. If heard in the dark, then the rustle of its foraging is augmented by the slight rattle of its quills. These drop off fairly regularly, and are ften found in the bush.

The porcupine's diet is varied, and they are fairly opportunistic when it comes to food. Roots and tubers are favourites, as is the bark of certain trees; they will also eat meat and small reptiles or birds if they have the chance.

Similar species Also spiky, the **southern African hedgehog** is found in north-central areas, including the Kaokoveld and Owamboland. This species is much smaller than the porcupine (about 20cm long), but is also omnivorous. They are not common.

Rock hyrax *Procavia capensis* Shoulder height 20–30cm. Weight 4kg.

Rodent-like in appearance, hyraxes (also known as dassies) are claimed to be the closest living relative of elephants. The rock hyrax and similar **Kaokoveld rock hyrax** (*Heterohyrax welwitschii*) are often seen sunning themselves in rocky habitats, and become tame when used to people.

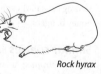

Rock hyrax

They are social animals, living in large groups, and largely herbivorous, eating leaves, grasses and fruits. Where you see lots of dassies, watch out for black eagles and other raptors which prey extensively on them

Scrub hare *Lepus saxatilis* Shoulder height 45–60cm. Weight 1–4.5kg.
This is the largest and commonest African hare or rabbit, occurring everywhere in Namibia except the far west and south. In some areas a short walk at dusk or after nightfall might reveal three or four scrub hares. They tend to freeze when disturbed.

Ground squirrel *Xerus inauris* Shoulder height 20–30cm. Weight 400–700g.
This terrestrial rodent is common in most arid parts of Namibia, except the far west of the desert. The ground squirrel is grey to grey-brown with a prominent white eye ring and silver-black tail. Within its range, it might be confused with the meerkat, which also spends much time on its hind legs. Unlike the meerkat, ground squirrels have a characteristic squirrel mannerism of holding food in their forepaws.

The ground squirrel is a social animal; large groups share one communal burrow. It can often be spotted searching for vegetation, seeds, roots and small insects, while holding its tail aloft as a sunshade.

Ground squirrel

Bush squirrel *Paraxerus cepapi* Total length 35cm. Weight 100–250g.
This common rodent is a uniform grey or buff colour, with a long tail that is furry but not bushy. It's widely distributed all over southern and east Africa, and occurs where there are moist woodland habitats in Namibia. Bush squirrels are so numerous in mopane woodlands that it can be difficult to avoid seeing them – hence its other common names, the mopane squirrel or the tree squirrel.

Bush squirrels live alone, in pairs or in small groups, usually nesting in a drey of dry leaves, in a hole in a tree. They are diurnal and venture to the ground to feed on seeds, fruit, nuts, vegetable matter and small insects. When alarmed they often bolt up the nearest tree, keeping on the side of the trunk away from the threat, out of sight as much as possible. If they can find a safe vantage point with a view of the threat, then they'll sometimes make a loud clicking alarm call.

Appendix 2

LANGUAGE

There isn't the space here to include a guide to Namibia's many languages, although, if you are staying in a community for longer than a few days, then do try to learn a few local greetings from your hosts. To get you started, here are the essentials in the major languages that you'll come across. Note, too, that the Afrikaans *moro* has been widely adopted to say 'hello' to tourists – especially among the Himba.

	Damara/Nama	**Herero/Himba**	**Ovambo**
Hello; How are you? (to older man/woman)	*Matisa*	*Perivi*	*Wa le lepo (tate/meme)*
Answer 'Fine' ('Khaingya')	*!Gâi-i-a*	*Nawa*	*Ondili nawa*
Thank you	*Kai-aios, Kai-gangans*	*Okuhepa*	*Ndagi, Ondapandula*
Goodbye	*!Gâitses* *Karee nawa* (stay well)	*Gainga nawa*	*Bye bye,* or *Kalapo nawa*

Do note, too, the cultural guidelines on pages 26–7, and notes on pronunciation of the 'click' languages on page 447. For background details on language, see *Chapter 2*.

While travelling, you are likely to come across unfamiliar words that are in common use in southern African English, many of Afrikaans origin. These include:

apteek	chemist or pharmacy (most towns have one)
bakkie	pick-up truck, with open back
berg	mountain, or mountain range
boerewors (or *wors*)	sausage – an essential component of any *braai*
boma	traditional enclosure, often used at safari camps to mean the area around the fire where everyone gathers.
braaivleis (*braai*)	barbecue
the bush	generic term for any wild area, usually implying some thick vegetation cover
bundu	the bush (see above) – more often used in Zimbabwe
cuca shop	bar
dam	manmade lake
donga	small ravine, sometimes caused by water erosion
dorp	small rural town, though often implies a place with small-minded, reactionary attitudes
kantoor	an office
klippe	rock or stone (as used in *klip*springer)
kloof	ravine, often with a small river at the bottom

kopje (or *koppie*)	rocky hill, often alone in an otherwise flat area
kraal	cattle enclosure or group of African huts (Owambo)
lekker	good, nice – now slang, typically used to describe food
mielie	corn or maize, the staple for most of the subcontinent
mieliepap	maize flour porridge, often eaten for breakfast
mokoro	dugout canoe (plural *mekoro*)
orlag	war
pad	road or track
ompad	diversion, often used on road signs
omuramba	dry river-bed
rivier	river
robot	traffic lights (ie: '*robot* ahead', or 'turn left at the *robot*, then…')
rondavel	traditional African hut (usually round)
tackies	running shoes or trainers
veld	grassland – like 'the bush', this term is used for wide open wilderness areas, but implies mostly low vegetation cover
vlei	depression, valley, lake or low-lying place where water gathers, this term is used throughout the subcontinent
wato	type of dugout canoe
werft	traditional settlement (often Herero)

Appendix 3

FURTHER INFORMATION

BOOKS AND JOURNALS Many of these books are quite widely available, while others may be found only in Namibia. A useful source is the website of the Africa Book Centre, www. africabookcentre.com.

History

Andersson, Charles John *Lake Ngami* and *The River Okavango* Originally published in the late 1850s; republished as a facsimile reprint by Struik, Cape Town, 1967. These two fascinating books record Namibia in the 1850s through the eyes of one of the first traders and hunters in the area.

Baines, Thomas *Explorations in South-West Africa* London, 1864. Although linked more with the countries further east, the travels of Baines, as he accompanied Livingstone and others, make fascinating reading.

Camby, Robert *The History of Rehoboth* A very useful pamphlet for understanding Rehoboth's history.

Cocker, Mark *Rivers of Blood, Rivers of Gold: Europe's Conflict with Tribal Peoples* Jonathan Cape, London, 1998. This highly readable book explores four colonial episodes: the conquest of Mexico, the British onslaught in Tasmania, the uprooting of the Apache in North America, and the German campaign in South West Africa during the early 20th century. It gives an excellent, detailed account of the 1904–07 war, and examines the conflict, and the main characters, in the context of contemporary world politics.

Davis, Ronald, PhD and researchers at Stanford University 'Y chromosome sequence variation and the history of human populations' *Nature Genetics*, November 2000.

Dunbar, R I M 'Why gossip is good for you' *New Scientist*, 21 November 1992.

Gordon, Robert J *The Bushman Myth: The Making of a Namibian Underclass* Westview Press Inc, Colorado and Oxford, 1992. If you, like me, had accepted the received wisdom that Bushmen are the last descendants of Stone Age man, pushed to living in splendid isolation in the Kalahari, then you must read this. It places the Bushmen in an accurate historical context and deconstructs many of the myths we have created about them.

Katjavivi, Peter H *History of Resistance in Namibia* Co-published James Currey, London; OAU in Addis Ababa; UNESCO Press in Paris. Rather more scholarly than *Namibia – The Facts*, it's impressive in its detail.

Mossolow, Dr N *Hansheinrich von Wolf and Duwisib Castle* Society for Scientific Development, Swakopmund, 1995. This neat 20-page account of the castle and its founder is half in German and half in English, and often available from the castle itself. The middle eight pages are black-and-white photographs of the castle and its characters. Worth buying while you are there.

Namhila, Ellen Ndeshi *The Price of Freedom* New Namibia Books, Windhoek, 1997. A biographical account of 19 years spent in exile by a young Namibian woman.

Olusoga, David, and Erichsen, Casper W *The Kaiser's Holocaust* Faber and Faber, London, 2010. While the title of this new history may be seen as inappropriate, there is no doubt that – in the pursuit of land – the colonial German powers were responsible for the deaths of countless Nama and Herero people in the early years of the 20th century. Whether the parallels drawn between their atrocities and the Nazi policies of later years are justified is a matter for considerable debate.

Parsons, Q N 'Franz or Klikko, the Wild Dancing Bushmen: A Case Study in Khoisan Stereotyping' *Botswana Notes & Records*, vol. 20 (1989), pp. 71–6.

Reader, John *Africa: A Biography of the Continent* Penguin Books, London, 1997. Over 700 pages of highly readable history, interwoven with facts and statistics, to make a remarkable overview of Africa's past. Given that Namibia's boundaries were imposed from Europe, its history *must* be looked at from a pan-African context to be understood. This book can show you that wider view; it is compelling and essential reading.

Natural history

Burke, Antje *Wild Flowers of the Central Namib* Namibia Scientific Society, 2003.

Carruthers, Vincent *Wildlife of Southern Africa* Random House Struik, 2008. Features more than 2,000 plants and animals likely to be encountered on a touristic visit.

Craven, Patricia, and Marais, Christine *Damaraland Flora* Gamsberg Macmillan, Windhoek, 1992. Similar to the *Namib Flora*, and equally well illustrated, this volume covers Spitzkoppe, Brandberg and Twyfelfontein, but is invaluable anywhere in the Kaokoveld.

Craven, Patricia, and Marais, Christine *Namib Flora* Gamsberg Macmillan, Windhoek, 1986. This delightful hardback covers a small area 'from Swakopmund to the giant *welwitschia* via Goanikontes', though many of the plants that it beautifully illustrates will be found elsewhere.

Grunert, Nicole *Fascination of Geology* Klaus Hess Publishers, Namibia.

Lovegrove, Dr Barry *The Living Deserts of Southern Africa* Fernwood Press, South Africa, 1993. A beautifully illustrated book with a scholarly text that is both informative and accessible.

Main, Michael *Kalahari: Life's Variety in Dune and Delta* Southern Books, Johannesburg, 1987. Though primarily concerned with Botswana, this is a superb, highly readable treatise on the Kalahari. It covers the origins and ecology of this thirstland and even tackles some of the more sticky political and human questions facing the region. The many marvellous details in the book, and Main's general clarity on the issues, come from personal experience – he's lived in Botswana and travelled there very extensively. But even if you're heading for Namibia's Kalahari, it's still worth getting a copy. The only problem is that it will, of course, captivate you and make a subsequent visit to Botswana essential.

Newman, Kenneth *Birds of Southern Africa* Southern Books, South Africa; published in numerous editions from 1983. Probably the best identification field guide to birds in southern Africa, including Namibia.

Rothmann, Sakkie and Theresa *The Harsh and Forbidden Sperrgebiet Rediscovered* Swakopmund ST Promotions, Namibia, 1999.

Seely, Dr Mary *The Namib Desert* Research Foundation of Namibia, Windhoek, 3rd edn 2004. A detailed work on the desert's origins, with descriptions of many sites and the animals and plants that live there. This paperback is well worth getting when you arrive in Namibia. Also in this series is *Waterberg*.

'Shipwreck in the Forbidden Zone' *National Geographic*, October 2009. An absorbing article about the discovery in 2008 of the oldest shipwreck to be found in sub-Saharan Africa.

Sinclair, Ian, Hockey, Phil, and Tarboton, Warwick *Sasol Birds of Southern Africa* Struik, South Africa, 3rd edn 2002. First published in 1993, this is particularly useful for the illustrations of birds at different stages of their development, and in flight.

Stuart, Chris and Tilde *Field Guide to Mammals of Southern Africa* Struik Publishers, South Africa, revised 2007.

Unwin, Mike *Southern African Wildlife: A Visitor's Guide* Bradt Travel Guides, UK, 2011. A compact, single-volume guide to the habitats, identification and behavioural characteristics of the region's wildlife. A well-written text, which includes sections on tracks and signs, is matched by exceptionally good photographs.

Van der Walt, Pieter, and le Riche, Elias *The Kalahari & its Plants* Pretoria, 1999.

Art and culture

Breuil, Abbé Henri *The Rock Paintings of Southern Africa* Trianon Press Ltd, Paris, 1955–60. These large volumes cover some of Namibia's major rock-art sites, including the controversial 'white lady' of Brandberg.

Lilienthal, Adelheid *Art in Namibia* National Art Gallery of Namibia.

Malan, Professor J S *Peoples of Namibia* Rhino Press, Pretoria, 1995.

Mans, Minette *Ongoma! – Notes on Namibian Musical Instruments* Gamsberg Macmillan, Windhoek, 2000. This resource book for teachers on traditional instruments deserves a wider readership.

Rural Art in Namibia Rössing Foundation of Namibia, 1993. A 25-page colour booklet, categorised by region, illustrating traditional Namibian arts and crafts, including interviews with artists about their work.

Photography

Bannister, Anthony, and Johnson, Peter *Namibia – Africa's Harsh Paradise* New Holland, London, 1990. Yet another for the coffee table, this covers the whole country and concentrates on the Bushman and Himba people.

Coulson, David *Namib* Sidgwick & Jackson, London, 1991. This stunning coffee-table book doubles as a readable travelogue. Published 18 years after Coulson's first visit, its insight tells much of his love for Namibia's wilderness.

Marais, Chris, and du Toit, Julienne *Namibia Space* Struik, 2006. One of several coffee-table books showcasing the beauty of Namibia's landscapes.

Schoeman, Amy *The Skeleton Coast* Struik, Cape Town, 2003. Involving, well-informed text and superb photographs make this an excellent read, and easily the definitive work on the coast. Amy's late husband was the legendary Louw Schoeman, and she remains involved with Skeleton Coast Fly-in Safaris, though she now concentrates on travel writing and photography.

Travelogues

Martin, Henno *Sheltering Desert* First English edition published William Kimber, London, 1957. The story of two German geologists who lived out World War II by hiding in the Kuiseb Canyon – holiday reading if you're visiting the Namib-Naukluft National Park.

van der Post, Laurens *The Lost World of the Kalahari* First published Hogarth Press, 1958, subsequently many reprints by Penguin. Laurens van der Post's classic account of how he journeyed into the heart of the Kalahari Desert in search of a 'pure' Bushman group – eventually found at the Tsodilo Hills. His almost mystical description of the Bushmen is fascinating, so long as you can cope with the rather dated turgid prose. You then need to read Robert J Gordon's very different book (see *History* above) to put it in perspective.

Guidebooks

Bulpin, T V *Discovering Southern Africa* Discovering Southern Africa Productions, South Africa, 1970. In this part guidebook and part history book, Bulpin covers mainly South Africa but also extends into Namibia and Zimbabwe. A weighty tome with useful background views and information, written from a South African perspective.

Health/reference

Dodwell, Christina *An Explorer's Handbook – Travel, Survival and Bush Cookery* Hodder & Stoughton, London, 1984. Over 170 pages of both practical and amusing anecdotes, including chapters on 'unusual eatables', 'building an open fire' and 'tested exits from tight corners'. Practical advice for both plausible and most unlikely eventualities – and it's a great read.

Wilson-Howarth, Dr Jane *Bugs, Bites & Bowels* Cadogan Books, London, 2006. An amusing and erudite overview of the hazards of tropical travel.

Wilson-Howarth, Dr Jane, and Ellis, Dr Matthew *Your Child Abroad: A Travel Health Guide* Bradt Travel Guides, UK, 2005. Full of practical first-hand advice from two leading medical experts. An indispensable guide if you plan to travel abroad with young children.

Fiction

Andreas, Neshani *The Purple Violet of Oshaantu* Heinemann, London, 2001. A Namibian woman's perspective on love and marriage in the context of traditional values and beliefs.

Brink, André *The Other Side of Silence* Vintage, London, 2003. The story of Hanna X, who joined a group of women sent to German South West Africa in the late 19th century to service the needs of the new colony's men. By turns brutal and uplifting.

Hiyalwa, Kaleni *Meekulu's Children* New Namibia Books, Windhoek, 2000. Reads more like a biography of a child growing up during Namibia's struggle for independence than a novel. Powerful stuff.

WEBSITES

www.airnamibia.com.na Air Namibia's site includes schedules and fares.

www.grnnet.gov.na The official website of the Namibian government.

www.holidaytravel.com.na Links to various tourism magazines, including *Flamingo*, the in-flight magazine of Air Namibia.

www.met.gov.na Ministry of Environment and Tourism website.

www.nacobta.com.na Overview of the community-orientated tourism projects run under the auspices of NACOBTA.

www.namibian.com.na *The Namibian* newspaper online.

www.namibiatourism.com.na Namibia Tourism Board's official site.

www.namibweb.com A rather ramshackle site focused on travel around Namibia.

www.nbc.com.na The government-sponsored Namibia Broadcasting Corporation (NBC).

www.nwr.com.na Namibia Wildlife Resorts (NWR). Essential for booking accommodation in national parks.

www.swakop.com Details useful information for tourists to Swakopmund and Walvis Bay.

Index

Page numbers in **bold** indicate major entries; those in *italic* indicate maps

INDEX OF ADVERTISERS